THE GROWTH OF LITERATURE
VOLUME II

THE
GROWTH OF LITERATURE

BY

H. MUNRO CHADWICK

AND

N. KERSHAW CHADWICK

VOLUME II

CAMBRIDGE
AT THE UNIVERSITY PRESS
1936
REPRINTED
1968

Published by the Syndics of the Cambridge University Press
Bentley House, 200 Euston Road, London, N.W. 1
American Branch: 32 East 57th Street, New York, N.Y. 10022

PUBLISHER'S NOTE

Cambridge University Press Library Editions are re-issues of out-of-print
standard works from the Cambridge catalogue. The texts are unrevised
and, apart from minor corrections, reproduce the latest published edition.

Standard Book Number: 521 07423 1
Library of Congress Catalogue Card Number: 33–6470

First published 1936
Reprinted 1968

First printed in Great Britain at the University Press, Cambridge
Reprinted in Great Britain by John Dickens & Co. Ltd, Northampton

To

ALFRED CORT HADDON

IN GRATEFUL RECOGNITION OF THE
ENCOURAGEMENT WE HAVE CONSTANTLY
RECEIVED FROM HIM

CONTENTS

Part II. YUGOSLAV ORAL POETRY

Part III. EARLY INDIAN LITERATURE

PART IV. EARLY HEBREW LITERATURE

PREFACE

IN the first volume of this work we attempted a survey of the ancient literatures of Europe, in so far as they appear to be of independent (native) growth. In the present volume we complete our survey for Europe by an examination of two of the modern oral literatures, and then pass on to an examination of two of the ancient literatures of the East. The next—and final—volume will be occupied with an examination of certain modern oral literatures from Asia, Africa and the Pacific, and with a summary of the results of the whole survey.

The examination follows in general the same lines as in Vol. 1; but each literature is now treated separately. The same plan will be followed in Vol. III. This difference of treatment is necessitated by the fact that the two authors are not alike familiar with the whole of the material, as was the case in Vol. 1. In the two later volumes the literatures are distributed between us.

In the introductory chapter of Vol. 1 (p. 4) it was pointed out that a comprehensive survey of the medieval and modern oral literatures of Europe was out of the question. A selection had to be made, and for the reasons given (*ibid.*) our choice fell upon Russian and Yugoslav. These are the fullest and most varied of the modern oral literatures known to us. Moreover they have maintained their vitality to a certain extent down to our own times, and consequently supply abundant evidence as to the way in which an unwritten literature is preserved and cultivated. At the same time we were naturally influenced by the fact that we had already some knowledge of these literatures. For some time before we undertook this work we had come to realise the importance of the Russian and Yugoslav material for the study of heroic poetry, and consequently had paid a good deal of attention to it. This made it possible for us to treat the literatures in a way which we could not have done, if we had had no previous knowledge of them.

We realise that in making this choice we have laid ourselves open to criticism. The Russian and Yugoslav languages are rather closely related; and the diction of oral literature in both has a good deal in common. Moreover both literatures have been subject to similar ecclesiastical influences; and in certain genres further affinities can be traced, even in relation to secular subjects. But these common elements must not be overestimated. In narrative poetry—or at least heroic narrative poetry—which is the most highly developed genre in both literatures, they are virtually wanting. The principles of metre too are wholly different. And in any case the considerations pointed out above seem to us to outweigh the disadvantages arising from these affinities.[1]

The ancient literatures discussed in Vol. I date from times when written literature was a more or less recent innovation; the earliest works, at least in Greek and Norse, were doubtless composed before it existed. In Russia and Yugoslavia on the other hand written literature —of foreign (ecclesiastical) origin, but in a language not very different from the vernaculars—had been cultivated for centuries before the time of the earliest oral literature which we can trace. It may naturally be expected therefore that the influence of written literature will be stronger than in the ancient literatures.

This influence is most clearly perceptible on the negative side. Oral literature in Russia and Yugoslavia is practically limited to literature of entertainment and literature of celebration (e.g. wedding and funeral poetry). Literature of thought, whether relating to the past or to the observation of nature or general philosophy, is very poorly represented. Creations of native mythology are hardly to be found, except in the Yugoslav 'Vila of the Mountain', who, curiously enough, maintained her position down to the end. Even stories of 'the wise'—wizards,

[1] We should have liked to include English ballad poetry in our survey. This contains without doubt a large amount of material, varied in character, which is valuable for the study of oral literature. Thus, heroic poetry is well represented in the Border ballads, which supply interesting analogies to Yugoslav heroic poetry of the later periods (cf. p. 325 ff.)—analogies due doubtless to the prevalence of similar political conditions—while the transition from heroic to 'post-heroic' may be illustrated by other ballads, from Scotland and the north of England. Literature of thought is hardly to be found, except in riddle ballads; but these, though they are seldom or never of native origin, furnish interesting parallels to the riddle catalogues noticed in this volume (pp. 212 f., 410, 560 f.). For the study of variants ballads afford abundant material. But the subject cannot be treated adequately except by specialists, owing partly to the immense amount of documentary evidence which has to be taken into account, and partly to the difficulty of distinguishing between native and foreign (international) ballads. The latter, apart from a few theological pieces, belong properly to the 'unspecified' (timeless-nameless) category; but in this country they have often adopted English names, as in 'King John and the Bishop'. On the other hand there may be many ballads of native origin which have lost most of their names and perhaps borrowed motifs from foreign ballads.

In the summary of our survey, which will be included in Vol. III, we shall refer occasionally for illustration to ballads which are clearly of English origin; and the volume will also include a note explaining our classification of these. But, for the reasons given above, we dare not undertake a comprehensive treatment of the subject.

seers and sages, other than Christian saints—seem to be extremely rare. The literature of thought as a whole is surrendered to written literature, i.e. to ecclesiastical learning.

On the positive side the influence of written literature may be seen in stories of saints—which are apparently more frequent in Russia than in Yugoslavia. Otherwise this influence is in general not very obvious. Religious formulae, which are derived ultimately from ecclesiastical literature, are of common occurrence in oral poetry; but the poems as a whole usually show little trace of this influence, especially in Yugoslavia. Some scholars hold that Russian heroic poems relating to early times derive their subjects from chronicles; but we have not met with any convincing evidence in support of this view. It would seem rather that, just as in Ireland, Wales and Germany, chronicles not unfrequently show the influence of heroic poetry.

Some scholars also hold that literary influence from the West is to be found in both Russian and Yugoslav oral poetry; but here again the evidence is in general far from convincing. The influence of the Renaissance is perceptible in some poems from the Adriatic coast; but it is of an indirect character and not very marked. In Novgorod Western influence may have been felt at an earlier date, and possibly to a greater extent. Moreover throughout both Russia and Yugoslavia modern folktales and folksongs have borrowed motifs from the West, as from other quarters. But we see no reason for accepting the view that Russian or Yugoslav heroic poetry derives its inspiration from Western romances.

According to our view, apart from the ecclesiastical element and a not inconsiderable element in folksongs, Russian and Yugoslav oral poetry represents an earlier phase of literature than the romances of the West. In modern times its analogies are to be found eastwards, as we shall see in the next volume. Its closest Western analogies are to be found in the ancient literatures treated in Vol. i. But these belong to the past. The medieval poetry which took their place sometimes preserved themes from the earlier phase. But this poetry was not purely oral;[1] and its form universally, and its subjects usually, represent a

---

[1] Medieval romances, at least as a rule, cannot properly be regarded as oral literature. Usually they seem to have been written by their authors, although at first they were doubtless intended for recitation, perhaps from memory, rather than for a reading public. Ballads on the other hand do in general belong to oral literature, though they are sometimes derived from written sources. This is true even of the remote Faroes; cf. Kershaw, *Stories and Ballads of the Far Past*, p. 166 f. The ballads peculiar to this country (cf. p. x, note), as also those which are peculiar to

revolution, due to the influence of written literature. In literature, as in civilisation generally, the east of Europe has lagged behind the west.

As we have remarked above, heroic narrative poetry is on the whole the most important genre in both Russian and Yugoslav oral literature. In the extent and variety of this no other oral literature known to us can compare with either of the two. In Yugoslavia the history of an original creative poetry of this kind can be traced back, more or less continuously, for some four or five centuries. Moreover the abundance of variants and the fullness of information obtained from both countries as to the procedure and technique of the minstrels (or reciters) are of the utmost value for the general study of this class of literature.

It may be added here that oral literature as a whole was most intimately connected with the intellectual life of both peoples. Until recent times it was the only form of literature or of intellectual activity known to the overwhelming majority of the population. What we think of as poetry of entertainment in reality served various other purposes also, e.g. that of political propaganda. It must be regarded as the Russian (or Yugoslav) counterpart, not merely of the folksongs and ballads, but also of the whole written literature, of the Western peoples. Until recently written literature in both countries was an exotic product, with a very limited range of circulation.

We have made no attempt at an exhaustive survey of the material. In view of its extent indeed such an attempt would hardly be practicable. Many of the collections and also many works bearing upon the subjects have been inaccessible to us.[1] We hope, however, that what we have done will be sufficient to give the reader at least a general conspectus of the material.[2] So far as we are aware, no such survey has been attempted in English before for either of the two literatures.

The whole of the Russian material has been treated from the original texts. In the Yugoslav use has been made of English—occasionally also of German—translations, where such were available. But these cover only a small fraction—perhaps one fifth or sixth—of the material

Denmark or other countries, afford some interesting analogies to the literatures we have discussed; but the very large 'international' element—the affinities of which lie with folktales—renders this subject difficult, as we have noted.

[1] It is much to be regretted that so few books relating to these subjects have found their way into English libraries. We have had to buy nearly every book—including the collections—that we have used, except a few which have kindly been lent to us; and Russian books are not always easy to obtain.

[2] Mohammedan Yugoslav poetry is not represented so fully as we could have wished.

treated.[1] References are given in each case to the translations which
have been used. No translations in other languages have been accessible
to us.

The translations which we have given from both languages are our
own throughout, except in one or two passages where the originals
were inaccessible. We do not profess to be experts in these languages,
and have had no special facilities for learning them. Incidental inaccuracies may therefore be expected; but it is hoped that these will not
seriously affect the interpretation of the texts, or give an erroneous
impression as to their character.

The ancient Oriental literatures which occupy the latter part of this
volume show in several respects a striking contrast to those which we
have been discussing. Literature of entertainment—in particular heroic
poetry or saga—is by no means wanting; but on the whole it is definitely of secondary interest in both cases. The chief interest in both
lies in the literature of thought, especially perhaps on the mantic side.
Such literature was not, as in Europe, displaced by a foreign written
literature; it appears to have developed freely on its own lines.

Oriental scholars will doubtless be of opinion that work of this kind
should not have been undertaken, except by specialists. Our reply to
this criticism is that in such a survey as ours the ancient literatures of
the East cannot be ignored without loss to the subject as a whole. We
are writing not for Orientalists,[2] but for readers interested in comparative literature; and our object is of course not to propose new
interpretations of these ancient literatures, but to bring their evidence
to bear upon the general history of literature.

At present it is the prevailing fashion in works of this kind to treat
the literature—as also the history, etc.—of various peoples in a series
of volumes or chapters, each of which is entrusted to a specialist. This
plan has the obvious advantage that by it one obtains as good an
account as can be got of each literature within its own limits. It has,

---

[1] It is remarkable that the very interesting collections of poems preserved in
MSS. of the eighteenth century and earlier seem to have been almost entirely
neglected by English scholars.

[2] Parts I and II are intended for Orientalists, Parts III and IV for Slavists, all
four Parts for Hellenists, Celtists and Teutonists.

As we are not writing for Orientalists, we have generally avoided the use of
diacritical marks, except for the length of vowels in Indian names. In Part IV we
have followed the usage of the English Bible, except that we write 'Jehovah' for
'the LORD'. This form of the name, though doubtless incorrect, is probably more
widely known than Jahweh or Yahweh.

however, the disadvantage that it does not bring to light so clearly as might be wished the parallels and differences between one literature and another. We believe that for comparative purposes there is room for accounts of literature written with this as their primary object, by students who are not specialists in this or that literature, but whose interest is distributed over a considerable number of literatures, or rather over literature in general. The defects which such a plan inevitably involves in the treatment of the literatures individually may, we think, be counterbalanced to some extent by the observation of the presence or absence of features common to various literatures.

Early Indian literature is of supreme importance for the study of oral tradition. Some difference of opinion prevails as to the date at which it began to be written down; but there can be no doubt that by this time an extensive and varied literature had long been in existence. Writing indeed seems to have played a comparatively unimportant part in the history of this literature—a feature which, among many others, may be commended to the attention of students of European literature. The decline of interest in the ancient literatures of the East is a fact which is in our opinion much to be deplored.

It may be observed here that much diversity seems to have prevailed in the character of Indian oral tradition. Sometimes it takes the form of strict (verbal) memorisation; sometimes again it appears to have been as free as that of the Russians or the Yugoslavs.

We venture to think, however, not only that the ancient literatures of the East may throw light on the early history of literature in Europe, but also that in their turn they may themselves receive some light from the study of the latter. We cannot doubt that the study of early Norse literature is able to contribute materially to the explanation of Hebrew literature—especially in the use of saga, the nature of which seems not to have been fully appreciated by Hebrew scholars.

In Part III translations have been used throughout; the original texts have been consulted only where the actual wording was of importance. The translations given are our own, except in a few cases, where it is otherwise stated. We do not pretend to be experts in the language, but hope that they are substantially correct. In Part IV we have used the Revised Version of the Old Testament throughout. Our knowledge of the Hebrew language is negligible.

We may repeat here what we said in the Preface to Vol. i, that we have made no attempt to consult the voluminous modern literature bearing upon these subjects. If we had done so, we should doubtless have avoided many errors and inaccuracies, and our work, so far as it went, would have profited greatly thereby; but it would never have seen the light. As in the preparation of Vol. I, we have read some books which happen to have come in our way; and to some of these we refer occasionally.

In conclusion we must express our indebtedness to Professor E. J. Rapson for allowing us to quote the passage printed on p. 617 and to consult him on several questions, especially relating to the Purānas; to Professor A. Mazon for sending us copies of important articles, of which we should not otherwise have known (cf. p. 456), and for allowing us to quote the passages printed on p. 247 f.; to Professor E. H. Minns and to Mrs V. Scott-Gatty for the loan of books; to Mr N. G. L. Hammond, Fellow of Clare College, for bringing to our notice an important account of Albanian oral poetry (cf. p. 455 f.); to the Editors of the *Slavische Rundschau* for permission to translate the passage printed on p. 241 ff., below. Above all we are indebted to Dr C. E. Wright of the Department of MSS., British Museum, who has most kindly read through the whole volume in proof and thereby, as in Vol. I, saved us from many oversights and obscurities. To the University Library and its staff we are under the same obligations as in the past, especially in the preparation of Parts III and IV. To the Syndics of the Cambridge University Press, and also to the staff— including Mr E. H. Taylor, who has prepared the Index—we must repeat the thanks which we expressed in the Preface to the previous volume.

A list of Addenda et Corrigenda for Vols. I and II will be given in Vol. III. We may take this opportunity, however, of calling attention to certain corrections in the present volume:

P. 22, l. 33, and p. 52, note 1. For 'harp' read 'zither'. In the *gusli*, as in a zither, the sounding-board is parallel to the strings, not at a right angle to them, as in a harp. The Yugoslav *gusle* is a stringed instrument of quite different character; cf. p. 303, note 2.

P. 37 f. For *polênitsa* read *polenitsa*.

P. 195, l. 8. For 'Vol. III' read 'Part II'.

P. 252, l. 17. Read '...to his son, and also to his grandson, Terenti Ievlev'.

H. M. C.

N. K. C.

August, 1936

PART I

RUSSIAN ORAL LITERATURE

NOTE. In this volume reference will be made from time to time to certain types of literature which were defined in Vol. I (pp. 28, 42, 60, etc.). It will be convenient therefore to repeat these definitions here. Type A: narrative poetry or saga, intended for entertainment. Type B: poetry (very rarely prose) in the form of speeches in character. Type C: poetry or prose intended for instruction. Type D: poetry (seldom prose) of celebration or appeal, especially panegyrics, elegies, hymns, prayers and exhortations. Type E: personal poetry (very rarely prose) relating to the author himself and his surroundings. These types apply only to literature relating to persons, not to impersonal literature.

By 'saga' we mean prose narrative preserved by oral tradition.

CHAPTER I

INTRODUCTION

ORAL TRADITION AND WRITING

RUSSIA is rich in the possession of a large body of poetry which is still carried on by oral tradition. Traditional prose narrative is also a living form, but the nature and extent of the cultivation of saga have never received as much attention from collectors or scholars as the poetry. We shall therefore not be in a position to treat of the history or distribution of the prose with anything like the same fullness. The available material is much less, and even of the collections and critical material which are available in Russia very little has been accessible to us. The traditional oral poetry, on the other hand, had aroused a certain amount of interest in the west before the Russian Revolution of 1917, and a number of collections had found their way into English libraries, both public and private.

The oral literature which we propose to consider in this chapter has been collected in the main from Great Russia and Siberia. Rich collections of oral poetry have also been made from Little Russia. These, however, are in a different language, and the epic poetry of Little Russia has a different history. The lyrical poetry of Little Russia is a wholly distinct body, differing fundamentally in subjects and in traditional form, metre, and diction from that of Great Russia. The two areas are therefore quite distinct from one another as regards literary tradition, and would require separate treatment. We have selected Great Russia as being the area offering on the whole the richer field of study, and a body of literature of which the narrative portion at least has a much longer and more interesting history.

The oral narrative poems of Russia which are concerned primarily with secular subjects are called *byliny* (sing. *bylina*), or *stariny* (sing. *starina*). The word *bylina* is said to be derived from the past participial form (*byl*) of the verb *byt*, 'to be', and to signify 'that which has been', 'past occurrences'. The term is, however, commonly applied also to poems celebrating contemporary events, and to folk-songs which are narrative in form and composed in the metre and diction of the *byliny*. According to Professor Mazon[1] the word was first applied to the oral

[1] *Bylines*, p. 679.

narrative poetry of Russia by Sakharov, who misunderstood the opening passage of the *Slovo o Polky Igorevê*, in which the word *byliny* (*'po bylinam'*) occurs—probably with reference, not to poems, but to 'events of past times', 'true histories'. Indeed it is commonly stated[1] that the only term in use among the singers on Lake Onega in the former Government of Olonets is *stariny, starinki*, 'stories of long ago' (*stary*, 'old'). Rybnikov, however, represents the people of this region as using the word *byliny* commonly,[2] and we have therefore ventured to retain the term throughout this Part, the more so as it is now generally familiar and has gained a wider currency in critical literature than *stariny*.

In addition to the *byliny*, or *stariny*, a body of oral narrative poetry is also current in northern Russia which is chiefly devoted to religious subjects. These poems are known as *stikhi*,[3] 'poems', 'poetry' (sing. *stikh*, lit. 'verse', 'stave'). They relate principally to the Gospel stories, and to Biblical and Apocryphal stories generally, to lives of saints, and to religious legends of both Greek and native Russian origin. The subjects of the *stikhi* are derived in the main ultimately from books. The poems have, however, had a long life in oral circulation, quite divorced from written literature, and many versions show wide variants from any parallel form of the narratives, exactly as we should expect to find in oral tradition. These songs are sung by groups of itinerant peasants, known today as *kalêki perekhoʒie* (lit. 'itinerant cripples'). The singers are generally cripples, the great majority being blind, so that the modern Russian word *kalêka*, 'cripple', has been generally substituted for the archaic *kalika*, originally a different word, meaning 'pilgrim', 'itinerant begging singer of religious songs'. Rybnikov generally retains the older form, but modern writers, such as Speranski, generally adopt the term *kalêki* as being the one more familiar.

The Western student is not wholly without guidance in beginning a study of the oral narrative poetry of Great Russia. Rambaud's French work on the subject, *La Russie épique*, is an admirable and delightfully written survey of the field, and although published as early as 1876, soon after the appearance of the first great collections, it still remains the standard work on the subject. It contains an admirably selected series of summaries and translations within the text. Three years after the ap-

---

[1] Mazon, *loc. cit.*; cf. Brodski, etc., p. 70, footnote.
[2] Rybnikov, I. p. lxxviii.
[3] For an account of these *stikhi* see Bezsonov, IV. p. i ff.; Speranski, *R.U.S.* p. 358 ff.

pearance of Rambaud's work, the German scholar Wollner published his *Untersuchungen über die Volksepik der Grossrussen*, which contains useful summaries of the *byliny*. Among the earliest translations in English are the small selection contained in Talvi's *Historical View of the Languages and Literature of the Slavonic Nations*, and in Morfill's *Slavonic Literature*. Hapgood's *Epic Songs of Russia*, first published in 1886, and again in 1915, consists of translations of conflate texts of a selection of *byliny* from the oldest cycles, and contains a brief introduction relating to their literary history. In 1932 a volume of English translations of *byliny* of all periods was published by N. K. Chadwick, also with a critical introduction. Translations of a small number of *byliny* relating to the historical period have been published by Eisner in *Volkslieder der Slawen* (Leipzig, 1926). In 1931 L. A. Magnus published a critical account of this poetry, entitled *The Heroic Ballads of Russia*. Critical accounts of the narrative poetry as a whole, and also of individual poems and singers (*skaʒiteli*, sing. *skaʒitel*, lit. 'a reciter'), have appeared from time to time in periodicals, such as *Russkaya Mysl*, *Archiv für slavische Philologie*, *Slavische Rundschau*, *La Revue des Études Slaves*, *The Slavonic Review*, etc. A number of translations of individual poems have also appeared, among which we may mention Kate Blakey's translations of versions of two from the Novgorod Cycle, published in *The Slavonic Review*, III. 1924–5, p. 52 ff.[1]

Oral poetry other than narrative has attracted less attention. Ralston published an interesting and very readable account, *The Songs of the Russian People*, in 1872. The work contains many translations. Unlike many of the works mentioned above, however, it relates to both Great and Little Russia, and contains translations from the poetry of both areas. In 1926 Paul Eisner published his *Volkslieder der Slawen*, a very useful collection of German translations of oral poetry from a number of Slavonic countries, including Russia. Very little popular prose has been translated into English. The most important collection of prose stories is a selection of Russian folk-tales translated by L. A. Magnus[2] from the great collection of Afanasev, to which we shall refer later.

Scientific interest in Russian popular poetry is of comparatively recent date, even in Russia itself. Before the beginning of last century such poetry was neglected and almost unknown. The opening up of Russia to western influences under the stimulus of the Romantic Revival aroused a great interest in popular poetry among Russian men of letters

[1] Fuller details of the editions cited above will be found in the List of Abbreviations at the conclusion of this Part. [2] See List of Abbreviations.

such as Pushkin and Lermontov, and later, among the more intellectual of the official classes; and there can be no doubt that Percy's *Reliques* and Macpherson's *Ossian* acted as strong incentives to the collection of Russian oral literature. The scientific collection and investigation of oral poetry as a living form has therefore been carried on under peculiarly favourable conditions in Russia. The lower classes, backward and illiterate, wholly untouched by the new education and culture, continued to derive their entertainment from the old traditional forms of poetry, while the officials and landed gentry of the more progressive type, especially those in the neighbourhood of Moscow and St Petersburg, acquired the literary outlook of the Romantic Revival, simultaneously with the scientific and critical methods which in western Europe followed on the newly awakened interest in popular poetry only after an interval. Owing to these fortunate circumstances the great Russian collections offer for our purposes a peculiarly valuable field of research. We shall give some account of the precise circumstances under which these collections were made, and the manner in which oral tradition was carried on in northern Russia, in the chapter on 'Recitation and Composition'.

Some few MS. collections of popular poetry had already been made before the great collections of last century; but these were made for the most part by individuals for their own use, and not for publication. It is interesting to note that the earliest known collection was made by an Englishman, Richard James, a graduate of Oxford, who in 1619, while serving as chaplain to the English merchants in Moscow, wrote down, or induced a friend to write down for him, six poems on contemporary events, of the kind known today as *byliny*. These poems were written on a few sheets put loosely into a note book, which is preserved in the Bodleian Library at Oxford.[1] They are, as Bezsonov observes,[2] particularly interesting as affording rare examples of Russian popular poetry composed contemporaneously with the events celebrated, and recorded during the earliest stages of its recitation in the place where it was composed, before it had suffered deterioration from oral transmission. Later in the same century (1688) a further small collection of *byliny* treating of contemporary events was made; but both this collection and that of James remained unpublished till long after the more recent collections had seen the light.

---

[1] They have been published by the St Petersburg Academy, and by Bezsonov in his edition of the collections made by Kirêevski and others. See his edition of Kirêevski's collection, VII. p. 58.   [2] Kirêevski, *loc. cit.*

During the eighteenth century a collection of *byliny* was made by a certain Kirsha Danilov from the workers connected with the Demidov mines in the former Government of Perm, in the neighbourhood of the Urals. It is a matter for regret that little is known of Kirsha himself. He has been called the true originator of the modern interest in traditional oral narrative poetry. It is possible that recent research in Russia may have succeeded in unearthing details relating to him which have not been accessible to us. In the absence of further information, however, we see no reason to regard his collection as differing, either in object or scope, from those which were occasionally made last century by the few singers of *byliny* who were able to write, and who wrote down their collections for their own personal use; and it is not impossible that Kirsha's object in making his collection was similarly practical.

A selection of twenty-five poems from Danilov's MS. was published in 1804 by Yakubovich under the title *Les anciennes Poésies russes*, which created considerable interest. In 1818 the famous Russian editor Kalaidovich published a more complete edition from the same collection, comprising sixty poems. In 1819 a collection of *byliny* was published anonymously at Leipzig, apparently the work of a German resident in Russia, under the title *Fürst Wladimir und dessen Tafelrunde, alt-russische Heldenlieder*. The collection is of especial interest as containing, besides German translations of some of Kirsha Danilov's *byliny*, some additional pieces of which the Russian originals have not since been found.[1]

The interest of the Russian public was now thoroughly aroused, and from the middle of last century onwards many thousands of poems were recorded from the recitation of peasants in various parts of Russia, more especially the north. From 1852–1856 M. Sréznevski edited narrative poems or *byliny* as they were still sung in the provinces of Olonets, Tomsk, and Archangel. The first of the important collections of oral poetry of modern times was made by Rybnikov in 1859 and 1860 among the peasants of Olonets on the shores of Lake Onega. This collection was published in four volumes during the years 1861–1867.[2]

The wealth and range of Rybnikov's collection created so much interest that in 1871 Gilferding set out to the same region in the hope of

---

[1] Rambaud, *R.É.* p. 1 f.; Hapgood, *Songs*, p. xxii.

[2] The original edition is very scarce. A new edition was edited by Gruzinski in three volumes at Moscow in 1909, under the title *Pêsni Sobrannŷa P. N. Rybnikovym*, 'Songs collected by P. N. Rybnikov'. Our references are to Gruzinski's edition throughout.

supplementing Rybnikov's work. He penetrated, as a matter of fact, much farther to the north, and into more inaccessible regions than Rybnikov had done, and was able to add much valuable new material, which was afterwards published in three large volumes.[1] Moreover Gilferding also interviewed many of the same singers whom Rybnikov had heard, and again recorded their *byliny*. A comparison of the variant versions thus obtained affords much valuable material for the study of the composition and recitation of oral poetry and the circumstances of oral transmission.

While Rybnikov was making his researches in person among the peasants in the neighbourhood of Lake Onega, Kirêevski was publishing *byliny* collected from all over Great Russia, from Archangel to Moscow, from Novgorod to Siberia. Some of the *byliny* in his collection had already been published from Kirsha Danilov's MS. Others were obtained from albums and private MS. collections. While many of them relate to ancient times, and are identical with, or variants of those of Rybnikov and Gilferding, the majority relate to more recent times. It is, in fact, the most representative collection of Russian *byliny* which has appeared. It was first published at Moscow in four parts, during the years 1860–1862.[2]

Each of these three great collections has a special interest of its own. Rybnikov, as a pioneer collector of the narrative poetry relating to the Russian Heroic Age, will always hold the first place. His work is also extremely valuable for the collection of lyrics and ceremonial songs which it contains, and for the large amount of interesting information which he recorded relating to the singers themselves, both men and women, from whose recitation he noted down his texts. Gilferding's is the most comprehensive collection of *byliny* relating to Heroic Russia which we possess, affording, as it does, an enormous number of narratives and variant versions. Kirêevski's collection is the most interesting

---

[1] His collection was published at St Petersburg in 1875 under the title *Onezhskÿa Byliny zapisannÿa A. F. Gilferdingom*, 'Byliny of Onega recorded by A. F. Gilferding'. A new edition appeared, also at St Petersburg, and in three volumes, in 1894 under the same title. Our references throughout this Part are to the latter edition.

[2] Kirêevski's collection was published at Moscow by P. A. Bezsonov in 1860 under the title *Pêsni Sobrannÿa P. V. Kirêevskim*. Bezsonov also included in the edition valuable supplementary and editorial matter. The edition was afterwards reprinted without change by Bezsonov in ten parts at Moscow during the years 1868–1874 under the same title. This enlarged edition is referred to in this volume as Kirêevski.

from both a geographical and an historical point of view. Not only does it contain, as we have said, *byliny* recorded from singers scattered over the whole Great Russian world and many parts of Siberia, but the subjects are drawn from all periods of Russian history. Rybnikov and Gilferding each obtained some examples of poems relating to modern times, but Kirêevski was the first to show the real wealth of popular poetry relating to historical events. In his volumes we have, as it were, the oral records of Russian history composed from the viewpoint of the unlettered classes, which supply a popular supplement to the more professional forms of historical record.

From the same period as Rybnikov's *Pêsni* we have the great collection of *stikhi*, or oral religious poems, published by P. Bezsonov in three volumes at Moscow in 1860–1864, under the title *Kalêki Perekhoçhie*. The collection represents the répertoire of the *kalêki*, the itinerant groups of peasant singers of religious songs, to whom reference has already been made. In the past *stikhi* have attracted less attention than *byliny*, but in recent years they have been made the subject of special study by Speranski and others. The *Dukhobors*, and other backward religious sects of Russia have also preserved much traditional oral religious poetry from the past, which promises to throw interesting light on the history of Russian religious thought, but which is at present very little known, even in Russia itself.[1]

In addition to these collections of traditional verse, chiefly of a narrative character, large collections of lyrics have also been made from the same area—indeed from all parts of the Russian Empire. With the rich collections from Little Russia we are not concerned here. Among pioneers in folk-song collecting in Great Russia we must again mention Rybnikov himself, whose great collection of *Pêsni* contains many wedding, funeral and personal songs. In the same district Barsov made an important collection of funeral songs which he published at Moscow in 1872.[2]

Since the publication of the great collections already mentioned, a number of others have appeared from time to time of almost equal interest and importance.[3] These for the most part contain collections

[1] A valuable though brief account of the whole subject is given by Speranski, *R.U.S.* p. 358 ff.
[2] See List of Abbreviations. For a fuller list the reader is referred to the bibliography appended to Ralston's *Songs*, p. 437 ff.
[3] For an outline of the history of the collections, and an account of their character, and the areas from which they have been obtained, see Speranski, *R.U.S.* p. 3 ff. A valuable bibliography will be found at the end of the same work.

made within limited areas, and are therefore of great value, not only as adding to the number of available poems and variants, but also as enabling us to study the local répertoires of these areas. Of special interest in this connection are collections of *byliny*. We may instance among many others those of Markov from the shore of the White Sea, of Grigorev from the neighbourhood of Archangel, of Onchukov from Pechora on the shore of the Arctic Ocean, the recent collection from Olonets made during the expeditions of the Sokolov brothers, the Siberian collections of Gulyaev from Barnoul, and a number of *byliny* recorded from the descendants of Russian settlers on the R. Kolyma in the north-east of Siberia, and published by V. F. Miller. Other collections have been obtained from the area around Moscow, from Samara in south-eastern Russia, from the district around Novgorod, and even from the Caucasus. The material thus obtained has been further supplemented to some extent from reprints of texts contained in private MS. collections, old note-books, and account-books, etc., and scattered in various journals and periodical publications, as well as from some few written texts contained in MSS. of the seventeenth and eighteenth centuries.

Such collections are of the greatest value for comparative purposes, as well as for the light which they throw on the history of versions and redactions, and, ultimately, of the *byliny* themselves. Indeed the full importance of the study of area and distribution in relation to répertoire and version is perhaps only now coming to be fully appreciated. In general it may be said *byliny* have been collected[1] from areas where Russian settlers formed pioneer communities among a non-Slavonic population during the sixteenth and seventeenth centuries, and where they have lived during the intervening centuries as self-contained communities in social and political backwaters, having little or no intercourse with the more progressive centres of population. Since the origin and history of these colonies is generally fairly well known, it follows that these local collections are invaluable for the study of the relative chronology of the variant versions of the *byliny*.

Very little information has been accessible to us relating to the collecting and editing of prose narratives, and very little is known in western Europe of Russian oral prose. Many thousands of stories have been collected from oral recitation in modern times, however, from all parts of Great Russia. Some sagas are also contained in Russian medieval

[1] For an account of the geographical distribution of the *byliny*, see Speranski, *R.U.S.* p. 181 ff.

MS. collections, while others have been incorporated in Chronicles and Lives of Saints. Some of these have been embodied in the histories of Russia by Solovev and Karamzin, where they are perhaps most easily accessible. These 'inset' sagas, related for the most part in summary form, are not numerous. They often appear to be derived in the last instance from written authorities, but they bear the stamp of literature which has passed through a stage of oral transmission. The great storehouse of Russian prose of a purely oral character, however, is Afanasev's *Narodnÿa Russkÿa Ska₂ki* ('Russian Popular Tales'), which was collected during the latter half of last century. The collection contains hundreds of folk-tales, and also a number of examples of prose sagas relating to the early periods of Russian history and tradition. Unfortunately his notes as to the sources from which they were obtained are very brief. The vast majority of the stories contained in his collection are pure folk-tales which appear to have been recorded in modern times from recitation. Reference has already been made to the selection from Afanasev's collection which has been translated into English by L. A. Magnus.

The poetry recited by the Russian peasants, including the *byliny* and the *stikhi*, is purely oral in character, and its history is the history of oral tradition. The mould in which it is cast was made long ago; but the traditional form still continues to circulate, and, to some extent, to undergo re-creation with each fresh generation of reciters. In certain remote districts such poetry will no doubt continue to be the popular form of entertainment for some time to come. The *stikhi* are still widely sung, or were until the Revolution of 1917.[1] In the province of Irkutsk, where the *byliny*[2] have retained a particularly archaic form, it is said that even today one can still hear on the banks of the River Kolyma ancient Russian songs and legends couched in diction now obsolete in European Russia, and akin to the diction of the *Slovo o Polky Igorevê*.[3]

Our fullest and best evidence for the cultivation of *byliny* in modern times comes from the former Government of Olonets, in the neighbourhood of Lake Onega, and from the White Sea. In these districts the largest, and, on the whole, the best collections have been made. By the middle of last century *byliny* relating to the early periods of Russian

[1] See Speranski, *R.U.S.* p. 358 f.
[2] A number of *byliny* recorded in this district are included by Miller in *Byliny*. See List of Abbreviations at the close of the present Part.
[3] Shklovsky, p. 12.

history were believed to be almost extinct. Sreznevski and Rybnikov found them still flourishing in the north, especially among the singers of Olonets. This discovery was at first treated by the educated world with a scepticism similar to that which greeted Macpherson's *Ossian* in our own country. Even in Olonets—the district from which the great majority of the *byliny* have been collected—the practice of singing *byliny* was limited in area. Yet at Petrozavodsk in this same district, at the time when the early collections were made, the old men related how, fifty years earlier, it had been the custom in their little town for the *chinovniks* or officials, no less than for the bourgeoisie and merchant classes, to meet together in the evenings to listen to the singing of *byliny*.[1] Nowadays such poetry is restricted to the peasant class, and is doomed to pass away with the spread of education. Even today, however, it is still cultivated among the people of Olonets. During the years 1926–1928 the Sokolov brothers were able to make an important collection of *byliny* from this area, and to note down on their phonographs the tunes to which they are sung. No longer ago than February 1932 in this same region, Jean Porcher, under the guidance of Yury Sokolov, was enabled to hear a number of old women singing some of the best known of the *byliny*,[2] and some of the greatest of all the *skaʒiteli* are still to be found here. We do not know if fresh *byliny* are still composed on modern subjects, but we should expect this to be the case in remote districts both in Olonets and elsewhere.[3]

It will be seen that Russian oral poetry is not a recent development. During the last three centuries we have continuous testimony to the singing of *byliny*, and it is clear from a comparison of the poems written down in the early part of the seventeenth century in James's note-book, and those collected by Kirsha Danilov in the eighteenth century, with those written down last century, that no change took place in the form of the poems during this period. When we compare the poems on contemporary events in James's collection with poems collected during last century, but relating to events which took place during the seventeenth century, we find no fundamental difference in style or treatment. Some of the poems recorded by Rybnikov and by Kirêevski might equally

---

[1] Rybnikov, i. p. lxxxvi.   [2] Mazon, *Bylines*, p. 681.

[3] Russia contains many remote pockets. Even today there are said to be communities living in the Urals who know nothing of the Soviet and have no knowledge that the tsar is not still living. (See the review by Sir J. C. Squire, 'Ballads and Folk-Songs of the Russian People', in the *Daily Telegraph*, August 23rd, 1932.) Such areas must still be rich in traditional oral poetry.

well have been recorded by James. The results of such a comparison afford strong testimony to the fidelity of oral tradition in Russia during the last three and a half centuries. Moreover, though *byliny* relating to the last three centuries of Russian history have been collected from all over Great Russia, they grow more and more scarce everywhere for periods approaching our own days, while *byliny* relating to more remote times are only to be found in remote areas. This chronological and geographical distribution suggests that the *byliny* which relate to the oldest periods are older, and were once far more numerous than those relating to modern times.

Beyond this point the antiquity of the *byliny* has been disputed, and a fuller discussion of the subject must therefore be left to a later chapter, when we come to consider the question of authorship. It may be mentioned here, however, that the *byliny* contain a large body of narrative relating to characters who belong to the period before the fourteenth century, and some appear to belong to much earlier times. Some of these characters are known from historical sources. Further indications of ancient date are to be found in the diction and in the references contained in the poems themselves. These also will be discussed later.

Oral narrative prose has also been widely cultivated in Russia for some centuries, though our evidence is not so full or so valuable as for oral poetry. Prose sagas have been written down by collectors both from oral recitation and from private MSS. or 'albums'. All evidence goes to indicate that these manuscript collections have been made from oral recitation. The authors are not known or named, and we are not told the date, place or circumstances of composition. The stories do not appear to have for the most part any written sources. In the majority of instances of stories obtained by collectors from oral recitation, the reciters—frequently the audience also—were unable to read or write. Their intercourse with a reading public, with a few exceptions, may be regarded as negligible. There can be no doubt that the prose sagas of Russia, like the *byliny*, have a long history behind them, and in earlier times we may be certain that they formed the basis of an appreciable portion of the early written chronicles of the country.

Notwithstanding the vitality and longevity of oral tradition, writing has long been known and practised in Russia. It was probably not unknown at the court of Kiev in the time of Olga, who was baptised at Constantinople in 957. It was certainly established there when Vladimir I, the Great, and his court were baptised in 988. The language and script employed were those of Cyril and Methodius.[1] The language differed but little from the Russian current at the time. Written literature in Russia begins in the eleventh century, with the possible exception of one or two documents which may be earlier. It is, for the most part, ecclesiastical; several manuscripts of the Gospels are known to have been written in this century.

Besides Gospels, other forms of ecclesiastical literature, such as sermons and chronicles, also date from the same period. From the first half of the eleventh century we have the *Instructions* written by Luka Zhidyata, bishop of Novgorod, for his congregation; and from a few years later in the same century we have the *Eulogy on St Vladimir*, which is composed in Russian, and appended to a sermon by Ilarion who became metropolitan of Kiev in 1050. The earliest chronicle[2] which we possess was compiled c. 1110. It has been traditionally ascribed to Nestor, a monk of the Pechersk monastery at Kiev (c. 1056–1114); but it is now recognised that this chronicle has undoubtedly incorporated earlier written annals,[3] and that the final compilation was the work of Sylvester, Abbot of the Vêdubitski Monastery of Kiev. The Synodal transcript of the Chronicle of Novgorod[4] is said to be founded on an historical compilation made by a priest named Herman Voyata, of the Novgorod church of St James, who was appointed to his office in A.D. 1144, and who died in 1188. This compilation is believed in its turn to be based on early ecclesiastical annals compiled at Novgorod; and, in fact, there are clear indications that chronicle writing at Novgorod is as old as the eleventh century.[5]

Writing was already used in the eleventh century to some extent for other than ecclesiastical purposes. It is at the close of this century that Vladimir Monomakh, Grand Prince of Kiev, is believed to have composed his *Pouchenie Dêtyam*, 'Instruction to Children', which is generally thought to embody a considerable amount of autobio-

---

[1] The 'apostles of the Slavs' who converted Moravia and Hungary in the ninth century, and introduced writing. The language which they employed was a form of Southern Slavonic, which, in consequence of their translations, became, and has always remained the ecclesiastical language of the Orthodox Slavs. But the 'Glagolitic' alphabet (derived from Greek cursive) which they introduced was displaced about a century and a half later by an alphabet derived from the Greek uncial, which has been in use ever since, and is erroneously called 'Cyrillic'. For an account of their work, see Murko, *G.ä.s.L.* p. 36 ff.; *ib. S.L.* I. ix. p. 197 ff.

[2] See List of Abbreviations, *s.v.* Ancient Chronicle.

[3] See Michell, etc., p. xxxvii; cf. also Klyuchevski, p. 13 ff.

[4] This transcript is so called because it is in the possession of the Synodal Library at Moscow.   [5] See Michell, etc., p. xxxvii f.

graphical matter. Earlier in this century also, in the reign of Yaroslav the Wise, son of Vladimir I, the first codification of the Russian laws (*Russkaya Právda*) is believed to have taken place, though the compilation was actually continued into the twelfth century.[1] They are modelled to a considerable extent on earlier Byzantine codes,[2] but the close analogy which they show to the Teutonic laws, notably those of the Anglo-Saxons, is very striking. They are written in the Russian vernacular, and preserved in a MS. of the Chronicle of Novgorod. From the beginning of the twelfth century we have an interesting account by the Abbot Daniel the Palmer, of his sojourn in Jerusalem during Easter, and his visit to the Holy Sepulchre. There is, however, nothing to indicate that the use of letters was at all widely understood or practised anywhere outside the church and the monasteries for many centuries.

In spite of the paramount importance of Scandinavian influence in Russian political life at the time when 'Russia' first enters the pages of written history,[3] Russian culture looks to the east rather than to the west. From the time of her conversion to Christianity under Vladimir I, and her inclusion in the Greek Church in 988, Byzantine tradition directed the course of Russian educated thought. A certain amount of western influence has left its mark on the Slavonic literature which has come down to us. We may point to the Slavonic translations of such medieval romances as those of Tristan, Lancelot, and Bevis of Hampton.[4] But the schism between the eastern and the western churches, and the preoccupation of Russia with the Tatar invasions retarded to a considerable extent the progress of Russian intellectual life for many centuries.

This intellectual backwardness is manifest in all classes of the laity. From the thirteenth to the seventeenth century even the courts of the Russian princes were barbarous, and the coarse and unlettered Russian nobility afford a strong contrast to the polished and educated Polish

[1] Klyuchevski, p. 133.   [2] *Ib.* p. 134.

[3] The great antiquity of most of the sites in the valley of the Dnêpr, which were formerly believed to be of Scandinavian origin, is now well known. There can be no doubt that the traditions pointing to the Scandinavian origin of the *Rus* recorded in the Ancient Chronicle were composed in the interests of the Scandinavian rulers, as a critical reading of the text shows. Opinion is, however, divided as to the amount of importance to be attached to the Scandinavian elements in Russia as a whole. In any case the area actually in Scandinavian occupation cannot have been relatively very great, though Scandinavians no doubt occupied the headwaters of the Volga and the Kama at an early date—as early, if not earlier, than the valley of the Dnêpr. See Schröder, *G.R.M.* VIII (1920), p. 209; Braun, p. 150 f.

[4] Murko, *G.ä.s.L.* p. 183 f.

aristocracy. Of Dimitri Donskoy, Grand Prince of Moscow, who fought successfully against the Tatars at the Battle of Kulikovo in 1378, it is frankly stated that he had little knowledge of books. Other princes are said to have been wholly illiterate.[1] On the other hand learned ecclesiastics were numerous in medieval Russia, and their knowledge of letters was extremely valuable to the illiterate princes. Evidence is not lacking to show that a certain amount of education, even in Greek learning, was carried on orally by these ecclesiastics, and that laymen as well as clerics profited by this oral instruction. Thus we are told of Cyril, bishop of Rostov, that the people used to flock together from the neighbouring towns to listen to his instruction from holy books; and the author of this information tells us that he himself used to be stationed in a sequestered corner of the church, and to write down the words of the preacher.[2] It is not improbable that many medieval sermons and addresses have been similarly noted down during their delivery.

The first advance towards an educated upper class appears to have been made by Ivan III (1462–1505), whose Byzantine wife brought many scholars and manuscripts with her to Moscow. Ivan IV (1533–1584) was, for his time, a well-read man, and some of the letters and memoirs of the period, notably the famous correspondence between Ivan himself and the nobleman Kurbski, show that a certain amount of intellectual activity was present among the nobility, at least in court circles. But education spread very slowly in the country. Even the introduction of French culture and the culture of western Europe generally in the seventeenth century does not seem to have greatly affected the country as a whole, apart from the large towns. In the reign of Katharine II (1762–1796) it was apparently still exceptional for a nobleman to be able to read and write. Her farces, as well as those of Griboêdov and Derzhavin, are largely directed against the ignorant and unlettered aristocracy, and readers of Aksakov will remember the passage in which he describes his grandfather, an eighteenth-century landowner of the noble class in the province of Simbirsk:

"Ignorance was general among the landowners of his day, and he had received no sort of education. He could hardly read and write Russian. But while serving in the army, and before he was promoted to the rank of officer, he had learned the elementary rules of arithmetic, and how to calculate on a reckoning-board, and he was fond of referring to this, even in his old age."[3]

[1] Solovev, col. 1305.   [2] *Ib.* col. 1306.
[3] Aksakov, *Sem. Khron.* p. 13; cf. *Russian Gentleman*, p. 5.

Aksakov's grandmother, of course, who also belonged to a noble family, could neither read nor write.

In the towns education was more advanced; but even there progress was slow. Dearth of books seems to have been the greatest drawback to education in the eighteenth century. At the beginning of last century the scholars in the high-school, afterwards the university, at Kazan were sometimes obliged to copy out every word of their text-books in manuscript.[1] The peasantry of the period were of course wholly illiterate. Even in 1872 Gilferding found that in the neighbourhood of Lake Onega, where the population was, to some extent, in touch with St Petersburg, out of seventy peasants, only five could read or write.[2] The two best reciters of *byliny* interviewed by the Sokolovs in their expedition to the same region in 1926–1928 were both illiterate.[3]

In such a country oral literature was bound to flourish and die hard, and from the eighteenth century onward we have abundant evidence of extensive cultivation of oral literature in Russia. Aksakov remembered hearing in his youth the maid-servants in his grandfather's house at Aksakovo in the province of Ufa, singing their peasant songs at their spinning, or during their leisure in the evenings. He remembered, too, being taken to see queer old-time plays, in which the actors made strange noises, dressed and masked as animals, and acted rude comedy with dancing and poetry.[4] Pushkin spent much of his time on his country estate, listening to the folk-lore and tales of his old nurse, who told him stories of the *rusalka*, the Russian water-nymph, and sang folk-songs to him—perhaps the *bylina* of Ksenÿa, the daughter of Boris Godunov, the hero of Pushkin's greatest drama, whose family estate was only two miles from his own home. Many of the literary works of the period, such as Lermontov's *Cossack Cradle Song*, were clearly composed under the influence of popular poetry.

Aksakov's *Family Chronicle*, to which we have already referred, is really a family saga committed to writing by himself. He refers to himself as 'an honest chronicler of oral tradition'.[5] The history which he actually relates is carried back no farther than the time of his grandfather, but his statement that his grandfather 'lived in the government of Simbirsk on his own ancestral property, granted to his forefathers

[1] Aksakov, *Sem. Khron.* p. 275; *Schoolboy*, p. 112.
[2] See Rambaud, *R.É.* p. 18.
[3] *Slavische Rundschau*, IV (1932), p. 465 ff.
[4] *Sem. Khron.* p. 250 ff.; *Schoolboy*, p. 88 ff.
[5] *Russian Gentleman*, p. 240.

by the Tsars of Muscovy'[1] suggests that a certain amount of family tradition had been preserved from earlier times. Elsewhere he adds that his grandfather was a descendant of the great Shimon. Tolstoi's *War and Peace* is a more ambitious and elaborate work of the same form. Though a work of fiction, Tolstoi's 'novel' is composed in the form of a family saga, and actually embodies many of the characters and experiences of the families of his own father and mother. With such an example of family history and family fiction before us, we can hardly doubt that family saga, of the type with which we are familiar from early Iceland, was a flourishing form of oral literature in Russia down to the latter half of last century.

All the popular poetry of Russia, and all the saga which can properly be called popular, are anonymous. The reciters are only able to give the names of those from whom they themselves have heard them. The original authors in all cases are absolutely unknown. Even in rare cases where MS. collections have been made by the reciters—a point to which we shall return later—no authors are assigned to the poems. We shall see that a distinction is sometimes drawn in regard to the narrative poems between *babi stariny* and the rest of the *stariny*; but this distinction has reference to the subjects favoured by men and women for recitation, and not to authorship of the poems.

The literature of thought is but scantily represented in Russian oral tradition. Gnomic and didactic poetry can hardly be said to exist, and descriptive poetry is not abundant. Mantic poetry exists,[2] but has not been accessible to us. We doubt, however, if it can be very abundant. Poetry and saga relating to heathen deities are either wholly absent, or have been so transmuted that the divinities have become unrecognisable. The influence of the Church is no doubt responsible for this in Russia, as elsewhere, and we have seen that Christian narrative poetry is abundantly represented. By far the largest proportion of Russian popular poetry, however, consists of poetry relating to well-known heroes and historical characters, and to nameless individuals. Of these categories Russia offers an abundance and range which is probably unparalleled.

---

[1] *Sem. Khron.* p. 1.

[2] A collection of divination and conjuration formulae, ritual poetry, popular drama, etc. is contained in Vol. III of *Russki Folklor*, published by Y. M. Sokolov in 1931 (see List of Abbreviations, *s.v.* Sokolov, *R.F.* at the end of this Part). The work has not been accessible to us, and we are indebted for a notice of the contents to *R.É.S.* XII (1932), p. 257.

The great majority of these poems are narrative in form. Even folk-songs are commonly composed in the form of narrative. Poetry of Type B is not found in relation to the early periods, but makes its appearance in relation to poetry of the sixteenth and following centuries, where it seems to have encroached on elegiac poetry. Type C is practically unknown with the exception of one or two examples relating to Christian learning. Poetry of celebration and elegy is very common, especially in the poetry of social ritual. No examples have survived relating to early times, but the conservative character of the form shows that it is not a new development. Personal poetry of the advanced character of the Greek examples discussed in Vol. 1 is unknown, though personal poetry of a more or less stereotyped form is very common among the modern peasantry. Advanced oral saga is rare, but folk-tales are exceedingly common.

Very little scientific work has been done on the metres of the popular poetry of Great Russia. The metre of all poetry of this kind is identical with that of the *byliny*. In modern studies of the history and provenance of the *byliny* the subject is generally silently ignored. Three studies of metre are cited in Prof. Mazon's Bibliography of useful works on the *byliny*;[1] but the first (by Korš) dates from 1897, while the third, published at Leningrad in 1925, consists of only five pages. These unfortunately have not been accessible to us. Speranski, writing in 1917,[2] recognised the importance of the study of native music for the proper understanding of metre, and the insufficiency of the data relating to such music. Fortunately these data have since been increased by the recent expedition of the Sokolovs to the reciters in north Russia, in the neighbourhood of Lake Onega. Their results have not as yet, however, so far as we are aware, been made available to the general public.[3]

Those who have heard the *byliny* recited generally describe them as a kind of rhythmical chant. The lines vary to some extent in length within the poem, but on the whole they tend to be composed in approximately equal length throughout. For example, we may refer to one *bylina* relating to the healing of the great hero, Ilya of Murom, recorded by Kirêevski[4], which is composed of long lines, while the lines of

[1] Mazon, *Bylines*, p. 694.
[2] See *R.U.S.* p. 139.
[3] Our efforts to obtain specimens of their phonograph records from Moscow have not been successful.
[4] Kirêevski, i. p. 1; translated by Chadwick, *R.H.P.* p. 57 ff.

another *bylina* on the Tatar *bashkak* or tax-collector Shchel Kan Dudentevich,[1] are much shorter. It is interesting to note that different localities favour different lengths of line. Poems obtained to the east of Lake Onega, e.g. from the district of Pudoga, are generally composed in short lines of 5 or 6 syllables, whereas the same poem to the west of the lake is generally in long lines of 8 or 9. Rhyme is wholly absent from the *byliny*.

Gilferding distinguished three types of singers of *byliny*:[2]

(1) singers who accurately observe a regular metre in every *bylina*;

(2) singers who observe metre, but not always accurately;

(3) singers who in general do not observe metre.

A certain amount of variation appears to exist between the metres of the *byliny* according as they are sung or recited. In the latter case it was noted by Gilferding that the metre almost entirely disappeared. It has also been observed that I. T. Ryabinin, in reciting *byliny*, frequently abandoned the metrical form for several lines consecutively, reciting in pure prose. He appears to have done this more especially in reciting the speeches of his characters. It may be noted that I. T. Ryabinin recited a generation later than Gilferding's minstrels, and probably represents a more advanced stage in the metrical disintegration. It is this breakdown in the metres, resulting in prose paraphrases of the *byliny*, which gives us a unique form of heroic saga in Russia—the *pobyvalshchiny* or prose versions of *byliny*, in which the poetic diction and conventions are preserved intact.

Although the character of the metre cannot be said to be established,[3] it is impossible to doubt that metre in some form exists. The *byliny* are quite different from ordinary prose, and their rhythmical character at once becomes apparent if we compare them, e.g., with these *pobyvalshchiny* or 'broken-down' *byliny*. The following points are not without significance for determining the metrical character of the *byliny*:

(1) There is a rough approximation in the length of the phrases, unless they are swelled by the addition of (*a*) adjectives, (*b*) nouns joined by a conjunction, (*c*) particles; i.e. the 'sentence ideas' are roughly equal in length.

(2) Such equality is obtained by the general use of simple, and the avoidance of compound, sentences.

---

[1] Kirêevski, v. p. 186 ff.; translated by Chadwick, *R.H.P.* p. 57 ff.

[2] Gilferding, I, p. 41.

[3] For some general observations on this point the reader may consult Gilferding, I. p. 39 ff.; Lyatski, p. 25 ff.; Magnus, *Ballads*, p. 14 ff.

(3) When a sentence or phrase would fall short of the normal length, it is frequently made up to the norm by repetition in the first half of the sentence of the closing half of the preceding sentence.

(4) When lists are recited, or words or sentences repeated, they are not given, as they would be in prose, in the briefest possible form, but each item is drawn out by the repetition of superfluous words, till the item represents the normal line length. This is not a natural prose convention. It suggests that

(5) The line length is governed by some mechanical agency, such as musical cadence; and it is in a scientific investigation of the musical accompaniment that we shall probably find the key to the *byliny* metres.

(6) We may note that the term regularly in use for reciting a *bylina* is *pêt*, lit. 'to sing'. All recorders habitually speak of the *byliny* as sung, and several attempts have been made to record the tunes which accompany them. This 'singing' or 'chanting' of the *byliny* is the more remarkable as no instrument is in use in modern times in north Russia. To this subject we shall return later.

The break-down of metres appears to go hand in hand with the deterioration in musical accomplishment. Although the *byliny* are now sung without accompaniment in the north, it may be doubted if this was always so. The loss of the instrumental accompaniment may have been partly caused by the poverty of the singers, and the consequent lowering of standard and disintegration of the poetry. We are told that the airs generally possess a certain monotony, the variety in the performance being obtained by the amount of expression put into it by the singers. Even the best singers have generally only one or two tunes. Yet there are exceptions, and Yakushkov, perhaps the greatest of all the singers, knew a different tune to almost every *bylina*, and of the latter he had the largest répertoire on record. The evidence as a whole, therefore, suggests that Russian popular music has riches in store for the investigator.[1]

The importance of the musical accompaniment in regard to metre is strikingly attested by Gilferding's experience among the Olonets reciters. Seeking out Abram Evtikhiev, who had formerly sung the *bylina* of Mikhailo Potyk to Rybnikov, he followed with Rybnikov's printed text while the *skaʒitel* sang him his *bylina*.

"I was amazed by the difference, not in the subject matter of the narrative, but in the versification. In the written text metrical structure is expressed only by the dactylic endings of the line; inside the line there

[1] Speranski, *R.U.S.* p. 139 f.

is no sort of metre whatever. Yet when Abram Evtikhiev sang there was clearly discernible, not only the musical cadence of the air, but also the fact that the line consisted of feet marked by tonic accents. I resolved to write down the *bylina* afresh; the *ska\u0173itel* offered to recite (*ska\u0173at*) it to me word by word (*po slovesno*) without song."

Gilferding then wrote down the *bylina* of Mikhailo Potyk; the metre had disappeared, leaving nothing but broken prose like that of Rybnikov's version.

"I tried to arrange this disjointed (*rublennaya*) prose into lines (*stikhi*), making the *ska\u0173itel* sing it repeatedly; but this proved impracticable because... the reciters alter the *bylina* to some extent with every fresh recitation, transposing words and passages, now adding, now leaving out some lines, now employing different expressions. Having listened for some days... and made vain efforts to write the *bylina* down perfectly exact, with the metre preserved, as it is sung, I tried to get my rhapsodist friend to sing (and not to recite merely by words) the *bylina*, with such pauses between each line that it could be written down. This was easily explained to Abram Evtikhiev, and I once more attempted to write down his *bylina*. The air preserved the poetical metre... and the *bylina* got on to paper as it was actually sung."

Gilferding tried the same plan with the other singers and almost always with success.[1]

It has been observed that in northern Russia, and more especially in Olonets, Russian oral poetry has generally been sung in modern times without musical accompaniment. No instrument is in use to accompany the *byliny* or *stikhi*. Elsewhere in Russia, however, musical instruments[2] are still in use, and in the south and west the *kalêki* still sing *stikhi* to the accompaniment of the lyre and the *bandura*. The latter is a kind of lute, or large fiddle with more than twenty strings, played with an arched bow, which is said to have been introduced into Little Russia from Poland in the sixteenth century.

The instrument frequently referred to in the *byliny* as in use by the heroes of Kiev and Novgorod is the *gusli*, a kind of recumbent harp, played on the knees. It is now extinct in Great Russia.[3] Its place has

---

[1] Gilferding, I. p. 39 ff.

[2] An account of the musical instruments in use in Russia today and in the past, together with a number of illustrations, will be found in Lavignac, p. 2486 ff.

[3] An interesting account of the Russian *gusli* and a series of pictures of the instrument will be found in an article by Väisänen. See the List of Abbreviations at the close of this Part, *s.v.*

been taken in many parts by the three- or four-stringed *balalaika*, a kind of guitar with a triangular box, which is played by plucking the strings with the fingers.

The airs to which the *byliny* are sung, like the metres, still await scientific investigation. Unfortunately the music has hitherto completely baffled musical experts. The article by Delange and Malherbe in Lavignac's *Encyclopédie de la Musique*, Vol. v, Pt. i, p. 2486ff. contains some interesting specimens of folk-tunes and notes on Russian peasant instruments, but makes no attempt at serious musical analysis or comprehensive treatment. Kirsha Danilov noted down a large number of airs in the collection of *byliny* from Perm, which he made in the eighteenth century, and these are accessible in Sheffer's edition.[1] In 1895 Lyatski also published some tunes recorded from Olonets;[2] but as the system of scales followed by the singers differs widely from that employed in modern systems of notation, it is obvious that such attempts can give only a partial and unsatisfactory idea of the originals. In our own day the Sokolovs have obtained phonograph records from the singing of the peasants of Olonets, which should produce interesting results for the history of Russian music when they are made available.

The evidence of the medieval Russian chronicles suggests that heroic conditions have appeared in different areas of Russia at different periods. While it would be misleading to speak of a Heroic Age of Russia as a whole, we can distinguish a series of Heroic Ages or Heroic Phases with different centres of activity at different periods. The first of which we have record is that of the Scandinavian supremacy, having its centre at Kiev. This was, of course, only one development of the Viking activity, which took place over a great part of northern and western Europe between the eighth and the tenth centuries, and which is generally referred to as the Viking Age. But in Russia, or at least in south Russia, this activity seems to have assumed heroic characteristics, if we may judge from the records. The so-called chronicle of Nestor, more properly known as the Ancient Chronicle,[3] which is our chief authority for the early period of Kiev, has manifestly been composed in the interests of the Scandinavian dynasty, and, in the earlier portions,

---

[1] The edition of Sheffer to which reference is made was published at St Petersburg in 1901.　　　　　　　　　　　　　　　[2] Lyatski, *ad fin.*

[3] For the convenience of western readers references are given throughout to Léger's (French) translation. See the list of abbreviations at the close of this Part, *s.v.* Ancient Chronicle.

appears to have been derived largely from heroic saga or poetry, the spirit of which it has preserved very carefully. As a literal record of fact the early entries of this chronicle leave much to be desired; but they create an impression that heroic conditions prevailed in Kiev at the period to which the early entries relate, and that from this period a large body of heroic tradition survived to be transcribed in the written records at a later date.

The Ancient Chronicle covers, roughly speaking, the period from the middle of the ninth to the fourteenth century, and it is to this period, and more especially to the earlier portion, that the heroic traditions of Kiev are ascribed by the annalist. In the oral poetry of Russia these heroic traditions are centred in Prince Vladimir of Kiev—whether Vladimir I (980–1015), or Vladimir II (1113–1125). It is an interesting fact, however, that already in the time of Vladimir I a definite movement was made in the direction of civilisation by the adoption of Christianity in the year 988. At the same time, the marriage of the Prince with a Greek wife must have introduced a considerable amount of Greek culture into the country. Heroic traditions, nevertheless, seem to have flourished at Kiev down to a much later date. Moreover the internal family relations of the ruling dynasty, and the political relations of Kiev with the northern cities show little or no advance beyond heroic conditions, and such temporary advances as were made from time to time by the more enlightened rulers were checked by the Tatar inroads from the south, notably the invasion by the Pechenegs in the time of Vladimir I, and that by the Polovtsy in the eleventh and twelfth centuries. The disturbed conditions consequent upon the Tatar menace must have tended to foster and revive the heroic elements in the community, which evidently persisted down to the Tatar invasion of 1228 and the sack of Kiev in 1240.

During the period of the supremacy of Kiev there also existed a number of city states in northern and central Russia, some of them nominally dependent on Kiev, others virtually independent, and struggling for regional supremacy according to the rank, ambition, and ability of their rulers. Among others we may mention Chernigov, Suzdal, Pskov, Ryazan, Tver, Vladimir. Each of these communities was no doubt at some period a small centre of heroic activity. We shall see in the chapter on 'Historical and Unhistorical Elements' that some of the heroic stories originally belonging to these cities have at a subsequent period been adopted into the Cycle of stories associated with early Kiev.

The most important of the cities of northern Russia in the early period was Novgorod. Novgorod had, however, long ago emerged from heroic conditions. A Heroic Age had no doubt existed in Novgorod at an early period, when the Scandinavian Vikings first entered Russia from the north-west and settled Novgorod and Ladoga and the regions to the north. Echoes of this heroic phase, especially relating to the settled areas to the north-east of the Great Lakes, as well as to Scandinavian settlements in Finland, make themselves heard in the Old Norse *Fornaldar Sögur*. But when we first read of Novgorod in the pages of the Russian chronicles she has already left the Heroic Age far behind, and become a rich trading community, with distant colonies and outposts reaching as far as the White Sea in the north and the province of Tobolsk in Siberia in the east, and possessing a cosmopolitan population, and an advanced and highly individual constitution. Nominally she owed fealty to Kiev (from c. 880–1169); but she had long resented interference from the southern state on the Dnêpr. During most of this time the Grand Prince of Kiev appointed rulers to Novgorod, but not infrequently her proud citizens 'made their bow and showed them the road'. When the Grand Prince Svyatopolk proposed to appoint his son as prince of Novgorod against the will of her citizens they said promptly: "Send him here if he has a spare head!" They styled themselves "My lord Novgorod the Great" (*Gospodín veliki Novgorod*), and the question used to be asked humorously: "Who can stand against God and my lord Novgorod?" If we may judge by the written records, the economic conditions of Novgorod seem to be considerably in advance of those of Kiev at the beginning of the historical period; but here again the 'heroic' and partisan character of the Ancient Chronicle may be misleading.

The long struggle between royal Kiev and mercantile Novgorod came to an end in 1228. In this year the disruption of Kiev, which was already far advanced owing to incessant struggles with neighbouring princes, was completed by the disastrous defeat of the Russians at the hands of the Tatars on the River Kalka. Novgorod, on the other hand, was sheltered behind her marshes, and so was spared the Tatar scourge. She was the only Russian city of consequence which remained immune.

But a new power was coming into being in the east in the growing importance of the principality of Moscow. During the earlier periods of Russian history, when the power of Kiev and Novgorod were at their height, Moscow was merely an unimportant little forest-girt city on the

River Moskva, a tributary of the Klyazma,[1] wholly absorbed in petty relations with her mighty western neighbour, Novgorod. Owing, however,
to her favoured geographical position, Moscow had long been receiving
an influx of immigrant agricultural colonists from the devastated areas
round Kiev and elsewhere, and had gradually developed into a political
centre of some consequence. Surrounded by forests which offered unfavourable conditions to the tactics of the mounted Tatars, she was also
admirably placed for communication with the great river systems, the
only roads of Russia. Partly owing to these factors, partly owing to her
central position, and perhaps more than all owing to the politic and
ambitious character of her princes at the time of the Tatar Conquest,
Moscow became virtually the tax-collectors for the Golden Horde, and
did not hesitate to make the most of her position to aggrandise herself
at the expense of the other states. Under a series of able and politic
rulers Moscow gradually emerged to a position of authority over the
rest of the Russian principalities. Her period of military activity was
to follow. In 1378 Dimitri of the Don, Grand Prince of Moscow, won
the first considerable victory over the Tatars on the plain of Kulikovo.
Later, with the conquest of Kazan by Ivan the Terrible in 1552, the
power of the Tatars in Russia was broken. A series of conquests, some
of them earlier, under Ivan III, others to follow later, under Ivan IV,
made the Muscovite kingdom supreme in Russia, and the city of Moscow continued to be the focus and centre of Russian power till the
removal of the capital to St Petersburg under Peter the Great.

[1] The Klyazma is itself a tributary of the Oka, which flows into the Volga.

CHAPTER II

HEROIC POETRY

THE *BYLINY*

SECULAR oral narrative poems (*stariny*, *byliny*) are exceedingly numerous. Scores, if not hundreds, of themes and stories occur, most of them in several variant forms. The subjects of these poems offer a wider range of motif and treatment than any other literature with which we are familiar. The majority group themselves into Cycles, and these Cycles are associated for the most part with prominent Russian rulers of the past, and the cities in which they lived. All the *byliny* appear to relate to Christian times. It has been commonly supposed that certain poems relating to the so-called 'Older Heroes', date from the heathen period, but, as we shall see later, there is no satisfactory evidence for assigning to them so early a date. The pure narrative form is the one in which these poems are most commonly composed, and indeed it is the only form in which *byliny* relating to the earlier periods are found. The majority of the *byliny* are heroic in style, but non-heroic elements are numerous and pervasive.

The relationship of the form of the *bylina* to the story, of story to version, of both story and version to the group of stories connected with a particular hero, and again of this group to the Cycle in which it occurs, is a complicated one, and it is perhaps in this relationship that the oral poetry of Russia differs most essentially from that of the Yugoslavs. It is not merely that the tone or 'tendency'—the signs of the milieu in which a *bylina* has taken form—may vary indefinitely. The shape and scope of any given *bylina* also admit of almost indefinite variation. While one *bylina* may consist of a single incident, related elaborately and at length, and rounded off, another *bylina* may consist of a variant version of this incident, together with other incidents leading up to it or arising from it. A third may relate a totally different series of incidents associated with the same hero. Yet another may relate a whole cycle of stories associated with him, narrated in more or less summary form, according to the length of a *bylina*, and the memory, or mood, or skill of the reciter. These incidents may be organically connected with one another; but they may, on the other hand, be more or less independent.

In the latter cases, the only unity is supplied by the person of the hero. They are stories of a person rather than of events. Indeed every hero of the great Cycles relating to the earlier periods is himself the centre of a group of stories from which the reciter selects at pleasure the incidents to be related at each recitation. This aspect of the reciter's art will be considered more fully in the chapters on 'The Texts', and 'Recitation and Composition'.

We will now give some account of the subjects of the *byliny*. These, as we have said, tend to fall into Cycles, associated with particular periods and localities. Of these the Cycle which has generally been considered the earliest in regard to subject is the one which includes the heroes Volga, Mikula, and Svyatogor, with whom also is associated, and partly confused, the Biblical hero Samson. Of the first three nothing appears to be certainly known from other sources. The fourth has undoubtedly borrowed some of his exploits, as well as his name, from the hero of the Old Testament. This group is generally known as the 'Older Heroes'. There is, however, no valid reason for assigning special antiquity to any of them except Samson himself, as we shall see when we come to consider the question of historical elements in the *byliny*. The heroes themselves, and in general the feats which they perform, have their nearest affinities in folk-tales. They have, however, very little in common with one another.

The stories relating to the hero Svyatogor narrate four important incidents in the life of the hero.[1] The story of his marriage is found only in a *pobyvalshchina* (cf. p. 20 above), and in a *bylina* of which the hero's name is Samson. Both these versions are recorded from reciters of the same village. The story, which relates to an intrigue between Svyatogor's wife and Ilya of Murom, is also rare, occurring in three versions only, two of which are in prose, the remaining one in verse. A third story relates how Svyatogor, despite his vast strength, fails to lift a bag carried by his fellow-traveller, which proves, upon examination, to contain the weight of the whole world. Of the seven versions which have been recorded of this story, four are in verse, two in prose, and one partly in verse, partly in prose. Of the fourth story, which relates the death of Svyatogor in a fatal coffin, thirteen versions have been recorded, of which eight are in verse, four in prose, and one partly in verse, partly in prose. Like the *byliny* of Mikula, all these versions, prose and verse alike, belong to the north of Russia in Europe. The motifs of which the

---

[1] A study of the *byliny* relating to Svyatogor, and full references to all versions, has recently been made by A. Mazon, 'Svjatogor ou Saint-Mont le Géant', *R.É.S.* XII (1932), p. 160 ff.

first two stories are composed are found widespread also in folk-tales elsewhere, and both these stories are believed to have been associated with Svyatogor only in recent years.[1] The story of Svyatogor and the bag, and that which relates the death of the hero, are more distinctive and more interesting, though analogies to both are to be found in other literatures, notably in the neighbourhood of the Caucasus.[2] Versions of both have been translated into English.[3] It will be seen that these two stories are of far more frequent occurrence than the two preceding ones, and they are much more frequently found in the form of *byliny* than of prose stories.

The figure of Svyatogor is strangely nebulous, and his origin and identity have hitherto evaded the curious scrutiny of many scholars. He lacks the distinctive personal traits of Mikula the husbandman to whom reference will shortly be made, and who appears as his fellow-traveller in certain versions. On the other hand he is in no sense a heroic figure, though he is brought into close association with Ilya of Murom, and also, sporadically, with other heroes of Kiev and Novgorod, though the two latter associations are obviously adventitious. He resembles the giant of folk-tales, whose character seems to consist wholly of vast strength. He is, indeed, definitely styled a giant (*velikan*)—one of the few supernatural beings who are heroes of *byliny*—and his name is thought to mean '*Holy Mountain*'. The stories associated with him— whether prose or verse—are wholly lacking in local associations or local colour. It is stated in several versions that 'he was not allowed in holy Russia: damp mother earth could not bear his weight'. He dwells

> On the lofty mountains, on the holy mountains,

but his vast strength is a sorrow to him:

> He was heavily burdened, as if with a grievous load;
> He could not control his heroic strength.
> And he threw away his steel club,
> Which vanished out of sight above the clouds,
> And caught it again in his white hand:
> "If I should take to walking on the earth
> I would fasten a ring to heaven,
> I would bind an iron chain to the ring,
> I would drag the sky down to mother earth,
> I would turn the earth on its end,
> And I would confound earth with heaven."[4]

[1] See Mazon, *loc. cit.* p. 176 ff.   [2] *Ib.* pp. 175, 190.
[3] Chadwick, p. 50 ff. Unless otherwise stated, the references to Chadwick throughout the footnotes of this Part are to English translations of the *byliny* cited in the text.
[4] Dormidontov, p. 217; cf. Rybnikov, I. p. 6; etc.

Yet no great achievements are attributed to him in Russian tradition, and all the stories which we possess represent the hero as balked or in some way rendered impotent. The most interesting is the story of his inglorious death. He is represented as journeying with Ilya of Murom and as finding a stone tomb or coffin. Ilya lies down in the coffin, but it does not fit him. Svyatogor in turn lies down in it to test it, but once the lid is lowered it can never again be raised. The giant breathes some power into Ilya before he dies which suggests that he may have been regarded in the light of a magician; but we are told that had he been allowed to breathe with his full dying force his breath would have been death to the hero. Professor Mazon suggests that this malicious attempt of the dying giant on the life of his companion allows us to suspect that in the original version of the story Svyatogor had been imprisoned in the tomb by some trick or act of bad faith on the part of Ilya.

Another hero who is generally classed in the so-called early group is Mikula Selyaninovich, 'Mikula the villager's son'. The principal *bylina* of which Mikula is the subject relates to his exploits as a superb field labourer and ploughman. The characteristic features of this hero are his tremendous strength and his knowledge of husbandry and agriculture. He is a typical 'strong peasant'. This *bylina*[1] has been found only in the north of Russia in Europe. It is recorded in four important versions, and some thirteen versions which are either inferior or fragmentary. Of the four principal versions, the one recited by Kasyanov, the 'educated' (*gramotny*) *skazitel*, to Gilferding[2] is held to be the most complete, if not the best, while of the other three, two are recorded from the recitation of the elder Ryabinin, and a third, which closely resembles them, from that of his son. The *bylina* recited by the elder Ryabinin to Rybnikov has been translated into English.[3] We will therefore give here a short account of the version of Kasyanov. It will be seen that his version does not differ greatly from those of Ryabinin and his son.

The *bylina* opens with an account of the birth of another hero, Volga Svyatoslavovich, and tells of his early education in shape-changing and animal lore. After he has collected a *druzhina*[4] he rides over the open plain to take possession of his cities, and as he does so he hears the grating of a plough against the stones. For two days he follows the

[1] For a recent study of this *bylina* and an account of the extant versions, see an article by A. Mazon, 'Mikula le Prodigieux Laboureur', *R.É.S.* xi. p. 149.

[2] Gilferding, ii. p. 517 ff.   [3] Chadwick, p. 44 ff.

[4] This is the name of the group of personal attendants and immediate followers, especially military followers, of the Russian princes in early times.

sound, but cannot come up with the ploughman. At last on the third day he succeeds in overtaking him. The appointments of the plough are fine and costly, and the mare is a superb steed. The ploughman himself has curly hair which falls about his shoulders like pearls; he has bright eyes like those of a falcon, and sable brows, and he wears green morocco shoes with high heels and pointed toes, and a robe of brocade. Volga hails him and tells him that he is riding to take possession of three cities which have been bestowed on him by Prince Vladimir—Kurtsovets, Orêkhovets, and Krestyanovets. Mikula warns him that the citizens are unfriendly and have destroyed the foundations of the bridge leading to the town. He tells him that he was there three days ago buying salt, and the citizens demanded an extortionate price for it: but he gave them a drubbing. Volga at once invites Mikula to join him as travelling companion, and Mikula consents, and proceeds to unharness his mare from the plough. Mikula desires that his plough be thrown behind a bush for the use of peasants and countrymen, but five of Volga's *druzhina* cannot lift it, nor even ten; even the whole twenty-nine cannot move it. But the ploughman seizes it lightly in one hand and flings it behind the bush and rides away. His mare moves forward at an easy pace, while Volga's horse gallops, yet cannot keep up with him. Volga cries out to Mikula that if his mare had been a horse he would have offered him five hundred roubles for it. Mikula replies that he gave that price for the mare as a young foal; had it been a horse it would have been priceless. Volga then enquires the name of his ploughman companion, and they ride together to the city of Kurtsovets. The occupants of the city are astonished at the transformation of their visitor who only three days before had been a 'muzhik', and they approach him bowing low and making excuses for their previous conduct. Then Volga turns to Mikula and appoints him his governor in the three cities, bidding him collect the tribute. It may be observed that this incident is absent from the versions of Ryabinin and his sons; but it is the logical conclusion of the preceding incidents, and probably formed a part of the original story.

Professor Mazon holds that this *bylina* is wrongly entitled Volga and Mikula, and that it should rather be 'Mikula the stupendous labourer' (*Mikula le prodigieux laboureur*), since Mikula is obviously the hero. There can be no question that in its final redaction the *bylina* is primarily concerned with the glorification of Mikula. Yet Volga is equally essential to the story, which would fall to pieces without him. The point is of some importance since it affects the relationship of this *bylina* to the one next to be considered. The following points should therefore be noted as significant: (1) In the *bylina* of Volga and Mikula the figure of Volga is constant. The only exception,[1] which occurs in one of the versions of secondary value,[2] is obviously due to inadvertence; (2) The *bylina* almost invariably opens with an account of the birth and early training of Volga. Professor Mazon suggests that this opening has been transferred from the *bylina* of Volga next to be considered, but if this is the case, the consistency with which this transference is effected itself requires explanation; (3) The picture of Volga is distinctive, unique, and consistent. It is remote from the figure of folk-tale, or the 'type', such as is usually found when it is thought necessary to supply a framework for the principal hero; (4) In the best versions of the *bylina* (those of Ryabinin and Kasyanov) Mikula at once recognises Volga and addresses him by name, whereas Volga has to enquire the name of the ploughman—surely an admission that the former rather than the latter belongs to the original nucleus of the *bylina*. For these and other reasons which will appear presently, it would seem reasonable to regard the part of Volga in this *bylina* as integral and significant.

In addition to the *bylina* of Volga and Mikula, there is one other *bylina* in which Volga plays an important rôle. Here, indeed, he is the sole hero, and the *bylina* is devoted wholly to the story of his intellectual gifts and protean character on the one hand, and to his practical exploits on the other. The versions of this *bylina* are, so far as we know, all derived from the north of Russia in Europe and from Perm. They are not numerous, and differ very little from one another. The most important is the version recited by Ryabinin to Rybnikov and Gilferding. The former has been translated into English.[3] It relates the birth of the hero, and, like most versions of this *bylina*, and of that which relates to Volga's comradeship with Mikula, it takes note of the state of the elements and external nature at the time of Volga's birth, as if these bore some special relationship to the character or mental and spiritual endowments of the hero. Even in his youth the birds and beasts flee from him in terror, and as he grows up he learns all tongues and all handicrafts, and becomes proficient in supernatural wisdom. He collects a brave *druzhina* of twenty-nine bold youths, and orders them to hunt and snare wild creatures; but the *druzhina* are unsuccessful in their efforts

---

[1] In the version recited by Lyadkov (Gilferding, III. p. 316 ff.) Ivan Godinovich has been substituted for Volga. [2] See Mazon, *loc. cit.* p. 150.

[3] Chadwick, p. 33 ff. Kirsha Danilov's version is held to be the most perfect example of this *bylina*, but it is incomplete. See Mazon, *R.É.S.* XI. p. 152.

till Volga transforms himself into a lion and rounds up all the animals. Then he orders his *druzhina* to go fowling; but again they are unsuccessful till Volga transforms himself into a bird and flies away to the sky and collects all the birds together. His *druzhina* try fishing, but they catch nothing till Volga transforms himself into a pike and drives together all the other fish. Thus far the hunting of Volga. He next turns his attention to military matters. He wishes to send a messenger to the land of the Turks (or, variously, the Golden Horde), to discover the intentions of the Turkish 'tsar' in regard to Russia; but he comes to the conclusion that none can be trusted to carry out the mission with the requisite speed save himself. Indeed as we read this *bylina* we feel that Mikula is right when he tells Volga that the members of his *druzhina* are a negligible band. He accordingly transforms himself into a bird and flies to the window of the palace of the Turkish 'tsar', and overhears the 'tsar' and 'tsaritsa' arguing as to the advisability of invading Russia. As the 'tsar' seems firm in his intention, despite the dissuasions of the 'tsaritsa', Volga transforms himself into a wolf and tears the throats of the 'tsar's' horses; into an ermine, and ruins his weapons; and finally once more into a bird, and then returns to Russia. Naturally the ensuing battle is an easy victory for Volga and his *druzhina*. In the version in which Volga is represented as flying to the Golden Horde, no battle takes place. When Volga, in the form of a bird, overhears the conversation between the 'tsar' and the 'tsaritsa' in the Golden Horde, he upbraids the 'tsar' roundly and orders him to be gone, and the 'tsar' is fain to return along the road by which he has come.

In the *bylina* of Volga and Mikula the balance is almost equally maintained between the heroic and the non-heroic elements. Despite the supernatural features attributed to Volga at the opening of many versions, he figures throughout the action as a heroic prince devoid of any supernatural power. Mikula, on the other hand, is primarily endowed with the characteristics of a peasant—physical force, speed and skill in husbandry. He is the glorification of the peasant ideal. In the *bylina* devoted wholly to Volga, heroic and non-heroic characteristics are again equally balanced, this time in the person of the hero himself. The non-heroic characteristics are not those of a peasant, however, but resemble closely those of the Siberian shaman. He stands in intimate relationship with the world of nature and the elements. He is full of wisdom, but his wisdom is occult, the supernatural knowledge of nature. Like a shaman he possesses the power of changing himself into all creatures of animate nature, and into whatever order of nature he transforms himself he is supreme. He is also a military chief and a great hunter. In this triple function of shaman, hunter, and heroic chief, Volga stands alone among the heroes of the Russian *byliny*. For analogies we must look to the oral literature of the Turkish and Turko-Finnish and Ostyak tribes of northern Asia, especially those on the western watershed of the Yenisei, whose narrative poetry is contained in the second volume of Radlov's collection; though the nearest actual parallel occurs in the Kara-Kirghiz poem *Joloi* (cf. Vol. III). The affinities of Volga will become clearer when we come to speak of the literature of the Tatars in the following volume.

By far the largest Cycle of *byliny* relates to the district in and around Kiev. The earliest of the heroes to whom a date can be assigned with any probability is Vladimir I, the last of the 'Scandinavian' princes of Kiev, who was baptised in 988, and who was commonly referred to by the historians of last century as the founder of the Russian Empire. Round him by far the largest number of stories are loosely grouped, much as the legends of the knights of the Round Table are grouped round the person of King Arthur. But like King Arthur himself, Vladimir is never the principal figure of the stories, though he is the *Solnyshko* ('Little Sun', or 'Dear Sun')[1] round whom the other planets revolve. The minstrels who composed the *byliny*, however, have not distinguished him from Vladimir Monomakh who died in 1126, and have attributed to the former prince many of the features which belong to the latter. Vladimir I was constantly engaged in hostilities against the Pechenegs, as Vladimir Monomakh was against the Polovtsy. In the *byliny* the enemies are the 'Tatars'.

The poems of this Cycle relate the adventures of the members of Vladimir's *druzhina*, or body of personal followers. They are primarily stories of adventure and of practical action, but incidents and scenes from domestic life are also common. The range of subjects consists for the most part of feasts, journeys, single combats, trials of skill in arms, sports, or horsemanship, acts of insubordination followed by punishment and reconciliation, and expeditions against the Tatars and other neighbouring peoples. Incidents of domestic life are also common, such as courtships, marriages, and infidelities. Quarrels between heroes also

---

[1] The origin of the epithet is unknown, though many derivations have been suggested, mostly of a romantic character. It is perhaps worth remarking that the word 'Sun' is commonly applied to the heroes in Tatar epic poems, as the word 'Moon' is to the heroines, and here the words seem to be used in the sense of 'son' and 'daughter'. We suspect that the Russian epithet is of Tatar origin.

occur as a natural consequence, though they are not common, and rarely very serious. In the combats the object is generally treasure or 'tribute', or else women, or, less frequently, personal aggrandisement. Head-hunting for its own sake is rarely referred to[1]; cattle-raiding, never. Sea voyages on mercantile enterprises, curiously enough, are not rare in the early Cycles. Disguise and impersonation are surprisingly frequent, both by men and women. The element of the marvellous and the superhuman is not rare, but in general it is chiefly confined to exaggeration, and though supernatural elements occur, they are usually subordinate to the heroic narrative of adventure, and to incidents of domestic life. The style of the *byliny* is wholly conventional, however, and there is no attempt at realism.

One of the few *byliny* in which Vladimir himself figures in an important rôle is 'The Marriage of Vladimir'. In the version sung by Chukov[2] Vladimir sends his two brothers, Fedor Ivanovich and Vasili Ivanovich, to woo on his behalf Nastasya, the daughter of the king of Lithuania. In the variant version recorded by Kirsha Danilov[3] from Perm, the emissary is Ivan Gostinoy Syn, one of Vladimir's *druzhina*. The king is not favourable to the match, but when the usual threat is expressed that if his daughter is not given honourably she will be taken ignominiously, his daughter comes out and addresses the messengers from her staircase[4] as follows:

> Greetings, Vasili Ivanovich!
> Greetings, Fedor Ivanovich!
> If you have any sense in your heads,
> You will take my father,
> The beloved king,
> Drag him into the open plain,
> Bury him in the damp earth,
> Bury him to his white breast;
> Perchance the king will then come to his senses,
> Perchance the king will then regain his wits,
> Perchance he will then give me, the princess Nastasya,
> To the Prince Vladimir.

[1] A possible instance is to be found in the version of the slaying of Tugarin the Dragon's Son by Alyosha Popovich recorded by Kirsha Danilov, in which Alyosha is represented as cutting off Tugarin's head, piercing his ears, binding the head to his horse, and bringing it to Kiev, where he flings it into the midst of the royal courtyard. See Kirêevski, II. p. 70 ff.; Hapgood, *Songs*, p. 65.

[2] Rybnikov, I. p. 142.   [3] Kirêevski, III. p. 70 ff.

[4] The external staircase leading to the living apartments, including the women's quarters, on the first floor. The famous 'Red Staircase' in the Kremlin is a survival of this early architectural feature. See Chadwick, plan facing p. 288.

> Although I was never in the city of Kiev,
> Yet I know all its wealth and splendour.
> This Prince Vladimir has
> A gorgeous palace,
> And rich lands;
> Whereas my own father,
> The beloved king,
> Has only a bare dwelling,
> And very poor land
> Very poor land, very unproductive.[1]

At this point the king her father, who has been eaves-dropping behind his oaken doors, comes forward on hearing Nastasya's speech, and urges them to place her on horseback and away forthwith. They bring her to Kiev, and Vladimir meets them in his most precious jewels and his bravest attire. He takes her 'by her white hands, by her gold rings', he lifts her from her mettlesome steed, and kisses and embraces her, and conducts her into his palace of white stone, all gaily decorated. He makes a great feast in her honour, plying the guests till they are replete, and giving wine to the wooers till they can drink no more, and all his subjects begin to boast:

> What a prince is our dear sun Vladimir,
> Vladimir, prince of royal Kiev!
> His like is not in the whole of Russia,
> His like there is not in stone-built Moscow.[2]

The same singer also recited to Rybnikov another *bylina* of Nastasya,[3] relating to her earlier life at her father's court in Lithuania, in which she is represented as saving the life of her lover who is condemned to death by the king for boasting of his familiarity with her.

One of the most important of the heroes of Kiev is Dobrynya Nikitich, who is sometimes represented in the *byliny* as a nephew of Vladimir. He is a man of polished manners and courteous bearing, and is frequently employed by Vladimir on diplomatic missions. The most important of Dobrynya's adventures relates to the slaying of a great dragon with twelve tails, which inhabits a cavern on a river—in some versions the R. Pochay, in others the Smorodina, the Safat, etc. Many

---

[1] Rybnikov, I. p. 144 f.
[2] The last line is a form of anachronism very common in the *byliny*. At the time to which the stories of Kiev relate, Moscow had not yet come into existence. The stone buildings of 'Moscow of the white stone walls' (*bêlokammenaya Moskva*) have made a great impression on Russian singers accustomed only to wooden buildings.
[3] Rybnikov, I. p. 223 ff.

versions of this exploit have been recorded. In the version recited by Chukov to Rybnikov[1] we are told that at the first encounter Dobrynya contents himself with cutting off the dragon's tails and letting it go on a promise of good behaviour in the future. When next he goes to the court of Kiev, however, he learns that the dragon has carried off Zabava Putyatichna, Vladimir's niece, and hidden her in a cavern. Dobrynya makes his way to the cavern, and this time he hews the dragon's body into small pieces.

As he is escorting Zabava back to Kiev he comes upon the tracks of a *polênitsa*, or warrior maiden of great strength, riding in the open plain. He seeks to overcome her, but she seizes him by his yellow curls and twists him from his horse and drops him into her leather pouch. Eventually she grants him his life on condition that he promises to marry her. Her name also is Nastasya. She is the sister of Vasilisa, the warlike wife of Stavr of Chernigov, who visits Vladimir's court (cf. p. 258 below). Her father is generally said to be Mikula Selyaninovich, of whom we have already heard (p. 30 ff. above), though in an alternative version she herself says that she is daughter to the Polish king Mikula.

Bold Alyosha, or Alexander, the 'priest's' son, from Rostov, is one of the most active and prominent members of Vladimir's *druzhina*, though he is not the subject of many independent stories. A rare *bylina*[2] relates how he set out from his own home in Rostov, with the blessing of his father, the priest of the city, and accompanied by his *druzhina*. The party arrives at a point where three roads meet, the first road leading to the city of Kiev, the second to the city of Chernigov,[3] and the third to the blue sea. They decide to avoid Chernigov with its luxuries,[4] and to ride to Kiev to pray in God's churches, and to pay their respects to the holy monasteries. In this way Alyosha comes to be a member of Vladimir's court, where he becomes the sworn brother of Dobrynya Nikitich.

Alyosha proves false to his compact with Dobrynya, and a favourite subject of the *byliny*[5] relates how he comes to Kiev during Dobrynya's absence, and spreads false reports of his death in order to persuade his wife Nastasya to marry him. Nastasya, as she appears in this story, is a

[1] Rybnikov, I. p. 147 ff.; Kirêevski, II. p. 23 ff.

[2] Sokolov, *Byliny*, p. 69 ff.

[3] Chernigov is on the Desna, a left tributary of the Dnêpr. In early times it was one of the most important cities in Russia.

[4] An interesting touch of genuine tradition, since for many centuries Chernigov has been a place of no particular wealth or importance. See note 3 above.

[5] One version is translated by Chadwick, p. 80 ff.

gentle domestic character, and a great contrast to the *polênitsa* or amazon called Nastasya whose wooing by Dobrynya has already been referred to. Alyosha is also the central figure of a small number of *byliny*[1] which are believed to be late, and which belong more properly to the class referred to below (p. 45) as *babi stariny*. In these also he appears in a sinister light. It is clear that the authors of these stories have no love for the 'priest's' son. They represent him as a mocker of women, and as one who loves to smirch their honour and then betray them, holding them up to abuse and punishment. These versions gloat openly when Dobrynya returns to avenge himself, and the 'priest's son' is discomfited.

Alongside this unfavourable portrait of Alyosha, however, there exists also another traditional portrait of a very different kind—one, indeed, which is so directly contradictory in all respects that it is impossible to doubt that the contradiction is deliberate, and that we are dealing with two opposed traditions which have been carefully fostered by schools of reciters with diametrically opposed views and interests in regard to the Church. The most important of all the *byliny* in which Alyosha appears as the central figure is that which relates his exploit in slaying the winged Tugarin Zmêevich, 'the Dragon's son'. And it is important to note, that the fullest, and in every respect the best version of this *bylina* is the one recorded by Kirsha Danilov.[2] This version may be summarised briefly as follows:

As Alyosha Popovich and his servant Ekim Ivanovich ride from Rostov to Kiev they meet a kalêka who tells them that he has seen Tugarin, 'the Dragon's son':

> Tugarin is three *sazhens*[3] high,
> Between his sloping shoulders is a span of one *sazhen*,
> Between his eyes is the width of a tempered arrow,
> The steed beneath him is like a ferocious wild beast,
> From his jaws pour burning flames,
> From his ears issues a column of smoke.

The description is certainly more appropriate to a fiery dragon than a man, though no wings are mentioned here. In the encounter between him and Alyosha which follows, however, Tugarin does not appear other than a human adversary. Alyosha changes clothes with the

---

[1] Kirêevski, II. p. 64 ff.

[2] The text will be found in Kirêevski, II. p. 70. A translation of the first part is given by Chadwick, p. 74 ff.; the whole is paraphrased closely by Hapgood, *Songs*, p. 58 ff.

[3] A Russian *sazhen* is rather more than seven English feet.

kalêka in order to be able to put his unsuspecting enemy off his guard. As he approaches Tugarin he can hardly walk for the noise of his roaring. When Tugarin addresses him, Alyosha bids him come nearer, pretending to be deaf,[1] and suddenly smites him on the head, so that he falls to the damp earth. Tugarin beseeches him to swear brotherhood with him, but Alyosha distrusts him, and cuts off his head; and then, dressing himself in Tugarin's valuable clothes, he sets off to rejoin Ekim and the *kalêka*. Ekim and the *kalêka* are naturally startled at the sight, and slay him, mistaking him for Tugarin. When, however, they discover their error, they revive Alyosha with a 'drink from beyond the seas', and Alyosha and Ekim ride on to Kiev.

Vladimir gives them welcome, and presently twelve mighty heroes bring in Tugarin on a sheet of pure gold, and place him in the most important seat next to the princess Apraxya. Here Tugarin's coarse and gluttonous habits give great offence to Alyosha, and he cannot bide quietly while the Dragon's son takes liberties with the princess:

"My father, the priest of Rostov," cries Alyosha "had an old cow who painfully dragged herself[2] into the kitchen, and drank beer until she burst."

This speech displeases Tugarin. He flings his steel dagger at Alyosha, but Alyosha dodges it, and Ekim catches it, and Alyosha challenges Tugarin to meet him on the following day in single combat.

> Then Tugarin went forth,
> He seated himself on his good steed,
> And soared on his paper wings, flying up to the sky.

Meanwhile Alyosha and Ekim ride forth to the river Safat; but Alyosha spends the whole night in prayer to God, and his prayer is as follows:

> Send, O God, a heavy cloud,
> A heavy cloud, and pouring rain.

And God sends pouring rain which soaks Tugarin's paper wings, so that he falls 'like a dog' to the damp earth. As he glances for a

---

[1] The *kalêki* frequently suffer from some bodily defect.

[2] This seems to be a mocking reference to the disablement which Tugarin has suffered at his hands, which may also account for Tugarin's entry on what appears to be an impromptu stretcher of gold. The latter may, however, be an allusion to the custom among the Tatars and kindred people, according to which a ruler is supposed never to put his foot to the ground. We may refer to the account of the de-nationalised ruler on the Volga in 923 given by the Arabic writer, Ibn Fodlan. It will be noticed that in the *byliny* the episode of the beheading has either been forgotten, or was not intended to be taken literally.

moment behind him—the reason has been omitted in this version [1]—
Alyosha springs forward and cuts off his head—his head which is 'like
a beer kettle'. He pierces his ears and binds the head to his horse and
carries it in triumph to Kiev. Apraxya bemoans the loss of her lover,
but Vladimir rejoices greatly, and takes Alyosha into his service.

A prominent member of the Kiev Cycle is Dyuk Stepanovich from
rich Galicia, whose visit to Vladimir's court is a favourite subject with
the reciters. [2] The story relates that Dyuk comes to Kiev to discover for
himself whether the stories are true which have been told him of the
splendour of the court of Kiev. But he finds the conditions there
inferior in all respects to those of Galicia, and gives himself such airs
in consequence that his behaviour exasperates Vladimir's seneschal
Churilo Plenkovich. Churilo accordingly challenges Dyuk to a competition as to which of them can produce the greatest number of fine
new clothes, and when he finds that he has got the worst of it he again
suggests to Dyuk that they shall each jump across the R. Dnêpr on their
steeds. Dyuk is in despair, for Churilo's steed is a good one, and fresh,
being carefully tended by his groom in his own home, whereas he himself has only a jaded mount in Kiev. His steed, however, bids him take
heart, promising to carry him across the Dnêpr on invisible equine
wings, and so he does. With a single equine bound he leaps across the
river and a whole *verst* [3] beyond, while Churilo falls splash into the midst
of the river, and Dyuk has to return and gallantly pull out his discomfited rival by his golden curls.

It is curious that the *bylina* of Dyuk should be one of the most popular
among the singers. The hero is a foreigner whose consistent attitude is
that of contempt for all that he finds at Kiev. His defeated rival and
opponent is a member of the court, though only a temporary one. It is
not easy from the story, as we have it, to see how the scornful boaster
has succeeded in so greatly endearing himself to the minstrels whose
heroes are the subjects of his scorn. There is, however, another rare
bylina in which quite a different motive is assigned for Dyuk's visit to
Kiev. In this *bylina*, recorded by Rybnikov, [4] we are told that Dyuk
comes to Kiev with the express purpose of fighting Shark Velikan, a
terrible foe to Russia. Shark Velikan is described as a monster pouring

---

[1] The reason generally given is a deceitful remark by Alyosha. It will be noticed
that our version is favourable to Alyosha throughout, and the incident is accordingly
suppressed.
[2] One version is translated by Chadwick, p. 101 ff.
[3] A *verst* is about two-thirds of a mile.
[4] Rybnikov, II. p. 697 ff.

out scorching flames on the Christian heroes, mincing them with his steel sword, and trampling them underfoot with his iron clad feet. When Dyuk catches sight of him his spirited heart grows faint, and his heroic steed draws back; but he bravely accepts Shark Velikan's challenge to single combat, and, having prayed to God, he succeeds in overcoming him.

It has been suggested[1] that this *bylina* has been borrowed from some MS., and that to some extent it shows literary characteristics. Yet some such story as this would more satisfactorily account for Dyuk's presence at Kiev than the motive of mere curiosity. Moreover Rybnikov has preserved another *bylina* of Shark Velikan[2] in which Churilo Plenkovich is represented as his friend and guest. Such a tradition, taken in connection with the one above referred to, would account for the unexplained enmity between Dyuk and Churilo. It is not easy, without such traditions, to explain why, from among all the heroes of Vladimir's court, it should be only Churilo, the unwilling temporary seneschal, who should concern himself to vindicate the honour of Kiev against the wealthy stranger from Galicia; or why the haughty foreigner should have endeared himself to minstrels devoted to the heroes of Kiev.

One of the most interesting, and surely the most fantastic of the *byliny*, is that which relates to Mikhailo Potyk. The story is very popular among the reciters, as we may see from the large number of versions on record. We will give here as briefly as possible the version recited by Kalinin to Gilferding,[3] which is one of the best and fullest. Later, when we come to the chapter on 'The Texts', a brief summary will be given of the variant version of the *bylina* recorded by Kirsha Danilov.

At a great feast Vladimir gives commissions to Ilya of Murom, Dobrynya Nikitich, and Mikhailo Potyk[4] to go each on a separate expedition to collect the tribute which has long been overdue. The three set off, and at the parting of their ways they swear brotherhood together, promising to meet at the same spot when they have executed their commissions. Mikhailo sets off to Poland, and having collected the tribute by force of arms, he proceeds to take his pleasure on the river, shooting geese and swans with his arrows. He catches sight of a

---

[1] See editor's footnote to the text, Rybnikov, *loc. cit.*
[2] Rybnikov, ii. p. 701 ff.   [3] Gilferding, i. p. 63 ff.
[4] In the version from the R. Kolyma in north-eastern Siberia, Mikhailo's companions are Dobrynya Nikitich, Sukhan Domantevich, and Alyosha Popovich. Miller, *Byliny*, p. 205 ff.

white swan and draws his bow; but the swan cries out and begs him to
spare her, declaring that she is no swan but a fair maiden, Marya of
Poland, the daughter of the Polish king, and willing to be received into
the Orthodox Church and to become his bride. Mikhailo accordingly
returns to Kiev with Marya and the tribute, and the marriage is duly
celebrated. It is a curious fact that in this and other versions of the
bylina it is Marya herself who insists on her change of faith. At the
wedding the pair swear a mutual oath that whichever of them shall die
first, the other will accompany the corpse into the tomb alive, and remain
there for three months.

Shortly afterwards Tsar Bukhar from beyond the sea comes to levy
tribute from Vladimir. Mikhailo goes to meet him and plays at chess
with him, the tsar staking among other things the tribute due to him,
while Mikhailo stakes the White Swan. Mikhailo wins the stakes, but
as they are playing Dobrynya enters and announces that the White
Swan is dead. Mikhailo accordingly returns to Kiev and orders a
chambered tomb to be constructed, with room inside to sit, or stand, or
lie down; and he furnishes it with torches and bread and water to last
for three months; and taking with him iron tongs, and three iron rods,
he goes inside, into the 'damp earth' for three months. Other versions
add that Mikhailo's steed also enters the mound with him, and that
afterwards yellow sand is heaped over the tomb, and grass sods are laid
over all. And when it grows dark the hero lights a wax torch and waits.
On the second day of his vigil a monstrous snake glides up with twelve
little snakes about her tail. He seizes the monster snake with his tongs,
and beats it with his rods till it promises to bring the water of life to
restore his White Swan. On her return he sprinkles Marya three times
with the precious water, and on the third occasion she wakens, crying
"Fu, fu, fu, what a long sleep I have had!" Thereupon Mikhailo cries
out so loudly that he is heard in the city, and his companions come and
dig him out of the damp earth.

Before long the White Swan sends a secret invitation to the prince of
Lithuania to come and carry her away. When Mikhailo hears of her departure, he disguises himself as a woman and follows the fugitives, but
Marya recognises him and presents him with a goblet of magic wine
which turns him to stone. Three years pass by, and Mikhailo's sworn
brothers, Ilya and Dobrynya, set off to seek him, and in the guise of
kaléki, or itinerant religious singers, they visit the Lithuanian prince,
accompanied by a genuine *kaléka* whom they meet on the way. Marya
recognises them, and by her advice they are received hospitably; but

when they ask Marya for Mikhailo Potyk, she replies that she also mourns for him, and that she does not know what has become of him. They set out for Kiev, and on the way they pause beside the stone figure of Mikhailo to divide the wealth which the prince has bestowed on them. The heroes are surprised to find that the *kalêka* is dividing the wealth into four parts. They question him, and he says that the fourth portion is for him who shall raise the stone. Ilya and Dobrynya each essay it in vain, but the old *kalêka* lifts it without difficulty, saying: "Where the stone stood, let Mikhailo Potyk Ivanovich stand!" The stone splits asunder, and there stands Mikhailo Potyk. The *kalêka* bids him build two churches as a thank offering, and then departs; but Mikhailo again sets off to the king of Poland, disguised as an aged *kalêka*. Again Marya offers him wine, and again his old love of drinking proves his undoing, for he empties the goblet and falls in a stupor, and Marya drags him into a cellar and nails him to the wall. But she has only four nails, and a fifth nail is needed for his heroic heart, so Marya runs off very, very quickly to the market to buy a fifth nail. Meanwhile Nastasya, the king's daughter, draws out the nails, carefully nailing a Tatar to the wall in Mikhailo's place and removing Mikhailo to her private apartment. Marya on her return does not notice the exchange, and drives the nail through the heart of the Tatar. Meanwhile Mikhailo recovers, and takes Nastasya to Kiev where she is converted to his faith and becomes his bride. Mikhailo, moreover, fulfils his promise to the *kalêka* and builds two large churches. And so ends the '*starina*' of Mikhailo Potyk Ivanovich.

We have dwelt somewhat at length on this *bvlina* or '*starina*' because we shall have occasion to refer to it later. Meanwhile it will be observed that while heroic in framework and in style, it also contains a considerable proportion of non-heroic elements. It is obvious that Mikhailo Potyk depends for his success more on his wits than his prowess. He never fights, though he beats and hangs the Polish muzhiks, and is ready to cut off his wife's head. He cheats the Tatars, and gets the better of Tsar Bukhar by luck and guile. In some versions, it is true, he cuts off the heads of forty princes who come to steal his wife; but he deals with them seriatim, catching each one unawares and by guile. He cheats his wife of a part of their death compact. His most glorious feat is catching her unawares in her swan disguise and carrying her off to Kiev. He is a confirmed drunkard in this version, and is only saved from utter destruction by the good offices of a *kalêka* and a woman.

The theme of the *bylina* also is predominantly non-heroic. The central point of the original story would seem to be the death compact and the double burial, and Marya's resuscitation. This is the event which brings forty princes to seek her in marriage, since it is believed she cannot die twice. Moreover Marya is herself an essentially 'non-heroic' figure. She can change herself into a swan; she is learned in drugs, and an enchantress, as we see from her treatment of her husband. The only figure in the *bylina* whose power exceeds her own is the *kalêka*, and it is interesting to note that he succeeds where Ilya and Dobrynya have also failed. Whatever the origin of the *bylina*, there can be no doubt that ecclesiastical influence has made itself felt on the story in its present form.

The principal hero of early times and the favourite alike of reciters and audience is Ilya of Murom, whose life is spent in warfare against the enemies of Russia. He is somewhat of a free-lance, and not permanently attached to Vladimir's *druzhina*, though he is constantly associated in his exploits with the heroes of Kiev. He is also constantly referred to as the 'peasant's son', and the 'Old Cossack'. The *byliny* are not in entire agreement in this, however, as we shall see later. Ilya is always represented as possessing a horse and weapons which is hardly consistent with peasant rank. On the other hand he is only rarely represented with a personal attendant or a *druzhina*, and in a *bylina* which relates to his youth[1] his parents are said to be absent in the forest felling trees. This *bylina* relates that in his youth Ilya was feeble or paralysed for thirty-three years, till one day Christ and two apostles come to him disguised as *kalêki perekhozhie*, or itinerant religious singers. They bestow strength upon him, and bid him go forth to fight as a great warrior, prophesying that he will not die in battle.

One of the favourite stories of Ilya[2] relates to his journey from his parents' home in Murom to Vladimir's court at Kiev, and his encounter with Solovey the Robber, whom he overcomes and binds to his stirrup, and takes as a prisoner to Kiev. Although frequently found at the court of Kiev, Ilya is not always on good terms with Vladimir. Another *bylina*[3] relates that Vladimir omits to invite Ilya to a feast, and that in consequence the Old Cossack goes through Kiev despoiling the churches of their gold ornaments, till Vladimir succeeds in conciliating him by the most assiduous attentions.

The heroes of the Kiev Cycle are constantly represented as on good terms with the *kalêki*, and as effecting a temporary exchange of garments

---

[1] Kirêevski, I. p. I ff.; Chadwick, p. 57 ff.
[2] Rybnikov, I. p. 15 ff.; Chadwick, p. 66 ff.
[3] Gilferding, II. p. 38 ff.; Chadwick, p. 61 ff.

with them in order to carry out their enterprises in disguise. An interesting example is the story—found in numerous versions—of the encounter of Ilya of Murom with Idolishche, in which we are told that Ilya exchanges garments with a *kalêka*, and goes to Jerusalem to slay Idolishche who is destroying the Holy City and bullying the Emperor Constantine. We have already seen that a similar disguise is effected by Alyosha Popovich in the *bylina* relating to his encounter with Tugarin the dragon's son (cf. p. 38 f. above). By means of this disguise he is able to approach his unsuspecting enemy at close quarters. In most versions of the story of Mikhailo Potyk, Ilya and his sworn brother Dobrynya Nikitich disguise themselves as *kalêki* in order to visit the Lithuanian prince. The motif is an interesting symbol of the history of these *byliny*, whose heroic origin is thus effectively disguised in a non-heroic garb. By this means the martial achievements are transformed into deeds of guile, and the heroes themselves are made directly dependent on the good will and assistance of their ecclesiastical allies.

Rybnikov refers [1] to certain of the *byliny* as *babi stariny*, which he says the women are specially fond of singing, but which are less popular among male singers. The examples which he cites from the Kiev Cycle are Churilo Plenkovich and Katerina Mikulichna, generally known as 'The Death of Churilo'; Khoten Bludovich; and Ivan Godinovich. Examples from later Cycles are Dimitri Vasilevich and Domna Aleksandrovna; Prince Mikhailo; Kastryuk; and Grishka and Marina. The name *babi stariny* recalls the *ženske pjesme* of the Yugoslavs, but the two classes seem to have little in common, since the latter denotes chiefly stories approximating to folk-tales in character, and resembling them also in that the heroes are, in general, virtually unnamed. Rambaud, in referring to this passage from Rybnikov, translates the phrase as "vieilles histoires de femmes", and adds that they are stories in which "les femmes jouent en effet un rôle plus important, et qui, sans perdre tout à fait le caractère épique, touchent cependant au fabliau".[2]

Actually, *babi stariny* more probably signifies 'women's stories', i.e. stories favoured by women, rather than stories about women. Some of the examples cited, such as the 'Death of Churilo Plenkovich' approximate to the *fabliau*. On the other hand in other examples of *babi stariny*, such as the story of Kastryuk, the feminine interest is reduced to the minimum. It may be pointed out also that all the '*babi stariny*' of the Kiev Cycle cited here by Rybnikov, as well as the *starina*, or *bylina* of Kastryuk, are favourite subjects among the male singers also, as is

[1] Rybnikov, I. p. lxxxii. [2] *R.É.* p. 10.

shown by the number of versions recorded in Rybnikov's own collection. On the whole, therefore, it would seem that no exclusive class of poems is indicated by Rybnikov's remark, but merely the fact that the women tend to favour stories and versions in which feminine interests are prominent, and that some of the male singers tend to deprecate these subjects in favour of sterner stuff. Perhaps we need not press the examples too far.

Recent researches carried on by the Sokolov brothers in the country formerly traversed by Rybnikov and Gilferding have tended to confirm Rybnikov's observations in regard to *babi stariny*. The Sokolovs found that the proportion of women reciters has greatly increased in recent years, and they recorded a corresponding increase in the number of *byliny*, or versions of *byliny*, in which feminine interest predominates:

"La voilà entrée dans le répertoire féminin, qui se compose surtout de chansons lyriques et de chansons de mœurs, et auquel l'épopée est étrangère: elle n'y trouvera guère sa place dans la mesure où elle s'inspire d'une tradition belliqueuse et héroïque."

The orientation of interest in the *byliny*, they tell us, has changed accordingly:

"Ce sont les bylines de contenu romanesque, réalistes, familières, souvent du type des fabliaux, qui ont la faveur du moment, et non pas, il fallait s'y attendre, les bylines racontant les exploits héroïques des bogatyrs.... Il est instructif de constater que la byline de Salomon et Vasily Okulovich, celle de l'enlèvement de la femme de Salomon, toute pleine d'intrigues et d'aventures, est entièrement absente du recueil de Hilferding, alors que nous en avons entendu, pour notre part, 11 variantes. La byline héroïque de Dobrynja et le Dragon, cédant à la même tendance, a visiblement perdu de sa popularité: nous n'en avons recueilli que 4 versions contre 9 de Hilferding."[1]

We will give here a brief account of three of Rybnikov's '*babi stariny*' belonging to the Kiev Cycle.

The *bylina* of Ivan Godinovich is an interesting instance of a story composed wholly of the elements which go to make a typical heroic narrative. The story is preserved in many versions, which only differ slightly from one another in points of detail. In the version recited by Trofim Romanov to Rybnikov,[2] Ivan Godinovich, who is here and elsewhere represented as Vladimir's nephew,[3] relates at a royal feast in

[1] Sokolov, 'À la Recherche des Bylines', *R.É.S.* (1932), p. 207 ff.
[2] Rybnikov, II. p. 326 ff.
[3] Cf. the version recited by Nikifor Prokhorov, II. p. 116 ff.

Kiev that he has been 'across the glorious blue sea' to the city of Chernigov, to the white-stone palace of the merchant Dimitri to woo his daughter Nastasya, but that he has received a refusal. He begs four hundred men and golden treasure wherewith to make a second offer, and again he departs to Chernigov, only to be again refused. This time, however, he is determined, and he makes his way to Nastasya's apartment and carries her off by force. As he is departing with his bride, Dimitri the merchant comes out and tells him that his daughter is already espoused to Koshchey the Immortal, who will cut off his rebellious head. Ivan replies with defiance, and rides away with speed, and on drawing near to Kiev he dispatches his troop of followers to the city, while he himself pitches his white tent to take his pleasure with Nastasya. But at that moment, like a storm sweeping, like thunder rumbling, Koshchey the Immortal comes flying through the air. Koshchey roars with all his might, so that damp mother earth shakes, and the damp oaks tremble, and he orders Ivan to come forth from his white tent. Ivan comes out and addresses Koshchey as 'evil flying crow', and the heroes fight together for three hours, and then Ivan overcomes his enemy and sits on his white breast, and he calls to Nastasya to hand him his steel dagger wherewith to dispatch his enemy; but at the same time Koshchey also calls to her, reminding her that if she marries Ivan her status will be that of a peasant, whereas if she marries him she will be a princess. Upon hearing this Nastasya seizes Ivan by his yellow curls, and drags him away from Koshchey. Then they tie Ivan to a damp oak and enter the tent together. Meanwhile two doves perch on the oak above Ivan, and begin to coo, and Koshchey asks Nastasya to hand him his bow and arrow to shoot them. Nastasya complies, but begs him not to shoot the doves, but to shoot Ivan. The arrow, however, instead of piercing Ivan strikes the damp oak and rebounds into the heart of Koshchey himself. Then Nastasya approaches the damp oak, intending to cut off Ivan's head herself, but her hand fails of its stroke, and instead she inadvertently severs the bonds wherewith Ivan is bound. No sooner is he freed than he seizes Koshchey's sharp sword in his hand and mutilates Nastasya with the utmost savagery, after which he makes his way alone to Kiev, and conveys to Vladimir the homage of the dead hero Koshchey. The cruel vengeance which Ivan takes on his bride is one of the rare cases in the *byliny* of extreme brutality practised on a woman.

The most important of the heroes of the *babi stariny* is Churilo Plenkovich, who is one of the most bizarre and attractive figures in the strange assortment composing Vladimir's court, and a favourite subject of all the singers. Churilo, however, like many of the other heroes, is not a permanent resident at Kiev. His home, or rather that of his father Plenko, is some distance from Kiev. A delightful *bylina*[1], of which there are many versions, relates how, owing to the depredations made by the 'very young' Churilo and his *druzhina* on Vladimir's property, Vladimir visits him in his own home and invites him to serve a term as his seneschal in Kiev. We may interpret the invitation as a command, since Churilo goes unwillingly. But his yellow curls and fine clothes prove too distracting to the ladies of Kiev, and especially to the Princess Apraxya, and Vladimir is glad to shorten his term of service and send him back to Old Plenko. A second *bylina*—one of the *babi stariny* mentioned above—is also current in several versions and relates to Churilo's death. This *bylina* has not been translated. It tells how Churilo sets out one day dressed in his usual finery, his hood embroidered, his shoes of seven silks, his heels as sharp as awls. Thus arrayed Churilo arrives at the house of a certain Velma Vasilevich,[2] and enquires in a loud voice if the master is at home. His wife Katerinushka replies that he has gone to church, but invites the visitor in, and sets before him sweet food and honeyed drinks, and then ensconces him in a bed of down. But Velma has a maid servant who sees that something is amiss.

> The maiden ran to the Church of God,
> The maiden cried at the top of her voice:
> "Alas, Velma Vasilevich!
> You are standing, Velma, in the church of God,
> You are praying, Velma, to the Lord God,
> You are bowing, Velma, to the damp earth,
> You see not the misfortune which has come upon you.
> You have at home an unwelcome guest,
> Eating, and drinking, and taking his ease,
> And diverting himself with your wife."

The tone of light comedy which in all versions has characterised the career of Churilo now deserts him. Velma hurries home and is met by his wife, who tries in vain to persuade her husband that Churilo's hat belongs to her brother. Velma finds the hero lying fast asleep in his bed, and with his sharp sabre he hews off his 'turbulent head'.[3]

The *bylina* of Khoten Bludovich has not been translated into English. One of the best versions of the story given by Rybnikov is that sung by Vasili Lazarev.[4] The *bylina* opens with a feast given by Vladimir to his

---

[1] Rybnikov, II. p. 524 ff.; Chadwick, p. 91 ff.
[2] In other versions his name is given variously as Bermyag, Bermyata.
[3] Rybnikov, II. p. 415.   [4] Rybnikov, II. p. 15.

princes and boyars, at which two widows are present, the rich old lady Chasova, and the less fortunate Bludova, mother of Khoten. Chasova has a daughter Ofimya whose hand Bludova asks for her son in marriage; but the rich widow seizes her goblet of green wine and dashes it in her face, saying that her daughter's hand shall be for a prince or a boyar, and not for Khoten:

> For my family is rich and eminent,
> An eminent family, and of princely rank.

Bludova leaves the feast abashed, and tells her son Khoten what has occurred, and how her mantle has been spoilt with the wine. Full of indignation Khoten rides to the house of Chasova, and is met by her daughter who comes out on to her staircase and mocks him. He replies that if she will not marry him he will carry her off as a serf, and lays about him with his steel club, destroying the property. Chasova is obdurate. She hires mercenaries to oppose him, and also sends her nine heroic sons against him, and Khoten arms himself and rides against them in the open plain, while the obdurate Chasova watches the proceedings through a telescope. When she sees her sons overcome, she runs to her 'brother', Prince Vladimir, and begs the help of the princes and boyars at the feast. In some versions Vladimir lends her some troops, but these also are defeated. Finally Vladimir is fain to offer Chasova's daughter to Khoten in marriage. But Khoten is not easily appeased, and the humiliated Chasova has to load forty carts with gold and silver and bring these and other treasure to Khoten before he at last consents to take her daughter in honourable marriage. In general the various versions [1] of this story recorded by Rybnikov differ little except in detail. In the version sung by Ryabinin, however, Ofimya welcomes the arrival of Khoten and gladly consents to become his wife.

Before leaving the Kiev Cycle mention must be made of the *bylina* of Tsar Kalin, which relates to the last great battle of the heroes of Kiev against their Tatar foes. The *bylina* is one of the most popular with the singers, and exists in a number of variant versions. These versions differ considerably among themselves, but they are in general agreement in regard to the main theme of the story, which relates the descent of a vast Tatar host on the city of Kiev, the challenge sent by the Tatar leader to Vladimir, Vladimir's appeal to his *bogatyri* to defend Kiev, and the heroic prowess of one, or sometimes three, or seven, of the

---

[1] For a summary of the contents of some of the variants, see Magnus, *Ballads*, p. 106.

bogatyri who attack the Tatar host. It is chiefly in the identity of the *bogatyri* who fight the Tatars that the variants occur. Very frequently the hero who shows most courage is Ilya of Murom; but in several versions the credit is given by a strange anachronism to Ermak Timofeevich, the intrepid youth who gained fame for his victory over Mahmetkoul and the capture of his capital Sibir in 1582.

Both Ilya and Ermak are at times represented as encountering the Tatars single-handed. When Ermak is the hero, other heroes linger at a distance, unaware that he has ventured forth alone to encounter the Tatar army. The reciter, Kuzma Romanov,[1] represents Ilya of Murom, Dobrynya Nikitich, and Alyosha Popovich as waiting together, and Ilya sends Dobrynya to try to dissuade Ermak from attacking the host. The version breaks off at this point; but in the parallel version of Nikifor Prokhorov,[2] Ilya's companions, Dobrynya Nikitich and Mikhailo Potyk, ride together to the Tatar host to seek Ermak, and Ilya succeeds in overcoming and dismembering Tsar Kalin. In the version sung by Trofim Romanov,[3] Ilya rides alone to Tsar Kalin and obtains a brief respite in which to make preparations, and then rides to the Faraonski Mountains to seek the hero Samson Manoilovich, who is represented in this *bylina* as his uncle.[4] Samson delays, and Ilya rides alone against the Tatar host; and as he is encountering the host at their last entrenchment his horse falls into the trench. Though the horse succeeds in making good his own escape, Ilya is taken prisoner and bound. As the Tatars are about to cut off his head Samson rides up with his *druzhina* and rescues his nephew, overcoming the Tatars. In this version Tugarin, who is here simply described as a 'pagan Tatar' of great strength, is employed by Tsar Kalin (in this version *Kain*) as his envoy.

A third Cycle, which cannot properly be called heroic, relates to 'heroes' of a different period and a very different political milieu—the citizens of the wealthy trading city-state of Novgorod. This is a much smaller Cycle, chiefly occupied with the adventures of only two important heroes, Sadko the 'rich merchant', and Vasili Buslaev. Of these the former must have been a very popular hero, since a large number of *byliny* are extant in which he is the leading figure. Other *byliny*—those of Terenti Danilovich, commonly known

---

[1] Rybnikov, I. p. 264 ff.   [2] *Ib.* II. p. 104 ff.   [3] *Ib.* p. 304 ff.

[4] The term used (*dyadyushka*) need not be pressed to imply actual blood relationship; but this seems nevertheless to be implied, since Samson refers to Ilya as his nephew (*plemyannichek*).

as Terenti Gost, 'Terence the Merchant', and of Akundin—appear to have been little sung by minstrels. The story of Terenti seems to be derived ultimately from a French source[1], but the setting and milieu are local and belong to Novgorod. The *bylina*[2] relates a humorous domestic contretemps of bourgeois life. Although heroic in metre and—to some extent—in style, it is quite Chaucerian in atmosphere and plot, and in its attitude to women. Like Sadko it presents a lively picture of the wealth and activity of Novgorod at the height of her prosperity.

The atmosphere and style of this Cycle as a whole differ considerably from those of the Kiev Cycle. They offer a relatively larger range of episode, increasing the number of incidents and narrating them in summary form. While retaining many of the characteristics of heroic narrative, the framework of the story is drawing closer to the style of the medieval metrical romances. Terence the merchant is frankly bourgeois in character. Like Sadko, Vasili Buslaev belongs to the burgher class, and his exploits reflect the clashing interests of a rich trading community. In passing from the combats of the Kiev heroes to those of Vasili Buslaev, we pass from the single combats of Homer or Beowulf to the encounters of the Montagues and Capulets in the streets of Verona. Moreover a new element has entered into these poems—the element of burlesque. The reciter of the Novgorod *byliny* does not regard his hero seriously, and even the Church is not exempted from satire. The treatment of Vasili and his exploits is invariably playful in tone, while in some versions his godfather the monk appears wearing the bell of the cathedral of St Sophia as a helmet, and using the clapper as a walking-stick.[3]

The variant versions of the story of Sadko differ considerably in detail; but the main outline and order of the episodes which constitute the *bylina* can be ascertained with tolerable certainty. The most complete versions on the whole are those recited by Sorokin to Rybnikov and Gilferding.[4] These vary somewhat in length,[5] but the contents are substantially the same.

This *bylina* relates how Sadko comes by the riches with which he is enabled to undertake his trading enterprises. In early life he is a poor man who goes about to banquets held in the city of Novgorod, and enter-

[1] See the note by A. Mazon, *R.É.S.* XII. (1932), p. 247.
[2] An excellent version of this *bylina* was recorded by Kirsha Danilov. Kirêevski, v. p. 54 f.   [3] See *S.R.* III. p. 56.
[4] Rybnikov, II. p. 243 ff.; Gilferding, I. p. 541 ff.
[5] The version recorded by Rybnikov consists of 387 lines; that by Gilferding of 601 lines.

tains the guests by playing on his *gusli*.[1] At last a day comes when he is no longer invited to play at the feast. Again and again this happens, and each time the musician repairs to the shore of Lake Ilmen, and sits on a stone and plays his *gusli* in solitude. One day as he plays, the lake suddenly becomes rough, and the *tsar morskoy*, the 'tsar of the sea', appears and thanks Sadko for his music. He tells Sadko that he has been giving a great banquet, and that Sadko's minstrelsy has given great delight and entertainment to his guests. He promises to reward him richly, and advises Sadko to lay a wager with the citizens of Novgorod, staking his head against all their riches, that he will catch fish of pure gold in Lake Ilmen, and with these the tsar of the sea undertakes to furnish him. It is with this wealth won by his wager that Sadko is enabled to build for himself his fine fleet of thirty 'falcon ships'.

This same *bylina*, and others recited by Leonty Bogdanov[2] and by Fedotov[3] to Rybnikov, relate how Sadko commands his *druzhina* to take golden treasure and buy up all the merchandise in Novgorod; and when Novgorod is completely empty Sadko has ships built and loaded, and he and his *druzhina* sail away over the blue sea. What follows is related with only slight variation in many versions, and the version recorded by Kirsha Danilov has been translated into English elsewhere.[4] Sadko and his thirty ships sail away on trading ventures; but while twenty-nine ships sail before a favourable breeze, Sadko's vessel lies becalmed and motionless. Sadko suggests that lots shall be cast to discover which of the crew is the cause of the unfavourable conditions, and the lot falls upon Sadko himself. Accordingly the silver gangway is lowered, and Sadko takes his resounding *gusli* and his precious golden carved chessmen, and he seats himself on his chessboard, and the crew lower him into the blue sea, and the ship speeds on its way like a white hawk. In the version recited by Vasili Lazarev, Sadko also carries in his right hand the image of St Nikolai.[5] Presently Sadko finds himself in the dwelling of the tsar of the sea with whom he remains for twelve years. At the end of that time his host commands him to play on his resounding *gusli*, so that he may dance to his music; but St Nikolai appears to Sadko in a dream, and bids him cast away his *gusli*, for his music and the tsar's dancing have rendered the sea rough, causing many wrecks and much loss of life. Eventually by carefully observing these and other commands of the saint, Sadko finds himself on the bank of the

---

[1] The *gusli* is a kind of harp. See p. 22 above.
[2] Rybnikov, I. p. 332 ff.   [3] *Ib.* p. 376 ff.
[4] Chadwick, p. 134 ff.   [5] Rybnikov, II. p. 27.

River Volkhov, close to Novgorod, just as his fleet sails into port laden with wealth.

Kirsha Danilov has also recorded another version of this *bylina*[1] in which Sadko appears as a stranger from the region of the Volga, who comes to Novgorod to seek his fortune in trade. As he leaves the Volga, the river begs him to convey her greetings to her brother, Lake Ilmen. Accordingly on his arrival in Novgorod he goes to the lake and recites his message, whereupon a fine youth appears to him from Lake Ilmen and asks who he is. On learning that the hero has spent twelve years on the Volga, and knows the river from source to mouth, he gives him advice similar to that which is given in other versions by the tsar of the sea, and by carefully observing it Sadko is similarly enriched so that he is enabled to purchase all the goods in Novgorod and build three churches. The *tsar morskoy* is absent from this version of the story, and there is no hint of Sadko as a musician. Speranski[2] regards this as representing the original form of the story.

Despite the fact that the two great Novgorod heroes are ascribed to the same century, the atmosphere of the *bylina* of Vasili Buslaev is very different from that of Sadko. Mythology, romance, folk-tale—whatever it is that endows the great Novgorod merchant with so much glamour and mystery—are absent from the account of Vasili's exploits. Instead we have a realistic setting in the city, and a clumsy, powerful hero, a figure of burlesque, despite the piety of his latter days.

The *bylina* of Vasili Buslaev consists of two stories which are virtually independent of one another, though they are occasionally found combined in a single poem. The first tells of the early life of the hero in his native city of Novgorod of which his father was *tysyatski* or *posadnik*, 'governor,' during his lifetime; the second, of his pilgrimage to Jerusalem for the purpose of expiating his own sins and arranging for prayers for the souls of himself and his relatives. Both stories are found widespread in the north of Russia in Europe, and are also to be found in the collection of Kirsha Danilov from Perm; but the story which relates the early life of the hero is the more popular of the two. The versions of this *bylina* of Vasili's life in Novgorod as recorded by both Kirsha Danilov,[3] and also by Fedotov of Olonets,[4] have been translated into English.[5] Kirsha's version of Vasili's pilgrimage will be found in the English version given by Hapgood.[6]

The *bylina* of Vasili's early life, and his exploits in Novgorod as

---

[1] Kirêevski, v. p. 47.   [2] *R.U.S.* p. 291.   [3] Kirêevski, v. p. 14 ff.
[4] Rybnikov, I. p. 368 ff.   [5] Chadwick, p. 141 ff.   [6] *Songs*, p. 236 ff.

recorded by Rybnikov from the recitation of Fedotov, opens with the death of old Buslaev, and the early education of young Vasili, who is brought up under the care of his mother. Early in life he begins to show his unruly nature, and even in his youth his habits when playing with other children are such as to cause consternation to parents:

> Whoever he seized by the arm, that arm came off at the shoulder;
> Whoever he caught by the leg, that leg was no more.

He collects a *druzhina* from among the townspeople and the local gentry—apparently a somewhat motley crew—and with these he goes as an uninvited guest to a feast given by the citizens of Novgorod. During the course of the evening he lays a wager with the citizens that he and his *druzhina* will defend the bridge over the Volkhov against them all on the following day. His mother does her best to undo her son's foolish boast, but in vain. The citizens, who have their own grievances against her truculent son, welcome this opportunity to pay off old scores. The combat accordingly takes place, and is generally described with much humour and verve. Vasili lays about him with his club of red elm wood:

> Where he struck, a street was formed through the fallen,
> Where he brandished his club, a lane was made.

Panic-stricken, the citizens run to Vasili's mother, begging her to control her son. Then his 'heroic' mother makes haste after the manner of the *byliny*:

> She thrust her shoes on to her bare feet,
> Flung her sable cloak over one shoulder,
> And sped to the bank of the Volkhov.

Here she flings her cloak over her son, or, according to some versions, pinions him from behind with her arms, and bears him off to his own home, to the relief of the entire city.

The second *bylina*, as recorded by Kirsha Danilov,[1] opens with a picture of Vasili's ship at rest on Lake Ilmen, while Vasili and his *druzhina* go ashore to take leave of the hero's mother before setting off on his pilgrimage to Jerusalem. The widow gladly speeds them on their way, for the cause is good, and she supplies them with all their needs for the journey. There is a covert reproach for many past misdeeds in her words:

> If you go on a good errand,
> I will give you a heartfelt blessing;
> But if, my son, you go on piracy,
> I will not give you a heartfelt blessing.

[1] *Loc. cit.*

Vasili and his *druzhina* sail away, and when they come to the Soro-chinski[1] mountain Vasili kicks a skull, which thereupon protests against his contemptuous act, and tells him that he shall himself be buried on the same spot. On the top of the mountain is a stone bearing an inscription to the effect that whoever shall amuse himself by leaping from end to end of the stone shall break his turbulent head thereon. Vasili and his *druzhina* amuse themselves by leaping across it from side to side only, and then proceed on their journey, passing through the Cossack community on the Caspian, and at last come to Jerusalem. Here Vasili serves masses for his own soul and those of his parents, and says prayers for the good bold youths who have robbed and slain, and then sets out on his homeward way. When he comes to the Sorochinski mountain he cannot resist the temptation of climbing it once more and leaping over the stone, this time from end to end; but in doing so he falls and breaks his turbulent head, and his brave *druzhina* bury him on the spot where the skull lies, and return sadly to Novgorod to bear the tidings to Vasili's mother. The similarity of the incident of the skull to the account of the death of Oleg in 912 as related in the Ancient Chronicle, and to that of the death of Örvar-Oddr in the Norse saga which bears his name is very striking.

In Kirsha Danilov's version we can discern an attempt to transform Vasili into a reputable figure. According to this he was taught both to read and to write in his youth, as well as to sing church music. In all Novgorod there was not his equal in church singing, till he took to evil pursuits. Even then Kirsha is careful to tell us that his hero makes liberal contributions to the tradesmen's guild on the vigil of St Nikolai. Moreover he does not wish to quarrel with the citizens at the vigil feast. Indeed he tries to part the combatants; but they box his ears. This is recognisably the same hero who in later life makes the pilgrimage to Jerusalem in order to expiate his past sins and to pray for the souls of the living and the dead.

Vasili Buslaev, as we have said, belongs to the burgher class, and the *bylina* of which he is the hero reflects vividly the party feeling and stormy politics which were a prominent feature of the city life of the rich trading republic during the Middle Ages. His exploits are of a less romantic nature than those of Sadko, and in his early life partake of the nature of street brawls between himself and his *druzhina* on the one hand, and groups of truculent citizens on the other. In contrast to the *byliny* of

---

[1] Lit. 'Hill of the Saracens', one of the many static 'heroic' localities which have not been identified.

Sadko supernatural elements are very slight, save in the folk-motifs introduced into the account of Vasili's foreign travels. Instead we find humorous exaggeration, and the treatment of the hero partakes largely of the nature of burlesque, though these features vary according to the taste and personality of the reciters. Despite its humorous character, the *bylina* which relates to Vasili's life in Novgorod perhaps contains more local colour and local interest than any other of the early *byliny*, and its hero is the most completely individualised. These elements are almost absent from the *bylina* which relates Vasili's journey to Jerusalem. In the latter the elements borrowed from folk-tale, and the strong moral tone differentiate this poem wholly from the first. This is particularly striking in the series of portents which the hero encounters and which lay a series of tabus upon him. It is the violation of these tabus which brings the hero to his death. All these elements—the individualism, the local colour, and the humour in the first *bylina*, and the moral tendency of the second—are definitely post-heroic, though the conventions are those of heroic poetry throughout. The combination has resulted in a delightful mock-heroic poem, unique in Russian popular literature.

It is a curious fact that we have hardly any *byliny* which can be attributed with even approximate certainty to the period intervening between the twelfth and the sixteenth centuries. During almost the whole of this long period Russia was under the Tatar rule. As if conscious of the strange blank in their oral poetical record, the popular poets have brought the heroes of the Kiev Cycle into touch with the Tatars, more especially with their *khans* Batu, Mamai, and the Golden Horde in general. The anachronism is the more strange in view of the consistency with which, in general, the *byliny* Cycles are kept apart. We have already referred to the *bylina* in which Mikhailo Potyk cheats the Tatar 'Tsar Bukhar' of his tribute, and to that of Vasili Kazimirovich, in which three heroes from Kiev, sent by Vladimir with tribute to Tsar Batu in the Great Horde, are represented as vanquishing the Tatars in various trials of skill, and returning to Kiev without paying any tribute. In the Siberian version of the *bylina* of Tsar Kalin the heroes of Kiev are all slain by the Tatars under their ruler Kalin, and so the Cycle comes to an end. The popular singers make no distinction between the Polovtsy raiders of the eleventh and twelfth centuries, and the Tatars or Mongols who overran Russia in the thirteenth century.

One interesting *bylina* breaks the silence of the Tatar period proper.

This is the *bylina* known as 'The Princes of Tver', which relates to Shchel Kan Dudentevich, who was made *bashkak*, or tax-collector for the Tatars by their Khan Azvyak, and who was massacred by the citizens of Tver in 1327.[1] The incident is related in a straightforward and literal manner. The absence of epic features, especially epic diction, and the sobriety and restraint of this poem, are in striking contrast to the *byliny* of the Kiev and Novgorod Cycles.

A small number of *byliny* have been regarded as having reference to heroes of the principalities of Russia during this period. It is true that the heroes bear names which can be found among these princes; but the names themselves are, for the most part, such as are in common use, while the *byliny* themselves are brief and slight in content. They narrate a single incident, or series of incidents, in summary form, and resemble *byliny* which relate to unspecified individuals (cf. p. 219 below). The *byliny* on Prince Dimitri,[2] Prince Vasili,[3] and the *bylina* which relates how the mother of Prince Mikhailo murders his young wife during his absence,[4] belong rather to the milieu of folk-tale and folk-song than to that of heroic poetry,[5] and the occurrence of the names of well-known medieval princes carries no conviction, and adds no impression of verisimilitude to the bizarre contents. A little *bylina* on the death of Prince Mikhailo[6] apparently belongs to the same series.

Similar in character are some of the *byliny* on Prince Roman and the *bylina* on Prince Danilo, who have been identified with some probability as Roman and Daniel, the two famous rulers of Galicia, who lived at the close of the twelfth and during the first half of the thirteenth centuries. More recent opinion favours an identification of Prince Roman with a Livonian prince who lived during the second half of the thirteenth century. This identification will be discussed later (p. 127 below). The *bylina* on Prince Danilo relates that a certain Prince Danilo tries to make himself popular among the young girls in order that they may compose favourable songs about him; but instead they deride him, and when he orders them to be punished the people rise and slay him. The poem is interesting on account of the reference which it contains to the

---

[1] Kirêevski, v. p. 186; Dormidontov, p. 225. See Solovev, col. 1314 f. A translation of the poem is given by Chadwick, p. 159 ff.

[2] Kirêevski, v. p. 63 ff.   [3] *Ib.* p. 66 f.

[4] *Ib.* p. 68 f.

[5] Translations of these poems and those next to be considered will be found in Chadwick, p. 164 ff. Brief mention is made of them by Rambaud, *R.É.* p. 234 f.

[6] Kirêevski, v. p. 77 f.

singing of popular narrative poetry (*pêsni*) by troops of girls (cf. p. 261 below).

The most interesting of the *byliny* associated with Prince Roman—and indeed, perhaps the most interesting of the *byliny* generally regarded as relating to this period—is that which tells of his warfare with the two Lithuanian princes, nephews of King Tsimbal. The story is actually told of a Prince Roman of Moscow; but, as Rambaud points out, there never was a Prince Roman of Moscow at any time, and it is probable that the Roman in question is one of the medieval princes of this name. The *bylina* is too long to be related here. The reader is referred to the excellent paraphrase by Rambaud (*R.É.*, p. 236 ff.). Two other *byliny* on Prince Roman are discussed in the chapter on 'The Texts'.

These so-called 'medieval *byliny*' belong to a different literary tradition from either the 'Older Cycle' or the Kiev and Novgorod Cycles. The difference of their diction and style is apparent even in translations. Moreover they share common characteristics of their own, both in regard to diction and style, which suggests that they originated in a common poetic milieu. These characteristics may best be summed up as simplicity, brevity and literalness, though exception must be made, as suggested above, for certain of the *byliny* relating to Prince Roman. We shall see presently that these characteristics are shared by the Muscovite school of the seventeenth century.

It is believed that the Cycle of songs relating to the Cossacks of the Don and Volga also began during the medieval period, though the best known early examples are those which are concerned with Ermak Timofeevich, the Conqueror of Siberia,[1] who was drowned in the R. Irtish in 1584. The *byliny* which narrate the exploits of the Cossacks of the Don and Volga are scarcely separate from those of the Moscow Cycle (cf. p. 59 below). Their form is the same, and the same characteristics sometimes appear, owing to the close historical relations of the Don and Volga Cossacks with the Muscovite rulers, especially after the capture of Kazan from the Tatars in 1552. The Cossack poems are remarkable, however, for their fidelity to history. The authentic exploits of such adventurers as Ermak in the sixteenth, Stenka Razin in the seventeenth, and Pugachev in the eighteenth centuries left little to be desired in the way of incident, even by the most accomplished minstrel or the most exacting audience. But indeed it may be said of the *byliny* as a whole that each fresh Cycle becomes progressively nearer to his-

[1] Kirêevski, vi. p. 36 ff.; Chadwick, p. 199 ff.

torical fact as it approaches our own time, though the atmosphere of the poems becomes further and further removed from that of the court.

The Princely Cycle of Moscow undoubtedly reached its highest development in the time of Ivan the Terrible, who ruled at Moscow from 1533 to 1584, and who, like Vladimir, has become the central figure of a wide circle of narrative *byliny*. The novel offensive of Ivan's struggle against the Tatars, and the romance of the Conquest of Siberia by a handful of heroic adventurers, are in themselves sufficiently akin to the bizarre adventures of Vladimir's own community on the Dnêpr to fit naturally into the old framework and to wear naturally the old dress.[1] The Muscovite *byliny*, however, at times keep surprisingly close to fact, and the spirited *bylina* which relates the capture of the town of Kazan,[2] the great Tatar stronghold in Russia, in 1552, reads almost like a versified dispatch or war bulletin. A *bylina* composed in a more exalted and artificial style relates a successful expedition undertaken by the great *boyar*, Boris Godunov, and the tsarevich, Fedor Ivanovich, against an invading army of Tatars from the Crimea under their Khan Devlet-Girei in 1571.[3] In a brief *bylina* of 34 lines the poet manages to narrate or suggest the high hopes of the 'mighty cloud' of Tatars and their ignominious discomfiture and flight. The crispness and terseness of its aphoristic style is perhaps due in part to the fact that it was written down only forty-five years after the actual event.

The *bylina* on Ermak the Cossack and the Conquest of Siberia perhaps reaches the highest level of the warlike *byliny* of this period. Few, if any, of the versions preserved are complete.[4] Yet even in their fragmentary or abridged form one is struck by the martial spirit, the reckless daring of the little band of Cossack freebooters, outlawed for their deeds of violence.

> I will go in person to the White Tsar,
> I will put on a cloak of sable,
> I will tuck my cap of marten-skin under my arm,
> I will offer submission to the White Tsar;—
> "O you are our hope, Orthodox Tsar!
> Do not bid them slay me, bid me speak a word;—
> For I am Ermak Timofeevich,

[1] See the series of versions of the *bylina* on 'Ermak the Cossack, Conqueror of Siberia' published by Kirêevski, VI. p. 39 ff.

[2] Kirêevski, VI. p. 1 f.; Chadwick, p. 187 ff.

[3] Kirêevski, Supplement to VII. p. 56; Chadwick, p. 190 ff.

[4] The version published by Kirêevski, VI. p. 39 ff. has been translated by Chadwick, p. 199 ff.

I am the robber Hetman of the Don;—
It was I who sailed the blue sea,
The blue sea, the Caspian,
And I it was who destroyed the dark grey ships;
But the ships did not bear the Russian Eagle.
And now, our hope, Orthodox Tsar,
I bring you my rebellious head,
And with my rebellious head I bring you the Empire of Siberia."
Then our hope, our Orthodox Tsar begins to speak,
The terrible tsar, Ivan Vasilevich:
"Hearken, Ermak Timofeevich!
Hearken, you Hetman of the Cossacks of the Don!
I pardon you and your band;
I pardon you for your services,
For your trusty service to me,
And I grant you, Ermak, as an inheritance the glorious silent Don!"

Ivan's many matrimonial alliances, and the consequent arrival of strangers at his court, give ample scope for the introduction of many of the static motifs of the *byliny* of the Kiev Cycle—the 'honourable feast', the rivalry between the native *druzhina* and the guests, with boasting, challenges, and single combats. The *bylina* of Kastryuk[1] relates the marriage of the tsar Ivan Vasilevich to the Circassian princess, Marya Temryukovna. It is generally included, as we have already seen, among the *babi stariny* (cf. p. 45 above), though the feminine interest in the story is little developed, the chief part being played by the bride's brother Kastryuk. Kastryuk sits sulking at the marriage feast, and casting a gloom over the proceedings, till the tsar asks the cause, when Kastryuk replies that he wishes to challenge a Muscovite to wrestle with him. The tsar has the challenge proclaimed, but only opponents of low rank come forward. Their names vary considerably in different versions. In some versions Kastryuk successfully overcomes one or two of these opponents before he is finally subdued; in others the first Muscovite who tackles him throws him over the roof. In all versions the boastful Circassian is overcome by the Muscovites and stripped ignominiously. It is a typical heroic story save for one or two humorous touches, and in all versions resembles the *byliny* of the Kiev Cycle so closely that if the proper names were changed it might pass for a story of one of Vladimir's feasts. The subject of the story also recalls the story told in the Ancient Chronicle of the young Pecheneg

---

[1] Many versions of this *bylina* have been recorded in all the big collections. It has not been translated into English; but some extracts have been translated into French by Rambaud, *R.É.* p. 254 ff., where some account of variants will also be found.

who challenged a member of Vladimir's *druzhina* to wrestle with him. None of Vladimir's men were found who were willing to volunteer, and the king was in despair, when an old serving-man of his household came forward and volunteered that his youngest son should be brought. His strength was such, he said, that he would be able to overcome the Pecheneg. Vladimir consented joyfully, and the young peasant overcame the foe of royal Kiev, and was taken into Vladimir's *druzhina*.[1]

This affinity of the *bylina* of Kastryuk with the Kiev Cycle is the more remarkable since the marriage which it celebrates is a historical fact, and the *bylina* has preserved many authentic details.[2] Ivan IV married as his second wife—

> Not one of us in holy Russia,
> Not one of us in stone-built Moscow,
> But one from a heathen land,
> The land of the Circassians,
> Marya Kastryukovna,
> Marya Temryukovna,
> Receiving as her marriage portion
> Three hundred Tatars, and five hundred Don Cossacks.[3]

Marya was the daughter of Temryuk, a Circassian prince. She was a Mussulman, baptised on the eve of her marriage, and she brought with her her brother, the fierce Kastryuk. These Circassians, whom the singers do not distinguish from Tatars, were hated by the Muscovites, and Kastryuk was impaled later on the charge of having poisoned Ivan's third wife. This strange marriage of Ivan with the barbarian princess, and the advent of her entourage at Moscow, must have supplied admirable material for epic poetry, and the wrestling match which forms the central theme of the *bylina* on this royal marriage may well reflect the kind of entertainments which took place on the occasion.

One of the most picturesque *byliny* of this picturesque Cycle is the one which generally bears the title: "The Tsar resolves to slay his son".[4] In actual fact Ivan the Terrible accidentally slew his eldest son in 1581 during a momentary burst of anger, though in the *bylina* he is represented as deliberately ordering the execution of his son as a penalty for treason.

In this Cycle, in addition to pure narrative *byliny*, we find poetry in which a single emotional situation is portrayed in detail. These poems

[1] Ancient Chronicle, p. 102.
[2] For an account of the historical background of this *bylina*, see Rambaud, *R.É.* p. 254 f.
[3] Rybnikov, II, p. 568.
[4] Kirêevski, VI. p. 55 ff.; Chadwick, p. 193 ff.

are generally largely occupied with speeches, not unfrequently a monologue, sometimes a dialogue, though there is generally a brief narrative
introduction, and very frequently a few lines of narrative are introduced
again between the speeches. The affinities are therefore with the poetry
of Type B, though the form appears to be derived ultimately from poetry
of Type E. Poems of this kind very frequently purport to be spoken
by a woman. As an example we may refer to the *bylina* entitled 'The
Tsar sends the Tsaritsa into a Convent',[1] which opens with the announcement that the tsar is banishing the tsaritsa to a convent, and then passes
to a dialogue between the tsaritsa and the grooms who are about to
drive her away, and concludes with an account of the arrival of the
tsaritsa at the convent, and her address to the abbess and nuns. Apart
from their brevity the chief respect in which these poems differ from
narrative poetry is that they are composed almost entirely in the present
tense.

A number of poems of Type D date from this period, especially elegies.
The *bylina* composed on the 'Death of the Terrible Tsar Ivan Vasilevich'[2] describes the scene in the Uspenski Cathedral, the tolling of the
great bell, the assembling of the princes and boyars before the new
coffin of cypress-wood in which lies the body of the dead tsar.

> At his head stands the life-giving cross,
> Beside the cross lies his royal crown,
> At his feet his sharp, terrible sword.
> To the life-giving cross each makes his prayer,
> To the golden crown each makes his bow;
> Each looks at the terrible sword, each feels dread.

This particular poem contains no speeches, but the majority of the
elegiac poems of this and succeeding centuries, like the poems of
Type B just referred to, consist of speeches, generally introduced by
a few lines of narrative. These elegies fall for the most part into
two classes. The first consists of elegies purporting to be recited by
widows, such as the 'Lament of the Tsaritsa for the death of Ivan the
Terrible'.[3] We shall see presently that similar elegies are attributed to
successive tsaritsas down to our own day, and that the form of such
elegies does not differ essentially from certain elegies attributed to widows
whose names are unrecorded (cf. p. 162 below). These Russian elegies
differ from laments ascribed to widows in Irish and Greek literature

---

[1] Kirêevski, VI. p. 202 f.; Chadwick, p. 203 f.
[2] Kirêevski, VI. p. 206; Chadwick, p. 206.
[3] Kirêevski, VI. p. 207; Chadwick, p. 208 ff.

in that they contain a slight narrative element. The second class of elegies consists of *byliny* purporting to be recited by the troops, such as the 'Lament of the troops on the death of Ivan the Terrible'.[1] This elegy, like the one mentioned above, is the first of a long series of martial laments for dead tsars. Like the former elegy, also, it resembles closely elegies recited in memory of unnamed individuals, and doubtless embodies a certain ritual element. We know of no close parallel for these martial laments in Greek, Celtic, or Teutonic literature, but the description of the funeral obsequies for Beowulf makes it not improbable that such poetry may have been in existence among the heathen Angles and Saxons.

Both narrative poetry and short objective poems of situation composed in the present tense, are found throughout the Period of Troubles and the reigns of the Romanovs, but examples are not very numerous, the entire collection occupying less than a hundred pages in Kirêevski's collection.[2] Moreover very few extend to a hundred lines, and the majority are much shorter. The commonest type of poem is one in which the poet celebrates a contemporary event—generally a momentous or tragic situation—by narrating it in the present tense as if it were actually in progress. In these brief poems the old heroic metre is still kept, and also, in a large measure, the diction. In the attitude of the poet to his subject, however, a change is noticeable. The events and characters are not always lifted on to the same exalted plain as in the earlier *byliny*. The heroic spirit has given place to a spirit of criticism, often of frank censure. The adjective *slavny*, 'glorious', 'exalted', applied to all heroes of the earlier *byliny*, is at this period often replaced by *zloy*, 'evil', 'accursed', 'wicked', which is even applied to crowned heads such as Boris Godunov. In this period it is a static epithet of the boyars.

In these *byliny* on the political troubles of the early seventeenth century the atmosphere is post-heroic. They represent the views of the Muscovite citizens on contemporary events. They are astonishingly outspoken. Many of them read like articles from an evening paper in a country where censorship of the Press is unknown. Nothing could illustrate better than these *byliny* the change which came over the political situation in the period following the death of Ivan the Terrible. The old autocracy has gone, the unity, stability, and oppressive rule of the old tsarist régime. The bourgeoisie has become a power and articulate; but it is not as yet stabilised. We shall have occasion to return to these post-heroic poems later.

[1] Kirêevski, VI. p. 212; Chadwick, p. 210.　　　　[2] Kirêevski, VII. p. 1 ff.

Poems of Type B are not rare in this period. The Lament or Laments [1] of Ksenÿa, daughter of Boris Godunov, are simple monologues introduced by two lines of statement:

> The little bird laments,
> The little white quail:
> "Alas that I so young must mourn," etc.

and again:

> The tsarevna laments in Moscow,
> The daughter of Boris Godunov:
> "O God, merciful Saviour!
> Why hast Thou overturned our throne?" etc.

This type of *bylina*, like its prototypes of the sixteenth century, consists largely of speeches, most commonly, though not exclusively, purporting to be recited by women. It may be doubted if the form was really new even in the sixteenth century. The second version of the Lament of Ksenÿa is so similar in form to the 'Lament of Yaroslavna' contained in the *Slovo o Polky Igorevê* that we may suspect the type to have had a continuous history.

It is impossible to be certain how far the elegiac and personal poetry of the sixteenth and seventeenth centuries was actually composed by the people who purport to be the speakers. We know that in modern times similar poems composed by private individuals sometimes achieve a wide circulation (cf. p. 288 below). On the other hand, the majority of the poems of this period, such as the laments on the tsars, have the appearance of obituary and 'Press' notices, and were probably composed by 'street poets' like our own ballad mongers of the same period. These people were no doubt important retailers of news, and would naturally model their compositions on traditional poetical forms. Speech poems composed in celebration of contemporary events are naturally often devoid of proper names and composed in the present tense. In the course of time, however, such poems would lose much of their significance, and so the addition of a brief narrative introduction, and the necessary proper names, would be essential if the poems were to have a continued circulation after the events which gave rise to them.

References to panegyric poetry are not wanting in this period. Olearius stated in his account of his visit to Russia in 1633—'When we were sitting at dinner there came two Russians with lutes and *gudkas* ('fiddles') who made their bows to the ambassadors, and began

[1] For a note on the relationship of the two versions of the Lament of Ksenÿa, see p. 160 f. below; cf. also Chadwick, p. 221.

to play and sing about the mighty sovereign and tsar Michael Theodoro-vich".[1] In Kirsha Danilov's version of the *bylina* on the death of Skopin[2] we are told that in the celebrations held in Moscow after Skopin's victory over the Lithuanians, etc., the Muscovites held a ban-quet and sang a *Slava* in his honour. Even if we are to interpret this as merely a traditional rhetorical figure, it shows at least that the tradition of panegyric poetry such as is found in the *Slovo y Polky Igorevê* was not forgotten, even in the seventeenth century.

Under Peter the Great the narrative *bylina* again springs to life, though in general it lacks the splendour which it had known under Ivan the Terrible and in the 'earlier' Cycles. It is generally short and simple in style and diction, like the *byliny* of the sixteenth century, though the conventions of the 'early' Kiev Cycle are still common. We still find the same heroic epithets, the same heroic simplicity of outlook, the same straight issues in the theme, and Peter, 'our sovereign tsar', behaves like an irresponsible *bogatyr* surrounded by his *druzhina*.

The *byliny* of the time of Peter the Great fill an entire volume (Vol. VIII) in Kirêevski's collection. They are by no means uniform in style. On the contrary most of the forms with which we are already familiar are represented here. The traditional narrative styles of the earlier *byliny* are again found in the *bylina* on Peter's wrestling match with the dragoon in his boyhood,[3] and the *byliny* which relate to the Capture of Azov,[4] and to Peter's Journey to Sweden.[5] The *bylina* which shows us Peter holding his council and writing a protocol—'not on common paper, but paper with the eagle stamp'[6] is an admirable instance of purely heroic treatment applied to a singularly unpromising theme.

In this collection also we find the type of *bylina* in which an event is commemorated in narrative form during or immediately after its com-pletion. Many celebrate incidents in the life of the tsar himself, such as the little poem on Peter's birth, with the making and decorating of his cradle, the freeing of the prisoners and the royal celebrations.[7] Others

---

[1] Olearius, *The Voyages and Travells of the Ambassadors sent by Frederick, Duke of Holstein, to the Great Duke of Muscovy, and the King of Persia*, transl. by J. Davis (London, 1669), p. 7.
[2] Kirêevski, VII. p. 11 f.; Chadwick, p. 229 ff.
[3] Kirêevski, VIII. p. 37 ff.; Chadwick, p. 257 ff.
[4] Translated into French by Rambaud, *R.É.* p. 300.
[5] Kirêevski, VIII. p. 164 ff.; Chadwick, p. 260 ff.
[6] See the French translation of the first part of this *bylina* by Rambaud, *R.É.* p. 322.
[7] Kirêevski, VIII. p. 1 ff.; Chadwick, p. 255 ff.

are concerned with the death of Alexis and the nomination of Peter as his heir;[1] and with Peter at sea.[2]

These *byliny* are for the most part, however, reactionary in tone. The return to an autocratic monarchy has brought about a return to the old heroic attitude. The note of criticism and protest is silenced. It is a notable fact that several of the *byliny* of the reign of Peter are based on *byliny* originally composed for Ivan the Terrible. It has often been remarked how similar are many of the features of the two reigns—even incidents in the private lives of the two tsars; and these similarities have facilitated the adaptation of the older *byliny* to the new incidents, or the composition of new *byliny* on the old models. Thus we again find in the reign of Peter a *bylina* commemorating the banishment of the tsaritsa to a monastery; but it is significant of Peter's suppression of popular speech that the name of the tsaritsa does not occur in the poem. The tsar had issued an order that her name must never be mentioned.[3]

Byliny were still composed on contemporary events throughout the eighteenth and nineteenth centuries. The tenth volume of Kirêevski's great collection is devoted exclusively to *Nash Věk*, 'Our own times', i.e. the nineteenth century—principally the first half of the period. It includes *byliny* relating to the Napoleonic Invasion of 1812;[4] the entry of the Russian troops into Paris in 1814;[5] the capture of Warsaw by the Russian general Paskovich in 1831;[6] the Crimean War of 1854–6;[7] an interesting but somewhat difficult poem on the attack by the English on the Solovetsk monastery in the White Sea;[8] and a host of other subjects. As an example of the narrative poetry of the period we quote the following brief *bylina* on the Napoleonic Invasion of 1812 recorded from the territory of the Don Cossacks.[9]

> It happened in the land of France,
> Our dog of an enemy, King Napoleon, appeared.
> He collected an army from various lands,
> He loaded his galleys with various goods,
> And these various goods were lead and powder;
> And he wrote a dispatch to the Tsar Alexander:
> "I beg you, Tsar Alexander, I beg you, do not be angry,
> Prepare for me a lodging in the Kremlin of Moscow,
> Prepare your royal palace for me, the French king."

---

[1] See the French translation by Rambaud, *R.É.* p. 296.　　[2] *Ib.* p. 307.
[3] See Bezsonov's note, Kirêevski, IX. p. 105; cf. Rambaud, *R.É.* p. 316, footnote 1.
[4] Kirêevski, X. p. 2; Chadwick, p. 287 f.
[5] Kirêevski, X. p. 25 ff.　　[6] *Ib.* p. 472; Chadwick, p. 292 ff.
[7] Kirêevski, X. p. 484 f.　　[8] *Ib.* p. 487 f.　　[9] *Loc. cit.*

The Tsar Alexander sat down in his chair to reflect,
The expression of his royal countenance changed;
Before him stood a general—Prince Kutuzov himself:
"Fear not, fear not, Tsar Alexander, do not be dismayed!
We will welcome him half way—that dog of a foe.
We will prepare him delicacies of bombs and bullets,
As an entrée we will offer him cannon balls,
As a side-dish we will present him with deadly grapeshot,
So that his warriors will march home again under their banners."
Then our Tsar Alexander rejoiced greatly,
The Tsar Alexander cried out and proclaimed in a loud voice:
"Exert yourselves to the utmost, you warrior Cossacks,
And I will richly reward your horsemen,
I will confer high rank upon your officers;
I will discharge you, my children, to the glorious silent Don."

The following picturesque *bylina*[1] of Type D, is a piece of popular poetical journalism. Its purpose is to announce and lament the death of the Tsar Alexander I. The tsar died at the Spa of Taganrog in South Russia in 1825. While preserving some of the old poetical conventions, the poem shows in its general originality of treatment that the art of composing *byliny* was not yet wholly dead.

Our Tsar Alexander has gone to review his army;
Our Tsar Alexander has promised to come to the house of Rozhestov
Everybody is out on holiday—Alexander is not at home.
"I will go,[2] I will climb the tower—the highest tower of all,
I will gaze in the direction where my Alexander has gone!"
Along the Piterski road the dust rises in columns,
The dust rises in columns—a young courier is running.
"I will go, I will question the courier: 'Whither, courier, are you running?
Can you give us tidings, courier, of the Tsar Alexander?'"
"Throw off your crimson shawls, put on your mourning-weeds,
I have tidings of the Tsar Alexander for all you loyal souls.
Our Tsar Alexander has died at Taganrog,
And twelve generals act as bearers to our tsar,
While two officers lead his raven steed,
And four guardsmen march with banners."

It will have been observed that the intellectual outlook of the Russian *skaziteli* has hardly kept pace with the dignity of their subjects. As we pass from the Kiev Cycle to those of more modern times we are conscious of an increasing disparity between the subject and the treat-

[1] Kirêevski, x. p. 197.
[2] From the variants recorded by Kirêevski (*loc. cit.*) it appears that it is the tsar's mother who speaks.

ment by the popular poet—a disparity which becomes most obvious when we come to the last considerable body of heroic poetry which Great Russia has produced—that on the Napoleonic Wars. The history of the *bylina* as a literary type is to be regarded, therefore, as the history of an art in its decline. Its characteristic features were acquired at a time when the minstrels moved in court circles and shared the intellectual outlook of their patrons. The greatest Cycle of the heroic poetry of Russia is admittedly that which relates to Kiev. The Kiev Cycle of *byliny* has set the standard in heroic narrative style in Russia which has persisted down to our own day.

While the Cycle of Moscow produced many fine *byliny* of a similar form and technique to those of the Kiev Cycle, this Cycle also contributed a new literary form to the *byliny*. The short popular song, consisting largely of speeches, which we know to be already a fully developed form at the time when the *Slovo o Polky Igorevê* was composed, was developed in Moscow into a literary form admirably suited to the celebration of contemporary events and to the expression of popular feeling. When this form is combined with narrative, it is equally well adapted to the transmission of contemporary or recent news. It is curious that the form is hardly ever applied to the themes of the Kiev Cycle. It is reserved for contemporary history. The Muscovite singers never developed, as did the Norse poets, their ancient epic themes as subjects for the special study of emotional situations, or the development of poems concentrating on a single event or scene.

It will be necessary to turn to the Kiev Cycle in order to analyse the qualities of style and technique which characterise Russian heroic poetry. It is certainly the *byliny* of this Cycle which have set the standard in heroic narrative style—a style which has persisted to our own time. This style and technique have influenced the *byliny* of all the succeeding periods in a greater or lesser degree, and in general it may be said that the measure of the artistic success of the *byliny* of more 'recent' Cycles is proportionate to their approximation to the style and technique of the Kiev poems. It will therefore be best to take the *byliny* of this Cycle as the starting point for our analysis of the characteristic features of Russian heroic poetry as a whole.

It will have been observed that the analysis of the characteristics of Greek and English narrative heroic poetry given in Vol. 1, p. 20 ff. is also true in great measure of the *byliny* relating to Kiev.

(1) Narrative poetry preponderates. In Cycles relating to the early period it is almost the only type represented. Type B appears as a

fully developed type in relation to events of the sixteenth century, but seems to be confined to contemporary events. Type D also appears as a fully developed type for the first time in relation to events of this period, but there are reasons for suspecting that it had long been in vogue. In both these types, however, a narrative element is generally found.

(2) The majority of the early poems either narrate stories of adventure, or imply a life of adventure as their background. Settled conditions and an ordered routine are wholly absent. A considerable number, however, even of these early poems, relate to domestic life. During the more modern period any important public event, whether relating to the domestic life of the tsar, or to affairs of national or international importance, may be made subjects of *byliny*.

(3) Poems of the early period are always intended for entertainment. From the sixteenth century onwards, however, many of them are designed to convey information relating to contemporary occurrences. Such *byliny* constitute a kind of oral journalism in poetical form and embrace *byliny* of Types A, B and D.

(4) The poems of the Kiev Cycle relate to the tenth or eleventh centuries, which, if we may trust the picture of this period as presented by the Ancient Chronicle (cf. however, p. 23 above) constituted the Heroic Age of Russia. Other cycles, such as that of Novgorod, while sharing many of the characteristics of the Kiev poems, relate to a community which had left the Heroic Age far behind. From time to time heroic conditions make their appearance in various parts of Russia, and these periods undoubtedly gave a fresh impetus to the production of *byliny*. Such heroic phases are particularly marked during the sixteenth century. But *byliny* continued to be composed in the traditional Kiev style long after heroic conditions had ceased everywhere.

(5) The *byliny* are invariably anonymous. Some of the poems assigned to Type B contain personal details, and may have been composed by the people to whom they relate; but as there is no indication of authorship in any poem of Types A or D known to us, it would be unsafe to assume it for poetry of this Type on internal evidence only. As in the *narodne pjesme* of the Yugo-Slavs, a reciter can, in general, give only the name of the person from whom he learned the *bylina*, and, occasionally, one or two steps further back.

(6) In regard to metre, the *byliny* are invariably composed in the unrhymed measure already discussed (p. 19 f. above). While this metre

varies somewhat, particularly in regard to the length of the lines, as between one locality and another, and between one school of singers and another, yet no change is discernible in this respect between the *byliny* of one Cycle and another, or between those which are known to have been composed in the early seventeenth century and those of the present day.

(7) The *byliny* are invariably, or almost invariably, characterised by an unbroken flow of verse. No form of stanza or refrain appears to have been used, at any rate before the seventeenth century at the earliest.[1] The lines are generally end-stopped. Enjambement is rare, but a common device is the repetition of the last half of a line as the first half of the following line.

(8) Speeches are very common everywhere in the *byliny*. Not infrequently they occupy the major portion of even poems of Type A. In *byliny* relating to the Period of Troubles, to that of Peter the Great, and to more modern times, letters are not unfrequently mentioned and quoted at length. As examples we may refer to the letter written by Prince Mikhailo Skopin Shuyski to Charles IX of Sweden, begging for assistance during the siege of Moscow in 1608–1610 at the hands of the insurgent army of the Pretender Peter;[2] to the insulting letter written by Charles XII of Sweden to Peter the Great,[3] and to the letter of challenge written by the Emperor Napoleon to the Tsar Alexander I.[4]

(9) Like the Greek and Anglo-Saxon heroic poems the *byliny* are rich in lengthy descriptions, and a spirit of leisure pervades the narrative, even when rapid action is the subject. A hero may be setting off on a journey or some urgent mission, but the reciter rarely misses the opportunity of describing minutely the hero's costume and weapons and the equipment of his horse. The poet loves to dwell on minutiae of costume, which are often of great interest to students of the date and provenance of the *byliny*. Something more will be said on this subject in the chapter on 'The Heroic Milieu'.

Even the most commonplace actions are described minutely. In the *bylina* of Solovey Budimirovich[5] we are told how Vladimir's niece Žabava arose—

---

[1] Something in the nature of a refrain occurs in the Lament of Ksenÿa Borisovna recorded by James in 1619 (cf. p. 64 above).
[2] Kirêevski, VII. p. 11 f.; Chadwick, p. 229 f.
[3] French translation by Rambaud, *R.É.* p. 320 f.
[4] Kirêevski, x. p. 2; Chadwick, p. 287 f.; cf. also p. 66 above.
[5] Gilferding, I. p. 517 ff.; Chadwick, p. 116 ff.

When it was still very early dawn. . .
She washed herself with water till she was quite clean,
She dried herself on a little towel till she was quite dry,
She said her prayers to the Lord God,
And then she looked out of her little window.

The poet is at pains to hold our attention in expectation of what is about to happen by dwelling on the commonplaces of a banquet:[1]

Princes and boyars assembled,
Powerful mighty heroes,
And all bold women-warriors;
The feast was half over,
The banquet was half consumed,
The boyars had nearly eaten enough,
The boyars had nearly drunk their fill.

(10) Static adjectives are of very frequent occurrence. They are often found in static combinations, and sometimes as compounds, e.g. 'damp mother earth' (*mat-syra zemlya*); 'free open plain' (*razdolitsoe chistoe pole*); 'white stone city' (*bêlokamenny gorod*); 'good heroic steed' (*dobry kon bogatyrski*); 'glorious gentle Don' (*slavny tikhi Don*).

More often the static adjectives are found singly. These are frequently identical with the Yugoslav, e.g. 'white palace or town' (*bêlaya palata* or *bêly gorod*); 'white hand' (*bêlaya ruka*); 'white face' (*bêloe litse*); 'bitter tears' (*goryuchÿa slezy*); 'good steed' or 'hero' (*dobry kon* or *bogatyr*); 'illustrious prince' (*laskovy knyaz*); 'nimble feet' (*rêzvÿa nogy*). Static adjectives which differ from the Yugoslav are 'rebellious head' (*buynaya golova*); 'green wine' (*zelenoe vino*); 'damp earth' (*syra zemlya*); high mountain (*krutaya gora*); 'red' or 'fair' sun (*solntse krasnoe*).

We may instance further 'sweet food' (*yastva sakharnÿa*); 'honeyed drink' (*pite medvyanoe*); 'silken bowstring' (*tetiva shelkovaya*); 'dark forest' (*lês temny*); 'holy Russia' (*svyataya Rus*); 'white Tsar' (*bêly tsar*).

Certain of the heroes of the *byliny* have their own particular static adjectives with which their names are usually associated; e.g. 'the terrible tsar, Ivan Vasilevich' (*grozny tsar, Ivan Vasilêvich*); Vladimir prince of royal Kiev (*Vladimir knyaz Stolno-Kievski*); Ilya of Murom, the Old Cossack (*stary Kazak Ilya Muromets*); Sadko the merchant, the rich stranger (*Sadko kupets, bogaty gost*).

---

[1] See the *bylina* entitled 'The Tsar resolves to slay his son', Kirêevski, VI. p. 55 ff.; Chadwick, p. 193 ff.

Standing formulae and stock motifs and situations are very common. As in Teutonic and Greek heroic poetry, common actions and events, especially such as occur frequently in daily life, tend to be described in identical terms.[1] Thus the formula for setting out in a hurry is as follows: "He flung his boots on to his bare feet, his fur cloak over one shoulder, his sable cap over one ear." The formula generally used of a person's entering a building is "He bowed on two (three, four, all, etc.) sides". When strangers meet they commonly ask the following question: "By what name do they call you, and how are you known in your native country?" Speeches are almost always introduced by the phrase: "Dobrynya, (Churilo, etc.), spoke such words" (sc. as follow).

Guests at a feast are usually described as seated round a table of oak or cypress wood, as eating 'sweet food' or the white swan, and as drinking green wine or honeyed drinks. The hero generally begins his adventures by "mounting his noble, heroic steed and riding over the free, open plain". Introductory formulae are also common. Thus in poems of Type B, we frequently find the opening lines occupied with an address to the bright moon, which seems to bear no relationship to what follows.

In addition to the formal characteristics enumerated above, the *byliny* employ a number of conventions of a somewhat elaborate character which would seem to have a long history behind them. Not unfrequently they open with an invocation to the sun and moon, or to nature under various aspects. Sometimes in the place of invocations we have observations on the weather, which is then generally described as if it reflected the mood of the characters or incidents in the poem, as e.g. in the various *byliny* containing laments of the troops for the dead tsars.[2] Metaphors are commonly introduced, and are sometimes sustained for some length. We are struck by the large number drawn from bird life, as in the *Slovo*. We may refer to the opening lines of the Lament which purports to be spoken by Ksenÿa, the daughter of Boris Godunov:[3]

> The little bird laments,
> The little white quail:
> "Alas that I so young must mourn".

Similes introduced by 'like' or 'as' (*kak*) are not common in the *byliny*, though they are not unknown. We have however a curious device which is neither quite a simile nor a metaphor, but which is something

---

[1] See Mazon, *Bylines*, p. 682; Rzhiga, *R.É.S.* XII. (1933), p. 213 ff. Cf. also p. 246 below.
[2] Cf. Chadwick, pp. 210 f., 273 ff., 284 f., and the references there cited.
[3] Kirêevski, VII. p. 58 f.; Chadwick, p. 218 ff.

between the two—a comparison introduced by a negative. This form is very common, and appears to have arisen with the loss of the earlier figurative diction. A striking illustration of the use of this so-called 'negative comparative' will be found in the opening lines of the *bylina* on the murder of the Tsarevich Dimitri:[1]

> It is not a whirlwind rolling along the valley,
> It is not the grey feather-grass bending to the earth,
> It is an eagle flying under the clouds,
> Keenly he is eyeing the River Moskva,
> And the palace of white stone,
> And its green garden,
> And the golden palace of the royal city.
> It is not a cruel serpent rearing itself up,
> It is a caitiff dog raising a steel knife.
> It has not fallen into the water, nor on to the earth,
> It has fallen on to the white breast of the tsarevich...
> It is not a whirlwind rolling along the valley,
> It is not the grey feather-grass bending to the earth,
> It is the terrible wrath of God sweeping
> Over orthodox Russia.

Not unfrequently we are introduced to the speech of a hero by such words as the following:

> It is not a golden trumpet resounding,
> Nor a trumpet of silver; it is someone speaking in a loud voice,
> It is Ermak Timofeevich [or some other hero] speaking.[2]

Repetition is used even more freely than in Greek or Teutonic heroic poetry. It is, indeed, one of the most characteristic features of the *byliny*. It occurs with especial frequency in speeches. Very commonly we find long passages repeated with hardly any variation, very much as we do in the west European ballads. Such repetitions are often used with considerable skill to hold the imagination in check and prepare for the effect of a new announcement—the climax. Hence they commonly occur before important statements or in situations of emotional stress. Typical examples occur in Ryabinin's version of the *bylina* of Dyuk Stepanovich[3] and Chukov's version of the *bylina* of Staver.[4] The latter is quite shameless in the liberality of its repetitions of speeches, but by no means unskilful in the use of slight variations which give piquancy to these same speeches, and serve to keep the attention in a state of expecta-

---

[1] Kirêevski, VII. p. 1; Chadwick, p. 216.   [2] Chadwick, p. 200.
[3] Rybnikov, I. p. 98 ff.; Chadwick, p. 101 ff.
[4] Rybnikov, I. p. 202 ff.; Chadwick, p. 123 ff.

tion. The repetition of long passages is no doubt due to the poet's desire to make his story last as long as possible, coupled with a knowledge that such devices have a certain cumulative effect.

(11) The length of time covered by the action varies very greatly. In the Kiev and Novgorod Cycles it frequently extends over a number of years. In Chukov's version of 'The Absence of Dobrynya'[1] the action is extended over twelve years, though the attention is focussed on the two scenes at the beginning and the close of the period. In Kirsha Danilov's version of Mikhailo Potyk[2] the story extends over many years, though the scenes which occupy almost the whole *bylina* apparently took place in a few months. In many versions of the *byliny* of Sadko and Vasili Buslaev the narrative covers the greater part of the lives of the heroes, though here also the greater part of the *byliny* is occupied with a few important events, the rest being narrated summarily. The siege of Kazan by Ivan the Terrible is narrated as if it took place during the space of a few days, whereas actually it lasted for six weeks. We have seen that many of the *byliny* relating to the sixteenth century and all succeeding periods are concerned with events which can only have occupied a few moments.

When a lapse of time has to be accounted for it is frequently artificially abbreviated, as in folk-tales. Thus Ilya's journey from Murom to Kiev is represented as taking place between Matins and Mass on Easter morn, owing to the exaggerated fleetness of his horse.[3] In Kirsha Danilov's version, Sadko's twelve years' sojourn with the tsar of the sea are passed over almost in silence, the narrative concentrating on the events of a few hours.[4]

Sometimes lapse of time is frankly admitted, as in the case of the imprisonment of Ilya of Murom, of Vasili Buslaev, of Sukhan, and of Stavr. In such cases the length of time is generally greatly exaggerated, thirty years being a static period. Not unfrequently the action falls into two main parts with a considerable interval between. We may refer to the version of the *bylina* of the 'Absence of Dobrynya' recited by Chukov to Rybnikov,[5] which is almost wholly occupied with two such scenes. In the first we have Dobrynya's leave-taking and departure, in the second his return, after an interval of twelve years. In these devices we may observe a developed sense of form and structure, an advanced technique.

---

[1] Rybnikov, I. p. 162 ff.; Chadwick, p. 80 ff.
[2] Kirêevski, IV. p. 52 ff.   [3] Cf. however, p. 117 below.
[4] See Kirêevski, v. p. 41 ff.; Chadwick, p. 134 ff.
[5] Rybnikov, I. p. 162 ff.; Chadwick, p. 80 ff.

(12) The distance in the time of the action in relation to the poet is seldom, if ever, expressed in the *byliny* of the early Cycles. This is all the more remarkable as we generally find at the beginning of the folk-tales a tacit recognition that some pronouncement on this point is expected by the audience. And we may add that it is the more remarkable also in view of the realisation on the part of the modern singers of the *byliny* that the events narrated, in the case at least of the two early cycles, happened very long ago. Rybnikov and Gilferding found that if they or any of the audience expressed scepticism in regard to the super-human feats of the heroes, the minstrel, or even a member of the audience versed in such matters would reply: "Ah, but the men of that time were not as the men of to-day." Sometimes however a vague indication is given in the *bylina* that the story relates to the far past. We may refer to the opening lines of a *bylina* of the healing of Ilya of Murom:

> Who is there who could tell us about the old days,
> About the old days, and what happened long ago,
> About Ilya, Ilya of Murom?[1]

The manner of recitation for the most part, however, is dramatic rather than historic, and the present tense is used almost as commonly as the past. In poems relating to the sixteenth and following centuries, as we have seen, the events are very frequently represented as actually taking place, or just completed, at the time of composition. The *bylina* recorded by James in 1619 on the invasion by the Khan of the Crimea in 1571 opens with the words:

> It is not a mighty cloud which has gathered,
> Nor mighty thunder rumbling:
> Whither goes the dog, Crimea's tsar?[2]

The *bylina* 'The Tsar sends the Tsaritsa into a convent' opens with the question:

> Why is all so sad here in Moscow,
> Why are they tolling the great bell?[3]

Kirsha Danilov's version of 'The Death of Skopin'[4] is a rare instance of a *bylina* opening with an exact statement of the date of the occurrence about to be narrated.

The persistence and conservatism with which the *byliny*, collected from all over Great Russia and northern Asia, have retained the con-

---

[1] Kirêevski, I. p. 1; Chadwick, p. 59.
[2] Kirêevski, Supplement to VII. p. 56; Chadwick, p. 192.
[3] Kirêevski, p. 202; Chadwick, p. 204.
[4] Kirêevski, VII. p. 11; Chadwick, p. 229.

ventions associated originally with the *byliny* of the Kiev Cycle, are all the more remarkable in view of the fact that all trace of this Cycle has disappeared in precisely the district where it is believed to have grown up. In the valley of the Dnêpr round Kiev, where the court of Vladimir was held, and the heroes performed their exploits, scarcely a trace remains of their names or deeds. The disunion among the Russian princes of the Dnêpr, followed by the destruction of Kiev by the Tatars in 1240, and the consequent stream of migration northwards, are no doubt initially responsible in part for the wide distribution of themes and *motifs* derived from the poetry of this Cycle. In the meantime changing political conditions in and around Kiev inspired fresh schools of heroic poets to fresh efforts. The old themes were superseded in their native district by a totally new cycle of poems celebrating the exploits of the heroes of the rising community of the Zaporogian Cossacks and the Republic of Little Russia. This new school looked to the west for its literary traditions, and composed in rhyming strophic verse quite distinct from that of the *byliny*.

CHAPTER III

THE HEROIC MILIEU

INDIVIDUALISM IN THE HEROIC POEMS

THE milieu of the great majority of the *byliny* is heroic. There are, as we have seen, certain exceptions. The milieu of the *bylina* of Volga and Mikula is partly heroic, partly non-heroic, while that of certain of the *byliny* of the Novgorod Cycle, notably of Vasili Buslaev and of Terenti Gost, are post-heroic, the former even mock-heroic. Certain of the *byliny* relating to the seventeenth century are also post-heroic in tone. These non-heroic and post-heroic *byliny* differ from the heroic *byliny* of the Kiev Cycle chiefly in regard to their outlook, though there are also certain differences perceptible in the personnel, as we shall see. All, or almost all the *byliny* have retained the heroic form and style.

The milieu of the *byliny*, like that of the other heroic poetry and saga already considered, is mainly aristocratic in character. Dyuk Stepanovich is the son of a prince of Galicia. The heroes of the Kiev Cycle are not, for the most part, of princely rank, however. Both Dobrynya Nikitich and Ivan Godinovich are sometimes represented as 'nephews' of Prince Vladimir, though in one *bylina* recorded by Kirsha Danilov Dobrynya is said to be the son of a rich merchant of Ryazan.[1] Alyosha Popovich is the son of a priest of Rostov, the great ecclesiastical centre of north Russia in ancient times. Churilo Plenkovich is the son of a man of wealth and substance, sometimes also described as a merchant. Ilya of Murom is said to be a peasant's son, though he has horse and weapons, and seems to be rather in the nature of a country squire. Khoten Bludovich is the son of a merchant of Kiev. Solovey Budimirovich is a wealthy seafaring merchant, and Stavr is a merchant of Chernigov. In the Novgorod *byliny* Sadko is a great trader, a rich merchant; Vasili Buslaev is the son of the *tysyatski*, i.e. the chief of the mercantile half of the city of Novgorod. But though his rank is hereditary, and his prestige high, he does not belong to a princely family. In these early Cycles, therefore, it would seem that the majority of the heroes belong to the wealthy mercantile class though they are attached to Vladimir's court. Stavr is spoken of in some versions as being poorly clad and not

[1] Sheffer, p. 147; Kirêevski, II. p. 49.

4

well set up in life,[1] but the *byliny* are not wholly consistent on this point, and in any case he is only a messenger on a mission to Vladimir's court. For the most part the heroes live the life of a rich, leisured aristocracy. It is clear that they at least belong to the highest rank of society known to the poets, and mix on an equal footing with the princes, with whose families they intermarry. They recognise no social superiors and live like princes themselves, enjoying a life of ease and leisure, and apparently lacking none of the accessories of people of the highest rank, as we shall see.

Women are constantly referred to in the *byliny*, and they play an important part in the narrative. They are in general of the same rank as the men. They are represented as wiser than men, and sometimes possess second sight and the power to interpret dreams. These gifts are attributed to the wife of the Turkish Tsar Santal in the *bylina* of Volga, and to Domna Faleleevna, the affianced bride of Prince Dimitri in the little *bylina*[2] which bears the name of this prince, and which has been thought to have reference to the medieval period. References to witches are not rare. Marya the White Swan, the wife of Mikhailo Potyk, is a witch of Polish or Lithuanian origin. Marina, of whom Dobrynya Nikitich is enamoured, and who almost proves his undoing, is also a witch; and in the seventeenth century we have another Marina, the Polish wife of the false Dimitri, who possesses the power of shape-changing.

Very few young girls appear in the *byliny* of the early Cycles. Zabava Putyatichna, Vladimir's niece, and the young princess Apraxya are represented as naïvely frivolous. In her spiteful and dishonourable treatment of Kasyan Mikhailovich, the leader of the 'Forty and One *Kalêki*', Apraxya plays a despicable rôle; but here and elsewhere it is difficult to distinguish the traditional character of the person in question from a character in a given story which has come to be attached to her—perhaps at a later period—and again from the elements which have accrued to it from the milieu in which it has circulated. In general the traditional character of Apraxya is presented to us as giddy and undignified, but not as actively mischievous, and we have little doubt that the story of Kasyan and the *kalêki* had originally nothing to do with Apraxya or Kiev. The theme is a common motif of folk-tale.

The mothers of the heroes, on the other hand, whether of the Kiev or Novgorod Cycles, are represented as uniformly wise, far-sighted, prudent and practical. They are a notable society in themselves. We may

---

[1] E.g. Gilferding, II. p. 406, line 32 ff.
[2] Kirêevski, v. p. 63 ff.; Chadwick, p. 179 ff.

refer to the mother of Dyuk Stepanovich who warns her son against drunken boasting, and then saves him from the effects of his rashness; to the rich and forceful widow Chasova, the mother of the girl whom Khoten Bludovich marries; to the mother of Dobrynya Nikitich who warns him against Nevêzha, the dragon of the mountain, but later encourages him to destroy it; of Solovey Budimirovich who is active in her son's welfare, sharing his trading expeditions, and passing her leisure in prayer for his welfare; of Vasili Buslaev whose mother wisely locks him up in a strong room to save him from his own folly; and many others. It is a curious fact that the two chief heroes of the Kiev Cycle who come to a bad end—Alyosha Popovich and Churilo Plenkovich—do not appear to have mothers. The heroes enumerated above as particularly blessed in their mothers appear to be fatherless. It is still more curious that it appears to be very rare for a hero to possess two parents. Exceptions are Ilya of Murom and Sadko; but even here the parents are barely referred to.

In this community a number of military women, known as *polenitsy*, are frequently mentioned. They are sometimes occupied in military pursuits, and are frequently mentioned among the guests at Vladimir's feasts. One of the most prominent is Nastasya, the wife of Dobrynya Nikitich, whom Dobrynya first encounters riding alone in the open plain, and whom he only succeeds in making his wife after she has forced him to acknowledge her superior strength and fleetness on horseback.[1] Yet curiously enough in the *bylina* which relates to their married life Nastasya figures as docile and conventional. She is said to be a sister of Vasilisa, the wife of Stavr of Chernigov, and a daughter of Mikula. These *polenitsy* correspond in many features to a similar class of warrior women who play a more prominent part in Norse literature, especially in the *Fornaldar Sögur* and in the narrative poetry of the Tatars, to which reference will be made in the next volume.

In these early Cycles the poorer classes are rarely mentioned—never by name. Of the people as a whole, or their occupations, we are told hardly anything. The only servant who appears to be clearly individualised is the servant of Alyosha Popovich, who is variously known as Ekim or Torop and who is said to be able to read. As Alyosha himself is the son of a priest of Rostov, the chief centre of learning and education in northern Russia, his servant is obviously a clerk, and no doubt he belongs to one of the lower orders of the church.

[1] Reference may be made to the *bylina* recited by Chukov to Rybnikov, I. p. 147 ff.

In the *byliny* which relate to Volga, Mikula and Svyatogor the merchant class disappears completely. The achievements of these heroes, especially those of Mikula and Svyatogor, are such as characterise the peasantry. Strength rather than skill are the characteristics of Svyatogor and Mikula, though the last is an exceedingly skilful ploughman. His furrows are straight and well turned; he clears the ground of all roots and stones; he has a good heavy plough horse. His little wallet contains the weight of the whole world. Svyatogor is so strong that his power to destroy can only be restrained with difficulty. Volga is eminently successful as a hunter, a fowler, and a fisherman. He is skilful, and full of knowledge. Nevertheless none of these heroes are true peasants, and they are not without wealth. Volga is a hero of aristocratic rank, who exalts the peasant Mikula to a place in his *družhina*. Mikula, it has been pointed out, has harness of silk, a plough of maple wood, and his horse is a highly bred steed with a 'noble equine pedigree'. Mikula must therefore be pictured as a man of substance. Svyatogor is perhaps hardly to be classified according to ordinary standards of rank, but his horse and tent, his weapons and way of life would seem to entitle him to a place in the same rank as Volga. His companion is Ilya of Murom. The peasants of this group, therefore, like so many peasants in folk-tales, are introduced only to be exalted.

In the later Cycles, with the exception of the Period of Troubles, the *byliny* are chiefly concerned with members of the royal family. This is particularly striking in regard to Ivan the Terrible and Peter the Great, though in Peter's reign, and in the eighteenth and nineteenth centuries, great generals and statesmen also play a prominent part. Throughout the period from the sixteenth to the nineteenth century also important Cossack chiefs such as Ermak, Stenka Razin, and Pugachev are celebrated as heroes. Such men are not always of aristocratic birth, but the poet does not concern himself too closely with their origin, provided always that they have attained to rank or fame or high prestige. During the Period of Troubles men who are not of high rank occasionally occupy the position of heroes of *byliny*, but such instances are rare. Grigori Otrepev, the first pretender, is introduced to us as an 'unfrocked priest', but he is treated with little sympathy by the poet. He is the villain rather than the hero of his *bylina*. Another person of the middle class who figures as the hero of a *bylina*[1] is Kuzma Minin, the famous butcher of Nizhni-Novgorod, who took a prominent part in the restoration of the monarchy in 1613. There can be little doubt, however, that

[1] Kirêevski, VII. p. 21 ff.; Chadwick, p. 241 ff.

he owes his fame in heroic or post-heroic poetry to the assistance which he rendered to 'the glorious magnificent house of Romanov'. In general it may be said that during the historical period the heroes are almost invariably princes or aristocrats, while in the Cycles relating to earlier times, when they are not of this class they are generally of the rank and resources of country squires, and merchant princes, who associate as equals with members of the royal family, and even intermarry with them. The people of the poorer classes are rarely mentioned.

Unlike the Teutonic and Celtic heroic stories the Russian *byliny* are, for the most part, associated with large cities; so much so that in mentioning the early Cycles it is usual to refer to them by the name of the city with which they are connected—the Kiev Cycle, the Novgorod Cycle, the Moscow Cycle, etc. Neither Svyatogor nor Mikula are directly connected with any such centres; but they move on the periphery of the circle of Kiev, and Volga is directly connected with several cities of which the names are preserved in the *bylina* of Volga and Mikula. The scene is generally laid either in the royal palace or in the 'open plain' (*v chistom polê*). In the latter case we are often introduced to the 'white tents', both of the heroes and of their enemies. Less frequently the scene is laid in a foreign court or open country, such as Lithuania, Poland, or Galicia, or in the palace of the Turkish tsar; but in these cases the picture presented to us does not differ in any respect from that of Kiev, or the Russian plains and rivers, or Vladimir's court.

In the Novgorod *byliny* the background is somewhat more varied. The *byliny* of Sadko the merchant carry us from the banks of the Volga to the shore of Lake Ilmen, again on to the Baltic among the streets and booths of Novgorod, even into the customs house, and again into the palace of the 'tsar of the sea'. Vasili Buslaev wanders from his mother's house through the streets of Novgorod to feast with the guild of St Nikolai and to drink in the taverns, and again along the river bank to fight his battle on the famous bridge over the river Volkhov. In later life he journeys to Jerusalem, but his route lies over the mythical Sorochinski hills and down the Volga.

In the *byliny* of Ivan the Terrible and those of later times the scene is generally laid either in the palace or its vicinity, or else on the battlefield. The palace and general mise-en-scène of the Kiev Cycle reappear with little variation, though certain features of the Kremlin, such as the Red Staircase, the lime-wood block where executions were carried out, and the Great Bell figure rather more commonly. Sometimes the principal

streets of Moscow are referred to by name, and we begin to hear of the
great churches of the Kremlin, the Uspenski Sobor, the Blagovêsh-
chenski Sobor, and the Church of Michael the Archangel. During this
period, as we have seen, we have for the first time *byliny* devoted wholly
to women, and as a natural result the scene is sometimes laid in the
terem or upper storey, with its 'floor of white hazel-wood'; or shifts to a
convent and its cell with three windows,

> The first looking on to God's Church,
> The second on to the green garden,
> The third on to the open country.[1]

But we never pass into the interior of a house of the middle or lower
classes, and in the modern *byliny* even the inns become rare. The poet
restricts his outlook rigidly to the aristocratic quarter.

Inside this restricted and highly conventionalised framework the
heroes are pictured as leading the life of a wealthy and fortunate little
community of adventurers. Practical needs, and questions of ways and
means, trouble them not at all. The days are spent in warfare, or in
sports, both outdoor and indoor, or adventures of various kinds. The
evenings are spent in feasting. By far the commonest opening of a
bylina of the Kiev Cycle, and also of the narrative poems of the Moscow
Cycle, is a royal feast attended by 'princes and boyars and all bold
women warriors (*polenitsy*)'. Unlike the Yugoslav poems, the *byliny*
invariably insist on the food as well as the drink as elements of the
banquet. The menu from the earliest times to the seventeenth century
or later consists of 'the white swan', 'sugared food', 'sweet drink',
'green wine', 'sweet mead'; and occasionally *kalachi*, little rolls of
white wheaten flour, are mentioned. Meat is never mentioned.

The conduct of the banquet is somewhat similar to that of the Teutonic heroic poems. Prince Vladimir invariably presides in the Kiev
poems, Ivan the Terrible in those of Moscow. The prince walks up and
down his apartment, and occasionally looks through his windows over
the open plain to see if any new comers are arriving. When the heroes are
half way through the feast they proceed to make their boasts, each
attempting to outdo his fellow in big talk, and it is from these boasts that
the adventure about to be related generally arises. It is in this way that
Sukhan Domantevich undertakes to bring to Vladimir a white swan
alive and uninjured; in this way too Stavr boasts that his young wife
Vasilisa will outwit all Vladimir's princes and boyars. By means of

[1] Kirêevski, VIII. p. 107.

these boasts the tragedy is often brought about. In the *bylina* which relates how Ivan the Terrible resolves to slay his son, we see how the poet turns heroic custom to literary account by a touch of irony:

> The terrible tsar Ivan Vasilevich was making merry,
> He was walking through his apartments,
> He was looking out through his glazed window,
> He was combing his black curls with a small-toothed comb,
> He spoke the following words,
> He addressed his boyars: "Drink and take your ease,
> But you cannot boast about your own exploits.
> It is I who have banished treason from my own country,
> It is I who have brought the imperial purple from Tsargrad."[1]

Even the banquet at which Prince Mikhailo Skopin Shuyski is believed to have been poisoned in 1610 is described in similar terms:

> When the feast was half over,
> And the princely banquet was half consumed,
> Those who were drunk began to boast
> The strong boasted their strength,
> The rich boasted their wealth.[2]

Minstrelsy is rarely if ever mentioned at what we may call these routine banquets of the *byliny* of the Kiev and Muscovite Cycles. In the Novgorod *byliny* of Sadko, on the other hand, we are told that in early life the hero has been a professional minstrel, who used to entertain the people of Novgorod with his *gusli* at their banquets, till a time came when they grew tired of his music. Again, when he is the guest of the 'tsar of the sea', he is bidden to play on his resounding *gusli*, and immediately afterwards we are told that the 'tsar of the sea' plies him with drink till he falls into a deep sleep. It is possible, therefore, that his performance formed the entertainment at the tsar's banquet, and that the Novgorod tradition differed from that of Kiev in this respect. Several of the heroes of Kiev appear nevertheless to be accomplished minstrels. Churilo Plenkovich and Solovey Budimirovich can play on the *gusli*, and Dobrynya Nikitich and Stavr Godinovich are especially skilled in the art. The two latter are represented as entertaining the company at marriage feasts with a wide répertoire. We shall discuss this subject more fully in the chapter on 'The Skaziteli'.

The daily occurrences of life are conducted with much ceremonial.

---

[1] Kirêevski, VI. p. 55; Chadwick, p. 194.
[2] Kirêevski, VII. p. 11; Chadwick, p. 233.

The wooing of princes is done by an emissary on their behalf. The *byliny* which relate the wooing on behalf of Prince Vladimir,[1] and the mock wooing of Vasilisa disguised as an emissary of the Polish prince,[2] give a detailed picture of the leisurely and ceremonious negotiations of the *svath* or professional match-maker. On the other hand Zabava, Vladimir's 'niece', is represented as wooing Solovey with naïve directness on her own behalf—a forthright way of going about it for which Solovey gravely chides her.[3] In this *bylina*, and still more clearly in the *bylina* on the 'Absence of Dobrynya',[4] it would seem that Vladimir claims the right to dispose of the hands of the unmarried women and widows at his own discretion. In the latter *bylina*, and in Kirsha Danilov's version of the *bylina* of Kastryuk,[5] we have detailed pictures of the whole ceremony—the wooing by the *svath*, the service in church, the feast which follows, and the music and sports and general entertainment which accompany it.

The *dobry kon* ('good steed') is an important element of the Russian heroic milieu. The heroes of the Kiev Cycle are all mounted, and a close sympathy exists between the horse and its master. When a point of dispute or difference arises between them, however, the horse is invariably in the right, and one gets the general impression that the horse is always a finer hero than its master. References to hunting are not unknown in the *byliny*, but they are not common. Fowling appears to be one of the favourite occupations of the heroes of the Kiev Cycle, and Mikhailo Potyk, Churilo Plenkovich, Sukhan Domantevich, and, at a later period, Prince Roman are all represented as occupied in shooting 'geese, and swans, and little grey feathered ducks'. The weapons used appear to be only the 'taut bow with silken bow-string' and the 'tempered arrow'. References to tame hawks or falcons are not common, though they occur. In one version of the *bylina* of Vasili Kazimirovich[6] Vladimir orders Dobrynya Nikitich and Vasili Kazimirovich to take as tribute to Tsar Batu in the Great Horde '20 bright hawks, and 20 bright ger-falcons'. Hounds used for hunting appear to be rare

---

[1] The version recited by Chukov will be found in Rybnikov, I. p. 142. For Kirsha Danilov's version, see Kirêevski, III. p. 70 ff.

[2] There are many versions of this *bylina*. The version recorded by Rybnikov from the recitation of Chukov is translated by Chadwick, p. 124 ff.

[3] Gilferding, I. p. 517 ff.; Chadwick, p. 116 ff.

[4] The version referred to is recorded by Rybnikov from the recitation of Chukov, I. p. 162 ff.; Chadwick, p. 80 ff.

[5] Kirêevski, VI. p. 143 ff. Cf. p. 60 above.

[6] Kirêevski, II. p. 83.

or unknown. Indeed we know of very few references to dogs of any kind in the *byliny*. House dogs are referred to incidentally in the *bylina* of Dyuk Stepanovich (cf. p. 88 below); and in a version of Dobrynya and Marina recorded from Simbirsk Marina is transformed into a grey bitch running about among the dogs.[1] The word 'dog' rarely occurs, however, except as an opprobrious term of the Tatars.

One of the commonest activities of the heroes is fighting; and in this they have little to dread, for the poets have no hesitation in making a single Russian hero victorious over an entire army. It is thus that Suk-han Domantevich overcomes single-handed an invading host of thirty thousand Tatars. Similarly also Mikhailo Potyk overcomes a vast army of invaders in the north. In the Olonets versions of 'Tsar Kalin' three Russian heroes are able to withstand the whole Tatar host for several days. Ilya has on a previous occasion overcome by his own efforts a vast Tatar host under the walls of Chernigov. In later times Ermak and a handful of Cossack outlaws succeed in surprising and overcoming Kuchum Khan in his stronghold of Sibir—a feat which has furnished material for one of the finest of the *byliny*. Yet the sum total of the *byliny* leave on one the impression that warfare is an unpleasant necessity rather than a choice to the heroes. They do not glory in fighting for its own sake like the Yugoslav heroes. The warfare is almost wholly defensive. Volga alone carries out a policy of aggressive warfare against the Tatars, attacking them on their own ground. Of feuds among the Russians themselves we hear little or nothing. When Alyosha deceives Dobrynya and steals his wife, the injured husband does not stab the culprit with steel weapons, or cut off his turbulent head:

> He seized Alyosha by his yellow curls,
> He dragged Alyosha over the table of oak,
> He flung Alyosha over the brick floor,
> He seized his riding whip,
> And set about belabouring him with the butt-end.[2]

But such feuds are exceptional, and never end very seriously in the early Cycles. One hears on the contrary of many compacts of sworn brotherhood, and these compacts are in general faithfully adhered to. The general impression left by the Kiev *byliny* is that the heroes focus their attention on casual encounters and aimless journeys in search of adventure or sport, and only enter into serious fighting when necessity

---

[1] Kirêevski, II. p. 40 ff.; cf. *ib*. II. p. 43 f.
[2] Rybnikov, I. p. 162 ff.; Chadwick, p. 81.

calls for it. But the *byliny* have undoubtedly passed through various phases before they achieved their present attitude, and the predominance of peaceable and domestic preoccupation may be due to the nature of either the reciters or their audience, whether in the seventeenth century or in modern times.

The heroes are only lightly armed. Mail-coats and suits of armour are rare or unknown. The shield is apparently not used. The commonest weapons are swords, bows and arrows, and a kind of 'travelling whip' (*shalyga dorozhnaya*), consisting of a leather strap weighted with lead at the end. Spears and lances are sometimes mentioned. The latter is the weapon with which Tugarin the Dragon's son threatens to dispatch Alyosha Popovich. The weapon of Svyatogor is a steel club (*palitsa*) which he hurls; but Ilya uses the same club for striking. The weapon of Vasili Buslaev is

> a club of red elm,
> With a core in the centre
> Of weighty lead from the east,
> This elm club weighed twelve *pud*.[1]

It is interesting to note the absence of any reference to firearms or other similar anachronisms in the early Cycles.

Elaborate descriptions of costume are introduced so frequently and with such fullness that we can form a fairly complete idea of the costume of the men of the Kiev Cycle—their sable caps for daily use, with sun and moon decoration for parade occasions, their cloaks of marten skins, their fantastic chased buttons 'like apples of Siberia', or 'in the semblance of youths and maidens', their morocco boots with high heels and toes pointed like awls, their patterned or flowered robes (*plate tsvêtnoe*). The costume of the *kalêki* too is no less minutely described, and seems to have been even richer, if we may judge from the accessories of the leader of the 'Forty and One *Kalêki*,' with his bag of velvet and his stick or 'crutch' tipped with ivory. In the later Cycles the references to costume are not so full, and are introduced only incidentally, but the details are still the same. The dress of the women is generally referred to incidentally in the same terms as that of men, though it is never described with any fullness.

It would, of course, be unsafe to assume that either the weapons or the costume necessarily represent any great antiquity. The costume of

[1] Kirsha Danilov's version, Kirêevski, v. p. 14 ff.; Fedotov's version, Rybnikov, I. p. 368 ff. A *pud* is a weight of 40 Russian pounds, or rather more than 36 English pounds.

the heroes may represent that of any period down to the time of Peter the Great, when an edict was issued forbidding the Streltsy to continue to wear the semi-oriental habit and the ancient long-skirted costume of tradition. The costume of the *kalêki* is certainly not more recent; but to what precise period they are to be assigned could only be ascertained by considerable research. Equal uncertainty invests the question of the exact date of the weapons.

Social standards or moral judgments are very rarely expressed, either by the poet himself, or by the characters in the *byliny*. Courage, loyalty, and generosity, so frequently alluded to in Teutonic heroic poetry, are rarely if ever alluded to in the *byliny*. Courage, indeed, is not a very marked feature of the early heroes. When Vladimir calls for volunteers to attack the enemy we are told not infrequently that 'the greater hid behind the lesser, and the lesser for their part were speechless.' Indeed the heroes often seek to evade an encounter. When Dobrynya is commissioned by Vladimir to go and rescue his niece Zabava from the dragon Nevêzha, he goes to his home in the deepest gloom, and it is his mother who encourages him and seeks to give him confidence. Similarly when Vasili Buslaev has made a wager with the citizens of Novgorod that he and his *druzhina* will fight them all on the following day, the hero returns to his mother overwhelmed with gloom and fear. Yet this absence of courage is not incompatible with naïve recklessness and disregard of warnings and sober council.

The loyalty of all the heroes to Vladimir is implicit. In general also they are faithful to their compacts with one another, though many flagrant breaches of honour are recorded in the *byliny* of the early Cycles. Sworn brothers can generally be depended upon to help one another at need. Mikhailo Potyk's sworn brothers, Dobrynya and Ilya, are untiring in their efforts to rescue the hero from the enchantments of the White Swan; and Alyosha Popovich recognises that it is his duty to go and seek and restore to life his sworn brother Dobrynya, when the latter is slain by a Tatar.[1] Yet he deals treacherously with Dobrynya in persuading his wife falsely that her husband is dead, and in marrying her during his absence. None of the heroes appear to have any scruples in breaking their word to women.

The formality and ceremony with which life is invested in the Kiev *byliny* has already been emphasised. The heroes do not fail to follow certain observances on arrival and departure. On entering a building, the hero ties up his horse, tucks his cap under his arm and enters the

---

[1] See the Siberian version of Tsar Kalin, Kirêevski, IV. p. 108 ff.

apartment, bowing on all sides, and in particular to his host and hostess. The more punctilious ask leave of the porters and door-keepers as they pass through. If the new arrival is unknown, his host courteously and in formal speech enquires his name and parentage and his place of origin, and being satisfied, he politely invites him to take his seat at the table of oak, to eat sweet food and drink honeyed drink. In spite of these and many other formalities, however, both heroes and heroines not infrequently lapse into childish and even boorish conduct, and the well-ordered feast may end in an unseemly brawl. The widow Chasova does not hesitate to fling her goblet of green wine in the face of the widow Bludova when the latter presumes to ask her daughter in marriage for her own son Khoten. We have already seen Dobrynya drag Alyosha by his yellow curls over the table of oak and fling him about the brick floor. The deportment of Dyuk on his arrival as a guest at Vladimir's hall is open to criticism:

> Rolls of millet flour were handed round.
> Dyuk Stepanovich, the prince's son,
> Took his millet roll in his hand,
> Took a bite of the outer crust,
> And threw the middle to the dogs...
> They poured out a goblet of green wine,
> And handed it to Dyuk Stepanovich;
> Dyuk Stepanovich, the prince's son,
> He took the goblet in his right hand,
> And lifted it to his delicate lips;
> That liquor did not please him,—
> He cast it all forth across the golden table,
> Over the glorious hall.[1]

It will be remembered that the coarse and gluttonous habits of Tugarin and Idolishche give great offence to the more polished heroes of Kiev.

Instances of coarseness of speech, or references to subjects not mentioned in polite society, are strikingly absent at all periods.[2] Enemies as well as friends are in general treated with reserve and respect. Atrocities and the horrors of war are rarely mentioned, or but lightly touched on. It is clear that as a general rule the audience has no taste for brutality. It is interesting to observe that the *byliny* give no hint of the terrible cruelties which history attributes to Ivan the Terrible and Peter the

---

[1] Rybnikov, I. p. 98 ff.; Chadwick, p. 103 ff.

[2] Exceptions are rare. We may refer to Kirsha Danilov's version of Ivan Godinovich, Kiréevski, III. p. 25, line 192.

Great, though some reminiscence of them may linger in the static description of

> The place of execution, the lime-tree block,
> Where eyes are put out of their sockets,
> Where tongues are torn out from their roots.

In general it is enough to say that the executioner 'cut off his rebellious head from his sturdy shoulders'. In particular the treatment of, and references to women are reserved and dignified. Exceptions occur, especially in the earlier Cycles. We may refer to brutal treatment meted out by Ivan Godinovich to his wife; and to the *bylina* of Prince Roman, recorded by Kirsha Danilov,[1] which perhaps offers us more which is macabre than any other *bylina*. In general, however, there is little in the *byliny* which could offend the most fastidious taste, and from the six-teenth century onward practically nothing.

Perhaps the feature in which the society of the *byliny* differs most widely from any of the heroic literatures hitherto considered is its extreme naïveté. In regard to the men this is most clearly observable in their boasting and self-conceit. In the *bylina* of Volga recited by Kuzma Romanov to Gilferding the Turkish tsar tells the tsaritsa that he proposes to go and raid in Russia and will bring back for her a costly mantle; but when she prophesies his failure,

> He struck her on one white cheek,
> And then he turned and struck her on the other,
> And he flung the tsaritsa on the brick floor,
> And again he flung her a second time.
> "I shall go into holy Russia,
> I shall take nine cities,
> I shall bestow them on my nine sons,
> I shall bring for myself the costly mantle!"[2]

This might, indeed, be cited as an instance of the brutal treatment of women if it were not so manifestly a humorous touch on the part of the poet. But the naïveté remains. Similarly ingenuous is the boast ascribed to Prince Mikhailo Skopin Shuyski (1610), who makes the following announcement at the feast held in his honour:

> You foolish people, and senseless,
> You are all boasting of mere trifles!
> Now I, Prince Mikhailo Vasilevich Skopin,
> I can indeed boast,

---

[1] Kirêevski, v. p. 108 ff.; Chadwick, p. 164 ff.
[2] Gilferding, ii. p. 172; Chadwick, p. 37 ff.

> For I have purged the Muscovite kingdom
> And the mighty Russian realm;
> Moreover they are singing a paean in my honour,
> Both old and young,
> Both old and young in my honour.[1]

In the women this naïveté generally assumes the form of a startling frankness in the matter of their affections, however fleeting the fancy:

> Marvel not at me, my gentlewomen,

cries the Princess Apraxya as she carves the white swan at the banquet—

> In that I have cut my fair right hand;
> I was gazing on the beauty of Churilo,
> On his golden curls,
> On his gold rings,
> And my bright eyes were dazzled.[2]

When Vladimir's niece, Zabava Putyatichna, hears Solovey's *druzhina* playing on the *gusli* of maplewood,

> She seated herself on the newly hewn bench
> And sat there the whole day from early morn,
> All day from early morn till eventide,
> And from eventide till midnight,
> And from midnight until broad daylight.

And when Solovey himself enters—

> Zabava sprang to her nimble feet,
> Zabava bowed to the very ground:
> "Greetings to you, bold noble youth,
> Young Solovey Budimirovich!
> You are a youth as yet unmarried,
> And I am a marriageable maid."[3]

Even in the seventeenth century the maidens still appear as unsophisticated, for in the *bylina* of Ksenÿa, daughter of Boris Godunov, Ksenÿa herself speaks:

> I do not wish to be shorn a nun,
> Or to keep monastic vows.
> The dark cell must be thrown open
> So that I may gaze upon the fine youths.[4]

There can be no doubt, however, that the naïveté is in reality due largely to the manner in which the literary tradition has been trans-

[1] Kirêevski, VII. p. 11; Chadwick, p. 229 ff.
[2] Rybnikov, II. p. 524 ff.; Chadwick, p. 99.
[3] Gilferding, I. p. 517 ff.; Chadwick, p. 116 ff.
[4] Kirêevski, VII. p. 58 f.; Chadwick, p. 218 f.

mitted, and in particular to the humble rank of the poets and reciters, and the humble milieu to which, in modern times, the latter generally belong. This literary naïveté is manifest in the standards of affluence recognised by the poets, as we see in the nature of the bribes offered and the prices paid for favours asked. Such bribes and payments generally take the form of 'a bowl of pure silver, another of red gold, and a third of round pearls'. The same literary naïveté is manifest also in the inappropriateness of some of the attributes of the heroes, especially of the great men of modern times. We may refer to the behaviour ascribed to Frederick the Great when the Russian army with Krasnoshchokov, the Cossack general, at its head, enters Berlin. "Tell me, king's daughter", Krasnoshchokov enquires, "Whither has the Prussian king fled?" "I called out to you," replies the daughter of the greatest monarch in Europe, "but you would not hearken, I waved my silk kerchief, but you would not look;

> He has perched on the window as a blue pigeon,
> The Prussian king is sitting under the table as a grey cat,
> He has flown from the hall as a free bird,
> He has alighted on the black quagmire as a black crow,
> He has plunged into the blue sea as a white fish,"[1] etc.

It is clear that the poet has forgotten his hero, and the shamanistic catalogue of Volga or his like has run away with him. But he is at all times a little uncertain in his touch when depicting incidents in the lives of modern sovereigns, especially incidents for which the early Cycles provide no literary precedent. In the *bylina* which relates the journey of Peter the Great in disguise to Sweden, 'the land of Stockholm', when the king's daughter suspects his identity,

> She brought out the portraits of the tsars of seven lands,
> She recognised the White Tsar from his portrait.[2]

When the Emperor Napoleon is about to invade Russia,

> He wrote a dispatch to the Tsar Alexander:
> "I beg you, Tsar Alexander, I beg you, do not be angry,
> Prepare for me a lodging in the Kremlin of Moscow,
> Prepare your royal palace for me, the French king."[3]

It is not easy to disentangle this literary naïveté, which is doubtless to some considerable extent a thing of modern growth, from the barbaric setting and elementary social outlook of the actual heroic milieu.

[1] Kirêevski, IX. p. 154 ff.; Chadwick, p. 281 ff.
[2] Kirêevski, VIII. p. 164 ff.; Chadwick, p. 260 ff.
[3] Kirêevski, X. p. 2; Chadwick, p. 287.

At one moment the heroes are conducting the most casual actions and encounters with elaborate and stereotyped ceremony; at another they are behaving on occasions of the utmost solemnity, in august or sacred buildings, like ill-bred children or tavern brawlers. Much of this inconsistency is doubtless inherent in barbaric society everywhere; but in the *byliny* it is greatly increased by the change which has taken place in the milieu in which the poems themselves have been preserved. The style and conventions of the poems, as we have seen, are at once highly elaborate and highly conventional, and a comparison of them with the style of the *Slovo o Polky Igorevê* convinces us that in the past the *byliny* have formed the répertoire of poets whose function it was to entertain a courtly audience. Yet in modern times neither reciters nor audience are familiar with court circles or high social standards. The picture of heroic life in the early Cycles has been in process of disintegration for many centuries, and traces of its degeneration are, as we have seen, clearly discernible. Nevertheless it cannot be too strongly emphasised that, considering the length of time in which the *byliny* have been in circulation, and considering the ignorance and poverty of the peasants to whom we are indebted for their transmission, the most astonishing feature about the *byliny* is their conservatism—not what has been lost, but what has been preserved. We hope to demonstrate the general fidelity of the *byliny* tradition in the chapter devoted to 'Historical and Unhistorical Elements'.

As in the heroic literatures already discussed, nationality plays little part in the *byliny*. Indeed in the early Cycles it is not easy to see how this could be otherwise, since nothing corresponding to Russia had as yet been formed in the period to which this Cycle refers, and the rivalry between the various cities, many of them governed by members of the same family, was not conducive to the sense of unity and stability indispensable to the growth of a spirit of nationalism. Still less were the Tatars likely to present to the Russians a picture of a stabilised political unit. Their mobility, their celerity, and their whole organisation and general way of life were calculated to convey an impression of an army of occupation rather than a state. Their capital is said to have resembled a camp rather than a town. It is true that the *byliny* frequently make mention of Russian and Tatar, but it is doubtful if these terms have any ethnographical or political significance.

For the poet of the *byliny* the chief distinction between the Russians and the Tatars is a military one. They constitute two opposing camps.

But though this is the chief distinction, it is not the only one. The poet is also aware of religious distinctions. The Russians are statically referred to as *pravoslavnÿe*, 'Orthodox', and Russia as *svyataya*, 'holy'. The Tatars are commonly referred to as Murmans, i.e. Mussulmans, and *paganÿe*, 'heathen', and as *zly*, 'evil', while the Jews are referred to as *nechestivÿe*, 'unclean', the Poles as *proklyatÿe*, 'accursed'. Yet here again it may be doubted how far distinction of doctrine is clearly apprehended. 'Orthodox' and 'heathens' constitute two opposing parties, and it is the interaction of these two parties which interests the poet and his audience.

There is no suggestion in the poems that the Russian heroes regarded the Tatars as foreigners. They have no difficulty in conversing freely with them, and no hint is ever given of a difference of language. They commonly refer to the Tatars as 'dogs' (*sobaki*), and Mamai, the Tatar khan, is naïvely addressed to his person as 'heathen dog Mamai'; but no offence appears to be either taken or intended by this brusque mode of address. We do not hear of any national characteristics, whether virtues or vices, ascribed to the Tatars as such, or any special distinction of dress, or habit, or way of life. Such physical distinctions as have left traditional traces on the *byliny* are so distorted as to be almost unrecognisable (cf. p. 119 below). The Russians frequently visit their camp, it may be only on diplomatic or hostile missions; but once there they are generally found engaged in sports and pastimes with the Tatars, and whiling away the time by no means unpleasantly in their company.

In the *byliny* of the Kiev Cycle, the sympathy is uniformly on the side of the Russians, and we never find members of the Tatar horde who have any claim on our sympathy. Indeed the *byliny* not infrequently represent the opponents of the heroes in an unfavourable light. This is especially the case with those to whom superhuman features are attributed. These superhuman foes have been identified with the Polovtsy. On the other hand the references to the Tatars proper are comparatively liberal, and free from abuse, and it is not often that the latter are represented in a strikingly unfavourable light. The poet never leaves us in any doubt, however, as to where his sympathies lie. He always represents the Russians as victorious in their contests with the Tatars, whether in warfare or sports, though he often represents the latter as gaining an advantage at the outset.

There is no suggestion that the Russia of the *byliny* of the early Cycle extended beyond the valley of the Dnêpr, or that the Russian heroes are to be found outside the orbit of Kiev. This is the more remarkable in view of the fact that the poems give no hint of the recognition of the existence of any other nationalities settled in their midst or in their vicinity. The *byliny* never mention the Finnish and Mordvin tribes of the north and east, or the Scandinavians of the Dnêpr. They never hint at linguistic boundaries between one area of Russia and another, or of linguistic barriers between different classes of the population. Foreigners sojourning in Kiev for however short a time become, for the poet, 'Orthodox Russian heroes', and experience no difficulty in conversing with the heroes of Vladimir's court or with one another. It is a significant fact that the hero who undertakes to oppose Shark Velikan, one of the heathen foes of Orthodox Russia, is Dyuk Stepanovich, the son of a prince of Galicia, whose sojourn in Russia—i.e. Kiev—is a purely temporary one (cf. p. 40 above). The other hero who is concerned to vindicate the honour of Kiev against Shark is Churilo Plenkovich, whose provenance is not clearly known, but who is certainly a stranger to Kiev, and whose name looks suspiciously Polish. Moreover the heroes of the Kiev Cycle are drawn from widely separated districts, not only outside Russia, but also from distant parts of Russia itself. Ilya is a native of the Mordvin district of Murom in the east in all modern versions of the *byliny*;[1] Alyosha comes from Rostov in the north; Dobrynya from Ryazan in the centre. Yet there is no suggestion that their interests are at variance in any respect with those of Kiev, or that they owed any responsibilities to their own communities. There is no hint of a clash of interests between one community and another. Indeed outside the court of Kiev no community can be said to exist as such in the poet's world.

One of the chief claims of a hero to a place in heroic poetry in Russia, as elsewhere, is success in warfare. The warfare may be either single combat, or a battle in which large numbers of the enemy take part; but on the Russian side it is all the same. Whether the heroes are opposing a single enemy or a whole army, we never hear of more than a handful at most on the Russian side, and in the great majority of cases the hero fights alone. Thus it comes about that strategy or the science of war, or good generalship, has no place in the *byliny*. The qualities most admired in a hero are personal strength and exaggerated and foolhardy recklessness. With these he is ready to overcome single-handed any number of the foe. When the citizens of Volga's three cities claim two kopecks from Mikula for the two bags of salt which he is carrying away, he lays about him with his travelling whip:

[1] See, however, p. 117 below.

Whoever was standing I left sitting,
And whoever was sitting I left prostrate,
And whoever lay prostrate would never rise again.[1]

When the River Dnêpr complains to Sukhan Domantevich that she is oppressed by a Tatar army of thirty thousand men, Sukhan uproots an oak-tree with which to lay about him, and of all that Tatar host he leaves no more than three alive. This is heroic warfare indeed! Or is it not nearer to folk-tale? There can be little doubt that these gigantic exaggerations of victory are a popular feature of the *byliny*, and due to the uncritical standards of an ignorant audience. In all probability they are a comparatively modern development. It has already been mentioned that in all the versions of Tsar Kalin from Olonets recorded by Rybnikov, Ilya and one or two companions are represented as victorious over the Tatar host. But in the version recorded by the poet Mey from the recitation of an old Siberian Cossack,[2] the battle is represented as a signal defeat for the Russian heroes. It is true they might have overcome the Tatar host which had come to destroy Kiev, had it not been for the fact that for every Tatar slain two living Tatars sprang up to take his place. By such a device of poetic diction some ancient poet has sought to symbolise the overwhelming numbers of the Tatar army, and the odds encountered by the little band of Russians on the lower Dnêpr. But the importance of this version lies in the fact that the last great battle of the Russian heroes is here represented as a defeat, like the great battle of Kosovo in Yugoslav epic poetry. There can be little doubt that this Siberian version represents an older redaction of the story than the versions current in Olonets.[3] We may compare the heroic raid of Prince Igor and his brother narrated in the *Slovo o Polky Igorevê*, which also ends in a defeat for the Russian heroes.

The warfare of the Kiev Cycle is almost wholly defensive, and consists in warding off the inroads of the Tatar armies, and the raids of individual dragon and monster heroes, who, as we shall see, are sometimes frankly admitted to be Tatar chiefs. It follows that the usual incentives to war, such as personal motives, vengeance for wrongs or insults, quarrels with relatives, desire of glory, and the like do not play so large a part in the *byliny* as in the heroic poetry of the Greek and

[1] Rybnikov, I. p. 10; Chadwick, p. 47.
[2] Kirêevski, IV. p. 108 ff.
[3] Bezsonov regards the Siberian *bylina* as corrupt, and there are undoubtedly certain discrepancies in the narrative. There are nevertheless cogent reasons which need not be discussed here for regarding this version as representing the most conservative form of the tradition.

Teutonic peoples. Head hunting for its own sake appears to be unknown. In certain versions of Tsar Kalin the Tatar sends an envoy to
demand that the Princess Apraxya be given up to him, and it is in answer
to Vladimir's appeal that his honour and that of the princess shall be
vindicated that the heroes ride forth to encounter the Tatar host.
Similarly Churilo Plenkovich goes forth to single combat against Shark
Velikan in defence of the Princess Apraxya—an incident which may be
a variant of the preliminary episode of the story of 'Tsar Kalin'. Not
infrequently the cause of war is 'tribute overdue'. It is for this cause
that Tsar Bukhar leads an army against Prince Vladimir, and for this
also that Vladimir sends Mikhailo Potyk to the north, where he overcomes the 'muzhiks' in battle and obtains the tribute. Sometimes the
tribute is said to consist of water birds, but these appear to be 'White
Swans', in other words slave girls (cf. p. 123 below). Volga alone of
the early heroes wages offensive warfare against the Turkish tsar. There
can be no doubt that in this case the object is booty.

> They went into the Turkish land,
> And took the Turkish host prisoners.
> "My brave, my bold druzhina!
> Let us now begin to divide the spoil."
> What was a dear bargain,
> And what a cheap?
> Good steeds went for seven rubles,
> And a steel weapon for six rubles,
> Sharp swords for five rubles,
> Steel clubs for three rubles;
> But the cheap bargain was the womenfolk,—
> Old women were priced at a quarter of a kopeck,
> And married women at half a kopeck,
> And fair maidens at a halfpenny.[1]

The most striking and spectacular narratives of single combats in the
byliny are fought between Russian heroes and superhuman enemies of
Kiev. Of these we have a fine series. We may instance the two combats
fought between Dobrynya Nikitich and Nevêzha, the serpent or dragon
of the Mountain, the first on the bank of a river in the Steppe or plains to
the south of Kiev, the second at the mouth of the mountain cavern
where the dragon has its home. In some versions Nevêzha is described
as a black crow,[2] in others as an ordinary *bogatyr*.[3] Again he is said to be

---

[1] Gilferding, II. p. 172; Chadwick, p. 33 ff.
[2] Rybnikov, II. p. 590 ff.   [3] *Ib.* II. p. 402 ff.

capable of assuming all these forms[1]. Both Churilo Plenkovich and Dyuk Stepanovich are represented as fighting Shark Velikan (cf. p. 40 f. above); but it is Dyuk who slays him. Ilya of Murom seeks out and slays the Tatar Idolishche, who is represented as having conquered a Christian city and stabled his horses in the holy Churches. Finally we may refer to the two great combats against Tugarin Zmêevich, Tugarin 'the Dragon's Son', which are variously attributed to Dobrynya[2] and Alyosha,[3] and in which Tugarin is slain. Other instances of such combats between the heroes of Kiev and their superhuman or supernatural foes might be cited. Supernatural features are attributed to most of their enemies. They hiss like serpents, roar like aurochses, so that the glass windows are shivered, and people fall stunned at the sound. Burning flames pour forth from their mouths, and they are furnished with paper wings which are nevertheless strong enough to carry them through the air.

It will be seen that the Russian heroes, who are in general without supernatural and superhuman attributes, are at a disadvantage in their single combats. It is to this disadvantage no doubt that we are to attribute the serious want of fair play in their relations with their enemies. This absence of fairness often takes the form of downright trickery. Examples are numerous. One of the commonest of these tricks is disguise. It would seem that the kalêki are sacrosanct in the eyes of the enemy, and accordingly the Russian heroes are in the habit of approaching their enemies in the guise of kalêki in order to put them off their guard. It is in this way that Alyosha Popovich approaches Tugarin in the version ascribed to Kirsha Danilov, and so also Ilya of Murom approaches Idolishche. At other times the hero, unable to overcome his enemy by force of arms, throws his kalêka cap at him, and at the touch of the sacred headdress the strength of the dragon-hero collapses. It is not easy to see, however, how the heroes could have coped with foes who are capable of flying through the air without superhuman aid.

[1] *Ib.* II. p. 590, line 71.
[2] Rybnikov, I. p. 79. Fragments of a *bylina* in which Dobrynya appears as the slayer of Tugarin are also recorded by Chulkov in his collection of Russian *skazki*. The same collection contains a *skazka* which also represents Dobrynya as the hero of the exploit. See Bezsonov's note, Kirêevski, II. p. 79. We may compare also the version from Simbirsk which describes Dobrynya as fighting a dragon of this name. *Ib.* II. p. 40 ff. Cf. *ib.* p. 49, where the dragon slain by Dobrynya seems to be Tugarin.
[3] The exploit is attributed to Alyosha in Kirsha Danilov's version, and in a prose story published by Afanasev, II. p. 257 f., and elsewhere.

Accordingly the evening before a contest is usually spent by the heroes in prayer that a heavy shower of rain may fall to wet the enemy's 'paper wings', so that he may 'fall like a dog on to the damp earth'. Even when Tugarin is thus disabled Alyosha has not the courage to meet his enemy in fair fight. He distracts him by a false statement so as to make him turn momentarily to look behind him, and during the moment that he is off his guard Alyosha springs upon him and dispatches him, cutting off his head, which he carries back in triumph to Kiev. It is only fair to add that the dragon-heroes for their part appear to have a very irresponsible attitude to their own plighted word. Nevêzha has no sooner given a promise to Dobrynya that he will never more enter the city of Kiev or carry off Russian maidens than he comes flying over Kiev and carries off Vladimir's niece Zabava to his cavern in the mountains; but then, as the poet does not omit to explain to us, 'the dragon was a perfidious dragon'.

In spite of the shameless breaches of honour to which we have just referred it is clear that certain standards are observed, and certain codes and regulations accepted in matters of warfare and single combat. Even after Tugarin has thrown a dagger at Alyosha, and Idolishche at Ilya of Murom, the Russian heroes do not rush upon their adversaries without due notice given. In each case the Russian arranges to meet his adversary early on the following morning in the open plain and there to fight hand to hand. Despite the fact that Alyosha's honour is badly smirched by his behaviour in regard to Dobrynya's wife during his absence, yet he fulfils the requirements of honour when the latter is slain by the Tatar, and goes himself to seek Dobrynya and fight the Tatar who has slain him. Indeed the heroes not unfrequently show a chivalrous spirit in their dealings with one another. Dyuk Stepanovich, after successfully leaping the Dnêpr on his horse, does not fail to turn back to rescue his defeated rival who is struggling in the middle of the river.

The picture which the *byliny* present of the individualistic outlook of the heroes and of their standards and methods of warfare, like that of the heroic milieu, is to be accepted only with reserve. Once more we must remind ourselves that the *byliny* have been transmitted to us by an isolated and scattered population, whose political ideas can only be very elementary, and who know nothing, or next to nothing, of warfare. The only prose literature on which their ideas can be modelled consists of *skazki*, or oral folk-tales. It is only to be expected, therefore, that interchange of influence will have taken place to a considerable extent between these two literary forms, and the influence of the *skazki* on the *byliny* is nowhere more marked than in the tendency to exaggeration, to lose touch with reality and verisimilitude in matters of heroic prowess, to substitute the hero's strong right arm for the assistance of a *druzhina*. And there are other influences which have contributed to place the *byliny* at a definite remove from heroic tradition. Among the chief of these we may refer to the inevitable tendency of the peasants to interpret literally the figurative diction of the traditional style of court poetry, which has resulted in an extensive growth of supernatural features in the heroic narrative. Chief among these we may instance the modern representation of the chief enemies of Kiev as fiery dragons.

Yet in spite of these reservations the picture of the society of Kiev is, on the whole, a picture of a heroic community, both in peace and in war. The society is formed of a prince surrounded by his *druzhina*, a wealthy and leisured class, irresponsible, fond of display, proud and boastful, recklessly daring and generally successful. Political thought is undeveloped, the outlook is individualistic and acquisitive, the warfare consists chiefly of single combats carried on by a few of the leading heroes. Love of adventure is their predominating characteristic. In this society the strong and the boastful, the wealthy, and the beautiful are destined to success and glory. In some respects Ilya of Murom may be thought of as an exception, but there can be little doubt that his peasant attributes are comparatively recent and intrusive (cf. p. 118 below). The interest is distributed with an approximation to impartiality over a considerable number of heroes, each of whom is himself the centre of a heroic adventure or a series of adventures. Moreover these heroes are depicted, not in isolation, but in close relationship with one another. All this is the material of heroic poetry and the picture of a heroic society, not of folktale. We hope in the following section to show that it is a picture derived from heroic tradition which has a historical basis.

There is yet another factor which has tended to change the atmosphere of the heroic stories and detract from the high seriousness which we are accustomed to associate with court poetry. This is the element of humour, which is rarely far away from the *byliny*, and is often introduced with considerable effect. By this device the singers succeed in humanising their narratives, and enlisting the sympathetic attention of the modern audience for stories which without it would soon grow jejune, and would at all times be remote from modern interests. Instances come crowding to the memory too numerous to quote—Kastryuk crawling on all fours under the stairs after his sorry failure in the wrestling bout; Vladimir's dilemma between his fear of angering the envoy Vasili and his apprehension of losing his prisoner Stavr; Mikhailo's rejection of Vladimir's offer of towns and villages as an alternative to the privilege of free drinks; Nastasya the *polenitsa* tucking her defeated pursuer comfortably in her pocket; Mikula's treatment of the extortionate *muzhiks*. More often the humour is seen in static but telling phraseology —as a sign of fear:

> The greater hid behind the lesser,
> And the lesser for their part were speechless;

—as a sign of total defeat:

> Whoever was standing he left sitting,
> Whoever was sitting he left prostrate,
> And whoever lay prostrate would never rise again;

—as a sign of heroic strength which we are not asked to take too seriously,

> Whoever he seized by the arm,
> That arm came off at the shoulder;
> Whoever he caught by the leg,
> That leg was no more.

It shows itself also in the daring exaggerations—the very abandon of high-spirited fun:

> The youths wore kaftans of scarlet cloth...
> The boots on their feet were of green morocco,
> The points were like the points of awls, and the heels high,
> Round the tips an egg could be rolled;
> Beneath the instep a sparrow could fly
> A sparrow could fly, could flit to and fro.[1]

In these passages of poetical shorthand the heroic singer tiptoes over our credulity. His high-spirited and reckless exaggerations resemble those of Tatar heroic poetry and no other, and it is difficult to dissociate both from the mentality of a people familiar with horses in full career across the Steppe. To call it humour is too literal, and to call it exaggeration is sesquipedalian. Here the critical faculty is out of place. The singer compels the listener to his own mood, he gives us the high-spirited irresponsible abandon of the poetical imagination in full gallop. The listener holds his breath in suspense, but he need not fear a stumble. There is no bathos in the *byliny*.

[1] Rybnikov, II. p. 460.

CHAPTER IV

HISTORICAL AND UNHISTORICAL ELEMENTS IN THE *BYLINY*

THE later Cycles of *byliny* relate to times for which ample historical evidence is available. It is clear that they frequently distort historical fact, and that they also introduce elements manifestly unhistorical. But in general there can be no doubt that the characters are historical persons, and that the events recorded in connection with them have some foundation in fact. The earlier Cycles, however, relate to times for which the available historical evidence is limited. Many of the characters still remain unidentified, and such historical evidence as bears directly on these is late and fragmentary. Moreover such identifications as have been suggested are, more often than not, of a highly controversial character, and the evidence consists largely in a balance of probabilities. We propose, therefore, in the following chapter to concentrate primarily on the historical elements in the early Cycles. We shall also have something to add on the unhistorical elements in both the early and the modern Cycles. When we reflect on the wide field covered by the Russian *byliny*, and the number of characters involved, it is clear at the outset that we cannot hope in this brief survey to cover the whole field. The most that we can hope to do is to select a few of the most important and representative of the *byliny* of various Cycles for discussion.

We will take the Cycles in the order which is commonly regarded as chronological, beginning with the so-called 'Older Heroes', then passing to the Kiev and Novgorod Cycles, and concluding this portion of our study with one or two of the 'medieval' *byliny*. In each Cycle we will first consider the personnel and their relation to history. A word will then be added, where relevant, on the political geography of the poems, and the conservatism with which the milieu has been preserved. In the case of the Kiev Cycle certain elements generally regarded as supernatural and unhistorical claim some attention, since we think that in some cases their origin and definite relation to history can be demonstrated. We will conclude with a brief discussion of some of the unhistorical elements in the cycles which have relation to more modern times, from the sixteenth century down to our own day.

No serious claim to historicity has ever been made for Svyatogor, and the history of the group of stories relating to him is still obscure.[1] Nor has any historical foundation been established for Mikula. The *bylina* relating to him is believed to be of Novgorod provenance,[2] and it has been suggested with considerable probability that the person of the hero is derived from a certain Mikula of Pskov, who is said to have been a strong and powerful man of the peasant class (*kerls*), who greeted with defiance the invading army of Ivan the Terrible. A Bulgarian Bogomil legend of a certain Prince Prov who meets Christ working at the plough as he is on his way to collect his revenues, and invites him to accompany him, may well be a variant of the motif which has formed another element in the story of Mikula.[3]

The question of the identity and historical origin of Volga has probably aroused more interest and controversy than that of any other hero; yet there has been no agreement among scholars as to his prototype.[4] It is now generally held that in the *bylina* of Volga, two *byliny*, originally distinct, have been combined, one relating to the supreme hunter Volga and another, wholly independent of it, relating to the expedition of a hero (Volkh) into a foreign land.[5] V. F. Miller[6] held that the story of Volga the hunter originated in the *skazanie* or prose saga of the great hunting expeditions of the Princess Olga incorporated in the Ancient Chronicle, with whom his name was originally identical. On the other hand in Russian literature the combination of the power of shape-changing and occult familiarity with the animal world is not infrequently attributed to historical characters of early times, and notably to important military princes. It is ascribed to Prince Oleg, brother of Rurik, who figures in the Ancient Chronicle as leading his *druzhina* against Byzantium, like Volga himself, and who is said to have been known as *Vêshchi*, the Sage or Sorcerer, on account of his wisdom. It is also ascribed to Vseslav,

---

[1] A fine study by Prof. Mazon (*R.É.S.* XII. 1932, p. 160 ff.), has recently given us the data for a fresh approach to the subject on scientific lines. The net result is to strengthen our belief in the unhistorical origin of the hero.

[2] V. F. Miller, *Ocherki*, I. p. 168 ff.; cf. III. p. 38. Cf. Mazon, *Bylines*, p. 153 f.

[3] Prof. Mazon has recently made a study of the *bylina* of Mikula (*R.É.S.* XI. 1931, p. 149 ff.) in which an account of the Bogomil legend, and of the person of Mikula of Pskov are also given.

[4] A useful summary of some of the earlier suggestions which have been made will be found in an article by Schröder, *G.R.M.* VIII. (1920), p. 287 ff. See also Chadwick, p. 33 ff.

[5] This suggestion was first put forward by Shambinago. See Miller, *Ocherki*, III. p. 18. [6] *Loc. cit.*

prince of Polotsk, in the *Slovo o Polky Igorevê*, and also to Prince Roman of Galicia, both in certain of the *byliny*, and in the so-called Chronicle of Volhynia.[1] It is a significant fact that the characteristics attributed to Roman, both in the Chronicle and in the *bylina*, are almost identical with those attributed to the hero Volga, the common variant of whose name (*Volkh*) might perhaps be connected with *Vlakh*, the Slavonic translation of *Roman*.

On the whole the historical element which can be traced in the *byliny* of Svyatogor, Mikula, and Volga may be regarded as negligible. It is doubtless largely because of the unhistorical character and supernatural features of these *byliny* that they are commonly regarded as having reference to an earlier period than any other Cycle. There is, however, no clear evidence which points to such a conclusion, and in regard to Mikula it is not even probable that it is correct. The date of Volga's historical prototype, if he had one, is still problematical, but we have little doubt that the element of the marvellous entered into the tradition in comparatively modern times—not earlier than the fifteenth century, and probably later—and is due to a literal interpretation of the highly figurative diction which was current in the traditional narrative style of the Kiev school. The association of this figurative diction with Volga in itself makes it probable that the hero belongs to this area, and to a period not much later than the composition of the *Slovo o Polky Igorevê*.

We will next turn to the Kiev Cycle, which undoubtedly has some connection with history, and with one of the two Vladimirs who ruled in Kiev, though it cannot be regarded as settled whether the Cycle originally had reference to Vladimir I who was crowned in 980 and died in 1015, or to his great-grandson who ruled from 1113 to 1125. Many of the heroes of the *byliny* of this Cycle are mentioned in the Chronicles, though the Chroniclers are not always in agreement as to the period, or even the century, to which they belonged. These references have generally been accepted in the past by Western writers, both as a guarantee of the historical existence of the heroes, and also of their original association with the events in connection with which they are named. Researches carried on in Russia during the last half century, however, especially in connection with the early chronicles and with the historical sagas (*povêsti* and *skazanÿa*) which they frequently incorporate, have shown that these references to the early heroes are of very unequal value.

[1] The exploits of Prince Roman and his brilliant punitive campaign against the Lithuanians are related in the Chronicle, s.a. 1196. See Rambaud, *R.É.* p. 239.

Of all the heroes of the Kiev Cycle, Alyosha Popovich is the one for whom we possess the fullest and most satisfactory—though not the earliest—historical evidence. The Chronicles are not in entire agreement in regard to this hero, and their evidence is of very unequal value; but the evidence of the Chronicle of Tver (or, more properly Rostov)—an authority of prime importance[1]—makes it clear that according to Rostov popular local tradition current in the thirteenth century, Alexander or Alyosha was originally in the service of the grand prince Vsevolod Yurevich ('Big-Nest', 1176–1212) of Rostov. After the death of Vsevolod, when his son Constantine obtained the city of Rostov, Alexander passed into the *druzhina* of Constantine, and is frequently mentioned in the Chronicle as assisting Constantine in the defence of Rostov against his elder brother Yuri. His servant Torop is also mentioned as assisting in the fighting. In these dissensions between the brothers, Alexander performed such great exploits against Yuri's followers that after the death of Constantine he thought it expedient to flee to Kiev, together with his servant, and there 'to serve the only Grand Prince in the mother city of Kiev'. Having arrived in Kiev Alexander, we are told, together with his *druzhina*, 'beat his forehead'[2] to the mighty prince Mstislav Romanovich, and the Grand Prince prided himself and boasted greatly concerning them.[3]

These adventures of Alyosha and his *druzhina* are related in the *Povêst* or saga (incorporated in the Chronicle of Rostov) directly before the account of the Battle of Kalka, concerning which the Chronicler tells us:

"There took place the slaughter of the wicked for our sins, and there took place the victory over the Russian princes, the like of which had never taken place since the beginning of the Russian land."

This battle is generally believed to be reflected in the *bylina* of Tsar Kalin[4] (cf. p. 49 above). Enumerating those who had perished in the battle, the writer of the Chronicle adds:

[1] Our information relating to this Chronicle and to the notices which it contains of Alexander Popovich is derived from Miller, *Ocherki*, III. p. 74 ff.; the extracts quoted below are from the texts contained in Brodski, etc., p. 105. Complete texts of the Russian Chronicles, with the exception of those of Kiev and Novgorod, have not been accessible to us.

[2] I.e. offered his submission, entered his service.

[3] Brodski, etc., p. 105; Miller, *Ocherki*, III. p. 74 f.

[4] The name *Kalin* is thought to be derived from the name of the river (Kalka) on which the great battle was fought between the Russians and the Tatars in 1228.

"And Alexander Popovich was slain there with seventy other heroes (*khrabrÿe*)."

A still earlier mention of the destruction of Alexander Popovich with his companions occurs in the Academy transcript of the Chronicle of Suzdal. Here, however, the information is quite isolated, and wholly unconnected with what precedes or what follows, and it is not explained who the hero was, the implication being that he is quite a well-known figure.[1]

Miller has shown that these notices of Alyosha Popovich are derived from contemporary local tradition, and has stressed the value of the whole narrative of the Chronicle for the history of the *byliny*. "We have," he writes, "no evidence more valuable for the history of our native epos, generally so poor in written documents. These entries carry us into the spirit of Rostov in the thirteenth century, with its precious traditions of its local hero, Alexander Popovich."[2] The inclusion of the thirteenth-century local hero of Rostov in the Kiev Cycle is no doubt to be accounted for by his final journey to Kiev, and the position which he held in the *druzhina* of the Grand Prince. His death in the Battle of Kalka against the Tatars would materially assist this inclusion.

If the tradition of the Chronicle of Tver relating to Alexander Popovich of Rostov be accepted as authentic, the results are of interest in relation to the setting of the *byliny* in which he figures. He is at times represented as the slayer of Tugarin, 'the Dragon's Son', though in variants his place as a protagonist is generally occupied by Dobrynya Nikitich. Now it is generally agreed[3] that Tugarin the Dragon's Son is no other than Tugor Kan, one of a number of leaders or *khans*[4] of the Polovtsy. According to the Ancient Chronicle, Svyatopolk II made a treaty with him in 1094 and married his daughter.[5] Vladimir Monomakh also married his son Andrey to Tugor's grand-daughter; but these marriages did not deter Tugor from further incursions. In

---

[1] Brodski, etc. p. 109.
[2] *Ocherki*, III. p. 76.
[3] See Kirêevski, IV. p. cxv; cf. Miller, *Ocherki*, III. p. 41 ff.
[4] *Kan* is a dialectal variant form of the Tatar word *khan*, 'a chief'. The Polovtsy, or Kipchak Turks occupied the steppe and harassed the borders of the southern Russian states on the Dnêpr during the latter part of the eleventh and beginning of the twelfth centuries. They are better known among European writers as *Cumani*. For an account of their history see A. Bruce Boswell, *The Slavonic Review*, VI. p. 68 ff.
[5] Ancient Chronicle, p. 189.

the year 1096, encouraged by a successful attack made by the Polovtsy
under Bonyak and Kurya, he led an army to besiege Pereyaslavl.
Syvatopolk, likewise undeterred by close ties of marriage, together
with his cousin Vladimir Monomakh, marched against Tugor. The
Polovtsy were surprised and defeated. Many of their princes were
slain, and both Tugor and his son were killed in the ensuing battle.
Tugor's body was discovered next morning, and Syvatopolk gave
orders that it should be brought to Kiev and buried near Berestovo.[1]
Such is the account of Tugor Kan in the oldest source which we possess.
This account, which seems to imply that Tugor was killed in honourable
warfare, was accepted by Solovev.[2] According to L. A. Magnus, the
'Chronicles' state that Tugor and his son were murdered by the
princess, i.e. his own daughter: which may be a later version of the
story.

This account of Tugor corresponds well enough in its main features
with the Tugarin of the *byliny*. It makes him a contemporary of
Vladimir II. Tugarin, stripped of his supernatural features, may well
represent the Steppe nomad, whose marriage relations would suggest
that he was in the habit of frequenting Kiev on friendly terms, but
whose coarse habits and offensive table manners might naturally be
distasteful to the city-dwelling Russians. It is clear, also, that Tugor
was killed on Russian soil. But when we try to equate the slayer of
Tugarin in the *byliny* with historical fact we are in a difficulty; for
Tugor was killed in 1096, while according to our best authorities
Alyosha Popovich of Rostov lived more than a hundred years later, and
was killed in 1224. If, therefore, Tugarin 'the Dragon's Son' is to be
identified with Tugor Kan, as there seems no room to doubt, he cannot
have been killed by Alyosha Popovich. We may remember, however,
that a rival though less famous tradition ascribes the slaying of Tugor,
not to Alyosha, but to Dobrynya Nikitich, who may well have been a
contemporary of Tugor K(h)an, as we shall see (cf. p. 110 below).
Indeed there are cogent reasons for regarding the latter tradition as the
more authentic.

Dobrynya Nikitich has generally been regarded as a historical figure,
though his actual historical prototype has never been clearly established.
The early historical records of Russia mention several Dobrynyas. The
earliest occurrence of the name is in the Ancient Chronicle, where a
certain Dobrynya, uncle of Vladimir I, plays a prominent part as a

[1] Ancient Chronicle, p. 193 f.
[2] Vol. III. col. 342.

zealous heathen and governor of Novgorod. The second person of this name is Dobrynya Raguilovich, *voevoda* of Mstislav Vladimirovich, prince of Novgorod, who, according to the same authority, fought in 1096 on behalf of his prince against Oleg and Yaroslav. He is probably to be identified with the Dobrynya referred to in the Synodal transcript of the Chronicle of Novgorod, s.a. 1117, where it is stated that 'Dobrynya, Posadnik of Novgorod, died on December 6'.[1] A third Dobrynya is mentioned as living in the thirteenth century, but on less satisfactory authority. Solovev tells us that a medieval Russian work is still extant which records the journey of one Dobrynya Yadreykovich to Tsargrad in 1210,[2] and the Chronicle of Nikon refers to one Dobrynya of the Golden Belt of Ryazan, who is here stated to have perished in the Battle of Kalka, with Alyosha Popovich and others.[3]

It will be seen that three independent traditions are recorded in the Chronicles, according to one of which Dobrynya lived in the time of Vladimir I, according to another in the time of Vladimir II, whereas according to a third he is to be placed in the early part of the thirteenth century. As regards the third tradition, it may be suggested here, however, that the reference in the Chronicle of Nikon can hardly be regarded as independent of heroic poetry; and indeed in one of Kirsha Danilov's *byliny* devoted to Dobrynya[4] the hero is described as the son of a rich merchant (*bogaty gost*) named Nikita, of Ryazan, a town on the River Oka, which is a tributary of the Volga. When it is remembered that Nikon was born at Nizhni Novgorod, at the junction of the River Oka with the Volga, in 1605, and that Kirsha Danilov's collection was made in the Province of Perm during the first half of the eighteenth century, the close correspondence between the entry in the Chronicles and the opening lines of Kirsha Danilov's *bylina* need cause no surprise. Moreover it seems not impossible that the journey of Dobrynya Yadreykovich to Tsargrad in 1210 referred to in the 'medieval work' mentioned by Solovev is a reminiscence of Dobrynya's journey to Tsargrad narrated in the *byliny*, and that this passage also is not independent of heroic oral tradition. The patronymic *Yadreykovich* looks suspiciously like a popular (oral) corruption (with metathesis of *r* and change of *g* to *d*) of the name *Raguilovich*, ascribed in the Ancient Chronicle to the second Dobrynya, who is represented as a contemporary of Vladimir II.

---

[1] Michell, Forbes and Beazley, *Chronicle of Novgorod* (London, 1914), s.a. 1117.
[2] Vol. III. book I, col. 762, footnote I.
[3] Brodski, etc. p. 105.
[4] Kirêevski, II. p. 49.

We will now turn to the first Dobrynya. In the poems Dobrynya is represented as the nephew of Prince Vladimir, and on the basis of this close relationship many scholars have sought to identify him with Dobrynya, the uncle of Vladimir I, who is several times referred to in the Ancient Chronicle. Thus s.a. 6478 (A.D. 970) we read that Vladimir was a son of Svyatoslav by Malusha, a serf and housekeeper to Olga, and also sister to Dobrynya; that is to say, Dobrynya was Vladimir's uncle, and the close association between them is emphasised in the Chronicle. In the same annal we read that when the men of Novgorod demanded a prince, Dobrynya suggested that Vladimir should be sent, 'and the men of Novgorod took Vladimir, and Vladimir went to Novgorod with his uncle Dobrynya'. Later (s.a. 6486–8), when Vladimir came to the throne of Kiev, he established his uncle Dobrynya at Novgorod. Here, we are told, Dobrynya set up an idol to Perun on the bank of the Volkhov. Yet again later (s.a. 6493) we hear of Dobrynya going with Vladimir by sea to make war on the Bulgarians, and helping him with his prudent counsel.

The story of Dobrynya's activities in Novgorod on behalf of Perun need not be regarded very seriously. The whole crude story of the conversion by Vladimir I as related in the Ancient Chronicle is regarded with complete scepticism by all serious historians,[1] though some form of oral tradition—no doubt of a highly popular character—undoubtedly lies behind it. With this story the story of Dobrynya and Perun is closely bound up, and apparently of no more historical value.

Dobrynya is also associated with Vladimir I in the Ioakim Chronicle,[2] as well as in certain other Chronicles composed in modern times, such as the so-called Chronicle of Nikon.[3] The Ioakim Chronicle, however, represents Dobrynya as a zealous Christian, and offers us a vivid and

---

[1] See Klyuchevski, I. pp. 12, 16, 22; Laehr, p. 87 ff.; cf. also Braun, pp. 158, footnote 1, 177 f.

[2] The so-called Ioakim Chronicle is incorporated in the first volume of Tatishchev's *History of Russia*. It was held in the past that its author availed himself of the earlier portion of the Chronicle of Novgorod which has not come down to us, and which he attributes to Ioakim, the first bishop of Novgorod, though he does not state on what grounds he makes this attribution. See Solovev, III. i. col. 794.

[3] Solovev points out (I. vii. 172, footnote 1) that the account of the conversion of Novgorod in the Ioakim Chronicle is in no way at variance with the account incorporated in the Chronicle of Nikon, though Nikon mentions two missions, whereas Ioakim specifies only the one in which he himself took part, telescoping the narrative so that the two events are run into one.

detailed account of the conversion of Novgorod by Dobrynya, with the help of a certain Putyata, who is described as *tysyatski* of the city of Vladimir.[1]

The account is strangely at variance with the notice already cited from the Ancient Chronicle, which would seem to represent Dobrynya as a devotee of Perun. If the account were genuine, we should have to suppose, either that two contradictory traditions were current, or else that the conversion of Dobrynya himself intervened between his setting up the idol of Perun, as recorded in the Ancient Chronicle, and his forcible conversion of the men of Novgorod as recorded in the Ioakim Chronicle. Despite the fact that the credibility of the Ioakim Chronicle used by Tatishchev has been impugned in recent years,[2] the testimony of this document, together with that cited by Solovev (cf. p. 108, footnote 2, above), makes it clear that traditions of the conversion of Novgorod by Dobrynya were current in variant forms before the middle of the seventeenth century.

In the Ancient Chronicle also Dobrynya is found as a contemporary of Putyata. Here Putyata figures in connection with events which are strangely similar to those related in the Chronicles of Ioakim and Nikon. In the Ancient Chronicle, however, these events are represented as taking place, not in the time of Vladimir I, but in that of Vladimir II. We must turn, therefore, to examine the data for the second tradition before attempting to decide to which of these two reigns the original Dobrynya, the prototype of the hero of the *byliny*, actually belonged.

It must be confessed that until the Slavonic works impugning the authenticity of the Ioakim Chronicle are accessible, no such conclusion can be wholly satisfactory, and perhaps a final judgment of the matter must be postponed until such works are available to us. In the meantime, however, two important facts are clear. The first is that the portion of the Ancient Chronicle which refers Dobrynya and Putyata to the close of the reign of Svyatopolk and the beginning of the reign of Vladimir Monomakh is a contemporary document of unimpeachable authority, while on the other hand it is now generally agreed among Russian historians that much of the material relating to the earlier

---

[1] The Old Slavonic text of the passage under discussion is given by Brodski, etc. p. 96 f. A modernised Russian version will be found in Solovev, i. vii. col. 171 f.

[2] See Miller, *Ocherki*, i. p. 145. For further references to Slavonic works on this subject the reader may consult a note by Laehr, p. 143.

periods represented in the Ancient Chronicle is of a legendary character. The second is that a careful reading of the portions of this Chronicle which relate to the reign of Yaropolk and his sons makes clear the nature of the events which led to the circumstances in which Dobrynya and Putyata were involved, and shows these circumstances to be the natural result of a long chain of events culminating in the early years of the twelfth century. The authenticity of the narrative is all the more probable in view of the fact that there is no hint in the record that the chronicler was aware himself of the operation of cause and effect in the events which he is recording.

According to the Ancient Chronicle (s.a. 6604 = A.D. 1096) a certain Dobrynya Raguilovich was *voevoda* of Mstislav Vladimirovich, prince of Novgorod, sometimes called Mstislav the Great. The same entry also makes mention of one Nikita who is said to have been bishop of Novgorod at this time. In the year 1117 the Chronicle of Novgorod records the death of Dobrynya, a *posadnik* of the city, who in view of the rarity of the name, may doubtless be identified with Dobrynya the '*voevoda*'. In the entry in the Ancient Chronicle referred to above, Dobrynya Raguilovich is said to have been in charge of an expedition organised by Mstislav against the Russian princes in the north, who refused to join Svyatopolk and Vladimir Monomakh in an alliance which they were forming at this time to oppose the aggression of the Polovtsy in the south. It is an interesting fact that the year 1096 to which Dobrynya's activities are referred was also the year which saw the death of Tugor Kan in the great Polovtsy attack on Pereyaslavl. This attack has generally been regarded as a raid; but the conduct of the princes Oleg and Yaroslav, both at this time and in previous years, suggests that concerted action was planned between them and the main Polovtsy body in the south, and that the simultaneous action of Mstislav of Novgorod in the north, and of Svyatopolk and Vladimir Monomakh on the southern Dnêpr, was planned in order to cut off the Polovtsy from their northern allies. Thanks to the vigorous and successful offensive of Dobrynya, backed by the able support of Mstislav, and thanks also, we are told, to the prayers of the holy bishop Nikita, this plan was completely successful. The check given by Dobrynya to the movements of the northern princes at the very moment when the southern Polovtsy were attacking the cities of the Dnêpr doubtless accounts for the disaster suffered by the Polovtsy at Pereyaslavl and the death of Tugor Kan. We have seen that according to one version of the tradition Dobrynya Nikitich, and not Alyosha Popovich, was the slayer of Tugor Kan. There are cogent reasons[1] for regarding this form of the tradition as the original one, and the achievement of Dobrynya against the allies of the Polovtsy in the same year as that which saw the death of the Polovtsy chief in battle would support such a conclusion. We have no historical evidence, it is true, that Dobrynya fought against the actual Polovtsy; but his association with Mstislav, the son and close ally of Vladimir Monomakh in the great struggle against the Polovtsy aggression, would satisfactorily account for the inclusion of Dobrynya in the Kiev Cycle. It seems to us not improbable that Dobrynya's rare patronymic Raguilovich has been forgotten in popular tradition, and that the singers have substituted the more familiar name of Nikita of Novgorod, who was a contemporary of Dobrynya, and who is mentioned by the writer of the Ancient Chronicle as assisting Mstislav and his *voevoda* with his prayers. Nikita doubtless stood officially to both Dobrynya and Mstislav in the position of spiritual 'father'.

Dobrynya Raguilovich is also a contemporary of a certain Putyata who was *voevoda* of Kiev at the accession of Vladimir II. Of this Putyata the Ancient Chronicle has much to tell us, furnishing circumstantial details, not only of his own career, but also of that of his brother, his father, and his grandfather. This evidence is valuable, since this portion of the Chronicle is a contemporary document. Since Dobrynya and Putyata are thus contemporaries in both the Ancient and the Ioakim Chronicles, and closely associated together in the latter and in the Chronicle of Nikon, and since they are Christians in all three, we may conclude that the account in the Ancient Chronicle is probably reliable, especially as they are here represented as contemporaries of the Chronicler himself.

Putyata is generally thought to be the prototype of the father of Zabava Putyatichna, who is commonly referred to in the *byliny* as Vladimir's 'niece'. He appears in the *byliny* only rarely, but he is shown in an unfavourable light, as a crafty and unscrupulous councillor. We may refer to the *bylina* of Danilo Lovchanin,[2] where Putyata advises the prince to send Danilo to the island of Buyan in order that the prince himself may take possession of his beautiful wife. Further instances are cited by Miller.[3] Putyata's daughter Zabava has an important place in the court of Kiev and plays a not inconsiderable rôle in the *byliny*.

---

[1] The reasons are literary rather than historical and cannot be given here. They are the result of a critical examination which we have made of the variant versions of the *byliny* relating to the slaying of Tugarin Zmêevich.

[2] Kirêevski, III. p. 28. [3] *Ocherki*, II. p. 29.

Miller held[1] that the unfavourable light in which Putyata appears in the *byliny* is due to the unpopularity of his master Svyatopolk as indicated to us in the account given in the Ancient Chronicle; but the events as there related make it clear that Putyata himself belonged to an unpopular family and an unpopular party; and the story of Putyata as related in the Ioakim Chronicle, though a widely different tradition and referring to a different period, only serves to strengthen this impression.

In connection with certain entries cited above from the Ancient Chronicle which assign Dobrynya to the time of Vladimir I, reference may perhaps be made to the hero Khoten Bludovich, whose patronymic has been generally regarded as identical with that of Blud, the *voevoda* of Prince Yaropolk, to whom reference is made in the Ancient Chronicle. Here we are told (s.a. 6486) that while Yaropolk was ruling in Kiev and Vladimir in Novgorod, Vladimir marched against Kiev. Yaropolk shut himself up in Kiev with his *voevoda* Blud and all his people. Vladimir sent messengers to Blud, promising him that, if he would betray Yaropolk, and join his interests to his own, Vladimir would 'take him as father'. Blud consented to betray his master, and with his help Vladimir obtained possession of Kiev. No other Blud is known in Russian historical records, and the close association of Blud, *voevoda* of Yaropolk, with Vladimir makes it not improbable that he is the father of the Khoten who is one of the few heroes represented in the *byliny* of this Cycle as a native of Kiev. It is interesting to observe that there is evidence for regarding the names Khot, Khotov as peculiar to Novgorod in historical times.[2]

The Chronicle of Novgorod makes mention of a certain Stavr, who was a *sotski* of the city in the time of Vladimir Monomakh. According to the Synodal transcript, which is the oldest existing transcript of the Chronicle,[3] Vladimir made all the boyars of Novgorod come to Kiev to take the oath of allegiance in consequence of certain disturbances which had taken place in their city, after which he dismissed them to their homes. Others, however, including the *sotski* Stavr, he detained, and subsequently drowned in punishment for their having plundered two of the citizens of Novgorod.[4] Solovev makes no mention of the drowning; and he understood the passage to mean that the boyars, as well as Stavr and

---

[1] *Ocherki*, II. p. 28 ff.; III. p. 35.   [2] See Miller, *Ocherki*, II. p. 384.

[3] See the note on the texts of the Chronicle by A. A. Shakhmatov in the English translation of the Chronicle by Michell, Forbes and Beazley, *ed. cit.* p. xxxvii.

[4] Michell, Forbes, etc., *Chronicle of Novgorod*, s.a. 1118.

his party, were guilty of the robbery.[1] Miss Hapgood, in a note on Stavr Godinovich, mentions that, according to the Chronicle of Novgorod, "Vladimir Monomachus...summoned all the nobles of Novgorod to Kiev, and made them take an oath of allegiance to him. Some he permitted to return home; others—among them Stavr—he sent into exile in wrath at some of their exploits."[2] It would seem, therefore, that variant versions of the Chronicle assign different punishments to Stavr, though they appear to be in agreement that he belonged to Novgorod, and that he incurred Vladimir's displeasure and suffered imprisonment. This tradition is apparently the only occurrence of the name Stavr in Russian written records. The name is not Slavonic in form. The form would be quite regular in Norse, though we do not know the word as a proper noun in Norse. Stavr may, nevertheless, be a descendant of one of the Norse settlers at Novgorod. There can, we think, be little doubt that he is the historical person from whom the hero of the *bylina* is derived, and the picture presented by the poets of the presence of the hero in sulky and depressed mood at Vladimir's court, and of his subsequent imprisonment, may well be a reflection of his detention in Kiev referred to in the Chronicles. The substitution of Chernigov for Novgorod in the *byliny* is not unnatural, seeing that Chernigov was, after Kiev, the most important city in Russia in early times, and figures incidentally in the *byliny* of the Kiev Cycle, whereas Novgorod is practically outside their orbit. It is a curious and interesting fact that in the Synodal Transcript of the Chronicle of Novgorod, s.a. 1117, immediately before the annal quoted above, we find the entry already cited (p. 107 above) referring to the death of Dobrynya, *Posadnik* of Novgorod.[3]

Miller with great probability includes Stavr in a group of heroes who belonged originally to Novgorod and Novgorod tradition, but who were incorporated at an early date into the Kiev Cycle.[4] To this group he also assigns, among others, Dobrynya Nikitich, and there can be little doubt that this hero probably belonged originally to Novgorod. The non-heroic *bylina* which relates the journey of the 'Forty and One *Kalêki*' to Jerusalem (cf. p. 188 f. below), of which the hero is Kasyan Mikhailovich, is also ascribed by Miller to this group of Novgorod traditions.[5] In his opinion the framework of the journey is derived from the expedition of a party of forty from Novgorod, which took place in

---

[1] Solovev, II. iv. col. 372 f.; III. i. col. 770   [2] *Songs*, p. 267.
[3] Michell, *Chronicle of Novgorod*, s.a. 1117.   [4] *Ocherki*, III. p. 36 f.
[5] *Ib.* p. 37 ff.—though in some versions of the *bylina* the 'Forty-One *Kalêki*' are stated to belong to Galicia.

the time of John, archbishop of Novgorod, during the reign of Rostislav in Kiev († 1168), according to an account which has come to us from the end of the sixteenth and the beginning of the seventeenth century. On to this apparently historical tradition of the journey, extraneous unhistorical tradition, and perhaps earlier historical traditions also, have been grafted. In the earliest versions of the *bylina* Prince Vladimir is represented as engaged on a hunting expedition beyond Kiev, and Miller points out that the incident probably reflects Monomakh's love of travel and sport. Rostislav himself has been forgotten.

No historical prototypes of Dyuk and Churilo have been satisfactorily established, but Miller has shown grounds for regarding the *byliny* relating to these heroes as embodying a group of traditions and proper names derived from Galicia and Volhynia. To this group he assigned also Dunay Ivanovich and Mikhailo Potyk, or Potok. He held that these names, and the stories associated with them, were incorporated into the Russian epos during the brief political and economic prosperity enjoyed by Galicia and Volhynia in the twelfth and thirteenth centuries; and he assigned the composition of the *bylina* of Dyuk to the end of the twelfth or beginning of the thirteenth century, i.e. shortly after the period of Yaroslav Osmomysl of Galicia, a time when Galicia was in particularly close touch with Byzantium.[1] This would, of course, preclude the association of Dyuk with Sharu Khan (cf. p. 119 below) if the original *bylina* of Dyuk was derived from a contemporary, or almost contemporary work. Miller is doubtless right in regarding the name Churilo, with its variants, as of Galician or Polish origin, though we are in the dark as to his exact milieu. Miller pointed out that the *byliny* relating to him show, in their present form, traces of the sphere of cultural influence of Novgorod. He held that the entire group of Galician poems have been grafted on to the Vladimir Cycle, perhaps at a time when the cultural traditions of Kiev passed westwards into Galicia on the downfall of Kiev, and that they then again passed north into the sphere of Novgorod and perhaps into Suzdal also, through the medium of trade and other channels.[2]

During the closing years of last century A. N. Veselovski and V. F. Miller[3] showed that the person of Mikhailo Potyk was historical, and that his adventures were founded on fact, and in one of his latest studies Miller made it clear that he still adhered to his original opinion.[4] If

[1] *Ocherki*, I. p. 97 ff.; III. pp. 50, 54.   [2] *Ib.* I. p. 187 ff.; III. p. 50 f.
[3] *Ib.* I. p. 122 ff.; cf. II. p. 16.
[4] *Ib.* III. p. 52 f. The article here referred to was probably written in 1912, but was not published till 1924, eleven years after his death.

they are right Mikhailo Potyk is to be identified with St Michel de Potuka, a Bulgarian saint, who is believed to have lived in the second half of the ninth century. He must therefore have been among the earliest Christians in Bulgaria. According to the traditional life of the saint, he fought as a young man in the Byzantine army, and when the Greeks were driven back in an encounter with an invading pagan force of 'Agarians' and 'Ethiopians', Michel and his *druzhina* rushed to their rescue, boldly hurling themselves on the foe whom they utterly routed. As he was returning to his home in the town of Potuka he chanced to pass by a lake where a dragon lived and preyed on the children sent by lot from the neighbouring town. On this occasion a maiden sat awaiting her doom. Michel boldly slew the dragon and rescued the maiden, but in the encounter he received a mortal wound and died shortly afterwards. In the town of Potuka where he was buried miracles were worked at his tomb, and in 1206, when the Bulgarian Tsar Kaloyan captured the town of Potuka, he ordered the relics of the saint to be transferred to his new capital of Trnovo. The transference was carried out with great pomp, and Miller suggested that it was at this period, when the legend would naturally receive a renewed vogue, that the fame of St Michel of Potuka spread across the Bulgarian frontier and reached Russia by way of Galicia, whose possessions on the lower Danube actually marched with Bulgaria at this period.[1]

It will be seen that the story corresponds to the *bylina* of Mikhailo Potyk in many respects. Both relate to a hero whose name is identical. Both heroes are great warriors, who fight and overcome a great army of pagan invaders. As they are journeying along a lake they find an un-protected maiden who comes under their power or protection. At some point in the story they encounter a dragon or serpent which comes to claim or devour the maiden, and over which the hero is victorious. They themselves enter the tomb while still young—whether alive or dead. After entering the tomb they obtain supernatural power—the power to work miracles. This miraculous power is certainly connected with the dragon or serpent in the *byliny*, and would seem to be at least very closely connected with the slaying of the dragon in the life of the saint. Several of these common features are commonplace enough, and can be widely paralleled both in folk-tale and in hagiographical literature. Yet their occurrence in close juxtaposition, and, with the exception of the encounter with the dragon, in almost identical order in both literatures, and in connection with a hero of identical name, is very striking.

[1] *Op. cit.* I. p. 125.

Dumézil has recently challenged[1] Miller's conclusion that the Russian story is derived from the Bulgarian, and suggests that it originates rather in an Indo-European myth; but his arguments cannot be considered convincing, and Miller's conclusions are now generally accepted.[2]

Certain of the heroes have been identified with historical figures of a later period than those hitherto discussed. We may refer to Dunay Ivanovich and Sukhan Domantevich. The name Dunay is found frequently in the records of the wars of Prince Vladimir of Volhynia during the thirteenth century. Thus the Ipatêvski Chronicle records the fact that in 1281 Dunay led the *druzhina* of his prince against the Poles. In the following year he is referred to as the *voevoda* sent by Vladimir to enrol the Lithuanians as allies. He plays a striking part in the events recorded in 1287. When Konrad Semovitovich succeeded to the government of Cracow on the death of Prince Leshko Kasimirovich, he sent to Prince Vladimir, on whose help he was in part dependent, and who was himself incapacitated by a wound, asking him to send his *voevoda* Dunay as his representative in order to secure Konrad's position. The request was granted. The incident is a striking testimony both to Dunay's fame and to the high trust in which Vladimir held him. The correspondence in the name, the fact that both Dunays serve a Prince Vladimir, and both occur in close relationship with a Polish prince, suggested to Miller[3] that the name of the Volhynian prince Dunay may have been preserved in local traditions and in the poems of the *druzhina* in connection with the name of Prince Vladimir whom he served, and thus have been incorporated in the course of time into the Kiev Cycle, where he appears in *byliny* as the hero Tikhi Dunay Ivanovich.

Miller has shown[4] that Sukhan Domantevich (cf. p. 139 ff. below), more frequently referred to in the *byliny* as Sukhmanti, has certain features in common with Domant, Prince of Pskov, who is frequently mentioned in chronicles and early historical documents, and who died in 1299. Domant defended the city of Pskov against a large host of pagan invaders, as Sukhan defended Kiev against the Tatars. Like Sukhan he was heavily outnumbered by the opposing forces, and like Sukhan he boldly crossed the river (Dvina) and defended it against the enemy who were trying to cross. Many similar battles are attributed to him, and the entries in the Chronicles refer to him in a tone of exaltation, and with the exaggeration and lack of verisimilitude reminiscent of heroic poetry. Such exploits are, of course, common enough in the records of the time,

[1] *R.É.S.* v (1925), p. 205 ff.   [2] Cf. Mazon, *Bylines*, p. 691.
[3] *Ocherki*, I. p. 130 ff.; cf. III. p. 53.   [4] *Ib.* III. p. 167 ff.

as well as in heroic poetry; but the correspondence in the names is all the more striking in view of the fact that both Sukhan and Domant are rare. Miller considered that the exploits of Prince Domant have been transferred to his son by the popular singers, and he hints that in the *byliny* of Sukhan we may possibly possess the last relics of the popular oral tradition of Pskov, though he obviously regards the last suggestion as hazardous.

Many other identifications have been suggested, too numerous to mention here. We may refer, among others, to Miller's collection of data bearing on the identity of Vladimir's wife.[1] He points out that her name appears in a number of forms in the *byliny*, and that these forms are all variations of two distinct names, Apraxya and Evfrosinÿa, the former being the commoner in modern oral tradition. The name Apraxya is, in his opinion, an amalgamation of two traditions, one of her names being derived from Evpraksi, the wife of Prince Theodore of Ryazan, who plays a prominent part in early accounts of the Tatar invasion under Batu in the first half of the thirteenth century. The name Ofrosini (Evfrosinÿa) he regards as derived from St Evfrosinÿa (1101–1179), a princess of Polotsk.

We have left Ilya Muromets (Ilya of Murom), the most important of the heroes, until the last because the question of his identity is closely bound up with that of Prince Vladimir. Ilya is mentioned in various Russian written records from 1574 onwards,[2] and Miller has shown[3] that a comparison of these early notices with the early versions of the *byliny* makes it clear that the original name of the hero was not Muromets, but Murovets, and that the home of the hero was not Murom in central Russia, but the ancient Morovsk (Morovisk), in the valley of the Dnêpr, which belonged to the principality of Chernigov in the twelfth and thirteenth centuries, and is frequently mentioned in the Chronicles as a dependency of Chernigov. We may suppose that Karachaevo or Karachoro made its appearance in the poem as a reminiscence of the more southerly city Karachev, the ancient seat of the princes of Chernigov, mentioned in a Chronicle in the beginning of the twelfth century. Neither the epithet 'old', nor the epithet 'Kossack', belong to the earliest versions of the *byliny* of Ilya, and they appear to have been first applied to the hero in the seventeenth century.[4]

---

[1] *Ocherki*, II. p. 359 ff.; and cf. *ib.* I. p. 321 ff., and the references there cited.

[2] These notices have been brought together in a careful summary in Russian by V. F. Miller (*Ocherki*, III. p. 68 f.) and, more recently in German, by E. Studer, p. 24 ff.

[3] *Ocherki*, III. pp. 3 ff., 61 ff., 118 ff.   [4] *Ib.* III. pp. 91 ff., 136 ff.

German tradition, as represented by the early Norse text of the *Thiðreks Saga af Bern*, and the Middle High German poem *Ortnit*, both composed during the thirteenth century, show that already before this period oral traditions were in existence relating to a Russian hero of the name of Ilias, who was of high rank, and a close relative of a certain prince Valldimar (Vladimir). It would seem natural to suppose that the German tradition has incorporated some early version of a tradition relating to Ilya of Murom, or, more correctly, of Murovsk; but such an identification has not met with general acceptance. Veselovski regarded the Valldimar of the *Thiðreks Saga* as relating to a certain prince Vladimir of Polotsk, who lived at the close of the twelfth and beginning of the thirteenth century,[1] and in a more recent study of the whole question Prof. Mazon[2] expresses himself unable to see any serious ground for the identification of the Norse or German stories with the hero of the *byliny*.

Yet it may be pointed out that both heroes are located in Russia; both are great champions; both are contemporaries of Vladimir (Valldimar) and closely associated with him; and both render him assistance by their wise counsel and prowess in arms. If we are to suppose, with Prof. Mazon, that the Russian Ilya is not the same person as the western Ilyas, we are reduced to assuming that two Russian heroes called Ilya, closely related to two Russian princes called Vladimir, and possessing certain common features, flourished at some period before the middle of the thirteenth century, and that while one of these Russian heroes was sufficiently famous to have found a place in Norse and German tradition of the thirteenth century, the other was sufficiently famous to have made for himself a place in Russian tradition which has lasted down to our own time. The most probable view on the whole would seem to be that the name and tradition of the Ilyas of the *Thiðreks Saga* and of *Ortnit* are derived from south-west Russian oral tradition at some period prior to the middle of the thirteenth century.[3]

[1] Miller, *Ocherki*, III. p. 82 f.   [2] *Ib. Ilya*, p. 669 ff.

[3] In the early Norse *Völsungasaga*, ch. 32 the names *Valdamarr* and *Jarisleifr* (i.e. *Yaroslav*) occur in a passage which is derived from *Guðrúnarkviða*, II, str. 20. The text of the latter as we have it has *Valdarr* for *Valdamarr*, and also a third name *Jariʒscáre* which seems to be Russian. *Valdarr* or *Valdamarr* is in both cases associated with Denmark or the Danes. But both passages would seem to make it clear that Russian princes were familiar in Norse heroic poetry in the thirteenth century. Both Vladimir (I and II) and Yaroslav were, of course, familiar enough in Scandinavia from historical saga. But the milieu here is clearly that of minstrel poetry. Cf. also *Hervarar Saga*, ch. 12.

We will now turn attention to the group of heroes or monsters who are represented as in opposition to the heroes of Kiev. Despite the supernatural fea ures which are persistently attributed to them, many of these monsters have been identified with the Polovtsy leaders. It would be interesting, if time permitted, to examine these supernatural features with a view to ascertaining how far they are due to the traditional figurative diction in which the minstrels loved to clothe those characteristics of their enemies which struck them as most bizarre and remote from their own experience. We may, indeed, refer to one or two instances. We have already seen that Tugor K(h)an is to be identified with the Polovtsy leader of the same name, though he is represented in the *byliny* as the son of a dragon, and as flying through the sky on his paper wings. Miller and others have also pointed to references in the *byliny* and prose traditions to his contemporary, the Polovtsy chief Konchak, who figures in the Ancient Chronicle and in the *Slovo o Polky Igorevê*, as well as to his father Otrok (more correctly Atrak). In a prose narrative from Archangel, Konchak and his two brothers are represented as so strong that while far apart they are able to hurl cauldrons to one another as if they were balls.[1] We may refer also to Shark Velikan, who, according to a rare *bylina*, was the friend and ally of Churilo Plenkovich,[2] and who, according to another rare *bylina*, was slain in single combat by Dyuk Stepanovich.[3] He is described as half man, half horse, who is unable to walk against his enemy, but rolls now to one side, now to another. Rambaud, commenting on these features, observed: "C'est un reptile plutôt qu'un héros; on sent que ce géant doit être quelque brouillard ou quelque nuée d'orage."[4] It is now generally believed, however, that the original of this humorously grotesque portrait[5] was Sharukan or Sharu Kan 'the old', another great Polovtsy chief, and ally of Bonyak, with whom he raided Pereyaslavl and laid siege to Lubny on the Sula in 1107. His daughter was the wife of David, son of Svyatoslav II, grand prince of Kiev.[6] Sharu Kan was severely defeated in 1111 by the Russian princes Svyatopolk, David and Vladimir in a great battle in the neighbourhood of the R. Don. If the name of Shark Velikan is actually derived from that of Sharu Kan, it is possible that the adjective *Veliki*, 'great', has been habitually inserted in popular speech as a standing epithet (?Sharu Veliki Kan), and that his title has then undergone certain phonetic changes—perhaps pro-

---

[1] Miller, *Ocherki*, III. p. 43 f.
[3] *Ib.* p. 697.
[5] Kirêevski, IV. p. cxv.

[2] Rybnikov, II. p. 701.
[4] *La Russie épique* (Paris 1876), p. 45.
[6] Miller, *Ocherki*, II. p. 377.

lepsis and haplology. The minstrels have been impressed by the Polovtsy chief's expert horsemanship and his reluctance to leave the saddle, and his discomfort when on foot, and they laugh, like many modern travellers, at the awkward and rolling gait of the Tatar when he is compelled to the unfamiliar exercise of the pedestrian.

One of the most interesting of the supernatural or supernormal of the foes of Kiev is Solovey Rakhmatovich or Rakhmanovich, otherwise known as Solovey Razboynik, 'Nightingale the Robber'. It is to be observed that the patronymic is found only in versions from Olonets and Archangel, while versions from other parts of Russia and Siberia know only Solovey Razboynik. Miller has shown cogent reasons for regarding the patronymic as derived from the form *Akhmatov, Akhmatovich*, to which an initial *r* has become attached from the epithet *vor*, 'thief', 'robber'; and indeed Kirêevski[1] actually records a version from Archangel in which the form *vor Akhmatovich* occurs. Miller further points[2] to the name of a certain Tatar *khan* Akhmat, who was renowned for his campaign against Moscow and his lengthy encampment on the R. Ugra in 1480. It is very possible that, as Miller suggests, about the beginning of the sixteenth century the memory of Khan Akhmat's expedition and his subsequent flight may have caused his name to be attached to another robber Solovey. This conjecture is perhaps strengthened by the fact that in one *bylina* Solovey figures as a Mussulman and a destroyer of monasteries.

We have now considered a certain amount of evidence which should be of assistance in helping us to determine the identity of Vladimir, 'Prince of royal Kiev', who is present throughout the Cycle as the constant central figure. It will be remembered that at least three Vladimirs have been laid under contribution by the minstrels; but no one, we suppose, would seriously consider Dunay's prince, the thirteenth-century Vladimir of Volhynia, as the prototype of the Vladimir of the *byliny*. Opinion has varied greatly as to whether Vladimir I, who is credited in the Ancient Chronicle with the Conversion of Russia in 988, or Vladimir II, who ascended the throne in 1113, is the person originally indicated. Both were princes of outstanding importance for Russian history; both were constantly engaged in defending the Christian state of Kiev against the inroads of the pagan tribes of Turkish stock—Vladimir I against the Pechenegs, Vladimir II against the Polovtsy. Both entered into diplomatic relations with Byzantium.[3]

[1] I. p. 77 ff. [2] *Ocherki*, III. p. 133.
[3] See further the parallels adduced by Zhdanov, cited by Miller, *Ocherki*, III. p. 33.

Nevertheless there can in our opinion be little doubt that the cycle of stories, as distinct from the actual *byliny*, in its present form and as a unity, originated, or at least has to some extent undergone reconstruction in the time of Vladimir II, and perhaps at subsequent periods also.[1] The considerations which point to this conclusion are many and varied. In the first place the evidence which assigns heroes of *byliny* to the reign of Vladimir II or a later period is on the whole of a more satisfactory character than that which relates to the time of Vladimir I. Of the list of heroes who have been selected for consideration as representative of the Cycle as a whole, Blud, the hypothetical father of Khoten Bludovich, is the only hero who can be related to the period of Vladimir I with any show of credibility; while to the period of Monomakh, or that which closely precedes or follows, there are good grounds for ascribing Dobrynya, Putyata (the hypothetical father of Vladimir's niece, Zabava Putyatichna), Stavr, Evfrosinẏa (Apraxya), perhaps Ilya of Murom, and possibly also Dyuk; and the Polovtsy chiefs Tugor, Shark Velikan (Sharu Khan), Konchak and Otrok. To the following century are probably to be ascribed Alyosha Popovich, Mikhailo Potyk, Dunay Ivanovich, Apraxya, and possibly Sukhan Domantevich. Others whom we have not mentioned might be added, such as Kazarin, Ivan Gostinny Syn, etc. Solovey Razboynik appears to be still later.

The Cycle of *byliny* relating to Kiev and Prince Vladimir was certainly not completed in the reign of either prince of this name. New subjects were added, and new heroes included, at least as late as the thirteenth century, and perhaps later. Modern Russian scholars are in agreement that in the *bylina* relating to Tsar Kalin and the destruction of the heroes of Kiev, we have a reminiscence of the disastrous battle on the Kalka, in which the Russians were overthrown by the Tatars in 1224. However this may be, there can be little doubt that some of the principal heroes of the Cycle make their first appearance in history during the thirteenth century.

The political geography of the *byliny* of this Cycle is surprisingly conservative. It has preserved with considerable fidelity the memory of the city-state on the Dnêpr, and the local and restricted sphere of its influence. It knows nothing of Russia in the modern connotation of the word, or of any Russian cities except those in the valley of the Dnêpr, and the ancient ecclesiastical city of Rostov in the north. Chernigov is

---

[1] Miller considered that during the sixteenth century, and notably during the latter half, the subjects of the old *byliny* underwent a restoration, bringing them into conformity with contemporary conditions. See *Ocherki*, III. p. 168.

at the height of its power and importance, and the rivalry between the two neighbouring cities of Kiev and Chernigov is reflected in more than one *bylina*. Novgorod is outside the orbit, and Moscow has not yet come into being. Ryazan is mentioned rarely.

Among the historical elements preserved in the *byliny* we must also mention the natural features and physical geography of south Russia. The singers make constant reference to the characteristic features of the south Russian landscape which neither they nor their immediate ancestors have ever seen—the 'open plain', the 'feather-grass of the steppe', the 'aurochs' which has long been extinct. The use of obsolete words also suggests that the *byliny* have retained traces of some earlier actual milieu. A hero is known as *khrabry* and *bogatyr*,[1] the latter word being later than the former, and borrowed from the Tatars at some period of the Tatar inroads. The *byliny* frequently mention the *polenitsy* or heroines who fight like men, though the term has been forgotten for many centuries in current Russian and was unknown even to lexicographers. Many of the features which are doubtless genuine historical reminiscences are retained in an obscure form which almost evades detection. We may refer to the mutual oaths sworn by Dobrynya Nikitich and the 'dragon of the Mountain', by which Dobrynya undertakes never more to ride in the open plain, or bathe in the river, or molest young 'dragons', or rescue Russian captives, while the 'dragon' undertakes never again to fly over Kiev and carry off young maidens. This compact suggests the ancient though short-lived division of south-west Russia between the Russians and the Polovtsy, by which the Polovtsy occupied the southern steppe, and necessarily set enormous store by their rights over the rivers, while the Russians occupied the cities and the upper valley of the Dnêpr.

Yet on the whole it must be confessed that the contact of these early Cycles with ascertained historical fact is slight, and, in general, problematical. The nature of the stories would seem to render any detailed discussion of their unhistorical elements otiose. These elements consist for the most part, as we have seen, of exaggeration rather than of supernatural features, though the latter are not absent. We have no evidence for the introduction of deliberate fiction. The rarity of the overlapping of the different Cycles suggests a considerable amount of literary conscience on the part of the reciters in regard to the integrity of their material. To this subject we shall refer later.

The most considerable element of manifestly supernatural material in

[1] The word is said to be identical with the Turkish *bohadyr*, 'a champion'.

the *byliny* lies in the frequent introductions of dragons and white swans. The 'dragons', however, have been shown in the majority of cases to be no other than Polovtsy or Tatar chiefs, and there can be little doubt that in many cases their supernatural features have come to be ascribed to them largely, though not wholly, in consequence of the epithet, as in the case of Tugarin, Shark Velikan, Idolishche. In some cases the supernatural features have no doubt been introduced from folk-tale motifs, in which dragons figure largely. Where the theme of such folk-tales originally bore some resemblance to that of the *bylina*, the introduction of the former into the latter can easily be accounted for, as in the case of Mikhailo Potyk. In other cases again the epithet of dragon is still remembered by many of the reciters to be merely a term of poetic diction for a 'Tatar' (? Polovtsy) chief. This is so in regard to the dragon of the mountain slain by Dobrynya. The fact that the term 'dragon' is never applied to Russian chiefs, but is reserved exclusively for their enemies, has no doubt been of material assistance in aiding the introduction of supernatural attributes and episodes.

The 'white swan' seems to have had a somewhat similar history to the 'dragon'. Like the latter the term 'white swan' clearly originated as a term of figurative diction. It is used as a poetical or figurative epithet of a maiden in the *Slovo o Polky Igorevê*, and also in modern poetry relating to unspecified individuals and social ritual. In the *byliny* it seems to be applied, like the term 'dragon', exclusively to foreigners, especially to the western neighbours of the Russians, whether Lithuanians, Poles, or others. The conception as we have it in the *byliny* is strikingly similar to that of the *vile* of the Yugoslavs, and the *samovilen* of Bulgaria, more especially to the latter, who, like the white swans, are invariably represented as mischievous in intention. The maidens described as white swans in the *byliny* generally possess supernatural powers, such as shape-changing, and the ability to transform the shapes of others. Here again the application of the term to foreigners, and especially to races inimical to the Russians, has no doubt facilitated the introduction of supernatural features. The fact that the white swan figures largely in folk-tales is also no doubt to some extent responsible for the introduction of supernatural elements and episodes in connection with them, as we have seen to be the case in regard to the dragons. Here again we may instance the case of Mikhailo Potyk, and also of Ivan Godinovich. It is a curious and interesting fact that the dragon and the white swan appear to be commonly found in the same *byliny*, and to be in some way associated together.

A historical origin has generally been claimed in the past for the two principal heroes of the Novgorod Cycle, though here, as in the Kiev Cycle, the accretion of myth and legend appears to be far greater than the historical kernel. Sadko is generally regarded as identical with a famous Sadko who is mentioned in the Chronicles of Novgorod and Pskov as the founder of the Church of Saints Boris and Glêb in Novgorod. According to the Synodal transcript—the oldest existing transcript of the Novgorod Chronicle[1]—in the year 1167 "Sedko Sitinits founded the stone church of the Holy Martyrs Boris and Glêb under Knyaz Svyatoslav Rostislavits".[2] Stone churches were still rare in the twelfth century, and the name of this historical founder (who in the annals of the Cathedral of Saint Sofia is called Sotko *bogaty*, 'Sadko the wealthy')[3] recalls the *byliny* in which Sadko, the wealthy merchant (*bogaty gost*) of Novgorod, likewise appears as a builder of churches.[4]

It is generally held that around the person of the historical rich merchant of the twelfth century a number of other stories have collected, quite unhistorical in character. The version in which Sadko figures as a guest of the tsar of the sea, and that in which he is enriched by a nymph of Lake Ilmen, have been thought to be derived from Finnish oral sources,[5] and Speranski points to the existence of an early form of the *bylina* of Sadko from which the tsar of the sea is absent, and in which Sadko appears to be neither a musician nor a native of Novgorod.[6] Further, an episode very similar to the casting adrift of Sadko is found in an Old French romance *Tristan de Léonois*, and the similarity is the more striking since the incident is associated with a hero of the same name, *Sadoc*. The name *Sadko, Sadok* is said to be Hebrew (Zadok), and there can be little doubt that the story has reached both countries from a Hebrew milieu, such as that which exercised a marked influence on Novgorod during the early Middle Ages.[7] The coincidence of the name perhaps accounts for the association of this story with the wealthy and prominent Novgorod citizen.

The only evidence known to us for the historicity of Vasili Buslaev is a solitary reference in the compilation of Nikon.[8] Here, in an entry

---

[1] Michell, p. xxxvii.   [2] *Ib.* p. 25.

[3] Miller, *Ocherki*, I. p. 287.

[4] We may refer, e.g. to Kirêevski, v. p. 47 ff.

[5] See Miller, *Ocherki*, I. p. 296 ff.   [6] *R.U.S.* p. 280 ff.

[7] Miller, *Ocherki*, I. p. 303 f.

[8] For the reference to Nikon, and a discussion of the problem of the historicity of Vasili Buslaev, see Bezsonov's note, Kirêevski, v. p. lxv.

for the year 1171, we find the following brief notice: "This year the *posadnik* Vaska Buslaevich died at Novgorod." This entry has generally been considered by western writers as valid evidence for the association of the hero with a historical person of Novgorod;[1] but the absence of any reference to the hero in the versions of the Chronicle of Novgorod which have survived make one feel some hesitation in accepting Nikon's entry on its face value. The absence of reference in the Novgorod Chronicle is the more surprising in view of the fullness of the information which it affords on other local matters of this period, especially in regard to the *posadniki*. Bezsonov rightly emphasised the absence of the name of Vasili Buslaev from the list of the *posadniki* of Novgorod.[2]

On the other hand the wording of the entry in the compilation of Nikon implies that the hero is an important person. He is referred to as a *posadnik*, and he is mentioned amid events of the greatest importance in the life of Novgorod. In the opinion of Sobolevski, *Buslav* is a derivative from *Boguslav*, with a reduction of *g* to *h*. The latter appears to be an ancient pan-Slavonic name which was in general use in antiquity, like *Bogukhval*, *Bogumil*, and appears to have been specially common among the Czechs and Poles.[3] There is record of a *boyarin* of Novgorod called Boguslav in the thirteenth century. The earliest Chronicle of Pskov speaks in the entry for the year 1500, of a *posadnik* Foma Buslavich.[4] Possibly, therefore, Bezsonov was right in suggesting[5] that the name Vasili, with its nickname Vaska, has been substituted for the original name of some *posadnik* of Novgorod. The name Buslavlya is recorded as the name of a village in the seventeenth century, and a village Buslaevo exists to-day in the government of Kostroma.[6]

The *bylina* of Vasili's life in Novgorod in its present form is reminiscent—despite its satire and exaggerations—of the conditions which prevailed in Novgorod when at the height of its power, during the fourteenth and fifteenth centuries. To this period, accordingly, Shambinago attributes the composition of the *bylina* in its present form. He suggests, moreover, that the *bylina* has perhaps come down to us through a *skomorokh*[7] tradition, and that it is strongly coloured by seventeenth-

---

[1] See Rambaud, *R.É.* p. 144; Hapgood, *Songs*, p. 281, and cf. Magnus, *Ballads*, p. 142.
[2] *Loc. cit.*; cf. also Speranski, *R.U.S.* p. 318.
[3] Bezsonov, *loc. cit.*; Brodski, p. 109 f.   [4] Brodski, *loc. cit.*
[5] *Loc. cit.*   [6] Brodski, p. 110.
[7] For the *skomorokhi* (sing. *skomorokh*) see p. 261 ff. below.

century features. The merry tone, rough humour, and good-humoured if somewhat clumsy burlesque support this suggestion, and remind one of similar features in the *bylina* of Terenti Gost, which is almost certainly a *skomorokh* product in its present form, though the story is said to be based on a French original.[1] Possibly some slight traces of a more serious picture of the hero Vasili Buslaev are preserved in the version of Kirsha Danilov (cf. p. 54 f. above), though the humorous tone of the poem as a whole is equally well sustained in Kirsha's version. In any case there can be little doubt that in Vasili Buslaev we have an example of a purely local hero, and, in the *bylina* of his Novgorod brawls, an example of a composition of Novgorod provenance.

It will be seen that the evidence for the historicity of the heroes of the Novgorod Cycle is hardly superior to that of Kiev. Yet some of the characteristic features of early Novgorod have been preserved, and the atmosphere of the poems is very different from that of the Kiev *byliny*. The peculiar and individual local topography and political organisation of medieval Novgorod are not forgotten, or its turbulent citizens, its constant brawls, its *posadnik*, its *tysyatski*. The circumscribed nature of its interests are hinted at. The Novgorod *byliny* know nothing of the Tatars, nothing of Kiev. The *byliny* suggest no less clearly than the Chronicle that the preoccupations of Novgorod were chiefly with civil strife at home and commerce abroad. The two chief heroes, and the rest of the citizens also,[2] can read and write. The personnel consist of citizens and tradespeople, and the scene is laid in the streets and guildhall.

The historical element in the poems of the Cycle which is generally regarded as having reference to medieval times does not appear to be great. The most convincing identifications are those which relate to the *bylina* of the Princes of Tver and to the *byliny* of Roman. Of the former there can be no doubt. The *bylina* refers to the murder of the Tatar *bashkak*, Chol Khan, at the hands of the citizens of Tver in 1327. We have related the circumstances more fully elsewhere.[3] The popular singer has forgotten the cruel consequences of the murder however, for he states in the last line[4] that

No-one was made to answer for the deed,

whereas in reality Alexander, the Prince of Tver, who had led the insurrection in person, was forced to flee for his life to Pskov, and Tver

[1] See A. Mazon, *R.É.S.* XII (1932), p. 247.
[2] See Kirsha Danilov's version, Kirêevski, v. p. 14 ff., line 60; Chadwick, p. 152.
[3] Chadwick, p. 159. [4] Kirêevski, v. p. 186 ff.

was cruelly ravaged by 50,000 Tatars in a punitive expedition led by Ivan of Moscow.

The question of the identity of Prince Roman, and the origin of the story relating to him have never been satisfactorily solved. Korobka,[1] followed by Sobolevski and Markov, identified him with a certain Prince Bryanski Roman Mikhailovich, who ruled 1263–1288, and suggests that the events narrated in the *byliny* contain echoes of the Lithuanian-Russian relations of the thirteenth century, and that the *bylina* which relates the attack on his home during his absence by two Lithuanian princes was composed to commemorate the first attack on this prince by the Lithuanians in 1263. On the other hand Zhdanov identifies him with Prince Roman of Galicia who was ruling at the end of the twelfth and the beginning of the thirteenth century. The name Manuelo Yagailovich, which occurs in the version recorded from Archangel,[2] is, in his opinion, reminiscent of Polish-Lithuanian history, perhaps a reference to the Jagellon dynasty. Miller identifies the name Manuelo, however, with the Byzantine emperor Manuel Komnenos. It may be added that he has shown good reason elsewhere for believing that the great emperor was remembered in the *byliny*, that his name was especially popular in Galician oral traditions, and that already in the thirteenth century such traditions represented Manuel Komnenos as a contemporary of Vladimir Monomakh. All these identifications, it would seem, receive considerable support from the evidence of the *byliny*, and it is not impossible that a transference has taken place, and that both the historical Romans have been called into requisition.

Before leaving the subject of the historical and unhistorical elements in the heroic poems, a word may be said on the later periods, from the time of Ivan the Terrible to the present day. The relationship of these poems to historical fact varies greatly. Nor is the variation a chronological one. The *bylina* which relates the capture of Kazan from the Tatars in 1552 is much closer to history than that which tells of the capture of Berlin by the Cossack Krasnoshchokov in 1760.

The most important factor in the unhistorical elements in the *byliny* of the modern period is the prevalence of the tradition of the Kiev Cycle. Wherever this is prominent, unhistorical elements abound, and where it

---

[1] The works cited below have not been accessible to us. For summaries of the views expressed we are indebted to Miller, *Ocherki*, I. p. 114 f.; II. p. 364 f.; III. p. 58 f.

[2] Kirêevski, v. p. 92 ff.; Chadwick, p. 168 ff.

is absent the *byliny* at least symbolise fact, even when they do not actually reflect it. This will become clearer as we proceed. In the modern period exaggeration is a less important factor than in the earlier Cycles. Where the unhistorical elements are not due to the prevalence of the heroic tradition, or to the introduction of themes derived from folk-tales, or to extraneous literary (oral) motifs, they are generally to be attributed partly to the telescoping of events, partly to their transference and artificial grouping round a few well-known names, partly again to the ignorance of the singers as to the details of the occurrences which they celebrate.

Adopting the classification followed in Vol. I, ch. VIII and in the Yugoslav section, we will first give one or two examples of incidents and situations in these later Cycles which are at variance with reliable historical evidence. In general the *bylina* which relates the capture of Kazan by Ivan the Terrible[1] keeps surprisingly close to history. Errors of detail occur, however, as is not surprising in oral poetry. The ruler of Kazan at the time of its capture was Ediger. He was not blinded by Ivan as the *bylina* states, but baptised under the name of Simeon, and became a great lord in the Muscovite court. The siege lasted, not for 'eight years' as in some versions of the *bylina*, or for 'thirty-three years' as in others, but for six weeks. The *byliny* not infrequently transpose the names of the Tatar khans. In the *bylina* which relates the Conquest of Siberia by Ermak the Cossack[2] in 1581 the name of the Tatar khan is given as Kuchum, whereas it was in reality Mahmetkoul.[3]

The *byliny* show no exact knowledge of what was happening in the Kremlin either in this period or in the Period of Troubles. A striking instance of the misrepresentation of historical fact—whether deliberate or inadvertent—occurs in the *bylina* which relates how 'the Tsar resolves to slay his son'.[4] Ivan IV did, in actual fact, slay his own much-beloved son. The rescue of the tsarevich in the nick of time by Nikita Romanovich as related in the *bylina* is wholly unhistorical. But what the singer represents as a deliberate sentence for treason was, in reality, an accident. Ivan in momentary anger struck his son on the temple with the iron point of his stick. He never intended to kill him, and was inconsolable after his death.

Similar inaccuracies are observable in the *byliny* relating to the

---

[1] Kirêevski, VI. p. I ff.; Chadwick, p. 187 ff.
[2] Kirêevski, VI. p. 39 ff.; Chadwick, p. 199 ff.
[3] Rambaud, *R.É.* p. 248, footnote 2.
[4] Kirêevski, VI. p. 55 ff.; Chadwick, p. 193 ff.

troublous period following Ivan's reign. In Kirsha Danilov's version of the *bylina* of Grigori Otrepev and Marina,[1] the *streltsy* are represented as hostile to the usurper, while the Tsaritsa repudiates him. In actual fact it was the boyars who opposed him while the *streltsy* gave him their support, and the Tsaritsa actually acknowledged him as her son, though she seems to have failed to make good her recognition of him when the tide set strongly against him.[2]

A number of other *byliny* also illustrate popular misconceptions of the course of events, dimly apprehended, which are occurring in the Kremlin. In the *bylina* of Vasili Shuyski[3] the people of Moscow appear loyal to the tsar and suspicious of the boyars, and are aware of the disturbance at the palace and of the tsar's absence, but ignorant of the precise circumstances. They assemble in the Red Square, anxiously enquiring why the blinds are drawn in the palace, and why all is in commotion. A bold youth tells them that it is because the 'evil boyars' have sent the Tsar Vasili to Siberia. As a matter of fact Vasili was never sent to Siberia, but he was forced by the boyars and their Polish allies to abdicate, and was carried a prisoner to Warsaw where he died.

In the *bylina* of Prokofi Lyapunov[4], who was in charge of the troops in Moscow during the Period of Troubles, and was murdered by the Cossacks in 1611, both the opinion expressed on the hero and the facts narrated conflict with what is commonly accepted. The hero is now generally regarded by western historians as primarily a self-seeking adventurer. But in his own day he was looked upon as a champion of the Christian faith by the Russian cities, who were anxious for a union with Moscow against the Poles, and it is not unlikely that contemporary opinion was right, and that his fumbling advances towards unity and nationalism have been misunderstood by modern writers. The singers of the *bylina* have no doubts on the matter:

> One boyar, the wise governor, sturdily defended the faith,
> Sturdily defended the faith, and drove the traitors away:
> Now this wise governor was Prokofi Lyapunov.

The statements in the same *bylina* that Sigismund III of Poland had established his dwelling in Moscow, and was subsequently strangled

---

[1] Kirêevski, VII. p. 5 ff.; Chadwick, p. 223 ff.
[2] For a discussion of this curious and obscure phase of history, and of the part played by the Tsaritsa, see Rambaud, *R.É.* p. 278 f.
[3] Kirêevski, VII. p. 17 ff.; Chadwick, p. 226 ff.
[4] Kirêevski, VII. p. 17 ff.; Chadwick, p. 238 ff.

there, are quite unhistorical. Sigismund was never in Moscow himself, and he lived till 1632.

Even in times nearer our own the popular singers are singularly ill-informed. The *bylina* on 'Krasnoshchokov and Frederick II'[1] which relates to a raid on Berlin in 1760 by a Russian force of Cossacks and Kalmuks, represents the Cossack general, Krasnoshchokov, as entering Berlin alone in disguise, and purchasing powder and lead in the merchant's row, after which he succeeds in making his way into the royal palace. Here he slays the Prussian queen and takes captive the princess who tells him that on his approach the Emperor Frederick transformed himself into a number of creatures, such as a grey cat, a black crow, a white fish, etc.

The *byliny* relating to modern times are not often at variance with one another as regards serious matters of fact. We may therefore pass on to consider the second class of unhistorical evidence, namely, incidents and situations which are in themselves incredible. Chief of these are supernatural elements.

Supernatural beings are rarely if ever introduced into the *byliny* of modern times, though human beings are occasionally credited with supernatural power, especially the power to change their shapes. When the Pretender, Dimitri Otrepev, was attacked in his palace in 1606 by Vasili Shuyski and a party of boyars with their followers, we are told in the *bylina* that

> His wicked wife, Marinka the godless,
> Changed herself into a magpie,
> And away she flew out of the palace.

We have just seen how, on the entry of Krasnoshchokov, the Cossack general, Frederick II is represented as changing himself into a grey cat, a black crow, a white fish, etc. Such passages as these appear to be a heritage from the *bylina* of Volga and the Kiev Cycle, and are strangely at variance with the more literal narrative which generally characterises the *byliny* of modern times.

The modern *byliny* do not offer many examples of incidents, motifs, etc., which can be stated with certainty to have been taken from some other story, and still fewer which appear to be due to invention. As we have already seen, however, there can be no doubt that the stories and motifs of the Kiev Cycle have affected the themes of the later *byliny*. The *bylina* of the marriage of Ivan the Terrible to Marya Temrukhovna,

---

[1] Kirêevski, IX. p. 154 ff.; Chadwick, p. 281 ff.

and the exploits of her brother Kastryuk (cf. p. 60 above) have undoubtedly been influenced by the marriage feasts and the games and
festivities which accompany them in such *byliny* of the Kiev Cycle as
Stavr Godinovich. Similarly the *bylina* which relates the brilliant
services rendered by Prince Mikhailo Skopin Shuyski to the Russians
besieged in Moscow by the Poles and their allies, and the account
of the feast at which he was poisoned at the instigation of his jealous
uncles[1], shows traces of the same traditional treatment. But so far as
we are aware the actual themes and incidents of earlier poems and stories
are rarely inserted in modern *byliny* where they are not justified by
actual analogous historical occurrences.

Nevertheless it is clear that a certain amount of transference, or rather
of adaptation, has taken place. It is thought that certain of the achievements attributed in the *byliny* to Ivan the Terrible were originally
proper to his grandfather, Ivan III, and his father Vasili, whose campaigns and foreign achievements have been overshadowed and even
incorporated into the Cycle of the Terrible.[2] It is thought that the
bylina which relates to the banishment of the wife of Ivan the Terrible
into a convent may have been inspired by, or even formed on the model
of, an earlier *bylina* commemorating the banishment of Solomonÿa, wife
of Ivan III, to a convent; but so far as we are aware there is no evidence of
such an earlier *bylina*. On the other hand such banishments are not rare
in Russian history, and *byliny* composed on the theme are commonly
found. We have discussed the subject elsewhere,[3] and shall treat of it
again more fully in the present volume in the chapter on 'The Texts'.

Byliny of Type B relating the laments of the *tsaritsas* and of the troops,
composed on the deaths of various tsars, are neither at variance with
historical record, nor do they differ in any respect from what we should
expect to find had they actually been composed by the speakers. There
can be no doubt, however, that they are not wholly independent of one
another, and the situations and speeches which they record are to some
extent conventional. The nature of their relationship will be discussed
more fully later, also in the chapter on 'The Texts'.

The most important class of unhistorical elements in the modern
byliny are those which are neither at variance with historical record nor
in themselves incredible, but which we nevertheless regard with
scepticism for one reason or another. A number of *byliny* relating to
Peter the Great may be included under this heading. A whole Cycle of

---

[1] Kirêevski, VII. p. 11 ff.; Chadwick, p. 229 ff.
[2] Rambaud, *R.É.* p. 239 f.   [3] Chadwick, p. 203 f.

byliny and *skazki* has sprung up relating his exploits. The north of Russia is especially rich in memories of the great tsar, and has retained a great wealth of tradition, both in prose and verse, relating to his remarkable character and habits, and to his early years.[1] It must be confessed however that the historical value of these traditions is not on a high level. What impressed the popular imagination was not so much Peter's greatness as his eccentricity—his tall and powerful figure, his habit of associating with peasants, his foreign travel, his love of foreign importations—folding-tables, telescopes, embossed note-paper—his mechanical hobbies. All these things appear in the *byliny* in unnatural combinations and fantastic association, transporting us into the atmosphere of a kind of Russian Alice in Wonderland. At times elements derived from adventures in the *byliny* of the Kiev Cycle are attached to Peter, at times features of the *bogatyri* themselves, or the supernatural power of the heroes of the 'Older Cycle'. Thus it comes about that while a large proportion of the *byliny* are quite unhistorical in their main facts, they yet reflect those spectacular features in Peter's life and character, especially in his early days, which impressed themselves on the people of Russia in his own time. We may refer to the *bylina* which relates how Peter challenged a young dragoon to wrestle with him,[2] and was overcome, and how well he took his beating. We need not believe that the actual occurrence took place; but it was the kind of thing he would be likely to do.

The variation between the different versions of the *bylina* which relates Peter's voyage to Stockholm[3] will be discussed later (p. 156 f. below). In one of these versions the departure of Peter over the sea is described as accompanied by disturbances in the world of nature analogous to those which accompany the birth of the hero Volga. Another version, which is in general comparatively free from the marvellous, has nevertheless completely distorted the facts. Actually Peter set out in 1697 to travel through western Europe, passing through Livonia where the Swedish governor of Riga took advantage of the *incognito* under which Peter travelled to insult him. In the *bylina* the scene is shifted from Riga to Stockholm, and the place of the hostile governor has been taken by the Swedish queen, who

> Brought out the portraits of the tsars of seven lands,
> And recognised the White Tsar from his portrait.

---

[1] See the admirable chapter on Peter the Great by Rambaud, *R.É.* p. 287 ff.
[2] Kirêevski, VIII. p. 37 ff.; Chadwick, p. 258.
[3] Kirêevski, VIII. p. 164 ff.; Chadwick, p. 260 ff.

The atmosphere is that of folk-tale, but the element of fiction, of pure invention, is undeveloped or wholly absent here as elsewhere. The popular singer, ignorant alike of political geography and of the usages of royalty, but with a mind stored with many a *bylina* of court life and royal personages of the past, has kept as close to history as he knew how to do, and related the incident in the diction and manner traditionally sanctioned to such themes.

A *bylina* of more recent years which bears a somewhat analogous relation to historical fact, and which is entitled 'The Invasion by the French under Napoleon (1812)',[1] describes how Napoleon sends a dispatch to the tsar Alexander I, bidding him make ready the royal apartments in the Kremlin for his reception. The tsar is represented as receiving the news with dismay. It is only when he is reassured by Kutuzov that he recovers his spirits and addresses encouraging words to his army. The unhistorical nature of all this requires no demonstration. The brilliant and courageous part which the Emperor played personally in the campaign of 1812 has been wholly forgotten, both here and elsewhere in the *byliny*. The Battle of Borodino has also been forgotten, and few of the Russian generals are mentioned by name except the great Kutuzov, the hero of the people. The principal facts have not been wholly forgotten however, and are dimly reflected in our *bylina*. Napoleon presumed to covet Moscow and hoped to rule in place of the Russian tsar, but was thwarted largely by the dogged determination and generalship of Kutuzov. This *bylina* has been quoted on p. 66 above.

In estimating the fidelity and the shortcomings of Russian oral tradition it is of importance to note that there is hardly any overlapping between the different cycles. A poem is recorded by Rybnikov[2] which represents Vasili Buslaev of Novgorod as feasting with Vladimir in Kiev. A *bylina* recorded by Gilferding[3] represents Sadko as associated with Volga, while another *bylina*, also recorded by Gilferding,[4] associates the same hero with Svyatogor. Svyatogor himself is also found in association with Ilya of Murom. Irmak Timofeevich, who conquered Siberia in 1581, figures as a member of Vladimir's court in several versions of the *bylina* of Tsar Kalin. Cases of contact between the cycles are, however, not common when we take account of the great number of poems under discussion, and in the later Cycles, from the time of Ivan the Terrible to the present day, they are practically unknown.

[1] Kirêevski, x. p. 2; Chadwick, p. 287 f.   [2] Rambaud, *R.É.* p. 131, footnote.
[3] *Loc. cit.*   [4] Gilferding, ii. p. 297. Cf. Rambaud, *R.É.* p. 152.

CHAPTER V

THE TEXTS

THE *byliny* offer an enormous choice of variants. Not only is the choice very extensive numerically, but we also have variants from regions which are separated from one another by many thousands of miles. *Byliny* from the north-east of Siberia offer us variants of *byliny* from Novgorod and Olonets in the north-west of Russia in Europe, and *byliny* from Archangel on the White Sea offer variants of *byliny* from Astrakhan and Saratov and even the Caucasus.

On the other hand we have no MS. texts of Russian *byliny* as early as that of the two poems published by Hektorović in 1556 from the Island of Hvar in Dalmatia, and no considerable collections comparable to the Yugoslav MS. collections dating from the beginning of the eighteenth century. The earliest MS. texts of Russian *byliny* known to us are the half dozen texts written down by Richard James in 1619, and preserved in the Bodleian Library at Oxford; but unfortunately these texts appear to be unique. We know of no duplicates or variants of them from any period. Later in the same century (1688) a further small collection of *byliny* treating of contemporary events was made, but this collection has not been accessible to us, and we do not know if it is yet published. The collection made by Kirsha Danilov from the miners in Perm during the eighteenth century has already been referred to frequently. The miners doubtless came from all parts, and it would be misleading to suppose that this collection represents local variants exclusively. Its principal value is chronological, and it offers us a wealth of early versions with which to compare the modern texts from elsewhere. In addition to these collections, we have a number of other texts recorded, often at random, in notebooks, account books, and other odd places by various people, such as early settlers in Siberia. These have been collected to some extent in modern times, and published by students of Russian oral literature.

We may refer again here to the German translation of a collection of *byliny* published anonymously in 1819, of which mention has already been made (p. 7 above), and which contains some versions not known from other sources. All these early versions, from whatever source, are of great value for comparative purposes, and enable us to some extent to restore the early forms of the personal names—a very important factor in the study of the historical elements—and the redactions[1] of the *byliny* from which our modern variants are more or less directly descended. Unfortunately we have no evidence for Russian variants comparable to that supplied by the Yugoslav eighteenth-century MS. collections of poems called *bugarštice*, which offer such an interesting series of parallels to the modern versions composed in a totally different metre.

The nature of the Russian variants differs greatly. In many cases they are merely inconsiderable details of text, and this is sometimes the case even when the variants have been collected from areas which are hundreds of miles apart. In other cases the stories themselves differ considerably, though it may be clear nevertheless that they are derived from a common prototype. Again it frequently happens that stories recognisably identical are preserved in versions which differ so widely as to make us doubt if they do not represent two traditions which have been distinct from the start. A more difficult and important question is that of static motifs and formulae, stock situations ready made and easy of insertion, of which the composers always have a large stock-in-trade` ready for re-use. A hero is to marry—the cue is sufficient; the wedding is brought forward and moved into its place; a previous lover advances prior claims to the bride—the situation has many a precedent, the pursuit, the flight, the duel are all ready to be transferred bodily into the new position; the treachery of the bride must needs follow, and the final triumph of the hero. But has the author of the *bylina* 'borrowed' his properties from another story? Has he adapted his own original story to another well-known theme? Or has he drawn from his rich traditional store of motif, incident, situation, formulae and diction to produce a new story with a familiar family likeness to others which we have previously known? In regard to poems of Types B and D the problem is still more complex. Poems which are sometimes almost identical, yet which at other times differ considerably, though containing closely corresponding passages—are such poems 'borrowings', or 'refurbishings', or 'variants', or are they more or less independent compositions following a traditional 'idea' or 'ritual'? These are some of the questions which arise in considering the varying degrees of similarity and disparity in the variant versions of poetry which has been carried on for many centuries by oral tradition. We cannot hope in the following pages to do more than give examples of

---

[1] By 'redaction' we do not mean to imply the existence of a written text.

different kinds and degrees of variants, and some suggestions which have occurred during the course of our study as to the manner in which such variants may arise.

We will first consider some narrative *byliny* relating to the Kiev Cycle, and then pass on to *byliny* of comparatively modern times, concentrating chiefly on Types B and D. In regard to the former a few general variations in regard to textual points will first be considered, after which we will pass on to examine some closely similar versions of the *bylina* of Sukhan Domantevich, in which again the variants are merely textual. Next we will turn to variants where incidents of the story have been altered and transposed, after which we will take wholly distinct *byliny* which appear to be variants of a common original poem, selecting as our examples the *byliny* of Sukhan Domantevich, Mikhailo Potyk, and Ivan Godinovich. Two distinct *byliny* will then be compared from a later Cycle, relating to Prince Roman, which do not appear to be derived from a common composition, but from two distinct compositions based on a common original theme or historical occurrence.

Turning next to the seventeenth century we will compare two *byliny* on the murder of the Tsarevich Dimitri, which appear to be variant versions of a common original poem, though one version in its present form is a narrative poem, while the other is approximating to Type B. From this we will pass on to compare the opening lines of two variants of a single *bylina* on the voyage of Peter the Great to Sweden, which differ from one another widely in diction, though not in the actual course of the narrative. Finally we will consider the nature of the relationship of a number of *byliny* of Types B and D which have reference to people and events of widely different periods, but which resemble one another closely, at times so closely as to be almost identical.

We will begin with narrative *byliny* belonging to the Kiev Cycle. As an example of variation in textual points we may compare some passages in various *byliny* recited to Gilferding by the *skaʒitel* Ivan Feponov of Pudoga with those of other reciters. Feponov, as became a *kalêka* (cf. p. 248 below), tended to introduce Christian references into his poems, representing his heroes as constantly praying to God. We have therefore selected some of the passages containing such references for comparison with other versions, as having an interesting bearing on the passages in the Anglo-Saxon poem *Beowulf* which are commonly regarded as 'Christian interpolations'. These passages will serve to illustrate the way in which the personality of the reciter colours the narrative without encroaching on it or obtruding itself in any way.

In Feponov's account of the journey of Ilya of Murom from his native village, when the hero arrives at the city of Bekeshov,

> He entered the church of God.
> And all the citizens of Bekeshov
> Had assembled in the church,
> Confessing their sins and praying to God,
> And preparing for their death.[1]

Ilya learns that a Tatar host has surrounded the city, and this is the cause of their panic. He accordingly defeats the host and sets off to find the dwelling of Solovey the Robber. The incident recurs in many versions of the story, generally in connection, not with Bekeshov, but with Chernigov, but without any reference to the assembly of the citizens in church. Thus in Ryabinin's version Ilya defeats the pagan host which is surrounding the town of Chernigov before he enters the city, and then rides up to the town:

> The men of Chernigov came to meet him,
> And opened to him the gates of the city of Chernigov
> And invited him to become the governor of Chernigov.

Ilya, however, declines the invitation, and asks the way to the home of Solovey the Robber.[2]

In Feponov's version of Kalin Tsar, when Vladimir sends for Ilya of Murom, whom he himself has previously buried in a deep vault, and whom he believes to be dead, the hero is found sitting alive in the tomb,

> Burning a wax candle,
> And reading the Gospels.[3]

We may compare the parallel passage in a version recorded by Gulyaev and published in Kirêevski's collection, where we are merely told that when Vladimir's messengers come to Ilya's tomb,

> They cried in a loud voice,
> "Ho, bold, noble youth,
> Are you alive or no?"
> Then Ilya of Murom replied to them,
> And they lowered a ladder to him,
> In his deep vault:
> God's daylight reached Ilya Muromets,
> And the messengers brought him to Prince Vladimir.[4]

---

[1] Gilferding, I. p. 417, line 46 ff.
[2] Rybnikov, I. p. 15, line 15 ff.; Chadwick, p. 66 ff.
[3] Gilferding, I. p. 427.   [4] Kirêevski, I. p. 69.

Feponov's tendency to introduce and emphasise Christian elements is seen further in line 178 ff. of the same poem, where Ilya declares that he will go and oppose Tsar Kalin:

> But not for the sake of Prince Vladimir,
> And not for the princess Apraxya,
> But for the sake of the holy land of Russia,
> And for the sake of the Orthodox faith,
> And for the sake of the great churches,
> And for the sake of Our Lady.[1]

And a few lines later (line 239 ff.), as the Tatars are leading Ilya captive past a cathedral to the place of execution, Ilya offers up a prayer to all the saints, whereupon his steed comes running up from the open plain, and frees his master from his bonds. These Christian touches are not found in any other versions, so far as we are aware.

We may refer further to Feponov's account of Dobrynya's preparations before setting out on the morning after his first encounter with the dragon:

> He arose in the morning early,
> He washed himself very white in spring water,
> He dried himself on a linen towel,
> He prayed to the Lord God
> That the lord, the Saviour, would deliver him.[2]

Again in Feponov's account of the departure of Dobrynya to rescue Vladimir's 'daughter'—in other versions generally his 'niece'—from the dragon, we are told that having collected all his weapons together Dobrynya prepared to set out; first however,

> He prayed to the Lord God,
> He prayed to St Mikula,
> That the Lord, the Saviour would deliver him.[3]

With these passages we may compare Chukov's account of Dobrynya's preparations and departure on the same quest:

> He arose in the morning very early,
> He washed himself in the morning very white,
> He dressed himself with special care,
> He saddled his good steed,
> Swiftly he mounted his good steed.[4]

---

[1] Gilferding, I. p. 430, line 181 ff.
[3] Ib. p. 447, line 308 ff.
[2] Ib. p. 442, line 122 ff.
[4] Rybnikov, I. p. 151, line 140 ff.

We will next study an example of closely allied texts of a single *bylina*, selecting as an example the *bylina* of Sukhan Domantevich[1] which is of comparatively rare occurrence, though a few versions have been preserved. It has been recorded from the district of Pudoga near Lake Onega in the present Soviet republic of Karelia in north-west Russia by Rybnikov,[2] Gilferding,[3] and the brothers Sokolov,[4] and from the neighbourhood of the White Sea by A. V. Markov.[5] Markov's version differs from that of Rybnikov astonishingly little, and that only in unessential details, while that of Gilferding corresponds for the most part in the main outline of the narrative, though it is corrupt in parts. A fragment of a version from Saratov[6] has been recorded which also seems to follow the lines of the northern version, though the conventions differ somewhat. Sukhan also figures prominently in a *bylina* of especial interest from the R. Kolyma in north-eastern Siberia,[7] though Mikhailo Potyk ('Potok Mikhailovich') is the actual hero. A number of other notices of unpublished *byliny* relating to Sukhan are given by S. Shambinago.[8] We will begin by giving a comparison of the closely allied texts of Rybnikov, Gilferding and Markov, which for the sake of convenience we will refer to as A, B and C respectively.

The versions given in A and C are remarkably close. In both these versions the story relates that at Vladimir's feast Sukhan is silent and sulky until Vladimir invites him to make his boast with the rest. Sukhan then boasts that he will capture and bring to Vladimir a white swan alive and uninjured. He goes forth, and in A passes successively three rivers, but makes no attempt to shoot geese or swans or ducks. In C we are merely told that when he comes to the R. Pochay he can find

---

[1] V. F. Miller has shown cogent reasons for regarding this as the original form of the name. See *Ocherki*, III. p. 170. It is the form which occurs in a *skazanie* dating from the eighteenth century and in the collection of Kirsha Danilov, as well as in a *bylina* recorded from the R. Kolyma in north-eastern Siberia—a region which has preserved exceptionally pure and archaic forms. In Rybnikov's version of the *bylina* the name appears as *Sukhmanti Odikhmantevich*, in Gilferding's as *Sukhman Dolmantevich*. Sokolov also apparently found the form *Sukhman* in the same region. In Markov's version from the White Sea the name appears as *Sukhmaty Sukhmatevich*; in a fragment from Saratov, as *Sukhan Ivanovich*.

[2] II. p. 338 ff.   [3] I. p. 468 ff.

[4] In the expedition to Pudoga, the brothers Sokolov recorded in 1928 a third version of the *bylina*. This version has not yet been published so far as we are aware. See the article 'A la Recherche des Bylines', by B. and Y. Sokolov, *R.É.S.* XII (1932), p. 212.   [5] Markov, p. 86 ff.

[6] Miller, *Byliny*, p. 132 ff.   [7] *Ib.* p. 205.

[8] *I.P.S.S.* p. 503.

none. In both versions, accordingly, he proceeds to the R. Mother Dnêpr. The river, which is personified as a woman or maiden, is troubled and disturbed. In both versions she addresses Sukhan in human voice, and laments that she is oppressed by a vast host of Tatars on her further bank. Each day they labour to build a bridge with which to span her, each night she destroys their work. Sukhan leaps across the Dnêpr, and in A tears up an oak tree and encounters and utterly destroys the vast Tatar army, using the oak-tree as a club. On his return to the Dnêpr he is shot by the arrows of three Tatars who are hiding by the river. He staunches his wounds with poppy petals, and slays these three Tatars also, after which he returns to Kiev, but does not bring the white swan in fulfilment of his promise. In C the events are practically the same, but the hero is here said to tear up the oak-tree to use as a club after he has received his own death wound, apparently in the midst of his onslaught. In C only one Tatar is said to shoot the fatal arrow, not three as in A, and no ambush is mentioned; and after staunching his wound the hero goes on fighting till not one Tatar remains. On his return to Kiev in both versions he boasts of his great deed to Prince Vladimir, but is cast into a deep pit or dungeon (*gluboki pogreb*, A; *temnitsa temnaya*, C); and Dobrynya is sent to verify his story. When Dobrynya returns and testifies to the truth of Sukhan's report, the hero is released, and Vladimir desires to reward him; but Sukhan goes forth into the open plain, and tearing from his wounds the petals of the poppy flower with which they are staunched (A; grass, C) he allows the blood to gush forth again, and so dies.

The version recorded by Gilferding (B) differs from A and C in a few important respects only. (1) The river is not personified and does not speak; (2) On his arrival in Kiev without the white swan, Sukhan is buried alive for thirty years in a '*pogreb gluboki*', a '*temnitsa temnaya*'; (3) Ilya of Murom goes to the Dnêpr at the end of this period to verify Sukhan's story, whereas in A and C Dobrynya Nikitich—not Ilya of Murom—is sent as soon as Sukhan is imprisoned. Ilya of Murom and not Sukhan here has the second encounter with the surviving Tatars lying in ambush, who are here stated to be two in number, and here it is clearly stated that they are the only survivors from the host slain by Sukhan, and that they escaped and lay concealed in the bushes. Here, however, the interview takes place, not immediately after the battle, but when Sukhan has been buried alive for thirty years, and while Ilya is visiting the site of the battle to verify his story. The treacherous attempt, therefore, is here made, not on the life of Sukhan, but on that of Ilya, though the attempt proves unsuccessful. B is manifestly inferior to A and C at this point; for here a stock motif from the *byliny* of the slaying of Tugarin or Idolishche has been substituted for the wounding of Sukhan, whereas Sukhan's own wounds are left unexplained. The period of thirty years, during which he is buried alive, is manifestly a purely conventional figure.

It will be seen that A and C are much closer than A and B, though the two former are separated by many hundreds of miles, while the two latter were recorded in the same district. It will be interesting to see where the affinities of Sokolov's version lie, since this was recorded in the same district as A and B some sixty years later. In the meantime A and C permit us to realise the fidelity of the Russian peasant memory in the *byliny* tradition, despite the freedom allowed and the partial recomposition which takes place with each fresh recitation.

The fragment from Saratov,[1] which we will refer to as D, opens with a picture of Sukhan (*sic*), who is here not called Domantevich, or any variant of this patronymic, but Ivanovich. He is riding away over the open plain, his horse richly caparisoned, and he himself finely dressed. He rides until he comes to a damp oak on which sits a wise (i.e. talking) crow. Sukhan draws his bow and places his arrow in position, intending to shoot the crow, but the crow addresses him in human speech: "Do not shoot me, Sukhan, but ride instead to the R. Jordan. There stands a Tatar army." The fragment breaks off at this point, but it is not difficult to see its relationship to the other versions. The *bylina* evidently opens at the point where Sukhan has left Vladimir's court and set out on his quest. In the present version he finds the damp oak at an earlier stage in the poem than in the previous versions, and it is introduced for a different purpose. The talking crow here takes the place of the talking river in A and C, and the Jordan has been substituted for the Dnêpr. Here we have an interesting illustration of the Russian attitude to their great river as a barrier between their Christian heroes and the infidel Tatars. Sukhan's quest is here represented as something in the nature of a crusade. Some of these new conventions are southern and comparatively local in character. The damp oak and the talking crow which addresses the hero as he is about to shoot are characteristic features of the southern *byliny*. Despite these differences of detail, however, it is easy to see that the outline of the narrative, in this version, corresponds to that of the versions previously considered.

The conventions and diction of these versions are full of interest for

[1] Miller, *Byliny*, p. 132 ff.

the study of the variant versions and the genesis and history of the *bylina*, though space does not permit us to enter here upon a full discussion of their importance. The dialogue between Sukhan and the R. Dnêpr recalls the dialogue between Prince Igor and the R. Donets in the *Slovo o Polky Igorevê*, in which the R. Dnêpr is said to have 'closed its dark banks' (*zatvori Dnêpr temnê berezê*) to the youth Rostislav Vsevolodich.[1] We may perhaps compare a *bylina* recorded from Simbirsk[2] which relates a dialogue between Dobrynya Nikitich and the R. Smorodina, in which the river is referred to as a 'gentle, fair maid'. The river addresses him in human speech, and permits him to ford her, but afterwards drowns him in consequence of his vaunting words. This *bylina* is said to be very late;[3] but the motif of the dialogue between a hero and a river, in which the latter is personified as a maiden or woman, is older than the *Slovo o Polky Igorevê*, where the form of the dialogue between Yaroslavna and the R. Dunai suggests that the convention was already stereotyped. We may refer also again to the dialogue in the *Slovo* between Igor and the R. Donets, in which the latter is addressed as a maiden preparing a bed for her lover.[4] It is perhaps worth noting that in the same work the minstrel or author complains that the R. Sula no longer flows with silvery current, and the R. Dvina flows sluggishly amid the shouts of the pagans.[5] The poetic conventions of the *bylina* of Sukhan, therefore, are to be traced to the poetic milieu of the *Slovo*. The convention is not a common one in the *byliny*, which know nothing of the *rusalka* ('water-nymph') of modern Russian folk-lore, and, in general, neither personify their rivers nor people them with personified spirits. In modern oral narrative poetry, the convention in Sukhan is comparable rather with a Yugoslav poem on the building of the bridge at Višegrad in Bosnia,[6] in which the builders are hindered in their building operations by the *vila* or spirit maiden of the river. The *vila* is, of course, absent from the Russian poem, the personified river taking her place. It is interesting to note how in the *bylina* of Sukhan the fundamental part played by the R. Dnêpr in the political history of ancient Russia is reflected in the partizan attitude which the river is represented as adopting in the struggle between the Russians of Kiev and the Tatars.

Although personifications of rivers are not common in the *byliny*, it is,

---

[1] *Slovo*, line 694 ff.
[2] Kirêevski, II. p. 61 ff.
[3] Magnus, *Ballads*, p. 54.
[4] *Slovo*, line 694 ff.
[5] *Ib.* line 531 ff.
[6] This poem will be noticed later, in Part II.

as we have seen, by no means rare to find a maiden referred to as a
white swan. We have seen that the personification of a river as a maiden
is a common poetic convention of the *Slovo*. In the *Slovo* also we find
the maiden identified with the white swan, and associated with the river
in a manner which suggests the river *vila* referred to above. The passage
is obscure in certain features, but appears to be clear enough in this
respect. It may be provisionally translated as follows:

Scorn rose high among the hosts of the descendants of Dazhbog. She[1]
entered as a maiden into the land of Troyan, she splashed with her swan
wings, bathing in the blue expanse of the Don, and aroused a period of
trouble.[2]

It is, we think, in the light of this diction, as found in the *Slovo*, that
the personification of the river and the disappearance of the white swan
from the *bylina* of Sukhan are to be explained.

We will now turn to the *bylina* from the R. Kolyma in far north-
eastern Siberia in 1895 under the title of 'Potop Mikhailovich (Ivan
Godinovich)'.[3] This *bylina* opens with an account of the arrival of
Sukhan Domantevich at Kiev. His appearance is noted with the
usual formulae attached to a hero. It is not a black crow, or a bright
falcon flying, it is Sukhan riding a fiery steed, and he sits in his saddle
like a grey eagle, with eyes bright as the falcon's, brows black as two
sables, and a turbulent head like a great beer cauldron. He does not
pause to pass through the gates but leaps over the iron fence on his
steed. He does not hand his steed to a groom, or ask leave of the porters
or address the attendants, but boldly makes his way through every door
till he finds himself in the presence of the prince and princess, whom he
greets in the usual courteous manner. They welcome him, and a place is
made for him at the table, and food is set before him, and they ask him
where he has been journeying. Sukhan replies that he has been far away
across the open plain, and farther still, beyond the blue sea, where he was
in the presence of Zakhar Makarevich, where he saw Zakhar's daughter,
the lovely white swan. She was as white as snow, her eyes were as
bright as the falcon's, her brows as black as two sables as they lay on her
white cheeks. It is clear that the white swan is simply a fair girl. At this
point of the story Potop Mikhailovich, who is seated at the table, springs
to his feet and bows low before Vladimir, and begs the prince to send

---

[1] Edd. generally assume this to be *Obida*, 'scorn', 'contumely'. Could it not,
however, have reference to Dazhbog, who is here referred to as standing for all her
descendants? [2] *Slovo*, line 285 f.
[3] Miller, *Byliny*, p. 205 ff.

him to woo the white swan. This hero is more generally known as Mikhailo Potyk Ivanovich, and for the sake of convenience we will refer to him by the latter name, though it is not the one by which he is known in this *bylina*. From this point (line 34) Mikhailo is the foremost figure in the *bylina* and Sukhan takes only a secondary place. The prince grants his request, and Mikhailo sets off, accompanied by Dobrynya Mikitevich (more usually *Nikitich*), Sukhan Domantevich, and Alyosha Popovich. On the way they meet a *kalêka*, and Dobrynya and Sukhan each try unsuccessfully to force him to change costumes with them, till Mikhailo takes him in hand. At this point there is a break in the narrative, where the reciter appears to have forgotten, or the editor omitted a portion. The *bylina* takes up the narrative again (line 84) with the arrival of the heroes at the abode of Zakhar Makarevich, and Mikhailo sends his three companions to sue for the hand of the fair white swan. Zakhar Makarevich replies that his daughter is already betrothed to Koshel Trepêtoy (better known elsewhere as Koshchey the Deathless or the Immortal). Alyosha Popovich retorts that if he will not give her willingly they will take her by force, whereupon Zakhar Makarevich consents. Again the heroes ride forth, and again we have a break in the narrative, but apparently only a brief one, for at line 104 Mikhailo appears to be in the act of sending his three companions to Kiev to bid them come to welcome him and his bride at dawn. Then Koshel comes flying to Mikhailo and his bride, and overpowers the hero in his sleep, and binds him with iron chains. Koshel takes his bow, and places his arrow in position, and shoots it at Mikhailo. The white swan forbids him to shoot, explaining that the arrow of the hero cannot enter Mikhailo's flesh; but it is too late, and the arrow breaks through all Mikhailo's bonds, and Mikhailo frees himself, and seizes his sharp sabre, and makes an end of Koshel. Then we are told that Mikhailo rides away, but he does not take his bride with him, and Alyosha greets him with ironical words which seem to mean that though his wooing has been successful, yet the hero returns alone.

It is obvious that this story has a considerable element in common with the Russian *bylina* of Sukhan. Both stories have as their theme a mission sent from Vladimir to bring to his court a white swan. The white swan, as her name suggests, lives on the edge of water—the Dnêpr in the Russian, the blue sea in the Siberian. The same hero plays a part in both stories, and the beginnings of the two stories seem to supplement one another, though they are not identical. According to the Siberian version it is after viewing the white swan that Sukhan comes to Vladimir's court and tells the prince of her beauty. In the Russian versions Sukhan is first introduced to us at Vladimir's feast, where he boasts that he will bring the white swan alive and uninjured. We are not told that he has already seen her himself; but perhaps this may be inferred. In both versions a hero at once goes to obtain the white swan. In the Siberian version the white swan is a maiden, as in many Russian *byliny*. In the Russian versions of Sukhan the white swan is never introduced to us in person, and she appears to have dropped out of the story inadvertently; but in two of these versions the river is personified as a fair maiden, who seems in some way to have taken the place of the white swan. In the Russian versions the hero who goes to seek the white swan is Sukhan, while in the Siberian it is Mikhailo Potyk, which seems less natural, seeing that in this same version we are told that it is Sukhan and not Mikhailo who has seen her and brings the report of her to Kiev. Is it possible that in the Siberian version the position of the two heroes has been transposed, and that the better-known hero has usurped the original function of the more obscure? In favour of such a suggestion we may refer to Sukhan's patronymic Ivanovich, which belongs more properly to Mikhailo Potyk, and the substitution of which for Domantevich would seem to suggest that there has been some confusion between the two heroes in the Siberian version. It may be further added in favour of this suggestion that in the best Russian versions only two heroes are associated with Mikhailo as his sworn brothers, whereas in the Siberian there are three, making a very unusual grouping of four, and suggesting that one of them is a comparatively recent introduction.

In both stories the hero has to cross a sheet of water and to fight a battle before the White Swan can be his. This is, of course, not unusual; but it is curious that in both stories the life of the hero is attempted by an ambush, his enemy shooting an arrow while the hero is off his guard. In the Russian version this results in Sukhan's mortal wound, while in the Siberian version the result is different. It is not the hero who dies, but his enemy. Yet it is again curious that in both stories, while the hero is represented as victorious, he returns without his prize, the white swan—a fact which is left wholly unexplained. We are not told her ultimate fate in either story. This part of the Siberian version is obscure and obviously imperfect. The latter part of the *bylina* has not been well remembered. On the whole a comparison of these two stories would seem to suggest that they are derived ultimately from a common original; and that the opening and early part of both *byliny* have been comparatively well remembered in both traditions, but best in the Siberian, while the latter part has not been perfectly remembered in either, though it would not be difficult to show how each could be utilised to supplement the other. Before forming any definite conclusion on this point, however, we will next compare the Siberian version of Mikhailo Potyk with a Russian *bylina* relating to the same hero.

The *bylina* of Mikhailo Potyk is a favourite subject among the reciters of north Russia, and is found in a large number of variants. The story is a long one and contains an unusually large number of incidents. It is therefore the more surprising that the modern versions differ little from one another save in the proper names, and in the order of events, which are sometimes transposed. Otherwise the variations, even in details, are, for the most part, inconsiderable. This would seem to suggest that all the modern north Russian versions of Mikhailo Potyk—and perhaps the earlier versions also[1]—are derived from a single common redaction at no very remote date. Among the best of the modern versions—though not the longest[2]—is the version recited by Kalinin to Gilferding, which consists of 971 lines. It is interesting to observe that although the actual outline of the two narratives corresponds, the abridged version recited by Kalinin to Rybnikov's emissary[3] consists of only 504 lines. The same reciter was able, in fact, to recite the same *bylina* in a compass double the length without material alteration of his narrative. The discrepancy is the more striking in view of the fact that Kalinin twice recited the *bylina* in the form recorded by Rybnikov, apparently practically without alteration.[4] We will take as the basis for our comparison of this *bylina* with the Siberian version the version recited by Kalinin to Gilferding. As a summary of this version has already been given (p. 41 ff. above), we will refer the reader to this passage to avoid repetition here.

It will be seen that the Russian tradition of Mikhailo Potyk as represented by this version has much in common with the Siberian *bylina* discussed above. In both versions Vladimir at a royal feast dispatches Mikhailo Potyk on an embassy to the home of the white swan. It is not stated in the Russian version under discussion that Vladimir was himself aware of the existence of the white swan; he

[1] Cf. Dumézil, *R.É.S.* v. p. 205 ff.

[2] The longest contained in the collections of Rybnikov and Gilferding is the one recited by Petr Prokhorov to the latter, which consists of 1129 lines.

[3] It appears that Rybnikov never interviewed Kalinin himself. See the editor's note, Rybnikov, II. p. 54 f.

[4] See the footnote to line 13 of Ryabinin's version of the *bylina* of Mikhailo Potyk, Rybnikov, II. p. 55; cf. also editor's note prefixed to this *bylina*.

merely sends three heroes—among them Mikhailo—to collect tribute in different quarters. But in the version recorded by Kirsha Danilov we are told that the tribute is to take the form of water birds,[1] while in one version recorded by Rybnikov[2] Vladimir tells his heroes that in sending them ostensibly to collect tribute, his true intention has been that they should procure wives for themselves. We may doubtless assume, therefore, that a Russian tradition existed in which Vladimir had sent one or more of the heroes to obtain tribute in the form of white swans. In both the Russian and the Siberian versions Mikhailo obtains his White Swan by force. In the Siberian version she is already betrothed to another hero, Koshchey the Deathless. This is not stated in the Russian version, but the consistent hostility of the White Swan to her deliverer in all versions after the scene in the tomb is exceedingly difficult to explain, as is also her attachment to the Lithuanian prince—or his counterpart in other versions—and could most naturally be accounted for if he had had some prior claim on her affections which had been violated by Mikhailo in the first instance.

In both the Russian and the Siberian versions a joint attack by Mikhailo's enemy and the White Swan herself is made on the life of Mikhailo when he is asleep, though in the Russian version this is developed into an elaborate series of encounters. In both versions the hero is rendered helpless before his enemy makes the attack—in the Siberian by iron bands, in the Russian by a magic potion. In both versions, however, Mikhailo is restored to freedom and consciousness by miraculous means, and in both he is enabled to destroy his enemy, perhaps the White Swan also, though in the Siberian version this is not actually stated. In both versions, at any rate, Mikhailo, though victorious in the duel, returns without his prize, the White Swan. It is noteworthy that in both versions Mikhailo's enemy uses bow and arrow, while Mikhailo cuts off his head with a sharp sabre. It may be added that there are other incidents which correspond in the two versions, the most striking being the introduction of the *kalêka* and the change of dress. The lacuna in the Siberian version at this point has doubtless robbed us of several other identical or similar features in the two versions.

There can be no question that the Siberian tradition of Mikhailo Potyk is a variant of that which relates to the Russian hero of the same name. It has already been shown that there are cogent reasons for regarding this Siberian tradition as a variant of the Russian tradition of

[1] Kirêevski, IV. p. 52; cf. also a version from the White Sea cited by Dumézil, *R.É.S.* V (1925), p. 208.   [2] II. p. 609.

Sukhan. It would therefore be tedious to compare the Russian tradition of Mikhailo with the Russian tradition of Sukhan, though such a comparison is not without interest, and has been made by us elsewhere. Here we may take it for granted, in view of what has been said above, that a certain relationship between the two undoubtedly exists. It would be of interest for the study of the growth of variants if we could indicate the nature of this relationship and the relative chronology of the two versions. It has been shown above that the diction and the conventions of the *bylina* of Sukhan belong to the same poetic milieu as the *Slovo o Polky Igorevê*. We may therefore infer that this *bylina* is conservative in form. It has also been observed, on the other hand, that the relatively close correspondence between the Russian versions of the *bylina* of Mikhailo Potyk argues a comparatively recent origin for this redaction, though this may nevertheless mean a date prior to the seventeenth century. It remains to see if any other literary evidence can be found in the Russian *bylina* of Mikhailo Potyk which will throw light on the period to which the present form of the Russian *bylina* tradition is to be assigned.

Despite the points of similarity between the *bylina* of Mikhailo Potyk noted above and the *bylina* of Sukhan, there are certain points of difference which require explanation. Of these the most important is the strange mutual oath sworn between Mikhailo and the White Swan in the *bylina* of Mikhailo, and the ensuing encounter with the dragon in the tomb. There are also some curious features in the former *bylina* which are not well motivated, and which also require explanation. We may instance Marya's implacable hatred of her lover after her deliverance from death, and her anxiety to remain with a strange husband who has suddenly appeared, comparatively late in the story, and carried her off from Mikhailo. In the Siberian version of the combined story of Sukhan and Mikhailo we are told that Marya was already affianced to Koshchey the Deathless when Mikhailo carried her off, and this would, of course, account satisfactorily for both phenomena. But there is no hint of this in the Russian versions of the story, in which the encounter with the dragon appears as so prominent a feature.

Now there can be no doubt that in its present form the encounter with the dragon is a common folk-motif which is found in many lands, as Dumézil pointed out in 1925.[1] Five years later Dumézil, without reference to the *bylina* of Mikhailo Potyk, published in a collection of songs of the Ossetes and neighbouring peoples in the heart of the Caucasus a story which has so striking a resemblance to the incidents

[1] *R.É.S.* v (1925), p. 219 ff.

of Mikhailo Potyk under discussion as to constitute in our opinion another variant. At the same time it helps to explain the curious and inexplicable features in the Russian story noted above.

Here is the story as it is current among the Kabardes and the Ossetes: "Sosruko [one of the early heroes whose exploits are still recited by their minstrels] avait une maîtresse, nommée Nart-Žan. Un jour, en la quittant pour aller prendre part aux jeux des Nartes, Sosruko échangea avec elle un grand serment: ils résolurent de ne point se survivre l'un à l'autre. Or, trois jours plus tard, quand il revint, on lui annonça l'affreuse nouvelle: Žan, sa Žan était morte et ensevelie. Il alla jusqu'à la tombe, enleva une à une toutes les pierres dont les Nartes avaient couvert la fosse, il se jeta sur le cadavre et sanglota amèrement. Au bout de quelques minutes, il vit s'avancer dans la tombe deux serpents qui se mirent à se battre, et finalement l'un tua l'autre. Le survivant disparut, puis revint, traînant une feuille verte dont il frotta son adversaire: aussitôt le serpent mort se ranima et tous deux s'enfuirent. Sosruko ramassa la feuille, en frotta le cadavre de Žan: à peine avait-il achevé ce travail que Žan resuscita. Par la suite il l'épousa."[1]

In a variant the husband of the bride, on seeing her resuscitated, claims her as she and her deliverer leave the tomb; but the hero points out that by burying her, the husband has relinquished his claims on her.[2]

It will be seen that the incident is very similar to the parallel episode in the Russian *bylina*, even in the games in which, in many versions, Mikhailo is engaged when the news of the death of the White Swan is brought to him. It is interesting to observe that in neither of these versions is the dead woman the wife of the hero. Is it possible that in the original Russian version, as in the Caucasian and the Siberian, the White Swan already had a husband when Mikhailo found her? In this case it would be natural that she should subsequently rejoin him when opportunity permitted.

However this may be, there can be no doubt that the entire episode is a common folk-motif. We shall therefore probably be safe in regarding it as either wholly intrusive, or else as a transformation of some other incident which originally stood in its place in the *bylina*. The Siberian tradition has no hint of it, and the *bylina* of Sukhan has no real parallel. It is found in the version of Kirsha Danilov, however, and as this version is said to be virtually identical with seventeenth-century versions

[1] Dumézil, *Légendes sur les Nartes* (Paris, 1930), p. 102.
[2] *Loc. cit.*

we may presume that the incident is found in them also. We may suppose, therefore, that it belongs to a redaction of the *bylina* which is later than the *bylina* of Sukhan and prior to the seventeenth century. And this is the conclusion to which, as we have seen, a general comparison of the modern Russian versions has already led us.

Before leaving the *bylina* of Mikhailo Potyk with its curious history we will compare the eighteenth-century version recorded by Kirsha Danilov[1] with the modern Russian version utilised above, in order to illustrate the chronological change in the *bylina* during the intervening period, and also in order to illustrate the difference in tone and colour in the two narratives as representing the different mentality of the reciters, or the tradition which they follow.

At a feast given to his princes and boyars Vladimir gives orders to Mikhailo to go and shoot geese and swans and ducks for his royal table. Mikhailo sets off at once, and on reaching the 'blue sea' (*sinee more*) proceeds to shoot a number of birds. As he is about to leave he sees a fair White Swan, and is going to shoot her, but she begs him to desist and approaches the shore. She tells him that her name is Avdotya Likhovidevna, and beseeches him to marry her, and to promise her that whichever of them shall first die shall be accompanied by the other alive into the tomb. Mikhailo replies that they will go forthwith to the cathedral in Kiev, where the bells are ringing for Vespers, and there they will be affianced. Then he rides away to Kiev, and the White Swan flies there and arrives before him. Mikhailo goes to the royal court, and tells Vladimir that he has brought him the grey ducks and swans as he was bidden, and for himself a fair maiden whom he desires to marry forthwith. Accordingly they go to the cathedral and are duly married, taking their strange oath together before the cathedral clergy, and in the evening Vladimir gives a great marriage feast in their honour.

Six months later the White Swan suddenly falls ill and dies. Mikhailo goes immediately to the cathedral to inform the clergy, and they tell him to place the body on a sledge and to bring it at once to the porch of the cathedral. Then they dig a deep and wide grave, and when it is ready they let down the corpse, and they place Mikhailo in it also with his horse and his armour. Then they cover the burial chamber with planks of oak, and heap golden sand above it, and on the top they place a wooden cross. But in one spot they insert a rope which is tied to the cathedral bell. And there Mikhailo remains with his good steed from mid-day till midnight, and he lights a taper of pure wax. And when

[1] The text of Kirsha's version will be found in Kirêevski, IV. p. 52 ff.

midnight comes, numbers of dragons assemble, and there comes one great dragon in particular, stinging and scorching with its fiery flame. But Mikhailo is not afraid. He seizes his sharp sword and kills the evil dragon, and cutting off his dragon head he anoints the corpse of Avdotya with it. Then she, 'the heretic', comes to life; and Mikhailo pulls the bell rope. All the Orthodox people assemble and marvel; but Mikhailo cries out from within the tomb in a loud voice. And they break open the tomb with all speed, and take out Mikhailo and his good steed and his young wife, and tell the news to Prince Vladimir and the cathedral clergy, who revive them with holy water, and bid them live for ever. And when Mikhailo grows old and dies, then the priests bury him according to their original promise, and with him they bury alive in the damp earth his wife Avdotya Likhovidevna.

It will be seen that Kirsha's version is less comprehensive than any of the other versions which we have considered. Only one hero is mentioned, and the only incidents which are narrated with any degree of fullness are the meeting of Mikhailo and the White Swan, their burial, and the incident in the tomb. As regards the actual incidents related, Kirsha's version is nearer to the Caucasian story than to the Siberian or the remaining Russian versions.

On the other hand the tone of the narrative is far removed from either that of folk-tale or of heroic poetry. A strong ecclesiastical bias pervades Kirsha's version of this strange story. The hero is attentive to the cathedral bell ringing for matins; it is before the assembled clergy that the strange oath is taken, and it is in the cathedral that the hero and the White Swan are married. Immediately on her death the hero again repairs to the cathedral, and the obsequies are carried out under direct ecclesiastical supervision. It is the clergy who dig the grave and enclose Mikhailo alive with the corpse. Yet all is carried out in due order. Wax tapers are lighted beside the corpse, and means are placed within the hero's reach by which he can communicate with the clergy in case of need. They assemble at once when Mikhailo rings the cathedral bell, and release him and his bride from the tomb, and sprinkle them with holy water. At a subsequent date the clergy once more enforce the fulfilment of the oath. Throughout this version Mikhailo appears as a zealous member of the Orthodox Church. There can be no question but that an early tradition existed in which Mikhailo is almost more of a saint than a *bogatyr*.

Before leaving the *byliny* of Sukhan and Mikhailo Potyk and their variants we may pause to call attention—as others have often done—to

the close similarity between the latter *bylina* and that of Ivan Godinovich. A summary of the latter story has already been given (p. 46 f. above)
and need not be repeated here. We would call attention however to the
main points of resemblance in the two stories, and more especially to the
Siberian version, including the first part of the latter, in which Sukhan
plays a part. In both a hero goes to a distant place 'beyond the blue
sea' where they see a White Swan, and come back to Kiev full of her
praises, and then obtain an escort from Vladimir wherewith to woo her;
but on arriving, their suit is refused, on the ground—in both versions—
that she is already betrothed to Koshel (Koshchey) the Immortal. In
both Koshel (Koshchey) is represented as 'flying'; and in other respects
also he resembles Tugarin and Idolishche. In the Russian versions of
Mikhailo Potyk it is not definitely stated that the White Swan has been
betrothed to Koshchey before she is carried off by Mikhailo, but we
have seen that it is implied by her subsequent anxiety to join him. In
both, the first lover—apparently in his dragon form—surprises Mikhailo and the White Swan as they are alone, and is killed in the combat
with the hero which follows. In both the White Swan shows implacable
hatred to the hero, at least from the point of the story when Koshchey
comes to claim her. In both the hero returns to Kiev without the
White Swan.

It has generally been assumed that confusion has taken place between
the stories of Mikhailo Potyk and Ivan Godinovich; but it is by no
means clear what exactly are the elements confused. The story of Ivan
Godinovich contains practically nothing which does not occur in either
Mikhailo Potyk or Sukhan. We have seen that there is reason to believe
that into the former story a folk-motif has been introduced, doubtless
because it bore a resemblance to some element in the original story.
Here the attack of the dragon lover on the hero and the White Swan
in the tent at night is sufficiently close to the arrival of the dragon in
the tomb at night where Mikhailo and the White Swan are alone to
account for the substitution of the latter motif for the former. It is
interesting too that in one *bylina* the hero's name is Ivan, whereas in
the other this is the hero's patronymic. We suspect that we have before
us an instance, not of 'confusion' but of transference, the entire story
having been transferred from the father to the son—as is suggested in
regard to Sukhan (cf. p. 117 above)—though the process may possibly
be the reverse. In any case we have little doubt that the *bylina* of Ivan
Godinovich is merely a variant version of that of Mikhailo Potyk
Ivanovich..

A number of *byliny* published in variant versions in Kirêevski's collection relate to Prince Roman and his relations with his wife, Marya, the White Swan. It is not easy to say whether these *byliny* are variants of one original theme, or whether they are derived from two originally distinct stories which have influenced one another very considerably in certain details.[1] In one of these *byliny* an obscure hint is given in the opening lines of the murder of Marya the White Swan by Prince Roman, in consequence of her dream that she lost the ring from her right hand—a dream full of foreboding. After this, however, we have no further reference to bad relations between them. The White Swan is carried off by raiders, but escapes to a mountain where she effects a disguise, and after fording a shallow stream, and crossing a still bigger river on a tree-trunk, she eventually reaches Russia, where she is re-united to her husband. A second *bylina* contains no obscure hints. It relates how Prince Roman rends his wife in pieces and casts her into the river; how an eagle carries her hand with its gold ring, and drops it in the garden where her daughter is walking; and how her remains are ultimately found and buried by the daughter and her maids.

It will seem at first sight that the stories have little in common. It is curious, however, that the first *bylina* should open with the obscure statement that Prince Roman dismembered (*lit.* 'cut up') his wife in consequence of her foreboding dreams. Is this intended merely as a static description of Prince Roman, a manner of intimating to the reader which Prince Roman the following story refers to? It is a commonplace of Russian heroic poetry that the prince ill-treats his wife when her dreams forebode evil to him. The motif occurs e.g. in certain versions of the *bylina* of Volga. On the other hand the river plays a prominent part in both poems; in both cases Marya's body is entrusted to it, in one case alive, in the other dead. Similarities of detail may also be mentioned, such as the prominence of the gold ring, and its loss; the walk in the 'green garden' with the maids. The general impression left on the mind is that we are dealing with variant accounts of a single original story, which have had a long enough history in oral tradition to have lost most of their common features.

We will next compare two very brief poems relating to comparatively recent times, recording the murder of the Tsarevich Dimitri, the youngest son of Ivan the Terrible, at the hands of the regent, Boris Godunov, in 1591. As is very common in Russian oral poetry of the last three or

[1] One version of each of the two principal themes is translated by Chadwick, p. 164 ff.

four centuries, the Types are not clearly differentiated; but the first of the two poems about to be considered is approximating to a poem of Type B, the second is clearly a narrative poem. The form of the poems would suggest that their prototype was composed shortly after the event which they celebrate; but they differ from one another considerably in style, and it is not at first sight obvious whether the two poems represent variant traditional versions of a single original composition, or whether they represent two poems originally distinct, each composed in the conventional style traditionally associated with such themes. The first poem, which was published by Dal,[1] is as follows:[2]

> It is not a whirlwind rolling along the valley,
> It is not the grey feather-grass bending to the earth,
> It is an eagle flying under the clouds;
> Keenly he is eyeing the River Moskva,
> 5   And the palace of white stone,
> And its green garden,
> And the golden palace of the royal city.
> It is not a cruel serpent rearing itself up,
> It is a caitiff dog raising a steel knife.
> 10 It has not fallen on to the water, nor on to the earth,
> It has fallen on to the white breast of the tsarevich,
> None other than the tsarevich Dimitri;
> They have murdered the tsarevich Dimitri,
> They have murdered him in Uglich,
> 15 In Uglich at his play.
> Then dark night fell upon the palace.
> A kite built a nest for its nestlings!
> Now this eagle is the tsarevich Dimitri,
> While the kite is Boris Godunov.
> 20 Having murdered the tsarevich, he seated himself on the throne,
> And he reigned, the villain, for seven whole years.
> It is not a whirlwind rolling along the valley,
> It is not the grey feather-grass bending to the earth,
> It is the terrible wrath of God sweeping
> 25 Over orthodox Russia.
> And the kite has perished in his nest,
> His plumage is wafted to the clouds,
> His blood has been poured down the River Moskva.[3]

---

[1] We do not know from what district Dal's text is recorded. A second text differing only very slightly from Dal's was also published by Minyaev.

[2] See Kiréevski, VII. p. 1. For the following translation and a note on the circumstances narrated in the poem, cf. Chadwick, p. 215 ff.

[3] Boris's wife and son were murdered by the adherents of the 'False Dimitri', and Boris himself died in 1605 as the usurper was actually approaching Moscow. It was believed that his death was not without violence.

The second poem, which was recorded from the recitation of an old woman from Tulsk in 1834, is as follows:[1]

> O, my brothers, in years gone by, in times long past,
> In times long past, under the tsars of old,
> The times were evil, and wretched.
> An evil time befel under the tsar of long ago, under Fedor Ivanovich;
> 5 And when our orthodox tsar Fedor Ivanovich died,
> Our Russia fell into villainous hands,
> The villainous hands of the boyars and nobles.
> One turbulent head rose up among the boyars,
> One turbulent head, Boris Godunov himself.
> 10 Now Godunov duped all the boyar folk,
> He resolved to govern our foolish Russia.
> He seized all Russia, and usurped the throne of Moscow,
> And he seized, moreover, the realm of the dead tsar,
> Of the glorious dead tsar, the holy tsarevich Dimitri.
> 15 Then that robber Godunov collected his band,
> He collected accursed folk, evil robbers;
> And having collected them, he spoke accursed words to them:
> "Robbers, you bold youths!
> Will you go and murder the tsar Dimitri.
> 20 And come back, saying: 'We have murdered the tsar?'
> If you do me this service I will reward you with gold and silver."
> Then the accursed folk went, the rascal robbers,
> They went into the sacred place, into the glorious city of Uglich,
> And there they murdered the holy young tsarevich Dimitri,
> 25 And then returned, and told it to Boris Godunov.
> When Boris heard it, he rejoiced at the evil deed.
> And Boris ruled as tsar for exactly five years;
> Boris killed himself with the bitterness of a snake's venom,
> A snake's venom, a sharp dagger.

It will be seen that while the two poems narrate precisely the same event in almost identical compass, they differ considerably both in substance and in style. The text published by Dal, which is very close to that of Minyaev, we will call for convenience, I; that from Tulsk, II. The first difference between the two versions, which strikes us at the outset, is the difference of tense in the opening lines. I pictures the event as actually occurring at the moment, II is a narrative poem in the past. In I the scene of the murder of the tsarevich is represented as taking place before our eyes, the narrator acting as a kind of Mentor, though the reference to the length of the subsequent reign of Boris throws the scene back into the past at the close. In II the entire incident is represented at the outset as taking place in a distant age.

[1] The text will be found in Kirêevski, VII. p. 2 f.

I represents the murder of the tsarevich as the work of an eagle; but as the tsarevich is himself described as an eagle later in the poem, and Boris, the murderer, as a kite, the poet would seem to have confused his metaphors. The plural of the verb is used of the actual murderers, however ('They have murdered', etc.). In II, Boris is said to have bribed others to murder the tsarevich, and it is stated that he himself rejoices when he hears that it is successfully carried out. In I, Boris is said to have reigned for seven years, though five years are stated in Minyaev's version; and in II, for five years. In I, Boris is merely said to perish in his own home by a violent death; in II he is said to have stabbed himself with a sharp dagger. In I, the style is figurative throughout, the narrative being conducted by a series of negative metaphors, each followed by its literal interpretation, giving a staccato effect characteristic of Russian oral poetry. In II the narrative is direct and literal, and the style cursive. There is, however, one exception. In II the dagger with which Boris killed himself is described as a snake, and it is interesting to notice that the same metaphor is used in I of the dagger with which the tsarevich is murdered.

This feature alone would make it probable that the two versions are not wholly independent of one another, and the number of common features in the two poems renders this still more probable. The compass of the poems is practically the same, and the aspects of the incident selected for the narrative or for comment also correspond closely for the most part. We may refer to Boris's part in the murder of the tsarevich, his usurpation, the reference to the length of his reign, and his violent death, with which each poem closes—all these suggest an identical prototype for the two poems which have passed into oral tradition and been modified and refashioned according to the divergent tastes and literary environment of the popular singers.

We will next compare the opening lines of two variants of a *bylina*, also recorded in modern times, which gives an account of the departure of Peter the Great from Russia in 1697 to travel in western Europe. The first version, which we have translated below, is incomplete, as are also two other variants composed in a closely similar style. This fragment is recorded from the Government of Saratov.[1]

> It is not a cloud of dust which has gathered,
> It is not a mist arising from the sea,
> It is geese and swans which have risen from the sea,
> Geese and swans and grey ducks;

[1] Kirêevski, VIII. p. 162 ff.

5   The geese and swans are flying with their goslings,
      The little grey ducks are swimming with their ducklings;
      The geese and swans have risen from the sea,
      And the blue sea is full of agitation,
      The white fish have all dived to the bottom,
10   All dived to the bottom, to quiet waters,
      To quiet waters, to shady pools,
      To shady pools, to safe retreats.
      For over the sea, the blue sea,
      The blue sea, the Khvalinsk,[1]
15   There sailed, there sped just thirty ships.
      And one ship sped before the rest,
      Before the rest, as a falcon flies.
      Bravely was the ship adorned.
      The sails were all of taffeta,
20   The rigging all of silk,
      The awning of brocade,
      And there on that ship sits the orthodox tsar,
      With his glorious generals,
      With his heroic officers.
25   Now our father, the orthodox tsar, cries out,
      The orthodox tsar, Petr Aleksêevich,
      "Ho, my gentle sailors,
      Climb the ship's mast,
      Look out through the telescope:
30   Are we far from the city of Stockholm?
      We will go to the city of Stockholm this evening,
      We will carry off the citizens of Stockholm at daybreak."

With this we may compare the opening lines of a poem from Nizhegorod[2] which narrates the same journey of Peter:

      No one knows, no one can say
      Whither our sovereign tsar is preparing to go.
      He has loaded his ships with pure silver,
      He has furnished his vessels with bright gold.
      He is taking with him very few men—
      No one except the Preobrazhenski grenadiers.[3]
      Our father the White Tsar has commanded thus:

---

[1] The collectors observe that the singer once substituted 'Baltic'; others two or
three times substituted *Vereyski*, i.e. no doubt, Varangian, or Norse.

[2] Kirêevski, VIII. p. 164 ff. The whole poem is translated by Chadwick, p. 260 ff.

[3] So called from the village of Preobrazhenskoe near Moscow, where Peter lived
as a boy. The Preobrazhenskoe regiment developed out of the *druzhina* or body of
personal followers whom Peter collected round him during his boyhood. In this
regiment Peter himself held a commission as captain of the gunners.

"Hearken, officers and soldiers!
Do not address me as your tsar or sovereign,
Address me as a merchant from overseas."
Now our sovereign tsar has set off to amuse himself at sea.
When the White Tsar had been crossing the sea for a week,
He continued for a second week;
On the third week he reached the country of Stockholm,
The realm of Sweden....

It will be seen that the style of the two poems is wholly different. The version from Saratov is ambitious and highly figurative in style. It is composed in the stereotyped diction of the Kiev *byliny*, and is rich in traditional imagery, though this imagery has not always been set in its correct connotation. A critical audience might observe that the action here ascribed to the fish is one which is more appropriately, and more usually ascribed in Russian popular poetical convention to the ducks. The description of the fleet setting out, and the tsar's falcon ship outstripping the rest is strongly reminiscent of the description of the departure of Sadko's fleet in the Novgorod *bylina*, while the description of the falcon ship itself is equally traditional, and recalls the vessel of Solovey Budimirovich. The archaic and highly artificial 'negative comparative' is used, and the static adjectives *slavny* ('glorious'), and the still more archaic *khrabry* ('heroic').

In contrast to this the Nizhegorod version is simple and direct, almost bare, and the reference to the silver and gold with which the tsar's vessel is furnished is the only departure from verisimilitude. There is no hint of a fleet to disturb the quiet waters and put wild nature into a panic. Personal details of Peter's life are remembered—the name of his favourite regiment which he had formed himself, and in which he had held a commission in early life; the incognito under which the tsar travelled on his western tour, and the small number of his attendants. The form and the manner of the narrative have left the traditional style of the Kiev *byliny* far behind, and with them the elaborately embroidered diction, and have substituted the modern cursive narrative style, and an artistic attitude characterised chiefly by its naïveté.

There is a series of poems of Type D belonging to the last four centuries which resemble one another very closely, but of which the term 'variant version' can only be used with great caution. This series consists of laments or elegies on dead tsars which are ascribed to the troops, and which purport to voice their grief for their dead sovereign.

Some account of these poems has already been given (p. 62 above).[1]
They generally open with a *pripêvka* or overture, which consists of a
brief address to some natural object, such as the moon, the rough winds,
or a berry or bunch of flowers or grasses. This *pripêvka* has no direct
connection with what follows, but often delicately expresses the mood
—regretful, wistful, or distressed—of the reciter or composer of the
poem which follows. Following the *pripêvka* there are usually a few
lines introducing us to a poem of Type D. These lines state as a rule
that a young soldier is standing on guard beside the grave or coffin of
the dead tsar, or at the door of the cathedral where the body lies in state.
The lines are generally expressed in the past tense, and the poem then
passes on to report the words which grief forces from the young soldier.
With this speech the poem closes. The speech itself is particularly interesting because in all cases it follows very closely a fixed traditional
formula which is also found frequently in popular elegies relating to
unnamed individuals. The poems are generally quite short, varying
from twenty lines to fifty.

It will be seen that these laments are composed in a traditional framework which consists of three parts (1) the *pripêvka* or overture; (2) the
narrative of the young soldier's bearing; (3) the soldier's speech. The
chief examples known to us are the laments for Ivan the Terrible, Peter
the Great, Katharine II, and Alexander I. They range over a period,
therefore, of two hundred and forty years. It is difficult to use the term
variant of such poems, and one even hesitates to assume that any one
poem is based directly on one of the preceding. A variant of the
Lament for Peter the Great translated by Morfill[2] resembles very
closely the Lament for Ivan the Terrible, especially in the opening
lines; but a variant of this from Saratov published by Kirêevski[3] shows
considerable modification, and suggests that the poet is following a
different traditional form of elegy. Again, both the opening and the
closing lines of the Lament for Alexander I show a variation from the
earlier laments, though the opening lines are a traditional formula. It is
only in the speech of the soldier that the tradition appears to be absolutely fixed. Here the variations are merely verbal, and correspond
closely, moreover, with the speeches in the popular timeless-nameless
laments referred to above. It would seem probable, therefore, that these
speeches are derived from some ancient traditional formula used in the

---

[1] Translations of a representative series of examples will be found in Chadwick,
passim.

[2] *Russia*, p. 168.   [3] VIII. p. 278 f.; Chadwick, p. 274 f.

obsequies for the dead. It is not improbable that the figure of the young soldier may also be derived from some such ritual. On the other hand the possibility of some pre-eminent artistic prototype for the whole series is also to be taken into account. For obvious reasons elegiac poetry rarely survives in oral tradition for long periods, and it is not surprising that no specimens of Type D relating to the Kiev period have been recorded in modern popular tradition. Such poems must nevertheless have existed, and may well have created the traditional formulae for succeeding generations, even while the prototypes themselves perished comparatively early, owing to the ephemeral interest of their subject.

Finally we will refer to another series of poems relating to identical situations, but ranging over several centuries. This series consists of Laments of tsaritsas and princesses who are forced to take the veil. As examples[1] we may mention the Lament of the wife of Ivan the Terrible who is named in the song Marfa Matvêevna;[2] the two Laments of the princess Ksenÿa, the daughter of Boris Godunov; and the Lament of Evdokÿa Fedorovna Lopukhina, the wife of Peter the Great, whose name is not mentioned in the poem.[3] All these ladies are represented as lamenting their impending fate immediately before departing to the convent. A fifth example may also be mentioned which has reference to an unnamed wife of a certain Prince Vasili. The prince himself has been drowned at sea, but scholars have not succeeded in ascertaining his identity. In this last example the confinement would seem to be voluntary; but the point is by no means clear, and the poem is obscure in this and many other features.

The two Laments[4] of Ksenÿa Borisovna appear to be variant versions. They refer to her fears that the Pretender, Grigori Otrepev, will send her to a convent, as we know actually happened shortly after his accession in 1605. The two poems were recorded by Richard James (cf. p. 6 above) in 1619, and are therefore especially interesting in

---

[1] Translations of the examples mentioned below will be found in Chadwick, *passim*, where references to the texts are also given.

[2] On the name and the identity of the *tsaritsa* with whom the poem is concerned, see Chadwick, p. 203 f.

[3] After Peter's return from his foreign travels he divorced his wife and issued an edict that her name was never to be mentioned; cf. p. 66 above.

[4] It is possible that these are, in reality, one continuous poem (not two versions). They are printed as such in Wiener's *Anthology of Russian Literature*, I. p. 132 f., and by Morfill, *History of Russia*, p. 101. We think it more likely that the two poems are separate, as printed by Bezsonov in his edition of Kirêevski, Supplement to VII. p. 58 f.

view of the short time which intervened between their composition and
James's record. It is clear that a definite relationship exists between the
two poems. One line is found identical in both:

> The tsarevna laments in Moscow.

In each poem Ksenÿa addresses the house she is about to leave, and asks
who will live there after her departure. Thus in one she cries:

> Alas our pleasant halls!
> Who will dwell within you,
> After our living there as kings,
> And after Boris Godunov?

and in the other:

> O you dear ones, our lofty mansions!
> Who will be your owners
> After our living there as kings.

In each poem she foretells that Grigori will send her to a convent. In
one she cries:

> When the traitor comes to Moscow,
> Grisha Otrepev, the unfrocked priest,
> He will make me prisoner,
> And having imprisoned me he will shave off my hair,
> And impose monastic vows upon me.

In the other she cries:

> And when the unfrocked priest comes to Moscow,
> He will destroy our halls,
> He will seize me, the tsarevna,
> And send me to Ustyuzhna Zhelêznaya;
> He will shear me, the tsarevna, and make me a nun,
> And enclose me in the cloister behind the grille.

In each poem she declares her inability to accept her lot. In one she
cries:

> I do not wish to be shorn a nun,
> Or to keep monastic vows.
> The dark cell must be thrown open
> So that I may gaze upon the fine youths.

and in the other:

> How can I pace the dark cell,
> In the convent of the Orthodox mother superior?

It seems probable that these are variant versions of a single original
poem, whether originally composed by Ksenÿa herself, or, more likely,

by a contemporary poet, and that the variations in the passages quoted above, and in other parts of the poems, are due to the thirteen or fourteen years of oral transmission through which they have passed.

The other Laments of royal ladies referred to above also possess certain features in common with one another and with those of Ksenÿa. Like Ksenÿa, the wife of Ivan the Terrible addresses the house she is about to leave:

> Alas, you hall of stone,
> Hall of white stone, and faceted![1]
> Can it be that I shall no more wander about you, dear palace?

May we assume from this that such apostrophes were commonplaces of farewell laments? We have little doubt that the apostrophe is a static poetic formula commonly introduced in poems composed for similar situations. It constitutes, in fact, one of the static formulae, like tesserae of a mosaic, to which we have already referred (p. 72 above), the *parties mobiles*, as Prof. Mazon aptly styles such formulae, of which the *byliny* are in a large measure composed.

Finally we may point out the common features between the Lament of the wife of the unidentified Prince Vasili on the one hand and the Laments of the wives of Ivan the Terrible and of Peter the Great on the other. In their general outline and style these Laments differ widely from one another. Yet the static formulae and identical motifs introduced into all these poems suggest that there was a traditional form associated with poetry composed on such themes, and that this traditional form was never wholly lost sight of. We may point to the reference to the cell with its three aspects mentioned in the Lament of the wife of Prince Vasili, and in that of the wife of Peter the Great. The former lady is represented as saying to the abbess on her arrival at the nunnery:

> O reverend abbess,
> Shave me as a nun.
> Build me a little cell,
> Pierce three windows:
> The first window
> To look towards the Blessed Annunciation,[2]

---

[1] A reference to the old *gridnya* or audience chamber in the Kremlin, known as the *Granovitaya Palata*, i.e. the 'faceted' or 'rusticated hall' or 'chamber', on account of the facets into which the outer face of the stone was cut—the process known to architects as 'rustication'—on the façade facing the Cathedral Square. The hall was built towards the close of the fifteenth century, and is still standing.

[2] We do not know if a church of this name is referred to.

> The second window to look
> Over my native land,
> And the third window
> Over the blue sea.

And Peter the Great is represented as addressing his wife thus:

> Go and get shorn as a nun, you who are not dear to me,
> Go and take the habit, you whom I abhor!
> To be shorn as a nun I will give you a hundred roubles,
> To take the habit I will give you a thousand.
> I will build you a new cell,
> In a green garden under an apple-tree;
> I will pierce three windows,
> The first looking towards God's Church,
> The second on to the green garden,
> The third on to the open country.

More striking than such common formulae, and more interesting for the history of oral transmission is the sequence of actual motifs in the Lament of the wife of Prince Vasili and in that of the wife of Ivan the Terrible. In both poems the lady is represented as instructing her attendants to drive her on her journey. In both her arrival at the convent is noted, and her reception by the reverend mother superior. The words spoken on her first arrival at the convent are almost identical in both poems. In the first the speaker is a young nun:

> Reverend Mother,
> It is not a guest who has arrived,
> It is a postulant who has come to us,
> To be a permanent inmate.

In the other the speaker is the tsaritsa herself:

> Abbess and nuns,
> It is not for an hour that I have come to visit you,
> It is not for one dark night that I have come to lodge,
> I have come to you to remain for ever.

Again it is difficult to doubt that these Laments, like the Laments of the troops for the dead tsars, are following a poetical tradition derived ultimately from some prototype of which all record has vanished.

CHAPTER VI

SAGA

THERE is good reason for supposing oral narrative prose to have been much cultivated in Russia in early times. In this connection it is interesting to observe the large number of technical terms denoting different kinds of oral prose narratives (sagas) which are current today, e.g. *skazka, skazanie, povêst, slovo, pobyvalshchina*, etc. In the great collections of oral literature from which our examples are mostly drawn, and to which reference has already been made, the sagas are for the most part unclassified and undated, at any rate in the modern editions which have been accessible to us. There is an unfortunate lack of specific information as to the period and the sources from which the collectors obtained them. 'Old manuscripts', or 'Government of——' is frequently the only indication given as to their source. In both these respects we are in a much poorer position to offer a scientific classification of the sagas than of the poetry.

In our own day, although the *skazki*, or 'folk-tales' are extremely numerous and widespread, the longer and more ambitious sagas appear to be comparatively rare and confined to a limited area. Examples have been obtained from north Russia from the same area as the *byliny*, and we have reason to suspect that they are not wholly restricted to this area; but our evidence is scanty and defective. It is greatly to be doubted whether the same amount of interest has ever been devoted to the collecting of prose stories in Russia as to the recording of *byliny*. Large collections of the former are comparatively few, and of these the *Skazki* of Afanasev are the only collection which has been available to us. Fortunately, however, this collection is very varied. It contains, in addition to the *skazki*, a number of examples of more ambitious sagas. It is to these examples, and to a few contained in Rybnikov's collection, and some other individual examples cited in critical works, that we are chiefly indebted for such slight knowledge as we possess of the nature of modern oral saga in Russia, while a certain amount of information relating to earlier times is available in the Russian Chronicles and other written sources. It need hardly be added, therefore, that these remarks are intended to be merely suggestive, and that anything in the nature of exhaustive treatment is out of the question.

The subjects treated in Russian prose sagas extend over a long period of time. The sagas themselves vary greatly in length, but we have not observed that this variation bears any relation to the subjects treated. Historical narratives, such as those telling of the voyage of Peter the Great to Sweden, may be quite brief, whereas others dealing with trivial occurrences to unknown people may occupy many pages. We find sagas representing very varied stages of artistic development, from the brief anecdote, related sometimes in summary form, sometimes with picturesque detail and carefully elaborated 'point', to the long and elaborate saga with numerous characters, minutely reported speeches, and embroidered style.

There exists in Russia a form of traditional oral prose narrative for which we know of no exact parallel elsewhere. This form of saga is known as a *pobyvalshchina* (pl. *pobyvalshchiny*). It is believed to be derived from the *byliny* of the Kiev Cycle, of which it is a broken down relic.[1] Nevertheless the *pobyvalshchiny* are the most elaborate Russian sagas which we possess, and frequently extend over several pages. Their scope, in fact, corresponds to that of the *byliny* of the Kiev Cycle, and varies similarly. Sagas of this type resemble in many respects the rhythmical 'poetical' prose of early Polynesian sagas, though there is no evidence, so far as we are aware, that the latter is derived from metrical form. The *pobyvalshchiny* on the other hand are reminiscent in a remarkable degree of their poetical origin.

This is evident in their style, their subject-matter, and the milieu in which they are found today. Although the metre has disappeared for the most part, the *pobyvalshchiny* frequently fall into a form of rhythmical prose which suggests the fluid metres of the *byliny*, and their poetical origin can even be traced, and occasionally reconstituted, where the conservative phraseology has preserved whole lines intact from the poetical original, the phrase length in the prose version corresponding approximately to the line length of the *byliny*. In such cases alliteration is frequently preserved. The elaborate and artificial style is also identical with the style of the *byliny* of the Kiev Cycle. The epic diction, the static formulae, the repetitions, the entire conduct of the narrative, corresponds exactly with the latter. Moreover the subjects treated are the same as the subjects of the Kiev Cycle of *byliny*, though the proper names have at times disappeared. The *pobyvalshchiny* have been obtained for the most part from the same districts, the same milieu, and often the same reciters as the *byliny* themselves.

[1] See Rambaud, *R.É.* p. 21 f.

The *pobyvalshchiny* vary considerably, however, in regard to traditional verbal exactitude. That is to say, some have preserved more closely than others their relationship to the poetical original from which they are directly or indirectly derived. Among the best examples we may mention those which relate to Ilya of Murom. A fine *pobyvalshchina* is given by Afanasev[1] which relates the hero's journey from his native village of Karachoro to Kiev by way of Chernigov, and the slaying of Solovey Razboinik. The most complete version is derived from a chapbook, but a variant is also given from an eighteenth-century MS.,[2] while other prose stories relating to the same hero are said to occur in MSS. dating from the seventeenth and eighteenth centuries.[3]

It is interesting to compare the *pobyvalshchina* on the 'Healing of Ilya of Murom', recorded by Rybnikov[4] from the *kalêki*, and the variant of the same story given by Sakharov,[5] with the *bylina* to which they are closely related, and which was recorded from Simbirsk, and published by Kirêevski.[6] The correspondence between the poetical and the prose versions is especially close in the early part of the *bylina*. The latter appears to have been paraphrased so closely, line by line, that it is difficult to believe that the resultant 'prose' version is due to lapse of memory.[7] The diction and phrases are frequently identical; the same repetitions and inversions are reproduced; nothing but sustained rhythm is required to transform our *pobyvalshchina* into a *bylina*.

A similarly close relationship is observable between the *pobyvalshchina* of 'Alyosha Popovich and the Slaying of Tugarin' and the *bylina* recorded by Kirsha Danilov (cf. p. 38 above) which narrates the same exploit. The *pobyvalshchina* was recorded from Shenkursk in the former Government of Archangel, and published by Afanasev.[8] A translation is given by Magnus.[9] The proportions and alternations of the speeches and narratives contained in the *pobyvalshchina* are identical with those of the *bylina*, and the relative length and proportions of the whole correspond closely.

A number of briefer *pobyvalshchiny* relate to *byliny* and stories of other cycles. In relation to the hero Svyatogor, as we have seen, the *pobyval-*

---

[1] II. p. 246.   [2] *Ib.* p. 248.   [3] Miller, *Ocherki*, III. p. 91.
[4] II. p. 581.   [5] Printed in Afanasev, II. p. 249.
[6] I. p. 1.

[7] The subject seems to be a rare one. In general we do not cite specific references to the precise version of a *bylina* on which a *pobyvalshchina* is based, since such references would manifestly be misleading where the original is an oral version of no fixed verbal tradition.

[8] II. p. 257.   [9] *Ballads*, p. 74.

shchiny actually preponderate over the *byliny*, and the relationship of the former to the latter is illustrated in an interesting manner by such versions as that of the elder Ryabinin,[1] in which the opening and concluding portions are of prose, while twenty-three lines of poetry of the ordinary form of *bylina* intervene. In the story of Samson, which was recorded by Rybnikov from the same reciter,[2] and which incorporates stories of Svyatogor, we again have prose passages introduced into the midst of the *bylina*. On the other hand Leonty Bogdanov, from whom we have two valuable complete *pobyvalshchiny*,[3] recited no other prose apart from these, but only *byliny*.

Not infrequently we find a type intervening between the *bylina* and the *pobyvalshchina*. We may refer to the *bylina* of Dyuk recited by Latyshev to Rybnikov,[4] which contains brief passages in prose. Rybnikov's collection also contains a recitation of Permian provenance[5] relating to Ermak Timofeevich (cf. p. 59 above), of which the first half consists wholly of prose, the second half of poetry. In a note to the conclusion of the prose portion we are told that although the rest of the story was 'sung', the reciter frequently forgot the words of his poem. Here, as elsewhere, the relationship between the *pobyvalshchiny* and the *byliny* is clearly demonstrated.

Perhaps we may include among the *pobyvalshchiny* brief stories based directly on *byliny*, and closely following them in style and phraseology, though in a somewhat summary form. As an example we may refer to the brief saga of Vasili Buslaev published by Afanasev.[6] This little story, which closely follows some versions of the *bylina* which we actually possess on the same hero, is nevertheless so much condensed as to have lost many of their incidents and episodes, though the turn of phraseology remains. It will be remembered, moreover, that the *bylina* of Vasili Buslaev is itself simpler and more direct in style than those of the Kiev Cycle.

There are other *pobyvalshchiny* which differ much more widely from the type described above. The milieu may be heroic, and the style and diction of the *byliny* may still be preserved in part. But along with this we find more or less numerous elements derived from folk-tales—both formal elements and motifs. Nameless characters are introduced; indeed the principal character sometimes has no name. As an example of a *pobyvalshchina* of this type we give a brief account of the *Dvoryanin*

[1] Rybnikov, I. p. 8.
[2] *Ib.* p. 4 f.
[3] *Ib.* p. 318 f.
[4] II. p. 641.
[5] II. p. 719.
[6] II. p. 256 f.

Bezschastny Molodets, 'The Unfortunate Young Courtier', of which the fullest version known to us is contained in Rybnikov's collection.[1]

The story tells how Vladimir sets an impossible task to a member of his *druzhina*. The youth succeeds in accomplishing the task with the help of an old woman—a typical folk-tale motif—whose lovely daughter he afterwards marries, and Vladimir himself bestows his blessing on the nuptials. One day, however, the youth unwisely boasts of his wife at the feast, whereupon a certain Fedka 'the Mocker' springs up and vows that he has lived with her secretly for three years, and when Vladimir insists that he shall prove his words he obtains her necklace by guile. Her angry husband sells his wife to a foreign merchant, but she eventually makes her way back to Kiev, loaded with riches and honour, and makes herself known to her husband. Fedka the Mocker is punished, as is only right and proper—they cut off his head and present it to the lady.[2]

It will be seen that the story contains a variant of the theme of the *bylina* of Stavr, together with other equally well-known motifs from folk-tales. The story of Stavr and his clever wife would seem to have been very popular, to judge from the large number of versions which have been recorded. The three stories published by Afanasev under the titles of 'Danilo the Unfortunate',[3] 'Vasili the Tsar's Son and Helen the Fair',[4] and 'Vasilisa the Priest's Daughter'[5] appear to be variants of the same story.

Although none of these versions follow the *bylina* of Stavr as closely as the *pobyvalshchina* on the 'Healing of Ilya of Murom' follows the *bylina* on the same subject, nevertheless the poetical original is clearly traceable in the diction, phraseology, and repetitions, as well as in a certain degree of consistency in regard to these details. In general the diction and phraseology differ in a marked degree from the diction, etc., of folktales. 'The Unfortunate Young Courtier' in particular shows a marked affinity with the *byliny* of the Kiev Cycle. The names Vladimir, Apraxya, and, in one version, Alyosha Popovich, occur, and the scene is laid in Kiev. The mise-en-scène is that of the Kiev *byliny*—the feast, the rash boasting, the character of the personnel. There can be no doubt that this *pobyvalshchina* was composed in a milieu in which the strongest literary tradition was that of the *byliny* of Vladimir's court at Kiev.

[1] II. p. 656.
[2] A much fuller account of this story—in fact an abridged translation—is given by Rambaud, *R.É.* p. 117 ff.   [3] II. p. 259 ff.
[4] *Ib.* p. 261 ff.   [5] *Ib.* p. 269 ff.

On the other hand, certain features of the story as we have it in one version and another point to the breakdown of the purely heroic traditional form, and the encroachment of folk-tale elements—a breakdown and an encroachment which are also traceable in many of the *byliny*, and are not confined to the prose versions. We may point to the fact that in no instance in the prose versions is the hero's full name given. He is called variously 'the unfortunate young courtier', 'Danilo the unfortunate', 'Vasili the Tsar's son', etc. In one version, the name of the mischievous person who brings about the catastrophe is given as Alyosha Popovich.[1] In Rybnikov's version he has become simply Fedka the Mocker, which is really no more specific than the name of the hero himself.

Folk-tale elements are also encroaching on the incidents of the narrative. The task which Vladimir assigns to the Unfortunate Young Courtier, and the impossibly short time in which it is to be accomplished, are common motifs in folk-tale. Characteristic of folk-tale also are the description of the old woman and the maiden, and the part which they play in the story; and it is precisely in these respects that the variant versions of the story offer the most marked divergences. At times the formulae common to folk-tale appear in the midst of those characteristic of the *byliny*, striking a strangely alien note. This is especially arresting in 'Vasili the Tsar's Son'. We may refer, e.g. to such phrases as: "They went a long way, and whether it was long, whether it was short, whether it was high, whether it was low, they came" etc.; and the opening phrase: "In a certain kingdom, in a certain government, there lived, there was", etc. The variant versions of the *pobyvalshchina* of 'The Unfortunate Young Courtier' are thus of special interest as enabling us to trace stage by stage the transition from the style of the *bylina* to that of the folk-tale.

Other *pobyvalshchiny* in the collection of Afanasev show the characteristic features of the heroic tradition interspersed with folk-tales. The story of Baldak Borisevich, recorded from the Province of Novgorod,[2] follows very closely the framework and style of a *bylina* of the Kiev Cycle, from which many of its motifs are manifestly derived. The story opens at the court of the royal city of Kiev, where Prince Vladimir is giving a 'noble feast'. He commissions Baldak Borisevich to go and insult the Turkish sultan, and bring away his horse with a golden mane. The opening theme thus resembles the *bylina* of Mikhailo Potyk and Vasili Kazimirov. Baldak arrives at the dwelling of the sultan by night,

[1] In 'Vasili the Tsar's Son'.　　　　　[2] Afanasev, II. p. 265.

and cuts down a number of trees in the garden, and pitches his tent in the clearing. In the morning, very early, the Turkish sultan awakes. At once he looks out on to his beloved garden, and no sooner has he looked than he sees that all the trees have been cut down, completely cleared, and thirty white tents now stand in his garden in their place.

The whole incident and what follows closely resembles the well-known motif in the *bylina* of Solovey Budimirovich, while the latter part of the story bears a close resemblance to other *byliny*, notably that of Stavr. The closing scene in which Baldak Borisevich blows his horn to such effect that the Turkish sultan and all his followers become spellbound recalls several episodes in the *byliny*, such as that in which Solovey Razboinik whistles with his full power, against the express command of Ilya of Murom.

As an example of a saga which is obviously closely related to a *bylina* of the Kiev Cycle, though it has lost both the proper names and the diction characteristic of heroic poetry, we may refer to the story of Nikita Kozhimyaka, 'Nikita the Courier', recorded from the Government of Tambov in the upper valley of the Don.[1] This story is nothing more or less than a variant of the *bylina* of Dobrynya and the serpent or dragon of the mountain. It relates to a serpent who dwells in the neighbourhood of Kiev and carries off and devours young maidens. At last he carries off the tsar's daughter, but owing to her beauty he marries her instead of eating her, and when he goes on his depredations he leaves her shut up in his cavern. But the maiden writes a letter, and ties it to the tail of her dog, and sends it to the tsar in Kiev. The tsar sends back a letter by the same messenger, bidding her find out who is stronger than the serpent. The maiden discovers that Nikita the Courier is stronger. Nikita succeeds in overpowering his enemy; but the serpent, like Dobrynya's adversary, is wily. He begs for mercy, pointing out that he and Nikita are the two strongest beings in the world, and ought to divide the land between them. Nikita consents, and a dyke is made from Kiev to the Caspian; but Nikita insists on continuing the division through the water, and in the midst of the sea Nikita dispatches his foe. The story concludes with an interesting piece of local antiquarian speculation, telling that the dyke is still to be seen, and is two *sazhens*[2] high. Agriculture is carried on on both sides of it, but the dyke itself is left untouched, 'and those who do not know who built it call it a vallum'.

[1] Afanasev, I. p. 196.
[2] For a *sazhen*, cf. p. 38, footnote 3 above.

A saga is recorded from Olonets which relates to Ivan the Terrible,[1] and which tells 'How Treason came to be introduced into Holy Russia'. The story is, therefore, ostensibly another antiquarian tradition, though its theme has affinities with folk-tales, as is not rare in stories of antiquarian form. On the other hand the formulae common to folk-tales are absent from our text, and the editor (Barsov)[2] is of the opinion that its true affinities are with the 'stariny', and that the text as we have it has been considerably 'edited'. If Barsov is right, the true form of the story is that of a pobyvalshchina. The abridged translation of the text given by Rambaud will give the reader a fair idea of the style of the original.[3]

The story relates that the subject kings refuse to pay tribute to the tsar, Ivan the Terrible, and threaten to dethrone him unless he succeeds in solving three riddles. An old man whom the tsar meets building a church offers to solve the riddles if he is rewarded by a cask of gold. The answers given, the tsar saves his throne, but deceives the old man in the matter of the gold. The old man, who is God Himself in disguise, informs the tsar that by his deception treason has been introduced into Russia for all time.

A large number of early oral prose sagas were incorporated into the Russian medieval and early modern chronicles, and written in other MSS., especially such as contain material relating to early Russian history. These sagas are generally referred to under the names of *slova* (earlier *slovesy*, sing. *slovo*), *povêsti* (sing. *povêst*), and *skazanya* (sing. *skazanie*). The two former are more generally applied to events and traditions belonging to the south, the latter to the north. This division is, however, by no means universal. A more fundamental distinction is the all-important fact that the *slovo* and the *povêst* represent the traditional form of oral saga in medieval Russia, the *skazanie* represents what appears to be a later stage in the history of saga. That is to say it represents a critical and synthetic use of oral material, generally by an educated person. The style of the *skazanie* is therefore naturally more closely akin to that of western Europe than that of the *slovo* or the *povêst*, being modelled on the literary style, and more especially the diction, of the best medieval historical writings.

The *skazanya* are found chiefly in written sources, and we know of no evidence for the recitation of really good examples of *skazanya* in

[1] Rybnikov, II. p. 715.   [2] *Ib. loc. cit.* footnote 1.
[3] *R.É.* p. 269.

modern times which have not been derived more or less directly from books or MSS. Yet the connection with oral saga is very close. The *skazanie* on Alexander Nevski, prince of Novgorod (1263), is known to have been composed by a contemporary who was on intimate terms with Alexander himself. Indeed Alexander is said to have himself related the narrative of the battle on the Neva to the author.[1] Miller has shown that the *skazanya* of the heroes of Kiev contained in the chronicles are derived from oral tradition, possibly, as he suggests, from the panegyric poetry preserved by the *druzhiny* or personal followers of the princes.[2] An example of a *skazanie* of this kind is that of Alexander Popovich, preserved in the Chronicle of Pskov already referred to. Elaborate *skazanya* were also composed on Prince Domant of Pskov (cf. p. 116 above), and on the invasion of the Tatar khan Batu, on the sack of Ryazan, and the tragic fate of its royal house,[3] and indeed on a host of other subjects. *Skazanya* on the northern princes are especially numerous.

The *skazanya* are of great interest for the history of oral literature, and the fact that they have come to us in written form detracts from their value no more than it does in the case of the Icelandic sagas. Indeed in their fullness of description and detailed portrayal of events, as also in their simplicity and directness, they resemble the saga style of Iceland closely, though the *skazanya* never developed the study of personality such as we find in the 'Sagas of Icelanders.' They give us the 'official' record of personal and political events as opposed to the 'domestic' record of the Icelanders. It is interesting to find this native Russian saga style combined in the Russian chronicles with the annalistic form derived ultimately from Eusebius. As an example of the *skazanie* style we give a translation of a part of the story of the 'Foundation of Moscow and the death of the mighty prince Daniel Alexandrovich', which relates the murder of Tsar Daniel at the instigation of his faithless wife, and the foundation of the city of Moscow on the site of the fortified village in which his brother Andrey Alexandrovich, Grand Prince of Suzdal, avenged his death. The story has come down to us in two versions. The first is contained in the manuscript of the Chronicle of Novgorod belonging to the Olonets Seminar.[4] The second is written in a late

---

[1] Solovev, col. 1315.   [2] *Ocherki*, III. p. 55, and *passim*.
[3] Solovev, col. 1318. With this *skazanie* from the Moscow Chronicle we may compare the variant *skazanie* of the destruction of Ryazan and Vladimir, given in the Chronicle of Novgorod, s.a. 1238.
[4] Rybnikov, III. p. 236 ff.

seventeenth- or early eighteenth-century hand in another MS. of the same Chronicle.[1] Both texts were probably first written down before the close of the medieval period. We translate an extract (abridged) from the first of these versions:

"Prince Daniel galloped...on his horse into the depth of the forest; and he fled...along the River Oka, abandoning his horse...And he was obliged to make for a ferry, but he had nothing with which to pay for his crossing except a gold ring on his hand, and this ring he gave to the ferryman.... The ferryman came across close to the bank from the far side of the River Oka, and when he was opposite to Prince Daniel he reached out his oar to the prince and said: 'Put the ring on the oar, and then I will take you across.' And Prince Daniel, believing him to be an honest man, and not suspecting that he was lying, placed his gold ring on the oar, whereupon the ferryman took the ring on the oar from the prince, and drew away from the bank. And Prince Daniel fled along the river, fearing his pursuers; and the day drew towards evening, and he had nowhere to shelter, having reached a desolate spot in a wooded ravine. And...he found...a grave of some dead man, and the prince rejoiced at this pit and hid in it, forgetting his fear of the dead, and slept through the dark night till dawn.

The sons of the boyar Stepan Ivanovich Kuchka[2] fell into lamentation and grief and mighty sorrow that Prince Daniel had escaped alive out of their hands, although wounded, and they began to repent, saying to themselves:

'It would have been better for us if we had not plotted this deed of death on the prince, since he has escaped from us wounded into Vladimir to his brother Andrey Alexandrovich; and we shall get cruel punishments and death, many and cruel at their hands, and Queen Ulita will be hanged....'

But in the morning Queen Ulita gave a dog to her lover and commanded saying:

'Where you find Prince Daniel, deal death to him.'

And those wicked assassins...took the dog, and set out to the place where they hoped to slay the prince; and from that spot they sent the dog ahead of them. And the dog ran on in front, and they followed him quickly, and the dog ran along the bank of the River Oka, and came to the pit where Prince Daniel lay hidden. When the dog caught sight of Prince Daniel, he began to rejoice over him, leaping on to his neck and wagging his tail; and his pursuers caught sight of the dog rejoicing over

---

[1] Rybnikov, III. p. 244 ff.   [2] I.e. Prince Daniel's pursuers.

7

him and wagging his tail, and they leapt forward and discovered the pit, and found there Prince Daniel Alexandrovich, and slew him at once, piercing him through the ribs with their swords and spears. And they cut off his head, and put his body back into the pit, and buried it."[1]

The style of the *slovo* and the *povêst*, unlike that of the *skazanie*, is essentially a spoken style, and for its proper appreciation requires to be addressed to an audience rather than to be read in a study. It is rhetorical, highly figurative, and poetical in diction, closely resembling the written medieval *Slovo o Polky Igorevê* and the *Zadonshchina*. Indeed one is often tempted to wonder in reading a *povêst* on some subject connected with medieval Russian history whether it is not in reality a paraphrase of some lost medieval form of *bylina*—a sober paraphrase with the poetic diction retained, but with the repetitions omitted and the speeches curtailed. The *povêsti* and *slova* which have formed the basis of many of the written *skazanÿa* can often be traced in the style of the latter, especially *skazanÿa* having reference to persons of early times, such as the heroes of the Kiev Cycle.

A great body of sagas composed in this highly elaborate form of poetical prose refers to the Tatar invasion of the thirteenth century, and to the relations of the Russians and the Tatars in the following centuries. Again most of our information comes from written sources. There is, however, a fine *povêst* on the Battle of Kulikovo which has been recorded from oral recitation in modern times from Shenkursk in the Government of Archangel.[2] According to Afanasev this *povêst* has made use, as one of its sources, of a famous '*skazanie* of the battle with Mamai',[3] which he says was well known to the people both from old MSS. and from paper editions. The saga is nevertheless worth quoting as it gives us an admirable idea of this style of Russian narrative prose at its best.

The Battle of Kulikovo, which was fought in 1380, is famous throughout Russian history as the first serious reverse suffered by the Tatars at the hands of the Russians, under the leadership of Dimitri of the Don, Prince of Moscow, of whom we shall have more to say in a later chapter. The Shenkursk *povêst* relates how the Russian envoy, Zachary Tutrin, goes to the court of Mamai the Tatar khan, on behalf of Dimitri, Prince of Moscow, and there bids him defiance. He leaves the Tatar camp, pursued by Mamai's emissaries, most of whom he slays, and he sends a message to Prince Dimitri, bidding him prepare for battle with the Tatars. The second part of the story tells how Dimitri collects his

[1] Rybnikov, III. p. 245 ff.
[2] Afanasev, II. p. 272.   [3] *Ib.* p. 275, note.

forces and marches to meet the Tatars on the Plain of Kulikovo in the neighbourhood of the Don. He and the envoy, and other Russian generals, then make arrangements as to the disposition of the forces and the order of attack. They meet the Tatars in fierce battle, which ends in a brilliant victory for the Russians, though their losses are heavy, and Dimitri himself is severely wounded. The narrative gives no hint that other states besides Moscow are engaged, though the names of five other leaders are mentioned.

"The Russian envoy, Zachary Tutrin, understood his work thoroughly. He caught twelve bright falcons and thirteen white gerfalcons. First of all he tore up the yarlik of the pagan Mamai, and wrote on his writing paper. Having written, he secured it to a bird's tail and said: 'Bright falcons and white gerfalcons! Fly away to Prince Dimitri Ivanovich in stone-built Moscow, and tell the Zadonski Prince Dimitri Ivanovich to collect a vast army from city and village and distant hamlet. Leave at home only the blind and halt, and young ungrown children to take care of them. And tell him that I am going to my own country to collect the hairy, bearded Cossacks of the Don.'

At dawn, at sunrise, clouds spread over the clear sky, bringing in their train rapid, fine showers, with raging whirlwinds. In the roar, in the thunder, nothing could be heard except the resounding voice from the royal dwelling.[1] The Zadonski Prince Dimitri Ivanovich was ordering a proclamation to be made throughout the whole of white-stone Moscow:

'Gather yourselves together, all princes, and boyars, and valiant men, mighty heroes and all bold women warriors,[2] to the prince in the hall of the bright dwelling.'

All the princes and boyars, the valiant men, the mighty heroes and all bold women warriors gathered together from all parts of white-stone Moscow to the prince in the hall of the bright dwelling, to hear his prudent words, and most of all to gaze upon his bright eyes. Like a stout oak among slender juniper bushes, its summit mingling with the clouds, so stood out the mighty prince among his princes and boyars. It is not a golden trumpet resounding, it is the Zadonski prince Dimitri Ivanovich who has begun to make a speech:

'My beloved warriors! I have not summoned you to a drinking

---

[1] The word is *terem*, lit. the attic, or upper part of a dwelling. In the *byliny* and the traditional prose compositions the word is regularly used of a dwelling, including a royal dwelling.

[2] *Polenitsy udalÿa*. The *polenitsy* are the warrior-women frequently referred to in the *byliny* of the Kiev Cycle (cf. p. 37 above).

banquet, nor for a joyful feast are you assembled before me. It is on account of mournful tidings that you are assembled before me: Mamai the Godless, the stinking dog, with all his heathen hordes is coming to make war on holy Russia. It will be a bitter cup that we shall get to drink from Mamai, the dog. Let us go, my beloved warriors, to the great sea, let us prepare our light barks and then let us hasten from the ocean-sea into the Khvalinsk Sea to the Solovetsk wonder-worker: there we will surround him, and nothing will Mamai the Godless, the stinking dog, get from us; otherwise he will take us prisoners, put out our eyes, and inflict an evil death upon us.'[1]

The princes and boyars made answer, inclining their turbulent heads:

'Zadonski Prince, Dimitri Ivanovich! One sun rolls across the sky—one prince rules over orthodox Russia. We have not come to gainsay your mighty word; with your good will we will keep our compact when we have.to settle accounts with Mamai the Godless, the stinking dog. Zadonski Prince, Dimitri Ivanovich! We will go to the great sea, we will hew light craft, we will launch what we cut down in the great sea, we will collect a mighty armed force, and we will fight with Mamai the Godless, the stinking dog, to the last drop of blood—and we shall triumph over Mamai the Godless.' What is that noise? What is that thunder rolling through the hall? It is the Zadonski Prince, Dimitri Ivanovich speaking.... The Zadonski Prince, Dimitri Ivanovich, gave strict injunctions to collect an innumerable mighty force reckoning a city with its suburbs, a village with its estates, and all the distant hamlets, but that they should leave the blind and the halt, and young ungrown children at home as defenders. From all sides of orthodox Russia they collected a mighty force. They consolidated a force throughout white-stone Moscow. The force was apportioned by lots among Simeon Tupik, Ivan Kvashnin, the Russian envoy Zachary Tutrin, and the seven brothers Byelozerets. The force marched to the Field of Kulikovo."

Oral prose sagas relating to the sixteenth century and the succeeding periods in general bear no relation to the *pobyvalshchiny*, or to the other elaborate forms of saga discussed above. They appear to have begun their existence in prose form, but of a comparatively humble kind, and show no trace of having been derived either from poetic originals, or

---

[1] The geography is not clear. In the word 'great- (lit. ocean-) sea' (*okian-more*) the first element seems to be used intensively merely to denote size. The word *Khvalinsk* occurs constantly in the *byliny*. The Solovetsk monastery is the famous stronghold of the Old Believers on the White Sea.

from the works of educated people. They are for the most part composed
in a simpler diction and less elaborate and artificial style. Many of them
show the influence of the *skazki* or folk-tales. Indeed it may be said that
few of the oral sagas which have come down to us relating to known
characters are free from this influence. It is clear that they belong, in
general, to the milieu of the *skazki* themselves, which have largely
moulded their diction, form, and style.

The commonest type of these sagas on historical persons is the brief
summary narrative or historical anecdote similar to those found in
Herodotus. Such stories are not always developed to their fullest
artistic possibilities. They deal for the most part with a single situation,
and consist of a simple story, a single strand of narrative, with a strictly
limited personnel. The speeches are few and generally brief. It is
probable that such stories have been remembered in outline only, and
that verbal tradition, if it exists, is confined to the speeches. We do not
often find in the Russian sagas of this type the clever turn of phrase
which gives 'point' to the anecdotes of Herodotus, and which is to be
attributed to a more sophisticated milieu than any which has existed in
Russia.

A number of these short historical anecdotes have been recorded
from the north. Barsov in particular has made an important collection
dating from the seventeenth and early eighteenth centuries relating to
Peter the Great.[1] This work unfortunately has not been accessible to us,
but Rambaud has left us an interesting account of many of the stories.[2]
Some of them are merely reminiscences and the briefest anecdotes, and
in these we see Peter leaping from his carriage to talk with peasants,
eating their black bread, and drinking their brandy, learning their way
of life, and taking part in the events of their lives.

Rybnikov records[3] one of these brief anecdotes from the recitation of
a boatman of Pudoga in Olonets. Despite its affinities with folk-tale the
story is very characteristic both of the tsar himself, and of the kind of
traditions which still circulate about him among the peasants of the
north. It relates how one day, as the tsar is riding alone in the forest, he
meets an old peasant felling trees. The tsar greets him, and asks him
about his family and his means. The man's answer, which is couched in
the riddling diction dear to folk-tale, pleases the tsar, who compliments
him on his wit, and asks him to guide him across the steppe, as he himself does not know the way. The peasant is induced to accompany the

[1] *Peter the Great in the Traditions of the North.*
[2] *R.É.* p. 324.
[3] II. p. 368.

stranger in return for payment. As they journey along the stranger asks his guide if he has ever seen the tsar. The peasant replies that he has not, and the stranger bids him look, for the tsar is on the steppe.

"But how shall I recognise the tsar?"

"Everyone will be running without cap. Only the tsar will be wearing his cap."

When they reach the steppe the people catch sight of the tsar, and everyone takes off his cap and runs as hard as he can. But the peasant's eyes open wide: only they two keep their caps on. And he says:

"But which is the tsar?"

And Petr Alekseevich replies:

"Manifestly one of us two is the tsar."

Side by side with these brief anecdotes there are also fictitious sagas in which Peter appears as a being of supernatural powers ordering the forces of nature and the elements. One of these stories has assumed an antiquarian form, and tells how it comes about that Lake Ladoga is less stormy than of yore. Originally, we are told, Lake Ladoga was a calm lake, wholly free from storms, till one day the divine wrath aroused it against an impious race, after which it never regained its repose till Peter the Great ordered the waves to be beaten. From that time the lake has been tranquil.[1] This is only one of many stories in which Peter figures as master of the elements, and it is significant that many of these stories have reference to the sea—the stormy sea and lakes of the north.

Side by side with historical and personal anecdotes and fabulous sagas such as those just referred to, we find also that Christian and hagiological legends have become attached to the name of the great tsar. In one of these he is represented as visiting the Solovetsk monastery in the White Sea, and examining the bones of the saints to see if they are genuine relics. When he leaves the island on which the monastery is situated a tempest arises, and for eight days his ship tosses on the sea. On the night of the ninth day he has a dream. "Tsar," says a voice, "you have been in the monastery of Solovetsk. Why did you not secure the reliquary of the saints with your sovereign hands?" The tsar awakes, and relates his dream to his sailors. All at once, in the midst of his recitation, the heavens grow bright, and they behold the Solovetsk monastery only three *versts* away. Peter lands, celebrates a liturgy in honour of the saints, secures their reliquary with his sovereign hands, and carries the key away with him.[2]

[1] Rambaud, *R.É.* p. 326.   [2] *Ib. loc. cit.*

The sagas of Peter the Great clearly bear the impress of the peasant milieu in which they have been preserved. They offer a strange picture of treatment by peasants of material eminently unsuited to uncultivated story-tellers. Nevertheless they also bear the impress of a careful and self-conscious art, and, full though they are of credulous and self-conscious episodes, they are nevertheless sometimes carefully worked up, couched in traditional diction, with conversations fully related, and with the proportions of the story carefully preserved. The peasants who narrate these sagas clearly aim at a certain standard in saga-telling, and follow to some extent the conventions derived from sagas of a more ancient period. At the same time they are familiar with the *skazki*, the conventions and motifs of which they naïvely combine with the traditional heroic themes and style. The result is as bizarre as some of the *byliny* relating to modern times, and, from the literary point of view, on no higher level.

It will be seen that the art of the composition of prose saga in Russia, like that of the composition of *byliny*, is an art in its decline. It is clear from the *povêsti* and *skazanÿa* incorporated in the medieval chronicles, as well as those which have an independent existence, that oral prose narratives which relate to early times—many of them certainly composed in early times—are far superior as works of art to the brief anecdotes and inconsiderable sagas which relate to the modern period. Many of the latter are but little removed from folk-tales. We shall see in the later chapters that there is evidence that the art of saga-telling, no less than that of minstrelsy, was highly appreciated in early times, and in the sixteenth century at least was encouraged by Ivan the Terrible himself. Saga, like poetry, flourishes best in a leisured and wealthy milieu, and deteriorates even more rapidly than poetry in poverty and neglect.

CHAPTER VII

NON-HEROIC POETRY

THE *STIKHI* (1)

ADOPTING the classification employed in Vol. 1 we may distinguish three classes of non-heroic stories in Russian oral literature. In the first class we include stories relating to native Russian saints, as opposed to the saints of the Greek Church, who will be discussed in the chapter devoted to 'Poetry relating to Scriptural Subjects and to the Saints of the Greek Church'. Of these native saints we have a considerable number of stories in Russian poetry. The second class consists of stories of prophets or wizards and other persons possessed of supernatural power or knowledge. To this class belongs the hero Volga; but for reasons already given we have treated the stories relating to him with the rest of the *byliny*. We shall see further that Egori Khrabry, 'St George the Brave', is at least as much a shaman as a Christian saint; but owing to the Christian milieu in which the poems relating to him have reached us, we have postponed our discussion of him till we come to consider the saints of the Greek Church in Chapter VIII below. We have no further examples of non-heroic poems of the second class, and we may doubtless regard them as having been banished in early times, or so transformed under Christian influence as to be unrecognisable. Of non-heroic stories relating to persons not included in either of these categories we have a rich harvest in Russia. They relate not only to royal persons and ecclesiastics, but also to semi-religious confraternities, such as the *kalêki perekhozhie*. We shall confine our discussion in this chapter, therefore, to stories of Class I and Class III.

Russian oral religious poetry, of whatever kind, and whatever subjects, is known collectively as *dukhovny stikh*. A poem of this kind is also known as a *dukhovny stikh* (plural, *dukhovnye stikhi*). *Dukhovny stikh* is included in the répertoires of both the *kalêki* and the *skaziteli*, but is sung much more extensively by the former than the latter. The principal collection of poetry of this kind is contained in Bezsonov's great corpus entitled *Kalêki Perekhozhie* (2 vols., published at Moscow in 1861 and 1863); but it is by no means confined to this collection. Indeed Bezsonov's volumes are said to contain only a small fraction of the great wealth of religious oral literature still current even today among the Russian peasants.[1] The 'Old Believers', the *Dukhobors*, the so-called 'New Israelites', and other backward sects are said to be especially rich in such Christian oral literature.[2]

The most important recent account of poetry of this kind is that given by Speranski in his *Russkaya Ustnaya Slovesnost*, published at Moscow in 1917.[3] From a comparison of this account with the texts published by Bezsonov we can distinguish two different kinds of oral religious poetry. One of these consists of *stikhi* which are mainly narrative in character, and which correspond in form and diction to the *byliny*; the other, of *stikhi* which are, in the main, not narrative, but 'lyrical' in character, and which consist largely of adaptations of psalms and chants of the Orthodox Church. They are characterised by a rhymed strophic form, like the narrative poetry of Little Russia, to which we have referred above (p. 3). The former class of *stikhi* are believed to be of earlier origin than the latter, and while comparatively rare in the south, they are widespread over northern Russia, like the *byliny*, which they resemble. *Stikhi* having the rhymed form are rare in the north, where they are believed to be intrusive; but they are the prevailing form in central and southern Russia, where they have developed in the full current of western influence. In our present study we are concerned only with the northern or more especially native class. This class consists for the most part, as we have said, of narrative poems which resemble the *byliny* in form, metre, style and diction, and are, indeed, indistinguishable from them save in their subject matter. They include both stories relating to native Russian saints, and non-heroic (Christian) poems relating to other classes of religious persons, such as the *kalêki*, ecclesiastics, and such of the early Russian princes as are traditionally believed to have distinguished themselves as defenders of the Christian (Orthodox) faith against the Tatars.

The extent to which such poetry is dependent upon books varies very greatly. That of north Russia is said to be much further removed from the original 'book' inspiration than that of the south, and in north Russia the themes current in oral poetry have moved further away from their original source. Here local conditions have introduced a large amount of local colour, and the original literary theme is transmuted and transformed under the influence of the local literary tradition.

[1] Speranski, *R.U.S.* p. 364, footnote 1.
[2] *Ib.* p. 389.
[3] *Ib.* p. 358 ff. A brief notice will be found also in Rambaud, *R.É.* p. 225 ff.

This oral Christian literature has indeed developed for several centuries in an intellectual milieu which has largely overlapped with that of the *byliny*, and which has been to some extent identical with it, *byliny* and *stikhi* frequently forming the répertoire of the same individual. The relatively greater distance of the poetry of the north from book tradition, as compared with that of the south, is doubtless due in the main, however, to the fact that the north is more conservative, and has kept alive the more ancient forms, as the metre shows. The *stikhi* of the north have, in fact, had a longer life in oral tradition, and consequently more protracted opportunities of modification and approximation to oral secular types.

Those Christian poems which have preserved their original literary form more or less intact need not concern us here. They hardly belong at this stage to the study of traditional oral poetry, even though their setting is of a popular character, as in the extensive series of poems inspired by the parable of Dives and Lazarus[1] (*Lazari*), and most of the other stories which draw their inspiration directly from Biblical or Apocryphal literature. The more literary stories of the saints will similarly be excluded from the following study. We will confine our attention to poetry composed on religious subjects which has been so transformed by popular tradition that its original inspiration from Christian book learning need no longer be considered.

One of the finest examples of *stikhi* relating to Russian saints is the poem on the vision of Dimitri Donskoy, the hero who inflicted the first serious defeat on the Tatars in their military campaigns against Russia. The famous battle in which Prince Dimitri led the Russians to victory was fought on the plain of Kulikovo to the south of Tula in the neighbourhood of the River Don in 1378. In memory of the victory Dimitri was known ever after as Dimitri Donskoy ('Demetrius of the Don'), and has become a national saint and hero. The following poem relates to a vision which appeared to the saint on the anniversary of the battle of Kulikovo. The poem is composed in the form of a narrative, though it probably relates only to a brief moment. It is a perfect short story in verse, despite the antiquarian touch in the concluding lines.

The Vigil of St Dimitri

On the vigil of the Sabbath of St Dimitri,
In the holy cathedral of the Assumption,
Saint Cyprian was singing mass;
And at this mass Prince Dimitri was present,

[1] Bezsonov, I. p. 43 ff.

5   With his Orthodox Princess Evdokÿa,
    With his princes and boyars,
    With his glorious generals.
    Suddenly something happened:
    Prince Dimitri ceased to pray;
10 He leant against a pillar—
    He was rapt in contemplation.
    His spiritual eyes were opened,
    He beheld a marvellous vision.
    It is not the candles burning before the ikons,
15 It is not the precious gems sparkling on the golden images,
    It is not the sacred chanting that he hears;
    What he sees is the open plain,
    The open plain of Kulikovo.
        The plain is strewn with corpses
20 Of Christians and Tatars:
    The Christians are like shining candles,
    And the Tatars are like black pitch.
    Over the plain of Kulikovo
    Walks the most holy Mother of God,
25 And behind her the Apostles of the Lord,
    The archangels and the holy angels,
    With gleaming candles.
    They are chanting the requiem over the relics of the Orthodox warriors
    It is the blessed Mother of God herself who waves the incense over them
30 And crowns descend from Heaven upon the dead.
    And the blessed Mother of God has made enquiry:
    "But where is Prince Dimitri?"
    The Apostle Peter answered her:
    "Prince Dimitri is in the city of Moscow,
35 In the holy cathedral of the Assumption.
    He is attending Mass
    With his Princess Evdokÿa,
    With his princes and boyars,
    With his glorious generals."
40 Then said the blessed Mother of God:
    "Prince Dimitri is not in his place;
    He must conduct the choirs of the martyrs,
    And his princess must be in my train."
    Then the vision faded.
45 In the Church the candles gleamed,
    On the images the gems sparkled,
    Prince Dimitri came to himself,
    And his tears fell.
    He uttered these words:
50 "Ah, now you may know that the hour of my death is near.

Soon I shall be laid in my tomb,
And my princess will become a black-robed nun!"
And in memory of the wondrous vision
He instituted the Sabbath of St Dimitri.[1]

By far the most popular of the stories of Russian saints is that which relates to the martyrdom of Boris and Glêb, the two sons of Vladimir I, who were murdered by their elder brother Svyatopolk. The incident is related in full in the Ancient Chronicle. Bezsonov[2] gives no less than thirteen versions of this poem, and a comparison of these with the Ancient Chronicle shows that the popular singers have departed from their literary sources in several material details of the narrative. Our version opens with an account of the division of the kingdom by Vladimir I among his three sons, and of his death. To his eldest Svyatopolk he bequeaths Chernigov, and to his two youngest, Boris and Glêb, Kiev. Svyatopolk, however, hopes to inherit the whole of his father's dominion, and treacherously invites his two young brothers to a memorial feast in honour of their dead father. The mother of the two youths is represented as lamenting sorely when the invitation arrives, for she suspects the plot, and beseeches her two young sons to refuse; but they will not listen, and set off at once. Svyatopolk meets them out in the open country, and a graphic picture of the scene which takes place is presented to us by the popular poet. Svyatopolk is fully armed, and the two young brothers fall on their knees before him, beseeching him to spare their lives, and offering to serve him as his slaves —an aspect of the story for which there is no warrant in the literary source. Svyatopolk is ruthless, and having slain his brothers, he orders their bodies to be dragged away and thrown into the woods, where they remain for thirty years, uncorrupted and untouched by bird or beast. At the end of this period a white stone pillar[3] is seen stretching from earth to heaven. The priests and patriarchs assemble at the pillar to hear the divine command; the blind are healed and the deaf are made to hear, and the bodies of the two saints are interred in Kiev.

It has been mentioned above that in addition to the *kalêki*, the 'Old Believers' also have preserved many *stikhi*. Among the poems recorded

---

[1] Bezsonov, I. p. 673 ff. The saint would not, of course, have instituted his own saint's day. But the *kalêki* are perhaps not well versed in ecclesiastical procedure.

[2] Bezsonov, I. p. 625 ff. An interesting notice of this and several of the poems to follow will be found in Rambaud, *R.É.* p. 226 ff.

[3] We may compare the references to such a pillar in the *byliny* of Kolivan recorded by Gilferding, II. p. 665; III. p. 374.

from their recitation is the single version of 'Alexander Nevski' in Bezsonov's collection.[1] This great Novgorod prince obtained his epithet *Nevski* in memory of his victory over the Swedes on the River Neva in 1240. The popular singers, however, do him too much or too little justice in speaking of him as 'beating and driving off the pagan Tatars'; for Alexander strenuously opposed offering battle to the Tatars, and went in person on four several occasions on diplomatic missions to the Tatar headquarters in his endeavours to obtain immunity for his people. On the fourth occasion he died on the return journey. The poem, which consists of only fifty-nine lines, represents the invasion of the 'Krimean Tatars' as a punishment sent to Russia from God for their sins, and the immunity of Novgorod as due to the piety of its citizens and the fine leadership of Alexander. We may perhaps conclude from this naïvely partisan 'tendency' that the poem originated in Novgorod. It should be added that in Bezsonov's opinion neither this poem nor the two which follow can be regarded as purely popular.[2]

Bezsonov held that the poem last discussed originated in the same milieu as the two following poems on Mikhailo and Fedor of Chernigov and Peter the Metropolitan, on the grounds of their general similarity. The former,[3] which consists of twenty-one lines only, was recorded in the Government of Novgorod from the recitation of an old woman. It opens with an apostrophe to Russia by her people, and dwells on the miseries which she is now suffering under the Tatars, and appeals to one and all to repent and pray for a merciful release. In answer to their prayers there appear in Russia two valiant men with fiery swords, Mikhailo and Fedor of Chernigov, wearing Russian diadems, who deliver holy Russia, and themselves depart to the Horde, where they meet the death of martyrs. As Rambaud observed,[4] it is evident that the popular singers prefer holy valour to humane prudence, for the picture of the two princes as fiery and militant instruments of God is remote from the historical record, which pictures them as making the journey of submission to the Tatar headquarters.

The *stikh* on Peter the Metropolitan consists of eighteen lines only, and was recorded from the recitation of an old man in the Government of Ryazan. As in the case of the last two poems, Bezsonov records only one version of the text.[5] The poem belongs to Type B. It opens with an appeal in the second person spoken by Peter the Metropolitan of

[1] 1. p. 669.
[2] See p. 699, note; and cf. p. 678, note.
[3] Bezsonov, I. p. 671 f.
[4] *R.É.* p. 228.
[5] Bezsonov, I. p. 672 f.

Moscow in the time of Prince Simeon Ivanovich (1340–1353). The appeal is made to the people in general to pray to the saints in order that the burden of the Tatar yoke under which they live may be removed. The words of the prayer follow, and also a brief prayer by the prince himself, and the poem concludes with the statement that God hearkened to their prayer and freed the city from the peril which overshadowed it.

It will be seen that all the saints whose stories we have been considering lived between the beginning of the eleventh and the close of the fourteenth centuries, and the majority belong to the thirteenth and fourteenth. It would seem, however, that in this respect Bezsonov's collection is hardly representative, even making allowance for the small number of poems relating to native saints included in it; for according to Speranski,[1] the majority of native saints celebrated in *stikhi* belong to the fifteenth and sixteenth centuries. Bezsonov clearly suspects, however, that the poems on Alexander Nevski, Mikhailo and Fedor of Chernigov, and Peter the Metropolitan are comparatively late in origin, and this is certainly supported by the curious perversion of fact in the poems themselves, whereby far-seeing and prudent rulers who sought to avoid suicidal warfare against the Tatars are represented as belligerent and victorious crusaders. This perversion of truth would be best explained as the efforts of the citizens of Novgorod, Ryazan and of the ecclesiastical party in Moscow in a later age to make good some claim to a share in the overthrow of the Tatar power. Such efforts on the part of even the boldest singers could hardly have begun till some time had elapsed after the victory of Prince Dimitri Donskoy in 1378.

We have, however, one interesting *stikh* in Bezsonov's collection[2] relating to a later period, viz. the ' Solovetsk Monastery'. This *stikh* is a rare, though not a unique,[3] example of a *pêsn* referring to the reign of the Tsar Alexis Mikhailovich (1645–1676), the father of Peter the Great. Three versions of the *stikh* are given, the longest consisting of sixty lines. These *stikhi* relate to the famous and protracted resistance offered by the great Solovetsk monastery in the White Sea to the imposition of the corrected texts of holy Scriptures, and to other ecclesiastical reforms, ordered by the tsar and the patriarch in 1654. This monastery was a stronghold of the 'Old Believers' (*Starovêry, Staro-obryadtsy*), and was

[1] *R.U.S.* p. 263; and cf. p. 205 below.
[2] I. p. 675 ff.
[3] For further examples we may refer to e.g. the poem on the birth of Peter the Great, Kirêevski, VIII. p. 1 f. (translated by Chadwick, p. 256) and to the poem entitled *Zemski Sobor*, Rybnikov, I. p. 218, and there are others.

one of the last to accept the reforms. Indeed the opposition of the monks was not overcome till the monastery was actually stormed by the royal troops. The *stikhi* give us a vivid picture of the reluctant *voevoda* directing his cannon against the holy monks, of the monks themselves gazing from the walls of the monastery as the royal troops approach, conjecturing as to whether the visit of the troops has a pious or a hostile object, and finally of the storming of the monastery, the overthrow of the 'Old Belief', and the punishment of the obdurate monks.

We will now turn our attention to the third class of non-heroic stories, relating to persons other than ecclesiastics or people of mantic pretensions. The poetry of this class is more interesting than that which we have been considering, because it is, on the whole, less dependent on direct inspiration from books. For this class our evidence relates largely to the *kalêki perekhozhie*, who, as has already been mentioned, are a body of itinerant religious singers, men and women, who travel about the country singly, or more often in small groups, singing *stikhi*. The *kalêki* are generally cripples, blind people being especially common. Today they are generally so poor that they have earned for themselves the alternative and more commonly used title of *nishchaya bratya*, 'poor brethren'; but evidence is not lacking to show that in early times they were wealthy, and of comparatively high social status. We shall have more to say of these religious singers later, but a few words have been required here as introduction to the *stikhi* which the *kalêki* sing about themselves and their predecessors.

The first poem which naturally claims our attention is entitled 'The Origin of the Kalêki'. This is the best example of a purely antiquarian poem known to us in Russian oral literature. Bezsonov[1] gives three versions of the *stikh*, the longest consisting of 134 lines. We give a translation of one of the shorter versions below:[2]

What the Kalêki Perekhozhie sing of themselves.
The first appearance of the Kalêki Perekhozhie.
Ascension. Ivan Bogoslov.

(Sung in the Governments of Perm and Novgorod)

When Christ ascended to Heaven
The 'Poor Brethren' lamented,
The poor and the needy, the blind and the halt:
"Hearken, true Christ, Tsar of Heaven!
How shall we 'Poor Ones' be fed?
How shall we 'Poor Ones' be clothed and shod?"

[1] Bezsonov, I. p. I ff.   [2] *Ib.* p. I f.

Then answered Christ, the Tsar of Heaven:
"Do not weep, Poor Brethren!
I will give you a mountain of gold,
I will give you a river of mead:
You shall have food and drink,
You shall be shod and clothed."
Then Ivan Bogoslovets spoke:
"But hearken, true Christ, Tsar of Heaven!
Do not give them mountains of gold,
Do not give them rivers of mead:
The strong and the rich will take them away;
Then there will be much murder,
Then there will be much bloodshed.
Give to them your holy name:
Then your name they will repeat,
And your name they will extol,
While they themselves will have food and drink,
And they themselves will be shod and clothed."
And Christ, the Tsar ôf Heaven, replied:
"Hearken, Ivan Bogoslovets,
Hearken, Ivan of the Golden Mouth!
You have uttered a true word,
You have spoken and said well;
Your mouth shall be of gold,
And your festivals shall recur from year to year."

The best known example of a narrative poem relating primarily to
the *kalêki* themselves is the *bylina* entitled 'The Forty and One Kalêki'
(*Sorok Kalik So Kalikoyu*; cf. p. 113 f. above). Of this poem Bezsonov
gives three variants, one from the collection of Kirsha Danilov,[1] one recorded by Rybnikov from the recitation of Ryabinin, and one from the
collection of Dal. None of them, therefore, appear to belong to the
répertoire of *kalêki* or other religious singers, and this is consistent with
what we know of the poem in other collections, where it is frequently
found among the *byliny* sung by the *skaziteli* of Olonets and elsewhere.
The background of the poem is the court of Kiev, and Vladimir,
Apraxya, Alyosha Popovich and other well-known persons of the Kiev
Cycle play a prominent part in the story. The hero is Kasyan Mikhailovich, the head of a party of *kalêki* who halt at the court of Vladimir
in the course of their pilgrimage, and there can be little doubt that a
story, perhaps a folk-tale, associated at an early date with the *kalêki*,
and originally independent of Kiev, has been attracted into the Great
Cycle.

[1] III. p. 81 ff.

In its formal characteristics the poem is indistinguishable from a *bylina*; but its tone is definitely that of Christian morality rather than of heroic virtue, and its purpose is evidently cautionary, despite the heroic setting. This cautionary tendency is visible not only in Kirsha's version, which is perhaps the most persistently edifying, but also to a less extent in all the versions. We have therefore decided to treat it here rather than in connection with the Kiev Cycle, though the personnel of the poem would seem to entitle it to a place in the latter.

The story[1] relates how forty *kalêki* (earlier, *kaliki*) and their leader, Kasyan Mikhailovich—or, in one version,[2] Thomas Ivanovich—take a vow of chastity and poverty and general discipline, and set out on pilgrimage to Jerusalem by way of Kiev. In some versions they set out from a religious house, such as the Hermitage of Efimev, at the Monastery of Bogolyubov,[3] or the Hermitage of Danilov, 'from the city of Volintsa (Volhynia), from Galich (Galicia)', and under the auspices of the king.[4] In others they are simply called *bogatyri*, heroes who voluntarily make a vow, and go on pilgrimage to atone for their sins. We may compare the story of Vasili Buslaev, who, in some *byliny*, is represented as going on pilgrimage to the Holy Land shortly before his death. When the *kalêki* come to the country near Kiev they meet Vladimir and beg alms of him, but he, being in the open country, refers them to his wife Apraxya who is in Kiev.

Apraxya falls in love with their leader, Kasyan Mikhailovich, and when he repels her advances, she secretly places in his bag Vladimir's golden bowl.[5] Next day, when the *kalêki* have resumed their journey, the loss of the golden bowl is discovered, and Apraxya, out of spite, suggests that messengers be sent to search the *kalêki*. Alyosha Popovich is first dispatched, and he rides truculently up to the *kalêki*, ordering them in abusive terms to give up the stolen cup. But Kasyan threatens to belabour him, and Alyosha retreats discomfited. Dobrynya is then sent, and Dobrynya, as his manner is, entreats them courteously to stop and search their bags, lest perchance the cup has inadvertently dropped into one of them. And Kasyan, as courteous as Dobrynya himself, orders them to pause and search. The cup is, of course, discovered in his own bag. Kasyan declares his innocence, and surmises that the bowl has

---

[1] The story is translated by Miss Hapgood, *Songs*, p. 66 ff.
[2] Kirêevski, III. p. 84.   [3] *Ib.* p. 90.   [4] *Ib.* p. 81.
[5] In the version recorded by Kirsha Danilov, Alyosha Popovich makes advances to Kasyan on behalf of Apraxya, and it is he who places the bowl in Kasyan's bag. The bowl is of silver.

been put there by Apraxya; but he reminds the *kalêki* that by the terms of their vow they have pledged themselves not to steal, and urges them to punish him according to the manner which they had agreed on when the vow was made. Accordingly they take leave of him with tears, and then

> They drove him forth into the open plain,
> They dug a deep pit,
> They buried him in the damp earth,
> In the damp earth to his white breast;
> His eloquent tongue they plucked out,
> And his bright eyes from their sockets,
> His high heart from between his shoulders;
> And they have left the bold youth Kasyan
> In the open plain.

Then the *kalêki* go on their way. But Mikula of Mozhaisk (St Nikolai) appears to Kasyan and restores him to his former health, bidding him resume his pilgrimage. He overtakes his companions late that night and goes to Jerusalem with them. When they come to Kiev on their return journey they find that Apraxya has been ill from grief ever since she heard of the punishment which had befallen Kasyan. Then Kasyan raises her up and pardons her, and they all feast and make merry. The pilgrims depart each to his own land, and none of them ever again rides over the open plain seeking adventures, or stains his white hands with blood; and when young Kasyan comes to his own land he raises a Cathedral Church to Mikula of Mozhaisk.

The non-heroic—we might almost say anti-heroic—character of this *bylina* is very striking. Heroic deeds are represented as matter for repentance and expiation, and finally to be abjured. The *kalêki* are represented as faithful to their vow, even to the uttermost, and their suffering leader is blessed by St Nikolai himself. The princess Apraxya is disgraced, while young Kasyan is exalted. Finally Apraxya is restored to health, and happiness is restored in Kiev by the magnanimity and purity of the *kalêka* whom she has injured.

We know of no other narrative poems in which the *kalêki* constitute the principal personnel, though they play an important rôle in many *byliny*, especially those of the Kiev Cycle. Not infrequently the turning-point in the action, which secures success for the hero, is effected by them. More frequently the hero attains success by changing clothes with a *kalêka*, and impersonating him. Some examples of these motifs have already been cited (p. 97 above). Whether such motifs originally formed an integral part in heroic stories, and at what period the *kalêki* came to play so important a rôle in the *byliny*, is an interesting subject worthy of investigation.

Stikhi of Type D are not rare in the répertoire of the *kalêki*, and consist chiefly of prayers. A little *stikh* of four lines consists of a prayer of the *kalêki* as they sit by the road-side on pilgrimage.[1]

> Our Father, our spiritual Father!
> Grant, us, Lord, good health!
> Bring us, O God
> To the Troitsko-Sergiêvskaya monastery.[2]

The *kalêki* have also a little prayer for alms[3] (ten lines) to be recited 'at the threshold and under the windows'. Another *stikh* of this class is a thanksgiving to be recited by the *kalêki* when they have received alms or food:[4]

> We poor brethren,
> We needy folk,
> Must pray to God,
> Must beg alms of Christ,
> For food and drink;
> For he gives us to eat and drink,
> He gives us shoes and clothing,
> And we must give glory to Christ.
> Save us, and have mercy upon us,
> O Christ, the Tsar of Heaven, etc.

This *stikh* is a more ambitious composition than the last, and consists of forty-two lines. There is also a *stikh* consisting of the prayer of the church collectors (thirty-five lines) for blessing and prosperity on the household from which they receive a donation.[5]

The *kalêki* also sing poems about themselves which have the form of poetry of Type E, that is to say of personal poetry, but which cannot be regarded as the expression of individual emotion or experience. They are, in fact, rather the expression of the feelings and ideas of a community, the product of a class rather than of any one *kalêka*, although of course the work of individuals. As an example we may refer to a single poem of which Bezsonov gives two versions,[6] and which is something in the nature of a manifesto of the *kalêki*. It represents a *kalêka* as speaking

---

[1] Bezsonov, I. p. 26.
[2] Or to some other place of pilgrimage (Ed.). The Troitsko-Sergiêvskaya monastery is the famous monastery situated about forty miles from Moscow. It was founded in 1340, and is one of the most interesting and important convents in Russia.
[3] Bezsonov, I. p. 26. [4] *Ib.* p. 34 ff.
[5] *Ib.* p. 38. [6] I. p. 25 f.

in the first person, telling us that he has no estate, or home, or possessions, that he plies no trade, and serves no prince or boyar. He is
merely a sinful soul, and in the two concluding lines he prays God that
he may partake of the blessed sacrament before his death.

The history of the *dukhovny stikh*, or spiritual poetry, is closely bound
up with that of the *byliny* or *stariny*. The two forms of *dukhovny stikh*
current in Russia—the rhymed strophic form of the south, and the unrhymed, non-strophic form of the north—correspond exactly with similar
forms in the secular poetry, that of the north being known as *byliny*,
stariny. The literary devices and conventions which they employ are
likewise identical. It is clear, therefore, that the *stikhi* and the *stariny*
have been current in the same milieu from early times. There is some
slight evidence for the existence of *stikhi* at an earlier date than any
which we possess for the *stariny*, though this evidence has an important
bearing on the latter. This subject will be considered more fully at
the close of the following chapter.

CHAPTER VIII

POETRY RELATING TO SCRIPTURAL SUBJECTS AND TO THE SAINTS OF THE GREEK CHURCH

THE *STIKHI* (2)

RUSSIAN oral literature has practically no poetry or saga relating to the gods or demons of heathen times. Such literature doubtless existed in the past. Certain passages in the *Slovo o Polky Igorevê* have been held to contain references to ancient Russian deities, but a more critical view of the text is tending to reduce the number of such passages,[1] and we may feel some doubt as to how far those deities which remain are exclusively or even specifically Russian. Moreover the literature of northern Russia—the area with which we are primarily concerned—does not appear to possess poetry or saga relating primarily to spirits.[2]

Natural objects, especially rivers, are sometimes personified as a maiden, and speak with a human voice, as in certain versions of Sukhan Domantevich (cf. p. 140 f. above) and of the 'Death of Dobrynya Nikitich'. In this they resemble the river *Vile* who are occasionally found in the oral literature of the Yugoslavs; but Russia has naturally no mountain *Vile* corresponding to the widespread mountain *Vile* of the latter. While the personifications of rivers in particular are not very rare, they are never prominent, and so far as we are aware they never supply the principal motif or the framework of a poem; and, unlike the Yugoslav, they do not appear to be used for didactic purposes.

There are two classes of supernatural beings which figure largely in Russian oral poetry. These are 'dragons' and 'white swans'. They never play the principal rôle in the poems in which they appear, and we do not find poems in which they form the sole personnel, as supernatural beings sometimes do in Greek, Norse, and Irish sagas. The dragons and 'white swans' appear to be introduced rather as foils for the heroes. The dragons are generally, though not invariably male, while the 'white

---

[1] We may refer to the work of V. J. Mansikka and references there cited *passim*.
[2] It is possible that our information may be defective on this point. Recent collections, such as that comprised in *Russki Folklor* by B. and Y. Sokolov, may contain some material of the kind. But it is improbable that any very important body of such poetry would have escaped the previous collectors.

swans' are invariably female. In the latter feature, as in many others, the 'white swans' differ from the deities of other peoples and approximate to the *Vile* of the Yugoslavs. They resemble the latter also in the fact that they always appear singly and do not form a community. Both the dragons and the 'white swans' are invariably 'unsympathetic' characters, and are in all cases overcome by the hero, or forced to obey him. In this respect they fulfil the same function as the demons and monsters of other literatures.

The use of the term 'white swan' in reference to a maiden appears to be already stereotyped when the *Slovo o Polky Igorevê* was composed; but the dragon does not appear in that work. We have tried to show elsewhere that the term 'dragon' is commonly applied in modern oral poetry to a Tatar chief, while the 'white swan' appears to be in reality a foreign, more particularly a Polish, maiden. In oral poetry these beings are depicted sometimes as actual dragons and swans, sometimes frankly as Tatar chiefs and Polish maidens respectively, the terms 'dragon' and 'white swan' being no more than forms of diction. At times, again, a transformation from the dragon and swan to their human forms is depicted as taking place in the course of the narrative. There can be no doubt, therefore, that two forms of tradition have been current for some time; according to one the dragon and the white swan are human beings (foreign), while according to the other they are evil spirits. The conception is, in fact, a definitely heathen one. We have shown elsewhere that the 'white swans' correspond to the *Vile* of the Yugoslavs, while we have Norse evidence for the existence of the 'dragon' conception in north Russia at least as early as the first half of the twelfth century.

As in Yugoslav, the part played in heathen literatures by the gods is filled in Russian oral literature by the Christian saints and other prominent figures in the ecclesiastical records of the Orthodox Church. Some account of the Christian oral literature of Russia has already been given (p. 180 ff. above). We have seen that in northern Russia poetry of this class shares the formal characteristics of the *byliny*, and represents, in general, an older type than that of the south. The former is predominantly narrative, and derives its subjects principally from Biblical and Apocryphal literature, especially from the New Testament, from the lives of saints and other prominent persons who figure in the annals of the Greek Church, as well as Russian princes and ecclesiastics, and native Russian saints. The Christian oral poetry of the south is predominantly of Type D, and consists largely of popular adaptations of the psalms and chants of the Orthodox Church. It is, of course, with the northern class that we are chiefly concerned here.

The stories and poems connected with these religious subjects are frequently popular in character, sometimes even familiar. We shall find that in this respect Russian oral Christian poetry resembles that of the Yugoslavs. On the other hand, we have not found in Russian popular poetry the humorous element and total absence of dignity which characterise some of the Yugoslav stories to be referred to in Vol. III. This may perhaps be due to the nature of our evidence. The only remains of Russian popular Christian literature which have been accessible to us are, as we have said above (p. 180) contained in Bezsonov's collection *Kalêki Perekhozhie*; but we have seen that there is a vast store of such poetry still current among the Russian peasants which still awaits publication. Moreover, the collections of Russian traditional oral saga include many examples of stories exactly similar in tone to the most naïve and crude of the Yugoslav Christian narrative poems. It is quite possible, therefore, that poetry similar in tone exists also in Russia in connection with the saints and other prominent figures of the Orthodox Church.

It is consistent with the somewhat more dignified tone of the Russian series that we do not find in the collection of Bezsonov examples of poems in which the scene is laid in Heaven, and which relate to the great saints of the Christian Church or to Biblical characters. Such poems actually exist in connection with native Russian saints, however, as we may see from the poem on the Vigil of Dimitri Donskoy quoted above; and from this we may again raise the question as to whether the absence from Bezsonov's collection of such a mise-en-scène in connection with the saints of the Christian Church may be due to accident, or to the selective process of the collectors or the editor. We may refer to the Russian Christian oral sagas, in which scenes laid in Heaven are not rare. In such Russian sagas, however, when the scene is laid on earth, the localities are, in general, left vague, whereas in the narrative poems under discussion the localities are almost always clearly stated. It would seem probable on the whole, therefore, that in Russia the phase of Christian oral literature which corresponds most closely to this phase among the Yugoslavs consists of saga rather than of poetry.

Of the stories which form the subjects of narrative poetry,[1] it has

---

[1] For a general account (in Russian) of this religious poetry, and summaries of the poems referred to below, see Speranski, *R.U.S.* p. 358 ff. A brief chapter on the subject, containing summaries of several poems, will also be found in Rambaud, *R.E.* p. 370 ff.

already been said that those derived from Biblical stories retain their original features in general in such a way that, despite their popular treatment, their source is easily recognised. These and other stories derived thus directly from book sources hardly come within the scope of this chapter. Even in such stories as these, however, there is often a great difference between one variant and another in regard to the amount of local colour and popular features introduced. We may instance the Old Testament story of Dives and Lazarus, which has given rise to a whole class of poems known as *Lazari*.[1] The original nucleus is always easily recognisable; but the treatment is generally highly popular in character, and enriched with all the dramatic power and force of characterisation to which the situation lends itself. The unlettered reciter is fully aware of the possibilities of contrast and dialogue afforded by the situation in the parable. Accordingly we find that while the majority of the *Lazari* are composed in the form of Type A, all are rich in dialogue which occupies a large, sometimes the largest part of the poem, while several versions, by reducing the narrative to the minimum and increasing the dialogue, have become poems of Type B.[2] The great vogue of this story is doubtless due to its exceptional possibilities as a vehicle for propaganda. The *kalēki* depended for their subsistence on alms, and the cautionary tendency of the story, the picture which it presents of the rich uncharitable man brought low, and the poor and needy in the place of glory in Heaven, offers an admirable vehicle for begging in narrative form, and none of the possibilities of the story, whether artistic, didactic, or utilitarian are lost on the 'poor brethren' who have made it a kind of manifesto of their order.

The stories derived from the lives of saints of the Greek Church, whether apocryphal or genuine, have sometimes retained their Christian character intact, and the narrative, though homely, is not necessarily undignified. The localities are generally carefully noted, as well as the names of the principal characters. We may refer to the story which relates to 'Alexis, the Man of God',[3] the son of a Prince Ephimian, who lived in Rome in the time of the Emperor Honorius. The poem, of which there are many variants, tells how Alexis leaves his bride on the night of his marriage and sails to Odessa, changing clothes with a *kalēka* on the way, like many of the heroes of the *byliny*, in order to hide his identity. Arrived at Odessa, he enters the principal church,

---

[1] Bezsonov, I. p. 43 ff.   [2] E.g. Bezsonov, I. p. 55 ff.

[3] The version which we have summarised below will be found in Bezsonov, I. p. 98 ff.

where he remains as a professional beggar for many years. His parents, who greatly mourn for him, send in search of him, but the messengers who come to Odessa, and even to the very church, fail to recognise him. At last Alexis receives a command from Heaven to return to Rome to receive the blessing of his parents and convert them to the Christian faith. When he comes to Rome his parents do not recognise him, but since he brings them news of their son, they honour him and build him a cell to live in, and give him attendants; but his enemies persecute him, and, feeling his end draw near, he sends messengers to the prince asking for writing materials. Then the saint writes an account of his lineage and his life, and dies with the completed MS. in his hand. The prince and the clergy assemble at the cell of the man of God, and the prince orders the life of the saint to be read. It is then for the first time that the prince and princess realise that Alexis, the man of God, was their own beloved son.

In contrast to the sober and decorous poem of 'Alexis the Man of God', the poem of 'St Fedor Tiryanin'[1] approximates closely to the *byliny*, both in style and content. The poem opens with a message which Tsar Constantine receives during evening prayer from the Tsar of the Jews, threatening, in a formula common in the *byliny*, that if he will not give up the city of Jerusalem peaceably it will be taken by force. Tsar Constantine summons his followers and calls for a volunteer, but, again as in the *byliny*, the greater hide behind the lesser, and the lesser are speechless. Then Constantine's young son Fedor comes forward and offers to defend the city. The tsar protests that he is too young, but Fedor insists, and succeeds in destroying the pagan host single handed. Then, as in the *bylina* of 'Dobrynya and the dragon of the Mountain', the blood of the pagans rises to his horse's mane, to Fedor's silken girdle, and threatens to engulf them; but Fedor thrusts his sharp sword into the damp earth, opens the Gospels, and prays. His prayer, however, is practically identical with Dobrynya's prayer, when the blood of the slain serpent rises in flood around him. It consists of an adjuration formula to 'damp mother earth' to open on all four sides and swallow up the blood. And the earth opens and swallows all the blood of the Jews. Then the youth returns home. His father is watching for him, and greets him joyously, and takes him by his white hands, by his gold rings, and seats him at the table of oak. His horse is securely tied to a ring attached to a pillar in the courtyard, and his master eats, and drinks, and takes his pleasure. The second half of the *bylina* relates how a fiery dragon

---

[1] The version summarised below will be found in Bezsonov, I. p. 527 ff. A notice of this poem is given by Rambaud. *R.É.* p. 370 f.

carries off the hero's mother to its cavern, and how the hero rescues her and brings her safe home. This latter story bears so striking a resemblance to the story of Dobrynya's rescue of Vladimir's niece—or, according to a variant, his own (Dobrynya's) aunt—from the fiery dragon of the mountain, that it is impossible to believe that the two accounts are independent of one another.

Unlike the last poem, that of St Dimitri of Solun approximates in subject matter rather to a *skazka* than to a *bylina*. It tells us[1] that 'Tsar Mamai', the Tatar general, is harassing and destroying the town of Salonica, and the people in terror are evacuating the city. Two angels appear to St Dimitri and bid him go forth and destroy the Tatar army, and the saint gladly obeys the summons, and rides forth alone, slaying untold numbers, and Tsar Mamai is forced to withdraw to his own land. As he goes, however, he takes with him as prisoners two Russian maidens—no other than the daughters of St Dimitri himself. Mamai summons the two maidens and enquires of them the name of the Russian hero who has defeated him, and on learning that he is their own father, St Dimitri, he commands them to embroider the likeness of the saint on a carpet that he may dishonour and insult it. When the maidens refuse he threatens to cut off their heads from their 'sturdy shoulders'—a touch of heroic diction—but the maidens beseech him naïvely:

> O you wretch, you dog, heathen Tsar Mamai,
> Do not cut off our heads
> From our sturdy shoulders.
> Grant us until this evening,
> And we will embroider for you on a carpet
> Saint Dimitri, the miracle worker of Salonica,
> We will deliver up his blessed likeness to be insulted.

The two maidens embroider the holy countenance on the carpet, weeping and praying to St Dimitri, until at last they fall asleep. Then a miracle takes place. By the command of God, and at the prayer of St Dimitri, a great storm arises, and transports the carpet on which the two maidens are sleeping into the cathedral church in the town of Salonica. The popular singer is not content to relate this common incident of Oriental folk-tale in its bare outline. He gives a dramatic picture of the astonishment of the sexton who comes to unlock the church for matins, and finds the two girls asleep on the carpet before the throne. The sexton hastens away from the church and goes to arouse the priest. Finding him asleep he wakens him, and bids him rise, telling

---

[1] The version summarised below will be found in Bezsonov, I. p. 588 ff.

him what he has seen. The priest rouses himself from sleep, washes his face in holy water, puts on his outdoor clothing, and goes straight to the church, and wakens the two girls, who, unaware of their situation, address him as 'Wretch, dog, heathen Tsar Mamai'. It will be seen that the reciter makes the most of the dramatic possibilities of his stereotyped theme. Of course the priest at once reassures the terrified girls, and a great thanksgiving service is held in the Cathedral in honour of St Dimitri.

A large number of *stikhi* and *skazki* celebrate the glory of the most popular of all the Russian saints, St Mikula. The story of Vasili of Antioch,[1] like a large proportion of the stories relating to St Mikula, closely resembles a *skazka*, and, in fact, introduces a theme similar to the one just related in the *stikh* of St Dimitri. The poem begins by telling of the reverence habitually shown by Agricola of Antioch to St Mikula. One day he sends his son Vasili into the Church of St Mikula in Antioch, and as his son is praying in the church the Saracens fall upon the city and carry off many prisoners, and among them Vasili himself. The outraged parents abstain from prayer and from all church services, and refuse to show honour to St Mikula for three years. At the end of that time they again decide to pray to the saint for the release of their son. At this point we are transported into the presence of the Saracen prince 'in his palace of white stone'. Before him stands Vasili in Saracen costume, officiating as a slave, a flagon in one hand and a cup of gold in the other. Suddenly, by unseen and unknown means, he is transported from the palace of white stone and finds himself in his father's courtyard. Agricola, hearing the commotion of the dogs, sends his servants to find out who is there. They can see no one, but when Agricola and his wife go to look they see their dear son Vasili, in Saracen dress, holding the flagon and the golden cup. They ask him how he has come there, and he tells them that when he was transported from the white stone palace of the Saracen prince to his own courtyard he saw no one save St Mikula himself.

Probably the most widely celebrated of all the *stikhi* are those which refer to Egori Khrabry, 'George the Brave, or the Hero', or St George. A far greater proportion of space is allotted to him in Bezsonov's collection than to any other hero. He is chiefly known from what appears to have been originally a single poem, of which Bezsonov gives a large number of variants. In this poem, unlike the last two of which we have given an account above, the saint is himself the hero and the

---

[1] The following summary has reference to the version in Bezsonov, I. p. 559.

principal actor. Other poems also exist relating to him, and to these we will return later. Here we will give some account of the poem which appears to be the most widespread, and which is generally regarded as the chief account of the saint current in oral poetical tradition. We have selected the variant recorded by Bezsonov, I. p. 440 ff.; but the variants are, on the whole, singularly well preserved, and offer surprisingly little variation considering their number; and many other versions are equally or almost equally complete.

St Egori (George) is the son of the Tsar Fedor and the blessed Tsaritsa Sofÿa, and his home is the city of Jerusalem. He has three sisters. At birth his legs are of pure silver as far as the knees, his arms of pure gold as far as the elbows, and his head is wholly of pearl. The first incident relates to an attack on the city by the Tsar Demyan, who destroys the town, and slays Tsar Fedor, and carries off his son and his three daughters as captives into his own country. The tsar threatens his prisoners with death unless they will accept his faith, which is naïvely styled as both Latin and Mussulman. The three maidens yield to the tyrant and abandon Christianity, but Egori holds fast to his faith. A large proportion of the poem is occupied with the vain efforts of Demyan to torture the saint; but the teeth of the saws are blunted by divine agency, the 'German' axes grow dull, despite their double edges, the boots with iron nails will not hurt him, or boiling pitch scald him, and the saint sings hymns of praise throughout his ordeals. At last the tyrant has a deep pit dug, into which the saint is lowered, and in which he remains for thirty years, while the tyrant rejoices that the saint is "no longer in holy Russia,[1] and cannot behold the white light, or gaze upon the red sun, or see father, or mother, or hear the Church bell, or hear God's word". And when thirty years are passed the saint beholds a vision; the bright sun shines in his deep pit, and the blessed Virgin appears before him and promises him the joy of Heaven as a reward for his sufferings. Then a violent storm arises, tearing up the coverings of the pit, and once more the saint is free to wander over holy Russia. He returns to Jerusalem where he finds his mother praying for him in church. This incident, therefore, is not essentially different from the dénouement in the last

[1] This passage has an important bearing on certain passages in the *bylina* of Svyatogor, of whom it is said that 'he was not allowed in holy Russia.' The expression is generally taken to mean that he was located outside Russian territory; but there are features in his story which suggest that he was originally regarded as a chthonic being, and that the expression "not in holy Russia" signifies, not that he lived in another territory, but that his home was underground. Ilya's great achievement would thus be in securing him in his proper sphere, whence he had escaped.

two *stikhi* discussed above. With the reunion of the saint and his blessed mother the first part of the poem, the preparation of the saint for his life's work, may be said to close.

Egori next obtains his mother's blessing, and resolves to wander over Russia, preaching the Christian faith. In the land of Russia the dreaming forests impede his progress; but he bids them spread apart, and wave their branches over the land of Russia, so that he may build churches from their trunks, and the great forests grow strong and thick throughout the land, exactly where they are bidden. Then he rides to the swift rivers, but he cannot go forward. He orders the rivers to flow throughout the land of Russia, through steep, high mountains, and through the dark, dreaming forests, and at the command of God and the prayer of St Egori the rivers flow in the course commanded. The mountains next impede his progress, forming a close, dense barrier, and Egori bids them stand for ever that he may build churches on their summits. He next visits the abode of swift wolves, and here he finds his three sisters acting as herdswomen. Their bodies have grown like the bark of fir-trees, their hair is like feather-grass. And St Egori scatters the wolves in packs and pairs and singly throughout the steppes and the dark forests. After other similar encounters St Egori makes his way to the white stone palace of his former master Demyanishcha:

> Tsarishcha Demyanishcha caught sight of him,
> Demyanishcha the Mussulman, the godless dog;
> He shrieks like a wild beast,
> He hisses like a serpent,
> He was minded to kill Egori the brave.

But the saint is not dismayed. He rides him down on his swift steed, and with his sharp sword he cuts off his accursed head from his sturdy shoulders. Then he takes his three sisters to bathe in the Jordan, and as they do so the coarse grass falls from them, they shed the pine bark, and St Egori restores them to their own lady mother, Sofȳa the Wise:

> Many are the adventures of Egori,
> Great was his suffering.
> He suffered manifold tortures,
> All for our sinful souls.
> We sing the glory of St Egori,
> St Egori the bright, the brave,
> His glory shall stand for ever,
> For ever and ever, Amen!

With these words the pious *kalêki* end their *stikh.*

We have treated the *stikh* of Egori the Brave at some length because it is one of the most interesting and instructive of the *stikhi*, illustrating, as it does, the astonishingly naïve coalescence of Christian tradition and heathen lore. In the first part of the *stikh* the saint does not differ essentially from scores of other Christian saints of whom our medieval records have many similar stories to tell. In the second half of the poem, however, St Egori has become a wizard of the Asiatic type, a shaman, of whom our nearest European prototype is the *bylina* hero Volga. Both are shown to be supreme over each individual kingdom of nature, the chief differences being that while Volga is at once a hunter and a shape-changer, assuming the form of a member of each of the animal kingdoms in turn in order to control them, St Egori is a civilising influence, and, while retaining his human form, directs nature, both animate and inanimate, to be subservient to the needs of the Orthodox Church. His powers are, however, far more universal than those ascribed to any other saint known to us. It would almost seem as if, in the popular imagination, he has assumed the attributes of deity, and adopted methods which are an improvement on those detailed for us in the early chapters of Genesis.

One of the favourite stories of the Old Testament current among the *kalêki* is the story of Joseph the son of Jacob, better known to popular tradition as Osip Prekrasny, 'Joseph the Fair'. A considerable number of narrative poems (Type A) are current relating to him, some based directly on the Biblical version of the story, others so far removed from it as to be classed by Bezsonov as 'purely popular'. Independent of these narrative poems, a rich crop of poems of Type B[1] are also current in connection with the same hero. Many of these are laments which purport to be spoken by Joseph himself.

One of these laments[2] is described by Bezsonov as derived directly from books. In two of the texts which he gives, the lament proper (*plach*) forms a kind of overture to the *byl* or narrative poem which follows, and which relates a portion of the life of Joseph. The *plach* is composed wholly in the first person. It represents Joseph as lamenting his sins and the hard fate which he has suffered at the hands of his brothers, and concludes with the words:

> Earth, earth,
> Who cried out to God for Abel,
> Cry out now to Jacob,
> To my father Israel!

[1] Bezsonov, I. pp. 187 f., 191 f.   [2] *Ib.* p. 188.

Two other versions of the same *plach*, also spoken by Joseph, are given by Bezsonov[1] independently, and he adds a note[2] to the effect that the *plach*, in various forms, constitutes the introduction to *stikhi* of which the main subject may be emotional, spiritual, literary, didactic, etc.

Among the poems classed by Bezsonov[3] as those which are purely native and popular (*stikhi chisto-narodnye*) are the series known as the 'Tsarevich Josaph the Hermit'. Of these Bezsonov gives a large number of versions. Many of them consist of a few lines of narrative telling us of the decision of the prince to become a hermit, and of his arrival at the hermitage. The rest of the poem consists of a dialogue between the prince and the hermitage, personified as a woman, in which the latter sets forth to the prince the hardships and discipline of the life eremitical. A further series[4] consists of addresses of the tsarevich to the hermitage. Such poems also are apparently technically known as *plachi* (pl. 'laments'). Yet a third series[5] consists of the prayers of St Joseph after he has entered the hermitage.

An interesting example of Christian oral poetry of Type C is the widely popular *Kniga Golubinaya*, 'The Book of the Dove', of which Bezsonov gives seventeen versions. The setting of this poem is sufficiently removed from Biblical authority to merit a place in popular oral poetry. The poem tells us[6] that during a violent storm the 'Book of the Dove' falls on the 'life-giving cross', and many tsars and princes assemble at the spot to learn its contents. The chief initiative is taken by the Tsar Vladimir (Volodýmir, Volodemir, Volodimir, Volotomon, Volontoman, etc.). Vladimir asks the assembled princes which of them is able to read, and will discover to the rest the contents of the book,

> And tell us of the white light:
> Whence has come our white light,
> Whence came our red sun,
> Whence came the pale new moon,
> Whence came the innumerable stars,
> Whence came the bright red glow,
> The red glow of dawn and of eventide?

All the tsars are silent save the wise David, the son of Esau, who volunteers to expound to them the contents of the book. The princes thank him, and the rest of the poem consists of groups of questions put

---

[1] I. p. 204 f.   [2] I. p. 205, note.
[3] I. p. 205 ff.   [4] I. p. 240 ff.   [5] I. p. 259 ff.
[6] We are following the *stikh* in Bezsonov, I. p. 293 ff.; but the versions do not differ materially from one another.

to David by them in the form of a series, and his answers, likewise in groups and in the form of a series. The convention resembles the riddle sequences which we shall see later to be common in Russian folk-poetry; but the questions are not riddles, since the meaning is never veiled. This dialogue occupies almost the whole of the poem, which varies in length from thirty lines to over nine hundred lines, the setting occupying a few lines only at the beginning and end.

After enquiring as to the origin of the universe, the princes next enquire as to the origin of the various social classes of mankind, such as tsars, boyars, muzhiks, etc. Satisfied on these points, they enquire as to who is the chief tsar of all the tsars, and which is the chief of all cities, and are told that the 'White Tsar' of Russia is the chief of tsars, because he professes the Christian faith, and Jerusalem is the chief of cities, because the Holy Sepulchre is there. Then follow questions on geography, of the kind with which we are familiar in secular poetry of didactic and antiquarian learning, such as 'which sea is the mother of all seas, which lake the mother of all lakes?' The answers, however, show the reciters to be better endowed with spiritual than with intellectual gifts, since they do not shrink from declaring, among other analogous statements, that Ilmen is the chief of lakes because the River Jordan flows out of it. They are not wholly without intellectual scruples, how-ever, for they hasten to add that it is not the Lake Ilmen beside Nov-gorod which is in question, but the Ilmen[1] which is beside Jerusalem. We are next told in succession the chief of each of the animal kingdoms, of the mountains and the trees; allegorical questions follow, approxi-mating closely to riddles. Finally David interprets Vladimir's dream as portending the future marriage of his own daughter with David's son Solomon; and with this personal touch the poem ends.

It will be seen that the poem is analogous in form to the Old Norse poem *Sigrdrífumál*. In each the framework of the poem represents a dialogue as taking place between a character famous in heroic poetry and a non-heroic individual famous for wisdom and knowledge. The body of the Christian poem, however, is occupied, not with spells and heathen lore, but with antiquarian and learned matter transformed into Christian lore. In this respect it resembles the Anglo-Saxon dialogue poem of *Salomon and Saturn*. There can be no doubt that the poem is a traditional type of great antiquity which has lent itself readily to adapta-tion as a vehicle of popular Christian instruction.

[1] *Ilmen* is the Finnish word meaning 'lake'. Is the reciter or composer of the poem aware of this?

The history of *dukhovny stikh*, or spiritual poetry, so far as we can trace it, appears to be in many respects similar to that of the *byliny*. *Dukhovny stikh* seems to have existed in a form similar to that in which we now have it already as early as the fifteenth century,[1] for in a MS. dating from that period we find the unique, and famous *dukhovny stikh* of 'Adam', which was written down at the close of the fifteenth century. During this century also we find a reference to a *dukhovny stikh*, analogous in content to the *stikh* of 'Adam'. Its title is especially interesting. It is called 'a *stikh*—a *starina* for the ale-drinking'. The expression 'for the ale-drinking' probably means that this *stikh* was sung at dinner time, when, in accordance with monastic rule, ale was drunk. The identification of the *stikh* with the *starina* is particularly interesting, for *starina* is, as we have seen, the customary name in north Russia for a *bylina*, and the occurrence of the word in connection with a *dukhovny stikh* suggests that already in this early period the *dukhovny stikh* and the *starina* are identical in form. On the other hand according to Speranski the majority of the *dukhovnÿe stikhi* of a pre-eminently historical character, i.e. relating to the Russian saints, have reference to the fifteenth and sixteenth centuries. We may with probability conclude, therefore, that this was the period, if not actually of the first appearance of such poetry, at least of the first vigorous growth and expansion of *dukhovnÿe stikhi* in their present form.

From the middle of the seventeenth century we have very rich material for the study of poetry of this kind. Fragments of such *dukhovnÿe stikhi* are found in MSS. dating from this period, and from the close of the century we have whole collections, which were copied and added to throughout the eighteenth century.

The conclusions which we may draw from these written *stikhi*, both the earlier and later, may be summarised briefly as follows. The spread of *dukhovny stikh*, i.e. religious poetry which, despite its original inspiration from books, had an independent life in oral transmission, began approximately with the fifteenth century. In the history of this poetry, however, we can distinguish two phases,[2] which appear to correspond to the history of the *byliny*. The earliest phase introduced *stikhi* which are mainly narrative in character, and which correspond in form and diction to the *byliny*. We may suppose that they were composed when the *byliny* are believed to have first assumed their present form, i.e. from the late fifteenth to the seventeenth centuries, and in a similar milieu. We may also conclude that, like the latter, they have

[1] Speranski, *R.U.S.* p. 363.   [2] *Ib.* p. 364.

always consisted for the most part of narrative. The *stikhi* of this phase, like the *byliny*, have had a continuous history down to the present day.

The second phase appears not to have been introduced into northern Russia until the second half of the seventeenth century, from which period it also has had a continuous history. Poetry of this second kind is characterised, as has been said already, by a rhymed strophic form, and has developed in the full current of western influence. Before this period rhyme is believed to have been unknown in northern Russia. Both these forms flourish side by side in Russia today, but the earlier form continues to predominate in northern Russia, the later in southern, though both are found to some extent in the same areas.

CHAPTER IX

POST-HEROIC, ANTIQUARIAN, GNOMIC, AND DESCRIPTIVE POETRY AND SAGA

POST-HEROIC poetry may be said to have hardly begun in the oral traditional poetry of Russia. The traditional heroic style has persisted down to our own day, and examples of original post-heroic themes are rare and practically confined to *byliny* relating to the seventeenth century. Even here the literary features of style are generally those of heroic poetry. The post-heroic elements in these poems are chiefly to be found in the more advanced political thought expressed by the speakers. At times a post-heroic element has also been introduced into *byliny* of other Cycles, originally heroic, and can be discerned in the sophisticated outlook of the reciter, or of the milieu in which he has received his répertoire.

Post-heroic features hardly appear in the *byliny* of the early Cycles. Exceptions are, however, to be found occasionally. The *bylina* of *Terenti Gost*, 'Terence the Merchant', in the Novgorod Cycle is post-heroic in subject and in tone, though even here the style and metre are heroic throughout (cf. p. 51 above). Some of the *byliny* of Vasili Buslaev are also post-heroic in treatment, especially those in which burlesque is most obvious. Indeed we have already seen reason to regard the Novgorod Cycle as a whole as far removed from the original heroic impetus. Vsevolod Miller long ago pointed out that the action of the Novgorod epos is for the most part unheroic in character, and he reminds us that the term 'heroes' (*bogatyri*) was not originally applied to the personnel of this Cycle, but came into the répertoire of the Olonets *skaziteli* from the heroic *byliny* of Kiev and Suzdal.[1]

Post-heroic poetry as a definite genre makes its appearance for the first time in the seventeenth century in the Period of Troubles. Reference has already been made to the censorious tone assumed in regard to Boris Godunov in the poems composed on the death of the Tsarevich Dimitri. These poems, and still more the poems on Vasili Shuyski and on Kuzma Minin and Pozharski, contain an element of criticism, the expression of a strong feeling of dissatisfaction directed against the boyars, who are regarded as betraying the country.

[1] *R.M.* IX. p. 150.

In the latter poem, in addition to the political consciousness expressing itself in a tendency towards party faction, we meet for the first time an appeal to action addressed primarily to the bourgeoisie, who are called upon to assume serious responsibilities of citizenship. Moreover a change is noticeable in the attitude of the poems towards Russia, which is no longer regarded merely as a geographical area, as in the earlier cycles, but stands rather for a conception of the Russian people as a whole, perhaps more especially the aristocracy and the merchant classes. This newly attained national consciousness is the natural outcome of a political situation which was to terminate in the patriotic rise of the citizens under the leadership of Minin, the butcher of Nizhni Novgorod. A brief satirical narrative poem on the Priest Simeon also exists[1] which shows that the spirit of enlightenment was expressing itself in a critical attitude even towards the church itself.

These few short poems which have survived from the Period of Troubles throw an interesting light on the state of popular feeling with regard to Muscovite politics in the seventeenth century. It will be observed that all the *byliny* of this period, heroic and non-heroic alike, are strongly royalist in sympathy. This feeling is expressed particularly strongly in the *bylina* on *Kuzma Minin and Prince Pozharski* which celebrates the election of

> Michael Fedorovich
> Of the glorious heroic House of Romanov.[2]

Indeed it is difficult to escape the conclusion that the *byliny* of this period were exercises in political journalism, and perhaps we may even suspect that their composers were not without party support and encouragement.

When we turn to examine the *byliny* dating from the period intermediate between the Period of Troubles and the present day we are struck by the absence of political feeling and party politics. Bezsonov regards the first of the variants which he records of the *bylina* on the death of the Empress Katharine II as inspired by party feeling directed against the Emperor Paul.[3] But the frank censure characteristic of the *byliny* of the preceding century has been replaced by innuendo. Plain speech is absent, and we do not think that even such a half-hearted spirit of censure as this poem may be supposed to contain is common.

---

[1] See Rambaud, *R.É.* p. 283 f.
[2] Kirêevski, VII. p. 21 f.; Chadwick, p. 241 f.
[3] Kirêevski, IX. p. 265.

We have already referred to the royal proscription of references to certain proper names—a proscription which may have affected the *byliny* more widely than we realise. But whatever the immediate cause may be, the almost total absence of political feeling in these *byliny*, in contrast to those of the previous period, as well as their tone of personal loyalty to the tsars and tsaritsas, are particularly instructive as indicating the strength and longevity of the heroic tradition in Russian popular poetry, and the close ties which to the end united the interests of the minstrels to the tsarist régime.

Nevertheless alongside the traditional type of heroic poetry which again comes into favour in this period we find post-heroic poetry of a somewhat different character from that which we have been discussing. We may instance the *byliny* on the two great battles of Ehresfer[1] and Poltava[2], fought between the Russians under Peter the Great, and the Swedes. In these poems the issue is clearly conceived as depending on the united action of whole armies rather than of individual heroes. We may refer also to the *bylina* in which defiance is offered to the Swedes by the Russians before Poltava,[3] and in which again regiments rather than individuals are represented as deciding the issue in combat. In the later *bylina* on the capture of Smolensk[4] national consciousness is fully developed. These poems are analogous to the Anglo-Saxon poem composed on the Battle of Brunanburh, in which, in spite of many echoes of heroic poetry, we have a clear conception of national consciousness and a realisation of the importance of the army as a whole.

Antiquarian poetry is rarely met with in the répertoires of the *skaziteli* or the *kalêki*. We have no doubt that its place has, in general, been usurped by Christian historical poetry such as the Lives of the Saints. Occasionally, however, antiquarian touches are introduced, even into Christian religious poetry, as we see in the last two lines of the *stikh* on the 'Vigil of Saint Dimitri' (cf. p. 184 above). The boldest flight of antiquarian speculation known to us in Russian oral poetry is the little poem which claims that the organisation of the *kalêki perekhozhie* was instituted by Jesus Christ himself on Ascension Day. This poem has already been noticed in connection with non-heroic poetry, and translated on p. 187 f. above.

As we have already seen, heroic prose stories and stories of the tsars

---

[1] Kirêevski, VIII. p. 125 ff.; Chadwick, p. 270.
[2] Kirêevski, VIII. p. 168 ff.   [3] Rambaud, *R.É.* p. 320 f.
[4] Kirêevski, X. p. 23 f.; Rambaud, *R.É.* p. 353 f.

not unfrequently assume an antiquarian form. We may refer once more to the story of Ivan the Terrible, in which treason is said to be introduced into Russia for all time, as a result of his act of perfidy (cf. p. 171 above). In another story we are told that Lake Ladoga was originally calm, till roused by God's anger against the human race, after which it was invariably stormy till pacified by Peter the Great (cf. p. 178 above). The story of Nikita Kozhimyaka and his fight with the serpent, clearly identical with the story of the slaying of the serpent by Dobrynya, concludes with an antiquarian speculation on a great vallum in south Russia, traces of which still remain (cf. p. 170 above).

Indeed where antiquarian speculation exists in Russian popular literature it is found chiefly in the form of local and ecclesiastical tradition, and undoubtedly for the most part in the form of prose. For at least four hundred years the name of Ilya Muromets has been attached to one or other of the bodies preserved from early times in open coffins in the crypts at Kiev. While this claims to be, and has generally been regarded as genuine historical tradition, there can be little doubt that the identification is due to medieval ecclesiastical speculation. Further, in the village of Karachoro in the province of Murom, which has come to be traditionally associated with Ilya—doubtless through confusion with Murov—there is a family known as the Ilyuchni, who claim direct descent from the *bogatyr*. Here again similarity of name has no doubt led to genealogical speculation and speculative identification. Local legends abound which are associated with various incidents in the life of the hero.

The local traditions of Kiev associate the bodies preserved in the caves with other *bogatyri*, in addition to Ilya of Murom. Such identifications probably originated in learned speculations on the etymology of the word *bogatyr*, which was explained by a spurious etymology[1] as 'Champion of God', and the term was no doubt applied indifferently to saints and heroes. It is possible, therefore, that the tradition of the caves of Kiev merely indicates that saints and heroes such as St Ilya are believed to be buried there. There is, indeed, a rival tradition which associates the burial-place of the heroes of Kiev with quite a different locality. The work of a Russian traveller of the sixteenth century contains the statement that about ten *versts*[2] from Kiev, on the opposite bank of the Dnêpr, lies the city of Pereyaslavl, where the Russian *bogatyri* are buried, and adds that very large stones lie in the burial-

[1] For the true affinities of the word see p. 122, footnote 1 above.
[2] For *verst*, cf. p. 40 above, footnote 3.

ground.[1] We do not know if the reference here is to boulders or to Christian tomb-stones. It is particularly interesting, however, in view of the fact that according to one version of the *bylina*, recorded from the recitation of an old Siberian Cossack,[2] the heroes of Kiev fled to the hills above Kiev after the great battle against the Tatar 'Tsar Kalin', and were turned to stone. Has this version of the *bylina* been influenced by the local tradition, or has the tradition arisen from the attempts of local antiquaries to identify the spot referred to in the *bylina*? It is difficult to say. But to describe burial in a Christian cemetery with Christian headstones as being 'turned to stone' would be quite in accord with the traditional figurative diction characteristic of the *byliny*, which is responsible for the growth of so many of their supernatural features.

Gnomic and didactic poetry or saga are equally scantily represented in the collections before us. We are almost wholly in the dark in regard to the native learning of the ancient Russians. We have already noted the absence of poetry of Type C apart from rare examples of Christian *stikhi* of this kind. It is natural to suppose that the influence of the Church has to a large extent taken the place of the development of both popular ethics and popular learning. Such relics as we possess of poetry of this kind have generally been transmuted, as is not uncommon in Christian countries, into popular entertainment literature or popular games.

Popular learning is represented chiefly by the echoes which survive in the *zagadki* (sing. *zagadka*). The word is generally translated 'riddle' or 'dark saying'. It does not appear, however, that the *zagadki* are always expressed in the form of riddles, and many of them appear to correspond to the *kennings* familiar to us from Celtic and Teutonic literature. They consist for the most part of statements or questions, couched in highly figurative terms, about the weather or natural phenomena— the sun, moon, stars, the winds, the sea, the sky, rocks, death, etc.; e.g.

Riddle: "There is inscribed a writing on blue velvet, and to read that writing is given neither to priests, nor to deacons, nor to wise muzhiks."

Answer: "The starry sky at night."[3]

In all probability many of the actual *zagadki* are of foreign origin.

According to Khudyakov,[4] in the Government of Pskov, on the occasion of a marriage, the bridegroom and his friends are obliged to

---

[1] Studer, p. 26.   [2] Kirêevski, IV. p. 108 ff.
[3] Ralston, *Songs*, p. 348.   [4] *Ib*. p. 353.

answer all the riddles put to them by the bride's friends before they are allowed to enter the bride's cottage. It is stated that in one of the villages in the Government of Yaroslav, 'riddles' are asked by the 'seller of the bride' instead of coin, and are answered, as payment, by the grooms-man, in gestures instead of words.[1] On the other hand, in the poem quoted below, which was heard by Buslaev in Moscow, it is the bride-groom who asks riddles of the bride.[2] The custom is also found in folk-tales. Ralston quotes a story—not of native origin—in which a princess tests her suitors by riddles, beheading those who are unable to answer them, and marrying the suitor whose intelligence is equal to the ordeal.[3] Parallels in other folk-tales could be multiplied indefinitely, and the motif occurs also in Tatar oral saga.

The following folk-song, recorded by Buslaev in Moscow and trans-lated by Ralston, relates a riddle wooing of this kind. Here the riddle sequence is encased in a slight framework of narrative:

A maiden fair was strolling in a garden,
Gathering rosy flow'rets was the maiden;
By that way a merchant's son came driving:
"Now may God be with thee, beauteous maiden,
God be with thee, rosy flow'rets gathering!"
"Many thanks! O merchant's son! Thanks many!"
"Shall I ask thee riddles, beauteous maiden?
Six wise riddles shall I ask thee?"
"Ask them, ask them, merchant's son,
Prithee ask the six wise riddles."
"Well then, maiden, what is higher than the forest?
Also, what is brighter than the light?
Also, maiden, what is thicker than the forest?
Also, maiden, what is there that's rootless?
Also, maiden, what is never silent?
Also, what is there past finding out?"
"I will answer, merchant's son, will answer,
All the six wise riddles will I answer.
Higher than the forest—is the moon,
Brighter than the light—the ruddy sun.
Thicker than the forest—are the stars.
Rootless is, O merchant's son, a stone.
Never silent, merchant's son, the sea,
And God's will is past all finding out."
"Thou hast guessed, O maiden fair, guessed rightly,
All the six wise riddles hast thou answered.
Therefore now to me shalt thou be wedded,
Therefore, maiden, shalt thou be the merchant's wife."[4]

[1] *Loc. cit.*   [2] *Ib.* p. 354 ff.   [3] *Ib.* p. 356.   [4] *Ib.* p. 356 f.

It is interesting to observe that the riddles are asked in a series, and the answers are also delivered in a series. In this they form a contrast to the Latin and Anglo-Saxon riddles, each of which is self-contained and supplied independently with its answer. The Russian form recalls some of the Early Norse Riddles of Gestumblindi in the *Hervarar Saga*, e.g.:

> What lives in high mountains?
> What falls in deep valleys?
> What lives without breathing?
> What is never silent?
> King Heiðrekr, read me this riddle.

Heiðrekr replies:

> Your riddle is a good one, Gestumblindi,
> I have guessed it.—
> A raven always lives in high mountains,
> And dew falls in deep valleys,
> A fish lives without breathing,
> And the booming waterfall is never silent.[1]

Traces of the same form are found also in Irish. In the *Amra Choluim Chille* (cap. 63)[2] we have a fragment of a riddle sequence.

> What life is worse than death?
> What empty is heavier than full?
> What lake is broader than any sea?

We shall see in the following volume that the same form of riddle sequence is characteristic also of the riddles of the Tatars. It will be observed that in all these examples—Russian, Norse and Irish—the sequence of answers, read independently of the riddles which prompt them, form a set of gnomic verses closely resembling the Cottonian and Exeter gnomes of Anglo-Saxon literature.

The parallels between the Norse and the Russian riddles extend beyond the external framework. Many of the Russian *ʒagadki* recall in detail of both form and style some of the Early Norse riddles. We may perhaps compare the form of the following riddle of Gestumblindi:

I went from home, I made my way from home, I looked upon a road of roads. A road was beneath me, a road above me, and a road on every side[3]— with a riddle asked by a suitor of the princess in the Russian story referred to above:

As I came to you, I saw on the way what was bad, and I struck the bad with a bad thing, and of what was bad the bad died.[4]

---

[1] Kershaw, *Stories and Ballads of the Far Past*, p. 117.
[2] Ed. and transl. W. Stokes, *Revue Celtique*, xx. p. 258.
[3] Kershaw, *op. cit.* p. 115.
[4] Ralston, *Songs*, p. 355.

It is no doubt significant that the subjects treated in Gestumblindi's riddles chiefly have reference to natural phenomena, and offer almost the same range of theme as the Russian riddles referred to and quoted by Ralston. We shall see in the following volume that in this respect also the Russian and the Norse riddles bear a close resemblance to those which occur in the oral literature of the Tatars.

The evidence afforded by the *zagadki*—whether we consider the nature of their contents, the circumstances in which they are introduced, or the sagas in which they form a motif—suggests that they were used in the past as 'intelligence tests', or 'education tests', in the 'oral examination' which appears to have formed a part of the general examination usually held as a part of the proceedings connected with peasant weddings. As the preliminary part of this transaction the parents or their representatives meet and discuss the circumstances of both parties. Erman observed[1] that in western Siberia early last century the second, or practical, stage of the proceedings was a mutual inspection of one another's appearance by the prospective bride and bridegroom. We have already seen that in certain districts the marriage is said to have depended on the ability of the bride, or, more often, the bridegroom, to answer a series of questions on matters relating to popular natural science, philosophy, etc. In folk-tales failure is said at times to prove fatal. It would seem therefore that the riddle, whether of native or foreign origin, is regarded as an ordeal, intellectual in character, which those who aspire to matrimony must pass to the satisfaction of the other party. In other words, it is a test of the culture of mind of the aspirant. The conduct of the princess who orders the unsuccessful suitors to be put to death becomes intelligible if we consider that mere uneducated boors, in no wise qualified for polite circles, are presuming to offer themselves as suitors for the royal hand. We shall see in the following chapter that a large amount of the poetry which relates to unnamed individuals is directly connected with social ritual. If our suggestion as to the original function of Russian riddles is correct, it is interesting as showing that, so far from being, in the first instance, a social recreation or mere artistic form, they have their origin in social ritual, and serve an economic purpose.

Philosophical and reflective poetry can hardly be said to have developed far in Russia as an independent composition. Examples are not wholly wanting in which these elements predominate, but the frame-

[1] Erman, I. p. 388.

work is generally that of some other type of poetry. Dormidontov cites (p. 242) an address to grief, a timeless-nameless apostrophe embodying a series of philosophical descriptive gnomes. The whole forms an effective composition in figurative style, concluding:

> Ah grief, grief, bitter grief!...
> I flee from grief into the dark forest,
> But grief is always there before me;
> I flee from grief to the honourable feast,
> But grief is there, seated beside me;
> I flee from grief into the tsar's tavern,[1]
> But grief is waiting for me, and steals my beer.
> When I was naked he mocked at me.[2]

Descriptive poetry is not uncommon, though many of the examples cited in anthologies and collections may have been originally composed as a part of the wooing or marriage or other ceremonies of social and ritual solemnity. We may cite the two following which are published by Dormidontov (p. 241) as 'Descriptions in poetical form'.

The Dandy

> He dresses himself up, he dons his attire,
> He draws on his boots of morocco leather,
> He gets into his long coat of fox-skin.
> His coat of fox-skin rustles like the forest,
> And his gold ring glistens like live coals.
> He wears a cap of brocade velvet.
> In his right hand is a slender cane
> And on the cane is a crimson ribbon.

The Belle

> Dunyasha, the darling,
> Has a white face, all painted...
> Her cheeks flame crimson,
> Her black eyebrows are pencilled.
> Her rebellious head is smoothly combed,
> Her flaxen plait is finely braided,
> In the flaxen plait is a crimson ribbon.

---

[1] In former times spirits were a monopoly of the Crown in Russia, and formed a part of the royal revenues. The inns bore the royal arms, the Russian eagle.

[2] Dormidontov, p. 242. For a variant, recorded by Shein, see Glazunov, *R.N.L.* p. 60, translated by Ralston, *Songs*, p. 30.

CHAPTER X

POETRY RELATING TO UNSPECIFIED INDIVIDUALS

POEMS and sagas relating to unspecified individuals are very numerous. The latter consist mainly of folk-tales, and with these we are not prepared to deal. Very many of them have a wide international circulation. They must be regarded as 'international' rather than 'national' literature, and their origin is quite uncertain. Russian folk-tales indeed appear to have some individual characteristics, e.g. certain conventional motifs, formulae, openings, conclusions, etc. But to indicate what is specifically Russian even in these would require a knowledge of the popular literature of the neighbouring peoples, and of folk-tales in general, to which we can make no claim. Moreover, the subject is far too extensive and complex to be treated here, except in a perfunctory way. We shall therefore confine our attention to poetry of this class.

A large number of poems are published in Rybnikov's collection from Shungsk and Olonets, and the regions of Lakes Ladoga and Onega generally.[1] Others are published in the new series of the collection of Kirêevski, and in the collections of Sakharov, Tereshchenko, Shein, etc. The complete works of the three last-named collectors have not been accessible to us, but extracts are given in Glazunov's *Russkaya Narodnaya Lirika*, in Dormidontov's *Kratki Kurs Istori Russkoy Literatury*, and in *Istoriko-Literaturnaya Khrestomatÿa* by Brodski, Mendelson and Sidorov. English translations of a number of poems, chiefly in an abridged form, or merely extracts, are to be found in Ralston's *Songs of the Russian People*. A more recent series of German translations has been published by Paul Eisner in *Volkslieder der Slawen*.

Narrative poetry which has reference wholly to unspecified individuals appears to be not very common. A large number of folk-tales and folk-motifs have been incorporated into the heroic poems, as we have seen, especially into poems of the Kiev and Novgorod cycles, while many others have become attached to the names of well-known historical figures. Poems which simply narrate a folk-tale of an unnamed person, or a person unknown beyond the limits of the story, are

[1] Rybnikov, III. *passim.*

not very frequently to be found in collections of Russian oral poetry, though they are not unknown. It is quite possible, however, that our evidence is defective on this head, and that more stories of nameless characters exist than have been accessible to us.

Poems of Type B are exceedingly common. The majority relate to women, and are composed in the form of a 'complaint'; but a large number also relate to men. The poems of this type are occasional in character, and are generally limited to a narrow domestic environment. Many of them are perhaps in origin poems of Type E, but we are often ignorant of the exact circumstances of composition. Poems of Type D are also common, especially elegies and laments.

The form and conventions characteristic of heroic poetry are surprisingly tenacious in Russia. The great majority of the poems which relate to unspecified individuals have adopted the metre, diction and formulae of heroic poetry. The long line is in general use and is end-stopped. The strophic form appears to be rare or entirely absent from Great Russia, offering a marked contrast to the varied metres of Little Russian lyrics. Many of the poems are, indeed, heroic in all respects except in the lack of proper names. Such poetry is distributed all over north Russia and Siberia, and the provenance does not appear to differ from that of ordinary heroic poetry.

The narrative poetry of this class is related solely for purposes of entertainment, and shares in its general style the heroic characteristics of the narrative *byliny*, though it is commonly briefer and less ambitious in scope than the latter. The time covered by the action is usually quite short, the characters introduced are few in number, and the action is commonly, though not invariably, confined to a single episode or situation. The actual stories narrated in poems of this class are very often of the level and character of folk-tales.

Yet pure narrative poems which relate a true folk-tale are, as we have said, surprisingly rare in the collections which have been accessible to us, and such poems as contain stories of the intellectual level and character of folk-tales are usually quite brief. It would seem that the Russians do not possess any considerable body of poetry analogous to that of the Yugoslavs, in which the heroic form seems to have attracted into itself a number of such motifs as are usually associated elsewhere with folk-tales. In Russia motifs of this kind are generally to be found, not in sustained narrative poems, but in short popular prose *skazki* or folk-tales. This contrast between the usage of the Russians and the Yugoslavs may be compared with the contrast in regard to their treatment of the saints of the Greek church. Among the Yugoslavs stories of these saints, related in familiar, humorous and homely vein, are embodied in the form of narrative poetry, whereas in Russia such stories appear to be confined in general to the *skazki*.

Although Russian narrative poems relating to unnamed persons are, in general, less ambitious in form and scope than those of the Yugoslavs, they resemble the latter in the nature of many of the subjects treated, as is to be expected in motifs which are similar to those of folktales. We may refer to a poem which relates how a band of robbers attack a man and his wife and child as they are preparing food by the sea in the course of a journey. It is not till after the robbers have slain the man and drowned the child that they learn that the woman is their own sister.[1] This motif of the sudden recognition of a brother and a sister after long absence is not unknown in Russia even in heroic poetry, and has even made its way into the cycle of stories associated with Alyosha Popovich.[2] It is, however, believed to be late and intrusive,[3] and is more commonly to be met with in Yugoslav poetry.

A poem recorded by Sakharov and translated by Ralston[4] relates how a sister attempts to poison her brother, and how he discovers her treachery by accident and takes summary vengeance. The narrative is very brief, and both the brevity and the savagery are alien to Russian heroic narrative poetry. The motif, details and treatment are more akin to the Yugoslav *narodne pjesme* than to the *byliny*, and Ralston was of the opinion that the poem is of foreign origin;[5] but Russian parallels, both to the subject and to the treatment, are by no means lacking. We may compare the story related in a group of poems recorded in Kirêevski's collection among the 'Poems of the Don Cossacks',[6] in which a hero is represented as dismembering his own wife. But, while the former story bears all the impress of a folk-motif, the latter is merely a version of the *bylina* of Prince Roman to which reference has been made above (p. 153). Moreover, there can, we think, be little doubt that the association with Prince Roman is an original and not an adventitious one, since certain *byliny* which relate the murder of his wife appear to be independent poems composed on the same subject, or at least versions which became variants at a very early date.[7]

---

[1] A translation is given by Ralston, *Songs*, p. 49 f. The text of this poem has not been accessible to us.

[2] See the version recorded by Sokolov (Kirêevski, II. p. 80 ff. and p. 82, footnote).

[3] See Miller, *Ocherki*, III. p. 77.   [4] *Songs*, p. 394.

[5] *Ib.* p. 23.   [6] Kirêevski, v. p. 113 ff.

[7] See Chadwick, p. 168.

As further illustrations of poems of this class we may refer to a series of poems or versions recorded in Kirêevski's collection, in which an unnamed youth is represented as slaying in ignorance his own wife and children at the evil instigation of his mother. Bezsonov connected[1] this theme with that contained in the *bylina* of Prince Mikhailo (see p. 57 above), and regarded both as connected with that of the *bylina* of Prince Roman.[2] The similarity of the themes is undeniable, and the 'nameless hero' may well be ultimately derived from Prince Roman. On the other hand we have to take into account the encroachment of motifs of a 'folk-tale' character into the domains of heroic poetry. This encroachment generally tends to increase as heroic tradition declines, and there can be no doubt that atrocities such as the dismembering of a wife by a husband at the instigation of his mother is more in accordance with the atmosphere of folk-tale than with that of heroic poetry. The process may in actual fact be inverse, therefore, and the crude motif may conceivably represent a folk-motif which has become attached at an early period to a heroic figure, perhaps suggested by some remote resemblance to an actual occurrence.

This brings us to a small class of poems which we have treated more fully in the section on *byliny* (p. 57 above). This class comprises poems in which pure folk-tales, or stories of the intellectual level of folk-tales, have become attached to names which purport to be historical, though they have never been successfully identified with any known historical characters. We have already mentioned the poems on Prince Mikhailo which perhaps belong to this class. We may refer here also to the little poems on Prince Dimitri and Prince Danilo. In the former the hero is represented as beating his affianced bride 'till she was half dead' because she had mocked his ugly appearance and ungainly carriage. The poem on Prince Danilo has already been discussed (*loc. cit.*).

It is possible that we ought to include in the class of poetry having reference to unidentified heroes, and close affinities with folk tales, at least some of the *byliny* of the so-called 'Older Cycle', e.g. those of which the hero is Svyatogor, and possibly Mikula also. These heroes, however, of whatever origin, have certainly acquired by courtesy and long tradition a conspicuous place among the great heroes of *byliny*. Moreover, Svyatogor is closely associated with Ilya of Murom and with

---

[1] See Editor's note in Kirêevski, VII. Supplement, p. 25. See also Kirêevski, New Series, p. 72, no. 1903.

[2] See also Kirêevski, New Series, p. 5, no. 1620.

Mikula, while Mikula is associated with Volga, who claims, in his turn, to hold his cities under Vladimir of Kiev. Further, the *byliny* devoted to Svyatogor, and more especially to Mikula, are, in general, much longer and more ambitious in form than the *byliny* of the class which we have just been discussing. They are, in form, identical with the *byliny* of the Kiev Cycle, sharing their scale, scope, literary style and conventions, and we have no doubt that for many centuries they have been recited in the same milieu.

Next we may refer to poems which relate to known historical events, and events which have the appearance of actuality. In such poems witchcraft, magic, sudden transformations and the usual stock-in-trade of folk-tales play hardly any part. Supernatural elements are absent except for exaggeration and an occasional tendency to overstep the natural limits of time and space, which rarely goes beyond what is commonly allowed in literary poetry to be poetic licence. A considerable body of poetry relating to individuals who are not named appears to have reference to the robbers and Cossacks of the Don and Volga,[1] and many poems are thought to have been composed in celebration and commemoration of rebellions, raids, and political executions, especially those of Stenka Razin and of the Streltsy in the seventeenth century, and of Pugachev in the eighteenth. Reference has been made above to the poem on the 'Execution of the Prince, the Great Boyar',[2] which is thought to have reference either to the son of Stenka Razin himself, who was executed at Moscow in the Red Square in 1672, or to the execution of the leader of the rising of the Streltsy in 1679. In such cases we have little doubt that many of the characters whose names are not mentioned are actual historical characters. Sometimes we can be fairly certain as to their identity; sometimes the data are insufficient to allow of this.

An example of poetry of this class is summarised and partly translated by Ralston from Sakharov's collection. The original text has not been accessible to us, but the poem appears to be a narrative. It relates that a great boyar (Ralston suggests that this is probably a certain Prince Dolgoruki) starts from Moscow for the R. Don, boasting that he will hang all the Cossacks. They, suspecting his intention, meet together and form a great circle, in the midst of which the boyar takes his stand and reads to them the tsar's ukazes. When he mentions the tsar's royal titles the Cossacks all doff their caps, but the boyar omits to do so,

---

[1] See Ralston, *Songs*, p. 41.
[2] Kirêevski, VIII. p. 22; Chadwick, p. 264 f.

Thereupon they rose in commotion,
Flung themselves upon the Boyar,
Cut off his proud head,
And threw his white body into the quiet Don.[1]

Since the majority of such poems are very brief, and were, we may presume, composed in the first instance shortly after the events which they celebrate, the absence of proper names requires no explanation. On the other hand we have reason to suspect that in many cases the names were deliberately suppressed from motives of prudence. We have seen (p. 66 above) that in the 'Lament' which purports to be recited by the tsaritsa Evdokÿa Fedorovna Lopukhina, the first wife of Peter I, the name of the tsaritsa does not appear, though Peter's own name is mentioned at the close of the poem. The omission of the tsaritsa's name might be explained by the fact that the poem is a speech poem in the first person, and contains no narrative. On the other hand we know that after Peter had divorced his wife he issued a royal edict that her name must never be mentioned, and for a long time songs which contained her name were prohibited.[2] Even in songs composed on the death of General Lopukhin in 1757 in the war against Prussia, the popular singers frequently preferred to omit the name. We may well believe that the popular singers would hesitate to introduce the names of rebel heroes and others who had not found favour with the crown.

In Little Russia the poetic convention of referring to individuals under the guise of birds has proved a useful device for poems with a dangerous political significance. Ralston translates[3] a *khorovod*[4] song recorded by Tereshchenko from this region which illustrates this convention very well. The Russian text has not been accessible to us, and we are uncertain whether Ralston has translated the poem in its entirety. No proper names are mentioned, but a number of individuals are referred to under the guise of specific birds, from among whom the bullfinch is represented as choosing a bride. The poem appears to be a brief narrative poem as given by Ralston, but we are told that the song is sung during the dancing of the *khorovod*, and that the person representing the bullfinch wanders about inside the *khorovod*, seeking his bride among its members, who sing the song meanwhile. The song is said to

[1] Ralston, *Songs*, p. 42.
[2] Kirêevski, ix. p. 104 f. (Bezsonov's note).
[3] *Songs*, p. 12.
[4] The *khorovod* is a combination of song and circular dance. It was especially popular in Little Russia before the Revolution, but was also widespread in Great Russia. See Ralston, *Songs*, p. 2.

have been composed during the reign of Ivan the Terrible, and to have been prohibited for a time because it contained allusions to the life of a certain influential boyar. The convention of referring to people under the guise of birds is in origin, however, a poetic one, and was already ancient when we first meet it in the *Slovo o Polky Igorevê*.[1]

In poetry relating to unnamed people, as in the heroic *byliny*, the distinction between narrative poetry and poetry of Type B tends to be somewhat arbitrary, owing to the brevity of the former poems, and the tendency of poems of Type B to coalesce with them in form. The distinction may be said to disappear altogether when, as very often happens, the tense changes from past to present, or the whole episode is represented as taking place before our eyes. In such poems speeches generally play a large part. We may refer to the *bylina* on the 'Execution of the Prince, the Great Boyar', in which a proud youth walks up the road leading to the scaffold, followed by his weeping relatives, and proudly declines to humble himself before the tsar and ask for mercy.[2]

The following poem, recorded by Sakharov, relates undoubtedly to the labour enforced by Peter the Great in the construction of the Ladoga Canal—labour involving the transportation of large numbers of Russian peasants from their distant homes:

> At day-break, early, very, very early,
> At the peep of dawn,
> At the red sunrise,
> It is not geese, my brothers, or swans,
> Rising from the pools and lakes,
> It is noble youths arising,
> Noble youths, the free people,
> All the labourers of the lower river,
> On the canal of Ladoga,
> On the royal task.
> They are escorted, those noble youths,
> By fathers and mothers, and young wives,
> And with them their little children.[3]

---

[1] We may compare the description of the funeral ceremony of Ame-waka-hito, the 'Young Sky-Lord' in prehistoric Japan, as related in the early Japanese chronicle the *Nihongi*, in which various classes of birds are represented as taking the part of mourners and singing dirges. The editor cites the analogy of the Death of Cock Robin. See *Nihongi*, I. p. 65 f., *Chronicles of Japan* (English translation by W. G. Aston, London, 1896, 2 vols., published as a Supplement to Transactions and Proceedings of the Japan Society, London).

[2] Kirêevski, VIII. p. 22; Chadwick, p. 265.

[3] Glazunov, *R.N.L.* p. 70, no. 112.

In such poems as these the semblance of oral journalism which we noted in *byliny* relating to the seventeenth century, is very marked.

The commonest kind of poetry of Type B is folk-songs. These may be said, in general, to correspond to the narrative poems embodying folk-tales and folk-motifs. It will be noticed that many of them are composed in the form of a dialogue. The best examples approximate to such Anglo-Saxon poems as *The Wife's Complaint* (cf. Vol. I. p. 425).

> "Do not sit, my beloved, late into the evening,
> Nor burn the candle of pure wax,
> Nor linger for me till midnight.
> Alas, have they departed, departed, our bright days?
> Has the rough wind carried away our joys,
> And sown them broadcast over the open plain?
> My dear father has willed it,
> My dear mother has bidden me
> That I should marry another wife!
> Two suns do not blaze in the heavens,
> Nor two moons shine,
> One cannot twice love a fair maiden.
> Yet will I not disregard my father;
> My dear mother I will obey,
> I will wed another wife,
> Another wife, an early death,
> An early death and violent!"
> The fair maid shed bitter tears,
> And through her tears she cried;
> "Alas, my darling, my beloved!
> I cannot live in the white world
> Without thee, my hope!
> The dove does not mate with two doves,
> Or the swan with two swans.
> I cannot take to myself two lovers!"
> The candle of pure wax is burning,
> On the table lies a new coffin of deal,
> In the coffin lies the fair maiden.[1]

The following little dialogue is a typical folk-song. The opening lines belong to the conventional openings of poems of Type D:

> "Pear-tree, my pear-tree,
> My green pear-tree!
> Why art thou sad?

[1] Dormidontov, p. 235. For the opening formula, cf. also Glazunov, *R.N.L.* p. 59, no. 96.

Wert thou not planted in spring-time,
Hast thou not been watered,
Or hast thou not been sheltered?
Beautiful maiden, my darling,
Dost thou love me, my joy?"
"How, dear one, could I do other than love thee", etc.[1]

So also the following:

O thou, my grass,
My silky grass!
In springtime didst thou grow,
In summer didst thou mature,
In autumn, O grass,
Didst thou begin to wither,—
Thy dearly beloved
Didst thou begin to forget;
His beloved he has made to pine and grieve,
His heart has grown cold,
And he has driven me
Out of my wits.[2]

To judge from their form these poems might have been composed by a
professional *voplenitsa* as part of wooing and funeral ceremonies (cf.
p. 286 below).

Many of the short lyrical poems recorded by Sakharov and Shein are
speech poems introduced by a few lines of narrative, like the Anglo-
Saxon poem, *The Wanderer*. We may give as an example the following
poem recorded by Shein:

It is not a falcon flying through the air,
It is not a falcon shedding its grey plumage,
It is a youth speeding along the road,
And shedding bitter tears from his bright eyes.
He has bidden farewell to his country,
To his native country on the lower river,
Where it flows into fair mother Volga;
He has bidden farewell to a fair maiden;
He has left her, as a reminder of himself,
A precious jewelled ring,
And has taken in exchange from the fair maiden
A gold wedding-ring.
When they exchanged them he addressed her:
"Do not forget me, my darling,
Do not forget me, my heart's dearest,

[1] Dormidontov, p. 234 (1).   [2] *Ib.* p. 235 (2).

> Gaze often upon my ring,
> And often will I kiss thy wedding ring,
> Pressing it to my eager heart,
> In remembrance of thee, my beloved.
> When I think of another love
> May the gold wedding ring break;
> If thou weddest another
> May the stone fall out of the jewelled ring."[1]

It will be observed that the form and diction are in the direct tradition of the heroic *byliny*. Even in the following example, which has reference to a peasant girl, the same tradition prevails:

> When to the bubbling spring,
> To the cool well,
> A noble youth rode up,
> A fair maiden was drawing water,
> She drew her water and set it down;
> And having set it down she grew wistful,
> And growing wistful she began to weep,
> And weeping she uttered a word:
> "Well is it for him who lives in the world
> Having father and mother,
> Father and mother, brother and sister,
> Brother and sister, alas! his dear family.
> Whereas I, a fair maiden,
> No father have I, nor mother,
> No brother, nor dear sister,
> No sister, nor dear family,
> No friends whom I can love."[2]

Examples of poetry of this class abound in the collections of Russian oral poetry. For a recent collection the reader is referred to the new issue of Kirêevski's collection *Pêsni Neobryadovÿe* (Moscow, 1929). Throughout these poems, as in Type B elsewhere, feminine interest preponderates over masculine.

Much of the poetry of Type B, like the narrative poetry already referred to, appears to have reference to historical events. We may cite the little poem on Prince Vasili in Kirêevski's collection.[3] The poem opens with five lines of narrative in which we are told that Prince Vasili was drowned in the blue sea 'through the weight of his gold crown', the remainder of the poem consisting of the speeches of his widow. The identity of Prince Vasili is unknown.

[1] Glazunov, *R.N.L.* p. 58.   [2] *Ib.* p. 56.
[3] Kirêevski, v. p. 66; Chadwick, p. 182 f.

In many cases the proper names have not been recorded because they were of no great importance, though the poems nevertheless may well refer to an actual occasion which has taken place in the past. We may refer to the following address of a dying man, probably a Cossack, to his companions, recorded by Aristov:

> Ah, my brothers and comrades,
> Take me, brothers, by the white hands,
> Raise me up, brothers, on my nimble feet,
> Lead me into the Church of God,
> Give me Communion, brothers, and shrive me;
> Place me in a coach,
> Bear me forth, brothers, into the open plain,
> Into the open plain, into the broad open space,
> Lay me, brothers, where three roads meet,
> At my head erect the life-giving cross.[1]

We may mention also a poem recorded by Rybnikov[2] in the Government of Archangel which has reference to the recruiting officers who go to fetch the widow's only son. We are told, however, that the poem is commonly recited by the relatives of the young soldier leaving his home for the army, and is thus actually recited as a lament, amid tears and sobs.

Some of the finest examples of poetry of this Type consist of poems which, like certain of the narrative poems, have reference to a definite event, but of which the proper names have been forgotten or suppressed for political reasons. As examples we may refer to the poem in which a boyar is represented as addressing his own head as he awaits execution on the scaffold.[3] The poem is thought to have been inspired by the executions following upon the revolt of the *streltsy*, the old Muscovite palace guard, which took place during the foreign tour of Peter the Great between 1697–8. Such poems do not, however, differ essentially from such *byliny* as the 'Lament of Ksenÿa' referred to above, save that accident has put us in possession of the identity of the speaker of the latter poem.

Since all these poems, whether of Type A or B, are brief, it naturally follows that the time covered by the action will be short. Speeches form a large proportion of poetry of this kind. Indeed it would be safe to say that the speech far outweighs the narrative portions, and the first person

---

[1] Glazunov, *R.N.L.* p. 74, no. 119.
[2] III. p. 158.
[3] Kirêevski, VIII. p. 24; Chadwick, p. 267 f.

is the one most commonly used. Static epithets are universal, but they appear to be of a simple type and narrow range. They are in general identical with those of heroic poetry, e.g. 'stone-built Moscow', 'bright moon', 'damp earth', 'green wine', 'mighty beer', 'bright eyes', 'brave youths', 'red sun', 'green garden'. Rhetorical repetitions also frequently occur, especially where the poet wishes to lead up to a climax. The figures, similes, especially such as are drawn from nature, and the metaphors of heroic poetry, the curious use of *ne* to form comparisons or strong contrasts, the invocations and adjurations to nature, and the artistic use of the 'pathetic fallacy', are all introduced here as freely and effectively as in the *byliny*. Elaborate figures of speech are as common and as well sustained as in heroic poetry. We may instance the habit of referring to ladies as 'white swans', or 'cuckoos', to boys as 'falcons', to parents as 'suns'. The figure is often sustained through several lines. We know of no more elaborate metaphor in the heroic poems than that of the following extract from one of the Cossack songs recorded by Sakharov:

> Beyond the glorious river Utva,
> In the Utvinsk hills,
> In a broad valley,
> A cornfield was ploughed.
> Not with a plough was the cornfield ploughed, whether of steel or wood,
> But with the keen spears of the Tatar princes.
> Not with a harrow was the field harrowed,
> But with the swift feet of horses.
> Not with rye, nor with wheat, was the field sown,
> But that cornfield was sown
> With the rebellious heads of Cossacks.
> Not with rain was it watered,
> Not with heavy autumn showers—
> The field was watered
> With scalding tears of Cossacks.[1]

With the figure sustained throughout this passage we may compare that of the *Slovo*, l. 583 ff.

In Vol. 1, Type E (personal and occasional poetry) was found only in a later phase of intellectual development than that which is represented in the oral poetry of Great Russia today. It might be argued that much of this Russian poetry is the village equivalent of Type E, and that it expresses the opinions and emotions of persons of the peasant class as

[1] Glazunov, *R.N.L.* p. 68 f.

faithfully as the poetry of Type E treated in Vol. I reflects those of more advanced and educated persons. This is true enough; but there is a difference. In the Russian peasant poetry the form is stereotyped and conventional. In general the original element in any given poem of this class is comparatively slight. Such poems might be called 'pattern poems', or mosaics. They are, in fact, the poems of a class rather than of an individual. And this is equally true of the poems of Types D and B which relate to domestic life and social functions. Whether the laments and other poems of domestic life are composed by the principals and reciters on their own behalf, or whether they are composed for them by a more gifted friend, or relative, or professional composer, the form, style, and, in general, the content of the poem varies only within a strictly limited range, dictated by tradition.

That the custom of composing personal and occasional poetry is very widespread in Russia there can be no doubt. On the subject of the extempore composition of personal poetry, the English traveller Coxe made some interesting observations in the latter half of the eighteenth century. He tells us that the peasants frequently compose extempore songs relating to their past experiences or their present situation, among other subjects, even chanting, in dialogue with one another, their ordinary conversations. The account is given in his own words more fully on p. 285 below. It may, however, be doubted whether many of these informal personal compositions survive a single recitation, or whether such poetry ever passes beyond the limits set to its form, diction, or sentiments by well established tradition. We have, of course, in Russia as elsewhere, vast quantities of personal poetry which have reference to individuals and occasions in private life which are in no sense social functions, but the poems in which these individuals express themselves are none the less stereotyped and objective.

The most interesting body of poetry in this category is undoubtedly that which is connected with social ritual (Type D). The conservative and conventional character of this social ritual has given rise in Russia to an equally conventional body of poetry, celebrating, or more frequently lamenting, the various occasions of ceremonial gravity which occur in the life of individuals and communities. Much of this poetry is, as we have already remarked, composed by the individuals who recite it, while again much is composed by more gifted friends or relatives, or by professional composers, on their behalf. We are singularly fortunate in possessing a considerable amount of information relating to the circumstances under which this formal village poetry is composed in

Russia, but we must leave further discussion of these details till we come to our final chapter on 'The Popular Poet and Story-Teller'. Here we will confine ourselves to a few examples of the actual poetry belonging to this class.

We will first give examples of elegiac poetry, such as are recited at various stages in the ceremonial proceedings which follow upon a death in the Onega district. Rybnikov recorded a number of examples of dirges and laments which formed a part of the social ritual connected with the funeral practices of this area. He tells us[1] that in the backward and more conservative districts every woman can give expression to her grief in poetical form, either by composing a new *zaplachka* ('lament'), or by adapting one already in existence to the new circumstances. He records four examples from the recitation of a young woman of Pudoga, which, though cruder than the compositions of the professional *voplenitsa*, lit. 'mourner', see p. 286 f. below, yet retain enough of the original diction to convince us that even these personal and private dirges follow traditional lines. The first is a lament by a mother for a dead baby, consisting of forty-two lines:

> I must go in my sorrow
> To my own, my loved one,
> To my own heart's dearest...
> On such a day as this
> The sun does not burn as in the summer time,
> It does not warm as in the spring:
> I have suffered a heavy loss,
> I have let fall a great treasure—
> My own darling.
> To-day, this day,
> I will draw near, sad and weeping,
> To my own beloved:
> "Tell me, my dear one,
> Why have you deceived your mother,
> Your mother forlorn?
> I can get no answer,
> Not one secret word
> For my troubled heart.
> Hearken, my heart's dearest,
> My own, my darling baby"....

[1] Our information regarding the poetry of social ritual is largely derived from the Introduction to the first volume of Rybnikov's *Pésni*, and from his running commentary on the poetry of social ritual contained in the third volume of the same work.

> But I am indeed a mother forlorn:
> Like a cuckoo in the dark forest,
> Like one astray in the damp pine wood,
> I also am a sad waif.
> In my white hands
> The red gold has changed to copper,
> The silver to iron.[1]

The second is a slightly shorter lament for a dead mother, to be recited when the corpse is removed. The opening lines are recited by the whole family, the rest by her daughter, who laments in traditional archaic diction the privations and hardships which will befall the orphan, deprived of 'sugared foods'—the traditional phrase of the Kiev poems—and mocked at by all honest folk.[2] We may refer also to the translation of another of these orphan songs published by Ralston.[3] Elsewhere Ralston also gives laments of orphans which are recited at a later period than the dirge proper.[4]

The third song in the little group recited to Rybnikov by the woman of Pudoga is a brief lament by a wife for a dead husband,[5] and the fourth is a more ambitious lament of over seventy lines which was improvised by a young woman on the death of her first cousin. We shall have occasion to refer to this poem later. The concluding lines may be translated as follows:

> I feel blame and anger,
> Reproach and indignation,
> Against my own mother,
> Who did not send me, unhappy that I am,
> To the dear loved one,
> To my own cousin.
> I would have sat in grief
> By the bed of pain and sickness,
> I would have sadly besought
> My own cousin
> To speak to me in my sorrow,
> Though it were but one secret word;
> Then grieving I would have told it
> To my aunt, dearly beloved.
> Unhappy that I am, I would have given
> To swift, fleet-footed death
> Even my patterned robe.
> I would have laid aside my happy way of life,
> And all my golden treasure without stint,
> Rather than give up my cousin.[6]

---

[1] III. p. 122 f.   [2] *Ib.* p. 123 ff.   [3] *Songs*, p. 334 f.
[4] *Ib.* p. 293.   [5] III. p. 125.   [6] *Ib.* p. 126 f.

The following lament is composed to be recited by a widow of the poorer class after the body of her husband has been washed and dressed and laid on the table. As in the orphan's lament referred to above, the lament proper is prompted by a brief introduction in the form of a series of questions from the relatives. The whole is composed in an archaic form of diction which proves the form to be traditional, and probably ancient.

Turning to the widow the relatives ask her:

> Were you sitting by the bed of sickness,
> Were you present at the passing of the soul,
> When the soul passed from the white body?
> And in what guise did swift Death come to you?
> Did she come as a 'poor' one, a wandering *kalêka*,
> Or as a 'bold, brave, good youth',
> Or as a glorious workman from Petersburg?

If the deceased were a poor man, the widow (or the professional mourner on behalf of the widow) answers as follows:

> If I had been living amid riches and plenty,
> Then I should have been sitting by the bed of sickness,
> I should have seen swift death;
> If she had come as a wandering *kalêka*,
> I would have placed bread and salt upon the table,
> I would have fed the wandering *kalêka*,
> And she would have left me my wedded spouse;
> If she had come as a 'bold, brave, good youth',
> I would have clad her in a patterned robe,
> I would have shod her in kid boots,
> I would have given her a silken girdle;
> If she had come as a glorious workman from Petersburg,
> I would have bestowed on her countless golden treasure,
> And she would have left me my wedded spouse.
> But since I live in wretched and miserable conditions,
> My little children cause my heart great care:
> We have no bread and salt for the table,
> We have no sugared food,
> No fine clothes for a youth,
> Nor kid boots for the feet;
> We have no countless golden treasure.
> And so I did not see my wedded spouse
> When the soul passed from the white body.
> The peasant woman's labour is too great for her strength,
> Her wretched cares are too heavy for her to think on,
> And I have well-nigh lost my wits,
> And the light fades untimely from my eyes.

How shall I rear my dear little ones
Without my wedded spouse?
Shall I lose myself in the dark forest,
Or plunge into a little round lake,
Or drown myself in a swift current?
Where can I divest myself of my great misery?...
Split open, damp mother earth,
Open, O new coffin planks,
And come flying from heaven, angels and archangels,
And place the soul in the white breast,
And speech in the wise head,
And white light in the bright eyes.
Rise up again, my wedded spouse,
I have begged thee from the Lord God....
Assuredly it cannot come about
That a dead man should come back again from the grave.
I must be bereaved of my wedded spouse.[1]

Rybnikov also recorded a similar lament composed to be sung in well-to-do households.[2] Both poems are composed in the highly figurative style and diction with which we are already familiar from heroic poetry.

Further laments, known as *prichitanỹa*, composed in rhetorical, if not rhythmical prose, are recorded by Sakharov and by Tereshchenko. They are sung by relatives of the deceased, or by a professional mourner (cf. p. 286 below) beside the grave, as a part of the *pomniki*, 'commemoration' of the dead, a ceremony which takes place at some period subsequent to the funeral. Translations of two examples of these *prichitanỹa* are given by Ralston.[3]

The most important poetry of social ritual is that which is connected with the marriage ceremonies. Russian peasant weddings in the Onega district and other backward parts are accompanied by a long and elaborate ceremonial. They begin with the formal proposal, made by deputy, which is followed by the betrothal. Other ceremonies succeed one another rapidly. One of their most important features consists in the recitation of appropriate poems at each stage of the proceedings. These poems are sung by various persons taking part in the ceremonies—the *svath* or professional male matchmaker, the *svakha* or professional female matchmaker, the bride, the bridegroom, the *voplenitsa*[4] or mistress of ceremonies (who is often identical with the professional mourner of the funeral songs), the bride's mother, her girl friends, and

---

[1] Rybnikov, III. p. 115 ff. The complete poem is translated by Ralston, *Songs*, p. 338 ff.   [2] III. p. 118 ff.   [3] *Songs*, p. 343 f.
[4] The important rôle which she plays in Russian peasant weddings will be discussed later (p. 286 f. below).

others. The songs, though highly conventional and traditional in style, are largely extempore. Some are recited in solo, some in dialogue, some in chorus. A collection of such songs was recorded by Rybnikov[1] from the recitation of a *voplenitsa* in the Onega district, and Tereshchenko has devoted a whole volume of 618 pages to this subject, giving a detailed account of the marriage ceremonies in nine distinct Russian provinces.[2] A number of other examples of these wedding songs are also recorded by Sakharov and others from various parts of Russia. English translations of a few specimens have been made by Ralston,[3] who also devotes an admirable chapter to the ceremonial and wedding customs generally. The series of songs given by Rybnikov, which follow closely the ceremonial of one of these weddings, constitutes something very like a ritual drama.

The actual betrothal is generally negotiated by the matchmakers, and many of the songs purport to be sung by the bride, expressing her dismay at sight of their approach. Several of these songs are translated by Ralston from the collections of Tereshchenko, and a number are recorded by Rybnikov. In the first of Rybnikov's series[4] the bride appeals in turn to her father, her mother and her brothers; in another she implores her compassionate relatives to retain her, and use her as an outdoor servant in the garden, or barn, or threshing floor:

> I will be a trusty servant to you,
> I will be your faithful handmaid.[5]

A third poem in which the girl expresses her dismay at the arrival of the matchmakers opens in narrative form:

> It is not two crows who have flown together in the dark forest,
> Or two warriors who have met in the open plain,
> It is two matchmakers who have met together in my home,
> In the glorious honourable ikon corner.[6]
> The tall matchmaker is my sire,
> The second is a matchmaker from elsewhere;
> They have taken deep counsel together,
> They have lighted candles of pure wax,
> Before the wonder-working ikon.
> They have touched their bright eyes with the cross,
> They have struck hands on the bargain.[7]

[1] III. p. 6 ff. A large and valuable body of such poetry is published in various Russian collections. An English translation of a complete series, such as that recorded by Rybnikov, would be valuable.

[2] See Ralston, *Songs*, p. 263. The work of Tereshchenko has not been accessible to us.   [3] *Ib.* p. 262 ff.   [4] III. p. 6.   [5] *Ib. loc. cit.*

[6] Lit. 'the great corner', the place of honour, where the ikons are kept.

[7] *Ib.* p. 7 f.

Two days after the match is agreed upon comes the ceremony known as the *poruchenie* or *blagoslovenie*, 'betrothal'.[1] During the interval the future bride makes a round of visits among her relatives, attended by some ten or twenty of her unmarried friends, singing various songs and laments on her impending loss of liberty. The note of sadness and regret, even of violent grief, which was expressed in her opening songs, sung on the arrival of the matchmakers, is typical of all the songs sung by the bride, and many of those also which are sung by her friends. The songs sung on this round of visits are concerned chiefly with regret for the impending loss of girlhood and independence, and are full of gloomy foreboding for the future of the young bride, who will have to leave her father's dwelling and go to live in a distant part of the country with her husband's harsh relatives. The following is an example of one of these songs sung by a girl who laments that her mother is dead and will not be able to give her her blessing at the nuptials.

> There stands a green oak on a mountain;
> It is moving without wind,
> It is dripping without rain;
> Many are the sprays on the oak,
> Many the sprays and branches,
> Many the green sprays,
> Many the curly fronds;
> Only the damp oak
> Has no golden summit,
> No gilded finial,
> Such as would now be fitting,
> Now, on this occasion,
> Or in the golden Summer,
> Or in the generous Spring.
>
> Many, many are the kith and kin
> Of the maiden fair;
> Many are the relatives and kinsfolk,
> Many the dear friends,
> And the near neighbours;
> But the fair maiden
> Has no dear mother,
> Whom now she stands in need of—
> Now, on this occasion,
> For the great betrothal.
> I shall not lack food or drink,
> But I shall miss the blessing....

[1] Rybnikov, III. p. 14.

In a case where the girl has no mother and a father only, the company sing:

> Her father will bless her
> With her mother's cross.[1]

During various other formalities, such as visiting her husband's relatives in the *izba* or peasant's dwelling, which will be her home in the near future, the bride continues to chant her formal songs. Two days after the preliminary arrangements referred to above, the bridegroom and his friends come to the bride's house where the formal betrothal takes place. As the bride is led forward, her girl friends stand in a corner chanting *pripêvalnÿa pêsni*:

> You are going, my child, to marry
> A lovely fair maid;
> The maidens will sing songs for you,
> For you, sir, accompanying the bride.[2]

After the party have eaten bread and salt and drunk *vodka*, the *voplenitsa* chants a long poem[3] which opens with a prayer for blessing on the happy pair, but quickly passes into a mournful chant in the first person, as if the bride were herself lamenting the loss of all her girlhood's pleasures and freedom. Meanwhile the bride sits on a bench apart in feigned grief, while the women of her family lament over her, expressing regret at her departure into a family of strangers, after which the bride becomes somewhat more composed and sings yet a further lament (*zaplachka*) herself, beginning:

> I can not spare time to sit here at my leisure
> Talking and chatting:
> The time for mowing has come, and for hay-making,
> The season for work is here.[4]

Numerous points of ceremonial are observed in succession, each of which is accompanied by its appropriate chant sung by the bride, the *voplenitsa* and other members of the party.

Sometimes after the betrothal two or three *vecherinki* or 'evening parties' ('At Homes') take place, in which all the bride's relatives assemble, and the bride's unmarried friends sing songs of lamentation and consolation in her presence. On the last evening before the wedding her friends unplait and comb her hair and then replait it again, adorning it with ribbons; and during this process, or on the following morning,

---

[1] *Ib.* III. pp. 15, 128 f.   [2] *Ib.* III. p. 24.
[3] *Ib.* III. p. 25 ff.   [4] *Ib.* III. p. 34 f.

the bridegroom's brother or the *tysyatski* (i.e. the leader of the bride-groom's party) enters and bargains for the bride's plait, her *kosa*—the sign of her unmarried state. Meanwhile the bride again addresses her plait in mournful song. A great many of these *kosa*-songs have been preserved and have found their way into collections of popular poetry.[1] After the wedding ceremony, which takes place in the church, the young couple proceed to a feast at the house of the bridegroom's parents, when further ceremonies and poetical addresses take place, which continue again on the following day, and recur at intervals during the following weeks. Examples of this ceremonial poetry will be found translated by Ralston.[2]

From the literary point of view, among the most interesting aspects of this Russian peasant wedding poetry are its traditional archaic conventions, motifs, and diction. Although it is a common custom for the young couple to come together by meeting and taking a liking to one another at the *posidêlki*, or evening parties, or some other recognised social gatherings held among the young peasants on summer evenings out of doors, or on winter evenings in an *izba*, yet many of the songs imply that the bridegroom has never seen the bride's face until the betrothal. In this, as in other respects, we see not only the ancient traditional motifs in these Russian peasant wedding songs, but also the aristocratic milieu in which they originate, and which has never been modified in the diction of the poetry recited by the poorer classes on these occasions. Traces of the same aristocratic milieu are also to be found in the titles *knyaz*, 'prince', *knyazhna*, 'princess' (unmarried), *knyaginya*, 'princess' (married), under which the peasant bride and bridegroom of today are referred to; in the references to the great riches bestowed on the bride's father as the price of the bride—'towns with their suburbs, villages with their estates', when in reality a small sum of money is all that is paid; in the references to the great numbers accompanying the bridegroom, with a *tysyatski* (lit. chief over a thousand men)[3] at their head, the total number probably amounting only to ten or twenty of the bridegroom's personal friends.

The diction with which we are familiar from the heroic poems of the Kiev Cycle pervades these songs, which also employ the same metre.

---

[1] An example, translated into English, will be found in Ralston, *Songs*, p. 288.

[2] *Songs*, p. 262 ff., and *passim*.

[3] In Yugoslav heroic poems relating to weddings the bridegroom's party frequently consists of a thousand men. Instances may be found in Low, *The Ballads of Marko Kraljević*, pp. 64, 162, 170. But the bridegrooms are usually princes.

The bride refers to her brother as 'fair sun' (*krasnoe solnyshko*), 'bright falcon', etc., and her father tells the matchmaker that he has 'a daughter, a white swan'. Even in speeches which are recorded by Rybnikov in prose form, the heroic diction remains unchanged, striking a peculiarly artificial and exalted note. Thus the people who first come to woo the bride on behalf of the bridegroom—whether his parents, brothers, or professional matchmakers—always announce in the words of Vasilisa in the poem of Stavr in the Kiev Cycle that they have come 'on an honourable mission' (*za dobrym dêlom*), viz. 'to woo' (*za svatovstvom*).[1]

[1] Rybnikov, III. pp. 4 (footnote 2), 5.

CHAPTER XI

THE RECITATION AND COMPOSITION OF HEROIC POETRY AND SAGA

THE SKAZITELI

RUSSIAN oral poetry is of especial interest, not only for its vast compass, and for the long period of time covered by its subjects, and the early date to which some of the Cycles have reference, but also because it has continued as a living art down to our own time. New *byliny* were composed on contemporary events as late as the reign of Tsar Nicholas I, while in remote districts, notably in the region of the Great Lakes and in the Province of Archangel, the old *byliny* relating to ancient heroic themes are still recited today. It can hardly be claimed that the *byliny* represent an art which is actually in a flourishing condition, or that it is, or has been in modern times, the expression of a contemporary Heroic Age. The Heroic Age, or Heroic Ages, which, at different periods, have been enacted in different parts of the vast Empire, are all long past. The *byliny* composed in modern times represent a traditional form rather than a direct expression of heroic conditions.

In modern times the *byliny* are restricted to peasant circles in backward and remote districts, and this circumstance has inevitably affected their form, and made in some measure for disintegration and decay. The reciters, known as *skaziteli* (sing. *skazitel*), are among the poorest and most ignorant class of Russian peasantry. We have seen that this was not always so, and that even as late as the beginning of last century the *byliny* and the *stikhi*, like the Danish ballads in the sixteenth century, formed the entertainment of the country gentry and the official classes. It is clear from both the style and the internal evidence of the *byliny* themselves that they did not originate in a peasant milieu. It is only within the last hundred years that they have become restricted to peasant circles.

The great wealth of the *byliny*, and the peculiar interest which attaches to them as living traditional heroic poetry, invest their reciters with especial interest, and we are fortunate in possessing a rich store of reliable first-hand information in regard to the recitation of such poetry in Russia. Rybnikov and later collectors have left us much

circumstantial detail of the milieu in which he found the *byliny* recited.[1]
Rybnikov was an officer in the Russian Civil Service, a *chinovnik*,
stationed at Petrozavodsk on Lake Onega. He had reason to believe that
byliny relating to the ancient heroes of Russia were not wholly dead
among the peasants of the Olonets Government, the district which has
since come to be known among Russian scholars as the 'Iceland' of
Russian epic,[2] and when in 1860 he was ordered to obtain statistics in
that district on behalf of the Government, he was enabled to make per-
sistent enquiries for singers familiar with *byliny*. He constantly heard of
the great reputation of a travelling tailor known as 'the Bottle', who was
a famous singer of *byliny*, and whose work took him throughout the
whole of the trans-Onega district; but his efforts to find either 'the
Bottle' or other singers were unsuccessful for a long time. The peasants
feared and distrusted a *chinovnik*, and even in that backward region it
was not easy to come upon people who were actually familiar with poetry
of the kind he was seeking. Success came unexpectedly one day when
he and his companions were overtaken by a storm as they were crossing
Lake Onega in a crazy boat, and took refuge on an island. His account
of the romantic incident is as follows:

"On the island there was a smoky shelter, a shed, where in the summer
and autumn time, in calm, in contrary, and in stormy weather the people
take shelter at night. Round the wharf were many boats from the north
of the Onega, and the shelter was full of people to the point of over-
flowing. To speak the truth, it was excessively smelly and dirty, and
although it was very cold, I felt no desire to go in and rest. I lay down
on my bag beside the meagre wood fire, made some tea for myself over
the embers, drank it, and ate some of my travelling supply, and then
becoming warmed by the fire, I gradually fell asleep. I was awakened
by strange sounds. Up to now I had heard many songs and religious
poems, but such singing as this I had not heard. Vivacious, fantastic,
and gay, now it grew quicker, now it slowed down, and recalled by its

---

[1] The information in the following pages is largely drawn from Rybnikov's
own account of his experiences in north Russia in the neighbourhood of Lake
Onega, reprinted in the second edition of his *Pêsni*, I. p. lxi ff.; also from Gilferding's account of his own experiences, *Oneẓhskÿa Byliny*, Vol. I; from the
account of the recent expedition of the brothers Sokolov in the same region published in *R.É.S.* XII (1932); from Lyatski's brochure *Skaẓitel Ivan T. Ryabinin i ego
byliny*, 'The reciter Ivan T. Ryabinin and his byliny' (Moscow, 1895); and from
various other studies referred to in the following footnotes and the List of Abbreviations at the end of this Part.

[2] See Sokolov, *R.É.S.* XII (1932), p. 202; *Slavische Rundschau*, IV (1932), p. 466.

tune something very long ago, forgotten by our generation. For a long time I was unwilling to awaken, and listened to every word of the song—so happy was I to remain totally overpowered by this new sensation.

As I dozed, I could see that three paces from me some peasants were sitting, and an old man sat singing, with a bushy white beard and bright eyes and kindly expression of face. Squatting on his heels beside the dying fire, he turned first to one neighbour, then to another, and sang his song (*pêsn*), breaking off now and then with a smile. When the singer had finished he began to sing another. Then I made out that he was singing the *bylina* of 'Sadko the Merchant, the Rich Trader'. Needless to say I was on my feet in a moment, and prevailed upon the peasant to repeat his song, and wrote it down from his lips. I began to question him as to whether he did not know anything else. My new acquaintance, Leonti Bogdanovich from the village of Seredka, Kizhski district, promised to recite many *byliny* to me—of Dobrynya Nikitich, Ilya of Murom, Mikhailo Potyk Ivanovich, of the noble Vasili Buslaevich, of Khotenushka Bludovich, of the 'Forty and One Kalêki', of the hero Svyatogor; but he knew only incomplete versions, i.e. he could not complete the narratives. Consequently I wrote down in the end only such of his *byliny* as served to supplement other versions by their details, or such as offered wholly new matter. For the rest, on the first occasion I wrote down somewhat reluctantly and preferred to listen. In the course of time I listened to many rare *byliny*; I recollect ancient, superb melodies. The singers sang them with exquisite voices and masterly declamation, but to be perfectly honest, I never experienced again that fresh sensation which the wretched versions of the *byliny* conveyed to me, sung by the broken voice of old Leonti in Shuynavolok."[1]

Thirty years after Rybnikov had sat listening to old Leonti Bogdanovich on the island in Lake Onega, a lady was present in a crowded Olonets *izba* when the *Skazitel* Nikifor Prokhorov (nicknamed Utka), was reciting *byliny*, and she also has left us a rapid sketch of her impression of what took place:

"Utka coughed. Everybody became silent at once. He threw his head back and glanced round with a smile at those present, and seeing their impatient, eager, expectant expressions, he at once began to sing again. Little by little the face of the old singer changed; all its cunning disappeared, and it became childlike and naïve. Something inspired appeared in it; the dove-like eyes opened wide, and began to shine. Two

[1] Rybnikov, I. p. lxix f.

little shining tears sparkled in them; a flush overspread the swarthiness of his cheeks; occasionally his nervous throat twitched.

He lived with his beloved *bogatyri*; grieved in tears for the infirmity of Ilya of Murom, when he sat paralysed for thirty years, gloried with him in his triumph over Solovey the Robber. Sometimes he broke off of his own accord, interpolating his own remarks. All the people present lived with the heroes of the *byliny* too. At times an exclamation of wonder involuntarily escaped from one of them; at times the laughter of another resounded through the room. From one fell tears which he involuntarily brushed away from his lashes. Everybody sat without winking an eye while the singing was going on. Every sound of this monotonous but wonderfully gentle tune they loved."[1]

During the expedition of the Sokolovs to Olonets in 1928–9 they found the peasant singers of today no less devoted to their art, and they have left us memorable accounts of the performances of two singers in particular, the wealthy peasant Konashkov, and the destitute Yakushkov, the latter the greatest of all singers whose names are on the roll of honour as reciters of oral poetry. As soon as the Sokolovs heard Konashkov's recitation of the *bylina* of Stavr Godinovich they realised that they had found a man who knew and loved *byliny*, and one who had a fine voice and varied melody.

"He did not simply sing the *bylina*—he enjoyed it. Very often he interrupted the course of his recitation to introduce comments....In deep silence, quite entranced, we sat and wrote until one o'clock in the morning, as the night was a northern 'white', and no artificial light was necessary. Weary and contented we lay down on the floor to sleep, our sail-cloth covering serving as mattress. At three o'clock we were awakened by the impatient reciter. 'Stand up! we will sing some more *stariny*. Otherwise I must go on the lake.' We were on our legs in a minute. After we had drunk raspberry tea we again sat down to work. The old man did not go to the lake; and again we wrote until the depth of night."[2]

The Sokolovs invited Konashkov to come to meet Yakushkov, and induced the two artists to engage in friendly rivalry in singing their *byliny*—a singing contest which must have required great tact on the part of the directors of the function. Meanwhile the phonograph recorded, and the singers were afterwards enabled to hear the reproduction of their own rendering.

---

[1] Quoted by Lyatski, p. 11.   [2] *Slavische Rundschau*, IV (1932), p. 469.

"The reciters greeted one another.... The conversation soon turned on *byliny*. We began by recording a melody on the phonograph. Konashkov sang first. The record was an admirable success.

'Perfect! How it sings the melody! It gives a correct reproduction!' rejoiced Konashkov.

Yakushkov sang next. Whether he was excited, or whether the phonograph functioned badly—whatever the cause, the reproduction was very defective.

'Bad,' triumphed Konashkov; 'mine went quite smoothly.'

Yakushkov was silent.

Then we suggested that they should each in turn sing *byliny* on the same subject, so that we could make an exact comparison of texts and melodies.

Konashkov began by singing the *bylina* of Stavr Godinovich. He sang as was his wont, with his head slightly inclined towards the right, keeping an eye on us to watch what impression he was making.

Yakushkov listened in silence and very attentively. His eyes had a penetrating and sombre expression.

Konashkov came to an end.

Then Yakushkov began.

The strangely beautiful melody, and the masterly performance quite abashed his rival, who nevertheless shrugged his shoulders hastily over some details in the narrative of the *bylina* which he had just heard.

'I want to know whatever it is about? Now why is the terrible tsar here and Nastasya there? It is supposed to be dealing with Stavr!' He turned to us with a deprecating wave of the hand.

'It is quite wrong. I don't understand it.'

Yakushkov was manifestly taken aback by this remark. 'Perhaps I have made a mistake,' said he guiltily.

The conversation turned on another *bylina*.

'I know a *starina* which takes me a whole half day to sing,' exclaimed Yakushkov. 'Do you know the *bylina* of Ilya and Mikhailo Potyk?—Where Mikhailo went down under the earth?' We decided, however, that it would be better to omit *byliny* of such length from the competition. We agreed on the romantic *bylina* of Churilo and Katerina.

Again Konashkov sang first. He sang interestingly and smoothly, but to a monotonous tune.

'I will take it in hand,' said Yakushkov eagerly.

And he rendered this strange *bylina* in a loud voice and with an extremely vivacious, varied and original melody.

Konashkov saw himself beaten. He began to carp at certain words. 'You make the counterpane of silk, whereas I make it of sables. I call the old man Velma Grigorevich; what about you?'

'Pah', Yakushkov cut him short; 'everyone sings after his own fashion.'

Konashkov was mollified and they came to an agreement.... '*Byliny* are sung variously.'

In spite of all his ambition and rivalry, Konashkov listened to Yakushkov's performance with pleasure. Although he was several times called home to dinner, yet he did not go until he had heard the *bylina* of Dobrynya and the Dragon to the end.

'I must get hold of the *starina* and the tune.'

Finally when he was obliged to go he again turned back almost immediately to say to Yakushkov: 'Sing them the poorest ones in the meantime, and wait with the best until I come back.'

The competition between the two reciters was taken up afresh later, and for a long time they spread their treasures before us, and although there was no doubt which of the two was the greater artist, we listened to their performance with the same absorption."[1]

The *byliny* are generally sung, or rather recited, in a kind of recitative, wherever the peasants are gathered together—in inns, round camp fires, in one another's huts. They are frequently sung in Olonets in an *izba* or peasant's wooden hut, crowded with eager listeners, who sit about on the bedstead, the wooden benches, the table, indeed wherever they can find room. No instrument is in use in Olonets, though in Perm, in the southern Urals, as well as in Simbirsk and elsewhere, the *byliny* are sung to the accompaniment of the *balalaika* and other stringed instruments.[2] The singers of Olonets are called *skaziteli*, i.e. lit. 'story-tellers', 'narrators'; but the tradition of musical accompaniment is clearly indicated in the current expression 'to sing (*pêt*) a *bylina*'.

In general few tunes are known to any singer. The elder Ryabinin, one of the best of the singers of *byliny*, knew only two tunes; another of the best singers, Kuzma Romanov, knew only three; 'the Bottle', another good singer, knew only one.[3] Yakushkov, the greatest of all singers of *byliny*, however, had a different tune to almost every *bylina*,

---

[1] *Slavische Rundschau*, IV (1932), p. 475 ff.

[2] The article of Delange and Malherbe in Lavignac's *Encyclopédie de la Musique*, Vol. V, part 1, p. 2486 ff., contains some interesting notes and pictures of the musical instruments.

[3] Rybnikov, I. p. xciii.

and he recited 37 to Sokolov in 1928–9. Lyatski, writing in 1895, says that musical specialists who had listened to the younger Ryabinin, had not succeeded in obtaining any reliable versions of the tunes.[1] Specimens of these tunes, so far as they are capable of notation by our modern system of scales, were recorded by Kirsha Danilov,[2] and, more recently, by Lyatski himself.[3] In our own time, however, the phonograph records taken by the brothers Sokolov should form the basis for a scientific analysis in the future. Undoubtedly the tunes retain some earlier system of scales than that which is in general modern use.

The tunes are said to be in general very monotonous. Speaking of the reciters of Olonets, Mazon tells us that "Le chanteur...chante d'une voix lente, souvent un peu traînante, à la manière rituelle d'un chantre d'église; la mélodie, d'une grande simplicité et infiniment monotone, donne une impression d'antiquité saisissante: on s'imagine reporté à quelques siècles en arrière."[4] Nevertheless there is a considerable amount of variation in the rendering of the tunes. Rybnikov found that the same musical theme was very bright if accompanying the story of Stavr, melancholy for Mikhailo Potyk, solemn for Volga and Mikula.[5] The elder Ryabinin held that the *bylina* of Stavr must be chanted rather heavily (*tolshche*), that of Mikhailo Potyk lightly (*tonshe*). Kuzma Romanov is said to have sung on three notes only, yet the vibrations of his voice enabled him to vary his singing to an astonishing extent.[6]

The singers of the Olonets district, both men (*skaziteli*) and women (*skazitelnitsy*), are mostly peasants, but it is interesting to observe that they are not as a rule primarily agriculturists. They belong for the most part to the artizan class, and are occupied in net-making, fishing, inn-keeping, tailoring, etc. Gilferding gives the people's own explanation of this fact:

"The peasants themselves explained to me that, sitting for a long time in one spot at monotonous work sewing or plaiting nets, they felt a wish to sing *stariny*; and they then easily mastered them. On the other hand the *krestyanstvo* (i.e. agriculture) and other heavy work not only does not allow time for this, but it deadens in the memory even what they have committed to memory and sung in the past. For the rest, the

[1] Lyatski, p. 25 f.
[2] *Sbornik*, ed. Sheffer (St Petersburg, 1901), *passim*.
[3] Lyatski, *ad fin*.   [4] See Mazon, *Bylines*, p. 682.
[5] Rybnikov, i. p. xciii.
[6] At the present day the Carmelite nuns in our own country sing only on four notes. Yet no sense of monotony is felt by the listener, and the music seems infinitely varied.

reader must bear in mind that the arts of which I speak are by no means the only ones practised by those who sing *byliny*. Each of them is at times an agriculturist, and works in summer at his peasant farming. The difference is merely that in their spare time in winter they busy themselves with such arts as are favourable to the preservation of epic poems, while the practice of others, and especially of hunting, forest labour, carting, etc. does not allow leisure for rhapsody."[1]

The peasants, however, are not the only people who sing *byliny*. Gilferding says further:

"They told me that the wife of the priest of the place, a worthy person,...was a native of the place, and she and her sister, having been forbidden by their father, a very strict man, to sing Christmas and dancing songs, had learnt *byliny* from an old peasant tailor, to pass the time."[2]

She still remembered many of these *byliny* in later life and recited them to Gilferding.

On the other hand the internal evidence of the *byliny* is overwhelmingly in favour of the belief that they circulated in early times in a wealthy and, in some degree at least, an aristocratic milieu. Much of this evidence has already been considered in the chapter on the heroic milieu, where it has been shown that the minstrel presupposes in his audience aristocratic tastes, and familiarity with a life of luxury and leisure. We may refer once more to the frequency with which the *byliny* open with a great feast, and details of rich food and drink. We shall presently have occasion to refer also to one or two of the instances in which the poet addresses his audience directly, and from which we may deduce some definite facts regarding both the minstrel himself, and the audience before whom these particular versions were recited.

It is not easy to draw a clear distinction between the author and the reciter of a *bylina* today.[3] Each recitation is, in some measure, a creative work. Gilferding observed that among the peasants of Lake Onega a singer never sang a *bylina* twice alike.[4] He tells us that in general the speeches of the heroes are remembered and transmitted verbally, and these vary less. On the other hand the narrative is not remembered by heart, but reconstituted afresh with each recitation from the singer's fund of epic material. In neither respect is usage consistent

---

[1] Gilferding, I. p. 18.
[2] *Ib.* p. 19 f.
[3] Rybnikov, I. p. xciv ff.
[4] Gilferding, I. p. 32.

however. The *bylina* of Volga, as recited by Kuzma Romanov to Rybnikov, consists of 187 lines, whereas the same *bylina* recited by the same singer to Gilferding consists of 206 lines, more than half the difference being accounted for by variation in the speeches contained in the poems.[1] On the whole, however, the two *byliny* differ surprisingly little considering the period of time which had elapsed between the two recitations. On the other hand the text of the *bylina* of 'Volga and Mikula' as recited to Rybnikov by the elder Ryabinin varies considerably from the same *bylina* recited by the same singer to Gilferding.[2] When Konashkov asked Yakushkov why he sang some *byliny* with different details from himself, Yakushkov replied: 'Everyone sings after his own fashion.'[3]

The poetry of the *skaziteli* of north Russia is, indeed, of particular value to students of oral poetry as representing a stage intermediate between exact verbal tradition and extempore composition. The reciters are not creative poets in the strict sense of the term. Yet extempore composition is widely practised. The artistic process in the mind of the singer, and the large extempore element in his performance are greatly facilitated by the conventional character of the poetry. We have already seen, both in the chapter on the '*Byliny*' and also in the chapter on 'The Texts', that static adjectives, static formulae, and static phrases—the latter often of considerable length—are extensively used throughout the *byliny*. But the static elements are not confined to these features. They are equally evident in the actual incidents which form the very texture of the *byliny*. These consist of a limited range of incidents, themes and motifs, which recur constantly in varying combinations, like the tesserae of a mosaic. Thus the elder Ryabinin is said when reciting to have 'combined various ready-made motifs, and to have worked them up afresh, in one place heightening the colour, in another omitting one or two details.'[4]

The conventional character of the treatment as a whole has been carefully analysed by V. F. Miller in two papers on the composition and recitation of the *byliny*.[5] In addition to the purely verbal conventions and epic formulae, he points out that the entire narrative is composed

---

[1] Cf. Rybnikov, I. p. 258 ff. with Gilferding, II. p. 172 ff.
[2] Cf. Rybnikov, I. p. 10 ff. (Dormidontov, p. 219 ff.) with Gilferding, II. p. 5 ff. Rybnikov's version is translated by Chadwick, p. 44 ff.
[3] *Slavische Rundschau*, IV (1932), p. 476.
[4] Lyatski, p. 9; Gilferding, I. p. 32.
[5] *Ocherki*, III. p. 1 ff.

of a series of conventions, stock situations described in static terminology, which are introduced in various combinations. He further distinguishes local peculiarities in the conventions employed in the *byliny*, pointing to local schools of composition. He quotes as an instance a conventional opening which does not occur in a single *bylina* from Olonets in the collections of either Rybnikov or Gilferding, but which is found in the *byliny* from Simbirsk.[1]

The process of composition has been admirably described in the recent paper on *byliny* by Prof. Mazon to which we have referred already:

"La byline est comme une matière molle dont le chanteur, suivant sa personnalité, fait ce qu'il veut. Le chanteur est en quelque manière un improvisateur. Il dispose d'un sujet et d'un certain nombre d'épisodes et de formules typiques propres à ce sujet (par exemple, telle déclaration invariable du héros): c'est là le fond auquel il ne peut guère toucher, à moins qu'il n'emmêle deux sujets ou que, par confusion, il ne transporte un ou plusieurs épisodes d'un sujet à un autre, ou bien encore qu'il ne modifie, par son interprétation personnelle, le sens original d'un épisode. Mais à côté de ce fond presque immuable, il dispose aussi d'un arsenal de parties mobiles dont il use à sa guise: prélude (*pribautka*), entrée en matière (*zachin*), formules à épithètes d'une constance homérique, scènes toutes faites le héros selle son cheval, la mère donne sa bénédiction au héros qui s'en va, le héros lance une flèche, la rencontre d'une jeune fille, le salut du passant au héros, le même d'un festin, les vanteries après boire, etc., etc....L'art du chanteur se mesure, pour une bonne part, à l'usage qu'il sait faire des parties mobiles."[2]

The 'parties mobiles', as Mazon calls the stock situations which recur in various combinations in the *byliny*, have recently been made the subject of a study by V. Rzhiga, who shows that they are themselves subject to modification according to the milieu in which they are found. Thus the 'parties mobiles' and the static formulae of the *byliny* found in the collection of Kirsha Danilov, while they bear a general resemblance to those of the modern collections, yet differ in some interesting particulars. In Kirsha's collection the heroes not unfrequently drink hydromel from an aurochs horn—a feature borrowed from conditions of life in pre-Tatar Russia; whereas in the modern collections this feature occurs only once. Again, in Kirsha's versions the hero does not saddle his own steed; this duty is performed for him by his squire, and

[1] *Loc. cit.* p. 155.
[2] Mazon, *Bylines*, p. 682, cf. also Lyatski, p. 9; Gilferding, 1. p. 32.

the fact is, in general, briefly noted. In the modern versions, which have been affected in this, as in other matters, by the peasant milieu in which they now circulate, the hero generally performs this office for himself, and the reciter expends a wealth of detail on each stage of the process.[1]

Despite the conventional and static character of the *byliny*, there can be no doubt that the personality of the reciter colours to some extent the character of his narrative. A man of a passionate temperament is said to emphasise the warlike incidents and expressions, accompanying his recitation with great force and bravura of manner, while one of a gentler temperament tends to tone down the narrative. Gilferding tells us[2] that the *kalêka* Ivan Feponov, generally known as 'blind Ivan',[3] when reciting *byliny*, tended to give a religious colouring to his narratives, representing the heroes as constantly praying to God (cf. also p. 137 ff. above). Mazon,[4] citing Boris Sokolov, notes that "Tel chanteur...est si dévot que les héros de ses bylines n'entreprennent rien sans force signes de croix et pieuses inclinations; tel autre, pareillement dévot, farcit les bylines de mots d'église; tel autre, qui fut domestique en sa jeunesse, ne manque pas de faire s'arrêter ses héros dans l'anti-chambre; tel autre, qui est tailleur, fait sauter la tête d'Idolishche, le Païen, sous les coups d'Ilya 'comme le bouton d'un vêtement'". The personal element in the *byliny*, however, though undoubtedly present, is never in great evidence.

More important than the potential variation of a given *bylina* is its constant entity. But since the *byliny* differ in some degree with every fresh recitation, and since its potential variation is almost unlimited, this constant entity is very difficult to define. When we are told that Potap Antonov learnt his *byliny* from his grandfather, and the elder Ryabinin from Kokatin, what exactly are we to suppose that they learnt? Certainly not the exact words, nor the motifs, nor the exact order of events, for these are all variable. It was not even the story, for this also varies, not merely by omission and transposition of events, but also in their selection and combination. It would seem, then, that what one singer transmits to another is in the first place the *bylina* technique, and in the second, the sphere of action within which the hero's activity is confined, the group of activities to which he may be committed, the outstanding traits of character which he may exhibit, the milieu, in the narrower sense, as apart from the Cycle, to which he belongs. When a pupil has been initiated into this knowledge his equipment is complete. Established

---

[1] Rzhiga, *R.É.S.* XIII (1933), p. 213.   [2] See Gilferding, I. p. 32.
[3] *Ib.* p. 413.   [4] *Bylines*, p. 684.

tradition, contemporary practice, and his individual talent are hence-forth his only guides and his only checks. He will know certainly what his hero may not do, what episodes he may enact and those from which he is excluded; which heroes may come to his aid and which may fail him; how his hero may be expected to act, and the kind of remarks which he may make. He will know, in fact—and this is all important—the nucleus of the various stories associated with each of his heroes.

Gilferding, who probably heard a larger number of *byliny* of the early cycles in a shorter time than any other collector, was particularly struck by the extreme fidelity of the ancient traditions—traditions which had consistently preserved the typical features of each of the individual heroes, and the principal incidents of the stories with which each is associated; Churilo Plenkovich, Mikhailo Potyk, Dobrynya Nikitich, Alyosha Popovich, and the rest. Throughout the variant versions, and throughout the many stories in which they play their parts, they are rarely found, as we have observed already, to depart from their own particular characteristics or functions, or to encroach on one another's spheres.[1] It has already been pointed out that the poems contain frequent references to plants and animals unfamiliar to people living in the far north, e.g. the 'stout oaks', the 'aurochs'—an animal of the open grasslands of the south, extinct in modern times—the 'feather-grass' which is characteristic of the steppe, and which is referred to more appropriately in the early work, the *Slovo o Polky Igorevê*. Indeed the life described is that of the open steppe-lands of the south, and not of the northern forests, and these conservative features can only be due to the long and retentive memories of many generations of *skaziteli*.

Again, as we have seen (p. 122 above), words and phrases are fre-quently retained of which all meaning has been forgotten in the south, and which represent conditions of life long superseded anywhere. A particularly interesting example is the word *polenitsa*, which was long glossed incorrectly in dictionaries as 'giant', but which the peasants of the Onega district all know to mean a female warrior or amazon.[2] In matters of this kind the *byliny* are exceedingly conservative. Gilferding found that whenever he questioned either singer or audience about a word not in common use in their province, the answer which he in-variably received was: "So it is sung", "So the people of the past sang it, but we do not know what it means." Occasionally a *skazitel*, singing some poem of Prince Vladimir which was very disrespectful to him,

---

[1] Gilferding, I. p. 24 f.   [2] *Ib.* I. p. 30.

asked to be excused for this—"For we know ourselves that it is not right to speak in this way of a saint;[1] but what can we do? Our fathers sang it so, and we received it so from them."[2]

The poems vary greatly in length. In general, as we have seen, those which relate to the early period are longer than those of more modern date, and as we approach our own time the *byliny* grow briefer. Those of recent origin are generally comparatively short, the majority consisting of less than a hundred lines, though many, of course, are longer. On the other hand it is to be observed that great freedom is allowed in the recitation.[3] A poem as recited by one minstrel may consist of eleven hundred lines,[4] while another will recite what appears to be in nucleus the same poem in 100; or, more frequently, he will select only certain episodes from the many which relate to a given hero, and recombine them into a single briefer *bylina*. Very often a single episode constitutes a complete *bylina*.[5] The disparity in length between one *bylina* and another is often to be largely accounted for by the amount of repetition which they contain. Vsevolod Miller estimated that in the long *byliny* the repetitions constitute no less than a third of the whole.[6] Such liberal use of repetition must have been of the greatest assistance in extempore composition.

Gilferding made the interesting observation that the singers all over north Russia, and in particular around Lake Onega, were divided into two groups. In the villages to the west of the lake the poems were always longer, and the lines generally consisted of seven, eight, or nine feet (*stopy*; sing. *stopa*). In those to the north-east, repetitions and digressions were avoided. The poems were much shorter, and the lines generally consisted of five or six feet.[7] Within these groups he distinguished further schools with their own particular usages in diction and style, and their own vogues with regard to the choice of heroes to be

---

[1] A reference to Vladimir I, who was baptised in 988 and later canonised.

[2] Gilferding, I. p. 28.

[3] See Rybnikov, I. p. xciv f. An interesting instance of the free use made of the poetical material by the *skaʒitel* E. T. Ryabinin will be found on p. 9 ff. of the paper by Lyatski to which reference has already been made.

[4] See e.g. the text of the *bylina* on Dobrynya Nikitich as recited by Kalinin, Gilferding, I. p. 31 ff.

[5] See e.g. the text of the *bylina* relating the marriage of Dobrynya's wife during his absence, as recorded by Chukov ('the Bottle'), Rybnikov, I. p. 162 ff.

[6] See Mazon, *Bylines*, p. 683 f.

[7] Gilferding, I. p. 34 f.

celebrated.[1] Lyatski also points out that the singers of the Kizhsk 'school' (in particular the younger Ryabinin, Ivan T.) concentrated in their *byliny* on the outline of the narrative; those of the Tolvuisk 'school' (e.g. Kalinin) gave much attention to the details of the story, with full epic diction and picturesque colouring.[2] It is interesting to note that Russian scholars, such as Lyatski and others, who have made a close study of different singers and their technique, are of the opinion that liberal use of 'epic' features—epithets, similes, figurative speech, repetitions, etc.—are chiefly made use of by singers of defective memory in order to gain time for thought. Singers like the elder Ryabinin, who recall and follow unhesitatingly the outline of their narrative, have no need of such devices, and use them more sparingly.[3]

The Russian *skazitel* can vie with the best of the Yugoslav minstrels in the extent of their répertoires and the length of their recitals. The minstrels of our own day appear even to excel those of last century. The best of the earlier reciters, the elder Ryabinin, recited nineteen *byliny* to Gilferding, comprising in all more than 5000 lines. During the expedition of the Sokolov brothers to the Onega district in 1926–8, F. A. Konashkov also sang nineteen *byliny*, some of which were very long. The recitation of his *bylina* on Ilya Muromets lasted more than two hours. The finest répertoire on record, however, is that of Yakushkov, who, during the same expedition of the Sokolovs, sang thirty-seven *byliny*, consisting in all of some ten thousand lines.[4] He recited to the Sokolovs continuously for three days and nights, with only very brief pauses, and even at the end of this time they were convinced that his répertoire was not exhausted. His *bylina* of Mikhailo Potyk alone filled a whole half day. Yakushkov was also quite remarkable in the range of his tunes. As already stated, he sang almost every *bylina* to a different air.[5]

We know of no evidence which might lead us to suppose that the *skaziteli* of modern times ever compose poems on new subjects. Their répertoires seem to be restricted to subjects of past history, though they sometimes recite *byliny* which narrate comparatively recent events, and also *stikhi*.[6]

The *byliny* are all anonymous. We do not know the name of the author of a single *bylina*. There are no secular professional minstrels in north Russia. The communities are too poor to support such a class, especially in the Olonets district. Indeed there does not appear to be

[1] *Ib., op. cit.* p. 37 f.   [2] Lyatski, p. 22.
[3] *Ib.* p. 23.   [4] *Slavische Rundschau*, IV (1932), p. 468.
[5] *Ib.* pp. 471 ff.   [6] *Ib.* p. 473.

anywhere in Great Russia an extensive class of what we should call
secular professional minstrels, i.e. people who earn their living exclusively by minstrelsy. A high degree of specialisation exists, however,
and we have seen that certain singers enjoy a relatively high reputation.
Wherever Rybnikov went in his search for *byliny* in the Olonets
district, he heard of a singer called 'the Bottle' (cf. p. 239 above), who
travelled from district to district in pursuit of his trade as a travelling
tailor, and who was a famous singer of *byliny*.[1] From him Rybnikov
took down many *byliny*.[2] Among the great names of *skaziteli* we may
instance the elder (Trofim G.) and the younger (Ivan T.) Ryabinin,
father and son, and their descendants in our own generation; and
also Konashkov and Yakushkov from the same region; Tupitsyn the
Siberian; and Marya Krivopolênova from Archangel.[3]

Sometimes the reciters are blind. We may instance Ivan Feponov,
Kuzma Romanov and Petr Kornilov, from Olonets. Frequently the art
of singing *byliny* is handed on from father to son. Thus Ilya Elustafev
bequeathed his art and his répertoire to his son Iev, and he in turn to his
son Terenti Ievlev. Being himself something of a public entertainer
among the peasants, Ilya had other pupils as well as his own descendants.
Among them were Kuzma Romanov and Trofim (the 'elder') Ryabinin, who were two of the best singers of *byliny* when Rybnikov and
Gilferding visited Olonets. The last four generations of the Ryabinin
family have all been *skaziteli*—the fourth still reciting when Sokolov
visited Kizhi on Lake Onega in 1926-7.[4] Potap Antonov, an old man of
seventy, who also recited *byliny* in Pudoga to both Rybnikov and Gilferding, had learnt his *byliny* from his grandfather, who died at the age of
ninety-seven. His grandfather had learnt them from a blind *kalêka*,
Mina Efimov, who had travelled much and had been in Moscow, and it
was in Moscow, according to Antonov's account, that he had acquired
his *byliny*. This Mina enjoyed a great reputation for his wisdom.
Antonov remembered him in his childhood. He had died sixty years
previously.[5]

During the expedition of the brothers Yuri and Boris Sokolov to the
districts in which Rybnikov and Gilferding had collected their *byliny*
(that is to say, in the north-east of what was known at that time as the
Government of Olonets, but which now constitutes the autonomous
Soviet Republic of Carelia) they found that the region of Pudoga is

[1] Rybnikov, I. p. lvi.   [2] *Ib.* pp. lvi, lxxxiv, xci.
[3] Mazon, *Bylines*, p. 684.   [4] Sokolov, *R.É.S.* XII (1932), p. 203.
[5] Gilferding, I. p. 468.

today, as it was formerly, the chief refuge of the *byliny*. They attribute its present pre-eminence to the great *skaziteli* of the days of Rybnikov and Gilferding, who may be said to have established a 'school'. It is represented in our own day by a few great singers such as F. A. Konashkov, and more especially G. A. Yakushkov.[1] The latter died suddenly in 1929 at the age of sixty-nine, when he was preparing to assist Yuri Sokolov in a series of conferences in Paris, Berlin, and Prague. Konashkov recited in 1929 and 1930 in Moscow and Leningrad. The names of these singers, add the Sokolovs (to whom we are indebted for this information), may henceforward be inscribed in the history of the *byliny* in succession to those of the Ryabinins.[2]

Konashkov, an old man of seventy who is still alive, is a fisherman, and not badly off as things go in that district. He learnt his own *byliny* as a child from his grandfather and his uncle. He tells Sokolov that *byliny* have been sung in his family for 300 years, since the time of Ivan the Terrible. "They have been handed down from generation to generation." His grandfather and uncle were obviously very good reciters, for Konashkov declares that more than thirty fishermen used to collect in their *izba* to listen to their recitations.[3] Konashkov's own répertoire comprises not only *byliny*, but also wedding and ceremonial songs (cf. p. 287 below) and *stikhi*, and his skill in improvisation and knowledge of traditional practice make him greatly in demand on ceremonial occasions in the Russian peasant life of his district.

The greatest of all the *skaziteli* was Grigori Alekséevich Yakushkov. He was one of the poorest of men. His parents died early, and the child was cast adrift on the world very young. His *byliny* have an excellent pedigree, though it is not confined, like Konashkov's, to his own family. He was steeped in the love and knowledge of *byliny* himself, which even in his childhood had a great fascination for him. He attributed the singular riches of his répertoire chiefly to the fact that in his wanderings he had come into contact with the three best reciters in the Onega district, reciters famous in the collections of Rybnikov and Gilferding. His first teacher of *byliny* was his uncle on his mother's side, P. T. Antonov, whom Gilferding had known as an old man of 70. We have already seen that Antonov had learnt them from his centenarian grandfather, and he in his turn from the famous reciter, the blind *kalêka*

---

[1] Portraits of both these singers are given in the article by Boris Sokolov already cited: 'Zwei Bylinenrezitatoren', in *Slavische Rundschau*, IV (1932), p. 465 ff.

[2] 'À la Recherche des Bylines', *R.É.S.* XII (1932), p 212 f.

[3] *Slavische Rundschau*, IV (1932), p. 469.

Mina. Thus it is clear that Yakushkov's *byliny* go back to the beginning of the eighteenth century. As a child Yakushkov also learnt *byliny* from Nikifor Prokhorov, or Utka as he was called (cf. p. 240 f. above), a fine reciter who also lived to be close on a hundred years of age. "I filched money from my father," declared Yakushkov, "and took it to him so that he would sing for me." Finally he learnt a few *byliny* from Ivan Feponov the blind *kaléka*, who sang religious poems (*stikhi*) and *byliny* for alms. "He had a powerful voice." Yakushkov's comment on Feponov's voice is interesting because the exceptionally powerful voices of the *kaléki* are always emphasised in the *byliny*. It is also especially interesting to note that two of Yakushkov's three teachers sang for money, and that the *byliny* of two of his three teachers constituted the répertoires of *kaléki* (i.e. those of Antonov and Feponov).[1] It is not surprising that Yakushkov himself sang *stikhi* in addition to *byliny*, 'though unwillingly'.[2]

The singing of *byliny* is by no means confined to those who have made a special study of the art, however. Rybnikov observed that in many parts of the country round Lake Onega, every intelligent old man carried one or two *byliny* in his memory.[3] Gilferding found that almost all the peasants, including the women, knew some *byliny*.[4] During the recent visit of the Sokolov brothers to the same district they ascertained that during the sixty years which have elapsed since the visit of the pioneer collectors "les bylines, ou tout au moins certaines d'entre elles, sont devenues un bien plus largement commun, qui a cessé d'être l'apanage de quelques chanteurs forts de leur expérience et de leur maîtrise, et peu à peu, a passé à la foule. Le fait est confirmé par le nombre même des chanteurs qui a presque triplé". On the other hand they found that the number of subjects treated in the *byliny* had dwindled during the intervals, and, moreover, that the extent of the individual répertoires had become smaller. "Le genre de la byline a gagné en diffusion, mais sa vitalité productrice ne s'est pas accrue."[5]

The Sokolovs also ascertained[6] that the proportion of women reciters had greatly increased since Gilferding's researches were made. Gilferding recorded *byliny* from only nine women singers, whereas the Sokolovs recorded in 1926–8 from eighty-five. It is calculated that

---

[1] Feponov's own teacher of *byliny* was one Méshchaninov, a singer with an exceptionally fine répertoire consisting of some 70 *byliny*. (Rybnikov, II. p. 499.)

[2] *Slavische Rundschau, loc. cit.*   [3] I. p. ci.

[4] I. p. 18 f.; cf. Rybnikov, I. p. lxxii.

[5] Sokolov, *R.É.S.* XII (1932), p. 204.

[6] *Loc. cit.*

in Gilferding's time the proportion of women singers to men was eighteen per cent., as against sixty-three per cent. in 1926–8. It is to be remembered, however, in considering these figures, that Gilferding's reciters for the most part came to recite to him in his hut, whereas the recorders in the Sokolov expeditions travelled through the various villages, and visited the singers in their own homes. It seems to us that by this method the recent expedition would naturally increase the proportion of *byliny* recorded from women, since it would in general be more difficult for the women to leave their homes than the men; and those whose répertoires were confined to one or two *byliny* would hardly be likely to think it worth while to do so. The figures are therefore possibly somewhat misleading, though the proportion of women reciters may have increased to some extent; and this would seem to be borne out by the increase in the proportion of *babi stariny* recorded in 1926–8, and the decrease in the number of heroic *byliny*.

The custom with regard to payment varies greatly. Rybnikov observed that in the boat on Lake Onega the peasants gladly took turns to do Leonti's share of the rowing in order to persuade him to sing to them.[1] Indeed he noticed that where money was not offered the peasants generally took turns to do the singer's share of the labour in order to get a song from him. Sometimes payment was made in kind. Both Rybnikov and Gilferding found that money was frequently refused by some singers, whereas others demanded a fixed price of so much per song. Rybnikov found that in the country round Onega the *skaziteli* sang for the love of their art, in contradistinction to the *kalēki*, who sang as a profession and as a means of obtaining a livelihood.[2] Gilferding remarks that the only *skazitel* whom he met in north Russia who regarded himself as a professional singer was Kuzma Romanov, who set a price on his *byliny*.[3] It has already been stated, however, that Yakushkov used as a child to give money to Nikifor Prokhorov in order to induce him to sing *byliny* to him, and the same *skazitel* told Sokolov that the blind *kalēka*, Ivan Feponov, also sang *byliny* for alms, in addition to *stikhi*. This graded custom with regard to payment probably corresponded to the varying degrees of specialisation as much as to the financial circumstances of poet and audience. Those *skaziteli* whose poems had their price, such as Kuzma Romanov and Ilya Elustafev, and others already mentioned, still retain many of the characteristics of professional performers, though Ilya's chief source of livelihood was fishing.

[1] Rybnikov, I. p. lxxxix. [2] *Ib.* I. p. ci. Cf. also *ib.* p. lxxxix.
[3] Gilferding, I. p. 15.

The *byliny* are all carried on by oral tradition. There appears to be no evidence that any of the poems have been derived in the first instance from written sources, and scarcely any of the singers can read or write, nor can they refer to any known authors of the poems. They recite merely what they have heard from one another. Very rarely we hear that someone has formed a manuscript collection, but only as a mnemonic for himself. This was done by Kokatin, an innkeeper in St Petersburg, who taught Ryabinin some of his songs.

So far we have considered only the modern evidence relating to the recitation of the *byliny*. We have seen that in modern times the *byliny* are recited almost exclusively by peasants to a peasant audience. We have seen also that there is no evidence for supposing that the peasants ever compose the stories or themes of the *byliny*, though the act of recitation is always in some measure a creative process, and is inseparable from the art of extempore composition. This applies, of course, only to a *bylina* in what we may regard as its final stages. The nucleus of each *bylina*, from which the several variants derive their source, was composed in the past. The modern singer selects his theme from a circumscribed répertoire of known and approved motifs. The style of presentation alone varies. We know of no evidence for the composition of new themes relating to the past among the peasants who recite *byliny* in modern times. *Byliny* composed on modern themes are assimilated to the ancient tradition, fitted to the old framework, tricked out in the old heroic diction, often, as we have seen, with bizarre and even ludicrous results. But of the authorship of either the modern or the ancient *byliny*, or of the circumstances under which any *bylina* has been composed, we know absolutely nothing, either from the internal evidence of the *byliny* themselves or from external sources.

Taking into account the absence of creative ability among the peasant singers, combined with the elaborate and highly artificial diction of a strictly conventional character, and the rigidly conventional framework, we may be sure that we must look elsewhere, and among people of a more specialised training, for the original authors of the *byliny*. These features suggest, indeed, that the original *byliny* were composed by professional minstrels, and were transmitted to their present humble milieu in comparatively modern times. The evidence of the *byliny* themselves can teach us something as to the milieu in which they circulated in the past, though the value of literary evidence of this kind is particularly difficult to estimate, and is full of pitfalls. Historical sources also have something to tell us of the minstrels and entertainers of Russia from the sixteenth century onwards. From such evidence as we have, therefore, we will proceed to state what we can deduce as to the conditions in which the *byliny* have developed. Our conclusion, however, will at best be a balance of probabilities, and the results must be regarded as conjectural and provisional.

We will consider first the evidence of the *byliny* themselves. We are well aware, as we have said, of the danger of literary evidence of this kind, and if Prince Mirsky were correct in associating the style of the *byliny* with Byzantine models,[1] and in deriving their acquaintance with Kiev and Prince Vladimir from written sources,[2] it would not be easy to prove that the information furnished by the *byliny* relates to minstrelsy as it was actually practised on Russian soil. Yet even allowing, with Stasov, for the introduction of certain Oriental elements, and, with Mirsky, for the influence of Byzantine themes and style, the pictures which the *byliny* present are on the whole too much in accord with historical record and local conditions to be so lightly dismissed. With this subject we have already dealt and we will therefore pass on to a brief examination of the evidence which the *byliny* afford us as to their own history.

The *byliny* contain no references to authorship or to the composition of *byliny*, but they have several allusions to recitation and minstrelsy. None of the heroes of the so-called 'Early Cycle' are represented as practising minstrelsy, but a number of the heroes of the Kiev Cycle appear to have played the *gusli* and sung songs. At Kiev, as in Heorot in the Anglo-Saxon poem *Beowulf*, and in Scheria in the *Odyssey*, the feast is the favourite occasion for such recitations. When Dobrynya Nikitich disguises himself as a *skomorokh* (entertainer; see p. 261 below) and returns to Kiev, he sings to the accompaniment of the *gusli* at the wedding feast in which his own wife Nastasya is about to be married by Prince Vladimir's orders to Alyosha Popovich.

> He began to wander over the strings,
> He began to lift up his voice...
> And all who were at the feast sat still and grew silent,
> They sat and watched the *skomorokh*...
> And everyone at the table became pensive,
> And everyone listened to his playing...
> Such playing had never been heard in the world,
> In the white world, the like playing had never been known...

[1] *S.R.* III. p. 89.   [2] *Ib.* p. 78, footnote 1.

> Dobrynya played mournfully,
> Mournfully, softly,
> So that every one, even princes and boyars,
> Even those Russian heroes,
> They were all deceived:
> "Ah, young *skomorokh*, [said the Prince],
> For your glorious playing,
> For your sweet delights,
> Drink green wine without measure,
> Accept golden treasure untold."[1]

Dobrynya is further said to have sung beautiful tunes from overseas, to have touched the strings to airs from Kiev, Tsargrad (Constantinople) and Jerusalem; or, variously,

> He sang an air from Novgorod,
> A second he sang from Tsargrad,
> The third time he began to play,
> He related all his adventures.[2]

It will be remembered that Dobrynya, as envoy to Vladimir, was a great traveller. In the version of the *bylina* of Dobrynya and Vasili Kazimirov recited by the elder Ryabinin to Rybnikov, Dobrynya's sworn brother, Ivanushka Dubrovich, is shown to us playing on Dobrynya's *gusli* of maplewood with such skill that

> All the *igroki* at the feast grew silent,
> All the *skomorokhi* listened,
> Such minstrelsy had never been heard.[3]

In a similar scene in a *pobyvalshchina* of the Kiev Cycle,[4] Baldak Borisevich plays his horn to such effect that the Turkish sultan and all his followers are spellbound, and Baldak and his *druzhina* are enabled to overcome and slay them.

Stavr, the merchant (*gost*) from Chernigov, is an accomplished minstrel. His wife, who comes to Kiev disguised as an ambassador, says that her husband is 'an expert player on the *gusli* of maplewood'.[5] At the feast held by Prince Vladimir in honour of herself in her guise as ambassador, and of his other noble guests, she sits and sulks because no one plays on the *gusli* (cf. p. 262 below). It is, of course, her object to have her husband brought out of his prison into the assembly. Her

---

[1] Miller, *Ocherki*, I. p. 59 f. For parallel passages in other versions see the references in footnote 1.

[2] *Ib.* For references to parallel passages in other versions, see footnotes 2, 3.

[3] I. p. 56; cf. *ib.* p. 64.   [4] Afanasev, II. p. 567.

[5] Rybnikov, I. p. 210.

attitude, however, suggests that a guest would naturally feel dishonoured if no minstrel was present at the feast to entertain him. In the version recited by Chukov to Rybnikov,[1] when Stavr is at last brought forward and asked to play, we are told that "he began to play on the *gusli* of maplewood, he made merriment (*razveselilsya*)".[2] The phrase recalls the *veselÿe lyudi* or public entertainers of the Middle Ages, as we shall see presently.

The feast is not the only occasion for the display of heroic minstrelsy. Churilo Plenkovich, in his capacity of groom of the bed-chamber to Vladimir and the Princess Apraxya, is said to "sit beside the high pillow and play on his *gusli* of maplewood to divert Prince Vladimir, and Queen Apraxya more particularly".[3] Solovey Budimirovich, the rich merchant prince, who marries Vladimir's 'niece' Zabava Putyatichna, is also an accomplished minstrel, and practises his art both on sea and land.

> Solovey played on his resounding *gusli*,
> He tuned his strings in accord;
> He played and sang airs,
> He sang a song from Novgorod,
> And another he sang from Jerusalem,
> And all the little lilts from over the blue sea,
> The blue sea of Volhynia,
> From the Kadolski island,
> From the green headlands.[4]

It is interesting to note that neither Vladimir nor Apraxya are said to practise minstrelsy, nor, apparently, Dyuk Stepanovich, the prince's son, nor Alyosha the priest's son, nor Ilya of Murom, the 'peasant's son'. The heroes who practise minstrelsy all appear to have mercantile interests. Stavr is a merchant, and Solovey Budimirovich, and Churilo appears to be a merchant's son, since old Plenko his father is described as a *gost*, 'stranger', 'merchant'. Dobrynya's origin is not clear, but in at least one version (see p. 107 above) he is described as the son of a rich merchant of Ryazan. The evidence of the Kiev poems, slight though it is, seems to represent amateur minstrelsy as a polite accomplishment of the wealthy merchant class. Even Solovey the Robber, an accomplished musician in his own way, has his 'nest' above the high road traversed by merchants passing from Chernigov to Kiev.

Turning now from the Cycle of Kiev to that of Novgorod, we again find that both Sadko the rich merchant, and Vasili Buslaev the *tysyatski*

---

[1] *Loc. cit.*
[2] *Ib.*
[3] *Ib.* II. p. 463.
[4] *Ib.* p. 345.

or *posadnik*, (cf. p. 125 f. above) of this rich mercantile city are accomplished musicians. Vasili, who is reported to have been a well educated man who could read and write, was also well trained in church music. In the words of the *bylina* recorded by Kirsha Danilov,

> His dear mother sent him—
> The venerable widow Amelfa Timofeevna—
> She sent him to learn church singing,
> And he mastered the art of singing.
> And never had we had singing
> In glorious Novgorod
> To compare with that of Vasili Buslaev.[1]

We have already seen (p. 51 f. above) that in the versions of the *bylina* of Sadko, the rich merchant of Novgorod, recited by Sorokin to Rybnikov and Gilferding, Sadko is described in terms which leave no doubt that in early life he was a professional musician, a poor man who attended at feasts in Novgorod, entertaining the company by playing on the *gusli*, till the time came when he was no longer invited to the banquets. We have also seen how, when overtaken by a storm at sea, he descends into the waves on a golden chessboard with his *gusli* under his arm, and is able to entertain the tsar of the sea until St Nikolai appears and discourages him. The story suggests that perhaps Sadko's minstrelsy was a little out of date in busy Novgorod, but was welcomed by the more backward Finnish communities in the country districts round Lake Ilmen; but this, of course, cannot be pressed seriously. We have also seen (p. 53) that in a version recorded by Kirsha Danilov, Sadko is said to have been a stranger in Novgorod, and to have spent the early part of his life on the Volga; but this version knows nothing of him as a minstrel, though it emphasises his mercantile prosperity and wealth.

The evidence of the *byliny* themselves, therefore, suggests that in the past minstrelsy was largely cultivated and patronised by rich merchants and wealthy men. Such men may or may not have sometimes belonged to the princely class, but certainly were not necessarily of royal or even of noble blood. Such evidence does not prove that in this respect the *byliny* have preserved a faithful record of the state of minstrelsy in either ancient Kiev or Novgorod; but at least it is very probable that the tradition of minstrelsy which they embody reflects faithfully the custom or the current traditions of the period when the nucleus of our *byliny* assumed their present form.

References in the *byliny* to playing the *gusli* are practically confined

---

[1] Kirêevski, v. p. 14 f.

to the Cycles of Kiev and Novgorod. The later Cycles do not appear to recognise the instrument. It is a striking fact that the *bylina* of Kastryuk, which narrates the marriage of Ivan the Terrible to the Circassian princess, does not refer to minstrelsy or to the *gusli*, though in general this *bylina*, and in particular the description of the wedding feast, bears a close resemblance to those of the Kiev Cycle. On the other hand no reference is made in the Cycle of either Kiev or Novgorod to the recitation of *byliny* (*stariny*). Indeed practically nothing is told us of the nature of the songs sung. It would seem that either the words or the tunes—it is not clear which—are frequently foreign, and rarely local.

The only reference known to us which relates to the recitation of *byliny* (*pêsni*) occurs in a little *bylina* which relates to quite a different milieu, and has nothing in common with the Cycles of either Kiev or Novgorod. This *bylina* relates to a certain Prince Danilo, who is unknown elsewhere in the *byliny*, and who has been thought, on very slender evidence (cf. p. 57), to be identical with Prince Daniel of Galicia who was crowned in 1254. The prince, as we have seen, is represented as wandering through the streets and saying pretty things to the girls whom he meets. He invites them to sing him a *pêsn* (i.e. a popular song) 'about Ilya of Murom, or Egor the tsar's son, and other heroes'. They reply that they cannot sing *pêsni* on any of these heroes, but threaten to sing a scurrilous *pêsn* of which he himself is the subject.

This little *bylina* is of great interest. Ilya of Murom is the chief hero of the *byliny*, and Egor the tsar's son is no other than Egori Khrabry, George the Brave, the chief hero of the *stikhi*. The prince is asking the girls to sing him *byliny* or *stikhi*, and so far as we know this is the only reference in popular poetry—in oral tradition—to either. Its testimony, then, is of considerable importance. It suggests that the prince had reason to expect such songs, not from professional minstrels and *gusli* players, but from popular singers, of whom some at least are women.

In addition to the amateur and merchant minstrels, and the popular reciters already discussed, the *byliny* also contain a number of references to a class of professional performers, known as *skomorokhi*, to whom we have already referred. The origin of the word is unknown, but both the word itself, and the class of people to whom it refers, are thought to be of Byzantine origin. The *skomorokhi* were a confraternity of public entertainers, actors, wandering minstrels, dancers, singers, wrestlers and buffoons, who from the late Middle Ages onwards took an active and prominent part in Great Russia in all festivals, especially weddings, and feasts. They were not confined to Great Russia, however, but appear in White Russia as minstrels, in Poland as leaders of bears.[1]

As we have seen, the *skomorokhi* are referred to not infrequently in the *byliny* of Kiev and Novgorod, both under this title, and also under the terms *veselӗe lyudi* (lit. 'joyous people'), *dobrӗe molodtsy* ('bold youths', 'good companions'). Reference has already been made to the part played by Dobrynya Nikitich, disguised as a 'bold *skomorokh*', at the wedding feast of his own wife Nastasya. It is clear that the 'bold *skomorokh*' occupies a seat of honour and enjoys a high status. We have seen also that *skomorokhi* and *igroki* (lit. 'players', sc. on the *gusli*) are also referred to in Ryabinin's version of the *bylina* of Dobrynya and Vasili Kazimirov, where they are said to grow silent with admiration at the minstrelsy of Ivanushka Dubrovich.

In Kirsha Danilov's version of the *bylina* of Stavr,[2] the hero's wife, disguised as an envoy, asks Prince Vladimir the following question:

> How, Prince Vladimir, do you amuse yourselves in Kiev?
> Have you 'joyous youths' (*veselӗe molodtsy*)?

Prince Vladimir then sends to seek on all hands for such people, and "collected the *veselӗe lyudi* in the prince's palace". Then he makes a joyous feast to entertain the great folk, but the ambassador sits joyless, saying to the prince: "Have you no one to play the *gusli*?" Then it is that Prince Vladimir sends for Stavr 'the *boyarin*', the *gost* from Chernigov.

The *skomorokhi* are also referred to in Kirsha Danilov's version of the *bylina* of Vasili Buslaev.[3] The hero, as we have seen, is trained by his mother to sing in a church choir; but although he appears to respond readily to the discipline of the training, the poet immediately passes on to tell us that he joined a band of drunken *veselӗe lyudi*, his qualification being presumably his voice. We are not expressly told the subjects of their songs, but from the subsequent conduct of the troop we may assume that they were not ecclesiastical in character.

In the *bylina* of Terenti Gost, 'Terence the Merchant', the *skomorokhi* are represented as roaming in a band about the streets of Novgorod, apparently in search of someone who will give them employment. They take an active part in Terence's domestic affairs, revealing to him the infidelity of his young wife. To this end they are shown to us arriving at Terence's house, where his young wife lies in bed with her paramour, but feigning sickness. They are invited to come in and sit together on a

[1] Mazon, *Bylines*, p. 686.
[2] Sheffer, p. 55.   [3] *Ib.* p. 391.

bench in the hall and sing to the accompaniment of the *gusli*. In this instance their song is extempore and topical, and consists of an address to the deluded husband whom they have hidden in a great muff, and to whom they quote in their song the disparaging terms in which he is referred to by his young wife. The *bylina* shows the *skomorokhi* as quick-witted and accomplished rogues, well practised in an art which is nevertheless not of a very high order. Their song is referred to as a *pêsn*.

In the *bylina* of Kastryuk, wrestlers are called in to provide the principal part of the entertainment at the marriage banquet of the tsar Ivan the Terrible. It is generally assumed by scholars that these wrestlers are *skomorokhi*, though the identification seems to us somewhat uncertain. It is doubtless due to the terms *bortsy*, *dobrÿe molodtsy*, by which they are referred to. In one version of this *bylina*, however, recited to Rybnikov in Pudoga,[1] an actual *skomorokh* is referred to as playing the part of messenger (*posol*) and announcing the approach of the bridal party.

From these references it would seem that according to the evidence of the *byliny*, alongside the wealthy amateur minstrel there were also guilds or associations of professional performers. These men were also minstrels, players on the *gusli*, accomplished musicians. Their répertoire may be supposed to have been identical with that of the wealthy amateur, since Dobrynya could so readily assume the rôle. Like the amateurs also (e.g. Dobrynya, Ivanushka Dubrovich, Stavr) they give performances at feasts. They appear to have been held in high esteem, and to have enjoyed an honourable status, and they are represented as mixing as equals with the members of the court of Kiev. Here again we need not assume that their order reaches back to the period to which the *byliny* refer; but here again we may be sure that they reflect conditions at least as early as the period of the original composition of the *byliny*.

It will have been observed that the internal evidence of the *byliny* relating to the *skomorokhi* overlaps to a considerable extent with that of the minstrel heroes. Dobrynya plays in the guise of a *skomorokh*, and Ivanushka Dubrovich and Stavr play in the presence of, or in emulation of, *skomorokhi*. Vasili Buslaev—the educated singer—appears to identify himself with the *veselÿe lyudi*. It is a striking fact that direct references to the *skomorokhi* in the *byliny* virtually end with the Novgorod Cycle. From the later Cycles they are practically absent. It is not clear that the *skomorokh* to whom reference is made in a single version of the *bylina* of Kastryuk is a musician or an entertainer.

[1] *Ib.* II. p. 688.

It does not seem to be stated anywhere that the *skomorokhi* composed or sang narrative poetry (*byliny, stariny*). We have seen that when Dobrynya sings to the *gusli* disguised as a *skomorokh*, his *tontsy* (? 'airs') are largely, though not exclusively, foreign. The *skomorokhi* in the *bylina* of Terenti Gost sing a purely occasional poem (*pêsn*) addressed to Terenti himself. So far as we are aware these are the only positive statements made in the *byliny* as to the répertoire of the *skomorokhi*. There are, however, some passages in the opening, and more especially in the concluding, lines of certain *byliny* which seem to claim that they form the subject of recitation by the *skomorokhi*.

These passages are especially common in the versions recorded by Kirsha Danilov—a circumstance which has lent colour to the suggestion that this collection is based on their répertoire. One of the longest and most interesting of these passages is rendered by Prof. Mazon as follows:

> Telle est notre vieille histoire, notre histoire vraie,
> Notre histoire à réjouir la mer bleue...
> A distraire les bonnes gens,
> A se passer de bouche en bouche, entre jeunes compagnons,
> A faire notre joie de joyeux drilles,
> Assis à converser de bonne manière,
> Buvant hydromel et eau-de-vie.
> Où l'on nous donne à boire, là nous rendons honneur,
> Nous rendons honneur au grand seigneur,
> Au bon maître de la maison.[1]

Here the picture would seem to be of oral recitation by the professional minstrels known as the *dobrÿe molodtsy*, or *veselÿe lyudi*, at a feast given by a wealthy householder whom they are at pains to thank and compliment.

For further examples of such 'tags' we may refer to the concluding lines of Kirsha Danilov's version of the *bylina* on the death of Skopin.[2] A number of instances are also cited by Miller,[3] and English translations of several are given by L. A. Magnus.[4] It is generally supposed, and indeed it would seem to be very probable, that in such passages as these the *veselÿe lyudi* and the *skomorokhi* make claim to be the reciters of the *byliny*.

Our fullest information for the history of minstrelsy in general comes, not from the *byliny*, but from historical sources. It is clear from numerous allusions in both native and foreign authors that the *skomo-*

---

[1] Mazon, *Bylines*, p. 685.
[2] Kirêevski, VII. p. 11; Chadwick, p. 229.
[3] *R.M.* X. p. 1 ff.; *Ocherki*, I. p. 59 ff. [4] *Ballads*, p. 173 ff.

rokhi were in high favour at the Muscovite court during the sixteenth century. Sir Jerome Horsey, the English ambassador to Ivan the Terrible, has left us an account in his diary of the court at Moscow as he saw it at the close of the sixteenth century.[1] It contains a curious entry which states that the Emperor went into the bath, and "sollaced himself, and made merie with pleasant songs, as he useth to doe". Fletcher gives it as Ivan's custom that "after his sleepe he goeth to evensong…and thence returning, for the most parte recreateth himself with the empresse till supper time, with jesters and dwarfes, men and women, that tumble before him, and sing many songs after the Russe manner. This is his common recreation betwixt meals that hee moste delightes in".[2] Earlier in the same century Osepp Napea, the Muscovite ambassador, reported that "in the dinner time there came in sixe singers, which stood in the midst of the chamber, and their faces towards the Emperour, who sang there before dinner was ended three severall times, whose songs or voices delighted our eares little or nothing".[3]

Side by side with notices in the works of foreign travellers relating to 'buffoons', 'tumblers', and 'singers' at the Muscovite court, we find plentiful evidence in Russian history and legal documents for their popularity, under the name of *skomorokhi* and *veselÿe lyudi*, 'joyous people'. They are represented as singing to the *gusli* and the *gudka* ('fiddle') among other accomplishments, and they are constantly associated with fiddlers. The Russian noble and man of letters of the reign of Ivan the Terrible, Andrei Mikhailovich Kurbski,[4] tells us that after the Tsar Ivan Vasilevich had drunk, "he began to dance and feast with *skomorokhi* in *mashkarakhi* ('masks')".[5] In a Chronicle of Novgorod s.a. 1571 we read: "At this time in Novgorod, and throughout all the cities and districts in the government, they received the *veselÿe lyudi*"; and immediately afterwards it is stated that "there drove from Novgorod in carts to Moscow on Saturday…the *skomorokhi*".[6] It will be remembered that in the *bylina* of Terenti Gost, 'Terence the Merchant', the *skomorokhi* are represented as wandering in a band about the streets of Novgorod.

For the seventeenth century our information relating to the *skomorokhi* is even more abundant. Olearius mentions in his account of Russia that he saw and heard *skomorokhi* in Ladoga on the outskirts of

---

[1] Horsey, p. 201.   [2] Fletcher, p. 142.
[3] Osepp Napea, p. 358.   [4] Born 1528; died 1583.
[5] Famintsyn, p. 15; Miller, *R.M.* x. p. 13; *Ocherki*, I. p. 56.
[6] Miller, *loc. cit.*

the earlier Novgorod dominions in 1634, and that they sang panegyric poetry. When he and his companions were sitting at dinner there came two Russians with lutes and *gudkas* ('fiddles'), who made their bows, and began to play and sing about the great mighty sovereign and tsar Michael Fedorovich. Then they danced and made strange gesticulations.[1]

The reference is to the Tsar Michael Romanov I, who reigned 1613–45. It is interesting to know that stringed instruments were still used for the accompaniment of such songs. This contemporary notice by Olearius suggests that the short contemporary *byliny* which rose to prominence in Moscow in the sixteenth and seventeenth centuries formed a part of the répertoire of the *skomorokhi*. It was possibly on some such occasion, and from similar people, that Richard James in 1619 made his little collection of contemporary *byliny*.

The widespread popularity and high patronage enjoyed by these variety entertainers converted them into formidable bodies of rich and unruly folk. Sometimes settled in permanent homes, sometimes wandering about various districts in companies, already by the fifteenth century they had become a serious menace to ecclesiastical and civil authorities alike. A company of the 'joyous people' frequently consisted of "between sixty and a hundred people, who seized their food and drink by force from the country people, and stole their food from the larder, and robbed in the streets".[2]

Their troublesome and unruly conduct gave colour to the hostile representations of the ecclesiastical and monastic authorities, and from the sixteenth and seventeenth centuries a series of repressive *ukaʒes* were directed towards curbing and curtailing their power. In particular we may refer to the Council of Stoglov held in 1551, in which they were solemnly condemned.[3] As the popular proverb has it, *Skomorokh popu ne tovarishch*, "Skomorokh and priest are no comrades".[4] Under Michael Fedorovich (1613–45) the persecution never took a very serious form. The official ban however was finally given to the *skomorokhi* under Alexis Mikhailovich (1645–76), the father of Peter the Great, whose relentless persecution of the wandering *skomorokhi* of every sort throughout his reign finally brought it about that they gradually disappeared, and from this period onwards references to them grow rarer. The strong ecclesiastical prejudice is perhaps reflected in the *bylina* of Sadko, where St Nikolai is represented as bidding Sadko cease

[1] Olearius, p. 7.
[2] Miller, *R.M.* x. p. 14; *Ocherki*, I. p. 57.
[3] Solovev, II. col. 418 ff.
[4] Mazon, *Bylines*, p. 686.

playing and fling away his *gusli*, as it is causing destruction to mankind.

It will have been observed that the period covered by this wealth of historical evidence, testifying to the singing of songs by the *skomorokhi* to the accompaniment of musical instruments, corresponds to the period of which the *byliny* themselves have little to tell us in regard to the heroic minstrel. The disappearance of the courtly minstrels of the Kiev and Novgorod Cycles coincides with the beginning of the historical evidence for troops of 'joyous people'. Moreover, soon after the persecution of the *skomorokhi*, etc. in the seventeenth century by the upper classes, we begin to have collections of *byliny* from the peasantry. These circumstances and the evidence already cited have led Vsevolod Miller and other scholars to regard the *skomorokhi* as the professional class from whom the peasants received their répertoire. The disappearance of the *skomorokhi* as a professional class from the extensive regions of Great Russia in which they had been distributed in itself makes it probable that the last traces of their répertoire will be found in outlying districts. It is, as we have seen, from such districts that our collections of *byliny* have been drawn. If it could be shown that the *skomorokhi* and the *veselýe lyudi* were actually associated with the singing of *byliny*, there would be considerable ground for regarding Miller's view with favour.

Such evidence is not wholly lacking, though it is slight in quantity, and dates from comparatively recent times. It is found in the well-known passage written by the historian Tatishchev, who lived 1685–1750.[1] The notice is as follows:

"I heard in the past from the *skomorokhi* ancient songs about Prince Vladimir, in which they make mention of his wives by name, as well as of those glorious men Ilya of Murom, Aleksêy Popovich, Solovey the Robber, Dolk (? Dyuk) Stefanovich, and glorify their deeds; but of history, very little or nothing."[2]

From this it seems clear that at least in the early part of the eighteenth century the *byliny* formed a well recognised and important part of the répertoire of the *skomorokhi*, the *veselýe lyudi*, who were, we have no reason to doubt, at least part heirs of the traditional court minstrelsy. From them, it may be regarded as certain, the peasants have in some degree received their répertoire in more recent times. It is less easy to demonstrate the second part of Miller's proposition that they were also the authors of the *byliny*; nor indeed is it clear to us that Miller himself

---

[1] Tatishchev was the first Russian to write a history of Russia.
[2] See Miller, *R.M.* x. p. 19; *Ocherki*, I. p. 63.

intended to press this view with regard to the *byliny* of the Kiev Cycle, which embrace strictly heroic traditions. On internal evidence, however, he urges that the *byliny* which have as their subjects scenes from domestic life, whether in the court of Kiev, or in the streets and houses of Novgorod, must have been composed by the 'joyous people'. Indeed it cannot be denied that the atmosphere of such *byliny*, and more particularly their broad humour—a humour coarser than we are accustomed to associate with court poetry—is precisely such as we should expect to get from the *skomorokhi*.

Finally, the question has often been asked: who else could have composed them? We have seen that the *skomorokhi* are versatile people. We have met them as wrestlers, dancers, tumblers, buffoons, minstrels, singers, fiddlers. We have found them termed variously *skomorokhi*, *veselÿe lyudi, veselÿe molodtsy, dobrÿe molodtsy*. It is clear, therefore, that their functions were wide and not strictly delimited, and that the above terms were used loosely of any public entertainers. If, as we believe, the *byliny* as a whole were composed by illiterate but highly trained minstrels, it is natural, in view of the lack of evidence to the contrary, to suppose that some at least were composed by the only highly trained secular artists and popular entertainers whom we know, i.e. the minstrels whom Tatishchev heard singing them; and a number of *byliny* offer strong internal evidence of such an origin. We shall see later, however, that there are reasons for believing that the *skomorokhi* were not the only composers of *byliny*, and we greatly doubt if it is to the *skomorokhi* that the majority of the *byliny* are originally indebted. We are inclined to attribute the prototypes of the *byliny* of the Kiev Cycle to the *kalêki*. This subject will be discussed more fully in the next chapter.

It may be regarded as certain, however, that when the Olonets *skaẓitel* sings his *bylina* in a corrupt metre to two or three tunes, without accompaniment, losing that metre entirely when he abandons his singing for recitation, we are in the presence of the last flicker of the genuine secular 'minstrel' tradition in north Russia. When those last few tunes have been forgotten, we have abandoned minstrelsy and poetry for the *pobyvalshchina* or traditional heroic saga. This is no doubt the reason why it appears that there are few, if any, *pobyvalshchiny* relating to subjects which are not connected in some way with the medieval heroic cycles of Kiev and Novgorod. The sagas relating to Peter the Great and to other comparatively modern heroes bear no trace of having been paraphrased, or, indeed, of having existed in any other form.

Of the recitation and composition of prose saga very little is known. Neither the collectors nor the texts which they record have much to tell us. In modern times the art of saga telling, like that of the recitation of *byliny*, has become almost wholly restricted to peasant circles, and sagas proper, i.e. traditional oral prose narratives of an elaborate kind, circulate today in the same circle as the *skazki*. Such sagas are, however, as we have seen, far less numerous than the *skazki*, which doubtless accounts for the meagre character of the evidence relating to their circulation.

Nevertheless we doubt very much if saga-telling is of humble origin in Russia. We know from Nestor's own account that he was indebted to the *slovesy* of one Yan for much of his information, and it seems probable on the whole that prose narratives are implied.[1] Yan, as we learn from the references in Nestor, belonged to one of the leading families in the country. Moreover, there is ample evidence that certain types of narratives such as *skazanya* were composed by ecclesiastics, and even by men who were high in royal favour; cf. p. 172. In all probability the mention of these aristocratic composers of saga is only due to the accidental circumstance of their compositions having been committed to writing. We shall see later, in the chapter on 'The Popular Poet and Story-teller', that there is evidence that story-telling was encouraged in the households of noble families in Russia in the eighteenth century, and even by Ivan the Terrible himself in the sixteenth.

Such evidence as we possess relating to the circulation of sagas in modern times again points to the north of Russia as the region where the art is chiefly cultivated. Here last century were recorded specimens of the elaborate poetical sagas known as *pobyvalshchiny*, a modern development from the *byliny*—in fact non-metrical *byliny*. One of the longest and best preserved of these was recorded by Rybnikov from the recitation of a peasant who by profession was a *kaleka*,[2] but who, upon occasion, also sang *byliny*.[3] (Cf. p. 167 above.) The *pobyvalshchina* on 'The Healing of Ilya of Murom'[4] was recorded from the recitation of 'decrepit old men', in other words the *kaleki*.[5] Barsov and others have collected many sagas from the older peasants of the north relating to Ivan the Terrible and Peter the Great.[6] We have no evidence from modern times, however, which suggests that these or other sagas form the exclusive or specialised répertoire of any class of reciters.

[1] The word is commonly used in medieval Russian texts with reference to sermons.
[2] Rybnikov, I. p. lxxxviii f.; II. pp. 583 f., 656 ff.
[3] *Ib.* p. 632.
[4] *Ib.* p. 581.
[5] *Ib.*
[6] *Ib.* I. p. lxxvi; II. p. 715 f.

CHAPTER XII

THE RECITATION AND COMPOSITION OF RELIGIOUS POETRY

THE KALÊKI

WHATEVER part the *skomorokhi* played in regard to the *byliny*—whether that of reciters only, or of composers also—is now a matter of ancient history. Since the beginning of the eighteenth century they have been a mere memory. There is, however, another class of professional singers who are widespread throughout Great Russia, and who, down to our own time, have carried on the recitation of *byliny* alongside the amateur peasant *skaziteli*. The professional singers of this second class are the *kaliki perekhozhie*, or, as they are called today, the *kalêki perekhozhie*.[1] The *byliny* are said to be in general, however, only of secondary importance in their répertoire, at any rate in modern times. Their recitations consist chiefly of *dukhovnie stikhi*, or oral narrative religious poems. Unfortunately all too little evidence regarding the *kalêki* themselves is accessible at present to western scholars, and we shall therefore treat this subject very briefly.

The *kalêki*, as we have already noted (p. 4 above), are a confraternity of itinerant religious singers. They are—or appear to have been in the past—in some way loosely associated with religious institutions. In contrast to the *skaziteli*, the *kalêki* are professionals, having no other means of livelihood. In contrast to the *skaziteli* also they do not live, in modern times, in fixed habitations, and are free from labour and social ties.[2] In one of the poems which professes to recount the origin of their corporation (cf. p. 187 f. above) they claim to have received divine sanction for their art, and to have voluntarily abrogated riches and worldly possessions.

As their name implies the *kalêki* are generally cripples, the majority being blind. In modern times they are very poor,[3] mendicants in fact, and generally more or less ragged. Singly or, more commonly, in small groups of blind singers, led by a child or someone who has sight, they wander from village to village, and from one great house to another, and attend fairs, singing and begging alms. Their disabilities doubtless

---

[1] For a discussion of the two terms, see p. 272 below.
[2] Rybnikov, I. p. xci. [3] *Ib.* pp. xxxix, cii.

make it desirable for them to travel in small parties rather than separately. They are sanctioned by the Church, but they have no status and do not belong to any ecclesiastical organisation. The *kalêki* (*kaliki*) whom Rybnikov found in the Olonets Government in 1859 were accustomed to resort to Shungsk Fair, where they used to sit by the churchyard and sing to crowds of listeners.[1] Even in our own day they may still be found at fairs and church festivals and in the neighbourhood of monasteries, and in many districts their wailings still form an essential part of all funerals.[2]

The *kalêki* consist of both men and women, but if we may judge from the pictures contained in Bezsonov's corpus of their songs,[3] the men and women generally travel in separate groups. They carry bags which are frequently shaped like our own rucksacks, only rather larger, and which contain their provisions. The bags hang from the shoulders by cords, and sometimes they are pointed at the lower end, and one is worn on each side, the straps crossing from right to left. Sticks also are carried, and each group has a common cup in which to receive alms. The men wear no hats, but a long coat, or, in milder weather, a short smock and girdle, and rough shoes. Their appearance is unkempt. The women wear a kerchief over their heads and tied under the chin, long wide coats and girdles, and rough shoes. The women's costume is almost identical with that of our modern Carmelite nuns in England except for the absence of the veil. In the south and west of Russia one member of each group (probably of the men only) usually carries a lyre or *bandura* with which to accompany their songs.[4] In the north, however, the *kalêki*, like the *skaŗiteli*, sing without accompaniment. Bezsonov gives two pictures, each of a single man who appears to be blind, and who is seated and playing a musical instrument, one a *bandura*, a stringed instrument somewhat resembling a guitar, characteristic of Little Russia; the other, a kind of lyre.

Their songs consist chiefly of *stikhi* or religious narrative poems about

---

[1] Rybnikov, i. p. lxiv.

[2] In 1850 the police prohibited the *kalêki* from singing as they went along the roads, and in 1859 and 1860 Rybnikov had difficulty in finding them, even at the Shungsk Fair (Petrozavodsk), where they had been accustomed formerly to resort in large numbers. By the good offices of Rybnikov the local authorities were prevailed upon to withdraw their interdict, and the *kalêki* reappeared on the Fair ground. (Rambaud, *R.É.* p. 4.)

[3] *Kalêki Perekhoŗhie*. The reader may also refer to Rambaud's description of the picture in the private art collection formed by Tretyakov in Moscow, *R.É.* p. 13.

[4] Brodski, etc., p. 232; cf. Speranski, *R.U.S.* p. 140.

saints or biblical heroes. Not unfrequently, however, as we have said, they sing *byliny* also. In Olonets especially many *byliny* have been recorded from the recitation of the *kalêki* (*kaliki*). We have seen that Rybnikov obtained one or two of his first *byliny* from two *kalêki*[1] who attended the Shungsk Fair in the Onega district. Later he obtained nine *byliny* from another *kalêka* in a neighbouring district[2] and more than twenty from a third.[3] He tells us that the *kalêka* Latyshev wandered about from fair to fair singing for money. On the shores of Lake Onega, where many Old Believers were to be found who hate worldly music, this *kalêka* sang chiefly *dukhovnie stikhi*, 'spiritual songs'; but in the Government of Archangel, where rich peasants lived in the villages, and in the neighbourhood of the towns, the merchants and officials enjoyed hearing narratives about the heroes. Latyshev had learnt his *byliny* chiefly from the centenarian *kalêka* called Gergush, who also taught him a fine *pobyvalshchina*.[4] Here, then, we have yet another (cf. p. 254 above) répertoire of *byliny* directly derived from an eighteenth-century *kalêka*.

Like the *skomorokhi*, the *kalêki* (*kaliki*) have preserved their anonymity. So far as we are aware, in no instance does the name of an author or reciter appear in connection with any of their poems. We know nothing of the circumstances under which they composed their poems, and very little of the means by which they acquire and transmit them. They appear to be wholly uneducated people, and we know very little as to the exact sources from which they have obtained their knowledge of the subjects of their poems, the majority of which are, as we have seen, derived ultimately from books.

According to a brief account of the *kaliki* by Maslov[5] the institution of the *kaliki* dates from the early years of the Christian era; but his brief notice of their history is somewhat disappointing in its absence of dates and precise references, and the exact date or place of the origin of the *kaliki* is not discussed. It is now generally held that there have been, from comparatively early times, two classes of *kaliki perekhozhie*. The first class, which has long been extinct, consisted of comparatively well-to-do people who undertook specific pilgrimages from motives of devotion. The second consisted of poor people and cripples—the true forerunners of the *nishchaya bratya* or 'poor brethren', and *kalêki* or

---

[1] In Rybnikov's notes on these singers the archaic form *kaliki* is invariably retained, and is probably still in use in Olonets.
[2] Rybnikov, I. p. xci.   [3] *Ib.* p. lxxxviii f.
[4] *Ib.* p. lxxxix.   [5] Brodski, etc., p. 231 f.

'cripples' of later times—who adopted the calling of wandering pilgrims as a permanent way of life. The similarity of the two words (*kaliki, kalêki*) has brought it about that the original distinction between the two classes has been lost, and all alike are popularly referred to in modern times as *kalêki* without any direct reference to bodily infirmity. Some scholars, such as Rybnikov and Maslov, retain the obsolete or archaic form *kaliki*. We have preferred to use the modern term, especially in reference to our own time, as being of wider application and more general use. Probably the distinction between these two classes of *kaliki* ought not to be pressed too far, even in relation to earlier times, and it is certain that numbers of people of all classes attached themselves to both types. Indeed the personnel of both these classes of pilgrims was extremely varied, and included run-away serfs, people of no status and no permanent homes, as well as clergy.

The monasteries served as centres whither the *kaliki* flocked together, and where they were always assured of a reception on the ground that in the foundation of the Russian Church attributed to St Vladimir the *kaliki* were included in the list of people in holy orders. From the monasteries they derived their knowledge of spiritual things, which they disseminated among the people. In this way, travelling through Russia and adjoining countries, many of them even reached Byzantium and the Holy Land. Sometimes on their return they would revert to their former calling. Sometimes they adhered permanently to an itinerant life. It is obvious that on their travels the *kaliki* would acquire much material of both secular and ecclesiastical interest with which to store their memories, and which would ensure them a welcome as reciters on their wanderings. It is not surprising that it has been found difficult to trace the immediate source of most of their music and their poetry.

The *kaliki* probably reached their zenith in the reign of Alexis Mikhailovich (cp. p. 266 above), when they attained to high prestige and greatly increased in numbers. Among the many circumstances favourable to them about this time, doubtless the most important was the proscription of the *skomorokhi* and other secular musicians. In this reign, the house of amusement of the tsar was abolished and devoted to the poor, who sang to the tsar stories of the past, songs of *Laẓar* (cp. p. 196 above), and other religious songs. Even at the feast of the tsar himself the old gay traditional songs were replaced by *stikhi*. The wealthy boyars naturally followed the tsar in this respect, and large numbers of houses were devoted to the poor and cripples. This encouragement in high circles, and the ease of a life of alms, brought about a great increase in the number of the wandering poor, who fell heirs to the répertoires of the genuine *kaliki* pilgrims. The succeeding government attempted to check the increase of vagrancy by drawing a distinction between the poor and the cripples on the one hand and the healthy and capable on the other. By this means the genuine *kaliki*, i.e. pilgrims by conviction, disappeared.[1]

The *kaliki* are mentioned frequently in the *byliny*—more frequently, indeed, than the *skomorokhi*. And unlike the *skomorokhi* they are frequently introduced into the *byliny* as individuals, and as playing a definite—sometimes even an important—rôle. In several versions of Mikhailo Potyk, the rescue of the hero from the enchantments of the White Swan is brought about by a *kalika*. In the *bylina* of the 'Healing of Ilya of Murom', Christ and two disciples visit the house of Ilya's parents during their absence in the guise of *nishchaya bratya*, 'poor brethren', which is the popular term for the *kaliki perekhozhie*. They beg Ilya to give them a drink, and in return prophesy good fortune and health to him—quite in the manner of the professional beggar.

In general, however, the *kaliki* as they appear in the *byliny* are wealthy and richly dressed imperious people, in striking contrast to the 'poor brethren' of the latter *bylina* and to the *kaliki perekhozhie* of today. The fullest picture of a group of *kaliki* is given in the *bylina* of the 'Forty and One *Kaliki*' already discussed, where they are shown to us as *bogatyri* who have voluntarily taken a vow to go on pilgrimage to atone for their sins, and as setting out in a body from a religious house and under ecclesiastical and royal auspices. Their costume and equipment are rich and splendid, and their bearing and behaviour are as polished and imperious as those of the heroes themselves. They set out on their long pilgrimage to Jerusalem by way of Kiev, wandering along the high-road begging alms—

> For the love of Christ, the Tsar of Heaven,
> For the love of the holy Mother of God.[2]

Their procedure does not seem to differ greatly from that of their modern representatives. Standing in a circle, they beat with their sticks upon the ground to demand attention, and sing their *stikhi*, apparently without the accompaniment of any musical instrument, at least when they perform in groups. With their leader, Kasyan Mikhailovich, 'a stalwart, fine young man', the Princess Apraxya falls in

---

[1] Maslov (Brodski, etc. p. 231 ff.).
[2] Kirêevski, III. p. 82.

love, but, true to the *kalika* vow of chastity, the party pass on and decline to take advantage of Apraxya's weakness. When they have left Kiev, and are overtaken and questioned in discourteous fashion by the first party of the queen's pursuers, they show themselves of a martial bearing, and well able to defend themselves. They respond instantly to the courteous advance of the second party of pursuers, and, 'standing in a circle', as their custom is, proceed at once to justice. The poem is interesting as showing a system of summary justice, self-imposed, among the *kaliki*, and a kind of self-government which must have contributed greatly to the toleration by society of such wandering troops of pilgrims.

The heroes of the *byliny* are frequently represented as exchanging clothes with the *kaliki* in order to effect a disguise and to purchase immunity for themselves. The frequency of this device suggests that the persons of the *kaliki* were regarded as sacrosanct. Thus in certain versions of the *bylina* of Mikhailo Potyk, Dobrynya Nikitich and Ilya of Murom disguise themselves as *kaliki* when they go to visit the King of Poland to enquire for Mikhailo Potyk. In one version[1] of the story of Alyosha's marriage to Dobrynya's wife, Dobrynya arrives at the wedding disguised, not as a *skomorokh*, but as a *kalika*. The variation is significant.

The *kaliki* disguise is adopted with especial frequency by the Russian heroes in their encounters with the Tatars, and the consistency with which the Tatars are represented as respecting the *kaliki* costume is very striking. In the *bylina* which recounts the slaying of the Serpent of the Mountain by Dobrynya Nikitich, Dobrynya wears the *kaliki* hat and costume when he goes to bathe in the forbidden waters, and it is only when he is stripped of these garments that the fiery dragon attacks him. In Kirsha Danilov's version of the *bylina* of the slaying of Tugarin the Dragon's Son by Alyosha Popovich, the Russian hero, in his *kaliki* dress, is permitted to approach his enemy at close quarters and so attack him off his guard. In a similar disguise Ilya of Murom is invited into the palace of the Tsar Alexander, which is also occupied by his enemy Idolishche, and there he is hospitably treated. We know from historical sources that the Tatars were in general tolerant to the religion of their enemies, and spared its votaries. The evidence of the *byliny* is fully in accord with history; it suggests, however, that the Tatar generosity in this respect was frequently very ill requited by the Russians.

[1] From Olonets; Kirêevski, II. p. 11.

The incidents which show the heroes disguised as *kaliki* generally afford a good opportunity for introducing an elaborate description of the *kaliki* costume, which, in contrast to that of modern times, is rich and elaborate. Their hats are said to be of Greek manufacture; their shoes are composed of seven silks; their bags are of velvet and 'rustling silk'; their staffs, which are sometimes of cypress-wood, are heavily mounted with gold and tipped with ivory; their hands are resplendent with jewels, and, as we have seen, the Russian heroes, in their guise of *kaliki*, frequently visit the courts of princes in foreign lands. There is no hint in the poems of the Kiev Cycle that these religious singers are in any way deformed, or blind, or outcasts, like the *kaliki* of today.

From what has been said, it will be seen that the *kaliki* are much more prominent in the *byliny* than the *skomorokhi*. They constitute the chief personnel of one *bylina*—that of the 'Forty and One *Kaliki*', which is devoted to their interests, and seeks to exalt them at the expense of the Princess Apraxya. They are the real heroes of the *bylina* on 'the Healing of Ilya of Murom', in which the *kaliki*, by an adroit device, are made responsible for the career of the greatest of all the heroes of *byliny*. It would not be difficult to see the hand of the *kaliki* themselves in the composition of such *byliny* as these.

The prominence of the *kaliki* is not confined to *byliny* of which they are the most conspicuous characters. We have seen that the dénouement of the *bylina* of Mikhailo Potyk is brought about by a *kalika*, though he is absent from some versions, notably that of Kirsha Danilov, and his presence looks suspiciously adventitious. The substitution of the disguise of Dobrynya as a *kalika* for that of a *skomorokh* in the single version of the 'marriage of Dobrynya' referred to above is certainly adventitious. We have seen that it is in the guise of *kaliki* that the heroes frequently perform their greatest feats—the slaying of Idolishche by Ilya of Murom; of Tugarin the Dragon's Son by Alyosha Popovich; of the Serpent of the Mountain by Dobrynya Nikitich. Examples might be multiplied. Are we really to believe that in the original versions of the heroic stories of the Kiev Cycle the principal heroes were wholly dependent on the aid of the *kaliki* in the performance of their heroic deeds?

The traces of the *kaliki* in the *byliny* are not restricted to the personnel or to their influence on the action, nor are they confined to the modern versions. The prominence of ecclesiastical interest in the *byliny* recorded by Kirsha Danilov is difficult to account for unless we suppose that many of his versions have come under the influence of the *kaliki*.

Prof. Mazon holds that Kirsha's collection represents the répertoires of the *skomorokhi*,[1] and in this he is no doubt partly right: we can well believe that the broader and more sophisticated versions have been obtained from such sources, especially those of the *byliny* of Kiev and Novgorod. We are inclined, however, to think that the prominence of religious and ecclesiastical elements in Kirsha's collection has been underrated, both by Prof. Mazon[2] himself and by other scholars.

If we take at random Kirsha's versions of *byliny* relating to the modern period, we cannot fail to be struck by the prominence of ecclesiastical elements and of references to religious practice. We may refer to the *bylina* on 'Grigori Otrepev and Marina', which opens with the cry:

O God, God our merciful Saviour!
Why hast Thou grown angry with us so soon?

and lays stress throughout on the Pretender's apostasy, on Marina's heresy, on their neglect of religious observances, stressing in contrast the devoutness of the Russian princes and boyars, and enlarging on the memorial services held on all feast days for the murdered Tsarevich Dimitri, son of Ivan the Terrible; and all this in a *bylina* of 68 lines. Again, in the account of the death of Prince Simeon Romanovich Pozharski, the account of the treatment of the dead hero has a strong ecclesiastical flavour:

They carried Pozharski away to the city of Konotopa.
In the city of Konotopa a bishop officiated,
He assembled bishops, priests and deacons,
And sextons of the church;
And...he gave orders to wash the body of Pozharski.
And they laid the remains of his body together in a reliquary of oak,
And covered it with a lid of white oak;
And then the people marvelled,
For his body grew together again.
When they had chanted through the requiem appointed,
They buried his white body in the damp earth,
And sang a mass for the eternal welfare
Of the soul of Prince Pozharski.

Even in the *bylina* on the 'Death of Skopin', which concludes with the lines which have been already referred to (p. 264 above), and which

---

[1] Referring to the *skomorokhi*, he writes: "Les 'vieilles poésies russes' rassemblées par Kirsha Danilov étaient, sans doute aucun, de leur répertoire....Le ton moyen du recueil de Kirsha Danilov est frappant à cet égard: c'est celui du fabliau plutôt que de la chanson de geste." *Bylines*, p. 686.

[2] He refers to the *bylina* of the 'Forty *Kaliki*' as "la seule byline du recueil de Kirsha Danilov où apparaisse une note religieuse sincère". *Bylines*, p. 688.

appear to claim that our version belongs to the *skomorokh* répertoire, features appear which would seem to be of a very different origin:

> And in the morning early, very very early,
> Skopin heard matins in the Cathedral,
> He heard matins, and then he set off on his journey.
> He hoisted the royal banner,
> And on the banner was stamped
> The miraculous Saviour and Redeemer;
> And on the reverse side was stamped
> Mikhailo and Gabriel the archangels,
> With all the heavenly host...
> God's help be with him!

And the poet proceeds to tell us of the form taken by the celebrations of Skopin's victory—the masses that were recited, and the Te Deums, 'and the whole of the great liturgy'.

It is not only in the *byliny* relating to the century immediately preceding his own that Kirsha's versions frequently betray a strong ecclesiastical bias. This feature is even more prominent in certain of his versions of the *byliny* of the Kiev and Novgorod Cycles. Perhaps the most striking instance is his version of Mikhailo Potyk, of which we have given some account, and in which the ecclesiastical tone has come to predominate throughout the *bylina* to an extent which is truly astonishing when we compare it with any other version of the story. We may refer also to Kirsha's version of the *bylina* of the slaying of Tugarin by Alyosha Popovich in which the hero overcomes his enemy in the guise of a *kalika*, and spends the whole night before the final encounter in prayer to God. Here also the name of Alyosha's servant is given, and we are told that he was 'a man instructed in letters', i.e., we may assume, a clerk or person in some kind of minor orders. Turning to the Novgorod Cycle we find that Kirsha's version of Vasili Buslaev represents the hero as a champion of Christianity and a great benefactor of the Church, who makes liberal contributions to the Guild of St Nikolai, and in later life makes a pilgrimage to Jerusalem to atone for his sins and pray for the souls of the dead. In both of Kirsha's versions of Sadko the religious element is very marked. In one (cp. p. 52 above) the hero is rescued from the tsar of the sea by the intervention of St Nikolai, whose commands he is careful to obey. In the other he is represented as a great builder of churches.

We have dwelt somewhat at length on the traces left by the *kaliki* on the *byliny* as a whole, and on Kirsha Danilov's collection in particular, because it seems to us that there has been a tendency among scholars to underestimate the part which the *kaliki* have played in the history of the *byliny*. In view of the positive testimony of the *kaliki* themselves to Rybnikov; in view of certain *byliny* of which they form the principal personnel, and of others in which they supply the dénouement; in view of the many instances in which the heroes of Kiev perform their most important feats in the guise of *kaliki*; and in view of the strong ecclesiastical bias of a great number, if not of the majority of the *byliny* as we have them, it becomes clear that at some period of their history the *byliny* have been widely current among the *kaliki* themselves, and have been at least very widely influenced by them. Indeed we have no doubt that the peasants of modern times have acquired their *byliny* from the *kalêki* (*kaliki*) more directly, and to an even greater degree than from the *skomorokhi*. And we know as a certain fact (cf. p. 252 ff. above) that a number of the most important répertoires of *byliny* on record are derived directly from *kalêki*.

How has this come about? We have seen that while the *skomorokhi* were extremely popular, both at court and among the laity as a whole, during the sixteenth and seventeenth centuries, they were held in grave disapprobation by the Church. Under the Tsar Alexis (1645–1676), whose sympathies were strongly ecclesiastical, they were officially banned, and after this they gradually disappear from history. Not so the *kalêki*. Although shorn of their former splendour, we have seen that these people still in the days of our grandparents, and no doubt even in our own day, wander along 'the great road, the long road' begging alms, 'for the sake of Christ, the Tsar of Heaven'. We have seen also that the *kalêki* are patronised by the Church, whose interests are in no way at variance with their own. There can be no doubt that the loss of the *skomorokhi* was the gain of the *kalêki*. The *kalêki*, like the *skomorokhi*, are professional singers and reciters of oral narrative poetry, and like the *skomorokhi* they are expert extempore composers. Their technique is identical. The subjects alone might be supposed to have originally differed. When, however, the wealth and prestige of the *skomorokhi* began to diminish about the close of the seventeenth century, would it not be natural that the *kalêki* (*kaliki*) would endeavour to improve their means of livelihood by stepping into the vacant places left by the disappearance of the *skomorokhi*? We know, indeed, of a certain blind *kalêka* of the name of Mina, who sang *byliny* early in the eighteenth century, and bequeathed to his pupils what must have been one of the finest among the répertoires of *byliny* (cf. p. 253 above). And it is clear that other *kalêki* of the same century also sang *byliny* (cf. p. 272 above). As sanctioned by the Church, the *kalêki* must retain the *stikhi* as the principal part of their répertoire; but with the removal of the *skomorokhi* the *kalêki* were free to treat of subjects of secular interest in addition, and without competition, and thereby to increase their own popularity with the laity.

Did the *kaliki* recite *byliny* as well as *stikhi* before the decline of the *skomorokhi*? On this point we have no direct evidence; but it is difficult to believe that the influence of the *kaliki* on the *byliny* was restricted to the brief period between the proscription of the *skomorokhi* under the Tsar Alexis, and the collection of *byliny* made by Kirsha Danilov about the middle of the eighteenth century. Moreover, as we have seen, the *stikhi* are obviously identical with the *byliny* in much of their diction and many of their stylistic characteristics. Indeed in all matters relating to form the *byliny* and the *stikhi* are virtually indistinguishable. It is natural to suppose, therefore, that the *byliny* or *stariny* were known to the reciters of the *stikhi* at an early date. Are we really justified in assuming that these two great bodies of poetry belonged originally to totally different milieus?

We do not think that it has ever been seriously suggested that the *kalêki* were originally responsible for the composition of the proto-types of the *byliny* of the Kiev Cycle, though much might be urged in favour of such a view. We have seen that in recent centuries at least the *kalêki* have been in the habit of reciting these *byliny* for money no less, or hardly less, than *stikhi*, tactfully adapting their répertoire to their audiences. We have also seen that such evidence as we have points to the practice being at least as strong in the eighteenth century. It is difficult to see where the *kalêki* could have found so decorous a Cycle of secular stories as those which had as their central figure a prince whose name was identical with that of the great Vladimir, saint and founder of the Russian Church, founder also of the great ecclesiastical centre of Kiev, and—perhaps most important of all—credited with having included the body of the *kalêki* in holy orders, thereby gaining for them the permanent hospitality and patronage of the Church and monasteries.

Moreover it might be pointed out that the ecclesiastical bias of Vladimir is never lost sight of. He is constantly represented as attending matins in the cathedral church of Kiev, and his *druzhina* consists of *bogatyri*, who, as we have seen, are represented as little less than crusaders, defending holy Russia against the heathen Tatars. The only people who are at times represented in the poems as their superiors are the *kalêki* (*kaliki*) themselves. It is difficult to see where the *kalêki* could have found a group of secular characters and a cycle of secular stories so likely to have been handed down in oral tradition in ecclesiastical circles, or so little likely to be frowned on in monastic circles as a part of the *kalêki* répertoire. These facts, taken together with the identity of form of the *byliny* and the *stikhi*, suggest that the former originally constituted the secular portion of the *kalêki* répertoire, the latter the ecclesiastical, rather than that the former originally constituted the répertoire of a totally different and by no means ecclesiastically minded class of minstrels.

We have seen that Russia has little or no heroic poetry in the strict sense of the term. The heroic stories have almost all reached us through a non-heroic milieu. At the same time, despite this present non-heroic atmosphere, there can be no doubt that the personnel of the *byliny*, the stories themselves, and the whole milieu originated in a heroic age. It is impossible to believe that the Kiev Cycle of stories, as distinct from the Kiev Cycle of *byliny*, originated in ecclesiastical circles. Its aristocratic, its military, and its strong mercantile personnel and preoccupations are all against such a supposition.

But we have seen that the institution of the *kaliki* is itself believed to have consisted originally chiefly of aristocratic elements. The *byliny* indeed represent the *kaliki* as in all particulars identical with the heroes themselves—as, in fact, heroes who have voluntarily and temporarily adopted a non-heroic calling, and are living in a non-heroic milieu. If this is true, it is easy to see how the *kaliki* might have come into the possession of a Cycle of traditional heroic stories. Such stories would, indeed, in all probability, constitute their normal literature (oral) of entertainment in secular life. At the same time it would be natural to them in their pilgrimages to give an ecclesiastical bias to their recitations of even secular subjects, and this bias would be further emphasised by such of the *kalêki* as adopted the life of pilgrims as a permanent calling. The *kalêki* of modern times, poor and disabled, would, it need hardly be said, be unlikely to be the authors of the Kiev *byliny*, but no such disabilities seem to have rested on the members of their order in early times.

It is not, of course, intended to suggest that heroic stories and poems as such relating to Prince Vladimir and the heroes of Kiev originated with the *kaliki*, still less that the *kaliki* are responsible for the origin of the *bylina* as a literary form. This is extremely unlikely. We know from the evidence of the *Slovo o Polky Igorevê* that Cycles of heroic poetry were also current in the Middle Ages relating to Galicia on the one hand, and to Putivl, and doubtless to other cities of the Dnêpr also on the other; and that these Cycles celebrated a number of heroes of whom the Kiev *byliny* know nothing. But while all other heroic poetry has perished, leaving its traces only in the *Slovo* and in prose paraphrases and traditions, the stories of Vladimir have been perpetuated and given a new life and an increasing and wider currency. What we think the *kaliki* were responsible for is the selective process which singled out Prince Vladimir and a number of heroes associated in one way or another with early Kiev; for the synthesis which grouped them together into a single Cycle; and for the composition of the immediate proto-types of our modern *byliny*.

Both the immediate sources from which the subjects of the *byliny* are derived, and the origin of the *bylina* as an artistic form are difficult and disputed questions which lie outside the scope of the present work, and to discuss them even briefly would require more space than we have at our disposal. There has been a growing tendency in modern times to derive both the stories and the form of the *byliny* of the early Cycles from literary (written) sources. The chief arguments adduced in favour of this view are the absence of contemporary or early references to the singing of *byliny*, and the occurrence of certain stories and motifs of the modern *byliny* in early written (i.e. learned) records, such as the Chronicles.

It has been shown in Vol. 1, however, in connection with Anglo-Saxon heroic poetry, how little value negative evidence really has when the question is one which relates to oral literature. Nor can we regard the occurrence in the Chronicles and other learned works of stories and motifs found in the *byliny* as evidence that the latter are indebted to written sources. Russian medieval Chronicles and other written records are manifestly frequently indebted to oral recitation for their material, as the Chronicler at times tells us himself, and as the nature of the texts makes clear. Similarly in the West we find Jordanes' history, and the Annals of Quedlinburg drawing upon heroic poetry for their accounts of the death of Ermenric, while the early Irish annals contain numerous entries which are obviously derived from heroic sagas.

We must confess further that we have great difficulty in accepting the view that the form of the *bylina* is of literary origin. The metres are virtually confined to the north, and it is probable that in this, as in other respects, the north is conservative, and has preserved in a more or less disintegrated condition a form of metre which in the past was widespread also in the south. Even accepting Miller's view that the *byliny* in their present form originated in the Province of Novgorod, it is probable that the form had reached this district from the cultured cities of the Dnêpr. The diction is practically that of the *Slovo o Polky Igorevê* and the *Zadonshchina*, and we have little doubt that Mazon is right in regarding these as representing an earlier form of the *bylina*.[1] But the *Slovo* and the *Zadonshchina* are avowedly works composed for oral recitation, and follow directly in the artistic tradition of an older school of oral poetry, which flourished on the Dnêpr and in Galicia in still earlier times. It is, we think, probable that the form of the *bylina* is of similar origin and that neither the form nor the subject matter have any direct connection with learned sources.

[1] *Bylines*, p. 691.

CHAPTER XIII

THE POPULAR POET AND STORY-TELLER

THE most widely cultivated form of oral poetry is undoubtedly poetry relating to unspecified individuals, generally known as folk-songs, which appears to be recited in peasant circles throughout all parts of the country, especially by young people. Little is known of the authorship of such poetry in general, but some observations have been made by early travellers on its composition and recitation, and a few words will be said on this subject later.

A class of poetry which is of peculiar interest and importance in Russia is the poetry of social ritual, more especially poetry recited at weddings and wakes. We have seen that this poetry is of a very elaborate character, and is cultivated with a high degree of specialisation. Such poetry appears to have continued in a flourishing condition down to the third quarter of last century in Little Russia and in many parts of Great Russia, notably in the Government of Olonets. A collection has been made in our own day by the brothers Sokolov.[1] Owing to the extempore character of such poetry, and to its close association with the events which call for its recitation, it is difficult to treat of the authorship and composition apart from the poetry itself, and we have therefore already discussed these subjects to some extent in the chapter on 'Poetry relating to Unspecified Individuals'. The section of the present chapter which deals with this subject, therefore, is to be regarded as merely supplementary to what has already been said in the previous chapter.

The extempore composition of popular poetry by non-professional people was very widely practised by the Russian peasants in the eighteenth and nineteenth centuries, and no doubt continues to be so still in remote districts. In 1824 the German traveller Erman found that in the neighbourhood of Tobolsk the Russian groom accompanied the alternate bounding and rattling of the carriage "with ever-varying, apposite addresses to the horses separately, always in rhyme, partly with songs of considerable length".[2] He tells us that the horses are adjured, in heroic fashion, "not to flag on the road which constantly grows shorter, but to bound without delay from hill to hill". Reference

---

[1] *R.F.* Vol. III (1931). Our efforts to obtain a copy of this work have met with no success. [2] Erman, I. p. 314.

has already been made (p. 228 above) to the account given by the English traveller Coxe, during the latter part of the eighteenth century, of the universal practice of turning the discourse of every-day life into poetry, and the proficiency of the Russian peasants in extempore composition of this kind. The passage however deserves to be quoted at length here because it is full of interest for the study of the genesis and milieu of village poetry:

"In our route through Russia I was greatly surprised at the propensity of the natives to singing. Even the peasants, who acted in the capacity of coachmen and postilions, were no sooner mounted than they began to warble an air, and continued it, without the least intermission, for several hours. But what still more astonished me was, that they performed occasionally in parts; and I have frequently observed them engaged in a kind of musical dialogue, making reciprocal questions and responses, as if they were chanting (if I may so express myself) their ordinary conversation. The postilions *sing*, as I have just observed, from the beginning to the end of a stage; the soldiers *sing* continually during their march; the countrymen *sing* during the most laborious occupations; the public-houses re-echo with their carols; and in a still evening I have frequently heard the air vibrate with the notes from the surrounding villages.... The words of the songs are mostly in prose, and often extempore, according to the immediate invention or recollection of the singer; perhaps an ancient legend, the history of an enormous giant, a declaration of love, a dialogue between a lover and his mistress, a murder, or the description of a beautiful girl....I have been also informed that the subject of the song frequently alludes to the former adventures of the singer, or to his present situation; and that the peasants adapt the topics of their common discourse and their disputes with each other to this general air; which, altogether, forms an extraordinary effect; and led me to conjecture, as I have before expressed myself, that they chanted their ordinary conversation."[1]

As we have seen, Rybnikov found the compositions of the village poets flourishing in a peculiarly high degree in the Onega district. In addition to the two volumes of *byliny* which he recorded from this area, a third volume is occupied with occasional poems and poems of social ritual, as well as some slighter poems or typical folk-songs. It is, of course, in the nature of things that poetry of this kind is ephemeral, and the great majority of such compositions perish unrecorded. The elements which survive and reappear in each fresh composition are the conven-

[1] Coxe, I. p. 441 ff.

tional form and formulae of many types of such compositions. What might almost be called the Platonic 'idea' of a given type of poem survives from generation to generation. Occasionally, of course, individual poems are also perpetuated, though how long they would retain their verbal identity is doubtful. Rybnikov quotes a *zaplachka* composed by a young woman on the death of her cousin, which, on account of its excellence, "immediately acquired notoriety, and was adopted by other women, who now sing it whenever a similar calamity befalls them" (cf. p. 230 above).

Rybnikov has recorded many interesting data in regard to the recitation and composition of such poetry in the Onega region. The social milieu in which it is current is today identical with that of the *byliny*. Rybnikov obtained a number of poems of this class in the Province of Olonets from the identical singers who also furnished him with the *byliny*, and a large number of poems of social ritual were obtained by him from the women of the same class and region. He noted that the women had their own range of themes and styles of poetry as specialised as those of the men, but different.

He was impressed by the practice prevalent in the Onega district of composing poetry on every important occasion in the life of an individual. "Almost every woman", he says, speaking of the neighbourhood north of Lake Onega, "can give expression to her feelings of distress either by improvising a new lament (*zaplachka*), or by adapting an old one to the circumstances."[1] When the individual did not feel able either to compose or to adapt some composition already in existence, she called in a specialist, or a professional poet, to compose one for her. It is chiefly due to the professionals that the ancient traditional form and diction of this popular ritual poetry have been so faithfully preserved in North Russia. In districts where the professional no longer exists, these ancient forms and formulae have almost disappeared.[2]

In Great Russia, in the districts from which Rybnikov obtained most of his material, and from which much of our most interesting information on this subject is derived, the professional is generally a woman. In the neighbourhood of Lake Onega she is known as the *plakalshchitsa*, or *voplenitsa*, 'wailer', from *plakat*, 'to weep', and *vopit*, 'to lament', or 'wail'. Rybnikov became acquainted with a *voplenitsa* who enjoyed a great reputation for her knowledge of traditional ritual and her proficiency in extemporising songs, and who was frequently

[1] Rybnikov, I. p. lxv.   [2] Ralston, *Songs*, p. 341.

summoned to remote parts to officiate at ceremonies. From her he obtained a number of wedding and funeral songs.[1]

The *plakalshchitsa* or *voplenitsa* is a person of great importance and prestige, and is in great demand. She it is who supervises social ritual and acts as mistress of ceremonies at important social functions, such as weddings, funerals, and commemoration feasts. On such occasions she must see to it that the traditional rites are observed, must settle the details of the ceremonial, and chant appropriate songs on behalf of the principals concerned, in which, standing by their side, she gives expression in improvised song to the sentiments which they may be expected to feel on such occasions, or—alternatively—prompts them to song and action on their own behalf. At weddings it is her function to prompt the bride; at funerals, the widow and the orphan.

Her labours are often sustained through a considerable period of time. On the day of betrothal she attends the bride, singing *zaplachki*, laments expressive of the sorrow felt by the girl at leaving her home, and the dread inspired by the prospect of a life among strangers. She accompanies the girl on the prescribed visit to her relatives, bewailing her coming separation. Through all the numerous ceremonies which precede the actual wedding in the church she attends and prompts her, supplying her with songs suited to every step in the elaborate ritual.

It is interesting to find that the *skaziteli* of Olonets are sometimes equally expert at extemporising the songs chanted according to ancient custom on occasions of social ritual. We learn from Sokolov that one of the great *skaziteli* of our own time, Fedor Andreêvich Konashkov, is also a great expert in north Russian wedding rites, especially the utterances proper to the master of ceremonies at a north Russian peasant wedding. "In this capacity he is famous throughout an exceedingly wide circle, and is invited to the most remote villages. With a kerchief over his shoulder he rides at the head of the wedding procession and entertains the guests with his observations. His speech throughout must consist of improvisations. Readiness of speech and wit, combined with dignity, must attain to their highest degree of excellence. Konashkov adapts to this purpose the rich verbal and pictorial treasures which he has got from the *byliny*, and this circumstance makes his part in a wedding all the more valuable."[2]

It has been shown (p. 228 f. above) that a striking feature in the life of

---

[1] For Rybnikov's account of the *voplenitsa* and her répertoire, see I. p. lxv f.; III. p. 3 ff. Cf. also Ralston, *Songs*, p. 341 f.

[2] *Slavische Rundschau*, IV (1932), p. 471.

the peasants of the Onega district is the large number of occasions on which such ceremonial songs appear to have been required by the exigencies of social etiquette. Indeed in the region to the north of the Lake, e.g. round Petrozavodsk, social life is exceedingly highly developed, and has become correspondingly ceremonial in character.[1] When the svakha (cf. p. 232 f. above) comes to consult the bride's father, the bride laments the impending separation in song. Songs of a lively or cheerful cast, such as are deemed suitable to the occasion, are sung at the feast which accompanies the betrothal. We have seen also that ẓaplachki are sung by the bride as she visits her friends and relatives on the days ensuing, when her plait is cut off and her hair bound up, when she receives the bridegroom, and on many other occasions during the ceremony. Similarly laments are sung by mothers over their sons who go to the army, by relatives over the dead, and by wives and mothers year after year at the graves of husbands and sons long dead. At times these laments are improvised on the spot. At times they appear to be handed on by oral tradition.[2]

Songs are sung also at social gatherings, the posidêlki and besêdy and vechery ('evening parties') being favourite occasions. In Olonets the Russian peasants, men and girls, assemble at an appointed iẓba with a large living room, often paying a small entrance fee, as if it were a clubroom. In some districts, such as Little Russia, and in the district south of the Urals, the girls sit and card and spin flax, singing at their work, much as Aksakov describes the maids doing at Aksakovo in Years of Childhood. Later in the evening, as the young men begin to drop in, the work is laid aside and dancing begins, sometimes to the accompaniment of songs sung by the girls. A man at the door takes the entrance fees, and music, when required, is paid for by general subscription. Ralston quotes the opening of one of the skaẓki in Afanasev's collection in which one of these vechernitsy or village soirées is described.[3] We are told that the party commences on November 30th, and lasts for a week. The girls brew and bake in preparation, and the boys bring music, and dancing takes place. It is interesting to note that on such occasions the songs are not chosen capriciously, but follow an established sequence.[4]

Such were the scenes of entertainment among the peasants of Olonets and elsewhere last century. Interesting descriptions of the posidêlki and

---

[1] Rybnikov, loc. cit.
[2] Rybnikov, loc. cit.; Ralston, Songs, p. 334.
[3] Ralston, R.F.T. p. 10.   [4] Ralston, Songs, p. 38.

of a *vecherinka* in the neighbourhood of Ekaterinburg and Tobolsk are given by the German traveller Erman,[1] who was present at some of these gatherings in 1828. They correspond substantially to those of Olonets and of Little Russia, except that the *balalaika* was frequently introduced to accompany the songs, tales, and character dancing with 'action songs', which form a part of the entertainment. Masking and fortune-telling or 'divining' also frequently took place.

The wealth of Russian *skazki* is enormous, and it is not surprising that we possess more information relating to their circulation than to that of saga proper. Yet even here our information is slight, while so far as we are aware we possess no information relating to the composition or initial circulation—what we may term the oral 'publication'—of a single *skazka*. The great collection of Afanasev contains hardly any direct (editorial) information as to the milieu from which his *skazki* are recorded. It is not improbable that in recent years more interest is taken in this subject than in the past; but if this is so the evidence has not yet been made available to western scholars. Fortunately some little information can be gleaned from the internal evidence of the *skazki* themselves, and from notices in Russian biographies of last century.

The *skazki* (folk-tales) themselves bear testimony that they are a popular source of entertainment in the *izba* or peasant's hut. Ralston refers to a story in Khudyakov's collection (Vol. II, p. 65) in which a boy who had been carried off by a Baba Yaga—a kind of witch monster—was found by his sister "sitting in an arm-chair, while the cat Jeremiah told him *skazki* and sang him songs".[2] In another story in Ralston's collection a *durak* (fool) is sent to take care of the children of a village during the absence of their parents, and is told to collect them in one of the cottages and tell them *skazki*[3]—in fact, a kind of impromptu *crèche*. A *skazka* referred to below relates to the recitation of *skazki* at night in the *izba* or household of people of humble class.

There is evidence to show that the sagas and even the *skazki*, like the *byliny*, formed at one time the entertainment of the upper classes. The Russian poet Zhukovski was preoccupied to the end of his life with the study of versions of native *skazki*.[4] Pushkin refers to the delight which he still felt in mature years in listening to the recitation of *skazki* by his old nurse. In one of his letters, written in 1855, we read: "I listen to *skazki*

[1] Erman, I. pp. 271 f., 312 ff.   [2] Ralston, *R.F.T.* p. 9 f.
[3] *Ib.* p. 10.   [4] Afanasev, I. p. xlvi.

in the evenings....How charming these stories are! Every one is a poem."[1]

Aksakov's evidence also suggests that in the eighteenth century the country gentry took an unsophisticated pleasure in listening to prose sagas. The cultivation of saga was certainly carried on in the household of Aksakovo, Aksakov's home during the time of his grandfather. The housekeeper, Pelageya by name, was regularly employed by the old man to send him to sleep by telling him stories at night.[2] She had been for some time in Astrakhan, and had learnt many stories (*skaʒki*) from the merchants congregated there. One of her stories—apparently an Oriental folk-tale—is narrated by Aksakov in full.[3] Aksakov tells us that her special qualifications as a story-teller were her extensive répertoire, and her ability to keep awake all night.

Aksakov appears to attribute Pelageya's proficiency as a story-teller, as well as the richness of her répertoire, to her sojourn among the eastern merchants in Astrakhan; but the habit of telling stories to induce sleep had been practised in Russia for many centuries, and the Aksakov family in this, as in other respects, was conservative, and no doubt typical of the more backward among the landed gentry. Rambaud mentions the fact that in the sixteenth century, "the rich never went to sleep without being lulled by tales told by some popular story-teller. Ivan the Terrible always had three, who succeeded each other at his bedside."[4]

We have traditional evidence for the same practice in a *skaʒka*, which suggests that the habit was a common one. According to this story, a peasant had a wife who was so fond of stories that her husband is said to have found it 'rather costly'. One day a wayfarer called and begged a night's lodging, and the peasant asked if he could tell stories. The peasant replied that he could tell stories 'all night long'. The delighted peasant invited him in, and when supper was over, they lay down to sleep, and the stranger began to tell his stories.[5]

It is interesting to observe that the guest is regarded as especially expert because, like Pelageya, he can tell stories 'all night'. In this story, as at Aksakov's home, and as was the case also with Ivan the Terrible, it is only after they have had supper and lain down to sleep

[1] See Afanasev, *loc. cit.*

[2] *Sem. Khron.* p. 209; *A Russian Schoolboy*, p. 45 f.

[3] The story is called 'The Scarlet Flower', and is printed as an appendix in *Years of Childhood*, p. 415 ff.

[4] *History*, 1. p. 321 f.   [5] Magnus, *Folk-Tales*, p. 333.

that the story-telling begins. We are not told whether Ivan's story-tellers were professionals or merely household servants with a gift for story-telling. Pelageya herself was a serf. The *skazka* just referred to seems to suggest that among these night story-tellers every man had his price, and that, moreover, the custom was not confined to the rich.

From what has been said it will be evident that story-telling has been a source of entertainment in Russia for many centuries. Like the *byliny*, the sagas have suffered a decline from the high esteem in which they were once held, both at court and also in the monasteries. The introduction of printing and the circulation of books have brought 'enlightenment' and culture and a wider circle of interests, and the sagas have become the entertainment chiefly of old folk and children on winter evenings. The spread of education, tardy though it has been in Russia, is finally killing the saga as surely as it is killing the *bylina*.

LIST OF ABBREVIATIONS

Books and periodicals are referred to under the name of the author, sometimes followed by one or more prominent words of the title of the book, or the initial letters of the words forming the titles of books or periodicals. A list of the periodicals referred to will be found immediately following the list of books given below.

AUTHOR AND TITLE OF BOOK	ABBREVIATION
AFANASEV, A. N. *Narodnÿa Russkÿa Skazki* ('Russian Popular Tales'). 3rd ed. 2 vols. Moscow, 1893.	Afanasev.
AKSAKOV, S. T. *Semeinaya Khronika i Vospominanÿa* ('Family Chronicle and Reminiscences'). Moscow, 1856.	Aksakon, *Sem. Khron.*
—— The above, translated by J. D. Duff (from the edition published at Moscow in 1900), under the titles of	
A Russian Gentleman (Oxford, 1923).	Aksakov, *Russian Gentleman.*
Years of Childhood (Oxford, 1923)	Aksakov, *Childhood.*
A Russian Schoolboy (Oxford, 1924).	Aksakov, *Schoolboy.*
BEZSONOV, P. A. *Kalêki Perekhozhie* ('Wandering Kalêki'). 6 parts. Moscow, 1861–4. See also under Kirêevski.	Bezsonov.
BLAKEY, K. 'Folk Tales of Ancient Russia (Byliny of Lord Novgorod the Great)'. In *S.R.* III (1924–5), p. 52 ff.	Blakey.
BRAUN. 'Das Historische Russland im Nordischen Schrifttum des X–XIV. Jahrhunderts.' In *Festschrift für Eugen Mogk*. Halle an der Saale, 1924.	Braun.
BRODSKI, N. L., MENDELSON, N. M., and SIDOROV, N. P. *Istoriko-Literaturnaya Khrestomatÿa*. Pt I. Moscow and Petrograd, 1922.	Brodski, etc.
CHADWICK, N. K. *Russian Heroic Poetry*. Cambridge, 1932.	Chadwick.
Chronique dite de Nestor, traduite…avec introduction et commentaire critique par Louis Léger. Paris, 1884. Publications par l'École des Langues orientales vivantes. 11e Série, Vol. XIII.	Ancient Chronicle.
COXE, W. *Travels into Poland, Russia, Sweden and Denmark*. 3 vols. London, 1784–90.	Coxe.
DANILOV, KIRSHA. *Sbornik Kirshi Danilova*. Ed. Sheffer. St Petersburg, 1901.	Sheffer.

AUTHOR AND TITLE OF BOOK	ABBREVIATION
DORMIDONTOV. *Kratiki Kurs Istori Russkoy Literatury*, Pt I ('Short Course in the History of Russian Literature'). Tallinna Eesti Kirjastus-Uhisus, 1923.	Dormidontov.
DUMÉZIL, G. 'Les Bylines de Michajlo Potyk.' *R.É.S.* v (1925), p. 205 ff.	Dumézil, *R.É.S.*
—— *Légendes sur les Nartes*. Paris, 1930.	Dumézil, *Nartes*.
ECK, A. *Le Moyen Age Russe*. Paris, 1933.	Eck.
EISNER, P. *Volkslieder der Slawen*. Leipzig, 1926.	Eisner.
ERMAN, G. A. *Travels in Siberia*..., translated from the German by W. D. Cooley. 2 vols. London, 1848.	Erman.
FLETCHER, G. *Russia at the Close of the Sixteenth Century*. Comprising the treatise 'Of the Russe Common Wealth' by G. F., and the travels of Sir J. Horsey, now for the first time printed entire from his own manuscript. Ed. by E. A. Bond. Hakluyt Society, London, 1856.	Fletcher. Horsey.
GILFERDING, A. F. *Onezhskÿa Byliny*. 2nd ed. in 3 vols. St Petersburg, 1894–1900.	Gilferding.
GLAZUNOV, I. *Russkaya Narodnaya Lirika*. St Petersburg, 1910.	Glazunov.
GRUZINSKI, A. E. See Rybnikov.	
HAPGOOD, I. F. *Epic Songs of Russia*. 2nd ed. London, 1915.	Hapgood, *Songs*.
—— *Russian Rambles*. London, 1895.	Hapgood, *Rambles*.
HORSEY, J. See under Fletcher.	Fletcher. Horsey.
JENKINSON, A. *Early Voyages and Travels to Russia and Persia*. Edited by E. D. Morgan and C. H. Coote. Hakluyt Society, London, 1886.	Napea.
KIRÊEVSKI, P. V. *Pêsni Sobrannÿa* ('Collected Songs'). Ed. P. A. Bezsonov. 7 parts. Moscow, 1860.	Kirêevski.
—— Second edition (unchanged). Moscow, 1868, etc. (We have made use of both editions, but generally the second. Unless otherwise indicated references are to the latter.)	Kirêevski.
—— *Pêsni Sobrannie. Novaya Serÿa*. Vol. II, Pt II. *Pêsni Neobryadovÿe*. Ed. M. N. Speranski. Moscow, 1929.	Kirêevski, *N.S.*
KLYUCHEVSKI, V. O. *History of Russia*, translated by C. J. Hogarth in 3 vols. Our references are to Vol. I, London, 1911.	Klyuchevski.
LAEHR, G. *Die Anfänge des Russischen Reiches*. Berlin, 1930.	Laehr.

Author and Title of Book	Abbreviation
LYATSKI, E. *Skaẓitel Ivan T. Ryabinin i ego Byliny.* ('The Reciter Ivan T. Ryabinin, and his Byliny.') Moscow, 1895.	Lyatski.
MAGNUS, L. A. *The Heroic Ballads of Russia.* London, 1921.	Magnus, *Ballads.*
—— *Russian Folk-Tales.* London, 1915.	Magnus, *Folk-Tales.*
—— *The Tale of the Armament of Igor.* Oxford, 1915.	Magnus, *Igor.*
MANSIKKA, V. J. *Die Religion der Ostslaven.* Vol. I. *Quellen Suomalainen Tiedeakatemia.* Helsingfors, 1922.	Mansikka.
MARKOV, A. V. *Bêlomorskÿa Byliny.* Moscow, 1901.	Markov.
MAZON, A. 'Le Centaure de la Légende Vieille— Russe de Salomon et Kitovras.' In *R.É.S.* VII (1927).	Mazon, *Kitovras.*
—— 'Mikula le Prodigieux Laboureur.' In *Ib.* XI (1931).	Mazon, *Mikula.*
—— 'Svjatogor ou Saint-Mont le Géant.' In *Ib.* XII (1932).	Mazon, *Svjatogor.*
—— 'Les Bylines russes.' In *Revue des Cours et Conférences,* 3 March 1932 (Paris).	Mazon, *Bylines.*
—— 'Il'ja de Murom dans l'Épopée Germanique.' In *Mélanges offerts à M. Nicolas Iorga.* Paris, 1933.	Mazon, *Ilya.*
MICHELL, R., FORBES, N. and BEAZLEY, C. R. *The Chronicle of Novgorod.* London, 1914.	Michell.
MILLER, V. F. *Ocherki Russkoy Narodnoy Slovesnosti.* Vol. I, Moscow, 1897; Vol. II, Moscow, 1910; Vol. III, Moscow, 1924.	Miller, *Ocherki.*
MILLER, V. and TIKHONRAVOV. *Byliny Novoy i Nedavney Zapisi iẓ Raẓnykh Mêstnostey Rossi.* Moscow, 1908.	Miller, *Byliny.*
MIRSKY, Prince D. S. 'Old Russian Literature.' In *S.R.* III (1924-5), p. 74 ff.	Mirski.
MORFILL, W. R. *Russia.* London, 1890.	Morfill, *Russia.*
—— *A History of Russia from the birth of Peter the Great to the death of Alexander II.* London, 1902.	Morfill, *History.*
—— *Slavonic Literature.* London, 1883.	Morfill, *S.L.*
MURKO, M. *Geschichte der älteren südslawischen Litteraturen.* Leipzig, 1908. Die Litteraturen des Ostens. Bd. v, Abt. 2.	Murko, *G.ä.s.L.*
—— 'Die Südslawischen Literaturen.' In Hinneberg, *Die Kultur der Gegenwart: Die Osteuropäischen Literaturen,* I. IX, p. 194 ff.	Murko, *S.L.*
NISBET BAIN, E. *Slavonic Europe.* Cambridge, 1908.	Nisbet Bain.

AUTHOR AND TITLE OF BOOK ABBREVIATION

OLEARIUS, A. *The Voyages and Travells of the Am-* Olearius.
bassadors, sent by Frederick, Duke of Holstein, to
the Great Duke of Muscovy, and the King of
Persia...rendered into English by J. Davis.
2nd ed. London, 1669.

PARES, Sir BERNARD. *A History of Russia.* London, Pares.
1926.

RALSTON, W. R. S. *Russian Folk-Tales.* London, Ralston, *R.F.T.*
1873.

—— *The Songs of the Russian People.* 2nd ed. Lon- Ralston, *Songs.*
don, 1872.

RAMBAUD, A. *The History of Russia from the earliest* Rambaud, *History.*
times to 1877.... Translated by L. B. Lang.
2 vols. London, 1879.

—— *La Russie épique.* Étude sur les Chansons Rambaud, *R.É.*
héroïques de la Russie.... Paris, 1876.

ROZNIECKI, S. *Varaegiske Minder i den russiske Hilte-* Rozniecki.
digtning. Copenhagen, 1915.

RYBNIKOV, P. N. *Pêsni Sobrannÿa* ('Songs'). Ed. Rybnikov.
Gruzinski. 3 vols. Moscow, 1909–10.

RZHIGA, V. 'De l'Évolution des pièces mobiles dans Rzhiga, *R.É.S.*
les bylines.' In *R.É.S.* XIII (1933).

SCHRÖDER, F. R. 'Skandinavien und der Orient im Schröder.
Mittelalter.' *G.R.M.* VIII (1920), pp. 204 ff.,
281 ff.

SHAMBINAGO, S. 'Istoricheskÿa Perezhivanÿa v Shambinago,
Starinakh o Sukhanê.' In a Collection of articles *I.P.S.S.*
presented to V. O. Klyuchevski. Moscow, 1909.

SHEFFER, P. N. *Sbornik Kirshi Danilova.* St Peters- Sheffer.
burg, 1901.

SHKLOVSKY, J. W. *In Far North-East Siberia.* Trans- Shklovsky.
lated by Edwards and Shklovsky. London, 1916.

SOKOLOV, B. *Byliny, Istoricheski Ocherk, Teksty i* Sokolov, *Byliny.*
Kommentari. Moscow, 1918.

SOKOLOV, B. and Y. *Russki Folklor.* 4 vols. Moscow, Sokolov, *R.F.*
1929–32. (For further details of this publication,
see *R.É.S.* XII (1932), p. 257.)

—— —— 'À la Recherche des Bylines.' In *R.É.S.* Sokolov, *R.É.S.*
XII (1932).

—— —— 'Zwei Bylinenrezitatoren'. In *Slavische* Sokolov, *Slavische*
Rundschau, IV (1932). *Rundschau.*

SOLOVEV, S. M. *Istorÿa Rossi s Drevnêyshikh Vremen.* Solovev, col. —.
2nd ed. St Petersburg, 1895, etc. (The columns
are numbered continuously throughout the
volume. The pagination is not numbered.)

AUTHOR AND TITLE OF BOOK	ABBREVIATION
SPERANSKI, M. *Istorÿa Drevney Russkoy Literatury.* Moscow, 1914.	Speranski, *I.D.R.L.*
—— *Russkaya Ustnaya Slovesnost.* Moscow, 1917.	Speranski, *R.U.S.*
STENDER-PETERSEN, Å. *Die Varägersage als Quelle der Altrussischen Chronik.* Leipzig, 1934.	Stender-Petersen.
STUDER, ELLA. *Russisches in der Thidreksaga.* Bern, 1931.	Studer.
VÄISÄNEN, A. O. 'Das Zupf-instrument gusli bei den Wolgavölkern.' In *Juhlakirja Yrjö Wichmannin,* published as Vol. LVIII of the Mémoires de la Société Finno-Ougrienne, Helsingfors, 1928, p. 303 ff.	Väisänen.
WIENER, L. *Anthology of Russian Literature from the earliest period to the present time.* 2 parts. London and New York, 1902–3.	Wiener.

PERIODICALS

Archiv für slavische Philologie. Berlin, 1876.	*Archiv s.P.*
Etnograficheskago Oboʒrenÿa.	*E.O.*
Germanisch-Romanische Monatsschrift. Heidelberg, 1909, etc.	*G.R.M.*
Revue des Études Slaves.	*R.É.S.*
Russkaya Mysl.	*R.M.*
Slavia.	*Slavia.*
Slavische Rundschau.	*Slavische Rundschau.*
Slavonic Review.	*S.R.*
Viestnik Evropy, 1868.	*V.E.*
Zeitschrift für slavische Philologie. Leipzig, 1924– .	*Z.S.P.*

PART II

YUGOSLAV ORAL POETRY

CHAPTER I

INTRODUCTION

LITERATURE AND WRITING

UNLIKE the peoples whose literatures were discussed in the first Volume the Yugoslavs[1] possess a large body of poetry[2] which is still—or was until very recently—carried on by oral tradition. Before the beginning of last century comparatively little of this poetry seems to have been committed to writing. Since that time, however, the number of poems which have been published must amount to several thousand, though very many of them are variants.

The collection of this large body of poetry is due in the main to the fortunate circumstance that Yugoslav scholars who were interested in it got to work while the conditions of life which prevailed in many parts of the country were still 'barbaric'. Indeed Vuk Stjepanović Karadžić,[3] the greatest of all the collectors, published his first volume in 1814, when Serbia was under Turkish rule; and other volumes were published not much later. Towards the end of the century large numbers of poems were collected in Bosnia and Hercegovina within twenty years after the Turks had evacuated those regions. The other districts which seem to have yielded most material are Montenegro and the old 'Military Frontier'. The latter had continually been receiving refugees from Serbia and Bosnia, while the former was in a state of more or less constant guerilla warfare, as we shall see later. With these exceptions, not very much seems to have been obtained from the lands which had always, or for a long time past, been free from Turkish rule.[4] There are,

[1] We use the term 'Yugoslav' in the restricted sense of Serbo-Croatian. There is also a large amount of Slovenian oral poetry; but we have made no study of it. We understand that it is of a very different character.

[2] A good deal of saga (including heroic saga) is also said to be preserved. But nothing of this kind has been accessible to us, except translations of folktales.

[3] As regards the pronunciation of the letters—c corresponds to Engl. ts, č to ch (in child), h (final) to Scot. ch (in loch), j to Engl. y (in year), š to sh, ž to Engl. ž, ž to s in measure; ć represents more or less the initial sound in Engl. tune. We follow Croatian orthography, which very often has je or ije for Serbian e; otherwise the differences are very slight. Dj and gj are often used indifferently, especially in the name 'George'.

[4] Apart from ženske pjesme (see below), in which some of these districts, especially on the coast, seem to be rich.

however, some older collections of poetry, especially from Ragusa and southern Dalmatia, preserved in MSS. of the seventeenth and eighteenth centuries.

Oral poetry—*narodne pjesme*, lit. 'poems of the people'—as distinct from written poetry, is still current in some parts of Yugoslavia;[1] and new poems relating to events of the day are said to have been composed during the Balkan Wars of 1912–13 and the Great War. We have not seen any of this recent poetry; but we understand that it follows traditional lines. Owing to the progress of education, however, no part of Yugoslavia is now dependent upon oral tradition for its literature. Oral tradition indeed, in the strict sense, will probably soon be a thing of the past, though many of the poems will doubtless be remembered through the medium of books, owing to their popularity. In general we shall confine our attention to poems which were composed before 1860.

Yugoslav oral poetry is not a thing of recent growth. References to the recitation of heroic poetry occur in records which date from the early part of the sixteenth century; and there are much earlier references to oral poetry of other kinds. Many heroic poems are concerned with persons and events of the fourteenth and fifteenth centuries, though some scholars hold that this kind of poetry did not originate before 1500. This is a question which we shall have to discuss later. The oldest texts of oral poetry which have been preserved are two heroic poems included in Petar Hektorović's *Ribanje* ('Fishing'), written in 1556, which the author states that he had heard from fishermen in the island of Hvar (Lesina).

In spite of the prevalence of oral poetry (and saga) written literature was at no time wholly unknown in any of the Yugoslav lands. Indeed the history of writing in these lands can be traced back to much earlier times than that of oral poetry. This is true not only of Greek and Roman writing, which survived in certain districts from the sixth century, before the Slavs crossed the Danube. The language of the Slavs themselves was committed to writing by the missionary saints Cyril and Methodius, c. 860, and during the following centuries both the early Slavonic alphabets—first the Glagolitic, and later the Cyrillic—were widely used for ecclesiastical purposes. In the thirteenth century Serbia became the chief centre of Slavonic literary activity; and writing

---

[1] Cf. Murko, *Rev. des Études Slaves*, XIII. 16 ff., where an interesting account is given of the present conditions. In remote districts the tradition seems sometimes to be still strictly oral. In other places this kind of poetry is fairly widely cultivated —often by educated people—but printed collections of poems are used.

now was not wholly unknown even to the laity, at all events to members of the princely families. Two of the rulers themselves are known as authors, Stephen (Stjepan) the First-Crowned (1196–1228), who wrote the life of his father (Stjepan Nemanja), and Stjepan Lazarević (1389–1427), to whom are attributed many translations, as well as some original works. The literature, however, continued to be essentially of ecclesiastical character. The most important exception was the code of Laws promulgated by Stjepan Dušan in 1349.

The western districts, Dalmatia and Croatia, came under the ecclesiastical influence of Rome in the tenth century; and the use of the Slavonic language by the Church was maintained only with difficulty, though it lasted down to the age of printing. In other respects also these districts[1] came gradually more and more under Western influence. The Roman alphabet was used for writing Slavonic, except for liturgical purposes, from the fifteenth century; and even before this there seems to have been a good deal of religious poetry written in Glagolitic, but based on models derived from Italy. Some translations of romances also were made in the fourteenth century—likewise derived, in part at least, from Italian sources. Then, late in the fifteenth century, the influence of the Renaissance began to be felt, especially in Ragusa, where a voluminous literature was produced, of very varied character but almost wholly in poetry and based on Italian models.[2] The same influence was felt, though to a slighter extent, in other Dalmatian towns and in western Croatia—indeed wherever Roman writing and print had come into use. The northern districts were also affected by the Reformation.

In Ragusa and the greater part of Dalmatia the course of civilisation was at no time seriously interrupted; and literary activity never ceased, though after the seventeenth century it declined somewhat. The same is true of western Croatia, though the civilisation here was less advanced. But all the eastern Yugoslav lands, which included almost the whole of the Orthodox population, were conquered by the Turks—Serbia in 1459, Bosnia in 1463, Hercegovina in 1482, the (Hungarian) lands north of the Danube, together with Belgrade, in 1561–26. In these lands such progress in civilisation as had been made during the previous centuries seems now to have been lost; and they were practically unaffected by

[1] It is to be noted that Dalmatia was for the most part under Venetian rule from c. 1000. About a century later Croatia was conquered by the Hungarians. Soon afterwards they obtained a footing also in Dalmatia, for the possession of which they contended with the Venetians for the next three centuries.

[2] Cf. P. Popović, *Jugoslovenska Književnost* (Cambridge, 1918), p. 17 ff.

the influence of the Renaissance. A few religious books were printed during the first century after the conquest; but this came to an end before the close of the sixteenth century, and for the next two centuries the monasteries were still dependent upon MSS. The whole of this period was sterile, apart from a few chronicles and religious works on traditional lines. Outside the monasteries there was no education.

Towards the end of the seventeenth century the Turks were expelled from Hungary by the Austrians. This event soon brought the Yugoslavs who lived north of the Danube and the Sava into contact with Western civilisation, and led to a considerable development of educational and literary activity on modern lines in the latter part of the eighteenth century. From this quarter the movement spread to Serbia after the Wars of Independence. It is said that neither Kara-Gjorgje, who led the first war (1804–13), nor Miloš Obrenović, who ruled—with intervals—from 1815 to 1860, was able to read. In Montenegro there seems to have been little provision for education before the reign of Nikola (1860). Bosnia and Hercegovina remained isolated and out of contact with the civilised world until the Austrian occupation (1878).

From what has been said above it will be seen that the various Yugoslav lands have had a very different history during the last five centuries. The western districts, which were not conquered by the Turks, remained in contact with Western civilisation, and participated, at least to some extent, in the intellectual and literary movements of the times. The most advanced place was Ragusa (Dubrovnik), which had a separate and peculiar history. The Ragusans accepted Turkish sovereignty, but secured internal independence. By this course they acquired more or less a monopoly of trade between the Turkish dominions and the west. In wealth and culture Ragusa was far in advance of the Venetian possessions in Dalmatia, and comparable rather with Venice itself. In striking contrast with this culture was the state of the more eastern and larger part of the Yugoslav area, which was under direct Turkish rule for periods varying from two centuries, in the north, to four centuries or more, in Bosnia and the extreme south. During the periods in question—perhaps more especially during the seventeenth and eighteenth centuries—the conditions of life throughout this area were those of barbarism. Such education as there was seems to have been restricted on one side to ecclesiastics, on the other to a limited number of officials, who were mostly Mohammedans; but the two systems had nothing in common except mutual hostility.

As we have seen, it is from this eastern area that most of the *narodne pjesme*[1] are derived—apart from those which are preserved in old MSS. The great bulk of them come from the regions in which Turkish rule lasted until the nineteenth century. Within certain limits, which will be noted later, it may be said that oral literature was characteristic of the Yugoslavs who were under Turkish rule, written literature of those who lived outside the Turkish borders.

One exceptional case is that of Montenegro. The Montenegrins themselves maintain that they have always been independent; but this claim is not generally allowed by historians. Apparently the ruling family embraced Islam about the beginning of the sixteenth century, following the example of most of the Bosnian aristocracy; and the greater part of the country then came under Turkish rule. But it may be that the rugged and barren western district was never effectively occupied. At all events it was able to maintain its freedom from the close of the seventeenth century. But its history, as revealed in the numerous *narodne pjesme*, seems to have been one of almost continuous raiding and border warfare. Down to the middle of the nineteenth century education was practically limited to the family of prince-bishops; but the last of these, Peter II, is generally recognised by the Yugoslavs as their greatest poet. It is of interest to note that this bishop established a printing-press at Cettinje, after an interval of nearly three centuries and a half; but before many years it was converted into bullets.

In this book we are concerned only with *narodne pjesme*, not with written literature of ecclesiastical or cosmopolitan affinities. For the former we have used the term 'oral poetry', and there can be no doubt that this description is generally correct. Most of the reciters from whom the poems were obtained were unable to read; some of them were blind. But we do not know to what extent the poems are now preserved by oral tradition; for conditions have greatly changed. Most of those who now recite the poems have probably learned to read, and printed copies are easily purchasable.

With the character of the recitation we shall have to deal in a later chapter. It may, however, be noted here that *junačke pjesme*—which include heroic poems (see below)—are usually accompanied by a stringed instrument, either the gusle or the tambura,[2] and that very

---

[1] In particular the 'men's poems' (see below). 'Women's poems' (*ženske pjesme*) seem to have had a wider circulation; large numbers have been obtained from the Adriatic coast.

[2] The gusle is a kind of primitive fiddle with only one string, but resembling a

great freedom is allowed in the treatment of the subject. Variants are extremely numerous and sometimes show little or no verbal resemblance to one another. Indeed a man cannot repeat a poem in exactly the same words; the faculty cultivated by the reciters or minstrels is improvisation rather than memorisation.

The authors of the poems are usually unknown; the reciters can give the names only of those from whom they themselves heard them. Karadžić[1] suspected that two of the Montenegrin poems which he collected were derived from poems of Bishop Peter I (St Peter), which had gradually been transformed into *narodne pjesme* and rendered unrecognisable. Occasionally, as we shall see, the history of a poem can be traced back for centuries by the help of variants in the MS. collections. We do not know whether minstrels' books have ever been found; but there appear to be more or less trustworthy records of soldiers who had collections of poems in Turkish writing. Such cases, however, must have been quite exceptional among an almost entirely illiterate population.

With regard to the collections of poems contained in MSS. of the eighteenth century and earlier, it is to be noted that many of the poems, known as *bugarštice*, have a different metre from that which is regularly employed in modern narrative *narodne pjesme*. The latter consists of a uniform decasyllabic line with caesura after the fourth syllable.[2] The *bugarštice* on the other hand have an irregular and much longer line—usually, though by no means always, eight syllables in the second half (after the caesura), and a more variable number (but usually between six and nine) in the first half. Moreover the continuity of the metre is in many poems interrupted by the introduction of short lines—usually of six syllables, but sometimes less—at regular or irregular intervals. In one type the second, fifth, eighth, eleventh (etc.) lines are short, and in such poems stops occur most frequently after the third, sixth, ninth, twelfth (etc.) lines. The short lines are not refrains, though often they are not essential to the sense. The *bugarštica* seems to have gone completely out of use in the course of the eighteenth century.

banjo in appearance. A picture of a man playing this instrument is given by Subotić, *Yugoslav Popular Ballads*, facing p. 165. The tambura, which is used only by Mohammedans, seems to be a kind of mandoline with two strings.

[1] *Srpske Narodne Pjesme*, IV (Vienna, 1862), p. 68, note.

[2] The decasyllabic poems preserved in MSS. of cent. xviii at Ragusa and Perast almost all contain a number of irregular lines. Many other forms of metre occur in *ženske pjesme*; for an account of these see Subotić, *op. cit.* p. 26 ff. It may be observed here that rhyme (which is usual in literary poetry) is of fairly frequent occurrence in *ženske pjesme*. In 'men's poems' it is extremely rare.

It has been disputed whether the *bugarštice* are properly to be regarded as *narodne pjesme*, or whether they were of literary origin. The total number of these poems, which have been preserved, is said to be about a hundred; and of these there are several which have the appearance of literary compositions.[1] But many others give quite a different impression and bear unmistakable traces of oral transmission. Frequently indeed this is placed beyond reasonable doubt by the existence of variants. In other cases we meet with expressions which are characteristic of oral poetry. Sometimes the poem ends with a wish for the happiness of the master of the house or those who are present. Hektorović records the melody or rhythm (*način*) of the chant with which the fishermen's poems were rendered. The literary *bugarštica* must at least be regarded as the exception rather than the rule.[2] It may be observed here that the term *bugarštica*[3] is doubtless connected with the verb *bugariti*, 'to chant or lament'—the word used by Hektorović for the chanting of the poems— as well as with *bugarka*, 'elegy, dirge'.[4] Three of the poems, however, contained in a Zagreb MS., dating from c. 1700, bear the title *bugarska* or *pjesan bugarska*, an expression which originally can hardly have meant anything else than 'Bulgarian poem'; and it is likely that the other words are of similar origin. A difficult problem arises here, which will require notice later. For the present it will be sufficient to observe that the original significance of the words must have been forgotten even in the sixteenth century; for Hektorović describes the rhythm of the poems he obtained as 'Serbian'. Indeed it would seem that early writers use the word *bugarštica* in much the same sense as *narodna*

[1] Cf. Bogišić, *Narodne Pjesme iz starijih...Zapisa*, Introd. p. 2, who regards three of the seventy-six *bugarštice* published by him as of literary origin.

[2] The theory, which we believe to be mistaken, that the *bugarštica* is of (foreign) literary origin, will be noticed later, in Ch. x. It may be remarked here that the interest and importance of the *bugarštice* seem not to have been sufficiently appreciated by modern writers. Most English writers seem to have neglected them. We may also observe that we have frequently found a good deal of difficulty with their language, especially the vocabulary.

[3] This is only one of a number of similar words which are used by early writers in the same sense. Hektorović uses *bugarskica* and *bugarkinja*. Our information is derived from Bogišić, *op. cit.* Introd. p. 29 ff., where further details and quotations are given. Hektorović's work is not accessible to us.

[4] The word *bugarka* was perhaps once used as equivalent to *bugarštica*. In MS. Yugoslav. Acad. (Zagreb) 638 it is applied to a *bugarštica*, of which the text is given (No. 11) in Bogišić's edition; cf. Miklosich, *Denkschr. der k. Akad. d. Wiss.* (Vienna), *Phil.-Hist. Cl.* 1870, p. 57. According to Miklosich (*ib.*) all these words are derived from the name 'Bulgarian'.

pjesma is now used,[1] i.e. to distinguish such poems from literary poetry.

It should be observed that the evidence for the *bugarštica* is much earlier than that for the poem in decasyllabic metre. The former, as we have seen, is known from 1556; the latter does not occur until towards the end of the seventeenth century, and is believed to have come into existence not long before that time. Presumably therefore the public recitations of heroic poetry, which we hear of from time to time in the sixteenth and early seventeenth centuries, were those of *bugarštice*. On one occasion at least the reciter is said to be blind. To this subject we shall have to refer again in the last chapter.

It is the custom to divide *narodne pjesme* into two classes—*junačke pjesme* ('heroic poems') or *muske pjesme* ('men's poems') and *ženske pjesme* ('women's poems'). But this classification is not very satisfactory. *Ženske pjesme* are not recited or sung exclusively by women; and among *iunačke* (*muske*) *pjesme* there are many poems to which we should not apply the term 'heroic'. Musical accompaniment is said to be unusual with the former class—many of them are sung at work or recreation— but customary with the latter, which are intended primarily for the entertainment of a party. But we do not know how far this distinction is to be pressed. We shall classify the material according to the scheme followed in Vol. 1.

Literature of thought, as represented by the antiquarian, gnomic, descriptive and mantic categories and by Type C in other categories, occurs but rarely in the collections. This is doubtless no accident; for the same phenomenon is found in the modern oral literatures of other Christian and Mohammedan peoples. On the other hand heroic poetry is very largely represented, while non-heroic poetry seems to be by no means rare. There is a little poetry which corresponds apparently to the poetry and saga relating to deities found in the ancient literatures. Poetry relating to unspecified individuals is abundant, though the characters commonly bear names.

Perhaps the most distinctive feature of Yugoslav oral poetry is the prevalence of Type A, which tends to encroach upon the other Types, especially Type D. The latter occurs in its proper form, though we have not found it easy to obtain examples. Type B is by no means rare, but

[1] It would probably be more correct to define *bugarštica* as a poem in the form of a *narodna pjesma*, i.e. without the conventions (rhyme, etc.) observed in literary poetry.

usually contains an element of narrative. We have not found any certain examples of Type E; but we have no doubt that it is cultivated.[1]

The distinction drawn in Vol. I between 'non-heroic' poetry, relating to the Heroic Age, and 'post-heroic' poetry, relating to times later than the Heroic Age, cannot be drawn on strict chronological lines in the case of Yugoslav oral poetry. In point of fact there is a not inconsiderable amount of poetry corresponding to the poetry found in both these categories, and as a rule the two can be distinguished as easily as in the ancient literatures; but the distinction here seems to be geographical rather than chronological. The close of the Heroic Age may be equated with the end of Turkish rule and the introduction of modern civilisation, and may be dated c. 1880 in Bosnia, Hercegovina and Montenegro,[2] about sixty years earlier in Serbia, and farther north again much earlier. But the 'post-heroic' poetry which we know comes from the Dalmatian towns and relates to events of the sixteenth and seventeenth centuries; much of it is preserved in MSS. not later than c. 1700. There are no records, so far as we know, of a Heroic Age in these places; the heroic poems preserved there relate to other regions. If such a period ever existed on the Dalmatian coast, it would seem to have come to an end before the sixteenth century. The plan we shall follow therefore is to treat all non-heroic poetry in the same chapter. It will be seen that some of the Serbian non-heroic poems relate to earlier times than any of the heroic poems.

Most of the non-heroic, as well as the heroic, poems are conventionally included among the 'men's poems'. The great majority of the 'women's poems' relate to unspecified individuals (Ch. VII), though they frequently contain names. Sometimes the names are those of famous heroes. But in many cases there is reason to suspect that a poem existed before the hero's name became attached to it. Indeed not unfrequently we find variant texts of such poems, one of which contains the name of a famous hero, while another is nameless, or has some other name.

We shall devote our attention in the main to the 'men's poems'. The timeless nameless poems—relating to unspecified individuals—seem in general to be of a less distinctive (Yugoslav) character. Analogies are

---

[1] Cf. Murko, *Zeitschr. d. Vereins f. Volkskunde*, 1909, p. 22, note, where quotations are given from letters between a Slavonian corporal in the Austrian army and his wife, written in 1897. Many of the sentences form regular decasyllabic lines and may be regarded as typical examples of love-poetry (of Type E).

[2] Montenegro was independent, at least from c. 1700; but the conditions of life were governed by the fact that it was almost surrounded by Turkish territory.

often to be found, especially for the non-narrative poems, in the folk-songs of the other Slavonic peoples, and even in more distant parts of Europe. We are under the impression that poetry of this kind spreads and overcomes even linguistic barriers rather easily. For a satisfactory treatment of Yugoslav folksongs one would require a knowledge of the popular poetry of all the surrounding peoples, including Italian and probably also Turkish and Hungarian—knowledge to which we can make no pretensions. The 'men's poems' too are not wholly without external affinities; but these seem to be much more limited. On this subject we shall have a few words to say at the end of the last chapter.

CHAPTER II

HEROIC POETRY

IT has been mentioned that the amount of heroic poetry which has been preserved is very large. There must be at least several hundred different poems; and many of these are preserved in several variant forms. Type A (narrative) is by far the most common; but Type B and Type D (cf. p. 2) also occur. The poems vary in length from under a hundred lines to over four thousand—perhaps much more.

The Heroic Age may conveniently be divided into three main periods, as follows: I. The period of full or partial independence, before the Turkish conquest was complete. This period may be said to end c. 1500. The stories treated in the poems seem to extend over rather more than a century and a half before this date. II. The period of Turkish rule, from c. 1500 to c. 1700 in Montenegro, to c. 1800 in Serbia. III. The period of Montenegrin independence, after 1700, including the wars of independence in Serbia (c. 1800–1820).

All the poems which relate to Period I, so far as we know, are derived from Christian sources. The poems which relate to Period II are partly Christian, partly Mohammedan. In the latter, historical elements are more obvious than in the former. In Period III the Christian poems seem to be in a considerable majority. The Mohammedan poems, relating to both these periods, come chiefly from Bosnia and Hercegovina.

The themes of the poems are in general very similar to those of heroic poetry in other lands—battles, raids, quarrels, marriages, etc. Cattle-raiding is less frequent than one would expect, just as in the Teutonic poems, though treasure is often mentioned. The heroes, however, are as a rule, out for the lives of their enemies, rather than their property. Head-hunting is the dominant principle. On the other hand marriages are also a popular subject—corresponding to the 'Courtships' of Irish saga, especially as exemplified in the 'Courtship of Ferb' (cf. Vol. 1, p. 48). The bridegroom usually sets out with a company at least a thousand strong, including the most famous heroes he can get; and the wedding festivities are regularly followed by a fight on a big scale either with the bride's relatives or with some enemy who waylays the party on their return journey. In this class of stories characters and motifs are often borrowed freely by one poem from another, in defiance of chronology.

A good number of stories relating to Period I are treated in *bugarštice*. Many of these are identical in substance with later poems, and are of interest as early variants of the latter. Some *bugarštice*, however, are concerned with stories which do not occur elsewhere, so far as we are aware.

The earliest time to which any heroic stories known to us relate is the reign of Stjepan Dušan (1331–1356). Of these the most famous is the 'Marriage of Dušan'.[1] Here also we may mention certain poems relating to Vukašin, who was a contemporary of Dušan and succeeded him in part of his dominions. The best known of these are the 'Marriage of Vukašin'[2] and the 'Walling of Skadar (Scutari)'.[3] All the stories relating to this period are of an imaginative or legendary character. The 'Marriage of Vukašin' is largely concerned with Momčilo's winged horse, which is disabled by his faithless wife. In the 'Walling of Skadar' Vukašin contrives to get his brother's wife immured as a foundation sacrifice to the Vila. This poem, however, cannot properly be regarded as heroic, though it is concerned with heroic characters.

Next we may take a large group of poems relating to Marko Kraljević, the most famous of all Yugoslav heroes. Not much is known of him from historical sources. He was a son of the Vukašin mentioned above, who was killed at the battle of the Marica in 1371; and some time after this, apparently in 1385, he submitted to the Turks. As a Turkish vassal he seems to have kept the castle of Prilep in Macedonia, together perhaps with some portion of his father's dominions. He is said to have been killed at the battle of Rovine, in 1394, while fighting for the Turks against the Rumanians.[4] It is a remarkable fact that a man with such a record has come to be the great national hero of the Serbians. In the poems themselves his connections with the Turks are frequently mentioned. We may refer (e.g.) to 'The Sister of Leka Kapetan', 461 f., where he is taunted with being a Turkish minion (*pridvorica*) and with fighting for the Turks. There are many other passages in which he takes the heads of individual Turks; but he seems to be always in the Sultan's service, and more or less loyal to him.

[1] Transl. (paraphrase) by Petrovich, *Heroic Tales and Legends of the Serbians*, p. 150 ff.

[2] Transl. by Low, *The Ballads of Marko Kraljević*, p. 1 ff.; Petrovich, *op. cit.* p. 186 ff.

[3] Transl. by Morison in Subotić's *Yugoslav Popular Ballads*, p. 40 ff.; Petrovich, *op. cit.* p. 198 ff.

[4] Cf. Low, *The Ballads of Marko Kraljević*, p. xxii.

It is unnecessary to describe this group of poems, since most of them are translated in Low's *Ballads of Marko Kraljević.*[1] It will be seen that Marko is not a very attractive hero, according to modern ideas. Especially in his treatment of women, he is sometimes more of an ogre than a hero, tearing out their eyes and chopping off their hands. Physical strength and heavy drinking are among his chief characteristics. He owes much to his horse Šarac, which he feeds on wine.

Here it will be sufficient to refer to a few poems which are not included in Mr Low's collection. In 'Marko's Revenge for the Death of his Brother Andrija'[2] the hero and his brother are hunting in the mountains, and Andrija is overcome with thirst. He goes to a tavern where thirty Turks are drinking, and the barmaid asks him in. He begins to drink; but the Turks cut off his head. Then Marko comes to look for him. The barmaid denies that she has seen him; and Marko enters the tavern and begins to drink heavily. The Turks attack him; but he kills them all. Then he puts out the barmaid's eyes, ties her to a horse's tail, and drives it over the hills.

One of the two poems (*bugarštice*) preserved by Hektorović[3] (cf. p. 300) gives a story which is entirely inconsistent with this. Here Marko and Andrija (Andrijaš) seem to be brigands. They have captured three horses, and quarrel over the division of the spoil. Marko plunges his sword into his brother's heart. This narrative is told very briefly—in seventeen lines—and is merely introductory to Andrija's dying speech, which occupies the rest of the poem. He asks his brother not to withdraw his sword until he has made certain requests. First he begs him not to let their mother know what has happened. If she asks why his sword is bloody, he is to say that he has met a stag which would not make way for him; if it had turned aside he would not have killed it. If she asks where his brother Andrija is, he is to reply that he has fallen in love with a maiden in a land from which he cannot return. She has given him magic food; and he comes no more to join his brother in his adventures. Then he bids Marko himself to call upon his name, when he is attacked by brigands; he cannot come to his help, but the enemy will take to flight on hearing his name.

[1] The texts will be found in Karadžić, *Srpske Narodne Pjesme,* Vol. II.

[2] The text will be found in *Hrvatske Narodne Pjesme* (publ. by the Matica Hrvatska), I. ii. 126 ff. There are many variants; cf. *ib.* 390 ff. Cf. also Bogišić, *Narodne Pjesme,* No. 89.

[3] It is publ. also (from Hektorović) in the collections of Miklosich (*op. cit.* p. 64 f.) and Bogišić (*op. cit.* p. 18 ff.).

This poem shows a striking contrast to the modern poems relating to Marko. The subject is treated with dignity and restraint; and the sense of tragedy arising from a hasty act is sustained throughout. Grotesque and brutal features are wanting. The diction is more careful and artistic than in later poems.

Next we may take one of the poems called 'The Marriage of Marko Kraljević'.[1] Marko goes hunting or hawking on the hills, but meets with no success and becomes exhausted. While he is resting, he sees in the distance Vile—supernatural female beings—dancing the *kolo* (round dance), which is led by Nadanojla, chief of the Vile. He tells his falcon to go and swoop down upon Nadanojla and seize her wings and head-dress, and bring them to him. He promises to reward the falcon handsomely. The falcon carries out his orders, in spite of Nadanojla's appeals, and Marko sets off home with the spoils. Nadanojla follows him; and when the guards at the gate, and then his mother, remark that he has been lucky in capturing the Vila Nadanojla, he replies at her request that it is not the Vila Nadanojla, but a shepherdess whom he has found on the hills, and whom he intends to marry. She brings luck to the house and bears him a son; but on one festive occasion he boasts that his wife is a Vila—at which she is much displeased. She persuades his sister Barbara to ask Marko to let her have her wings and headdress, so that she may dance the *kolo* in front of the house. Marko consents; and the Vila dances three rounds, and then flies away, saying that she has left him because of his disobedience. Not long afterwards, however, he sees her again; and again succeeds in catching her through his falcon. He makes his peace with her; she brings up the child, and they live together happily afterwards.

In another poem called 'The Birth of Marko Kraljević'[2] practically the same story is told of Vukašin, Marko's father. There is no falcon; Vukašin finds a Vila, called Mandalina, asleep and steals her crown and robe. She appeals to him to restore them; but he refuses. Then she follows him home; he marries her, and she bears him two sons, Marko and Andrija. Nineteen years later he celebrates the marriage of Marko, and a *kolo* is danced. Mandalina asks for her crown and robe, so that she may take part in the dance. He consents; but after two rounds she flies up into the clouds. He appeals to her to return for the sake of their

[1] Publ. by the Matica Hrvatska in *Hrvatske Narodne Pjesme*, 1. ii. 61 ff. This is a wholly different story from the poem of the same name transl. in Mr Low's book.

[2] Publ. in *Hrvatske Narodne Pjesme*, 1. ii. 1 ff.

young son Andrija; but she promises only to come at night to feed him. Vukašin never sees her again.

It will be seen that in one of these stories Marko is the husband, in the other the son of a Vila. The latter story cannot have been generally accepted, for Marko's mother is introduced or mentioned in numerous poems, without any hint of her supernatural origin. She is often called Jevrosima, in accordance with 'The Marriage of Vukašin' (cf. p. 310). In this story she is Momčilo's sister; and Vukašin marries her when he has killed Momčilo and his faithless wife. Yet the story given above is not peculiar to 'The Birth of Marko Kraljević'. It is found also—very briefly—in a poem[1] preserved in the Franciscan MS. at Ragusa, which dates from the middle of the eighteenth century. We may note further that in another poem, likewise preserved in an early MS.,[2] the story of Momčilo, with his winged horse and his faithless wife, occurs in a form very similar to 'The Marriage of Vukašin', but without reference to Vukašin himself, whose place is here taken by a *ban* ('governor') from Germany. All this illustrates the freedom with which stories of Marko have been treated, at least during the last two centuries.

Another important group of poems centre round the first battle of Kosovo, in which the Serbian prince Lazar was defeated and slain by the Turks, in 1389. Lazar was a contemporary of Marko Kraljević; but the latter does not figure in these poems. The two cycles are quite distinct, except for the fact that a few of Lazar's heroes, especially Miloš, are sometimes introduced, as minor characters, in stories relating to Marko. In the Kosovo poems this Miloš—called Kobilović in the *bugarštice*, but Obilić in the later poems—is the leading hero. He kills the sultan Murad; and this seems to be a historical fact, though practically nothing more is known of him from early sources. But in these poems the interest is much more widely distributed than in those of the Marko Cycle. On the whole it is centred chiefly in Milica, the wife of Lazar; but there are poems in which she is not mentioned. A curious feature of the story is the treachery attributed to Vuk Branković, Lazar's son-in-law. This has never been quite satisfactorily explained, so far as we know. From historical sources it appears that he continued to carry on the struggle against the Turks for some years after Lazar's son Stjepan had made peace.

Apart from the fact that one cycle is concerned with a single individual,

---

[1] Publ. by Bogišić, *op. cit.* p. 231 f. (*ad fin.*).

[2] Publ. by Bogišić, *op. cit.* p. 265 ff. We think it is taken from the same (Franciscan) MS.; but if so there is a misprint in Bogišić's introduction, p. 131, lines 15 ff.

the other with several, there are remarkable differences in the character of the two sets of poems. They relate to the same period; yet the Kosovo poems give the impression of a much more advanced and cultured milieu. They represent human beings—of the heroic type, but still quite human; the crude and ogre-like element is wanting, and the fantastic rare, even in the modern poems. There is a general underlying resemblance to the 'Battle of Maldon', which may be due to the historical circumstances[1]; but the feminine element, which is very prominent here, though wanting in the latter, has its analogies in Norse heroic poetry. It is to be observed that several of the poems properly belong to Type B, while the narrative poems tend to approximate to this Type.

Naturally the Kosovo poems appeal to the modern mind much more strongly than those of the Marko Cycle. They are better known in this country than any other group of *narodne pjesme*, and have frequently been translated into English.[2] We shall therefore confine our attention practically to the *bugarštice*, which are less well known than the modern poems. In regard to the latter, however, one or two points may be noted here. 'The Fall of the Serbian Kingdom'[3] is a poem of Type C; it is an example of the utilisation of a heroic theme for the treatment of a religious motif. Lazar receives a message from Jerusalem bidding him choose between 'the heavenly kingdom' and the 'earthly kingdom'; and he chooses the former. This poem stands quite apart from the rest of the group, though the introduction of—more or less mystical—religious motifs occurs occasionally elsewhere in *narodne pjesme*.[4] It should be observed that there is no reference to national feeling, as in some of the other (modern) Kosovo poems. The latter part of the poem (47 ff.) is a catalogue—largely unhistorical—of the forces engaged in the battle, and can hardly have belonged to it originally.

'The Girl of Kosovo'[5] is a poem of Type B, of which the central character is a girl, not named, who is betrothed to Toplica Milan, one of Miloš' companions, and comes to the battlefield to look for him. She is presumably a fictitious character; and the poem is of interest as a very effective example of the use of a special type of fiction. A 'girl of

---

[1] For an account of the early historical works and documents relating to the battle the reader may be referred to Subotić, *Yugoslav Popular Ballads*, p. 74 ff.

[2] Cf. Mijatovich, *Kossovo*; Rootham, *Kossovo*; Subotić, *Yugoslav Popular Ballads*, p. 57 ff. (selections). Only the first of these contains the *bugarštice*.

[3] Karadžić, *S.N.P.* II. 295 ff. (No. 46).

[4] E.g. Karadžić, II. No. 34 (Low, p. 13 ff.). Karadžić, II. No. 95 (cf. Petrovich, p. 177 ff.) has a religious tone; but it is not mystical.

[5] Karadžić, II. 315 ff. (No. 51). Transl. by Morison in Subotić, *op. cit.* p. 70 ff.

Kosovo', perhaps taken from this poem, is introduced also in 'Musić Stefan' (106 ff.) and gives that hero news of the battle.

Another poem,[1] said to be a fragment, describes the banquet given by Lazar to his nobles before the battle—at which he charges Miloš with disloyalty. This piece is of special interest owing to its antiquity. An anonymous Italian translation of Ducas' History, dating from about the end of the fifteenth century, contains a rather long passage—not found in the Greek original—which seems to be derived from it. Several sentences show verbal coincidences with the poem, which cannot be due to accident.[2]

The longest of the *bugarštice*[3] relating to Kosovo embraces the themes of several of the later poems. First it describes the departure of Bušić Stjepan, which forms the subject of Karadžić's 'Musić Stefan' (ii. No. 47). Then it passes on to Milica's request that Lazar should leave one of her brothers behind with her—as in 'King Lazar and Queen Milica' (*ib.* No. 45). Next it tells the story of the accusation of Miloš by Lazar at supper. Lastly, it relates Miloš' attack upon the Turkish king, and the deaths of Miloš and Lazar. Part of this poem will require discussion in a later chapter. We may, however, note that Miloš and Vuk Branković are here clearly represented as personal enemies. It is Vuk who first accuses Miloš of disloyalty, in the supper scene; and later, in the battle, when Miloš calls out to Lazar for help, Vuk replies and charges him with fighting on the Turkish side.

In another poem[4], which seems to have no modern counterpart, Milica is sitting at a window talking to her two daughters, one of whom is married to Vuk Branković, and the other to Miloš. The daughters begin to compare their husbands; and an angry scene takes place, in which Vuk's wife strikes her sister and tears her face with a ring she has on her finger. Miloš' wife runs out into the garden to hide herself. While she is crying and mopping up the blood, Lazar comes home with his sons-in-law. Miloš goes to look for his wife, and she tells him what has happened. He flies into a rage and attacks Vuk, throwing him down

---

[1] Karadžić, ii. 50. iii. Transl. by Seton-Watson in Subotić, *op. cit.* p. 65 f.

[2] Cf. the note on p. 341, below, and Chadwick, *The Heroic Age*, p. 314 f., where these passages are quoted.

[3] Publ. by Miklosich, *op. cit.* p. 73; and by Bogišić, *op. cit.* p. 3 ff.

[4] Publ. by Miklosich, *op. cit.* p. 71; transl. by Mijatovich, *Kossovo*, p. 49 ff. A variant of this poem was evidently known to Orbini, *Il Regno degli Slavi* (Pesaro, 1601), p. 314, where the two daughters are called Mara and Vukosava, as also in Karadžić, ii. 49. In the *bugarštica* now referred to they are not named; but in Bogišić, No. 1, Miloš' wife is called Danica.

and kicking out two of his teeth. The action here clearly takes place some time before the battle, to which there is no reference. But the poem, or at least the version of the story which it represents, is connected with the one last noticed; for in the latter (209), when Vuk calls out to Miloš during the battle, he says that he (Miloš) will now have to pay for his teeth. One poem supplies a motif for the other. In the poem relating to the wives there is no suggestion of treachery. The hostility of the heroes arises from the quarrel between their wives. An interesting analogy is to be found in the story of Guðrún and Brynhildr.

Another *bugarštica*[1] describes Milica visiting the battlefield. She lights upon a mortally wounded hero, who makes himself known to her as her son-in-law, Miloš. He asks her to give to his wife his gold and a cap which she has embroidered for him, and also to set free upon the hills a horse covered with silk trappings. This poem represents a form of the story different from what is found in the long poem; for in the latter (*ad fin.*) Miloš is beheaded by the Turks and buried at the Turkish king's feet. In the piece we are now discussing, which is a poem of Type B, the hero is called Miloš Dragilović.

In addition to the group of poems noticed above there are a few others connected with the battle of Kosovo or with the heroes who took part in it. We may refer in particular to the story of Strahinja Banović, which is treated in a *bugarštica*, as well as in later poetry. Other poems are of a non-heroic character; and with these we shall have to deal in the next chapter.

The next large group consists of poems relating to the times of Despot[2] Giorgje or Djuro (Branković), who reigned from 1427 to 1456. This group includes a considerable number of *bugarštice*. The modern poems published in Karadžić's collection are not numerous; but we believe that others are current and have been published in more recent collections, which are not accessible to us. Very few poems of this group seem to have been translated into English.

As a whole this group of poems has less unity than either of the two which have been discussed above. It is not centred either in one individual or in one event. Some poems are concerned with Despot Djuro and his wife Jerina, others with various Serbian heroes of the time, others again with Hungarian heroes. The last named are the most numerous, especially in the case of the *bugarštice*. Indeed Sibinjanin Janko, i.e. the Hungarian leader John Hunyadi, is the most prominent

---

[1] Publ. by Miklosich, *op. cit.* p. 78 ff.; by Bogišić, *op. cit.* p. 10 ff.
[2] A Byzantine title adopted by Serbian rulers of cent. xv.

hero of the whole group. He and his comrades are recognised as being Hungarians, especially in the *bugarštice*, in which he is frequently called Ugrin Janko, 'Janko the Hungarian'. But he is not regarded as an alien. He is commonly represented as at enmity with Despot Djuro, the Serbian prince, but the sympathy is entirely on his side. Djuro generally appears as an old man and no warrior, and is treated with little respect, while his wife frequently acts on her own authority and is represented as a most detestable character. From historical records it would seem that the Despot's position, between the Hungarians and the Turks, was uncertain; but he kept possession of his territories until his death. The Turkish conquest of Serbia—apart from Belgrade, which now belonged to Hungary—took place in 1459.

There is indeed one *bugarštica*[1] which makes Janko to be of Serbian origin. In this poem Stjepan Lazarević, who ruled over Serbia from 1389 to 1427, is said to marry a girl (not named) of Sibinj (Hermann-stadt, in Transylvania) at the request of the nobles of that place. On the day after the wedding he sets off to Kosovo and is slain there; but in due course his wife bears twins, who are Janko and his sister Rusa. From historical sources nothing certain seems to be known of Janko's origin; but he was presumably a Magyar. Despot Stjepan was a well-known scholar; but he is very seldom mentioned in *narodne pjesme*. He was not killed in battle, nor indeed was any battle fought at Kosovo during his reign. It would seem that the poem has confused him with his father, Lazar. We have not met with any reference to this story elsewhere; and consequently we doubt whether it can have been generally accepted.

Fiction without doubt plays a great part in poems relating to this period. 'The Marriage of Djuro of Smeredevo'[2] seems to be a purely fictitious work. Jerina is here said to be a daughter of Mijailo, king of Ragusa.[3] Djuro decides not to go for the bride himself, but sends in his place Marko Kraljević—who was dead long before this time. With him he sends Janko, together with Miloš and other heroes of the past. An attack is made upon the wedding party in Ragusa; but Marko and his companions satisfactorily dispose of the assailants and return with the bride.

In the *bugarštice* such anachronisms are as a rule wanting, though we

---

[1] No. 8 in Bogišić's collection (p. 25 ff.), from the Zagreb MS.
[2] Karadžić, *op. cit.* II. 469 ff. (No. 79); transl. by Low, *op. cit.* p. 159 ff.
[3] According to Orbini (*Regno d. Slavi*, p. 276) she was a daughter of Matthias, son of the Greek emperor Ioannes Cantacuzenos. Her mother was a daughter of Vukašin. Jerina represents Irene.

may suspect the presence of a good deal of fiction in other respects. 'The Marriage of the King of Budim'[1] (i.e. the king of Hungary) forms the subject of two *bugarštice*, which seem to be variants of one original poem. Curiously enough neither poem gives the names of either bridegroom or bride, though the latter is said to be the daughter of the *ban* of Kruševo (Kruševac). The king's chief sponsors are Janko and Despot Djuro. At the feast which takes place—in one poem (A) before the bridegroom sets out, in the other (B) at the wedding itself—Janko refuses to join in the general merriment. In answer to the king's question he says that he cannot bear being in the presence of his enemy, the 'faithless' (A) Despot Djuro. In A he wants to use his sword. The king begs him not to spoil the festivities, and suggests a plan for showing his feelings towards Djuro later on—which Janko duly carries out. When they arrive at Kruševac they are not admitted until certain feats of shooting and horsemanship have been performed; but Janko has no difficulty with these. Then twelve girls come out, among whom the bride has to be identified. Janko produces a number of gold rings and draws his sword, saying that if anyone picks them up except the bride, he will take off her head.[2] When the feast is over, they set out on their return journey; and at Smeredevo (Semendria) Jerina comes out upon the walls with her ladies to watch them. Then Janko, following up the king's suggestion, grabs Djuro by his gray beard and beats him with a cudgel. The humiliation of an unpopular character in his wife's presence is a motif which occurs elsewhere in *bugarštice*.

A number of poems relate to the second battle of Kosovo, which was fought between John Hunyadi and the Turks in 1448. We may refer here to a strange and apparently widespread story which is known to us from two variants in Karadžić's collection,[3] as well as from a *bugarštica*[4]; but there may be other versions of it not accessible to us. In the later versions the story is, in brief, as follows. Janko collects all the warriors he can muster, including his youthful nephew Sekula (John Székély), and sets out for Kosovo. Sekula's sisters beseech him to leave their brother behind; but he refuses. On their arrival at Kosovo Janko goes to sleep, and Sekula makes his way to the tent of the Turkish king.

[1] Bogišić, *op. cit.* Nos. 9, 26 (pp. 28 ff., 72 ff.).

[2] Similar tests occur elsewhere, e.g. in 'The Marriage of Dušan' (Karadžić, II. No. 29).

[3] *Op. cit.* Nos. 85 f., pp. 506 ff. (A) and 509 ff. (B). B is fragmentary. Karadžić (p. 513) refers to another story, in which the Despot's enmity to Janko is inspired by fear that he means to enforce Catholicism.

[4] Bogišić, *op. cit.* No. 19 (p. 56 ff.) from the Zagreb MS.

Before starting he tells his uncle that he is going to turn into a six-winged snake, and that he will bring the Turkish king in his teeth in the form of a falcon. He does as he has said; and the two creatures fly to Janko's tent. Janko awakes and—in A—debates with himself what he shall do. Then he takes his bow and shoots the snake, which falls to the ground; but the falcon flies away to the Turkish camp. In B he consults Despot Djuro, and at his advice shoots the snake. Three times he hits it; and then it vanishes, and the falcon flies away. Then Sekula is brought to him mortally wounded; and he tells his uncle that he has hit him three times, first breaking his arm and then his leg and, lastly, shooting him in the heart. A is less detailed, and it is not clear how Sekula makes his appearance; but in both versions he blames Janko for not following his instructions, and then dies.

The *bugarštica* begins with Sekula's departure to the Turkish camp. He gives no instructions to Janko, but the latter tries to dissuade him from going. When he arrives at the king's tent, he produces from his own bosom both a winged snake and a falcon; and they fly off to Janko's tent. Janko is drinking with the Hungarians, and asks them which he shall shoot with his bow. They reply that he must shoot the falcon; but ill luck makes him shoot the snake. Then Sekula rides up, disfigured in appearance. Janko asks him whether he has been drinking, and other questions; but he answers that he has been shot in the heart by his uncle's arrows, and that his wounds are incurable. Then he dies.[1]

Curiously enough not one of these three poems refer to Janko's defeat in the battle. Yet it seems likely that this story was originally connected with some attempt to account for it. Note should be taken of the fact that in one version the responsibility for the unfortunate deed is thrown upon the unpopular character Despot Djuro.

There are several other poems connected with the second battle of Kosovo, which do not mention this incident. We may refer here to a *bugarštica*[2] which describes how Janko, Svilojević and Sekula come to ask the king of Budim (Buda) to give his sister to Sekula. The marriage is celebrated; but very soon afterwards Janko is summoned to meet the Turks at Kosovo, and Sekula with him. Sekula makes an attack upon the Turkish king's tent against Janko's orders; but he is mortally wounded and dies soon after his return to the camp. A more imaginative

---

[1] This form of the story, which is more than two centuries old, suggests derivation from an account of a kite-flying competition. For such competitions and for the idea that a kite could embody its owner's soul see Chadwick, *Journ. R. Anthr. Inst.* LXI. 455 ff.   [2] Bogišić, No. 20 (p. 59 ff.).

account of the same events is given in another *bugarštica*.[1] King Vladi-slav's sister looks out from her window upon the plain of Kosovo—several hundred miles away—and sees three Vile mounted on stags. She calls her brother, who chides her for her folly and says they are not Vile; they are the three *banove* (governors), Janko, Mihaile (Svilojević), and also Sekula—to whom she is now betrothed. They give her presents, and then set off with the king to Kosovo, where they all perish. The poem ends with a monologue by the king's sister, who asks herself for whom shall she make lamentation. Janko, Mihaile and Sekula all have mothers or sisters or wives to lament for them; but Vladislav has neither mother nor wife. She will therefore lament for her brother. The statements of this poem, however, are unhistorical. Only Sekula was killed at Kosovo. Janko was wounded and Svilojević captured by the Turks according to other poems.[2] King Vladislav IV was killed at the battle of Varna, four years before this.

In another *bugarštica*[3] Janko has been wounded at Kosovo and is making his way home. He tries to pass through Smeredevo, Djuro's capital; but the Despot has him arrested and put in prison. He writes to his wife Margarita, and asks her to come to him with their two young sons. She brings them, against the advice of Svilojević, her brother, and persuades the 'faithless Despot' to exchange them for her husband. As soon as Janko has left the city he calls out to the guard that, unless he gets his children back by the evening, he will return with his Hun-garians and destroy the place. Djuro then releases the boys. In the meantime his own young son Lazar has gone to play with them in the prison and, in the course of a quarrel, has been killed by Janko's son Matthias. When Djuro hears of this he gives orders for the fugitives to be pursued; but they make good their escape.

There are a number of other *bugarštice* relating to Janko and other Hungarian heroes and also to the king. The king seems usually to be Vladislav IV (1440–1444); but he is not distinguished from Vladislav V (1444–1457). We may, however, refer here to two *bugarštice*[4] which describe the royal election of 1457, after the death of the latter. The Hun-garian lords assemble under the presidency of Janko. Three times he throws the golden crown into the air; and each time it comes down upon the head of his son Matthias, who is then recognised as king. But in reality John Hunyadi was dead before his son's election.

In Karadžić's collection note may be taken of a short poem called

---

[1] Bogišić, No. 21 (p. 62 ff.).   [2] Cf. Bogišić, Nos. 25, 46 (pp. 71 f., 120 ff.).
[3] Bogišić, No. 10 (p. 31 ff.).   [4] Bogišić, Nos. 30 f. (pp. 80 ff., 84 ff.).

'Jerina, Wife of Djuro'[1] which has an interest as illustrating certain motifs. Jerina asks her grandson Maxim Grgurević for advice as to the marriage of her daughter. There are three suitors—Vilip the Magyar, the king of Moscow, and the Turkish king. Maxim advises her to choose first the Magyar, and next the Muscovite. He adds that if she chooses the Turk, he will claim possession of the country and the castles. She is furious at the answer and strikes him in the face, knocking out four teeth; and he falls to the ground. But he repeats that with her daughter she is giving the country and the castles to the Turks; and the poem adds that thus it came to pass. Jerina is therefore made responsible for the betrayal of the country.[2]

Among the Serbian heroes of this period Radosav seems at one time to have been the most famous; but he does not figure in many of the later poems which are accessible to us, and we do not know his story. One of the two *bugarštice* recorded by Hektorović[3] gives an account of his fate. He is described as a *vojvoda* ('general'), and at the beginning of the poem he is bidding farewell to his castle, Sjeverin. Then he falls into the hands of the *vojvoda* Vlatko, by whom he is treacherously put to death. Possibly this is to be identified with the Vlatko Mladenović who in another *bugarštica*[4] is said to be intercepting wounded Hungarians and despoiling them of their arms, and who is entrapped and slain by Janko.

Radosav himself is the central figure of one poem in Karadžić's collection.[5] Two ladies appeal to him on behalf of their husbands who have been imprisoned by Jerina. He goes to Despot Djuro and obtains his consent to their release; but he is only just in time, as they are about to be hanged. Jerina comes forward with the ladies of the court and threatens to hang Radosav together with Vuk the 'Dragon-Despot', who is not otherwise mentioned in this poem; but Radosav strikes her to the ground with his whip, and sets free the imprisoned nobles. He appears also as a great fighting-man in another poem in the same collection.[6]

The last considerable group of poems to be noticed here is concerned chiefly with Vuk the 'Fiery Dragon' or 'Dragon-Despot' and the

---

[1] Karadžić, *op. cit.* II. 479 f. (No. 80).
[2] According to M. Orbini, *Il Regno degli Slavi*, p. 325, Jerina did persuade Djuro to marry their daughter to Murad II. But he does not indicate that she was influenced by any motive other than political prudence.
[3] Bogišić, No. 49 (p. 126 ff.).   [4] *Ib.* No. 24 (p. 70).
[5] II. 499 ff. (No. 83).   [6] II. 445 ff. (No. 75).

Jakšića. Vuk is said to have ruled in Srijem—between the Danube and the Sava—from 1471 to 1485; his home was at Kupinovo on the Sava. He was a grandson of Despot Djuro and Jerina. One of his brothers, named Maxim, who apparently became a bishop, has already been mentioned. Vuk's chief friend in the poems is Dmitar Jakšić, who, with his brother Stjepan, holds the castle of Belgrade. This was within the Hungarian dominions; but the rest of Serbia had now become a Turkish province. The two brothers are frequently spoken of together as Jakšića (dual).

The poems relating to Vuk provide interesting material for studying the growth of unhistorical features. He is generally represented as a great warrior; but some of the later poems attribute to him supernatural properties, suggested perhaps by a desire to account for his surname. According to one (Bosnian) poem[1] he is found as a new-born babe with his head covered with wolf's hair,[2] with living fire blazing from his mouth and blue flame darting from his nose, and with arms red up to the shoulders. But the wildest story forms the subject of a poem in Karadžić's collection.[3] Here Vuk is made a contemporary of Lazar, who fell at Kosovo nearly a century before his time. Milica is troubled by the attentions of a fiery dragon which comes from the mountain Jastrebac and visits her at night in her tower. Lazar advises her to ask the dragon if there is anyone he is afraid of. He replied that Vuk in Srijem is the only person he fears. Then Lazar sends for Vuk, who lies in wait for the dragon. When he arrives and finds Vuk, he flies up into the sky. Vuk follows him and breaks his wings with a club. Then he falls to the ground, and Vuk cuts off his head.

There are other stories, however, of a less extravagant character. In a poem in Karadžić's collection (II. No. 93), called 'Porča of Avala and Vuk the Fiery Dragon', Porča is drinking in his castle at Avala, above Belgrade, with Djerzelez-Alija, who comes from Sarajevo. His guest taunts him with not having a waitress to serve and amuse them. Porča says he will go to Belgrade and get one; and then Djerzelez-Alija asks him if he is not afraid of the Jakšića. Porča replies that he has no fear of them. He has some fear of Vuk; but Kupinovo is a long way off, and he is not likely to meet him. So he sets off. But at this time Vuk happens to be drinking with the Jakšića; and he catches sight of the horseman, and asks them who he is. They tell him, and say that Porča is constantly

---

[1] Publ. with Germ. transl. by Krauss, *Slavische Volkforschungen*, p. 333 f.
[2] Suggested by the name *Vuk*, 'Wolf'.
[3] II. No. 43 (p. 255 ff.). Transl. by Petrovich, p. 129 ff.

killing their men and carrying off captives. Then they set a trap for him. They dress a girl up in fine silk clothes, and post her on the bank of the Sava. When Porča arrives she offers him a drink, and he seizes her; but Vuk pounces upon him, and he takes to flight. Djerzelez-Alija sees two horsemen approaching the castle at full speed, and orders the gates to be closed. Three times Vuk pursues Porča round the castle; and at last catches him and cuts off his head. Djerzelez-Alija thanks God that the gates were closed, and returns to Sarajevo.

Next we may take 'The Marriage of Vuk the Dragon-Despot'. In the poem contained in Karadžić's collection (II. No. 92) the bride, who is called Rosanda, is daughter of the *ban* of Venice. In response to a letter from her he brings twelve hundred followers; for she expects an attack from Djerzelez-Alija. When the wedding is over he lingers behind in Venice to bid farewell to the *ban* and his wife. Then a messenger comes to say that his men have been slaughtered by Djerzelez-Alija, though the Jakšića are still defending the bride. Vuk hurries to the scene, and after a stiff fight succeeds in shooting his enemy with an arrow.

A very different account of Vuk's marriage is given in certain *bugarštice*—Nos. 12 and 13 in Bogišić's collection.[1] Here the bride is called Barbara, as in other *bugarštice*. In No. 12 she is sister of the *ban* of Bosnia, in No. 13 of the *ban* of Poljice.[2] In the former she has befriended King Matthias, when he was in prison; and he has promised to marry her. But when the *ban* writes to remind him of this, he says he cannot marry her, because she is his *kuma*.[3] He invites her, however, to a feast, at which she may choose a husband from the assembled nobles. She accepts the offer, and chooses Vuk.

In No. 13 the marriage is treated very briefly. The *ban* offers Vuk a military escort to take them home; but Vuk replies that he has a good friend Alibego at the Dunaj. But when they arrive at the river, Alibego, who is a Turk, wants first to see the bride, and then to have her on his horse with him. Vuk consents, and then Alibego dashes into the river. Vuk is unable to catch him up; but one of his companions, Gredeljica

[1] No. 12 is from the Zagreb MS., No. 13 from the Franciscan (Ragusa) MS.

[2] We are not clear about the geography of this poem. The only place called Poljice known to us is not far from Ragusa. We do not know what river is meant by *Dunaj* (*Podunaj*) here.

[3] A *kum* (masc.) or *kuma* (fem.) is a person with whom one has entered into a fictitious blood-relationship, which precludes marriage. The word occurs very frequently in descriptions of weddings, where the *kum* is the chief sponsor; cf. Low, *op. cit.* p. 184.

Radosav, succeeds in overtaking him, and strikes his horse with a cudgel. Then Alibego drops the lady, and makes off across the river. Vuk calls out to the Turk that within six months he will raid his house and carry off his wife; and when he has got his bride safely home he fulfils his promise.

There are several other *bugarštice* relating to Vuk's adventures. We may refer here to No. 16 in Bogišić's collection (from the Franciscan MS.). Vuk comes back from the border badly wounded and shuts himself up in his room, without saying a word to his wife or his mother. His wife, Barbara, suspects that he has captured a girl and got her with him. She goes and looks through the door and sees a white mountain Vila washing and attending to his wounds. She tells Vuk's mother what she has seen, and the apparition (*znamenje*) at once flies away. Vuk then calls her into the room, and asks her why she has poisoned him. She denies having done anything of the kind; but he says she has poisoned him, not by seeing the Vila, but by speaking to his mother of having seen her. Then he asks her to summon Mitar Jakšić, who is to bring a monk with him. He makes known to Mitar what he wishes to be done with his property, and the monk shrives him.[1]

A number of poems—both *bugarštice* and later poems—are primarily concerned with the Jakšića. At least one of the latter, 'The Captivity and Marriage of Stjepan Jakšić', has been translated into English.[2] It relates how one morning, before dawn, a Vila from Mount Avala calls out to Mitar Jakšić that the Turks are at hand. He has just time to make his escape; but the castle and his brother Stjepan are captured by the enemy. Eventually Stjepan is imprisoned at Novi Pazar. Here the Pasha's daughter falls in love with him and enables him to escape. She accompanies him to Belgrade, and they marry. In this poem the religious element is unusually prominent. Stjepan is repeatedly pressed to become a 'Turk', but stedfastly refuses to give up the Christian religion. In the end the Pasha's daughter is baptised.

In some poems the two brothers are represented as quarrelling over their wives. Yet in one *bugarštica* (Bogišić, No. 43) they perish unmarried. They are discussing the possibility of marriage while they ride

---

[1] Vuk's last conversations with his wife and with Mitar Jakšić and his dying injunctions to the latter form the subject of a *bugarštica* publ. by Novaković, *Arch. f. slav. Philol.* III. 641 ff. from a Ragusa MS. of the early eighteenth century, not used by Bogišić. This poem seems to be of a more historical character and says much about Vuk's relations with King Matthias, whose vassal he was. There is no reference to the Vila.

[2] Cf. Petrovich, *Heroic Tales and Legends of the Serbians*, p. 177 ff.

together, and they are overheard by Vile of the mountains. The Vile decide among themselves that whichever of them can bring about a quarrel between the brothers shall be their queen. One Vila undertakes the task and presents herself before the Jakšića. Mitar is so overcome by her beauty that he tells her they are unmarried and asks her which of them she will have. She replies by choosing Stjepan, and Mitar thereupon turns upon his brother in fury and slays him. Then he is immediately overwhelmed with remorse and takes his own life, telling the Vila that she is responsible for the fate of them both.

II. Heroic stories relating to the second period of the Heroic Age (c. 1500–1700) differ in general from those of the earlier period in the fact that they are not concerned with the doings of princes and their noble followers; neither are they centred in events of national importance. There are, it is true, a number of poems which relate to important events in Turkish and Venetian history—sometimes indeed to events which took place in distant lands, e.g. the battle of Lepanto in 1571, the fall of Candia in 1669, and the relief of Vienna in 1682—but these poems cannot properly be regarded as heroic. No Yugoslav princes now survived, so far as we know. The greater part of Yugoslavia was under Turkish government, while the rest, apart from Ragusa, was subject to Venice or Austria. On the border between the two areas, in Dalmatia and Croatia, there was much frontier warfare, which is often celebrated in poetry. But a good deal of this poetry also, especially what comes from southern Dalmatia, cannot properly be treated as heroic; with this we shall have to deal in the next chapter. The heroic poems are concerned chiefly with the doings of local chiefs in Croatia, Bosnia and Hercegovina, and with the adventures of brigands (*hajduci*) and outlaws (*uskoci*) in Turkish territory. The fighting which is described is therefore usually on a small scale.

The battle of Muhač (Mohacs) in 1526, which brought about the Turkish conquest of Hungary, seems not to be clearly remembered in the poems, though it is evident enough that the disaster made a lasting impression. In one *bugarštica* (No. 28 in Bogišić's collection) Janko is made to interpret a girl's dream as foreboding the fall of Buda and the death of King Vladislav; and it is added that the disaster took place as soon as he had spoken. But here there is obvious confusion with the death of Vladislav IV at Varna in 1444. Janko himself died about seventy years before the fall of Buda. A somewhat clearer reminiscence is preserved in another (decasyllabic) poem (*ib.* No. 115), in which a sister of King Rakocija describes to her brother a dream she has had. This dream has much in common with the last—clouds and lightning over Buda, etc.—but she also describes various birds which she has seen descending upon the plain of Muhač. The king interprets the dream as presaging his own and his kingdom's ruin, and identifies the various birds with the emperor Suleiman, the grand vizier Cuprilić, the Janissaries, and other elements of the Turkish army. As soon as he has spoken, a letter comes from the emperor demanding his surrender. He refuses, and goes to meet the Turks at Muhač, where he loses his life and his kingdom. In this case the confusion is with the defeat of George Rakoczy II, prince of Transylvania, in 1657. The king slain at Muhač was Louis II. Suleiman was the conqueror at this battle; but Cuprilić was the opponent of Rakoczy. The defeat of the latter is the subject of certain Mohammedan poems, which we shall have to notice in the next chapter.

Another *bugarštica* (No. 36 in Bogišić's collection) deals with the defence of Siget (Szigetvar) by Miklauš Zrinjski (Nicholas Zrinji) against the emperor Suleiman in 1566. In view of the confusion relating to the battle of Muhač it is somewhat remarkable that this, less important, event is much more accurately remembered. A number of details regarding the siege and the final sortie are recorded, and these seem to be more or less in accord with what is known from historical sources.[1] One is inclined to suspect that the poem—which is preserved in a Zagreb MS.—may have been copied from an earlier text, written perhaps within memory of the disaster.[2] After this time references to events in Hungarian history seem to become less frequent, except in Mohammedan poems.

A much larger number of poems are concerned with the doings of heroes who appear to have been of merely local importance. The materials for identifying these persons are not accessible to us; but many of them evidently lived in the western borderland during the period under discussion. As an example we may take Ivo (Ivan) of Senj, on the

---

[1] An account of this siege will be found in Vambéry, *Hungary* (Story of the Nations), p. 311 ff.

[2] In a decasyllabic poem (Bogišić, No. 112) preserved in the Franciscan MS. a certain *ban Zrinjenski* becomes involved in a deadly feud with a *beg* named Malkoč. The *ban* is supported by the emperor, and the *beg* is slain by Janissaries. The superscription in the MS. calls this *ban* 'Nikola Zrinski', presumably identifying him with the hero of the poem noticed above; but there is nothing in the poem itself to suggest this. The superscriptions in the MSS. often seem to be wild guesses; and we have usually ignored them.

Adriatic (Quarnerolo), who figures in a number of poems. The warfare described in these is of a ruthless character. It seems to be essentially private—without reference to the action of any higher authorities.

In one poem[1] (No. 108 in Bogišić's collection) Ivo is drinking with the warriors of Senj, when the mother of one of his friends named Mihajlo Desančić begs him to rescue her son, who is imprisoned by Asan-aga. He advises her to invite him and his companions to a feast; and there they pledge themselves to the undertaking. Ivo posts his men in hiding, and makes his way to Asan-aga, concealing his identity. He begs from Asan-aga, saying that he has been imprisoned by Ivo of Senj. Asan-aga gives a him trifle and allows him to go to his house to beg more. Then he goes to the tower where Desančić is imprisoned, and ascertains from him how access is to be attained. On the following night, having put Asan-aga off his guard by false information, he surrounds the tower and rescues his friend.

A somewhat similar adventure forms the subject of another poem (*ib.* No. 109). A certain Ivan Latović, while hunting, is captured by the sons of a pasha and brought to their father, who declares that he will hang him. Ivan contrives to send a letter to Ivo of Senj; and the latter sets out with his followers. They succeed in rescuing the captive, make a slaughter of the Turks, and hang the pasha's sons.

In another poem (*ib.* No. 110) two men (presumably Turks) who have been captured by Ivo appeal for help to Asan-aga. The latter writes to Ivo to arrange a ransom. Ivo replies that he will not take gold or silver, but demands the castle of Jajce. Thereupon Asan-aga challenges him to single combat. Ivo sets out with his men, encounters Asan-aga on horseback, and throws him to the ground. Then his men make an attack, slay the Turks and carry off the Turkish women as booty. The Turkish ladies beg him not to drive them barefoot over the stones, since they have not been used to it. But he takes no heed of their complaints; he beats them with cudgels and brings them back with him to Senj. He sells the younger captives into slavery and puts the older ones to the sword. The same event forms the subject of another poem (*ib.* No. 111); but here the castle of Asan-aga, captured by Ivo, is called Belgrade.[2] There is no reference to the treatment of the women.

[1] The metre of this poem is irregular, some lines having ten syllables, others twelve. The following poems are decasyllabic (with occasional irregularities).

[2] The confusion is perhaps due to the fact that *bio grad* ('white castle') is a static term applied to any castle or fortified town. In No. 110 it is applied to Jajce.

The death of Ivo is the subject of another poem.[1] He has been raiding in Italy, and on his return is ambushed and mortally wounded, though he succeeds in making his way home. His enemy, Asan-aga—if it be the same person—figures in the famous 'Lament' of his wife, which was, we understand, the first of the *narodne pjesme* to be translated into English.

Some of the poems of this period are of a more romantic or imaginative character than those which have been noticed above. For an example of this kind we may refer to Bogišić, No. 99. Alajbeg Čengić has in his prison a certain Božo Rajković, whom he refuses to put to ransom, until he sees his sister and wife before him. Word of this comes to Rajković's sister, and she persuades the wife to give her her brother's horse and to dress her up in his accoutrements. Čengić's wife wakes her husband and tells him that a magnificent looking warrior has arrived; he must go out to greet him. He does so; but the horse kicks him and throws him down, and then Rajković's sister seizes and binds him. Then she beats him with a cudgel, and demands the keys of the prison. Čengić's wife brings the keys, and when she tries to prevent the release of Rajković the stranger strikes her with them. Then she sets her brother free and takes him off with her, and also Čengić as a prisoner. On the way she asks her brother if he recognises the horse and accoutrements; and he confesses that he knows them to be his own. But he does not know his sister, whom he believes to be a man. He supposes that his wife has been compelled to sell his accoutrements to a warrior unknown to him. On their arrival home she makes herself known. Then she beats Čengić with a cudgel; and he begs to be allowed to ransom himself. He writes to his wife; and she sends his horse and a large quantity of treasure. As soon as this has arrived Rajković's sister cuts off Čengić's head and fastens his body to his horse, which she sets free. The horse gallops home; and Čengić's wife, seeing it coming, believes her husband to be returning, and calls to her ladies to welcome him. When she sees the body she laments that she has lost both her husband and her treasure.

In two other poems in Bogišić's collection (Nos. 63 and 64) mention is made of an Alajbeg Čengić, governor of Hercegovina, who fought with the Venetians in 1654; but we do not know whether this is the

---

[1] The originals of this poem and also of the 'Lament' are not accessible to us. The former is transl. (by Seton-Watson) in Subotić, *Yugoslav Popular Ballads*, p. 47 ff. For the latter see *ib.* p. 224.

same man.[1] It should be mentioned that a variant of No. 99 occurs in No. 98, in which the rescued man is called Rašković. But here no name is given to the unfortunate Turk; he is spoken of merely as 'the vizier'.

Mohammedan poems relating to this period are numerous, though many of them cannot properly be described as heroic. As an example of the heroic class we may take the following.[2] The chief characters are said to be well known historical persons of the seventeenth century. Ćejvan Aga is drinking with his nephew Ibro Nukić and a party of friends, when he receives a message from the Sultan, ordering him to arrest a brigand named Vuk Gnjatijević. They prepare to set out; but Ibro begs for a day's respite, as he is to be married. The wedding takes place; but he sits up all night, singing and playing the guitar (tambura). Then he gives his bride a large sum of money, and rejoins his uncle. Ćejvan calls for a volunteer who will track the brigand to his lair, and only Ibro will undertake the dangerous duty. He finds the brigands, thirty in number, in a defile of the mountains, rushes upon them single-handed with his sword, and slays all of them except Vuk, whom he binds to a tree. He is himself too badly wounded to move, but he fires two shots to attract Ćejvan's notice. When the latter arrives with his party, Ibro tells him that he is mortally wounded, and gives him his clothes and weapons for one of his friends. Then Ćejvan takes the prisoner to Sarajevo and claims all the credit for himself. Hasan Pasha Ćoso enquires after Ibro; and Ćejvan says he is being married. But now Vuk convicts him of lying; and the Pasha puts them both in prison. In the meantime three Vile come to Ibro and tend his wounds. He soon recovers, and then makes his way to Sarajevo. There he obtains the release of his uncle, and is rewarded with a sword of honour for his exploit.

One of the most famous Mohammedan heroes is the beg Ljubović, who belongs to Hercegovina, though we do not know his date. In one poem[3] he is said to have a great number of cattle, which he sells advantageously in Dalmatia. Then he makes his way to Zara, in spite of warnings from his foster-brother Stjepan Majković and others, who tell him that Turks are prohibited from entering that city by an agreement between the Turkish and the Austrian emperors. He insists upon

---

[1] The death of an Alajbeg Čengić is celebrated in Karadžić, IV. 49 ff. (No. 8); but this would seem to be a different person.

[2] Publ. with German translation by Krauss, op. cit. p. 394 ff. The events are said to have taken place about 270 years before the date of publication (1908).

[3] Publ. with German transl. by Krauss, op. cit. p. 310 ff.

visiting the place, and surveys the buildings and fortifications. Then he is observed by the *ban* (governor), who orders his men to attack him and cut off his arm. The *ban's* page undertakes the duty. Ljubović at first takes no notice of him, but when the page strikes him he turns and cuts him in two. Then he is attacked by the *ban's* troops; but he succeeds in fighting his way out through the gates and escaping. Now the *ban* writes to the Pasha at Banjaluka, sending him rich presents and demanding the punishment of Ljubović. The Pasha despatches his officer, named Erdo, to Nevesilje (Nevesinje), the home of Ljubović; but the *beg* is away hunting. Erdo puts to death both his child and his mother, and then sets out on his return to Banjaluka. When Ljubović and Majković, who lives with him, come home and discover the outrage, they start at once to intercept the murderers. Erdo is captured and sent back to the Pasha after he has been half flayed; the rest are killed. Then the Pasha appeals to the Sultan, who sends an officer with a strong force to arrest Ljubović. On the arrival of these Ljubović and Majković give themselves up; but immediately afterwards a message comes from the Sultan, calling for a champion to defend him against the challenge of a black Arab. Majković takes up the challenge, goes to Constantinople and slays the Arab. He will not accept the Sultan's offers of treasure or the hand of a princess. He asks only for a grant of baronial rights and the death of the Pasha—whom he subsequently captures and flays.

We do not know who Ljubović was, or when he lived. There may have been more than one *beg* of this name. But it may be observed that he is a 'Turk', i.e. a Mohammedan, whereas his foster-brother Stjepan Majković, who lives with him, is evidently—from his name—a Christian. But there is no trace of any feeling of religious antagonism in the poem. The reciter, from whom it was taken down, was a Christian, and so also was the man from whom he had learnt it; and it may be due to this that Majković appears on the whole to be the greater hero of the two. But the fight with the Arab may well be an accretion to the story; for very similar incidents are related of Marko Kraljević and other heroes. It is not clear to us whether the poem was originally Christian or Mohammedan; it may have circulated among both communities. The heroes have no respect for any authorities, whether Christian or Turkish, except the Sultan himself.

III. Lastly, something must be said with regard to the numerous poems relating to Montenegro in the eighteenth and nineteenth centuries and to the Serbian wars of independence. The great majority of the poems of this period are concerned with warfare against the Turks. Poems of purely domestic interest seem to be very rare. The heroes of the Montenegrin poems seem usually to be men of the same class as Ivo of Senj; the rulers, whether bishop or prince, seldom play a leading part. But the fighting is often on a much larger scale; the forces engaged are sometimes armies rather than bands. This remark is true also of the poems relating to Serbia. Here the leading hero is Gjorgje or Gjoko (Djoko) Petrović (Kara-Gjorgje), who was for some years (1804–13) the de facto ruler of Serbia, and from whom the present royal family are descended. An important part is also played by Miloš (Obrenović), who subsequently succeeded in establishing himself as prince. It may be observed that in some poems, especially those relating to Montenegro, the achievements or adventures of the heroes tend to be lost in those of the army as a whole, though hardly to the same extent as in Mohammedan poems. More often, however, heroic characteristics are well preserved.

The poems relating to the Serbian war of independence also vary a good deal in character. Although some are definitely heroic, others approximate more to 'post-heroic' standards; national interest is preponderant, while the personal element is sometimes comparatively slight. Among these we may perhaps notice here an important poem (Karadžić, IV. 24)[1] on the rising of 1804, though it can hardly be regarded as heroic in the strict sense. The Turks in Belgrade are dismayed by portents in the sky—obscurations of the sun and moon, thunder and lightning in the winter, accompanied with earthquakes. The seven leading men ascend a tower with a glass of water from the Danube by means of which they seek to interpret the portents; but it reflects their deaths. Then they send for learned men, to ascertain what is to be found in the scriptures; but they find that the time is now come for the peasants to rise and for Turkish dominion to be overthrown. Mehmed Aga, one of the leading men, announces his determination to take stern measures against the Serbians and to put to death their leaders. The oldest of the Turks endeavours to dissuade him, and recommends a conciliatory policy; but the others follow Mehmed Aga. Then several of the Serbian leaders are trapped and beheaded; and a party of Turks is sent to arrest Kara-Gjorgje. But he escapes, and arms the men of his farm. They attack the Turks, kill half of them, and give pursuit to the rest.

[1] Nearly the whole of this poem (except the first 41 lines) is transl. by Morison, *Slavonic Review*, VI. 646 ff. Very few of the poems relating to this period seem to have been translated into English.

Then Gjorgje calls the Serbians to arms throughout the country. A general rising takes place, and the Turks are overcome and slaughtered everywhere.

In other poems the individual element is more prominent. We may take as an example a short poem, No. 40 in Karadžić's collection (IV. 310 ff.), which describes Kara-Gjorgje's departure in 1813. It is a poem of Type B, in the form of two dialogues between the hero and a Vila, or rather perhaps two different Vile. The Vila calls to him first from Mt Rudnik and asks him what he is doing, taking his leisure while the Turks are overrunning the land. Gjoko tells her to be silent, and says that he has no fear of emperor or vizier while his lieutenants hold their positions. The Vila replies that his lieutenants are either killed or cut off, and that the Turks are close upon him; and she tells him to take to flight. He then flees to the land of Srijem, beyond the Sava, and bids farewell to his country; but he says that he will return within a year. The Turks now devastate the country. When a year and a half have elapsed (65 ff.) a Vila from the neighbourhood of the Sava calls to him, telling him that his home has been laid waste and reminding him of his promise. In reply Gjoko sends greeting to his country and to Miloš, and wishes for their success. He says that he will supply plenty of ammunition; but he is himself going not to his country but to the emperor of Moscow, to serve him for a year.

'Prince Miloš' Revolt against the Turks', No. 45 in Karadžić's collection (IV. 341 ff.), is a much longer poem, likewise of Type B. The framework is cast in a traditional mould. Two ravens fly from (Old) Serbia southwards to Skoplje, and alight at the castle of Ćaja Pasha. They tell the Pasha's wife that they have brought news; and she questions them, expecting to hear an account of his victories. They say that at first he was successful; and she runs off to tell the news to the guests in the castle. But they call her back to hear the continuation of the story, which occupies the rest of the poem. The Pasha had acted with great tyranny against the inhabitants, and they had appealed for protection to Miloš, whose co-operation the Pasha had hoped to secure. In answer to their petition he consented to lead a rising, and went to obtain munitions of war. The Pasha was victorious in the first encounter—and on hearing this the lady again runs off to tell the good news, but again the ravens call her back. Then they go on to relate how in the next engagement the Turks were defeated and the Pasha killed. Another battle followed in which their forces were utterly routed, and most of the leaders slain. The ravens narrate the course of events in detail, and dwell with evident pride upon the prowess and success of the Serbians. At the conclusion they leave the Pasha's wife overwhelmed with grief.

It will be seen that this poem cannot be described as purely heroic. The patriotic element is much in evidence, while the interest is centred more in the Serbian army as a whole than in Miloš himself. The events described took place in the year 1815.

The great majority of the Montenegrin poems of this period are occupied with fighting and the preliminaries of fighting. Women are rarely introduced, except members of the princely family, and these only in the very few poems which are not concerned with fighting. But the heroic element would seem to be on the decline. In the poems contained in Karadžić's fourth volume, which comes down to the death of Bishop Peter II (1851), it is usually much in evidence. But in the fifth volume, which covers the reign of Prince Danilo (1851–1861), examples are less frequent; the interest in individual heroes tends to be subordinated to the national interest, or rather to the doings of the whole body of Montenegrins involved in the action. The leading characters indeed sometimes figure rather as commanders than as combatants, though they take part in the fighting. Much of the poems is occupied with letters and speeches before the action.

Heroic features, however, are by no means wanting. As an illustration we may take 'The Death of Djulek' (Karadžić, v. 2). A priest named Luka receives a letter from a friend called Zimonjić Bogdan, who lives at Gacko in Hercegovina, telling him of the tyrannous doings of Djulek, an imperial major (*bimbaša*), who has recently come from Constantinople. The letter states further that Djulek means to establish himself at Nikšić—which at that time belonged to Turkey—and begs the priest to help in intercepting him on his way. The priest promptly writes to various friends, apparently leading men of the neighbouring districts, to assemble their followers and meet him on the way to Gacko. Having assembled his forces he joins Bogdan; and they ambush and surround Djulek, who has a large body of Albanians with him. Djulek draws his sword and challenges the Montenegrins to combat; but he is shot down, and so also is a 'black Arab' who tries to defend him. Then three Montenegrins, whose names are given, attempt, one after another, to get Djulek's head; but they are all shot down by the Albanians. Next, the Montenegrins make a charge; and now a fourth man succeeds in cutting off the head, while a fifth, one of the leaders, gets that of the

12

black Arab.[1] Then the Turks take to flight. The Montenegrins pursue them, and take off sixty heads. Much booty is captured, in the form of weapons and horses, and divided among the conquerors. But the ladies of Djulek's harem are sent home—an incident which occurs elsewhere and which shows a marked improvement upon the ways of earlier times. The best rifle is given to the priest, as the prize of honour. The heads are brought to Cetinje, and the town is decorated with them. The prince receives the warriors graciously and gives them silver medals.

A good deal of typical heroic matter occurs in Karadžić, v. 3, which describes 'Omer Pasha's attack upon Montenegro', in 1852–3. The poem is too long to be summarised here, but we may cite a short series of passages (891 ff.). The Turks are attacking a church, which is defended by a party of Montenegrins. A Turkish officer named Alo Verizović calls out and asks if Krco Petrović is there—whom he accuses of seizing his estates at Župa. Krco, who is a relative of the prince, replies from the church and challenges him to single combat, in which they shall divide Župa with the sword. The Turk is to choose whether they shall fight on foot or on horseback. After this (923 ff.) the famous hero Cerović Novica begs Mirko, the prince's brother, not to let anyone fire until he has had the first shot. He takes aim at Omer Pasha, but misses him though he hits his standard-bearer. Then, a little later (948 ff.), we have a description of Mirko himself, the commander-in-chief, mounting a spirited horse and with drawn sword inciting his men, one after another, to heroism, and calling upon them to hold the church until reinforcements arrive. Similar heroic features are much in evidence also in the poems (*ib.* v. 12 f.) on the 'Sack of Kolašin'.

In conclusion we may note two poems in the same collection (v. 17 f.) which relate to the death of Prince Danilo (in 1861). The first called 'The Lament of the Dragon on the Lovćen', properly belongs, at least in part, to Type D, though it has the form of Type B. The poem begins with a rhetorical question in the form of the—not uncommon—inverted simile. The Black Mountain is echoing. Is it the rushing of the wind over the heights, or the whistling of the pines, or the distant booming of cannon at Cetinje, or the beating of the waves upon the shore? No, it is none of these things—it is a wounded dragon on the top of the Lovćen[2] groaning over the loss of his wings. A white Vila

---

[1] Presumably this was a negro slave. But the Yugoslavs of the past seem to have had a peculiar dread of coloured people.

[2] The Lovćen (5700 ft.) rises above Cattaro, guarding the approach to Cetinje. The Durmitor (8295 ft.) is in the north of Montenegro.

from the Durmitor calls out and asks him the cause of his grief. He replies (36 ff.) that he has lost both his wings, one many years before at Grahovo, and now the other, with which he had still been able to fly, near Cattaro.[1] Now he is helpless. The Vila answers him, comforting him and saying that, though he has lost his wings, he has produced a fierce snake,[2] who will have the wings of a falcon, and round whom the falcons will gather. She tells him further that he has ten brothers—personifying the various divisions of the Yugoslav nation—who will come to his aid and drive the national foes from the land. Then (161 ff.) the poem goes on to say that this was not really a dragon but Mirko the *Vojvoda* ('general'), who is lamenting the death of his brother, Prince Danilo. He is consoled by his young son Nikola. It may be noted that the speeches of the Vila in this poem show a strongly developed national interest.

The other poem (*ib.* v. 18), called 'Sorrow and Joy at the Death of Prince Danilo', differs in form from all other heroic poems known to us. It consists wholly of speeches, connected by brief narratives in prose, and is divided into five parts. In the first part the scene is laid in the Biljarda[3] at Cetinje, after the funeral. The prince is lamented first by Darinka, his wife, next by Stana, the wife of Mirko, then by the various generals and senators in order. After the lamentations Darinka declares Nikola to be prince; and he is acclaimed by the assembled company and congratulated by the foreign representatives. The second, third and fourth parts describe—again wholly in speeches—the reception of the news in Turkish gatherings, first at Skadar, then at Onogošt in Hercegovina, and finally in the imperial court at Constantinople. The fifth scene is laid in Paradise, where the kings and national heroes of the past —Dušan, Lazar, Miloš Obilić, Peter II, and many others—are assembled in council. Danilo arrives and is welcomed by them. It will be seen that in its general plan this poem may be compared with the *Hákonar-mál*,[4] while for the final scene an analogy is to be found also in the *Odyssey*, xxiv. 15 ff., though the reception of Danilo is of course honorific.

[1] Prince Danilo was murdered near Cattaro, where he was taking a holiday. His brother Stefan had been killed in battle by the Turks at Grahovo in 1835.

[2] Regarded as the young of the dragon. The reference is to Mirko's son Nikola, who succeeded Danilo, his father's brother, as prince. In 1910 he took the title of king.

[3] The state-room in the old palace. It derived its name from the billiard-table installed in it by Bishop Peter II.

[4] Cf. Vol. I, p. 344 f.

The last four scenes of this poem obviously belong to Type B, and the same is perhaps true of the first scene, though this is not quite so certain. The poem was supplied to Karadžić with many others by Kapetan Savo Martinović, who figures prominently as a hero in a number of poems, and who had been attached to the prince's service for some time. But he left Montenegro, apparently before the prince's death, and in 1862 he was living at Zara.[1] Savo was a poet himself, as we shall see later; but it is not clear to what extent he actually composed the poems attributed to him, though he was probably responsible for their final form.[2] In this case the question is whether the whole poem, including the first scene, was a purely imaginative work, composed by him at Zara, or whether it was based on letters or verbal report from Montenegro. In any case, however, it would seem likely that the first scene follows more or less traditional lines—that it represents what the members of the court might be expected to say.

It may be noted that the speeches of the generals and senators are in the ordinary decasyllabic metre; but those of the royal ladies, Darinka and Stana,[3] are in a different metre, which we have not observed elsewhere in heroic poetry, though we suspect that it was in common use for dirges.[4] Each line contains twelve syllables, with a caesura after the eighth syllable, as well as after the fourth; and the last four syllables stand in no syntactical relationship to the sentence. These two speeches are dirges in the strict sense. We may quote the opening lines of Darinka's speech, though it is difficult to render the broken sentences in English: "The lords have assembled—young prince!—around thy throne—young head! But thou art not in the palace—my wounds!—nor upon thy throne—golden crown! The golden crown has been torn off—illustrious prince! For a little while, but not for long—long grief!—thy throne stands forsaken—now I am forsaken! The lords have been brought low—now I am disfigured! Everyone around the palace mourns—now I am mourning!..." The scene described in the prose narrative is of a highly emotional character. In its general features we may

---

[1] This is stated in the Preface to Vol. IV. Karadžić does not say when Savo left Montenegro; but his words imply that he had at least retired from the prince's service some time before 1861.

[2] Internal evidence suggests that some of the poems, especially v. 1, are largely Savo's work.

[3] Darinka belonged to a wealthy family in Trieste, and had presumably received a European education. But she might be expected to follow the customs of the country. We do not know the origin of Stana.

[4] Cf. p. 439 f., below.

compare the lamentation of the royal ladies over Hector in the *Iliad*, XXIV. 723 ff.[1]

We have not seen any examples of heroic poetry later than these; but we are under the impression that it was still cultivated in Montenegro during at least the first half of Nikola's reign. After that the opportunities for heroic exploits were much reduced, partly through the Austrian occupation of Bosnia and Hercegovina, and partly by the improvements in education and communication introduced under Nikola. It is said, however, that new heroic poems were composed during the wars of 1912–18, even in Serbia. One instance may be given.[2] In 1914 a *guslar* ('minstrel') was entertaining the wounded in a military hospital at Kragujevac, when news came that the surgeon's son had been killed. At the request of his audience the minstrel at once produced a poem on the subject. He had practically no knowledge of the circumstances, but followed time-honoured conventions. Two ravens fly from the field of battle and alight at the barracks, where they are questioned by the commanding officer. A few days later the same minstrel was heard repeating the poem, but with full details which he had apparently acquired from someone who had been present. The poem would seem to have been in narrative form; but we may probably regard it as an example of Type D, since it was composed more for the purpose of showing sympathy with the surgeon than for entertainment.

We may now summarise briefly the characteristics of the heroic poems, in accordance with the scheme outlined in Vol. I, p. 60 ff. (cf. p. 20 ff.):

(1) The narrative type (Type A) is decidedly the most prevalent. Type B is also of frequent occurrence, and so also probably is Type D in modern poems, though we have not seen many examples.[3] But poems which belong to either of these types almost always contain a narrative element.

(2) Adventure of some kind seems to be involved everywhere, either in the action itself or in the antecedent circumstances. A few modern

---

[1] For other parallels see Vol. I, p. 634, and note.

[2] For this illustration we are indebted to Gesemann, *Studien zur südslavischen Volksepik*, p. 65 f.

[3] We have not seen any heroic poetry of Type E; but something as to its character may be inferred from the song sung by Ibro Nukić on his wedding night (cf. p. 329): "Is my uncle at the foot of the mountain? Is he already expecting Nukić the standard-bearer?" For the 'types' see p. 2.

Montenegrin poems may perhaps be regarded as exceptions; but we doubt if these can have had a long life.

(3) As in the literatures treated in Vol. I, poems of Types A and B seem always to be intended for entertainment, those of Type D primarily for celebration. Didactic heroic poems (Type C) appear to be very rare (cf. p. 314), and though narrative poems occasionally show a religious colouring, this would seem to be due to a feeling of what we may call 'religious loyalty' rather than to any didactic tendency.

(4) In some of the Yugoslav lands, especially Montenegro, the Heroic Age comes down to recent times. Heroic poems, apparently on traditional lines, are said to have been composed even later. We have not seen any of these; but we are under the impression that their composition was due to special circumstances.

(5) Anonymity is regular. When a poem was first produced, its author must of course have been known, as in the case of the minstrel at Kragujevac in 1914 (cf. p. 337). But it was not the custom to introduce any remarks of a personal character; and consequently, if the poem became popular and was acquired by other minstrels, his name was soon forgotten. It is only in very exceptional cases that the original author of a poem can be conjectured.[1] A minstrel can usually give only the name of the man from whom he learned a poem, though less frequently he may be able to trace its history one step further back.

(6, 7) The metre which has been almost invariably used for heroic poetry in modern times is a uniform decasyllabic line, with caesura after the fourth syllable, and without rhyme or stanza; but—in contrast to Anglo-Saxon heroic poetry—stops seldom occur in the interior of a line. This metre has been in use for more than two centuries, as may be seen by MS. collections. But the poems preserved in early collections—at least those in the Franciscan (Ragusa) and Perast MSS.—almost always show a number of irregularities—lines with more or less than ten syllables and variable position of the caesura. The regularity, therefore, which characterises the modern metre can hardly have belonged to it

---

[1] Karadžić suspected that two of the poems (Nos. 10 and 11) contained in his fourth volume were originally the work of Bishop Peter I, though transformed in popular use; see his note, ib. p. 68. As regards the authorship of some of the poems contained in Vol. v see above, p. 336. None of these poems can have been current more than about a dozen years before they were printed. It may be observed that no authority is cited for 'The Lamentation of the Dragon', though this poem cannot have been composed more than three years before the publication of the volume.

from the beginning. In some poems (especially Bogišić, Nos. 105, 108, 113) lines of twelve and thirteen syllables are frequent, and some contain even more, suggesting a transition from the *bugarštica*.

The *bugarštice* in general belong to an earlier period, and are known only from MSS. (and books) of the eighteenth century and earlier. In the Perast collections we can see *bugarštice* converted into decasyllabic poems, as will be noticed later. So far as we are aware, they never deal with events later than the seventeenth century. Their normal line is of variable length—usually between fourteen and seventeen syllables—but much shorter lines are often introduced at intervals, as noticed on p. 304. In some collections[1] almost all the poems, whether heroic or not, consist regularly throughout of groups of three lines—long, short, long—which may practically be regarded as stanzas. In the Bocche di Cattaro this type seems practically to have ousted all others. The largest collection of all—the Franciscan MS. at Ragusa[2]—shows considerable diversity. Out of thirty-seven poems in all twenty-three have a uniform long line, while three others contain only one short line each. Nearly all these are heroic poems, mostly of Type A. Of the eleven poems which introduce short lines more frequently not more than six are heroic, mostly of Type B. This evidence, so far as it goes, rather suggests that the uniform long line was the prevalent metre for heroic poetry of Type A. But we say this with all reserve; for we believe that there are a number of *bugarštice* in existence which have not been accessible to us.

(8) Speeches are seldom, if ever, wanting in heroic poems. In poems relating to the more modern periods letters also are of very frequent occurrence. In narrative poems speeches and letters usually occupy at least a third of the whole.

(9) The fullness of detail in the description of action which characterises Greek and English heroic poetry is a common feature also of Yugoslav heroic narrative poetry. The poems vary of course in length

---

[1] Two MSS. in the Zagreb Academy, which are believed to have come from the Bocche (cf. Bogišić, Introd. p. 136) and the earlier MS. at Perast, also in the Bocche. The metre is found also in Bogišić, No. 37, a fragmentary poem in the Ragusa MS., and *ib.* No. 46, which is thought to have come from Croatia. A different stanza, consisting of seven lines—five long, one short, one long— is employed regularly in the two poems (*ib.* Nos. 6, 49) obtained by Hektorović (cf. p. 300) in the island of Hvar.

[2] This MS. really contains three different collections (cf. Bogišić, Introd. p. 130 f.), all of which have poems with the uniform long line. The seventeen poems supplied by Jodzo Betondić are all of this type.

very greatly; but the conciseness characteristic of Norse heroic poetry is in general foreign to these poems.

(10) Static epithets are as frequent as in Greek and English heroic poetry. Thus mountains are regularly 'green' (*zelen*), hands 'white' (*bio*), wine 'cool' (*hladan*), relatives and friends 'dear' (*mio, drag*), the earth 'black' (*crn*). Epithets containing nouns in apposition with personal names also occur, though hardly so often as in Greek and English. We may instance Karadžić, v. 12. 127 f.: "Then spake the spiritual head, the Archimandrite", or *ib.* 2. 65, where a certain Novak Krstović is described as 'swift champion (lit. 'plumed man') of Montenegro'. Occasionally one meets with more ambitious examples, as in *ib.* 11. 45. 4 (and elsewhere), where Lazar is described as 'golden crown of Serbia'. Heroes are often described as 'falcons'. Repetitions are of constant occurrence and frequently extend over long passages. Speeches are introduced in much the same way as in Greek and English heroic poetry.

(11) The length of time covered by the action usually amounts to no more than a few days. Poems relating to early times, however, sometimes fall into two or more scenes, which may be separated by long intervals. In 'The Captivity and Marriage of Stjepan Jakšić' (cf. p. 324) the intervals altogether must come to nearly two years. In 'The Marriage of Maxim Crnojević' (Karadžić, 11. No. 89), 183 ff. nine years elapse; but the part of the poem which precedes this passage is merely preliminary to the main action.

(12) The time of the action relatively to the poet[1] is seldom, if ever, expressed. There can be no doubt that the modern poems were composed soon—sometimes immediately—after the events with which they are concerned. Whether this was the case in earlier times also is a question which we shall have to consider later. All that need be noted here is that there was no convention, as there was in Norse heroic poetry, of stating that the events happened long ago.[2]

It may be added here that the heroic narrative poetry (Type A), taken as a whole, presents hardly any features which strike the student of Greek and English heroic poetry as unfamiliar, although certain groups of poems have some special characteristics of their own in metre or diction. Poems of Types B and D tend to approximate to Type A more

---

[1] Poems occasionally give the dates of the events with which they deal; e.g. Karadžić, v. 3, *ad init.*

[2] In the epilogue to one of the poems published by Krauss (*op. cit.* p. 248) the minstrel says that 'we' did not see (the events), but have heard of them from our elders.

closely than in Norse, while they have little in common with their Welsh and Irish counterparts.[1] In general the outstanding feature of Yugoslav heroic poetry of all types, as compared with the ancient literatures, is the greater simplicity of its language and diction. With Russian heroic poetry the relationship seems to be somewhat closer. The two languages are of course nearly related; and the diction of oral poetry in general has much which is common to both. On the other hand there is no connection in the heroic stories, as in English, Norse and German heroic poetry; there are no themes or characters common to the two. The metres also are wholly different. There is, however, a certain similarity in the style of the narratives; and occasionally we meet with conventional passages, e.g. in the openings of poems, which seem to indicate a connection, not merely in poetry generally, but even in heroic narrative poetry. Some of these conventions may be due to communication between Russian and Yugoslav poets in the sixteenth and seventeenth centuries; but others may be much older.

NOTE. The following are the more important sentences in the translation of Ducas,[2] relating to the banquet before the battle of Kosovo, as noted on p. 315. The connection with certain passages in Karadžić, II. 50. iii (translated by Seton-Watson in Subotić's *Yugoslav Popular Ballads*, p. 65 f.) is obvious enough.

"El zorno precedente a quello che seguì la iniqua et infelice bataglia, Lazaro convocati tutti i signori et principali del suo imperio,[3] comandò che se aparechiasse una sdraviza secondo la usanza dela sua corte; in laquale, come gratioso et benigno signore, a tutti porse la sdraviza con sua mano. Quando la volta toccò a Milos, se fè dar una grande taza d' oro piena de pretioso vino,[4] la qual porzendoli disse a Milos: 'Excellentissimo cavalier, prendi questa sdraviza, che con la taza te dono...sdravize per amòr mio. Ma molto mi doglio che ho inteso una mala novella, che al tuo dispoto sei facto ribello'.[5]

---

[1] Darinka's lament (cf. p. 336) has something in common with Welsh and Irish elegies, but it is much simpler.

[2] Cap. 15; p. 353 in Bekker's edition (*Corpus Script. Hist. Byzant.*).

[3] Cf. Karadžić, II. 50. iii. 2. 3 f.:
Svu gospodu za sofru sjedao (*scil.* Lazare),
svu gospodu i gospodičiće.

[4] *Ib.* 3. 13: Car uzima zlatan pehar vina, etc.

[5] *Ib.* 4. 31 ff.: Zdrav Milošu, vjero i nevjero!
prva vjero, potonja nevjero!
Sjutra ćeš me izdat' na Kosovu,
i odbjeći Turskom car-Muratu;
zdrav mi budi! i zdravicu popij:
vino popij, a na čast ti pehar.

Al qual Milos, reverentemente presa la taza con chiara faza, disse: 'Signor dispoto, molto te ringratio della sdraviza et taza d' oro che m' ai donata. Ma molto mi doglio dela mia dubitata fede.[1] Doman de matina, se dio darà effecto al' alto pensier mio, se cognoscerà se io son fidele o ribello dela tua Signoria'."

An account of the banquet and of the events which followed, very similar to that contained in the translation of Ducas, may be found in Ludovicus (Cerva) Tubero's *Commentarii*,[2] which were written c. 1522. But it is not taken from the translation; both seem to be derived from the poems. In one passage at least (p. 144 f.) Tubero shows a closer connection with the *bugarštica* (Bogišić, No. 1): *Lazarus, Dardanorum rex, duces suos ad coenam uocat, obiecturus inter coenandum Miloni, ex purpuratis uni, proditionem, cuius a quodam aemulo per inuidiam apud se erat criminatus.* In the poem (118 ff.) Vuk Branković accuses Miloš of treachery; but the accusation is made to Lazar at the banquet itself. In the descriptions of Miloš' and Lazar's deaths the Italian is much nearer than Tubero to the *bugarštica*, though both of them, as against the latter, represent Miloš as going alone to the Turkish camp.

A somewhat different account of the banquet is given in Benedict Curipeschitz' *Itinerarium*,[3] in an entry dated 24 September, 1530. Miloš is here said to be an old man. The account of his death, however, shows some resemblance to the *bugarštica*. Note may also be taken of the same author's statement[4] that many songs are still sung in Croatia and the Frontier about Miloš' exploits.

In view of the evidence given above there can be no reasonable doubt that heroic poems relating to Miloš were widely current at the beginning of the sixteenth century, and that by this time his exploit was already celebrated in a number of variant forms. The first poems on the subject—including an account of the banquet—must clearly have been composed at a much earlier date. It is also worth noting that, if we may judge from the early authorities cited above, the account of the banquet given in Karadžić's poem seems to be more conservative than the one in the *bugarštica*, though the latter is a much older text. Analogies for this will be noticed later.

[1] *Ib.* 5. 39 ff.:

> Vala tebe, slavni knez-Lazare!
> Vala tebe na tvojoj zdravici,
> na zdravici i na daru tvome;
> al' ne vala na takoj besjedi; etc.

[2] Edition publ. at Frankfort, 1603.
[3] Ed. Lamberg-Schwarzenberg, Innsbruck, 1910.
[4] "Milosch Khobilovitz...von welches ritterlicher thatten noch yetzt in Crabaten und der ennde vill lider gesungen werden" (p. 47).

CHAPTER III

NON-HEROIC POETRY

AS pointed out on p. 307 the division which we made in Vol. I between 'non-heroic' poetry relating to the Heroic Age and 'post-heroic' poetry cannot conveniently be followed in the classification of Yugoslav oral literature. In point of fact both categories are represented; but the division here is geographical rather than chronological. There is also a certain amount of material which must be regarded as transitional or intermediate between the two. We shall therefore attempt to treat all non-heroic poetry in this chapter. We will deal first with poems whose affinities lie with the non-heroic poetry and saga discussed in Vol. I, Ch VI, then with poems which seem to belong to the post-heroic category. In the former we will follow the classification adopted *ib.* p. 96 ff., viz.:

(1) Stories relating to Christian saints.

(2) Stories relating to prophets, wizards, and persons, other than ecclesiastics, who are credited with abnormal or supernatural powers and knowledge.

(3) Stories relating to persons not included in either of these categories.

(1) A distinction must be drawn between stories relating to native (Yugoslav) saints and those relating to saints of earlier times who are recognised by Christendom in general. The latter are for the most part similar to the stories of supernatural beings discussed in Vol. I, Ch. IX, and will be noticed in Ch. VI, below.

We have met with very few stories of the former class. As an example we may take 'Simeun the Foundling' (Karadžić, II. 70 ff., No. 15). An unnamed emperor or king (*car*) marries a girl called Janja against her will. When she bears a child she throws it into the sea, clothed in a vest. It is discovered by the Serbian princely Patriarch St Sava,[1] who brings it up and calls it Simeun (Symeon) the Foundling. When Simeun is grown up he sets out to look for his parents. The king has just died, and the queen is sought in marriage by the chief nobles. She proposes a

---

[1] Son of Stjepan Nemanja, the founder of the dynasty, and first archbishop of Serbia (c. 1220). The poem describes him as Patriarch.

contest to settle her choice: she is to throw a golden apple and to marry the man who catches it. Simeun accomplishes the feat, and she marries him; but while he is away hunting she finds the vest and realises that she has married her own son. When Simeun hears what has happened he appeals to St Sava for absolution. But the saint replies that no absolution is possible for such a sin. He immures him in a tower, and throws the keys into the sea. Thirty years later the keys are found in a fish. Then St Sava opens the door of the tower, and finds that Simeun is dead and has become beatified.

It would seem from the closing lines of the poem that the church of Vilendara recognised a saint corresponding to this Simeun. But the story has all the appearance of a folktale. It may be observed that a variant version is to be found in Karadžić, No. 14 (II. 63 ff.). In this a nameless monk takes the place of St Sava, and a queen of Hungary that of Queen Janja. The child is found in the Danube, and there is no contest.

We do not know whether there are any Mohammedan poems of this class.

(2) We do not know of any poems relating to prophets or wizards. This class of stories indeed belongs properly to heathen times, in spite of the Irish and Welsh examples given in Vol. I. But we may perhaps cite here a story which in part turns upon the wisdom attributed to an architect, though we are not at all certain that it does not properly belong to No. 3, below. We know the story only from the abstract given by Gesemann, *Studien zur südslavischen Volksepik*, p. 98 f.[1]

Mehmed Sokolović, a wealthy Pasha, decides to build a bridge over the Drina at Višegrad, in Bosnia. He summons an architect named Mitar, and tells him to engage three hundred builders and a thousand workmen, without regard to expense. Mitar rides into the middle of the river, to test its depth; but there the horse comes to a stand and refuses to move. The Pasha throws his amulet to the architect; and the horse then springs out of the water, dragging with it a Vila, whose hair has become entangled round its feet. Mitar means to kill the Vila; but she begs for her life and promises her help in making the bridge secure. Now for seven years he toils at the bridge; but the work which is done in the day is undone at night. At length Mitar, at the Pasha's request,

---

[1] The text is publ. in Hörmann, *Narodne Pjesme Muhamedovca u Bosni i Herce-govini* (Sarajevo, 1888), which is not accessible to us. Gesemann (*ib.*) gives a number of interesting parallels.

appeals to the Vila. She will not come herself, but she advises him to immure 'Stoja and Ostoja'[1] in the bridge. This is done—though apparently no explanation or details are given—and the work is soon completed. But now the river becomes turbid, and a fir dashes against the bridge and makes it shake. The architect calls out to the Pasha that he has made no present to the Drina, and bids him to scatter gold into it with a silver shovel. In explanation of this the poem adds that he wanted to see whether the Pasha grudged the gold—though it may be doubted whether this was the original point of the incident. When the Pasha has thrown a good deal of gold into the river, Mitar stops him, and chops the fir with an axe. Then blood spurts from the trunk, and a voice from it declares that the bridge over the Drina will now stand for ever.

This poem is of interest as illustrating the imaginative form which a historical event—of not too promising a character, one would think—can assume in oral poetry. Mehmed Sokolović was a famous man, to whom we shall have to refer again later. The bridge still stands, and bears a Turkish inscription, stating that it was built by him in the year 1571. Nothing seems to be known of the architect, though his name indicates that he was a Christian.

(3) Non-heroic stories relating to persons who do not belong to either of the classes noted above seem to be of more frequent occurrence. As an example we may take a poem in Karadžić's collection, II. No. 20 (p. 93 ff.). The Serbian emperor Stjepan[2] keeps the feast of his patron saint and invites a large number of ecclesiastics—three hundred priests, twelve bishops and four great abbots. He gives his guests a most honourable welcome, waits upon them himself, and hands the wine-cup to each in turn. But the ecclesiastics protest that he should not do so; they beg him to sit down with them and let his men serve them. He gives way to their entreaties. But the Archangel, who has been standing beside him, caressing his cheek with his wing, while he served his guests, now strikes his cheek and then takes his departure from the palace. He is observed, however, only by one old monk, who tells the doorkeepers what he has seen. They make it known to the emperor; and all join in beseeching the Archangel for forgiveness.

[1] These names are clearly to be connected with 'Stoja and Stojan', described as a sister and brother, in 'The Walling of Skadar'. The Vila orders Vukašin to find these persons and immure them in the foundations; but his messenger is unable to discover them.

[2] We do not know whether Dušan is meant, or one of the earlier kings. Most of the medieval kings of Serbia were called Stjepan.

Another example is to be found in No. 21 (*ib.* p. 96 ff.). A general (*vojvoda*) named Todor, who is imprisoned, apparently at Ragusa,[1] begins to lament as the day of his patron saint, St George, approaches. He begs Petar Mrkonjić, who has charge of the prison, to allow him to go out to the market. There he sells some gilded silver knives, the only things of value that he has, and buys food and wine with the money. Then he returns and gives a feast to his fellow-prisoners, and calls upon St George to release him. At this point someone calls to Todor from outside the prison, telling him to come and speak to him. He replies that he cannot, as the prison is locked; but the stranger says that the gates are open. Todor then comes out, and finds a finely accoutred hero on horseback, who tells him to make his escape and advises him to take to the mountains, avoiding the sea because of the Latin guards. Todor turns to give the hero a drink of wine; but both horse and rider are gone. Then he relates what has happened in the prison, and all make their escape. When he arrives home his wife is celebrating the feast with his friends and neighbours, and beseeching the saint for his safe return.

Some poems of this class relate to well-known heroes. For an example we may refer to 'Uroš and the Mrnjavčevići',[2] in which the leading character is Marko Kraljević, and which has obvious affinities with the stories just noticed. At the death of the emperor (Dušan) his young son Uroš' claim to the throne is disputed by Vukašin and his two brothers, Uglješa and Gojko, each of whom desires it for himself. The four claimants with their followers meet beside the church of Samodreža on the plain of Kosovo; and Vukašin writes to the ecclesiastic who gave the last sacrament to the emperor, summoning him to come to them. But the ecclesiastic disclaims all knowledge of the emperor's intentions, and refers the messengers to Marko Kraljević, Vukašin's son, who had been secretary to the emperor. Vukašin is confident that his son will decide in his favour; and when Marko shows from the books that Uroš is the heir, he bursts into fury and attacks him with a dagger. Three times he pursues his son round the church. Then a voice from the church calls to Marko to take refuge within. As the door closes behind him, Vukašin strikes through it with his dagger, and the woodwork drips with blood. Vukašin thinks he has killed his son, and is

[1] The beginning of the poem speaks of the castle (*grad*) of Sokol, which is unknown to us. Neither do we know anything of the persons who figure in the poem.
[2] Karadžić, *op. cit.* II. 189 ff. (No. 34). Transl. by Low, *The Ballads of Marko Kraljević*, p. 13 ff.

seized with repentance; but a voice from within declares that it is not Marko but an angel of God whom he has struck.

It will be seen that all these stories contain a didactic—or at least an 'edifying'—element. The two latter, however, seem to be intended primarily for entertainment and may be regarded as examples of Type A. The story of Stjepan and the Archangel (p. 345) obviously belongs to Type C.

Stories of this class without ecclesiastical colouring are also probably to be found, though we cannot recall any very satisfactory examples. The story of the building of the bridge at Višegrad, noticed under No. 2, above, should perhaps rather be included here. We may mention also 'The Walling of Skadar'.[1] Vukašin and his brothers try to fortify Skadar; but their work is destroyed each night by a Vila. After three years the Vila calls out to them that the walls will never stand, unless they immure a sister and brother, named Stoja and Stojan, in the foundations. They seek for these persons, but are unable to find them. Then the Vila calls out again that they must immure one of their wives, whichever of them comes out to bring the workers their dinner on the following day. They agree to keep the matter a secret from their wives; but Vukašin and Uglješa break the covenant. Gojko behaves honourably, and his wife has to be immured. She suckles her child for a year through a hole in the wall; and milk still continues to trickle there.

This story seems to be derived from a variety of a widely distributed folktale. We may compare a Bulgarian poem[2] which is evidently a modified form of the same story. An architect, named Manoil, tries to build a bridge; but it will not stand. He suggests to the workmen that they shall immure one of their wives in the foundations—the one which shall come to bring them their breakfast next day. It is his own wife who comes; and he will not keep to the bargain. In place of his wife he immures a reed. The wife goes home, and immediately falls ill and dies. But her spirit haunts the bridge; and when her child cries her sisters-in-law take it there, and milk flows from the masonry to feed it.

Next we may take poems the affinities of which seem to lie with 'post-heroic' poetry. In Vol. I, Ch. XIV, we saw that, apart from sur-

---

[1] Karadžić, II. No. 26. Transl. by Morison in Subotić, *Yugoslav Popular Ballads*, p. 40 ff.
[2] We know this poem only from the transl. by Eisner, *Volkslieder der Slawen*, p. 482 f. There is of course a secondary motive here, the attempt to get out of a bargain—originally, it would seem, to cheat some supernatural being of his due.

vivals of the heroic category, post-heroic poetry was usually concerned either with the personal experiences and feelings of the poet himself (Type E), or with the interests of the community to which he belonged. For Type E we know of no recognisable illustrations in *narodne pjesme*,[1] though it is possible that some of the timeless nameless poems which we shall have to notice in Ch. VIII may be of such an origin. On the other hand poetry of communal interest is well represented, at least in the older MS. collections; and it is to this that we must now turn our attention. We have no doubt that such poetry is of similar origin to (Greek and other) ancient poetry of communal (political) interest. But the relationship is largely obscured by the fact that what is preserved of the latter is almost wholly poetry of exhortation or celebration (Type D), whereas the Yugoslav poems belong almost without exception to Type A or Type B. With the communal interest is often combined a major or minor interest in individuals concerned in the events which are described.

By far the most important material known to us comes from the coast region, Ragusa and southern Dalmatia.[2] The poems relating to these districts are preserved, as we have seen, in MSS. of the eighteenth century or earlier. It is of importance to observe that there are apparently no heroic poems concerned primarily with persons who belong to these districts. This is all the more striking from the fact that the earliest texts of heroic poems are preserved in MSS. (or printed works) which come from the districts in question. Indeed heroic poems and poems relating to the coastland are sometimes preserved in the same MSS. Yet the heroic poems are concerned with the interior, while the poems relating to the coastland are not heroic. It is in complete accord with these facts that when heroic poems—in later texts—refer to Ragusa, which is not unfrequently the case, they treat it as an alien, and indeed often as a hostile, place. The coastland lies clearly outside the area of the Heroic Age, though it has preserved early texts of heroic poems which have drifted there. It may once have had a Heroic Age of its own; but owing to the mixed character of the population this is a difficult question, into which we need not enter. The essential fact for our purpose is that the poetry of the coastland which has been preserved is that of town

[1] It is to be borne in mind that in Ragusa and Dalmatia there was a flourishing written lyric poetry from the fifteenth century onwards.

[2] We mean especially the Bocche di Cattaro. We do not know what evidence is available for northern Dalmatia. Heroic conditions seem to have prevailed at one time even in the maritime part of Croatia (cf. p. 326 f.).

communities. Owing to this fact its analogies are to be found in post-heroic Greece, rather than in the other ancient literatures. Sometimes the interest is centred more in individuals, sometimes more in the community; but even in the former case it is of a different kind from that of heroic poetry. Often it is of an unfriendly character.

(a) Poems relating to Ragusa differ a good deal from the rest—a fact which is due doubtless partly to the greater wealth and civilisation of that city, and partly to its peculiar political position (cf. p. 302). These poems are largely concerned with individuals; but it is not their heroic or martial exploits which are celebrated. If the individuals are Ragusans or friends of Ragusa, the poems usually serve as illustrations of their cleverness or astuteness; if they are aliens, they suffer for their stupidity. Occasionally this tendency is carried so far that one might almost think the poet wanted to confirm a proverbial saying which occurs sometimes in Serbian poems—'the Latins are old hands in deception'. But the motif of communal or patriotic interest is seldom, if ever, entirely wanting. On the whole the poems have something in common with the Greek sagas recorded by Herodotos of the tyrants and others who lived in the seventh and sixth centuries, when Greek post-heroic poetry was flourishing.

In one poem, No. 80 in Bogišić's collection, the magnates of Ragusa hold debate, and appoint Jakob Maruškovič to be their envoy to the Turkish court. On his arrival he makes his bow and offers tribute from the city. But the emperor says he wants no tribute, but the keys of the city. He charges the Ragusans with increasing their fortifications, and says he has heard that their territory possesses many attractions, parkland and fountains, which would be convenient for his army. In reply Jakob pleads that the city has been obliged to increase its fortifications from fear of the Doge. He says that the emperor has been wrongly informed as to the attractions of Ragusa, which would be of no use for the support of the emperor's army. And he adds that the Ragusans would never give up the keys of the city. If driven to desperation they would rather transfer their allegiance to the king of Spain. On hearing this reply the emperor's attitude becomes threatening; but Jakob has a good friend at the court, Sokolović Pasha, who gives him a hint to ride off. The Pasha now tells the emperor it is an unheard of thing that injury should be done to a Ragusan envoy; and he says that news of his threat will be published in all directions. The emperor replies that the Pasha is to do what he thinks best, though he suggests that he has received a good bribe from the magnates of Ragusa. A party of Turks are now sent after

Jakob to bring him back and effect a reconciliation. But Jakob prefers to continue his journey home.

We may cite also another *bugarštica* in the same collection (No. 79). The emperor raises an army and sets off against Ragusa. Amongst others he summons a Pasha (unnamed) who asks him the reason for the expedition. The emperor in reply describes the attractions of Ragusa; but the Pasha tells him that he has been misinformed. Then the emperor charges him with having received a bribe from the magnates of Ragusa; but he denies the charge, and says that he has served in the city for nine years, and consequently knows the place well. He persuades the emperor to give up the expedition and to send him to Ragusa instead. The magnates receive the Pasha with great honour and give him rich rewards for what he has done; and in return he makes peace for them at Carigrad (Constantinople). Strictly this poem is 'timeless-nameless'; but it probably relates to the same persons who figure in No. 80, apart from the envoy.

Next we may perhaps take a decasyllabic poem (*ib.* No. 119) of quite a different character. The chief figure is Herceg[1] Stjepan, ruler of Hercegovina—which takes its name from him—about 1435–1466. The poem opens in conventional heroic style at Stjepan's castle at Blagaj, where a lady named Jelina—who must be Stjepan's wife—is conversing with a swallow. She asks the bird if it has come from Carigrad and whether it has seen her son Vladislav. It replies that it has seen Vladislav; but he is now called Mehmed Pasha. He has asked the Sultan for three hundred Janissaries, and has promised to bring him the keys of Blagaj and all Herceg's riches. Then the Pasha himself appears and demands the keys; but his mother tells him that Herceg has gone to Mostar and taken the keys with him. The Pasha now returns to Sarajevo to collect a force; but Herceg packs up all his wealth and takes it in three caravans to Ragusa. When he arrives at the gate, a clever nobleman tells him to write down that he has not arrived or brought his property.[2] Herceg allows himself to be persuaded and goes away for a short time. On his return he asks for his property; but the Ragusans refuse to give it up. They use it for charitable purposes.[3]

[1] He had assumed the title 'Duke (*Herzog*) of St Sava'.

[2] The poet seems to have in mind some kind of banking transaction, which he does not understand, but regards—and evidently admires—as clever cheating.

[3] The facts seem to be that Herceg Stjepan deposited his money at Ragusa and that it was afterwards paid to his sons, in accordance with his will. One of his sons, Vlatko (Ahmed) dishonestly obtained double payment. Cf. Villari, *The Republic of Ragusa*, pp. 252, 258. The poem seems to have confused two of the sons. According

Mention should perhaps be made here of a short poem of Type D (Bogišić, No. 81), in the form of an address to Ragusa. This poem is believed to be of literary origin, though it is preserved in one of the (Zagreb) MS. collections of *narodne pjesme*. But it is of interest as expressing the Ragusan ideal of peace, in contrast with the heroic and military character of the neighbouring communities.

(*b*) Among the towns under Venetian rule Perast offers by far the most interesting material. This is a place at the entrance to the Bay of Risan in the Bocche di Cattaro. So far as we know, it has never been a town of any great size or importance. But two of the houses possess MS. collections of *narodne pjesme*—one (A) a collection of *bugarštice* written about 1700,[1] the other (B) a collection of decasyllabic poems written more than half a century later. The latter are variants or adaptations of the former, the differences as a rule being very slight.[2] These poems are wholly concerned with events of local history. They present a most interesting contrast to the poems relating to Ragusa; for they are products of a much more backward community. There is no less local patriotism than in the Ragusan poems; but the patriotism here is of the militant kind. The poems indeed are full of fighting, though it is not fighting of the heroic type. The exploits which they celebrate are those not of individuals, but of the fighting men of Perast collectively.

First we may take Bogišić, Nos. 59 (from A) and 60 (from B). A Spanish general named Don Karlo occupies Novi Grad[3] and among other tyrannical doings mishandles two servant girls from Perast. The men of Perast, on hearing the news, hold debate, and send a spy to Novi Grad. A week later he returns and says that Don Karlo is going to set out with his followers the next morning. During the night the men of Perast make their way over the strait, and lie in wait for Don Karlo near a spring. When the Spaniards arrive they open fire and then attack them with their swords, killing forty-three of them. Don Karlo and his wife are captured alive, and a savage vengeance is taken upon them. The poem ends with a remark that the warriors of Perast performed this

to Orbini, *Il Regno degli Slavi*, pp. 273, 387, Helena (Jelina) was a granddaughter of Andrija, the brother of Marko Kraljević. She was Stjepan's second wife, but not the mother of his sons.

[1] This MS. also contains a number of early decasyllabic poems, which have not been accessible to us.

[2] But it is clear from various passages that B is not derived from the written text of A; cf. p. 353, notes.

[3] We are not clear whether this means the walled city now called Herceg Novi or Castelnuovo or a castle, now called Spagnuolo, upon the hill behind it.

exploit so as to prevent any reproach against them; and several of the other poems likewise end with remarks looking to the future of the town. In MS. A it is stated that the events took place in the year 1573.

The next poems, Nos. 61 (A) and 62 (B), are occupied with a rather sorry story of strife between the men of Perast and those of another maritime place or community called Paštrovići, which we cannot identify.[1] A man of Perast named Nikola, who is returning in a small craft from Albania, stops to visit a friend in Paštrovići. There he encounters a young lady who declares that on a previous visit he had promised to marry her. An altercation arises in which he says that he would not marry her if she brought him half Paštrovići as a dowry. Then she calls upon the men of the town to avenge her wrong, and they give chase to Nikola; but he escapes in his boat. Not long afterwards she persuades a certain Djuric Davidović to go with a party of twelve armed men to Perast. They find Nikola in front of the Church of St Nikola and shoot him dead, and then run for the shore. But the bell rings, and the men of Perast assemble and give chase. They soon overtake and slay the raiders, and they chop Djuric to pieces. The poem reflects on his want of forethought. No man of Perast, except Nikola, is mentioned by name.

The next two poems, Nos. 63 (A) and 64 (B), approximate more nearly to heroic poetry in theme; but the treatment is not heroic. The poems open with a reference to a Turkish victory over the Venetians at Knin, in 1654. Then Mehmed Aga Rizvanagić of Risan begs Ali Pasha to lend him troops, so that he may raid Perast. He undertakes to get seven hundred captives, and among them the three daughters of Tripo Burović. Neither the emperor nor the Doge has girls equal to these; if they can get them Ali Pasha will be promoted to be Grand Vizier and Mehmed Aga to be Pasha of Bosnia. The Pasha agrees, and a Turkish army arrives at Risan by night. In Risan the men of Perast have a spy, who quickly makes the news known to Krilo Vicković, the Kapetan of Perast; and by dawn the latter has all the towers manned by his men. Mehmed Aga makes straight for Tripo's house and, finding it deserted, sets it on fire. But Tripo espies him in the garden from one of the towers, and fires and wounds him. Then, as he is trying to avoid a further shot, Tripo comes up and asks him why he has set his house on fire. Mehmed Aga surrenders at once and offers to give up his two sons, together with a large amount of money. The two men are evidently friends, and Tripo has no wish to cut off his head. But unfortunately a body of the

---

[1] It would seem to be somewhere on the coast between Bar (Antivari) and the Bocche.

defenders arrive at this moment and compel their leader, Krilo Kolović, to cut it off. In all they take seventy-four Turkish heads and seven banners. The poems dwell with pride upon this achievement of the men of old; for there were only forty-three of the men of Perast then at home, the rest being away in Albania.[1]

The MSS. contain several other poems of the same type. The group as a whole is of outstanding interest as forming a body of poetry of purely local reference and belonging to a very small community. The events described extend over a period of well over a hundred years; and the records are still—or were until recently—preserved only in the place itself. The poets of Perast were of course familiar with the *narodne pjesme* cultivated elsewhere in their times. That is obvious enough from the diction of the poems. We may also refer to the story of the dream with which No. 66[2] opens—one of the most popular conventions of *narodne pjesme*. But the patriotic interest which dominates the poems is of the most strictly local character—concentrated wholly in the 'famous place on the edge of the sea'.

It would be of interest to know whether other maritime places possessed similar bodies of poetry peculiar to themselves. If so they have perished; and it is likely enough they were never committed to writing. We may, however, cite one (fragmentary) poem of local interest, though it is of quite a different character—being concerned exclusively with the affairs of individuals. In Bogišić, No. 76, we hear that Ivan Voihnović made a fine bet in Kotor (Cattaro) with the 'providur[3] of Kotor'. He undertakes to throw a club of a certain weight over a church which was a hundred feet high. The stakes are three hundred gold ducats and half of the city. It is stated that Ivan has no relatives in Kotor; but he writes to his uncle Ivan Crnojević in Montenegro— presumably the man who figures in 'The Marriage of Maxim Crnojević' (cf. p. 340), and who was ruler of Montenegro towards the close of the fifteenth century. His uncle replies, telling him not to draw back and wishing him good luck. Ivan succeeds in throwing the club over the church; but unfortunately it comes down upon one of the nobility of the city on the far side of the church, and injures and blinds him. For this he is arrested and imprisoned; and now he writes to his uncle,

---

[1] The statement relating to Albania occurs only in B (64. 108). It may be observed that the text of A (No. 63) is not well preserved in this poem. There is clearly an omission after line 98.

[2] This passage occurs only in B. A (No. 65) has an entirely different introduction.

[3] This word seems to represent *Provveditore*, the title of the Venetian official (governor or agent) at Kotor.

saying that he has carried out his bet, but met with misfortune. At this point unfortunately the text comes to an end.[1]

Lastly, we may notice a poem (No. 57), again of very different character, which likewise may come from the Bocche di Cattaro—or possibly from Šibenik (Sebenico)—though it is preserved in the Franciscan MS. It is concerned with an event of European importance, the battle of Lepanto, which took place in 1571; but the details are of an imaginative character, based perhaps to some extent on popular rumour. The emperor (Sultan) writes to the Doge, bidding him lend him three harbours—Šibenik, the Bocche di Cattaro, and Venice itself. The Doge weakly consents, and then writes to a Venetian hero, named Kanaleti, and tells him what he has promised. Kanaleti is overwhelmed with grief, dresses himself and his galley completely in black and sets off to the Doge. When the Doge enquires why he has done so, he replies by asking what is now to become of the Doge's fleet. Then he persuades the Doge to write to the king of Spain, telling him that the emperor has seized his harbours and begging for his assistance. The king writes back to say that he cannot come over the blue sea himself, because he has had a darling child born; but he will send his brother Domdžovan.[2] The Spanish and Venetian fleets meet and encounter the (Turkish) fleet from Carigrad; and Domdžovan captures two sons of Sokolović Pasha. Their mother writes to him and begs him to release them. She offers in ransom a spear of pure gold, a countless amount of good money, and a fine big horse which has no equal in all Turkey. The text breaks off as he begins to write a reply to her letter. But it seems unlikely that anything more was said about the battle or its results. The poet is interested only in personal details.

This is not the only example which the early MSS. preserve of poems concerned with distant wars. Other instances will be found in No. 58, a *bugarstica* (from one of the Zagreb MSS.) on the relief of Vienna in 1683, and in No. 113, a poem in irregular decasyllabic metre (from the Franciscan MS.) on the fall of Candia in 1669. On the former subject also at least one poem has been taken down in recent times. It is clear then that in the sixteenth and following centuries the inhabitants of the coastal districts—not Ragusa only—were interested in foreign politics, even if their interest tended to take a personal form. Such interest was

---

[1] A story closely related to this occurs in Karadžić, II. No. 37, which will require notice later.

[2] This name seems to have been acquired in Italian form—Dom Giovanni, i.e. Don Juan of Austria, brother of Philip II.

doubtless stimulated by the employment of Yugoslav troops in the Venetian and other forces. Even in Perast, where feeling seems to have been parochial enough, evidence for such interest is not altogether wanting. We may refer in particular to No. 65, which gives an account of the contingents sent by the various powers—the Pope, the Grand Master of Malta and the Grand Duke of Tuscany—to the expedition against Novi Grad.

Apart from the early Dalmatian MS. collections noticed above we have no personal knowledge of *narodne pjesme* which are definitely 'post-heroic' in character. We are under the impression, however, that a good deal of poetry with such characteristics has been produced in the western districts of the interior—Bosnia, Hercegovina and Montenegro—during the last half century. Thus it is said[1] that the new poems current during the years before the War were concerned occasionally with small affrays, but more often with weddings, courtships and love affairs of every kind, and also with punishments for poaching, with elections, and with journeys of emigrants to America. Even appeals and complaints to the authorities were treated in poetry at considerable length. Not all these subjects of course are necessarily 'post-heroic'; but the inventory as a whole leaves no room for doubt. The Heroic Age had come to an end; new themes for heroic poems were no longer available. But education had not yet advanced so far or become so general that books and newspapers could take the place of that oral poetry which had hitherto been the intellectual activity of the country. This 'post-heroic' poetry, as elsewhere, is to be regarded largely as the journalism of a transitional age. We do not know whether any collection of such poems as those noted above has been published.

One would expect that poetry on somewhat similar lines may have been cultivated in Serbia in the course of last century; but we do not know whether there is any evidence to this effect. One interesting incident, however, has been recorded.[2] In 1873–4, when the Parliament (*Skupština*) was discussing the Budget and a bill for introducing a new monetary system, the debates were reproduced by a peasant Deputy in poetry to audiences outside the building. If such poetry as we have been discussing was current at the time it is hardly necessary to regard this performance as anything eccentric.

[1] Cf. Murko, *S. B. d. k. k. Akad. in Wien*, CLXXVI. 43 (1914–15).
[2] Cf. Mijatovich, *Kossovo*, p. 40. The same author remarks (p. 38) that peasant Deputies not unfrequently speak in 'blank verse' when their "feelings are roused to an exalted pitch". This book was published in 1881.

Although we have not seen any of the more recent poetry, the beginnings of the movement towards journalism may be seen clearly enough in some Montenegrin poems of the reign of Danilo (1851–1861) —published in the fifth volume of Karadžić's collection. Political events and issues are frequently treated at considerable length, much as in newspaper reports and articles. It has already been remarked (p. 333) that in many of these poems heroic interest is subordinated to communal or national interest, though not to the same extent as in the Dalmatian MS. poems. And there are other features which the two groups of poems have in common. Turkish leaders are made to propound ambitious schemes of conquest—sometimes at great length. Much interest is also taken in foreign politics, though in both cases these assume a very personal form. For instances we may refer to Karadžić, v. 1 (*ad init.*), where the dying bishop expresses his views as to the relations of Montenegro with Austria and Turkey, and to *ib.* 3. 2205 ff., where in a letter to Danilo the Austrian emperor speaks of the troubles by which he is beset in his own dominions. It is evident that even by this time the Montenegrins, poor and illiterate as they were, already had an intelligent interest in international politics.[1] Yet, as we have seen, it would hardly be true to say that the Heroic Age had come to an end. The poetry is of a transitional character—from heroic to post-heroic, though the former element is perhaps still dominant in the majority of the poems.

We do not know how far any similar transition can be traced in Mohammedan poetry. The question here seems to be more complex. It is said that the Mohammedans are much devoted to poems relating to the past, especially stories of the seventeenth century, and that they care less for modern themes. But their old stories appear to be not so uniformly heroic in character as those of the Christians. As an example we may take a poem on the war against Rakoczy in 1659–60.[2] The poem is concerned primarily with the adventures of the Bosnian contingent, which may be summarised briefly as follows: They set out from Sarajevo under an aged and wise leader named Džanan. In order to cheer his men, as they are leaving home, Džanan tells Ibro, his young standard-

---

[1] Cf. also Karadžić, v. No. 12. 78 ff., and No. 13. 79 ff., where the leaders of the attack upon Kolašin recognise quite clearly that the prince will not allow them to undertake such enterprises, owing to pressure from the consuls of the four Powers. In 12. 761 ff., after the town has been sacked, the Sultan writes letters of complaint to the Russian emperor, the Caesar of Vienna, the French king and the queen of England.

[2] Publ. with German transl. by Krauss, *Slavische Volkforschungen*, p. 197 ff.

bearer to sing a song. What he sings is virtually a last farewell, and has the effect of depressing the troops. Džanan is very angry, strikes him and takes the banner from him, and sends him home. Then he himself sings that they will gain greaty booty in the war, which will enable them to rebuild their wretched ruined houses. When they are approaching the Turkish camp, his men begin to shout and fire their muskets; but he tells them, as soon as they enter, to look downwards and appear thoroughly depressed. The Pashas and Viziers ask him why they are acting like this; and he explains that they feel their extreme poverty when they are faced with so gorgeous an array. By this means he succeeds in obtaining a large sum of money for his men. Now Ćuprilić, the commander-in-chief, asks for suggestions for a plan of campaign; and Džanan is the only one of his subordinates who can give any advice. A general attack is to be made in three days. But in the meantime Džanan and his men make a night attack independently, and completely rout the Magyars, though their own numbers are reduced by half. In the morning the Turks see that the Bosnians have left their positions; and one Pasha accuses them of desertion. But he is refuted by a Vila from a cloud; and Ćuprilić cuts off his head. Then the Turks advance, and find that Džanan has won the battle and captured all the leaders of the enemy, together with an immense amount of booty. As a reward for their achievement Džanan demands charters of land-possession for all his men, both the survivors and those who have fallen, and for himself half of the imperial seal.

The scholar who obtained this poem found also an interesting variant of it from a distant part of the country.[1] We may call the two versions A and B. The following are among the chief variations in the latter. The young standard-bearer, here called Ibro Fazlagić, is not sent home after his unfortunate song; he is one of the most prominent figures in the story. The Bosnians arrive in the Turkish camp not with a look of depression but in great disorder, raging desperately against one another and especially against Džanan himself. This ruse, however, serves the same purpose as the other; for Džanan explains that they have spent all their money, and thereby secures liberal supplies for them. After the battle no Vila intervenes; Ćuprilić himself sees from the look of the battlefield what has happened. When he overtakes the Bosnians, Ibro Fazlagić, who has led the attack, is missing; and Džanan is grieving

---

[1] Publ. with German transl. by Krauss, *op. cit.* p. 229 ff. This poem (B) came from near Brčka, in the extreme north-east of Bosnia, whereas A was obtained near Mostar and could be traced to Nikšić.

for his loss. Soon afterwards, however, he appears, bringing Rakoczy and his wife with him as prisoners. Then the Sultan arrives, and Džanan is brought to him. Džanan declares that the victory is due to Fazlagić; and both of them are rewarded with high honours. It is Fazlagić who asks for the granting of charters to the soldiers, both the living and the dead.[1]

The differences between the two versions are remarkable. B may be regarded as a heroic poem; for Ibro Fazlagić, who is prominent throughout, is a typical hero. But in A he disappears at once; and Hasan, who takes his place, is mentioned only twice. The subject is martial in both poems alike. But the dominant feature of A is the sagacity of the old leader Džanan and his care for his followers. We have not met with any parallel to this before—at least not as the dominant or central feature of a poem—and we are inclined to suspect that in Yugoslavia it is specifically Mohammedan.[1] It is not in accordance with heroic standards, unless we are to use the term 'heroic' in a wider or less definite sense than we have done hitherto. Its affinities are rather with post-heroic poetry. But we shall see later that such features are not necessarily limited to times later than the Heroic Age;[2] and therefore we prefer the term 'non-heroic'.

One would like to know which of the two versions was more true to the form of the original poem. Krauss, who published both of them, pointed out[3] that Bosnian custom is represented in B more faithfully than in A. Yet in regard to the differences noted above we are inclined to think that a transformation of A to B is more easily intelligible than the reverse change. However that may be, we must take note of the interesting fact that one of two versions of a poem is largely—not wholly—heroic; the interest is divided between a wise man and a hero. In the other the heroic element is wanting; there is no hero, and the interest is centred in the wise man. The contrast is striking enough to suggest a considerable difference in intellectual outlook between the circles in which the two versions assumed their present forms.

---

[1] If Despot Djuro's policy was really guided by patriotic motives, as historians seem to think, the poems relating to him are instructive as showing how such policy can be interpreted in a heroic society.

[2] In the literature treated in Vol. I communal or national interest seems to occur only in post-heroic and antiquarian records. But we shall see later that this limitation does not hold good for all literatures. Sometimes we find an active opposition between heroic and non-heroic elements.

[3] *Op. cit.* p. 226.

The characteristics of heroic poetry, as pointed out on p. 337 ff., hold good in the main also for the poetry treated in this chapter. Most of the poems are narrative poems and intended—with certain exceptions—primarily for entertainment. With regard to the limits of the Heroic Age enough has been said above. Both series of poems are anonymous, and their formal characteristics are in general similar, though non-heroic poems are usually shorter and less detailed. The essential differences between heroic and non-heroic poetry will require notice in the next chapter.

CHAPTER IV

THE HEROIC MILIEU

INDIVIDUALISM

IN Vol. 1, Ch. IV, we discussed the milieu of heroic stories under the following headings: (1) the social standing of the personnel; (2) the scenes of the stories; (3) the accessories of heroic life; (4) the social standards and conventions observed in heroic poetry and saga. We may now examine briefly the Yugoslav evidence bearing upon the same subjects.

(1) In regard to personnel a difference is clearly to be observed between the medieval and the modern stories. The personnel of the former—i.e. of poems relating to the medieval period—is almost exclusively aristocratic.[1] It includes kings and princes and their families, nobles, who are sometimes intermarried with the princely families, and the squires of princes and nobles; but squires never play more than a subordinate part in a story. The leading characters are usually either members of princely families or persons closely connected by marriage with such families—like Miloš Kobilović, who is said to be Prince Lazar's son-in-law. The exceptions[2]—Strahinja Banović, Bušić Stjepan, and one or two of the Hungarian heroes—are neither numerous nor very important. The Jakšića are more important, if they are real exceptions; but we do not know their family connections. They are rulers of Belgrade and intimate friends of Despot Vuk; but that is all we know of them. Persons of lower rank than the squires of nobles seem not to be mentioned by name, except in poems relating to Marko Kraljević, many of which are more akin to folk-tale than to heroic tradition.

In stories relating to the nineteenth century the case is different. The heroes of the Serbian wars of independence are said to have been

---

[1] In modern versions of the stories this fact tends to be obscured; the heroes are represented as living more or less like peasants—the only form of life known to the minstrels. Often we hear of no court; sometimes there seem to be no servants. In the poem on the birth of 'Fiery Vuk' (cf. p. 322), the hero's father, 'Blind Grgur', apparently builds his own house. But he was really a prince, one of the sons of Despot Gjorgje who had been blinded by Sultan Murad II. The same features are prominent in poems relating to Marko Kraljević.

[2] If they are really exceptions. We do not know the origin of either Strahinja or Bušić Stjepan. The wife of the former is a sister of Milica, the wife of Prince Lazar.

peasants, though some of them were probably as well off as any Christians could be in Serbia under Turkish rule. The leading Montenegrin heroes were for the most part persons who bore the titles *vojvoda*, *senator*, or *serdar*.[1] They appear to have been chiefs of districts; but we have no precise information as to their position, e.g. as to whether it was in any sense hereditary. We suspect that it is misleading to describe such persons as peasants—though they were doubtless very poor—and the society in which they lived as democratic; but in practice there must have been a considerable difference between their position and that of the earlier heroes.

For the heroes of the intermediate period, the sixteenth and following centuries, we have much less information. Heroes such as Ivo of Senj seem to act as if they were independent chiefs; and they can muster forces sufficient to take such strong fortresses as Jajce. Actually they must have been Hungarian or Austrian subjects, presumably with some recognised position; but the country was doubtless much disorganised. The same remarks apply apparently to the Turkish *age* and *beži* opposed to them. Other heroes, however, whether *beži* or *hajduci* would seem to be adventurers, without any recognised authority. The *beg* Ljubović respects the orders of the Sultan, but defies all other authorities, whether Turkish or Austrian. But the poems do not suggest a democratic society.

The Dalmatian MS. poems give quite a different picture. The *braća* ('brotherhood') of Perast debate and avenge their wrongs. There is a *kapetan*; but he is seldom mentioned. When the luckless Mehmed Aga is disabled and captured (cf. p. 352), he offers one third of his ransom to the *zbor* ('assembly') of Perast. Here we do seem to have a democratic society, though it consists of seafarers rather than peasants. And it is likely enough that other maritime places had similar organisations, though their poetry happens not to have been preserved. Ragusa of course stands quite apart from the rest, with a republican organisation of a more advanced type. But we have seen that heroic poetry appears to be foreign to the whole of the coastland.

(2) As in the heroic stories treated in Vol. 1, the scene is usually laid either in the house of a prince or noble or on the battlefield or other place of adventure. In the former case the scene is as a rule a drinking-scene, as in Vol. 1. In modern Montenegrin poems heroes meet for drinking at the tower of one of the chief men, or less frequently at a church; ladies

---

[1] Members of the princely family also figure prominently in some poems. It is to be remembered that the ruler was a bishop until 1851.

are never present. Occasionally in stories relating to early times one hears of heroes drinking in a tavern, as in the story of the death of Andrija, brother of Marko Kraljević (cf. p. 311). But it may be doubted whether this is in accordance with ancient heroic usage. A much older poem, as we have seen (*ib.*), represents Andrija as slain by Marko himself on the hills.

When visitors are received by a prince, the poems seldom fail to notice the bows and formal greetings exchanged by host and guest. Such receptions are hardly described as fully as in Greek and English heroic poetry, except perhaps in connection with marriages and proposals of marriage. For an example of the latter we may refer to 'The Sister of Leka Kapetan', 216 ff.

(3) As regards the accessories of heroic life, drinking plays at least as prominent a part as in any of the ancient heroic literatures. Wine is regularly the beverage. It is strange, however, that one seldom if ever hears of minstrelsy—or any other diversion—during the drinking. Yet heroes sing on other occasions—during the march of a wedding procession[1] or of an army (cf. p. 356 f.), and even on the field of battle, as in Karadžić, v. 3. 1378 ff., where Savo Martinović is said to be singing all the time that he is firing. But all these cases seem to refer to poetry of Type D. Ibro Nukić sings to the *tambura* throughout his wedding night; but this is for his own diversion (Type E). Yet historical records, as we shall see, refer to the singing of heroic poems at banquets, even as far back as the sixteenth century.

A hero's most valued possession is his horse. Marko Kraljević who is a great drinker shares his wine equally with Šarac. The horse is an invaluable ally to him and occasionally even speaks, as in 'Marko and Philip the Magyar', 149 ff. The same is said of Momčilo's winged horse, in 'The Marriage of King Vukašin', 201 ff. Strahinja Banović is assisted by both his horse and his dog in his fight with Vlah Alija. For the close relations between a hero and his horse we may refer also to 'The Death of the Mother of the Jugovići',[2] 40 ff., where Damjan's horse cries, not from hunger or thirst, but because it misses its master.[3] In the poem on the battle of Lepanto (cf. p. 354) the poet no doubt shows a knowledge of heroic custom when he makes the wife of Sokolović Pasha offer a horse and golden spear in ransom for her sons.

Weapons also are greatly prized, though references to them are hardly so frequent as in ancient heroic literatures. The value attached to

---

[1] Cf. Karadžić, v. 968 ff.   [2] Karadžić, II. No. 48.

[3] Ibro Nukić's horse cries and refuses to eat when its master is going into danger.

a sword, sentimental as well as actual, in early times may be illustrated by the two poems called 'Marko Kraljević recognises his Father's Sword'. We may refer also to the list of treasures in 'The Marriage of King Vukašin', 270 ff., which the faithless wife of Momčilo brings to his slayer, and which include helmet, sword and mail-coat. Again, in 'The Marriage of Maxim Crnojević',[1] 764 ff., the gifts presented by the bride's relatives include a golden sword, a jewelled head-dress (*kalpak*) and a golden robe, together with a horse and a falcon. Gorgeous robes and head-dresses are mentioned elsewhere also, much more frequently than in the ancient heroic literatures. But in poems relating to modern times such splendour is seldom if ever thought of. Mohammedan heroes of the seventeenth century win swords of honour (cf. p. 329), as prizes for exceptional valour. But in the middle of the nineteenth century the prize given to the priest Luka, the leader of the successful force in 'The Death of Djulek' (cf. p. 333 f.), is merely a good *dževerdan*—a musket of some kind.

(4) Social standards or indeed moral judgments of any kind are rarely expressed in heroic poetry, though they occur in the (post-heroic) Perast poems, as well as in other non-heroic poetry. There can be no doubt, however, that courage and loyalty are the qualities most prized in the heroic character.

Obscenity seems to be entirely wanting in heroic poetry. In this respect Yugoslav heroic convention falls in no way short of the Greek and English heroic standards; indeed we have never met with any passage which could offend the most fastidious taste. On the other hand the Perast poems, though they are moral enough, do not shrink from unpleasant details.

In other respects, however, and especially in regard to temper the behaviour of both heroes and ladies is open to criticism. Milica's daughters have an unseemly quarrel (cf. p. 315), which is subsequently taken up by their husbands, with disastrous consequences. Jerina knocks her grandson Maxim down (cf. p. 320 f.), and in another poem she is herself knocked down by Radosav (cf. p. 321); but she is an exceptionally unpopular character. On most of these occasions teeth are scattered. Marko Kraljević is a heavy drinker; and it would seem that Serbian heroes in general were credited by the Latins with the same propensity. At all events the prospect of their presence at weddings is regarded with some apprehension—as may be seen (e.g.) from 'The Marriage of Djuro of Smeredevo' (cf. p. 317), 12 ff., where the king

[1] Karadžić, II. No. 89.

of Ragusa begs the bridegroom to invite Greeks and Bulgarians, not Serbians, as his guests, 'for Serbians are heavy drinkers and fierce brawlers'. The same description is applied to the king's nephews in 'The Marriage of Dušan',[1] 44 f. In 'The Marriage of the King of Budim' (cf. p. 318) one of the two principal guests pays off an old grudge against the other with the bridegroom's connivance, and when they are both apparently sober.

The worst feature, however, in the earlier heroes is their brutality towards women. Marko Kraljević is the worst offender of all, especially in 'The Sister of Leka Kapetan'. But other heroes, e.g. Miloš in 'The Marriage of Dušan', 575 ff., at least threaten to cut off girls' arms. And Ivo of Senj beats the Turkish ladies without mercy. It should be observed that in regard to barbarities of this kind there is sometimes a striking difference between the old *bugarštice* and the later poems collected by Karadžić. Thus in the story of Strahinja Banović, when the hero brings his faithless wife back to her home, in the *bugarštica* (Bogišić, No. 40) her brothers at once dispatch her with their swords; in Karadžić's poem (II. No. 44, *ad fin.*) they are dissuaded from doing so by the hero himself. Again, in the story in which the Jakšića test the generosity of their wives, the wife who fails in the test in the *bugarštica* (Bogišić, No. 41) has her head cut off on the spot by her husband; in Karadžić's poem (II. No. 100) the husband tries to throttle her, but is stopped by his brother. It would seem then that the ferocity of early times was not always approved of by later poets or their audiences.

On the other hand it may be remarked that women sometimes wield great influence. This is especially noteworthy in the case of Jerina, the wife of Despot Djuro. Maxim Crnojević's bride has no difficulty in bringing about a deadly struggle between her bridegroom and the man he has allowed to personate him. Mention may also be made here of the stories—which are not uncommon (cf. p. 328)—in which a girl herself takes arms and acts as a hero. In heroic *bugarštice* the interest is very often centred in women.

Taking the evidence as a whole, it is clear that the Yugoslav heroic milieu in early times—down to c. 1500—differed little from what we found in the ancient heroic literatures. It is essentially an aristocratic milieu; the interest is concentrated in princes and their noble followers, and the appurtenances of aristocratic life. From the sixteenth century onwards, when Yugoslav princes no longer existed, the interest is centred in local chiefs, who carried on heroic warfare on their own account, and

[1] Karadžić, II. No. 29.

even in outlaws (*uskoci*). In the nineteenth century it is centred in the Serbian leaders of the wars of independence and in Montenegrin local chiefs. In these later periods the milieu is not aristocratic—at least not in the sense in which we apply that term to the early period; but neither can it properly be called democratic. A truly democratic milieu seems to be found in the (non-heroic) poetry of Perast, dating from the sixteenth and following centuries.

The subject of individualism was treated in Vol. 1, Ch. v, in connection with (i) nationality, (ii) heroic warfare. We came to the conclusion that the prominence of the individual appears to be an essential characteristic of heroic stories and of the Heroic Age itself.

(i) In Vol. 1 we saw that ancient heroic poetry and saga in general yielded little evidence for any feeling of nationality, apart from the fact that the poets' world is divided into two hostile camps both in the *Iliad* and in Welsh poetry. In the *narodne pjesme* we find a similar and permanent division prevailing throughout between the Christian world and the Turkish world. The religious aspect of the division is not very often expressed; but it is quite exceptional to find Christian and Turkish heroes acting together in perfect accord, as in the story of the *beg* Ljubović(cf. p. 329 f.). Marko Kraljević is loyal to the Turkish emperor; but his relations with other Turks are often unfriendly.

This distinction is more religious—or rather 'politico-religious'[1]—than national in the strict sense. Most of the 'Turks' mentioned in the poems are Mohammedan Yugoslavs. But Mohammedan poems do not in general distinguish between Mohammedan Yugoslavs and true Turks or Albanians. And, similarly, Christian poems do not in general distinguish between Christian Yugoslavs and Christians of other nationalities. Some of the leading heroes are Hungarians. It is true that 'Latins' are sometimes regarded with suspicion; but this term includes Dalmatian and Ragusan Yugoslavs, as well as Venetians, and would seem to be religious or political rather than national.

What we have been speaking of is the consciousness of a barrier rather than the definite assertion of nationality. In regard to the latter

[1] The line of division is not rigidly according to religion. In early times we find Marko Kraljević on the Turkish side. In the nineteenth century the poems often mention among the Turkish leaders a Marko Kapetane, who was presumably a Christian—perhaps an Albanian. Smail Aga has a friend called Djoko Malović, as well as a groom called Martin. In several early stories Christian and Turkish heroes are friends, though the latter are said to act treacherously.

13

great differences are to be found between the different periods and groups of poetry. In poems of the nineteenth century it is frequently expressed. Montenegrins speak of themselves sometimes as *Crnogorci* (Montenegrins), sometimes as *Srbi* (Serbs); and, in spite of the persistence of the heroic element, patriotism flourishes, both in the narrower and the wider sense of the term—as applying to all Christian Yugoslavs. The most pronounced illustration is 'The Lament of the Dragon on the Lovćen' (cf. p. 334 f.).

In poems relating to the early period there is by no means the same uniformity. The Cycle of Marko Kraljević naturally gives little scope for the expression of nationality; for it is generally recognised in the poems that Marko was a Turkish vassal. The conception of him as a patriotic hero would seem to be modern and due to his popularity. But the question is how an unpatriotic character—one who was liable to be called a 'Turkish minion' (*pridvorica*)—could attain such popularity.

The Kosovo Cycle on the other hand has usually been regarded as essentially national and patriotic. Yet this description is only true in part. The passages which show national or patriotic feeling in the strict sense are few in number. The most important of them is the solemn imprecation in 'Musić Stefan',[1] 21 ff., 76 ff., pronounced by Lazar upon him "who is a Serbian and of Serbian stock, of Serbian flesh and blood, and comes not to battle at Kosovo". The curse of barrenness is invoked both upon him and upon his land. Far more numerous are the passages which attribute a religious significance to the struggle. We may quote a fragmentary poem,[2] which we believe to be very old in substance (cf. p. 315). Miloš, replying to the charge of disloyalty brought against him by Lazar, solemnly denies the charge and adds: "Tomorrow I intend to die for the Christian faith at Kosovo".

But in the old MS. poems preserved at Ragusa the heroes are not said to be animated by feelings of either patriotism or religion. Here the guiding principle is personal loyalty of the true heroic type. In Bogišić, I. 31 f., 43 f., which correspond to the first of the passages cited above, there is no reference to any curse or declaration by Lazar. Bušić Stjepan (i.e. Musić Stefan) merely states that he will not desert the army of Prince Lazar, the Hungarian lords and the brothers Ugovići. Again, later in the same poem, when Miloš has been charged by Lazar with

---

[1] Karadžić, II. No. 47 (p. 298 ff.); transl. by Morison in Subotić, *Yugoslav Popular Ballads*, p. 58 ff.
[2] Karadžić, II. No. 50. iii (p. 310 ff.); transl. by Seton-Watson in Subotić, *op. cit.* p. 65 f.

disloyalty, he declares (139 ff.) that he will not betray him at Kosovo. He vows in the presence of all the lords to make his way to the Turkish camp before sunrise on the morrow and to slay the emperor there. But he says nothing about dying for the Christian faith. The motives stated or implied in this poem—as also in the other early MS. poems relating to Kosovo—are always of a personal character. Vuk Branković's treachery or desertion arises out of his refusal to help Miloš, against whom he bears a bitter animosity owing to the loss of his teeth (cf. p. 315 f.).

Further, it may be observed that the name 'Serbian' does not occur in these poems.[1] The only national names found are the 'Turks' and the 'Hungarian lords' (*Ugarska gospoda*). It has been suggested that by the latter term—which occurs several times—we are to understand Hungarian allies of Lazar. But the suggestion has not been generally accepted; for it is obviously unlikely that such allies[2] would be the only persons mentioned, apart from the prince and his brothers-in-law. There can be little doubt that the poem reflects the political conditions of the fifteenth century, especially the latter part of it, when the unconquered Yugo-slavs carried on the struggle against the Turks under Hungarian leader-ship. But if so, we must infer that no great importance was attached to nationality in these times.

This inference is fully borne out by the large number of poems in the MS. collections which are concerned with Hungarian kings and heroes. It is obvious that the poets and their audiences were much interested in these persons; and there is no indication that they regarded them as aliens, in spite of such expressions as *Ugrin Janko* ('Hungarian John'). One poem (cf. p. 317) indeed makes Janko (John Hunyadi) to be a son of Stjepan, son of Lazar. But even here the name 'Serbian' does not occur, while the scene is laid at Sibinj (Sibiu or Hermannstadt), which was never a Yugoslav town. The poets' intention was presumably to claim for Janko not Serbian nationality so much as a distinguished ancestry with which they were themselves familiar. There is no evidence

---

[1] It does seem to occur, however—in the form *sarsku* (for *Srpsku*)—in a *bugar-štica* from a Ragusa MS. publ. by Novaković, *Arch. f. slav. Philol.* III. 648 ff. Here it is applied apparently to the Hungarian nobles.

[2] Lazar had allies from various quarters; but we are not aware that there were Hungarians among them. It may be observed that in Bogišić, I. 106 ff., Lazar says the Ugovići have vowed to the Hungarian king (*kralju Ugarskomu*) that if the sky shall fall to the earth they will catch it on their spears. It is not clear to us whether he means himself; elsewhere in these poems he is called *knez*, not *kralj*. The passage may have suffered in the course of oral tradition; but we think it is to be taken in connection with political conditions of cent. xv.

that they had any knowledge of Hungarian history before Janko's time —a fact which is the more noteworthy because the coastal districts, from which the MSS. come, had been partly under Hungarian protection down to 1420. But it is only after this date that the interest in Hungarian heroes begins.

In these MS. poems the attitude towards the Hungarian heroes is regularly sympathetic. Even when Janko is in conflict with the Serbian ruler Despot Djuro, the poems always take the side of the former. Moreover this attitude is not peculiar to them. There are a number of Serbian poems collected in later times and included in Karadžić's collection which also deal with Hungarian heroes; and here too the attitude is usually, though not always, sympathetic. We may refer in particular to Karadžić, II. No. 86, noticed on p. 318 f., which is entirely sympathetic to Sekula and makes the Despot responsible for his death. The only poem we have noticed which takes the opposite view, i.e. friendly to the Despot and hostile to Janko, is No. 81, 'The Death of the Vojvoda Kaica'; and it can hardly be due to accident that this poem speaks throughout of the Magyars. In the other poems Janko and his men rarely if ever have any national name applied to them.

Lastly, it may be mentioned that we have not observed any traces of national feeling in the Cycle of poems dealing with the Jakšića and Vuk the Fiery Dragon, though references to personal relations between these heroes and a king of Budim (Hungary) are not rare. More than one of these poems, however, shows a strong religious interest.

From what has been said it will be seen that throughout the early period interest in nationality must be regarded as exceptional. The modern collections contain a few striking examples, especially in 'Musić Stefan' and 'The Death of Kaica'; but even here it is not widespread. In the old MS. collections it seems to be entirely wanting. If we take into account, further, that the MS. poems regularly, and the modern poems sometimes, sympathise with Hungarian heroes against the native Djuro, and that the most popular of all the early heroes, Marko Kraljević, is a loyal vassal of the Sultan—it is difficult to avoid the conclusion that the early poets and their audiences were not interested in nationality, and that where this element occurs in the poems it has been introduced in later times.

The religious interest is of somewhat more frequent occurrence and may be older. Indeed to some extent it may have been attached to the Kosovo Cycle from the beginning. But the evidence does not suggest that this was what primarily interested the early poets. If we take the *bugarštice* and the later poems together it would seem that the primary motives were of a purely personal nature—the disastrous quarrel between Lazar's sons-in-law and the fate of Milica's brothers. The quarrel between the wives was doubtless invented to explain the former motif. And likewise in the rest of the stories which relate to the early period we see no reason for doubting that interest in the heroes as individuals was the dominant element from the beginning, just as in the heroic poetry and saga discussed in Vol. I.

We regret that our knowledge of the large body of heroic poetry relating to the period c. 1500–1800 is not sufficient to allow us to speak of it with any confidence; but we are under the impression that the same remark is true here also in general. There are indeed a number of Mohammedan poems (cf. p. 356 ff.) of which it is clearly not true; but we do not think that these are properly to be regarded as heroic. In Christian poems the religious element seems to be more important than in the earlier period; and the same may probably be said of the national (patriotic) element. We suspect, however, that the importance of the latter dates from towards the close of the period.[1]

Finally, it is to be borne in mind that from the sixteenth and seventeenth centuries we have a good deal of poetry, preserved in MSS., which is dominated by patriotism of the narrowest kind, and in which little importance is attached to the individual. Especially instructive are the poems from Perast, 'the famous little place on the edge of the sea'. We regard these poems as essentially non-heroic (post-heroic). We think also that the Mohammedan (Bosnian) poems alluded to above are best referred to the same category.

(ii) Heroic warfare among the Yugoslavs seems on the whole to be much the same as elsewhere. Attention is usually concentrated upon the courage and strength of individual heroes. In poems relating to the early period, battle scenes are not of very frequent occurrence. Much more often the subject is an exploit carried out by a hero alone or with one or two companions. Thus Miloš Obilić is accompanied by two companions, Milan Toplica and Ivan Kosančić, who seem originally to have been his squires.[2] Marko Kraljević is most often alone. Sometimes,

---

[1] It is probably to be connected with the growth of national feeling in cent. xviii, especially among the Serbians north of the Danube and the Sava. This in itself may have been largely due to a similar movement among the Magyars, while the latter again seems to have been religious in origin. These, however, are historical questions, into which we need not enter.

[2] Cf. Bogišić, 1. 146, where Miloš' squires (*sluge*) bear similar, though not identical, names.

however, he is accompanied by one or two famous heroes, including even Janko, who belonged to a later generation. No historical value of course can be attached to such associations. Vuk the Fiery Dragon is usually unaccompanied. But in one of the poems on his marriage (cf. p. 323) there is a battle on a large scale; and it is of interest to see how the issue depends wholly on the prowess of the two principals. The rest of the combatants count for nothing.

In modern Montenegrin poems long passages are often devoted to descriptions of the gallantry of individual heroes, who charge the enemy sword in hand, in spite of the general use of firearms. Sometimes the poet will describe the gallantry of two or three heroes in succession, very much as in the battle-scenes in the *Iliad*; and the presence of their followers is ignored, just as in the latter. A typical scene of this kind will be found in Karadžić, v, No. 12 (499 ff.), one of the poems on the Sack of Kolašin, in 1858. Shorter passages of similar character from other poems were noticed on p. 334.

Vows and boasting before an action occur just as in the heroic poetry and saga of other peoples. We have already (p. 367) referred to the rhetorical vow of the Jugovići and to the vow of Miloš Kobilović, which he actually carried out. In modern poems challenges are frequently offered in the course of a battle; instances will be found on p. 333 f. Such challenges seem as a rule to be ignored, probably owing to the use of firearms; but they are doubtless in accordance with traditional usage. Heroes are also said to boast of their own achievements in the past, especially when wine is beginning to take effect upon them; cf. Karadžić, v. 13. 12, 116 ff.

In view of the characteristics noted above it is not surprising that, as in the heroic stories of other lands, wars and raids are often said to be due to personal motives. In Karadžić, v. 13, it is the Vojvoda Milan who is responsible for bringing about the attack upon Kolašin, and his chief motive is to avenge his brother. In IV. 58. 62 ff., 95 ff., Bishop Peter II is represented as encouraging Cerović Novica to attack Čengijć Smail Aga owing to his own desire to obtain vengeance for his nephews. It may perhaps be questioned [1] whether the bishop, who was a very cultured man, was really animated by such a feeling; but there can hardly be any doubt that the poem truly represents how both Turks and Montenegrins expected him to feel.

---

[1] In the poem itself (cf. No. 57. 61 ff.) the statement is represented as coming from a man in the Turkish service; but Karadžić (IV, p. 459) seems to have believed it to be true. The poem was supplied to him by a high official in Prince Danilo's household.

More frequently perhaps the incentive comes from the hope of booty and of glory. When the priest Luka summons his friends for the attack upon Djulek (cf. p. 333), he says there is plenty of treasure and glory to be obtained. Actually the booty seems to consist of horses and fire-arms. At the sack of Kolašin an enormous amount of livestock is said to have been captured; cf. Karadžić, v. 12. 608 ff. In an earlier attack upon the same place the men who send out the summons say (ib. iv. 53. 8 ff.) they have marked a fine spoil—which eventually they succeed in securing (ib. 618 ff.). The plundering of the sheepfolds is a great object of desire. A raid of this kind, on a big scale, forms the subject of iv. 54. It is arranged to take place during a Mohammedan festival.

But the desire for glory was greater even than that for booty. In Yugoslavia, as in ancient Ireland, this took the form of head-hunting. The practice is found in poems relating to the earliest times, e.g. 'The Marriage of Dušan' and 'Marko Kraljević and Philip the Magyar', and it continued in full use down to the latter part of the nineteenth century in the border warfare between the Montenegrins and the Turks of Hercegovina. We have already seen (p. 333) how one hero after another falls in the attempt to get the head of Djulek—a scene which may be compared with a passage in the *Iliad*, where the Trojans and Achaeans fight for the body of Patroclos. Head-hunting itself, however, is foreign to the *Iliad*, whereas to the Montenegrins the heads were the symbols and proofs of their prowess. We may refer to a passage in Karadžić, v. 3 (1673 ff.), where it is stated that—in the course of the battle against Omer Pasha—every hero gains glory. One gets one head, another two heads; but the standard-bearer Djuro Martinović brings four heads. The Serdar's heart is rejoiced; and Petrović (Mirko) roars with laughter, as they bring the heads to him; and he embraces and kisses each of the warriors. Again, at the end of one of the poems on 'The Death of Čengijć Smail Aga' (ib. iv. 58. 514 ff.) we hear that the Serbians return singing and firing their guns. They bring the heads of Smail Aga and the Begs with them to the king of Cetinje (Bishop Peter II). The king receives them graciously and presents a gold medal to Cerović Novica —whom he promotes—a silver medal to Mirko, and other suitable rewards to the rest of the warriors. Similar passages occur elsewhere; indeed decapitation is the conclusion of practically every exploit.

In connection with these passages it may be of interest to quote here an extract from the diary of Sir J. Gardiner Wilkinson, the famous Egyptologist, who visited Bishop Peter II shortly before the death of

Smail Aga. The passage is dated 17 June, 1839:[1] "The same day after dinner the Vladika (bishop) ordered that every one should bring his heads to the plain of Cettigne, and forming a great circle Monsignore placed himself in the midst with the President and all the Senate; called out the warriors one by one; and embracing each hung round his neck a silver medal by a red cord."

It was the custom at Cetinje to impale the heads on stakes and set them up on a round tower behind the monastery. Many of them were seen there by Wilkinson, while others lay on the ground below. At Mostar, where a similar practice was observed, the stakes were fixed on the walls. It is said that in the days of Ali Pasha Rizvanbegović, Peter II's contemporary, there were always a hundred and fifty heads to be seen there. Most of these had been cut off the Pasha's Christian subjects.

In Montenegro the Heroic Age can be studied at closer quarters than in any other of the literatures we have examined as yet; but it is not a typical specimen. The absence of an aristocracy possessing any kind of wealth and the strength of the feeling for nationality are abnormal features. The first was due to the poverty of the country, the second to the fact that it was almost surrounded by an enemy of infinitely greater resources. To the same causes we must attribute the almost exclusive preoccupation with warfare shown in the poems. The heroes seem to have no other interest.

The survival of the Heroic Age down to so late a time was due doubtless in part to the constant insecurity of the frontier. But there was another cause, no less important, namely the fact that the country was cut off from communication with the civilised world, except by one mountain road. On the shores of the Bocche, only a few miles away, there were communities whose civilisation three centuries previously was comparable with that of the Viking Age, and far in advance of the Montenegrin. A little further along the coast there were cities which had shared the full civilisation of the Renaissance. It would be difficult anywhere else to find so great diversity in so limited an area —at least without linguistic barriers.

In the early part of the Heroic Age—down to c. 1500—the stories relate to a much wider and richer area. Here the conditions seem in general to be very similar to those we observed in Vol. 1. The milieu is aristocratic, and interest in the individual is paramount. The stories are by no means exclusively concerned with fighting; and women frequently

[1] J. Gardiner Wilkinson, *Dalmatia and Montenegro* (1848), p. 495.

play a prominent part in them. Indeed it can hardly be said that the position of women—especially the queens, such as Milica and Jerina—compares unfavourably with what we find in heroic stories elsewhere. There are some crude and brutal features, such as head-hunting and atrocities committed against women. In the latter respect indeed the early period is much worse than the nineteenth century;[1] Montenegrin usage shows a great improvement (cf. p. 334), while later versions of the early stories often eliminate the atrocities (cf. p. 364). But these brutalities and atrocities are found also in the Heroic Ages of other lands. Head-hunting is a regular practice in Irish sagas; and the worst atrocity of all—tearing women to pieces by tying them to the tails of horses, as in 'The Marriage of King Vukašin'—is found also among the Teutonic peoples, both in heroic stories and in historical records.[2] All that can fairly be said against the Yugoslavs is that, owing to their geographical situation, their civilisation in the early part of the Heroic Age was some centuries behind that of western Europe. The Turkish conquest delayed progress for several centuries more.

[1] It is incorrect therefore to attribute these atrocities to Turkish influence, though Turks also doubtless perpetrated them. Such atrocities were usually due to passion or resentment for insult, whereas typical Turkish atrocities were more deliberate and on a larger scale. It is as well to remember that for the latter type some of the western nations have an ugly record for the sixteenth and seventeenth centuries. But the Turks kept up these practices much longer.

[2] We may refer to the story of Eormenric and also to the death of the Frankish queen Brunihildis in 613. Cf. also Gregory of Tours, *Hist. Franc.* III. 7.

CHAPTER V

UNHISTORICAL ELEMENTS IN
HEROIC POETRY

IT is unnecessary to demonstrate the existence of historical elements in Yugoslav heroic or non-heroic poetry. There can be no question that the events related in the modern poems are in general historical, at least in their main outlines. It is clear too from evidence which is beyond suspicion that very many of the persons and events recorded in stories of earlier periods are likewise historical. We may therefore confine our attention to unhistorical elements.

We must confess at once that we have not the requisite knowledge for a detailed study of this subject; nor are the records necessary for such a study accessible to us. It must suffice to take a limited number of examples, in which the evidence is more or less clear. Even these, we venture to think, will yield a good deal of instructive material. Most of our illustrations will naturally be taken from stories of the earlier periods. The unhistorical elements which occur in modern stories seem usually to consist of exaggerations and distortions of facts; and it would require the knowledge of a specialist to check these.

In Vol. I, Ch. VIII, we classified unhistorical elements as follows: I. Incidents and situations which are in conflict (*a*) with reliable historical evidence or (*b*) with other heroic stories. II. Incidents and situations which are in themselves incredible. III. Matter of various kinds which is neither in conflict with other evidence nor yet in itself incredible, but which, at least in its context, is certainly or probably to be regarded as unhistorical. The invention of characters was treated in connection with the last of these sections.

I. In poems relating to early times heroes who belonged to different ages are frequently brought into association with one another. This is especially noticeable in the case of Marko Kraljević, who is often found in various relations, friendly or hostile, with Janko of Sibinj, i.e. John Hunyadi. Marko lived in the latter part of the fourteenth century. His father was killed in 1371, and he himself is believed to have been killed in 1394. But John Hunyadi belonged to the middle of the fifteenth century. He is seldom, if ever, mentioned before 1437; and he can hardly have been more than an infant, even if he was born, in Marko's lifetime. Yet this unhistorical association is found not only in the poems published in modern collections, such as those of Karadžić and the Matica Hrvatska, but also in early texts preserved in MSS. Thus in 'Marko and Mina (Minja) of Kostur'[1] the former hero receives an invitation from Janko to come and christen his child or children; and this feature occurs not only in Karadžić's version, but also in the earlier text of the same poem preserved in a Zagreb MS. (cf. p. 305). It must date back therefore to the seventeenth century. Again, in a decasyllabic poem[2] preserved in the Franciscan (Ragusa) MS., which dates probably from before the middle of the eighteenth century, Marko fights a duel with Janko, and cuts off his head.

Janko is by no means the only hero who is incorrectly associated with Marko. In 'The Marriage of Djuro of Smeredevo' (cf. p. 317) we find a medley of fourteenth and fifteenth century heroes; but the chief part is played by Marko. Despot Djuro himself, however, was a contemporary of Janko, and died in 1456. This poem indeed seems to be wholly fictitious, apart from the name of the bride. But it would probably not be difficult to find even more striking anachronisms. The name of the emperor associated with Marko is sometimes given as Sulejman; but the first of that name succeeded to the throne in the year 1502.

There are perhaps more anachronisms in poems relating to Marko Kraljević than in any others, owing to the great popularity of this group. But equally glaring examples are to be found elsewhere. We may refer to 'The Empress Milica and the Dragon of Jastrebac', where Vuk the 'Dragon-Despot' (or 'Fiery Dragon') comes to the aid of Milica, wife of Lazar, by a supernatural adventure (cf. p. 322). This Vuk lived nearly a century after the time of Lazar and Milica.

In bugarštice relating to Hungarian heroes we find not only anachronisms but also incidents and situations of various kinds which are contrary to historical fact. Thus in Bogišić, No. 21 (cf. p. 320) Janko and King Vladislav are made to fall at Kosovo with Sekula. Another poem (ib. No. 28), represents Janko as living down to the capture of Budim, and makes King Vladislav to be slain in its defence. In reality John Hunyadi died in 1456, while Buda was not captured until 1526; during the interval Hungary was at its greatest strength. Again, there was no king called Vladislav reigning in 1526. It would seem that the tradition of the bugarštice had combined all Janko's battles against the Turks in the

---

[1] Karadžić, II. No. 62; transl. by Low, *The Ballads of Marko Kraljević*, p. 91 ff. The Zagreb text will be found in Bogišić, No. 7, and in Matica Hrvatska, *Junačke Pjesme*, II. No. 47.   [2] Bogišić, No. 88.

second battle of Kosovo—which was fought in 1448—and all the kings of Hungary, except Matthias, in 'King Vladislav'. The latter mistake was of course facilitated by the fact that three kings bore this name in the fifteenth century; and these are not distinguished from one another in the poems. Lastly, we may recall here another *bugarštica* (Bogišić, No. 8), noticed on p. 317 above, in which it is stated that Janko was the son of the Serbian prince Stjepan, son of Lazar, and that the latter also was killed at Kosovo. Neither of these statements seems to be in accordance with historical fact.

In poems relating to the first battle of Kosovo (in 1389) anachronisms of this kind seem to be much less frequent. In Karadžić, II. No. 46, however, we find included among those who fell in this battle Vukašin, who was killed eighteen years before, and Erceg Stjepan, who lived nearly a century later. But the passages in which these heroes are mentioned occur in the second half of the poem, which is merely a catalogue of forces and apparently unconnected with the first half (cf. p. 314).

After what has been said above it is perhaps hardly necessary to give examples of discrepancies between one poem and another, where the historical facts are unknown. A striking instance will be found in the different accounts of the death of Andrija, brother of Marko Kraljević, noticed on p. 311.

In modern poems we have not observed anachronisms and unhistorical statements of the kind noted above; and we should be inclined to doubt the possibility of their occurrence in relation to recent events. Curious discrepancies, however, between one poem and another do occur occasionally. Thus in one of the poems (Karadžić, v. No. 12) on 'The Sack of Kolašin' the instigators and leaders of the attack are three in number—Cerović Novica, Milan the Serdar, and Dimitrije the Archimandrite, all of whom seem to be equally prominent in the story. But in the other poem on the same subject (*ib.* No. 13) no mention is made of Dimitrije. Yet the two poems would appear to be not wholly independent of one another. And they cannot have had a long life; for the event took place in 1858, only seven years before the publication of Karadžić's collection. The case is of interest therefore, as showing how quickly such discrepancies may arise—whatever may be the cause.

II. Among incidents and situations which are in themselves incredible we may begin with (*a*) the introduction of supernatural beings. By far the most important of these are the Vile—female supernatural beings, whose nature will require notice in the next chapter.

Vile are frequently introduced in heroic poems of all periods and sometimes in poems which cannot properly be regarded as heroic. In 'The Walling of Skadar'[1] a mountain Vila throws down the new walls every night, undoing all the work that has been done in the day.

Vile figure prominently in several poems relating to Marko Kraljević. In 'Marko Kraljević and the Vila'[2] the hero is riding with Miloš, and asks him to sing. Miloš replies that on the previous night he has been drinking with the Vila Ravijojla, and that she has threatened to shoot him if he sings. He gives way, however; and the Vila first sings against him, and then shoots him in the heart with an arrow. Marko gives chase to her, and eventually catches her and beats her with his mace. She persuades him to let her seek for healing herbs; and with these she brings Miloš back to life. There are many variant forms of this story. In one[3] Relja is Marko's companion. The Vila is one of three, who are offended that the silence of their mountain should be broken by the singing. She is sent by the two others, and shoots the offending hero; but she is caught by Marko and made to restore him to life. As soon as Relja comes to himself, he kills her.

More striking is the story noticed on p. 312, in which Marko captures a Vila and marries her. On one occasion she escapes; but he recovers her. She bears him a son. To this story also there is a variant—if such it can be called—according to which (cf. p. 312 f.) it is Vukašin who captures and marries the Vila. Marko and Andrija are her sons. In 'The Death of Marko Kraljević'[4] it is a mountain Vila who warns him that his last hour is come.

Another case of marriage with a Vila occurs in a *bugarštica*, Bogišić, No. 39. The husband here is Novak; and she escapes from him just as in the stories cited. The hero Grujica is her son.

In the *bugarštica* which recounts the death of Vuk the Dragon-Despot (cf. p. 324) a mountain Vila comes to tend the hero's wounds. His wife, however, catches sight of her, and tells his mother. Then the Vila disappears, and Vuk dies soon afterwards.

In 'The Captivity and Marriage of Stjepan Jakšić' (cf. p. 324) a Vila calls out to Mitar from the mountain Avala, and warns him of the approach of the Turks. In a *bugarštica*, likewise relating to the Jakšića

---

[1] Karadžić, II. No. 26; transl. by Morison in Subotić, *Yugoslav Popular Ballads*, p. 40 ff.

[2] Karadžić, II. No. 38; transl. by Low, *op. cit.* p. 21 ff.

[3] Publ. with German transl. by Krauss, *Slavische Volkforschungen*, p. 373 f.; other variants follow. Yet another variant will be found in Matica Hrvatska, *Junačke Pjesme*, II. No. 3 (cf. also *ib.* p. 332 ff.).

[4] Karadžić, II. No. 74; transl. by Low, *op. cit.* p. 174 ff.

(cf. p. 324 f.), Vile appear in a less favourable light. One of them, instigated by her companions, brings about a deadly quarrel between the brothers, in which they both lose their lives.

The story of the building of the bridge at Višegrad by Mehmed Pasha Sokolović (cf. p. 344 f.) seems to be one of the most interesting of all, though it may have lost some of its original features. It has elements in common with 'The Walling of Skadar'; but the Vila here is evidently connected in some way with the river Drina.

Vile are introduced not only in Bosnian stories like this, in which the religious milieu is indefinite, but also in definitely Turkish (Mohammedan) stories. We may refer to the incident noticed on p. 357, where a Vila calls from a cloud and proclaims the loyalty of the Bosnian army.

Another Turkish example has been noted on p. 329, where Vile come to the help of the wounded Ibro Nukić and restore him to health.

It will be observed that in many of these stories Vile play an active part in the action. In poems relating to the nineteenth century, however, their activities seem to be limited, so far as we have noticed, to exhorting and remonstrating with heroes and, more especially, to warning them of impending danger. Examples of both kinds, first of warning and then of remonstrance, are to be found in 'Kara-Gjorgje's Farewell to Serbia', cited on p. 332.

In Montenegrin poems we find Vile calling out to heroes to warn them or rouse them to action, even as late as the reign of Danilo (1851–61). Examples will be found in Karadžić, v. 6. 1 ff., 10. 195 ff., 1031 ff. The most elaborate instance, however, occurs in 'Omer Pasha's Attack upon Montenegro' (*ib.* 3. 472 ff.). The Vila of Mt Šara (beyond Prizren) calls out to the Vila of Mt Kom (Komovi), and bids her put on her wings and fly to the Lovćen and warn Prince Petrović (Danilo) to arise and collect his army; for the Turkish emperor is sending a vast host against him. The second Vila does as she is bidden, calling out to the prince from the Lovćen, over the plain of Cetinje. But the prince tells her to be silent, and says that he has confidence in his Montenegrins and in the friendship of the Russian and Austrian emperors. Then the Vila warns him not to trust in false hopes; and now she succeeds in rousing him to action.

We have not met with any later examples than these, though they are probably to be found. The introduction of the Vila of the Durmitor in 'The Lament of the Dragon on the Lovćen' (cf. p. 334 f.) is a rhetorical device of a more sophisticated kind.

Supernatural beings other than Vile are of comparatively little account. Dragons occur sometimes—in one story[1] Marko Kraljević kills a three-headed specimen—but they are not treated at any great length. The dragon of Jastrebac and Momčilo's winged horse Jabučilo[2] may be included in the next section.

(b) The attribution of supernatural powers to human beings or animals is not rare. Some heroes are credited with the power of transforming themselves into snakes or dragons. Such is the case with the Hungarian hero Sekula (cf. p. 318 f.), and also with Vuk the Dragon-Despot or Fiery Dragon (cf. p. 322). It would seem that Vuk's opponent, the dragon of Jastrebac, was also regarded as a human being with similar powers.[3]

Marko Kraljević is credited with absurd feats of strength; and exaggerations of various kinds occur in stories of other heroes. But on the whole the *narodne pjesme* are comparatively free from reproach in these respects.

Animals[4] are sometimes credited with supernatural powers. Marko's horse Šarac and Momčilo's horse are able to speak on occasion. The latter also has wings with which it can fly. Falcons too can perform incredible feats in stories of Marko. One has the power of speech;[5] and another carries off the wings and crown of a Vila (cf. p. 312). Ravens frequently bring news of disaster from a battlefield (cf. pp. 332, 337). Indeed this is one of the most common conventions of battle-poems. In Vol. IV of Karadžić's collection no less than six poems begin in this way.

(c) In Vol. I (p. 216 ff.) we treated stories relating to the birth or childhood of heroes as a separate group. In Yugoslav *narodne pjesme* we have observed only one instance of this kind—the story of the birth of Vuk the Dragon-Despot, noticed on p. 322. Some other heroes are credited with supernatural or unnatural parentage. In one story, noticed above, Marko Kraljević is said to be the son of a Vila, while in 'The Sister of Leka Kapetan', 473 ff., Miloš is reproached with having been

---

[1] Matica Hrvatska, *Junačke Pjesme*, II. No. 50.

[2] Jabučilo's sire seems to be a supernatural being. It inhabits a lake, like Irish supernatural horses. Cf. Karadžić, II. p. 106, note; Low, *op. cit.* p. 9. But we do not know whether this creature is ever mentioned in poems.

[3] It is tempting to think that this story arose out of an attempt to explain Vuk's surnames. Both stories are possibly influenced by kite-flying of some kind; cf. p. 319, note.

[4] Occasionally also inanimate things, as in the action of the Hungarian crown at the election of King Matthias; cf. p. 320.

[5] Karadžić, II. No. 54; transl. by Low, *op. cit.* p. 58.

born from a mare (*kobila*). The latter statement is obviously due to an attempt to explain his surname *Kobilović*—as is also the statement in the *bugarštica* noticed on p. 315 that he was suckled by a mare.

As regards poetry relating to heroes after their deaths it has already been pointed out[1] that the last scene of the poem on Prince Danilo's funeral (Karadžić, v. xviii. 1774 ff.) presents an interesting parallel to the opening scene in Book XXIV of the *Odyssey* and to certain Norse poems.

III. Among unhistorical elements which fall under neither of the main headings treated above we distinguished in Vol. I (p. 221 ff.) between (*a*) incidents, motifs and characters which seem to be taken from some other story, and (*b*) incidents, etc., which seem to be invented—or perhaps adapted from some idea or source which cannot properly be called a story.

(*a*) The borrowing of incidents, etc., by one story from another seems to be extremely widespread. It is most obvious in the 'Marriages'. In these stories the friends of the bridegroom often have to perform certain feats. One is to shoot an apple; another is to leap over a number of horses, which sometimes have spears fastened upright to their saddles; a third is to pick out the bride from a number of girls, who are all dressed alike. All of these occur (e.g.) in the two *bugarštice* on the marriage of the king of Budim (Bogišić, No. 9 and its variant No. 26) and in 'The Marriage of Dušan'; the two former also in 'The Marriage of Djuro of Smeredevo'. It is likely enough that some such feats were proposed at marriage; but we find it difficult to believe that the stories are independent, especially the ruse employed for identifying the bride in the third feat (cf. p. 318).

There can be no question as to the existence of a connection between 'The Marriage of Djuro of Smeredevo' and 'The Marriage of Stojan Popović'.[2] In both stories the personnel of the bridegroom's suite is mostly the same, though it consists of persons who belonged to different periods. In both cases we find a request from the bride's father not to invite Serbians, followed by a letter from the bride herself or her mother advising the bridegroom to disregard this request. In both cases the bridegroom submits the question to his mother, who decides in favour of the lady's advice. A request from the bride's father not to invite certain persons occurs also in 'The Marriage of Dušan'. It is remarkable how often the marriage takes place in 'Latin' cities, especially

---

[1] Vol. I, p. 221; Vol. II, p. 335.
[2] Karadžić, II. No. 89; transl. by Low, *op. cit.* p. 168 ff.

Venice and Ragusa. Apart from the three stories just mentioned this applies to 'The Marriage of Vuk the Dragon-Despot' and 'The Marriage of Maxim Crnojević'. Yet in all these cases the bridegrooms seem to be Orthodox; and such marriages must surely have been somewhat unusual.

Sometimes we find a substantially identical 'marriage' story told of different heroes. Thus the story of Marko Kraljević's marriage with the Vila (No. 19 in the Matica Hrvatska collection), noticed on p. 312, is practically the same as the story of Vukašin's marriage (*ib.*) contained in the Ragusa MS. Again, the story of Momčilo preserved in the same MS. (cf. p. 313) is practically identical with 'The Marriage of Vukašin' in Karadžić's collection (*ib.*), though in the former story Vukašin's place is taken by a '*ban* of Njemac'. In these cases virtually the whole theme is borrowed by one story from another, or possibly by both from a common source.[1]

Apart from 'Marriages' the most striking instance of borrowing that we know occurs in 'Miloš among the Latins' (Kradžić, II. No. 37). Lazar sends Miloš Obilić to collect tribute from the Latins. They receive him courteously, but show him their church of St Dimitrije, and say that there are no churches in Serbia equal to it. Miloš will not allow this, and enumerates a long list of churches. Then he lays a wager that he will throw a heavy club over this church. He succeeds in his effort; but the club falls down upon the palace of the *ban* and kills his two sons, with four generals and twelve other nobles. Miloš is then put in prison; but he obtains writing materials from a gipsy, and sends word to Lazar. The prince immediately demands his release and heavy compensation for his imprisonment.

The scene of this incident is not stated in the poem. But Karadžić appends a note saying that the people of Kotor (Cattaro) declare it took place in their city and point out the spot where the *ban*'s house had stood. There can hardly be any doubt that the incident is the same as that related in Bogišić, No. 76 (cf. p. 353), where the hero is called Ivan Voihnović. The latter seems to have lived about a century after the time of Lazar and Miloš. The poem therefore is a good example of the transference of a story from a person who was little known to one who was famous.

(*b*) Invention of incidents, motifs and characters is of course difficult

---

[1] Both the stories of Momčilo are unhistorical. He is said to have been killed in battle by the Greeks in 1345; cf. Murko, *Geschichte d. älteren südslaw. Litteraturen*, p. 201.

to prove, when (a) presents so many possible openings. Strictly speaking, one ought to take a case which stands by itself. And such a case seems to be supplied by the motif of treachery ascribed to Vuk Branković in the story of the first battle of Kosovo. Actually what is involved here is apparently not so much deliberate invention as the growth of an unhistorical motif. The historical facts are that Vuk escaped from—or at least survived—the battle and that he continued the war against the Turks. The later poems represent him as a traitor; but the *bugarštica* on the battle (Bogošić, No. 1. 218) merely states that he fled to the green mountain, when Lazar was attacked. That does not necessarily imply treachery, perhaps not even cowardice if the situation was hopeless. But in the tradition of the *bugarštice*—two poems are affected (cf. p. 315 f.)—the story is complicated by two other motifs, (i) the deadly quarrel between Vuk and Miloš, and (ii) the charge of treachery brought by the former against the latter. The first of these motifs is obscured in the later poems; and we do not know whether it has any historical basis. But it is an essential element in the *bugarštica*, where Vuk's resentment against Miloš is given as the reason for his charge against him and also, later, for his seeking to prevent Lazar from going to rescue him. On the other hand the *bugarštica* does not, like the later poems, represent Miloš as charging Vuk with treachery. It would seem then that two distinct stages can be traced in the growth of the story. In the first, represented by the *bugarštice*, Miloš handles Vuk roughly, owing to a quarrel between the wives, who are sisters; and Vuk in revenge accuses him of treachery, and afterwards prevents him from being rescued. In the second stage, represented by the later poems, Vuk is himself a traitor to Lazar and is denounced as such by Miloš before the battle. We do not know how far the earlier form is unhistorical;[1] but we suspect that it contains a considerable element of fiction.

Many of the anachronisms, discrepancies and impossible happenings noticed earlier in this chapter are doubtless due to fiction in one form or another. We may instance the slaying of Janko (John Hunyadi) by Marko Kraljević and the story of the dragon of Jastrebac; so also the deaths of the Jakšića, while unmarried, at the instigation of a Vila—especially if this story be compared with several other stories in which they quarrel about their wives.

As an example of the extreme freedom with which stories can be

---

[1] The story is told, with only slight variations from the poems, by M. Orbini, *Il Regno degli Slavi* (Pesaro, 1601), p. 314. But he may have derived his information from poems. He gives the names of the wives as Mara and Vukosava (*Vucosaua*).

treated we would call attention to a decasyllabic poem (Bogišić, No. 101) preserved in the Franciscan (Ragusa) MS. It contains, we think, more unhistorical features than we have met with in any other poem, though they may be due to borrowing rather than to invention. The emperor Sulejman writes to General Bergentinović, challenging him to battle. The general has a nephew (sister's son), called Sekuo (Sekule), who is captured by the Turks. The emperor questions him about three great warriors, whom he has seen in the general's army. He replies that the first is Hrelja (Marko Kraljević's companion), the second Miloš Kobilović, and the third himself. The emperor then asks him how he is to put him to death. Is he to throw him into the river, or to burn him alive, or to hang him? Sekuo answers that he is not a fish that he should swim, or a tree that he should burn, or a thief that he should be hanged; he should be treated as a hero. He asks the emperor to set him on a packhorse, girded with his sword, but with his hands bound and his feet fastened beneath the horse, and three hundred Janissaries in pursuit of him. His horse should be given to the one who secures his head. The emperor grants his petition; but the hero prays to God, and his hands are freed. Then he seizes his sword and makes a great slaughter of the Janissaries. After this he returns to his uncle's camp, and tells him to attack the Turks at once. The general gains a great victory.

We cannot identify General Bergentinović; but his sister's son Sekuo[1] (i.e. Sekul) can hardly be separated from the famous Sekula, who is regularly known as sister's son of Janko. Miloš and Hrelja (Relja) are often associated as companions of Marko Kraljević. Consequently we have here representatives of at least three different periods of history.

In Karadžić's collection (II. No. 52) there is a poem which can hardly be regarded otherwise than as a variant of this, though the beginning is different. A certain Jurišić Janko, whom we cannot identify, is imprisoned by the emperor Sulejman in Stamboul. He begs the emperor in vain to allow him to ransom himself. Then the emperor asks him who were the three generals who destroyed his army at Kosovo. The rest of the story is practically identical with the one given above, except at the end, where the hero rides away home, and there is no general battle. The three heroes mentioned in this case are Marko Kraljević, 'Ognjan'—presumably Vuk the Fiery Dragon—who is called Marko's sister's son, and Janko himself. So here again we have characters belonging to three different periods. The battle is said to be at Kosovo.

[1] A variant form of *Sekula*. *Sekule*, *Sekulo* are Voc. forms of *Sekuo*, *Sekula* respectively. The Voc. is frequently used for the Nom. in *narodne pjesme*.

A much earlier variant is to be found in a *bugarštica* (Bogišić, No. 46), which is said to have been written down in 1663.[1] The prisoner is here Svilojević, who figures in other *bugarštice*; but the Sultan (*car*) is nameless. The three heroes are Marko Kraljević, Sekula, and Svilojević himself. The Sultan asks him what form of death he will choose, but makes no suggestions. He chooses as in the other versions, except that he has his own horse. The three hundred Janissaries attack him; but one Turk unbinds him, saying they would be disgraced if they slew a bound Kaffir. All the Turks are slain except one wounded man, who reports to the Sultan how they have killed the prisoner.

From a comparison of the various versions it seems probable that in the original form of the story, which must go back at least to the first half of the seventeenth century, the three heroes were Janko of Sibinj (John Hunyadi), Sekula, his sister's son, and Svilojević (Michael Szilagyi), his wife's brother, and that the battle was the second battle of Kosovo, fought in 1448. In Bogišić, No. 21, we find these three heroes riding off together to Kosovo; and they are said to perish there—which is unhistorical. But in No. 25 Sekula only is killed and Michael (Svilojević) captured—which may be true.[2] The story, however, with which we are now concerned, is clearly a work of the imagination; and it is worth noting that the latter part of it is a frequent theme in timeless, nameless stories,[3] of course with slight variations. The hero or heroine sometimes invokes a Vila, sometimes a saint. In some cases he takes revenge on the Sultan.

In conclusion we may consider briefly the poems relating to Marko Kraljević, who is the central figure of more stories than any other hero. If variants be ignored, these poems seem to furnish about thirty or forty distinct stories. About half a dozen of these are different 'Marriages', in which Marko is the bridegroom. Yet, so far as we know, he is never said to have had more than one wife. It would seem therefore that not more than one of the 'Marriages' can have any historical foundation. We doubt very much if the proportion of fiction—of one kind or another—is less in the remainder of the stories. In the stories of Marko indeed the problem is to point out historical rather than unhistorical elements—apart from the mere existence of the hero. Even the story of his death is remote from the truth. He was killed at the battle of

---

[1] Cf. Bogišić, Introd. p. 125 f. It may be observed that the language is of a peculiar type, approximating to Slovenian.

[2] He was regent of Hungary under Matthias, about ten years later.

[3] E.g. Matica Hrvatska, *Ženske Pjesme*, II. Nos. 4 and 6.

Rovine, in 1394, while fighting for the Sultan Bajazit against the Rumanian prince Mirčeta.[1]

Yet Marko could never have attained his fame if he had not been credited with striking exploits—or at least one striking exploit—from the beginning. It is remarkable therefore that the stories which are the earliest authenticated and most widely known are seldom concerned with such exploits. The earliest (c. 1550) is the poem which describes how he killed his own brother Andrija (cf. p. 311); and it is entirely sympathetic to the latter. Four other *bugarštice* are preserved in MSS., of which two are occupied with love incidents, one with the killing of the Arab lady who had befriended him—a confessedly shameful deed— and one with the story of Minja of Kostur. Obviously only the last of these comes in for consideration here. Again, seven (irregular) deca-syllabic poems are preserved in the Franciscan (Ragusa) MS., in which they are said to have been written c. 1758. Of these[2] two are concerned with the story of Minja (Mina) of Kostur,[3] one with the (unhistorical) slaying of Janko (cf. p. 375), one with the avenging of Andrija (cf. p. 311)—as against the *bugarštica* noted above—two with the violation of the fast of Ramazan, and one with the robbing of the Sultan's treasure. We have not met with the last of these stories elsewhere; but the story of Minja is represented by numerous variants,[4] and that of the breaking of the fast by a good many.[5] It would seem that these are the only stories found in collections prior to 1800, which could have been responsible for Marko's reputation. The story of Minja may be regarded as the one which on the whole offers the most promising opening for our purpose.

The main features of this story, as told in Karadžić's text (II. No. 62), which is translated by Low (p. 91 ff.), are as follows. While Marko is away fighting for the Turkish emperor against the Arabs, he receives a message saying that his castle has been burned down, his wife Jela

---

[1] According to Orbini, *Regno d. Slavi*, p. 279, he was put to flight and took refuge in a wood, where he was shot in the throat with an arrow by a Rumanian (Vlah), who thought he was a wild animal. Orbini, who was a Ragusan, seems not to have regarded Marko as a great hero.

[2] These are respectively Nos. 86–90, 92, 91 in Bogišić's collection.

[3] It may be observed that No. 86 seems to be in some respects more original than the *bugarštica* (*ib.* No. 7), though the latter is closer to Karadžić's text (II. No. 62; transl. by Low, p. 91 ff.). The Hungarian element is wanting in No. 86.

[4] Cf. Matica Hrvatska, *Junačke Pjesme*, II. 419 ff.

[5] *Ib.* II. No. 8 and p. 344 f.

carried off, and (in this text) his mother killed by a certain Mina of Kostur. He appeals to the emperor, who gives him three hundred Turkish warriors. These he sends to Kostur—Castoria in Greek Macedonia—disguised as labourers, and tells them to wait there for him. But he himself sets off to the Holy Mountain (Athos), where he puts on the black garb of a monk and grows a beard. Then he rides to Kostur, and is admitted to the castle. But his horse Šarac excites attention—in some texts it is recognised by Jela. He explains to Mina that he had found Marko Kraljević dying, and had been presented with the horse by him. Mina is greatly pleased to hear of his death, and begs the monk to marry him to Jela, which he does. Then he gives him wine, while Jela brings him a large amount of gold and his old sabre. Then the monk begins to dance, so that the castle shakes. He cuts Mina's head off with the sabre; and the Turks rush in and plunder and burn the castle. Marko returns to Prilep with his true wife and Mina's treasures.

The story told in Bogišić, No. 86, is in the main substantially the same, though it contains a number of additional details, whereas No. 87 is shorter and simpler. The bugarštica (ib. No. 7[1]) resembles Karadžić's text more closely in some respects; but it describes 'Minja Kosturani' as a Magyar, and lays the scene in the 'land of the Magyars'—apparently not knowing where Kostur is.

In connection with this story account should be taken of a passage in Orbini's Regno degli Slavi, p. 290, where it is stated that after Vukašin's death his son Marko Kraljević held Castoria, together with Ochrida and also Argos in the Morea. He attached himself to the Turks, and constantly advanced their interests. His brother-in-law Balsa (Baoša II), prince of Zeta (Montenegro), was greatly displeased at this, and came against Castoria with a small army. Marko was away, but his wife Helena was in the city. She is represented as a woman of flighty character, and on bad terms with her husband. Baoša entered into an intrigue with her, promising to marry her and put away his present wife, a daughter of Lazar; and she then handed the city over to him. Hearing of this, Marko hastened to the scene with a considerable force, both his own men and Turks, and laid siege to the city. Baoša, however, sent

---

[1] These three poems (Nos. 7, 86, 87) may also be found in the Matica Hrvatska's *Junačke Pjesme*, II. pp. 206 ff., 210 ff., 424 f. No. 7 is taken from a Zagreb MS. which is believed to have come from the Bocche di Cattaro and was written c. 1700. The features which it has in common with Karadžić's poem must therefore go back at least to cent. xvii. The relationship with No. 86 is evidently more remote, as will be seen below.

word to his brother Gjorgje, who set off to the rescue with a larger force; and Marko had to retire. Then Baoša returned home with his new wife; but soon found her conduct intolerable. First he imprisoned her, and then sent her away in an insulting manner.

This is a very different story from the one told in the poems; but there can be little doubt that it relates to the same events. The scene is the same, and so are the personnel, except that the historical prince Baoša takes the place of the unknown Mina. Jela is the usual abbreviation of Helena. We do not know the source of Orbini's story; but it must go back at least to the sixteenth century, since his book was published in 1601. The event is dated apparently after 1376 and before 1379, when Gjorgje died. Baoša himself was defeated and killed by the Turks in 1383; but we do not know whether Marko was present at this battle, though one of his brothers was killed on Baoša's side.

How did Mina come to take the place of Baoša? Most of the versions of the story contain an introduction, in which it is stated that Marko receives three letters. One is always from the emperor (the Sultan), summoning him to war. The others are sometimes from a king of Hungary (Matthias or a nameless king) and Janko. Sometimes, however, one of them is from Mina. Thus in Bogišić, No. 86, where there are only two letters, Mina writes that he had heard that Marko is going to serve the emperor. "If thou goest to serve the emperor, Marko, I will burn down thy palace and carry off thy wife as a slave." Here Mina appears more or less in the character of Baoša; he regards Marko as a traitor. We may remark that the story could hardly have acquired currency among the Christians of the west if Baoša's name had been preserved—at least so long as it was remembered that Baoša had lost his life fighting as a leader of the Christians against the Turks. Yet in all the earlier forms of the story Mina is clearly a Christian—from which we may probably infer that it originated in a milieu which was more or less Turcophil.

In Orbini's account Marko gets little glory from the incident, while his true wife cuts a sorry figure. The discrepancy with the poems is great, though hardly greater than what we have found in the different stories of Andrija's death (cf. p. 311). A hint that Marko was at first baulked in his revenge may be preserved in the long delay, during which his Turks remain idle. But for all we know Orbini's account, which comes presumably from Ragusan sources, may itself be biassed; it seems to admit that Marko eventually recovered the city, though not his wife.

At all events it is clear not only that the story contains both historical and unhistorical elements, but also that two widely different views of Marko were current in the coastland, as far back as the sixteenth century. In one he was regarded as a hero, in the other as a traitor. Our earliest recorded poem (cf. p. 311) already represents him as a solitary brigand. But the story of Mina preserves an earlier representation, in which he appears as a commander of Turkish troops. There can be no reasonable doubt that this story was derived from the interior.

But what we would call attention to in particular is the growth of the Cycle. Many of the stories are obviously fictitious. Many others are not impossible in themselves; but they would hardly have attracted the attention of poets if Marko had not become famous. It is instructive to find one such story current in the island of Hvar, hundreds of miles from Prilep, before 1556. The development of the Cycle therefore had begun without doubt in the fifteenth century. It is probable enough that Marko has appropriated stories which were originally told of other heroes, and also timeless, nameless stories; but to trace these would require more knowledge than we possess. We may note, however, that the story of the Vila wife is told also of his father Vukašin and of Novak (cf. p. 377). Even the story related of Sekula and others (cf. p. 383 f.), about the prisoner choosing his own death, is told also of Marko.[1] Such transferences may sometimes be quite recent; for the treatment of the poems was very free, as we shall see later, even down to the end of last century. But the growth of the Cycle doubtless extended over several centuries. In general we suspect that the attitude which a story shows towards the Turks may be taken as a rough criterion of its antiquity. If the attitude is friendly, as in 'Marko and Mina of Kostur', or if Marko's loyalty to the Sultan is emphasised, such a story is likely to date from an early period, before interest in the individual hero was affected by religious and national feeling.

We have said nothing about the invention of characters, because the records accessible to us are insufficient for a satisfactory study of the question. We are under the impression, however, that in poems relating to the nineteenth century such invention does not occur. In the earlier periods we have little doubt that minor characters, such as squires and servants, were freely invented. In Bogišić, No. 1, Bušić Stjepan has a squire called Oliver—a rare, and perhaps unique, example of a name taken from French poetry, which can hardly have been current except in a few of the coast towns. It is not unlikely too, if we may judge

---

[1] Matica Hrvatska, *Jun. Pjesme*, II. 344 f. Cf. the *ženske pjesme* referred to on p. 384, note.

from the frequency of certain names, that women characters were sometimes invented. But were any of the important heroes invented—say
Novak or the Jakšića?[1] That is a question which we fear we can only
ask. In the early period, down to c. 1500, we think such cases must be
rare. They may well be more frequent in stories relating to *hajduci* (çf.
p. 327 ff.), in the sixteenth and seventeenth centuries. But this impression
also may be due to the lack of records.

NOTE. We wish to call attention here to a passage in Petrovich's *Hero-Tales
and Legends of the Serbians*, p. 64 f., note, which is of considerable interest as
bearing upon the occurrence of the marvellous in heroic stories. The passage
relates to an incident in the Balkan War. Early in November, 1912, a
Serbian army advanced against Prilep, Marko Kraljević's castle, which was
held by a considerable Turkish force. The general gave orders that the
infantry were not to attack until the Turkish guns had been silenced. But the
troops, moved by a sudden impulse, and disregarding their officers, charged
and carried the position by storm. After the battle the general addressed them,
and pointed out that this action might have led to disastrous consequences.
In reply thousands of soldiers shouted that they had been led by Marko
Kraljević—"Did you not see him on his Šarac?" For further details and the
names of some of the officers concerned we may refer to the passage cited.
    The incident affords striking testimony to the influence of the stories of
Marko. It is to be remembered that he had long been regarded as a national
hero, and indeed as a future deliverer of the country. But indirectly the
incident also has some bearing upon the marvellous elements which occur in
heroic stories themselves. If in a moment of tension such an impression as this
could overcome a highly disciplined army, we must not assume that these
marvellous elements are necessarily to be dismissed either as late additions to
the stories or as items in a conventional literary apparatus.

[1] It has been questioned whether Miloš Obilić was a historical person. But this
is carrying scepticism to an unreasonable length; we may refer to the summary of
the records given in Subotić, *Yugoslav Popular Ballads*, p. 75 ff. Whether he was
really a son-in-law of Lazar is of course a different question.

CHAPTER VI

POETRY RELATING TO SUPERNATURAL BEINGS

IT is remarkable that supernatural beings of definitely heathen character should play so prominent a part as the Vile do in the poetry of a people which had been Christian for several centuries before the earliest times to which any existing poems relate. Doubtless their frequent appearance in the poems is due in the main to poetic convention, like the appearance of deities in the Homeric poems and elsewhere. But this convention rests ultimately upon belief; and indeed the belief in Vile is still—or was until yesterday—widespread in some parts of Yugoslavia.[1] We have not met with any instances of actual worship; but that is due probably to the inadequacy of our information.[2]

Vile differ from the deities of other peoples in two important respects. In the first place they are always female. Secondly, they are credited with little or nothing in the way of corporate life. As a rule they appear singly, though we hear not seldom of groups of three. Larger groups are rare, except in connection with the dancing of the *kolo* or round dance. It is on an occasion of this kind that Marko catches the Vila Nadanojla (cf. p. 312), who is described as mistress (*gospodja*) of all the Vile. Usually, however, a Vila has no name given to her.

Vile are most frequently connected with mountains—to such an extent indeed that 'belonging to the mountain' (*planinkinja* or *od planine*) is a static epithet of a Vila. In poems relating to the nineteenth century this connection seems to be almost invariable; each big mountain seems to have a Vila of its own. In stories of earlier times, however, Vile seem to be associated sometimes with rivers and springs. In Bogišić, No. 85, Vukašin plunges with his horse into a lake to catch a Vila, whom he marries.

[1] Cf. Low, *The Ballads of Marko Kraljević*, p. 21, note: "A man who was in the service of my wife's family in Serbia saw a Vila on several occasions, and was reduced each time to a pitiable state of terror...." On popular beliefs regarding Vile cf. Krauss, *Slavische Volkforschungen*, p. 34 ff. and *passim*. They have much in common with witches, but seem always to be supernatural beings.

[2] Bishop Danilo, the liberator of Montenegro, is said—apparently in a poem—to have prayed to the Vila of Mt Kom, when the Turks invaded Montenegro in 1712; cf. Temperley, *History of Serbia*, p. 151. This poem has not been accessible to us.

As will be seen from the stories noticed in the preceding chapters, Vile are sometimes malevolent, but more often helpful to heroes. In modern poems they do little more than exhort them or warn them of danger; but in early times they frequently play a more active part in the story. There are no poems, however, so far as we are aware, concerned with the affairs of Vile alone—like the stories of Greek, Irish and Norse gods. Sometimes we find short passages occupied with discussions between Vile; but such passages are merely preliminary to their intervention in the affairs of some hero.

Personifications of nature are of not very rare occurrence in the *narodne pjesme*. In general they may be regarded as rhetorical figures; but some of them may ultimately be derived from mythological conceptions. Such is perhaps the case with the personification of heavenly bodies,[1] as seen in Karadžić, II. 98, a poem which is concerned with the relations of the Jakšića. The framework is a dialogue (Type B) between the Moon and Danica (the Morning Star). The Moon asks Danica where she has been, where she has spent the last three days. In answer to him Danica says she has been watching the Jakšića dividing their patrimony; and the rest of the poem is occupied with her account of what she has seen. In Bogišić, No. 46 (cf. p. 384) a girl appeals to the Moon to tell her if he has seen Svilojević; and the rest of the poem is occupied with his answer.

A much more sophisticated example of personification is to be found in a poem[2] which consists of a dialogue—or rather altercation—between Earth and Heaven (Sky). Earth complains of the bad weather sent by Heaven, which ruins her trees and fruits and harasses the life of mankind. Heaven replies that he has every reason to be wroth with her, owing to the sins of mankind, which he briefly recounts. The framework is that of Type B; but there is obviously a (moral) didactic purpose—so we may class the poem under CB. For the didactic element in the poem an analogy will be found in the first example treated in the next section. For its sophisticated character we may compare 'The Lament of the Dragon on the Lovćen' (cf. p. 334f.); but in the latter the dragon

---

[1] It is difficult to doubt the existence of some connection in the past between these personifications and those of the same heavenly bodies which are found in Lithuanian poems or songs; but the mythological element in the latter is more definite.

[2] Matica Hrvatska, *Ženske Pjesme*, II. No. I. German transl. by Eisner, *Volkslieder der Slawen*, p. 341 f. Other personifications will be found *ib.* p. 399 f.

seems to represent Mirko, the prince's brother, while the interest is national, rather than moral.

Even in unsophisticated narrative poetry natural objects are sometimes personified to the extent that speeches are addressed to them. We may quote from one of the poems on the 'Sack of Kolašin' (Karadžić, v. xii. 555 ff.): "Would thou couldst see the Serdar Milan, how mightily he raged—what strength the Serdar showed! He seized the Turks by their white throats, two and four of them at a time, and dashed them down from the wall of the fortress; and the clear stream of Tara bore them off. The Serdar cried with the full force of his lungs: 'Tara, thou rolling stream, devour the awful Turks of Kolašin.'"

Apart from heathen conceptions and personifications of nature the mythological instinct has also been busy with saints and other characters who figure in ecclesiastical records of ancient times. A number of poems[1] are concerned with the doings of these characters. They are treated in a familiar style, not unlike what we find in stories of the Greek, Irish and Norse deities. The scene is laid sometimes in heaven, sometimes on earth; but in the latter case no indication is given that it is in Yugoslavia. This fact distinguishes them from the non-heroic stories of native saints noted on p. 343 f. The latter also seem to be much more definitely ecclesiastical in tone than the poems now under consideration.

In 'The Saints divide the Treasures'[2] the scene is laid in Heaven. A number of saints, St Peter, St Nicholas, St John, St Elias and St Pantelia, are 'dividing the treasures'—an expression which is explained later—when Maria the Blessed arrives, weeping bitterly. Elias the Thunderer asks her what is the cause of her trouble, addressing her as 'our sister'. She replies to him, as 'my brother', that she has just come from the accursed land of Indjia,[3] where lawlessness is rampant. She gives a list of the sins prevalent there, which seems to be merely a longer variant of the list given by Heaven in the poem noticed above. Then Elias asks her to wipe away her tears, and promises that, as soon as they have divided their treasures, they will go to God's court and

[1] We have seen very few stories of this kind. We do not know whether there are many of them in existence.

[2] Karadžić, ii. No. 1; transl. (free) by Petrovich, *Hero-Tales and Legends of the Serbians*, p. 195 ff. Karadžić, ii. No. 2 is a variant.

[3] Indjia (*Indjija*) presumably means the district round the place now called Indija, in Srijem, about thirty miles to the north-west of Belgrade.

beg for the keys of heaven, so that they may close the heavens and prevent the fall of any rain or dew. In the meantime they divide among themselves their 'treasures' (*blago*). Peter takes wine and wheat and the keys of the kingdom of heaven, Elias lightnings and thunders, Pantelia great heats, St John takes brotherhood and fellowship and crosses of holy wood, Nicholas the waters and ships. Then they make their way to God's court and after three days' prayer obtain the keys of heaven. They seal up the clouds, so that no rain or dew falls for three years; and famine and plague destroy the people, until the survivors repent.

There is a Montenegrin variant of this poem (Karadžić, ii. No. 2), in which a larger number of saints figure. Here Maria, called 'the Fiery', takes the lightnings and thunders; but it is Elias who has visited the accursed land—which seems to be the whole earth. There is no reference to locking up the heavens; but each saint uses his or her 'treasure' against the land, with the same effect as in the other variant. It is in Srijem that the people begin to repent. As Indjia is in Srijem, we may perhaps infer that the original poem was composed in that district. It would seem to have been composed for some moral didactic purpose (Type C), like the dialogue of Earth and Heaven, with which it can hardly be unconnected. The motif of the saints dividing their treasures may, however, have been taken over from older poems.

Next we may take Karadžić, ii. No. 17, 'The Emperor Duklijan[1] and John the Baptist', another Montenegrin poem, but one which is evidently intended merely for entertainment (Type A), at least in its present form. John and the emperor are drinking wine together on the sea shore—the locality is not further specified. Then John suggests that they should go and play, he with an apple and the emperor with his crown. St John soon throws his apple, and it falls down to the bottom of the sea; and he begins to cry bitterly. The emperor tells him not to cry; he will get the apple back for him, if John will not take his crown. John swears by God that he will not take it; and then the emperor swims out for the apple. Then John flies to Heaven, and asks the Lord if he may swear falsely by him and take the crown. The Lord replies: "John, my true servant! You may swear falsely by me three times, but not by my name."[2] St John now flies back to the shore, just as the emperor is returning from the sea with the apple. They resume their games; but the apple again falls into the sea, and again John begins to cry. The emperor says:

[1] According to Subotić, *op. cit.* p. 142, this is Diocletian.
[2] This seems to be the literal meaning of the words; but we do not understand the distinction.

"Fear not, dear comrade! I will recover the apple for you; but do not steal my crown." John swears by God three times that he will not take it. Then the emperor covers the crown with his cap, sets a bird 'of evil news'[1] to watch it and again dives into the blue sea. St John now makes the sea to freeze, seizes the golden crown, and flies up to Heaven. But the bird croaks; and the emperor hears it, and rises from the bottom of the sea. After great difficulty he succeeds in breaking through the ice; and then he puts on his wings and sets off in pursuit of John. He overtakes him at the gate of Heaven, and seizes him by the right foot— "what he gets hold of, that he tears off". John comes weeping to the Lord, bringing the bright 'sun'[2] to Heaven. He bemoans how the emperor has paid him out. Then the Lord says to him: "Fear not, my true servant! I will do thus for everyone."

In explanation of this poem, and especially of its somewhat obscure conclusion, Karadžić (*ib.* p. 84 f.) gives the following story, which he says he had heard in his childhood. When the devils had been expelled from Heaven they took the sun with them, and the emperor of the devils carried it fixed on the end of a spear. The earth complains to God that it is all being burnt up; so he sends the Archangel to get it back from the devils. The Archangel makes up to the emperor; but the latter suspects what he wants. They go to the seashore to bathe, and the Archangel suggests they should try which can dive furthest. He dives first, and brings up sand from the bottom. Then the devil dives; but before doing so he makes a magpie out of his spittle and sets it to watch the sun, which is fixed on his spear. The Archangel now makes the sea to be covered with a thick coating of ice; and then he seizes the sun and runs off to God. But the magpie croaks; and when the devil hears it he rises and by great efforts breaks through the ice, and gives chase. Just as the Archangel gets one foot in Heaven, the devil catches him and tears off a large piece of flesh from the sole of the other foot with his finger-nails. The Archangel comes wounded to God with the sun and asks what he is to do after such a wound. But God tells him not to be afraid; he will bring it about that all people shall have a similar small hollow under the sole of the foot. The story ends with the remark that in consequence of this all people still have a small hollow under the soles of both feet.

---

[1] Is this a kenning for 'raven'? With *zloglasnica* we may compare *zlokobnica* ('of evil omen'), applied to a raven in Bogišić, No. 82. 54, 58.

[2] The text has *tunce*, which is a misprint for *sunce* ('sun'), as noted in the Corrigenda at the end of the volume.

A modern reader might be inclined to regard 'The Emperor Duklijan and John the Baptist' as an attempt made by some enemy to bring ridicule upon the Christian religion, though it is hardly credible that such a work could have found its way into circulation among *narodne pjesme*. But the story just noticed shows that it has a history behind it. There must be some relationship between the two; and the poem is not likely to be in general the older version. Not only is its conclusion hardly intelligible without the other; but as a whole it is more remote from anything that we know of ecclesiastical legend. Perhaps John the Baptist and the emperor Duklijan have taken the places of the Archangel and the emperor of the devils. But we do not know whether the story of the theft and recovery of the sun is found outside Yugoslavia.[1] The point which interests us here is that a story which in some form or other must be founded ultimately on ecclesiastical legend has in course of time come to be transformed into a mythological poem of entertainment, with a very low standard of morality. This fact may not be without significance for the interpretation of ancient mythological stories in which deities are presented in an ugly or ludicrous light. Perhaps the closest analogy is to be found in the story of Othin's theft of the mead (cf. Vol. I, p. 249 f.).[2]

We know only of one or two other poems which may properly be said to belong to the series under discussion.[3] Among them we may perhaps include a poem on the 'Birth of St Pantelija',[4] apparently from Gacko (cf. p. 333) in Hercegovina, close to the Montenegrin border. There were two sisters who had no brother; but they tried to make one out of spikenard and white silk. Then the materials are given in detail. They make his heart of box-wood, his head from a golden apple, his scalp from tufts of silk, his eyebrows from a sea-leech, his teeth from a string of pearls, and so forth. Then they bring him drink and food; but his mouth is unable to eat, and his tongue cannot speak. Two angels watch what is happening so intently that they are late in returning home, and God asks them what has detained them. When he hears their

---

[1] The subject seems to have been discussed by Dännhardt, *Natursagen*, I. 136 ff., which we have not seen; cf. Dumézil, *Bibl. de l'Inst. franç. de Leningrad*, XI. 193.

[2] This passage (from the Hávamál) belongs of course to a far more advanced stage of literature than the poem noticed above. It may be observed that in the more popular form of the story (as told in the Skaldskaparmál, cap. 1) Othin is chased by Suttungr, both of them being in the form of eagles.

[3] 'Maria the Fiery in Hell' (Karadžić, II. No. 4) is another example.

[4] Publ. with German transl. by Krauss, *Slavische Volkforschungen*, p. 349 ff.

story, he sends them back to earth, to infuse life into the lifeless man and give him the name Pantelija. He is to give his sisters in marriage and to live forty years. They carry out his orders; and it comes to pass as he has said. Pantelija dies at the end of forty years. For this story a close parallel is to be found in a timeless, nameless poem from Bosnia.[1]

Lastly, we may notice here a poem called 'The Holy Crosses' (Karadžić, II. No. 18), which belongs to a different class from those we have been discussing. The emperor Kostadin (Constantine the Great) is drinking wine in Constantinople with the Apostles Peter and Paul. He asks them where the holy crosses now are and what emperor possesses them. They reply that they are in the Hebrew land; and they tell him to raise an army and ravage that country. He is to capture the Hebrew emperor and torture him; but the latter will die before he tells them where the crosses are. Then Kostadin is to seize the empress' child and place it between two fires till it hisses like a snake; and the empress will then disclose the secret. He acts according to the Apostles' directions, captures the Hebrew emperor and tortures him to death, and then scorches the child between two fires. The empress first promises, and then withdraws; but when the child is again brought to the fires she gives full information as to the crosses. The rest of the poem follows the usual tradition.

This story is one which was familiar to the greater part of the Christian world. The form in which it is given here has some peculiar features, especially the opening scene with the Apostles. Constantine plays the chief part, instead of Elena, who is barely mentioned; and the torturing of the Hebrew chief is greatly magnified—he is stripped of hands, feet, eyes and teeth. The torturing of the child also seems to be a new element, as far as we know. But in spite of all this the story remains perfectly recognisable. It stands on quite a different footing from the other stories noticed above.

Yet all the stories we have been discussing may in some sense be regarded as of ecclesiastical origin, like most of the non-heroic stories noticed on pp. 343 f., 345 f. 'The Holy Crosses' has changed com-

---

[1] Transl. by Eisner, *Volkslieder der Slawen*, p. 411 f. The first part of the poem seems to be merely a variant of the one given above; but it develops differently. Another variant, likewise timeless, nameless but very brief, is to be found in Karadžić, I. No. 307; cf. Bowring, *Servian Popular Poetry*, p. 213. It may be observed that the 'Lives' of St Pantaleon (Pantelija) are said to have nothing in common with the story given above (cf. Krauss, *op. cit.* p. 349).

paratively little from its original form; possibly it has not had a very long life as a *narodna pjesma*. The others have been assimilated by the native minstrelsy and transformed to such an extent that their original form or character seems impossible to determine. In one case even the personnel has apparently been changed; and something similar may have happened with 'The Birth of St Pantelija'. In their present form these poems can only be regarded as examples of popular mythology.

CHAPTER VII

POETRY RELATING TO UNSPECIFIED INDIVIDUALS

BOTH poetry and saga of this category are abundant. The saga accessible to us, however, consists either of folk-tales—some of them widely distributed folk-tales—or stories of similar character. We shall therefore confine our attention, as usual, to the poems. In these all the possible types (A, B, C, D) are represented.

In Type A we include not only poems which are strictly nameless but also, as in Vol. I, poems relating to persons with names in common use which are insufficient—and presumably not intended—to convey any means of identification. Some of them contain geographical names; and it is always possible that such poems may originally have been concerned with persons known from other sources. But unless definite evidence to this effect is available we think it better to treat them as relating to characters existing only for the moment.

First we may take Bogišić, No. 38, a poem preserved in the Franciscan (Ragusa) MS., where it is described as an account of an event of about the year 1380. It gives the impression, however, of being a purely imaginative work. Ivan the Croatian has a Turkish servant (unnamed), who serves him for nine years, not for the sake of money, but for the sake of Ivan's sister. Yet he never sees her until the end of this time, when he catches sight of her at a window. As he is unable to get possession of her, he goes to the Turkish emperor and persuades him to lend him his horse, a sword with silver hilt, and a hundred ducats wherewith to buy silk—in return for which he promises to bring him the girl. Then he returns to Croatia and sets up a tent; and the ladies come to buy his silks. Ivan's sister comes also; and as soon as she arrives, he mounts his horse and carries her off to the mountains. Then he asks her how he is to get past the emperor's palace. She tells him to give her his yellow boots, his silk turban, his silver-hilted sword and his horse, and to stand beside her as an attendant. The Turk thinks she is advising him in good faith and does as she asks. But as soon as she is mounted (and dressed as a man), she turns the horse towards Croatia and makes off. He calls after her, to bring the horse back; but she takes no heed. When she arrives home she finds that Ivan has assembled the

Croatian lords to go in pursuit of her. He does not recognise her, and she asks him to invite her to dinner. Then she tells him that she has met a renegade Vlah carrying off a Croatian girl as a prisoner. Her brother begins to weep, and she makes herself known to him.

Several poems of this class are contained in Vol. II of Karadžić's collection. We may first take No. 11, 'Mujo and Alija', a poem from Montenegro, which seems to be derived from a 'Turkish' source.[1] Two brothers, Mujo and Alija, go fowling. They come to a lake, where they see a duck. Mujo sets his falcon upon it, and Alija his crane; and Mujo is vexed because the crane catches it. Then they drink wine under a pine, and go to sleep. Three Vile see them; and the eldest says she will give a hundred ducats to any Vila who will make the brothers quarrel. The youngest Vila flies over Mujo's head and pours hot tears down over his face. He springs up as if he was mad, and sees the girl. Then he calls out to his brother, who likewise springs up and replies: "May you not come to a bad end! Two girls to you,[2] and not one to me!" Mujo in anger stabs him to the heart. Then he mounts his horse, lifts up the girl behind him, and makes for home. Now Alija's horse begins to cry, and the dying man begs his brother not to leave it abandoned on the mountains. He therefore places the girl on it, and they set out. On the way they meet with a raven which has lost its right wing; and he asks the bird how it manages without it. The raven answers that it is like a man who is without a brother—"like you without Alija". Now Mujo begins to repent of the heroism he has just shown. The Vila tells him to turn back, saying that she was once a healing Vila and that she would heal his brother. He turns back; but when he arrives at the lake he looks round and sees that the horse behind him is riderless—the Vila has gone. He runs up to his brother; but Alija is already dead. When Mujo sees this he draws his sword and plunges it into his own heart.

This story is of special interest owing to the resemblance which it bears to a poem describing the deaths of the Jakšića, noticed on p. 324 f., above—a *bugarštica* preserved in one of the Zagreb MSS. Indeed the general parallelism between the two poems is so close that in a sense one might perhaps be inclined to regard them as variants. Now it was pointed out on p. 324 that the Zagreb poem is irreconcilable with

[1] The characters are presumably to be identified with two brothers named Muji and Halili, who seem to be much celebrated in Albanian oral poetry; cf. Lambertz, *Volkspoesie der Albaner* (Sarajevo, 1917), p. 7 ff.

[2] Karadžić was uncertain whether this means that Mujo is married or that there are two Vile beside him.

most of the other poems relating to the Jakšića; for it represents these heroes as perishing unmarried, whereas the other poems are largely concerned with their wives. It would seem therefore that this is a fairly. clear instance of a heroic story derived from a timeless, nameless story.

Some of these poems contain an 'edifying' element, and one is in doubt whether to treat them under Type A or Type C. As an example we may take Karadžić, ii. No. 5, a poem which has been translated into English[1] and may therefore be noticed very briefly. Jelica, who is un-married, has a married brother named Paul, as well as another married brother who hardly comes into the story. Paul's wife is jealous of Jelica; and in order to bring about her undoing she kills her husband's horse, and tells him that the deed has been done by his sister—who denies the charge. Then she kills his falcon, and finally her own child. At this Paul is so enraged that he will not accept Jelica's denial; and she tells him, if he will not believe her, to tie her to the tails of horses. He does so; and flowers spring up wherever her blood is shed, and a church arises at the spot where she dies. Then Paul's wife falls ill with a loathsome sickness. She begs to be taken to Jelica's church; but a voice from the church says she is not to come there—the church will do nothing for her. Then she tells her husband to tie her to the tails of horses. Where her blood falls thorns spring up; and at the spot where she dies a lake appears. In this a horse is seen swimming and drawing a cradle, which contains a falcon and a child, with its mother's hand holding a knife at its throat.

Poems of this class occur more frequently among ženske pjesme (cf. p. 306). A good number of examples will be found in Vol. ii of the collection published by the Matica Hrvatska.[2] Most of them are of a simple and childish character, and quite short. One or two specimens will be sufficient.

In No. 3 a girl is gathering flowers on the mountain. She falls asleep; and when she wakes she says to herself that she will drink no wine, nor kiss a man's face, nor eat mutton.[3] She thinks no one hears what she says; but she is overheard by two servants of a Pasha, who go and tell their master what she has said. He orders them to go back and seize and bind her, and bring her to him; and they do so. Then the Pasha asks her

---

[1] By Petrovich, *Hero-Tales and Legends of the Serbians*, p. 206 ff., under the title 'The Stepsisters'. Surely it ought to be 'The Sisters-in-Law'?

[2] Vol. i of Karadžić's collection also contains a considerable number—many of them very short.

[3] Does this mean a wedding-feast?

if it is true what they have reported, and she confesses that it is. Next, he asks if she will become a Turk, and be his wife. She replies that she will not—she prefers the mountain to his court. The Pasha then puts his hand in his pocket, takes out a thousand ducats, which he presents to her, and sends her back to the mountain.

No. 4 begins with the same motif. The girl, who is here called Mare of Zara, is minding sheep on the mountains. She tells them to feed without fear of the emperor or his servants, while she goes gathering flowers. Two servants of the emperor (Sultan) hear her and report to their master, who orders her to be brought and questions her, as in the preceding poem. She admits the charge; and he then asks her whether she prefers to be trodden down by horses or burned with fire or slain with a sword. She replies that she is not grass to be trodden by horses, nor wood to be burned with fire, nor a tree to be cut down with a sword. Then, as in the story of Sekuo (cf. p. 383), at her request he has her bound and placed on an old horse, with six hundred Turks in pursuit of her. Then she calls for help to St Tekla, St Nedjelja and the Vila of the mountain, her comrade. She is at once freed and her horse rejuvenated; and she turns upon the Turks, kills most of them and puts to flight the rest. Then she dashes into the palace, seizes the emperor and ties him to the horse's tail, and rides off home.

No. 28 is a short poem with quite a different theme. Bogdan has nine vineyards, nine water-mills and nine horses, and has to part with them all in order to pay his debts. But even then he does not get clear; and he decides to sell his old mother. His wife tells him it would be much better to sell her. He will get a better price for her than for his mother, and at the same time incur less disgrace. Bogdan agrees, and takes his wife to Novi Pazar, where he sells her to a Turkish Janissary for three hundred ducats. The Turk takes the wife by the right hand and lifts her on to his horse behind him, and goes home singing; but Bogdan goes home wailing.

This poem comes from Sibinj. There is a much longer variant (No. 29), from the island of Šipan, in which the husband is called Ljutica Bogdan, while the man who buys his wife is called Beg Filipović. The latter discovers that the lady is his long lost sister—a not uncommon denouement in stories of this kind—and the incident ends happily. This poem cannot properly be assigned to the category now under discussion; for several of the characters have quite distinctive names. The description also given by Jela (the lady) of her family and home at Karlovac is quite precise. On the other hand No. 28 may well be regarded as practically timeless-nameless; for the only names which occur in it are the man's name Bogdan, which is fairly common, and the place-name Novi Pazar. The obvious relationship between the two poems is therefore of some interest, though its nature is not clear. Has No. 28 come into our category by losing—perhaps by forgetfulness—its termination and most of its names? Or has No. 29 been developed out of the timeless-nameless story seen in No. 28 by attaching to it a rather popular motif? We do not know whether any of the characters are known from other sources.

Type B of this category seems to be of frequent occurrence in short poems of a simple character, many of which resemble the modern folksongs of other European peoples. Longer examples are apparently somewhat rare; but the following instances may be noted.

First we may take the 'Prayer of a young Vlahinja', a *bugarštica* published in Bogišić's collection (No. 83) from one of the Zagreb MSS. Apart from three lines of introduction and one of epilogue it consists wholly of a speech. She prays God not to kill her with vital longing, to pierce her with cruel darts. May she have the full love of a proud hero— wearing upon her head a green garland of olive and seeing upon her hand a gold ring of countless value. But if God will kill her, may he turn her into a slender pine upon the mountain, and make fine clover of her fair hair and two springs of clear water from her dark eyes. When her lord comes to hunt upon the mountain, may he take his rest beneath the pine and refresh his horses with the clover and at the springs. The poet adds that she obtained what she prayed for. It will be seen that in form this poem bears a certain resemblance to the Anglo-Saxon poem 'The Wife's Complaint'; but the study of character and the subtlety of conception which distinguish the latter are of course wanting here.

Another *bugarštica*, No. 82 in the same collection, is a composition of more advanced type. This also is preserved in one of the Zagreb MSS.; but Bogišić's text is taken from Baraković's *Vila Slovinska*, which was written before 1625, though not printed until 1682. A swallow is piping plaintively at the gate of Zara. It is piping late; the sun has set and the moon has risen. But it is no swallow. It is Majka Margarita ('Mother Margaret'), the old mother of Ivan, calling for her son and her brother. A white Vila from the mountains comes to her and asks her why she is lamenting—what trouble is causing her tears to flow. She replies that she has two cruel wounds in her heart, from which she cannot recover. She has had a young brother Peter and a dear son Ivan, and brought them up to the age of manhood. But a bright dawn summoned them, and she committed them to the dawn. Now she does not know whether they are alive or dead. But she has seen a sorrowful portent—a raven perched upon the parapet of the walls of Zara, with its black wings all stained with blood. She has tried to make friends with the raven, asking it to explain the portent and promising to cool its weary wings with her tears. But the evil bird would not look at her. It has flown away to the mountain and left her weeping. The Vila asks her what price she is willing to pay for the release of her brother and son, if they have fallen into the hands of the Turks. She replies that she will give her head for her brother and be burned with fire for her son. Then the Vila says she will tell her the truth. They have not been imprisoned by the Turks. A Greek girl has fallen in love with her brother and given him drink from the water of oblivion, so that he will remember his sister no more. Her son, at parting with whom her heart was turned to stone, has gone to the 'Coastland'.[1] There fair Cvite of the Coastland has found him. She has woven a garland of magic acanthus. At sight of one another they fall in love, and she crowns him with the garland, so that he will never return to his mother. Now she must lament and grieve and shed bitter tears—never drying the tears from her face. She will neither be able to address her brother nor to expect her son.

The central feature of this poem is an unexpected denouement. The introduction of the raven, which flies away without speaking, is a parody of a traditional motif, very widespread in heroic poems, which makes ravens bring to a woman news of the slaying of her husband or son. And the attitude of the Vila—as indeed of the poem as a whole—can hardly be regarded otherwise than as cynical in the highest degree. The affinities of the poem therefore are 'post-heroic', as might be expected in a composition originating in one of the coast towns. For analogies we may turn to Greek poets like Archilochos or Norse poetry of the Viking Age, especially the *Hávamál*.

The modern poems of this type known to us are often short dialogue (conversational) pieces, of a simple and trifling character. It is difficult to give abstracts without conveying an impression of banality, which is unfair to the originals. We may take an example from the collections of the Matica Hrvatska, *Ženske Pjesme*, II. No. 99, which describes the sparring of a boy and a girl. A youth is sauntering through Karlovac, weary and thirsty, with his head full of girls. He is smoking a pipe and

[1] Perhaps southern Dalmatia is meant.

playing a mandoline of pure gold, with strings made of girls' hair and a peacock's feather for a plectrum. A girl sees him from a window, and he asks her why she is watching him. He is a hero and will not have her until he sees her white hands. Does she know how to spin and use a needle? He has heard she is a spinner, and so he will send her a small bundle of yarn, for her to make a shirt and breeches. What is left of the yarn she can use for her clothes, and then she can boast to her friends that her lover has put together her clothes. The girl answers that she has heard he is a goldsmith; so she will send him some gold tinsel, for him to make her a complete weaving apparatus.[1] With what is left he can shoe his horse, and boast to the heroes of his village that his sweetheart has shod his horse. The same collection contains a number of similar poems, e.g. Nos. 57, 77 f., 87 ff.

Short monologue poems of this type are also not uncommon. As an instance we may cite Karadžić, i. No. 361, a poem from Ragusa. The speaker, who is a girl, compares the attraction of lovers to that of certain herbs,[2] and then goes on to complain that her own lover has left her. "My lover has gone to Venice. I will write to him a sheet of thin paper, to tell him that he is to have no love-making with the girls of Venice, but to come back to his white house. But if he will not come home, I will give my young heart to another, who is handsomer and better than he." The majority of such poems contain a short narrative element, by way of introduction; but exceptions, like the one cited here, are not rare.

As noted above, many of these short poems show a closer approximation to the folksongs of other European peoples. We are under the impression that poetry of this type is peculiarly subject to external influence. This is a question, however, which we must leave to those who have a knowledge of the popular poetry of the neighbouring peoples, especially perhaps Slovenian and Italian.

Type C in this category seems hardly to be so common as one might have expected. But the distinction between Type C and Type A here is not very clearly marked; and perhaps we ought to include under the former such poems as Karadžić, ii. No. 4, which was noticed on p. 400. The poems which have now to be noticed all contain a religious element.

---

[1] We do not know the exact meaning of the technical terms used here, nor even that of their English equivalents. If we are right in translating *tetrejika* (*titreika*) as 'tinsel', the whole passage must be taken in a playful sense—the materials specified being (probably in both cases) ludicrously inadequate. The vocabulary of these poems presents a good many difficulties.

[2] Basil and *cmilje*. The latter is said to mean 'Sandruhrkraut', but is unknown to us.

The moral is not always obvious, if there is one at all. The denouement is sometimes different from what one would have expected.

We will take first the Matica Hrvatska, *op. cit.* No. 2. A pretty girl is sewing and singing to herself that she fears no one but God—neither the emperor (Sultan) nor his sons. She would found three churches with golden altars and silver doors. The story then proceeds on conventional lines (cf. p. 400 f.). She thinks nobody hears her; but two of the emperor's servants are listening, and report to their master what she has said. He sends them back to arrest her. If her hair is over two feet long, they are to bring her to him; if not, they are to cut off her head. She passes the test, and is brought to the palace. The emperor asks her if the report is true; and she confesses that it is. Then he tells his servants to lock her up in a prison, with cold water reaching to her knees and green weeds up to her shoulders. After nine years he sends them to bring her bones. But they find the prison brightly lighted, as if the sun was shining. In front of her is a golden table, and beside her three angels of God. They run to tell him the news; and he sends them again to bring the girl and ask her who has provided her with food, who has washed her face and plaited her hair. They bring her to the palace, and she tells the emperor her story—how God had sent three of his angels. Then the emperor marries her to his son, and she bears him a fine family of two daughters and four sons.

Another poem (No. 5) in the same collection ends in a way which is more to be expected. A mother boasts over her child, called Dijan, that when he grows up he will deprive the emperor of his kingdom. She is overheard, and the story proceeds as before. The child is shut up in prison; and after nine years the emperor sends his servants to bring out his bones. They find Dijan praying and the prison brightly lighted. He tells them that God has given him bread, Marija wine, and that St Peter has taught him to write. Then the emperor orders him to be burned to death; but angels fly down from heaven and take Dijan back to heaven with them. The poem ends with the reflection that God is more powerful than all emperors.

It can hardly be doubted that these poems originated in ecclesiastical circles. But the ending of No. 5 is obviously more appropriate than that of No. 2. The marriage of a Christian girl, who is evidently very religious, with a Mohammedan prince, after angels have intervened to save her, is not an ending which would appeal to religious circles. It would seem then that No. 2 has changed its sphere of currency and assumed its present form in circles which were little concerned with religion. Such changes, even from Christian to Turkish circles or vice versa, are not very rare (cf. p. 399).

Here also we may take a poem from Karadžić's collection, ii. No. 3. A deacon named Stevan goes out early on Sunday morning to work in the fields. He meets two old tramps, who ask him what he is doing on the holy day. Is he out of his mind, or has he become a Turk? He replies that he is forced to work by sore necessity, owing to his helpless family. He has nine dumb and nine blind children; and God will forgive his sin. Then the tramps go to his house, where they find his wife preparing bread. They ask her the same question, and she gives them the same answer. Then they ask her to give them a male child out of its golden[1] cradle. They will kill it and draw blood from its flesh, to sprinkle the house. All that are dumb will be able to speak, and all that are blind able to see. After some hesitation she consents to give it up; and they do as they had said. Then the rest of the children are able to speak and see. The tramps now take their departure; but the wife turns round and sees her child sitting in its cradle, playing with a golden apple. It tells her that the strangers were not really old tramps but angels of God. The moral of this poem is not very obvious to us; but we see no reason for doubting that it originated in religious circles.

Type D of this category occurs, so far as we know, only in songs (folksongs) which belong to social or domestic ritual. Vol. i of Karadžić's collection contains numerous poems of this type; and a number of translated specimens will be found in Eisner's *Volkslieder der Slawen*. It may be observed that none of the Croatian poems contained in the latter book, with one possible exception (p. 333), belong properly to Type D.[2] But this would seem to be due to accident; for several of them presuppose the existence of such poems, and one or two are very close to Serbian examples of this type. The book also contains examples from other Slavonic languages.

The Serbian examples consist of cradle-songs or lullabies (p. 351 f.), wedding songs (p. 390 ff.) and elegies or dirges (p. 415 ff.). Of the wedding songs[3] three or four seem to belong to Type D—i.e. they have a form which would be appropriate to the occasion—and these are all quite short. The elegies are all of this type. The two last seem to have a form identical with that of Darinka's elegy for Prince Danilo, noticed on p. 336.

[1] A good example of the meaningless use of this word—which is extremely frequent (cf. p. 404).

[2] The majority of Karadžić's poems seem to come from the southern part of the Adriatic coast, especially Risan and its neighbourhood.

[3] We may compare the Russian wedding songs quoted above, p. 233 ff.

CHAPTER VIII

THE REMAINING CATEGORIES

1. ANTIQUARIAN POETRY

IN this subject we shall follow the same scheme of classification as in Vol. I, Ch. x; but it must be confessed at the outset that the evidence we have been able to collect under the various headings is meagre and disappointing. This is due in part to the defects of our own information and of the records accessible to us. But we doubt very much whether material comparable with what is found in the ancient literatures exists in Yugoslavia. In all countries where Christianity or Islam prevails, in anything more than name, there is an educated class with a written literature, whether in the native or some other language; and the learning of the nation tends to be concentrated in this class. In Ireland and the North, it is true, the traditional unwritten learning was able to maintain itself independently for some time. But the Yugoslavs had been Christians for several centuries before the earliest date to which their native traditions refer; and there seems to be no trace of the survival of any such native learning or of a class of persons devoted thereto. The activities of their intellectual men had been devoted to ecclesiastical literature and, later, to some extent (in the west) to that of the Renaissance. We are not concerned with these activities, but with the learning, such as it was, of the mass of the population which remained illiterate—not wholly uninfluenced by ecclesiastical learning, but apparently without any inherited native learning comparable with what is found in ancient literatures.

I. We have not met with any genealogies;[1] but this may well be due to the defectiveness of our information. We should be surprised to learn that genealogies are not preserved in any part of Yugoslavia. Are they ever preserved in metrical form? It would seem not to be the custom to introduce genealogies in narrative poems or poems of Type B.

II. Catalogues are not of a very rare occurrence in heroic poetry; but they are usually quite short. The most frequent type consists of an

[1] Except in Orbini's work, which was published in 1601. Most of these are quite short.

enumeration of the guests present at a banquet or wedding. As examples we may cite the lists of guests at Lazar's banquet before the battle of Kosovo (Karadžić, II. No. 50, iii),[1] and at the marriages of Djuro of Smeredevo (*ib.* No. 79) and of Stojan Popović (*ib.* No. 87). Similar enumerations occur in the latest poems, e.g. the list of Montenegrin heroes drinking together in Karadžić, v. 14 (*ad init.*). A short, but quite unhistorical, catalogue of the leaders and forces engaged at the battle of Kosovo occurs *ib.* II. 46 (cf. p. 314); but it has nothing to do with the first part of the poem.

In poems which are not heroic, catalogues seem to occur rather more frequently. Karadžić, II. No. 1 contains a short list of saints (cf. p. 392), No. 2 a slightly longer list. One short poem[2] consists of little more than a catalogue of churches and monasteries founded by the early kings of Serbia. Similar catalogues are contained in Karadžić, II. Nos. 35, 36 and 37. It would seem that the song sung in Karadžić, II. No. 38 (28 ff.)[3] by Marko Kraljević's companion—Miloš in this version—when he is attacked by the Vila (cf. p. 377), is a poem of this kind. We may also compare the long catalogue of substances out of which St Pantelija is formed (cf. p. 395).

III. Speculations on the origin of personal names are found occasionally. We have seen (p. 379 f.) that Miloš' original surname *Kobilović* is explained more than once by a story that he had been born or suckled by a mare (*kobila*). The name of Vuk the Fiery Dragon seems to have been prolific in producing such speculations. In one story (cf. p. 322) he is born with wolf's hair upon his head—the word *vuk* means 'wolf' —and with flames darting from his mouth and nose. It is very probable also that the story of his fight with the dragon of Jastrebac (*ib.*) arose from some similar speculation.

We have not observed any such speculations upon place-names; but we are not prepared to say they are not to be found. In Bogošić, Nos. 59 (83 ff.) and 60 (93 ff.) it is stated that the spring at which Don Karlo's followers were slaughtered (cf. p. 351) has ever since been called 'the grave of the Spaniards'. But this may be an authentic tradition. At all events the name is doubtless a reminiscence of the time when the Spaniards occupied Castelnuovo.

---

[1] A longer form of this list is to be found in Karadžić, II. No. 36, which can hardly be regarded as a heroic poem.

[2] Publ. with German transl. by Krauss, *Slavische Volkforschungen*, p. 187 f.

[3] Transl. by Low, *The Ballads of Marko Kraljević*, p. 21 ff.

IV. We have not noticed any examples of speculation upon the origin of institutions or ceremonies.

V. Traditions or speculations relating to the foundation of churches and monasteries seem to have been fairly common. We have referred above to a short poem which consists of a catalogue of churches founded by the Nemanjići, the early kings of Serbia, and also to catalogues of such foundations contained in three other poems. Two of these (Karadžić, 11. Nos. 35 and 36) are concerned with the foundation of the church of Ravanica by Lazar. The passage cited from 'Marko Kraljević and the Vila' suggests that this subject was a popular theme of poetry.

Traditions or speculations relating to the origin of secular buildings seem to be of less frequent occurrence. We may instance 'The Walling of Skadar' and the story of the building of the bridge at Višegrad (cf. p. 344 f.). The former seems to be a purely imaginative work; but the latter is based on authentic tradition, so far as the main fact is concerned, though it has been treated imaginatively. It may be observed that the immuring of human beings is involved in both cases.

VI. We have not met with any traditions or speculations upon the origin of the nation in *narodne pjesme*; and we are inclined to doubt if such are to be found. But in modern poems references to ancient history and the glories of the past are not rare. Sometimes also we find a recognition of the relationship between the various Yugoslav peoples. The most striking example of this occurs in the 'Lament of the Dragon on the Lovćen' (cf. p. 334 f.). But instances are to be found elsewhere also; it is recognised (e.g.) by a Turkish speaker in Karadžić, v. 3 (*ad init.*). For a passage relating to the glories of the far past we may refer to *ib.* 8 (*ad init.*), where the Serbian (Montenegrin) generals are drinking wine in the prince's palace at Cetinje. As they become more cheerful, they begin to talk about heroic deeds, about Serbian warrior heroes, about Miloš and other generals, how they waged glorious war under Dušan and the emperor Lazar, and extended the empire with Serbian swords—their dominions reaching to three seas. In *ib.* 11 (*ad init.*) the Sultan refers to Murad and Kosovo, noting that five centuries have now passed since the establishment of Turkish sovereignty.

VII. Cosmological speculation seems to be foreign to the *narodne pjesme*. The nearest approach to it known to us is the dialogue between Heaven and Earth noticed on p. 391, especially the speech of Earth.

But the speech of Heaven has affinities in a different class of poems, as we have seen (p. 392 f.); and it is possible that the dialogue as a whole owes its inspiration ultimately to an ecclesiastical source, analogous perhaps to the 'debates' found in the West.

2. GNOMIC, DESCRIPTIVE AND MANTIC POETRY

Gnomes seem not to be of frequent occurrence in *narodne pjesme*; but we meet with them occasionally at the end of poems. As an example we may cite Karadžić, 1. 313, a short timeless-nameless poem of Type B, in which a girl is speaking of her love troubles: "Wealth consists neither in silver nor in gold, but rather in what is dear to one." Poems also which celebrate successes gained over bands of Turks or other enemies sometimes end with a gnomic reflection upon the presumption or folly of the beaten enemy.

We have not found any poems consisting wholly of gnomes, nor even any lists of gnomes in what can properly be regarded as *narodne pjesme*. Short 'gnomic-descriptive' lists are not unknown, as answers to riddles. An instance occurs in Karadžić, 1. 285, a short timeless-nameless poem, where a girl is sitting on the seashore and talking to herself. She asks herself: "Is there anything broader than the sea, or longer than the land, or swifter than a horse, or sweeter than honey, or dearer than a brother?" A fish in the water replies: "The sky is broader than the sea, the sea longer than the land, eyes swifter than a horse, sugar sweeter than honey, a lover dearer than a brother." Norse and Irish examples of such riddle catalogues have been noticed in Vol. 1, p. 414; in Russian, as we have seen (p. 212), they are more common. They are of course closely related to gnomes of the variety which applies to beings other than human (Type 11 (c); cf. Vol. 1, p. 377 ff.).

Poems of a wholly descriptive character, such as we noticed in Vol. 1, Ch. XIII, seem to be somewhat unusual; but very many poems begin with a short descriptive passage. A favourite opening for timeless-nameless poems is to speak of a pine, beneath which something happens or some persons are sitting. Less frequently poems begin with a short description of dawn or moonlight. In longer narrative poems the 'inverted simile' is a not infrequent opening. Thus in Karadžić, v. 9, the poet begins by stating that a beautiful rosetree was growing in the city of Trieste. Then he goes on to say that this was not a rosetree but Darinka, the daughter of Jovan Kvekić—whose marriage with Prince

Danilo is the subject of the poem. This kind of opening is common also in Russian, as we have seen (p. 72 f.).

As instances of poems which are wholly descriptive we may cite two examples from Eisner's *Volkslieder der Slawen*, the originals of which we have not seen. One (p. 357 f.) gives short descriptions of a (typical) married and unmarried man. The former is described as easy to recognise. His moustache is unkempt, his hair in a mess. As he walks along, he looks straight before him with bent head, as if he had lost a precious ring. The unmarried is still easier to recognise. His moustache is curled, his hair trimmed. As he walks along he glances in all directions. To right and left he looks up at the windows, like a hawk circling over a wood, to see if there is any prey to be got.

The other (*ib.* p. 338) describes a tom-cat lying at rest on a window-sill and blinking his yellow eyes. His sister comes and asks him what is the matter. He says that women have been slandering him for eating their cheese—which he has never seen, even in a dream. All he will admit is that he has been creeping along the pantry shelves and finding something there—which may have been cheese or anything else—which he liked the taste of.

Spell-poems are hardly as much in evidence as one would have expected; for such poetry is evidently cultivated by both the Bulgarians and the Slovenians,[1] and prose spells are known among the Yugoslavs themselves.[2] The fact that we have not found any satisfactory examples of such poetry may be due in part to the defectiveness of our information. But it is rather curious that among the *ženske pjesme* contained in Karadžić's collection (Vol. 1) we have noticed—even among the lullabies and spinning songs—hardly anything in the form of a spell.

We may cite one short narrative poem, apparently of Mohammedan provenance, in Eisner's collection (*op. cit.* p. 388 f.). A widower, called Ali, meets two girls, Huma and Emina, who mock him. When he comes home, he writes out three spells, one of which he throws into water, and another into the fire, while he lays the third under his pillow. All are to the same effect—that the senses of the proud Emina are to be carried away, or burnt, or lulled to sleep, so as to make her come to his house at midnight, clad in nothing but her shift.

Curses are very common; but as a rule they amount to no more than wishes for bad luck. They occur most frequently in short poems dealing with lovers, e.g. Karadžić, 1. 443, where a youth curses a girl who has

---

[1] Cf. Eisner, *Volkslieder der Slawen*, pp. 286 f., 471 ff.
[2] Cf. Krauss, *Slavische Volkforschungen*, p. 164 ff.

proved faithless to him. May she never marry! and if she does, may she never have a male child!

Prophecies and forebodings of misfortune are of frequent occurrence in all periods. Usually, but not always, they take the form of dreams. In Bogišić, No. 29, the death of King Vladislav is proclaimed before the walls of Buda by a 'white Vila of the mountains'. In modern poems we find political prophecies which speak of the reunion of the Yugoslavs (and other Christian peoples) and the expulsion of the Turks. The most striking example of this kind is the 'Lament of the Dragon on the Lovćen' (Karadžić, v. 17); cf. p. 334 f.

In this chapter, as in Ch. VII, we have made no attempt to give more than a very cursory notice of the short timeless-nameless poems included among *ženske pjesme*. Many of them, though not all, are properly folksongs, and to deal adequately with these would require a wider knowledge of folksongs in general than we possess. We suspect that poetry of this kind has more than any other in common with the similar poetry of neighbouring, and indeed even of more distant, peoples—in short that it is specially open to external influence.

CHAPTER IX

THE TEXTS

IN the preceding chapters we have frequently had occasion to refer to variant versions of poems. These exist in very great numbers. They are a natural and indeed inevitable result of the manner in which *narodne pjesme* are preserved and recited, as we shall see in the next chapter. Sometimes the variations are quite slight; thus in some of the Perast poems the variations are hardly more than verbal, though there is a change of metre (cf. p. 351). In other cases the differences are so great that we may be in doubt whether we have to do with variant versions of a common original or with poems of independent origin, though they may relate to the same event. Sometimes again it may be suspected that poems which show partial resemblances may be of independent origin but subsequently influenced by one another.

We will begin with a detailed analysis of two modern Montenegrin heroic poems (Karadžić, iv. 57 f.), which are obviously derived from a common original. They describe the death of the powerful Turkish nobleman Čengijć Smail Aga in the year 1840. The story therefore had not had a long history. No. 57 was sent to Karadžić in 1846. We are not told when he received No. 58; but this volume was published in 1862. It may be mentioned here that the next poem, No. 59, which is very short, relates to the same event; but it seems to be unconnected with the others. On the other hand Karadžić (p. 502, note) says that he had four more poems on the story, all of which differed very little from No. 57.

First we will give an abstract of No. 57:

1–104. Letter of Djoko Malović[1] to Smail Aga. He charges (11 ff.) certain leading men (*bans*) of his district, Drobnjak (Drobnjaci) in Hercegovina, with disloyalty—namely Novica Cerović, Mirko Damjanović and Šujo Karadžić. They have been to the bishop at Cetinje, complaining of Smail Aga's tyranny. Their speech is given in 24–52; the bishop's reply in 54–66. The bishop says he will reward anyone who brings Smail Aga's head; but he makes no reference to the battle of Grahovo. 67–89. The three *bans* make a solemn vow to kill Smail Aga. 90–104. Djoko advises Smail Aga to come to Drobnjak with a small army and take them by surprise.

[1] Evidently a Christian of Hercegovina, but loyal to the Turkish authorities.

105 ff. Reflections of Smail Aga.

123–140. Letter of Smail Aga to Ali Pasha at Mostar, asking him to send his son Miralaj with a hundred picked horsemen.

141–170. Smail Aga writes to Ahmet Bauk at Nikšić, asking him to bring troops to his assistance.

171–191. Smail Aga writes a similar letter to Mujaga Mušović at Kolašin.

192–212. March of Miralaj. 213–229. March of Ahmet Bauk and of Mujaga.

230–261. Smail Aga goes to meet Miralaj.

   249–254. Speech of Smail Aga. 258–261. Speech of Miralaj.

262–289. They march to the castle of Djoko Malović.

290–303. The three *bans* hear of their march and discuss the situation.

293–298. Speech of Novica.

304–340. Novica advises Šujo to go to see Smail Aga.

   318–323. Hypothetical speech of Smail Aga upon seeing Šujo; he will charge him with intriguing with the bishop. 325–340. Suggested reply of Šujo, protesting loyalty, offering to collect tribute, and charging Djoko with lying.

341–372. Šujo sets off to see Smail Aga and finds him at Djoko's house.

   358–362. Speech of Djoko (just before Šujo arrives), urging the destruction of the *bans*. 365–372. Šujo surprises them both by doing obeisance to Smail Aga.

374–379. Speech of Smail Aga to Šujo, identical with 318–323.

381–394. Reply of Šujo, more or less identical with 325–340.

395–426. Smail Aga believes Šujo. They set off to Smail Aga's camp together; and then, at Šujo's suggestion, move on to Mletičak. 419–423. Speech of Šujo, asking for tobacco and persuading Smail Aga to let him keep guard on a mountain.

427–447. Šujo addresses his men (speech 430–440), calling for a volunteer to summon Mirko and Novica.

448–471. Novica is debating with his men (speech 454–459), when the messenger arrives.

472–492. Novica assembles three hundred and eighty men, holds a religious service (speech 485–488), and joins Šujo on the mountain by night.

493–524. The night is cold and wet. A priest's wife comes to Smail Aga and warns him (506–509). He says he has no fear of Vlahs (511–517), and ill-uses her. She curses him (522–524).

526–545. A Hodža (Mohammedan priest) comes to warn Smail Aga (531–533); but the latter repeats (535–539) that he has no fear, and ill-uses him. The Hodža curses him (544 f.).

546–559. The day is now breaking; and Mirko and Novica advise that they should wait until the following night (549–554). But Šujo says he will attack at once (557–559).

560–582. They attack the camp. The Aga calls to his groom Martin for his horse (576); but the latter says (578 f.) that they have taken it. Then he mounts the groom's horse.

583–599. Men say he could have escaped. But he turned his horse and drew his sword, to make a fight. Mirko shoots him and cuts off his head.

600–614. Novica and Šujo cut off the heads of other leading Turks. In all they take eighty heads. Then they make off to Cetinje and present Smail Aga's head and horse to the king (bishop), who rewards them well.

No. 58 is as follows:

1–126. Djoko Malović writes to Smail Aga, accusing (11 ff.) nine leading men of disloyalty, among them Novica Cerović, Mirko Damjanović, Šujo Karadžić, and a priest named Golović, who writes letters for them to the bishop—also called king—at Cetinje. Novica also has visited the bishop, charging Smail Aga with tyranny. 34–58. Speech of Novica to the bishop. 61–105. Reply of the bishop. He speaks at length on the battle of Grahovo and the death of his nephew Stefan, for which he desires vengeance. 108–110. Reply of Novica, promising vengeance. 113–126. Advice of Djoko to Smail Aga to come with small army to Drobnjak.

127 ff. Reflections of Smail Aga.

134–168. Letter of Smail Aga to the Vizier Stočević, asking him to send his son Miralaj with six hundred Turks.

169–178. Smail Aga writes to Amet Bauk at Nikšić, asking him to bring men of the garrison to his assistance.

179–189. Smail Aga writes a similar letter to the Beg Mušović at Kolašin.

190–201. Arrival of Miralaj.

202–221. Smail Aga marches to the castle of Djoko Malović.

222–230. Šujo hears of his arrival and sets off to see him.

231–249. Smail Aga is conversing with Djoko, who advises him (235–249) to arrest Novica and Šujo, to put the priest Golović to the lash and cut off his right hand, and to fine the other leaders.

250–256. Šujo arrives in time to overhear this speech, and salutes the Aga.

257–284. Conversation of Šujo with Smail Aga, who (258–260) charges him with disloyalty. 262–266. Šujo denies the charge and accuses Djoko of lying. 268 f. Smail Aga enquires about Novica. 271–277. Šujo replies that he is at his home and has been collecting tribute for him. Smail Aga replies (279) that Novica is to go to Pošćenje. 280 ff. Šujo offers to prepare quarters for the Aga at his own home (Petnić); and the Aga assents.

285–298. Šujo returns home and writes an urgent letter (291–298) to Novica, telling him to come to Drobnjak.

299–305. Novica, on receiving the letter, calls his cousin Sekuo; and they set off to Drobnjak.

306–320. They find Šujo weeping. He tells them that Smail Aga has cruelly beaten the priest Golović.

321–329. Novica vows vengeance, and proposes that they should start for Pošćenje.

330–341. They come to Smail Aga at Pošćenje. Šujo kisses the Aga's hand; but Novica merely scowls. The Aga asks him (339 ff.) why he is acting thus.

342–372. Speech of Novica. He is angry because the Aga has doubted his loyalty and ill-used the priest. He has not been able to collect the tribute; the peasants threatened him. He reports a speech he had made to them (365–368), asking them to wait till he has seen Smail Aga. Is he to take their cattle?

373–377. The Aga says he will receive whatever tribute Novica gets.

378–397. Novica offers to meet him on the morrow at Mletičak. When the peasants see the army they will pay. The Aga is to cut off his head if he does not act loyally.

398–405. The Aga agrees, and compliments him.

406–425. Novica goes home and writes letters to Mina Radović (413–417) and Mirko Damjanović (421–425), calling upon them to bring their men at once, in order to avenge the Petrovići (the bishop's relatives).

426–445. Novica assembles his own men; and when the others arrive they set out for Mletičak. In the meantime the Turks arrive there.

446–461. Novica's force is observed by Jelez, a Turkish captain, who runs to the Aga's tent and warns him that Novica is acting treacherously.

462–475. Šujo dissuades the Aga from believing the news, and asks him to give him forty irregulars, with whom he will go and keep watch. Smail Aga declares (470–475) that Novica will not betray him, and gives Šujo fifty irregulars—men of Drobnjak.

476–492. Šujo sets out and joins Novica. They decide to attack from the mountain Ivica; and they rest there for a time before doing so.

493–515. The Aga is preparing his coffee when the Serbians make a sudden attack. No details are given; but it is stated that Novica slew Smail Aga and Mirko cut off his head. In all a hundred and forty Turkish heads are taken, including those of forty Bezi; also a hundred horses and a large amount of booty.

516–529. They bring the heads of Čengijć and the Bezi to Cetinje. The king rewards them and promotes Novica (speech 525–527).

We have analysed these poems at some length, primarily for the purpose of illustrating the growth of variants. At the same time it is hoped that the analysis may serve to give the reader some impression of the construction of a class of poems, hardly any of which have been translated into English. It will be seen that, although they were composed so soon after the events which they recount, they are true heroic epics. They are quite short; but the sequence of events is treated in a well constructed scheme, with imaginative details and frequent changes of scene and personnel, as in the *Iliad*. They conform in all respects to the table of characteristics common to Greek and English heroic narrative poetry set forth in Vol. 1, p. 20 ff.; and they furnish conclusive evidence against the view that such poetry must be of literary origin. It may be added that these two poems possess no exceptional features, though they are good specimens of their class.

We have spoken of 'poems'; but the use of the plural is hardly correct. They are obviously variants derived from one original, though they have scarcely a single whole line in common, apart from static formulae. It will be seen that the divergencies in substance are comparatively slight at first, but increase as the poems proceed. Both begin with a long letter from Djoko Malović to Smail Aga; and the substance of the letter is the same in both cases. In both this letter is followed by three shorter letters from Smail Aga to the Turkish authorities at Mostar, Nikšić and Kolašin, though there is a difference in the name of the first of these. Then in both poems Šujo Karadžić comes to visit the Aga at Djoko's house; but in No. 57 he does so after discussion with Novica and at the suggestion of the latter, whereas in No. 58 he acts on his own initiative. In both cases he arrives in time to overhear Djoko advising the Aga to take strong measures against him and his confederates; and in both he protests that Djoko is lying. The chief divergence begins after this. In No. 58 Šujo summons Novica by letter; Novica comes himself to see Smail Aga, and from this point (299 ff.) to the end of the poem the action practically follows his movements. But in No. 57 Novica does not come to see the Aga; Šujo summons him—not for discussion, but to take action—after he has left the Aga. The rest of the poem is concerned more with Smail Aga than with Novica, who is not specially prominent. The fight is described in much greater detail.

The chief difference between the poems lies in the treatment of Novica. In both he is perhaps regarded as the most important of Smail Aga's enemies; and this may be historical fact. But in the older poem (No. 57) he is less prominent than Šujo. It is Mirko, not Novica, who kills the Aga; and no hero is mentioned individually in the account of the reception by the bishop at the end. In No. 58 we seem to see the 'development' of a hero. Novica has now become the most prominent figure in the story, except perhaps the Aga himself. He has taken over the chief share in the interviewing of the Aga. It is he too who kills the Aga, though Mirko gets his head. And the honours awarded by the bishop are directed primarily to him.

Of other features peculiar to one or other of the poems we may notice first the motif of the bishop's blood-feud in No. 58 (66 ff.), to which there is an implicit reference also at the end of the poem. Karadžić believed this to be the true cause of Smail Aga's death (cf. p. 370). The priest Golović and his cruel treatment at the hands of the Aga are also peculiar to this poem. On the other hand No. 57 introduces several minor incidents just before the final tragedy. The visits of the priest's wife and of the Hodža and the curses uttered by them look like rhetorical devices introduced in order to lead up to the climax. But we have no means of determining what elements are unhistorical, apart from the discrepancies between the two narratives.[1]

For the discrepancies noticed above analogies are to be found in other modern poems (Karadžić, v. 12 f.) on the Sack of Kolašin. In No. 12 there are three leaders in the attack—Novica Cerović, Milan the Serdar and Dimitrij the Archimandrite—all of whom are about equally

---

[1] Karadžić (p. 461) says he had heard that it was really an Orthodox priest (*pop*) who gave the warning to Smail Aga.

prominent. But in No. 13 the Archimandrite is ignored. Novica and Miljan (Milan) are the chief figures, though several others are more or less important.

The relationship between these poems is not the same as the relationship between the poems (IV. 57 f.) on the death of Smail Aga. There are common elements, e.g. in the opening scene, which suggest that one of them has been influenced by the other. But they can hardly be regarded as variants derived from a common original—the differences are too great. Nevertheless such a discrepancy as the one mentioned above is worth noting, because both poems must have originated very soon after the event. Kolašin was sacked in 1858; and the volume in which they are contained was published in 1865.

Next we will consider poems which relate to earlier times. In this case it will be convenient to take a text preserved in an early MS. and compare it with a text of the same poem contained in one of the later collections. Bogišić's edition presents a good number of examples available for this purpose, though it also contains many poems which are not to be found, so far as we are aware, in any modern collections. The example we will take is a *bugarštica* (Bogišić, No. 1), which we have had occasion to notice before (p. 315). It is preserved in the Franciscan (Ragusa) MS., and belongs to the group of poems supplied by Jodzo Betondić, who died in 1764; and it relates to the battle of Kosovo:

1–9. Bušić Stjepan bids his wife rise from her bed and open the windows, so that the light of dawn may brighten the house. He asks her whether the morning star has risen. Are the drums beating in front of Lazar's palace? Are the nobles assembling there?

10–24. She does as he bids, and tells him (20–24) that the day is breaking and that she hears the sounds of the army—repeating his words.

25–32. He rises, and bids her awaken his squire Oliver and tell him to saddle the horses and get ready the requisites for war—so that he may not be left behind by the army of Lazar, the Hungarian nobles and the brothers Ugovići.

33–40. She begs him not to go to war this day. She has had a grievous dream, in which she saw a falcon flying from the house, and coming back without its head.

41–44. Stjepan declines to stay behind.

45–49. Jela, his wife, then goes to awaken Oliver, and repeats to him (47–49) her husband's instructions.

50–58. Oliver carries out the instructions. Stjepan and he mount their horses and arrive at Lazar's palace. In front of the palace they meet many Hungarian nobles, and exchange greetings with them.

59 ff. Milica comes to a window to greet the nobles. There is no further reference to Stjepan Bušić. Milica talks with Miloš Kobilović.

99 ff. Milica begs Lazar to leave one of the Ugovići, her brothers, behind with her; but he refuses.

115 ff. Lazar, having arrived at Kosovo, gives a banquet to his chiefs, at which he accuses Miloš.

145 ff. Miloš sets off to kill the emperor. Then follows the battle.

With this poem we may compare Karadžić, ii. No. 47:[1]

1–5. Musić Stevan is drinking wine in his house at Majdan. His squire Vaistina is serving him.

6–28. He says he is going to bed; and he tells his squire to help himself to wine and watch for the dawn, when they must start for Kosovo. He repeats (21–28) the solemn curse pronounced by the prince upon any Serbian who should fail to go to the battle (cf. p. 366).

29–51. Vaistina watches for the dawn; and when he sees signs of it he fetches and saddles two horses. He also brings a standard, upon which are worked twelve golden crosses and the portrait of St John, Stevan's patron saint. Then he ascends the tower to awaken his lord.

52–63. Stevan's wife meets him and begs him not to wake her husband. She says she has had an evil dream, in which she has seen two falcons followed by a swarm of doves flying from the house. They flew to Kosovo and came down in Murat's camp; but they did not rise again.

64–85. The squire answers that he cannot act disloyally to his lord. He repeats (76–83) the curse pronounced by the prince.

86–89. He then goes to wake his lord, and tells him it is time to start.

89–103. Stevan rises, washes and dresses. He drinks a draught of wine to the glory of God. Then they mount their horses, unfurl the standards, beat the drums, and set out.

104–147. The day has dawned when they arrive at Kosovo. They meet a girl who is carrying a warrior's helmet; and Stevan asks her where she has found it. She replies that she has picked it out of the

---

[1] The first part of this poem is transl. by Morison in Subotić, *Yugoslav Popular Ballads*, p. 58 ff.

river, which was full of the bodies and accoutrements of warriors. Then Stevan realises that he has arrived too late, and that the prince's curse has fallen upon him.

148–169 (end). Stevan gives a present to the girl and hastens on to the Turkish camp, where he makes a great slaughter, but eventually perishes with his squire and a vast number of his troops—who have not been mentioned before.

There can be no question that the first parts of these two poems are variants derived from a common original. The relationship between them is naturally less close than between two variants which are more or less contemporary with the events, like the poems on the death of Smail Aga. But the fact of the relationship is clear from the general course of the narrative, and in particular from the wife's dream. It may also be observed that, so far as we know, Stjepan Bušić (Stevan Musić) is not mentioned elsewhere.[1] We do not know whether he has been identified from historical records.

The common element ends with the hero's departure from his home (54 in Bogišić's text, 103 in Karadžić's text). The earlier text now brings him to Lazar's palace, where he exchanges salutations with the nobles. After this he drops out of the story; the rest of the poem is concerned with Milica, Lazar and Miloš. The later text continues the story of Stevan; but it brings him to the battle direct, not to Lazar's palace. He arrives too late, and believes he has incurred the prince's curse.

We do not think that the curse is ancient, at least in its present form (cf. p. 368); yet it is difficult to doubt that the continuation of Karadžić's text has a better claim to represent the original than the continuation of Bogišić's text. In the latter Stjepan's story is left incomplete—indeed it can hardly be called a story at all. What follows in the poem has nothing to do with Stjepan. The next section leads up to Milica's request that one of her brothers should be spared to stay behind with her. This forms the subject of a separate poem (II. No. 45) in Karadžić's collection, though apart from the possession of the same motif the two pieces have hardly anything in common. The following section (115 ff.), dealing with the banquet, seems to be a variant of a third poem (II. No. 50, iii)—described as a fragment—in Karadžić's collection, though the resemblance is not very close. The last section (145 ff.) is concerned

___

[1] From Karadžić, II. p. 298, it would seem that a saga relating to him is (or was) in existence. But we have not seen this, and do not know whether it is independent of the poem.

with events which we have not seen treated at length in any later poem.[1] But these events were very famous; and it is difficult to believe that poems upon them were composed only in Dalmatia. In any case it may be noted that the *bugarštica* treats seriatim, in a connected narrative, a number of subjects which elsewhere are the themes of different poems, and that these poems stand in various degrees of relationship, sometimes near, sometimes remote, to the *bugarštica*.

As regards the relative faithfulness of the two traditions, the *bugarštica* frequently betrays the remoteness of its place of origin (Ragusa). It mentions only two geographical names, Kosovo and (the river) Marica; and the latter is a mistake for Sitnica, presumably owing to confusion with Vukašin's disaster. The use of the name 'Hungarian' is probably a reminiscence of the political conditions which prevailed during the fifteenth century. The name Oliver is doubtless due to the influence of the Romances, which were not unknown on the Adriatic seaboard. Features connected with the Orthodox Church, which are rather prominent in Karadžić's text (No. 47), do not appear in the *bugarštica*—probably because they had no meaning for Catholics. On the other hand we do not believe that the curse in Karadžić's text is ancient. And if Stevan's home was in the neighbourhood of Požarevac,[2] the hero's feat of arriving at Kosovo soon after daybreak shows an ignorance of geography almost equal to that of the *bugarštica*.

These details, however, are less important than the question whether we are to regard the *bugarštica* (Bogišić, No. 1), as an 'epic' formed by stringing together a number of originally separate 'lays'. The alternative explanation—viz. that Karadžić's poems were originally portions of a disintegrated epic—is improbable; for the great majority of Yugoslav heroic poems deal with single events, and possess a unity which is lacking to this *bugarštica*. There are exceptions, like Karadžić, II. No. 46, the first part of which is religious heroic (cf. p. 314) while the second is a catalogue; but these may be explained in the same way. The stringing together of poems would seem to present no serious difficulty, if one is ready to sacrifice to some extent the principle of unity. We do not of course mean to suggest that the poet[3] or minstrel responsible for our

[1] Two (or three) poems on the subject are in existence; but they are said to be not independent of literary influence.

[2] Cf. Karadžić, II. p. 298, note. The distance to Kosovo would be considerably over a hundred miles.

[3] It may be suggested that the poem in its present form may be the work of Jodzo Betondić (cf. p. 446), from whom the Franciscan MS. obtained it, and who was a learned man. But none of the other poems supplied by him seems to be of

bugarštica (Bogišić, No. 1) as a whole proceeded like the scholars of last century who tried to construct, or 'reconstruct', an epic of Kosovo from published texts. He doubtless used the same freedom in the treatment of his materials as he was accustomed to do in treating any other poems in his repertoire.

Variants of a kind very different from those we have noticed above are to be found among the Perast poems discussed on p. 351 f. The texts of the (irregular) decasyllabic poems contained in the later MS. are very close to those of the *bugarštice* preserved in the earlier one, in spite of the change of metre. Sometimes indeed the two differ merely in phraseology. If the variants really come from oral tradition, the latter must have been much more rigid at Perast than elsewhere. But we find it difficult to believe that this is the true explanation. The later texts are not taken from the existing MS. of the *bugarštice* (cf. p. 351, note); but we think they must be derived in some way or other from an earlier written text.

These remarks, however, are not true for all the cases. Thus in Bogišić, Nos. 73 f., the plan—the course of events portrayed—is the same, and there are some close verbal resemblances; but in general the details differ a good deal. The same is true of the latter parts of Nos. 65 f., which are concerned with the capture of Novi Grad by the Venetians in 1687. But the first parts of these poems are quite different. The *bugarštica* (No. 65) describes the gathering of the Venetians and their allies and the warnings sent to the city by the Ragusans of its impending danger. In place of this the decasyllabic poem (No. 66) relates how a girl of Novi Grad dreams that a violent storm falls upon the city, with lightnings and flying snakes, and tells the dream to her brother—a motif which occurs in other poems. The evidence of these poems seems to point to oral tradition of a rather conservative character.

The chief interest of the Perast poems, on the formal side, lies in the change of metre. The effects of this can of course be seen most clearly in those poems where there is little or no variation in substance. As an example of the changes in wording or phraseology we may take the opening lines of Nos. 69 and 70. The former begins as follows:

composite character; and neither this nor any of the others, so far as we have observed, shows stylistic features which differentiate it from other *bugarštice*. Indeed it seems more likely that Betondić obtained his poems in writing; for in his day (c. 1750) the composition of *bugarštice* was practically at an end. This question will require notice again in the following chapter.

Podiže se četa Turaka od Risna maloga mjesta,
carevoga mjesta,
i pred njima bijaše vrli Isa Rišnjanine.
I oni ti podjoše u zelenu Kostanjicu,
Risanske delije,
na bijele dvorove Nikole Daboviča.

"A band of Turks set out from the small town of Risan, a town belonging to the emperor, and in command of them was the illustrious Isa of Risan. And they made their way into green Kostanjica, the warriors of Risan, to the white house of Nikola Dabovič."

The beginning of No. 70 is as follows:

Podiže se Turska četa mala,
a od Risna mjesta malahnoga,
pred njima je Iža Rišnjanine;
ter podjoše ravnoj Kostanjici,
na dvorove Dabović-Nikole.

"A small Turkish band set out, even from the little town of Risan, and in command of them is Iža of Risan; and they made their way to level Kostanica, to the house of Nikola Dabović."

It may be observed that there is a tendency to reduce the number of static epithets.

Next we may consider certain parallels which are much less close. One may hesitate to treat stories as variants of one another when some or all of the chief characters are different persons. Yet it is impossible to doubt that 'The Marriage of Vukašin'[1] is a variant of Bogišić, No. 97, a poem in irregular decasyllabic metre—from the Ragusa MS.—which likewise tells the story of Momčilo and his faithless wife. The two narratives are identical in substance. But Momčilo is the only name they have in common. The faithful sister is called in one Jevrosima, in the other Andželija; but this may be merely a difference in name, though Jevrosima is well known from other poems as the mother of Marko Kraljević. More important, however, is the fact that the central figure in the story is in one poem a famous hero, King Vukašin, while in the other he is a nameless *ban* from Germany. We do not know how this discrepancy is to be explained.

Vukašin is not unknown to the poetry of the Ragusa MS. elsewhere. Another decasyllabic poem (Bogišić, No. 85) is concerned with his marriage; but this is a wholly different story from the one just noticed. He catches and marries a Vila—an incident which elsewhere, as we have

---

[1] Transl. by Low, *The Ballads of Marko Kraljević*, p. 1 ff.; cf. p. 313, above.

seen (p. 312), is related of his son, Marko Kraljević. In this case there is no resemblance in detail. On the other hand the latter part of this 'Marriage of Marko Kraljević' bears a close resemblance to a *bugarštica* (Bogišić, No. 39), in which the hero is not Marko Kraljević but Novak. The story therefore is told of three different heroes; and two of the poems which contain it are probably to be regarded, in part at least,[1] as variants. Was it originally a timeless, nameless story—perhaps a folktale?

Such seems to be the case with another story relating to a Vila, which likewise forms the subject of a *bugarštica* (Bogišić, No. 43), and was noticed on p. 324 f., above. This Vila brings about the deaths of the Jakšića, while they are still unmarried; and we pointed out (*ib.*) that it is inconsistent with most of the other poems relating to the Jakšića, which are largely concerned with their wives. But the story has a close parallel in the later poem 'Mujo and Alija', contained in Karadžić's collection (II. No. 11) and noticed on p. 399, above. The latter is practically a timeless, nameless poem. The resemblance between the two poems, however, is hardly of such a character that they can strictly be regarded as variants, though they are concerned with what is substantially the same story.

Portions of heroic poems—or at least what appear to be such—sometimes show closer resemblances to timeless, nameless poems. We may refer here to two poems noticed on p. 383, which can hardly be regarded otherwise than as variants. In one (Bogišić, No. 101) the hero is a certain Sekuo; in the other (Karadžić, II. No. 52) he is called Jurišić Janko. The latter hero is unknown to us elsewhere; and both poems without doubt contain a large element of fiction. The point, however, to which we would call attention is that the latter part of the story—from the point where the Sultan asks his prisoner what death he prefers—occurs also in timeless, nameless poems. In one poem in the Matica Hrvatska's collection (*Ženske Pjesme*, II. No. 6) the hero is called Marijan; he is the only person mentioned by name. In another (*ib.* No. 4) we find practically the same story,[2] but with a heroine, called Mare of Zara, instead of a hero; and here again none of the other characters are named. Both poems would seem to be variants, not only

---

[1] The beginning and the end of the story are wanting in the *bugarštica*. We suspect that this poem is incomplete—that the first part of the story, relating to the capture of the Vila, has been omitted. But the end, as told in the Matica Hrvatska's text, relating how the Vila was recaptured and then remained permanently with Marko, may well be a later addition.   [2] Cf. p. 401.

of one another, but also of the heroic (or quasi-heroic) poems just mentioned—so far as the latter part of these is concerned.

In such cases the heroic story may be derived from the timeless, nameless one—or, to speak more precisely, a timeless, nameless narrative poem may have been adapted to a heroic milieu. There are other cases, however, where heroes, even well known heroes, have had transferred to them stories which seem originally to have been told of other persons. We may instance a poem called 'Miloš among the Latins', in Karadžić's collection (II. No. 37), noticed on p. 381, above. Practically the same story is told in a (fragmentary) *bugarštica* (Bogišić, No. 76), of a certain Ivan Voihnović, a nephew of the Montenegrin prince Ivan Crnojević (cf. p. 353). Ivan Voihnović is unknown to us apart from this poem; but he must have lived a century after Miloš Obilić. Yet a comparison of the poems suggests that the *bugarštica* preserves an earlier form of the story, especially if Kotor was the scene from the beginning. Against the absurd damage and slaughter recorded in Karadžić's poem it describes an accident which might well have happened. It is a narrative in verse of an adventure of local interest, whereas Karadžić's poem seems to represent a variant which has wandered into some Orthodox district, and in which the story has been embellished, exaggerated, and transferred to a famous hero.

Lastly, it may be noted that heroic, or quasi-heroic, poems are occasionally derived in part from other poems of the same kind. Thus the first parts of 'The Marriage of Djuro of Smeredevo' (cf. p. 375) and 'The Marriage of Stojan Popović' [1] are obvious variants of one another. The common element would seem to belong properly to the former, if we may judge from what follows. This case then differs from the one discussed in the last paragraph; for Despot Djuro is a character well known both in poetry and history, whereas Stojan Popović seems not to be known except in this poem. Both poems alike, however, are full of anachronisms and may be regarded wholly as works of fiction.

Thus far we have been concerned with poems which must be regarded as, either wholly or in part, variants of one another, i.e. as derived from a common original, unless one is borrowed from the other, as perhaps in the last case. Something, however, must be said here with regard to poems which cannot be variants, but yet seem to have been influenced by one another. Illustrations of this process were noted

[1] Karadžić, II. No. 87. Both poems are transl. by Low, *The Ballads of Marko Kraljević*, pp. 159 ff., 168 ff.

in Vol. 1, p. 512 ff.; and in Yugoslav *narodne pjesme* examples may be expected to be frequent. But we must deal with this subject very briefly.

One probable instance has already been noticed (p. 376) in the two poems on the Sack of Kolašin (Karadžić, v. 12 f.). Both poems open with a long conversation between Cerović Novica and the Serdar Milan, who are drinking wine together beside the white church in Morača. Neither the speeches themselves nor the descriptions of the events which follow have much in common; but there are certain passages which suggest influence. Thus in No. 12, 67 ff. Novica says he is ashamed to meet the men of Cetinje because he has had no part in the battle of Grahovo, in which they won such glory; while in No. 13, 132 ff. the same hero relates how his boasting has been stopped by Mirko, the prince's brother, who declared that the glory won by himself at Grahovo was greater than any which Novica could claim.

It is in the opening scenes of poems that such influence seems to be most often traceable. Thus it can hardly be due to accident that the two poems on the battle of Grahovo itself (Karadžić, v. 10 f.) both open with a gathering of Turkish notables before the Sultan's divan in Constantinople, though otherwise they have little in common. In such a case one may suspect that the author of one poem borrowed the motif from the other, perhaps immediately after the events. On the other hand it is possible that both are based on common report or rumour.

A somewhat different case occurs in Karadžić, IV. 10 f. There is an obvious and close resemblance between the bishop's speech in No. 11, 96 ff. and the latter part of the same bishop's speech in No. 10, 110 ff. Otherwise these poems have little in common, though they deal with the same events—the war of the Montenegrins with Mahmut Pasha. It would seem therefore that either the original author or some later reciter of one of the poems had incorporated in his piece words which he had heard in the recital of the other. Here again, however, there is of course an alternative possibility, viz. that the authors of both poems may have recorded independently the words actually spoken by the bishop on this occasion.[1]

We have yet to consider certain formal characteristics of the *narodne pjesme*. Owing to the vast amount of material which has been published it is probable that no other country can supply greater opportunity for

---

[1] Karadžić was inclined to think (p. 68, note) that both these poems were originally composed by the bishop, Peter I (St Peter), though they had been taken over and transformed by lay minstrels.

studying the conventions observable in the structure of narrative poetry. Of this material we can of course make use of only an insignificant fraction. We shall therefore confine our attention in general to modern heroic poetry, with special reference to the conventions followed in the beginnings of poems.

The majority of these poems are concerned with raids or invasions. Such is the case (e.g.) with thirteen of the eighteen poems contained in Vol. v of Karadžić's collection. Of these thirteen poems four (Nos. 8, 12, 13, 14) begin with a sentence—varying in form—which states that two or more heroes are drinking wine together. The poem then goes on to recount their conversation. Two other poems (Nos. 5, 7) begin with a statement that a certain person wrote a letter, the contents of which are given. No. 3 follows the same scheme, though it is preceded by the date; and No. 2 is perhaps to be regarded as merely a more elaborate variant of the same opening. Two poems (Nos. 4, 15) begin with complaints made by Turkish inhabitants or officials to their governors—and recorded at length—about wrongs which they are suffering from the Montenegrins. Two poems (Nos. 10, 11), which are perhaps connected, open with the summoning of a Turkish council in Constantinople,[1] the proceedings at which are recounted in full. The remaining poem begins with a statement that a white Vila cried out from a high mountain. Her speech of warning follows.

Of the five poems which are not concerned with raids or invasions four begin with a religious formula—'Glory to God', or 'Dear God! a great marvel!'—though the poems themselves are not religious. In two cases (Nos. 9, 17) the formula is followed by an 'inverted simile' (cf. p. 334).

All these openings recur elsewhere. Thus Vol. iv of the same collection contains sixty-two poems; and of these eleven begin with the wine-drinking scene and the conversation which follows. It is possibly worth noting—though it may be mere accident—that this opening seems to occur more frequently when the scene is laid in a Serbian (Montenegrin) milieu; only in two cases are the drinkers Turks. Nine poems in this volume begin with a letter-writing formula; and to these we may perhaps add one (No. 36) which varies somewhat from the ordinary type. Only two poems (Nos. 10, 55) begin with the council of Turks, and only one (No. 18) with a complaint like those in Vol. v. On the other hand three (Nos. 21, 40, 49) open with a message called out by a Vila from a mountain, while in three others (Nos. 38, 43, 46) this

[1] In No. 10 this is preceded by the date.

opening follows the 'dawn' formula, which we have to mention below. The religious formulae 'Glory to God' and 'Dear God! a great marvel!' occur six times. In one case (No. 37) an 'inverted simile' follows.[1]

Vol. IV shows a number of openings which do not occur in Vol. V. First we may note a statement that 'Dawn had not yet grown pale, neither had Danica (the Morning Star) shown her face, nor was there any sign of day'—or variants to the same effect—when something took place. In three poems this formula introduces the call of the Vila, as noted above. In two others (Nos. 16, 34) it is used to indicate the early start of a hero or an army. Six poems (Nos. 2, 26, 30, 45, 52, 59) begin with the arrival of two ravens, which deliver a message of death and disaster to the wife or mother of a hero who has gone to battle. This opening belongs properly to heroic poems of Type B, though the story told by the ravens usually occupies the greater part of the poem. Among less frequent openings we may note the statements that a woman or girl dreamed a dream, which is found in three poems (Nos. 12, 27, 56), and that a small band of Turks set out from a certain place (cf. p. 424), which occurs twice (Nos. 20, 22). Lastly, note may be taken of the formula that someone is herding sheep, which appears in No. 47. This opening is very common in timeless, nameless poetry.

Several of the typical scenes noticed above, especially the wine-drinking, the complaint, and the arrival of the ravens, occur seldom, if ever, except at the beginning of poems, while others may be introduced later. Some of them again are capable of considerable expansion, especially the debates and letters. Not unfrequently also we find a series of such scenes following one another. By such processes the length of a poem may be greatly extended.

The first process may be illustrated by instances of the 'call of the Vila'. Sometimes, as in Karadžić, v. 6 (ad init.), the hero to whom she calls proceeds to act at once, in response to her warning. Very often, however, he disbelieves or disregards the warning, saying that he has complete confidence in his followers or allies. Then she will call again, telling him that his confidence is misplaced. Sometimes also the Vila's movements are described. A good example of this expanded treatment will be found in Karadžić, v. 6. 472 ff., noticed on p. 378, above.[2]

The 'letter' motif is capable of similar expansion, and to a greater extent. The recipient of the letter often despatches another letter or

---

[1] This is practically the case also in No. 1.
[2] For a fuller discussion of this motif and also of the 'ravens' and 'dream' motives see Gesemann, *Studien zur südslav. Volksepik*, p. 70 ff.

several letters to his friends. We have had an example of this kind in the poems on the Death of Smail Aga (cf. p. 413 ff.), where the Aga, on receiving a letter from Djoko Malović, sends off letters of his own to three Turkish chiefs. A similar case occurs in Karadžić, v. 2 (cf. p. 333), where the priest Luka receives a letter telling him of the movements of Djulek, and immediately writes to three of his friends, exhorting them to join him without delay in laying an ambush for him. Sometimes, as in this case, the letters are quite short; sometimes, like the speeches at debates, they argue all the bearings of the situation and even discuss international politics. Letters of this kind often occupy a considerable part of a poem. Verbal directions sometimes take the place of letters, especially on the part of a commander.

The 'complaint' motif may introduce a 'council' scene, as in Karadžić, iv. 18, or it may be followed by a letter to the Sultan, which will itself lead to the council scene. This latter scene not unfrequently contains a curious feature. The Sultan or Pasha at the close of the council issues a proclamation, calling for someone who will lead his army or execute some commission for him. In the event of success he promises great rewards, sometimes including the hand of his daughter in marriage. Usually some time elapses before anyone will undertake the commission.

As an illustration of a series of typical scenes and motives following one another in succession we may take Karadžić, v. 3, the long poem on 'Omer Pasha's attack upon Montenegro':

1–94. Letter of Osman Pasha at Skadar to the Sultan.

95–118. The Sultan calls a council, and issues a proclamation promising honours and his daughter's hand to anyone who will successfully carry out the expedition against Montenegro.

119–184. No one presents himself for fifteen days. Then the renegade Omer undertakes the expedition and is accepted by the Sultan.

185–200. The expedition starts.

201–471. Omer Pasha gives directions to his subordinates.

472–519. The Vile give warning of the expedition to Danilo (cf. p. 378).

520–623. Danilo gives directions to his subordinates.

624–641. A Montenegrin force sets out for Džupa.

642–679. Mirko, the Montenegrin commander-in-chief, sends letters to three other commanders, asking for reinforcements. Then he addresses the men of Džupa. It is only after this that the real action begins.

Thus far we have confined our attention to poems relating to recent events. In poems relating to the far past the proportion of stereotyped openings seems not to be so large. We may take the poems relating to Marko Kraljević in Vol. II of Karadžić's collection, translated in Mr Low's *Ballads of Marko Kraljević*. They are thirty-one in number. Among these there are only three examples of the 'wine-drinking' opening (Low, Nos. 14, 22, 28), of which two are in the singular, only two of the 'letter' (*ib.* 1, 17), of which one follows another opening, only one (*ib.* 20) of the religious formula, and one of the 'inverted simile' (*ib.* 8), referring to thunder and earthquake, as in Karadžić, IV. 37. In addition to these there is one very elaborate opening (*ib.* 6)—'since the world came into existence there has been no greater marvel,' etc.—which occurs also in Karadžić, IV. 5. But the total, it will be seen, is little more than a quarter of the whole number of poems. On the other hand we find a number of what seem to be conventional openings, but which apparently do not occur in Karadžić, Vols. IV and V. Such are the statements that two comrades were riding together, which occurs *ib.* 4, 15, 16, that someone rose early (*ib.* 12, 24, 31), and that Marko was sitting down to supper (*ib.* 11, 17).

Next, let us take the series of (irregular) decasyllabic heroic poems preserved in the Franciscan (Ragusa) MS., dating from c. 1750, and published in Bogišić, Nos. 85–119. Here, out of thirty-five poems eight begin with wine-drinking, seven with letters, one (No. 114) with an inverted simile, referring to thunder and earthquake, one (No. 115) with a dream, and one (No. 116) with the call of a Vila. News is brought by a bird in No. 119; but it is a swallow, not a raven. It may be noted that No. 122, a poem from the same MS., but not heroic, also opens with the call of a Vila, while No. 66, a poem from the later Perast MS., which belongs to about the same period (cf. p. 423) opens with a dream. It is also worth noting that two of Bogišić's heroic decasyllabic poems (Nos. 86, 92) correspond to two poems in Mr Low's collection, and that in both cases they have the same openings.

The evidence of the *bugarštice* is rather different. In seventy-six poems of this type contained in Bogišić's collection the 'letter' opening occurs five times (Nos. 15, 22, 30, 57, 71), but the wine-drinking only once (No. 55). There are three examples of the 'council' (Nos. 8, 31, 80) and one of the 'dawn'; but the latter is a different formula from what we find later. Once (No. 69) we find the expression 'a band of Turks set out'; and once (No. 36) a bird brings a message, but it is a falcon. The 'inverted simile' occurs three times (Nos. 6, 50, 82), though without reference to thunder or earthquake. There is no call of warning or exhortation from a Vila; but in No. 29 a mountain Vila comes walking to Buda and pronounces a dirge for King Vladislav in front of the castle. These are the only instances of the openings conventional in later times which we have observed in the *bugarštice*.[1] It would seem that in the age of the *bugarštice* most of the openings were only beginning to come into use, and some of them had not yet attained their final form.

The *bugarštice* are by no means without conventional openings; but most of these are different from what are found in later times. In seven poems somebody begins or proceeds to speak—introducing a speech. In six poems a lady (or Vila) goes walking, and in three two heroes go riding. In such passages the 'cognate accusative' is almost always used,[2] a construction which in later poems is preserved only in a few expressions, e.g. 'went hunting' (*lov lovio*). Not unfrequently, however, late poems relating to early times use simplified equivalents of these openings —a lady was walking,[3] or two heroes were riding (cf. p. 377). Various other openings of the same kind occur, e.g. (No. 28) 'cried a cry' (*kliku klikovaše*), where again the modern equivalent is simplified to 'cried'. Perhaps the most interesting case is *cvilu cviljahu* (*cviljaše*), used of the twittering of swallows; but both the passages in which it occurs (Nos. 50, 82) are instances of 'inverted simile'—the swallows being really women. Still more imaginative is the girl's appeal to the Moon, with which No. 46 opens. Lastly, it may be noted that the opening 'sat down to supper', which occurs in the poems of Marko Kraljević (cf. p. 431), appears also in *bugarštice* (Nos. 34, 40), though the word used here is *objed*, 'dinner'.

From what has been said above it will be clear that modern heroic poems usually begin with one or other of a limited number of conventional openings. In strictly modern heroic poems, i.e. in poems first composed in modern times, these conventional openings seem to be almost universal. But modern versions of old poems often have different openings, which occur also in *bugarštice*, though usually in a slightly different and more elaborate form. In such cases the modern version probably preserves an opening which the poem has had for

[1] The dream of a girl, portending disaster as usual, occurs in No. 28, but it does not actually begin the poem.

[2] Very often the word *lijep*, 'beautiful', is used in such expressions, e.g. (No. 2) *lijepu šetu pošeta*, lit. 'went a graceful walk'. But the expression has doubtless become merely conventional.

[3] In Karadžić, II. 80, *pošetala* is the later equivalent of *šetu pošeta* or *šedbu šetaše*. So in *ib.* II. 38 *pojezdiše* is the later equivalent of (*lijepu*) *jezdu jezdijaše*.

centuries.[1] Sometimes, however, it has substituted for the old opening one of the modern conventions, such as the 'wine-drinking'.[2] Nearly all the modern conventional openings seem to have been in use from the time of the earliest decasyllabic poetry, i.e. towards the close of the seventeenth century.[3] Indeed many of them can be traced even in *bugarštice*, though here their occurrence is sporadic, and sometimes they have a slightly different form. On the other hand *bugarštice* have, in addition to these, a number of conventional openings of their own. It may be observed that the openings found in the *bugarštice* do not vary, like the metres, according to the MS., i.e. according to the locality from which the poem was obtained. They would seem therefore to have been in general use on the Adriatic coast; and there can be little doubt that some of them go back at least to the sixteenth century. Indeed two of them occur also in Russian *byliny*—the two heroes riding together, and the inverted simile, referring to natural phenomena. The most frequent opening in *byliny*, however, is the banquet given by a prince (cf. p. 82). This also is to be found in Yugoslav poems, e.g. Karadžić, II. 20, 50. iii, 68. No. 50. iii can be traced back to the fifteenth century (cf. p. 341).

We have restricted our remarks in general to the openings of poems; but it must not be supposed that the conventional elements occur only in this position. Poems are largely built up from them; and they are always to be taken into account along with the freedom in the treatment of the text, which we noticed earlier in this chapter. In the next chapter we shall see that the Yugoslav minstrel works more by improvisation than by memory; but it is to be borne in mind that his materials are not single words but stereotyped phrases, passages and motifs.

NOTE. It has been suggested recently that the whole Kosovo cycle (cf. p. 419 ff.), including the *bugarštice*, is derived from a romance (cf. Note on p. 456). We can see no reason for tracing the origin of this cycle to a literary unit, whether romance or epic, any more than that of other Yugoslav cycles. The discrepancies between the poems seem to us to indicate that the story had been treated independently by various poets from the beginning.

[1] It is interesting to compare the openings of 'Marko Kraljević and Mina of Kostur' in Bogišić, Nos. 7, 86, and Karadžić, II. No. 62 (Low, No. 17). For 'letters' the *bugarštica* (No. 7) here has *glasa*, i.e. presumably verbal messages.

[2] As in 'Musić Stefan' (Karadžić, II. No. 47), as against Bogišić, No. 1.

[3] Apart from the decasyllabic poems in the Ragusa text, several of them seem to occur in the Erlangen MS., which dates from early in cent. xviii; cf. Gesemann, *op. cit.* p. 70 ff.

CHAPTER X

RECITATION AND COMPOSITION

THE POET

YUGOSLAV minstrelsy has a peculiar interest owing to the fact that it continued to be a living art down to our own times. Indeed it is said to be still widely cultivated, though we have no detailed recent information. We understand, however, that nearly everyone now can read and that printed collections of poems are purchasable everywhere, not to mention gramophone records and wireless performances. Moreover, even the most remote districts are no longer inaccessible to external influence. But the information which we have obtained applies properly for the most part to conditions which prevailed some thirty or forty years ago. We shall use the present tense; but it must be understood that what is said may now be true only in the case of old and exceptionally unsophisticated persons.

The value of the evidence lies not only in its abundance but also in the fact that in certain districts a living—perhaps even creative—heroic minstrelsy was still flourishing when it came to be studied at length by skilled observers. Our best information comes from Bosnia and Hercegovina, which were illiterate and more or less isolated from the civilised world until c. 1880. For Montenegro we have not such detailed information; but there can be no question that many of the records, such as they are, date from the Heroic Age itself.

In this chapter we ought to speak not only of minstrelsy, such as is intended for entertainment in some form or other, but also of the more or less casual recitation or singing of poetry, with or without musical accompaniment—and likewise of 'celebration' poetry, including elegies or dirges. Nearly all the information, however, which is accessible to us, comes under the first head; and we will begin with this.

English travellers and residents in Yugoslavia seldom seem to have interested themselves in this subject; but we have met with a few references which are perhaps worth noticing. Sir J. Gardiner Wilkinson, the famous Egyptologist, visited Bishop Peter II at Cetinje in 1839, at a time when heroic conditions there were still unimpaired. Smail Aga had not yet been killed, and many more of the poems discussed above were not yet composed. In his book *Dalmatia and Montenegro* (1848), Vol. I, p. 440, he says with reference to the music: "This instrument (*gúsla*)[1] is remarkable from having only one string, which is stretched over a long neck and narrow body covered with parchment; its general shape being rather like a guitar. It is played with a bow. The sound is plaintive and monotonous; and it is principally used as an accompaniment to the voice; the performer singing the glorious wars of Montenegrin and Servian heroes; of Tzerni George and Milosh Obrenovich; of Tzernoievich and Milosh Obilich; or of the far famed Scander-beg under whom their ancestors fought against the Turks.

It is interesting to see a custom of old times still retained while the deeds it celebrates are of daily occurrence; in other countries the bards and the subjects of their songs belong only to history and tradition, but in Montenegro they are both realities of the present day. There is not, however, any class of people who can properly be styled bards; the sturdiest warrior is in the habit of accompanying the gúsla; and the effect of the song is increased by the well known character of the performer."

Again, speaking of his visit to the Archimandrite at Ostrog (*ib.* p. 533), he says: "After dinner it was proposed that I should hear their gúsla or Slavonic violin and some of the songs of their bards; which on a frontier constantly resounding with the din of arms, are hailed with delight by every Montenegrin....I was glad to have the opportunity of witnessing the stirring effect produced by these songs. The subjects related to their contests with their enemies, the vain hopes of the Turks to subdue their country, and the glorious victories obtained over them both by themselves and the heroes of Servia; in some of which the armed bard may have had his share of glory. For like Taillefer, the minstrel of William the Conqueror, these men are warriors; and no one would venture to sing of deeds he could not emulate....The enthusiasm of the performer compensated for the monotony of the one-stringed instrument.

Pópé Yovan...returned during the performance; probably in time to hear some of his own exploits, recorded in the national songs of his countrymen."

This passage describes the entertainment provided in a monastery. An interesting account of the way in which an ordinary Montenegrin household used to spend its evenings—at a somewhat later date—is given by Denton, *Montenegro* (1877), p. 115 f. The men would tell

---

[1] The true form is *gusle*; cf. p. 303, note. An elaborately decorated specimen is described by Low, *The Ballads of Marko Kraljević*, p. xxxvi.

stories of the adventures they had experienced in battle, the older ones under the Vladika, the younger under Mirko. Then people returning from the market at Cattaro would arrive and tell the news, especially anything from Western Europe which was likely to affect them. Then other neighbours would drop in; the gusle was brought out, and lays sung about Ivan Beg, Miloš Obilić, and others. After this "songs of domestic love, of the deeds of the Hayduks, or weird lays of the Vila of the mountains, fill up the evening".

Sir A. J. Evans, *Through Bosnia and the Herzegovina* (1877), p. 136 ff., gives an account of a Catholic festival, at which he was present, on a mountain near Komušina. He says there was much music, both instrumental and vocal. One minstrel was entertaining an audience of girls. Then he saw "a larger gathering, forming a spacious ring lit up by a blazing fire, in the middle of which a Bosniac bard took his seat on a rough log". He tunes his gusle, and then "rolled out the ballad for hour after hour" until nearly sunrise.

If this recitation consisted of a single poem, it must have been of unusual length. Recitations of Mohammedan poems are said often to last all night; but Christian poems are seldom so long.

According to Wyon, *The Land of the Black Mountain*, p. 39, guslars are invariably blind. He adds: "their singing is execrable according to Western notions, a range of four or five notes in a wailing minor key making up their register". At the same time he points out that they are the history books of the country, and notes the importance of their songs.

By 'guslars' the author seems to mean those who are dependent upon minstrelsy for their living. Low, *The Ballads of Marko Kraljević*, p. xxvi, says that (in Serbia) the guslar is often blind. But he adds that there are now very few of these people; he had only met with three in the course of four years. There can be no doubt that somewhat before Wyon's time minstrelsy was a more or less general accomplishment in Montenegro. But probably no one could ever afford to devote his time exclusively to it, except those who were dependent upon charity. In Bosnia and Hercegovina the case may have been different, as will be seen later.

For these two provinces we have fuller and more precise information, especially from the investigations of Prof. M. Murko.[1] From his papers

---

[1] Cf. Murko, *Zeitschr. d. Vereins f. Volkskunde* (Berlin), 1909, p. 13 ff.; *Sitzungsberichte d. k. k. Akademie in Wien*, Bd. 176 (1914–15); also in *Travaux publiés par l'Institut d'études slaves*, No. x (Paris, 1929)—but this last has not been accessible to us.

and other sources we will attempt to give a summary account of the form of minstrelsy which prevailed there in the early years of this century.

1. Improvisation and memorisation. The minstrel depends more upon improvisation than upon memory. He need hear a poem only two or three times in order to reproduce it; but the reproduction is by no means given in the same words. To a certain extent every minstrel is a more or less creative poet. But a poem is never repeated in exactly the same words even by the same man; and in the course of years changes may be introduced which apparently render it almost unrecognisable. Cases are known of minstrels who have doubled and even trebled the length of poems which they had heard. It will be seen that these observations fully explain the existence of such variants as we noticed in the last chapter.

2. Speed of recitation. A good minstrel recites at a speed varying from 13 to 28 lines per minute. The normal rate is 16–20 lines. A good minstrel can keep this up for an hour, rarely up to an hour and a half; in long recitations a man usually wants a rest every half-hour.

3. Length of poems. Christian poems usually take not more than an hour to recite; but examples occur which run to as much as four and, according to report, even six hours. Mohammedan poems are as a rule longer; not seldom they take 3–5 hours and sometimes even a whole night.

4. Extent of repertoire. Some Mohammedan minstrels have a repertoire of as many as seventy or eighty poems. One Orthodox Christian could produce a poem every evening for three months, and claimed to have enough for a year. The most famous Mohammedan minstrel is said to have known over three hundred poems.

5. Old and new poems. Mohammedans prefer old poems, relating to times long past.[1] New poems, relating to recent times, are not unknown; but they are not popular, and often they are soon forgotten. Sometimes they were composed immediately after the events they celebrate. An elegy upon Smail Aga was composed by his standard-bearer while he was on his way home after the disaster. Christians generally prefer poems relating to recent times.

6. Occasions of recitation. Festivals and social gatherings, such as weddings, give minstrels their best openings. Some *Bezi* (Begs) have

[1] We understand that in the latest article this distinction—as between Mohammedan and Christian poems—is not fully maintained. Mohammedan poems relating to recent events have proved to be more common than was thought formerly.

minstrels to entertain them every evening, sometimes until daybreak, and even when they are quite alone. One Beg took a minstrel with him when he went to visit the spa of Rohitsch-Sauerbrunn in Styria, in 1913. Another is known to have had as many as six minstrels. We gather from Krauss' *Slavische Volkforschungen* and other accounts that it was possible thirty or forty years ago for visitors to get minstrels to recite to them for a small remuneration. But the general cultivation of minstrelsy as a regular amusement for every evening, such as we hear of in earlier accounts of Montenegro, seems by this time to have become a thing of the past.

7. Professional minstrelsy. Some of the minstrels who were in the service of Begs seem to have virtually become professionals. Apart from such service the rewards to be obtained now are so small that no one takes it up for a living, unless he is driven by destitution to earn anything he can—though in the past minstrels are said to have received handsome presents of horses, cattle, etc. Blind minstrels are said to be very rare. The majority of those who practise minstrelsy are shepherds and farm workers; but others are drawn from all classes, even the highest. Begs sometimes compete with one another in friendly contests.

8. Derivation of poems. Mohammedan minstrels can usually give the names of those from whom they have learned their poems, though occasionally they get them from wandering minstrels. Christian minstrels as a rule cannot give such information, unless they have learned them in their own homes. Murko mentions the case of a Catholic household where the father and three sons were all minstrels.

9. Written texts. Occasionally one hears of written collections of poems. Murko cites the case of a soldier who is said to have had one written in Turkish characters about 1875. But reading must have been a rare accomplishment at that time. In general the poems were first written down by Austrian and Croatian scholars in the late 'eighties.

10. Commercialising of poems. By the time when Murko wrote, oral tradition among the Orthodox Christians had largely been displaced by printed books of poems, owing to the enterprise of a printer in Nikšić. In the Montenegrin army there was a regular organisation of minstrels under a *kapetan od guslara*, or 'chief of the minstrels'. These men composed their poems collectively and sent them to the printer, who in his turn, apparently after some revision, supplied them with printed copies. Some kind of organisation seems to have been in existence as far back as the war of 1876; for Murko records the case of a man who in that year was visited by two representatives and told that

he could have his name brought into a poem—presumably as a hero—on payment of two plete, i.e. forty kreuzer, or about eightpence. The printer, however, can hardly have been established by this time; for Nikšić then belonged to Turkey.

In the poems themselves references to minstrelsy of entertainment seem to be extremely rare. Occasionally, however, we hear of heroes amusing themselves or passing the time with minstrelsy. An instance occurs in the story of Ibro Nukić (cf. p. 329), where the hero spends his wedding night singing to the tambura. So in Bogišić, No. 91, when Alil Aga wishes to wake Marko Kraljević, the only way in which he dares to do so is by playing the tambura. Singing is not mentioned in this case; but Marko seems to be sleeping with the instrument under his head.

Ženske pjesme (cf. p. 306) are said to be sung largely by women, without accompaniment, when they are amusing themselves or busy about their work. Men also used to sing much, especially shepherds out upon the hills. We hear of the improvisation of poetry even when fighting is in progress. An interesting case occurs in Karadžić, v. No. 3. 1379 ff., in the fighting at the monastery during the invasion of Omer Pasha, in 1852. Novica Cerović calls Mirko's attention to Savo Martinović, who is continually singing and at the same time firing with great effect: "He is singing of the illustrious prince and of the Serdar Milan, his relative, and of Djuro, his standard-bearer, and the rest of the comrades from Cetinje. Savo sings with the full force of his lungs, and cheers the rest of our company."

A large amount of singing takes place at weddings and other social functions. At weddings the ceremonies extend over several days;[1] and there seem to be appropriate songs for the various stages, though we do not know how far the words of these are fixed, or improvised. In Karadžić, v. No. 9. 968 ff., when the prince's bridal procession is making its way down to Kotor to meet the bride, two of his officers, Savo Ivanović and Savo Martinović, sing songs of rejoicing, which are evidently either improvised or composed for the occasion.

The poem on Prince Danilo's funeral (ib. v. No. 18), noticed on p. 335 f. above, seems to be typical of the poetry used on such occasions. The first two speeches are dirges, pronounced by the prince's widow and his sister-in-law; and these are in a special metre—lines of twelve syllables which should perhaps properly be regarded as couplets, of eight and four syllables. The same metre seems to be used in timeless

[1] A short account of them is given by Eisner, Volkslieder der Slawen, p. 528 f.

nameless dirges by female relatives,[1] and may be in general use for such occasions. We have not seen any other account of a funeral; but Wyon (*The Land of the Black Mountain*, p. 85) describes the singing of a somewhat similar dirge some time—apparently some months—after the funeral. He visited the widow of the Vojvoda Marko Drekalović in 1901 or 1902; and while he was there he saw four women, weeping and dishevelled, kneel down at the side of the grave. They sang, one at a time, extempore verses about the hero's life and deeds. One began as follows:

"Oh, thou grey falcon, who was so mighty a hunter as thou?
Who indeed shall now wield they bloodstained sword?
Oh, thou wolf, who is worthy to take thy place as our ruler and father?"

She went on until she was exhausted, while the rest were wailing, beating their breasts and tearing their hair. Then one of the others took her turn. It is not stated who these women were. The widow herself was not one of them, though she was present.

Hardly anything has been said above with regard to the authors of *narodne pjesme*, for the reason that they are very seldom known. It would seem that if a poem proved attractive enough to be taken over by other minstrels—for there was evidently no feeling for anything in the nature of copyright—the name of the original poet was very soon forgotten. Vol. v of Karadžić's collection covers the period from 1851 to 1861 and was published in 1865; yet out of the eighteen poems which it contains the origin of no less than six seems to have been unknown to him.

In a society where improvisation was so highly developed it might perhaps be expected that every minstrel was also an author, i.e. that he originated works of his own composition. But we are not clear that this is true;[2] at all events it is not suggested by any of the authorities we have

---

[1] Examples are given (in transl.) by Eisner, *op. cit.* p. 416 ff., where they are printed in couplets. The second of these dirges seems to be that of a mother.

[2] Jagić, *Arch. f. slav. Philologie*, IV. 236, quotes a very interesting statement by Joksim Nović, who lived in the middle of last century. The best reciter known to Nović was a certain Jovan of Gacko, who recited for Bishop Peter II. He had a hundred poems in his repertoire; but he would not allow that he had himself composed a single poem. "He disclaimed this faculty altogether, as almost all other reciters do, probably because he feared that a poem of his would not be received as favourably as if it were declared to come from 'our best and oldest' poets." Nović's explanation seems to be a conjecture of his own. Is it not possible that the minstrels were telling the simple truth?

read. We hear occasionally of minstrels who composed original poems. An interesting case is recorded by Karadžić.[1] He obtained several poems from a minstrel named Andželko Vuković, who came from Kosovo but had had to leave his home because he had killed a retired Turkish soldier. Once, when this man was travelling with Karadžić, the idea occurred to him of treating his adventure in a poem. He did so, and dictated it to a tradesman in Belgrade, who subsequently gave it to Karadžić. The poem is a purely imaginative work. The Turk is transformed into a mighty hero and robber, who has destroyed the peace of the country. Andželko, who goes to seek him in response to an appeal from the Pasha, appears as a kind of Marko Kraljević. They charge each other on horseback with spear and sword, before they use their pistols. The type of poem which the author took as his model seems to have been that of the earlier *hajduci* (cf. p. 325 ff.), rather than that of his own day. Perhaps he thought this would appeal more to Karadžić.

As regards the normal heroic poetry of the nineteenth century, it has been mentioned above that the origin of only twelve of the eighteen poems contained in Karadžić's fifth volume is known. Of these five are attributed to the Kapetan Savo Martinović and six to the Serdar Djuko Srdanović. Both these men were officers in high position at Cetinje.

Savo Martinović, in addition to his own poems, supplied Karadžić with several of those which are published in his fourth volume. He refers to himself fairly often in his poems; and he also figures as a hero in some of the anonymous poems, especially No. 3, the long poem which comes from Hercegovina. Here he is one of the defenders of the upper monastery at Ostrog and cheers his companions with his poetry, while he is fighting (cf. p. 439). He appears again as a poet in No. 9, the anonymous poem on Prince Danilo's marriage (*ib.*); his poem on this occasion is given in 9. 977 ff. According to No. 1, one of his own poems, he was one of the first people to attach himself to Danilo's cause, when the latter—whose claim was disputed—first arrived at Cetinje. At some later date, however, he left Montenegro; and in 1863 he was living at Zara.

Djuko Srdanović likewise supplied Karadžić with one of the poems contained in Vol. IV. But he seems seldom to be mentioned in poems himself. He refers to himself in one of his own poems, Vol. v, No. 5 (188 ff.)—a poem on Omer Pasha's invasion—where the prince tells

---

[1] We are indebted both for the story and the poem itself (in transl.) to Gesemann, *Stud. ʒ. südslav. Volksepik*, p. 85 ff.

him to bring into action the big cannon which his uncle had obtained from England. From the Preface to Vol. IV we learn that in 1862 he was chamberlain to the court of Prince Nikola.

This evidence, so far as it goes, suggests that the heroic poems composed about the middle of last century were largely the work of men of high rank. We have no further information;[1] but it is certainly a remarkable fact—and surely unparalleled in any other country in Europe —that three of the last four rulers of Montenegro, Bishops Peter I [2] and Peter II and King Nikola, were famous poets. We do not know whether Prince Danilo was a poet; but his brother, the Vojvoda Mirko (King Nikola's father), published a volume of poems, apparently heroic poems, which ran to a second edition in 1864.[3] The Vojvoda Marko Drekalović, who died c. 1901 (cf. p. 440), is also said to have been a poet.[4] Whatever may have been the nature of these poems, such a record as this is inexplicable, unless poetry was generally cultivated in the highest circles.

Thus far we have confined our attention to modern times. The evidence available for earlier times, whether from the poems themselves or from other records, is of course far less full and precise; but it is not entirely wanting for the *bugarštice*.[5]

In one of the Zagreb MSS. there is a very short poem (Bogišić, No. 84), containing only sixteen lines, alternately short and long, in the form of an address to the master of a house (Type D). It consists wholly of expressions of good wishes for his welfare and happiness and that of his

---

[1] The only other author recorded in Karadžić's fifth volume is Filip Srdanov, of whom we know nothing.

[2] It was suggested by Soerensen, *Arch. f. slav. Philol.* xx. 106 ff., that this bishop (St Peter) was the creator of modern Montenegrin heroic poetry. If it is true (*ib.* note) that he was fond of singing to the *gusle*, he may very well have influenced it, e.g. in its interest in the past and in external affairs. But if he had 'created' it, Karadžić, who was at work during his reign, would have been aware of the fact. Karadžić himself suspected the bishop of being the author of only two of the poems published by him (cf. p. 427, note).

[3] *Junacke Spomenek od Velekoga Vojvode Merka Petrovic*, Cetinje, 1864. We have not seen this work and owe the reference to Denton, *Montenegro*, p. 156.

[4] Wyon, *The Land of the Black Mountain*, p. 83.

[5] The origin of decasyllabic poems relating to early times is in general doubtless untraceable. It is worth noting, however, that there are said to be minstrels who specialise in legends of Serbian saints and churches (cf. Krauss, *Slavische Volkforschungen*, p. 186 f.). We suspect that such poems are as a rule derived ultimately from priestly circles.

friends. The person addressed seems to be a priest;[1] for he is called *Pope Gospodaru* ('Master Priest'). The occasion is evidently some domestic celebration, since he is wearing flowers on his head. There are other persons present, whom the poet addresses as 'proud heroes', with the wish that God may keep them in health. The poem concludes as follows: "Happy be all ye who are gathered around, may great God give you happiness. Dear gentlemen! the song is in your honour; health and happiness to us."

We think this short piece was probably composed as an epilogue to a recitation of poetry by a minstrel (or reciter). In the other Zagreb MS. one heroic poem (Bogišić, No. 5) ends with the words: "Happy be all ye who are gathered around, may great God give you happiness", while another poem (*ib*. No. 52) in the same MS. concludes as follows: "And now, gentlemen, the poem is in your honour. Dear gentlemen, the poem is in your honour; health and happiness to us." Modern Montenegrin poems not unfrequently end with somewhat similar expressions, e.g. Karadžić, IV. 43: "This poem is for all Serbians; the poem from me, from God health to you"; and *ib*. 47 (after the death of a hero: "May God grant him an abode in Paradise, and to us, brothers, health and happiness." We may also perhaps quote here another ending, which occurs, with slight variants, in three poems in the first Zagreb collection (Bogišić, Nos. 7, 11, 50): "This happened then (or 'once'), and now I call it to mind, my God who knowest (all)! Do thou, O God, also be mindful of my good health."

Certain *bugarštice* in the Perast collection have endings of a somewhat different character, which give the impression of having been composed for larger gatherings. One poem (Bogišić, No. 59) ends thus: "This was accomplished by the frontiermen and warriors, the good frontiermen (i.e. the local warriors of the past). Good health and happiness to the heroes of today!" In another (*ib*. No. 63) we find: "What was done by the men of old we call to mind as an example to heroes. But strike, ye heroes, as each is best able." This looks as if it was intended for recitation before a battle, though it may be of general reference. In any case the appeal is to local patriotism, as throughout this group of poems.

The endings of the two poems obtained by Hektorović from fishermen in the island of Hvar in 1556 and published by him (cf. p. 300) bring us back to the milieu of No. 84. One (Bogišić, No. 6) ends as follows:

---

[1] Possibly, however, two persons are addressed—first the master of the house, and then a priest who is present. Is the word *pop* applied to a Catholic priest?

"Happy be thou, master, and happy thy household, our master. May this poem be an honour to thy generosity." In the other (*ib.* No. 49) we find: "Now and for ever good luck be with thee, our master." The last line, which we cannot translate, seems to express a wish for health and happiness in our home. It is not made clear who 'our master' is in either poem. Hektorović's work is not accessible to us; and we do not know whether the phrase was applied to himself, as a term of respect, or to some nobleman or landowner, in whose service the fishermen were.

From the passages noticed above it is clear enough that the *bugarštice* —or at least many of them, which are drawn from various collections— were intended for recitation; and that the recitation took place sometimes on more or less private occasions, in the presence of some important person who is addressed as 'master', sometimes perhaps at larger gatherings. Unfortunately the amount of evidence available from external sources seems to be very limited. Only a few writers of the sixteenth and seventeenth centuries refer to heroic poetry—the earliest relating to the year 1531—and what they say is very brief. So far as they go, however, their statements are in full accord with the evidence of the poems.

The most important notices are the following.[1] Jurij Križanić, who wrote c. 1660, says that in his youth there survived among the Croatians and Serbians what he regarded as the imitation of a Roman custom, namely that soldiers stood behind the nobles and warriors at banquets and sang of the deeds of their ancestors and the glory of Marko Kraljević, Novak Debeljak, Miloš Kobilić, and some other heroes. Much earlier, in 1547, we hear of a blind soldier, who was conducted by his daughter, singing a song of Marko Kraljević at Splijt (Spalato), apparently to a large crowd, who accompanied him.

Taken as a whole the early evidence seems to indicate that poetry of this kind was cultivated in the sixteenth and following centuries very much in the same way as in recent times. Only one important element is lacking; we hear nothing of an instrumental accompaniment either in the poems or in the other records. The silence of the former counts of course for little or nothing; for references to such accompaniment even in modern poems are extremely rare. But we should have expected to hear something of it from Hektorović, if it was used by his fishermen, and

[1] The information given in this paragraph is derived from Murko, *Geschichte d. älteren südslawischen Litteraturen*, p. 204 f. (cf. *Arch. f. slav. Philol.* xxviii. 378). We regret that we cannot give references to the original authorities.

also in such references as those noted in the last paragraph. One cannot conclude with any confidence that instrumental accompaniment was unknown in these times—the amount of evidence is far too slight—but it would seem not to have been in universal, perhaps not even in general use. On the other hand the *gusle* does not look like a modern invention; and it is an instrument of the kind which is generally used elsewhere as an accompaniment to the voice.

The minstrels or reciters were perhaps as a rule men of more or less humble position, though we have no definite evidence except for Hektorović's fishermen. The address to the master of the house in Bogišić, No. 84, and the ending of *ib.* No. 52 (cf. p. 442 f.) rather suggest men, not necessarily professionals, who went to the houses of the rich to entertain for a consideration. The soldier who recited at Splijt in 1547 was blind. On the other hand the 'soldiers' who recited at banquets in Križanić's time were probably members of the military retinues of the noblemen whom they were entertaining. It is to be observed that practically all our notices except this last come from Dalmatia, where the upper classes generally cultivated Italian fashions and even spoke Italian to a considerable extent. The scope for the cultivation of traditional poetry was therefore limited.

On the question of authorship no evidence seems to be available; at all events the poems contained in Bogišic's collection are apparently all anonymous. We suspect that one of the *bugarštice* from Perast (No. 65) is the work of a priest, chiefly because of the strong religious (anti-Islamic) sentiments which it expresses towards the end; but it also describes the Venetian forces and their movements in a way which suggests an educated mind. One or two other poems may be of similar origin. But such cases seem to be exceptional.

There can be no doubt that most of the *bugarštice*—indeed we may say the *bugarštice* as a class—are to be regarded as *narodne pjesme*. This is shown not merely by the universal anonymity and by the endings of poems discussed above, which, it must be remembered, are found in various collections. Far more important is the prevalence of variants. Some *bugarštice* are variants of others (cf. p. 318); many more are variants of poems found in later collections. Indeed a large proportion of the themes treated in *bugarštice* belong to the traditional stock of *narodne pjesme*. Moreover the later variants often preserve features which are lost or obscured in the *bugarštice*. Instances will be found on pp. 385 f., 421 f.

It must not be assumed of course that all the *bugarštice* preserved in the various collections which we have noticed are derived from oral tradition. Bogišić himself (Introd. p. 2) believed that three of the poems preserved in the larger Zagreb MS. (Nos. 58, 77, 81) were of literary origin; and there may be more of such, though we are not convinced that this is the case. The poems which one is most tempted to suspect on internal grounds are the two recorded by Hektorović, owing to their careful and polished diction. Yet Hektorović's statements seem to be explicit enough. If he really composed or tampered with the poems himself, he deliberately misled his readers. He even indicates the tunes to which the poems were chanted.

Something more should perhaps be said about the *bugarštice* preserved in the Franciscan (Ragusa) MS., especially the collection supplied by Jodzo Betondić (cf. p. 422, note). This man, who died in 1764, was a Latin scholar and is described in the MS. as a 'distinguished Slavonic poet'.[1] We may therefore be inclined to regard his contributions with some suspicion. But this does not seem to be borne out by an examination of the poems. One poem from his collection (Bogišić, No. 9) is a variant of a poem (*ib.* No. 26) from one of the other collections in the same MS.; and the differences between the two are such as occur usually in variant versions of *narodne pjesme*. Both poems have been noticed above (p. 317 f.). The only special feature which we have observed in Betondić's collection is that one poem (*ib.* No. 1) covers the ground of three poems in Karadžić's collection, one after the other, as was noted on p. 421 f. above. The last part of this poem, describing the battle of Kosovo and the deaths of Murad, Lazar and Miloš, has no true parallel elsewhere among *narodne pjesme*, so far as we know. But it is in general very similar to the description of the same events given by Orbini (cf. p. 382). Orbini, it is true, might have got his account of the battle from historical sources; but the decisive point is the following. The last part of this poem is obviously connected with another poem in Betondić's collection, omitted by Bogišić but described on p. 315 above, which is concerned with a quarrel between Lazar's daughters. This story also is given, with slight variations, by Orbini: but it is clearly of imaginative (poetic) origin. It would seem then that some poem similar to Betondić's was in existence before 1601 (the date of Orbini's work), i.e. about a century and a half before Betondić's time. We may add here that we have not observed any noticeable differences in diction between

---

[1] *Vrijedni Slovinski spjevalac.* We do not know exactly what the last word means. He translated Ovid's *Heroides.* Cf. Bogišić, Introd. pp. 129, 133.

Betondić's poems and other *bugarštice*. Repetitions abound. In the first twenty-four lines of Bogišić, No. 1, seven lines are repeated (with slight variations), and four of these again a third time. This is hardly the way in which a literary poet would compose. Betondić may of course have been versed in oral poetry and in the traditional manner of treating it. But in this case his treatment of the poems in his repertoire need not be regarded as different from that of an ordinary reciter. On the other hand the poems may have been written down before they came to him; and in view of his date this is what we are inclined to think.

Almost all the *bugarštice*, including all the large collections, come from the Dalmatian coast; and consequently it is not surprising that they show features characteristic of that region, e.g. the use of Italian words in their vocabulary. The occurrence of the Romance name *Oliver*, borne by a minor character in Bogišić, No. 1, may doubtless be ascribed to the same Italian influence. Other features of the same kind are probably not rare. Is it possible that the Vila who carries a palm in her hand in Bogišić, No. 29, has been influenced by some figure of an angel, or perhaps some allegorical figure, seen in one of the coast cities?

But the *bugarštice* also show features which do not properly belong to the coast. It has been pointed out by several scholars that the religious milieu of the heroic *bugarštice* is that of the Orthodox Church.[1] Two poems in particular have attracted attention, Bogišić, Nos. 12 and 22, in which King Matthias and his father Janko (John Hunyadi) are represented as Orthodox. Why should well-known Catholic princes be represented as Orthodox in the poetry of Catholic cities? Clearly such poems must be derived from the Orthodox districts of the interior.

This consideration throws light upon another important fact, which likewise was pointed out long ago. The narrative *bugarštice* fall chronologically into two groups. The poems of the first group, almost all of which are heroic, relate to the fourteenth and fifteenth centuries, while those of the second, most of which are 'post-heroic', relate to the sixteenth and seventeenth, though the first half of the sixteenth century seems to be blank. The fact to which we would call attention is that the first group, with the exception of one post-heroic poem (Bogišić, No. 76; cf. p. 353), relate wholly to the interior, especially Serbia and Hungary, whereas the second group are almost entirely concerned with the

---

[1] Orthodox features seem to be sometimes omitted, as in Bogišić, No. 1, as compared with Karadžić, II. No. 47 (cf. p. 422). But we have not noticed any specifically Catholic features.

Adriatic coast. The inference again seems clear enough: the early history of this poetry is to be sought in the interior.

The part played in the poems by Hungarian heroes deserves special attention. A considerable part of Dalmatia had at one time been under Hungarian rule. But the poems preserve no remembrance of this period. Their interest in Hungary, or rather in Hungarian heroes, begins c. 1440 and continues not more than half a century. During this time, or at least the first half of it the Hungarian element is even more prominent than the Serbian, and the sympathy is with the Hungarian Janko as against the Serbian ruler Despot Djuro. The Serbian element dates back to an earlier time than the Hungarian, viz. to 1389 or a little earlier. But both elements cease about the same time; the latest event which we can date is the death of 'Fiery' Vuk (cf. p. 324), in 1485. There is no mention of the fall of Belgrade, in 1521; and though there are one or two hazy references to the fall of Buda, in 1526, no Hungarian king or hero is mentioned after Matthias, who died in 1490.

It should be observed that Hungarian and Serbian princes and heroes, Janko and Djuro, Matthias and Vuk, frequently figure in the same poems. In one poem (cf. p. 317) Janko is said to be a son of the (Serbian) prince Stjepan Lazarević. No consciousness of a feeling of nationality is ever expressed. Indeed the name 'Serbian' never occurs. In one poem (Bogišić, No. 1) the Serbian leaders seem to be called Hungarians (cf. p. 366 f.). On the other hand the Hungarian leaders are represented as belonging to the Orthodox Church—which is incorrect.

From all this it is clear that the group of poems which we are discussing represents a body of poetic tradition extending down to c. 1490. This tradition must be regarded as essentially Orthodox and Serbian, though it has incorporated a large but recent Hungarian element; but national feeling is entirely wanting. The interest throughout is individual and aristocratic. A considerable proportion of the poems are occupied with marriages and the domestic relations of princesses. Indeed, in contrast to poems relating to modern times, a strong feminine interest is usually present. Several of the poems correspond to what we now call light literature. It may be added that variants of many of the poems are to be found in modern collections, together with other poems relating to the same period. These show in general the same characteristics, though neither the Hungarian element nor the feminine interest is so strongly represented, and from time to time national feeling makes itself felt. The lighter elements have mostly disappeared.

It is a natural inference that the heroic *bugarštice* represent the 'literature' current among the Orthodox aristocracy at the time of the Turkish conquest. In some cases indeed we are hardly dependent upon inferences for this date. We have seen that the poems cannot have originated among the 'Latins' on the coast. But it is clear that some of them must have been widely known in Dalmatia in the early part of the sixteenth century. Poems upon Marko Kraljević and upon Radosav had penetrated before 1556 as far as the island of Hvar where Hektorović obtained them in Serbian rhythm (*Srbski način*). A poem on the banquet before the battle of Kosovo, which can be traced clearly enough in Bogišić, No. 1, and still better in Karadžić, II. No. 50. iii, must have been current somewhere on the coast before 1500; for it was quoted about this time by the Italian translator of Ducas (cf. p. 341). This brings us back to the time of the Turkish conquest, the date which is indicated by the internal evidence of the poems themselves. It is believed that about this time, say between 1459 and 1490, many noble families fled to the coast from the interior. They may very well have brought the poems with them, though other means of transmission are of course not impossible.

The history of the *bugarštice* then would seem to present little difficulty. Yet curiously enough a theory has obtained some currency that they represent a new form of poetry which came into existence on the coast c. 1500 through Italian—ultimately French—or Spanish influence, and that before this time the Yugoslavs possessed no heroic poetry. The evidence for the latter proposition is of course negative; there are said to be no references to such poetry before that date. This is an argument which, we fear, is not likely to convince anyone who has made a study of Anglo-Saxon heroic poetry. The written literature current in the interior of Yugoslavia before 1550 was essentially an ecclesiastical literature; and such literature seldom takes note of heroic poetry. England possesses a very large body of ecclesiastical literature, both Latin and vernacular, dating from before the Norman conquest; but, so far as we know, it contains only one definite reference—in one of Alcuin's letters—to poetry of this kind. Even so voluminous a writer as Bede never mentions it. The silence of the authorities proves nothing more than that the scholars of the day were not interested in such poetry.

On the Adriatic coast it may be agreed that the heroic *bugarštice* were comparatively new, though they were known there before 1500. But the argument for this is to be found not so much in the silence of the records as in the internal evidence afforded by the poems themselves, which shows that they are not native to the coastland.

Apart from negative evidence, various arguments for foreign influence have been adduced.[1] Different scholars indeed have given different reasons. One has called attention to the fact that a MS. of the *Chançun de Williame* was once preserved at Ragusa, others to resemblances between various passages in *narodne pjesme* (or *bugarštice*) and *chansons de geste*. Another lays stress on the warfare against a Mohammedan power which forms the background of both the *narodne pjesme* (including the *bugarštice*) and the French and Spanish romances, though this of course rests on historical fact, not literary convention.

We fear we cannot attach much importance to these considerations. The positive evidence for any influence of this kind upon the *bugarštice* seems to amount to very little; and we venture to think that it would never have been suggested but for the prevailing tendency to look for literary influence everywhere.[2] It is true that Ragusa—and to some extent other Dalmatian cities also—shared the intellectual life of the Italian Renaissance, and also that they were in frequent touch with Spain and other western lands. But we do not see how these facts can explain the origin of the *bugarštice*. When a country which is more or less backward or isolated comes under the influence of cosmopolitan literature or of any literature more advanced than its own, the usual result is that the native literature is submerged. This is what has happened in Yugoslavia during the last century; and the same thing happened in the twelfth century not only in England, where the conditions were peculiar, but also in all Scandinavian countries except Iceland. We suspect that it happened also in Dalmatia, long before 1500. In all these cases a new literature, of alien affinities, came into existence. Sometimes, however, as in south Germany, the native literature is not wholly killed; we find a partial revival of it transformed under the influence of the new. In such cases the effects of the latter are obvious enough in language, metre and style, if not in subject matter, just as in the medieval German epics. How could foreign influence in Dalmatia produce a wholly new heroic poetry, dealing with Serbian and Hungarian, not native (Dalmatian) themes—yet without any obvious resemblance to its (foreign) sources?

We may repeat here that the poet Hektorović, who was a cultured literary man, describes the rhythm of his fishermen's poems as Serbian.[3]

[1] Cf. especially Banašević, *Rev. d. Ét. Sl.* vi. 224 ff.; Subotić, *Yugoslav Popular Ballads*, p. 101 ff.

[2] It would seem also that scholars interested in this poetry have usually been more familiar with romance literature than with the heroic poetry of other peoples.

[3] An ingenious, though by no means convincing, attempt to explain away this difficulty is made by Cancel, *Rev. des Études Slaves*, i. 237, where it is suggested that

This expression may perhaps mean that he did not consider them to be properly native in his island. But it cannot possibly mean that he recognised them to be of Italian or Spanish origin. Yet if the poetry originated c. 1500, as is contended, this should have been within his memory, for he was born in 1487. On the other hand Hektorović's description is in complete accord with the Orthodox features of the poems. We have mentioned above that we cannot see why Dalmatian Catholics ('Latins') should wish to represent the Hungarians as Orthodox. But if the poems were originally Serbian the difficulty disappears. There is no pronounced feeling for nationality, as we have seen, and the Hungarian characters are not thought of as acting differently from the rest.

It is only as characters in poems that the Hungarian heroes could be represented thus; if they had been introduced into the poems in Dalmatia, from memory or historical records, such a mistake could not have been made. Indeed there can be little doubt that practically the whole personnel of the heroic *bugarštice* were introduced into Dalmatia as 'characters'. Why should Dalmatian poets concern themselves with the feelings of Vladislav's sister or Sekula's mother or even Barbara, the wife of Fiery Vuk—feelings which evidently were of more interest than the issues of national struggles? These persons can have become known in Dalmatia only as 'heroines' or items in a literary legacy brought from the interior.

Regarding the character of the poetry current before the Turkish conquest we have no information, except what may be inferred from a comparison of the *bugarštice* with the poems found in later collections. The milieu is essentially aristocratic, as we have seen (p. 360 ff.), and there can be little doubt that the poems of the day circulated among this class. *Bugarštice* show what we should regard as an excessive love of ceremony. On the other hand modern poems relating to this period sometimes represent even princes as living the life of peasants.[1] This is probably the word *srbski* was confused with a word *sebar(ski)*, equivalent to *rusticus* or 'vulgar'. But the reference to a passage in Križanić's *Poliglotta* is of interest. Križanić distinguishes two variants of a poem which he has composed (both Serbian) as *sarbski* and *latinski* respectively. The first seems to be a *bugarštica*, the other a poem according to Latin prosody. Križanić's use of *sarbski* (*srbski*) apparently coincides with Hektorović's and may therefore represent the general use of cent. xvi and xvii. The derivation of *bugarštica* from Ital. *volgare* referred to in the same article (p. 239) need hardly be taken seriously.

[1] A good example is to be found in a poem publ. by Krauss, *Slavische Volkforschungen*, p. 333 f., in which Grgur, the father of Fiery Vuk, is represented as a peasant and building his own house (cf. p. 360, note).

to be explained by the fact that in many parts of the country the Christians were not familiar with any other form of life after the conquest. We have not found anything of the kind in *bugarštice*.

Was minstrelsy cultivated? We have seen that it is not mentioned in *bugarštice* or in early records which refer to the recitation of poetry. But almost all these records come from Dalmatia. It would seem that instrumental accompaniment was not customary in this region. But one would hardly be justified without further evidence in inferring the same for the interior. The loss of the accompaniment might be accounted for by the fact that Dalmatia was permeated by foreign influence. It is likely enough that the primitive instruments of the Slavs had been wholly displaced by more modern types, which may not have been thought suitable for this purpose. For the interior no records are available. It is clear, however, from philological evidence,[1] as well as from occasional historical references, that the use of stringed instruments was ancient and widespread among the Slavonic peoples; and though the form of these instruments differs between one land and another, and the Yugoslav instrument must have undergone some change, e.g. through the introduction of the bow, in the course of time, there seems to be no reason for doubting that its use has been continuous. We cannot prove of course that heroic poetry was accompanied in the fifteenth century or earlier; but in view of the general use of such accompaniment in later times and the widespread prevalence of the same custom in other lands, we think it would be unwise to deny its existence, merely from the absence of evidence.[2]

In the course of our discussion we have had occasion from time to time to notice that the poems contained in modern collections, especially that of Karadžić, not seldom show earlier features or a better text than *bugarštice* which are variants of them. This is remarkable not only owing to their more recent date but also because they must have undergone a change of metrical form in the course of their existence. The invariable decasyllabic line, with caesura always after the fourth syllable,

---

[1] The word *gusle* seems to occur—for various stringed instruments—in all Slavonic languages (Church Slav. *gǫsli*, etc.). It has also many cognates, e.g. the verb *gudjeti*, 'to fiddle', Ch. Slav. *gǫsti*, 'to play the harp', etc.

[2] Mijatovich, *Kossovo*, p. 42, refers to a 'Serbian tradition' that the two sons of Despot Gjorgje Branković, who had been blinded by order of Sultan Murad II, took up the profession of wandering minstrels, and travelled, *gusle* in hand, singing songs of the good old time. We have not been able to trace the authority for this statement, except for the fact that two of the Despot's sons were blinded by Murad (cf. Orbini, *Regno d. Slavi*, pp. 326, 331). The Despot (cf. p. 316 ff.) died in 1456.

seems not to have been finally fixed before the middle of the eighteenth century. Poems written down during the first half of that century almost always show more or less variation, both in the length of the line and in the position of the caesura (cf. p. 338 f.). It would appear that in earlier times the line was both longer and more irregular. Moreover we may note that the versions of the heroic poems preserved in the (irregular) decasyllabic line in the Ragusa MS. compare unfavourably with their variants in Karadžić's collection. Evidently then the poems were less well preserved in Dalmatia than in the interior, either in early or in later times. Presumably they were better known and more widely cultivated in the inland districts, where heroic poetry was still a living and creative art.

We have no direct information as to the metrical form or forms in use before the Turkish conquest. So far as we know, no texts of poems written or printed before 1700 have been found except from Dalmatia and Croatia; and here the *bugarštica* seems to have been in general use until near the end of the period. Since *bugarštice* show little variation in metre between one poem and another, except in the presence and distribution of short lines, and since the earliest examples—given by Hektorović—go back to 1556, i.e. within about three-quarters of a century of the conquest, it seems likely that this was the form in which the poems were brought into Dalmatia; and Hektorović's expression *Srbski način* (cf. p. 449 f.) points to the same conclusion. The relationship of this metre to the one which succeeded it is not altogether clear;[1] but there seems to be no doubt that the latter came into existence in the seventeenth century.

The view that the *bugarštica* was in use throughout Yugoslavia at the time of the conquest is now, we believe, generally held except by those scholars who derive it from the west. On the latter theory sufficient has been said above. We need add only that, in regard to metre, it derives no support from the irregularity in the length of the line and the absence of rhyme in the *bugarštica*. Other scholars, however, hold a totally different view, namely that it came into existence in the southern parts of the country during the fourteenth century, and gradually made its way northwards.[2] This theory obviously has much more in its favour than the other. It makes heroic poetry begin, not in a land barren of heroic traditions, like Dalmatia, but in the country of Marko Kraljević, and pass on from there to the scene of the Kosovo poems, thus accounting

---

[1] It seems to be thought that the decasyllabic line arose in Dalmatia out of a line of 11–12 syllables; but cf. p. 339.　　[2] Cf. Popović, *Yugoslov. Književnost*, p. 58.

YUGOSLAV ORAL POETRY

for the two chief cycles of heroic story. Moreover it may help to explain the obscure terms *bugarštica* and (*pjesan*) *bugarska* (cf. p. 305). The latter can hardly mean anything else than 'Bulgarian poem', and the former is probably to be connected with the same name.[1]

We are inclined to be sceptical of any theory which would trace the heroic poetry of the Yugoslavs to a foreign origin; for they are a people who from all that is known of their early history might be expected to have cultivated such poetry for centuries. On the other hand it would doubtless be less difficult to borrow from a language like Bulgarian—which can hardly have differed appreciably from Yugoslav in the fourteenth century—than from an alien language like Italian. The true explanation may be, not that heroic poetry was new, but that innovations were introduced from this quarter. These innovations may have had to do with metre; the earlier Yugoslav poetry may have been more like Russian *byliny* in this respect. Any such innovations would presumably be connected with music in some way; and in this, as in other respects, the Bulgarians, owing to their geographical position, might be expected to be the first of the Slavonic peoples to feel the effect of foreign (Greek) influence. But it must be understood that we give these suggestions only for what they are worth; they are conjectures, and nothing more. So far as we are aware, nothing is known of medieval Bulgarian poetry, except such as is of a learned character. It seems to us clear that the Yugoslavs had already a flourishing heroic poetry at the end of the fourteenth century. This poetry preserves vivid memories of the battle of Kosovo in 1389; and it may be said to reach back to the death of Vukašin in 1371. But it has only hazy recollections of the time of Dušan, who died in 1356. Some change or new movement therefore may have taken place about this time.

Beyond this point we do not feel inclined to express any definite opinion. In practically all the works which we have consulted the origin of Yugoslav heroic poetry is treated as a purely Yugoslav question; but this cannot be correct.[2] The cultivation of heroic poetry seems to be by no means so widespread as that of 'women's songs' (folksongs) in this part of Europe; but it is not limited to Yugoslavia. It is found in a part at least—apparently the western part—of Bulgaria, in Greece, Albania

---

[1] These explanations have been current more than half a century; cf. Jagić, *Arch. f. slav. Philologie*, IV. 241 f.

[2] The necessity for comparative study of the oral poetry of the various peoples of the Balkans is pointed out by Gaster, *Slav. Rev.* XII. 173 ff. Unfortunately he does not distinguish between the different genres.

and Slovenia. On the other hand we are not aware that there is any evidence for the existence of Hungarian, Rumanian[1] or (Balkan) Turkish heroic poetry. But this may be due, in one case or another, to the defectiveness of our knowledge. What we wish to emphasise is that the question needs to be treated by someone who has fuller information of the facts. Account is also to be taken of the widespread cultivation of heroic poetry in Russia and of its absence in Italy.

No Bulgarian or Slovenian heroic poems have been accessible to us. We understand that they are known only from recent times, and that the former deal in part with heroes who are celebrated also in Yugoslav heroic poetry, at all events with Marko Kraljević and with Novak and his family. But we do not know whether the stories related of these heroes are the same as in Yugoslav poetry; neither have we any information as to the form and metre of the poems. There are said to be Slovenian poems relating to King Matthias and other Hungarian heroes of the fifteenth century; and indeed early references to the existence of such poems are known. But we are under the impression, rightly or wrongly, that the form and metre of these poems is under western influence.

With respect to Albanian heroic poetry we have derived some interesting information from Lambertz's *Volkspoesie der Albaner*. This poetry shows in many respects a close resemblance to Yugoslav heroic poetry. The poems cover practically the same period—at all events from the fifteenth century to the present time. The examples of early stories which are actually described give the impression of 'timeless, nameless' stories which have (secondarily) acquired names, rather than of historical stories; but in some districts there are said to be poems relating to Scanderberg, who died in 1468. More interesting is the account (p. 19 ff.) of the poems which celebrate more recent events— as late as the Balkan War of 1912—and which are doubtless of historical origin. They have much in common with their Yugoslav counterparts, though perhaps more with the poems relating to the Hajduci (cf. p. 325 ff.) of the seventeenth and eighteenth centuries than with more recent Montenegrin poems. They seem to be concerned with individual and family feuds far more than with fighting on a larger scale. Here also imaginative (unhistorical) elements are prominent. Heads speak after they have been cut off; and there is a supernatural being, the Sana, who is introduced not unfrequently. She is said to have something in com-

[1] We gather from Gaster, *ib.* p. 178 ff., that the themes of some Rumanian 'ballads' are derived from Bulgarian (or Yugoslav) heroic stories.

mon with the Vila; but she has also the interesting characteristic, apparently wanting to the latter, that she is the inspirer of poetry. The poems are regularly accompanied by a one-stringed instrument called *lahuta*, which is said to be similar to the *gusle*.

On the other hand there are evidently some striking differences between Albanian and Yugoslav poetry. The metres are different; and rhyme is universal, though it extends beyond pairs of lines. From the descriptions given it would seem that the poems are usually much shorter, though there are said to be poems which take an hour to sing. The sequence of events too is not described in so clear and orderly a manner, so that, unless one is familiar with the story, it is sometimes difficult to follow the action or to know who is speaking. In all these characteristics Albanian poetry seems to resemble Greek heroic poetry of the same period, rather than Yugoslav.

The history of Teutonic heroic poetry should make us hesitate to deny the existence of such poetry in times for which no evidence is available. This poetry has much to say about heroes who lived in the fourth, fifth and sixth centuries. One or two names go back to the third century; but they are hardly more than names. Yet a passage in Tacitus's *Annals* (ii. 88) shows that heroic poetry was cultivated in Germany even in the first century, though no trace of such poems has been preserved elsewhere. Among the Yugoslavs, as among the Teutonic peoples, the popularity of later poems may have brought about the extinction of the older. At all events we see no reason for supposing that heroic poetry was a new creation of the fourteenth century. The Yugoslav poetry, like the Russian, is typically representative of a class of oral literature which can be traced from England to the Altai.

NOTE. In a series of articles[1] published in *Revue des Courses et Conférences*, 1932, of which unfortunately we had not heard until this volume was in print, Prof. A. Vaillant has pointed out (p. 432) that references to Yugoslav heroic poets occur as early as 1415 in Polish records, and probably also in a Greek record dating from 1328. He thinks (p. 443 f.) that the *bugarštica* came from the south (as on p. 453 f., above), and that it was derived from Greek. On the other hand he holds (p. 641 ff.) that the Kosovo poems and also those of Marko Kraljević (p. 631 f.) are derived from (hypothetical) written romances or poems inspired by the Chansons de Geste—a view which seems to us highly improbable (cf. Note on p. 433, above).

---

[1] We are much indebted to the kindness of Prof. A. Mazon for sending us copies of these important articles.

PART III

EARLY INDIAN LITERATURE

CHAPTER I

INTRODUCTION

LITERATURE AND WRITING

THE ancient literatures of the East seem at first sight to present a striking contrast to those of the West. Students who have concentrated their attention on the latter cannot but be struck by the overwhelming preponderance of the religious element in the East. Yet in point of fact it will be seen that the same genres are to be found in the East as in the West; the difference lies mainly in the proportions of what has survived.

In India the earliest period of (surviving) literature is dominated by hymns, the next by ritual works, followed by works of a mystical (philosophical) character. All these forms of literature are but feebly represented in the West; but it is to be borne in mind that the native religions of the Celtic and Teutonic peoples were displaced by a new religion with a special (Latin) literature of its own. The native religions were banned.

On the other hand almost all the forms of poetry which chiefly invite attention among the ancient peoples of the West are represented also in ancient India, if only to a limited extent. But they have come down to us only through religious channels. In secular literature the genre which is best represented is heroic narrative poetry. A considerable amount of this has been preserved, but only in a later form and, in varying degree, transformed by—or embedded in—didactic religious elements. For this process we have of course an analogy up to a certain point in English heroic poetry; but in the Indian examples it has been carried immeasurably further. Saga is poorly represented in ancient India, though it was much cultivated by the Hebrews.

NOTE. Transliteration. In Sanskrit words, which are printed as such, the system followed is in general that of the *Cambridge History of India*; but *c*, *ch* are used in place of *ch*, *chh*, and *r* in place of *ri*. But in proper names we have not thought it necessary for the purposes of a work of this kind to use diacritical marks. As a rule therefore we do not distinguish between dentals and linguals, or between vowel and consonantal *r*, or the different varieties of *n*. It may be observed that *c* is the Anglo-Saxon palatalised *c* (Mod. Engl. *ch*), while *ç* denotes a *sh*-sound, but distinct from Skr. *sh* (*ṣ*). The vowel *r* (*ṛ*) must at one time have been pronounced as in Yugoslav.

The only literary genres which we have not been able to trace in ancient India are those which in Vol. I, Ch. XI, we included under the term 'Post-heroic poetry and saga'. We do not know of any personal poetry or poetry of national interest except, to a limited extent, in the earliest period. We cannot point with confidence even to narratives relating to times later than the Heroic Age. Consequently this Part contains no 'Post-heroic' chapter.[1]

India possesses a very large amount of ancient literature; but its history is difficult to trace. For the study of history as developed in Greece from the fifth century (B.C.) onwards, and eventually acquired by the rest of Europe from Greece, early Indian literature has no true parallel. From foreign sources hardly any information is available before the time of Alexander the Great, while native inscriptions begin somewhat later—in the early part of the third century. Some written literature is generally believed to have been already in existence, though its amount and date are difficult to determine. To this question we shall have to return shortly. It may be mentioned, however, that the earliest records of the Buddhists are thought to have been committed to writing at least half a century before Alexander's invasion. For the Buddha's own lifetime the dates generally accepted, though not quite certain, are c. 563–483, while Mahāvīra, the great prophet of the Jains, is believed to have lived c. 540–468. For times anterior to the Buddha, and to a certain extent down to c. 300 (B.C.) or even later, we are dependent upon genealogies and other traditional records, which are similar in general to those available for northern Europe before the times of written literature, though apparently less satisfactory.

There can be no question, however, that a large amount of literature of various kinds dates from before the sixth century; and in the absence of trustworthy historical records some conclusions of a general character can be drawn from the linguistic evidence which it yields. The language of the Vedic hymns, especially those of the Rigveda (Rgveda), is of a more archaic character than Classical Sanskrit. The differences between the two are comparable with those between Homeric Greek and Classical Greek of the fifth century, but somewhat greater. Stages intermediate between the (early) Vedic and the Classical languages are shown by the later hymns, especially those of the Atharvaveda, and by

---

[1] The reason for the omission of such a chapter in Part IV is not the same. In Hebrew 'post-heroic' personal poetry is by no means wanting, while national poetry is abundant. But both are bound up with mantic literature so closely that they will be included in the chapter dealing therewith.

the Brāhmanas—prose works mainly of a ritual character. On the other hand the Classical language itself is much more archaic than the earliest Prakrt or vernaculars. Yet the oldest inscriptions, which date from the third century (B.C.) are in the latter; indeed the vernaculars seem to have been used by the Buddhists and the Jains from the beginning. Apparently therefore even by the close of the sixth century Sanskrit was not the language of the general population. It had already come to be in some sense a literary language, or at least limited to an educated class or classes. Later its use came to be somewhat similar to that of Latin in the Dark Ages. Its form was finally fixed by the grammarians, especially Pānini, who lived probably in the fourth century.

The linguistic evidence then points to four stages or periods in the early history of the literature. Period I is represented by the earlier hymns of the Rgveda, Period II by the later hymns, especially those of the Atharvaveda. But many of the hymns contained in the Rgveda itself, especially in Book x, are also believed to date from this latter period. The formation of the four great collections of hymns—Rgveda, Yajurveda, Sāmaveda, Atharvaveda—is assigned to the same times. Period III is that of the Brāhmanas and the earlier Upanishads—prose works of a mystical and philosophical character, which are usually attached to the Brāhmanas. Period IV is that of Classical Sanskrit and the vernacular literatures.

To these periods the following dates are commonly assigned:[1] to I from (B.C.) 1200 to 1000, to II from 1000 to 800, to III from 800 to 600 or 550. The earlier Upanishads are believed to date from the close of the third period, perhaps c. 600–550. These dates, however, can only be regarded as more or less provisional. The evidence seems to point to the use of a type of language closely approximating to Classical Sanskrit in the sixth century—though the form was not absolutely fixed before the fourth—and also to the literary use (in some sense) of the vernaculars in the fifth century. But there appears to be little or no definite evidence for the earlier dates, apart from considerations of the length of time required for the changes in the language.

The early history of writing in India is still obscure. It was apparently used in the basin of the Indus as far back as the third millennium (B.C.). But there is no evidence to connect this early writing with the writing of historical times. It is still undeciphered, and the language is unknown. The early history of India is unknown; but there is no reason

[1] Cf. *Cambridge History of India*, i. 697.

for supposing that Aryan languages penetrated into the country until many centuries after this time.

The next writing which has as yet been found in India is upon coins dating from the time of Alexander the Great; but examples are rare before the following century. From c. 250 (B.C.) inscriptions upon stone monuments and copper plates (recording deeds and transactions of various kinds) begin to be numerous; and shortly afterwards many coins were minted with both Indian and Greek inscriptions. By means of these it has been possible to reconstruct in large measure the history of the centuries immediately before and after the beginning of the Christian era.

The language of the Indian inscriptions is Aryan—at first usually some form of Prakrt. The writing is of two varieties, Kharoshthī and Brāhmī. The former is derived from Aramaic—which was widely used in Mesopotamia and neighbouring lands under the Persian and late Assyrian empires—and, like Aramaic, it is written from right to left. It is believed to have been introduced into India in the fifth century. In the north-west of the country it had a long life, perhaps a thousand years, though its use seems to have been declining after the third century, A.D.

Brāhmī is believed to be derived from an earlier form of Aramaic— or possibly Phoenician—writing, though unlike all Semitic alphabets, it was almost always written from left to right. From the forms of the letters it is thought to have been borrowed c. 800 (B.C.) or even earlier; but this date seems to be regarded as somewhat conjectural. From Brāhmī are derived most of the alphabets of India, including Nāgarī or Devanāgarī, the alphabet in which Sanskrit is usually written.

There are said to be very few Indian MSS. earlier than the late Middle Ages in India itself; but in Chinese Turkestan and elsewhere many MSS. of the fifth century (and even earlier) have been found. The materials generally in use were of a very fragile nature, birch-bark and palm-leaves. Parchment seems never to have been employed, paper only in modern times.

The question which concerns us is when writing first came into use for literary purposes. It is generally agreed that its use at first was for purposes of trade; we may presumably add correspondence, as in Europe. But there is apparently no definite evidence for written litera- ture before the fourth century (B.C.),[1] and it seems to be the prevailing

[1] References to reading such as occur in translations of (e.g.) the *Chāndogya Upanishad*, VII. i. 2, must not be pressed. *Rgvedam adhyemi* (cf. *adhyāya*, 'chapter') need mean no more than 'I study the Rgveda' (from memory).

opinion that the use of writing for literary purposes did not develop before the fifth.[1] Down to that time literature is believed to have been preserved wholly by oral tradition. And even later—down to modern times, so far at least as the Vedas are concerned—written texts seem to have been of secondary importance. It is said that if all the written and printed copies of the Rgveda were to be lost, the text could be restored at once with complete accuracy.[2]

In the first volume we insisted repeatedly that the importance of oral tradition is under-estimated by modern scholars. We confess, however, that we are staggered by what is generally claimed for oral tradition in India. It is not so much the amount that was memorised. The Rgveda is said to be about equal in extent to the Iliad and the Odyssey combined.[3] More difficulty would be presented by the Brāhmanas, which are in prose; the Çatapatha Brāhmana is more than three times as long as the Iliad. But the really astonishing thing is that this tradition was strictly verbal; the texts were memorised in obsolete forms of language.

Oral tradition of a freer kind and in more or less modernised forms of language seems to be found in India, just as in Europe. Examples will be noticed later. And the preservation of the royal genealogies is apparently no better—indeed less good—than in Europe. But with the religious works which we are now considering the case is different. The text of the Rgveda is believed to have been finally fixed, without variants, c. 600 B.C.[4] Another text of the same collection, known as the Pada text, is thought to have been constituted not much later. In this text, which has also been preserved, each word appears in its (supposed) original form, unaffected by the final and initial changes which are regularly caused by following and preceding words. Further, it appears that oral commentaries on the text may be traced to the same period. A scholar named Yāska, who is believed to have lived in the fifth century (B.C.), refers to five collections of obscure Vedic words and gives the names of seventeen previous commentators.[5]

We know of no European parallels to such activities as these, except of course in written works, where they are common enough, especially perhaps in Ireland. The student of early Western literature is naturally inclined to suspect that too late a date has been assigned to the applica-

[1] Cf. Keith, *Cambridge History of India*, p. 141.
[2] Cf. Rapson, *Ancient India*, p. 37; Winternitz, *Gesch. d. ind. Litteratur*, I. 31 (where this statement is said to apply to a great part of Indian literature).
[3] Cf. Macdonell, *Sanskrit Literature*, p. 41.   [4] *Op. cit.* p. 50.
[5] *Op. cit.* pp. 61, 269.

tion of writing to literature, and that, in spite of the silence of the records, writing must have been in use for literary purposes when these activities began. Some scholars indeed hold that it was in use when the text of the Rgveda was fixed, and even when the collection was made.[1] In this connection it may be observed that the oral tradition postulated for the Vedas and for the Brāhmanas does not seem to be quite identical. The texts of both apparently represent the pronunciation of the Brāhmana period (Period III). But the texts of the Vedas are said—on metrical grounds[2]—not to represent exactly the pronunciation of the hymns in the times in which they were composed, i.e. in Periods I and II. This may point to some use of writing for literary purposes before the end of Period III, though the form of the literary language was not finally fixed until later.

The question involved here is of course one which only Sanskrit scholars can decide. But even if the earlier date for the use of writing should prove to be correct, the extent to which oral tradition was cultivated is remarkable enough, and in excess of anything which we have found in Europe. Possibly the Druids of Gaul may have attained an equal proficiency; but their learning perished with them.

In order to obviate any possible misunderstanding it ought perhaps to be mentioned here that there is evidence in the Vedas pointing to a time when oral tradition was more free. Variants in the text of individual hymns in the Rgveda are almost unknown; but there are hymns which are variants of other hymns in the Rgveda, while variants between different Vedas, e.g. the Rgveda and the Atharvaveda, are numerous. These will require notice later.

[1] Cf. Lanman, *Sanskrit Reader*, p. 354.
[2] We may refer (e.g.) to Whitney, *Sanskrit Grammar*, Sect. 329 f., 356a, b, and perhaps 135c, 209, 210a.

CHAPTER II

HEROIC POETRY

INDIA had a Heroic Age, similar in general characteristics to the Heroic Ages discussed in the previous volume. As usual, this age belonged to times which may practically be regarded as prehistoric. Its chronology indeed is perhaps even more difficult to determine than that of the Greek Heroic Age. We shall therefore begin with a brief account of the records. Only what may be called primary authorities can be noticed; but it should be borne in mind that heroic stories continued to furnish themes to poets and dramatists in later times, just as in Europe, and indeed for a longer period.

In this chapter we shall deal only with heroic matter. Non-heroic stories relating to the Heroic Age will be considered in Ch. IV. The records which require notice here consist of heroic poetry of Types A, C and D, and some antiquarian poetry. There appears to be no heroic poetry of Type E, and no heroic saga. This is worth noting,[1] because saga, combined with poetry of Type B, occurs in non-heroic stories and elsewhere. For these 'types' see p. 2.

Type D is directly represented only by one or two poems, which date from the Heroic Age itself. The other records, at least in their present form, date from much later times.

The great storehouse of heroic stories[2] is the Mahābhārata, a poem of prodigious length, containing about 100,000 couplets. The nucleus of the poem is the story of a certain family; but to this have been added[3]

---

[1] Several modern scholars have expressed the view that Sanskrit narrative poetry is derived from saga (in a free form), interspersed with poetry of Type B. They seem not to have distinguished between heroic and non-heroic. We believe this explanation to be true for the latter, perhaps also for stories of the gods; but we cannot find any evidence for it in the former case. It will be seen later that heroic and non-heroic poetry are of essentially different origin, except possibly in Type D.

[2] For further information on this subject, as also on those treated in Ch. V, we may refer the reader to Sidhanta, *The Heroic Age of India*. Prof. Sidhanta has treated these subjects more fully than it is possible for us to do.

[3] Evidence for the expansion of the poem is to be found in certain statements contained in it. In I. ii the number of couplets in the various sections is given in detail, and the total (including the Harivāṃça) comes to 100,000. But in I. i. 101 it is said to have originally contained 24,000 couplets, while another passage (I. i. 81) seems to imply 8,800 couplets—which is not much longer than the Iliad. To this question we shall have to return later.

numerous episodes, unconnected with the central theme, and a vast amount of didactic matter of various kinds, including theological and antiquarian elements and even laws. It is agreed by the great majority of modern scholars that the central theme was originally a heroic story; and in part it still retains this character, though it has itself incorporated a very large amount of non-heroic and didactic matter. Some of the episodes also are of heroic origin; and at least one of them preserves heroic features better than the central story. But most of the additions are non-heroic, and the poem as a whole is in its present form predominantly of this character.

It may be remarked here that the contrast between heroic and non-heroic elements is as a rule very clearly marked in early Indian literature. In general heroic stories are concerned with persons of the Kshatriya or princely caste, non-heroic stories primarily with Brahmans. References to the other castes are rare. But stories of princes whose fame is due to piety and asceticism, rather than to prowess, or who come to grief through impiety, must be regarded as non-heroic. They are doubtless of Brahmanic origin. This subject, however, will require to be treated in more detail in Ch. IV.

The chief events of the central story may be summarised briefly as follows:[1] Pāndu, a prince of the Kuru, whose territories lay in the upper basins of the Ganges and the Jumna, dies and leaves five sons, the chief of whom are Yudhishthira, Bhīma and Arjuna. His brother Dhrtarāshtra, who is blind, brings up Pāndu's sons with his own. The former soon distinguish themselves by their prowess, and Yudhishthira is designated as successor to the throne. But Dhrtarāshtra's sons are filled with jealousy, especially Duryodhana, the eldest, and contrive to turn their father against their cousins, though they are opposed by Bhīshma, the king's uncle, Drona, a Brahman who is also a warrior, and the judge Vidura, who is the king's illegitimate half-brother. The chief supporter of the king's sons is a famous warrior named Karna, who is not a prince but a charioteer's son. Eventually Duryodhana entices his cousins to a house made of inflammable materials, which is set on fire. The princes escape to the forest by an underground passage, together with their mother, Kunti; but they are believed to have perished.

For a time the brothers live, disguised as Brahmans, in the forest, where Bhīma, who is immensely strong, kills two cannibal monsters

---

[1] A much fuller summary is given by Winternitz, *Gesch. d. ind. Litteratur*, I. 275 ff.; an abridged verse transl. by R. Dutt, *The Ramayana and the Mahabharata* (Everyman). Complete (prose) transl. by M. N. Dutt, *The Mahabharata*.

(Rākshasa), somewhat similar to Grendel. Then they hear that Drupada, king of the Pancāla, a neighbouring people, is about to hold a svayamvara[1] for his daughter Krshnā, generally called Draupadī, and that all the princes of the country are making their way to his court. They set off with many other Brahmans to see the ceremony, supporting themselves by begging. The successful suitor has to string a certain very strong bow, and then to shoot through a lofty mark. The assembled princes, including the sons of Dhrtarāshtra, fail to accomplish the task. Only Karna succeeds in stringing the bow; but he is disqualified by Draupadī from proceeding further, on the ground that he is not a prince. Then Arjuna steps forward and successfully carries out both tasks. He is accepted by the bride and her father; but some of the princes are deeply angered at the prize being won by a Brahman. They make an attack upon the king, but are driven off by Bhīma and Arjuna. After this the heroes disclose their identity; and Draupadī is married to them all, in accordance with what they declare to be their ancestral custom.[2]

Drupada now brings about peace between his sons-in-law and their cousins; and Dhrtarāshtra cedes half his kingdom to Yudhishthira, with a new capital at Indraprastha, near Delhi. Arjuna unintentionally breaks the covenant which the brothers had made with regard to their relations with Draupadī, and insists on going into exile as a hermit for twelve years. During this time, however, he lives a rather active life, and even has several love-adventures. At her brother's suggestion he carries off and marries Subhadrā, the sister of his friend Krshna, a prince of the Yadu. By her he has a son named Abhimanyu. After his return home the family, by conquest and influence, acquire a dominant position among the peoples of northern India, and Yudhishthira offers a sacrifice which signifies the recognition of his supremacy.

After this Dhrtarāshtra's sons invite Yudhishthira to play dice with their mother's brother, Çakuni. Yudhishthira stakes all his property and even his own and his brothers' freedom, and loses everything. Dhrtarāshtra's sons claim Draupadī as a slave and insult her. The king eventually annuls the proceedings; but his sons again entice Yudhishthira to play. This time it is agreed that they are to go into exile in the forest for twelve years and to remain in concealment for a thirteenth year. They carry out the engagement, and spend the last year in the service of Virāta, king of the Matsya, a people to the south of the Kuru.

[1] The ceremony at which the bride chooses herself a husband from the assembled suitors.
[2] This custom will require notice later, in Ch. V (*ad fin.*).

At the end of the time they make themselves known; Arjuna defeats a great cattle-raid made by the princes of the Kuru. Virāta and Drupada now take up the heroes' cause, and demand the restoration of their kingdom. Dhrtarāshtra's sons refuse, against the advice of the older leaders, as usual; and both sides prepare for war. All the kings of northern India take part in it.

The battle is described[1] at very great length, and is said to last nearly three weeks. The Kuru army is commanded first by Bhīshma, then by Drona, then by Karna, and lastly by a prince named Çalya. All of these are killed, the three first by unfair means; and all the sons of Dhrtarā-shtra also are slain. The opposing army is commanded by Dhrshtady-umna, son of Drupada, who is killed at the end of the battle. Drupada himself also, Virāta, Abhimanyu and many other princes perish. The account of the battle is followed (XI. xvi ff.) by the elegy of Gāndhārī, the wife of Dhrtarāshtra, in which she laments her sons and describes the scene on the battlefield.

It is held by some scholars that the original poem ended with the funeral. At all events what follows contains little of a heroic character. Yudhishthira, now king of the Kuru, discovers that Karna was his brother, and offers a great horse-sacrifice to atone for the sin of his death. Finally, Yudhishthira gives up the kingdom to Parīkshit, son of Abhimanyu, and retires to heaven with his brothers and Draupadī.[2]

Even from the short summary given above it will be obvious that, apart from more or less irrelevant additions, the original story itself has been expanded from within by the repetition of motifs and incidents, such as the exile in the forest. Examples seem to be very numerous, and provide much interesting material for the study of variants. It can hardly be doubted too that many new incidents, both heroic and (more especially) non-heroic, relating to the heroes themselves, have been added in the course of time. In the abstract given above we have

---

[1] The description is in the form of a series of speeches by a messenger named Sanjaya, who returns from the battlefield from time to time and narrates to Dhrta-rāshtra what is happening.

[2] It may be remarked that the abstract given above does not claim to represent evenly the contents of the various Books. All the events down to and including the marriage of Draupadī are contained in Book I. Book II ends with the exile of the heroes after the dice-playing. Book III is mainly occupied with episodes related to Yudhishthira during his exile; Book IV with the adventures in Matsya; Book V with the deliberations before the battle. Books VI–X are occupied with the battle itself; Book XI with the lamentations and the funeral. The remaining Books are mainly didactic.

noticed only the more important—and probably older—elements in the story.

Next we may take the story of Nala,[1] which is related (in III. lii–lxxix) by a sage named Brhadaçva to Yudhishthira, during his exile in the forest. This story is of special importance, because it is much more free from Brahmanic influence than the central story. The interest is essentially heroic throughout, though it deals exclusively with times of peace.

The story falls into two parts, of which the first (I–v) deals with the hero's marriage. Nala, king of the Nishadha, sees some swans with golden plumage. He catches one of them; and it offers to be his envoy to the beautiful Damayanti, daughter of Bhīma, king of the Vidarbha.[2] The swans then fly to Vidarbha, where they find Damayanti with her maidens. She sends a suitable reply, and then falls into a deep love-sickness. Her father, though he knows nothing of the message, decides to hold a svayamvara for her; and the princes set out from far and wide in gorgeous array. In the meantime Indra finds that no heroes are coming to his abode—i.e. there is no fighting—and learns from the sage Nārada that they are all on the way to Damayanti's svayamvara. He and the other gods, Agni, Varuna and Yama, decide to go there too. On the way they meet with Nala and commission him to be their messenger to Damayanti. He is naturally reluctant; but when he learns who they are, he sees there is nothing for it but to obey. They enable him to make his way unseen into the presence of Damayanti. He tells her who he is, and gives her the message of the gods, saying she is to choose which of the four she will. She replies that she will have Nala himself; and when he points out the danger, she says he must come to the svayamvara, and then she will choose him in the presence of the gods. Then the ceremony takes place. In this case no feats are required; the lady seems to have complete freedom of choice. But when she enters the hall, she finds among the suitors five figures exactly like Nala, and is unable to make out which is the real man. Realising the trick played upon her by the gods, she prays to them to show the signs of divinity. They yield to her appeal, and she can now distinguish them —casting no shadows, their feet not touching the ground, their eyes motionless, their garlands not drooping. Nala alone remains without

---

[1] Transl. by Milman, *Nala and Damayanti*; Arnold, *Indian Idylls*; etc.

[2] Berar in the Central Provinces. The scene of this story seems to be located chiefly in central India. The Nishadha were perhaps the western neighbours of the Vidarbha—not very far to the N.E. of Bombay; cf. Sidhanta, *op. cit.* p. 13.

the divine attributes, and she lays her garland on his shoulders. The gods give them their blessings and depart; and the marriage takes place soon afterwards.

The second and much longer part of the story (VI to the end) follows after a long interval. Kali, a dice-demon, who has a grudge against Nala for his marriage, succeeds in getting possession of him after eleven years. He challenges his brother Pushkara, and stakes and loses everything that he has, except his wife. Damayantī does everything possible to avert the calamity, and finally sends away the children to her father. Then she accompanies her husband alone to the forest. Nala, who is beside himself with despair and shame, forsakes her while she is asleep, and divides the only cloak they have left. Damayanti's grief and despair, when she awakes, are described at length. She meets with a caravan of merchants and, after a disastrous attack by wild elephants, arrives safely at the city of the Cedi. Here she becomes maid to the queen, who is her aunt but does not know her. Meanwhile Bhīma has been sending Brahmans in all directions to make enquiries. Eventually they discover his daughter and bring her home. Then she sends them out again to search for Nala; and from the reports she suspects that he has become charioteer to Rtuparna, king of Ayodhyā (Oude). Now she sends word to Rtuparna that she is to have a second svayamvara. He sets out at full speed with Nala. He has a remarkable skill in counting, as Nala has in driving. On the way they agree to exchange these gifts, and the demon Kali is thereupon expelled from Nala. Nala is recognised by his wife, although his form has been changed. Now he regains his own form, and they are happily reunited. With his new gift he challenges his brother again, and wins back his kingdom and all his property.

It has often been remarked that this story—the second part of it—shows a general resemblance to the Odyssey. One must of course eliminate the maritime element in the latter, and also those portions which are concerned with 'fairy-land' and with folktales. Also it is to be observed that in the story of Nala, as in early Indian stories generally, the women are much stronger characters than the men, and indeed far superior to them in every way.

Mention may next be made of a short piece in v. cxxxiii ff., which seems to be taken from a heroic story.[1] It is related by Kuntī to Krshna, as a message to her sons. Its special interest lies in the apparently complete absence of Brahmanic influence. A prince named Sanjaya has been

---

[1] Cf. Winternitz, *Gesch. d. ind. Litteratur*, I. 328 ff., where a few passages are translated.

overthrown by his enemies; and the piece consists mainly of fiery exhortations by his mother Vidulā, bidding him rouse himself and encounter his foes again. Sanjaya tries to excuse himself on the ground that there is no hope of success; but in the end he is unable to resist his mother's scathing words. The theme has something in common with the Hamðismál, and also with the story of Ingeld, especially as related by Saxo.[1]

The story of Rāma is told in III. cclxxiii ff. It is a disputed question whether this account is taken from the Rāmāyana or from earlier poems, from which the latter itself is derived. In any case we may here give a brief account of this work.

The Rāmāyana[2] is another poem of immense length, containing c. 24,000 couplets. It is preserved in three different texts, which vary greatly from one another. The view now generally accepted is that it is in the main the work of one poet named Vālmīki, who is claimed as its author in the poem itself, and that it was composed some time between the fifth and the third centuries (B.C.). Certain portions, however, especially the first and last Books (I and VII), are believed to be additions made in later times, while the original matter is thought to have been greatly expanded. These additions must have taken place before the poem was committed to writing, for the extant texts, though they differ greatly from one another, all contain Books I and VII. The Mahābhārata, however, seems to have nothing corresponding to Book VII; and much of what is told in Book I is also wanting.

First we may briefly summarise what seems to be the original story, contained in Books II–VI. Daçaratha, king of Ayodhyā (Oude), has two wives named Kauçalyā and Kaikeyī. Kauçalyā has borne him his eldest son Rāma, Kaikeyī a second son named Bharata. He has also two other sons by a third wife. When the king grows old he decides to retire and give the kingdom to Rāma. All preparations are made; but when the ceremony is about to begin, Kaikeyī is roused to a frenzy of jealousy by her nurse, and demands to see the king. She reminds him that he has once given her his word that he will grant her any two requests she may make; and she now calls upon him to send Rāma into exile for fourteen years and appoint her own son Bharata in his place.

---

[1] The exhortations of Starcatherus, given in Latin verse by the latter, p. 251 ff. (204 ff.), are doubtless based upon vernacular poetry (cf. Beow. 2041 ff.).

[2] Transl. (Italian) by Gorresio; (Engl.) by Griffith (verse) and M. N. Dutt (prose). Abridged transl. (selections) by R. Dutt, *The Ramayana and the Mahabharata* (Everyman). Abstract by Winternitz, *op. cit.* I. 409 ff.

The king is overwhelmed with grief; but Rāma insists upon his keeping his word, and sets off into exile in the forest. He is accompanied by his wife Sītā, daughter of Janaka, king of Videha, and by his younger brother Lakshmana. Soon after his departure his father dies. Bharata, who has been away during this time, comes home, and has no mind to take his brother's place. He follows Rāma to the forest, and tries to persuade him to return, but without success. Then he takes Rāma's sandals, and places them on the throne, consenting to act as regent, though not in the capital, during his brother's absence. Rāma and his companions set off to the Deccan.

The rest of the story, contained in Books III–VI, can hardly be regarded otherwise than as romance. In principle it resembles the romantic part of the Odyssey, though it is largely concerned with fighting. Rāma and his wife and brother make their home in a forest on the Godāvarī, where they come into conflict with Rākshasas. A Rākshasa woman, whose advances to Rāma are repelled with scorn and injury, appeals to her brother Rāvana, the king, for vengeance. He carries off Sītā when the heroes are away from their hut, and flies away with her to his capital on the island of Lankā—later identified with Ceylon. Rāma, distraught with grief, sets off to look for her and meets with Sugriva, an exiled prince of the apes, whom he assists in recovering his kingdom. Sugriva has a wise councillor named Hanumat, who goes to search for Sītā, and eventually finds her imprisoned in Lankā. Rāma then sets out with an army of apes, who build him a bridge, and after long and desperate fighting, which is described in full detail, succeeds in capturing the island and slaying Rāvana. Sītā proves her fidelity by the ordeal of fire.[1] The time of Rāma's exile is now at an end, and he flies back to Ayodhyā with Sītā and Lakshmana in a car drawn by swans. Here he is joyfully welcomed by Bharata, who gives up the government to him.

Books I and VII show marked Brahmanic influence. In Book I the gods are much troubled by Rāvana and beg Vishnu to become incarnate in order to destroy him. Daçaratha offers a sacrifice for children, and by this obtains Rāma, who is Vishnu incarnate, and his other sons. Later there is an account of the svayamvara of Sītā, which involves the feat of stringing a mighty bow. In this story all Daçaratha's sons are married to daughters of Janaka, though in the subsequent Books Lakshmana is

---

[1] There is no ordeal in the Mahābhārata; but the gods (Vāyu, Agni, Varuna and Brahmā), together with Rāma's father, come to bear witness to Sītā's fidelity (III. ccxc).

unmarried. It is stated that Sītā was not an ordinary child, but sprang from a furrow when Janaka was ploughing.[1]

Book VII is largely occupied with antiquarian matter. Only a comparatively small part of it relates to Rāma, and in this he cuts a poor figure. He sends his faithful wife away to the forest owing to popular feeling against her, because she has been in the hands of Rāvana. Soon afterwards she bears him two sons named Kuça and Lava. She is sheltered by the hermit Vālmīki, who brings up the boys and teaches them the poem, of which he is the author. After many years Rāma offers a great horse-sacrifice, and during the festivities the boys recite the story of his adventures. Rāma recognises them as his sons, and invites Sītā, through Vālmīki, to come and clear herself by an oath. Sītā comes and adjures the earth-goddess to prove her fidelity. The earth then opens; the goddess appears on her throne, clasps Sītā in her arms, and disappears again with her. Rāma is left disconsolate.

The differences between heroic and non-heroic in Indian records are in general so clearly marked as to leave little room for doubt as to which of the two categories a story belongs to—even when a heroic story is deeply overlaid with non-heroic (Brahmanic) elements. There are, however, in the Mahābhārata certain cases where the original provenance is not obvious at first sight.

First we may take the famous story of Sāvitrī (III. ccxcii ff.). This story is so well known that it is hardly necessary to give an abstract here. It is commonly held to be of Brahmanic origin, though doubts have been expressed.[2] The tone is certainly religious to a high degree, and Brahmans enter much into the story; but they hardly influence the course of events. Indeed their presence with King Dyumatsena is more or less accidental; for he has fled to the forest as an exile and refugee. The essential and dominant feature of the story is the heroine's determination and resourcefulness, which causes the god of death (Yama) to desist from his purpose. This feature seems to us rather to suggest a heroic (Kshatriya) provenance, for women are not as a rule prominent in Brahmanic literature. Moreover Brahmanism has nothing to gain from the story. We suspect that, like certain Norse heroic poems (cf.

[1] The word *sītā* means 'furrow'. Personification is found even in the Rgveda, IV. 57; and in later literature Sītā appears as a genius of the ploughed field.

[2] Cf. Winternitz, *Gesch. d. ind. Litteratur*, I. 340. An abridged transl. will be found in R. Dutt, *The Ramayana and the Mahabharata*, p. 253 ff., where it is remarked that "the story is known by Hindu women...in all parts of India; and on a certain night in the year millions of Hindu women celebrate a rite in honour of the woman whose love was not conquered by death".

Vol. I, p. 599), it originated among women, presumably women of princely families.[1] Its religious character is hardly incompatible with such an origin. We think that, like the story of Nala, it is the product of a religious aristocratic society, not of a priestly class. But the dialogue between Sāvitrī and Yama (III. ccxcvi) has doubtless been much affected by Brahmanic influence.

Another story which should perhaps be noticed here is that of Çakuntalā, which is related in I. lxviii ff. She is said to be the daughter of the great seer Viçvāmitra and a nymph (Apsaras) named Menakā. She is deserted by her mother, and discovered and brought up by the seer Kanva. King Dushmanta, who has lost his way while hunting, comes to Kanva's hermitage and falls in love with Çakuntalā; but she will have no relations with him until he promises that her son shall be his successor. Some years later she comes to his court with her child, who is called Bharata, and claims the fulfilment of his promise. She pleads her cause at length; but the king will not recognise her until a voice from heaven declares that she is speaking the truth.

This story presents more than one problem. In the genealogies (I. xciv f.) this Bharata is referred to the remote past. He is the ancestor of the Kuru kings, Dhrtarāshtra, Yudhishthira and Janamejaya, who are frequently described as Bhārata, i.e. descendant of Bharata; and it is from him that the kingdom (dynasty) of the Bharata—very prominent in the Rgveda from the earliest times—derives its name. If the Bharata of the story is really this person, his origin is presumably to be traced to antiquarian tradition or speculation. It is possible, however, that his identification with the eponymos is secondary; for other persons of this name are known, e.g. the brother of Rāma. Again, the story in its present form is pronouncedly non-heroic. Çakuntalā is the daughter and foster-daughter of famous seers; and the gnomes attributed to her are not of heroic type, like those of Vidulā. Moreover Brahmanic tradition celebrates Bharata as a famous sacrificer.[2] But the evidence is not wholly conclusive; for another Brahmanic tradition describes Çakuntalā herself as an Apsaras.[3] It is possible therefore that the seers may have been introduced into the story, in order to claim a partly Brahmanic origin for Bharata.

---

[1] It is to such persons that Sāvitrī's position as an heiress (without brothers)—which entitles her to travel in quest of a husband—would most naturally appeal.

[2] In the poetry quoted in Ait. Br. VIII. 23. This refers to his victories on the Ganges and the Jumna, to elephants with golden trappings, etc.—all suggesting a not very early period.

[3] Çatapatha Brāhmana, XIII. 5. 4. 13.

In I.xcvii ff. we find another story which contains obvious Brahmanic features. A king named Çāntanu, a descendant of Bharata, marries a girl whom he meets on the bank of the Ganges. She throws all her children into the river as soon as they are born. The king at last intercepts her and saves one child, who is called Devavrata or Bhīshma; and she then leaves him, after revealing that she is Gangā, the goddess of the river. She explains at the same time that her children are deities who have been condemned to human incarnation; she has therefore befriended them by releasing them from the curse as soon as possible. Later, Çāntanu meets with another damsel named Satyavatī, whose father will consent to the marriage only on condition that her son shall succeed to the throne. The king is unwilling to pass over Bhīshma; but the latter settles the question by taking a vow of celibacy, though he continues to be a warrior. After his father's death Bhīshma seeks a wife for his half-brother Vicitravīrya; and hearing that the king of Kāçī (Benares) is holding a svayamvara for his three daughters, he goes there and carries them off, after a fight with the suitors. One of the princesses, named Ambā, who is already betrothed, is allowed to go to her fiancé. The other two are kept for Vicitravīrya; but he dies without leaving children. Bhīshma insists on maintaining his vow of celibacy; so Satyavatī calls in Vyāsa—the author of the Mahābhārata—a son whom she has previously born to the seer Parāçara, in order to provide heirs for Vicitravīrya. The princesses then give birth to Dhṛtarāshtra and Pāndu, while Vidura is born by one of the maids. Bhīshma himself, as we have seen, is commander of the Kuru army in the great battle, described in Book VI.

This story, as it stands, is clearly designed to claim a Brahmanic ancestry for the heroes of the Mahābhārata and their descendants, including Janamejaya. In Brahmanic poetry [1] it is apparently not easy for a prince to beget children, at least not without Brahmanic or divine assistance. The case of Vicitravīrya may be compared with that of his son Pāndu, who had to live as a celibate (I. cxviii ff.), because he had once killed a seer in the form of an antelope. His wives therefore at his request appealed to various deities—by means of a spell known to Kuntī—by whom they became the mothers of the heroes, Yudhishthira and his brothers. Yet the story is so complex as to suggest that it existed in some other form, before Vyāsa was introduced into it. Indeed some account of the heroes' family was presumably given or implied from the time when they first became a theme of poetry.

[1] Among other Brahmanic features in this story we may note the incarnation of deities—in the case of Vidura, as well as Gangā's children.

Apart from the main course of the story, Bhīshma's adventure in Kāçī has a sequel in the story of Ambā, which is related in v. clxxiii ff., and which seems to have been originally of heroic character, though it presents a number of peculiar features. It has been mentioned above that when Bhīshma had carried off the princesses of Kāçī from their svayamvara (cf. p. 475), the eldest of them, named Ambā, pleaded that she had already betrothed herself to a king called Çālva. Consequently Bhīshma released her, and she made her way to that king. But he repudiated her on account of the abduction. Then she betakes herself to a forest, where she finds her mother's father, a prince of the Srnjaya, with other ascetics. She refuses to return either to her own home or to Bhīshma, and thinks of nothing but vengeance upon the latter. At length she persuades the old Brahman warrior Rāma son of Jamadagni (Paraçu-Rāma)—not the hero of the Rāmāyana—to take up her cause. He tries first to make peace with Bhīshma; but when this fails he fights with him, and is defeated. Ambā is now thrown back upon her own resources, and devotes herself to austerities with a view to obtaining vengeance. Eventually the god Çiva tells her that, when she is born again, she will become a man, and slay Bhīshma. Then she piles up a funeral pyre, and immolates herself.

King Drupada, who is childless, beseeches Çiva to grant him a son, and receives the answer that he will have a daughter who will become a man. A female child is born, but is given out to be a boy and brought up as such. She is called Çikhandin. In course of time she marries the daughter of a neighbouring king. Then the truth comes to light; and her father-in-law, considering himself to be outraged, threatens Drupada with war. Çikhandin, however, contrives to persuade a Yaksha ('elf') to exchange sex with her; and friendship is restored with her father-in-law, who is satisfied that he has been misinformed.

This story is told by Bhīshma himself to Duryodhana on the eve of the battle, in explanation of his statement (v. clxxii. 16) that he will not fight with Çikhandin—for he has made a vow never to slay a woman. In the battle Bhīshma is killed either by Çikhandin or by Arjuna who is hiding behind him. There are discrepancies between different passages as to which of the two is the actual slayer—which can hardly have been the case in the original form of the story, especially in view of the pronouncements of Çiva. Other features [1] also suggest that the story has

---

[1] It is not clear why Drupada desires vengeance upon Bhīshma in v. cxc. On the other hand Çikhandin seems not to be concerned with Bhīshma until they meet in battle.

undergone a considerable amount of change; and one may perhaps suspect that originally it was less closely bound up with the main theme of the Mahābhārata. The fullness of detail with which it is related seems to point rather to its having once formed the subject of a separate poem.

The story has Brahmanic affinities in the asceticism practised by the heroine and in the idea of re-birth through sacrifice, for which we may compare the story of Janta in III. cxxviii. But these hardly prove that it is of Brahmanic origin. Ambā is not a Brahman; and the only Brahman who figures at all prominently in the story, Rāma son of Jamadagni, is defeated. Again, it resembles the stories of Nala and of Sāvitrī in the fact that the interest is centred in a woman. But Ambā has little in common with Damayantī or Sāvitrī except her resolute character; and the sympathy is not on her side. Her nearest analogy is to be found in Brynhildr;[1] and it may reasonably be inferred that the cultivation of her story has been inspired by a similar psychological interest, though rather, we think, from a man's point of view.

We may now briefly compare the characteristics of this poetry with those of Greek and Anglo-Saxon heroic poetry, as noted in Vol. I, p. 20 ff. We will confine our attention to the heroic elements in the main story and to the episodic stories of Nala, Rāma (together with Rāmāyana, II–VI), Sāvitrī and Ambā.

The first four characteristics noted in Vol. I seem to apply to these poems, just as much as to the latter. They are (1) narrative, and (2) concerned primarily with adventure. It is generally believed also that (3) they were originally intended for entertainment; and indeed this is doubtless still true in the main of the stories discussed above, in spite of the didactic matter which has become incorporated with them. (4) They may, we think, be said to relate to a Heroic Age, though this age is less easy to define than in the West, owing to the lack of chronological data. To this question we shall have to return later; but there can be little doubt that at the time when we first have definite evidence for their existence—say the fourth century (B.C.)—they were believed to relate to the past, probably a more or less distant past.

With regard to the remaining characteristics we may note:

(5) Like the Teutonic and (in our opinion) the Greek poems the Mahābhārata is generally regarded as anonymous. Vyāsa, it is true, is a much more definitely characterised person than Homer; but it is hardly

---

[1] Bhīshma might be expected to agree to Högni's words in Sigurðarkv. Sk. 45: "Let no man stay her from the long journey (sc. to the land of the dead)—from whence may she never be re-born!"

credible either that heroic poetry could be produced by such a man, or that any one author could be responsible for both the heroic and the Brahmanic elements in the poem. The commonly accepted view is that it is the work of many authors, and that its composition extended over a long period of time. On the other hand a large part of the Rāmāyana is believed to have been composed, though not written (cf. p. 471) by Vālmīki. Both in its diction and in its treatment of the subject-matter, and more especially in the amount of attention devoted to descriptions of scenery, this poem is less archaic than the Mahābhārata and approximates more nearly to the artificial (academic) poetry of later times. But Vālmīki himself seems to be as shadowy a figure as Homer, apart from the (presumably apocryphal) references to him in Books I and VII.[1]

(6) Like Greek and Teutonic heroic narrative poetry, the poetry we are considering employs a uniform line—at least if we may describe the half-çloka (see below) as a line. The usual metre is a line of sixteen syllables, with a caesura after the eighth. The last four syllables in each line are iambic, while the last four in each first half-line usually consist of an iambus followed by a spondee or trochee; in the remaining syllables quantity is disregarded. Two short syllables do not, as in Greek and Teutonic, count as equivalent to one long syllable; neither is there any alliteration or rhyme. This form of metre is said to be employed by about 95 per cent. of the verses in the Mahābhārata.

(7) The unit, however, is not the line but the çloka, which may be regarded either as a couplet of two lines or as a stanza of four half-lines, as described above. Modern editions are usually printed in lines. But according to the generally accepted view the latter description would seem to be more correct historically; for the çloka is believed to be derived from a stanzaic Vedic metre, called *Anuṣṭubh*. In this metre the stanza contains four lines, each of eight syllables and similar in form to the latter half of the çloka line. There are probably reasons for accepting this derivation, which we as non-specialists are unable to appreciate. But it seems to us strange that poetry of this kind should borrow its metrical form from a totally different type of poetry, which was cultivated originally, as we shall see later, by a different class of poets.[2]

---

[1] We are not clear why Vālmīki is identified with the fourth-century poet. The references to him in the later Books (I and VII) suggest a legendary figure of the far past (like Vyāsa), supposed to be contemporary with Rāma himself. But there may be evidence which we do not know.

[2] Unfortunately no heroic narrative poetry earlier than the epics has been preserved. In the Brāhmanas in place of narrative poetry we find stories told in the form of saga, with many of the speeches in verse, as in Irish sagas; and it is held by some

On the other hand if heroic narrative poetry was originally distinct from Vedic (i.e. Brahmanic) poetry, an assimilation of the former to the latter is what might be expected, when the cultivation of the former had passed into the hands of the Brahmans. We may compare the use of the stanza in Norse heroic narrative poetry, noticed in Vol. I, p. 30. Conventionally all Norse poetry is regarded as stanzaic (strophic). But as regards heroic narrative poetry—as also heroic poetry of Type B—it is only in what are thought to be the later poems that the (four-line) stanza is found regularly; and we believe that it has been borrowed from other types of poetry.[1]

In the poetry with which we are now concerned the couplet or stanza (çloka) seems to be much more regular, though çlokas of three lines are by no means rare. Breaks usually occur at the end of a çloka; but a sentence which begins in one çloka is frequently continued in the next. Less frequently, but not rarely, the break occurs within the çloka— usually at the end of the first line—instead of at the end of the çloka, as (e.g.) in Nala, II. 5 ff. (Mahābh. III. liv. 5 ff.): (5) "Her friends knew from the symptoms that she could not be well when she looked like this. Then Damayantī's company of friends to the lord of Vidarbha (6) made known that Damayantī was not well, Prince of heroes![2] Bhīma, lord of men, having heard this from Damayantī's company of friends, (7) considered that this was an important matter with regard to his daughter: 'How is it that my daughter is not looking well today?'" Passages like this cannot properly be described as stanzaic poetry in any sense. They are 'running' poetry, quite parallel to that of Beowulf and

scholars that this was the original form of narrative in India—that narrative poetry was of late growth. But all the stories told in the Brāhmanas are non-heroic stories. If saga was the usual form for these in early times—which is extremely probable—it must not be assumed that the same form was used for heroic stories. That could be admitted only if heroic and non-heroic stories were cultivated by the same classes of persons. The epics did eventually come into the hands of the Brahmans; but it is unlikely that the cultivation of heroic stories was theirs from the beginning. The use of the same metre for the heroic and non-heroic elements in the epics may well be a result of the annexation of the former by the Brahmans.

[1] It should be mentioned that some scholars believe Teutonic heroic narrative poetry to have been originally stanzaic. In view of the English and German evidence we have no hesitation in rejecting this view. It may be added that the amount of emendation needed to bring certain Norse poems (e.g. the Atlakviða or the Hamðismál) into four-line stanzas requires in very truth the bed of Procrustes. Such theories seem to proceed from an assumption that all the poetry of a given people must originally have been of uniform type. We do not see why there should not have been diverse types from time immemorial.

[2] This phrase is addressed to Yudhishthira by the reciter of the story.

the Homeric poems. It may also be observed that, as in the English poem, speeches very frequently begin in the middle of a line, i.e. at the caesura. Examples may be found in Nala, VI. 3 f., XV. 13.

(8) Speeches are of extremely frequent occurrence and occupy a large proportion of the space. We have no statistics, but are under the impression that the proportion of speech to narrative is in general not less than in Beowulf. In some parts of the main story it is probably as great as in the Homeric poems. Speeches are usually introduced with some more or less stereotyped formula, which occupies a whole line, just as in the Greek, English and Norse poems, e.g. Nala, IV. 5: "Thus addressed by the lady of Vidarbha, Nala said to her"—with which we may compare Beow. 1840: "Hrothgar made speech in answer to him." In place of such metrical formulae we find, less frequently, words like *Nala uvāca* ('Nala said'), which are extra metrum. Parallel phrases (e.g. *Atli kvað*) —likewise extra metrum—occur frequently in Norse, though not in English or Greek, heroic poetry. Such usage may be due to the influence of poems of Type B, where it is regular, e.g. in Helgakv. Hundingsbana II, Lokasenna and Alvíssmál.[1]

(9) The style is as a rule leisurely, with full description of details, just as in the Greek and English poems. The object is not to tell the story concisely, as in Norse heroic poetry, but rather to spin it out. As an example we may cite the account of Draupadī's svayamvara in I. clxxxiv ff.[2] Exceptions occur. There is not much superfluous matter in the first part of the story of Nala (I–V). But this story is no doubt properly to be regarded as preliminary to what follows.

(10) Static epithets are of frequent occurrence, as in Greek and English; but they are applied to human beings—persons of royal rank— much more freely than to any other objects. Epithets of heroes and princes are both substantival and adjectival, and sometimes very similar to what are found in the West, e.g. 'lord of men' (*nṛpati*), '(man) of mighty arm' (*mahābāhu*). More distinctively Indian are such terms as 'tiger of men' (*naraçārdūla*). The epithets applied to royal ladies seem to be usually adjectival and to relate to appearance, e.g. 'slender-

---

[1] These extra-metrical phrases have sometimes been brought forward as evidence for the derivation of narrative poetry from poetry of Type B; but we cannot see the point of the argument. They may be borrowed from Type B, as suggested above. Type B was certainly cultivated in India at an early date; for examples (not heroic) occur in the Rgveda. But often they may be late additions by a reciter or scribe. In Norse heroic poetry speeches are frequently introduced without mention of the speaker's name.

[2] Cf. R. Dutt's translation, p. 211 ff.

waisted' (*tanumadhyā*), 'long-eyed' (*āyatalocanā*), 'having a faultless figure' (*anavadyāngī*). Such epithets are especially common in the Vocative, in speeches addressed to princes and princesses. Sometimes one meets with strings of epithets, as in Beowulf, but of more extravagant length. Examples may be found in Nala, I. I ff., XII. 44 ff. Kennings like 'egg-born' (*aṇḍaja*) or 'moving in the air' (*antarīkṣaga*), applied to birds, are not uncommon.

(11) The length of time covered by the action extends in every case over a number of years. To speak more correctly, each story embraces several short periods, which are treated more or less fully, but separated from one another by long intervals. In the main story the length of time may have been increased by duplication of incidents.

(12) The time of action relatively to the poets is stated only in what are doubtless comparatively late additions to the poems. The Mahābhārata claims to have been recited by Vaiçampāyana to Janamejaya, whose father, Parīkshit, was born shortly after the battle. The recitation therefore takes place presumably rather more than half a century after the events. In the Rāmāyaṇa, Book VII, it is said that the author, Vālmīki, taught the poem to Rāma's sons, whom he had brought up. Both poems therefore claim to be contemporary; but such evidence need not be taken too seriously, especially in the latter case.

The correspondence with Vol. I, p. 20 ff., is in general very close. It is only in No. 7 (if the current explanation is correct) and in No. 11 that important differences are noticeable; and in the latter the stories of Nala and of Sāvitrī do not differ greatly from the Norse heroic poems. Again, we have not noticed any striking peculiarities in the Indian stories which are common to the whole group. But they differ very greatly from one another. To a reader who is accustomed to Western heroic poetry the story of Rāma appears strange, owing to the numerous fantastic elements which it contains. But that is not the case in the other episodic stories. Imaginative elements occur everywhere; but they are not of unfamiliar types, except here. On the whole Indian heroic narrative poetry is doubtless far more faithfully represented by the episodes than by the main story; for the latter has been engulfed in didactic matter and also apparently much expanded in other respects, e.g. by the duplication of incidents, as well as by extreme prolixity, especially in descriptions of fighting. On the other hand the story of Nala would seem to have suffered little or nothing from such processes. Didactic elements are less noticeable than in Beowulf.

The story of Vidulā is known only from the speeches (Type B), which naturally do not come in for consideration here; no narrative has been preserved. The story of Çakuntalā has been adapted to didactic purposes (Type C), if indeed it is properly to be regarded as a heroic story—which seems to us very doubtful. Large elements in the main story also belong to Type C; but these are generally believed to be accretions to the original story.

Type D (heroic) is not directly represented in the Mahābhārata. A secondary instance (BD), however, is to be found in Gandhārī's lament for her sons (xi. 16 ff.), which is doubtless based upon elegies or dirges in actual use. Apart from its length, it bears a general resemblance to European compositions of this kind. Heroic panegyrics are very frequently mentioned in the Mahābhārata; but apparently no examples are given at length. Some references will be noted in the last chapter.

A much earlier instance of Type D is to be found in the Atharvaveda, xx. 127, a poem which seems to consist of two quite independent panegyrics. The first celebrates the generosity of a certain Kaurama, king of the Ruçama, a people or dynasty occasionally mentioned in the Rgveda. Of Kaurama himself apparently nothing is known elsewhere. The second is a panegyric upon Parikshit, king of the Kuru, and describes the prosperity and peace which prevail under his rule. This king is in all probability to be identified with the Parīkshit, son of Abhimanyu and father of Janamejaya,[1] to whom we have referred above (p. 481). In the Mahābhārata (xiv. lxvi ff.) he is said to have been a posthumous child, born shortly after the battle which forms the climax of the story. It would seem then that this poem, which is doubtless a contemporary work, was composed in the generation immediately after the battle.

Somewhat similar poetry is preserved in the Rgveda. As a rule it consists of a few stanzas—usually from three to five—appended to hymns to Indra or other deities. These stanzas most commonly contain prayers or thanksgivings for victory on behalf of a prince, and also celebrate his generosity to the poet, who is evidently a priest. Occasionally, however, a whole poem is occupied with matter of this kind.

---

[1] Cf. Rapson, *Cambridge History of India*, i. 301 f., 306. Other scholars (cf. Zimmer, *Altind. Leben*, p. 131, Keith, *Cambridge History of India*, i. 120, 122) have identified the subject of the panegyric with a much earlier Parīkshit, who appears in the genealogies (in Mahābh. i. 94 f. and the Purānas), sometimes in connection with a Janamejaya. We are inclined to attach little value to these genealogies, which seem largely to be made up from doublets of heroic names.

We may note especially two poems, IV. 15 and V. 27, each of which, like the piece referred to above, consists of two separate and apparently unconnected invocations. The former consists of invocations for Srnjaya, son of Devavāta, and for Somaka, son of Sahadeva, who was apparently a descendant of Srnjaya.[1] These princes must have been regarded as ancestors of the royal family of the Pancāla, to whom the names Srnjaya and Somaka are sometimes applied in the Mahābhārata. Drupada himself also is sometimes called Saumaka.[2] In V. 27 the first invocation is for a certain Tryaruna, the second for a certain Açvamedha. We do not know of any relationship between these two princes; Tryaruna seems to belong to a later period than Açvamedha. The two parts of the poem are in different metres.

There is an obvious resemblance between some of these Vedic poems, especially perhaps Ath. xx. 127, and the Welsh heroic panegyrics upon Urien and other British princes, noticed in Vol. I, p. 38 f., which likewise are largely concerned with the heroes' generosity.[3] But it is doubtful whether the Vedic poems can properly be regarded as heroic. The Rgveda examples come from collections of poetry belonging to priestly families; and the generosity for which the princes are celebrated lies in the reward or fee (*dakṣiṇā*) paid to the priestly poet for his services in interceding with the deities. Their successes are due to the deities's favour, which is secured thereby. Hence the great value of the rewards—which consist of horses, chariots, female slaves, cattle and treasure of various kinds.

Account must also be taken of a passage in the Çatapatha Brāhmana, XIII. i. 5, where the horse-sacrifice is described. It is here stated that the praises of the prince, for whom the sacrifice is offered, are sung by ecclesiastical singers during the sacrifice itself, and by a royal minstrel (*rājanya*) afterwards, in the course of the evening. The former celebrate the prince's sacrifices and generosity (to priests), the latter his battles and victories. The panegyrics of the Rgveda clearly belong not to the latter

---

[1] Cf. Ait. Br. VII. 34, where Sahadeva is called Sārnjaya. Some scholars (cf. Keith, *op. cit.* I. 83 f.) take Srnjaya here as a national or dynastic name, the individual being Daivavāta. It is most difficult to distinguish between family and personal names in the Rgveda; but the Ait. Brāhm. passage seems to us to favour the latter here, especially in view of the association of Srnjaya with Nārada and Parvata in Mahābh. VII. 55 ff., XII. 29 ff. Another difficulty is caused by the fact that patronymics may mean either 'son of' or 'descendant of'.

[2] In the genealogies of the Purānas, whatever they may be worth, he is great-grandson of Somaka; but the latter's father Sahadeva is son of Sudās.

[3] For other early references to poetry of this kind see Vol. I, pp. 574 f., 582.

type, which is unquestionably heroic, but to the former. Poems such as
IV. 15, or rather its constituent parts, may have been composed as
'appendices' to previously existing hymns, in order to adapt them to the
occasion. In the case of the Atharva poem referred to above this is not
quite so clear. The series of poems (xx. 127–136) to which it belongs
seems to be of unknown derivation; and the panegyric on Parikshit at
least is hardly incompatible with a secular origin. In any case the passage
in the Çatapatha shows that the cultivation of heroic poetry of Type D
goes back at least to the Brāhmana period.

There may of course have been a time—before the caste system began
to develop—when heroic and non-heroic poetry of this type were less
clearly differentiated; but into this question we need not enter here. It
may be observed, however, that in the Rgveda, though the poems
themselves are not heroic, the prominence assigned to princes, and much
of what is said of them, seems to indicate a strong and probably dominant heroic element in society. We may therefore take the opportunity
here of adding a few remarks on the passages relating to princes contained in this collection.

First, in regard to chronology, it is possible to distinguish several
different phases in the period. In one family at least five generations
seem to be represented. In the earliest phase the most prominent person
is Divodāsa. Contemporary with him are a number of other princes,
among whom we may mention Srnjaya and Çrutarvan. In the next
phase the chief figures are Sudās and Trasadasyu. The former was a
grandson, or possibly son, of Divodāsa and a contemporary of the
famous seers Vasishtha and Viçvāmitra. Later phases are less easy to
distinguish; for references to princes seem to be much less frequent.
But in x. 32 f. we hear of three princes who appear to be son, grandson
and great-grandson of Trasadasyu. If these hymns are among the latest
in the collection, as seems quite likely, the whole time covered by the
Rgveda need not extend over more than about half a dozen generations.
The only ancestor of the Kuru mentioned in the Rgveda is Çamtanu,
who is clearly to be identified with the Çāntanu of the Mahābhārata (cf.
p. 475), the father of the old hero Bhīshma. The poem in which he
figures (x. 98) is an invocation for rain by his priest Devāpi, and is
likewise generally believed to be among the latest in the collection; but
it shows that the Rgveda reaches nearly to the times treated in the
Mahābhārata. On the other hand there are a number of references to
ancestors of the Pancāla, as we have seen. But neither the Pancāla nor
the Kuru are mentioned by name.

The earlier phases of the period have distinctive features of their own. The first phase is evidently a time of warfare—barbaric and apparently heroic warfare, carried on largely for the sake of plunder.[1] The enemies are chiefly people of a different race, known as Dāsa or Dasyu; they are frequently described as black, and once (v. 29. 10) as 'noseless'. The names of many of their chiefs—Çambara, Varcin, Pipru, etc.—are preserved in association with those of their conquerors, sometimes in the panegyric stanzas themselves, sometimes in later poems, which celebrate in catalogue form the great deeds performed by Indra or the Açvins in helping famous princes and seers of the past. The scholastic tradition of later times frequently regards them as demons—which is doubtless due largely to the highly figurative diction employed in the poems. It is often difficult to determine whether a poet really means actual human warfare or mythical incidents, such as the slaying of Vrtra, or elemental phenomena. The Dāsa are, however, now generally recognised to be the native (pre-Aryan) inhabitants of the land. It is not at all clear that they were a primitive people. In addition to cattle they have castles and abundance of treasure; indeed they may well have been more civilised than their conquerors. The prehistoric civilisation of north-west India seems to have belonged to much earlier times; but traces of it were perhaps still preserved.

After the first phase the Dāsa seem to be less prominent. Sudās' most famous battle is fought against a combination of other Aryan princes in the Punjab. He also fights (VII. 18, etc.) against a number of peoples who are seldom or never mentioned elsewhere, and who are commonly believed to have been non-Aryan; but this battle takes place on the Jumna. For the later periods there appears to be comparatively little evidence.

The geography of the Rgveda is quite different from that of the epics. Most of the princes, at least in the earlier phases, clearly belong to the Punjab. The rivers of that region are familiar; references to the Indus and the Sarasvatī are very numerous. But the Ganges and the Jumna are very rarely mentioned; and we hear nothing of the kingdoms in their basins, which form the scene of the Mahābhārata. Çamtanu may well have reigned on the Ganges; but he belongs to the end of the period. In Sudās' time this region seems to be occupied by unknown and probably non-Aryan peoples. In a poem of the earliest phase (iii. 23) the an-

---

[1] We may note the curious and apparently suggestive name Dasyave Vrka borne by a prince who figures much in the supplementary hymns (Vālakhilya) attached to Book VIII. This name can hardly mean anything else than 'Wolf to the Dasyu'.

cestors of the Pancāla are settled in the Punjab. And it would seem that the Kuru, as well as the Pancāla, claimed descent from the Bharata of the Punjab. The evidence is of course mainly negative, but so far as it goes it suggests that the Aryan conquest or Aryanisation of the Ganges-Jumna region took place during the later phases of the Rgveda period, i.e. not so very long before the time of the heroes of the Mahābhārata.

CHAPTER III

THE HEROIC MILIEU

INDIVIDUALISM

IN Vol. I, Ch. IV, we discussed the characteristics of the life portrayed in heroic stories under the following headings: (1) the social standing of the personnel; (2) the scenes of the stories; (3) the accessories of heroic life; (4) the social standards and conventions observed in heroic poetry and saga. It will be convenient to adopt the same classification here.

(1) As in the West the interest of the stories is centred in the doings of princes and princesses. Apart from them practically the only persons mentioned are their servants, who are not very prominent, and the Brahmans, who may be compared with the priests and seers of the West. Brahmans are far more important than the priests and seers of the Homeric poems, and more even than the Druids and *filid* of heroic Ireland. But their importance is in general limited to what seem to be accretions to the stories. In the main action they figure chiefly as agents of princes.

References to persons of other ranks, e.g. artisans and merchants, are rare and slight. When the heroes come to Draupadī's svayamvara, they are disguised as Brahmans and lodge at a potter's house; but nothing is said of this man, and his name is not mentioned. Again, when Damayantī is deserted in the forest, she joins a caravan of merchants. Several speeches by the leader and other members of the caravan are given (Nala, XII, 118 ff.), but their names are not mentioned; and the description of their behaviour after the disaster is hardly sympathetic.

There are certain exceptional characters who require notice here. Drona is a Brahman, but also a warrior. In particular he is an expert in archery, in which he instructs the young princes of the Kuru, including the sons of Pāndu. When the time comes for him to claim his fee, he demands the capture of King Drupada, against whom he harbours a special grudge. Arjuna accomplishes this task for him; and Drona now becomes king of part of the Pancāla kingdom. The story here seems hardly to be consistent; for apparently he remains at the

Kuru court. In the final battle, after the fall of Bhīshma, he commands the army of the Kuru.

Vidura, the judge of the Kuru, is a half-brother of the kings, Dhṛtarāshtra and Pāṇḍu; but his mother is a serving woman of low caste. He is said to be an incarnation of the god of justice. He is an honoured and influential member of the court, but seems not to be a warrior.

But the most interesting of these exceptional cases is Karna. He is a son of Pṛthā (Kuntī), and therefore half-brother to the sons of Pāṇḍu; but his father is the sun-god (Sūrya). His origin, however, is unknown to himself, or to anyone except his mother, who does not divulge the fact that he is her son until shortly before his death (vi. clxv). Throughout his life he passes as the son of a certain Adhiratha, a charioteer. Owing to his prowess he is welcomed by Duryodhana, who is jealous of Arjuna, and made king of Anga by him. At the svayamvara of Draupadī he appears with the other princes as a competitor, but is disqualified by the princess, who declares that she will not consent to marry a charioteer's son. He seems to remain at the Kuru court, and commands the army in the last battle, after Drona's fall.

(2) The scene of action is commonly, as in Western heroic stories, either a king's court or a battlefield or other place of adventure. Battle scenes are described at very great length, more fully even than in the Iliad. When the scene is laid in a king's court, we meet with the same love of ceremony as in Greek and English heroic poetry, though it takes the form of description rather than of action. Examples may be found in Mahābh. i. clxxxvii, cxcvi, ii. xxxiv f.[1] But the most distinctive feature of the Indian poems is the forest scene. Sometimes the forest is a place of adventure, as in the stories of Bhīma's encounters with Rākshasa (Mahābh. i. cliv ff., clxv). Here also we may refer to Damayantī's plight, when she is deserted by Nala, and the attack of the elephants (Nala, xi ff.). More frequently, however, we hear of forests as the homes of ascetics, and as places to which heroes retire, either for concealment or to carry out vows, as ascetics. A considerable part of the Mahābhārata is occupied with forest scenes, in which Yudhishthira converses with Brahmans. In general of course such scenes reflect the encroachment of the non-heroic upon the heroic milieu.

(3) In India, as elsewhere, warfare seems to be an essential rather than an accessory of heroic life. But it is hardly as chronic as in the West. Curiously enough the story of Nala contains no reference to

[1] For further examples cf. Sidhanta, *The Heroic Age of India*, p. 77 ff.

fighting of any kind, though there is some independent evidence, as we shall see later, that Nala was a warlike prince.

Feasting and drinking are not made so much of as in the West, though we hear of magnificent banquets in honour of distinguished guests. Religious festivals are sometimes (e.g. Mahābh. i. ccxxi) scenes of drunken revelry, in which even the king and queen participate. Rich presents are sent by one prince to another, and among these we find chariots, horses and elephants, as well as jewels and precious stuffs. A good idea as to the things most valued in heroic society may be gathered from Mahābh. i. cxciv. 11. When Draupadī accompanies the heroes to their lodging after her svayamvara, her brother Dhrshtadyumna follows at a distance, anxious to know who they are. They are disguised as Brahmans; but he contrives to overhear their conversations, and finds that it is all concerned with weapons, chariots, and elephants—from which he concludes that they belong to the princely (Kshatriya) caste.

It may be observed that, in spite of the frequent references to elephants, they do not seem to be used much by the greater heroes of the stories.[1] In actual practice the use of the chariot and horses is far more frequent, both in battle and on peaceful journeys. But the method of fighting is not that of the Iliad. The chief weapon is the bow, as with the Egyptians of the nineteenth dynasty and the Hittites, though the sword, battle-axe and other weapons are also often referred to. Princes are expected to be skilled in the management of horses; and sometimes, as in the Iliad, they act as drivers for other princes. Nala, when he is disguised and in exile, obtains a position as groom to Rtuparna. He is said to be unrivalled in swift driving. Arjuna offers to act as charioteer to Uttara, son of the king of the Matsya. Further examples will be noticed later.

Devotion to horses is perhaps the heroic feature most prominent in the Rgveda. References to horses occur everywhere; and whole hymns are occupied with the subject. This feature goes back to the earliest times. In viii. 57, which dates from the time of Divodāsa, one stanza (18) is devoted to the praise of a mare called Vrshanvatī.

Among indoor amusements we hear chiefly of music and dice. The former will require notice in a later chapter. The latter is the besetting sin of princes, and brings both Nala and Yudhishthira to ruin. We know nothing of this from the heroic stories of the West, though gnomic poetry and other authorities testify to its existence. Tacitus (*Germ.* 24), however, describes the gaming proclivities of the Teutonic nobility of

---

[1] Cf. Sidhanta, *op. cit.* p. 139 f.

his day in a form which is practically identical with what is found in the Mahābhārata.

(4) Statements of social standards are expressed in the Mahābhārata far more frequently than in Western heroic poetry. But this is due in the main to the very large didactic accretions which the poem has received. Indeed the extent to which the work has been subjected to Brahmanic influence renders it difficult at times to determine what the heroic standards were, except by what may be regarded as somewhat arbitrary judgment. Thus no virtues are more frequently commended than those of reverence and generosity to Brahmans. This may to some extent faithfully represent the feeling of heroic society. But there can be no doubt that Brahmanic influence is in the main responsible for such passages.

In general the qualities for which heroes are praised belong to the usual aristocratic type. The chief perhaps, as in the West, is prowess in arms, usually, if not always, combined with physical strength. Against this, however, stands another, essentially non-heroic, type of character, represented above all by Yudhishthira, which is distinguished by piety and reverence towards Brahmans. Common to both of these is a strict sense of honour, exemplified in adherence to a spoken word interpreted in the most narrowly literal sense. A hero may be involved in the most serious difficulties by promising, out of politeness, to accede to a request before he knows what it is. Through a remark of this kind Nala has to act as agent for the gods, when they are suitors for his intended. The situation is not unlike that of Pwyll at his wedding-feast. An absurd instance of this devotion to truth occurs in Mahābh. I. cxciii, where the marriage of Draupadī to the five brothers is attributed to a casual remark made by their mother, when they return from the svayamvara: thinking that they have been begging alms, she says that they must enjoy in common what they have acquired. There can be little doubt that this story is due to an attempt to explain the strange marriage. But in VII. cxci. 43 ff. there is an ugly story which is not so easy to account for. Drona appeals to Yudhishthira as a man of exceptionally high honour, to tell him whether his son has been killed. Yudhishthira, by muttering one word inaudibly, gives an answer which entirely misleads Drona, and brings about his death.

Unsympathetic characters are on the whole portrayed in a more unfavourable light than in Teutonic and Greek heroic poetry. Duryodhana's conduct to his cousins is malignant and treacherous throughout, while his brother Duhshasana treats Draupadī shamefully. On the other hand the best men sometimes behave badly—as in the Iliad, but even worse. Thus in Mahābh. I. cxxxiv, when Ekalavya, prince of the Nishāda, recognises Drona as his preceptor, because he has been practising archery before his image, Drona demands and takes Ekalavya's thumb as his fee, and renders him unable to shoot. We are reminded of the story of the *fili* Athirne, noticed in Vol. I, p. 98. It may be that the standard here, as in the Irish case, is not heroic; for Drona, though a warrior, is a Brahman. And, apart from this consideration, it is of course possible that both this case and that of Yudhishthira's equivoca-tion may have originated in the Brahmanic strata of the poem. In contrast to these cases the conduct of Rāma's brothers conveys a very favourable impression of Indian heroic society. But here again Brah-manic influence is possible.

Etiquette and courtesy are observed much as in Western heroic poetry, if we except the excessive reverence paid to Brahmans. Angry scenes occur from time to time, even at festivities. We may instance the fight which takes place at Draupadī's svayamvara, and more especially the scene at Yudhishthira's sacrifice, described in Mahābh. II. xxxvii ff., where Çiçupāla insults Krshna and Bhīshma, with its tragic ending. In general, however, such scenes are not very different from what we find in the Iliad.

The standard of decorum observed in the telling of a story is some-times, e.g. in the story of Nala, quite on a level with that of Teutonic and Greek heroic poetry; sometimes it is on a lower plane, comparable with that of Irish sagas. Not unfrequently we meet with descriptions of disgusting incidents. It would seem, however, that these are usually, if not always, of non-heroic origin. They certainly occur much more often in stories relating to Brahmans than elsewhere.

In its attitude towards individualism and nationality Indian heroic poetry differs little, if at all, from that of the West. The heroes are drawn from various kingdoms throughout the northern half of India; and there can be little doubt that within this area the stories had an international circulation. In the main theme of the Mahābhārata interest is centred in the kingdom of the Kuru, and it is to a later king of the Kuru, a descendant of Arjuna, that the story is first related. But princes of the Pancāla, the Matsya and the Vrshni are also prominent, while other heroes come from as far west as the Indus and as far east as Magadha. In the story of Rāma the hero belongs to Ayodhyā (Oude), while his adventures take place in the south of India. In the story of

Nala the scene is laid chiefly among the Nishadha and the Vidarbha, on the southern fringe of Aryan territory.

In every story of course there are certain leading characters who are specially 'sympathetic'. But the interest lies in them as individuals, not in their nationality; and the nationality of their opponents is seldom disparaged. Indeed the feeling for nationality is hardly more pronounced than in Teutonic and Greek heroic poetry. Krshna acts as charioteer to Arjuna in the great battle; but his relatives and the forces of his kingdom are ranged on the opposite side. It may be observed that, as in the West, the wives of kings and princes usually come from other kingdoms; and the part which they play in Indian heroic poetry is certainly not less important than elsewhere.

Even the opponents of the chief heroes are commonly treated with respect and even sympathy. The treatment of Bhīshma and Drona, the commanders of the enemy army, is entirely sympathetic; and even Karna, in spite of his bitter hostility to Arjuna, is always regarded at least with respect; indeed he is constantly represented as a much-wronged man. Among the leading characters of the story it is only the sons of Dhrtarāshtra who are portrayed in a wholly unsympathetic light; and even they bear honorific epithets and distinguish themselves by courage in battle. The blind king himself is a pathetic and kindly character, though too easily influenced by his sons.

In the story of Rāma the hero is banished in the interest of his brother Bharata. But Bharata himself is wholly guiltless, and does everything possible to preserve Rāma's rights. His mother Kaikeyī behaves very badly, but only after being instigated by a minor character. The only real hostility is with Rāvana and his Rākshasa or 'demons'. But even Rāvana has two brothers who try to dissuade him from his unjust conduct towards Rāma. One of them eventually fights on Rāma's side. The 'apes', with one or two exceptions, are wholly sympathetic. If the 'apes' and 'demons' really denote two peoples of southern India, one may infer some disparagement from the names, which may of course date from times anterior to the story; but otherwise there is no sign of any general feeling of hostility.

The story of Nala is concerned only with individuals; and there is no unsympathetic human character except Pushkara, who is not very prominent.

Heroic warfare, as in the West, consists mainly of single combats. Even in pitched battles the issue is decided by the prowess of individual heroes, though vast numbers of their followers are said to be slain. In combats warriors are expected to behave in a chivalrous manner;[1] and sometimes distinguished men refuse to fight weaker opponents. But in point of fact it happens not unfrequently that, just as in the West, even the greatest heroes act unfairly. Arjuna kills the aged Bhīshma by a contemptible ruse. And in the decisive combat between this hero and Karna neither heeds the appeals of the other for fair play; Arjuna's victory is due to an accident to Karna's chariot. The means by which Yudhishthira and Bhīma bring about the death of Drona are despicable to the last degree.

It has been mentioned above that the heroes regularly use chariots in warfare, as in the Greek and Irish heroic stories, though in India the chief weapon is the bow. Sometimes, as in the Iliad, the charioteer is himself a very distinguished man. Arjuna's charioteer in the great battle is Krshna, and to him he very largely owes his success. Karna, when he goes to encounter Arjuna, asks for and obtains as his charioteer Çalya, king of the Madra, who afterwards succeeds him as commander-in-chief. It is individual achievement as a warrior, rather than skill in generalship, which is looked for even in a leader; and consequently the charioteer is of prime importance.

Recklessness, boasting and self-glorification are as much in evidence in Indian heroic poetry as in that of the West. For an example we may refer to Karna's boasting before his encounter with Arjuna, who, he alleges, is hiding from him. For this he is derided by his charioteer. But Çalya himself later indulges in more extravagant boasts, saying that when he is angered he can fight with the whole world, deities, Asuras and men—and much more in the same strain.[2]

Thirst for glory seems to be as prominent a motive as in Teutonic and Greek heroic poetry. As an example we may cite Mahābh. III. ccxcix. 31, where Karna says that he longs for renown in this world even at the sacrifice of his life. But this sentiment is usually, as here, combined with the Kshatriya belief that by death in battle the hero will obtain eternal bliss in the next life.[3]

The causes of strife are always of a personal character. The great battle is due to the jealousy of the sons of Dhrtarāshtra, who are determined to exclude their cousins from a share in the kingship, and take

---

[1] Cf. Mahābh. v. vii. 30.
[2] Cf. Mahābh. VIII. xl. 3 ff.; IX. vii. 2 ff. For further examples cf. Sidhanta, *The Heroic Age of India*, p. 85 f.
[3] Cf. Sidhanta, *op. cit.* p. 82 f. Close analogies are to be found in Norse records; cf. Chadwick, *Cult of Othin*, p. 9 ff.

17

advantage of Yudhishthira's misfortunes with the dice to drive them into exile. The sons of Pāndu on their side are incited to vengeance by the insults offered to Draupadī. Karna's enmity against Arjuna is due largely to the slight put upon him by Draupadī at the svayamvara, when she accepted Arjuna as her husband. Even in the battle itself the desire for personal vengeance is often the guiding motive. Such is the case, e.g., in Arjuna's fight with Jayadratha and in the fighting between Drona and his son and the kings of Pancāla. Rāma's war against Rāvana is caused by the abduction by the latter of Sītā, Rāma's wife.

Other causes of strife are very similar to what we find in Western heroic stories. Among the chief of them is cattle-raiding. An example on a huge scale is described in Mahābh. iv. xxxv, where the princes of the Kuru take advantage of the absence of Virāta, king of the Matsya, to drive off his cattle to the number of sixty thousand. The same practice is frequently implied in the Rgveda.

Ambition and love of adventure likewise often lead to war. In connection with certain sacrifices we meet with what we may call regularised forms of provocation. Before the horse-sacrifice (Aśvamedha) it was customary to let the victim roam at will, attended by armed guards; and not seldom we hear of strife arising through its seizure by ambitious neighbouring princes. Again, in Mahābh. ii. xxv ff., when Yudhishthira is preparing to celebrate the Rājasūya sacrifice—the ceremony of his consecration as king—he sends his brothers out in all directions to demand submission and tribute. At the conclusion of the sacrifice (ib. xxxvi ff.) a gift of honour (arghya) is to be presented to the most distinguished of the guests—a custom which may be compared with the Irish 'champion's portion' (cf. Vol. i, p. 49 f.). Bhīshma decides in favour of Krshna; but his decision is disputed by Çiçupāla, and a quarrel arises, which ends in tragedy.

Again, we hear from time to time of marriage by capture—when a suitor, or someone acting on his behalf, carries off a princess, or more than one, perhaps from a svayamvara. We have already (p. 475) had occasion to mention Bhīshma's exploit, when he carried off the princesses of Kāçī, and the fight between him and the suitors which followed. In Mahābh. i. ccxxi ff. Krshna advises Arjuna to carry off his sister Subhadrā, and argues that this is recognised as an honourable act for a Kshatriya. Arjuna follows his advice and carries her off (ib. ccxxii). Her relatives are deeply angered, and prepare to pursue him; but Krshna pacifies them, and the matter is settled amicably.

In short the picture of society presented to us in the Mahābhārata is that of a princely class as self-willed and irresponsible as any of those we have met with in Europe. Perhaps the most striking case of all is the behaviour of Çalya. On the eve of the great battle he sets out with his troops to join Yudhishthira. But he is waylaid by Duryodhana, who persuades him to come over to his side. Then he meets Yudhishthira and tells him that he has joined the enemy; but promises that he will nullify the prowess of Karna. In the end he becomes commander-in-chief of the Kuru army, and is killed by Yudhishthira.

It is hardly necessary to summarise the evidence discussed in this chapter. Analogies with the heroic poetry and saga treated in Vol. I will be found at every turn. Indian heroic story is concerned, like that of Europe, with the doings of a princely class; and in both cases the salient feature is an unrestrained individualism. It is true that these characteristics are often obscured by Brahmanic influence, and also that the prestige enjoyed by the Brahmans dates from early times. But we see no reason for doubting what seems to be the generally accepted view, that the Brahmanic elements in the stories are secondary and due to constant encroachment upon the heroic.

We have confined our attention almost entirely to the Mahābhārata. The Rgveda frequently shows a very decided feeling for nationality, as between Aryan and Dāsa (cf. p. 485). The latter are usually regarded with deep aversion. But the Rgveda is non-heroic literature, and dates from a much earlier period.

CHAPTER IV

NON-HEROIC POETRY AND SAGA

THIS class of literature is very widely represented in ancient India and is found in nearly all Types of poetry and saga. Most of the references to (human) individuals which occur in the Vedas and Brāhmanas are of non-heroic character; indeed, in the Brāhmana literature, including the Upanishads, we do not know of any exceptions. The Mahābhārata had its origin doubtless in heroic poetry; but this has been largely transformed, and a vast amount of non-heroic matter added to it. Non-heroic, together with antiquarian, elements are predominant in the Purānas.

In Vol. I (p. 96) we classified the non-heroic material as follows: (1) Stories relating to Christian saints. (2) Stories relating to prophets, wizards, and persons, other than ecclesiastics, who are credited with abnormal or supernatural powers and knowledge. (3) Stories relating to persons not included in either of these categories. These persons are usually kings or princes. In ancient India the first of these classes is of course wanting; the same person is both seer and saint. Moreover both seers and kings figure in the great majority of the stories. We shall therefore take these classes together. First we will take examples from non-heroic stories and scenes in the Brāhmanas, the Upanishads and the Mahābhārata, where the circumstances are made more or less clear. After that we will notice references to seers in the Rgveda, where many of them speak as authors.

First we may take the story of Çunahçepa, which is told briefly, in the form of saga, in the Aitareya Brāhmana, VII. 13 ff. There was a king named Hariçcandra, who was childless. He consulted the seer (ṛṣi) Nārada, and by his advice prayed to the god Varuna to give him a son, whom he promised to sacrifice to him. The son is born and named Rohita; but the father keeps putting off the fulfilment of his vow until he is grown up. Then Rohita makes off to the forest, and his father, now unable to carry out the vow, is attacked with dropsy. Rohita is smitten with remorse; but Indra dissuades him from returning home. After five years he meets with a destitute seer named Ajīgarta, who has three sons and is willing to sell one of them for a hundred cattle. Rohita takes this son, Çunahçepa, home with him; and it is agreed by all, including

Varuna, that he shall be sacrificed in Rohita's place. But no one is willing to bind or slay him, until his father, Ajīgarta, offers to do so for two hundred more cows. Then Çunahçepa sings to the gods a number of hymns, by which his bonds are loosed and the king healed. This story, it is stated, is to be recited to a king on certain solemn occasions. The remunerations to be paid to the priests are very high. It may be observed that, in addition to a number of hymn stanzas quoted from the Rgveda, the story contains several speech poems (Type B). It must have had a long history, for references to it occur frequently in the Rgveda[1].

The story of Cyavana is told first in the Çatapatha Brāhmana, iv. i. 5. Cyavana, who was a decrepit and ghostlike seer, was pelted with clods by boys in the service of a king named Çaryāta. In wrath he causes discord in the king's following; and the king, to appease him, brings him his daughter in marriage. The Açvins try to persuade her to leave him; but she remains faithful, and induces them to restore him to youth. In return he instructs them how to obtain a portion in the sacrifices of the gods. The story is introduced in explanation of the origin of a certain sacrificial ceremony and, like the previous story, may be regarded as an example of saga of Type C. Its antiquity, as in the last case, is shown by references to it in the Rgveda.

The same story is told again (in verse) in the Mahābhārata, iii. cxxii ff., in a highly embellished form. Cyavana here is an ascetic of the most extreme kind, and remains motionless so long that an ant-hill grows up round him, and only his eyes are visible. The king's daughter comes to play at the ant-hill, and pokes out his eyes with a thorn. He refuses to be appeased until she is given to him in marriage. Later, when the Açvins have restored his youth, he offers soma to them on behalf of the king. Then Indra in wrath threatens him with the thunderbolt. But he disables the god's arm, and produces a monster, which makes ready to devour him, so that he cries for mercy.

Stories of this kind are very numerous in the Mahābhārata. The non-heroic element in this work has indeed developed to such an extent that even in the main theme the centre of interest has largely been diverted. It is generally agreed that the central figure in the story originally was the heroic Arjuna. But as we have it, this hero is on the whole subordinated to his elder brother Yudhishthira, who is not distinguished

---

[1] It can hardly have been known in its present form in Rgveda times; cf. Keith, *Rigveda Brahmanas*, p. 63 f. But there seems to be no reason for doubting that it was non-heroic from the beginning.

for heroic qualities, apart from his addiction to gambling; to the modern reader he seems a somewhat contemptible character. He is, however, extremely pious, and given to asceticism; and on this account he is much revered, and is sometimes able to effect what others cannot do. An example may be taken from an incident related in III. clxxviii ff. Bhīma, the second brother, is attacked in the forest by a monstrous snake, which turns out to be the ancient legendary king Nahusha, a great-grandson of the primeval Manu. According to other passages in the Mahābhārata (v. xi ff., etc.) Nahusha had once attained to such power that he even overcame the gods and usurped the place of Indra. He behaved with great insolence towards the (heavenly) seers, especially the great seer Agastya, who eventually cursed him. This brought about his fall, and he had to spend ten thousand years upon the earth as a snake. His only hope of release was to find someone who could answer all his (philosophical) questions. Yudhishthira succeeds in this task, and thereby not only releases Nahusha from the curse, but also saves his brother's life.

Among the non-heroic stories which are introduced as episodes we will next take an example relating to the remote past—the story of Yayāti (I. lxxv ff., etc.), which has special features of its own. Çukra, the priest of the king of the Asuras, has a daughter called Devayānī, who goes to bathe with Çarmishthā, the king's daughter. The two girls begin to quarrel. Devayānī claims precedence, as being the daughter of a Brahman; but Çarmishthā rejoins that her (Devayānī's) father's function is merely to sing the praises of her own father, the king. In the end she throws Devayānī into a well—from which she is rescued by King Yayāti, son of the Nahusha mentioned above. Çukra, enraged at the outrage done to his daughter, threatens to leave the king, to whom his services are indispensable. He therefore has to promise whatever Çukra demands; and the latter claims Çarmishthā as a handmaid for his daughter.

Devayānī again meets with Yayāti, who marries her. She takes Çarmishthā with her; and Yayāti promises to have no relations with her. Devayānī bears to Yayāti two sons, named Yadu and Turvasu; but after some years she discovers that he has also, in spite of his promise, had three sons—named Druhyu, Anu and Pūru—by Çarmishthā. She then complains to her father, who curses Yayāti, and brings decrepitude upon him. He allows him, however, to find a substitute to bear the curse for him. Yayāti then appeals to his five sons; but only the youngest, Pūru, is willing to undergo the punishment. After flourishing for a thousand years, Yayāti restores to Pūru his youth and gives him the throne, while he himself takes over his own decrepitude and retires to the forest as a hermit.

This story, as we have it, is clearly non-heroic (Type C). It is designed to show the superiority of the power of the Brahman over that of the king. But, just as clearly, it contains elements which point to a different origin. Yayāti's five sons are eponymoi[1] of five peoples or kingdoms, which are mentioned not unfrequently in the Rgveda and apparently form some kind of confederation. They are represented as occupying the greater part of the Punjab. The Turvaça and the Yadu, who bear the names of Devayānī's sons, seem to have been more closely connected than the rest. The Pūru are apparently the dominant people of the group in the Rgveda. In the heroic stories of the Mahābhārata, however, these peoples, except the Yadu, seem to be rarely or never mentioned, though some of the names, especially Pūru, reappear in the Purānas. It may be inferred therefore that this part of the story is derived from antiquarian tradition or speculation dating from Vedic times. In its present form additions have been made, probably at a much later date, for the purpose of illustrating the superiority of the Brahman over the Kshatriya. But the changes evidently had to be kept within certain limits. The dominant position is still retained by a son of the Kshatriya queen, though he owes it not to prowess but to filial piety.

Next we will take a story of purely non-heroic interest, illustrating (as usual) the superiority of Brahmanic to princely power. In III. cxcii a king named Çala goes hunting, and his horses are unable to overtake the stag. He hears that the seer Vāmadeva has horses of incomparable speed, and proceeds to borrow them; but afterwards refuses to give them back. The seer first sends a messenger, and then comes in person, to reclaim his horses; but the king is obdurate and says that such fine horses should not belong to a seer. Vāmadeva, regarding himself as insulted, produces four fearful Rākshasas, armed with spears; and as the king still refuses to give way, these kill him on the spot. His brother Dala, who succeeds him, likewise refuses to restore the horses; and when the seer again comes to reclaim them, he tries to shoot him. But the arrow kills his own son; he is unable to shoot at the seer, and consequently has to give in. Vāmadeva is presumably the seer to whom Book IV of the Rgveda is traditionally ascribed.

---

[1] Four of the sons have the same names as the peoples. In the remaining case the form *Turvasu* would seem to have been assimilated in its ending to the others. The variation between ç and s is not unknown in other names, e.g. *Kosala* and *Koçala*.

One of the best known of these stories is that which describes the deadly quarrel of the two famous seers Viçvāmitra and Vasishtha, to whom tradition ascribes Book III, and Book VII of the Rgveda respectively. According to this story (I. clxxvii; cf. IX. xl) Viçvāmitra was a prince, and came first by chance, when he was hunting, to Vasishtha's hermitage. The latter had a marvellous cow, which gave him whatever he wished. Viçvāmitra is eager to buy the cow, and offers up to ten thousand ordinary cows for it; but Vasishtha will not part with it. Then Viçvāmitra brings his followers to take the cow by force; but the cow—at Vasishtha's command, according to one version—produces a body of armed men, who drive the raiders off. Viçvāmitra is so much impressed with the superiority of mantic to royal power that he renounces his rank and devotes himself to extreme asceticism, by means of which he eventually becomes a great seer. He does not, however, forget his grudge against Vasishtha; for he afterwards brings about the death of the latter's sons.

A king named Kalmāshapāda, but more often described as Saudāsa,[1] i.e. son or descendant of Sudās(a), is cursed by Vasishtha's eldest son, Çaktri (Çakti), whom he has struck with a whip. Viçvāmitra causes a Rakshas or demon to enter the king; and this makes him kill and eat first Çaktri himself and then all his brothers. Vasishtha tries to commit suicide from grief, but afterwards bears his sorrow with patience. He finds the king roaming in the forest like a savage, and frees him from the curse. The king submits to him and is forgiven.

Apparently no early authority mentions a quarrel between Viçvāmitra and Vasishtha. In the Aitareya Brāhmana both of them are said to take part in the sacrifice of Çunahçepa (cf. p. 496 f.); and there is no doubt, as we shall see below, that they were contemporaries. The poetry, however, quoted in this story seems to imply that Viçvāmitra was a prince, as well as a seer. Again, the Kaushītaki Brāhmana, IV. 8, knows of a quarrel between Vasishtha and the sons (or descendants) of Sudās; he is said to have overcome them after his own sons had been slain by them. Some elements in the story given above are therefore fairly old. The relations of Vasishtha and Viçvāmitra with King Sudās himself will have to be noticed later.

Çaktri has a posthumous son born to him named Parāçara, who is brought up by his grandfather Vasishtha. When he learns the story of

---

[1] References to the cannibal king under this name are frequent. It is curious that XIV. lvi ff. is a variant of I. iii. 96 ff., where the king is called Paushya and is not a cannibal.

his father's death he becomes inflamed with the desire of wreaking ven-geance upon the world; but Vasishtha persuades him to content himself with a sacrifice of Rākshasa, whom he burns in a great fire (I. clxxx–iii). In I. cv (and elsewhere) he is the father of Vyāsa by Satyavatī, who later became the wife of Çāntanu (cf. p. 475). It may be mentioned that the Vishnu Purāna claims to have been narrated by Parāçara, whom it places in the time of Parīkshit. He can hardly be an invention of late times, as his name occurs repeatedly in the White Yajurveda. On the other hand the name *Parāçara* occurs in the Rgveda, VII. xviii, beside *Vasishtha*.

The Mahābhārata itself (I. i, and elsewhere) claims to have been com-posed by Vyāsa, also called Krshna Dvaipāyana, the son of Parāçara and Satyavatī; he is also said (*ib.*) to have arranged the Vedas. He is fre-quently introduced in the poem, and represented as a very great seer and ascetic. In I. cv he is called in by his mother to beget offspring for her younger son Vicitravīrya, who has died childless; and therefore Dhrta-rāshtra, Pāndu and Vidura are represented as his sons. He often visits his descendants, sometimes to console the sons of Pāndu during their exile, sometimes to dissuade Dhrtarāshtra from hostility towards them; but he seems not to influence the course of the action. In the introduc-tory part of Book I (lx, and elsewhere) he also visits Janamejaya, the great-great-grandson of Pāndu, when that king is celebrating the sacrifice of snakes. At his command his disciple Vaiçampāyana recites the Mahābhārata to entertain the king. It is commonly held that Vyāsa is a fictitious character, though both his name and that of Vaiçampāyana are recorded from early times.[1] Clearly neither the chronology of his life nor his claims as an author will bear examination; but that is all that can be said with confidence. We see no reason for denying that a learned ascetic of this name may have existed. But did he live in Janamejaya's time or about five generations earlier?

The story of the snake-sacrifice is one of the most curious incidents in the whole work. Parīkshit had hung a dead snake round the neck of a seer who refused to speak to him (I. xlix, *ad. fin.*); unknown to the king he was observing a vow of silence. The seer's son, infuriated at the insult, cursed Parīkshit, declaring that Takshaka, the king of the snakes, would kill him in a week. The king was warned by the seer and took all precautions; but Takshaka contrived to evade them all, and the king perished. In course of time his son Janamejaya determines to take vengeance; in I. iii (*ad fin.*) he is incited thereto by the seer Uttanka, who has a private grudge against Takshaka. Janamejaya now institutes

[1] In the Taittirīya Āranyaka, which has not been accessible to us.

a great sacrifice (1. li ff.), and the snakes in vast numbers fall into the fire. Takshaka is protected by Indra; but in the end he is brought to hover unconscious over the fire. At the last moment he is saved by the seer Astika, who is partly of snake blood and who begs as a boon from Janamejaya that the sacrifice shall be stopped. In 1. lviii. Janamejaya invites Astika to the great horse sacrifice which he is intending to celebrate. This horse sacrifice is frequently referred to in the Brāhmanas, and there can be little doubt that it is a historical event. But no early authority mentions the snake sacrifice, so far as we know.

The Brāhmanas and Upanishads preserve the names of a considerable number of seers who lived after the time of Janamejaya. Many of them take part in the debates with which the earlier Upanishads are largely occupied. Stories can hardly be said to exist. The narrative element as a rule amounts to not more than two or three sentences, explaining the circumstances under which the discussion arose. The debates themselves consist of speeches in character (Type B)—dialogues in which question and answer alternate. They are in prose, like most of the matter contained in the early Upanishads. The characters are Brahmans (seers) and learned kings. The occasion is sometimes a great festival (sacrificial) gathering, at which prizes are offered by the king for contests in learning; sometimes a private meeting between Brahmans or between a Brahman and a king.

The debates are often compared with Plato's Dialogues; but the resemblance is hardly more than superficial. The matter is clearly traditional. The same characters, and sometimes even the same debates, occur in more than one Upanishad; and there is nothing to show that the authors of the Upanishads, as we have them, are recording personal memories. Many of the characters are mentioned also in the Brāhmanas, which are believed to be older than the Upanishads. Yājnavalkya, the chief character of the Brhadāranyaka Upanishad, figures largely in the Çatapatha Brāhmana; and the preparation of the White Yajurveda, which is thought to be still older, is also attributed to him. But no dates can be given, owing to the absence of the feeling for chronology, which characterises all early Indian literature. All that can be said with confidence is (i) that most of the characters are represented as more or less contemporary with one another, and (ii) that they speak of Janamejaya and his family [1] as belonging to the past. But Janamejaya may have lived

[1] In Brhad. III. 3 Yājnavalkya is asked what has become of the Pārikshitas, and replies that he supposes them to have gone (in the next life) to where those go who have offered horse sacrifices. Unfortunately *Parikṣitas* can mean either Jana-

two centuries, or even more, before the time when the Upanishads, as we have them, were composed. Sometimes 'genealogies' are introduced; but these are genealogies not of flesh and blood, but of teachers, or rather doctrines. The chronological value of a 'generation' is therefore quite uncertain; it may mean no more than a few years, perhaps even less. In one short list found in Brhad. VI. 3. 7 ff. most of the teachers seem to be more or less contemporary. But the fact that in the longer genealogies Yājnavalkya's name usually appears far back in the list may probably be taken to mean that he was recognised to have lived not very recently.

The true analogies of the debates in the Upanishads lie in our opinion not with Plato's Dialogues, but with the contests between seers or learned supernatural beings which are treated in the earliest records of Europe. This is a subject which will require notice in Ch. X. Here it may be sufficient to point out that, although the Upanishads are not stories of adventure, the debates which they describe are not devoid of a certain element of danger. One speaker frequently warns another that, if he persists in a certain line of argument, he will lose his head; and on one occasion (Brhad. III. 9. 26) this sad fate does actually befall a competitor who is unable to answer Yājnavalkya. We are reminded of the fate of Calchas in the Melampodia and, still more, of the discussion in the Vafþrúðnismál (cf. Vol. I, p. 321 f.), where the learned giant Vafþrúðnir says to Othin (st. 19): "We have got to stake our heads in the contest of learning." At the end of the same poem Vafþrúðnir speaks of himself as doomed. Note may also be taken of the large rewards or prizes offered for success in these contests.

Many of the characters of the Upanishads figure also in the Mahābhārata; and here we hear something of the men themselves, as well as their doctrines. Of Yājnavalkya indeed we hear little more than in the Brhadāranyaka Upanishad, although he is made to enunciate his doctrines at considerable length in XII. cccxi ff. In the Upanishad we find him maintaining his claim to superiority over other sages in a contest for a prize awarded by King Janaka, and again paying private visits to the same king. We have also his farewell discourse to one of his wives when he departs to the forest. In the Mahābhārata we have only his discourses to Janaka; but in these, especially in XII. cccxix, he gives a little more in-

mejaya and his brothers or the dynasty as a whole. The second interpretation is the one commonly given; but in view of Yājnavalkya's reply this can only be correct if the whole dynasty—say each generation—were believed to have offered such sacrifices (cf. p. 515, note).

formation about himself. By his ascetic devotions he had won the favour of the Sun-god, who revealed to him the Yagus and promised him that Sarasvatī, the goddess of learning, would enter him. When he came home he thought of the goddess, and immediately she appeared before him 'adorned with all the vowels and consonants'.[1] With her help he composed the Çatapatha Brāhmana. As a teacher he attained great success; but this was displeasing to his maternal uncle, who possibly was Vaiçampāyana (cf. p. 514, note 3).

Among other learned Brahmans we hear perhaps most frequently of Uddālaka Āruni and his son Çvetaketu. They figure in debates in the Brhadāranyaka and Chāndogya Upanishads, and are referred to as authorities in Brāhmanas. Çvetaketu is represented as very young in the Upanishads. In Brhad. Upan. VI. 2 he is unable to answer questions put to him by a king called Pravāhana Jaibali, and refers them to his father. Uddālaka, who likewise cannot answer the questions, sets off to the king and begs to become his disciple. In the Mahābhārata Uddālaka Āruni is mentioned on several occasions. In I. iii he is the disciple of a seer named Ayoda Dhaumya. His teacher tells him to go and stop a drain; and he goes, but does not come back. When search is made for him he is found lying in the drain, which he says he could not stop otherwise. Çvetaketu is frequently mentioned. In III. cxxxii the seer Lomaça points out to Yudhishthira the hermitage of Çvetaketu, where he saw the goddess Sarasvatī in her heavenly form and begged her to endow him with the gift of speech. Another remarkable story is told in I. cxxii. A Brahman comes to Uddālaka's house and takes away his wife. Çvetaketu is greatly angered; but his father says that this is in accordance with ancient usage, a usage still observed by animals. Çvetaketu is then said to have established the law of conjugal fidelity.

Uddālaka is also said (III. cxxxii. 8 ff.) to have had a daughter—much older than Çvetaketu—who was married to one of his disciples called Kahoda.[2] The latter was devoted to learning but not proficient. On one occasion he is corrected by his unborn child, which he thereupon curses in his anger, saying it should be born as a cripple.[3] After this Kahoda

---

[1] It is to be noted that Sarasvatī is often identified with Vāc, i.e. 'Speech' (personified).

[2] He is presumably the Kahola Kaushītakeya who in the Brhad. Upan. III. 5 comes with Uddālaka and others to question Yājnavalkya.

[3] Lit. 'crooked in eight parts', i.e. in his whole frame, which was regarded as consisting of eight parts (cf. I. lxi. 1). This is perhaps an attempt to explain the name Aṣṭāvakra (from aṣṭau, 'eight', and vakra, 'crooked'). The story of the drain (above) may be due to a similar attempt to account for the name Uddālaka.

sets out to compete for a prize given by King Janaka; but he is defeated by a rival called Vandi or Vandin[1] and drowned. Soon afterwards the child is born posthumously, and named Ashtāvakra. When he is in his twelfth year, he learns from Çvetaketu for the first time of his father's death. He makes up his mind to go himself to King Janaka, accompanied by Çvetaketu. He has some difficulty in obtaining admission to the contest, owing to his age; but he eventually succeeds, and encounters Vandi (III. cxxxiv). The contest is in readiness of speech, as in the case of Ferchertne and Nede (cf. Vol. I, p. 467), and Ashtāvakra defeats his opponent. He and the Brahmans present then demand that Vandi (who is described as Sauti, i.e. 'son of a Sūta') shall be drowned. It is stated that the latter has brought this fate upon many of his competitors. These now return from the water restored to life, Kahoda amongst them, while Vandi goes to the water in their place and apparently drowns himself. Kahoda returns home with his son and shows him how to free himself from the infirmity which the curse has brought upon him. To the competition itself we shall have to refer again in Ch. X. For Ashtāvakra's precocious development we may compare the story of Taliesin's childhood (cf. Vol. I, p. 103 f.).

The examples given above will be sufficient, it is hoped, to convey some impression of the non-heroic stories preserved in the Mahābhārata. They are extremely numerous and varied. It will be observed that the stories relating to later times are of a more legendary character than the notices of the same persons found in the Upanishads and Brāhmanas. This is doubtless due largely to the fact that the Mahābhārata, as we have it, is a much later work. In famous seers, as in famous heroes, mythical elements tend to develop with the lapse of time.

The characteristics of the material discussed above are different in some respects from those of the heroic material, noticed on p. 477 ff. Most of it is narrative and concerned with adventure; but there is also a good deal of discussion practically without either narrative or adventure, Again, some of the narratives, as well as the discussions, are intended rather for instruction than for entertainment. On the whole there is perhaps more of Type C (both CA and CB) than of Type A. As regards the times to which the stories and discussions are referred, it has been mentioned that the Indian Heroic Age is difficult to date. None of the characters, however, so far as we are aware, belong to a period later than

---

[1] The name is perhaps identical with the word *vandin*, 'panegyric poet'. Possibly this word has been misunderstood as a proper name.

that of the philosophers who figure in the Upanishads; and there seem to be hardly any references to persons who lived after this time. The personnel of the non-heroic, as well as the heroic, elements in the Mahābhārata belongs apparently to times not later than the seventh century.

Most of the non-heroic material in the Mahābhārata has the same form and metre as the heroic. But it may have taken this over from the latter. The stories in the Brāhmanas (which are non-heroic) are in the form of saga (prose) with many of the speeches in verse, as in Irish sagas; and we see no reason for doubting that this was the usual form of non-heroic stories in early times.

In the Rgveda, references to the seers or sages who figure in the Mahābhārata are extremely frequent. Some of them, such as Cyavana and Çunahçepa, appear here also as characters of a legendary past; but others, like Vasishtha and Viçvāmitra, are persons of the present and claim the authorship of various hymns. On the other hand the persons who are introduced as speakers in the Brāhmanas and Upanishads are unknown, and it may therefore be inferred that they belonged to later times.

A difficulty is presented by the fact that the poet's name appears very often in the plural. Sometimes both singular and plural are used, indiscriminately it would seem, in the same poem. The explanation of this is said to be that names like Vasishtha are not properly individual names but surnames, derived from some remote ancestor. It is in accordance with this explanation that the name Kanva seldom occurs in the singular with reference to present time, though it is quite frequent in relation to the past, whereas the plural is very commonly used in relation to the present. The patronymic (Kānva) is also found, without any apparent difference in meaning. Again, in VIII. 22 the poet addresses himself as Sobhari, but in the same poem he speaks of Sobhari as 'our' father or ancestor. But we do not know whether this explanation will apply to all cases.

In poems which can be dated, by the panegyrics contained in them, to the earliest period (cf. p. 484) the only famous name[1] of this kind apparently is Bharadvāja. This name occurs in the singular in VI. 16 and in the plural in VI. 47—poems relating to Divodāsa and his contemporaries.

---

[1] A hymn which celebrates Çrutarvan (VIII. 63) seems to be claimed by a certain Gopavana. The names of the authors of other panegyrics belonging to this period seem not to be mentioned.

It also occurs, both singular and plural and mostly in reference to the present, in a number of other poems in Book VI, but not in connection with names of princes which belong to the later periods. In I. 59, however, it is found in the plural, apparently in reference to the present, with names otherwise unknown, which seem to be those of princes. Elsewhere in Books I and X it occurs only in reference to the past. So far as the evidence goes therefore, it would seem that this name belongs chiefly, if not exclusively, to the earliest period.

The names Vasishtha and Viçvāmitra appear first in connection with Sudās, i.e. in the next period. Indeed their princely connections are practically limited to this king. The former name occurs only once, so far as we have observed, in a reference definitely to the past, viz. in the catalogue poem I. 112, in which Bharadvāja and various other characters of the past are also mentioned. In references to the present the name Vasishtha, both singular and plural, occurs very frequently in Book VII and several times, in the singular, in Book X, while the plural form also (*Vasiṣṭhās*) appears in X. 122. The most interesting cases perhaps are VII. 18, 33 and 88. The first of these—to which we have already referred (p. 485)—gives an account of Sudās' victories on the Ravi and the Jumna, and of the rewards which the poet received from him. In VII. 33, which is a non-heroic poem of Type D, rather than a hymn in the ordinary sense, the same victories are referred to and attributed to the prayers of 'Vasishtha' (both singular and plural). Then (st. 7 ff.) the poet passes on to a panegyric upon the Vasishtha (plural) themselves, who here are evidently regarded as a family. A supernatural origin is claimed for them, though the details are not clear to us. 'Vasishtha', presumably the originator of the family, is here said to have been born by the Apsaras ('nymph') Urvaçī to the gods Varuna and Mitra. He is born at a sacrifice, and laid on a lotus-flower; but some part in the story is also played by the legendary seer Agastya. It may be remarked that in this poem (st. 1) the Vasishtha are described as wearing white robes and having their hair tied up on the right—which may have been characteristic marks of the family. In VII. 88 the poet (Vasishtha) says that Varuna had once taken him out to sea in a boat and there made him a seer. He had also entered Varuna's palace; but now, he complains, the god has become estranged from him.

To Viçvāmitra the scholastic tradition attributes most of the hymns in Book III; but the name seldom appears in the hymns themselves. The plural occurs in III. 18, 53; X. 89; the singular apparently only in III. 53. About half a dozen hymns, however, in Book III speak of the Kuçika (plural) as their authors; and from III. 53, as well as from the scholastic tradition, it appears that this was the name of Viçvāmitra's family. In all these hymns—where the names Viçvāmitra or Kuçika occur—the reference is to the present. But the celebrity of the poet or his family may be inferred from I. 10, where the patronymic *Kauçika* is applied to Indra. In III. 53 it is stated that Viçvāmitra was, or had been in the service of Sudās, and that it was to the influence of him and the Kuçika that the king's successes were due. But the most interesting poem of the series is III. 33, which consists of a dialogue between 'Kuçika's son' and the rivers Vipāç and Çutudrī (Beas and Sutlej), and is properly an example of Type B, rather than a hymn. In st. 2 f. the poet addresses the rivers, at which apparently he has just arrived. In st. 4 the rivers reply and ask him what he wishes. In st. 5 he asks them to take a rest. In st. 6 the rivers say that Indra dug their channels and let them flow, and ask the poet to celebrate them. Then he begs them to lower their waters; and they consent. He bids them flow on swiftly again, as soon as the Bharata—presumably Sudās' troops—have passed over them. Then (st. 12) follows a half-stanza of narrative, stating that the rivers assented to the poet's request, and that the Bharata passed over them. In conclusion he bids them fill their channels and speed on.

A slightly later time is perhaps represented by the poems of Sobhari in Book VIII. In VIII. 19 the poet celebrates Trasadasyu and in VIII. 22 Trkshi, son of Trasadasyu. The singular only is used; but in the latter poem the author speaks both of himself as Sobhari (st. 2), and also of Sobhari as his father (st. 15). In VIII. 5 Sobhari seems to be spoken of as a character of the past.

Çyāvāçva is another poet who belonged apparently to about the same period. There seems to be no reason for regarding him otherwise than as an individual; his name occurs only in the singular and in reference to the present. Several hymns in Books V and VIII claim him as their author. In VIII. 36 f. he refers to Trasadasyu, perhaps as a person of the past, while in V. 52 he says that he has himself acquired cattle and horses on the Jumna—possibly as a present from the spoils of war. The great advance of the Aryans in this region may have begun in his time.

In Book X the scholastic tradition gives the names of a very large number of authors, though some of these are merely 'characters' or speakers in poems of Type B. Of the remaining names comparatively few are recorded in the poems themselves, and of these again hardly any seem to be famous. Vimada occurs in several poems, both singular and plural, and in reference to the present—as also apparently in VIII. 9. A seer—or possibly hero—of the past with this name is referred to in several poems in Books I and X, usually in connection with his marriage. It is likely therefore that this is another of the old family names.

One poem, x. 98, to which we have already referred (p. 484), must be noticed again here, because it has given rise to a question of considerable importance. The author is perhaps a certain Devāpi Ārshtishena (i.e. son or descendant of Rshtishena. At all events this man is the speaker in st. 1–4 and again perhaps in st. 8–12. These stanzas are an invocation to various deities for rain, on behalf of Çamtanu (*Çaṃtanu*), who is evidently a king. The intervening stanzas (5–7) state that Devāpi was Çamtanu's priest, and that the rain came down in answer to his prayers. Now the scholastic tradition, which can be traced back to Yāska, c. 500 B.C., says that Çamtanu and Devāpi were brothers, and the same statement occurs in the Mahābhārata (1. xciv. 61 f., etc.). If this is true the hereditary principle of Brahmanism was not yet definitely fixed at this time—a prince could become a priest. But the poem itself gives no hint that the king and his priest were brothers. Moreover, the name Rshtishena does not occur among the ancestors of Çamtanu (*Çāntanu*) in either of the genealogies of this king given in the Mahābhārata (1. xciv f.). In both cases Çamtanu is son of Pratīpa; and in cap. xcvii there is a story which suggests that he was his eldest, if not his only, son—as against v. cxlix. 16 (cf. I. xcv. 44), where Devāpi is the eldest. But it may be observed that other names in *-sena* appear in both genealogies shortly before Pratīpa. In I. xcv. 41 his grandfather is Bhīmasena, son of Parīkshit. In xciv. 54 Parīkshit has six sons with names in *-sena*, though here he is not Pratīpa's great-grandfather, but a collateral. The evidence then, taken as a whole, rather suggests that in an earlier form of the story Devāpi was not Çamtanu's brother, but a more distantly related member of the royal family.

The Vedic seers are persons of very different character from those who bear the same names in the Mahābhārata. They are credited with being able by their invocations to influence the gods, so as to obtain blessings for their patrons. But they make no claim to be equal or superior to the gods. Indeed they do not seem to differ in any noteworthy respect from their counterparts in the West. Mythical elements occur only in stories of the past, e.g. in the story relating to the origin of the Vasishtha. Yet the Vasishtha and the Viçvāmitra of the Mahābhārata would seem to be those of Sudās' time, rather than their mythical progenitors. These at all events were certainly contemporaries, and it is not impossible that they may have been brought into hostility, as rivals for the king's favour, though the poems do not record anything of the kind. Neither do they record that Viçvāmitra was originally a prince. Perhaps in his time there would have been nothing remarkable in that—though there is some evidence, as we have seen, that he belonged to a prophetic family. It is hardly necessary to discuss the story which makes him father of Çakuntalā and grandfather of Bharata—the remote legendary ancestor of Sudās.

The life of the Vedic seers also seems to be very different from that which they lead in the epics. We hear nothing of asceticism or hermitages in the forest. The feature which perhaps strikes us most forcibly is the naive satisfaction with which they record the rich presents bestowed upon them by the kings. To these subjects, however, we shall have to return in a later chapter.

It is beyond our power to deal with the material relating to the seers and their genealogies contained in the Purānas. We believe this is generally agreed to be very largely a product of antiquarian speculation. The brief summaries given above will perhaps be sufficient to indicate the distinctive features of the material to be found in the Rgveda, the Brāhmanas and Upanishads, and the epics. It will be seen that the seers of the epics are, in name at least, largely identical with those of the Rgveda; and the same is true of the Purānas. But the seers and sages who figure in the Brāhmanas and Upanishads belong in general to a later period.

CHAPTER V

HISTORICAL AND UNHISTORICAL ELEMENTS IN HEROIC POETRY

IN Vol. I, Ch. VII, we saw that the early heroic poetry and saga of the Western peoples usually, if not always, seems to contain a considerable historical element. The evidence available for determining the existence of this element was classified as follows: (*a*) contemporary native records; (*b*) foreign records independent of native influence; (*c*) independent (native) traditions in different areas; (*d*) independent traditions in the same area; (*e*) the consistency of heroic tradition. The relative value of these various kinds of evidence is in general according to the order in which they are arranged. The most important is (*a*)—which may very well be conclusive—while (*e*) is of comparatively little value, if there is any valid evidence to the contrary. In addition to these we have to take account of (*f*) evidence from antiquities—material, social, religious, etc.—and (*g*, *h*) evidence from personal and local names.

For ancient Indian heroic stories evidence which comes under (*b*) seems to be wholly wanting. Evidence under (*c*) may very well exist; but we are not competent to deal with it. In regard to (*d*) the Brahmanical tradition, found in the Vedas and Brāhmanas is in general doubtless independent of heroic tradition; but the heroic tradition, represented in the epics, is very frequently, especially in the main story of the Mahābhārata, not free from the influence of late Brahmanical tradition. Evidence which comes strictly under (*a*) can hardly be said to exist; but the textual tradition of the Rgveda is so good that the poems may almost be regarded as coming under this heading. The evidence of the epics themselves and the Purānas is of course much inferior in value. The evidence available for this subject from the Brāhmanas and Upanishads is very small in amount; but these works are preserved in a much earlier form than the epics. Evidence from other literary sources, including Buddhist records, is hardly earlier than the fourth century (B.C.). Neither the archaeological evidence nor the local and personal names seem to have been investigated to any considerable extent, though some rather striking evidence has been noted in social usages and religion. On the whole therefore the material—so far at least as it is known to us

—is less varied than in the West, in spite of the vast extent and highly composite character of some of the records.

We need have no hesitation in treating the statements contained in the Rvgeda as historical, when they relate to the present. Reservations may be made in respect of the claims of certain seers, e.g. as to the success of their invocations in staying the course of a river; and there may be exaggerations here and there. Legendary elements appear in poems, especially catalogue poems, relating to heroes of the past. The evidence of the Brāhmanas is similar; but the legendary element is greater, because references to the past are more frequent.[1]

It is only in regard to the heroic stories contained in the epics that any discussion is necessary. But this is a subject which unfortunately, owing to the vast bulk and complex character of the material, it is quite beyond our power to treat systematically. It is generally agreed, as we have seen, that the kernel of the Mahābhārata is the heroic story of the battle and the events which lead up to it, and that this story has been amplified by the addition of other stories and didactic matter, which in its present form constitute at least four-fifths of the whole work. The different elements are very often clearly distinguishable; but this is not always the case. The heroic parts of the work seem frequently to have been expanded and recast under Brahmanic influence; and there is a large antiquarian element of uncertain provenance. Above all we are quite in the dark as to the age of the various elements. Variants and discrepancies abound.

It is the prevailing opinion now that the heroic story which forms the central theme of the Mahābhārata contains a historical nucleus,[2] though the events which gave rise to it took place several centuries before the beginning of what may properly be called the historical period. Such evidence as is available is thought to point to the eleventh or tenth centuries B.C., by those scholars who have recently expressed opinions on the subject.[3] The most definite evidence for such a date is supplied by the genealogies or successions of kings contained in the Purānas. It is true that only three of these lists are continued down to the historical period and that more than one of these has included a series of names

---

[1] The frequency with which the divine seers Nārada and Parvata are introduced, especially in association with kings, shows how extensively even early Brahmanical tradition was permeated by legendary elements.

[2] Cf. especially Rapson, *Cambridge History of India*, I. 307.

[3] The date indicated by the Purānas is reckoned at c. 950 by Pargiter, *Ancient Indian Historical Tradition*, p. 182; c. 1000 by Rapson, *op. cit.*, I. 307, 697; in century xi by Sidhanta, *The Heroic Age of India*, p. 41.

which do not belong to it. But when these errors have been removed it is noteworthy that the lists are of approximately the same length from the time of the battle of the Mahābhārata down to the beginning of the historical period. The three kings who were reigning in the time of the Buddha, c. 500 B.C., would seem to be the twenty-second, twenty-third and twenty-fourth respectively in succession from the kings who fought in the battle.[1] The actual date which is indicated for the battle depends upon the question whether these are really genealogies or lists of (reigning) kings—which unfortunately is not quite clear. In the former case it is difficult to believe that the date indicated can be much later than 1100; in the latter it might be as late as 900, or even later.

The Purānas unfortunately can hardly be regarded as satisfactory evidence. For times anterior to the story of the Mahābhārata one may suspect that they are largely products of antiquarian speculation; and even in later times they contain serious mistakes. It is of importance therefore that some corroborative evidence is to be obtained from the Brāhmanas. More than one of these works contain a list of kings who have offered the horse sacrifice (açvamedha). In this list are included the names of (i) Janamejaya and his brothers, the sons of Parīkshit, and (ii) a certain Çatānīka Sātrājita. It is generally agreed that this Jana-mejaya is the king to whom the Mahābhārata claims to have been first recited (cf. p. 501), and whose father Parīkshit is son of Abhimanyu, who is killed in the battle. Çatānīka Sātrājita in the Purānic genealogy, as also in the Mahābhārata (I. xcv. 85), is Janamejaya's son. The Brāhmanas give no dates; but they speak of these kings as persons of the past—which means probably at least not later than the eighth century.

Parīkshit himself, as we have seen (p. 482), is in all probability cele-brated in the Atharveda, xx. i. 27, which is evidently a contemporary panegyric. The poem describes the peace and prosperity which prevail during his reign, but gives us no particulars relating to the man himself, except the name of his kingdom (Kuru). Unfortunately also it cannot be dated.

There is some evidence, we think, in favour of a dating rather later than what is suggested by the lists of kings in the Purānas. Vaiçam-pāyana, who recites the Mahābhārata to King Janamejaya, is connected in the scholastic tradition, at least indirectly, with the Yajurveda. We need not take too seriously the statement of the Purānas that he was the author of this Veda. But several scholars who lived between the fourth

[1] Cf. Sidhanta, loc. cit.

and the second centuries (B.C.), including Pānini and Patanjali, state that the authors of certain early recensions of that collection were pupils of Vaiçampāyana. Such is said to have been the case with Kalāpin and Katha, the authors of the Maitrāyani Samhitā and the Kāthaka Samhitā, while Tittiri, the author of the Taittirīya Samhitā, is stated to have been a pupil of a certain Yāska Paingi, who was himself a pupil of Vaiçampāyana.[1] We believe that most modern scholars would regard a date c. 750–700 as probable for these recensions. Again, according to another authority of the same class the seer Aruna Aupaveçi, father of Uddālaka Āruni, was likewise a pupil of Vaiçampāyana.[2] Uddālaka is one of the two most prominent seers who figure in the Upanishads; the other, Yājnavalkya, is his contemporary and pupil. Neither of the two can be dated with certainty; but we believe that the Çatapatha Brāhmana, in which Yājnavalkya is the authority most frequently cited, would be attributed by most scholars to a period about a century later than the Samhitās of the Black Yajurveda mentioned above. Yājnavalkya[3] himself and Uddālaka may reasonably be thought to have lived between 750 and 650. All these considerations point to a date not earlier than c. 800 for Vaiçampāyana and Janamejaya. The grandfather of the latter is killed in the great battle of the Mahābhārata. Consequently the time to which the story relates would seem to fall within the ninth century.

It is to be observed that a number of uncertain quantities are involved here. Not one of the works referred to can be dated with certainty, though we believe that the dates given above are approximately what would be favoured by the majority of scholars. It is often uncertain how long a seer lived before the composition of a work in which he is quoted, or at least before it attained its present form. Vaiçampāyana is not mentioned in any very early work, i.e. in any work of the true Brāhmana period.[4] For the contemporaneity of Vaiçampāyana and Janamejaya we

---

[1] For references see Weber, *Hist. Indian Literature*, p. 93; v. Schroeder, *Maitr. Samhitā*, I. x f.; Keith, *Veda of the Black Yajus School*, p. xci.

[2] See Weber, *l.c.*; Keith, *l.c.*

[3] In Mahābh. XII. cccxix Yājnavalkya relates to Janaka how he was inspired to compose the (White) Yajurveda and Çatapatha Brāhmana and taught them to his pupils. He adds (st. 17) that thereby he displeased his great maternal uncle. In st. 19 he refers to a dispute with the same relative about a sacrificial fee. In the former passage Dutt's translation adds the name Vaiçampāyana. We do not know what authority there is for this relationship between Yājnavalkya and Vaiçampāyana.

[4] He is said to be mentioned first in the Taittirīya Āranyaka, the date of which is unknown to us.

are dependent upon the evidence of the Mahābhārata. In spite of these objections, however, we think that the evidence noted above collectively is on the whole to be preferred to that of the lists of kings in the Purānas, though we are not clear that the two are necessarily incompatible. The important point is that the period of the learned seers, from Vaiçampāyana to Uddālaka and Yājnavalkya, seems to be very short, though this is of value for the question under discussion only if we accept the contemporaneity of Vaiçampāyana and Janamejaya.[1] We are inclined therefore to the late dating suggested above; but in view of the total absence of fixed landmarks in the chronology we shall avoid the use of dates as far as possible.

It has already been noted that the Rgveda does not mention any of the heroes who figure in the main story of the Mahābhārata, though one— probably very late—poem (x. 98) relates to Çāntanu, the father of the old hero Bhīshma and grandfather of Dhrtarāshtra. There is therefore a gap of four generations between the two kings, Çāntanu and Parīkshit, for whom we have contemporary evidence, though the Mahābhārata makes Bhīshma to live on practically until Parīkshit's birth—and it is in this gap that the (main) story of the Mahābhārata falls. The gap must of course be reckoned at something over a century. Consequently, if we accept a date c. 900–850 for the battle and Parīkshit's birth, Çāntanu's lifetime must be placed in the tenth century. Then, according to the evidence noticed on p. 484 ff., the early hymns of the Rgveda will go back to the twelfth century, perhaps even to the beginning of it. On the other hand, if a date c. 1000 or c. 1100 be preferred for the battle, the

---

[1] There is one piece of early evidence which may indicate that Janamejaya did live about this time. In Brhad. III. 3 Yājnavalkya is asked "What has become of the Pārikshitas?" This is interpreted by many scholars to mean that the dynasty had already come to an end in some great disaster. If this is correct, we must of course reject *in toto* the evidence of the Purānas, which give Parīkshit a list of over twenty successors, coming down to the time of the Buddha. But Yājnavalkya's reply is that "they have gone whither horse-sacrificers go", and the context shows that a variety of heaven is meant. It would seem therefore that no more can fairly be inferred than that the Pārikshitas are dead. This name may mean either 'descendants of' or 'sons of Parīkshit'. In point of fact there is record of horse-sacrifices offered by Janamejaya and his brothers and also by Janamejaya's son Çatānīka. But there is no evidence, so far as we know, that such a sacrifice—which implies a kind of imperial power—was celebrated by any later king of this dynasty. It seems unnecessary therefore to assume that the dynasty had come to an end. The reference may be to Parīkshit's immediate successors. They had been powerful monarchs; but they have passed away—though not very long ago. They are still remembered.

other dates will likewise require to be moved back to a corresponding extent.[1]

Any such dating is of course based upon the assumption that the story of the Mahābhārata contains a nucleus of historical fact; but we believe that, in principle at least, this would now be admitted by the majority of scholars. Unhistorical elements of course abound; but we see no reason for supposing that in the combination of unhistorical with historical elements the story differs essentially from the heroic narrative poetry of the peoples we have already considered. The period during which it was preserved wholly by oral tradition must have been very long. Yet there is little trace of 'contamination' between it and the other heroic stories—of Rāma, Nala, Sāvitrī—which are introduced episodically. The leading characters do not betray a fictitious or mythical origin by their names or other obvious features. Supernatural beings are distinguished clearly enough from heroes and other human beings. The hypothesis that heroes are 'faded gods' has indeed been applied to the Mahābhārata, just as to the heroic poetry of other peoples; but the evidence seems to be no more satisfactory here than elsewhere. On the other hand the growth of myth may be traced, especially in the last book of the Rāmāyana, just as clearly as in the late stories of the childhood of Sigurðr.

So far as we are aware, only one serious argument has been brought against the story of the Mahābhārata, apart from details, namely the absence of reference to it in early literature. But it is not easy to see where references to it could reasonably be expected. The time to which it relates seems to be later than that of the Rgveda. The hymn (x. 98) in which Çamtanu figures may be one of the latest in the whole collection; at all events it is not clear that any of the other princes mentioned lived after him. The poems of the Atharvaveda were doubtless still being composed; but they very seldom refer to contemporary princes; and the same appears to be true of the other Vedas. On the other hand the Brāhmanas, and more especially the Upanishads, contain frequent references to princes of the not very remote past. But these are works of

---

[1] The uncertainties expressed in this paragraph are due to certain factors which are unknown to us but quite definite, and which may possibly be made clear, within certain limits, by future investigation. We see no adequate reason for the nebulous dating advocated by some scholars (e.g. Winternitz, *Gesch. d. ind. Litteratur*, I. 258). It is doubtless true that the history of Indian literature may in a sense go back to the third millennium B.C., or even earlier. But the same might be said of Greek, English, or Irish. We do not see how such an antiquity can be claimed for any existing poems.

essentially 'ecclesiastical' and learned character. No one who is familiar with early Western literature would expect to find references to heroic stories in such works, or to the heroes themselves, except by mere chance.

The times in which the Brāhmanas and Upanishads were composed were doubtless later than those in which the story of the Mahābhārata is laid; and if it is not pure fiction, the story must by then have already assumed some kind of 'literary' form—otherwise it would have been forgotten. The Mahābhārata itself claims to have acquired this literary form in the time of Janamejaya, which is not unreasonable. But why should the Brāhmanas or Upanishads refer to a heroic story? We have a very large body of ecclesiastical and learned literature, both Latin and vernacular, surviving from the Saxon period in England. But, as we have already remarked (p. 449), this literature preserves, so far as we are aware, only one direct reference to heroic poetry—in a letter, quoted in Vol. I, p. 556—though one or two other passages betray knowledge of it. Yet the learned literature of Saxon England abounds in references to kings, far more than the Brāhmanas and Upanishads, which indeed seldom mention such persons, unless they were famous as sacrificers, like Janamejaya, or patrons of learning, like Janaka of Videha.

If we were to argue from the silence of the ecclesiastical literature that heroic poetry was little known in England, we should go badly astray. But the evidence for its cultivation is to be found not in literary works but in registers of personal names and local nomenclature. Thus we know from the Durham *Liber Vitae* that in the seventh century—not long before or after Bede's birth—there were two members of the Lindisfarne community called Widsith and Beowulf; but Bede himself in all his voluminous writings never betrays acquaintance with heroic poetry. Such sources of information seem unfortunately to be wanting for ancient India. But is there any valid reason for doubting that in India, as in England, ecclesiastical and heroic literature ran in separate channels?

This expression, it is true, is not quite correct; for both in England and in India we find ecclesiastical literature encroaching upon heroic. The reverse process, however, does not occur. It is only quite rarely that we find acquaintance with heroic poetry betrayed by some mistake. For an example, not strictly of ecclesiastical character, we may refer to the *Historia Brittonum*, cap. 31, where in an English genealogy—derived from an English source—we find 'Finn son of Folcwald(a)' for 'Finn son of Godwulf'. This passage must have come through the hands of someone who was familiar with the famous Frisian hero Finn son of Folcwalda. An analogy to this is to be found, we suspect, in the Kāthaka Samhitā of the Yajurveda, where reference is made to a learned king named Dhrtarāshtra Vaicitravīrya. He is believed[1] to be identical with a Dhrtarāshtra, king of Kāçī, who attempted to celebrate a horse-sacrifice, but was prevented from doing so and then conquered by Çatānīka Sātrājita. The agreement of this double name with that of the blind king in the Mahābhārata can hardly be due to accident; for Dhrtarāshtra is not a common name, while Vicitravīrya seems to be quite rare. It is to be suspected therefore that the surname in the Kāthaka Samhitā is derived from some source familiar with heroic tradition.

Scholars who are more familiar with the sources than we are could probably produce further evidence for influence of this kind.[2] What we would emphasise is that in countries, like India and England, where the ecclesiastical and heroic spheres were sharply divided from one another, it is only by such indirect evidence, if at all, that one can hope to find any notice from the former of the existence of the latter.[3] The silence of the ecclesiastical authorities proves nothing, except the absence of connection between the two. In both cases the heroic sphere came to be invaded—in India dominated—by a kind of popular ecclesiasticism; but this was far removed from the academic ecclesiasticism of learned circles.

It is hardly necessary to point out the independence of the two traditions. The kings who figure most prominently in Vedic or in Brahmanic literature, such as Divodāsa and Sudās, are hardly more than names in the Mahābhārata. Janamejaya is the only one of whom much is said; and he belongs to the framework of the Mahābhārata, not to the story itself.

---

[1] Cf. Macdonell and Keith, *Vedic Index*, I. 403; *Cambridge History of India*, I. 119.

[2] Çikhandin Yājnasena in the Kaush. Br. VII. 4 strikes one as at least a strange coincidence; both this Çikhandin and his father seem to be seers. For Balhika Prātipīya, who is mentioned in Çat. Br. XII. 9. 3. 3, we may refer to Macdonell and Keith, *Vedic Index*, II. 63 f. As regards the Vāhlīka of the Mahābhārata it may be noted that he is not a prominent figure in the story, though he is mentioned fairly often. His age is not emphasised, like that of his nephew Bhīshma, though he fights and falls in the battle against the great-grandsons and great-great-grandsons of his brother. Some mistaken identification or chronological displacement seems not unlikely.

[3] Heroic stories may perhaps be included under the term Itihāsā Purāna in Ath. v. xv. 6 and elsewhere; but the name is doubtless applied also to non-heroic stories.

Moreover the events connected with him are not the same,[1] unless we are to suppose that the snake-sacrifice is a distorted reminiscence of the horse-sacrifice. With non-heroic (Brahmanic) stories of course the case is different. Many Vedic prophets and poets figure in the Mahābhārata. But the fantastic stories here told of them are quite foreign to the Vedas. These elements, if not wholly independent from the beginning, like the heroic elements, seem to represent the tradition of a type of Brahmanism different from what is found in the Brāhmanas and Upanishads.

We are not qualified to discuss the civilisation described in the Mahābhārata. But there is one feature which has attracted a good deal of attention, namely the polyandry associated with Draupadī. She is duly married not only to Arjuna, who has won her at the svayamvara, but also to his four brothers. Her father, when he first hears of the proposal, speaks of it (1. cxcvii. 27 f.) as an unheard of and sinful proceeding. But Yudhishthira replies (ib. 29) that "we follow the path successively trodden by our ancestors".[2] No such custom seems, however, to be known among the other princes of the Kuru, or in any of the numerous other royal families mentioned in the Mahābhārata; and it is foreign to Hindu law. But it is actually practised by some of the hill-peoples. Again, we may observe that not much is recorded of Pāndu, the father of the heroes. His sons are born after he has retired to the forest; and their existence is not known to the Kuru until after his death. From these facts it has generally been inferred that in the original form of the story the heroes did not belong to the royal family of the Kuru, but were of alien, presumably non-Aryan origin. Other explanations are of course possible.[3] Such a custom might arise (e.g.) through shortage of royal or noble women, in a land which has been recently conquered and settled. In any case, however, there can be little doubt that the story here preserves a very ancient feature, which must date back to a time when the Aryanisation of the land of the Kuru was recent or incomplete.

This conclusion is important, because in later times—indeed apparently even in the age of the Brāhmanas—the land of the Kuru seems to be regarded as the heart of Aryan India and the chief home of orthodox Brahmanism. Yet in the Rgveda the Jumna lies on the frontier of Aryan territory, if not beyond it. It is only in the latest poems,

---

[1] A reminiscence of Janamejaya's conquests is preserved in Mahābh. 1. iii. 22.

[2] We owe this transl. to the kindness of Prof. Rapson. Cf. also Winternitz, *Gesch. d. ind. Litteratur*, p. 283.

[3] Cf. Sidhanta, *The Heroic Age of India*, p. 121, where attention is called to the fact that Caesar (*Gall.* v. 14) notes the existence of a similar custom in Britain.

perhaps only in x. 98, that we hear of princes who probably ruled in the land of the Kuru, though this name is not mentioned. Çamtanu, the king mentioned in x. 98, is in the Mahābhārata the great-grandfather of the heroes. The conquest would therefore seem to have taken place not very long before their time. It may be of interest also in this connection to note that the stories, legendary as they are, represent Çamtanu as marrying women of the land. The case of Gangā, who is a divine being, should perhaps not be pressed. But Satyavatī[1] and her family, the 'fishing-people', are clearly native.

For the other heroic stories little evidence is available. They are all introduced in the Mahābhārata as stories told to Yudhishthira, and therefore relating to times anterior to the main story. Little weight, however, can be attached to this consideration.

Rāma and his father Daçaratha are referred in the genealogies of the Purānas to a remote antiquity, nearly thirty generations before the battle described in the Mahābhārata; but we need not take this evidence very seriously. A better clue is probably to be obtained from Janaka of Videha, the father of Sītā. A king Janaka of Videha figures frequently in the Upanishads, as the patron of Yājnavalkya and other seers of his time. In the philosophical parts of the Mahābhārata (XII. ccxviii f., ccciii ff., cccx ff., cccxxi) we hear of at least four kings of Videha with this name, all having much the same characteristics; from which it may perhaps be inferred that the name was dynastic, or perhaps a title.[2] In any case the evidence, for what it is worth, suggests that the story of Rāma relates to the age of the philosophical seers—the eighth or seventh century. We do not know of any evidence in the story itself which is incompatible with such a date.[3] It is not likely that the Aryanisation of these eastern kingdoms, Ayodhyā (Kosala) and Videha, goes back to very remote times.[4]

[1] In Mah. I. lxiii. 61 ff. and the Purānas she has a brother called Matsya, presumably the eponymos of the Matsya kingdom. This name ('Fish') may be compared with the Aja ('Goats') and Çigru ('Horse-radishes') mentioned in Rgv. VII. 18 among Sudās' enemies. Possibly such names are due to the substitution of familiar words for foreign names of similar sound.

[2] It is curious that the name *Janaka* is identical in origin with Norse *konungr*, 'king', and almost identical with our word *king*; but this may of course be accidental.

[3] In Rām. Vasishtha and other famous seers of the far past are occasionally introduced, along with seers of the Upanishads; but these incidents do not affect the course of events, and are doubtless embellishments of the story.

[4] In the Çat. Br. I. 4. I. 10, 17, Brahmanism is said to have been introduced into Videha by a certain Māthava Videgha; but unfortunately no indication of date seems to be given.

For the story of Nala the evidence is again limited, but somewhat more definite. The Aitareya Brāhmana, VII. 34, mentions Bhīma of Vidarbha in a list of princes who made offerings of soma, while the hero himself (Nala of Nishadha) is probably to be identified with a Naḍa Naishadha referred to in a verse preserved in the Çatapatha Brāhmana, II. 2. 3. 2. The verse says that Naḍa carries Yama southwards every day.[1] He seems to be compared with the god of death because of his conquests—apparently towards the south. It is to be observed that the Brāhmanas show no knowledge of the story of Nala. Their information is clearly derived from other sources, and quite independent. No indication of date is given by either passage, though the majority of the kings mentioned in the Brāhmanas seem to belong to times later than that of the main story of the Mahābhārata. And it is not at all likely that these southern regions came into Aryan hands in early times. On the other hand the Brāhmanas themselves are believed to date from the seventh century; and the poetry which they quote seems usually to be older. Bhīma is evidently a person of the past; for he is associated with the divine seer Nārada. We shall probably not go far wrong therefore if we assign these kings to a somewhat earlier period—say between the ninth and the seventh centuries.

The story of Sāvitrī relates to the kingdoms of Madra and Salva in the north of India. The chief characters of the story are apparently not mentioned in any early records; but that is in no way surprising, since the history of these lands is little known. It is clear that Satyavat (Sāvitrī's husband) and his father Dyumatsena are not characters created for the story; for they appear elsewhere (XII. cclxvii) in a wholly different connection. Here they are introduced as discussing the principles of punishment for law-breakers—a scene which certainly belongs to the Brahmanical portions of the work. There is no reference to Sāvitrī or her story. The evidence therefore falls under the variety (d) defined on p. 511; and it is probably a trustworthy example of independent traditions. As regards the period to which the story relates, the 'Discussion' would seem to suggest that of the philosophical kings, i.e. more or less that of the last three stories.

The story of Ambā is more complicated, though the Brahmanical element is, except at the beginning, not very obvious. The names of the three princesses carried off by Bhīshma recur in certain formulae used in the Rājasūya and Açvamedha sacrifices,[2] from which it would

---

[1] Cf. Macdonell and Keith, *Vedic Index*, I. 433.
[2] In the (Black) Yajurveda; see Keith, *Veda of the Black Yajus School*, II. 615 (cf. Vol. I. p. 118).

seem that they were titles of the wives—apparently the junior wives—
of the king of the Kuru. Ambikā and Ambalikā figure only in the incident where Vyāsa is introduced (cf. p. 475); and since Vyāsa, if he is a
real person, would seem to have belonged to a much later period, this
preliminary part of the story may be regarded as a (Brahmanical) fiction.
But the story itself deviates from heroic standards in some respects. The
heroine has no name other than Ambā, and no personal names are given
either to her father or to the prince to whom she is betrothed. Her
asceticism and re-birth are also unexpected in this connection, though the
metempsychosis is more of the Norse type than of the type usually
found in India. The introduction of the god Çiva perhaps points to a
late date. Suspicion may also be felt with regard to the Brahman hero
Rāma Jāmadagni, who elsewhere is introduced into what seem to be
late additions to various stories. All these considerations suggest a large
imaginative or 'romantic' element in the story. The motif is very remarkable, and it is difficult to avoid the suspicion that the story has been
re-cast under the influence of a folktale.

Upon the story of Bharata enough perhaps has been said in Ch. II
(p. 474). Here we need only note that, if the story contains any historical element, there must be some mistaken identification of the
eponymos with a later prince.

Historical elements are to be found, we believe, in all the stories
discussed above, except the two last—which are at least not purely
heroic. Of the rest the story of Rāma is probably the least historical.
But, taking the group as a whole, we see no reason for supposing that
Indian heroic poetry differs in this respect from that of the West.

It is to be remembered, however, that all the heroic material together
constitutes only a small fraction of the Mahābhārata. Historical elements
are not wanting also in the non-heroic narrative portions of the work.
There can be no reasonable doubt that Janamejaya is a historical character, whatever may be thought of his snake-sacrifice. Many of the seers
also are certainly historical persons. But we should seldom be prepared
to guarantee the historicity of what is related of them. They seem often
to be introduced without regard to chronology; and their adventures
and experiences in general can hardly be taken otherwise than as
products of fiction—like those attributed to the same class of persons in
the West.

From what has been said above it will be clear enough that the
Mahābhārata contains an immense amount of material for the study of

certain types of fiction. But any attempt to treat this systematically would be beyond our powers. We shall therefore confine our attention to a few typical examples of unhistorical matter, which occur either in the heroic portions of the work or in antiquarian elements which are closely connected with the main theme and may have been incorporated with it in early times.

For determining the existence of unhistorical elements certain criteria were specified in Vol. I, Ch. VIII. The first two of these need hardly be considered here. We have no historical documents by which to check the stories; the Rgveda relates to earlier times. Again, the various heroic stories are so little connected with one another, that evidence of a conflicting kind is hardly to be found in them, though discrepant and even contradictory accounts of an event frequently occur in the same story.[1]

Deities and other supernatural beings are introduced much as in the Homeric poems and in Irish heroic sagas. Sometimes they appear disguised as Brahmans. It is in this disguise that in Mahābh. III. cccviii (*ad fin.*) ff. Indra visits Karna and begs from him the armour and earrings with which he was born. Shortly before this (ccxcix ff.) Sūrya, the sun-god, who is Karna's father, has appeared to him in a dream, likewise disguised as a Brahman, and warned him of Indra's intentions. But in cccv. 8 f. Sūrya visits Kuntī, Karna's mother, without disguise—in his divine, though anthropomorphic, form. Indra and various other gods seem likewise to be without disguise in I. ccxxix f., when they fight with Arjuna and Krshna and are put to flight by them. In I. ccxxvii, Agni, the fire-god, presents these heroes with weapons—Arjuna also with a chariot and horses—which they afterwards use regularly. Similar incidents occur elsewhere not unfrequently.

One of the most interesting cases occurs in the story of Nala, ii ff. (Mahābh. III. liv ff.), where the gods Indra, Agni, Varuna and Yama hear of Damayantī's svayamvara and set off to it as suitors. On the way they meet with Nala and commission him, much against his will, to act as their messenger. Damayantī insists that she will have Nala himself; but when she comes before the assembled princes, she finds five figures exactly alike in the form of Nala. At her entreaty the gods display the divine characteristics by which she is able to distinguish them from Nala. Then they bestow blessings upon the bridal pair, and depart.

Gods are by no means the only supernatural beings introduced in the Mahābhārata. The divine seer Nārada is frequently introduced though

[1] For examples see Sidhanta, *The Heroic Age of India*, p. 17 ff.

he seldom influences the course of events. In I. clxxii, when Arjuna with his brothers is approaching the Ganges by night, on the way to Pancāla, he is attacked by Angāraparna, king of the Gandharva, who resents their disturbing his forest at such a time. Arjuna destroys his chariot, but spares his life; and the Gandharva then relates to him several stories of the far past. Apsarasas, or 'nymphs', appear not unfrequently. In I. ccxviii Arjuna releases five of them, who had been cursed by a Brahman and compelled to live in the form of crocodiles. Rākshasa, or 'demons', occur still more often. In general they correspond to the Norse Jötnar. The Rākshasa killed by Bhīma in I. clxv is a cannibal monster, very much like Grendel. But elsewhere, as in the story of Rāma, the word may be applied to human beings of alien race.

Supernatural birth and parentage is of very frequent occurrence. Reference has already been made to the case of Karna. His mother, Kuntī, has waited with great diligence upon a Brahman, and is rewarded by him with a spell, by which she can summon any of the deities. Out of curiosity she calls upon Sūrya, who immediately appears before her and insists upon her receiving his embraces (Mahābh. III. cccii ff.). She keeps the birth of her child, Karna, a secret, and sends it adrift in a basket on a tributary of the Ganges. The river carries it into the presence of the charioteer Adhiratha, who brings it up as his own child. Of the children born by Kuntī after her marriage with Pāndu, Yudhishthira is said to be son of Dharma (personified 'Duty'), Bhīma of Vāyu, the wind-god, and Arjuna of Indra, while Pāndu's children by his other wife, the twins Nakula and Sahadeva, are sons of the Açvins. We have already (p. 475) referred to the story of Çāntanu's marriage with Gangā (the divine personification of the Ganges), which is related in I. xcvii ff. Bhīshma is the son of this marriage. In I. lxxii Çakuntalā is said to be the daughter of Viçvāmitra and an Apsaras, named Menakā, who has been sent by Indra to tempt him. Even unions with the cannibal Rākshasa are not unknown. In I. cvii. 31 ff. Ghatotkaca is born to Bhīma by a Rākshasī named Hidimbā.

It is quite possible that some of these cases do not belong to the earliest strata of the poem. There seems to have been a widespread doctrine among Brahmans that princes (Kshatriya) could not produce offspring, at least unaided. In the case of Pāndu and his father Vicitra-vīrya this is expressly stated. The latter's sons are provided by a Brahman, the former's by various gods. But we see no reason for doubting the antiquity of the story of Karna's birth; and some of the others may be quite as old. It will be seen that more or less close parallels to most of them are to be found in the West. In Brahmanic belief, however, at least in its later phases, 'incarnation' (*avatāra*) takes the place of divine parentage; and for this we do not know of any satisfactory parallels in early Western literature,[1] though examples of metempsychosis, as from one human being to another, are not rare. Even in the Mahābhārata itself, as we have it, the incarnation of deities is nothing very unusual. We may refer (e.g.) to Vidura and the sons of Gangā. But the most notable instance is Krshna, whose divinity is dwelt upon at length very frequently, although there are many other passages, in which he seems to be merely a shrewd adviser.

The story of Rāma is of special interest as illustrating the growth of mythology. Rāma himself, like Krshna, is an incarnation of Vishnu; but in this case we meet with the conception in an incipient stage. In the Rāmāyana it seems to occur only in the later elements (cf. p. 471 f.). In the Mahābhārata it is found only in III. cclxxv, which is a preliminary rather than an essential part of the story.[2] Again, the identification of the heroine Sītā with the agricultural goddess or spirit of the same name likewise appears to be found only in the later elements of the Rāmāyana.[3] It does not occur at all in the Mahābhārata, so far as we have observed; she seems to be merely human. Rāvana's mythological connections, including Kubera's flying chariot, may be somewhat older, since in the Mahābhārata they are referred to in the story itself, as well as in the preliminary sections (III. cclxxiii–v). But there is no evidence, so far as we are aware, that Rāvana existed before—and independently of—the story of Rāma. His mythological character, in particular his defiance of the gods, may have been invented in part for the purpose of enhancing the glory of the hero. But when the process was started its extension evidently proved an irresistible temptation to the antiquarian mind. Even Manthara, the mischief-making maid of Queen Kaikeyī, is an incarnate spirit, specially commissioned for her purpose. To complete the unhistorical character of the personnel, we may add that most of the

---

[1] Neither do we know of any Western analogies for the birth of Dhrshtadyumna and Draupadī from the sacrificial altar.

[2] It occurs also in one or two passages in other parts of the Mahābhārata, not in connection with the story. We may cite III. xcix, where Rāma encounters his namesake Paraçu-Rāma, son of Jamadagni.

[3] It is remarkable that many scholars who accept the view stated on p. 471 f. as to the earlier and later elements in the Rāmāyana yet believe that the heroine Sītā is derived from the agricultural being. The literary evidence seems to us to leave no room for doubt that the folklore element is secondary.

famous seers of ancient (Vedic) times are introduced—Vasishtha and Vāmadeva even in the Mahābhārata—along with others who seem to belong to a later age.

The history of the unhistorical elements in the story would seem to have been, briefly, as follows. In its original form it was apparently a heroic story of a simple kind, describing the adventures of an exiled prince and his wife and brother in the forests of southern India. We can see nothing unreasonable in the popular view that the Rākshasa and the monkeys originally meant respectively the civilised Dravidian communities and the primitive forest peoples. But the use of these terms naturally gave a romantic colour to the story, if indeed this was not an inevitable result of the setting. Then some of the Rākshasa came to be connected with the demons of mythology, and other mythological beings.[1] The form of the story as preserved in the Mahābhārata (III. cclxxvi ff.) and in the earlier portions of the Rāmāyana represents the beginning of this stage. Next, the chief Rākshasa became regarded as incarnations of demons and the hero as the incarnation of the god Vishnu. This is the stage represented by the preliminary sections of the Mahābhārata (III. cclxxiii–v) and by the later portions of the Rāmāyana. Lastly, the heroine was identified with the agricultural goddess or spirit whose name she bore; but this took place only in the Rāmāyana. We are not prepared to discuss the case of Hanumat; it is possible of course that he may have been known independently of this story. But even if so the cult of Rāma, like that of Krshna, is sufficiently striking testimony to the influence of a popular heroic story.[2]

Natural beings—both men and animals—are sometimes credited with supernatural powers, much as in the West. We may instance the talking swans, which convey messages between Nala and Damayantī (cf. p. 469). More peculiar is the case of Karna, who is immortal so long as he preserves the armour and earrings, which are really part of his body. Ghatotkaca, the son of Bhīma and Hidimbā, can produce illusions of various kinds and even rise into the air (VII. clxxvi ff.). But the majority of the cases may perhaps be regarded as examples of exaggeration. We may refer to the speed with which Nala drives Rtuparna's chariot to Vidarbha, and the rapidity with which Rtuparna counts the leaves of a certain tree, during the journey (III. lxxii. 7 ff.; Nala xx. 7–11). In other connections we find exaggeration practically without limit. When

---

[1] The procedure is not essentially different from that of the Anglo-Saxon poet who made Grendel a descendant of Cain.

[2] The cults of some Greek heroes provide analogies to a certain extent.

it is stated how many warriors fight or fall in a battle the numbers given have lost all significance.

In non-heroic stories the possession of supernatural powers is far more frequent and striking. No king, however mighty, has a chance of resisting a great ascetic successfully; and even the gods themselves are at his mercy. It is perhaps unnecessary to give further examples. But the contrast between heroic and non-heroic stories in this respect is very noticeable. In the central story of the Mahābhārata, as well as in the heroic episodes, Brahmans play only a subordinate part, and hardly influence the course of events.

Even when no supernatural beings or properties are involved we hear not unfrequently of events and situations which are quite incredible. Such is the case with much of what is said of Bhīshma. It is not impossible that this old hero may have lived on into the days of the grandsons of his younger brother. But he cannot possibly have taken part, as an active combatant, in the battle in which Arjuna's son Abhimanyu was a doughty warrior. The longevity ascribed to Brahmans is, as usual, even more extravagant. In I. lx we find Vyāsa visiting Janamejaya, who is said to be his great-great-great-grandson.

There is some reason, as we have seen, for suspecting that the story of Ambā once existed in an independent form. It seems not to have been well preserved (cf. p. 476 f.). The general trend of the story leads one to expect that Bhīshma would lose his life at the hands of Çikhandin; but actually we are left in doubt whether he or Arjuna was the slayer. We suspect therefore that this story has been grafted upon that of the battle. There can be no question that other extraneous elements are to be found in the personnel of the latter. We need not consider the Yavana and other foreigners, who are doubtless late additions, like the Biblical peoples in Widsith. But it is of some interest to note that Vāhlīka, Bhīshma's uncle, is also present. In fact no less than five generations of the same family take part in the battle.

More important is the case of Pāndu. The view has frequently been expressed that the Pāndava were originally not a family but a people—a non-Aryan or at least non-Brahmanic people, who practised polyandry, like some of the backward hill-tribes at the present day. But we know of no evidence for a people called Pāndava; and the battle, so far as it can be regarded as a national war in any sense, is between the Kuru on the one side and the Pancāla and the Matsya on the other—though both parties have numerous allies. The Pāndava are merely exiled princes of the Kuru, whose cause has been taken up by the Pancāla [1] and the Matsya. The polyandrous marriage, however, is certainly remarkable; for it is quite alien to anything which can properly be called Hindusim, and the poets were evidently at a loss how to account for it. So far as we are aware it can be explained only as a custom taken over from the (non-Aryan) natives of the country, or as having arisen under special conditions, probably as a result of conquest. [2]

The fact that there is no trace of any such form of marriage in Dhrtarāshtra's family suggests that in the original form of the story this king and Pāndu were not brothers. Further, the introduction of Vyāsa into the story makes it likely enough that considerable changes have taken place in the part relating to the earlier generations, though we are not prepared to attempt any reconstruction. It is an essential feature of the story that the Pāndava have been deprived of their inheritance by the sons of Dhrtarāshtra. But it does not seem to us essential that the two families should be closely related.

There are a few facts which, so far as they go, rather tend to support the view that in the original story the Pāndava were a family of native or mixed stock. They are born far away in the mountains, to which their father has retired; and it is not until after his death that their existence is known. Later, they build their capital, Indraprastha, in a forest near the Jumna; and this is the part of the kingdom which they demand back on the eve of the battle. The story of Satyavatī would seem to show that this region was still largely non-Aryan. But without going into particulars, if the chronology adopted on p. 514 f. is correct, the Aryanisation of the whole of the Jumna and Ganges basins must have been comparatively recent in the times to which our story relates; and it is reasonable to expect that many native or half-native communities survived.

[1] The importance attached to Draupadī in the story is not to be overlooked. It is through their marriage with her and the influence of her powerful relatives that the heroes first attain their sovereignty. And in the last battle the army is commanded by Dhrshtadyumna, not Arjuna.

[2] Cf. the reference to the ancient Britons on p. 519, note. The two explanations do not perhaps necessarily exclude one another.

CHAPTER VI

POETRY AND SAGA RELATING TO DEITIES

IN poetry relating to deities the same Types are represented as in the West; but the distribution is very different. Type D is represented by a very large number of hymns, especially in the Rgveda. On the other hand narrative does not occur in the Vedas, apart from short incidental passages in the hymns. There is a little narrative saga in the Brāhmanas, but it is of the didactic type (CA). The Mahābhārata contains a good deal of narrative poetry, and some of it may perhaps be regarded as belonging to Type A; but here also CA seems to be more frequent. Type B is represented by a few poems in the Rgveda.

We will first take the hymns (Type D) preserved in the Rgveda. They are addressed to a considerable number of deities. The largest number (c. 250) is claimed by Indra. Next comes Agni with c. 200, then Soma with c. 120, then the Açvins with c. 50. Various deities have smaller numbers of hymns addressed to them. Sometimes more than one deity is invoked in a hymn, while a good number are addressed to all the gods collectively.

The hymns have little in common with the Homeric Hymns or with the theological poems of the Edda. In general they may be said to contain two main elements—(a) the description or celebration of the properties and might of the deity, (b) appeals for the welfare of the poet and his patrons, or perhaps all those who are taking part in the worship. The narrative element is insignificant. As might be expected, there is a good deal of repetition, both of formulae and of ideas. Each deity is credited with certain characteristic attributes and functions, as in the West; but they are by no means always clearly distinguished. Much difficulty is caused by the traditional and highly figurative diction which is constantly employed. To the modern mind it often seems as unnatural and meaningless as the kennings in Norse Skaldic poetry.

In hymns to Indra the following are perhaps the most constant and characteristic elements: (i) celebration of the god's prowess in slaying demons and in releasing the waters; (ii) the god's love of soma, which strengthens him for his exploits; (iii) appeals for victory and wealth, especially perhaps cattle and other booty. To the student of Western religion this combination of (i) and (iii) is unfamiliar. It is clear that Indra was at one time a thunder-god, as Zeus and Thor originally were.

The fights with demons are common to all three; but in parched lands like the earlier homes of the Aryans[1] the 'release of the waters' is a matter of more moment than in Europe. The other element, however, is not specially characteristic of Zeus, while in the North it belongs definitely to Othin, not Thor. Indra, like Othin, is the god of the warrior prince and the giver of victory. But the most peculiar feature of the hymns is that these two elements seem to be inextricably combined. Numerous passages make it clear that the dominating thoughts in the minds of the poets were those of victory and booty, usually at the expense of the natives. Indra is pictured as an Aryan prince driving to battle in his chariot and overthrowing the castles of the Dāsa. But this picture is commonly amalgamated and confused with the conventional description of Indra smiting the demons; and, owing to the traditional imagery employed by the poets, it is not easy to distinguish between the 'release of the waters' and a cattle-raid. In general, however, even when they are calling upon the god to smite Vṛtra, it is to be suspected that the practical object which they have in view is to get him to smite their human enemies.

Agni differs greatly from Indra; he is by no means completely anthropomorphised. The hymns addressed to him are usually of a descriptive character; for the name means 'fire', and the poets seem as a rule to have had a real fire in their minds. He is described as golden and blazing. The two fire-sticks are his mothers, whom he is said to eat; wood is his regular food. He is frequently said to be a priest and a messenger to the gods. Such terms as 'lord of the house' are also frequently applied to him. In all this the language of the hymns is not so very far removed from that of spells. But numerous passages also show the figurative diction to which we have referred above. Thus he is described as a bull, a horse, a bird, and as driving in a chariot; and his functions are not clearly distinguished from those of the other gods. On the whole, however—in contrast with Indra—he is more often appealed to for domestic welfare and offspring than for success in war.

Soma is the deity celebrated in all the hymns of Book ix and in a few other hymns. He is the personification of the intoxicating soma plant, and his anthropomorphisation is no more advanced than that of the fire-god. Indeed his hymns resemble spells even more than do those which are addressed to Agni. Many of them seem to be designed for singing while the juice is being extracted from the stalks and passed through

---

[1] At least the myth of the slaying of Vṛtra must date from times before the Indian Aryans left Iran, for the name *Verethraghna* (*Vṛtrahan*) occurs in the Avesta. Its origin cannot therefore be derived from Indian phenomena.

strainers. Much of what is said of Soma and his exhilarating powers has analogies in the Norse myth of Óðrerir, the mead of poetry (cf. Vol. I, pp. 249, 620), though the latter is not personified. Soma is 'lord of speech' and a poet, seer and sage. But he also gives physical strength, especially to Indra, and immortality. Apart from these special features he is often invoked for prosperity in general, like the rest of the gods. And the same obscure figurative diction is applied to him as to the rest; he is described as a bull, a horse, a chariot-rider, etc. In later literature he is generally identified with the moon, and most scholars believe that the beginnings of this remarkable idea are to be traced in some of the latest hymns in the Rgveda itself.

The Açvins (*Açvinā*), or '(pair of) Horsemen'—without notion of riding—belong to mythology of the more personal kind, like Indra. They are represented as young men, twins, driving in a chariot, which in the obscure diction of the hymns is often said to be drawn by birds, though this cannot be the original idea. They are celebrated chiefly as healers and deliverers from danger; and many hymns contain catalogues of the cures and rescues effected by them. Honey seems to be specially connected with their worship.

Among the deities who figure less prominently we may mention Ushas, or 'Dawn', who has about twenty hymns devoted to her. Here again the personification is only slight; the hymns are largely occupied with descriptions of the natural phenomena of dawn. As in the Homeric poems, she has her chariot and horses; but in the Rgveda she is an object of worship. She is invoked for protection, wealth and offspring.

Female deities receive very little attention in the Rgveda. Indeed there seem to be no truly mythological goddesses. Apart from the hymns just mentioned, there is one to Rātrī or 'Night' (x. 127), which is perhaps more a descriptive poem than a hymn. Earth (*Pṛthivī*) is addressed in one short hymn (v. 84), as well as in several others in which she is associated with Heaven (*Dyaus*). More important is Sarasvatī, the goddess of a river identified in later times with the Ghaggar, which loses itself in the Indian Desert. She is addressed in three hymns, in which she is besought to grant wealth and offspring. In later literature she is the wife of Brahmā and goddess of eloquence and wisdom.

Type B is represented by a few poems which consist exclusively of speeches in character—monologues or dialogues. There are also a few similar poems which appear to have a didactic purpose, and therefore properly belong to Type C (CB); but the two series may conveniently be taken together. Nearly all these poems are contained in Book x, and therefore probably date from towards the close of the Rgveda period.

We will take the monologues first. In x. 119 the speaker, apparently Indra, expresses the exhilaration he has received from offerings of soma. He has grown too big for heaven and earth, and is ready to smite the earth in his frenzy. Each stanza contains the refrain "Have I not drunk of soma?" In x. 48 and 49 the same god recounts the mighty deeds which he has performed. These consist in the main of successes which he has won for the Aryan peoples and individual Aryan heroes at the expense of the Dasyu. The first part of x. 27 seems to belong to the same series. Indra speaks in general terms of his exploits, though two stanzas apparently are addressed to him by the poet. But the latter part of the poem, from st. 11, seems to be a collection of riddles. Here also we may perhaps mention x. 125, in which a feminine being describes her qualities, much after the style of a riddle. The traditional interpretation is 'Speech' (personified); and this may be correct, though the sense seems at times rather to suggest an identification with 'Breath', or perhaps the spirit of life.

The dialogue poems show more variety. We may take first x. 10, in which the speakers are the twin deities Yama and Yamī. The latter appeals to her brother repeatedly to indulge in love with her. Yama rejects her advances, sometimes with persuasion, sometimes in anger, speaking of her as wanton and her proposal as sinful. This poem perhaps belongs to Type C (CB). Yama is not exactly the god of death in the Rgveda, but rather the leader of the 'Fathers' (ancestors) and, consequently, king of the dead. He and his sister are the first mortals, and progenitors of the human race.

A more certain example of the didactic type is to be found in x. 51, where the speakers are Varuna and Agni. The latter has been discovered hiding in the waters, in order to escape being used in sacrifices. He consents to being used on condition that the first oblations shall be granted to him. Other dialogue poems, however, resemble the monologues more closely. Thus in iv. 42 Varuna describes himself as ruler of the gods and establisher of law. Indra in reply boasts of his prowess as god of battle.[1] More peculiar is x. 108, a dialogue between Saramā, Indra's hound, and the Pani,[2] whose cattle she has traced. She threatens

---

[1] The relationship of the last three (historical) stanzas to the dialogue in this poem is not clear to us.

[2] This name (*Pani*) seems to be applied sometimes to the Dāsa (*Dasyu*), sometimes to malignant (niggardly) supernatural beings.

them with destruction from Indra, and demands that they shall give up their cattle. They refuse at first; and then try, without success, to persuade her to join them.

Some of these poems are probably to be taken as representing the lighter side of Vedic poetry. The same may be true of another poem, x. 86, which consists of a dialogue between Indra, his wife, and a third person called Vrshākapi ('Male Ape'). The lady is very angry with Vrshākapi, who seems to have damaged some of her belongings, and Indra is trying to make peace between them. Each stanza has a refrain expressing Indra's supremacy. The poem is now interpreted as a dispute over the misdoings of a tame monkey, but intended as a satire upon some contemporary prince, who is described as Indra. But it is far from clear; and the same may be said of one or two other poems (e.g. x. 28), which seem to belong to Type B.

It is only in poems of this type that one gets any pictures of the gods in relation to one another. In the hymns pairs and groups of deities are frequently associated; and we hear (e.g.) that the Maruts are children of Rudra and the Açvins of Dyaus, and that Vishnu helped Indra in the fray with Vrtra. So in the Wedding Hymn (x. 85) we find a large number of deities mentioned, though the treatment is mystical. But pictures of the social life of the divine community, such as one meets with in the *Thrymskviða*, the *Vision of Aengus* and the *Hymn to Hermes*, seem to be entirely wanting. This is doubtless due in the main to the total absence of Type A. But the fact that some of the deities, e.g. Agni and Soma, are only to a slight extent anthropomorphised is also to be taken into account. Truly anthropomorphic goddesses are hardly to be found.

In the Mahābhārata references to deities are extremely frequent. Often they are introduced into the action; often too the scene is laid in the divine world. Here we shall have to confine our attention to a few cases, which will be taken chiefly from narratives (Types A and CA).

The different parts of the Mahābhārata vary greatly in the divine personnel which they introduce. In stories or passages which are purely heroic we meet with the same gods as in the Rgveda. An instance may be found in the story of Nala (II–v; Mahābh. III. liv ff.), where the gods Indra, Agni, Varuna and Yama make their way to Damayantī's svayamvara. Their behaviour is somewhat irresponsible, but not malevolent; and the treatment of the episode shows an attitude towards them closely analogous to what is found in various Greek and Norse stories of deities. Indra is described as 'king of the gods' (*devarāja*). Elsewhere in the same story we hear of other Vedic deities, e.g. Vāyu, the Maruts (*Rudrās*) and the Açvins, as well as of some deities who are not mentioned in the Rgveda; but there is apparently no reference to Brahmā, Vishnu or Çiva.

The story of Nala is by no means peculiar in its treatment of the gods. Thus in the story of Sāvitrī (III. ccxcvi) Yama, the god of the dead, proves to be not inexorable to the persuasions of the heroine. And in the main story Sūrya, the Sun-god, when invoked by Kuntī (III. cccv f.) eagerly demands her embraces. A parallel to the spiteful treatment of heroes by deities in the Iliad is to be found in III. cccix, where Indra visits Karna, disguised as a Brahman, and begs from him the armour and ear-rings which make him invulnerable. Sūrya has warned Karna (his son) beforehand of Indra's intentions (*ib.* ccxcix ff.) and advised him to beg for an infallible weapon in exchange for what he gives up. We may note also that when Kuntī uses her spell on behalf of Pāndu (I. cxxii ff.)—a story which is not of purely heroic character—the deities whom she invokes are the Vedic gods Vāyu, Indra and the Açvins, as well as the later (abstract) deity Dharma ('Duty'). It will be observed that the deities who figure in the stories are almost always male, just as in the Rgveda. Savitrī's appearance in III. ccxcii is a rare exception.

But in the purely Brahmanic portions of the Mahābhārata the case is quite different. Here the supreme deity is Brahmā, who is frequently introduced and sometimes speaks at length. Vishnu also, who is only a minor deity in the Rgveda, is here regarded with the greatest reverence, especially in connection with his incarnations. In III. cclxxv he is born as Rāma, in order to free the celestials from molestation by Rāvana. And very many passages, all doubtless of Brahmanic origin, speak of his incarnation in Krshna. Rudra too, likewise a minor deity in the Rgveda, is of hardly less importance here. He is now generally known as Çiva ('friendly') or Mahādeva ('great god'); and when he comes upon the scene, he seems to be omnipotent. It may be observed that he appears twice in the story of Ambā and Çikhandin, which seems to us to have heroic features.

The attitude of the Brahmanic elements towards Indra is sometimes hostile and even contemptuous. In I. cxcix Vyāsa relates a story—how Indra met with Çiva and was treated by him with the utmost disdain. At a look from him he is paralysed and reduced to abject terror. Then, for his presumption, he is made to open up a cave, where he finds four other Indras, just like himself, imprisoned. They have all five to become incarnate at Çiva's orders. The story is told in justification of Draupadī's marriage.

Still more remarkable is the version of the slaying of Vrtra as related by Çalya in v. ix f. The god Tvashtr has a three-headed son, who devotes himself to asceticism to such an extent that Indra becomes afraid that he will displace him. He sends nymphs therefore to tempt him; and when this fails, he kills him with the thunderbolt. Tvashtr in revenge for his son's death creates Vrtra, who fights with Indra. The latter is repeatedly worsted in the most ignominious ways, but contrives to escape. The deities and the seers in heaven now become much alarmed and appeal for help to Vishnu, who advises them to make peace between Indra and Vrtra, though he intends to give victory to the former. Vrtra stipulates that he shall not be assailed by Indra in a list of ways which seems to be exhaustive—as in the story of Balder—but eventually Indra, by the help of Vishnu, contrives to slay him with his thunderbolt concealed in a mass of sea-foam. But now Indra is seized with dread at the thought of having killed a Brahman, and hides himself; and the gods appoint Nahusha to be their king for a time in his place.

It is not clear to us here whether the slain Brahman is Vrtra or the three-headed being. But there are many other references to the story. In xii. cclxxix ff. it is told at length again by Bhīshma, with considerable variations. No mention is made of Tvashtr or his son; but Vrtra has long devoted himself to asceticism. Indra is assisted by both Vishnu and Çiva; but the sympathy is again with Vrtra rather than with him. When Vrtra is slain the 'Sin of Brahmanicide' (personified) comes from his body and seizes upon Indra.

It is generally believed that the fight between Indra and Vrtra is a primitive story of a contest between the thunder-god and a demon; and, so far as we are aware, the Rgveda contains nothing incompatible with such an interpretation. At all events the story seems to date from a time before the Aryans entered India (cf. p. 530). There seems to be no trace of sympathy with Vrtra in the Rgveda; and the same is true of the reference to the slaying of Viçvarūpa son of Tvashtr in Rgv. x. 8.[1] The transformation of the story therefore, as seen in the above accounts, strikes the modern mind as absurd and childish. But it can hardly be due to late additions to the Mahābhārata; for something very much like the first account must have been known to the authors of the Aitareya Brāhmana. It is there stated (vii. 28) that Indra had been deprived of the soma-drinking because he had misused Viçvarūpa , son of Tvashtr,

---

[1] There seems to be no indication that Viçvarūpa is connected with Vrtra, though both are robbed of their cattle. Trita Āptya is associated with Indra in the former exploit.

and laid low Vrtra—together with various other offences. The change of feeling therefore can be traced back to very early times.

This change of feeling can hardly be interpreted as a religious revolution like that of the Avesta, where Indra has become a demon. He is still regarded as the king of the gods, not only in heroic stories, but also in the Brahmanic parts of the Mahābhārata, though here the real power lies with Vishnu or Çiva. But it is plain from the passage in the Aitareya Brāhmana just referred to, as well as from many passages in the epic, that Indra is viewed as the representative of the kingly power and the Kshatriya caste. The Brahman tolerates both the Kshatriya and his deity, but claims to be superior to them both. It may be observed that the population of heaven now includes seers, as well as gods, and the former are the more important.

Apart from deities we hear also a good deal of other supernatural beings, especially in the Mahābhārata. Among these we may note first the Gandharva, who are mentioned in the Rgveda, though not frequently, except in Book x. They seem to be guardians of the soma. Sometimes only one Gandharva is spoken of; sometimes the plural is used. In the former case we find also the name Viçvāvasu (x. 85, 139). In the Atharvaveda, II. 2, the Gandharva is invoked with the highest praises. In the Mahābhārata we hear more of these beings. In XII. cccxix Viçvāvasu, who is here called king of the Gandharva, consults Yājnavalkya upon his philosophy. But a much fuller account is given in I. clxxii ff. of Angāraparna, who is also called king of the Gandharva. He is enraged at the heroes' intrusion in his forests and attacks them; but Arjuna overthrows him and burns his chariot. He spares his life, however, and the Gandharva then relates to him a number of stories of the past.

Apsarasas or nymphs are not often mentioned in the Rgveda. On two occasions the reference is to Urvaçī. In VII. 33 she is said to have borne Vasishtha to Varuna and Mitra. Another poem, x. 95, consists of a dialogue (Type B) between the same nymph and the patriarch Purūravas, son (grandson) of Manu. The poem is obscure; but later accounts of the story show that it is concerned with a rather widespread motif— that of a man who has married a supernatural being upon some condition which he has subsequently broken.[1] In the poem Purūravas begs Urvaçī to return to him; but she only promises to send to him the child which she will bear. In the Atharvaveda, II. 2, Apsarasas seem to be the wives of the Gandharva. Like the latter they are invoked for success at

[1] For Yugoslav parallels cf. p. 312.

dice. In the Mahābhārata they figure rather frequently; and they are represented as sportive and amorous. In III. xlv f., at the instigation of Indra, Urvaçī sets out to try the effect of her charms upon Arjuna, but receives a rebuff from him. On other occasions Apsarasas are sent by the deities to tempt seers of whom they are afraid, in order to divert them from their asceticism. Thus in I. lxxi f. the Apsaras Menakā is sent by Indra to Viçvāmitra. The child Çakuntalā,[1] who is born from them, is deserted by her mother as soon as she is born. Here also we may refer to the Apsaras Bargā, who was turned into a crocodile with her four companions (I. ccxviii f.) by a seer whom they had tempted and mocked.

Among other supernatural beings we may refer in passing to the Yaksha who in v. cxciii f. exchanges sex with Çikhandin. Something more, however, must be said about the two 'divine seers' Nārada and Parvata. They seem to be unknown to the Rgveda, though they are mentioned fairly often in the Brāhmanas. In the Mahābhārata they are introduced very frequently, especially Nārada, both in the main story and in episodes. As a rule they are not distinguishable from human seers; but sometimes they carry news from the world to the gods. The chief story relating to them occurs in two variant forms, in VII. lv and XII. xxx. According to the latter, which seems to be the better version, Nārada and Parvata, who were uncle and nephew, set out on one of their visits to the earth, and made a compact that neither of the two should keep anything secret from the other. But when they visit a king named Srnjaya, Nārada falls in love with his daughter and conceals the fact from his nephew. The latter, however, finds out what has happened and is deeply angered. He curses his uncle, making him to have the face of a monkey. Nārada in return curses Parvata, declaring that he shall not get back to heaven. Eventually the two seers make up their quarrel; Parvata returns to heaven, while Nārada receives back his own face and stays with his father-in-law. It should perhaps be mentioned that this incident is only a part of the story of the seers' visit to Srnjaya. Another incident will require notice in a later chapter.

For a comparison of early Indian and European poetry of this category we are practically dependent upon the Mahābhārata; for the early hymn poetry which has been preserved in the West hardly presents a sufficient amount of material. It may, however, be observed that some of the most important gods are only partially anthropomorphised and

[1] In Çat. Br. XIII. 5. 4. 13 she is herself described as an Apsaras.

that little account is taken of (anthropomorphic) goddesses. We may also note the growth of priestly gods, who in the subsequent (Brāhmana) period become all-important.

In the Mahābhārata we have to distinguish between the heroic and the non-heroic elements. In the former the treatment of deities is in general similar to what is found in heroic stories and stories of the gods in Europe. Yet here again goddesses are seldom prominent—a fact which is the more remarkable owing to the prominent part usually played by women in Indian heroic stories. The Apsarasas may be compared with the youthful supernatural females of Europe—nymphs, Valkyries, Vile, etc.—but unlike the latter they seem to have no endowments or distinctive characteristics other than physical beauty. In the non-heroic parts of the Mahābhārata the representation of the gods has in general little in common with what is found in the European records which have come under our notice.

It is a characteristic of the non-heroic parts of the work that the distinction between human and divine beings tends to be obliterated. We have spoken of Nārada and Parvata as divine beings; but they are often introduced as if they were merely human seers, and this may have been their original character. Even more striking examples of such ambiguity are to be found in other seers, especially Kaçyapa, who is mentioned once in the Rgveda (ix. 114). Sometimes in the Mahābhārata (e.g. 1. xlii f.) he seems to be a (human) Brahman; but elsewhere (e.g. 1. lxv f.) he belongs to the world of myth and is the ancestor of various mythical beings. Much the same is said of Pulastya and others. Such ambiguities are presumably to be connected with the claims put forward by the Brahmans to equality with the gods.

There is no satisfactory evidence for any ambiguity of this kind in heroic poetry or tradition. We do indeed find Nārada and Parvata carrying news from mankind to the gods (iii. liv); but such passages doubtless represent merely the current beliefs or poetic conventions of the day. Heroic poetry seems to have been little concerned with seers. But we cannot admit the truth of a theory which found much favour among scholars of last century, that heroes themselves were by origin 'hypostases' of deities. This theory was applied to all early literatures; but we have never yet found an example which was satisfactorily substantiated.[1] In regard to India the case to which most importance has been

---

[1] It may happen, of course, that the name of a deity which has lost all its associations and attributes may eventually come to be regarded as that of a man—perhaps a king of the past. Lludd Llaweraint is a likely instance. But this is not what was meant by the theory noticed here.

attached is that of Arjuna, who is held to have been originally a hypostasis of Indra. Even in quite recent works this theory seems to be rather widely accepted. Yet there is nothing in the Mahābhārata to suggest that Arjuna was regarded as other than a man, though he is a son of Indra. In Indian, just as in European, heroic tradition a hero may be the son of a deity and may associate with deities—in which case he may be credited with fantastic experiences. In Brahmanic doctrine he may be the avatar of a deity. But the theory to which we are alluding—that a deity can come to be misinterpreted as a hero—is foreign to both heroic and Brahmanic ideas. In this case it is founded, we believe, more upon the hero's name [1] than upon his exploits and experiences. Yet the same name is borne by another hero, who is referred to fairly often in the Mahābhārata—Arjuna Kārtavīrya, a prince of the Haihaya but described as a tyrant and monster.

It may be suspected that in one respect heroic tradition did not clearly distinguish between human and supernatural beings, viz. in reference to the non-Aryan population. The word Rākshasa in the Rgveda seems originally to have denoted a monster [2] of superhuman strength and ferocity, like the Norse *jötunn*; but in the Mahābhārata, though this meaning is often found, there are many passages where the term is apparently applied to human beings of alien race. We may note in particular the story of Rāma—where this usage occurs also regularly in the Rāmāyana—and various incidents in which Ghatotkaca figures, especially his conflicts with other Rākshasa. With them may be mentioned the Yaksha, who are perhaps the spirits or deities of the indigenous population, rather than the people themselves. The god Kubera seems to belong to both classes. Into these questions we cannot enter; but we would note that the identification or confusion of alien peoples with demons is probably by no means peculiar to India.

[1] This is due especially to an obscure passage in Çat. Br. v. 4. 3. 7, where in a description of the Rājasūya sacrifice it is stated that the king mounts his chariot saying: "I, the inviolate Arjuna (mount) thee." The text goes on to explain that "Indra is called Arjuna, which is his secret name." The king then is supposed to be personating Indra. One text in place of *Arjuna* has *Phalguna*, a name which is often applied to the hero Arjuna in the Mahābhārata. One may perhaps be tempted to suspect that the king's words were originally a reminiscence of the hero, which later came to be misunderstood. But in any case the passage can hardly be held to prove the identity of the hero and the god, any more than the expression 'Zeus Agamemnon' can prove that Agamemnon was originally identical with Zeus.

[2] It is clearly a derivative of *rakṣas*, 'demon', a word frequently used in the Rgveda, especially for nocturnal demons.

CHAPTER VII

ANTIQUARIAN LEARNING

MOST of the works with which we have been dealing contain antiquarian elements. In the Mahābhārata they are very large. But in addition to these we have to take account here of the Purānas, a series of works which are primarily of antiquarian interest. The word *purāna* seems properly to mean no more than 'ancient story'; but in practice it has come to denote a collection of antiquarian lore.

The Purānas, which are eighteen in number, claim to deal with a common series of subjects, as follows:[1] (i) the origin of the universe; (ii) the reconstitution of the universe after its dissolution at the end of each aeon (*kalpa*); (iii) the genealogies of gods and seers; (iv) the *Manvantara* or periods (within the aeon) in which mankind is produced anew from a progenitor called Manu; (v) the history of the royal families reigning during the four ages (*yuga*) contained in a 'great age' (*mahāyuga*), which is itself a fraction of a Manvantara. But this scheme is merely traditional; it is not strictly adhered to in any of the existing Purānas. All of them show omissions; thus (e.g.) Sect. v is preserved in only seven Purānas. All of them also contain much extraneous matter of a didactic character.

The setting or framework is also traditional, and very similar to that of the Mahābhārata. Here again the author is Vyāsa, who has received his knowledge from Brahmā. The speaker is usually either Lomaharshana (the Sūta) or his son Ugraçravas (known as Sauti), to whom the Purāna has been imparted by one of Vyāsa's disciples. The scene is generally laid at the court of King Adhisīmakrshna, great-grandson of Janamejaya; but in the Vishnu Purāna it is at that of Parīkshit, Janamejaya's father. The history of the kings in Sect. v is continued—in three dynasties only—down to very much later times. But after the reign of Adhisīmakrshna it is expressed in the future, i.e. as prophecy, whereas the past is regularly used for the earlier kings.

It is now generally recognised that the Purānas have had a very long history, reaching back to a remote antiquity. But they have been added

[1] For further information on this subject see Rapson, *Cambridge History of India*, I. 296 f. For an account of the contents of the various Purānas cf. Winternitz, *Gesch. d. ind. Litteratur*, I. 450 ff.

to and transformed to such an extent that the history is difficult, if not impossible, to unravel. In their present form they seem to date from a period several centuries after the beginning of our era. Their history therefore is perhaps as long and complicated as that of the Mahābhārata. In point of fact the latter contains a very large amount of similar matter,[1] though here it is re-cast and grouped round the central theme, which is a heroic story. As the Mahābhārata is more generally accessible,[2] we shall refer to it, where possible, in preference to the Purānas.

It will be convenient to adopt the same classification of the material as in Vol. I (p. 270 ff.).

I. Genealogies form an important element in the Purānas. The genealogies of the kings contained in Sect. v are of immense length, extending from Manu, the first man, down to the great battle of the Mahābhārata. Most of the kingdoms of northern India seem to be represented. In three cases—the kingdoms of the Pūru (Kuru), Ayodhyā and Magadha—the genealogy is continued down to about the fourth century (B.C.), in Magadha until much later times. It would perhaps be more correct, at least in the later period, to speak of lists of kings; for they seem not to be genealogies in the strict sense.

The later stages of these three lists are probably derived in the main from genuine historical tradition, though they demonstrably contain some serious mistakes.[3] Then come in each line a considerable number of names which apparently we have no means of testing. Beyond these, the generations immediately following the battle of the Mahābhārata contain a number of names which are known from the Brāhmanas and Upanishads. For the period of the battle itself and (in some cases) a few generations earlier we have the evidence of heroic poetry, preserved in the Mahābhārata. Still further back the genealogies contain a good many names which occur in the Rgveda; but it is frequently difficult to reconcile the genealogies with the Vedic evidence. A remarkable fact is that the longest genealogies are those of the eastern kingdoms, such as Ayodhyā and Videha. There is no evidence that these regions were Aryanised in the Rgveda period, i.e. until a very few

---

[1] Cf. I. i. 63 ff. Sometimes (e.g. I. i. 85) the Mahābhārata itself is called a Purāna. The Harivamça, which is preserved as a kind of appendix to the Mahābhārata, is generally regarded as a Purāna, though it is not included in the eighteen.

[2] Only a few of the Purānas seem to have been translated: the Vishnu P. by Wilson, the Markandeya P. by Pargiter, the Bhāgavata P. by Burnouf (French), the Harivamça by Langlois (French).

[3] Cf. Rapson, op. cit. p. 310 ff.

generations before the battle; yet the genealogy of Ayodhyā gives about ninety generations from Manu to the battle, as against about forty-five for that of Pancāla (North Pancāla) during the same period. The details are hardly less surprising. Nala son of Nishadha occurs about twenty generations before the battle. This can hardly be anyone else than the Nala Naishadha (i.e. Nala of Nishadha) of the heroic story, whose home was far from Ayodhyā, though he visited it. His employer at Ayodhyā, King Rtuparna, is placed nearly twenty generations earlier still. Again, Trasadasyu and his father Purukutsa are known from the Rgveda to have been contemporaries of Sudās. But in the Puranic genealogy of Ayodhyā they appear about seventy generations before the battle, whereas in that of Pancāla Sudās (Sudāsa) is only five generations before Drupada. Lastly, it may be observed that the legend of Çunah-çepa[1] (cf. p. 496) is located at Ayodhyā and brought into connection with certain names—six or seven generations below Trasadasyu— which look like corrupt forms of names mentioned in Rgv. v. 27. It would seem that names and stories have been drawn into this genealogy from every side. At all events we cannot doubt that the Puranic genea- logies have cultivated antiquarian speculation on the most extravagant scale.[2]

The Mahābhārata also contains genealogies. In i. xciv f. there are two very long genealogies of the Kuru, which vary greatly from one another, and still more from the corresponding genealogy in the Purānas; but elements common to all three are not wanting. The Mahābhārata apparently does not give a genealogy of the Pancāla; but it contains a number of references to their past kings which, so far as they go, are compatible with the Purānas. As some of the names are certified by the Rgveda, we may believe that this genealogy preserves elements of genuine tradition for some little way beyond the battle of the Mahābhārata, though the connecting links are open to doubt. Un- fortunately neither the Vedas nor the Brāhmanas contain royal genealogies.

'Genealogies' are of frequent occurrence in the Upanishads; but they are genealogies of doctrine or information, not of flesh and blood (cf. p. 503). They are often of great length—sometimes more than fifty 'generations'. Usually they lead up to a divine being.

[1] For the growth of this story see Keith, *Rig-Veda Brahmanas*, p. 62 ff.
[2] For the contrary view see Pargiter, *Ancient Indian Historical Tradition* (passim), where the historical value of the lists is maintained with great learning. For the collection and presentation of the material this work is invaluable.

II. Catalogues, other than genealogies, are of very frequent occurrence both in the Mahābhārata and in the Purānas. As examples of different kinds we may cite the list of Dhrtarāshtra's hundred sons in the former work, I. lxvii. 94 ff. (cf. cxvii. 2 ff.) and the long list of incarnations of deities contained in the same chapter. A much longer catalogue is that of the holy places enumerated in III. lxxxii ff. But instances are common enough, especially in the Brahmanic parts of the work.

The Brāhmanas sometimes preserve lists of kings who were generous sacrificers and patrons of learning. Instances may be found in Ait. Brāhm. VII. 34, VIII. 21—both of which contain legendary elements. It would seem that lists of this kind were long cultivated by the Brahmans; for similar examples occur in the Mahābhārata, VII. lv ff., XII. xxix. We may also compare the list of kings who celebrated the horse-sacrifice, given in the Çatapatha Brāhmana, XIII. 5.

Short catalogues occur also in Vedic poetry. We may instance the list of rivers given in Rgv. X. 75. Short lists of deities, as in I. 22, are not rare. Longer examples may be found in the lists of persons of the past befriended by the Açvins or Indra (cf. p. 531), e.g. I. 112, 116 f., VI. 26.

III. Speculations upon the origin of names seem to be not at all uncommon in the Mahābhārata. As examples may be cited, for personal names I. xl. 1 ff., xcv. 45, 83, for a river-name I. clxxix. 9. This is of course a subject which must be left to specialists, who have a good knowledge of the language; but so far as we are able to judge, the evidence appears to be very similar to what is found in Europe. The examples we have noticed are all more or less isolated. We have not met with long series of such speculations—'etymological dictionaries'—of names, as in Ireland. The Indian counterpart to such activities seems to be the study of obsolete Vedic words, which began at a very early date. The study of grammar and phonetics also was evidently well advanced in the time of the earlier Upanishads.

IV. We have not the knowledge necessary for a discussion of speculations upon the origin of institutions, customs and ceremonies. The Brāhmanas have much to say about the origin of religious ceremonies; but this is material which only an expert can deal with. Upon the origin of institutions and customs a good deal is to be found in the Mahābhārata. Various, and quite incompatible, attempts are made to explain the marriage of the sons of Pāndu. In I. cxxii there is a curious story which attributes the establishment of the law of conjugal fidelity to the seer Çvetaketu. Book XII contains a number of such speculations. Thus sect. lix gives an account of the origin of kingship, which reflects a very sophisticated form of mythology.

It may be observed that Brahmanic tradition seems regularly to have maintained the doctrine that the Four Castes, together with the superiority of the Brahman, had existed from the beginning of the world. This doctrine is to be found once even in the Rgveda, in a cosmogonic poem (x. 90), which will require notice later. It is possible that the stanza (No. 12) in which this occurs was not an original part of the poem, for the doctrine seems not to be implied elsewhere in the Rgveda; but it was widely known from early times.

V. Speculations upon the origin of buildings and localities seem to be rare, unless we include very brief statements as to the association of holy places (*tīrtha*) with seers of the past—which are numerous enough. Book VII of the Rāmāyana attributes the foundation of certain towns to Rāma's brothers, and similar statements occur in the Purānas. But in the Mahābhārata and earlier works instances seem to be rare. We may perhaps cite the account of the foundation of Indraprastha by Yudhishthira and his brothers in I. ccix. 28 ff.

VI. Traditions and speculations relating to the origin of nations are connected in India, as in the West, on one side with the genealogies of royal houses, on the other with speculations upon the origin of mankind. Perhaps the most interesting example of this class is the story of Yayāti and his sons, to which we have already referred (p. 498 f.). It has been noted (i) that the names of the sons are those of five peoples mentioned—some of them very frequently—in the Rgveda; (ii) that the two peoples, Yadu and Turvaça, which bear the names of Devayānī's sons are often mentioned together, by themselves; (iii) that the Pūru seem to be the leading people of the group even in the Rgveda. We may add that the Rgveda very frequently refers to 'the five peoples' collectively; and it is clear that a group of Aryan peoples is meant. All this suggests that the political conditions upon which the story, in its original form, was founded were those of a very early period. The Bharata, who according to the genealogies were a branch of the Pūru, seem to have become an independent political organisation even by the time of Sudās, if not before.

A still earlier speculation of this kind can be traced in the Rgveda

itself. Here Manu seems properly to be the progenitor—and personification—of the Aryan peoples, as well as the institutor of sacrifice.
Often (as e.g. in VI. 21. 11) we find a distinction drawn between Manu
and Dasyu. Manu is clearly not the ancestor of the natives. He corresponds indeed to three consecutive generations in Greek speculation—
to Prometheus as institutor of sacrifice, to Deucalion in the (post-Vedic)
story of the flood, to Hellen as personified ancestor of the nation. But,
unlike Hellen, he is separated from the various sectional eponymoi by
four or five generations.

Many more eponymous ancestors are probably to be traced in the
genealogies. It is of course to be borne in mind that speculations of this
kind are ultimately based on actual usage, and that the person from whom
the family or kingdom claims its origin may have been a real person, as
we have seen in Britain (cf. Vol. I, p. 311). But in the case of ancient
royal families it is to be suspected that the deeds with which an eponymous ancestor is credited may often be very different from those
which he actually performed; even if he was a real person, his deeds may
be products of myth or fiction. In India the difficulties attending this
question are increased by the fact that the members of a royal family,
like those of a mantic family (cf. p. 506 f.), individually or collectively,
may bear the name of a real or reputed ancestor. Thus *Bharatas* (Nom.
sing.) may denote either the ancestor or any of his descendants—though
Bhāratas is more usual in the latter sense—while *Bharatās* (Nom. pl.)
denotes the descendants collectively. Now Bharata Dauhshanti may or
may not have been a real person. But if he was, as the genealogies say,
the ancestor of the Bharata (Bharatās)—who formed an important
kingdom even in early Rgveda times—he cannot have conquered the
lands of the Jumna and the Ganges (cf. p. 474); neither can he have been
a grandson of Viçvāmitra. If Bharata the conqueror is not a fiction, he
must have been a different person from Bharata the eponymos. Similar
difficulties arise in various other cases.

Most of the Puranic genealogies are traced back to the sons of
Yayāti, though there are a few which are derived from other descendants
of Manu. Thus the long genealogy of Ayodhyā is made to come from a
son of Manu called Ikshvāku—a name which occurs in Rgv. x. 60. 4,
though without reference to Manu or any other clear bearings. There
are no genealogies which claim any origin except from Manu; but it is
possible that such genealogies may once have existed. The kingdom of
the Matsya is one of those for which no genealogy has been preserved.
But the king called Matsya, whose birth is described in Mahābh. I. lxiii.

61 ff., may well have been the national eponymos.[1] He is the twin brother of Satyavatī; and they are born from an Apsaras who has been transformed into a fish. If this is correct it would seem that the Matsya were of non-Aryan origin, though they must have become Aryanised in course of time. It is a curious fact that in the Aitareya Brāhmana, VII. 18, various non-Aryan peoples, indeed 'most of the Dasyu', are said to be descendants of Viçvāmitra. The Purānas[2] also speak of Rākshasa who were descended from famous seers—which may point to a similar belief.

VII. Speculations upon the origin of mankind, the gods and the world are of very frequent occurrence in early Indian poetry. It will be possible to notice only a few of the more important features.

An account of the four ages (*yuga*) contained in a 'great age' (cf. p. 540) is given by the monkey-chief Hanumat in Mahābh. III. cxlix (cf. cxc. 9 ff.), and similar passages occur frequently in other parts of the work. The first age is called *krta*, the second *tretā*, the third *dvāpara*, the fourth *kali*. These names are taken from dice, and mean properly the four, three, two and ace respectively. It is in accordance with this terminology that the second age is only three quarters, the third half, the fourth a quarter of the length of the first. But there is a deterioration in virtue also; the first age is perfect, the last very evil. In this respect there is at least a remarkable coincidence with the Hesiodic scheme noticed in Vol. I, p. 318 f., though the terminology of the latter is taken from metals—apart from the Heroic Age, which we are inclined to regard as an addition. In the Purānas the royal genealogies run continuously through these ages. The first age begins with Manu, while the third ends and the fourth begins with the great battle of the Mahābhārata—i.e. at a date which is probably not very far removed from that of the beginning of Hesiod's last age. This may of course be a mere coincidence; but the possibility of a historical connection between the two schemes should not be entirely rejected. There seems to be no satisfactory evidence for any such scheme in Vedic literature.[3]

Manu, as we have seen, is known even in the Rgveda as the progenitor of the Aryan peoples and the institutor of sacrifice. The story of the flood, however, seems to be later. It is unknown to the Rgveda, and

---

[1] For the connection of this king with the Matsya cf. Pargiter, *Ancient Indian Historical Tradition*, p. 118 f. The word *matsya* means 'fish'.

[2] For references see Pargiter, *op. cit.* p. 241 f.

[3] Cf. Keith, *Rigveda Brahmanas*, p. 302, note 6.

there is only one, very doubtful, reference in the Atharvaveda (xix. 39. 8); but it is found in the Çatapatha Brāhmana, I. viii. 1, as well as in later works. In the Mahābhārata, III. clxxxvii, the story is told as follows: A small fish appeals to Manu for protection. He brings it up, and eventually transfers it first to the Ganges, and then to the sea. When it leaves him, it prophesies the destruction of the world, offers to save him, and advises him to build an ark and provide himself with various kinds of seed. He does so, and when the flood comes it reappears in answer to his appeal, now furnished with horns, and draws his ark safely through the waters for many years. At length it lands him on the Himalayas, and on its departure makes known to him that it is Brahmā. In this version of the story Manu is accompanied in the ark by the primeval 'Seven Seers' (Saptarṣi); but in the Çatapatha Brāhmana he seems to be alone. In neither case is there any reference to women in the ark. Idā (Ilā), daughter of Manu, is born later from the sacrifice which follows. In spite of such differences in detail, however, we can hardly doubt that this story is connected both with the story of Deucalion and with that of Noah. It may be observed also that a similar story is preserved in the Avesta (Vendidad, II. 21 ff.), though here the survivor, Yima, saves himself, with representative animals and plants, not in a boat, but in an earthen structure of some kind. The common source of all these stories is doubtless to be sought in Mesopotamia.[1]

Manu is occasionally said to be a son of Brahmā; but these passages may relate to previous incarnations. Usually he is son of Vivasvat, a relationship which can be traced back to the Rgveda. Now Yama is also son of Vivasvat; and this relationship is found also in the Avesta, where Yima is the progenitor of mankind, while Manu seems to be unknown. It is commonly held that Yama (Yima), which means 'twin', and his twin sister Yamī (cf. p. 532)—an Iranian counterpart of whom is found in late sources—were originally regarded as the original progenitors of mankind.[2] Manu may have taken over this function from Yama—if he was not originally identical with him—as the latter came to be more and more associated with death. The father, Vivasvat, is a rather obscure

---

[1] This question will require notice again in a later chapter. But it may be observed here that the fish which saves Manu would seem to be connected with the Mesopotamian water-god Enki or Ea, by whose advice Utnapishtim (i.e. Noah) builds the Ark and saves himself. This deity is commonly represented with a form which is partly that of a fish; cf. Langdon, Semitic Mythology, p. 103 ff. Can the 'Seven Seers' be connected with the 'seven wise ones' who are mentioned in an obscure reference to the Flood contained in an early Accadian story (ib. p. 139 f.)?

[2] Cf. Macdonell, Vedic Mythology, p. 173.

figure in the Rgveda, though in later literature he is identified with the sun; in the Avesta he is hardly more than a name. In the Brāhmanas, however, and apparently the Yajurveda, as also in later literature, he is counted among the Āditya, or children of Aditi—a group which in the Rgveda includes Varuna, Mitra, and sometimes Indra. This genealogy then would make the first human beings nearly related to the gods, just as in Greek antiquarian speculation.

Aditi in later literature is wife of Kaçyapa, who is either son of one of the primeval Seven Seers, named Marici, or else one of the Seven himself. He is frequently mentioned in the Atharvaveda, along with Vasishtha and other famous seers; but his name seems to occur only once (IX. 114) in the Rgveda, though many hymns are traditionally ascribed to him. On the other hand Aditi herself is often mentioned in the Rgveda, usually but not always in association with her children. In later literature she has numerous sisters, of whom one (Diti) is the ancestress of the Daitya, a second (Danu) the mother of the Dānava—including Çambara, Namuci and many others—a third the mother of Rāhu (see below), a fourth the mother of Vrtra and other Asura, a fifth the ancestress of various kinds of animals—deer, bears, lions, horses, etc. The genealogies contained in Mahābh. I. lxv f. are indeed even more comprehensive than those of Hesiod's Theogony.

In later literature Aditi is daughter of Daksha. The latter seems to be derived from an abstract idea, 'strength' or 'intelligence'; but he is personified even in the Rgveda. His relationship to Aditi here is apparently that of both father and son, according to x. 72. In Mahābh. I. lxvi. 10 f. Daksha himself is said to have sprung from Brahmā's right toe, and his wife from the left one—a story which may be compared with the generation of Ymir's children from his feet, related in the Vafþrúðnismál, st. 33 (cf. Vol. I, p. 323).

According to Mahābh. I. i. 29 ff. Brahmā, who is also called 'Grandfather' and Prajāpati ('lord of offspring' or 'lord of created beings'), was born from a great egg, which came into existence when all the world was darkness. Brahmā as a personal deity does not appear in the Vedas; but the name *Prajāpati* occurs six times in the Rgveda. Once it is applied to Savitr, the sun-god, once to Soma, and four times (in Book x) to a distinct deity, who is evidently regarded as supreme. In x. 121, of which Ath. IV. 2 is a variant, Prajāpati is the creator and sustainer of the world. He came into existence at the beginning as a 'Golden Germ' (Hiranyagarbha).[1] The Atharvaveda adds that the waters brought the

[1] Cf. Taitt. Samh. v. 5. 1.

embryo into being, covered with gold. In the Taittirīya Samhitā, VII. I. 5, it is said that in the beginning Prajāpati, becoming the wind, moved in the waters. He saw something and, becoming a boar, seized it. It became the earth; and from it he generated the gods.

Cosmology or cosmogony was a favourite subject with early Indian poets. The records vary greatly in character. Sometimes what we find is mythology of a childish enough kind, as will be seen from the above examples. A somewhat more advanced, but mystical (sacerdotal) conception is found in one poem in the Rgveda (x. 90) to which we have already referred. Here all things are fashioned out of a vast primeval Man (*puruṣa*), who is sacrificed by the gods. This poem, which will require notice again in Ch. X, bears a curious resemblance to a passage in the Norse Grímnismál (cf. Vol. I, p. 321). But there are other cases where mythology has altogether disappeared. Thus in Rgv. x. 129 the opening stanzas, which describe the formless void or chaos existing before the origin of the world, may be compared with passages in the Völuspá (st. 3 ff.) and in the Gylfaginning (cap 4 f.) which are concerned with the same theme (cf. Vol. I, pp. 321, 323). But the Norse passages introduce mythology in order to explain the change, probably on more or less traditional lines, whereas the Indian poet is content to ask who knows how it took place. He says (*ad fin.*) that the answer may or may not be known to a primal cause and governing power.[1]

Lastly, it may be noted that primitive explanations of recurrent natural phenomena occur in early Indian poetry, as elsewhere. We may instance the explanation of eclipses given in Mahābh. I. xix. The demon Rāhu had obtained access to a feast of Soma, disguised as a heavenly being. He was detected, however, by Candra and Sūrya (the Moon and the Sun) and pointed out to the gods; and thereupon Vishnu cut off his head. Ever since then the head has borne enmity against Candra and Sūrya and sought to devour them.

---

[1] The poems noticed in this paragraph (Rgv. x. 90 and 129) are transl. by Thomas, *Vedic Hymns*, pp. 120 ff., 127 f.

CHAPTER VIII

GNOMIC AND DESCRIPTIVE POETRY

INCIDENTAL gnomes are of frequent occurrence in the Rgveda, as in later poetry. Usually they belong to the second (non-Aristotelian) of the types[1] distinguished in Vol. 1 (p. 377), i.e. they are gnomes of 'observation', rather than of 'obligation'. As an example we may take x. 37. 2: "Every other thing which moves takes rest, (but) the waters and Sūrya (the Sun) are always in motion." As an illustration of human activities, which approximates somewhat to the other type, we may quote VII. 32. 9: "It is the zealous (i.e. he who is generous in offerings) who conquers, lives in peace, and prospers; the gods are not for him who is miserly."

In the Rgveda also, as in ancient European poetry, we find poems which consist wholly or mainly of gnomes. These poems, however, usually differ from those of the West in the fact that the gnomes are all connected and relate to the same object, faculty or quality. As a whole the poems amount to detailed descriptions of the things which are their subjects, and we shall therefore treat them under 'descriptive' poetry, below. The nearest approach to the Western type which we have observed is in Rgv. x. 117, the subject of which is Liberality. This poem contains gnomes relating not only to the liberal and the illiberal man, but also to the plough, the Brahman, animals, etc. One or two of the sentences also seem to be in the form of precepts. Even here, however, there is more unity than in Western gnomic poetry. Perhaps the nearest analogies are to be found in parts of Hesiod's *Works and Days*.

There is another poem (IX. 112), however, containing a short series of gnomes, which differs greatly from these; indeed we know of no parallel to it in early Indian literature. Its character may be seen from the following extracts:[2] "Diverse are our thoughts, (diverse) the

---

[1] Type I denotes gnomes of choice or obligation. In this we distinguish (*a*) moral (ethical) gnomes, (*b*) gnomes relating to religion or magic, (*c*) gnomes relating to industries, crafts, etc. Type II denotes gnomes of observation. Here we distinguish (*a*) gnomes relating to human beings, (*b*) gnomes relating to deities, fate and death, (*c*) gnomes relating to animals, inanimate objects, natural phenomena, etc. Gnomes of Type I are nearly related to precepts and can usually be converted into them. The affinities of Type II lie with descriptive poetry.

[2] A better translation will be found in E. J. Thomas, *Vedic Hymns*, p. 79 f.

desires of mankind. The joiner wishes for something broken, the doctor for someone injured, the priest for a worshipper. Flow round, Soma,[1] for the gratification of Indra!...I am a poet, my daddy[2] a doctor, my mammy[2] plies the quern. With diverse thoughts, (but) intent on livelihood, we go as it were in pursuit of cattle (i.e. wealth). Flow round, etc. The horse wishes for a light chariot to draw...the frog for water. Flow round, etc." One might be inclined at first sight to regard this as an occasional poem, of Type E, a Type which we have not found represented elsewhere in early Indian literature. But the refrain[3] shows that it is an 'occupation' song, presumably of Type B, for use during the preparation of the Soma. Its analogies are to be sought in weaving and grinding songs, on which the Norse poems Darraðarljóð and Grottasöngr are based.[4] Like them it is close akin to a spell, if it is not actually to be taken as such. But as regards the gnomes, with which we are concerned here, it is to be observed that they are all of the 'observation' type (Type II), and that the two last quoted belong to the variety (Type IIc) relating to observations of animals, etc., a variety which elsewhere seems to be rare in ancient India. The context in which they occur here is therefore worth noting. It is remarkable that such a poem as this should have been preserved in the Rgveda.

In the Atharvaveda the only example of gnomes we have noticed is XX. 128, one of the series of hymns known as *Kuntāpa*. In the Aitareya Brāhmana, VI. 32 ff., these poems are credited with a ritual interpretation, which is not easy to understand. But the natural interpretation of the poem to which we refer is gnomic or semi-gnomic, at least in st. 1–5. These stanzas distinguish between the pious, bold and liberal on the one hand and the incestuous, faithless, insolent and mean on the other, and the recompenses which both classes receive. The following stanzas again distinguish between persons and things which—one may infer— are regarded as commendable and their opposites; but it is stated merely that 'these things are ordered in the rules'. These lists include not only (e.g.) the liberal and the mean man but also the horse which is, or is not, under control and the pool where one can, or cannot, drink—instances

---

[1] The word used here (and very frequently elsewhere) is *indu*, the juice of the soma.

[2] The words used here are *tata* and *nanā*, terms used by children.

[3] The same refrain is found in the two following poems (IX. 113 f.), which otherwise have nothing in common with this. Words to the same effect occur very frequently in hymns to Soma.

[4] Cf. Vol. I, pp. 346 f., 449. We may also refer to the Greek fragment noticed *ib.* p. 429, note.

which again approximate to the variety of gnome which in Vol. i, p. 377 f., we classified under Type IIc. The rest of the poem (st. 12 ff.) has no gnomic affinities.

In the Brāhmanas themselves 'mystical' gnomes are extremely frequent, e.g. Ait. Br. iii. 39: "As in the ocean all streams, so in it (viz. the Agnishtoma rite) all the sacrificial rites are resolved" (Keith). Otherwise the gnomic element seems to be slight unless one includes under this head the statements of—and directions for—ritual observances, which form almost the whole of their substance. We think, however, that these are better referred to the timeless nameless compositions treated in the next chapter. But a certain amount of gnomic matter is contained in the poetry preserved in the Brāhmanas from sources other than the Vedic collections. We may instance the poetry quoted in the story of Çunahçepa (cf. p. 496 f.), in Ait. Br. vii. 13 ff. It is religious gnomic poetry (of Type IIa), relating to the advantages to be derived from having a son and from a life of retirement in the forest.

The earlier Upanishads likewise contain very little gnomic matter. Incidental gnomes occur occasionally, by way of illustration, as in the Chāndogya Upanishad, iv. xiv. 3: "As water clings not to a lotus leaf, so evil doing clings not to one who knows this." But the substance of the Upanishads—their philosophy—cannot properly be regarded as gnomic, unless one is prepared to include mysticism in this category. We prefer to treat it in Ch. X, below. There are indeed certain passages which may perhaps be regarded as gnomic, if they truly represent the current beliefs of the times. Thus in the same Upanishad, iv. iii. 1 ff., it is stated that the sun and moon at their setting, as also fire when it goes out and water when it dries up, pass into wind, while in sleep speech, the eye, the ear and the mind pass into breath.[1] But even with regard to this we are far from certain.

Mention must here be made of the Sūtras, a numerous class of works, which are likewise products of the Vedic schools. Like the Brāhmanas they are concerned with the observance of rites. But unlike these they contain no speculation or discussion; they consist of rules expressed in the briefest possible (prose) form for mnemonic purposes. The form is prevailingly gnomic. The chief varieties are (1) the Çrauta, which relate to the ritual of sacrifice; (2) the Grhya, which are concerned with the 'house' (*grha*) and devoted to such matters as household worship,

---

[1] Hume, *The Thirteen Principal Upanishads*, p. 217. A better example is perhaps to be found in the behaviour of the lover, described in the Brhadāranyaka Upanishad, vi. iv. 7 ff.; but the passage consists of spells.

marriage, the birth of children, education, funerals and offerings to the 'fathers'; (3) the Dharma which are concerned with law, and from which the (metrical) Law-books of later times, e.g. the 'Laws of Manu', are said to be largely derived. The interest throughout is essentially religious. This kind of literature is believed to have been cultivated for a long period; the earliest Sūtras are thought to date back as far as the sixth century (B.C.).[1]

The Mahābhārata contains an immense amount of gnomic poetry; but it is very unevenly distributed. In those portions of the work which can properly be regarded as heroic the gnomic element is usually very slight. This may be seen most clearly in the episodic stories of Nala and Rāma. Here we find only isolated gnomes; and these are by no means frequent. For one of the rare instances where two gnomes occur together we may refer to III. lxx. 8 f., where the disguised Nala, who is interviewing Damayantī's envoy, remarks: "Noble women, when misfortune befalls them, preserve themselves by their own efforts, attaining heaven without doubt by their loyalty. Even when forsaken by their husbands the best of women are never wrathful; they pass lives fortified by virtue." What he says after this applies to the special circumstances of the case.

On the other hand the speeches of Vidulā, in v. cxxxiii ff. (cf. p. 470 f.), abound with gnomes of a heroic character. Indeed they may be said to alternate between heroic gnomes and personal appeals to her son, to rouse himself to action. In general, however, gnomic elements are more prominent in the non-heroic stories. Instances may be found in the story of Çakuntalā, in I. lxxiv, and in that of Yayāti and his wives, especially I. lxxix ff. Çakuntalā's speeches, when she upbraids Dushmanta for repudiating her, alternate between gnomes and personal appeals, like those of Vidulā. But they are perhaps rather to be compared with Hesiod's *Works and Days*, for the gnomes are not of heroic character. The main story of the Mahābhārata varies greatly. At times the gnomic element is hardly more prominent than in the story of Nala; but very often the story has become merely a framework for didactic speeches, which are sometimes largely of gnomic character. Some of these are philosophical treatises, in which gnomic lore and mystical lore are combined, though usually the latter seems to be predominant. The most fully developed example of this kind is the Bhagavadgītā which

---

[1] We have not the knowledge to deal with the Sūtras more fully. We are under the impression that their value for a comparative study of literature is not very great; but this may be erroneous.

is spoken by Krshna to Arjuna on the eve of the great battle (VI. 26 ff.). Elsewhere the connection is with law, as in the long speech of the dying Bhīshma which occupies the greater part of Books XII and XIII. This is believed to be one of the latest elements in the Mahābhārata; much of it seems to be derived from the same sources as the Mānava Dharma Çāstra or 'Laws of Manu'. It is largely in gnomic form, though interspersed with many narratives and other matter of various kinds.

Among other collections of gnomes we may note the series spoken by the monkey Hanumat to Bhīma (III. 150), who has met him in the forest. They recognise themselves to be brothers, for both of them are sons of Vāyu (the Wind-god). The gnomes here, as in other collections, are concerned largely with the duties of the different castes and with advice to kings on the conduct of government; and there is nothing specially remarkable about them except their inappropriateness to the occasion. But it is rather curious that Hanumat's discourse as a whole consists of three elements—the doctrine of the 'Four Ages', brotherly admonitions, and the gnomes—which are found also in Hesiod's *Works and Days*.[1] The admonitions are doubtless an accidental coincidence; for the circumstances in the two cases are quite different. But the combination of the Four Ages with the gnomes is perhaps worth noting, especially as the former seem to be as much out of place here as the latter. We do not suppose that the gnomes themselves are ancient in their present form; nor do we doubt that the whole episode is a late addition to the Mahābhārata, derived from the story of Rāma. Yet it may contain early elements.

In III. cclviii a series of gnomes is delivered by Vyāsa, when he comes to comfort Yudhishthira. These are of a more strictly ethical character than most of the other series. Asceticism is praised, and it is laid down that the vicious will be re-born as beasts, while the virtuous will be rewarded in their next incarnation. But at the same time it is recognised that virtue brings its own reward in this life. Generosity is of course the greatest of virtues; but other virtues are not ignored.

Lastly, we may note the counsels given to King Dhrtarāshtra in I. cxlii by the Brahman Kanika, who is his minister or adviser. The king is becoming afraid of his nephews, the sons of Pāndu, and seeks advice as to how he shall deal with them. Kanika's discourse consists in the main of gnomes; but these are of a different character from those we

---

[1] Hésiod has five 'races'; but we doubt if the fourth of these belonged to the original scheme (cf. Vol. I, p. 318 f.).

have discussed above. The discourse is a speech in character, suited to the occasion; and Kanika realises that the king desires justification for dealing treacherously. Some of the gnomes are of a cynical character, superficially similar to what are found in the first part of the Hávamál (cf. Vol. I, p. 383 f.), though the element of humour seems to be wanting. We may cite st. 60, where it is stated that one should never trust the faithless and not put too much trust even in the faithful. But the majority of the gnomes relate to statecraft and recommend an unlimited employment of treachery in dealings with possible rivals. By way of illustration a fable is introduced, describing how a jackal cheated various other animals; and the king is recommended—apparently without any sense of humour—to take the jackal as his model. This fable will be noticed in the next chapter.

It is generally agreed that the long religious and legal 'treatises' noticed above are late additions to the Mahābhārata—later than the times which properly come within the scope of our survey. The gnomic elements in the story of Çakuntalā and in other non-heroic contexts may be of earlier date, in view of the poetry relating to Çunahçepa preserved in the Aitareya Brāhmana; and the same may be true of Vidulā's heroic gnomes. We should hesitate, however, to uphold the great antiquity of any of the gnomic collections contained in the Mahābhārata, in their present form.

The gnomes of the Mahābhārata belong to both of the types which we distinguished in Vol. I, p. 377 f. Both the Aristotelian type of gnome (Type I)—which implies the use of choice or judgment—and the gnome of observation (Type II) are of common occurrence. But the latter seems to be limited in general to human activities and experiences (IIa) and to the operations of fate and the gods (IIb). We have not noticed any gnomes relating to animal life and inanimate things (IIc), apart from occasional examples which are introduced in some relation to human beings. In view of the enormous extent of the Mahābhārata negative statements are not lightly to be ventured upon; but we think that 'natural history' gnomes, such as are found in Anglo-Saxon and early Welsh poetry, must be rare, if they occur at all. Enthymemes seem not to be common.

Descriptive poetry relating to specified persons, places or (individual) objects seems not to occur in the early period, except in the case of deities and their belongings. On the other hand typical descriptions, e.g. of animals, natural phenomena, and even abstract conceptions, are quite frequent, especially in the last book of the Rgveda. In these respects Vedic poetry shows the same characteristics as the early poetry of the West. The subjects treated in the poems are also often similar to what we found in the latter (Vol. 1, p. 407 ff.), though the treatment is fuller and the matter more homogeneous—free from an extraneous gnomic context. Sometimes the poems bear a certain resemblance to the early Riddle poetry of the West (*ib*. p. 412 ff.), though they are not themselves intended as riddles.

One poem (Rgv. x. 117) on Liberality, or rather the conduct of generous and ungenerous men, has already been noticed (p. 550). Akin to this in subject is x. 107, which deals with the 'Bounty' (*dakshiṇā*)[1] given by princes to the priests who perform sacrifices for them. It is a poem which well illustrates the more unpleasing side of Vedic poetry: e.g. (st. 2) "The bounteous abide on high in heaven; givers of horses are with Sūrya (the Sun); givers of gold acquire immortality; givers of robes prolong their lives." And again (*ib*. 7) "Bounty gives the horse, Bounty gives the ox, Bounty also gives gleaming gold", etc.

A short poem (x. 168) gives a description of the wind, which may be compared with the riddle contained in the Book of Taliesin, noticed in Vol. 1, p. 413 f. It celebrates "the might of the chariot of the Wind—destroying it goes, thundering its roar.…Hastening along paths in the air he comes not to rest on any single day. The friend of the Waters, first born and holy—where was he born, whence is he come? The breath of the gods, the germ of existence—this god moves as he will, His roars are heard, (but) his form is not (seen). Let us honour this Vāta (the Wind) with a sacrifice." Reference may be made here also to x. 127, the subject of which is Night.[2]

Descriptive poems upon animals are not unknown. As an instance we may cite 1. 163, which is intended for a horse-sacrifice, like the poem which precedes it (*ib*. 162); but much of it is occupied with the description of a typical chariot-horse. More interesting is a poem (VII. 103)[3] on the activities of frogs at the coming of rain. Their appearance and movements are described; and their croaking round the pool is compared to the chanting of Brahmans at an offering of Soma. The poem is

---

[1] This word properly means the priest's fee. We have used the word 'bounty', which is less strictly correct, because 'fee' to the modern mind rather suggests a fixed price, which seems to have been by no means what the poet intended. The poem is transl. by Thomas, *Vedic Hymns*, p. 106 f.

[2] Both these poems are transl. by Thomas, *op. cit.* pp. 90, 33 f.

[3] Transl. by Thomas, *op. cit.* p. 73 f.; 1. 162, *ib.* p. 100 ff.

believed to be intended as a spell for rain, for which the frogs are said to be responsible; but it may be noticed here, as its character is essentially descriptive.

Other poems of this class are concerned with human beings. The most striking of these is the description of a gamester, which forms the subject of x. 34. Dice-playing is noticed briefly in a descriptive passage in the Gnomes of the Exeter Book (182 ff.); but the Vedic poem describes it in detail and emphasises its disastrous consequences. Thus (st. 4): "Others embrace the wife of him whose possessions have been claimed by the conquering dice; his father, mother and brothers say 'We do not know him—bind him and take him away.'" And again (st. 10): "The forsaken wife of the gambler is consumed with sorrow, (and so also) his mother, as her son wanders from place to place. Covered with debt, living in fear, and seeking a subsistence, he makes his way by night to the dwelling of others"—whether as a thief or a beggar is not made clear. In st. 13 the poet passes on to a precept, to let dice alone and attend to the plough, after the manner of Hesiod. Several stanzas are occupied with the feelings and reflections of the gambler, in speech form, which makes the poem approximate to poetry of the next category. For a contrast we may compare x. 136, which describes briefly the life and appearance of a *muni* or religious devotee.

Mention may also be made here of vi. 75, which gives an interesting picture of the warfare of the Vedic period. The objects described are the bow, arrow, quiver, bracer, whip and body-armour. The warrior and charioteer, the horses and chariot are also noticed. There seems to be no reference to any weapons used in hand to hand fighting.

It has been remarked that most of the poems which belong to this class are found in Book x; they date therefore probably from towards the end of the Vedic period. There can be no doubt, however, as to the antiquity of the type, and also as to its importance in the early history of Indian poetry and thought. The hymns to the Dawn, which are fairly numerous and occur even in what are believed to be the oldest Books, must be regarded primarily as descriptive poems, like the poems on Night and Wind noticed above. In some of them indeed the descriptive element is still predominant,[1] though in others it tends to be obscured by references to the passage of time or to worship or the welfare of the worshippers.

[1] One short poem, x. 172, is little more than a description of the dawn, with the cows coming to be milked; but even here there is a reference to the morning sacrifice.

More important is the fact that some of the chief gods are not clearly distinguished from the objects and elements from which they are derived; the hymns to such gods consist largely of descriptions of the latter. Such is the case with Agni ('Fire'), whose hymns are very numerous and widespread. He is regarded as a priest and messenger to the gods, and invoked for various blessings; but the mythological conceptions relating to him are often of an elementary and more or less obvious character. Passages descriptive of (natural) fire and its workings are seldom if ever wholly wanting in hymns to him; and some hymns consist mainly of such descriptions. As an instance we may quote I. 65. 4: "When sped by the wind he spreads through the forests, Agni does indeed shear the hair of earth." So also v. 26. 3: "We would kindle thee, the bright summoner (of the gods) to the feast." Agni is sometimes said to be born at daybreak, when the fire is lighted, as in v. 1. 5: "Noble, he was born at daybreak, laid ruddy among the laid logs." Occasionally also, as in x. 79. 4, he is said to devour his parents —which seem to be the two fire-sticks.

The same remarks apply to Soma, to whom all the hymns in Book IX and several others are addressed. This god is hardly distinguished from the Soma plant and the intoxicating liquor, used at sacrifices, which was made from it; and the hymns largely consist of descriptions of the preparation and the virtues of this liquor. Thus Soma is said to have his home upon the mountains, from whence the plant was obtained; he is pressed with stones, by which the juice was extracted, and filtered through a woollen sieve. He boils or bubbles in the vessels.

True riddles are also to be found in the Rgveda. One long and very obscure poem (I. 164) seems to consist mainly of riddles. Among them are two 'year-riddles' (st. 11, 48), which were perhaps originally variants. The year is represented as a wheel, with twelve spokes or fellies and 360 or 720 minor parts, representing days or nights and days. Another, much shorter, poem (VIII. 29)[1] consists of brief descriptions of a number of gods, who are not named. The descriptions seem to be intended as riddles. Book x furnishes at least two examples. No. 27, a poem of Type B, in which Indra is the speaker, seems to contain a number of riddles, though it is very obscure. The same is true of No. 28, which is a dialogue poem of Type B. Another poem of the same type (*ib.* 125), in which the speaker is said to be 'Speech' (*Vāc*) personified, may also perhaps be regarded as a riddle (cf. p. 532). It has the form

[1] Transl. by Thomas, *op. cit.* p. 84.

found in many Anglo-Saxon riddles, in which the subject describes its own properties or powers.

In the Atharvaveda descriptive elements are by no means wanting; but they occur for the most part in poems which are primarily prayers or spells. We have not noticed any poems which can be regarded as wholly descriptive. On the whole possibly the nearest approach to this is a poem (XII. 1) which consists of a long series of invocations of Earth, alternating with brief notices of the various forms of activity, human, animal and elemental, which pervade it. We may also cite XI. 5, the description of a Brahmacārin (a Brahman student, who has taken a religious vow), which is neither a prayer nor a spell, though it contains much mystical matter. Here too mention should be made of XIX. 53 f., which are concerned with Time (*Kāla*), and of *ib.* 56, which is addressed to Sleep, both conceptions being more or less personified. A poem on the plough (III. 17) may practically be regarded as descriptive; but in form it consists of a series of prayers and wishes. The same may perhaps be said of III. 22, which is in the form of a speech by the princely owner of an elephant; but the description of the elephant is much less definite.[1] Brief descriptive passages are of frequent occurrence in spells.

Riddles seem to be rare in the Atharvaveda. A number of examples apparently occur in x. 8, an obscure poem dealing with cosmology; among them is a variant of the 'year-riddle', noticed above. Apart from this we have noticed instances only in the Kuntāpa series in Book xx, especially Nos. 133 f. These also are too difficult for us to deal with, though the obscurities are of a different kind from those found in the poem just mentioned.

In the Brāhmanas and early Upanishads descriptive passages seem to be rare. As an instance we may cite the invocation to a magical concoction (*mantha*) given in the Brhadāranyaka Upanishad, VI. iii. 4, in which the powers and qualities of the object addressed are enumerated. The passage has elements in common with some of the Rgveda poems noticed above.

Descriptive poetry in the Mahābhārata is naturally of a somewhat different character. Descriptions of places are by no means rare, though they are typical or conventional, not photographic, descriptions. The favourite subject seems to be a tropical forest. An instance may be found in III. lxiv. 1 ff., where Damayantī has been forsaken by her hus-

---

[1] Mention may also be made of VI. 109, which gives an account of the properties and history of the fruit of a certain tree, believed to be efficacious for healing wounds. This poem has not the form of a spell, though it may have been used as such.

band: "The lady of the lotus eyes, when she had slain the hunter, made her way to the awful desolate forest. It resounded with troops of crickets and was haunted by troops of lions, leopards, stags, tigers, buffaloes and bears. It was filled with numerous troops of birds and inhabited by barbarians and robbers. It was a network of bamboos" and various kinds of trees, a list of which occupies the next three *çloka*. Then "she saw hills[1] seamed with many different kinds of minerals, thickets resounding with song and caves of marvellous appearance, rivers, lakes and pools, with various animals and birds". Further details follow. Similar descriptions are to be found elsewhere; and the same is true of the Rāmāyana, where they are sometimes of great length.

Descriptions of persons also are not uncommon; and these too follow conventional lines. Examples may be found in the same section (III. lxiv. 44 ff.), where Damayantī describes her father and husband. The words differ, but the qualities specified—power, prowess, piety, liberality, personal beauty, etc.—are much the same in both cases. In lxviii. 10 ff. a much longer description is given of Damayantī herself, by the Brahman Sudeva. Here we have the picture of a beautiful and noble lady who has fallen into misfortune; but with this limitation the description is strictly conventional. He compares her, first, with the goddesses Çrī and Ratī and with the radiance of the full moon. Then he compares her form, besmeared with dust and dirt, with a lotus plant torn up by a mischance of fate from the lake of Vidarbha, and with a night at full moon when the moon has been devoured by Rāhu (the eclipse demon). Miserable and distraught with grief for her husband she is like a river whose waters have been dried up. Other similar comparisons follow.

Riddles seem not to be of frequent occurrence in the Mahābhārata. In III. cxxxiii, when Ashtāvakra comes to challenge Vandi at King Janaka's sacrifice (cf. p. 505), he finds at first some difficulty in obtaining admission, owing to his youth. The king asks him riddles in three couplets, to which he replies in three other couplets. The first is a form of the very common year-riddle. The second seems to refer to thunder and lightning. The third couplet contains four riddles in the shortest form, to which the answers are respectively 'fish', 'egg', 'stone', 'river'. The whole series bears a very close resemblance to the 'Riddles of Gestumblindi', noticed in Vol. I, p. 412. It may be observed that one of Gestumblindi's stanzas (No. 7) likewise contains four very brief riddles (raven, dew, fish, waterfall).[2] Russian and Yugoslav parallels have been noticed above (pp. 212, 410).

---

[1] The scene is laid in the Vindhya mountains.
[2] Cf. Kershaw, *Stories and Ballads of the Far Past*, p. 117.

Another, much longer, series occurs in III. cccxii. They are proposed to Yudhishthira by a Yaksha in the form of a crane—who turns out to be Dharma, the god of Duty, Yudhishthira's father. The heroes, who are overcome with thirst, have been forbidden to drink by the crane before they answer his questions; and Yudhishthira's four brothers have already dropped down dead. These riddles are all of the same composite type as the last of those just noticed, each couplet containing three or four. Most of them relate to religious and philosophical conceptions; but there are a few simple nature riddles—sun, moon, rain, etc. One (st. 61) is practically identical with the one given above.

CHAPTER IX

POETRY (AND PROSE) RELATING TO
UNSPECIFIED INDIVIDUALS

THIS category is well represented in early Indian literature, especially in Type D.

We will begin with Type B, to which probably may be assigned at least one poem in the last book of the Rgveda (x. 159). This is a monologue by a wife who has succeeded in obtaining the chief position in the harem. It appears to be a speech in character, similar to certain Anglo-Saxon poems, especially 'The Wife's Complaint' and 'The Husband's Message' (cf. Vol. I, p. 425)—a type which is represented also in Yugoslav poetry (cf. p. 402 ff.) and in Russian poems and folksongs (cf. p. 223 ff.). "(As) yonder sun has arisen, (so) my good luck has arisen. Clever, triumphant, I have won for myself my lord.... (Now) without rivals, having crushed my rivals, conquering, victorious, I have laid hold upon the glory and the goods of the other wives, as those of weaker beings. Victorious, I have conquered those rival wives, so that I shall have rule over this hero and his people."

There are other poems similar to this which have the form of spells. In x. 145 the speaker, again a woman, says she is digging up a certain herb, which has the property of driving off a rival wife and gaining the whole affection of a husband. She appeals to the herb to help her; and more than once she speaks of herself as already successful. In x. 166 the speaker, in this case a man, begs to be made conqueror of his rivals and slayer of his foes. In st. 3 he invokes Vācaspati ('Lord of Speech'), which seems to be a title of Brhaspati. But in spite of this the poem, which is perhaps accompanied by the drawing of a bow, looks more like a spell than a prayer. Three stanzas are addressed to his rivals. In st. 2 and again in st. 5 f. he speaks of himself as already victorious. The poem concludes as follows: "I have set my foot upon your heads. Speak to me up from below my feet, like frogs from the water."

In view of the resemblance between these three poems it may be thought that x. 159 should also be regarded as a spell; for spells often speak of the object as accomplished, in England and elsewhere, as well as in India. And this interpretation is quite possible. But we think on the whole it is more naturally to be taken at its face value, as a study of situation; for poems of this type (Type B) are found in the Rgveda in other categories (cf. 532 f.), and the descriptive poem on the gamester, noticed on p. 557, might almost be taken as an example in this category itself. As regards the other two poems, we see no reason to doubt that x. 145 is a true spell, i.e. a spell intended for actual use. According to our scheme therefore it belongs to Type D (see below). But we are not so sure about x. 166. In spite of the reference to the bow—which is not clear—it might be a speech in character in the form of a spell; in which case it is to be referred to Type B (BD). Poems of Types D and BD are of course often difficult to distinguish, especially in this category, where historical data are excluded.

The Atharvaveda contains a few poems which may be noticed here, though in every case the interpretation is open to some element of doubt. We may exclude III. 18, which is a variant of Rgv. x. 145, and also I. 14, which perhaps relates to a similar subject, but is difficult and obscure. There are, however, one or two poems on quite different themes which deserve consideration. In VII. 60 the speaker, who is a traveller, addresses the houses of a friendly village—whether it is his own village or not is not clear to us He wishes the inhabitants good luck and bids them not to be afraid of him. It does not seem to us very likely that this poem can have been intended for practical use, and therefore we are inclined to regard it as an example of Type B. With III. 15, which deals with a somewhat similar situation, the case is otherwise. The speaker here is a merchant, who is praying to Agni and other gods for success on a trading expedition; and the poem seems to be intended to accompany an offering.

Mention may perhaps be made here of a curious series of poems dealing with gambling at dice. Two of these (II. 2; IV. 38) are evidently spells, addressed to the Gandharva and the Apsarasas, who are credited with the power of granting success in gaming. Another (VII. 50) may likewise be intended as a spell; it contains invocations to Agni, the Maruts and Indra, and then addresses the opponent as already defeated. A fourth (VII. 109) is in the form of a prayer to Agni, accompanied by an offering of butter. A fifth (VI. 118) is an appeal to two Apsarasas by a man who has cheated and wishes to escape punishment, apparently in the next world. Some special circumstances, not clear to us, seem to be involved; and we are therefore inclined to suspect that this is a poem of Type B, rather than a genuine appeal. It should be added, however, that the naïveté which pervades the whole group suggests a mentality which it is difficult for the modern mind to appreciate. There is no trace of the censure which is expressed emphatically enough in Rgv. x. 34 (cf. p. 557).

The poem last mentioned is followed by another (VI. 119) which is somewhat in the same vein. The speaker represents himself as a dishonest man, who has incurred debts—not in gaming—and has no intention of repaying them. He appeals to Agni to absolve him from guilt. Here again we are faced with the choice between Type B and Type D. Is it a speech in character, by a knave, or a formula seriously prescribed for use in such situations?

Lastly, it may be noted that the Atharvaveda contains a number of love-poems. These are either spells or at least have the form of spells; and consequently they will require notice in the next chapter. In a few cases, however, this element is very slight, and perhaps no more than a traditional form. Such poems, especially VI. 8 f., approximate to modern love-songs (Type B), and it seems hardly necessary to suppose that they were any more restricted in use than the latter.

Type D is much more widely represented than Type B and, apart from the cases already noticed, most of the examples are free from doubt. Many of them, however, are spells, and these will in general be reserved for treatment in the next chapter. Of the poems which are not spells the majority seem to be designed for use on solemn occasions, at social festivities or funerals, or at political gatherings. Most of them contain a large religious element.

In the Rgveda we may notice, first, a group of funeral hymns, x. 14, 16–18, 154.[1] The first of these begins with an appeal to honour Yama (the king of the dead; cf. p. 532), 'who first discovered to us the way'. Then (st. 4 ff.) Yama is invited to come with the 'Fathers' to the ceremony. Next (st. 7) the dead man is exhorted to set out to where he shall see Varuna and Yama. In st. 9 demons are bidden to depart. In st. 10 the dead man is advised to hasten past the hounds of Saramā and come to the place where Yama is feasting with the Fathers. St. 11 is addressed to Yama, committing the dead man to his care. The rest of the poem is an exhortation to those present to worship Yama.

The next poem of the group (x. 16) is in the form of a prayer to Agni to convey the dead man to the Fathers. In this case the funeral is evidently by cremation. In st. 11 ff. Agni is besought to bring the

[1] Nos. 14 (except st. 3–6), 18 and 154 are transl., with interesting introductions, by E. J. Thomas, *Vedic Hymns*, p. 112 ff.

Fathers to the sacrifice. St. 3, 6 and 7 are apparently addressed to the dead man.

The next poem (x. 17) seems to be a composite work; only st. 3–6 relate to a funeral. In these Pūshan, Agni, Āyus (the spirit of life) and Savitar are invoked to bring the dead man to the Fathers.

The most striking poem of the group is x. 18. Here the funeral seems to be by inhumation. The poem begins with an appeal to Death to depart and not to harm the heroes (present) or their children. Then (st. 2–6) the mourners are addressed. They are described as returning from the dead, and they are to live to old age. They are also to be purified, and there is mention of dancing and merriment—whether the reference be to a wake or to a joyous life in the future. These stanzas are far from clear to us. Some act of ritual seems to be involved; a barrier is set up, and Death—does this mean the tomb?—is enclosed with a large stone. In st. 7 the married women are told to go forward with spices. In st. 8 the dead man's widow, who is lying beside him, is told to rise; she has entered into matrimony with him who takes her hand—presumably her husband's brother. In st. 9 the dead man's bow is taken from his hand, and wishes are expressed for the success of the survivors. The following stanzas contain an invocation to Earth not to press too heavily upon him, but to wrap him as a mother. There are references to propping up the earth and to a 'pillar' which the Fathers are invoked to hold up.[1]

The last book of the Rgveda also contains two poems (x. 173 f.) belonging to this category but relating to a very different occasion, viz. a political ceremony. The first of these[2] is the proclamation of a king. Various deities—Indra, Soma, Brhaspati, Varuna and Agni—are invoked; but the poem is not so much a prayer as a declaration and exhortation to the new king to maintain his authority firmly. The next poem (x. 174) looks rather like a sequel to this. It is a declaration by a king, apparently one who has just been proclaimed. He invokes Brahmanaspati for success in resisting his enemies. In the last stanza he makes use of much the same phraseology as we met with in x. 159, saying that he is now without rivals, his rivals slain, triumphant, so that he shall have rule over his people. Possibly the phraseology originated in speeches designed for such occasions as this.

[1] This poem deserves more attention than it has received from those who are interested in the funeral practices of ancient Europe. Possibly in certain points they would be inclined to suggest a somewhat different interpretation from what is given by Vedic scholars. The native scholastic tradition in this case is of doubtful value, because this kind of burial seems to have been given up at an early date.

[2] Transl. by Thomas, op. cit. p. 109 f.

The Atharvaveda contains a good number of poems corresponding to both the groups just noticed. Funeral hymns occupy the whole of Book XVIII. These are to a large extent variants of the hymns in the Rgveda; but the order of the stanzas is different, stanzas from different hymns are brought together, and many new stanzas are added.

Poems intended for political occasions, especially the proclamation of a king, are numerous. A variant to Rgv. x. 173 occurs in VI. 87 f., where it is divided into two poems. Other examples of the same type are to be found in III. 4 and IV. 8. Here also we may mention appeals to Indra, Agni and other gods to uphold and protect a new king; such are I. 9, 30, IV. 22, VI. 5, 54, VII. 35, XIX. 24, and perhaps VII. 78. In III. 3 special circumstances seem to be implied; the poem is apparently a proclamation of a king who is in exile, and an invitation to him to return. In this series we may also include III. 5, in which a man, who seems to be a king, binds upon himself an amulet in order to secure success, long life and the obedience of his subjects. This is no doubt properly to be regarded as a spell, though it is not intended for any specific purpose.

There are one or two other poems, which may belong to 'coming of age' ceremonies, rather than the assumption of office. Such is the case perhaps with I. 35, in which the speaker invests a man with an amulet of gold, in order to secure for him long life, valour and the fulfilment of his wishes from the gods.[1] A more certain example is to be found in II. 13, where a man—evidently a youth—is invested with a new robe. He stands upon a stone for the ceremony; and Agni and the gods are invoked to protect him and grant him long life and success. The ceremony is described in later literature. Another kind of initiation seems to be implied in VI. 133, which is evidently intended for the ceremony of investing with a sacred girdle.

Other poems seem to be designed for a ceremony corresponding somewhat to our Christening, though we do not know whether it was accompanied by the giving of a name. In II. 28 Mitra, Varuna, Agni and other gods are invoked to protect the child and to bring him to old age. In VI. 76 the company are described as sitting round the child, and a fire for sacrifice to Agni is burning. It is stated in gnomic form that the child of a Kshatriya, who is protected by Agni, will not fall into danger. In VI. 110 Agni is again invoked to grant long life to a child. This child was born on the 'Tiger's Day'—a reference to astrology. He will therefore be a hero; but he must not wound his father or disregard his mother.

[1] There are a number of spells for use at such investitures; cf. XIX. 26, 28–33.

For use at weddings a benedictory poem is to be found in VI. 78. The bridegroom is to treat his wife kindly and honourably. Tvashtr has made them for one another; let him grant them long life. In VII. 36 there is a poem consisting of one stanza, expressing a wish for mutual love and harmony. According to tradition it was to be pronounced by both the bride and bridegroom, when they have anointed each other's eyes. This is followed by another poem of one stanza (VII. 37), to be pronounced by the bride, when she robes the bridegroom. It is in the form of a spell, for the purpose of keeping him wholly devoted to her.

Lastly, note may be taken of two poems which are evidently intended for ceremonies at the opening of a new house. In III. 12 the house itself is first addressed. It is to stand firm and be rich in horses, cattle and children. In st. 4 various deities are invoked for prosperity. Then (st. 5) an appeal is made to the 'Queen of the home', apparently a deity, and after this an appeal to the roof-tree. In st. 8 the lady of the house is summoned to treat the guests. Then water is brought 'to kill Consumption', and the speaker enters 'with Agni' to take possession. A longer poem upon the same subject is to be found in IX. 3. This is of great archaeological interest; but the detailed description of the building presents a good number of difficulties, which we have not the knowledge to deal with. In the main it is addressed to the house, though the protection of Agni and other deities is invoked incidentally.

It will have been seen that several of the poems referred to above are really spells, quite similar to those which will require notice in the next chapter. Many others have in part, sometimes even wholly, the form of spells, though it seems to us uncertain how far they were intended for use as such. For similar expressions are in use among ourselves without any such meaning. Poems of Type D relating to social ritual would appear to be largely derived from spells; but it is difficult to determine at what point exactly the formula ceases to be intended as a spell.

In the Brāhmanas and Upanishads we have not noted any poetry of this type, though such may occur. But the directions used throughout the former—e.g. 'it should be recited', and even 'he recites'—seem properly to belong here. There is a close connection with spells, as will be seen in the next chapter.

We do not know of any narratives in the earlier literature which can be assigned with confidence to this category. We shall therefore take our illustrations for Type A and Type C (CA) from the Mahābhārata. Stories which are strictly timeless nameless and relate to human beings seem to be rare. Those we have noticed are quite brief and simple. An example occurs in a speech of Vidura to Dhrtarāshtra in v. lxiv. Two birds are caught in a net, but manage to fly up into the air, carrying the net with them. The fowler, who has set the net, gives chase; and a seer, who happens to be at hand, asks him why he does so—the implication being that his quest is futile. The fowler replies that they have taken his net by united action; but as soon as they quarrel they will come under his control. This soon happens; they fall to the ground and he catches them. The story belongs to Type C; it is told to inculcate a moral, the danger of disunion, as explained in the following stanzas. Vidura is trying to make the king exert his authority to prevent his sons from going to war against their cousins.[1]

We have not come across any examples of Type A—the narrative without a moral; but there is no reason for doubting that such stories were current. In III. lxvii Nala, transformed and disguised, comes to the court of King Rtuparna and is engaged to take charge of his horses. But every night he bemoans in verse the loss of his wife, wondering what has become of her. When one of the grooms questions him about his poetry, he replies: "A certain man of little intelligence had a wife who was greatly esteemed; but his own word was not sufficiently to be depended upon. For some reason this foolish man came to be separated from her...", and then in a few words, without giving his name, he depicts what has really happened to himself. The form used here points to derivation from timeless nameless stories of Type A—perhaps folktales—which must have been current when this narrative was composed.

In the didactic portions of the Mahābhārata there are some longer stories of Type C, which are almost without names. In III. ccv ff. we have an account of an irascible Brahman, who by his anger—acting apparently as a curse, though no words are mentioned—causes the death of a crane. His name is given as Kauçika;[2] but we do not know whether anything is recorded of him elsewhere. After this he goes to a house to beg and becomes extremely angry with the wife of the householder, because she waits upon her husband before attending to him. The lady tells him he ought to control his anger, and advises him to visit a fowler in the city of Mithilā, who is very learned and has his feelings

---

[1] Another didactic story, likewise told by Vidura, is that of the (nameless) Brahman who fell into a pit (XI. v). This is wholly allegorical and contains very little narrative; but it shows clearly enough that the principle was known.

[2] This name perhaps means a descendant of Viçvāmitra; cf. p. 507 f.

under control. He takes her advice and finds the fowler—who is really a butcher—to be a man of great learning and holy life, although he belongs to the lowest (Çudra) caste. After a long discourse the fowler explains to him (ccxiv. 21 ff.) that he had himself been a Brahman in a previous life, but he had been condemned to be reborn as a Çudra by the curse of a seer, whom he had unwittingly shot in the form of a deer. In this story the only persons mentioned by name are the Brahman and Janaka, king of Mithilā, to whose good government the fowler refers incidentally; no names are given to the fowler himself or the householder and his wife.

In Vol. I, p. 434 ff., we saw that some of the stories and incidents which are related in heroic poetry are commonly believed to be derived from timeless nameless stories, including folktales. In point of fact the incident last mentioned, the shooting of a seer in the form of a deer and the curse arising therefrom, has a close parallel in I. cxviii, where Pāndu is cursed with loss of progeny by a seer's son whom he has shot in the form of a deer. We have no heroic stories of Pāndu himself—this passage is clearly non-heroic—but he is the father of Yudhishthira, Bhīma and Arjuna.

To the story of Beowulf's encounter with Grendel the Mahābhārata presents a rather close parallel in I. clix ff. Bhīma and his mother Kuntī are staying in disguise, during their exile, at the house of a Brahman; and there they hear great lamentation. Kuntī learns from the Brahman that the town is terrorised by a cannibal Rākshasa, named Vaka, who has to be supplied by each household in turn with an offering of a cartload of rice, two bullocks and the person who brings the offering. Now the turn of his house has come. First he offers to go, then his wife, and afterwards his daughter offer to take his place; but Kuntī persuades him to let Bhīma, who is enormously strong, go instead. Bhīma sets out with the food to the place appointed, which is in a forest, shouts for the Rākshasa to come, and then sits down and proceeds to eat the food himself. The Rākshasa arrives in great fury, storms at Bhīma and strikes him; but Bhīma takes no notice until he has finished the food. Then they tear up trees and pitch them at one another, and after that fall to wrestling. Eventually Bhīma breaks the Rākshasa's back. His relatives and followers assemble, but Bhīma cows them all. Then he carries off the Rākshasa's body, and lays it down at one of the town gates. In the morning all the townspeople gather to see it, wondering who has done the deed. It may be observed that Vaka is somewhat more human than Grendel. He seems to be the head of a community; and both he and his people can speak. Elsewhere in the Mahābhārata, especially perhaps in the battle scenes in Book VII, it is very difficult to resist the suspicion that the term Rākshasa was applied to non-Aryan communities. Yet there can be no doubt that in general the use of the word was equivalent to that of Ang.-Sax. *eoten* and *þyrs* (N. *jötunn* and *þurs*), the generic terms for such creatures as Grendel.

The story of Bhīma's fight with Vaka belongs obviously to a class of stories which is widespread and familiar enough, especially in folktales. Two or three points, however, deserve notice. In the first place practically no names occur except those of Bhīma, Kuntī and Vaka. Yudhishthira and his other brothers do try to dissuade the hero from the adventure; but they are in no way essential to the story. No names are given to the Brahman and his family. Secondly, the incident has no bearing on the story of Bhīma and his brothers as a whole. Thirdly, the story is immediately preceded by that of Bhīma's encounter with another cannibal Rākshasa, called Hidimba. The two incidents are in general not unlike. But the adventure with Hidimba (I. cliv–vii) has some bearing upon the story of Bhīma and his brothers as a whole; for Hidimba's sister Hidimbā bears to Bhīma a son, Ghatotkaca, who subsequently plays a rather important part in the great battle. These considerations seem to us to suggest that the adventure with Vaka was not an original, or even an early, element in the story—that on the contrary it was introduced, whether as a variant or not, through the influence of the incident with Hidimba.

It would seem that in the case of Bhīma—and the same may well be true of Beowulf and Grettir—one story of adventure with demons led to another. A third incident of the same kind occurs in III. clvii, where Bhīma kills a Rākshasa called Jatāsura, who has carried off Yudhishthira, Draupadī and Nakula. The description of the actual fight is very similar; no weapons are used, and the business is settled by wrestling. Elsewhere, however, especially in fights with heroes, Bhīma uses the ordinary weapons, bow and sword, as well as a club, and drives in a chariot. Indeed in III. clx he kills a chief of Rākshasa with his club and many of his followers with arrows. But even in heroic warfare he is sometimes guilty of savagery, as in VIII. lxxxiii, when he drinks the blood of Duhshasana,[1] whose head he has just cut off.

Heroes like Bhīma and Beowulf, whose chief characteristic is physical strength, seem to be specially liable to attract folktales and other time-

---

[1] One is tempted to think of Hrólfs Saga Kraka, cap. 35. But there is historical record of such doings in human warfare; cf. Ammianus Marcellinus, XXXI. 16. 6.

less nameless stories of a somewhat crude kind. But we suspect that many of the incidents recorded of other heroes and also of seers are of similar origin. Such derivation is of course seldom capable of proof; but we may cite as a likely instance the story related in I. ccxviii f. Arjuna dives into a sacred pool, which is haunted by crocodiles. One of them assails him; but he drags it out, and it thereupon becomes a beautiful damsel. She explains to him that she and her companions are Apsarasas, who have been turned into crocodiles by the curse of a Brahman whom they had tempted. They were to remain in this form for a hundred years. Nārada had advised them to come to this sanctuary and told them that Arjuna would deliver them at the end of the century. It may be observed that the names of the Apsarasas are given, though not that of the Brahman.

There can be no doubt that the Mahābhārata contains an enormous amount of fiction. But it is not clear to us how far the 'art of fiction' is developed. Some of the most incredible stories relate to persons, like the seer Vasishtha or King Somaka, the son of Sahadeva, whose historicity is not to be doubted, while very many of them are concerned with characters well known from other stories. The question is whether the Mahābhārata knows the modern type of fiction, complete both in plot and personnel—a type which in Greece can be traced back to perhaps the sixth century (B.C.); cf. Vol. I, pp. 433 f., 444. It has been held, we believe, that the story of Sāvitrī (III. ccxcii ff.) belongs to this type; but the fact that some of the chief characters figure in a wholly different connection (cf. p. 521) renders this view improbable.[1] At all events the Mahābhārata in general shows little enough affinity with the modern world, or even with sixth-century Greece, which may be regarded as in some sense its beginning or precursor. It clearly belongs to a different phase; in the heroic elements its affinities lie with the Homeric and the Anglo-Saxon heroic poems, while the best analogies for the non-heroic elements are to be found perhaps in the Mabinogion. Indeed the characteristics which distinguish post-heroic poetry in Europe seem to be wanting in ancient India.

As an appendix to this chapter we ought perhaps to add a word about stories relating to animals, which are numerous in the Mahābhārata. Stories dealing with animals for their own sake, e.g. as illustrating the characteristics of the species, belong properly to a separate category,

[1] We think that the affinities of the story are to be sought rather in the story of Alcestis than in Stesichoros' romances.

and in principle no doubt ought to be treated as such. But in the great majority of the instances contained in the Mahābhārata the animal stories are introduced for the purpose of illustrating some moral bearing upon human relations. Usually they belong to Type CB rather than CA, i.e. the speech element outweighs the narrative. As an example we may take i. cxlii, where the minister Kanika is exhorting Dhrtarāshtra to employ an opportunist policy in his relations with his nephews. The greater part of his discourse consists of gnomes, somewhat in the spirit of the Hávamál (cf. p. 554 f.); but he illustrates his advice by the story of a jackal, who contrived to get a deer killed by a tiger with the help of a mouse, and then persuaded both the tiger and various other animals to leave the carcase to him. The characteristics of the different species are of course brought out in the discussion; but it is not Kanika's primary object to give the king a lesson in natural history. It may be added that discussions of this kind between animals occur not only in the Mahābhārata, but also in the Upanishads, where also we find similar discussions between the senses and inanimate objects.

The Mahābhārata, however, does occasionally introduce speeches by animals, in which no moral bearing upon human affairs is obvious. An instance occurs in iii. cxcix, where the sons of Pāndu ask the aged seer Markandeya if there is anyone living older than himself. He replies that he had once been asked the same question by a royal seer named Indradyumna. The latter had first asked him if he (Markandeya) knew him; and when he said he did not, he asked him if he knew anyone older than himself. He had replied that there was an owl in the Himalayas older than himself, and he might know Indradyumna. The royal seer then became a horse and carried Markandeya to the owl's home. He asked the owl the same two questions. The owl said that he did not know him, but that in a certain lake there was a crane, older than himself, who might know him. Then they made their way to the lake and asked the crane the same questions, with the same results. The crane, however, referred them to a tortoise, again older than himself, who remembered Indradyumna well. The lake in which he and the crane lived had been made by the feet of the oxen which Indradyumna had given away to Brahmans at his sacrifices. It may be observed that the animals have individual names, which seem to be descriptive.

This incident has a special interest owing to its resemblance to a passage in the story of Culhwch and Olwen.[1] King Arthur's envoys are searching for Mabon, son of Modron. First they come to the Ousel of

[1] P. 133 ff. in Lady Charlotte Guest's translation of the Mabinogion (Everyman).

Cilgwri, who dwells upon the great length of time she has been there; yet she does not know him. She knows, however, a race of animals created before her; so she takes them to the Stag of Rhedynfre. He also cannot answer the question; but accompanies them to an owl, which is said to be still older. The owl takes them on to an eagle, which he says is the oldest and most travelled animal in the world. The eagle has heard of Mabon, but takes them to a salmon for further information. It will be seen that the questions in the two stories are not identical, and also that in the Welsh story there seems to be some confusion between species and individual, apart from obscurities in other respects. Yet in spite of all this the parallelism is sufficient to call for explanation. We would suggest that both stories are due to speculation in natural history —on the question what animal lives to the greatest age. We may refer to a fragment attributed to Hesiod (fr. 207, Kinkel), in which the crow is credited with a life nine times as long as a man, while the stag is said to live four times as long as the crow, the raven three times as long as the stag, etc.

Occasionally animals are individualised more clearly than in the passage discussed above. Apart from supernatural beings, like the bird Garuda, the examples known to us are snakes. In III. lxvi the snake Karkotaka calls to Nala to save him from a fire. He is unable to move himself owing to a curse imposed upon him by Nārada. But the most interesting case is that of the snake which in III. clxxviii ff. seizes Bhīma and threatens to eat him. He tells his victim that he is the ancient king Nahusha (cf. p. 498) and that he has been turned into a snake by the curse of the sage Agastya. The curse is to remain operative until he finds someone who can answer his questions. Yudhishthira comes to the rescue and answers the questions, viz. 'Who can properly be called a Brahman?' and 'What is it which ought to be known?' He then proceeds to ask the snake further questions—at the end of which Nahusha is freed from the curse and liberates Bhīma. It may be observed that the scene generally bears a certain resemblance to that of the Fáfnis-mál, where Sigurðr and the dying Fáfnir question one another; but both the questions themselves and the circumstances are different. For the power of a seer to transform a person into an animal (cf. p. 571) good parallels are to be found in the Mabinogi of Math. In this story indeed, just as in many parts of the Mahābhārata, the power of the seer seems to have no limits.

CHAPTER X

MANTIC POETRY AND PROSE

IN Vol. I, Ch. xv, we included under 'Mantic Poetry' prophecies, spells and certain Welsh and Irish compositions of a mystical character—'declarations of bardic wisdom'—which have some affinities with these genres, but seem not to belong properly to either of them. It was observed that in the ancient literatures of the West, especially Greek and Norse, prophecy—or rather prophetic knowledge —relating to the future is not regarded as essentially different from knowledge of the past and the present which is derived from revelation or vision. It was also observed that prophecy and spell are not so remote from one another as they seem to be at first sight; the gap between the two genres is largely bridged over by blessings and curses.

Early Indian literature has preserved spells in great abundance; but prophecies, relating to specified persons and events, seem to be rare and late. On the other hand there is also a large amount of mystical literature, corresponding more or less to the 'bardic wisdom' of early Welsh and Irish records. The history of this is much fuller and clearer than that of the same genre in the West, and is able, we think, to throw a good deal of light on the latter. Prose is in more general use than in the West; but the great majority of the spells are in poetry.

A number of spells are preserved in the Rgveda, especially the last book. Two of them have already been noticed among the timeless nameless poems of Type B (cf. p. 562). In one, x. 145, a wife uses a plant, which she digs up, against her rival; and the spell is addressed to the plant. In the other, x. 166, the speaker is a man, who likewise is trying to get the upper hand of rivals; but no instrument seems to be used for the spell. Elsewhere also we find spells both with and without the use of accessories, such as plants or amulets. One poem, x. 97, is addressed to plants collectively, with a view to their power in banishing disease; the speaker seems to be a physician. We may perhaps compare with this the English 'Nine Herbs Spell' (cf. Vol. I, p. 447); but different kinds of plants are not specified, as in the latter. On the other hand in x. 163 there is no reference to any plant or other accessory. The speaker, who again seems to be a physician, enumerates all the various parts of his patient's body and repeats in each stanza the formula 'I drive away thy malady'.

Sometimes it is not clear whether a poem is to be regarded as a spell or a prayer. We may perhaps instance x. 155, a poem addressed to Arāyī, a spirit of distress, who is described as a one-eyed limping hag. The poet tries to frighten her away, and bids her depart upon a floating log. With this may be compared x. 164, which seems to be addressed to a spirit of evil dreams, bidding him depart. But both these poems invoke Brahmanaspati and other deities.

Of all the spells preserved in the Rgveda the most interesting perhaps is VII. 55, part of which is also found, together with other stanzas, in the Atharvaveda, IV. 5. This is a spell for sending a household to sleep, beginning—in the Rgveda version—with the dog. The Rgveda does not make it clear what the nocturnal visitor, who is the speaker, has in mind; but the Atharvaveda shows that he is a lover who is paying a clandestine visit to his lady.[1]

The Atharvaveda contains a very much larger number of spells than the Rgveda. Indeed the majority of the poems preserved in this collection are spells. Many of them are quite short. Parallels are to be found for most of the early spell-poems of the West; but the Atharvaveda covers a much wider range of subjects. It may be observed that spells not unfrequently contain invocations to deities. The distinction between spell and prayer seems not to be rigid.

Spells against diseases are perhaps the most numerous. Frequently these are addressed to some herb or amulet which was credited with healing powers. As an example we may quote I. 23, which seems to be intended for a doctor or medicine man attending a case of leprosy: "Thou wast born by night, thou black, dark and dusky herb. Rajanī![2] do thou colour this which is spotted and colourless. Make what is spotted and colourless and discoloured vanish from here. Let thy own colour come upon thee.[3] Make the white (spots) to fly away...." The

---

[1] The Rgveda version is transl. by E. J. Thomas, *Vedic Hymns*, p. 111. This poem is of interest both for the study of variants and as illustrating the tendency of Indian scholastic tradition to seek explanations in mythology or legend. Part of the poem according to the latter is said to have been recited by the legendary seer Vasishtha, when he came to visit Varuna to obtain food. The interpretation given above is, we believe, accepted by the majority of modern scholars, but not by all.

[2] *Curcuma longa*. There is a play of words between the name *Rajanī* and the word *rajaya* ('colour'), which immediately follows it.

[3] This sentence is believed to be addressed not to the patient but, like the context, to the herb, which is here thought of as working within the man.

concluding words represent the object of the spell as accomplished, as in the spells of other peoples: "By the spell I have made the white disfigurement to vanish."

With this may be compared another spell, II. 9, which is addressed to a herb or amulet[1] called Daçavrksha. The case for which it is invoked would seem to be something in the nature of paralysis. We may quote the first two stanzas: "Deliver this man, Daçavrksha, from the demon Grāhī, who has seized him in his joints, and raise him up, Lord of the forest, to the world of the living." The next stanza speaks of the patient as cured: "He has arisen, arisen, and come to the company of the living. He has become a father of sons and the most fortunate of men."

Next we may note a spell, II. 26, which seems to be intended for the recovery of straying cattle, a subject which is found also in English spells (cf. Vol. I, p. 448): "Hither let them come, the cattle which have been straying, in whose company Vāyu[2] has taken pleasure. Tvashtr knows their forms; may Savitr bring them back to this cow-pen. Together let them stream to this cow-pen. Let Brhaspati, who knows all things, lead them hither. Let Sinīvalī lead hither the leader of their herd; and when they have arrived do thou, Anumati, bring them in." It will be seen that in this case a number of deities are invoked, directly or indirectly, while there is no reference to herbs or other such accessories. Although the imperative is used for the cattle as well as the deities, the spell approximates to a prayer; but this is of such general application that it hardly amounts to more than the expression of a wish. The rest of the spell relates to prosperity in general.

Spells connected with agriculture are perhaps hardly as common as might be expected. As an example we may take VI. 142: "Spring up, Barley, and become massive in thy bulk. Burst all the vessels. Let not the thunderbolt of heaven smite thee. As we invoke thee, the barley, the god who hearkenest, spring up like the heaven, unlimited as the sea. Unlimited be the crops, unlimited the querns; unlimited be those who give and those who eat." This may be compared with an English spell (cf. Vol. I, p. 446), which was employed against the bewitching of the crops. Here also we may refer to a spell for abundant harvest (III. 24), and to the poem on the plough (III. 17), mentioned on p. 559, above.

---

[1] According to ancient authorities it is an amulet made of ten kinds of holy wood (cf. Griffith's note *ad loc.*)—though this may possibly be only an etymological guess (cf. *daça*, 'ten'; *vrkṣa*, 'tree').

[2] The Wind-god. The sentence is believed to mean that the cattle roamed as freely as the wind. The names which follow are those of deities.

A number of spells are love-charms. As an example we may take III. 25: "Let the 'Goader' goad thee on. Thou shalt have no rest upon thy bed. Dread is the dart of Love; and with it I pierce thee in the heart. . . . With a whip I drive thee hither, away from thy mother and father, so that thou shalt be in my power and submit to my will. Mitra and Varuna, shatter the thoughts of her heart and, having made her powerless, render her subject to my will." It is not clear that the word *uttudas* ('Goader') implies the use of any accessory here. But in some similar spells (I. 34, II. 30, VI. 102, and perhaps VI. 89) herbs or amulets are employed for the same purpose. Other poems of this kind (VI. 8, 9) seem to be more in the nature of love-songs. Examples of spells to be used by a woman for securing the love of a man are to be found in VI. 132, 139, VI. 38—in all of which accessories are employed. We may also refer here to certain spells (II. 36, VI. 60, 82), the object of which is to obtain a husband or wife.

There are also spells intended for various other occasions in human life. Some of these have been noticed in Ch. IX; for poems intended for social festivals sometimes have the form of spells. Some of the poems on the blessing of a child and on the opening of a new house (cf. p. 566 f.) may be regarded as belonging to either category. But there are other poems which can be intended only as spells, e.g. I. 11, which is a spell for the birth of a child. Possibly also we may include here a poem, III. 15, which is in the form of a prayer to Indra, Agni and other deities for success in a trading journey. This may be compared with the traveller's speech noticed on p. 563. Spells for success in battle, combined with invocations of Indra, are to be found in VI. 65–67, and to these may be added the invocations of the war-drum in v. 20 f., VI. 126. But the most interesting poems of this series perhaps are those which relate to gambling. Three of these (VI. 118, VII. 50, 109) have already been noticed (p. 563); they are on the whole perhaps rather to be regarded as poems of Type B (BD), though they have the form of spells or invocations. Another (IV. 38) is an invocation to the Apsarasas to grant success at dice, and may be intended for actual use. A fifth (II. 2) is an invocation of the Gandharva, who is here glorified in the highest terms, together with the Apsarasas, who are said to be his wives. The object of the invocation is not expressly stated.

Lastly, it may be observed that at least two of the poems relating to kings are in the form of spells. In II. 5 a king appeals to an amulet to grant him protection and success. In I. 29, which is a variant of Rgv. X. 174 (cf. p. 565), there are likewise references to the use of an amulet, though the Rgveda text speaks only of an 'oblation' (*havis*).

It is hardly necessary to give illustrations from other works. Spells for specific purposes occur occasionally in the Brāhmanas[1] and more frequently in the Upanishads. But in the former the great bulk of the matter might perhaps be regarded as coming under this head; for the ritual is treated throughout as possessing a magical property as well as a mystical significance, while the words of the hymns themselves are often interpreted in a (mystical) sense which cannot have been intended by their authors.

In the Upanishads spells are of rather more frequent occurrence; and occasionally the circumstances and accessories are described in great detail. As an example we may take Brhadāranyaka VI. 3, a shorter variant of which is to be found in Chāndogya V. ii. 4 ff. If a man wishes to attain greatness he is, first, to make certain preparations, which are described more fully in the former work. These include a mixed potion or mash, made of all kinds of herbs. In the former work the rite is to be carried out at a time fixed by astrology, in the latter on the night of the new moon. Then he pours ghee partly upon the fire, partly into the mash, at the same time saying *Svāhā* ('Hail') to a series of things, one after another. In Chāndogya the things enumerated are 'the chief and best' (breath[2]), 'the most excellent' (speech), 'the basis' (eye), 'success' (ear), 'the abode' (mind); but in Brhadāranyaka the list is much longer, including not only these but also Fire, Earth, Heaven, the Past, the Future, etc. Then (in Brhadāranyaka) he addresses the mash, describing its various properties—it is burning, firm, bright, powerful, food, light, etc. After this he eats the mash, addressing it with solemn words, which differ in the two works. In Brhadāranyaka they consist of quotations from the Rgveda, invoking blessings from rivers, plants, air, cattle, etc. Then he sits down behind the fire or altar. The Chāndogya adds that if he dreams that he sees a woman he may know that his sacrifice has been successful. The rite seems to be similar in principle to the *imbas forosnai* ascribed to Irish *filid* (cf. Vol. I, p. 659). We may also refer to the cauldron of Caridwen (*ib.* p. 103 f.). It may be observed that in Brhadāranyaka this spell is followed by a number of others.

---

[1] A very interesting example occurs in Ait. Br. III. 22; but we find the quotations, as usual, difficult to understand.

[2] These identifications are given in the preceding section. In Brhadāranyaka they are given in the spell itself, but are differently distributed—'the most excellent' is breath, 'success' is the eye, etc.

In the Kaushītaki Upanishad, ii. 3, there is a description of a some-what similar proceeding. Here the things (called 'deities') invoked with *Svāhā* are speech, breath, eye, ear, mind and knowledge—most of which are included also in the above lists. There is no mash, but only offerings of ghee. It is stated that when the man has inhaled the smoke and rubbed himself with the ghee, he is to depart in silence and declare his wish or send a messenger; and he will obtain his wish. The next section describes what is to be done by a man who wishes to become dear to any man or woman. The proceeding is almost the same; but he says: "I offer thy speech (ear, etc.) in myself; *Svāhā*." Then he is to depart in silence and try to come in contact with—or let the wind carry his words to—the person whom he wishes to love him.

Spells are also mentioned incidentally in the Mahābhārata, though here they are less frequent than what are more properly to be regarded as curses. The latter will require notice below. For an example of the spell proper we may refer to the story of Kuntī, the mother of Yudhish-thira, related in iii. cccii ff. Before her marriage, while she is still very young, she waits upon a Brahman, who in reward for her services teaches her a spell—apparently from the Atharvaveda—before he departs (ccciv, 16 ff.). The words of the spell are not given; but it is said to have the power of bringing to her any of the gods whom she may wish, even against his will. One day, while she is gazing at the sun (cccv f.) she decides from youthful curiosity to try the efficacy of the spell. Sūrya, the sun-god, immediately appears before her in majestic human form, and demands to be allowed to lie with her. She pleads that she has acted in childish ignorance; but he threatens to curse her and her family, and eventually she consents. The result of the union is the birth of Karna, which is kept a secret throughout his life.

Prophecy in the ordinary sense of the word, i.e. as relating to specific future events, appears to be less frequent in ancient Indian literature than in the West. In works of the earlier periods, the Vedas, Brāhmanas and Upanishads, we have not noticed any examples. Such may occur; but we do not think they can be very common.

In the Mahābhārata prophecies are not unknown, though they are not always easy to distinguish from blessings or curses. Thus, in the story last referred to, the god Sūrya describes to Kuntī (iii. cccvi. 18 ff.) the son whom she is to bear, and says that he will be a distinguished hero. But he gives her no information as to his fate; so this is probably to be regarded as a blessing rather than a prophecy. Again, there are cases which are perhaps equally capable of either interpretation, as in III. xxv. 18, where the sage Markandeya tells Yudhishthira that after his exile he will recover his kingdom from the Kauravas. But there are other passages, which can only be taken as prophecies. In III. ccxcii f. Sāvitrī goes to look for a husband, and on her return home informs her father that she has chosen Satyavat. The supernatural seer Nārada, who is present, says that the chosen bridegroom has one defect, namely that he will die within a year. Occasionally also we hear of prophecies of the disastrous struggle which was to take place between the Kauravas and the Pāndavas. In XI. viii. 34 f., the same Nārada is said to have foretold the struggle—a passage which is perhaps to be taken in connection with II. xxxvi. 19.[1] In the Purānas, as we have seen (p. 540), the lists of kings are given largely in the form of prophecies—for which analogies are to be found in early Irish and Welsh records (cf. Vol. I, p. 462 f.).

Blessings and curses seem to be of much more frequent occurrence than prophecies. Invocations for blessings, whether upon individual princes or upon the community in general, are to be found everywhere in the Rgveda. In the Atharvaveda also we find blessings of a general character, especially for long life, intended for use in festivities celebrating the birth of a child. But here we would call attention to blessings of more or less specific reference which, as we noted in Vol. I (p. 473), may be regarded either as spells or as prophecies which carry with them their own fulfilment. Two examples, which are hardly distinguishable from prophecies, have been noticed above. Another, which may be regarded either as a spell or a prophecy, occurs in III. ccxcii, where the goddess Savitrī arises from the altar and announces to King Açvapati that, as a reward for his piety, a daughter will soon be born to him. A somewhat similar but more curious case is to be found in the story of the sacrifice offered by the two Brahmans on behalf of King Drupada (I. clxix), which resulted in the birth—if such it can be called—of Drshtadyumna and Draupadī. We may also note here the promise given (in V. clxxxix) to Ambā by the god Rudra (Çiva), that she should be re-born and become a man.

The evidence for curses is similar. In the Atharvaveda, V. 17–19, we find curses of general reference upon those who take a Brahman's wife or a Brahman's cow. To speak more precisely, these poems are pronounce-

---

[1] Elsewhere we find more specific and detailed prophecies of the battle, as in V. cxliii where Karna has full knowledge of what is to take place and declares to Krshna who will be slain and who survive. Such passages are doubtless merely summaries of the following narrative, given in the form of prophecy; but they may be taken as showing that prophecy was widely recognised.

ments of the evils which will befall those who perpetrate or allow such outrages. Curses upon demons, wizards and diseases are fairly common. In the Mahābhārata curses upon specified human beings are of frequent occurrence. Sometimes they are of a general character, as in I. iii. 10, where the divine dog Saramā curses Janamejaya and his brothers for beating her son. Sometimes the nature of the curse is precisely specified, as in III. x. 30 ff., where the seer Maitreya declares to Duryodhana that in the war which the latter is bringing about Bhīma will break his thigh with a club. This is to be regarded as a curse rather than merely a prophecy; for the seer has been angered by an insult. Moreover when Dhrtarāshtra begs him to avert the curse, he says it will not take effect if Duryodhana makes peace with the Pāndavas. A similar case occurs in VIII. xlii. 39 ff., where Karna relates how he had shot a Brahman's calf. The Brahman then declared that when Karna was engaged in battle his chariot-wheel should sink into the ground and he should be overcome with fear—as actually took place in the great battle. In this case the Brahman refused to withdraw the curse, though he was offered great rewards if he would do so. In these instances, it will be seen, the curse comes into operation only in the future. In others, however, it takes effect at once, and consequently has the form of a spell rather than a prophecy. We may cite the story of King Kalmāshapāda, related in I. clxxviii. He strikes the seer Çaktri, son of Vasishtha, because he refuses to stand aside for him; and the seer in anger curses him so that he becomes a cannibal from that day. Here also we may refer to the story of Pāndu, as told in I. cxviii. He shoots a stag while it is mating; but the stag proves to be a seer in disguise and lays upon him the curse which brings about his death. Such spell-curses are not the exclusive property of seers. In III. lxiii. ad. fin., Damayantī curses a hunter who has insulted her; and he immediately falls down dead.

Supernatural beings, as well as men, are subject to curses. In I. ccxviii five Apsarasas are cursed by a Brahman for mocking and tempting him. They are turned into crocodiles for a hundred years, until they are rescued by Arjuna from their plight. So also in I. xcvi, the divine Vasavas tell Gangā (the Ganges personified) that they have been cursed by the seer Vasishtha and condemned to be born as men. At their request she consents to become the wife of Çāntanu and to bear them to him as her children. As soon as each child is born, she throws it into the Ganges.

It was pointed out in Vol. I, pp. 451 ff., 473, that the ancient peoples of the West did not clearly distinguish between prophecy, i.e. foreknowledge and foretelling, relating to the future and 'prophecy', in the sense of mantic knowledge and declaration, relating to the past and the present. Both faculties are possessed by the same persons, whether human seers or supernatural beings; and often the same terms are used for both. It is clear from the Mahābhārata and the Purānas that the same remark applies also to ancient India. These works, which are largely or mainly concerned with the study of the past, claim to have been composed by ancient seers, Vyāsa and others. In the form in which we have them they cannot of course be of great antiquity; but there can be little doubt that much of the tradition and speculation they contain must have had a long history.

The works, however, which have been preserved in early form, the Vedas, Brāhmanas and Upanishads, are little concerned with the study of the past, apart from cosmogony. The chief interest of the Vedic schools, as shown in the Brāhmanas and Upanishads, evidently lay in mysticism, relating in the former to the ritual of sacrifice, in the latter to the problems of human existence. This mysticism may be traced even in the Rgveda, in certain poems which deal with cosmogony. Thus in x. 90 we hear of a vast primeval 'man' (*purusa*), who was put to death by the gods, and from portions of whom the moon, sun, sky, earth, etc. were made. For this we have an analogy in the Grímnismál (cf. Vol. i, p. 321). But the Rgveda poem represents the slaying as a sacrifice[1]—a feature upon which it clearly lays great stress. It says that the ghee of this sacrifice was spring, the fuel summer, and the offering autumn. Again, it says that the Vedic hymns and metres were born from this sacrifice. These and other passages suggest that the author's interest lay not so much in the origin of the world—as is the case in x. 129 (cf. p. 549)—as in that of sacrifice. There are inconsistencies, however, which may perhaps point to changes or additions. As it stands the poem is generally believed to be one of the very latest in the collection. St. 12 is the only passage in the Rgveda which mentions the four castes.

It is beyond our power to deal with the mysticism of the Brāhmanas. The early literatures of the West preserve hardly anything analogous to these works. In the north of Europe at all events we know far too little of the ritual of sacrifice to determine how far mysticism was associated with it, though it can hardly have been entirely wanting. Perhaps it will be sufficient to repeat here that the ritual, which forms

---

[1] Snorri, *Gylfaginning*, cap. 8, says that Ymir was slain by the gods, and this is perhaps implied in the Grímnismál itself; but none of the records suggest that the act was regarded as a sacrifice. It would, however, be unwise, in view of the scantiness of these records, to lay much stress upon this.

the staple subject of the Brāhmanas, is interpreted throughout in a mystical sense. The same remark is often true of the quotations from the Vedas and even the use of the metres. As an illustration of the latter we may quote from a passage in the Aitareya Brāhmana, I. 5: "*Bṛhatī* verses should he use who desires prosperity and glory; the *Bṛhatī* is prosperity and glory among the metres.... *Triṣṭubh* verses should he use who desires strength; the *Triṣṭubh* is force, power and strength...."[1] It will be seen that, although we cannot cite precise European parallels, the phase of thought is the same as in the Sigrdrífumál, st. 6 ff. (cf. Vol. I, p. 449 f.), where the use of Runic letters is specified for various purposes: "Thou shalt know *Sigrúnar* ('Runes of victory'), if thou wilt have victory, and thou shalt inscribe them on the hilt of thy sword.... Thou shalt know *Brimrúnar* ('Runes of the sea'), if thou wilt have 'sailing-steeds' (i.e. ships) protected on the sea," etc.

There are two features, however, in the mysticism of the Brāhmanas, which can hardly be passed over. The chief deity is Prajāpati ('Lord of offspring'), a god who is not often mentioned in the Rgveda, though in one hymn (x. 121) he is said to be the creator of the world and supreme god. But in the Brāhmanas he is not only regarded as the chief deity; he is also identified with the victim of sacrifice and with the sacrifice itself. He has therefore something in common with the 'Man' of x. 90, discussed above, and is actually identified with him in several passages in the Brāhmanas. In addition to Prajāpati we have to take account of the conception called *brahma*.[2] This word originally meant 'prayer' or 'spell'; but in the Brāhmanas it is commonly used in the sense of 'holy power'.[3] In course of time this conception came to be personified, and the form of the word was changed from *brahma* (neuter) to *Brahmā* (masculine); and the new deity eventually became identified with Prajāpati. But in the works of which we are now speaking this last change has not yet taken place, though the personal *Brahmā* is mentioned occasionally in the later Brāhmanas.[4]

---

[1] Rigveda Brahmanas, transl. by A. B. Keith, p. 110. *Bṛhatī* and *Triṣṭubh* are two of the Vedic metres.

[2] We use this form (which is the nom. sing.) instead of *brahman* (which is the stem of the word) in order to avoid any possible confusion with the term for priest.

[3] Often contrasted with *kṣatra*, 'lordly power', in which case the two words denote the 'properties' of the Brahman caste and the Kshatriya (princely) caste respectively. The transl. 'holy power' and 'lordly power' are those of Keith.

[4] E.g. Kaushītaki Brāhmana, xv. 2; but here Brahmā is identical with Brahmanaspati or Brhaspati ('Lord of prayer'), a personification (deity) which is often mentioned in the Rgveda. The later personification (Brahmā) cannot be wholly independent of this earlier one.

The Upanishads are concerned in the main not with the ritual of sacrifice, but with the problems of human existence. Much of what they contain is philosophy; and with this we are no more qualified to deal than we are with the Brāhmanas. But they belong to a much more widely distributed class of literature, and cannot be passed over in a book like this, however ill qualified we may be to treat of them. They have often been compared with the 'Dialogues' of Plato; but we think that truer analogies are to be found in the early mantic literature of northern Europe, noticed in Vol. I (p. 467 ff. and elsewhere). Like the latter they probably owe their preservation, if not their composition, largely to educational use.

The Upanishads—at least the earlier ones, with which alone we are concerned—consist of enunciations of mystical lore in the form of series of homilies, or lessons, varying in length and relating to such diverse subjects as sacrifice, the Vedas and their metres, the gods, especially Prajāpati or Brahmā, the heavenly bodies and elements, and—perhaps most frequent of all—the senses and organs of sense (breath, speech, eye, ear, mind, etc.). Speeches and dialogues, consisting of question and answer, are frequently introduced. The speakers are sometimes men, specified or unspecified, sometimes gods, sometimes the senses and other animate or inanimate beings. Considerable portions of the longer Upanishads are occupied with dialogues among learned Brahmans or between them and kings. Sometimes these debates are of a private nature, e.g. between a Brahman and a king, sometimes they take place at great festival gatherings, at which the king has offered a prize for superiority in wisdom. It is rather curious that in private discussions the king not unfrequently proves to be wiser than the Brahman. In debates between Brahmans one speaker often threatens another that his head will come off if he persists in a line of argument and fails to answer questions; and in one case (Brhad. III. 9. 26) this tragedy actually comes to pass. How this happens is not stated;[1] but the context seems to make it clear that it is dependent in some way upon the will of the man who utters the threat—i.e. it is in the nature of a curse. We may refer to the story of Kahoda[2] in the Mahābhārata cited on p. 504 f., where the unsuccessful competitors are drowned, and to the Norse and Greek parallels noted on p. 503.

---

[1] Çatapatha Brāhmana (VII. 6. 3. 11), which gives part of the same dialogue, is a little more explicit. Yājnavalkya tells Çākalya that he shall die before such and such a day and that not even his bones shall come to his home. And so it came about; for his bones were stolen by robbers, who mistook them for something else.

[2] Kahoda (Kahola) is one of the speakers in the Brhad. Upan. (III. 5).

Certain Upanishads are connected with certain Brāhmanas. Thus the Brhadāranyaka Upanishad is connected with—indeed it is the continuation of—the Çatapatha Brāhmana, which is itself connected with the White Yajurveda. And in general the connection between the Upanishads and the Brāhmanas is very close. The Upanishads are not concerned with directions for ritual. But they are much occupied with mystical interpretations both of religious ceremonies and of the sacred books (the Vedas) and their metres, though less so in the (human) dialogues than elsewhere. And the cast of thought is 'ecclesiastical' throughout, such as could arise only from a training confined to hymns and ritual and speculations derived therefrom. Although the ecclesiasticism is less marked in the dialogues of sages than in the other portions of the Upanishads, it may be observed that many of the speakers are mentioned also in Brāhmanas. Thus Yājnavalkya, who is the most outstanding character in the Brhadāranyaka, figures prominently in the Çatapatha Brāhmana; and he is also said to be the author (redactor) of the White Yajurveda. Uddālaka Āruni and his son Çvetaketu, Satyakāma Jābāla and Budila (Bulila) Āçvatara Āçvi, all of whom figure in either the Chāndogya or the Brhadāranyaka or both, are cited as authorities upon ritual usages in either the Aitareya or the Kaushītaki Brāhmanas. There can be little doubt therefore that both series of works spring from the same milieu.

The Upanishads are not concerned with moral or natural philosophy. Gnomes of either of the types distinguished above (p. 550) are of rare occurrence, unless one is prepared to recognise 'mystic gnomes', which might be said to occur everywhere. Observations of social or political relations or of natural history are introduced only by way of analogy. Indeed the wisdom of the Upanishads seems to be the outcome not of observation, but of meditation and speculation along traditional lines.

The discussions between sages are largely concerned with the terms *brahma* and *ātmā* (*ātman*). It is beyond our power to formulate—or even to grasp—the conceptions denoted by these terms in the Upanishads. If we were to attempt to do so we should soon find ourselves entangled in the difficulties which brought about the tragic fate of the ancient sages. We can only try to give some approximate impression of them in popular language. In the Brāhmanas, as we have seen, the word *brahma* usually means 'holy power'; it also denotes the 'property' of the Brahmans, the holy caste. We might perhaps use the expression 'religious power' or 'religion'; but no deity is necessarily involved—the 'power' lies in the worship itself. The development of meaning would seem to be as follows: (i) (specific) prayer or spell; (ii) religious or mantic procedure, worship; (iii) the power inherent in such procedure. In the Upanishads, however, the word *brahma* seems to mean a power which pervades and comprehends the world and is itself self-existent (*svayambhu*). The development of this meaning[1] from 'prayer' or 'spell' is not easy to follow; but it is to be borne in mind that the line of thought is that of priests, who regarded their own functions and activities as all-important. The conception of the god Prajāpati, who is the chief deity and creator, as well as sacrifice, is to some extent parallel. The word *ātmā* in the Rgveda usually means 'breath', like the corresponding forms in the related languages (Ang.-Sax. *æðm*, etc.). But later it comes to mean 'soul, self'; and we hear of an *ātmā* of the world even in the Atharvaveda, x. 8 (st. 44).

As an illustration of the doctrines enunciated in the discussions we may quote a passage which is repeated several times in Chānd. vi. 8 ff., where Uddālaka Āruni is instructing his son Çvetaketu. He enumerates a series of objects—rivers, trees, salt, etc.—and adds in each case: "That which is the subtle essence, all that exists has this as its *ātmā*. It is the True. It is the *ātmā*; and you are it." In the same Upanishad, vii. 1 ff., we hear of persons who meditate on various things as *brahma*. The list is as follows: name, speech, mind, will, thought, reflection, understanding, power, food, water, fire (heat), space, memory, hope, breath (spirit). The benefits derived from each of these are noted; and it is stated that each one is better than the one preceding—speech than name, mind than speech, etc. Again, in Brhad. iv. 1, Janaka of Videha tells Yājnavalkya that he has been informed by one sage that speech is *brahma*, by another that breath is *brahma*, while others have said the same of sight, hearing, the mind and the heart. Yājnavalkya in reply comments upon and amplifies all these statements, saying of the first *brahma* (speech) that speech itself is its abode, space its basis, and that one should worship it as knowledge; and he gives similar descriptions of the others. He regards the heart as the highest *brahma*, saying that the heart itself is its abode, space its basis, and one should worship it as permanence. The following sections contain an exposition of Yājnavalkya's own philosophy. His favourite dictum, which recurs several times, is that the *ātmā* is to be described by 'No, no', or 'It is not' (this or that).

Apart from the catalogue form, which is found almost everywhere, the most characteristic feature of these utterances is the free play given

---

[1] Something of the kind seems to occur in the Atharvaveda, iv. 1; but here *brahma* is identified with the god Brhaspati, who was probably an early personification of it (cf. p. 583, note).

to the imagination. We constantly meet with such statements as (Chānd. VI. 7. 6): "Mind consists of food, breath of water, speech of heat." Many of these sayings are doubtless derived from the traditional learning inherited by the Upanishads. We may refer (e.g.) to the fantastic properties attributed to the Vedas, and more especially to the metres employed in them. So also the speculations which form the subjects of the discussions are doubtless largely based upon earlier speculations, such as we find exemplified in the cosmogonic poems in the Rgveda (Book x)[1] and the Atharvaveda, where also the same imaginative tendency is frequently to be found. But the freedom allowed to this tendency in the Upanishads, together with the fact that they are concerned with subjects upon which definite knowledge is unattainable, has led to the result that the dialogues are often in reality contests of skill in rhetoric—perhaps we might say rhetorical gymnastics. We may cite (e.g.) the dialogues between Yājnavalkya and Gārgī in Brhad. III. 6, 8. Skill in dialectic was obviously much cultivated. The account of the contest between Ashtāvakra and Vandi in the Mahābhārata, III. 134 (cf. p. 505)—in which each of the competitors has to name four groups of objects under each numeral[2]—may possibly be merely a travesty upon Brahmanical learning, though we see no reason for the necessity of such an interpretation. But at all events it shows how such learning was regarded in some quarters. We may also refer to another passage in the same work, II. xxxvi. 3 ff., where the discussions of the seers assembled at Yudhishthira's great sacrifice are noticed; and it is stated that some made the weaker arguments to appear stronger and the stronger arguments weaker. They were evidently regarded in much the same way as the Greek Sophists.

Etymological speculation occurs not unfrequently in the Upanishads, as in the learned literature of other peoples. The word which seems to have attracted most attention is *satyam*, 'the true' (neuter). In the Kaushītaki Upanishad, I. 6, we find even Brahmā, the supreme deity, propounding an etymology of this. Phonology, however, was more cultivated by the Indians than by any other ancient people known to us; and in the Upanishads it is applied to mystical purposes, with truly fantastic results. The most remarkable examples are to be found in the Aitareya Āranyaka, III. 2. 2, 5.

[1] We may compare (e.g.) the opening sections of the Aitareya Upanishad with the cosmogonic hymn, Rgv. x. 90, noticed on p. 582.
[2] Vandi comes to grief in the thirteens. He can specify only two groups of thirteen. Ashtāvakra completes the stanza by giving two more.

There is no special significance in the fact that the learning of the Upanishads tended to pass into rhetoric and pedantry. For this we have parallels enough elsewhere. The remarkable element is the all-pervading mysticism, which penetrated into every detail, as in the case just noted. In the Brhadāranyaka, IV. 2. 2, Yājnavalkya is represented as saying that "the gods love what is mysterious and dislike what is evident". And this element must be taken in connection with the spells, the curses, and the attention devoted to dreaming (as in Brhad. II. 1. 15 ff.; IV. 3. 7 ff., etc.). The spells do not, like the two latter, occur in the discussions of sages; but in Brhad. VI. 3. 7 ff. the long spell noticed on p. 578 is said to have been taught by a number of sages, including Uddālaka Āruni and Yājnavalkya. Each of these various sages is represented as saying that "if a man were to pour it on a dry stump, branches would grow and leaves spring forth"—a sentence which occurs elsewhere (Chānd. v. 2. 3), apparently as an expression of high commendation.[1]

There can be no doubt then that both in itself and in its connections this philosophy is essentially mantic. Indeed in the 'genealogies' included in the Brhadāranyaka it is traced back to the gods.[2] What distinguishes the Upanishads from other ancient expositions of philosophy is their exclusively mantic and mystical character. The gnomic element, as we have seen, is practically wanting. They are not concerned either with obligations, whether positive or negative, or with observations of human life or nature, except in so far as these can be interpreted in a mystical sense.[3]

It is obvious that this philosophy has much in common with the ancient European expositions of wisdom noticed in Vol. I. Both the Norse and the earliest Greek examples contain mantic elements. In the

---

[1] In Çat. Br. v. 5. 5. 14 it is stated that magic may be practised by a certain offering; and it is added that by this means Āruni bewitched Bhadrasena, son of Ajātaçatru. It would seem then that the leading sage of his time cultivated witchcraft.

[2] These genealogies are introduced symmetrically after the second, fourth and sixth parts of the Upanishad. It is not clear to us whether in each case they apply to all that has gone before, or only to some particular doctrine.

[3] It is not to be assumed of course that this philosophy, though evidently much cultivated in the Vedic schools, was the only type current in ancient India. Much evidence to the contrary is to be found in the epics. We may note in particular the uncompromisingly materialistic doctrine of Jābāli in the Rāmāyana, II. 108, though it is doubtless introduced as sophistry. If Jābāli is to be identified with Satyakāma Jābāla, it is curious that the poet should have taken for this purpose the name of a man who seems to have been rather prominent in the Vedic schools, especially in the Upanishads. But there were other seers of this name.

former especially these are important; and they are associated with other elements which are certainly mystical, though they cannot be interpreted satisfactorily. But in both Norse and Greek the manticism is usually associated with gnomes of obligation. Closer analogies are perhaps to be traced in early Irish and Welsh records; but here any comparison is rendered difficult by the fact that, owing to textual corruption and other difficulties, the interpretation of these, especially the latter, is possible at present only to a very limited extent. We have also to take account of the fact that the records were not committed to writing until these peoples had long been Christian, though the 'philosophy' itself was probably in large measure an inheritance from earlier times. It is clear enough at all events that the Irish and British sages, the *fílid* and the bards, shared the feelings of the Indian gods in their love of the mysterious and dislike of what is evident. There can hardly be any doubt that they cultivated mysticism. Moreover some of the questions which are asked in the Welsh mystical poems seem to be rather similar to questions which are asked in the Upanishads. Indeed certain obscure passages seem rather to suggest a doctrine of transmigration[1]—which is always implied in the latter. On the other hand, these poems contain no gnomic elements, though gnomic poetry was cultivated in early Wales. In Ireland gnomic compositions are attributed to *fílid*, as well as to royal sages; but gnomic elements are not found, so far as we know, in association with mantic compositions.

Perhaps the best analogy to the Upanishads is to be found in the Irish 'Colloquy of the Two Sages' (cf. Vol. 1, p. 467). At least it has the advantage of being the best preserved and most intelligible of the compositions of this kind which are known to us. The milieu is mantic, and one at least of the competitors is an adept in spells and curses. The dialogue itself also is for the most part mystical in form. On the other hand it is to be observed that the contest is really one of skill in the use of words—rhetoric rather than philosophy. But we have seen that the Upanishads themselves frequently show a tendency in that direction. It is a tendency which is not unnatural in a tradition which was essentially academic.

We are under the impression that the literary genre to which the

---

[1] Either transmigration (metempsychosis) or transformation during life; cf. Vol. 1, p. 459. Evidence for metempsychosis is found in early Norse and Irish records, as well as in notices relating to the ancient Gauls, but, so far as we know, only in the form of the re-birth of one male (female) human being in another male (female) human being. Stress must be laid upon the fact that our information on this subject, though definite enough, is very limited.

Upanishads belong is very widespread, though in Europe, owing to the change of faith and other circumstances, it is represented only by fragments which are at best only partly intelligible. It is to be hoped that further light may be thrown upon the Welsh and Irish records when they have received more attention from those who are experts in the languages. At all events the little that we know of the Druids of ancient Gaul suggests that they cultivated speculations of this kind—on *rerum natura* and metempsychosis—apparently in some definite literary (poetic) form. There is, so far as we know, no evidence for the mantic contest among them; but this is found, in one or other variety of mantic lore, in Britain, Ireland, Norway, Finland and Greece—in short whereever any considerable traces of native (heathen) learning have been preserved.

In Vol. I, p. 471, we described the Welsh and Irish compositions of which we have been speaking as 'declarations of mantic lore'; but they are very near akin to prophecy. The Upanishads, both the speeches and the rest of the matter, may, we think, be described as prophecy—not relating to specific persons or events, and not relating to past, present or future, but as 'timeless nameless' prophecy. We can hardly apply this description to the Welsh and Irish compositions; for in these the speaker, who seems usually to be a seer, speaks in the first person. But the difference is perhaps more apparent than real.

A word may be said here with regard to prophecy of general reference which relates definitely to the future. In the Irish 'Colloquy' Ferchertne's last speech describes at length the evils which are to come at some future time—famine, lawlessness, moral depravity, disorganisation of society, etc. We have not seen any instances of this type in the Vedas, Brāhmanas or Upanishads; but they occur in the Mahābhārata. In III. clxxxviii and again *ib.* cxc the immortal seer Markandeya gives to Yudhishthira a description of the *Kali*-Age, which rather closely corresponds to Ferchertne's speech even in details. The two passages (clxxxviii and cxc) would seem to be variants; and in both cases the description is introduced with a short account of the Four Ages (cf. p. 546). In the former version the Four Ages are treated as recurrent phenomena, and the last of the four (*Kali*) ends in an elemental catastrophe, which is described in some detail; the world is destroyed by fire and flood.[1] But the second version is concerned only with the next

---

[1] In this version the catastrophe ends in a universal flood, perhaps suggested by the story of Manu, which immediately precedes it (III. 187). Markandeya alone

coming *Kali*-Age in the future. In this case the elements seem to produce merely havoc, not complete destruction. It may be observed that the evil age of the Irish Colloquy leads up to the Day of Judgement, though there is nothing particularly strange in that, since the work dates, in its present form at least, from Christian times. But it is a much more curious fact that in the heathen Völuspá also the destruction of the world by fire and flood is preceded by a time of moral depravity.[1] Here, however, the elemental catastrophe is part of the story of Ragnarök.

Lastly, it may be added that 'prophecy' of specific reference relating to the present is not unknown in the Mahābhārata. Thus in III. lxxii Rtuparna, who is a king, not a Brahman, has the faculty of instantaneous counting; and he states correctly the number of leaves and fruits upon a certain tree, which he passes in his chariot. This is the faculty by which the Greek seer Mopsos overcame and brought death to Calchas, his rival (cf. Vol. I, p. 474). We may note that Rtuparna's faculty includes calculation at dice and that he is able to transfer this to Nala in exchange for the latter's faculty of swift driving.

In spite of the comparative rarity of prophecy in the ordinary sense, i.e. as relating to the future, there can be no doubt as to the very great importance of manticism in general in the early history of Indian literature. In the above short sketch it has been possible only to touch upon a few points. There is one question, however, which perhaps ought not to be passed over wholly in silence, viz. the relation between spell and prayer. The same word (*brahma*) is in general use for both of these; and it is not always easy to determine whether a given poem should be regarded as one or the other. The prevalent view seems to be that prayer belongs in the main to the earliest period, and that in course of time it was largely displaced and superseded by the spell. This view has in its favour that spells form the bulk of the Atharvaveda, whereas they are not numerous in the Rgveda, except in Book X, the latest part of the collection. It is also in accord with the supreme importance attached to ritual in the Brāhmanas, where the efficacy of the sacrifice

survives and is swallowed by Vishnu, who appears to him in the form of a child. The episode as a whole affords a good illustration of the process of accretion, which seems to be especially noticeable in the non-heroic elements contained in Book III.

[1] These passages also have frequently been explained as due to (direct or indirect) Christian influence. But the evidence is by no means convincing. We may refer to the doctrine attributed to the Druids by Strabo (cf. Vol. I, p. 328).

seems to depend on this rather than on the will of the deity to whom it is offered.

The second argument is doubtless valid, so far as the priestly tradition is concerned. The first, however, perhaps requires some qualification. The Atharvaveda is clearly a later collection than the Rgveda; but it does not follow that the matter contained in it is necessarily later. All that can be inferred with confidence is that in the circles by whom the poems of the Rgveda were preserved spells were not at first esteemed as highly as invocations of the gods. Moreover there is another consideration to be taken into account. We have seen that the hymns to certain deities, especially those to Agni and Soma, which are extremely numerous, often consist largely of descriptions of the way in which (e.g.) fire is produced or the Soma prepared. It is difficult to avoid the suspicion that the original invocations of these deities were properly spells. Indeed the spell-form seems to be preserved in such expressions as 'Soma, flow on', which are of very frequent occurrence. If so, spells must be of very great antiquity in India; and in this connection it may be noted that the cult of Soma (Haoma) existed among the ancient Iranians also. We see no reason for doubting that the spell is at least as old as the prayer. It would appear to have been less honoured than the latter in early times; but questions other than those of chronology may here be involved. A large proportion of the hymns of the Rgveda were clearly composed for sacrifices offered on behalf of princes, whereas the later literature is of more exclusively priestly interest. In any case, however, it seems likely that the appearance of priestly deities such as Agni, Soma, Brhaspati and Prajāpati, and the greater importance attached to ritual and spell mark phases in the development of priestly power.

CHAPTER XI

THE TEXTS

IN a literature which has been so much dependent upon oral tradition as that of ancient India the history of the texts is of course a subject of very great importance. To deal with it satisfactorily would require far more knowledge of both the literature and the language than we possess. But it is impossible to pass it over in silence in a book like this. We shall therefore venture a few observations on the subject in relation to the Rgveda, the early Upanishads and the Mahābhārata. We are aware that the Brāhmanas are at least as important as any of these for the study of textual tradition; but we dare not attempt to deal with them.

I. It has already been mentioned that the text of the Rgveda was fixed at a very early date and that practically no variants (in individual passages) are known. It has also been mentioned that much of the contents of the collection, both whole poems and individual stanzas, have been preserved also in other Vedas. More than nine-tenths of the Sāmaveda are to be found in the Rgveda; and the Atharvaveda also shares a very large amount of its contents with it. In these cases the same uniformity of text does not prevail. Thus in the Atharvaveda, while many poems (especially in Book xx) are identical throughout with poems in the Rgveda, many more show a greater or less amount of difference, sometimes in whole stanzas, sometimes in the wording of sentences. Much of the matter contained in Book xviii is found also in the funeral hymns in Book x of the Rgveda; but the arrangement differs greatly. Stanzas which belong to one hymn in the Rgveda are found in different hymns in the Atharvaveda, and vice versa.

It is the general opinion now, we believe, that wherever the Rgveda differs from the other Vedas, in passages which are obviously of common origin, the former has almost always the better text. At all events this is the case with the Atharvaveda, in which the common elements are thought to have undergone a large amount of change. Formerly some scholars held that the Sāmaveda often preserves a better text than the Rgveda; but we do not think that this view is now maintained.

The rigidity with which the text of the Rgveda was preserved, and which was doubtless bound up with its sanctity, can be traced back to very early times, probably not later than the seventh century (B.C.). But there is evidence that a freer treatment once prevailed. Though variants in individual passages are wanting, there are passages and even whole poems which are obviously variants of one another. The latter seem not to be of frequent occurrence. As an illustration we may take IX. 104 f. Both of these poems are hymns to Soma, each containing six stanzas. It will be sufficient to take three of these in each case.

No. 104 may be translated as follows:[1] (st. 1) "Friends, sit down; sing to him who is being purified (i.e. strained). Adorn him (Soma) as a child with sacrifices to grace him....(st. 5) Thou, Soma,[2] lord of our exhilarations, art the sustenance of the gods. As friend to friend be most attentive to (our) welfare. (st. 6) Put utterly away from us every devouring demon; defend us from him who is godless and treacherous, and from distress."

With this may be compared No. 105: (st. 1) "Sing to him, friends, who is being purified for your exhilaration. As a child they are gladdening him with sacrifices, with hymns....(st. 5) Thou, Soma, lord of our yellow (liquors) (art) the best sustenance of the gods. As friend to friend be gracious to men for (granting) their wishes. (st. 6) (Drive) utterly away from us every godless, devouring (foe). Victorious, Soma, thou shalt drive away[3] him who is treacherous." The stanzas (2–4) which have been omitted show about the same amount of variation.

Sometimes the parallelism between two poems does not continue throughout. One or more stanzas may be independent. Thus in IV. 13 f., hymns to Agni, each of which contains five stanzas, there is an obvious relationship between the two in st. 1 and 2, very similar to what we have just noticed. But st. 3 and 4 in each poem seem to be independent. The last stanza (5) in both is identical. It may be observed here that in Book IV hymns to the same deity frequently have a common final stanza, even when they are otherwise independent.

We are under the impression that single stanzas of common origin, though not (as in the last case) identical, are of fairly frequent occurrence. But we are not sufficiently familiar with the text to give sure examples. The resemblance may often be due to independent use of

---

[1] These passages have been translated as literally as possible. A better translation of No. 104 will be found in E. J. Thomas, *Vedic Hymns*, p. 75 f.

[2] The word used here (as frequently) is *indu*, 'juice' (of the soma plant), lit. 'drop'.

[3] This seems to be the meaning of the traditional text; but it involves the use of a verbal form which, we believe, many modern scholars will not allow.

traditional motifs and diction. For instances we may refer to I. 116–19, which consist in the main of catalogues of benefits conferred by the Açvins upon their various favourites. There are many resemblances; but we are not certain that any of the stanzas are, strictly, of common origin. The poets seem rather to be drawing upon a common store of poetic tradition.

Those who have made a study of the Rgveda could doubtless furnish better examples of parallelism than those which we have given above. These, however, are sufficient to show that the freedom with which the Atharvan poets treated the poems of the Rgveda is not to be regarded as an innovation. The text of the Rgveda itself gives evidence that it had not possessed rigidity from the beginning—that there had been a time when it was treated with the same freedom as the poetry of other oral literatures. The freedom shown by the parallels noticed above is of course much less than what is found in Yugoslav poetry (cf. p. 413 ff., above); but it is quite similar to some of the illustrations given from early Norse poetry in Vol. I, Ch. XVIII. The parallelism in IV. 13 f. is about the same as that between the opening stanzas of the Hamðismál and the Guðrúnarhvöt (*ib.* p. 515 f.).

II. In the earlier Upanishads recurrences of short passages—covering a few lines—are not at all infrequent. But we will confine our attention to examples of the recurrence of a complete scene or 'lesson' (*brāhmana*), where a dialogue is recounted or a doctrine stated in full.

First we will take two scenes from the Brhadāranyaka, II. 4 and IV. 5, which are for the most part practically identical. In the latter, though not in the former, there is a short introduction stating that Yājnavalkya had two wives, one of whom, named Maitreyī, was able to discuss intellectual subjects,[1] while the other was not. He is now about to retire to the forest for good. He tells Maitreyī of his intention—II. 4 begins at this point—and says that he will make a settlement for her and his other wife. She proceeds to question him on the subject of immortality; and he replies with a discourse upon the soul (*ātman*) and *brahma*. The differences between the two scenes are very slight and hardly more than verbal, though a few sentences found in IV. 5 are wanting in II. 4. The conclusion of the discourse is also wanting in the latter. In spite of these slight differences it cannot but strike the modern reader as remarkable that these two scenes have been preserved in the same work—a work of

[1] The word is *brahmavādin*, lit. 'speaking of mantic knowledge, power', etc.; cf. p. 585 f.

no very great length. Were they written down independently from different traditions? Or were they both preserved by the same tradition in the Upanishad before it was committed to writing?

Next we may take Brhadāranyaka VI. 1 and Chāndogya V. 1. These are two versions of a lesson on the functions of the senses or organs of sense—breath, speech, eye, ear, mind and (only in Brhad.) seed (or procreation). The lesson begins with a short series of mantic gnomes. Then the senses dispute as to which is the best of them. They appeal to Brahma (Brhad.) or Father Prajāpati (Chānd.) to decide; and he replies that it is the one whose absence will be most felt by the body. Then they all go away in turns, but find that they cannot subsist without breath. Except in a few points such as have been instanced, the two versions are substantially identical; but the Chāndogya is expressed more briefly throughout.

Parallel versions are again to be found in Brhad. VI. 2 and Chānd. V. 3. This scene is a dialogue. Çvetaketu, son of Āruni (cf. p. 504 f.) attends an assembly of the Pancāla and meets a prince named Pravāhana Jaibali, who asks him if he has been instructed by his father. He replies that he has. Then the prince asks him a number of questions—relating chiefly to the life after death. The questions are substantially the same; but Brhadāranyaka has one more than Chāndogya, followed by a quotation of poetry; Çvetaketu cannot answer a single question. Then the prince in Chāndogya asks him how he can say that he has been instructed; in Brhadāranyaka he invites him to stop with him. But in both versions he runs off to his father and either implicitly (Brhad.) or explicitly (Chānd.) blames him for not having given him sufficient instruction. He repeats the prince's questions to his father; and the latter confesses implicitly (Brhad.) or explicitly (Chānd.) that he could not answer them himself. Then Āruni, who is described as Gautama in both versions, sets off to see the prince himself. The prince receives him respectfully and offers him presents; but he says that he has not come for a present but to learn what the prince had spoken of to his son. The details here are different. Thus in Brhadāranyaka Āruni says that he is very well off and, later, that he comes as a student—and remains as such. In Chāndogya these details are omitted; but it is stated that Āruni makes his request to the prince on the day after his reception. After some hesitation, which is differently expressed in the two versions, the prince begins to instruct him. In the instructions which follow the differences between the two versions are in part about as great as those noticed above, in part somewhat greater. The Chāndogya is here the fuller of the two.

A somewhat similar dialogue is to be found in Brhad. II. 1 and Kaush. IV. 1. There was a learned man called in Brhadāranyaka Drptabālāki Gārgya, but in Kaushītaki Gārgya Bālāki. The latter enumerates the kingdoms he used to visit. He offers to speak on Brahma to King Ajātaçatru of Kāçi, who (evidently pleased) promises to reward him handsomely, saying that people will run to him and call him a Janaka. Gārgya specifies a series of objects and natural phenomena—the sun, moon, wind, fire, etc.—in which there is a person whom he worships (Brhad. adds 'as Brahma'); and the king comments upon each of them. The Kaushītaki has a longer series than the Brhadāranyaka, and the wording of the speeches is not the same; indeed the king's comments are in some cases substantially different. When Gārgya has finished, the king says he is dissatisfied. Then Gārgya asks to become his student. The king then takes him to a man who is asleep, and discourses on the nature of sleep. Here the parallelism between the versions is less close than before; and the differences become greater, until at the end there is nothing in common.

Another instance of parallelism between the Brhadāranyaka (VI. 3) and Chāndogya (V. 2. 4 ff.) is to be found in the spell[1] which was noticed in the last chapter (p. 578). Here the resemblance is less close than in the cases noted above, and the Chāndogya version is much abbreviated.

We have taken our illustrations from three of the earliest Upanishads. It is generally agreed that the Brhadāranyaka and the Chāndogya are the earliest of all. Dates of course cannot be assigned with any certainty; but there seems to be a general disposition to attribute both of these works to the sixth century, the Brhadāranyaka to the beginning or at least the first half of it. Now some scholars hold that by this time writing was already in use for literary purposes. It is possible therefore that the Upanishads, as complete works, were written down from the beginning. But in any case the existence of such variants as those which have been noted above seems to us to make it clear that they are composed of elements, including complete lessons and dialogues, which had been preserved by oral tradition. Unfortunately it seems to be impossible to determine how long they had been thus preserved[2] or how

[1] A similar spell occurs in the Kaushītaki (cf. p. 579); but we are not clear as to its relationship to this.

[2] It is to be observed that the Brāhmanas have elements in common with the Upanishads, and the former are in general older than the latter. An instance occurs in Brhad. III. 9, part of which is to be found also in Çat. Br. VII. 6. 3 (cf. p. 584). The Brhadāranyaka is a continuation of this Brāhmana, but is believed to be somewhat later.

long the interval was between the time of the characters of the dialogues and that of the (complete) Upanishads. But we may note that the circulation of the lessons and dialogues noticed above was not confined to any one school. The Brhadāranyaka belonged to the school of the White Yajurveda, the Chāndogya to that of the Sāmaveda, and the Kaushītaki to that of the Rgveda.

III. The Mahābhārata abounds in variants. Indeed repetition in one form or another is responsible to no small extent for the size of the work. But the differences are as a rule much greater than those we have discussed above.

The work begins (1. i. 1–21) with a short account of the arrival of Sauti (Ugraçravas son of Lomaharshana) at the sacred Naimisha forest, where many seers are gathered together to take part in the sacrifice held by Kulapati Çaunaka. The seers ask him where he has been; and he tells them he has been present at the great snake-sacrifice of King Janamejaya, where he has listened to the stories of the Mahābhārata composed by Vyāsa. He then asks them if they would like to hear a recitation of Puranic lore; and they reply that they would prefer a recitation of the Mahābhārata, just as it was recited by Vaiçampāyana at Vyāsa's direction. Then, after a short introduction dealing with cosmology, he describes how the work was composed by Vyāsa and written down by Ganesha, and from this passes on to an account of the contents of the work. This again is followed (1. iii) by an account of the circumstances which led to Janamejaya's sacrifice, which is interspersed with stories of the seers who lived in his time.

In 1. iv again we hear of Sauti in the Naimisha forest. He offers to give a recitation, and asks the seers what they wish to hear. They reply that Kulapati Çaunaka is busied with sacrificial duties; when he returns he will decide. Çaunaka asks for the history of the Bhrgu family, which Sauti thereupon proceeds to relate (1. v–xii). From this he passes on, at Çaunaka's request, to the story of Janamejaya's sacrifice and the history of the snakes, which leads to it (1. xiii–lviii). Then, in response to a further request from Çaunaka, he describes (1. lix f.) Vyāsa's arrival at the snake sacrifice and the recitation of the Mahābhārata by Vaiçampāyana. There is no reference to Ganesha or the writing of the work. After this (1. lxi) Sauti begins to repeat Vaiçampāyana's recitation of the story.

Even in this introductory section of the work (1. i–lx) there are a number of other instances of repetition, with more or less variation.

Sometimes a story is repeated in the form of a speech—for which of course analogies are to be found in the narrative poetry of other peoples. Thus the account of Parīkshit's death given in I. xl ff. is repeated, more briefly in a speech made by the king's ministers to his son in I. xlix f. But there are other cases where in a modern work such repetition would certainly be due to mere oversight, e.g. the descriptions of Jaratkaru's vision of his ancestors in I. xiii and I. xlv f. The differences between the two accounts are quite slight.

Similar repetitions are to be found frequently enough in other parts of the work. An interesting example occurs in VII. lv ff. and XII. xxix ff. In the former passage the story is told by Vyāsa to Yudhishthira, to comfort him for the death of Abhimanyu. It is as follows: Nārada and Parvata are staying with a king of old named Srnjaya. They are both smitten with love of the king's daughter. Nārada asks for her in marriage, and the king assents; but Parvata is angered and curses him, saying he shall not go to heaven when he wishes. Nārada replies that Parvata shall not go to heaven without him. Then the Brahmans of the place beg Nārada to grant the king a son; and he grants him one who can produce gold in various ways, which need not here be specified. The king now becomes extremely rich. But the child is killed by robbers; and the king's wealth disappears, and he is overwhelmed with grief. To comfort him Nārada gives him a long account of many famous kings who died in spite of their greatness and generosity. To this list we have already referred (p. 543). Then (VII. lxxi) Nārada restores the child to life.

The account of this story given in XII. xxix ff. is considerably shorter, and the matter is differently arranged. The reciter is at first Krshna, who is trying to console Yudhishthira for the loss of all his friends who have been killed in the battle. The story in this case begins with Nārada's speech to Srnjaya, comforting him for the loss of his son. The list of kings varies slightly from the previous account. At its conclusion Nārada promises to restore the child to life; but he mentions that the child had been granted to the king by Parvata, who has not been referred to up to this point. Then Yudhishthira asks Krshna why Parvata had granted the child to Srnjaya. Krshna replies that Nārada and Parvata, who were uncle and nephew, had left heaven for a journey on the earth, and had made a compact that they would keep no secrets from one another. The rest of this story, down to Parvata's departure, has been summarised briefly on p. 537. At this point Nārada himself comes to see Yudhishthira and continues the story. The gold-producing child is born, as in the other version; but here it is killed by a tiger, which in reality is the thunder-weapon in disguise, sent by Indra out of jealousy. The king is overcome by grief, but thinks of Nārada, who at once appears and after recounting the stories of the kings, restores the child to life.

Another, rather more complex story may be found in I. iii. 85 ff. and, somewhat more fully, in XIV. lvi ff. The latter account is as follows: A seer named Uttanka serves his teacher with great devotion until he reaches old age. His teacher, who is simply called Gautama, restores his youth and gives him his daughter in marriage. At his departure he wishes to give his teacher a reward. The teacher will not accept anything; but his wife asks Uttanka to get her the earrings of King Saudāsa's queen. Saudāsa is a cannibal—to whom we have had to refer before (p. 500) under the name Kalmāshapāda—but Uttanka sets out and meets him in a wood. The king wants to eat him at once; but he persuades him first to let him carry out his duty to his teacher. He begs the earrings from the queen, who gives them up when she ascertains that this is the king's wish; but she warns Uttanka never to let them touch the ground. This happens, however, when he is gathering some fruit; and a snake immediately carries them off into the ground. He digs in vain with his stick; but Indra appears, disguised as a Brahman, and imparts the force of thunder to the stick. By this means he penetrates into the world of the Nagas. There he meets a black horse, which tells him to blow into it. It explains that it is Agni, the fire-god, and it fills the home of the Nagas with fire and smoke. Then the Nagas, with Vasuki their chief, come out to propitiate him, and give him back the earrings, which he now takes safely to his teacher's wife.

In I. iii the story has quite a different setting. Uttanka's teacher is here called Veda; he is a friend of King Janamejaya and of a king called Paushya. When he offers to reward his teacher, on leaving him, it is the earrings of King Paushya's queen that the teacher's wife asks for. The main features of the story as told above recur here; but this version contains also many other incidents, which we must pass over. Paushya is not a cannibal, though Uttanka finds him difficult to deal with. The queen, however, gives him the earrings. Then they are stolen by a beggar, who, when chased by Uttanka, proves to be Takshaka, king of the snakes or Nagas, in disguise. Indra sends his thunderbolt to open a way through the ground; and what follows is much the same as in the other version, though there are a number of additional incidents. When Uttanka has handed over the earrings in safety to his teacher and bidden him farewell, he determines to have his revenge upon Takshaka. So he sets off for Hastinapura to stir up king Janamejaya to exact vengeance from the snakes for his father's death.

The different versions of this story have some interest as illustrating the freedom with which non-heroic stories can change their associations. If *Saudāsa* represents a real man, he must have lived many generations before Janamejaya. As a matter of fact in XIV. liii ff., just before the beginning of the first of the versions summarised above, Uttanka is brought into contact with Krshna—which refers him to a third period, intermediate between the other two. He figures also in another story (III. cc ff.), which seems to have no datable associations.

Repetitions such as we have noted above are by no means confined to narratives. They are to be found also in didactic passages. An instance may be seen in the discourses of Markandeya contained in III. clxxxviii, cxc. In both cases a brief account of the 'Four Ages' is followed by a long description of the evils which characterise the end of the Kali Age, though the conclusions are different and apparently under the influence of different doctrines. We may also refer to the two genealogies of the Kuru line contained in I. xciv f., the differences between which are very remarkable.

In the heroic portions of the work such repetitions are less obvious; they have been welded together so as to form a continuous narrative. They may be traced, however, sometimes without much difficulty, especially perhaps in battle scenes. As an instance we may cite VIII. iii–x, where a whole series of incidents are repeated—the appointment of Karna as commander, Duryodhana's speech on the occasion, Karna's fall, and Dhrtarāshtra's collapse on hearing the news. Indeed the principle must be deeply embedded in the structure of the main story as a whole. We may note the constant recurrence of scenes in which the older members of the court try to dissuade the king from giving way to his sons. It is hardly possible that so much repetition can have found place in a single heroic poem of entertainment (Type A). As in the cases noticed above, it is probably due largely to the incorporation of different versions.

It is in this way too that the repetition of motifs may most easily be explained. The question need not be discussed at length; for we can hardly get beyond conjecture in such a case. One example must therefore suffice. Three times in their career the heroes are found exiled or home-less in the forest. It is perhaps an integral part of the story that they were brought up there. But the other two incidents—their flight to the forest in I. clii ff. and their exile in III. i ff.—may originally have belonged to different versions of the story. The Rāmāyana provides a parallel in the two ordeals undergone by the unfortunate Sītā. It may be observed that the Mahābhārata has only one incident (III. ccxc) corresponding to these; and this is hardly an ordeal in the ordinary sense.

Something ought perhaps to be said here with regard to elements—scenes and dialogues—which are common to the Mahābhārata and Upanishads. But we have not the knowledge to deal with the subject; there may be intermediaries which are unknown to us. We may call attention, however, to the story of Naciketas, son of Uddālaka Āruni,[1] and his visit to the home of Yama, which is found in XIII. lxxi and in the Katha Upanishad, I. 1 ff. The resemblance is practically limited to the introduction in each case. The home of the dead in the former is a material Paradise, which is to be attained by generosity. The latter is a discussion of *ātman* and *brahma*, such as is usual in the Upanishads.

[1] The introduction to the Upanishad describes him as son of Vājacravas; but he is called son of Uddālaka Āruni in the poetry (I. 11). This story is preserved also in the Taittirīya Brāhmana, which has not been accessible to us.

CHAPTER XII

RECITATION AND COMPOSITION
THE AUTHOR

THERE can be no doubt, as we have seen, that oral tradition is involved in all the literature which we have had under discussion —Vedas, Brāhmanas, Upanishads and Mahābhārata. But the oral tradition varies much in character. In the Rgveda we find memorisation in the strictest form, whereas very great freedom seems to have been allowed in the Mahābhārata. In the Upanishads, and perhaps also the Brāhmanas, the treatment of the text seems to be intermediate between these extremes. In the former the most striking feature is the retention of sections which are obvious doublets, a feature which occurs also in the Mahābhārata. It would seem that the matter had been allowed to accumulate without much effort in the way of redaction. As regards the Rgveda, however, we have noted that strict memorisation cannot have prevailed from the beginning, as shown by the existence of variants, both in other Vedas and even in the Rgveda itself. The treatment of the text presumably became more strict as the hymns grew in sanctity.

All this literature may be described as priestly, at least in the sense that they have been preserved by Brahmans. It is true that the Mahābhārata contains large elements, including the central story of the work, which are evidently of different origin. Some of these elements appear to come from the same sources as the Purānas, as we shall see later. But there is no sufficient reason for doubting that the earlier records, the Vedas, Brāhmanas and Upanishads, owe their origin, as well as their preservation, to Brahmans. The fact that their history has been bound up from the beginning with a learned class is probably responsible for their being preserved in a more original form and a more archaic type of language.

How then was the literature preserved? It is to be borne in mind that the whole of it seems to have been used either for liturgical or for didactic or edifying purposes. The Rgveda was regarded as a verbally inspired Bible, and every poem contained in it as a hymn addressed to some deity or deified object. To every poem was assigned as 'author' or perhaps rather as 'publisher', a seer, who was supposed to have 'seen' it, i.e. in our terminology to have had it revealed to him. Not seldom these 'authors' are supernatural beings themselves. The Sāma-veda is a 'hymn-book', collected mainly from the Rgveda. The Yajurveda may be called a 'prayer-book'. It is concerned with the formulae muttered by the Adhvaryu and his assistants, the priestly officials who attended to the manual side of the sacrifices. The Atharva-veda consists of prayers and spells intended chiefly for private or social occasions.

All these works may be regarded as liturgical in some sense. But they were also used for 'educational' purposes. Not only Brahmans but also princes who made any claim to learning or piety are said to know the Vedas. We do not know what this means in actual practice; but we suppose that some knowledge of the Rgveda at least is involved.

The Brāhmanas and Upanishads are didactic, not liturgical works. The former consist of directions for the liturgy; but the matter is largely in the nature of commentary, and they may fairly be regarded as manuals of instruction for liturgical purposes. The Upanishads consist of instructions or expositions of doctrine for non-liturgical purposes. In both cases the tradition was presumably educational. Many, if not all, of the seers or sages of the time were teachers; and the teaching was passed on from the teacher to his pupils. It is generally believed that a number of these works have had additions made to them; thus (e.g.) the con-cluding parts of the Aitareya Brāhmana and of the Brhadāranyaka Upanishad are believed to be later in date than the preceding parts. Moreover there is reason for thinking, as we have seen (p. 597 f.), that much of the matter contained in the Brāhmanas and Upanishads is older than the existing works. The persons who are cited as authorities and who figure in the debates belong to the past; and there is no need to doubt that in some form or other the tradition goes back to their times. We see no reason for doubting also that in this earlier period doctrines were enunciated in debates between seers, as well as in the relations of teacher and pupil.

The tradition of the Brāhamanas was obviously priestly (Brah-manical), and we do not see how the Upanishads can be separated from them. But it is clear from the debates that it was regarded as nothing very unusual for princes to become proficient in the learning of the latter; and consequently we must infer that they were not excluded from the educational system with which these were bound up. From certain passages in the Brāhmanas (e.g. Ait. Br. VII. 27 ff.) it would seem that kings sometimes intervened even in matters of ritual.

The Mahābhārata was doubtless preserved in a similar way, by the instructions of teacher to pupils. According to the account which it gives of itself it was composed by Vyāsa and taught by him to his pupil Vaiçampāyana. But it was not intended merely for private or 'academic' circulation. At Vyāsa's own request Vaiçampāyana recites it before King Janamejaya and a large company assembled for his snake-sacrifice (1. 61). Sauti also recites it to a large gathering of Brahmans, who are attending a sacrifice (1. 1 and 4). In v. 141 it is prophesied that Brahmans will tell the world of the great battle. We understand that such recitations are still given at festivals. It is to be remembered that the Mahābhārata comprises both entertaining and didactic or edifying matter. It claims (e.g. 1. i. 268 ff.; ii. 380; lxii. 16 ff.) to be equal or superior to the Vedas and to have the power of purifying from sins those who hear or read it; it ensures their prosperity in this life and their salvation hereafter. But we do not know whether these claims were admitted by scholars of the Vedic schools.

On the subject of recitation the evidence is abundant enough, though not so clear as might be wished. Thus the Brāhmanas deal at great length with various sacrifices, but we have not been able to form a satisfactory picture of the procedure. The number of priestly officials who took part in the great sacrifices was at least sixteen, and several of these had speaking parts. The Adhvaryu had to 'mutter' formulae of the Yajurveda, while the Hotar seems to have recited hymns from the Rgveda; and there were others to sing hymns from the Sāmaveda. We do not know to what extent instrumental music was in use. It is mentioned in the Çatapatha Brāhmana, XIII. 1. 5. 6, 4. 3. 5, in connection with the horse-sacrifice; but it would seem to be used only to accompany the verses in honour of the sacrificing king, who is praised with righteous kings of old.

The Mahābhārata is recited evidently without instrumental accompaniment by Sauti and Vaiçampāyana; and the same is true of the heroic and non-heroic stories which are said to be recited incidentally in the course of the work by the seer Markandeya and others. Yet there are a number of passages which at least suggest minstrelsy. Thus in I. ccxx. 15 Arjuna, while staying with Krshna, is awakened by the sounds of the lute (*vīnā*) and the panegyrics of the poets; and again in VII. lxxxiv. 22 the same hero is greeted with the sounds of musical instruments and eulogies. These passages point to the use of stringed instruments as an accompaniment to heroic panegyrics (Type D). And for earlier times the same usage is placed beyond doubt by a passage in the Çatapatha Brāhmana referred to above. It is there stated that at the time of the horse-sacrifice, but during the evening, a man of princely rank (*rājanya*) sings to the lute three stanzas which he has composed in honour of the sacrificing king, celebrating the battles which he has won. Minstrelsy (with the *vīṇā*) is also mentioned in the Chāndogya Upanishad, I. 7. 6, but the character of the poetry is not made clear.[1] Elegies or dirges in the Mahābhārata seem not be accompanied, if we may judge from XI. xvi ff.; but this is the case in other lands also. We have unfortunately not been able to find any satisfactory instances of the recitation of spells or of public recitations of heroic narrative poetry by professional reciters, though in the former case the negative evidence of such an extensive collection as the Atharvaveda suggests that the use of music was at least not general. To the latter subject we shall have to return later in the chapter.

On the subject of authorship we have little direct evidence. A number of poems in the Rgveda contain personal references to their authors (seers), which may be compared with the personal references in Hesiod's poems. But in later literature anything in the nature of Type E seems to be entirely wanting. Contemporary information as to the authors is also seldom, if ever, to be found. We can therefore discuss only the circles or classes of persons from which the works seem to be derived.

We shall confine our attention in general to the Rgveda and the Mahābhārata. Regarding the origin of the Brāhmanas and the Upanishads we think there is little to be said, at least by those who are not specialists. Some of these works have authors assigned to them by tradition. Thus the Aitareya Brāhmana is attributed to a certain Mahidāsa Aitareya,[2] who is mentioned in the Chāndogya Upanishad and elsewhere. But it is clear that most of these works, including the one in question, are collections of learning which have accumulated in the course of time; and Mahidāsa can hardly have been more than a 'redactor', or at most a collector. The Black Yajurveda is preserved in several different recensions, representing different schools; but its origin

[1] Instrumental music does not seem to be much cultivated by seers; but in Mahābh. IX. 54 the divine seer Nārada arrives with a lyre—which shows that it could not have been unknown. In Indra's abode minstrelsy and panegyrics are cultivated by the Gandharvas (III. 43. 18, 28; 44. 9; 46. 27).

[2] Cf. Keith, *Rigveda Brahmanas*, p. 28 f., where the evidence is discussed.

is unknown. The White Yajurveda seems to be a redaction of this, attributed by tradition to Yājnavalkya. We do not know the history of the Sāmaveda or of the Atharvaveda. The latter seems to be a collection of prayers and spells coming down from various ages, comparable in this respect with the Rgveda. But, unlike the Rgveda, it seldom records the names of either seers or princes, and consequently its history is more difficult to trace.

The Rgveda, even as a collection (*Samhitā*) must be much older than any of the existing Brāhmanas. The hymns, including those contained in Book x, the latest portion, are always treated as sacred. Very often they are interpreted in a mystical sense, which the authors themselves cannot have intended; but everywhere they are credited with 'verbal inspiration' in the strictest sense. Every hymn, as we have seen, is attributed to a seer, to whom it was believed to have been revealed. Sometimes indeed these 'seers' are deities and other supernatural beings; for poems (of Type B) which are speeches in character seem not to have been distinguished from poems (of Type E) in which an author speaks in his own person. Among other considerations which point to a long lapse of time we may note that the Rgveda contains but one reference to the caste-system, whereas in the Brāhmanas the four castes are frequently mentioned and there is no indication that the system was of recent growth. The solitary passage in the Rgveda (x. 90. 11 f.) seems from the context (cf. pp. 544, 549) to be an addition to the poem. Even more striking are the differences in political geography and in geographical outlook.

The origin of the Rgveda, as a collection, is believed to have been as follows. Books ii–viii are attributed to certain families of seers and are sometimes called 'Family-Books'. Book viii is supposed to be somewhat later than the rest of these. Book i consists of a considerable number of similar but smaller collections. Book ix contains only hymns to Soma, which are believed to have been taken from Books i–viii and brought together. Book x is held to be a later supplement, drawn from various sources. The language here is commonly of a somewhat later type than in the other Books.

In many, though not the majority, of the hymns the seer's name or that of his family is recorded. All the rest have had the names of seers attached to them in the learned tradition of later times. It is a difficult question to decide how far this tradition is to be trusted; for many of the attributions are obviously incredible. The natural tendency of a modern reader is to doubt the existence of a genuine tradition reaching back to the times when the hymns were composed and to regard the attributions in general as due to speculation or guesswork. There are, however, among the names a considerable number of whom little or nothing seems to be known elsewhere; and, though some of them are doubtless fictitious, the possibility of a genuine tradition should perhaps not be excluded in all cases.

In most of the 'Family-Books' the great majority of the hymns are attributed by tradition to the founder of the family himself. Thus in Book III, which is said to belong to the family of Viçvāmitra, out of sixty-two hymns all except thirteen are attributed to Viçvāmitra himself. Of these thirteen four are attributed to sons of that seer and three to the god Prajāpati. In Book IV, the book of Vāmadeva's family, all the hymns except three, out of fifty-eight, are attributed to Vāmadeva. In Book VI, the book of Bharadvāja's family, all except sixteen, out of seventy-five, are attributed to Bharadvāja, and most of these sixteen to descendants of that seer. In Book VII, the book of Vasishtha's family, all the hymns, a hundred and four in number, are attributed to Vasishtha. In Book II, the book of Bhrgu's family, or of that of Grtsamada, a descendant of Bhrgu,[1] out of forty-three hymns thirty-nine are attributed to Grtsamada and the rest to another of Bhrgu's descendants. In Books V and VIII, the books of the families of Atri and of Kanva, the tradition shows no such approach to uniformity. In Book V only a few hymns are attributed to Atri, and in Book VIII none to Kanva, though in both cases many of them are attributed to their descendants. But many others are attributed either to supernatural beings or to persons who are more or less clearly fictitious.

Next let us take the evidence of the hymns themselves. In Book VII the name *Vasishtha*, in the singular, occurs in twelve hymns, usually, if not always, with reference to the present, and apparently meaning the poet himself. In the plural it occurs in eleven hymns, again probably always with reference to the present. In two hymns (Nos. 23 and 33) the name occurs both in the singular and in the plural, and we do not understand the significance of the change of number. Does the singular mean 'a Vasishtha', or is the same person—the famous seer of Sudās' time—always meant? The person whose mythical birth is described in No. 33 (cf. p. 507) is presumably an ancestor of the poet, or perhaps his father.

The same difficulty occurs again in Book III, where most of the hymns are attributed by tradition to Viçvāmitra; but here the proper

[1] According to Mahābh. XIII. 30 Grtsamada was a son of Vītahavya, a king who fled to Bhrgu for protection and became a Brahman.

names are not so frequent. We find the name *Viçvāmitra*, both singular and plural, and also the family name *Kuçika* (plural) in III. 53. Elsewhere the name *Viçvāmitra* seems to occur only in one hymn (in the plural) and the name *Kuçika* (plural) in five hymns.

In Book IV, as we have seen, almost all the hymns are attributed by tradition to Vāmadeva; but in the hymns themselves this name seems to occur only once (IV. 16), in the singular. The family name *Gotama*[1] is also very rare; we have noticed only one example in the singular and one in the plural. In the former case (IV. 4) the poet speaks of Gotama as his father. In Book II the name *Gṛtsamada* occurs in four hymns, but only in the plural. In Book VI the name Bharadvāja occurs in six hymns as singular and in seven as plural. In both cases probably the majority—though not all—of the examples relate to the present. For this name we may refer also to what was said in Ch. IV (p. 506 f.).

From this it will be seen that the amount of direct evidence available from the poems themselves as to their origin varies greatly from Book to Book. There are of course other considerations to be taken into account, besides the use of proper names. Thus the majority—over two-thirds—of the hymns in Book VII have a characteristic ending, addressed to the gods: "Do ye preserve us ever with blessings." In Book IV there are recurrent final stanzas, especially in the hymns to Indra. These cases in themselves prove no more than that the poems have at one time belonged to the same repertoire. But they may be taken as examples of a class of evidence which requires consideration. Those who have devoted more time to the study of the poems than we have could probably cite more important instances.

It would be of interest to know whether the hymns contained in each book are contemporary with one another. Unfortunately references to (living) princes occur only in a minority of the hymns. But all those which occur in Book VII seem to belong to one period, so far as we can judge. The same remark seems to be true of most of such references which occur in Book III and in Book VI. The former belong to the same period as those in Book VII, the latter to a period apparently about two generations earlier. One poem in Book VI (No. 20) may be somewhat later than the others; and one in Book III (No. 23) would seem to be two or three generations earlier than the rest of those contained in this Book. The latter is of some interest if we are to credit the tradition that Viçvāmitra's family was royal, not priestly; for it would then appear

---

[1] This name occurs more frequently in Book I, especially in two groups of hymns attributed by tradition to Gotama himself and his son respectively.

that the priestly families incorporated earlier poems in their collections. In general, however, the references in these three books, so far as they go, tend to show that most of the poems contained in each of them date from one short period. We are not clear that the same is true of the other books. In the case of Book VIII we should doubt it. But we think this is a composite collection.

Perhaps the most striking fact disclosed by a survey of this kind is the antiquity of the priestly families. Some of them had an established position in the time of Sudās, one of them even in that of Divodāsa, probably two generations earlier, while others claimed a still more remote, though legendary ancestry. These families professed to have the power of obtaining from the gods by their invocations success, especially in battle, for the princes who employed them; and the great rewards which they received show that their claims were admitted. An analogy is to be found in Greek mantic families, such as the Iamidai, members of which were in much demand as divining priests in time of war, even down to the fifth century. The 'Family-Books' consist of collections of such invocations, many of which evidently date from the earliest times.

We have not the knowledge necessary for discussing the question how far the different collections have influenced one another. They consist of hymns addressed to the same deities, and they are arranged in the same order, though this may be due to subsequent 'editing'. There is also a close general resemblance in diction and in the treatment of the matter. But the resemblances in detail between individual poems in different collections seem to us to be hardly close enough to prove influence on a large scale. This may of course be due to insufficient acquaintance with the poems. If not, one must conclude that the forms of this poetry were fixed in very remote times.

In any case there can be no question that beside the royal families a spiritual aristocracy, powerful and wealthy, and provided with its own sacred literature, existed long before we have any evidence for a Brahman caste—some centuries previously, it would seem. This aristocracy had apparently no central organisation, apart from the families themselves. Neither were its foundations fixed locally; for we hear nothing of permanent sanctuaries in this period. The families or their heads were doubtless as a rule attached to the service of kings; for a priest could obtain the richest rewards by becoming a *purohita* or 'chaplain' to a king. But we hear in the Kaushītaki Brāhmana (cf. p. 500) of a deadly quarrel between Vasishtha and the sons of Sudās, and the

Mahābhārata records many such quarrels. It may also be noted that in the 'Family-Books' themselves there are to be found hymns composed on behalf of more than one dynasty. Thus in Book VII, No. 96 and perhaps also No. 5 seem to have been composed for Pūru. But a number of other hymns were certainly composed for Bharata (Trtsu). In No. 19 the two kings are associated; but Nos. 8 and 18 are definitely hostile to Pūru. Did Vasishtha transfer his allegiance to Pūru?

Another possibility ought to be taken into account, viz. that the activities of the priestly families were 'international'—as seems to have been the case with the Greek mantic families. A careful examination of Books I and VIII might produce evidence to this effect. Thus at the beginning of Book VIII there is a group of poems composed for Turvaça or Yadu—which are usually associated—by the family of Kanva. And in both Books there are other groups of poems, coming apparently from the same family, which may have been composed for princes of other dynasties, apart from possible cases of alliance, as in VIII. 8. But we have not sufficient knowledge to identify the names. It may be noted that very few poems in the Rgveda seem to have been composed for Turvaça or Yadu, while Anu and Druhyu are, so far as we know, not represented at all, though in one passage at least (VII. 18. 6) the family of Bhrgu is apparently identified with Anu. To the more easterly kingdoms—Kuru, Pancāla, Kāçī, Kosala, Videha—which are the most prominent in the Brāhmanas, the Upanishads and the Mahābhārata, there seems to be no reference in the Rgveda, apart from the hymn for Çamtanu (x. 98). Presumably they did not come into existence until towards the close of this period. Yet it is here that we find the representatives of the great priestly families in later times. The explanation may be that these kingdoms were offshoots of Bharata or Pūru. And —as against what has been said above—the presence of a family in both Bharata and Pūru may be explained in the same way; for in the antiquarian speculations of later times Bharata is a descendant of Pūru.

We have spoken only of the ancient priestly families. But it is to be remembered that there are hymns attributed to seers who did not belong to these families. Such is the case with the hymn to which we have just referred, x. 98, the 'seer' of which (Devāpi) is said to have been a relative of King Çamtanu (cf. p. 509). The hymn is of importance as showing that at the end of the Rgveda period the priesthood was still open to members of royal families. In the learned tradition some hymns are even ascribed to kings, e.g. Trasadasyu; but such evidence perhaps need not be taken too seriously, since seers and kings seem to be confused not unfrequently. It is curious, however, that in later times Viçvāmitra is regularly said to have been a king; for it was hardly in accordance with the principle of the caste system to invent transfers from the Kshatriya to the Brahman caste. The Rgveda itself apparently gives no information as to Viçvāmitra's origin; but his royal position seems to be implied in the poetry quoted in the Aitareya Brāhmana, VII. 18.[1] We may also note here that the use of the name *Bhṛgu* for *Anu* in Rgv. VII. 18 (cf. p. 611) rather suggests that the former were regarded as belonging to the royal family of Anu.

This evidence is not very satisfactory; but it is probable in itself that before the caste system became fixed the priesthood was largely recruited from the ruling families. In later times we hear not unfrequently of the 'royal seer' (*Rājarṣi*), who was not a priest. But by now the caste system was fixed and regarded as eternal. The seer of the Rgveda is a priest, who takes part in the sacrifice. But there is nothing, so far as we know, to show that he could not be of royal origin. Analogous conditions seem to have prevailed among the Druids of Ireland. Our information regarding these persons is unfortunately very meagre. But they sometimes belonged to royal families, as did Cathbad; and sometimes the 'profession' tended to become hereditary (cf. Vol. I, p. 612).

The Mahābhārata contains both Brahmanical (priestly) and non-Brahmanical elements; but first we will consider the former. Among these are many long disquisitions upon doctrine or law, which need not be discussed here. We will confine our attention to (non-heroic) stories of seers and kings, such as were noticed in Ch. IV. These stories are very numerous and extend from the earliest times to the period of the seers who figure in the Upanishads.

With regard to these stories two features may be noted at once. In the first place the caste system is postulated throughout, as existing from the earliest times. Secondly, nearly all the stories which relate to early times—the period of the Rgveda and earlier—have one common motif, viz. the superiority of the Brahman to the Kshatriya caste. In stories relating to later times—the period of Janamejaya and that of the seers of the Upanishads—this motif seldom or never appears. Now the general impression one gets from the Brāhmanas and Upanishads is that by this time the relations of the castes had become settled, and the Brahman was recognised as possessing privileges which he could interpret as signifying his superiority. But the stories in the Mahābhārata which relate to

<hr/>

[1] Cf. Keith, *Rigveda Brahmanas*, pp. 66 f., 308 (note 8).

earlier times are very frequently occupied with a struggle for mastery between members of the two castes. No doubt there were at all times reckless and impious princes who were ready to insult and injure Brahmans. But the constant recurrence of this motif in the stories can hardly be explained by such sporadic cases. It seems rather to reflect the conditions of a time when the claims and privileges of the Brahman were not yet generally recognised.

We do not mean that the stories preserve a faithful historical record of the conditions of the Rgveda period. The Brahman is described as a poor man, possessing perhaps only a single cow. The more important characters are always ascetics, living in the forest. But the priests of the Rgveda, often the same persons, must have been wealthy; and we hear nothing of asceticism or of life in the forest.[1] We mean that stories relating to the Rgveda period, distorted and perhaps often fictitious, were current in the times between the end of that period and the reign of Janamejaya, and that owing to the growing claims of the Brahmans they assumed a certain colouring, which is reflected in the Mahābhārata.

As an illustration we may take first the story of Yayāti and his wives (cf. p. 498 f.), which relates to primeval times. This story is complicated by an antiquarian motif, which is quite distinct from, and probably earlier than, the Brahmanic, with which we are now concerned. But the contention between the wives turns wholly upon the question of superiority, as between Brahman and Kshatriya. More frequently we meet with a trial of strength between a seer (Brahman) and a prince. The latter insults the former, or injures him by force majeure; but in the end the power of the Brahman proves to be greater. Examples of this may be seen in the dealings between Vasishtha and Viçvāmitra, before the latter became a seer, and again in those between Vasishtha and King Kalmāshapāda (cf. p. 500), and so also in the story of Vāmadeva and the impious kings (p. 499).

In such stories the power of the Brahman is of course at first sight far inferior to that of the prince. He is generally a poor man, and lives by begging. But, as in the case of the Irish *fili*, his requests must not be refused, however extravagant they may be. If he cares to make use of his powers, especially his curse, he can disable or ruin his opponent in any way he wishes. We may refer to the Apsarasas who were transformed into crocodiles (cf. p. 581). Some seers have attained such

---

[1] In the Upanishads seers sometimes retire to the forest at a certain age. But little is said about asceticism, so far as we have observed. Sometimes they are evidently very well off, as in the case of Uddālaka Āruni (Brhad. VI. 2. 7).

power by their asceticism that even the gods live in dread of them. But the Brahman can do benefits, as well as injuries. This side of his power appears perhaps most often in the granting of offspring. One of the most frequently recurring motifs in the Mahābhārata is that of the prince who cannot obtain children by his own efforts. Sometimes, as in the case of Bhīma of Vidarbha (III. liii), the Brahman can grant them apparently merely by his blessing; but at other times he plays a more active part, as in the stories of Kalmāshapāda (I. clxxix) and Vicitravīrya. Occasionally he produces them forthwith from the altar of sacrifice, as in the case of Drupada's children (I. clxix).

The essential feature of the doctrine is that the prince is helpless without the Brahman, just as in the long run he is powerless to oppose or injure him. The doctrine naturally involved a change in the relations between the two. In the Rgveda the seer is an intermediary between the prince and the gods, and owes his influence to this position. But now he is himself the object of reverence and devotion. The pious prince is one who honours the Brahmans. In principle the gods have become superfluous.

It would seem that in practice princes continued to worship Indra and the other ancient deities. The Brahmans, however, had apparently come to regard Indra as a kind of divine Kshatriya; and the slaying of Vrtra is represented as Brahmanicide, the worst of all possible crimes. At an earlier date, before—though probably not long before—the close of the Rgveda period they had invented a god of their own, Prajāpati, superior to Indra. Yet they do not appear to have attached any great importance to orthodoxy in their theology. The extreme attention to formalism which we find in the Brāhmanas is balanced by great freedom of speculation in the Upanishads.

The existence of the Brahman caste[1] is perhaps what constitutes the chief difference between ancient India and the early civilisations of Europe. In ancient Europe also there were peoples among whom the intellectual element succeeded in establishing its ascendancy over the military. We may instance the Gauls. But the Druids did not form a caste; they were drawn, at least in part, from what would in India be called the Kshatriya. In other respects—the forest life, the educational activity, the character of the speculations, and perhaps also the attention which they gave to the law—there are close resemblances between the

[1] For the other castes—Kshatriya, Vaiçya, Çūdra—European analogies are by no means wanting. Sometimes, as among the Old Saxons, intermarriage was prohibited.

two cases. But the Druids of Gaul, unlike the Brahmans, had a centralised organisation.

It is doubtless due to the dominant position of the Brahmans that the whole of Indian literature which has survived from before Buddhist times has been preserved by them. They had not a monopoly of intellectual life. That is clear from the intellectual princes who figure in the Upanishads, and who seem to have been fairly numerous. But apparently, like the Druids, they had all education in their hands; and it is to educational tradition that we are wholly or almost wholly indebted for the preservation of ancient Indian literature.

The value of the Brahmanical elements in the Mahābhārata lies in the fact that they reflect, however remotely, the conditions under which the Brahmanical system became established. They preserve evidence which points to a transitional phase. It is related—against the principle of Brahmanism—that some priest-seers, including the famous Viçvāmitra, the founder of one of the great priestly families,[1] were of Kshatriya stock. On the other hand they have also much to say about certain Brahmans who were great warriors, especially Rāma, son of Jamadagni, who belonged to the family of Bhrgu, Krpa, a descendant of Gotama, and Drona, who was born miraculously to Bharadvāja and who became a king, as well as a warrior. Even if it be maintained that all these stories are products of fiction, it requires to be explained how such characters could be invented under the caste system. The natural explanation at all events is that they date from a time before the borderline between Kshatriya and Brahman families was rigidly fixed, and when exceptional cases were still not unknown.

The non-Brahmanical elements in the Mahābhārata consist of heroic stories and a certain amount of didactic matter, including genealogies and traditions of royal houses. It is a difficult question to decide how much of this didactic matter is to be regarded as non-Brahmanical. Indeed from the analogy of other lands one is inclined at first to doubt whether it is justifiable to deny the possibility of a Brahmanic origin for any of it. This element, however, is closely connected with the

---

[1] We do not know whether the priestly family who bore the name Daivāpi in Janamejaya's time claimed descent from the Devāpi of Rgv. x. 98 (cf. p. 611). Mahābh. ix. xxxix f. gives a list of four princes who attained the status of Brahman, viz. Ārshtishena, Devāpi, Sindhudvīpa and Viçvāmitra. The two first of these seem to be identical (cf. p. 509). In xiii. iv Sindhudvīpa is an ancestor of Viçvāmitra. In xiii. xxx there is a fifth instance, that of Vītahavya, who owed his change of status to Bhrgu.

Purānas, where the same problem arises. In the latter there is some definite, if not entirely satisfactory, evidence for derivation from a different class.

It will perhaps be best to begin with the heroic stories. One of these, the story of the sons of Pāndu, forms the central theme of the work, while the others are introduced episodically in the course of the action, and narrated by various characters. Three of them, the stories of Nala, Rāma and Sāvitrī, are narrated to Yudhishthira for the purpose of comforting him, while he is in exile in the forest. The narrators are the seers Brhadaçva and Markandeya. The story of Ambā is told by the old hero Bhīshma, in order to explain why he will not fight against Çikhandin. The speeches of Vidulā (cf. p. 470 f.) are quoted by Kuntī, in order to rouse Yudhishthira to action.

From this it would seem that both seers and members of royal families, including ladies, might be expected to be familiar with heroic stories. As regards the narrators individually, we may note that Markandeya is said to be immortal and that he recounts many stories of Brahmanic interest, as well as the stories of Rāma and Sāvitrī. He is known also to the Purānas, one of which bears his name. Brhadaçva is introduced briefly as a great seer, who visits Yudhishthira in the forest and relates to him the story of Nala (iii. lii). Before leaving him he imparts to him his knowledge of dice (*ib.* lxxix). It seems likely that he is to be identified with the king called Brhadaçva (*ib.* cci), who retired to the forest and became an ascetic. It has been pointed out[1] that the name is of a type more familiar in Kshatriya than in Brahmanic families. Bhīshma and Kuntī are of course leading characters in the central story.

There is other evidence that princes were supposed to be familiar with heroic stories. In i. ccxxiv. 29, when Arjuna and Krshna are sitting together near the Jumna during a festival, they amuse themselves by telling one another 'the glorious deeds of old and many other tales'.[2] It may be observed that the same two heroes on another occasion (xiv. xv. 5 ff.), while sitting together in the council-house at Indraprastha, relate not only 'tales of war and moil' but also 'genealogies of seers and gods'.

Frequently also we hear of professional poets or minstrels.[3] Usually,

---

[1] Sidhanta, *The Heroic Age of India*, p. 63.

[2] The translations of this passage and the next are taken from Hopkins, *The Great Epic of India*, p. 364.

[3] A number of references are given by Sidhanta, *op. cit.* p. 57 f.; cf. also Hopkins, *op. cit.* p. 366 f.

however, if not always, it is in connection with panegyrics—evidently
heroic poetry of Type D—that such persons are mentioned. One of
their functions is to chant panegyrics to a prince when he wakes in the
morning. Thus in I. ccxx. 14 Arjuna, when visiting Krshna, is awakened
by the sound of the lyre (*vīnā*) and the panegyrics of the bards. In III.
ccxxxv. 10 Dhrtarāshtra says that Yudhishthira used to be awakened
every morning by singers who chanted his praises. Sometimes these
panegyrics are said to include the praise of the dynasty, as in VII. lxxxii.
2 ff. In warfare, especially perhaps in the evening, a camp resounds with
such songs, accompanied with music and dancing (VII. lxxxv). They
greet a hero when he sets out to battle (*ib*. lxxxiv. 22 f.). Such panegyrics
are mentioned also on many solemn and festive occasions—when
Duryodhana returns home from an expedition (III. cclvi. 1), when
King Yudhishthira pays a visit of state to his predecessor (XV. xxiii. 7 f.),
when Abhimanyu's child (Parīkshit) is restored to life by Krshna
(XIV. lxx. 6 ff.).

These references and many others point rather to Type D than to
Type A; narrative poetry is seldom, if ever, specifically mentioned in
connection with performances of this kind. They would seem to have
more in common with the panegyrics delivered by the Rājanya at the
time of the horse-sacrifice, as described in the Çatapatha Brāhmana (cf.
p. 606), though they were often perhaps of a noisier character. Yet there
is reason for thinking that the panegyrists, or at least some of them, also
cultivated narrative poetry.

Among the numerous terms applied to the minstrels or poets who
pronounce the panegyrics we find occasionally the word *ākhyānaçīla*,
'versed in stories', which seems to imply narrative. The terms, however,
which occur most frequently are *sūta* and *māgadha*. According to Prof.
Rapson[1] "in the Brāhmanas the Sūta is the royal herald and minstrel,
and possibly also 'master of the horse'. He is one of the king's 'jewels'
(*ratniṇ*) and ranks with the commander-in-chief of the army and other
high officers of state; and in his character as herald he was inviolable.
In the law-books he is described as the son of a Kshatriya by the daughter
of a Brahman. The Purānas say that he was born to sing the praises of
princes and that he was entrusted with the care of the historical and
legendary traditions; but they state definitely that he had no concern
with the Vedas (*Vāyu Pur*. I. 1, 26–28). In later times he appears as the
king's charioteer," etc. It may be added that the statement as to the
origin of the Sūta is repeated in one of the legal disquisitions in the

---

[1] *Cambridge History of India*, I. 297; cf. also Keith, *ib*. p. 130 f.

Mahābhārata, XIII. xlviii. 10, where it is also stated that his duties are to recite eulogies and encomiums of kings and other great men. A little later (st. 12) the Māgadha or Vandin[1] is said to be the son of a Vaiçya father and a Kshatriya mother; and it is added that his duties also are to recite eulogies.

Apart from its occurrence in such references to panegyrics as have been noted above, the term *sūta* is applied to several characters who are mentioned more or less frequently in the Mahābhārata. One of these is Adhiratha, the charioteer who adopted and brought up Karna; the latter is often called 'the Sūta's son'.[2] Far more important, however, is Sanjaya, King Dhrtarāshtra's chief minister and confidential messenger. Before the great battle he acts as the king's envoy to the sons of Pāndu; and during the battle he reports to him the progress of events. He is the speaker throughout the greater part of Books VI–IX. When Dhrtarāshtra retires from the kingdom, Sanjaya accompanies him, though he has not approved of his policy; and he is the only man who remains with him to the end. In the introduction (I. i. 81) he is said to be one of the three (living) men who know the Mahābhārata. Elsewhere also he is represented as a man of great learning.[3] In VI. iv ff. he discourses at great length upon geography and cosmology, in order to entertain the king.

Next we may turn to the Purānas.[4] These works to a large extent follow a common scheme, as was noticed in Ch. VII (p. 540). In their present form they are late; but it is believed that they preserve elements of great antiquity. They seem to have originated as varieties of a tradition, known as Itihāsa Purāna, which was one of the recognised subjects of education in the time of the early Upanishads, and which is mentioned even in the Atharvaveda (xv. 6. 4). Now most of the Purānas claim to be recited by a Sūta named Lomaharshana or his son Ugraçravas, commonly called Sauti or 'the Suta's son', who have learned

---

[1] This word, which often occurs beside *sūta* and *māgadha*, though not so often as these, seems to mean 'panegyrist' (from the verb *vand*, 'to praise'); cf. note, below. The word *māgadha* is, we believe, generally thought to be derived from the name of the kingdom Magadha.

[2] The same term is applied in IV. 14 ff. to Kīcaka, the commander of Virāta's army. He seems to be the queen's brother and is evidently one of the leading persons in the kingdom (Matsya).

[3] It may be observed that in III. cxxxiv. 21 Vandi (or perhaps 'the Vandin'), who has brought Kahoda and many other Brahmans to their doom in contests of learning, is described as 'son of a Sūta'; cf. p. 505.

[4] For further information on this subject the reader may be referred to Rapson, *Cambridge History of India*, I. 296 ff., to which we are much indebted.

the subject from Vyāsa. The scene is sometimes laid at a great sacrificial gathering of seers in the Naimisha forest; and the time is usually the reign of Adhisīmakrshna, a great-grandson of Janamejaya.[1] This is of course practically the same setting as that of the Mahābhārata. The narrator here is Ugraçravas, usually called Sauti, who has learned the poem from Vaiçampāyana, the disciple of Vyāsa, its author. The scene and the occasion are the same. The time is not precisely stated; but Vaiçampāyana's recitation is given before Janamejaya himself. The Mahābhārata therefore shares the tradition of the Purānas. Moreover, though the dates given are not identical, this tradition is always referred to what may be called the Brāhmana period. Janamejaya's reign was apparently anterior to the time of any extant Brāhmanas, while that of Adhisīmakrshna would seem to coincide more or less with the time of Uddālaka Āruni and his contemporaries—probably c. 700 (cf. p. 514).

Many scholars would no doubt be unwilling to allow that either the Mahābhārata or the Purānas are to be traced back so far as this. Yet the fact that the composition and recitation of all these works is referred to that period requires some explanation. Moreover it is to be borne in mind that in the Mahābhārata we hear much of Uddālaka Āruni and his contemporaries, but practically nothing of any later seers or kings. There is abundant matter, doctrinal and other, which is doubtless of later date; but the latest personnel is substantially[2] that of the Brāhmana period—probably not later than the seventh century, and this seems to be true also of the (heroic and other) episodes, though these may well have been incorporated in much later times. We do not mean to suggest that anything like the Mahābhārata, as we know it, was in existence at such an early date. But we think it bears the imprint of some influence dating from that time. Perhaps it was then that heroic poetry first began to be cultivated by the learned.

It will be seen that both the Purānas and the Mahābhārata claim to be of Brahmanic origin. Vyāsa is the author; the Sūta or Sauti is merely the reciter. But the question naturally arises: Why should a gathering of Brahmans require such a person to recite to them the work of a Brahman? There are apparently only two other persons who know the Mahābhārata, and one of these is likewise a Sūta.[3] We are under the

---

[1] In the Vishnu Purāna the narrator is Parāçara (Vyāsa's father), and the time is that of Parīkshit, Janamejaya's father.

[2] Details such as the incidental references to Yavana need not be taken into account. Catalogue poetry (e.g. Widsith) is especially subject to such additions.

[3] Sanjaya (cf. p. 618). The other is Çuka, apparently the son of Vyāsa (I. 1. 81).

impression that most scholars now would be inclined to the view that in the original tradition the Sūta (Lomaharshana) was himself the author, and that he was reduced to the position of reciter in favour of the Brahman Vyāsa—perhaps in order to secure greater prestige for the works; for their preservation is doubtless due to Brahmans. At all events, like Sanjaya, he is regarded in the Mahābhārata as a learned man. In i. v his learning in the Purānas is known to Kulapati Çaunaka, who presides over the sacrificial gathering, and who asks his son (Sauti) if he also has studied them. In xii. cccxix. 21 Yājnavalkya tells Janaka that after he had acquired his knowledge of the Yajurveda he studied the Purānas with Romaharshana (Lomaharshana). He was evidently therefore a recognised authority on the subject.

It can hardly be doubted that the men who are described as 'versed in narrative' (cf. p. 617) belonged in part to the Sūta class—in other words that narrative, as well as panegyric, poetry was cultivated by this class. Sanjaya is a skilled narrator, and much of Lomaharshana's learning necessarily involves a knowledge of heroic stories. Indeed it is unnecessary to suppose that Types A and D, narrative and panegyric, were clearly distinguished. The Sūta class would seem to be the highest which could make a profession of poetry. We may add that in the Vishnu Purāna, i. 13, 'the Sūta' is said to have been produced in the juice of the Soma at a great sacrifice. The Māgadha is produced at the same time; and both are told by the seers that their special duty is to praise Prthu, son of Vena, in honour of whom the sacrifice is being performed. Similar passages occur in other Purānas.[1] The juice of the Soma is the liquor of inspiration.

It is important to note that the traditions relating to the origin of the Mahābhārata and the Purānas carry these works back to a period—the time of Janamejaya and his successors—when the caste system must in reality have been comparatively new, if indeed it had already acquired complete rigidity. How much truth the traditions contain we do not know; but the evidence of the Atharvaveda shows that something called Itihāsa Purāna was in existence about this time. But it is difficult to see how a Sūta caste (or sub-caste) can have existed before the Brahman and Kshatriya castes came to be rigidly separated from one another. Before that time we have to think rather of classes and families than of castes.

Now it is clear from the Rgveda that before the caste system became fixed there were a number of ecclesiastical families—perhaps we may say

---

[1] Cf. also Mahābh. xii. lix. 112 f.; but there is no reference to Soma here.

Brahman families—which must already have had a fairly long history, and which apparently possessed their own collections of hymns. We may also note that in the earlier Rgvedic period, the times of Divodāsa, Sudās and Trasadasyu, references to the generosity of kings occur frequently in the hymns, but that after these times such references become rare;[1] we cannot trace the history of the royal families, nor even count the generations. From this it would seem to be a legitimate inference that the old Brahmanic families became less dependent upon the kings. The claim to superiority which the Brahman caste maintained in later times may already have been beginning.

The Sūta and the Māgadha, as also the Rājanya mentioned in the passage from the Çatapatha Brāhmana cited on p. 605 f., doubtless represent different classes of intellectual persons connected by blood or service with the royal families. Such persons had presumably always had the function of composing panegyrics upon kings. They were also the persons best qualified for the cultivation of antiquarian learning in relation to the kingdoms; and we need not hesitate to add the cultivation of heroic stories, upon which this learning must to some extent depend. There was moreover a time, if we may believe the traditions, when the priesthood with its privileges was open to such persons—when the Brahman and the Kshatriya were not yet separated by barriers of birth—but this came to an end. The priesthood became reserved for those who were of Brahman blood, while those who were not retained the function of praising and entertaining kings and of cultivating such learning as related to kings. The old Brahman families, if the observation made above is correct, had ceased to be interested in learning of this kind; and the result was a cleavage between ecclesiastical and secular learning—each caste preserving its own (oral) literature. This cleavage was only temporary; for both the Mahābhārata and the Purānas have been preserved by Brahmans. We do not know when Brahmans adopted them. The tradition which connects the Brahman Vyāsa with them should perhaps not be wholly disregarded. But we are under the impression that Brahmans of the more conservative type, whose concern lay with the Vedas, have always regarded this learning with a certain contempt.

There can be no doubt that both the Purānas and the Mahābhārata, as we have them, have received very large additions from Brahmanic sources. Indeed it is possible that four of the five sections of which a

---

[1] Encomiums upon the munificence of the sacrificing king may still have been composed—as is implied in Çat. Br. XIII. 1. 5. 6—but they were apparently not as a rule preserved.

Purāna is traditionally said to consist (cf. p. 540), may come ultimately from such sources, though they can hardly be derived from the Vedas or any other extant Brahmanic works. But some of the learning seems to be of foreign origin. Such is probably the case with the doctrine of the 'Ages' which occupies the fourth traditional section in the Purānas and occurs frequently in the Mahābhārata. It has been mentioned above (p. 540) that every 'great age' (*mahāyuga*) consists of four recurrent 'ages' (*yuga*), each of which is worse than its predecessor. These ages bear the names Krta, Tretā, Dvāpara and Kali, derived from the 4, 3, 2 and ace of dice (cf. p. 546). They last 4000, 3000, 2000 and 1000 years respectively, thus making altogether a cycle of ten thousand years.[1] Sometimes the last age ends in a world-catastrophe, as in Mahābh. III. clxxxviii.[2] A much simpler form of this doctrine is known to Hesiod, as we have seen; but his ages are not recurrent, though each of them is worse than its predecessor, just as in the Indian scheme. On the other hand the conception of a recurrent 'great year' or cycle ending in a world-catastrophe seems to have been fairly widespread among Greek philosophers of the sixth century, though apparently little or nothing is known of its details. If the 'great year' was really estimated at ten thousand years, as is commonly supposed, the coincidence with the Indian scheme can hardly be accidental.[3] It may be then that the circles in which the Purānas and the Mahābhārata originated were more affected by external influence than the Vedic schools. But the date of such influence is difficult to determine.

The part played by women in Indian literature of the earliest periods is remarkably slight. Even among the deities the only important figure with any developed personality is Sarasvatī the goddess of speech and learning; and her identity with the River Sarasvatī, of which she is a personification, is generally remembered. Mortal women seem to be

---

[1] Cf. Mahābh. III. clxxxviii. 22 ff., where 'twilights' are included. Sometimes (morning and evening) twilights are added to each age, and these have the effect of increasing each 1000 years to 1200.

[2] Incidental references to the catastrophe also occur (e.g. VI. clxxvi. 26), which show that the idea was familiar.

[3] We suspect that the origin of most of these speculations is to be sought in Mesopotamia, and that they travelled east and west from thence, not all at once but in a series of 'waves of influence', beginning perhaps in the ninth century. It is apparently to the same quarter, and during the same period, that India owes the story of the Flood, the introduction of writing, etc. But we are not qualified to deal with the question.

comparatively seldom mentioned, except in spells, either in the Vedas or the Brāhmanas. Yet it is clear from the Upanishads that women, at least in the Brahman caste, were sometimes educated. Thus in the Brha-dāranyaka, IV. 5 (cf. II. 4), Yājnavalkya has two wives, one of whom has some knowledge of philosophy, while the other is without intellectual interests. Among the philosophers or seers who interrogate Yājnavalkya at Janaka's contest (cf. p. 503) there is a lady, named Gārgī Vācaknavī, who challenges him twice (ib. III. 6, 8).

In the Mahābhārata, especially the heroic portions, women are far more prominent. In the episodes of Nala and Sāvitrī, and perhaps also in that of Ambā, the chief character is a woman. The same is true of the shorter story of Çakuntalā and the speeches of Vidulā. In the central story Draupadī is one of the leading characters. These women are quite equal to the heroines of Western heroic poetry in their capacity for a vigorous initiative and sometimes far superior to their husbands in personality. Some of them, especially Çakuntalā and Vidulā, are skilful speakers.

It may be observed that the speeches in both these last cases are examples of gnomic wisdom of different kinds. The cultivation of manticism by women, apart from the mantic philosophy of the Upanishads, seems to be rare. Kuntī possesses a spell (cf. p. 579); but this has been given to her by a Brahman. She can hardly be regarded as a witch. Damayantī kills the hunter who insults her, apparently by her curse. Such cases, however, are uncommon, and we have not noticed any instances of professional witchcraft, or of prophecy by women. This would seem to point to a rather noticeable difference between early India and Europe.

To what extent was poetry cultivated by women? Royal ladies were evidently expected to recite elegies or dirges over dead relatives, just as in Europe. An example is to be found in Gandhārī's elegy for her sons in XI. xvi ff. Further, from the fact that Vidulā's speeches are recited by Kuntī it may be inferred that recitations of heroic poetry by such persons were not unfamiliar. But were these speeches, or any of the existing stories, composed by women? That seems to us not impossible; but it would be difficult to prove. We should be inclined rather to the view that, whoever may have been the authors, the stories of Nala and of Sāvitrī were composed primarily for the entertainment of royal ladies, or at least as much for them as for princes. It is clear from what Arjuna promises to do in IV. ii, when he wishes to enter Virāta's service, that stories were popular among the ladies of the courts.

On the subject of inspiration we have little to add to what has been noted incidentally in previous chapters. The hymns of the Rgveda were traditionally regarded as due to inspiration in the strictest sense. The poets were seers (*rṣi*),[1] to whom the hymns were revealed, or rather perhaps revealed themselves. In the Brāhmanas and very often in the Upanishads tradition is all-important. Sometimes, as in the Brhadā-ranyaka Upanishad, 'genealogies' are given, which trace doctrines through a long line of teachers back to the gods. New inspiration, however, seems not to be wholly wanting. It is to be obtained apparently by sitting in silence behind the altar after performing some rite (cf. p. 578). Instruction is given by various animate and inanimate things; but such incidents are hardly meant to be taken literally.

In the Mahābhārata we meet with a number of the same teachers who figure in the Upanishads; but here the inspiration takes a different form. Sarasvatī, the goddess of speech and learning, appears both to Çvetaketu and to Yājnavalkya; the latter is inspired also by Sūrya, the Sun-god. Usually, however, in the Mahābhārata the place of inspiration is taken by asceticism (*yoga*), an essential feature of which was the concentration of thought upon a particular object or idea. In course of time the *yoga* was developed into a very elaborate and complicated system, which need not be discussed here.[2] But the concentration of thought involved in it is usually found in association with mantic activities, in Europe[3] as well as in India. In the Mahābhārata it is credited with a magical power, for which the most extravagant and fantastic claims are made. The culti-vation of this faculty doubtless dates from a period before the growth of asceticism. For it is not essentially different from the meditations which we find in the Upanishads; and even in the Atharvaveda (XI. 5), the Brahmacārin[4] or 'devotee' is credited with properties similar to those which later are attributed to the ascetic. 'Asceticism' seems to have begun in the form of retirement to the forest on the part of elderly men. In the Upanishads this is found in the case of Brahman teachers;

---

[1] It may be noted that the word *kavi*, 'poet', also means 'seer'—which indeed is generally thought to have been its original meaning; in the pl. it denotes 'the wise', 'sages'. It is instructive to compare these meanings with those of Irish *fili* and Norse *þulr*; cf. Vol. I, pp. 602 ff., 606, 618 f.

[2] A short but instructive account will be found in the introduction to the trans-lation of the Bhagavad-Gītā by L. D. Barnett (Temple Classics), p. 29 ff.

[3] We may refer to the use of the word *þencan* ('think, meditate') and the phrase *þurh trumne geþanc* ('with steadfast thought, intent mind') in Anglo-Saxon spells.

[4] In the Mahābhārata this term is used for those who are under a vow of tem-porary asceticism, like the sons of Pāndu.

in the Mahābhārata it is a fairly common practice with princes, as well as Brahmans. But in the latter we hear also of children brought up as ascetics from their birth.

In Europe we observed that inspiration was very commonly associated with springs. For such association in early India we have not found any evidence, though sacred pools and rivers are not rare. In particular we may note the sacred river Sarasvatī, of which the goddess of speech and learning is a personification.

The inspiring drink which is found in various European lands (cf. Vol. I, p. 651 ff.) has an Indian parallel in the juice of the soma, which was very largely used in offerings to the gods. In the Rgveda Indra is represented as strengthened by these offerings for his combats with demons and alien enemies. The juice, which seems to have been of an intoxicating character, was drunk only by Brahmans, and apparently only at sacrifices. In the Purānas the Sūta is said to have been born from it (cf. p. 620). The personified Soma was regarded as a great deity, and all the hymns of Book IX of the Rgveda are addressed to him. The cult would seem to be very ancient, for it is found also in the Avesta.

For the use of music in this connection we have not been able to find any satisfactory evidence. The hymns of the Sāmaveda—most of which come from the Rgveda—were chanted at sacrifices; but we do not know whether there was any instrumental accompaniment. Neither do we know whether music, vocal or instrumental, was used for spells. For the other mantic accessories noted in Vol. I, p. 653 ff.—the seer's wand and chair—we have not found any early Indian parallels. The Mahābhārata has much to say about snakes; but they do not seem to convey inspiration.

PART IV

EARLY HEBREW LITERATURE

CHAPTER I

INTRODUCTION

LITERATURE AND WRITING

THERE can be little doubt that the earliest literature of the Hebrews, like that of India, is derived in large part from oral tradition. But both the nature of the records and the history of their transmission seem to be very different in the two cases.

In both literatures the religious element is predominant. But Indian literature begins with great collections of poems, consisting at first almost entirely of hymns. On the other hand the earliest Hebrew records are chiefly prose; very little hymn poetry is believed to date from the oldest period. The earliest Hebrew prose is occupied in part with ritual observances, like the Brāhmanas, the earliest Indian prose—but not to anything like the same extent as the latter. Saga, which occurs only in brief examples and incidentally in the Brāhmanas, forms the largest and most important element in the earliest Hebrew records. Narrative poetry, both religious and secular, is well represented in early Indian literature, though it is not preserved in very early form; but in early Hebrew literature it seems to be entirely wanting. One of the greatest difficulties in early Indian literature is the absence of historical records. In Hebrew on the other hand historical study, together with a keen sense for chronology, was cultivated from a very early period.

The forms of literature most fully represented in the earliest records seem to be heroic and (more especially) non-heroic saga, antiquarian learning of all kinds and mantic poetry. The three latter are closely connected, and on the whole antiquarian interest is paramount. It came to be combined with the study of historical records, and eventually provided the learned world with a scheme of universal history.

In regard to the transmission of early records Hebrew literary history seems to have differed very greatly from that of India. It is generally thought that early Indian texts have for the most part undergone but little change from the time when they were first committed to writing; but early Hebrew texts are believed to have had a complicated history. Even those which are best preserved, such as the prophecies of Amos, are said to have received a number of interpolations; in the prophecies of

Isaiah the additions are thought to amount to at least half, and probably very much more, of the whole collection.

It is, however, in the antiquarian and historical books with which the Old Testament begins—from Genesis to Kings—that the most important changes are believed to have taken place. These books must have existed practically in their present form in the third century, when the Greek translation was made. But it is thought that not long—probably not more than two centuries—before this time they had undergone a very great amount of change. The text of Genesis, Exodus, Numbers and Joshua is believed to have received its present form through the combination (conflation) of two parallel accounts, one of which, known as JE,[1] was of considerable antiquity, while the other, known as the 'Priests' Code' (P), was much later, though it was probably not the work of one author or of one period. Leviticus is attributed wholly to the latter, though it contains at least one considerable element which has a unity of its own. Deuteronomy is believed to have been originally a separate work; but it has incorporated in the later chapters (xxvii–xxxiv) a good deal from JE and a little from P. In Joshua the element derived from JE is thought to have been edited and augmented by a writer under the influence of Deuteronomy before it was combined with P. Lastly, it is held that JE itself was formed by the combination of two texts (J and E), which were originally distinct but contained parallel accounts of the same subjects and events. It is thought that different strata can be distinguished in each of these, and also that considerable additions were made to JE, after this conflate text had come into existence. But there is some difference of opinion as to how far these latter distinctions can be traced.

For the complex textual history involved in this analysis fairly close analogies are to be found in annals and chronicles of the Dark Ages. The early annals of the *Saxon Chronicle* will provide a good enough illustration. But the texts with which we are concerned here were not annals, but compositions of a character which would render such combination or conflation less easy to effect. It is indeed difficult for a student of early Western literature to resist the suspicion that this analysis has been carried too far. The process would of course be more

---

[1] J, E, JE, and P are the abbreviations regularly employed for the hypothetical texts postulated by modern critical writers. J and E are derived from the terms *Jehovah* (Engl. transl. 'the LORD') and *Elohim* (Engl. transl. 'God') applied to the deity in these two texts respectively. JE denotes the combination of J and E. P is called the 'Book of Origins' by some scholars.

easily intelligible if J and E had an independent existence only as oral variants—from which they are believed to have been derived—or if P were mainly of 'editorial' origin. But these are questions which must obviously be left to experts; and we understand that there is little difference of opinion in regard to the main features of the analysis. We shall therefore take it as our basis, where questions of textual history are involved.[1]

The next series of books, Judges, Samuel and Kings, are likewise believed to be of composite origin. The greater part of Judges—from ii. 6 to the end of xvi—is thought by many scholars to have been arranged or edited by a writer under the influence of Deuteronomy. But the first chapter and the last eight chapters are regarded as early fragments, which have not been affected by this influence. Other, and more recent, writers, however, hold that this threefold division of Judges applies properly only to its subject matter, not to its literary history. They believe the textual sources to be the same as in the Hexateuch, with the addition of a late form of E (E2). They limit the Deuteronomic element (D) to portions of cap. ii f.

The composite origin of Samuel is perhaps more apparent than that of any of the preceding books. The greater part of Book II, and probably also much of Book I, comes from a good early text, which some scholars regard as identical or connected with J. Among the other elements there is one—in the first half of Book I—which is commonly connected with E, and which seems to have been written originally as a continuation of the story of the Judges, perhaps as a sequel to the central portion of that book. The last four chapters of Book II are in the nature of an appendix, the introduction of which has broken into the continuity of the narrative derived from the earliest text. The continuation of cap. xx is apparently to be found in I Kings i f.

The rest of Kings (after the first two chapters) seems to have been compiled or edited by a writer under the influence of Deuteronomy. Cap. iii–xi of Book I are thought to be derived largely from the 'Book of the Acts of Solomon', referred to in xi. 41, while some of the material in the later parts is doubtless drawn from the 'Book of the Chronicles of the Kings of Israel' and the 'Book of the Chronicles of the Kings of Judah', both of which are frequently cited.

It must be understood that what has been said above applies to the textual history of the books specified, not to the character or ultimate

---

[1] Some remarks on this subject will be ventured in Ch. IX.

origin of the matter contained in them. The latter subject will need discussion in the following chapters. The Books of Judges, Samuel and Kings, which are of somewhat heterogeneous character, will be treated in Chs. II and III, the Hexateuch in Ch. VI.

The evidence for writing in Palestine goes back to remote times. The earliest examples apparently are monuments and objects of various kinds bearing Egyptian inscriptions. Under the Eighteenth and Nineteenth Dynasties—from the sixteenth to the close of the thirteenth centuries—the country was included within the Egyptian dominions. Indeed it was apparently not much before the middle of the twelfth century that Egyptian rule came to an end. Cuneiform (Assyrian) writing seems to have been even more widely known. Many letters in this script, written by princes and governors in Palestine during the early part of the fourteenth century, were found among the Egyptian archives at El Amarna; and similar letters have occasionally been found in Palestine itself.

Early evidence for writing in the native language is less easy to find. But it must have been in use even for literary purposes in the cities of the coast; for the Ras Shamra tablets, which date from the fourteenth and thirteenth centuries, preserve large fragments of poetry, inscribed in an alphabetic variety of cuneiform.[1] In the story of Wenamon, which relates to a time not long before 1100, the ruler of Byblos produces his family archives, though apparently neither the language nor the form of writing employed in them is recorded. He is said, however, to import papyrus rolls from Egypt. In the interior nothing in the native language has yet been found which can be dated before the ninth century, except a few fragments of inscriptions on broken pottery. The most important of these, in an early form of Hebrew alphabet, are painted upon vessels discovered at Tell Duweir, which is believed to be Lachish, and dating from the first half of the thirteenth century.[2] A small fragment from Beth-shemesh is thought to be still earlier. From the ninth century onwards examples seem to become rather more frequent; and there are a few stone monuments inscribed in the old Hebrew character. The most

[1] The language is commonly called Hebrew or Phoenician, but appears to be somewhat different. It was presumably the native language of the district before the Aramaean conquest, cf. Cantineau, *Syria*, xiii. 164 ff.

[2] Cf. *The Times*, 28 July 1934, 24 June 1935. Marston, *The Bible is True*, p. 262 and pl. The inscription on the tomb of Ahiram at Byblos is now ascribed to the same period. The Tell Duweir writing is thought by some to supply a connecting link with the much earlier inscriptions in the Sinai peninsula.

important of these is the one which commemorates the victories of Mesha, king of Moab (c. 850). From about the same time date numerous ostraka from Samaria—apparently pottery tickets, used for purposes of taxation, and inscribed with a reed pen.

In early Hebrew literature itself references to writing are common enough in works relating to the seventh century; and there can be little doubt that at that time it was widely known. Even in works and passages relating to the ninth and tenth centuries such references are not at all rare. Thus in II Kings x. 1 Jehu writes letters to the rulers of Jezreel regarding the children of Ahab. Again, *ib.* v. 5, the king of Syria sends a letter of introduction for his officer Naaman to Jehoram, king of Israel. In I Kings xxi. 8, Jezebel writes letters to the elders of Jezreel with reference to Naboth; she writes them in the name of her husband, Ahab, and signs them with his seal. In II Sam. xi. 14 f. David writes to Joab, instructing him with regard to Uriah, who is the bearer of the letter. In I Sam. x. 25 it is stated that Samuel wrote "the manner of the kingdom...in a book, and laid it up before Jehovah".

We may note, further, that in lists of court and state officials mention is sometimes made of one or more scribes. Examples occur in the lists of David's and Solomon's officials (II Sam. viii. 17, xx. 25; I Kings iv. 3), as well as in those of Hezekiah's time and later.

Lastly, it may be observed that writing is mentioned in a number of passages in the Hexateuch. Sometimes the reference is to the tables of stone inscribed by Moses or by the finger of God (e.g. Ex. xxxi. 18, xxxii. 15 f., xxxiv. 27 f.); but elsewhere Moses is said to write a book (*ib.* xxiv. 4, 7). All these passages are generally supposed to be derived from one or other of the hypothetical early texts E and J, chiefly from the former. Here also we may note Josh. viii. 32, where Joshua inscribes a copy of the Law upon the unhewn stones of an altar—presumably boulders. This passage is supposed to be late and due to the influence of Deut. xxvii. 1–8; but it is of interest as suggesting that the author was aware of such a custom.

There seems to be no decisive evidence for dating any of the early works, including the hypothetical texts, noticed above. But we understand that according to the views now most prevalent[1] both E and J

---

[1] But there is still much difference of opinion, some scholars preferring earlier, others later dates. Thus Albright (*Archaeology of Palestine and the Bible*, pp. 147, 154 ff., 213) ascribes J to the late eighth, E to the early seventh century, but dates the bulk of Deuteronomy to the ninth. The antiquity of all the elements in the narrative books, including J and E and the 'court-history' of II Samuel—at least in their present form—is doubted by Cook, *Camb. Anc. Hist.* III. 473 ff.

were written in the early part of the eighth century, the latter perhaps even in the ninth. The oldest element in Samuel, the narrative which occupies at least nearly half of Book II, is thought to be still older. Some scholars believe it to be almost contemporary with the events—which would carry it back to perhaps the middle of the tenth century.

From what has been said it will be clear enough that the use of writing for literary purposes was to all appearance much earlier in Palestine than in either Greece or India. And this conclusion is fully in accordance with the historical evidence. In Greece the eighth century can hardly be regarded as coming within the historical period; in India history begins much later. But the Books of Kings give us full lists of the kings of Israel and Judah, together with the length of their reigns and various other information; and it can be determined from occasional references in Egyptian and Assyrian records that the chronology is not seriously in error. The invasion of Judah by Shishak (Sheshonk I), king of Egypt, related in I Kings xiv. 25 ff., is known from a contemporary inscription at Karnak to have taken place c. 930. For the preceding reigns—those of David and Solomon—foreign evidence is wanting, owing doubtless to the fact that little is known of the neighbouring powers, or at least of their external relations, during that period. But in view of the character of the Hebrew records themselves, at least for David's time, we may regard the tenth century as a historical or semi-historical period in Palestine.

This can hardly be said of the earlier periods. The story of Samuel may preserve some historical information. But there is thought to be a discrepancy in the records in regard to his position. In one series of passages—representing one of the constituent texts noticed above—he appears to be merely a seer or prophet; in another series—which are believed to represent the later text—he is also the judge and ruler. The Book of Judges is generally recognised to be derived from traditions. Much of it must relate to the times when Palestine was under Egyptian rule; and the same is true of Joshua and the earlier Books. They are very largely concerned with political affairs; yet they never preserve any recollection of this rule—which must have lasted till within a century of Samuel's time.

The Book of Judges would seem to be derived from a number of stories (sagas), which were originally (more or less) independent, but were brought together and connected by an editor, or perhaps a series of editors. On the other hand the constituent elements in I Samuel, just as in the Pentateuch, are believed to have been more in the form of consecutive narratives. Yet the discrepancies between the narratives can hardly be explained except by derivation from variant forms of saga. And it may be observed that these discrepancies are not limited to the story of Samuel himself. Equally clear examples are to be found in the story of David, which follows. As an instance we may cite the different accounts of the first meeting between David and Saul. In xvi. 18 ff. they meet first when David is brought to Saul's court as a minstrel; he is described as "cunning in playing, and a mighty man of valour, and a man of war, and prudent in speech". But in the following chapter, when David fights with Goliath, he is described as a youth, evidently inexperienced in warfare; and Saul does not know who he is (cf. xvii. 55 ff.). A more serious discrepancy is to be found between this latter story and II Sam. xxi. 19, according to which Goliath was slain not by David but by a certain Elhanan, the son of Jaare-oregim the Beth-le-hemite.[1] It may be noted that the same description of Goliath's spear-shaft is given in this passage and in I Sam. xvii. 7.

A comparison between I Sam. xxiv and xxvi is still more important for the purpose of tracing the origin of these stories. In both cases Saul sets out with three thousand men in pursuit of David. In both cases he is surprised by his intended victim, who has him at his mercy but refuses to take his life. Then follows a conversation, in which the two accounts have a considerable element in common. In the details of the adventures there is much discrepancy; but it is clear enough that we have here a typical instance of saga-variants. We see no reason for doubting that many of the other discrepancies[2] are of similar origin—i.e. that the First Book of Samuel is largely, if not wholly, derived from saga.

Similar discrepancies are to be found in the Books of Kings, especially in the stories relating to the prophets Elijah and Elisha. Thus in I. xxi Naboth lives at Jezreel and is put to death there; and (ib. 19) Elijah prophesies to Ahab that dogs will lick his blood in the same place where they have licked the blood of Naboth. But in xxii. 38, where this prophecy is said to be fulfilled, the scene is Samaria, some five and twenty miles from Jezreel. The confusion is possibly due to Elijah's further

---

[1] Some scholars identify Elhanan with David. But the records profess to know the origin of the former, though they are not in agreement as to his father's name; cf. II Sam. xxiii. 24; I Chron. xx. 5. In the last passage the person slain by Elhanan is not Goliath, but his brother Lahmi.

[2] Sometimes one may hesitate to use the word 'variants', as in the accounts of David's two visits to Achish (I Sam. xxi. 11 ff. and xxvii), which have hardly anything in common. But it is difficult to believe that they can have belonged originally to the same story.

prophecy, given in xxi. 23, that Jezebel will be eaten by dogs in Jezreel —which is fulfilled, long afterwards, in II Kings ix. 35 f. Again, in I. xix. 15 f. Elijah, who is in Horeb, is said to be ordered by Jehovah to return to Damascus and anoint Hazael to be king over Syria; he is also to anoint Jehu to be king over Israel and Elisha to be his own successor as prophet. He sets off at once to find Elisha (*ib.* 19 ff.), who immediately follows him; but nothing more is said as to the rest of the commission. In II. viii. 13 Elisha prophesies to Hazael that he will be king of Syria— a prophecy which is fulfilled the next day, when he murders Ben-hadad. And in the following chapter (ix. 1 ff.) Elisha sends one of his followers to anoint Jehu. These discrepancies can hardly be due to oversight on the part of a compiler. They are clearly derived from divergencies in the tradition. But it is equally clear that the stories of Elijah and Elisha cannot fairly be regarded as a somewhat confused set of reminiscences. They bear all the marks of a very elaborate and artistic form of saga, in which a strong sense of dramatic propriety has been developed. We may refer (e.g.) to the dogs.

It has been mentioned above that the latter part of the story of David —in particular II Sam. ix–xx and I Kings i f.—is believed by some scholars to be a contemporary or almost contemporary literary work. So far as we are aware the chapters in question present no features incompatible with such an interpretation; but at the same time we know of no positive evidence in its favour, apart from the fullness of detail and the general verisimilitude and liveliness of the narrative. The style is that of saga, though this fact in itself is inconclusive—for a literary narrative style is often derived from saga. But it is worth noting that the narrative bears a rather close general resemblance to the 'Sagas of Icelanders' and to some stories in the (Icelandic) 'Sagas of Kings'—among which we may instance the Sagas of Ólafr Tryggvason and St Olaf in the *Heimskringla*. These sagas show the same verisimilitude and liveliness, together with fullness of detail, and in general, though they contain a large imaginative element, they may be regarded as historical authorities, in so far as they deal with countries which were intimately known; but they were not committed to writing within a century and a half—sometimes more than two centuries—of the events. It is extremely difficult, without external evidence, to distinguish sagas of this highly elaborate form from contemporary memoirs written in a saga-style. But in view of the evident use of saga in the early part of the story of David, it seems probable that the later part also is derived from saga rather than from memoirs. For the difference between the earlier and later parts many analogies can be found in Icelandic sagas. The early chapters of the latter frequently contain unhistorical elements.

For the story of David, unfortunately, external evidence seems to be wholly wanting. But we must not overlook the references to writing noticed on p. 632 f. especially those from Israelitish (Biblical) literature. The Phoenician evidence is less certain here; for it is very probable that civilisation was more advanced in the coast cities than in the interior. Account must also be taken of the written authorities cited in the Books of Kings, viz. the 'Book of the Acts of Solomon', the 'Book of the Chronicles of the Kings of Israel', and the 'Book of the Chronicles of the Kings of Judah'. But the date of these lost works is uncertain, so we will postpone discussion of this until later.

First we will take the references to writing in the Books of Samuel and Kings—before the seventh century. It will be seen that with one exception these all relate to letters. The only exception is the obscure passage in I Sam. x. 25, quoted on p. 633. This would seem to mean that Samuel entered Saul's appointment—or the terms of his appointment—as king in a register. It is hardly evidence for 'literature'. Moreover it is believed to come from the later of the constituent elements in the story of Samuel—the element which, as here, represents Samuel as ruler, and which is generally thought to date from a time between two and three centuries later than that of Samuel.

With the evidence of the letters we may take the references to scribes noted on p. 633. One of David's scribes, mentioned in I Chron. xviii. 16, is believed, from his name (Shavsha) to have been a Babylonian[1]— which may point to the use of cuneiform, though there can be no doubt that the Hebrew (North Semitic) alphabet was also known. The duties of such persons would presumably be chiefly in connection with correspondence and official records. But princes also are represented as able to read and write. In II Sam. xi. 14 f. David writes an extremely confidential letter to his commander-in-chief, which his knight, Uriah, who is the bearer, is evidently unable to read. The incident has been compared with a passage in the *Iliad* (VI. 168 ff.) relating to Proitos and Bellerophon, to which it bears an obvious resemblance, though unfortunately we do not know what the writing was in the latter case. But we may also compare a very similar story told by Saxo Grammaticus[2]—

[1] Cf. Hall, *Ancient History of the Near East*, p. 429; Cook, *Camb. Anc. Hist.* II. 334.

[2] Ed. Holder, p. 92 (p. 113 in Elton's transl.). The words are *literas ligno insculptas (nam id celebre quondam genus chartarum erat) secum gestantes*. With the incident we may compare *Atlamál*, st. 4, 9 ff., where Guðrún sends to her brothers a message of warning in Runic letters, which are tampered with by the messenger.

how Amlethus (Hamlet) was sent with a letter inscribed on wood instructing the recipient to put him to death. This story is not preserved in the vernacular; but the following words, "writing materials of this kind were much used in the past", leave no room for doubt that Runic writing is meant. It is of interest therefore to note that this kind of writing was in use in the North for perhaps a thousand years before the beginning of written literature, and also that princes and noblemen were expected to know it. The knowledge of reading and writing may be widespread, where there is no written literature; and consequently the references under discussion in the Hebrew records do not prove the existence of the latter.

We may now turn to the three (lost) works mentioned above which are cited in the Books of Kings. It is generally believed that these Books, apart from the first two chapters of I Kings, were compiled, at least in the main, from the works in question and from stories of the prophets. As to the source of the latter nothing seems to be known, though some of them would seem to be derived ultimately from saga, as noted above. The compiler, who brought together and edited these materials, was much influenced by Deuteronomy, and his additions are easy to distinguish owing to the peculiarities of his phraseology. It used to be thought[1] that the compilation must have been made after the year 621,[1] when a 'Book of the Law' was discovered in the Temple, as related in II Kings xxii. 8 ff.; but the identity of this book with Deuteronomy is now doubted,[2] and the date of Deuteronomy itself much disputed. At all events there can be no doubt that a written literature was in existence by this time. The 'book' was presumably a roll (of papyrus), such as is described, not much later, in Jerem. xxxvi. 4, 18, 23, and implied in Is. xxxiv. 4.

The story of Solomon contained in I Kings iii–xi is believed to be taken in the main from the 'Book of the Acts of Solomon', cited in xi. 41. If this is correct, the Book in question must have been of considerable length, and we may fairly regard it as an example of written literature. Unfortunately nothing seems to be known as to its date.

The other two lost Books mentioned above are very frequently cited.

---

[1] II Kings xviii. 5 would seem to suggest a somewhat earlier date; but we understand that the general opinion of Hebrew scholars is against this suggestion.

[2] Cf. Cook, *Camb. Anc. Hist.* III. 396. The book is read twice in a day, and consequently would seem to have been much shorter than Deuteronomy. Deuteronomy is now attributed by some scholars to the sixth century or later (*ib.* 484 f.), by others to the ninth century (cf. p. 633, note).

The 'Book of the Chronicles of the Kings of Israel' is referred to as an authority for the reigns of sixteen out of the eighteen kings of Israel. This also would seem to have been a work of some length. At all events it was more than a list of kings with their regnal years, such as we find in Anglo-Saxon records. We may quote I Kings xxii. 39: "Now the rest of the acts of Ahab, and all that he did, and the ivory house which he built, and all the cities that he built, are they not written in the Book of the Chronicles of the Kings of Israel?" Unfortunately it is not clear whether the Book was an original—perhaps official—record continued from time to time, or a compilation made from earlier records. It may not be without significance that one of the two reigns omitted is that of Hoshea, the last king. At all events it does not seem probable that such a work was composed after—perhaps we should say long after—the year 722, when the kingdom was destroyed.

The evidence available for the Hexateuch may be noticed here. It is commonly believed that the early constituent elements known as J and E were written in the first half of the eighth century, the former perhaps even earlier. Actual proof of this would probably be difficult to adduce.[1] Hosea, who prophesied not long after 750, seems definitely to imply (viii. 12) the existence of a written Book of the Law in his time. But it is not clear that his prophecies themselves were at once committed to writing.[2] More important perhaps is the fact that E is generally agreed to have been of northern origin. It came to be accepted in the southern kingdom (Judah) and to be combined with J, which is thought to have been of southern origin.[3] This is believed to have taken place before the production of Deuteronomy. Indeed the probability is that it took place some considerable time before; for Deuteronomy presupposes the growth of a tendency towards exclusiveness in religion. In particular we may note the laws contained in Ex. xxi f., which are attributed to E. These are presumably the laws of the northern kingdom; and their acceptance in Judah is more easily explicable at a time when the former kingdom was still in existence. In Vol. 1, p. 494, it was pointed out that written literature usually begins with the writing of the laws.

The evidence then, though it can hardly be regarded as decisive, tends

---

[1] Not much weight can be attached to the occasional references in Kings to a written 'Law of Moses'. In I. ii. 3 the context points to an addition by the compiler; and the other references may be of similar origin.

[2] They are supposed to contain a considerable number of 'interpolations', though the passage indicated is not generally included among these.

[3] The parallels with E are too close to allow of the supposition that the two were of wholly independent origin, but J may have been written down in the south.

as a whole to substantiate the accepted dates—which were arrived at, we believe, partly from linguistic considerations. The possibility of a much earlier date for the beginning of written literature is indeed not to be disregarded. The ostraka found at Samaria and dating from Ahab's time (cf. p. 633) were inscribed with pen and ink—which suggests that papyrus was known. At this time the conditions were favourable to Phoenician influence; the queen, Jezebel, was a Phoenician. The use of papyrus may well have begun then; but it can hardly have come into general use until much later. The stories of Elijah and Elisha, as we have seen, appear to be derived from saga. There is no evidence for a written collection of their prophecies, such as we have for the prophets of the eighth century—Amos, Hosea, Isaiah and Micah. The prophecies of these latter were written down, either by the authors themselves, or at a time when they were still more or less clearly remembered. In the case of Elijah and Elisha, however, we have only such prophecies as were preserved incidentally in the saga or sagas which narrated their doings. The evidence therefore, taken as a whole, would seem to indicate that the general use of written literature was a growth of the eighth century,[1] though its beginnings may go back even beyond the middle of the ninth.

From what has been said above it will be clear, not only that the literary use of writing began earlier than in the other literatures we have discussed, but also that the study of saga is here of primary importance. This applies of course primarily to the ninth and earlier centuries; but there can be little doubt that oral tradition in one form or another retained a certain force down to c. 700, or even later. Indeed the account of Sennacherib's invasion in the year 700, given in II Kings xviii (13 ff.) and xix, presents features which are difficult to explain, except by derivation from saga.

In the heroic, non-heroic and antiquarian categories saga is by far the most prevalent form of literature. The amount of poetry which has been preserved is small, though some of it seems to be very ancient. Non-heroic saga and antiquarian saga are closely connected and were doubtless cultivated in the same circles. The chief centres seem to have been

---

[1] It is of importance to notice that Assyrian sculptures of the eighth and seventh centuries sometimes depict a scribe, perhaps Aramaean, at work with roll and pen beside an Assyrian scribe, who is working with tablet and stylus. From the same period apparently dates a sculpture at Zenjirli in North Syria, which reproduces the ordinary Egyptian writing-outfit. Cf. Cook, *Camb. Anc. Hist.* II. 424.

the communities of the prophets and the Temple at Jerusalem, though for early times other sanctuaries may have to be taken into account. Heroic and non-heroic saga are as a rule very clearly distinguishable; they represent different elements in the population, which often were sharply opposed to one another. But in certain periods, especially the time of Elisha, there seems to have been some influence of the one upon the other.

Saga is found in all the various forms noted in Vol. i, p. 332 f. Sometimes a story is preserved only in the briefest possible form, perhaps in two or three sentences. The briefest example of all is what is said about Shamgar, son of Anath, in Judg. iii. 31; but this can hardly be called more than a reference to a saga. Even such specimens sometimes contain speeches, as in the story of Caleb and Achsah, related *ib.* i. 12 ff. Stories which occupy a chapter or a considerable part of a chapter and deal only with a single incident are of frequent occurrence; and these nearly always contain speeches. As an instance we may cite I Kings xiv. 1–20. Often they end with the explanation of a place-name or saying, as in I Sam. xix. 18 ff., which ends with an explanation of the saying, "Is Saul also among the prophets?"[1] Saga of a more elaborate and artistic form is to be found in a number of the stories related of Elijah and Elisha. But the most highly developed example of saga is the long and more or less continuous narrative which tells the story of David's later years and occupies the greater part of II Samuel. This narrative extends over a period of nearly twenty years; but attention is centred in a number of scenes, which are treated with a picturesque fullness of detail, very similar to what is to be found in the best Icelandic sagas.

In the remaining categories saga is unimportant. Theological saga— dealing with the adventures and experiences of deities—is practically excluded by the prevailing monotheism. Timeless nameless saga is slight and rare. 'Post-heroic' saga hardly occurs within our period.[2] Indeed this category as a whole seems to belong in Palestine to times when writing had come into general use for literary purposes; and we shall therefore omit it.

Early Hebrew poetry belongs to the mantic, gnomic and descriptive

---

[1] A different explanation of this saying is given in I Sam. x. 11.

[2] We do not mean by this that the Heroic Age extended down to the end of our period—say the reign of Hezekiah. But very little literature relating to contemporary events has survived from the eighth century, apart from the prophets. In point of fact the latter have elements in common with some of the 'post-heroic' literature of other countries, as will be seen later.

categories—apart from a number of poems and fragments, which are preserved incidentally in prose works. The mantic poetry presents very great difficulties, partly owing to its obscure and figurative diction, and partly because the texts, especially those of Isaiah and Micah, are believed to be largely interpolated. The gnomic and descriptive poetry is said to be late in its present form; and many scholars deny its antiquity, even in substance.

The characteristics of saga in general will require consideration in the next volume. But in view of the importance of the subject in Hebrew literature one or two preliminary remarks here may not be out of place. It is apparently the prevailing opinion now among Hebrew scholars that the early narrative texts were largely derived from saga. But at the same time there is evidently a good deal of misconception as to what is involved by this term;[1] it would seem that little attention had been paid to the study of those literatures, e.g. Irish, Norse and Polynesian, in which saga is best represented. Thus we find it assumed even by very recent writers that oral prose narratives cannot be preserved for very long, say not for more than three or four generations; but the literatures to which we refer supply abundant evidence that this is erroneous. Again, it is assumed that saga necessarily involves the presence of folklore elements. Such elements are of course of very frequent occurrence; but they are not essential. Their presence and frequency depends on the character of the milieu in which the saga is preserved.

On the other hand saga is sometimes credited with certain powers which, we think, it cannot justly claim. Thus the period of 430 years ascribed in Ex. xii. 40 f. (from P) to the sojourn of the children of Israel in Egypt has been attributed to saga, or at least to oral tradition; and the same origin has been suggested for the 480 years which in I Kings vi. 1 are said to have elapsed between the Exodus and the foundation of the Temple. We know of no analogies elsewhere in oral tradition for such figures; and the suggestions seem to us incredible. We are inclined even to doubt whether the shorter periods (of forty, eighty years, etc.) found in Judges are properly to be ascribed to oral

---

[1] This is due in part to the German word 'Sage', which has a much wider (less specific) meaning. The word 'legend', which is used by some writers, is open to more than one objection. It does not indicate that the story has a definite form; and it seems to us as inappropriate to the story of David's later years as to most of the 'Sagas of Icelanders'. A saga, at least in the early stages of its life, need not of necessity contain any unhistorical element, apart from the form (the conversations, etc.) in which it is presented.

tradition. There is some evidence for the recording of the lengths of kings' reigns. But more usually the only chronological evidence supplied by oral tradition, except for the recent past, consists of genealogies. We cannot but think that the Hebrew periods are the product of calculations made in the days of written literature, even if the data on which these calculations were based are not now traceable.[1]

Lastly, a word may be said here as to the relations between saga and narrative poetry. It is held by some scholars that certain stories, in particular the stories of the Patriarchs, have been converted from poetry into prose; Gen. xiv has been cited as a specially clear example. This is a question which must of course be left to specialists to decide. Analogies are to be found elsewhere both for the conversion of narrative poetry into saga and also for that of saga into narrative poetry. But it is quite erroneous to state, as has been done, that such conversions are universal or normal phenomena of oral literature. They occur, we think, only under certain conditions, which will require discussion in the next volume. The Hebrew literature of the Bible, as we have it, contains no narrative poetry, whether of Type A or of Type C. But it would hardly be wise to deny that such poetry may once have existed; for the fragments of mythological poetry found at Ras Shamra are usually described as 'epic' and in fact do contain a good deal of narrative, though speeches seem to predominate. On the other hand 'celebration' poems, like Judg. v, should not be cited as evidence for the cultivation of narrative poetry. Poetry of Type D is a more or less regular concomitant of saga, and seems to be best preserved where Type A is not cultivated (cf. p. 2).

There are still of course a good number of scholars who do not admit the use of anything which can properly be called saga among the sources of Hebrew literature. Some believe the written texts, or at least the earlier elements preserved in them, to be of much greater antiquity than is generally allowed. Others, while admitting the existence of 'traditions' of undefined form, hold that for practical purposes the books relating to early times are to be taken as reflecting the conditions and the thought of the times in which they were written, whether this took place in the eighth and seventh centuries or in later times; in other words these books cannot safely be regarded otherwise than as works of speculation or romance.

With regard to these widely divergent opinions we can only say that

---

[1] The remarkable reference to Zoan (Tanis) in Numb. xiii. 22 suggests acquaintance with some Egyptian record. We do not know whether there is any other evidence for the use of foreign chronological authorities.

as non-specialists we prefer to take as our basis the more commonly accepted views—which, so far as we can judge, seem to us as a rule well founded. We should not be greatly surprised, however, if some of the written texts should prove to have had a longer history than is commonly thought. On the other hand we would point out that saga is seldom, if ever, preserved in a rigid form. Normally it consists of an original composition plus the modifications and accretions which this has received in the course of time. The original composition may be derived from personal knowledge or from recent news; or it may be of a speculative or imaginative character. Its subsequent treatment depends upon the milieu in which it is preserved. It may be treated conservatively, or largely modernised; but it seldom or never reflects only the conditions and thought which belong properly to the last stage in its life—when it comes to be written down. To assume that a saga reflects only the conditions of its last stage is erroneous in principle, and involves the neglect of evidence which may be of value for literary or historical purposes. Every saga should be examined with the object of ascertaining what conditions it does reflect.

As regards the permanence or longevity of oral tradition other than what is preserved in saga or poetry we are inclined to be sceptical. Local traditions, which cannot properly be described as saga, sometimes have a long life; but we think they are always connected, directly or indirectly, with saga. These, however, are questions which will require more attention later.

CHAPTER II

THE HEROIC AGE

HEROIC SAGA AND POETRY

THE Heroic Age of the Hebrews is somewhat difficult to delimit, owing to the fact that only one story, or rather part of a story, has been preserved in pure heroic form. With the exception of the story of David we have only traces of heroic stories, or at best stories which were perhaps heroic originally but have assumed non-heroic characteristics. It is to be borne in mind that the whole of early Hebrew literature which has survived owes its preservation to non-heroic (religious) circles; and such circles naturally were not interested in heroic stories as such. That they preserved one such story—heroic and secular—was doubtless due to the fact that the hero was the founder of the national sanctuary.

It will be seen later that the Books of Kings, though they preserve no heroic stories in their true form, give some evidence which points to the cultivation of heroic saga. We think that the presence of heroic characteristics can be traced down to the latter part of the ninth century; but at the end of the century the evidence is slight and uncertain. Perhaps we may date the close of the Heroic Age about this time. Further back, we think that heroic saga can be traced in the Book of Judges. But the Books of Samuel are our chief source.

The story of David occupies the second half of I Samuel and the whole of II Samuel. It is clearly not all derived from one source; for there are discrepancies and even variant forms of saga, as we have seen (p. 635). As to the relationship of the various parts there are some differences of opinion; but it is generally agreed that II Sam. ix–xx form a single continuous narrative, together with I Kings i, ii. We will therefore begin with this narrative, which we may call the story of David's later years. But we are by no means clear that it is independent of everything that has gone before.

The narrative with which we are concerned begins (II Sam. ix) with David's reception of Mephibosheth. Next (x–xii) comes the war with Ammon, together with the death of Uriah, David's marriage with Bath-sheba, and the death of their child. This is followed (xiii) by the story of Amnon and Tamar. Then (xiv–xix) comes the story of Absalom and his rebellion, followed (xx) by the revolt of Sheba. In I Kings i, ii we have the account of the proclamation of Solomon and the deaths of David, Adonijah and Joab.

It has been mentioned above that some scholars believe this narrative to be a more or less contemporary memoir; and taken by itself it contains little or nothing incompatible with such an interpretation. But we shall then have to suppose that, according to the dates commonly approved, it was separated by a long interval from the rest of the literature; and we must regard it as extremely doubtful whether written literature existed at the time. Again, we cannot believe that the narrative is without connections in the preceding and intervening chapters. In point of fact some scholars hold that much of the preceding matter, in both Books, belongs to the same narrative; but the amount of 'dovetailing' involved by this view—on the assumption that a very ancient written text is concerned—seems to us incredible.

Other scholars give a totally different interpretation to the story, regarding it as a romance composed in later times. This of course disposes of the chronological difficulty; but in other respects it seems to us to have little in its favour. We presume that what is meant is a work of imaginative fiction, the subject of which is some well-known character or characters, historical or otherwise. It seems to be an essential feature of such stories that interest is centred almost exclusively in one or two characters, usually young, on whose behalf the sympathy of the reader or the audience is enlisted. Circumstantial detail and verisimilitude are wanting; the action takes place in a world of unreality. In the periods with which we are concerned romances are usually either developments of heroic stories or invented as additions to them; but they are distinguished from the heroic stories themselves by the features noted, which are doubtless due to distance, in time or place, from the original action. Intermediate stages are of course frequent enough. But the story of David's later years seems to have nothing in common with this genre.[1]

---

[1] The picture of David's court is not only detailed and intimate, but it also shows conditions different from those of later times. We may instance the absence of the chariot—to which we shall have to refer again later (p. 668 f.). We may contrast Samuel's speech in I Sam. viii. 11 ff.—a passage generally agreed to be late—where this anachronism actually occurs. The hardships described here as arising from kingly rule are those of a later time. Absalom seems to be the first prince recorded to have had a chariot and runners (II Sam. xv. 1); but this was to gain popularity. Apart

The resemblance of the story to the 'Sagas of Icelanders' is so close that it is hardly necessary to do more than give a reference to the latter. It may be observed that these also contain large imaginative elements, which it is impossible to control, except where external evidence is to be found. The essential feature, however, is that they have been preserved by a succession of skilled narrators from the time of the events which they relate. The first stage in the tradition may be illustrated by an incident in Njáls Saga, noticed in Vol. 1, p. 580. At a Christmas party given by Earl Sigurðr II of Orkney in 1013 the story of Njáll's death is related to the earl and the king of Dublin by one of those who had taken part in the fighting. For the next stage we may refer to the story (ib. p. 581) of the Icelander who recited to Harold Hardrada the account of that king's own exploits in foreign lands. He had got his story from a man who had been in the king's service. The sagas, as we have them, had a life of a century and a half or more in oral tradition before they were written down; and it is reasonable to expect that in the course of that time they underwent a considerable amount of change. But it is to be borne in mind that the audiences were familiar with them, so that drastic changes, especially in the relations of the personnel, would be difficult to carry out. Except for a partiality for ghost stories they preserve their verisimilitude; and the wealth of circumstantial detail is remarkable.

The 'Sagas of Icelanders' are not heroic stories. For heroic sagas we must turn to Ireland; and here the material is less suitable for comparison. The best and fullest Irish sagas relate to remote times—at least six or seven centuries before they were committed to writing. The stories of later times have for the most part been preserved only in rather brief form. Indeed they seem to have been much less in favour than the earlier ones.

We may note, however, that the story of David has also much in common with heroic narrative poetry. Most of the characteristic features of such poetry, as noted in Vol. 1 (p. 20 ff. and elsewhere), so far as they are applicable to saga, are to be found in this story. It is a narrative story of adventure, intended for entertainment, in the same sense as this may be said of heroic narrative poems. It is anonymous and full of speeches and descriptive details. More important than all this, however, is the milieu. It differs from all the other remains of early Hebrew literature in

from these considerations the references in the story to Joab seem to us quite irreconcilable with any theory of romance. This point will be noticed in the last chapter.

the fact that the view-point is, consistently, the court itself. It gives an intimate picture of the life and doings of the king and other members of the royal family; and the action usually takes place in their houses or in their presence. Elsewhere, as in the stories contained in the Books of Kings, this is only occasionally the case; the action usually follows the movements of prophets. The story may be described as court saga, just as heroic poetry in most countries may be described as court poetry. This is an essential difference between the story of David, which we call heroic, and the stories of Elijah and Elisha, which we call non-heroic.

On the other hand the story differs from heroic narrative poems, and from most heroic sagas, in its lack of unity. A heroic story, whether in verse or prose, is usually concerned either with a single adventure or with a series of adventures which are causally connected, though sometimes, as in the *Iliad*, the connection is very slight. The 'story' of David consists properly of a series or rather succession of stories, some of which are hardly connected with one another except by the personality of the chief character. In this respect it resembles the more strictly biographical Sagas of Icelanders—we may instance Egils Saga Skalla-grímssonar. Yet it may be questioned whether the difference between our story and very long heroic poems, such as the main story of the Mahābhārata and even the *Iliad*, is really essential. The latter may well have incorporated a number of stories which were originally treated separately. We may compare the long *bugarštica* on the battle of Kosovo (Bogišić, No. 1), discussed on p. 419 ff.

Another feature in which our story deviates from the heroic norm is the absence of a hero—at least in the part of the story with which we are now concerned. David is the central figure; but he is an elderly man. Stirring incidents abound; but he plays no active part in them. The absence of heroic deeds, whether by him or the other characters, is specially to be noted. 'Man-slayings' are by no means rare; but they are murders.

The heroic story without heroic deeds, though unusual, is by no means unknown. No heroic deeds are attributed to Nala or to Satyavat. Sigurðr is said to be a great hero; but in those Norse poems which can properly be called heroic (Types A and B), his function is to be mur-dered. The same is true of Noisiu and his brothers in the 'Exile of the Sons of Uisliu'. But all these cases differ from the story of David in the fact that the interest is centred in a woman—Damayantī, Sāvitrī, Guðrún or Brynhildr, Derdriu—whereas no woman plays a leading role in our story.

Notwithstanding this difference we think that the feature we have noted gives a clue to the original provenance of the story. We have seen reasons for suspecting that the stories of Nala and of Sāvitrī and most of the poems relating to Guðrún and Brynhildr are of feminine provenance; and the same may be true of the 'Exile', though in this case we are not prepared to speculate. Further examples may be found with some probability among the *bugarštice* noticed on p. 315 ff. (cf. also p. 448). By 'feminine provenance' we mean that the poems or stories in question have been composed either by women or for the entertainment of women. We suspect that much, though not necessarily all, of the story of David is of similar origin.

It is true that, in contrast with the cases noted above, no woman plays a leading part in the story; but taking the story as a whole, women, especially the ladies of the court, receive a great amount of attention. In II Sam. xi we have the account of David's passion for Bath-sheba, which involves what is practically the murder of her husband. It is surprising that this incident, discreditable as it is, should be treated so fully. Much more surprising, however, is the amount of attention given to the illness and death of the child, in the following chapter. What kind of audience was this intended for? Then in cap. xiii comes the story, likewise discreditable, of Amnon and Tamar. In xiv. 27 it is noted that Absalom had a beautiful daughter, also called Tamar; but his sons' names are not mentioned. More strange is the attention given to the concubines whom David leaves behind in his palace (xv. 16; xvi. 21 f.; xx. 3). We may also notice the prominence of the 'wise women' in cap. xiv and xx. 16 ff. Then in I Kings i f., Bath-sheba again comes to the fore; and a curious amount of attention is given to a young girl called Abishag.

This interest in the doings of women is by no means limited to the part of the story with which we are specially concerned. It begins in I Sam. xviii. 17 ff. with the account of Saul's daughters, Merab and Michal, and the marriage of the latter with David. In the following chapter (xix. 11 ff.) Michal enables David to escape from her father's emissaries. Cap. xxv is almost entirely occupied with an account of Abigail, who after her husband's death marries David. At the end of the chapter it is stated that David also married a certain Ahinoam of Jezreel; but Michal in the meantime had been given by her father to a man called Palti (Paltiel). In II Sam. iii. 2 ff. we find a list of the sons born to David in Hebron, with the names of their mothers, six in number. Next (*ib.* 7) we hear of Saul's concubine, Rizpah, and her relations with Abner.

When Abner seeks to come to terms with David, the latter stipulates (*ib.* 13 ff.) that Michal is to be restored to him. It is remarked that her husband Paltiel follows her weeping, until he is sent away by Abner. In v. 13 ff. it is stated that David took more wives and concubines after he had settled in Jerusalem; and another list of children is given. In cap. vi, where the bringing of the sacred Ark to Jerusalem is described, Michal reproves David for his undignified behaviour during the ceremony—at which David is evidently much annoyed. Lastly, we may notice the gruesome story told in xxi. 3 ff.—how David delivered up seven members of Saul's family to the Gibeonites, to be hanged. Two of these are sons of Rizpah, Saul's concubine, while the others are sons of his daughter Merab.[1] The story relates (*ib.* 10) how Rizpah watched and guarded the bodies for a long time.

The details recorded in a number of these passages are worth noting. We may refer (e.g.) to the passage (iii. 16) where Michal, when she is restored to David, is followed by her interim husband. The description of the conversation between David and Michal in vi. 20 ff. is of an intimate character. Still more striking is the description of David's grief at the illness of Bath-sheba's child in xii. 15 ff. Other intimate details of this kind, relating to the royal family, are recorded in the concluding part of the story (I Kings i f.).

We find it difficult to doubt that these narratives were intended in the first place for the entertainment of feminine audiences. This may not be true for the story as a whole. There are elements, e.g. II Sam. x, which suggest a different origin. But we think that the whole, or nearly the whole, of it can be satisfactorily interpreted as court saga, composed from stories current in the court, the majority of which were probably of feminine provenance.

This brings us to the question of the relationship between the different parts of the story. It is held by many scholars that considerable portions of the story from I Sam. xvi. 14 to II Sam. vi are derived from the same source as II Sam. ix–xx; indeed this element is believed to begin in I Sam. ix. The question of literary derivation is of course one which must be left to specialists, who can estimate the evidence of language and literary style. But we may perhaps say that we see nothing in the subject-matter of the portions indicated, which seems to us incompatible with derivation from the same saga-source as the later part of the story, whatever may be thought as to the literary channel. In particular, as we

---

[1] The name given hère (xxi. 8) is Michal; but cf. I xviii. 19.

have seen, the same lively interest in the doings of women is prominent in both.

Indeed we are inclined to suspect that more is derived ultimately from the saga than scholars will allow to have belonged to the hypothetical ancient text. We note specially that practically all catalogue matter is excluded from this element. Thus it is suggested that the lists of David's sons and wives in II Sam. iii. 2 ff., v. 14 ff., and of his officials in (*ib.*) viii. 16 ff., xx. 23 ff., and also the long catalogue of his heroes in (*ib.*) xxiii may be derived from registers. But lists of this kind are of frequent occurrence in the 'Sagas of Icelanders', and parallels are to be found in Irish heroic sagas and even in heroic narrative poetry. Such lists of course do not necessarily belong to the very oldest elements in a saga; but they may well be quite early accretions in this case. And we see no reason for doubting that they may have been added to the saga long before it was committed to writing.

The long catalogue of heroes in II Sam. xxiii. 8 ff. belongs to a series of chapters (xxi–xxiv) which is believed to be an insertion, and which interrupts the narrative contained in the preceding chapters and in I Kings i f. The contents of these chapters are of very varied character; but there seems to be no sufficient reason for denying that part of them —at least the catalogue of heroes[1] and the whole of cap. xxi[2]—may be derived from heroic (court) saga. It is unnecessary to suppose that the whole of this body of saga was collected and worked into a consecutive narrative at one time. On the contrary we have to think of the story which has been preserved as only a fraction of the amount of court saga which was once current. In this body of saga there were doubtless variant accounts of the same events, as well as actual discrepancies. It is in this way, we suspect, that the occurrence of variants such as I Sam. xxiv and xxvi is to be explained. The two accounts had come to differ so much that their identity was not recognised by those who collected or wrote down the stories. A similar case is perhaps to be traced in II Sam. viii. 3 ff. and x. 16 ff. As an instance of discrepancy we may cite the statements as to Absalom's sons in (*ib.*) xiv. 27, xviii. 18.

We do not mean to suggest that the whole of the story of David is

---

[1] We may compare the list of Eormenric's 'household force' (*innweorud*), enumerated in *Widsith*, 112 ff.

[2] Cap. xxiv is generally connected with xxi. 1–14; but it is distinguished from it by the prominence of the religious element and the introduction of the supernatural. Yet we are not inclined to deny the possibility that it may be derived from heroic saga. The scene is not very different from that of Book 1 of the *Iliad*.

derived from heroic saga. The religious poems in II Sam. xxii and xxiii. 1–7 are clearly of a different character; and the same is true of (*ib.*) cap. vii, which is likewise wholly concerned with religion. It is generally agreed, we believe, that both these passages are insertions made in later times. Both of them stand in positions where the narrative is interrupted by the inclusion of summaries and lists.[1] David was the founder of the national sanctuary at Jerusalem, and in later times at all events was regarded as the great champion and representative of the national religion. He was also credited with the authorship of a large number of hymns. Such insertions therefore are natural enough; for it is to be remembered that we owe to religious circles whatever has been preserved of early Hebrew literature. What is more surprising is that in general the secular character of the story has been so little affected. This fact would seem to indicate that it was written down—presumably in court circles—before it came into religious hands.

There are, however, some passages in I Samuel which may have had a different history. It is generally agreed that cap. xvi f. contains two accounts of David's introduction to Saul which are incompatible with one another. In xvi. 18 ff. he is brought to Saul as a minstrel or musician, and remains in his service in high favour. But in xvii, which describes the fight with Goliath, he is unknown to either Saul or Abner. In the former passage he is described as a warrior; in the latter he is a youth tending his father's sheep, and apparently not regarded as of military age. The former is generally agreed to belong to the earliest stratum of the story. As regards the latter there is some difference of opinion; some scholars believe the whole episode to be later, while others hold that parts of it belong to the oldest stratum, but that the Hebrew text[2] has been largely interpolated. The interpolation postulated is of a most elaborate character and seems to us hardly credible. Moreover it is to be borne in mind that the slaying of Goliath is elsewhere (II Sam. xxi. 19) attributed to a different hero, Elhanan.

---

[1] Cap. vii is immediately followed by a summary of David's wars, and this again by a short list of officials (viii. 16 ff.), as noted above. Both of these, we think, may have been derived from saga. In xxi–xxiv it would seem that insertions have been made repeatedly. The first insertion was apparently xxi. 1–14 and xxiv, the next xxi. 15–22 and xxiii. 8–39 (within the former insertion); then the religious poems (xxii and xxiii. 1–7) were inserted within the latter. All this matter, except the poems, may have been derived from current saga.

[2] The Greek transl. omits most of the passages which conflict with the preceding chapter. Hence some scholars hold that this transl. represents the original text. The view of those who think that the translator noticed and deliberately omitted the conflicting passages seems to us more probable.

Now cap. xvii has a strongly religious tone, which is entirely wanting in the other passage (xvi. 14 ff.). It appears also, however, in xvi. 1 ff.—the story of the anointing of David by Samuel. In this passage too—which is not thought to belong to the oldest stratum—David again is represented as a shepherd lad. Between the two narratives there is evidently no very close connection; but both bear a general resemblance to the kind of stories which everywhere tend to grow up round the childhood and youth of famous heroes. There is no suggestion of a court milieu in either case; indeed the story of the fight with Goliath is more like a folktale. Yet the prominence of the prophet in xvi (1–13) and the pronouncedly religious tone of xvii seem to point to a 'non-heroic' rather than a popular origin. And this is in full accord with the context of the former passage, which is clearly represented as the sequel to the 'rejection' of Saul, described in cap. xv.

The story of Saul is closely connected with that of David. As we have them, the two form a continuous narrative. From I Sam. xvi onwards David is the leading character, though some of the later chapters (xxviii and xxxi) are exclusively concerned with Saul. Here we will confine our attention to the earlier part of the story of Saul (I Sam. ix–xv).

It is generally agreed that these chapters contain two strands of narrative, which were originally quite independent. The earlier of the two is believed to be represented by cap. ix, x. 1–16, xi, xiii. 2–7, 15–23, xiv; it ends with—or is followed by—a short summary of Saul's campaigns and a list of his relatives (xiv. 47 ff.). The intervening sections,[1] together with cap. viii and xv, represent the later narrative. It will be seen that this analysis is in reality a division between heroic and non-heroic saga. The older narrative is not so intimate as the story of David, and the feminine element is wanting; but the interest is essentially personal and secular. The later narrative is typically non-heroic and religious; the central figure is not Saul, but Samuel. How the two narratives came to be combined in this way is not quite clear to us; but we believe the common view to be that the later narrative incorporated the earlier, when the latter was already in written form. At all events it would seem that the problem is the same as in cap. xvi f., where likewise we find two strands of narrative, one heroic and the other non-heroic, relating to David. The stories of Saul and of David have

---

[1] We have ignored one or two very short passages. We are inclined to think that in these analyses generally sufficient allowance has not been made for 'editorial' work.

therefore had the same literary history. Moreover from the fact that two narratives of Saul, without reference to David, are to be found in the later chapters, xxviii and xxxi—the former of which is out of place chronologically—we may infer with probability that the stories of Saul were collected in relation to those of David.

The history of the text may be that a number of heroic stories relating to Saul and David were at an early date collected and written down in the form of a continuous history, and that this history came later into the hands of a redactor who added other stories, of non-heroic character, in the earlier part of the work. But, however this may be, the important fact for our purpose is that heroic stories have been preserved relating to both these kings.

The first few chapters of I Samuel are concerned with the story of the prophet himself and show no heroic features. And elsewhere in early Hebrew literature the evidence for heroic saga is meagre and somewhat doubtful. Some possible instances, however, occur in the Book of Judges. The passage relating to Caleb and his daughter, in i. 12 ff., which occurs also in Josh. xv. 16 ff., might be a fragment of such saga; but it can probably be explained otherwise. Again, the story of Ehud, told in iii. 15 ff., might be a heroic saga in outline; but the account is so brief that one cannot speak with confidence. The story of Gideon and his son Abimelech, which is told at much greater length (cap. vi–ix), cannot be regarded as heroic saga in its present form. It shows, however, some obscure features, and apparently lacunae, which may indicate a change in its character; derivation from heroic saga is hardly impossible. The story of Jephthah in cap. xi f. may, perhaps with more probability, be derived from such a source, if allowance be made for preservation in non-heroic circles and a considerable amount of 'editing'. The story of Samson (cap. xiii–xvi), in addition to the religious element, which is found in all these stories, shows also 'popular' features, akin to those of folktales. If it is ultimately derived from heroic saga, it must have changed its character. The other stories present no distinctively heroic features, so far as we can see.

In the Books of Kings also—after the conclusion of the story of David in I. i f.—no saga which can properly be called heroic seems to be preserved. The account of Solomon's reign (I. iii–xi) presents a striking contrast to the story of David. Apart from two short narratives, illustrating Solomon's wisdom and wealth, and some catalogue matter, it is almost wholly occupied with a description of his buildings and with prayers and speeches made by him on various solemn occasions. Two different strata are generally recognised, much of the religious matter, together with the denunciation of Solomon's foreign marriages, being assigned to the 'Deuteronomist' redactor or compiler of the Books of Kings. The interests of the earlier and main element, which is of uncertain age, would seem to be antiquarian. There is no heroic element.

The same remark holds good for the rest of these Books. It would be hasty, however, to conclude from this that the Heroic Age was now at an end. In Ch. IV we shall see that there is a good deal of evidence for the prevalence of heroic conditions throughout the tenth and ninth centuries. The explanation may well be that, as in the case of the Book of Judges, the compiler was not interested in heroic saga. And in point of fact there is some positive, though slight and indirect, evidence for the existence of such saga. Some of the narratives relating to Elisha show in their details rather close resemblances to heroic saga. As an instance we may cite (II. ix) the account of the proclamation of Jehu and the proceedings which follow. This narrative and several others show a fondness for heroic (military) details; even the heroic attitude to the prophet is noted in ix. 11, without any real feeling of hostility. More important is the fact that the divine power sometimes (II. ii. 11 f., vi. 17) appears with military attributes. Such influence of the heroic upon the non-heroic may be explained by the rapprochement which took place between the two elements under Jehu, and indeed perhaps to some extent under his predecessor. It is now generally recognised that the moral judgments of the compiler do not represent the views of the early prophets. This is a subject which will require notice in the next chapter. But we may note here that Elisha's influence with the court seems to have been very great. The hostility towards the prophets of Jehovah which had existed under Ahab had completely passed away; and there is no need to suppose that the prophets, any more than the court, remained unaffected by the changed conditions.

Very little heroic poetry has been preserved—one poem, which is apparently complete, and a few fragments. All these seem to belong to Type D, i.e. either to elegies or panegyrics.

The only complete poem is David's elegy upon the death of Saul and Jonathan, preserved in II Sam. i. 19 ff. It is said in the text to be written in the 'Book of Jashar', which is generally thought to have been a collection of early Hebrew poetry. It is a typical heroic elegy, without any religious element. The possibility that it is really an example of

Type B (BD), i.e. a speech in character, put into David's mouth, cannot of course be excluded; but there seems to be nothing in the poem itself incompatible with the view that it is what it professes to be—a poem composed by David himself for the occasion, and preserved by oral tradition.

A short fragment of an elegy, likewise attributed to David, on the death of Abner, Saul's general, is preserved in II Sam. iii. 33 f. The little that is left suggests a poem of the same character as the preceding. In this case the elegy is said to be pronounced at the hero's funeral.

A fragment of a heroic panegyric—"Saul hath slain his thousands, and David his ten thousands"—is quoted in I Sam. xviii. 7 and xxi. 11. It is sung by women, with instrumental accompaniment, when Saul and David return from battle with the Philistines, and is said to have given great offence to Saul.

Lastly, we may refer here to a fragment of poetry, which seems to be heroic, preserved in the Book of Numbers xxi. 27 ff. The context apparently means that it is derived from a poem preserved by oral tradition, and implies that this was a poem celebrating a victory of Sihon, king of the Amorites, over Moab. And the fragment itself seems to have this meaning; but the last verse is obscure.

CHAPTER III

NON-HEROIC SAGA AND POETRY

THE non-heroic religious element is predominant in early Hebrew literature, and the amount of non-heroic saga which has been preserved is very considerable. Much of it, however, is primarily of national and antiquarian interest. Thus in what we may call the 'story of Moses', as contained in the Books of Exodus and Numbers, with the last chapters of Deuteronomy, the personal element is comparatively slight and in general quite subordinate to the early history of the nation and the origin of national and religious institutions. The Book of Joshua, again, is almost exclusively of national (antiquarian) interest; hardly anything of a personal nature is recorded of Joshua himself. The Book of Judges on the other hand consists in the main of a number of stories which are largely, though not exclusively, of personal interest. In the Book as a whole national interest is very prominent; but this is believed to be due in part to the compiler. We shall therefore include stories from Judges in this chapter, but reserve the stories of Moses and Joshua for notice in Ch. vi.

The combination of national with personal interest is one of the chief features which distinguish Hebrew non-heroic stories from those of India. In both cases the non-heroic element is essentially religious. And antiquarian interests of certain kinds are by no means wanting in India, though they are less prominent than here. But the feeling for nationality seldom finds expression in early Indian literature, except in the hymns of the Rgveda—where of course it is very prominent, as distinguishing the invaders (Aryans) from the native population of the country. In Palestine the same feeling appears in the earliest records; but it is never lost sight of, and in non-heroic stories it usually plays a very important part. The Israelites, like the Vedic Aryans, believed that their ancestors had come to the land as invaders; and they regarded the peoples who had previously inhabited the country as foreigners, although apparently they spoke the same language as themselves. Moreover this strong sense of nationality was closely bound up with the cult of the national god Jehovah. They believed that Jehovah had brought them to Palestine, and had ordered them to exterminate the native inhabitants. Most of the evils which befell them in the course of their early history are attributed to the influence of these natives; for they had carried out the order only to a limited extent. Yet instances of wholesale massacre, accompanied by the destruction even of the enemy's property and live-stock, are to be found not only in the Hexateuch, but also in later times, e.g. under the prophet Samuel (I Sam. xv).[1]

In conformity with this intense feeling for nationality and the national religion non-heroic (prophetic) saga frequently shows a warlike spirit, which is quite foreign to the non-heroic stories of (post-Vedic) India. The normal attitude of the prophets towards certain nationalities, especially the Canaanites and 'Amorites', and to all Israelites who came under their influence, is one of uncompromising hostility. They are often found rousing princes and people to battle also against foreign invaders. Indeed their influence would seem to be usually on the side of war, though they sometimes intervene to prevent warfare between different sections of Israel. It is only after the end of the period with which we are concerned that we find their influence exercised on the side of peace with foreign nations.

First we will take a story (Judg. iv f.) which we know both from a short saga and from a poem of Type D—a song of triumph—which follows it. The latter is believed to be the earliest piece of Hebrew poetry which has been preserved. The saga and the poem give somewhat different accounts of the story, which is that of a rising of the Israelites against Jabin, king of Canaan (or Hazor) and his general Sisera. Jabin is mentioned only in the saga,[2] and this describes only two tribes, Naphtali and Zebulon, as taking part in the rising, whereas the poem adds several others. Both versions, however, show strongly marked non-heroic features. Barak may perhaps be a prince of Naphtali—his position is not stated—but in the saga he will not consent to lead the rising, except under the guidance of the prophetess Deborah. There is no mention of heroic deeds by him or any other individual warrior in the army. Their action is inspired by religion. The final blow, Sisera's death, is due to a woman, the wife of an alien (non-Israelite). In the poem the motifs of religion and patriotism are dominant throughout;

---

[1] We have not noted any evidence for such complete destruction in the Rgveda; but parallels are to be found in the earliest records relating to the Teutonic and Celtic peoples. These are said to be due to religious vows, e.g. Tacitus, *Ann.* XIII. 57; Caesar, *Gall.* VI. 17; cf. also Orosius, V. 16.

[2] The saga seems to have confused the stories of two different wars. A war against Jabin, king of Hazor, ending with his death, is recorded in Josh. xi; there is no mention of Sisera. On the other hand the conclusion of the poem (Judg. v. 28 ff.) suggests that Sisera is regarded as an independent prince.

and fierce curses are invoked upon a district, which sent no contingent to the army. The speaker is the prophetess herself, at least in part, and perhaps throughout the poem.

The story of Gideon (*ib.* vi ff.) must be regarded as non-heroic in its present form, whatever may have been its original character. As we have it, patriotism and religion are the guiding motifs. Gideon is far more of a hero than Barak, and the interest is largely centred in his personality. But his religious inspiration is repeatedly emphasised; and he is not only a warrior, but also (vi. 25 ff.) a champion of one religion against another. In the story of his son Abimelech (*ib.* ix) also the non-heroic element predominates; but the story is told from an unsympathetic point of view.

The story of Micah and the men of Dan (*ib.* xvii f.) is another example of the unsympathetic kind. This story also would seem to have changed its character. We suspect that in its original form the interest was primarily antiquarian—relating to the foundation of the important sanctuary at Dan. But the form in which we have the story is presumably due to its preservation in circles, at Jerusalem or elsewhere, which regarded this sanctuary with disapprobation.

The last story in the Book of Judges (xix ff.) relates to the misdoings of the men of Gibeah and the war which arose therefrom. This is a story of somewhat different character. The interest is again tribal rather than individual; the only individuals who figure at all prominently are not named. But its antiquarian origin is by no means obvious. It may rather be founded upon the memory of some desperate intertribal conflict, which had become obscured in the course of time. Non-heroic connections may be traced in the insistence upon the punishment of immorality and in the organisation of the punitive action at the sanctuary of Mizpah.

The greater part of the Book of Judges is arranged according to a chronological scheme, which gives a succession of 'judges' or rulers of Israel. On various occasions the nation is said to have been subjected to foreign oppression on account of its sins. Then follows repentance and deliverance from the oppressors. The majority of the stories are concerned with these deliverances and the restoration of independence. The last two stories, however, fall outside this scheme, and would seem to refer to the early part of the period. Yet all the stories, whatever their origin—which may well have been very varied—contain certain non-heroic elements, probably due in part to the milieu in which they have been preserved.

The first half of I Samuel consists in the main of non-heroic saga. In cap. i–iii we have an account of the birth and childhood of the prophet Samuel, his dedication at the sanctuary of Shiloh and his first revelation, together with a description of the priest Eli and his family. In cap. iv–vii the sacred Ark is carried to battle; but the men of Israel are defeated by the Philistines, the Ark is captured, and the sons of Eli, who are in charge of it, are slain. Eli himself who is described as 'judge', dies on hearing the news. The Philistines, however, are smitten with plagues, and return the Ark to Israel; and it is brought to Kiriath-jearim. Samuel becomes judge of Israel, and a victory is gained over the Philistines. In cap. viii Samuel is an old man, and makes his sons judges; but the people demand a king. The request is regarded as sinful; but a king is promised.

There is much difference of opinion as to the literary history of these chapters. It is generally agreed that they are of composite origin; and the basis is commonly held to be a Life of Samuel, which has incorporated earlier material, relating to Eli and his family and the Ark. But there is some disagreement as to details, and also as to the date of the main narrative. Some scholars are inclined to connect this with the hypothetical text E of the Hexateuch, while others attribute it to a later date. Whatever may be the truth in regard to these points, non-heroic and religious interest is dominant throughout the whole narrative; and we cannot doubt that it is derived to a large extent from saga. Indeed we are inclined to ask whether the heterogeneous character of the narrative may not be in part inherited from the saga itself. Accretion is an extremely frequent phenomenon in saga everywhere. Biographical saga in particular consists as a rule of a collection of stories; and among these there are often enough some in which the subject of the saga does not figure personally. As regards specific cases, however, as here, the question can of course be decided only by experts.

An example of non-heroic poetry is preserved in the hymn said to be sung by Hannah, mother of Samuel, when her son was dedicated at the sanctuary (I Sam. ii. 1 ff.). It is clearly unsuited to the context in which it occurs, and is generally thought to have been composed originally for some occasion of national thank-offering, presumably during the period of the monarchy.

In I Sam. ix we come to the story of Saul, which appears to be heroic (cf. p. 653). But the (non-heroic) story of Samuel is not yet at an end. It would seem that the story of Saul, which is universally held to be the older of the two, has been incorporated in the latter. To the former are assigned cap. ix, x, 1–16, xi, parts of xiii, xiv, while the intervening passages are believed to come from the story of Samuel. According to the current view both stories or 'Lives' were in written form before they were combined; but the interweaving would be more easily explicable if this were true only of the earlier story. In the following chapters (xv–xvii) the non-heroic narrative is continued; but in cap. xvi the interest passes over from Samuel to David, and in cap. xvii is centred wholly in the latter. This suggests to us that the work in question, if it ever existed as a separate document, was not merely a Life of Samuel, but rather a collection of non-heroic stories relating to the times before David became king and brought together as an introduction to his story. But is the existence of this written work really certain? After cap. xvii non-heroic elements occur from time to time in the narrative, though we do not know of any long sections which can be described as definitely non-heroic. The evidence throughout suggests to us the work of a man who took the heroic stories—already written down—of Saul and David as his basis, and added to them much 'editorial' matter, as well as stories current in his own (non-heroic) circle. The occurrence of variants and discrepancies does not of course necessarily mean that one passage is of heroic, and the other of non-heroic, origin.

The non-heroic element in II Samuel is very slight. The chief passage is cap. vii, which is derived, we suspect, from 'Temple-saga'. Reference may also be made to the poetry in cap. xxii f. Elsewhere passages and expressions of a religious character are frequent enough; but they seem to us to prove nothing as to their origin. They may mean no more than that the Hebrew nobility, like the Indian, were much occupied with religion.

In the Books of Kings on the other hand non-heroic elements are predominant throughout, except in I. i, ii, which seem properly to belong to II Samuel. We may omit from consideration both these chapters and also iii–xi,[1] which, though doubtless of non-heroic origin, are mainly of antiquarian interest. The rest of the work consists of notices, generally short, of the reigns of the kings of Israel and Judah, set in a pronouncedly non-heroic framework and interspersed with non-heroic stories of kings and prophets. In the summaries of the reigns every king has a moral judgment passed upon his acts in accordance with the Deuteronomic standard; but we will confine our attention to the stories.

[1] Cap. xi, however, seems properly to belong to what follows. Both the matter and the treatment are analogous to what we find in the accounts of the subsequent reigns.

The first story is that of the revolt of Jeroboam, described in cap. xii. The interest here is at least as much national as personal, while on the personal side it is bound up with the story of Ahijah's prophecy, related in the preceding chapter. The next incident (xii. 22 ff.) is the intervention of the prophet Shemaiah, which prevents Rehoboam from attacking Israel. This again is followed by an account of Jeroboam's religious ordinances. Cap. xiii is occupied with the story of the two nameless prophets, which seems to date from the time of Josiah or later. Cap. xiv relates (1–20) how Jeroboam's wife consults the prophet Ahijah with regard to her son's illness; then (21 ff.) it gives a short account of the invasion of Judah by Shishak, king of Egypt, and the treasure he exacted from Rehoboam. It may be suspected that the last story is derived from the traditions of the Temple.

This short summary of the reigns of Jeroboam and Rehoboam will serve to illustrate the general character of the stories contained in the two Books. The interest is sometimes national rather than personal. Where it is personal it is usually centred in a prophet. There are indeed a large number of stories in which kings are the most prominent figures; but in these the interest usually lies not so much in their personal adventures or exploits as in their relations with prophets and their attitude to the religion of Jehovah.

We may next take the stories of Elijah and Elisha, which extend from I. xvii to II. xiii and form perhaps the most striking element in these Books. They are closely bound up with the history of the kings of Israel, Ahab and his successors. Some of these stories are very picturesque; the cultivation of saga has attained a very high standard. Elijah usually appears alone; he is represented as carrying on a long struggle single-handed against Ahab and his court. But Elisha is frequently associated with the 'sons of the prophets', societies of whom seem to have existed in various towns. He is also evidently held in much honour by the kings, even by Jehoram, son of Ahab, as well as by those of the following dynasty. We have already noted (p. 655) that the stories relating to this time show resemblances to heroic saga—which would seem to suggest that the prophetic circles, in which they presumably took shape, were then in more or less close contact with the court and military circles.

There are one or two stories relating to the times of Elijah and Elisha, in which neither of these prophets figures. The most striking of these is the story of Ahab's death. Elijah seems to be still alive; but he is not mentioned. The true prophet in the story is a certain Micaiah.

The story of Elisha's death (II. xiii. 14 ff.) seems to be the last instance of saga in the northern kingdom.[1] The accounts of the later
reigns consist of what are apparently historical notices, though they are
not free from chronological mistakes, especially in regard to the reign
of Pekah.

The amount of saga from the kingdom of Judah is much less. It is
non-heroic, but of a different kind from what we have been discussing;
prophets are seldom mentioned. The chief centre and home of saga, as of
tradition generally, was evidently the Temple at Jerusalem. This may
be seen by the frequent references to the treasures of the Temple, which
go back as far as the times of Rehoboam and Asa (I. xiv. 26; xv. 15, 18).
The first story, however, which is told at length is that of Athaliah
(II. xi). In this case the scene is laid wholly in the Temple. It is here ·
that the child Joash is concealed for six years, when the queen-mother
has destroyed the rest of the royal family. It is in the Temple too that
the dramatic scene takes place, when the child is proclaimed king by
the high-priest Jehoiada; Athaliah hastens in to know what is happening
and is carried away to execution. The next chapter gives an account of
the repairs to the Temple undertaken by Joash and Jehoiada.

In cap. xiv (8 ff.) a short story is told of Amaziah, son of Joash. He
sends a reckless challenge to Jehoash, king of Israel, to which the latter
replies with a disdainful reference to a cedar and a thistle. Amaziah
insists upon fighting, and is defeated. The challenge seems to preserve
an echo of heroic conditions; but the notice of the losses incurred by the
Temple, when it was plundered by the victorious king, again point to
saga originating in this quarter.[2]

The next story (xvi. 7 ff.) relates to Ahaz, grandson of Amaziah. He
goes to Damascus to meet Tiglath-pileser, king of Assyria, and sees there
an altar, of which he sends a model to the priest Urijah at Jerusalem. The
latter makes a copy of it for the Temple; and the account then goes on to
describe other changes in the Temple and its arrangements, which were
ordered by Ahaz. Again there can be no doubt as to the source of the
record.

By this time a written literature must already have been in existence.
Yet saga would seem to have been still cultivated in the reign of Heze-

[1] Except perhaps the short story of Amaziah's defeat (xiv. 8 ff.); see below.
[2] Some scholars take this story to be of northern origin, owing to the description
of Beth-shemesh in xiv. 11. The context is ambiguous; the reference to the losses of
the temple may have been added later. In II Chron. xxv. 20 Amaziah's defeat is
attributed to his idolatry; but this of course may represent a later view.

kiah, son of Ahaz; for it is difficult otherwise to account for the long story of Sennacherib's invasion, preserved in cap. xviii f. The account of the mission to Jerusalem is generally thought to have been duplicated, one version being given in xviii. 17–xix. 8, and the other in xix. 9–34; and it can hardly be doubted that the two passages are to some extent variants. And by this we do not mean merely that they are records of the same events. The connection between them is 'literary', as may be seen (e.g.) from xviii. 33 ff. and xix. 12 f.; they are derived from the same saga, though before they were written down they had come to differ so much that their identity was apparently not recognised by the compiler.[1] It may be noted that—in both versions—one scene is laid in the Temple —which suggests that this saga may have originated there, like the stories noticed above.

In cap. xx we find further stories of Hezekiah, while cap. xxii f. contain stories of Josiah. So far as form goes, these also might be derived, in part at least, from saga; but there is no definite evidence to this effect, as in the story discussed above. And there can be little doubt that the style of saga had been adopted into written literature before the time of Josiah.

It may be mentioned here that the Books of Chronicles contain a considerable number of stories relating to the period of kingship, in addition to those which they have borrowed from the Books of Samuel and of Kings. Like all the other matter contained in the Chronicles, these stories are concerned primarily with the kingdom of Judah. All of them are non-heroic, and composed or edited in the interest of the national religion—very frequently they refer to the Temple and priesthood at Jerusalem. In these stories we meet with a number of prophets who are not mentioned in the Books of Kings. Probably all of these belong to Judah; one of them (II. xxiv. 20) is a son of the priest Jehoiada.

The Chronicles are a very late work, hardly earlier than the third century (B.C.), at least in their present form; and their authority as a historical record is not rated high. But we find it difficult to doubt that they preserve a good deal of ancient tradition connected with the Temple. The subject is of course one which can be dealt with only by specialists; but it is of importance for the literary history, as well as the general history, of the period. There was at least one long break in the history of the Temple; but the organisation connected with it seems to

---

[1] The whole passage—including both versions of the story—is preserved also in Is. xxxvi.f.; but the language seems to show that this is derived from Kings.

have survived, and it is probable that to this in the main we owe the preservation of what has come down from the period of kingship. The Chronicles, even more than the Kings, point to intimate relations between the Temple and the Palace, which were adjacent buildings. Thus in II Chron. xxii. 11 it is stated that the princess Jehoshabeath, who saved the life of the child Joash, was the wife of the priest Jehoiada—a statement which certainly helps to explain the course of events. The existence of such relations will account for the preservation of the court saga which we have in II Samuel, and also for the fact that non-heroic saga (in Kings) shows in Judah a somewhat different character from what we find in the kingdom of Israel and elsewhere.

In conclusion reference should perhaps be made here to the Book of Ruth, though we do not think it is properly to be regarded as non-heroic saga. The majority of scholars now believe it to be a late work, though there are some who still maintain its early date. Its origin is perhaps to be compared with that of some of the Norse Fornaldar Sögur, or 'Stories of Ancient Times', in which a thin strand of tradition has been utilised to form the basis of an imaginative work. In short we should be inclined to regard it as a romance. The incentive to its composition may in the first place have been antiquarian—i.e. interest in the ancestry of David—just as in the case of some of the Fornaldar Sögur; but it can hardly be described as a didactic work, any more than these. It gives the impression of having been intended primarily for feminine circles.

NOTE. In the story of Samuel (p. 660 f.) we have followed in the main the commonly accepted analysis of the text (from cap. viii onwards), which appears to be well founded. Of the two constituent elements the (originally heroic) 'story of Saul' (cf. p. 653 f.) seems to be the earlier, though both may well be derived from collections of stories. But we are inclined to suspect that too much importance has been attached to the apparent discrepancies between the two elements in regard to the position of Samuel (cf. p. 634). A somewhat similar double rôle—of seer and ruler—is implied in the story of Moses; and in the course of our work we have met with analogies, not very rarely, elsewhere—especially perhaps in Africa. Some of these will be noticed in Vol. III.

CHAPTER IV

THE HEROIC MILIEU

INDIVIDUALISM

IN Vol. 1, p. 64 ff., we discussed certain characteristics of heroic stories under the following headings: (1) The social standing of the personnel; (2) the scenes of the stories; (3) the accessories of heroic life; (4) social standards and conventions.

The Hebrew evidence relating to these subjects is almost all contained in the Books of Samuel, especially the story of David. Some little evidence, however, chiefly of an indirect character, may be found elsewhere.

(1) The personnel of the story of David seems to be very similar to what we find in the ancient heroic stories of the West and of India. Most of the characters are members of the royal family, the court or the comitatus—a list of which is given in II Sam. xxiii. There are also certain ministers of state, together with priests and a prophet. In addition to these we meet with a number of persons whose rank is not stated; but persons not attached to the service of kings and princes are frequently nameless, as in the case of the wise women who figure in II Sam. xiv and xx.

In David's time kingship is said to have been a recent institution in Israel.[1] In Judges we hear of a long succession of rulers, only one of whom (Abimelech) is a king, while the rest are called 'judges'. But this historical scheme is believed by many to be the work of a late (Deuteronomic) editor. The stories themselves suggest that the authority of the various leaders was merely local. Several passages in Numbers (derived from P) and Chronicles speak of princes or chiefs of the tribes in the time of Moses; and though the authorities are late, it may be that each tribe had a ruler or ruling family of its own in early times. One of the names which occur regularly in the lists is Nahshon, 'prince of Judah', who according to the genealogies in Ruth iv. 18 ff., I Chron. ii. 10 ff. was an ancestor of David in the fifth generation. Possibly there-

---

[1] Kings of cities are frequently mentioned in the Book of Joshua, e.g. xii. 9 ff., where a list of thirty-one such kings is given. But these belong to the Canaanites and other native peoples. Abimelech's kingship at Shechem is perhaps to be regarded as primarily Canaanitish.

fore, if we may put any trust in the evidence, David's family had a hereditary right to rule in Judah. On the other hand, in I Sam. ix. 21, Saul is said to have belonged to an unimportant family in Benjamin. But the political conditions of the period before the institution of kingship are obscure.

In non-heroic stories, especially such as relate to prophets, the characters seem to be drawn from a wider circle. Some prophets, like Nathan, evidently have a recognised position at the court. But this is not the case as a rule with the prophets mentioned in the Books of Kings, at all events those who belong to the northern kingdom. Usually they are in opposition to the kings. As to their own position in life little information is given; but sometimes they seem to be associated with the 'sons of the prophets'. Elijah's origin is not stated; Elisha would seem from I. xix. 19 to be a well-to-do farmer. The evidence is perhaps too slight to be of much value; but it may be worth noting that Amos (vii. 14) describes himself as a herdsman and woodman.

(2) In regard to the scene of action little need be said here. In the story of David, as in the heroic stories of other lands, the scene is usually laid either in the house of the king or some other member of the royal family or on the field of battle or adventure. In non-heroic stories there is a wider choice; the action sometimes takes place in the house of a prophet or other commoner—who is often nameless—occasionally also in the Temple or some other sanctuary.

The scene of one very remarkable story (I Sam. xxviii) is laid in the house of a witch, who at Saul's request brings up the ghost of Samuel. In its present form at least this story is non-heroic; Samuel declares to Saul that his case is hopeless owing to his disobedience to the divine commands. The wording of the speech may of course be due to an editor; but it is not easy to see how Samuel could have been introduced for any essentially different purpose. For the incident as a whole we know no precise parallels in either heroic or non-heroic stories, though analogies for the various elements are of not infrequent occurrence.[1]

(3) The accessories of heroic life seem to be somewhat different from what we find in the West. Feasting is not so much in evidence. Adonijah gives a great feast (I Kings i. 9, 19, 41, etc.), when he makes himself king. In II Sam. iii. 20 David entertains Abner and his followers with a feast,

---

[1] Especially in early Norse poetry, e.g. *Vegtamskviða, Grógaldr, and Helgakv. Hund.* II. 40 ff. There may have been a tradition that Myrddin prophesied after his death, though the prophecies recorded under this title are very late (cf. Vol. I, p. 107). We may also refer to the consultation of Teiresias in the *Odyssey*, XI. 90 ff.

when they visit him. Feasting on a large scale is recorded in I Chron. xii. 39 f. But we do not hear of the constant feasting or drinking which seems to occupy every evening in the West. On the other hand much more attention is paid to the king's harem. Indeed it would seem that a king's reputation depended largely upon the number of his wives and concubines. Western analogies are of course not unknown—we may instance Priam, Attila and Harold the Fair-haired—but they are not very frequent. Certain passages, especially II Sam. xvi. 21 f., suggest that the appropriation of a king's concubines by an ambitious prince was regarded as an act of daring calculated to win adherents to his cause.

References to the weapons of heroes are curiously rare. This may be explained in part if, as we think, the story of David, or most of it, was intended in the first place for feminine circulation. But it is rather remarkable that so little should be said of weapons in such passages as II Sam. xxiii and I Chron. xi f. The sword captured from Goliath seems from I Sam. xxi. 9 to have been deposited in a sanctuary.

Horses and dogs are of no account in the story of David. For dogs this is true of all early Hebrew literature; they appear only as scavengers. But the evidence relating to the horse is interesting. From the time of Solomon onwards horses and chariots are regularly associated with kings and their troops. In a time of famine Ahab's chief concern is for his horses (I Kings xviii. 5 f.). When going on a journey or to battle a king always drives in a chariot. The wounded Joram has a chariot in readiness, in which he drives out, apparently a few hundred yards, to meet his general (II. ix. 21). At Jerusalem there was a special gateway for horses in the palace (*ib.* xi. 16). We have seen (p. 655) that in this period the divine power itself is said to be manifested in the form of chariots and horses. The armies of both Israel and Judah consist largely of chariotry.

David, however, is never represented as using chariot or horses. In the whole story Absalom is the only prince who provides himself with a chariot (II Sam. xv. 1), though on the field of battle he rides a mule (*ib.* xviii. 9). Only in the northern plains David seems to have had a small —but very small—force of chariotry; for in the Syrian war he is said (*ib.* viii. 4) to have destroyed all the captured horses, except what were sufficient for a hundred chariots. The use of chariot and horses by the Israelites[1] appears to be an innovation of David's or Solomon's time;

---

[1] The Books of Joshua and Judges contain a number of references to their use by the native peoples against the Israelites. Most of these relate to the northern part of the country, e.g. Josh. xi. 4, 9; Judg. iv, v. 22, 29. But in Judg. i. 19 we hear of them also in the south.

neither Saul nor any earlier leader is said to possess them. This is remarkable in view of the fact that the Egyptians and the Hittites had
carried on chariot warfare in Palestine, at least on the lower ground,
several centuries before David's time.[1] Possibly the roads had gone out
of use. Still more noteworthy, however, is the fact that the records have
so faithfully preserved the difference between the earlier and later
conditions. It confirms the antiquity of the heroic saga in the Books of
Samuel, and also gives good reason for believing that early saga is
preserved in the Book of Judges. The only anachronism in this respect
which we have observed occurs—in a definitely non-heroic context—
in I Sam. viii. 11 f., where Samuel speaks of service with horses and
chariots as one of the evils which the appointment of a king will in-
volve. The author evidently has in mind the conditions of a later day.
There is no evidence that Saul possessed either horse or chariot;
everything that we hear of him suggests that he was extremely
poor.

(4) In spite of the newness of the kingship we hear a good deal of
court etiquette. It is frequently recorded that when members of the
court and visitors come to see the king they do obeisance to him—much
as in Russian and Yugoslav heroic poems. The formalities observed in an
interview between Solomon and his mother are duly noted in I Kings
ii. 19.[2] In II Sam. xv. 1 ff. Absalom begins to live in state, when he is
aspiring to displace his father. He provides himself with a chariot and
fifty men to run before him, presumably in imitation of foreign kings.
David's life seems to be less ostentatious; but he entertains some men,
including a son of Jonathan, as perpetual guests in his household. We
hear also of embassies coming with presents from foreign kings (*ib.*
v. 11; viii. 10); but no details are recorded as to their reception.

In ethical standards there is much variety, such as one might expect
in a time of great political and social change. The heroic standard is well
represented by the Philistine Ittai of Gath, who enters David's service
shortly before Absalom's rebellion. When David has to leave Jerusalem,
he advises Ittai to return to his own land (II Sam. xv. 19 ff.). But the
latter firmly refuses to forsake him; and in the sequel (cf. I Kings i. 38,

---

[1] According to I Kings x. 28 f. Solomon obtained his horses and chariots from
Egypt; and the context seems to mean that the Syrians and Hittites likewise
obtained them from there. But see *Camb. Anc. Hist.* III. 256, 357. Was trade in
horses allowed only by special treaty? For Philistine chariots see I Sam. xiii. 5.

[2] It may be noted that in II Sam. vi. 16 David's wife Michal, daughter of Saul, is
annoyed at seeing her husband give way to religious ecstasy. When he returns, she
reproves him (*ib.* 20); and a quarrel ensues.

44) the Philistine mercenaries are evidently among the most reliable troops. At an earlier time David himself had served under Achish, king of Gath, and was regarded as loyal by him (I Sam. xxix. 3, 6 ff.).

A somewhat different and probably more primitive ethical standard may be seen in the case of Joab, David's nephew and commander-in-chief. Joab seems to be thoroughly loyal to David throughout, though the narrative is evidently biassed against him. But he is apt to take the law into his own hands, especially where wrongs to himself are concerned, as in the cases of Abner and Amasa. Family quarrels are common enough, e.g. in both Saul's and David's families. But it is a remarkable feature in David's character that he is reluctant to take vengeance. This may be seen not merely in his attitude to Absalom, but still more in the fact that he promotes Amasa, Absalom's general. He punishes the Ammonites for the insult done by them to his envoys. But it may perhaps be inferred that this was followed by a conciliatory policy; for one of their princes comes to his assistance when he is driven out by Absalom. Savage treatment of enemies seems to be rare; we hear nothing of wars of extermination,[1] such as occur so frequently in the Book of Joshua. Warfare of this kind is clearly a non-heroic characteristic. In I Sam. xv it is the prophet Samuel himself who kills Agag, when Saul has given him quarter.

In Vol. 1, p. 80 ff. we discussed the subject of Individualism under the two headings: (1) Individualism and nationality; (2) Heroic warfare.

(1) The contrast between individualism and nationalism is strikingly illustrated by a comparison of the heroic and non-heroic records discussed above. In reality, however, it is clear that sometimes the contrast lies not more in the attitude of the records themselves than in that of the persons with whom they deal. The kings and their adherents in general represent the individualism regularly associated with heroic conditions and ideals; the prophets usually stand for national interests and ideals.

David was regarded in the kingdom of Judah in later times as the national hero par excellence; but in the records of his life this characteristic is hardly to be found except in the account of his youthful

[1] Apart from I Sam. xxvii. 7 f., where he is said to have perpetrated a wholesale massacre in a raid towards the south. This, however, took place while he was in exile with the Philistines, before he became king, and a special, though perhaps not very adequate, reason is alleged for it.

exploit against Goliath, which has definite non-heroic and probably also legendary features. Elsewhere his actions are governed by the individualism characteristic of heroic kingship in other lands; he seems to be little influenced by national prejudices. When threatened by Saul he twice [1] seeks service under the Philistine Achish, king of Gath (I Sam. xxi. 11 ff., xxvii); and he follows this king to battle against Israel (*ib.* xxix), though the other princes of the Philistines insist on his withdrawing from the army. Again, both before and after he became king, he had foreigners among his most trusted warriors, including Hittites, like Ahimelech (*ib.* xxvi. 6) and Uriah (II Sam. xi), and Philistines, like Ittai of Gath (cf. p. 669), as well as Ammonites and others. In his later years he had a standing force of Cherethites and Pelethites, apparently Philistines, who were evidently among the most trustworthy troops he had. In his dealings with foreign rulers he seems to have followed much the same lines as other heroic kings, conquering some and entering into friendly relations with others. Savage treatment of enemies is but seldom attributed to him, as we have seen. He is said to have married at least one foreign wife (II Sam. iii. 3).

Solomon's kingship was evidently still more of an international, though hardly heroic, character. We hear of no wars in his reign; his activities and ambitions would seem to have been commercial, rather than military. He is said to have had an immense harem, recruited largely from the royal families of the neighbouring nations, and to have provided all his wives with sanctuaries for their national deities (I Kings xi. 1–8).

The later kings, at least in the northern kingdom, seem to have followed much the same policy as David, though their dominions were far less extensive. Sometimes they married foreign wives. Thus Jeroboam I is said [2] to have married an Egyptian princess, like Solomon, while Ahab's wife, Jezebel, was a daughter of the king of Sidon. The latter marriage seems to have been responsible for the introduction of the cult of the Phoenician Baal, which is vigorously opposed by the prophet Elijah. The revolution under Jehu may have been largely of a national character; at all events it is specially directed against this cult. In the smaller kingdom of Judah national feeling appears to be more prominent throughout, though Jehoshaphat and his family are closely associated with

---

[1] These two incidents have so little in common that they can hardly be regarded as variants. But we do not mean to suggest that both of them are historical, or even that they could originally have belonged to the same story.

[2] I Kings xii. 24 (Greek text).

Ahab and his sons. In II Chron. xix. 2 this friendship is denounced by the prophet Jehu, son of Hanani.

In earlier times Saul seems to be a more definitely national king than David. His reign apparently is almost continuously occupied with warfare against the Philistines. There is no record of his uniting himself or his family with foreign royal families by means of marriage, or indeed of his having any relations with foreign kings, though he had an Edomite (Doeg) in his service. The difference between his policy and David's may be seen in his treatment of the Gibeonites, a Canaanitish people, with whom the Israelites are said to have made a special treaty in Joshua's time (Josh. ix. 15 ff.). According to I Sam. xxi. 1 ff. a famine arose in David's time, which was believed to be due to the fact that Saul in his national zeal had made a slaughter of the Gibeonites. David offered them redress; and at their request gave up to them seven of Saul's family, to be hanged. Of course he may not have been too reluctant to get rid of possible rivals. On the other hand it is to be borne in mind that Saul himself was unwilling to put to death Agag, king of the Amalekites, who had surrendered to him, and that he incurred thereby the wrath of the prophet Samuel.

The prophets are usually, though not invariably, uncompromising nationalists; for the religion of Jehovah is generally regarded as essentially national. In I Sam. xv. 3 Samuel orders the complete destruction of the Amalekites—men, women, children, and even livestock. According to Ex. xvii. 14 ff. this people, who seem to have been a branch of the Edomites, had been made the object of a special curse, and denounced as the enemies of Jehovah for ever. When Samuel discovers that his orders have only been carried out in part, he cuts Agag in pieces, apparently with his own hand, and then declares to Saul that he has forfeited the kingdom by his disobedience.

Wholesale massacres and destructions of this kind, carried out in obedience to religious vows, are to be found among various other peoples.[1] In Hebrew antiquarian literature they are frequently recorded; but the victims are usually not external enemies but inhabitants of the land. According to their traditions the Israelites believed themselves to be invaders, and that they had received a divine command to overthrow and drive out the native peoples, the Canaanites and others, whom they held to be of different race from themselves, though they seem to have spoken the same language. In Ex. xxiii. 23 ff., xxxiv. 11 f. it is expressly forbidden to make any treaties with these peoples, to worship

[1] For instances among European peoples see p. 658, note.

their deities, or to have relations with their women. In accordance with this belief we hear in the Book of Joshua very frequently of wholesale massacres, in which the entire population of a city is slaughtered, though the cattle are usually—not always—appropriated by the invaders. Only once, in the case of the Hivites or Gibeonites mentioned above, is the prohibition against treaties explicitly transgressed; and this is said (Josh. ix. 3 ff.) to have been brought about by a stratagem of the Gibeonites. There are, however, several passages, especially Judg. i. 19 ff., 27 ff., which state that the Israelites failed to expel the natives from various places—a considerable number in all—and in most of these cases an agreement of some kind is implied. For this reason the Angel of Jehovah visits Israel in Judg. ii. 1 ff., and rebukes them for neglect of his commands, which will bring trouble in the future. Illustrations of this occur in the following chapters.

Samuel's sympathies are clearly national. But the stories recorded of him are concerned with external enemies, the Amalekites and Philistines, the latter of whom would seem to have conquered a large part of the country. We hear nothing of his attitude towards the native peoples, though Saul, as we have seen, is said to have persecuted them.

The attitude of David's prophets is evidently different. In II Sam. xii Nathan boldly rebukes the king for causing the death of Uriah the Hittite. The Hittites[1] are regularly included in the lists of proscribed peoples; but this fact is never alluded to in connection with Uriah. David is treated as guilty of an offence against Jehovah; and though it seems to be rather lightly forgiven (xii. 13), it was apparently thought of in later times as his one great sin. Jehovah is here regarded as the defender of what we should call ethical principles, independent of nationality. Again, on the occasion of the plague, David is ordered by his seer Gad to build an altar in the threshing-floor of Araunah the Jebusite, the place where the angel has appeared (II Sam. xxiv. 16 ff.). The Jebusites also regularly figure among the proscribed peoples; but they have evidently not been expelled from Jerusalem—at least not wholly. David's dealings with Araunah are friendly; and the angel does not shun his land.

These passages, together with the incident relating to the Gibeonites, noticed on p. 672, suggest that David, at least after he became king,

---

[1] Hebrew tradition seems to regard the Hittites as one of the native peoples of Canaan, where they are found even in the story of Abraham, though it knows also of Hittite kings in the north. The Hittites of Canaan were presumably descendants of early invaders, who had become assimilated to the natives of the land.

made little or no distinction in his treatment of Israelites and non-Israelites, and that his policy was accepted by his prophets. Solomon apparently followed the same lines to some extent, since he is said to have celebrated a great sacrifice at Gibeon (I Kings iii. 4 ff.); but elsewhere (ix. 20 f.) we hear that he raised a levy of bondservants from the native peoples. After this we have no further record of them within the borders of Israel;[1] and it would seem that they became amalgamated with the invaders. But Solomon's international policy, and in particular his marriages and the foreign cults introduced thereby, appear to have given rise to a recrudescence of national feeling, at least in religious circles. The denunciations contained in I Kings xi are believed to be late; but there is no need to doubt that Jeroboam's revolt was partly of a nationalist character.[2] According to xi. 29 ff. the first incitement came from the prophet Ahijah.

Prophets again appear as leaders of national feeling in the stories of Elijah and Elisha. Ahab's marriage with a Sidonian princess leads to the establishment of the cult of the Phoenician Baal; and the result is a religious struggle, involving massacres of prophets on both sides (I Kings, xviii. 4, 40). With the Syrian war, which is the chief feature of this period, Elijah is not said to be concerned—his activities are directed against the king's moral and religious offences—but the war policy is led by other prophets, three of whom (unnamed) are introduced in I. xx, and others again in I. xxii. Elisha, whose influence seems to have been very great, is consulted by Syrian princes on more than one occasion; but he also acts as adviser against them. His chief work, however, is the revolution which places Jehu on the throne. This brought an end to the religious strife by massacres which were remembered a century later by the prophet Hosea (i. 4, etc.).

In Judah the introduction of the cult of Baal by Ahab's daughter is said to have led to similar tragedies, though on a smaller scale. In this kingdom also the influence of the prophets seems to have been opposed to negotiations with foreign kings (e.g. II Chron. xvi. 7 ff.; II Kings xix. 6 f., 20 ff.; xx. 14 ff.), and even to intimate relations with Israel (e.g. II Chron. xix. 2; xxv. 7). But actual war between the two kingdoms is discouraged by the prophets on both sides (e.g. I Kings xii. 22 ff.; I Chron. xxviii. 9 ff.).

---

[1] Gezer was perhaps the last of these cities to lose its independence. According to I Kings ix. 16, it was captured by the Egyptians and given by them to Solomon as a dowry for his Egyptian wife.

[2] In addition to the burden of the industrial levies (cf. I Kings v. 13 ff., xii. 4).

In the works of the early prophets, Amos, Hosea, Isaiah and Micah, the feeling for nationality is still more marked than in the historical books. These prophets are seldom concerned with individuals, as were Elijah and Elisha. Sometimes their prophecies are directed specially against the ruling family and wealthy classes; but their interest lies in the nation as a whole. Frequently they speak of it as a personality—a figurative form of speech which makes their works, especially those of Hosea, difficult for a modern reader to understand. It may be noted that the kingdoms of Israel and Judah are not the only nations which are thus treated. Amos and Isaiah give a good deal of attention to foreign nations, and speak of them in much the same way.

(2) Illustrations of heroic warfare are hardly to be found in the latter part of the story of David. This part of the story shows little interest in fighting, for the reason, as we think (cf. p. 649 f.), that it was composed primarily for the entertainment of feminine audiences. Examples occur in the earlier part of the story; and these conform to the type found in other lands (cf. Vol. i, p. 85 ff.). The fighting consists largely of single combats. We may instance the story of Goliath (I Sam. xvii). This story has non-heroic and legendary features; but it illustrates the challenging and the boasting before the encounter, which is typical of this kind of warfare. We may also note Saul's offer of great rewards, including the hand of his daughter, to anyone who should overthrow the Philistine. The latter motif recurs *ib.* xviii. 25 ff., where Saul offers his daughter's hand in return for a hundred foreskins of Philistines; and David actually slays two hundred.

Short catalogues of heroic exploits, including single combats and combats against heavy odds, are to be found in II Sam. xxi. 15 ff., xxiii. 8 ff. To these we may add Jonathan's exploit described in I Sam. xiv. The two passages (I Sam. xxiv, xxvi) in which David surprises Saul, but spares his life, may also be mentioned here. Another typical heroic scene occurs in II Sam. ii. 13 ff., where the battle between Abner and Joab begins with a contest between twelve warriors on either side. During the battle Asahel, brother of Joab, is slain by Abner; and his death is subsequently avenged by Joab.

The non-heroic records show little interest in the details of fighting. It is recognised, however, that the great object in a battle is to kill the leader of the enemy. The Syrian king's orders (I Kings xxii. 31) are to "fight neither with small nor great, save only with the king of Israel". In II. ix. 24 Jehu shoots Joram with his own hand.

The causes of war seem to be much the same as in other heroic societies.

Great cattle raids are carried out both by David and by the Amalekites (I Sam. xxvii. 8 f., xxx. 1 ff., 18 ff.); women also are carried off by the latter. There is no record that the Israelites were head-hunters; but the Philistines cut off the heads of distinguished enemies as trophies (*ib.* xxxi. 9). David makes war upon Ammon (II Sam. x), to avenge the insulting treatment of his envoys. In II Kings xiv. 8 ff. Amaziah provokes war with Israel out of mere bravado.

CHAPTER V

HISTORICAL AND UNHISTORICAL ELEMENTS IN THE SAGAS

IN early Hebrew literature non-heroic saga is more extensive, and on the whole more important, than heroic. It is necessary therefore in this chapter to give as much attention to it as to the latter. In other respects the material will be treated according to the schemes adopted in Vol. I, Chs. VII and VIII.

I. First we will take the evidence available for demonstrating the existence of historical elements in the stories.

(*a*) Contemporary native historical records. These are not preserved in their original form. The only question is whether such records have been incorporated or utilised in the existing texts. This of course is a difficult question, and one which only experts can decide. Some scholars think that the use of contemporary records is implied in the lists of officials and warriors in the reigns of David and Solomon. But the evidence is far from conclusive; such lists often occur in heroic poetry and saga (cf. p. 651). It is true that anachronisms and imaginative elements are frequently to be found in the latter; but can it be proved that the Hebrew lists are historically accurate? Again, the existence of contemporary records in the later period is suggested both by the references to earlier chronicles (cf. p. 631) and by the synchronising of the kings of Israel and Judah. But the chronology is not correct, though on the whole it is not very far out. In particular we may note that Pekah, the last king but one of Israel, is given a reign of twenty years, which in view of the Assyrian evidence is much too long.[1] And this is not a mere mistake in figures, which could be attributed to a later copyist; for the synchronisms with the contemporary kings of Judah (II Kings xv. 27, 32; xvi. 1; xvii. 1) are based upon it, and must therefore themselves date from a time long after this king. There are some entries under Hezekiah (II Kings xviii. 9, 13) which we should be more

[1] Menahem seems to have been still reigning c. 739–8, while Pekah's downfall took place apparently not later than 732. According to II Kings xv. 22 ff. Menahem was succeeded by his son Pekahiah, who reigned two years before he was killed by Pekah.

inclined to derive from contemporary records.[1] But much of the account even of this reign seems to come from saga (cf. p. 663 f.).

(*b*) Foreign records consist wholly, or almost wholly, of contemporary inscriptions, celebrating the deeds of kings. These are of course invaluable, both as a check upon the chronology and because they show the relationship of Hebrew history to the general history of the times. Assyrian records mention many of the kings of Israel and Judah, from the time of Omri onwards, i.e. from early in the ninth century; and their evidence, so far as it goes, substantiates the succession recorded in the Books of Kings. References in Egyptian records are less frequent, but go back to an earlier time. Some scholars[2] identify the 'Zerah the Ethiopian', who in II Chron. xiv. 9 ff. is defeated by Asa, king of Judah, with Osorkon I, king of Egypt. The date of the battle is believed to be about the beginning of the ninth century. More certain is the invasion of Shishak (Sheshonk I), king of Egypt, which is recorded (I Kings xiv. 25 f.) in the time of Rehoboam. An inscription of Shishak contains a detailed account of this invasion, which would seem to have taken place c. 930. This is the earliest date for which foreign evidence is known as yet. For more than two centuries before this time foreign evidence seems to be practically wanting.[3] Apparently neither Egypt nor the kingdoms to the north were concerned with Palestine during this period. We hear of Egyptian activities in Palestine in the thirteenth century and earlier, and even in the early part of the twelfth; but Hebrew saga and poetry, except what is of definitely antiquarian character, hardly reaches back so far as this.

We are not certain whether the inscription of Mesha, king of Moab, should be mentioned here or under (*a*), above; for the language is said to be almost identical with Hebrew. It is a most valuable contemporary authority for the times of Ahab and his family. In it Mesha gives a detailed account of the victories he gained over Israel and the spoils which he won thereby. But he makes no reference to Joram, nor to

---

[1] It may be observed, however, that similar phrases (giving dates) occur occasionally in earlier times (I Kings xiv. 25; II. xii. 6). We do not know the explanation. The passages point to the Temple.

[2] Cf. Petrie, *History of Egypt*, II. 242 f.; Hall, *Camb. Anc. Hist.* III. 261. The battle is not mentioned in Egyptian records; and the identification of the names *Zerah* and *Osorkon* is not allowed by all scholars (cf. Cook, *ib.* p. 360). The chief argument for the connection is that in II Chron. xvi. 8 the army, like that of Shishak (*ib.* xii. 3), is said to have contained Lubim (apparently Libyans), as well as 'Ethiopians'.

[3] The story of Wenamon dates from this period (not long before 1100), but relates only to the Phoenician cities—which seem to be independent.

Judah or Edom; consequently the chronological relationship of the events to the war described in II Kings iii. 4 ff. is not clear.[1] But the date cannot be far from the middle of the ninth century.

(c) The existence of independent traditions in different regions. There seems to be no traditional material of any value, except what is preserved in the Old Testament. All of this, or at all events all that comes within our scope, has come down to us through Judaic channels. Much of the material, however, which is contained in the Books of Kings, is doubtless derived from the northern kingdom; and the same is probably true of Judges, and even of I Samuel. The northern and southern traditions may originally have differed in many respects. But the former, as we have them, often reflect the (southern) milieu in which they have been preserved. Thus the kings of Israel are without exception represented as evildoers; but it may be questioned whether this was the view even of the prophets in their own kingdom—at least in the case of Jehu. Jeroboam I also may have been regarded in a different light. In the form in which we have them therefore the two traditions cannot be regarded as strictly independent, though they doubtless preserve independent elements. The most important of these are perhaps to be found in the antiquarian saga and poetry, which will require notice in the following chapter.

(d) The existence of independent traditions in the same region. For the existence of different traditions—heroic and non-heroic—we have had abundant evidence. They cannot be described as wholly independent; for all the heroic material has presumably come down to us through non-heroic channels. But it is surprising that a large part of the story of David has so faithfully preserved its heroic character. This may be due to the peculiar nature of the non-heroic channel—the Temple, we suspect—through which the story has come down. In any case the contrast which it presents to the other (non-heroic) records of the period is so pronounced that it must be regarded as practically equivalent to an independent tradition. In the story of Saul heroic elements are not so well preserved, while in the stories of the 'judges' they are obscured, if they can be traced at all.

(e) The consistency of heroic tradition. In the heroic parts of the story of David the evidence is detailed and convincing. Even the non-heroic tradition, though inferior, is generally good of its kind. Inconsistencies are by no means rare—we may instance the discrepancy as to

[1] A full transl. of the inscription is given by Cook, *Camb. Anc. Hist.* III. 372 f., where it is dated shortly before or after the accession of Jehu (c. 841).

the slayer of Goliath, the existence of variants, the different accounts of the origin of the kingship—but taken as a whole and as reflecting the traditions of different districts and periods, they are such as tend rather to confirm the general credibility of the records.

(*f*) Archaeological evidence has become available, to any considerable extent, only in recent years; and we have not sufficient knowledge of the subject to deal with it. We need only remark that the description of Solomon's Temple is so detailed that valuable results may be hoped for from a comparison of the literary and archaeological evidence. It may, however, be noted here that the records seem to indicate differences in civilisation between the earlier and later periods. We may refer in particular to the use of chariots and horses, which was discussed on p. 668 f.

(*g*) and (*h*) The evidence of personal names and place-names. We cannot estimate the value of this evidence. To do so would require a knowledge of the language which we do not possess.

II. Next we may consider the unhistorical elements in the stories. Following the scheme adopted in Vol. 1 (p. 199 ff.), we may distinguish three main types of these.

(i) Incidents and situations which are in conflict (*a*) with good historical evidence or (*b*) with other stories. The amount of material available under (*a*) is not great, unless we include chronological mistakes—in the length of reigns—found in the Books of Kings. An instance of this kind has been noted above (p. 677). Some cases may of course be due merely to scribal error. As an illustration of quite a different kind we may take the striking contrast between the account of the war with Moab described in II Kings iii. 4 ff. and the contemporary inscription of Mesha. If the two records relate to the same events, the former must contain a large unhistorical element, whatever allowance be made for exaggeration in the latter. But it is possible that they are concerned with different phases of a long-continued war. Again, it is difficult to reconcile the story of Sennacherib's invasion given in II Kings xviii f. with the account of the same king's achievements in Palestine contained in his own inscriptions. Apart from the disaster mentioned in xix. 35, to which the Assyrian records make no reference, the former seems to imply that Sennacherib was slain very soon after his return home. Yet the events narrated apparently took place, in part at least, in 700, whereas Sennacherib was not killed until 681. Some scholars hold that he made a second expedition to Palestine towards the end of his reign; and though this is not recorded in his inscriptions, their silence is not conclusive, because the records for his later years are apparently defective. But in that case the Hebrew story would seem to have confused two different campaigns. This story, as we have seen (p. 663 f.), is probably derived from saga; for it appears to contain two variant accounts of the events. Such confusion or 'telescoping' of the history is therefore not unintelligible.

(*b*) Inconsistencies between one story and another imply of course the presence of unhistorical elements in at least one of the two. Such inconsistencies and discrepancies have already perhaps been sufficiently illustrated (p. 635 f.), in the discussion of variants. For examples we may refer to the slaying of Goliath (cf. p. 635), the occasions on which David takes Saul by surprise, the accounts of David's Syrian war. As an example relating to much earlier times we may note the discrepancy between Josh. xi and Judg. iv as to the date of the war with Jabin, king of Hazor. The discrepancies in I Sam. viii and ix regarding the beginning of the kingdom are perhaps not quite so striking at first sight; but they are thought to imply different conceptions of the political condition of Israel at the time.

(ii) Incidents and situations which are in themselves incredible. Following the scheme adopted in Vol. I (p. 204 ff.) we may first take (*a*) the introduction of supernatural beings. The 'angel' (messenger) of Jehovah appears on several occasions in visible form and converses with human beings. One of the most striking cases is Judg. vi. 11 ff., where Gideon finds the angel sitting under an oak. He appears also (*ib*. xiii) to Manoah and his wife, and converses with them (see below). In II Sam. xxiv. 16 f. David sees the angel standing by the threshing-floor of Araunah the Jebusite. Similar incidents occur in the Hexateuch. In II Kings ii. 11 a different form of theophany is introduced. Elijah is separated from Elisha by a chariot and horses of fire; and the former goes up into heaven by a whirlwind.

(*b*) Supernatural powers attributed to human beings. In the Book of Judges this feature is rare, except in the story of Samson, who has superhuman physical strength, so long as his hair remains unshorn. Among other feats he can rend a young lion without weapons and kill a thousand men with the jawbone of an ass. A parallel to the latter feat is attributed (iii. 31) to a certain Shamgar, who slays six hundred Philistines with an ox-goad. In stories of this kind numbers seem to be used quite recklessly. In the Books of Samuel supernatural powers are practically limited to manticism, which will be noticed in Ch. VII.

Indeed the story of David is almost free from supernatural elements, apart from II Sam. xxiv (noticed above). In the Books of Kings, on the other hand, prophets are frequently endowed with supernatural powers; but nearly all the examples belong to the stories of Elijah and Elisha. Both these prophets can produce a supply of oil, and restore a dead child to life—in which cases of course variant traditions may be suspected. Elijah has power over drought and rain, and can bring down fire. Elisha, like an Indian seer, can grant the birth of a child; he can also cure and produce leprosy, make iron to float, and work other wonders, which will require notice in Ch. vii. Apart from the stories of these prophets, examples are rare. We may note the incident of Jeroboam and the unnamed prophet in I Kings xiii. 4 ff. and that of Isaiah and the sun-dial in II. xx. 9 ff.

(c) Stories relating to the birth and childhood of great men. These are few in number. The most striking is the story of Manoah and his wife (Judg. xiii), when the angel visits them and prophesies the birth of Samson. Manoah offers a sacrifice, and the angel ascends in the flame of the altar. Samuel's birth and childhood are described at some length (I Sam. i ff.); but the supernatural element is slight. His birth is due to the blessing of the priest Eli; and he receives his first revelation while still a child, in the service of the same priest. It is somewhat curious that no stories of this kind are told of David's birth. All we hear is (ib. xvii. 34 ff.) that while still very young he killed a lion and a bear, in defence of his sheep.

Stories relating to the deaths of great men or to great men after their deaths are also very rare. We have already (p. 667) referred to the story told in I Sam. xxviii, where Saul wishes to consult the dead Samuel, and the witch brings up his ghost. For this we have found no precise analogies in the literatures which come within our scope. But the existence of similar beliefs is implied both in the *Odyssey*, xi. 90 ff., where Odysseus consults the ghost of Teiresias, and in the Norse poems Vegtamskviða and Grógaldr. But in the former case the scene is laid at the entrance to the home of the dead, and there is no witch, while in the latter instances—which belong to mythology and folklore—the witches are the dead persons themselves, consulted at their tombs. For the disappearance of Elijah, related in II Kings ii. 11, we know of no true parallels elsewhere. One can hardly compare the stories of supernatural beings who visit men and disappear mysteriously, often after the violation of some taboo.

(iii) Elements which appear to be unhistorical, though they are not necessarily incredible in themselves nor yet in conflict with other evidence. Under this head in Vol. I (p. 221 ff.) we treated (*a*) incidents, motifs and characters which seem to be taken from some other story. In the records we are now considering we have not noticed any important examples of this kind. It is possible, as we have seen, that some of the incidents which are related of Elijah and of Elisha were originally variants, and that they have been transferred from one of these prophets to the other. It is also quite likely that in Judg. iv Jabin, king of Hazor, has been taken from a different story. But we have not observed any longer or more detailed instances. Elements from folktales are probably to be found in the story of Samson, and perhaps in other stories in the Book of Judges; but we do not know their derivation.

(*b*) The invention of incidents, motifs and characters or of whole stories. Of all unhistorical elements this is of course the type most difficult to trace. In the records we are now considering we do not feel inclined to regard any stories as complete inventions, except perhaps one or two in which the chief characters are nameless. Such may be the case with the story (Judg. xix ff.) of the nameless Levite and the destruction of the tribe of Benjamin, though we confess that we cannot see how or why such a story should come to be invented. Another possible example is the story of the nameless prophet from Judah, who was killed by a lion (I Kings xiii). This story seems to be very late—not earlier than the closing years of the seventh century. It may have been suggested by a local story connected with a grave. Of course there may be other stories in which fiction may be suggested by the names or other circumstances. As regards names we have not the linguistic knowledge necessary for estimating the value of the evidence; but in other respects the case for postulating fiction does not strike us as at all obvious anywhere, except perhaps in stories relating to Samson. We cannot point out any obviously fictitious characters. There may, however, be stories in which, as they stand, the leading motif is an invention of later times. We may refer in particular to the discrepancies in stories relating to Samuel, in regard to his position and his attitude to the establishment of the kingship.

We have been speaking here only of stories in the Books of Judges, Samuel and Kings. In what appear to be later stories relating to the same period, contained in the Books of Chronicles and Ruth, the case for fiction is probably stronger. The story of Ruth, as we have seen (p. 665), may perhaps best be explained as a romance based upon some slight thread of (genealogical) tradition. In the Chronicles we may take as an instance the account of Abijah's war with Jeroboam (II. xiii). In Kings—where this king is called Abijam—it is merely stated (I. xv. 7) that such a war took place. But the Chronicles give the story at some length. They represent Abijah as a champion and preacher of the true religion, and ascribe to him a complete victory; the numbers both of the combatants and of the slain are, as usual, incredible. This story can hardly have been known to the authors or editors of Kings; otherwise they would not have reckoned Abijam (Abijah) among the evildoers. It may be observed that the Chronicles contain a good number of passages which, like this, represent the interest of the priesthood and the Levites. Many of them may be derived from priestly or Levitical tradition; but we do not know how old this was. The Chronicles frequently give information which is not found elsewhere and yet looks authentic.

Taking the material as a whole it would seem that the historical element is at least as great as in any of the literatures we have considered. The proportion, however, varies from one period to another. The stories preserved in the Books of Kings obviously contain large unhistorical elements; yet the general course of the history outlined in these books is at various points shown by contemporary foreign records to be substantially correct.

For the time of David such foreign evidence is wanting; we have to depend upon the Books of Samuel themselves. The latter part of the story of David is as detailed and circumstantial as the best of the 'Sagas of Icelanders'; and we see no reason for doubting that, like these, it is derived from more or less contemporary saga and is in the main historical, though it may contain a good deal of imaginative matter. This carries the history of Israel back to c. 1000—perhaps three centuries before the general use of writing for literary purposes.

For the times of Samuel and Saul also external evidence is wanting. We have a number of stories, which may well have a historical basis; but it is difficult to fix any dates, and even to determine the sequence of events. It is held by many scholars that Israel had been conquered by the Philistines, as a result of the defeat recorded in I Sam. iv. From the genealogy of the priests given in xiv. 3 (cf. xxii. 20) the date of this conquest has been calculated at c. 1080; for Abiathar, Ahitub's grandson was David's contemporary, and Ichabod, Ahitub's brother, is said (iv. 19 ff.) to have been born immediately after the battle—though the evidence of this passage would seem to be somewhat precarious. In vii. 7 ff. Samuel himself is said to have freed the country from the

Philistines by a subsequent victory. But this passage—which comes from the later (non-heroic) narrative—is in conflict with the evidence of the earlier narrative. Thus in x. 5 we hear apparently of some kind of Philistine authority, just before Saul becomes king, while in xiii. 19 ff. it is stated that hardly any of the Israelites possessed weapons, because the Philistines did not allow them to have smiths. These passages, taken together with the general course of the narrative in cap. xiii f., suggest that the war of liberation, if such it can properly be called, took place in Saul's time. His position may perhaps be compared with that of Kara-Gjorgje in Serbia during the early years of last century; but he probably had to deal with a less organised enemy.

The Book of Judges is arranged according to a chronological scheme, in which the judges follow one another in succession as rulers of Israel. The figures given for the various periods of rule and the intervals between them amount altogether to about four centuries. But it is generally recognised that this scheme is the work of those who collected or edited the stories. The stories themselves are unconnected with one another, except those of Gideon and Abimelech, and belong to different parts of the country; it is not clear that any of the judges rules the whole of Israel. The length of time covered by the stories as a whole is therefore quite uncertain. All of them seem to relate to times anterior to the reign of Saul; and some of them may go back as far as the twelfth century. The story of Deborah and Barak, which is placed among the earliest, has all the appearance—especially the poem—of a historical record; and we see no reason for doubting that most of the other stories contain historical elements. But here again no foreign evidence seems to be available.

Rameses III is recorded to have traversed Palestine with his armies in the early years of the twelfth century. The details of the conquests claimed by him are not generally credited—they are said to be copied from earlier lists—but it is believed that he fought in Phoenicia and probably at Kadesh on the Orontes, well to the north of Palestine. The country is thought to have been subject to him in some sense, though his troops may not have penetrated far into the hills. His inscriptions have much to say about the Philistines, Hittites and other peoples, but do not mention Israel. For a few years before this time—the last years of the thirteenth century— Egypt had been in a state of anarchy; but down to this time Palestine had long been included in the Egyptian dominions. In the reign of Merneptah (c. 1223) an unsuccessful rebellion is recorded to have taken place in Palestine. Among other geographical names, Askalon, Gezer, etc., we hear of Israel, which is said to have been exterminated by the king. This is the first known occurrence of the name. The inscriptions of Rameses II and Seti I, however, mention a people called Asher, which in Hebrew literature is the name of one of the tribes of Israel. The same name is known also from Egyptian letters. It is clear from both the inscriptions and the letters that Palestine was very well known to the Egyptians of the Nineteenth Dynasty. There are monuments of both Rameses II and Seti I even to the east of the Jordan valley. The northern frontier was fixed by treaty on the Orontes c. 1265, after long warfare with the Hittites. Under the Eighteenth Dynasty Egyptian territory had extended much further to the north.

Little information relating to Palestine is available for the half century before the accession of Seti I (c. 1314). From the first half of the fourteenth century, however, i.e. the later reigns of the Eighteenth Dynasty, we have most detailed information in the archives found at El Amarna. These archives contain many letters from governors or princes in Palestine, who were evidently in more or less regular communication with the Egyptian government. The letters show that the country was at that time in a state of much confusion, owing partly to quarrels among the governors, but partly also to the incursions of a predatory people called Habiru—a name which is now commonly identified with 'Hebrew'. Now the Israelites, according to their traditions, always believed that their ancestors were invaders, who had entered Palestine from the desert. These traditions will require notice in the next chapter. Here it will be enough to note that many scholars are inclined to identify the incursions of the Habiru with the invasion of the Israelites under Joshua. They point out that the general circumstances seem to be similar in the two cases. Moreover in one particular case a city (Jericho), which is said to have been destroyed by the Israelites, has been proved by excavation to have been destroyed about the beginning of the fourteenth century. On the other hand it is to be borne in mind that the archives of El Amarna never mention the name Israel or the names of any of the tribes of Israel, so far as we are aware. Unfortunately the archives cease at a point before the movements of the Habiru had achieved any decisive result. We do not know the sequel, unless it is to be found in the Hebrew traditions.

The fact, however, must not be overlooked that, though Palestine had been so long under Egyptian rule, Hebrew literature retains no remembrance of it. Apart from the story of the invasion, which will be noticed below, Hebrew tradition would seem not to reach back beyond the twelfth century.

CHAPTER VI

ANTIQUARIAN LEARNING

ANTIQUARIAN learning is very highly developed in early
Hebrew literature. Illustrations are to be found in all the records
discussed in the previous chapters. But in addition to these there
is a great body of literature, the Hexateuch, which is of essentially
antiquarian interest, comparable with the Indian Purānas.

In the classification of the material we shall follow the scheme
adopted in Vol. I (p. 270 ff.). It may be observed that illustrations of
Sections I–III are frequently to be found in the records already discussed,
whereas in IV–VII the material is derived almost wholly from the
Hexateuch. Something therefore will have to be said by way of introduction to the latter. But first we will take the evidence for I–III.

I. Genealogies are occasionally given in I Samuel; but they are not
frequent, and run only to four or five generations. As examples we may
cite those of Samuel (i. 1), Saul (ix. 1) and the descendants of Eli (xiv. 3).
These genealogies are never carried back to the times of Moses or the
patriarchs. At the end of Ruth, however, we find a genealogy of nine
generations, from Perez, son of Judah, to David. But the chief collection of genealogies is in I Chron. i–ix. Most of these begin with the
sons of Jacob. They contain many variants and discrepancies; and the
number of generations between terminal contemporaries differs at times
considerably. They do not seem to have been edited or compared with
any care by those who collected and wrote them down; but as to their
historical value we are not competent to express an opinion. Genealogies are also to be found in Genesis; but most of these relate to
primeval times, and will be noticed under VI, below. It is only rarely
that they come down to historical times, as in the lists relating to Edom
in Gen. xxxvi (cf. I Chron. i. 35 ff.).

II. Catalogues other than genealogies are rather more frequent.
Some of these have already been referred to (p. 651), e.g. the lists of
David's wives and sons and the long list of his comitatus (II Sam. xxiii).
A similar list of Solomon's officials is given in I Kings iv. In the
Chronicles such lists abound, both among the genealogies and later. In

Judg. i. 27 ff. we find a list of cities which were not depopulated by the Israelites. The Hexateuch again contains much catalogue matter. Thus Josh. xii gives a long list of the kings overthrown by the Israelites, while the following nine chapters are largely occupied with geographical catalogues, enumerating the places allotted to the various tribes.

III. Explanations of names, especially place-names, are also quite frequent. In I Sam. vii. 12 it is stated that, after a victory of the Israelites, "Samuel took a stone, and set it between Mizpah and Shen, and called the name of it *Eben-ezer* ('the stone of help'), saying, 'Hitherto hath Jehovah helped us'." Yet according to iv. 1 ff. a defeat had previously taken place at the same spot. We may compare II Sam. xviii. 18, where it is stated that Absalom reared up for himself a pillar in a certain place, to keep his name in remembrance—"and it is called Absalom's monument unto this day". Again, in (*ib.*) ii. 16 a place called *Helkath-hazzurim* ('the field of the sharp knives') is said to have got its name from the encounter between the followers of Abner and Joab, in which all the combatants were slain (cf. p. 675). Similar examples occur *ib.* v. 20, vi. 8, and in I. xxiii. 28. A number are to be found also in the Book of Judges. Thus in ii. 4 f. it is stated that at a certain place the children of Israel "lifted up their voice, and wept. And they called the name of that place *Bochim* ('Weepers')". Again, according to xv. 17, the name *Ramath-lehi* ('hill of the jaw-bone') was given to the place where Samson smote a thousand Philistines. Similar instances occur in vi. 24, xv. 19, xviii. 12. In the Hexateuch also examples are not rare. In Josh. v. 9 the name *Gilgal* ('Rolling') is explained as due to the fact that the Israelites were circumcised, while they were encamped at this place, because "Jehovah said unto Joshua, 'This day have I rolled away the reproach of Egypt from off you'". We may compare also vii. 26.

Some of these passages may of course preserve genuine traditions. Such is quite possibly the case with the pillar of Absalom, noticed in II Sam. xviii. 18. But the majority are doubtless products of speculation, like the European examples discussed in Vol. I, p. 283 ff. As a rule they are probably due to a tendency to connect places with famous persons or events; but occasionally the story itself may have been influenced by a place-name. We know of no collections of place-names, like those of early Ireland.

Explanations of personal names seem to be much less common. An instance occurs in I Sam. iv. 21, where the wife of Phinehas, whose husband has just been killed in a great disaster, calls her newly born child *Ichabod* ('No glory'), "saying, 'The glory is departed from Israel'". So also in Judg. vi. 32, when Gideon has broken down the altar of Baal, his father calls him Jerubbaal ('Let Baal plead'), "saying, 'Let Baal plead against him, because he hath broken down his altar'". In the latter case at least, if we were concerned with a European country, we should suspect that the story had been invented to explain the name. In countries like Iceland and Ireland, where surnames were much in use, one would not as a rule be inclined to attach much value to explanations of personal names, unless they were obvious. But with Hebrew names the case may be different; we understand that Semitic scholars are inclined to attach more significance to names.[1] It may be observed that names of the type we are considering (*Jerubbaal*) seem to be alien to the Indo-European languages. Yet the explanation of the name *Israel* given in Gen. xxxii. 28 is a clear case of antiquarian speculation. And the same may be said of the explanation of the name *Moses* in Ex. ii. 10. In reality this name seems to be Egyptian, not Hebrew.

Note may also be made here of a curious practice of substituting one element for another in compound personal names. Thus in II Sam. xi. 21 the name *Jerubbesheth* is used for Jerubbaal; and the names of Saul's son and grandson, *Ishbosheth* and *Mephibosheth*, are believed to have been substituted for Ishbaal and Mephibaal.[2] The second element, which means 'shame', has taken the place of a divine name which had become hated. Such substitutions are not unknown in Europe; but they are hardly due to the same principle. In Norse poetry they seem to be synonyms, e.g. Ásmóðr for Þormóðr,[3] and due either to metrical considerations or to the cultivation of enigmatism. The Hebrew examples, however, are perhaps to be ascribed to the pedantry of late scribes.

Traditions or speculations relating to the origin of customs, places, peoples, and the world itself belong almost wholly to the Hexateuch. This is a collection of essentially antiquarian character. It is of highly composite origin, as we have seen, and must have had a long history. The chief component elements—J, E, D (Deuteronomy) and P—have been noticed briefly on p. 630, above. The two latter are themselves

[1] Cf. Cook, *Camb. Anc. Hist.* II. 393 ff.

[2] Mephibosheth is generally identified with Merib-baal in I Chron. viii. 34, ix. 40. But the first elements of these names must also be different.

[3] The word *áss* ('god') is often used for Thor in poetry. It may be noted here that names with heathen associations were not discarded after the introduction of Christianity. Thus in England names like *Oswald* and *Aelfred*, compounded with *os* ('god') and *aelf* ('elf') were very popular.

believed to be composite; but they are too late to come within our scope, though P may contain early elements. It is with J and E that we are primarily concerned. From these are believed to be taken large parts of Genesis, Exodus and Numbers, a little of Deuteronomy (towards the end), and a considerable part of Joshua, though this last element is thought to have been edited and expanded by a Deuteronomist writer.

The contents of J and E are believed to have been very similar and to have covered much the same ground. It is commonly held that J belonged to Judah, and E to the northern kingdom. Different strata can be distinguished, it is thought, in each of the two; but both are supposed to have been based, to some extent at least, upon oral tradition. Eventually they were combined, the result being a conflate text (JE), drawn partly from one and partly from the other. This is thought to have taken place most probably in the seventh century, but before the introduction of Deuteronomic influence.

The subjects which are believed to have been included in each of the early texts, as well as in the conflate text derived from them, may be divided as follows:

(1) The Creation, the antediluvian period, the Flood, and a short sketch of what we should call the ethnography of the known world, treated genealogically, together with the account of the Tower of Babel. This corresponds in general to Gen. i–xi; but much of the existing text of Genesis here is believed to be derived from P. The text of JE in this section is thought to have been taken wholly from J.

(2) The story of the patriarchs Abraham, Isaac, Jacob, and the sons of Jacob—corresponding in general to Gen. xii–l.

(3) The story of Moses, the departure of the Israelites from Egypt, their wanderings in the desert, and the giving of the Law. This corresponds to large portions of Exodus and Numbers, together with the close of Deuteronomy.

(4) The conquest of Canaan by Joshua, and the distribution of the land among the tribes of Israel. This corresponds in general to the Book of Joshua. But this Book has been much edited and expanded; in the second half the amount which is believed to come from JE is not very great.

It is to be borne in mind that large portions of the present text of all the Books mentioned here, except Deuteronomy, are believed to be derived from P—from which also comes the whole of Leviticus. P is supposed to have contained a consecutive narrative, parallel to JE, from the beginning of Genesis to the end of Joshua.

The general likeness between the scheme outlined above and that of the Purānas (cf. p. 540) will be obvious enough. J and E may well have originated in variant forms of a Purāna. P also may be described as a Purāna, but of a somewhat different kind from the others. In the form in which it has been preserved it seems to have been a late and sophisticated work; and the material has been very freely treated. But it incorporates a large body of priestly tradition, much of which may have had a long history.

IV. Traditions or speculations relating to the origin of institutions, customs and ceremonies. A number of examples are to be found in the parts of Exodus which are believed to come from JE. A good instance occurs in xii. 21–7, which accounts for the origin of the feast of the Passover, and is to be taken in connection with the slaying of the first-born of the Egyptians, as stated *ib.* 29 f. Soon after this (xiii. 3–10) follows the institution of the feast of Unleavened Bread, which is to commemorate the escape of the Israelites from Egypt. The explanation is given in xii. 39: "They baked unleavened cakes of the dough which they brought forth out of Egypt, for it was not leavened; because they were thrust out of Egypt, and could not tarry, neither had they prepared for themselves any victual". In P (xii. 15) the institution of this feast is connected with that of the Passover. Then, in xiii. 11–16, JE goes on to prescribe the sacrifice or redemption of the first-born, which is explained by the story of the destruction of the Egyptian first-born. Again, in xvi. 4 f., 25–30 the institution of the Sabbath is explained by the story of the bread which fell from heaven for the use of the Israelites in the desert—a story which seems not to be completely preserved in JE. In P, from which the rest of this chapter is said to come, the story is told more fully; but in this text the Sabbath is carried back to the Creation (Gen. ii. 2 f.). Lastly, we may note the origin of the Law (xix ff.), which is said to have been given to Moses on Mt Sinai. Apart from this last case, which is derived wholly from JE, antiquarian subjects of this kind are usually treated more fully in P. Thus in xxv–xxxi we find a very long list of ritual regulations, which are said to be ordered at this time. It may be observed that all the instances given above from JE are connected with supernatural occurrences. Note may also be taken of the etymological element (xii. 23) in the explanation of the Passover.

In the Book of Joshua we may first notice the institution of circumcision, as described in v. 2 f., 8 f. The passage speaks of the incident as a repetition or revival of a custom which had fallen into abeyance; and this is explained by the intervening passage (*ib.* 4–7), which is believed to be a 'Deuteronomic' addition. In point of fact there is an obscure incidental notice of the rite in Ex. iv. 25 f., which is attributed to J. A still earlier reference occurs in Gen. xxxiv. 14 ff.; but the derivation of this passage is, we believe, disputed. In P the origin of the rite is traced to Abraham (*ib.* xvii).

The latter part of the Book of Joshua is largely occupied with the distribution of the land of Canaan among the various tribes of Israel, a subject to which we shall have to refer below. Two points, however, may be noted here. Cap. xx describes the institution of six 'cities of refuge'—three to the east and three to the west of the Jordan—for those who have been guilty of manslaughter, while cap. xxi gives a list of forty-eight cities allocated to the Levites, a tribe which had no separate district allotted to it in the distribution. But these chapters belong to P, though the former is said to contain Deuteronomic elements; and both are in accordance with the directions given in Num. xxxv, which like-wise comes from P. It may be observed here that, especially in Numbers, P has much to say regarding the privileges and duties of Levites, whereas JE, as we have it, seldom refers to this tribe, though it mentions that Moses and Aaron belonged to it.[1] This is a striking difference between the two sources.

Apart from the Hexateuch, traditions or speculations relating to the origin of customs seem to be rare. An instance occurs in Judg. xi. 39 f., where there is a reference to a custom—not made clear—in which the fate of Jephthah's daughter was celebrated or bewailed by girls for four days in every year. The context suggests that this rite took place on the hills.

V. Traditions and speculations relating to ancient buildings, graves, sanctuaries, and localities in general. Several instances occur in the first part of Genesis (i–xi); but these chapters probably have a separate history of their own. Elsewhere examples seem not to be frequent. The majority apparently relate to menhirs and (unchambered) cairns, which are said to have been set up or constructed in witness of agreements, or in commemoration of remarkable events or experiences. Thus in Gen.

---

[1] The 'Blessing of Moses', which is supposed to come from JE, speaks of Levi at length (Deut. xxxiii. 8 ff.); but JE is thought to have derived this poem from a separate source.

xxxi. 45 ff. Jacob raises both a pillar-stone and a cairn, which he and Laban invoke as witness of their agreement. It is not made quite clear whether these objects are familiar to the author, as in some of the cases noted below. Such may perhaps be the case with the pillar which (*ib.* xxviii. 18 f.) Jacob sets up at Bethel, in commemoration of his dream. A variant of the same story occurs in xxxv. 14 f., while at the beginning of this chapter he builds an altar at the same place. We do not know whether this is the same sanctuary as the one where Abraham builds an altar (*ib.* xii. 8; xiii. 3 f.). It would seem from Josh. xvi. 2 that the sanctuary lay outside the city of Beth-el (Luz), and that its name was in course of time transferred to the city (cf. Gen. xxviii. 19; xxxv. 6; Judg. i. 22 ff.). According to Gen. xxviii. 22 the name *Beth-el* ('house of God') referred originally to the pillar-stone.[1] An instance of the use of a menhir as a grave-stone—apparently known to the author—occurs *ib.* xxxv. 20, where Jacob sets one up at the grave of his wife Rachel: "the same is the Pillar of Rachel's grave unto this day".

Similar examples are to be found in Joshua, Thus, according to xxiv. 26 f., Joshua "took a great stone, and set it up there under the oak that was by (or 'in') the sanctuary of Jehovah. And Joshua said unto all the people, 'Behold, this stone shall be a witness against us'", etc. The scene here is Shechem; and the oak is presumably the one which is mentioned in the stories of Abraham and Jacob (Gen. xii. 6 f.; xxxv. 4).[2] Here too we may refer to the twelve stones, in cap. iv, which are taken from the bed of the Jordan and set up at Gilgal, and replaced by twelve other stones. Obviously these are not menhirs; but they serve a similar purpose—they are to be "for a memorial unto the children of Israel for ever". Cairns are thrown up over the malefactor Achan (vii. 26) and over the king of Ai (viii. 29). The use of the expression 'unto this day' in both these passages seems to imply that the cairns were known. In xxii. 10, 26 ff., etc. an altar is built—again as a memorial or 'witness' —by the tribes of Reuben, Gad and Manasseh, when they return home; but this passage perhaps comes from P. In viii. 30 ff. Joshua builds an altar of unhewn stones on Mt Ebal; and after sacrificing he writes on the stones a copy of the law of Moses. This passage is said to be Deuteronomic.

---

[1] The raising of menhirs for worship was specifically prohibited in later times (Lev. xxvi. 1; Deut. xvi. 22, etc.).

[2] Cf. also Judg. ix. 6, where Abimelech is made king 'by the oak of the pillar that was in Shechem'. The same locality is probably intended in Gen. xxxiii. 18 ff., where Jacob buys a piece of ground before the city and sets up an altar there.

The custom of setting up menhirs is recorded also in the Books of Samuel. Instances have already been given (p. 688). 'Absalom's monument' was evidently well known. It may be observed that a cairn is thrown up over the body of this prince (II Sam. xviii. 17).

Ancient graves are not very frequently referred to, except in connection with menhirs and cairns, as noted above. We may, however, mention the cave of Machpelah in the field of Ephron the Hittite, close to Hebron, in which the patriarchs are buried (Gen. xlix. 30 f.). The purchase of this field by Abraham is described at length in cap. xxiii. The references to this place might perhaps suggest that the locality was known; but apparently they all come from P. In xxxv. 8 Deborah, Rebekah's nurse is buried 'below Beth-el under the oak'; we do not know whether the sanctuary is meant. But in Josh. xxiv. 32 Joseph's bones are buried at Shechem, in a spot which is evidently the sanctuary founded by Jacob in Gen. xxxiii. 18 ff. (cf. p. 693 and note).

Sanctuaries have already been mentioned in connection with the pillar-stones set up at Bethel and Shechem. In Gen. xiii. 18 Abraham is said to build an altar by the oaks of Mamre (in Hebron), where he dwelt; and this also may indicate the foundation of a sanctuary. The same inference may perhaps be drawn from xxi. 33, where he plants a tamarisk tree at Beersheba. In xxvi. 23 ff. Isaac builds an altar and digs a well at the same place. It is rather curious that there seems to be no account of the foundation of the sanctuary at Shiloh. In Joshua there are references to a great assembly there; but only in P. But in the early chapters of I Samuel it seems to be the chief sanctuary of Israel, and possesses the sacred Ark; and this seems to be the case also in Judg. xviii. 31. An account—apparently not very sympathetic—of the origin of the sanctuary at Dan is given in the same chapter, and has already been noticed. The foundation of Solomon's temple need not be discussed here; but it may be noted that in II Chron. iii. 1 the temple is said to be built in the threshing-floor of Ornan (Araunah) the Jebusite—the place where David saw the angel. As in the case of other sanctuaries therefore, especially Beth-el, the foundation is connected with a vision.

It is remarkable that references to the foundation of cities in Palestine seem to be extremely rare. In Josh. xix. 50 Joshua is said to have built the city of Timnath-serah; but the passage is thought to come, at least in part, from P, and the expression might refer to re-building, as in I Kings xii. 25. In general the Israelites are clearly represented as appropriating the cities of the natives, built before the invasion, while their ancestors, the patriarchs, seem to live outside the cities.

VI. Traditions and speculations relating to the origin of nations. The Israelites devoted very great attention to the study of the origin of their nation, with which the national religion—the cult of Jehovah—was closely bound up. Practically the whole of the Hexateuch is concerned with these subjects. To repeat briefly what was said on p. 690, Genesis is occupied with the stories of the patriarchs, ending with the settlement of Jacob (Israel) and his sons in Egypt; Exodus and Numbers with the escape of the Israelites (Jacob's descendants) from Egypt and their wanderings in the desert; Joshua with the conquest of Canaan by them. Incidentally some attention is given, in Genesis, to the origin of the kindred nations.

Genesis differs greatly in character from the following books. The interest is centred in individuals, including women, who sometimes receive almost as much attention as the men. The narrative has perhaps more resemblance to the Mabinogion than to any other works we have discussed, with religion here taking the place of the magic which dominates the latter. The life which is portrayed is of a simple kind, not far removed from nomadism. The patriarchs are shepherds, and have distant pasturages; and they shift their abodes from time to time, though it is not clear whether this takes place periodically or only after the lapse of years.

But there is also a very large aetiological (eponymic) element in the stories. Jacob's sons and grandsons bear names which later are those of the tribes of Israel. Jacob himself is also called Israel, while his brother Esau is also called Edom. They have an uncle called Ishmael and other, more distant, relatives who are eponymoi of peoples. Among these we need only mention Moab and Ben-ammi, the sons of Lot, the latter of whom is said to be the father of the children of Ammon (xix. 38). It is clear then that we have the relationship of a number of tribes or peoples expressed in the form of a genealogy. It is true that elsewhere we do find kingdoms and dynasties (with their subjects) which bear the names of historical founders—in other words we find eponymoi who are, at least in all probability, historical persons. For instances we may refer to Vol. 1, p. 311. But in this case the eponymoi are far too numerous to allow of any such explanation; the evidence points to a carefully constructed scheme. The story of Jacob and his sons is of a very similar character to that of Yayāti and his sons, discussed on p. 498 f. The part played by Joseph may be compared with the part played by Pūru. The incidents of course have nothing in common; but each of the two is the ancestor of what was at one time the dominant people.

Eponymity, however, will hardly explain everything in this series of stories, any more than in India and elsewhere. It is not at all clear that the chief characters are eponymoi. In the cases of Abraham and Isaac there is no evidence for this explanation, so far as we are aware; in those of Jacob and Joseph it seems to be at least far from certain. So far as the Hebrew evidence goes,[1] the real eponymoi are Joseph's sons, rather than Joseph himself, while the identification of Jacob with the eponymos Israel may be secondary. It is quite possible then that the stories contain elements of genuine tradition, independent of the aetiological speculation. The latter may have been introduced into an existing saga, or the saga into the aetiological scheme. But, if so, what was the origin of the saga? The stories have much to say about the political conditions of Palestine. We find kings in various places. Hittites are settled in the land, even in the extreme south. Abraham and Isaac visit the Philistines in Gerar. On the other hand, though we hear frequently of Egypt and the Egyptians, there is no trace of Egyptian government in Palestine. It would seem then either that the stories were of an imaginative character from the beginning or that they have undergone a considerable amount of modification in the course of time.[2]

Whatever may be thought as to the origin of the stories, there can be no doubt of the truth of the second proposition. This is shown by the numerous variant versions of incidents which the stories contain.[3] It may be noted that in one account (cap. xx) of the visit to Gerar Philistines are not mentioned; but this is a matter of detail. What we would emphasise is that Egyptian government in Palestine had come to an

[1] Place-names which can be read as *Jacob-el* and *Joseph-el* occur in inscriptions of Thothmes III (early fifteenth century); and the former at least is clearly located in Palestine. Corresponding forms (*Ya'kubilu, Yašupili*) and also Jacob itself (*Yakubu*) are said to occur as personal names in Babylonian contract deeds of cent. xx. Some scholars take *Jacob* (*Ya'aqob*) to be an abbreviation of *Jacob-el*. Unfortunately the interpretation of the Egyptian evidence seems to be still uncertain. Can one infer that there were men (or gods?) called Jacob and Joseph in Palestine in cent. xv? The Babylonian evidence seems to render the supposition that they were gods somewhat unlikely.

[2] It may be noted that if the Mabinogion—we mean of course the 'Four Branches' —contain any historical element, the characters must have lived during the Roman period, or at least very soon afterwards. Yet they preserve no remembrance of the Romans or of Roman civilisation.

[3] Apart from the question of variants, there are certain passages which rather suggest that the patriarchs had once been represented as persons of a somewhat different and more warlike character. The most striking case is Gen. xlviii. 22, which almost approximates to the heroic. We might also refer to cap. xiv; but this is best left to specialists.

end by 1150, while the Philistines had arrived half a century or more before this time. We have an interval therefore of something like four centuries between these events and the time when the stories were committed to writing; and this allows ample time for previous conditions to be forgotten. Yet in spite of this the stories in general preserve very archaic features. Recent archaeological and topographical investigations have made it clear that the conditions which they reflect are not those of the period in which they were written down, but of very much earlier times.[1] Some recent writers indeed hold that they contain a considerable historical element; and it is at least unsafe to assume the contrary. But the question which more directly concerns us is the antiquity of the sagas; there seems to be no reason to doubt that the general lines of these go back to very early times. To this question we shall have to return shortly.

In striking contrast with Genesis the other Books show very little interest in persons; and even this is almost confined to the first half of Exodus. It is only here that we hear of Moses' wife and children. After this his sister Miriam is mentioned in three passages, and his brother Aaron frequently, but almost always in connection with religious observances and disputes. Otherwise there is practically nothing of a personal nature; and hardly any woman is mentioned by name. The case of Joshua is still more striking. We are not even told whether he had a wife or family; and we know nothing of his personality. Yet according to the story his importance in the history of the nation can hardly be regarded as less even than that of Moses.

The interest is concentrated almost wholly upon the fortunes of the nation and upon the national religion which is essentially bound up therewith. Much attention is given to the origin of institutions, as we have seen. To a modern reader these features are no doubt emphasised by the very long portions of these Books which are drawn from P, and which have practically no other interest. But the text of JE seems to have had the same impersonal character, if not quite to the same degree.

For this story also Western analogies are not wanting; but those which we know are only partial, and not preserved in early form. Parallels for the migration are to be found in the (Latin) accounts of the early history of the Goths and the Lombards (cited in Vol. I, p. 306), which are doubtless derived from native sources. We may also refer to the 'Return of the Heracleidai'. For the law-giving and the origin of

[1] This has been well pointed out by Albright, *Archaeology of Palestine*, etc. p. 130 ff.

institutions we may compare the stories of Numa Pompilius and Lycurgos. But the best analogy is probably to be found in the traditions of the (non-Teutonic) Prussians, whose religious and social institutions were believed to have been revealed to the legendary law-giver Bruteno by the thunder-god Perkuno.[1] This is said to have taken place in the sacred oak, which was their chief sanctuary.

The story of the Exodus has given rise to an immense amount of discussion, into which it is of course impossible for us to enter. It must suffice to note that the features upon which attention seems to have been chiefly concentrated are the numbers involved in the migration,[2] the route followed by it, and especially the date at which it took place. We may observe also that, except for the inroads of the Habiru (cf. p. 686), external evidence seems to be wanting,[3] though the history of Egypt in the fourteenth and thirteenth centuries is well known, while for Palestine there is a large amount of evidence available for the first half of the fourteenth century and a certain amount for the thirteenth. Lastly, it has been remarked that much of what is said in Genesis, especially perhaps with regard to sanctuaries, seems difficult to reconcile with a long separation between the land and the people. Against all this it has to be borne in mind that a knowledge of the story seems to be implied everywhere in early Hebrew literature, except perhaps in the story of David. Indeed there can be no reasonable doubt that it was generally believed, at least from the beginning of the eighth century.

We understand that at present the tendency is to the view that only a portion of the Israelites, perhaps only a few of the tribes, made their way to Egypt, and subsequently took part in the Exodus, while the rest had remained in Palestine all the time. Many scholars identify Joshua's invasion of Canaan with the inroads of the Habiru, and consequently date this event in the first half of the fourteenth century, while others still

---

[1] The fullest authority is Simon Grunau, *Preussische Chronik*, especially Tract. III. i. 2.

[2] The extravagant figures given in Numb. i and xxvi come from P. As to their origin an interesting suggestion is made by Albright, *Archaeology of Palestine*, etc. p. 158, viz. that they are derived from records of David's census. We are sceptical as to the preservation of any large figures by saga. In Ex. xii. 40 f. (P) the children of Israel are said to have sojourned 430 years in Egypt; but in Numb. xxvi. 59 (also P) Moses' mother is a daughter of Levi, while his father is frequently said to be Levi's grandson. This would indicate a period of less than a century for the sojourn.

[3] But there is now much archaeological evidence for the destruction of cities in cent. xiv and xiii.

prefer a date in the reign of Rameses II, about a century later.[1] Others again are inclined to connect the Exodus with bodies of foreign labourers called Aperu, who were employed in Egypt, especially in the time of Rameses III, nearly a century later still. This suggestion would account for the forced labour described in the story; but the escape of such a body would by itself hardly be sufficient to produce the effects recorded in the story. Moreover we are not aware that there is any widespread evidence for wholesale destructions in the twelfth century, as there is in the earlier periods. Lastly, the possibility may be borne in mind that—both in this story and in those of the patriarchs—the name 'Egypt' may be due to some misunderstanding. The story of the escape from Egypt might originally have been that of a rising against the Egyptian government in Palestine itself, and have changed its character in course of time, when the memory of Egyptian rule in Palestine had faded away. Few scholars would be willing to regard this as a satisfactory explanation of the story as a whole; but account must be taken of the possibility that it may contain elements of diverse origin, and such a misunderstanding is a factor which should not be overlooked.

In recent years great progress has been made with the excavation of cities said to have been destroyed by Joshua; but the date of the conquest is not yet agreed upon. It has been ascertained that three of these cities —Jericho, Ai and Hazor[2]—were destroyed about the same time. As regards the actual date of the destruction there has been some difference of opinion, some archaeologists attributing it to c. 1400, others to c. 1500; but the most recent evidence from Jericho seems to be decisive in favour of the former date, or even a little later.[3] This would seem to support the connection of the Israelite conquest with the movements of the Habiru, though the excavators themselves do not agree to this connection.[4] On the other hand the evidence from two other sites,

[1] The chief argument for this date is the reference to the store-cities, Pithom and Raamses in Ex. i. 11. Pithom seems to have been founded by Rameses II. But the passage may be an addition to the story, like many passages in the story of Joseph, which is believed to have been much edited by someone well acquainted with Egypt in the seventh century, or not much earlier. The reference to the destruction of Israel in Merneptah's inscription proves only that the Israelites were in Palestine by his time (c. 1223).

[2] Cf. Garstang, *Joshua and Judges*, pp. 146 f., 386 ff., 355 f., 381 ff.

[3] Scarabs of Amenhotep III (1411–1375) were found in the tombs. Very recently also some pottery perhaps later than 1400 has been found; cf. Marston, *The Bible is True*, p. 166.

[4] Cf. Garstang, *op. cit.* p. 255 ff. The grounds on which this connection is denied are not quite clear to us; cf. Marston, *op. cit.* p. 232 f.

which are in all probability to be identified with Lachish and Debir (Kiriath-sepher)—two cities likewise said to have been taken by Joshua —points to destruction about the middle of the thirteenth century, in the reign of Rameses II. This evidence in favour of the later date is supported by excavations and observations made in Edom,[1] which seem to show that that country had been unoccupied for some centuries before the time of Rameses II. In the fourteenth century the Israelites could not have been refused permission to pass through the country; there was no one to refuse it. But this objection affects only a detail of the story.

So far as evidence is available at present, it would seem that there were two periods of destruction in Palestine—separated from one another by an interval during which the Egyptian authority was maintained. The destruction of Jericho belongs to the earlier period; but in spite of the remoteness of the date Hebrew saga seems to have preserved a memory of the event. Whether Moses also belonged to the earlier period is a question which must be left for further investigation. It is possible that the saga has confused two separate movements. The Israelites, or at least part of them, apparently entered the country— presumably as semi-nomads—during the earlier period.[2] The later movement may have been in the nature of a rising, under religious influence, though perhaps supported by an influx of Bedouins. And a similar rising may have taken place still later, when the Egyptians finally evacuated the country.

The question, however, which primarily concerns us is the history of the story and its relationship to the story of the patriarchs. For both stories the literary sources are believed to be the same; both of them seem to have been included in both J and E, and in the composite JE derived from these, as well as in P—one story serving as the sequel of the other, just as in our present text. Moreover both of them are clearly of antiquarian interest and of non-heroic provenance. Yet, as we have seen, the differences of character between them are so marked that they can

---

[1] Cf. Glueck, *Illustrated London News*, 7 July 1934, p. 26, where it is noted that copper-mining on a considerable scale seems to have been carried on in the district from cent. xiii onwards.

[2] The name Israel itself has not yet been found before the time of Merneptah (c. 1223); but there are references to Asher, apparently in the territories assigned to it in Joshua, during the reign of Seti I—towards the close of cent. xiv. We understand also that a reference to Zebulon has been found very recently in the Ras Shamra tablets (cf. Marston, *op. cit.* pp. 177, 208 f.), though we are not clear as to the exact date. References to Simeon have also been suggested.

hardly have had the same history. The 'Hexateuch' of J and E—apart from the actual texts—would seem to have been a work of composite origin.

It is commonly thought that E belonged to the northern kingdom, J to Judah; and this may be correct for the written texts. But the differences between the two seem to have been so slight in substance that it is impossible to believe the stories themselves to have originated independently in the two kingdoms. One text must have been derived from the other—probably in unwritten form, though this is a question for experts to decide. J is thought by most scholars, we believe, to have been the earlier and more archaic of the two; but this of course does not prove that the work originated in the south. The story of the patriarchs clearly indicates an interest centred in Joseph; and in a story which so constantly has its outlook fixed upon the future this must mean that its origin is to be sought in one of the tribes which claimed descent from him, presumably Ephraim.[1] If the story had originated in Judah, the eponymos of this tribe would surely have had something more put to his credit than the incidents related in Gen. xxxviii.

For the original provenance of the story of the Exodus and the conquest of Palestine the evidence is not quite so clear. Moses and Aaron are said to belong to the tribe of Levi, while Joshua's origin is apparently not stated, except in P, where he is said to belong to Ephraim. But in Josh. xxiv. 29 ff. both Joshua and Eleazar, the son of Aaron, are buried in Ephraim, and it is added that Joshua and Phinehas, son of Eleazar, had their homes there. It may also be noted that in the ancient poem called 'The Blessing of Moses' (Deut. xxxiii), which is believed to have been incorporated in JE, Levi and 'Joseph'[2] receive far more attention than any of the other tribes. And in this connection we may observe that in the opening chapters of I Samuel the sacred Ark is kept at Shiloh in Ephraim, under the charge of a family of priests who seem to be descended from Aaron or Moses.[3] The evidence, therefore, though slight, points to the northern origin of this story, as well as the other. We know of no evidence to the contrary. It would seem then that the whole of the original 'Hexateuch' was, in substance, of northern origin.

---

[1] This is indicated only by one passage (Gen. xlviii. 13 ff.); but we know of no evidence to suggest a rival claim for Manasseh.

[2] Both Ephraim and Manasseh are mentioned (xxxiii. 17); but the former is evidently regarded as the more important.

[3] According to I Chron. xxiv they were descended from Ithamar (not Eleazar), son of Aaron.

J may perhaps represent a 'text' or form of the stories which came to the south in early times—presumably before they were committed to writing.

There can be little doubt that a large proportion of P is of southern origin. It has much to say (e.g.) about the privileges and duties of Levites, who in later times seem to have been chiefly congregated in Judah. But all such passages are presumably accretions. There does not seem to be any ground for supposing that the main narrative of P was derived from a source essentially different from JE.

The differences then between the two stories—the story of the patriarchs and that of the Exodus and the conquest of Palestine—can hardly be due to derivation from different regions. But they may be due to derivation from different tribes. The evidence for the former, as we have seen, points definitely to 'Joseph', and more particularly to Ephraim. The evidence for the latter, so far as it goes, points both to Ephraim and Levi, but more definitely to Levi than to Ephraim. It is true that most of the references to Levi in Exodus and Numbers come from P; but Moses and Aaron are Levites even in JE, and in one passage (Ex. xxxii. 26 ff.)—apart from the 'Blessing of Moses'—this tribe is specially commended for its fierce religious zeal. Now Levi was a tribe of religious character and without a territory of its own. In early times its chief sanctuary is said to have been within the territory of Ephraim. Such a derivation seems to provide an adequate explanation of the chief difference between the two stories. The interest in the later story lies not in persons, as in the earlier, but in an organisation; and that is what might be expected in a national sanctuary, like Shiloh. It will also serve to explain another noteworthy difference namely in regard to the treatment of the natives of the land. The ferocious treatment described and approved in the Book of Joshua is characteristic of religious warfare—the 'holy war'. On the other hand the relations of the patriarchs with the natives are more or less friendly. The only real outbreak of ferocity is the conduct of Simeon and Levi at Shechem (Gen. xxxiv); and this is condemned by Jacob both here and in the 'Blessing of Jacob' (ib. xlix, 5 ff.). It may be observed that this is the only incident in which Levi figures individually, and that the attitude towards him is far from favourable.

The derivation of the earlier story from Ephraim and of the later story from a sanctuary of Levi within the same district would seem to give a reasonable explanation of the differences between the two. It is natural enough that the sanctuary should use the story of the land as an introduction to the story of its own origin. The earlier story is presumably incomplete. It may have gone on to narrate the fortunes of the various tribal eponymoi, as in the case of Judah (Gen. xxxviii). At all events the story of Ephraim himself can hardly have been neglected; and though this is lost, a trace of its existence may perhaps be preserved in I Chron. vii. 20 ff., in a series of genealogies, which seem to preserve traces of other such stories. In this passage Ephraim is described as be-wailing the death of his sons, who have been slain by the men of Gath—not in holy war but in a cattle-raid. It is to be noted that Ephraim is here regarded as living in the uplands of Palestine, presumably the land of Ephraim. A story at variance with that of the Exodus is therefore implied; either Joseph himself or at least his son had returned from Egypt. Similar inferences may be drawn from other genealogies. Thus in the genealogy of Manasseh (*ib.* vii. 14 ff. and elsewhere) we meet with names of districts or communities, such as Machir, Gilead, Abiezer. These names, whether they be derived from tradition or from speculation, are presumably those of persons to whom the title of possession was traced. The story of the patriarchs may originally have served as an introduction to the traditions of the various tribes, for which in the Hexateuch, as we have it, the distribution described in Josh. xiii ff. has been substituted.

We have yet to discuss the antiquity of the stories. It is clear that both the story of the patriarchs and that of the Exodus were known to Amos and Hosea, the earliest of the prophets whose works have been preserved.[1] References are not so numerous or detailed that they can be proved to have known them in the form attributed to JE; but they were familiar at least with a number of the chief incidents. The stories then were in existence early in the eighth century. But they are probably much older. We cannot believe that anything so antipathetic and alien to modern feelings as the story of Moses can have originated in Israel so late as the eighth or ninth centuries. In its main lines this story is by no means incredible. Analogies are to be found in northern and eastern Africa, in regions fringing the desert, down to our own times. A holy man receives a revelation in the desert, and rouses the nomadic or semi-nomadic peoples around him to holy war against the settled inhabitants of a neighbouring country. But we cannot think that such a story was calculated to make much appeal to a nation which consisted in the main of agriculturists, merchants and townspeople. It may well have been

---

[1] These prophets do not mention Abraham; the first reference to him seems to be Is. xxix. 22. But evidence for the antiquity of his story may be found in Shishak's inscription (c. 930–925), which records a 'Field of Abraham', apparently in the south of Judah, among the places captured by the Egyptians.

accepted by them as a tradition coming down from the far past, under the sanction of a religious organisation; but, we think, not otherwise.

Apart from this general consideration both stories show plenty of features which are inconsistent with an eighth or ninth century origin. They must surely date from a time when the tribes were still of importance; and that does not seem to have been the case in the later history of the kingdoms. In the Books of Kings the tribes are seldom mentioned. It is stated that the founder of the first northern dynasty belonged to Ephraim, and the founder of the second to Issachar; but after this time—the early years of the ninth century—the tribes to which the dynasties belonged are not recorded. In I. iv. 7 ff. Israel is said to have been divided in Solomon's time into twelve fiscal districts, each under a special officer; but apparently only four of these districts correspond to tribes, though five tribes are mentioned. It is true that the prophet Ahijah promises to Jeroboam (*ib.* xi. 29 ff.) ten of the twelve tribes; but the ten are not specified, and it is not easy to see how so many can have been included in the northern kingdom.[1] The most likely explanation is that the passage dates from a time when some of the tribes had already disappeared as political units. On the whole then the evidence suggests that the tribal system had begun to lose its vitality soon after the establishment of the kingship.

There can be no doubt as to the antiquity of the system. In the 'Song of Deborah' (Judg. v. 14 ff.) eight of the tribes are named, while a ninth (Manasseh) is represented by Machir and Gilead. Those which are not named, Judah, Simeon, Gad, are among the most distant from the action. But the question which concerns us is the antiquity of the story; and in this connection there are two features which deserve notice.

In the first place the tribes are constantly said to be twelve in number. So also are the sons of Jacob, their ancestors; but the two sets do not exactly coincide. In place of the two brothers (half-brothers) Levi and Joseph we find two tribes claiming descent from sons of Joseph; Levi is not counted among the twelve, presumably because as a religious tribe it has no territory of its own. Yet it may be remarked that the references to Levi in Genesis do not attribute a religious character to him; indeed they practically preclude such an idea. In both cases (xxxiv. 25 ff.; xlix. 5 ff.) he is coupled with Simeon; and both of them are severely censured. In the 'Blessing of Jacob' they are cursed (xlix. 7), and it is stated that they shall be divided and scattered in Israel. Both these

---

[1] The arithmetic of the passage is at fault; but this may be due to an interpolation. According to xii. 14 Benjamin followed Judah; and it would seem that Judah had absorbed the territory of Simeon and probably the old territory of Dan.

passages seem to point to a tradition that Levi had been a tribe similar to the others, while the latter suggests that both it and Simeon had met with disaster and been expelled from their homes. Simeon appears to have been absorbed eventually by Judah; but the reference to Shechem in cap. xxxiv may indicate the lands of 'Joseph' as those from which the two tribes had been expelled. A trace of their former occupation may possibly be preserved in the possession of the sanctuary at Shiloh by a Levitical family. But all this is uncertain.

The second feature worth noting is the curious distribution of Jacob's family in Gen. xxix f. He has six sons by his first wife, two by his second and favourite wife, and two by each wife's maid. It is to be presumed that this arrangement reflects some kind of relationship among the tribes; but the nature of this is far from clear. It can hardly be geographical; for sons of the same mother, e.g. Gad and Asher, are widely separated. Possibly it may be chronological—indicating the growth of a confederation radiating out from some centre, such as Shechem. The illegitimate sons would then represent tribes recently or incompletely affiliated. But all this again is uncertain. What we would emphasise is that the stories contain elements which seem to be ancient and are not to be explained by any circumstances or conditions known to us.

The two antiquarian poems to which we have referred above are generally regarded as among the earliest remains of Hebrew literature. The 'Blessing of Moses' (Deut. xxxiii) seems clearly to be of northern origin (cf. p. 701). The honours here are divided between Levi and Joseph (Ephraim). Little is made of Judah; Simeon has disappeared altogether. On the other hand, in the 'Blessing of Jacob' (Gen. xlix) the honours are divided between Judah and Joseph; Simeon and Levi are cursed. Here again the balance of evidence points to the north; the honour paid to Judah may reflect the conditions of the undivided kingdom, under David or Solomon.[1] But the two poems are obviously of different provenance; the one points to a Levitical, the other to a non-Levitical origin—perhaps in a sanctuary or community of prophets, such as at Bethel.[2] We understand that the latter is commonly believed

---

[1] Additions may of course have been made to these poems from time to time; but in view of the very striking contrasts which they have preserved we think it safer to speak only of the texts as they stand.

[2] We know of no good evidence that Bethel was ever a Levitical sanctuary. Such passages as I Kings xii. 31 seem to imply that the Levites claimed exclusive right to the priesthood anywhere. But was this claim made and admitted in early times? From Judg. xvii. 9 ff. it may be inferred that the presence of a Levite as professional priest was desirable, but hardly that it was essential.

to be the older of the two. But it is to be observed that the opening of the 'Blessing of Moses' agrees substantially with a passage in the 'Song of Deborah' (Judg. v. 4 f.). Moses is not mentioned here; but there is a reference to a revelation at Sinai. Apparently too there is a movement from the south (Edom), as in the 'Blessing of Moses', but contrary to the account given in the prose story. It would seem then that, if we may take the passage as it stands, certain elements in the story of the Exodus may be traced back to a very early date, hardly later than the beginning of the eleventh century. And, though it is unsafe to lay much stress upon the exact interpretation of a single obscure passage,[1] it is clear at all events that the representation of the deity has something in common with the story, and more especially with the 'Blessing of Moses'. According to any interpretation he comes from beyond the southern border of Israel.

It would not be easy to show that either of the 'Blessings' dates from before the establishment of the kingdom, at least in anything like its present form. But the stories which they represent are doubtless much older than the poems themselves. The absence of any implication of kingship, and in particular the absence of any special honour paid to Judah or Benjamin, in either story must mean, we think, that the main lines of both were fixed before the times of Saul and David, though they may not have been current everywhere. Again, the story of Moses is connected with a type of sanctuary which belongs properly to nomads. The 'Tent of Jehovah' appears not only in early passages in Numbers, but also in the account of Solomon's accession, at the conclusion of the story of David (I Kings i. 39, ii. 28 f.; cf. II Sam. vi. 17).[2] This seems to imply a knowledge of the story that the nation or the national religion had come from the desert. On the other hand, the story of the patriarchs is connected with a different type of sanctuary, in which the chief feature is a menhir, usually set up beneath an oak. This type is not necessarily incompatible with the desert origin of the Israelites; but it gives no support to the idea that their national religion was imported from the desert as a corporate organisation. It was regarded with deep aversion by the prophets of later times. But its antiquity is guaranteed not only

---

[1] Many scholars regard the reference to Sinai as an interpolation, and interpret the passage to mean that Jehovah comes from Edom specially to assist Israel in the battle against Sisera.

[2] There are references (not early) to a temple at Shiloh in I Sam. i. 9, iii. 3. Against these may be set a (likewise late) passage (II Sam. vii. 6) where it is specifically stated that Jehovah has not occupied a house since the departure from Egypt.

by various passages in Genesis, but also by the story of Abimelech (Judg. ix. 6; cf. p. 693, note).

There can be little doubt then that both these stories go back at least to the eleventh century, in some form or other. How far they represent genuine tradition, what historical facts lie behind them, how far they are due to speculation—these are questions which we must leave to experts. Our object is to note the antiquity and the variety of Hebrew learning relating to the origin of the nation.

In conclusion we may observe that interest in antiquity was not limited to the origin of Israel itself. The origin of Edom, Moab, Ammon and other kindred peoples, is accounted for in the story of the patriarchs, as we have seen, while various other, more distant relationships are noticed in the early chapters of Genesis. The prophets also are interested in the origins of a number of foreign nations, as will be seen in the next chapter.

VII. Speculations upon the origin of mankind in general and of the world occupy the first eleven chapters of Genesis. A good deal of this section is believed to have been taken from P; but it may be doubted how far P is here independent of J. The two documents are distinguishable by their phraseology. But they seem to have covered much the same ground, except in cap. i; and, so far as we can see, most of what comes from P may have been taken originally from J and re-cast.

Perhaps the only considerable passage from P which seems to have been independent is the account of the Creation in cap. i and ii. 1–4. J appears to have had little to say upon this subject, except in relation to mankind.

Taken as a whole, cap. i–xi—or perhaps we should rather say ii–xi—differ from the rest of Genesis and from all the following Books in the fact that the matter with which they are occupied is mainly, if not wholly, of foreign origin. Some of it is indeed widespread; we have already met with it in Greece and India. But in those countries it has been naturalised much more thoroughly than in Israel. In Genesis the original (Mesopotamian) associations of the stories are still preserved to a large extent, both in place-names and in other respects. It is not likely therefore that their history in Palestine goes back anything like so far as that of the native stories we have considered above. Indeed, there is apparently nothing to show that they belonged to the common (oral) source from which J and E were derived. They must have become known, however, by the time of J, which is usually dated c. 800. It is apparently about the middle of the ninth century, under Shalmaneser III, that Israel begins to figure in Assyrian records; and communication between Palestine and Mesopotamia may well have become intensified about this time. More probably however they are derived from the Aramaeans of upper Meso-potamia, who may have acquired them much earlier. In Mesopotamia itself some of the stories were very ancient, and derived apparently from Sumerian records. But we must confess that we are not qualified to deal with this evidence—either the historical records or the stories themselves—and therefore we shall not attempt to give more than a passing notice of the latter.

The best known and most widespread of the stories is that of the Flood. What seems to be the fullest account[1] of this is preserved in an Assyrian text of the story of Gilgamish, dating from the seventh cen-tury, where it is introduced as an episode, narrated to the hero. The narrator, Utnapishtim, is also the chief character in the episode, and corresponds to Noah. The scene is laid at Shuruppak (Fara), about sixty miles to the north-west of Ur and nearly a hundred to the south-east of Kish and Babylon. This account shares with the story of Noah a number of features which are either wanting, or at least not clear, in the Greek and Indian stories.[2] Thus the flood is sent by a god (Enlil), apparently as a punishment for men's sins.[3] But other deities are not in sympathy with him; and it is another god (Ea) who warns Utnapishtim to build the vessel. He takes his family on board, but also a number of other people (craftsmen), as well as animals and birds; the vessel is of enormous size. A specially close resemblance occurs in the incident of the birds—here they are three separate birds, a dove, a swallow and a raven—which Utnapishtim sends out to explore. The raven finds food and does not return.

In the account given by Berossos, a Babylonian priest who wrote in Greek in the third century (B.C.), Utnapishtim is called Xisuthros, and in some Sumerian fragments, nearly two thousand years earlier, he is called Ziūsudra—which seems to be the same name. Both by Berossos and in Sumerian records Xisuthros or Ziūsudra is said to be the last of a series of ten kings who lived before the Flood. It is now generally be-lieved that the story arose from one of the great floods which took place

---

[1] We know this story from R. Campbell Thompson, *The Epic of Gilgamish*, p. 50 ff. An account of it and of other Babylonian records relating to the Flood will be found in Langdon, *Semitic Mythology*, p. 203 ff.

[2] Cf. Vol. I, p. 304, and above, p. 546 f.

[3] This motif seems to have been not unknown in Greece.

in Mesopotamia in the fourth millennium—the effects of which have been brought to light by excavations at Ur, Kish, and elsewhere. Possibly then Noah, Deucalion and Manu are all derived from a historical king.

In the Hebrew story Noah is immediately followed by the three ancestral brothers, who are his sons. In Greece they are Deucalion's grandsons. In India the brothers are five in number and removed from Manu by several generations. We do not know whether any feature of this kind has been found in Mesopotamia in connection with the story of the Flood. The closer resemblance between the Hebrew and the Greek stories suggests the possibility of a nearer relationship between them. Indeed, the latter may be derived from an early form of the Hebrew, though a common source in North Syria is also possible.

The origin of the rest of the stories contained in Gen. ii–xi is less obvious. The story of Adam has been brought into connection with various Mesopotamian stories; but the evidence is hardly convincing. The story consists of two parts: (cap. ii) the creation of man, followed by that of animals and birds and, lastly, of woman; (cap. iii) the incident of the serpent and the 'Fall'. The account of the creation itself is quite brief; for nearly half the chapter is occupied with a description of the Garden of Eden—which leads up to the incident related in cap. iii. It is not clear that the connection between the two parts of the story is essential or original, though it may have come to Palestine as a whole. The expression 'Garden of Eden' (*gan 'ēden*) means 'garden of delight'; but it is commonly thought, we understand, that the writing of the second word has been influenced by popular etymology. The original form of the expression may have been *gan 'eden*, the second part of which is a widespread name in Aramaean lands. We may instance the 'Sons of Eden', a North Syrian people mentioned in II Kings xix. 12, and the 'House of Eden' (*Bēth-'Eden*) in Amos i. 5, which seems to mean either the kingdom of Damascus or the Syrian peoples in general. The Assyrian form of the latter name (*Bīt-Adini*) is applied to an important Syrian kingdom on the upper Euphrates, in the neighbourhood of Carchemish, and also to a Chaldaean kingdom on the lower Euphrates, south of Babylon. It would seem then that, if this etymology is correct, the Garden of Eden was originally a legendary district or oasis which was regarded by one or more of these peoples as their ancestral home. The characterisation may have been influenced by the idea of a 'Golden Age'.

The story relates how the Garden of Eden was forfeited through the violation of a taboo connected with a tree, which may originally have been regarded as sacred. Apart from the name Eve (*Ḥavvāh*), which occurs only towards the end (iii. 20), it is a timeless nameless story, and has much the appearance of an explanatory folktale. Indeed, it may well be derived from a folktale beginning with some such formula as 'There was once a man who', etc. Various elements of folklore may be traced; but the chief object of the folktale was perhaps to account for the enmity which exists between mankind and snakes. It was due to the instigation of the latter that the Syrians of old lost their blissful abode.

The story of Cain and Abel is more obscure. It is not made clear why Cain's sacrifice is not accepted; and what follows is also difficult to understand. Above all, the special value attached to his life requires explanation.[1] The story hardly looks like a folktale. *Cain* seems to be a proper name. According to one theory he is the eponymos of the Kenites—which would point to Palestine, rather than Mesopotamia, as the home of the story. But Hebrew learning itself assigned quite a different origin to the Kenites; they were regarded as belonging to the family of Hobab (Jethro), i.e. as Midianites—who were themselves regarded as descendants of Abraham. Moreover, the Kenites seem to have been pastoral nomads, not agriculturists. On the other hand, some scholars identify the name *Abel* with Assyrian *ablu*, 'brother'—which again would seem rather to point towards Mesopotamia. On the whole, then, it is at least not clear that the story of Cain is of a different origin from the rest of cap. ii–xi.

The other stories or references to stories which occur in these chapters relate to Mesopotamia, so far as they can be located. We may instance the story of the Tower of Babel (xi. 2 ff.) and what is said of Nimrod (x. 8 ff.). Both these passages are instructive. It has often been remarked that the former gives a picture of a great building as viewed by nomads. In the latter it is not clear whether 'Nimrod' means some king of the historical period, such as Shalmaneser I, who is said to have founded Calah, or some legendary figure of the remote past. What seems clear is that this series of chapters (ii–xi) contains elements which in their origin were of different date and provenance, though they probably all

---

[1] In early European laws there is as a rule no vengeance or redress for homicide within the family or kindred, though the slayer often (not always) has to go into exile. Examples from various Teutonic and Celtic peoples will be found in Seebohm, *Tribal Custom in Anglo-Saxon Law*, pp. 30, 63, 164, 176, 241 f. But we do not know of any analogy for a sevenfold vengeance for a man who has been guilty of such a crime.

come from Mesopotamia. It may perhaps be described as an Aramaean collection, incorporating ancient stories, like that of the Flood, which were derived from the earlier peoples of that region.

As regards the date of the collection, if the name 'Ur of the Chaldees' (*Ur Kasdīm*) belonged to the tradition, we may ascribe it to the period between the eleventh and the ninth centuries; for the conquest of Ur by the Chaldees seems not to have taken place much before 1100. The name, however, may have been introduced in later times. And in any case it would seem to belong rather to the story of Abraham,[1] which follows, than to the preceding Mesopotamian elements. The latter have been utilised to form an introduction to the former, which is doubtless older (in Palestine). But the process is difficult to trace, because large portions of cap. x f. are taken from P. Cap. x contains Palestinian, as well as Aramaean learning. Possibly fresh discoveries at Ras Shamra or elsewhere may throw light on these questions. At present one can only say that the date suggested by the references to Ur of the Chaldees would seem not improbable on general grounds.

[1] This is a complicated question; for elsewhere the home of Abraham's family is 'Haran'. In xi. 31 P seems to have harmonised two discordant traditions. There is an ambiguity also about the position of Haran. The northern Haran, which, like Ur, had a famous lunar cult, was non-Semitic until c. 1350, when it was conquered from Mitanni by the Assyrians; and it seems not to have become Aramaean before cent. xiii. The southern Haran (near Damascus) doubtless became Aramaean somewhat earlier. But these questions hardly affect the origin of cap. ii–xi, unless the latter were bound up with the story of Abraham from the beginning.

CHAPTER VII

THEOLOGICAL AND MANTIC LITERATURE

THE theological literature of Israel differs from those of the other ancient peoples we have noticed, owing to its exclusive monotheism. Virtually this renders anything in the nature of narrative impossible, except what is concerned with the dealings of the deity with men. Neighbouring and kindred peoples, who were polytheistic, are known to have cultivated poetry relating to the divine community; and this poetry seems to have been partly narrative. Such is the case at all events with the very ancient fragments of poetry[1] found at Ras Shamra in northern Syria, dating from the fourteenth or thirteenth century. These consist largely of speeches; but some of them contain also a good deal of narrative. The poems would seem to have been, at least in part, of a didactic character. But we have not the knowledge necessary for dealing with the subject.

In the Old Testament itself a considerable number of deities are mentioned; but they are regarded as belonging properly either to the native peoples of the land or to external peoples. The national religion of Israel recognises no deity except Jehovah. Traces of anything resembling polytheism, which can strictly be called Israelitish, seem to be rare and somewhat faint. Perhaps the most striking instance is the vision of Micaiah in I Kings xxii. 19 ff., where the seer states that he has seen Jehovah "sitting on his throne, and all the host of heaven standing by him". The passage shows an interesting resemblance to certain passages in the *Iliad* (e.g. xx. 4 ff., xxii. 166 ff.), where Zeus consults the assembled gods with regard to the fate of a mortal. We may also compare the incident of the (personified) Dream sent by him to Agamemnon (*ib.* ii. 1 ff.). Elsewhere also, especially in the Psalms, Jehovah is represented as sitting on his throne and as a king above all other gods— expressions which are not strictly monotheistic in the modern sense. But the members of the heavenly court are never individualised, as in Greek and other references to divine communities; neither are they objects of worship. The feminine element seems to be wholly wanting.

---

[1] Cf. Virolleaud, *Syria*, xii. 193 ff., xiv. 128 ff.; *Antiquity*, v. 405 ff.; Gaster, *Journ. R. Asiat. Soc.* 1932, p. 857 ff.

The heavenly host is seen in a vision as an army of horses and chariots of fire in II Kings vi. 17 (cf. vii. 6).

In some stories Jehovah visits men in human form and, just as in some Greek and Northern stories, his supernatural nature is not recognised at first. Here also a trace of polytheism may be found in the fact that sometimes there appear with him—or, more often, in place of him—one or more unnamed persons described as 'messengers' ('angels'). The most striking example occurs in Gen. xviii. 2 ff., where Abraham sees three men approaching his tent. He gives them lunch, and then accompanies them towards Sodom. The conversation seems to imply that he recognises Jehovah before he leaves them. Then Jehovah himself departs; but the 'messengers' go on to Sodom, where they are not recognised. They spend the night with Lot, and rescue him in the morning, when the city is destroyed. A more obscure instance occurs *ib.* xxxii. 24 ff., where Jacob wrestles at night with God[1] and has his thigh dislocated. With this we may compare Ex. iv. 24 ff., which is still more obscure.

In the Book of Judges the messenger of Jehovah appears on several occasions. In ii. 1 ff. he comes from Gilgal to Bochim, and addresses the assembled people. In vi. 11 ff. Gideon sees him sitting under an oak and converses with him, but is slow to recognise him, until he produces fire in the sacrifice. The narrative here seems to identify the messenger with Jehovah himself. Again, in xiii. 3 ff. he appears first to Manoah's wife, and then to the wife and husband together. The wife is struck by his terrible appearance; but neither of them definitely recognise him, until he ascends in the flame of the altar. In this case too the messenger is identified with God (xiii. 22). An instance relating to later times is that of the messenger of Jehovah seen by David, in II Sam. xxiv. 16 f., at the time of the plague. In this case Jehovah addresses the messenger; the two therefore are quite distinct.

Lastly, we may cite Josh. v. 13 ff., where a man appears before Joshua with a drawn sword, and states that he is the 'captain of Jehovah's host'. Shortly afterwards (vi. 2) he is identified with Jehovah. It would seem then that he is a figure of the same character as the messengers.

The form of Type B—the speech in character—is of very frequent

---

[1] The use of this term, which is unusual in J, is perhaps due to the etymology of *Israel*, which is given (cf. p. 689). All the three instances noted here come from J. Such appearances are said not to occur in E, which prefers dreams and visions; but we may note the 'messengers of God', also called 'God's host', who appear to Jacob in xxxii. 1 f.

occurrence, especially with the prophets and in the Psalms. Strictly speaking, most of the examples belong to Type C (CB), for the substance is usually didactic. This form is of great importance in early Hebrew literature, in prose as well as poetry. Thus in the Books of Exodus, Leviticus and Numbers laws and directions of every kind are regularly expressed as divine utterances, and introduced by some such formula as "Jehovah said unto Moses". Instances from JE may be found in Ex. xx ff., xxxiv; but P also uses similar expressions. In the formulae employed by the prophets there is a good deal of variety; but most of the prophecies are represented, in one form or another, as utterances of Jehovah.

Type D is represented, in the form of hymns, by most of the Psalms and by a number of poems in other Books, some of which are variants of psalms. Prose prayers are also frequent. It is the prevailing opinion now that very little of the religious poetry dates from before the sixth century; much of it is thought to have been composed in the Persian period, or perhaps even later. We ourselves are not qualified to judge; but we understand that the language and diction preclude the possibility of a verbal tradition preserved from early times, such as is found in the Rgveda. We do not know, however, how far the possibility of a freer form of oral tradition has been considered. Evidence from many lands, as we have seen, shows that the substance of poems can be preserved when the form is modernised, though this is of course less likely to occur in poetry used for liturgical purposes. The Psalms contain a number of references to 'the king', which may most easily be interpreted as dating from the period of kingship—the seventh century or earlier—though they have been explained otherwise. Certain other features will be noticed in the next chapter. But the question as a whole must of course be left to specialists.

The mantic element in early Hebrew literature differs very greatly from what is found in ancient India. For spells, as apart from blessings and curses, there is but little evidence, though this may be due in part to the character of the surviving records. On the other hand, prophecy is very highly developed, and preserved in abundance. Again, mantic powers, whatever be their form, are seldom represented as proceeding from any innate or acquired faculty of the seer himself; usually they are due to revelation or direct action from Jehovah. Such spells as are to be found therefore have as a rule the form of prayers—which is rather exceptional in India. Lastly, the activities of the seer or prophet are very largely concerned with national or political interests—a feature which is found commonly enough in the Rgveda, but rarely in later India. Mystical speculation therefore takes a different form. In place of the attention there devoted to the relations between the individual and the absolute, we find the interest of the Hebrew prophets concentrated upon the relations between the nation and the national deity. In this connection the geographical and ethnographical differences between the two countries are to be borne in mind. Israel was constantly exposed to external danger, as well as to the influence of a native population who were regarded as aliens, though they spoke the same language. In general perhaps better analogies for Hebrew mantic activities are to be found in ancient Europe than in India.

Prescriptive spells are not easy to find in early Hebrew literature. The Book of Leviticus describes a good number of rites which contain elements of magic, in addition to hygienic and other practical considerations; but if set formulae were in use for such occasions, they are not recorded. The same remark applies to the rites described in the Book of Numbers, which likewise come from P. Here perhaps the nearest approach to a spell is in the formulae pronounced by the priest at an ordeal (v. 19 ff.), when a woman is charged with infidelity. Possibly, however, a fragment of a true spell may be preserved in the song sung by Israel in xxi. 17 f.: "Spring up, O well; sing ye unto it", etc.

In narratives, especially the stories of Elijah and Elisha, we hear not unfrequently of what may fairly be regarded as spells, though divine interposition is almost always invoked. The most interesting example occurs in II Kings iii. 11 ff. The kings of Israel, Judah and Edom have gone to war against Moab; but their army is in great straits through lack of water. They appeal for help to Elisha, who after some hesitation calls for a minstrel. "And it came to pass, when the minstrel played, that the hand of Jehovah came upon him. And he said: 'Thus saith Jehovah, Make this valley full of trenches. For thus saith Jehovah, Ye shall not see wind, neither shall ye see rain, yet that valley shall be filled with water'", etc. A somewhat similar case occurs in I Kings xviii. 36 ff., where fire descends upon the altar in consequence of Elijah's prayer. We may also compare (*ib.*) II. xiii. 15 ff., where Elisha on his deathbed tells King Joash to shoot an arrow through the window, and then to smite upon the ground with his arrows—by which he will obtain victory over the Syrians. Reference may also be made to the destruction of the soldiers by Elijah in II. i. 10, 12, and to Elisha's declarations to Naaman and Gehazi in II. v. 10 ff., 26 f. These last examples may be taken either as spells or as curses and blessings which have immediate effect; they are not expressed in the form of prayers.

Blessings and curses of the more usual type, i.e. such as take effect in the future, may be regarded, as we have seen, either as spells or as prophecies which bring about their own fulfilment. An example of this type may be found in Numb. xxiii f. The Syrian seer Balaam has been summoned by Balak, king of Moab, to curse Israel; but he can only declare what he is inspired to say. The king leads him from one hill-top to another, upon each of which he builds altars, offers sacrifices and recites short poems; but the poems are all blessings upon the enemy. It may be observed that the chapters in which this story is told come from JE, while the poems themselves contain references to Assyria which may perhaps point to the latter part of the eighth century.

Two poems which are probably still older, the 'Blessing of Jacob' and the 'Blessing of Moses', have already been noticed (p. 705 f.). The former (Gen. xlix) is addressed by Jacob to his sons on his deathbed, the latter (Deut. xxxiii) by Moses, likewise at the end of his career, to the children of Israel. The two poems follow more or less the same scheme, though the latter has a narrative introduction and a hymnic (panegyric) epilogue, which are wanting in the former. In detail they have little in common. The Blessing of Jacob contains what are practically curses, as well as blessings. It may be noted that the pronouncements contained in this poem, whether descriptions of the present or prophecies of the future are all alike expressed as statements of fact. In the Blessing of Moses, on the other hand, such pronouncements are varied from time to time by sentences expressed in the form of prayers.

Two more poems of this kind, but much shorter, are contained in Gen. xxvii. 27 ff., 39 f. In the former Isaac, who has become blind, blesses Jacob under the impression that he is Esau; in the second he blesses Esau, when he has discovered his mistake. The former is expressed in precative form, the latter in the future, as statement of fact; but no doubt is raised as to the fulfilment of the former, any more than the latter. The former is the greater blessing. It has been obtained by deception on the part of Jacob and his mother; yet Isaac himself recognises it to be irrevocable. In response to Esau's entreaty he can only give him an inferior blessing, which will not conflict with the other. He will have to serve his brother, though he will eventually free himself.

Blessings and curses upon nations are of not infrequent occurrence in the works of the early prophets; but on the whole these are perhaps best included among prophecies. Brief curses in prose are also not rare; we may instance the curse pronounced against the people of Amalek in Ex. xvii. 14 ff. An interesting example of a curse attached to a place occurs in Josh. vi. 26, where Joshua pronounces a curse upon the man who should rebuild Jericho. According to I Kings xvi. 34 this curse was fulfilled in the days of Ahab.

The literature of prophecy is very extensive. Indeed, this is the form in which Hebrew thought, or at least religious thought, chiefly found expression. In the intellectual life of the nation it may be regarded as occupying a position similar in a sense to that of the mystical philosophy of India; and it is rather curious that the most flourishing periods of both seem to have been more or less contemporary.

We have seen (Vol. I, p. 473) that in Europe, more especially in Greece and in the North, prophecy may relate to the past and the present, as well as to the future. It is the expression of mantic knowledge, whether by revelation or 'vision', irrespective of time. There can be no doubt that the same is true also of Hebrew prophecy at least as regards the present. Instances are not rare. Thus in I Sam. ix. 6 ff., when the young Saul is looking for his father's asses, his servant suggests to him that they should consult the 'man of God'. Saul hesitates at first, because he has not sufficient for a present (i.e. a fee) to the seer; but eventually they go to him. Samuel anoints him privately as king, but tells him incidentally (x. 2) that the asses have been found. Again, according to (ib.) xxii. 5, "the prophet Gad said unto David: 'Abide not in the hold; depart and get thee into the land of Judah'". It seems to be implied that, in virtue of his prophetic power, Gad has some knowledge of Saul's movements. A more specific instance occurs in II Kings vi. 11 f., where the king of Syria charges his servants with betraying his plans to the king of Israel, and one of them replies: "Nay, my lord, O king; but Elisha, the prophet that is in Israel, telleth the king of Israel the words that thou speakest in thy bedchamber". This is the same power which is possessed by Math, son of Mathonwy, in the Mabinogi which bears his name (ad init.).

The evidence for prophecy relating to the past is less definite and specific than in Europe. We cannot recall any passages in which revelation of the past is stated to be one of the prophet's functions. Yet it can hardly be doubted that this function was recognised at one time. Before the written texts acquired authority the knowledge of the past was dependent upon oral tradition. But who were responsible for the preservation of the traditions and, further back, for composing them or giving them shape? We believe that by many modern scholars these

24

activities are attributed to unknown prophets of the past. Some writers indeed describe the early texts J and E as 'prophetical' narratives, in contradistinction with P, the later 'priestly' narrative. From analogies in other lands we might ascribe the traditions either to prophetic organisations ('sons of the prophets') or to sanctuaries. But the distinction is perhaps not of vital importance; for there were prophets, as we shall see (p. 770), in some of the more important sanctuaries. To the question of authorship we shall have to return in a later chapter. But it may be noted here that the early prophets Amos, Hosea and Isaiah frequently refer to incidents in the Hexateuch, though it is uncertain whether they knew these from written texts or from oral tradition.[1]

At this point it is unfortunately impossible to avoid touching upon a question which properly requires linguistic knowledge, such as we do not possess. In the English Bible 'prophet' is a translation of Hebrew nābī', while 'seer' is used for two different Hebrew words, ro'eh and hozeh, both of which are closely connected with verbs meaning 'to see'.[2] We do not know what is the difference of meaning between these two words;[3] but the latter seems to be of rare occurrence in early works. The question, however, to which we would call attention is the relationship of these terms to 'prophet'. It would seem that, if not synonymous, the terms 'prophet' and 'seer' were applied to the same persons. Thus in I Sam. ix. 9, in what is evidently an explanatory note, incorporated in the text, it is stated that "he that is now called a Prophet was beforetime called a Seer (ro'eh)". Again, in II Sam. xxiv. 11 we hear of "the prophet Gad, David's seer (hozeh)". The same man is called prophet also in another passage, cited above (I Sam. xxii. 5). And both terms are applied to various other persons. Elsewhere a distinction is made, e.g. in I Chron. xxix. 29, between Samuel the seer (ro'eh), Nathan the prophet, and Gad the seer (hozeh); but the nature of the distinction is not made clear.[4] It is commonly held, we believe, that the prophet and the

---

[1] Some passages, e.g. Hosea xi. 8, are generally thought to be derived from authorities which are now lost.

[2] Just as Ir. *fili*, 'learned poet' (orig. 'seer') is connected with a lost verb 'to see' (W. *gweled*); cf. Vol. I, p. 606.

[3] According to some scholars the original function of the *ro'eh* was to 'inspect' the livers of sacrificial victims, that of the *hozeh* to read the signs of the heavens. But we do not know how far these explanations are accepted. They seem to leave out of account the chief attribute of the seer.

[4] We should be inclined to suspect that the descriptions are copied from the passages in the Books of Samuel where these persons are mentioned.

seer were originally distinct—the former being associated with ecstatic conditions—but that the terms eventually became synonymous, perhaps by the time of Elijah. It would seem at all events that Elisha had all the attributes which usually apply to either prophet or seer. He was closely connected with the 'sons of the prophets'. In what is said below, therefore, we shall not in general attempt to distinguish between prophet and seer, though the subject will require notice again in the last chapter.

One of the most striking features of Hebrew prophecy is that the prophet or seer commonly takes the initiative. Sometimes, it is true, a wrong impression may be conveyed by the brevity of the narrative. Thus in I Sam. xxii. 5, when Gad warns David to move his quarters, the warning may be an answer to a question, though this is not stated. But there are numerous examples where any such explanation would be extremely improbable. Elijah regularly takes the initiative in his dealings with Ahab. The same is true of the action of Shemaiah in I Kings xi. 22 ff., of Nathan in II Sam. xii, of the unnamed prophet in I Sam. ii. 27 ff. Even in the earliest times (Judg. iv. 6 ff.), the initiative against Sisera is clearly taken by the prophetess Deborah. Parallels for such initiative on the part of prophets are of course to be found among many peoples, indeed perhaps everywhere. But in most countries they seem to be exceptional. In the *Iliad*, 1. 68 ff., Calchas does not offer to explain the cause of the plague until a seer has been called for; but in II Sam. xxiv. 13, in a somewhat similar situation, Gad takes the initiative. Instances like *Od.* xx. 350 ff., where Theoclymenos unsolicited prophesies the doom of Penelope's suitors, are less frequent in Greece and elsewhere.[1]

We may now illustrate briefly the various forms of prophecy. First we may take prophecies on behalf of individuals. A simple example is to be found in II Kings viii. 7 ff. Benhadad, king of Syria, is ill, and sends his officer Hazael to Elisha with a large present, to ask him: "Shall I recover of this sickness?" Elisha replies: "Go, say unto him, 'Thou shalt surely recover'; howbeit Jehovah hath shewed me that he shall surely die." In the conversation which follows, other examples occur, e.g. when Elisha says (viii. 13): "Jehovah hath shewed me that thou shalt be king over Syria." Other instances may be found in Isaiah's prophecies (*ib.* xx. 1–6) with reference to Hezekiah's illness and troubles. We may also compare I Kings xiv, where Ahijah makes known to

---

[1] We may refer to an interesting passage in Rimbertus' *Life of St Ansgar* (cap. 26), cited in Vol. 1, p. 473.

Jeroboam's queen that her son's illness will prove fatal. It will be observed that in such cases the prophecy is sometimes a reply to an enquiry, sometimes spontaneous.

Next we will take prophecies on behalf of the nation. No rigid line of demarcation can be drawn between this class and the preceding; some prophecies may be interpreted as relating either to the king or to the nation. A very early example of this class is to be found in Judg. iv. 6 ff., where Deborah summons Barak to rise against Sisera. We may also take in this sense Samuel's speeches in I Sam. vii. 3 ff., though they contain little of what is commonly called prophecy, and the passage is believed to be late. Better examples occur in the account of Ahab's war with the Syrians (I Kings xx. 13 f., 28), where unnamed prophets prophesy victory for the king of Israel. Strictly these passages can be interpreted as prophecies on behalf of Ahab; but the cause is evidently national rather than personal. In this connection we may refer again to Elisha's dying injunctions to Joash (II Kings xiii. 15 ff.), though the passage resembles a spell more than a prophecy. Prophets seem frequently to have taken a leading part in stimulating resistance to foreign enemies. We may instance Isaiah's prophecies against the Assyrians, e.g. II Kings xix. 20 ff., Is. x. 24 ff. This is a feature for which analogies may be found in Europe. In particular we may refer to the Welsh prophetic poems noticed in Vol. I, p. 453 ff. (cf. p. 129).

Not unfrequently we find prophets reproving or denouncing kings. The reproofs are usually accompanied by prophecies of punishment. Saul is reproved or denounced by Samuel on three occasions; and in each case Samuel states that he will lose the kingdom. Two of these passages (I Sam. xiii. 13 f., xv. 16 ff.) come from the later account of Saul's life. In the third (*ib.* xxviii. 16 ff.), the origin of which is disputed (cf. p. 667), Samuel is already dead, and is called up from the grave to give a response to Saul. He denounces him unsparingly, and says that he will lose his life in a national disaster on the following day.

The fault for which Saul is denounced is that he has spared the life of Agag, king of Amalek, whom Samuel had ordered him to kill. In other cases kings are reproved or denounced for acts of flagrant injustice. Thus in II Sam. xii Nathan reproves David for causing the death of Uriah the Hittite. The reproof strikes us as not too severe, considering the nature of the crime; but it is accompanied by a prophecy of the humiliation which David will suffer through Absalom's rebellion. The incident is remarkable also from the fact that the prophet reproves the king for injustice to a man who is not an Israelite. In I Kings xxi. 20 ff.

Elijah denounces Ahab much more sternly for a very similar crime. Yet it is not clear that Ahab was personally responsible for Naboth's death, though he took possession of his property.

In later times Naboth's death was remembered as Ahab's greatest crime; but it was by no means the only cause of the hostility between him and Elijah. The root of the trouble seems to have lain throughout in his wife Jezebel, who was evidently regarded with horror by the prophets, both in her husband's lifetime and later. She is said not only to have acted tyrannically, as in the case of Naboth, but also to have persecuted the prophets of Jehovah. Indeed she would appear to have been fanatically attached to her own (Phoenician) religion. Other queens also are charged with introducing cults incompatible with that of Jehovah, though apparently only in the earlier part of the kingly period. But it is not clear that the early prophets were violently opposed to foreign influence, apart from religion. Elijah and Elisha were strongly patriotic; but this did not prevent them from visiting Phoenicia and Damascus.

The prophets do not rest content with reproofs or even with denunciations of kings whose doings had incurred their disapproval. On several occasions we find them prophesying, and indeed actively promoting, revolution. Samuel, as we have seen, prophesies the downfall of Saul and his family, and anoints David to take his place. Jeroboam's rebellion is said to be due to the action of Ahijah (I Kings xi. 29 ff.); but the same prophet later (*ib.* xiv. 7 ff.) prophesies the fall of his dynasty. The prophet Jehu, son of Hanani, prophesies the fall of Baasha's dynasty (*ib.* xvi. 1 ff.). Elijah similarly prophecies the destruction of Ahab's family (*ib.* xxi. 21 ff.); and the revolution which brings this about is directly instigated by Elisha (II Kings ix. 1 ff.). The political influence of the prophets seems to have been very great.

Thus far we have been concerned in the main with the pre-literary prophets—whose activities are known to us only from stories contained in the Books of Samuel and Kings. The activities of what we may for short call the 'literary' prophets—collections of whose works have been preserved—appear to have been of a somewhat different character, though it may be questioned how far the differences are due to accidents of transmission. So far as we can judge, the earlier prophets addressed themselves wholly or at least mainly to individuals. The majority of the stories relate to their dealings with kings, though there are others which are concerned with persons of humbler position, sometimes indeed such as were quite poor. But we seldom hear of appeals to the general public or to bodies of people, except in certain stories of Samuel, which are commonly believed to be very late. The story of the sacrifice on Mt Carmel (I Kings xviii) may be regarded as an instance; for Elijah appeals to the assembly (21 ff., etc.), though the king is presiding. But the appeal of Shemaiah (*ib.* xii. 22 ff.) is doubtless addressed primarily to the king, Rehoboam. On the other hand a clear example is to be found in II Chron. xxviii. 9 ff., where Oded appeals for the liberation of the captives. No king is mentioned here, though certain leading men are specified as taking the initiative. This case, however, relates to the period of the literary prophets.

The evidence for the literary prophets is very different. Amos can hardly be said to appeal to any individual, though he has an encounter with Amaziah, the priest of Bethel (vii. 10 ff.) and pronounces a prophecy or curse against him. Isaiah appeals both to Ahaz and to Hezekiah; and in one passage (xxii. 15 ff.) he prophesies against a high official. But the great majority of his prophecies relate to the nation collectively or to foreign nations. In Hosea's prophecies the name Israel occurs about forty times, and the name Ephraim almost as often, while Jacob and Samaria are also used in much the same sense; but no contemporary prince is mentioned, except in the title of the collection. The prophecies of Micah show the same, exclusively national, interest.

It is clear then that the prophets of the eighth century, in contrast with those of the ninth, make their appeal to the general public. They may have been enabled to do so by the more general use of writing. But we doubt if this is the true explanation. If the prophecies had circulated in written form from the beginning, the texts could hardly have come into the state of confusion in which we have them—more especially that of Isaiah. The explanation is more probably to be sought in changed political and social conditions. Such changes are found elsewhere at the close of the Heroic Age. There is no evidence indeed, so far as we know, for any post-heroic Hebrew literature of the individualistic type, such as we find in the poems of Archilochos and Egill Skallagrímsson; but such poetry is not the only product of early post-heroic times.

The Hebrew (literary) prophets were approximately contemporary with the early didactic poets of Greece, and in all probability also with the growth of philosophical (Upanishad) literature in India. This contemporaneity may not be without significance. But what concerns us more at the moment is that all three apparently represent phases of culture which have certain important elements in common. All seem to belong to times when writing was beginning to be used for literary purposes. Moreover all belong to early post-heroic times, though the interval which had elapsed since the end of the Heroic Age may have been longer in Greece than in the others.

The Hebrew prophets themselves have elements in common with both the Greek and the Indian works. With the latter they share their manticism, though the manticism is of quite a different character. Greek didactic poetry also was at least in part of mantic origin, though as a rule this element soon became forgotten, or survived only as a figure of speech. But in substance the Hebrew prophets have much more in common with the Greeks than with the Indians. They are concerned primarily with moral and social duties, or rather with the denunciation of moral and social evils, and with the relations between man, especially the nation, and God. All these interests are represented also in early Greek didactic poetry, though the treatment and the conceptions are different. But the Upanishads are not concerned with these subjects.[1]

Amos, the earliest of the literary prophets, belonged to Tekoa in Judah; but his prophecies relate almost entirely to the northern kingdom. Their date seems to be shortly before 750 B.C. in the reign of Jeroboam II. He says (vii. 14) that he was a shepherd and dresser of sycamores, but denies that he was a prophet or son of a prophet—by which he means presumably that he did not belong to any prophetic organisation. Apart from this we know nothing of his life, except that he visited or resided in Beth-el, where he had an encounter with the priest Amaziah.

The evils which Amos denounces seem to be in part of an economic nature—the oppression of the poor by the rich through the imposition of heavy burdens, and in particular by distraints for debt (ii. 6 ff., viii. 6). The rich live in great luxury, owing to their exactions from the poor (v. 11, vi. 4 ff.); their inanities, as well as their vices, arouse his wrath (vi. 5). The ladies of the aristocracy, whom he calls 'kine of Bashan' (iv. 1), are guilty of the same practices. But he also speaks of dishonesty and of injustice in the administration of the law—the use of false weights (viii. 5) and the taking of bribes (v. 12). Frequently he describes Israel—by which he seems throughout to mean the upper classes—as devoted to religious observances and to festivals at Beth-el, Gilgal, and elsewhere; but Jehovah will not accept their offerings. He

---

[1] Virtue and truth seem to be assumed in a philosopher; and a wise king is credited (*Chānd.* v. xi. 5) with permitting no vice within his realm. But specific moral injunctions (e.g. *Taitt.* i. xi) are very rare in the Upanishads, though common enough in later literature.

repeats again and again that disaster is coming; the cities and sanctuaries will be destroyed, and the country laid waste.

It is to be observed that the economic and social evils denounced by Amos are identical with those which we hear of in Greece at the beginning of the historical period. In many Greek states the seventh century was characterised by upheavals, which led to revolutions, dictatorships or cancellations of debts. The cause of these is doubtless to be sought, at least in part, in the opening or re-opening of Mediterranean lands to commercial enterprise and in the consequent raising of the standard of living. Before this time we have very little information; but it can hardly be doubted that the conditions which led to these movements were in existence to some extent in the eighth century. Greek commercial enterprise had begun to develop by the beginning of the eighth century, Phoenician enterprise much earlier. The latter had connections by land, as well as by sea[1]; and the luxury described by Amos shows that Israel, owing doubtless to successful warfare, had now become one of its important markets. The conditions then which we find prevailing in Greece and Palestine were probably not unconnected. The anarchy which followed the death of Jeroboam II—at least three violent revolutions in under twenty years—may be regarded as an earlier counterpart of the Greek upheavals. But in Israel the story was cut short soon afterwards by the Assyrian conquest.

For Greece of the eighth century Hesiod is almost our only contemporary authority; and it is of interest to compare the 'Works and Days' with Amos' prophecies, in regard to both the conditions described and the poets' attitude towards them. Hesiod's poem may be slightly the later of the two, possibly by a generation; but it is to be borne in mind that he belonged to a backward district, though his father had been a merchant of the Aeolic Cyme. The personal element in the poem—his admonitions to his brother Perses—need not be noticed here (cf. Vol. I, p. 357 f.).

Hesiod, like Amos, regards his age as one of outstanding depravity, far inferior to the days of old. Violence and injustice are rampant. In particular he denounces repeatedly the corruptness of the 'bribe-devouring' princes who administer the law. But of luxury he says little. Nor is the position of the poor agriculturist as hopeless as in Amos' prophecies. He can keep free from debt by hard work; and the latter part of the poem is mainly occupied with practical advice upon the

[1] We may refer e.g. to the silver platters, found in Italy, Cyprus and elsewhere, which depict both Egyptian and Assyrian scenes in concentric zones.

working of a small farm. The conditions of life in Hesiod's home were evidently more primitive than in Israel.

The poets have much more in common in their attitude to their subjects. Both of them are shepherds, and have received their inspiration while tending their flocks; and their attitude to society is doubtless coloured by their vocation. But they are by no means to be regarded as ignorant rustics; both of them are well versed in traditional (antiquarian) learning. Both of them are deeply impressed with the evils of the time, and bitterly hostile to the upper classes. But the outstanding ideas which both poets have in common are (i) the association of justice with the deity—Zeus or Jehovah—and (ii) the conviction that injustice and wickedness will lead to disaster. Amos is more specific in regard to the latter; he clearly has in mind the danger of foreign conquest, to which Israel, owing to its geographical position, was exposed. Hesiod's countrymen have only local wars, together with famine and plague, to fear. In one passage (*Works and Days*, 180–199) Hesiod himself represents the future as hopeless; but in another (*ib.* 223 ff.) he lays down that the city of the just will flourish, while that of the wicked will come to grief. He deals very largely in gnomes and gnomic precepts (cf. Vol. I, p. 390 f.)—of which Amos and the other Hebrew prophets make only sparing use. On the other hand he does not appeal to any intimate personal relationship between the state and its deity, like that between Israel and Jehovah, which forms the most prominent element in Amos' doctrine. His own inspiration is from the Muses, not from Zeus, and he evidently regards them as his patrons; but it is Zeus who governs the destinies of mankind. His attitude to religious observances would have brought stern denunciations upon him from Amos.

Hesiod's religious ideas, like the social conditions of his time, are of a more primitive character than what we find in Amos' prophecies. Yet there is sufficient resemblance to give ground for suggesting a connection in this case also; and a connection of some kind has in fact been proposed,[1] not only for Hesiod and the Hebrew prophets, but also for certain Egyptian official records dating from the same period, which show a noteworthy change of tone. The king (Piankhi), instead of the traditional glorying over the defeat of his enemies, discourses at some length upon his anxiety to show mercy. We may add that this record may be compared with the magnanimous conduct attributed to the leaders of Ephraim in II Chron. xxviii. 12 ff. The authority for the

---

[1] Cf. Petrie, *History of Egypt*, III. 276, where, however, Isaiah and Ezekiel, not Amos, are specified.

incident is of course late and uncertain, but hardly open to the suspicion of any partiality towards Ephraim.

This incident at all events suggests very distinctly that Amos' description of the ruling classes in Israel is one-sided, and that the feeling for justice and humane dealings was by no means limited to the prophets. Indeed one striking feature of the story is the readiness of the leading men to follow the prophet (Oded), just as in the days of Elisha. Moreover we have assured evidence to the same effect in the legislative activities of the period, both in Greece and in Israel. In Greece many states had their laws committed to writing in the seventh century; but in Israel this probably took place earlier, and apparently in the northern kingdom. The earliest Greek laws are not preserved; but those of Israel are clearly under religious inspiration. In this case at least a connection of some kind is more than probable—Greek writing itself was derived from Palestine—and consequently one cannot fairly deny the possibility of a similar connection in the movements of thought which make their appearance about this time in both countries.[1]

Modern scholars are inclined to attach great importance to Amos in the history of religious thought. He and the prophets who immediately followed him are often regarded as the 'creators of ethical monotheism'. In view of the fact that no earlier works other than narratives and laws have been preserved, this seems to us a somewhat hazardous proposition. Amos may be reflecting the religious thought of his time, though this is far more advanced than that of the narratives; for the latter were doubtless traditional, though they may only recently have been committed to writing. Hesiod retails much advice which is clearly secondhand;[2] and it cannot safely be assumed that his moral-religious views are original. Neither poet seems to us to show much insight in his treatment of social problems, except in certain details which may have come within his personal knowledge;[3] their denunciations are characterised by vigour rather than by discrimination. Could anything else be expected from shepherds?

It seems to us—and we speak with all reserve, as non-specialists— that two main elements may be distinguished in the populations of both

---

[1] There can of course be no doubt as to Oriental influence in early Greek antiquarian learning. We may refer e.g. to the story of the Flood and to the passage relating to Belos in *Catal.* fragm. 43 (Kinkel). In the sixth century evidence for Oriental influence is abundant.

[2] E.g. the directions for navigation (*Works and Days*, 617 ff.). He confesses that he had never been to sea.

[3] E.g. Amos vi. 4—the hardship of the demand for lambs and calves.

Israel and Greece. One of these was coastward or urban in its affinities, the other landward and pastoral. The former was open to every new wave of civilisation, with its increase of knowledge and its luxury, vices and follies. The latter was conservative, and regarded these innovations with abhorrence. In Israel this latter element seems to have been much under the influence of prophets, who cherished both a stricter morality and traditions of ferocity in their treatment of enemies. A century before Amos' time, under Ahab, the coastward element had been predominant. Then came a revolution, apparently by the landward element, who at first used their power ruthlessly. In Amos' own time a reaction had taken place, but gradually, not by further revolution; the coastward element had once more become predominant, and the prophets were again in opposition. But during much of the intervening period the two elements must have been in not altogether unfriendly contact; and we would suggest that it was at this time, when Elisha's influence stood high with the government, that Hebrew religious thought assumed that character which is reflected by the literary prophets.

If so, the original contribution made by these prophets themselves would seem to have been of a different character—mantic rather than philosophical. For several centuries Palestine and Syria had been free from serious molestation from the more powerful kingdoms to the north and south; but in the ninth century their freedom began to be threatened by the growth of the Assyrian empire. The Assyrian advance was slow; but throughout the first half of the eighth century it was a constant menace to Syria, and no thoughtful persons in Israel can have been free from apprehension for the future. The chief attention of the prophets is devoted to giving emotional expression to this sense of danger; they regard themselves as the mouthpieces of Jehovah and the impending disaster as a divine retribution for the nation's sins. In point of fact there can be little doubt that the catastrophe was hastened by the dissensions and the unsettled government which prevailed after the death of Jeroboam II. But the attitude adopted by the prophets strikes the modern reader as a strange way of dealing with such a situation, and likely to produce panic and demoralisation rather than social reform.

Hosea's prophetic activities are generally dated a few years later than those of Amos—shortly before and after the death of Jeroboam II, i.e. probably c. 745–735 B.C. He also is primarily concerned with the northern kingdom, to which he presumably belonged; most of the references to Judah are usually believed to be interpolations. Certain passages show that the period of dissensions had already begun. But nothing seems to be known of Hosea's personal history, apart from what he says about his unhappy marriage.

Hosea is much more difficult to understand than Amos, owing partly perhaps to the corrupt state of the text, which is believed to be extensively interpolated; but the chief source of difficulty lies in the extremely figurative character of his utterances. His work indeed is not of a kind which can be interpreted by a non-specialist; but at the same time it is too important to pass over without mention. One of the leading motifs in his prophecies seems to be the conception of Israel as the unfaithful wife of Jehovah. In the first chapter it is stated that the prophet at Jehovah's command married an immoral woman. An account of their unhappy married life follows; but much of this obviously applies to the nation, as the faithless wife of Jehovah, rather than to the prophet's own experiences. The question has been much discussed whether this story is to be taken as real autobiography or as didactic fiction; but the former seems to be the more commonly accepted view. It is certainly very remarkable; for this interpretation would seem to imply that the prophet turned his life into a kind of didactic drama, in which he played the part of Jehovah and his wife that of Israel. In later chapters much is said about 'whoredom' and adultery; and again it is not clear how far these terms are to be taken literally, and how far figuratively. In this case also it seems to be the prevailing view that the prophet had in mind real sexual immorality, perhaps especially in connection with religious festivals, as well as the religious infidelity of the nation. In his denunciations Hosea is both more impassioned and more specific than Amos. But he is uncertain whether the destruction will come from Assyria or from Egypt. The rulers of Israel seem to be negotiating with both these powers.

Isaiah presents at least as great difficulties. The Book which bears his name is a collection of prophecies, not more than half of which can well be his work. The latter part, from cap. xl, clearly belongs to much later times; and the same is true of not inconsiderable portions of cap. i–xxxix. These chapters also contain a certain amount of narrative, chiefly derived from Kings. Moreover it is not certain that all the early prophecies come from him; one short prophecy (ii. 2–4) is attributed also to Micah (iv. 1 ff.), his contemporary. The prophecies are not in chronological order; and the text is believed to be often corrupt or incomplete. Apart from these textual difficulties, the meaning is very frequently obscure, owing to the figurativeness of the language. Indeed we are well aware that Isaiah's prophecies, like Hosea's, are properly 'for experts only'; but—again like Hosea's—they are far too important to be ignored in a book of this kind, though we shall only attempt to notice a few examples.

According to the introductory words (i. 1) Isaiah's activities extended over a long period; and this is borne out by the text. Unlike the prophets already noticed, he is concerned with the kingdom of Judah, and especially Jerusalem, to which he evidently belonged. The earliest poem is probably cap. vi, where he receives his inspiration, in the year that King Uzziah died (c. 740). The inspiration comes to him in a vision; he sees the Lord (i.e. Jehovah) enthroned in the Temple, which is filled with his robes. Above him stand Seraphim with six wings, one of whom brings a hot coal or stone from the altar and touches the prophet's mouth with it. He receives his commission, which is a strange one—to obscure the understanding of the people, so that they will not realise the evils which are coming upon them. The land is to be utterly laid waste.

This attitude of complete hopelessness towards the future appears frequently enough in the prophecies; but it is not maintained consistently. Thus in cap. vii, when Ahaz is hard pressed by the armies of Israel and Syria, Isaiah tells him that the enemy are at the end of their strength and not to be feared; his prophecy here seems to be one of encouragement, though it is not well received. Even towards Assyria he sometimes adopts a bellicose, and indeed provocative, tone; we may instance x. 5 ff. and more especially II Kings xix. 21 ff. A number of prophecies probably, like the passage last cited, relate to Sennacherib's great invasion, in which Isaiah counselled Hezekiah to hold out, in spite of the devastation of the country. There are also many passages which speak of better times to come; but most of these are generally believed to have been added in later times.

Though Isaiah was in favour of holding out against Assyria, he seems, like other prophets, to have been strongly opposed to the policy of alliances with Egypt and other neighbouring states. Much of the evidence bearing upon this question is precarious, because a number of the prophecies which foretell the destruction of these states may be later, perhaps by centuries, than his time; but apparently his policy was to rely upon the protection of Jehovah alone. One of the most curious passages occurs in xx. 2 ff., where it is stated—though the text is not quite clear—that about the time of the fall of Ashdod (B.C. 711) Isaiah went about naked (perhaps half-clad) and without shoes for three years, to symbolise the disasters which are about to befall Egypt. The principle involved here is apparently the same as in the opening chapters of Hosea; the prophet turns his life into a kind of didactic drama. In this case, however, he personates not Jehovah but the unfortunate Egyptians, who are going to be carried away into captivity. The incident is the more remarkable because it is hardly to be supposed that he was greatly concerned at the fate of the Egyptians. His object is to demonstrate that, so far from being able to protect Judah or the Philistine states, Egypt itself will soon be overwhelmed by disaster. The parallelism between Isaiah's and Hosea's ideas may be illustrated by another passage (viii. 1 ff.), where the former gives his child a name derived from the disasters of Damascus and Samaria; we may compare the names given by Hosea (i. 6 ff.) to his children.[1]

The social evils denounced by Isaiah seem to be similar to those recorded by Amos; but the references are less specific, though injustice and bribery are mentioned. Like Amos he is indignant at the multitude of religious observances to which the nation is devoted, and demands a reform in place of them. Much is said about drunkenness, especially in Ephraim (xxviii. 1 ff.), but perhaps also in Judah (v. 11, 22). Isaiah also seems to share Amos' feelings towards the luxury and the inanities of the upper classes, e.g. the practice of minstrelsy at feasts (v. 12; cf. Amos vi. 5). He is especially severe upon the frivolities of the ladies of fashion; he specifies at length (iii. 16 ff.) their ornaments and the attractions which they cultivate, and prophesies, apparently not without some feeling of satisfaction, the horrors in store for them in the future. In general, however, the descriptive element is much subordinated to the denunciatory.

Nahum's prophecies belong to a time (c. 612 B.C.) which does not properly come within the scope of our work. But the contrast in tone is worth remarking. The prophecies consist largely of expressions of joy at the downfall of the great national enemy, Assyria, which is described in poetical language. The contrast with the earlier prophets lies not only in the political situation, but also, apparently, in the sentiments of the author, e.g. (i. 15) "Keep thy feasts, O Judah",—now that the danger is past.

The story of Jonah relates to an earlier time;[2] but it is preserved only

---

[1] Names of this kind are sometimes found elsewhere, e.g. I Sam. iv. 21. Isaiah himself (vii. 3) has another son, with a somewhat similar name.

[2] From II Kings xiv. 25, it would seem that he was an older contemporary of Amos, early in the eighth century. This passage also suggests that he had national interests.

in a late and legendary form. The chief point of interest is that Jehovah is represented as concerned about the fate of a foreign and hostile state, while the prophet tries to evade his instructions—apparently not so much from fear as from aversion to the thought that the Assyrians should be saved. Jehovah is no longer a deity of purely national interests; he is rather to be regarded as God of the World. Traces of the same conception occur in a number of passages in the Book of Isaiah; but we understand that all of these are believed to be later than Isaiah's time. A safer instance is probably to be found in Amos ix. 7, where Jehovah is said to have brought the Philistines and the Syrians, as well as the Israelites, from other lands. In some sense indeed the conception is implied—though only for certain peoples—in the story of Abraham and Isaac. It may therefore have been current in Jonah's time. On the other hand the true explanation may be that an author of much later times is utilising the old legend for the presentation of ideas in which he is interested.

Another question which is not clear to us is whether the early prophets ever have in mind a universal, elemental, catastrophe, such as we find in the Mahābhārata. There are several passages in Isaiah's prophecies which can be—and have been—interpreted in this way; but it is uncertain, we understand, whether any of them date from Isaiah's time. References to eclipse phenomena, e.g. Amos viii. 9, need not be interpreted thus; they may be regarded merely as omens of coming national disaster. In Zephaniah i. 2 f., 14 ff. the conception seems to be more clearly developed, though these passages are believed to be inspired by dread of some threatened invasion, towards the end of the seventh century. The development can perhaps be explained from the language of the prophets themselves. In popular usage the term 'Day of Jehovah' denoted an expected national triumph. But the early prophets use it for an impending national disaster (cf. Amos v. 18). Later it comes to mean a universal catastrophe, which will lead to the restoration of Jerusalem and the recognition of the supremacy of Jehovah by foreign peoples. But it may be questioned whether this development has not been affected by foreign influence. In India, where the evidence is doubtless much later (cf. p. 622), the conception of a universal catastrophe is connected with the doctrine of the Four Ages, which seems not to have been current in Israel. Unfortunately we do not know whether any evidence is available for the intermediate regions.

The same remark must be made with regard to the general characteristics of the early literary prophets. It is clear that a feeling for the need of moral and social reform in connection with religion was not limited to Israel during this period. Such a feeling is obvious enough in Hesiod, as we have seen, though in Greece generally the later development of the movement was political rather than religious. In Iran the religious element was stronger, and so too the importance attached to (divine) 'righteousness' (*aša*). Indeed the analogy with the prophetic movement in Israel is very striking, though the chronology of early Zoroastrianism is still uncertain. Evidence for somewhat similar movements of thought could also be found in more remote lands.

CHAPTER VIII

GNOMIC AND DESCRIPTIVE LITERATURE

LITERATURE RELATING TO UNSPECIFIED INDIVIDUALS

I. Hebrew gnomic literature is chiefly represented by the Book of Proverbs and the Book of Ecclesiastes. The Psalms also contain much gnomic matter; and a certain amount is to be found in Exodus and elsewhere, mostly in the form of precepts. The Book of Job belongs to the same class of literature, though the actual gnomic element in it is comparatively slight. A much closer resemblance to Proverbs is shown by two books which are not included in the Old Testament, the Wisdom of Solomon and the Wisdom of Ben Sirach (also called Ecclesiasticus), especially the latter.

Most of the 'wisdom' books date from a late period, which does not come within the scope of our work. Ben Sirach's book was written c. 190 (B.C.); and Ecclesiastes and the Wisdom of Solomon are generally believed to be no earlier. In regard to Job and Proverbs there is less agreement; but the former is commonly attributed to some time, earlier or later, within the Persian period. In the case of Proverbs, which is the most important of these works for our purpose, the discrepancy of opinion is much greater. It is obviously a composite work, consisting of a number of different collections. Many scholars believe several of these collections to be as early as the eighth or seventh century; but others attribute the whole to the Greek period, preferably the third century. If the latter view is correct, the work of course does not come within our scope. But since there is a difference of opinion, we have decided not to omit it, especially as there is very little gnomic material which can with confidence be assigned to any earlier time. We shall therefore give a brief summary of its contents. It may be remarked here that certain arguments which have been adduced in favour of a late date seem to us unsound. But there is some other evidence, of which we are not qualified to judge.

The chief constituent elements of the book seem to be as follows:

Cap. i–ix consist of discourses on wisdom in the form of instructions by a 'wise' father to his son—a widespread form of gnomic composition.[1] The prevailing form is that of the precept; but it is varied by gnomes,

[1] English, Norse and Irish examples will be found in Vol. 1, Ch. xii. For a probable Greek example we may refer to the fragment of Simonides quoted *ib.* p. 416.

chiefly of Type II a.[1] Examples of the former may be found in i. 8, 10, of the latter in i. 7. Enthymemes seem to be of frequent occurrence, e.g. i. 16; and the gnomes are commonly expanded into descriptions. Cap. vii–ix consist of a series of pictures similar to those in the Exeter Book (cf. Vol. I, p. 381), though some of them are of a more abstract character, comparable rather with the Vedic example referred to on p. 550, above.

Cap. x–xxii. 16 consist of gnomes of Type II a, arranged in couplets. In cap. x–xv the second member of the couplet usually presents a contrast to the first; but from ch. xv onwards[2] it tends, more and more frequently, to take the form of an extension or repetition, e.g. xx. 23.

At xxii. 17 begins a series of quatrains apparently described as 'the words of the wise'—which continue to xxiv. 22, though they are somewhat irregular. Like cap. i–ix, they seem to be in the form of instructions given by a father to his son. The prevailing form is again that of the precept. Enthymemes, giving the reason or purpose of the precept, are very common, e.g. xxii. 22 ff.; but sometimes the quatrain is filled up by expansion or repetition, e.g. xxiv. 3 f. This section shows frequent analogies with the *Hávamál*, though the cynical humour characteristic of a large part of the latter is wanting, as elsewhere in the Book of Proverbs. The first part of it (down to xxiii. 14) shows a still closer resemblance to an Egyptian gnomic poem, the 'Teaching of Amenemope',[3] with which indeed it is thought to have a definite literary connection.[4]

The remainder of cap. xxiv (from st. 23) seems to be in the nature of a supplement to the preceding section. It is introduced by the words: "These also are sayings of the wise." The matter is similar; but the quatrain form is not preserved. This short section ends (st. 30 ff.) with a picture of the idle man. Again we are reminded of the *Hávamál*.

---

[1] For the system of classification, see p. 550, note, and Vol. I, p. 377 f., where it is explained more fully. It should be noted that Type I a and Type II a are not always easy to distinguish. But gnomes of Type I seem not to be very frequent in Proverbs; their place is usually taken by precepts.

[2] Some scholars believe x–xv and xvi–xxii to be derived from two different collections, owing to stylistic differences.

[3] Transl. by Griffith, *Journ. of Egyptian Archaeol.* XII. 191 ff.

[4] Cf. Simpson, *Journ. of Egyptian Archaeol.* XII. 232 ff.; Oesterley, *The Wisdom of Egypt and the Old Testament*, p. 60 ff. There is some difference of opinion as to whether this section is derived from Amenemope, or both are derived from a lost (perhaps Hebrew source). The question depends to some extent upon Amenemope's relation to earlier Egyptian gnomic works (cf. p. 736 f., note), as to which we are not competent to judge. Affinities with Amenemope occur in other sections of the Proverbs.

In cap. xxv–xxix the couplet is again the prevailing form.[1] Most commonly the second member expresses a comparison with the first (e.g. xxv. 2); but there is a good deal of variety. Most of the sentences are gnomes of Type IIa, though precepts are not rare. Occasionally we find sentences relating even to animals and inanimate things (Type IIc), e.g. xxv. 23; but these are introduced, not for their own sake, as in Anglo-Saxon and Welsh gnomic poetry, but by way of comparison or as illustrations of gnomes relating to mankind (Type IIa), just as in the *Hávamál* (cf. Vol. I, p. 386).

Cap. xxx is of a somewhat varied character. It consists largely of gnomic catalogues, not unlike those which occur in the Exeter and Cotton gnomic poems and in the *Hávamál*, st. 81 ff. (cf. Vol. I, pp. 380 f., 383). They have also something in common with the catalogue riddles referred to *ib.* p. 414, and the Russian, Yugoslav and Indian compositions noticed in this volume (pp. 212, 410, 560 f.). Many of the gnomes contained in this chapter belong to Type IIc.

Cap. xxxi consists in part (st. 2–9) of instructions to a king by his mother, chiefly on the avoidance of wine and on merciful treatment of the helpless. The rest of the chapter (st. 10–31) is an alphabetic poem, occupied with a long description of the virtuous woman, with which may be compared the—much briefer—description of the queen given in the Exeter gnomes (cf. Vol. I, p. 381).

As regards authorship, we find in i. 1: "The proverbs of Solomon, the son of David, king of Israel"—a title which belongs presumably to cap. i–ix.[2] In x. 1 we find "The proverbs of Solomon", which may apply to the next section, down to xxii. 16. The section which follows is introduced by the sentence (xxii. 17): "Incline thine ear, and hear the words of the wise." The short section xxiv. 23–34 begins with the words "These also are sayings of the wise", as noted above. Then, in xxv. 1, as an introduction to the next section we find: "These also are proverbs of Solomon, which the men of Hezekiah king of Judah copied out." Cap. xxx begins with "The words of Agur the son of Jakeh; the oracle (or 'burden')". Cap. xxxi begins with "The words of King Lemuel; the oracle (or 'burden') which his mother taught him".

Nothing is known of the persons mentioned in the last two chapters,[2] which are perhaps to be regarded as supplements to the Book. The remaining sections—or rather collections—are attributed to Solomon,

---

[1] From stylistic grounds some scholars separate xxviii f. from xxv–xxvii. They think that xxviii f. is derived in part from the same collection as x–xv.

[2] Some scholars, however, take these words as syntactically connected with the following sentence, and not as a title claiming Solomon's authorship.

except the two short sections included in xxii. 16–xxiv, which are referred to 'the wise'. But it is generally agreed, we believe, by modern
scholars that this attribution is to be taken in the same sense as the
attribution of the Psalms to David. Solomon was traditionally famed
for his wisdom; in I Kings iv. 32 ff. he is credited with the composition
of three thousand 'proverbs', as well as a thousand and five songs and
much lore relating to natural history. It is not unnatural therefore
that anonymous collections of gnomic poetry should be attributed
to him.

Cap. i–ix are generally thought to be later than x–xxii. 16, and
perhaps composed as an introduction to the latter. Cap. xxv–xxix are
also believed by some scholars to belong to the older stratum, though
others date them later than cap. i–ix. The differences in date are not
thought to be great. Cap. xxii (from st. 17)–xxiv are generally referred
to about the same period, whether earlier or later than cap. i–ix. Indeed,
except for the last two chapters (xxx f.) and a few short passages elsewhere, no great differences in date seem to be proposed, as between the
various sections of the Book. But there is a very remarkable difference
of opinion as to the period in which it was composed—a difference
greater perhaps than in regard to any other work in the Old Testament.
Some scholars, as we have seen, believe the whole—with the few exceptions just noted—to date from the period of kingship, while others
attribute it to the third century, or perhaps rather the period between
350 and 250 B.C.

As mentioned above, some of the arguments which have been adduced
in support of the late dating seem to us by no means convincing. It is
surely unnecessary to attribute to Greek influence either the cultivation
of gnomic poetry or the esteem for 'wisdom', which is indeed virtually
implied in such poetry. The references given in Vol. i, Ch. xii, will be
perhaps sufficient to show how widely poetry of this kind was cultivated in ancient Europe. For the latter idea we may refer to the *Hávamál*,
which otherwise also has numerous elements in common with the
Proverbs. On the other hand the absence or rareness of gnomes in the
early prophets cannot prove that gnomic composition was unknown,
but only that it was not cultivated in prophetic circles. It would indeed
be a remarkable fact if such literature was unknown in a people which
had attained the civilisation and intellectual development of Israel in the
kingly period.[1] But the cultivation of prophecy and of gnomic literature

[1] In addition to the European material discussed in Vol. i, we may refer to the
early Indian evidence noticed in this volume, p. 550 ff. For Egypt there is far more

may well have belonged to different circles.[1] The frequent references in the Proverbs to town life and to trade may possibly give a clue to their original provenance, though we are by no means certain. In any case they are not incompatible with an origin in the eighth or seventh century.

A further objection to the antiquity of the Proverbs is based on the use of the words 'wise' and 'wisdom'. It is said that these words have no philosophical sense attached to them in the Old Testament, except in the 'Wisdom books' and a few Psalms. We cannot claim to speak with authority on this question; but it seems to us very doubtful if the characteristic denoted by the word 'wise' (ḥākām) in the Proverbs differs from the characteristic which it denotes in Jerem. viii. 8 f. and xviii. 18, or in II Sam. xiv. 2 and xx. 16. To take the word as referring to political sagacity in the former passages and cleverness in ordinary affairs in the latter appears to us arbitrary. In all these passages, just as in the Proverbs, the word surely has a half-technical sense. The 'wise' are those who have acquired not only knowledge but also the power of expressing it, especially, it would seem, in the form of generalisations. The qualification for which the 'wise' woman is chosen in II Sam. xiv. 2 is evidently rhetorical skill; and we may doubtless assume the same in (ib.) xx. 16. 'The wise' referred to by Jeremiah have obviously attained a reputation for sagacity—we do not see why this should be limited to political sagacity—but they are not likely to have attained this reputation by silence.

Rhetoric is intimately connected with gnomic poetry, if not essential to it. According to the *Hávamál*, st. 103, a man who wishes to be a great sage must cultivate speech, as well as memory. But there are of course different kinds of rhetoric. The rhetoric usually employed by the prophets is of an emotional type, very different from the reflective, generalising, character found in the 'Wisdom books'. But the gnomic type is not unknown even to the earliest prophets; we may cite Amos iii. 9 ff., Hosea viii. 7, x. 13, Is. i. 3.[2] Jeremiah himself (xxxi. 29) quotes a gnome current in his day (cf. Ezek. xviii. 2), though he seems to have no great

ancient evidence; cf. Erman, *Literature of the Ancient Egyptians*, p. 54 ff. The earliest gnomic compositions, including the 'Instructions of Ptahhotep', seem to date from the third millennium. The nearest resemblance to the Proverbs is shown by the 'Teaching of Amenemope'; but unfortunately there is great difference of opinion as to the date of this work—some scholars attributing it to the tenth century (or even much earlier) and others to the seventh, the sixth, or even the fourth century.

[1] This seems to be implied by Jerem. viii. 8 f.; see below.
[2] This passage may be compared with *Háv.* 21 (quoted in Vol. I, p. 383).

respect for this kind of learning. The passage in I Kings iv. 32 f.,[1] which describes Solomon's wisdom, may probably be taken as evidence for the existence of 'natural history' gnomes (Type IIc), traditionally attributed to Solomon. The speeches of the two ladies given in II Sam. xiv and xx cannot strictly be described as gnomic, though the former uses two gnomes; but they reflect a similar kind of wisdom. We need not doubt therefore that such wisdom and rhetoric were cultivated in the times of the kingship.

It would perhaps not be well to attach too much importance to the title of Prov. xxv, in which Hezekiah's men are said to have copied out the following proverbs; but we cannot allow that there is any true analogy between this title and the titles prefixed to certain Psalms, explaining the circumstances under which they were composed. Psalms were attributed to David in the same way as proverbs to Solomon; and when David's authorship had come to be accepted, it was not unnatural for scholars to speculate upon the circumstances of their composition. But the reference to Hezekiah's scribes cannot be explained in this way. There seems to be good reason for believing that Hezekiah's age was a time when much oral tradition was committed to writing; and if the collection contained in Prov. xxv–xxix is so old, the statement contained in the title is likely enough to be true. But what reason could scholars of the Hellenistic period have had for inventing such a statement? We know of no evidence which would suggest that they thought of Hezekiah's reign as a time of special literary activity.

Apart from the objections noticed above,[2] which seem to us unsound, the antiquity of the Proverbs is rejected by some scholars on the ground of their literary connections, more especially with the Book of Ben Sirach. This is a question which must be left to experts. But if the evidence is really decisive—and we gather that there is considerable difference of opinion on this point—we think that extensive use must have been made of earlier collections. We find it difficult to believe that gnomic poetry was not cultivated before the Hellenistic or Persian periods. The evidence for Egyptian connections seems to be much more definite; but their nature is not quite clear.

---

[1] Whatever may be the date of this passage, the latter part of it cannot be derived from the Proverbs as we have them.

[2] It is impossible of course for us to enter into all the arguments. Thus objection has been raised on the ground that idolatry is not referred to; but the Proverbs are not primarily concerned with religion. The frequent references to kings would seem to be of more significance.

After the 'Wisdom books' gnomic poetry is best represented in the Psalms. Unfortunately the literary history of the Psalms is more obscure even than that of the Proverbs. The present tendency is to date them as late as possible. We have a suspicion that many of them may have had a longer history than can be decided from the existing texts; but we are not prepared to discuss the question. The gnomic Psalms are commonly believed to be among the latest in the collection. Here we will refer only to one passage, Ps. xlix. 4. This psalm is commonly attributed to the Hellenistic period, and the passage referred to is thought by some scholars to be a still later addition. The poem as a whole is not strictly gnomic in form; but its affinities are with this kind of poetry, and it contains a number of gnomes. But the feature to which we would call attention is that it seems to be intended for accompaniment on the lyre. On the other hand, in spite of its title, it does not give the impression of having been composed primarily for liturgical use.[1]

Probably the earliest gnomic collections contained in the Old Testament are those which are preserved in the Book of Exodus. The 'Ten Commandments' (cap. xx) are gnomic precepts. The Laws also, which follow (cap. xxi ff.) are largely gnomic in form—either precepts or gnomes of Type I *a* and *b*. All this matter is said to be derived from E, which is commonly believed to have been written in the northern kingdom, hardly later than the middle of the eighth century.[2] The commandments contained in cap. xxxiv are precepts of a religious or ritual character, akin to gnomes of Type I *b*. These are believed to come from J, and are generally thought to be earlier than the commandments in cap. xx. It may be observed, however, that both these collections are of somewhat different character from the collections of gnomic poetry found in the Proverbs. The latter contain numerous precepts, usually much expanded; but the prevailing type of gnome, as we have seen, is Type II.

II. In the 'descriptive' category early Hebrew literature possesses one account for which we have not been able to find any parallel in the literatures previously discussed. This is the account of Solomon's temple and palaces given in I Kings vi f. It is commonly thought to be derived from the 'Book of the Acts of Solomon', mentioned *ib.*

---

[1] The opening may be compared with the first stanza of the *Völuspá*, where the introductory formula seems to be derived from that of a formal address. With 6t. 3 f. we may also compare the beginning of the Exeter gnomic poem, though the latter suggests derivation from a dialogue form.

[2] Some scholars, however, regard the Ten Commandments as a late addition to E—much later than the Laws; cf. Lods, *Israel*, p. 315 f.

xi. 41; but nothing definite seems to be known as to the date of this work.

The descriptions of buildings and localities which we have met with in other early literatures seem to be either imaginary or typical. But such can hardly be the case here, though the wealth of the buildings may be much exaggerated. Later chapters, in I and II Kings, contain frequent references to changes, spoliations and renovations of these buildings, which presuppose a knowledge of some such description. These references are presumably derived from records or traditions of the temple; and the lost 'Acts' themselves may have had the same origin. The interest would seem to be primarily antiquarian, but inspired by a desire not so much to explain the origin of the buildings as to celebrate their magnificence in the past. We find it difficult to believe that such an account could have been preserved by oral tradition in anything like its present form. On the other hand it gives the impression of having been composed while the buildings were still standing, or at least clearly remembered. It is of considerable interest in the history of art; difficult as it is to follow, at least in a translation, it seems to show features resembling those of Greek art in the Geometrical and Orientalising periods. We may hope that before long excavation will be able to throw light both on the credibility of the account and on the age of the buildings and objects which it describes.

Descriptions of typical persons and scenes, such as we have found in other early literatures, are not rare in Hebrew; but they are usually short and of uncertain date. One of the longest is the description of the virtuous woman in Prov. xxxi. 10 ff.: this may be compared with certain Indian poems noticed above (p. 557) and with some of the European examples referred to in Vol. I, p. 407 f. It is clearly a product of written literature; but it might date from a time when the writing of poems was still regarded as an accomplishment in which the author could take a good deal of pride.

The first part of the Proverbs (cap. i–ix) contains a number of descriptive pieces relating to Wisdom, which is personified. Thus in iii. 13 ff. we find a short poetical description of the blessings which Wisdom gives. Two other passages are speech poems, in which Wisdom is the speaker. In i. 20 ff. she declares the troubles which men incur by neglecting her. In cap. viii she describes her nature and properties at some length, and speaks of the advantages which will be gained by listening to her. We may compare the Vedic poems referred to on p. 556. Apart from these there are a few short descriptions of typical characters, such as we have found in other literatures. We may instance the 'strange woman' in v. 3 ff. and the 'foolish woman' in ix. 13 ff. The former passage is followed by a discourse on the advisability of avoiding such persons. In vii. 6 ff. there is a longer passage dealing with a similar character; but this is mainly occupied with a speech, and will be noticed in the next section. In vi. 6 ff. there is a very brief description of the ant; but this is given not for its intrinsic interest, but as a moral against idleness.

In the other sections of the Proverbs descriptive passages are rare and brief. We may, however, notice the description of the sad end of the idler in xxiv. 30 ff., which is followed by the same stanza as the passage last cited. In xxiii. 29 ff. there is a passage which is practically a description of the drunkard, though it is not expressed in the usual form of such descriptions. Lastly it may be noted that the latter part of cap. xxx consists largely of what may be called gnomic catalogues, somewhat similar to those which we have quoted in Vol. I, p. 418 ff.

The Psalms also contain a number of descriptive passages, though we do not know what period they date from. Among these we may note the long description of nature which occupies the greater part of Ps. civ.[1] But perhaps the most striking picture is that of the storm-tossed sailors in cvii. 23 ff. Brief pictorial similes are not rare. We may instance cxxiv. 7, where Israel is compared to a bird which has escaped from a trap, and xix. 4 f., where the sun is compared to a bridegroom.

In the early prophets examples of detailed description are not very common. In the collection of prophecies ascribed to Isaiah we may instance (iii. 16 ff.) the description of the ladies of Jerusalem and their finery; and so also (xxviii. 23 ff.) the work of the ploughman, and (v. 26 ff.) the approach of the invading army. Ideal conditions, when vicious animals shall become harmless, are sketched in xi. 6 ff. In v. 1 ff. there is a metaphorical description of a vineyard—representing the nation—which will yield only wild grapes. With this we may compare Hosea's account of his wife (ii. 5 ff.), which is in part descriptive, though the metaphor, if such it can be called, is not consistently adhered to. Brief descriptions, occupying only a verse or two, are more frequent. We may cite the ideal picture of peace in Micah iv. 3 f., part of which occurs also in Is. ii. 4. Most of the instances, however, are similes, e.g. Amos ii. 13, iii. 12, v. 24, ix. 13, or metaphors which may be taken as

---

[1] It has often been remarked that this psalm shows a striking resemblance to the Hymn to the Sun (*Aten*) found at El Amarna; transl. in Erman, *op. cit.* p. 289 ff. and in various other works. We cannot discuss the question of literary relationship.

similes, e.g. Hosea x. 1, 11. In Is. xxxi. 4 the simile, brief as it is, has some resemblance to the similes of the *Iliad*. But very often it is difficult to make out whether such descriptions are intended as similes or as statements of actual occurrences. We may refer e.g. to the series of visions recorded in Amos vii. 1–9, viii. 1 ff. We believe that these are usually interpreted as actual visions; and it is true that the vision in ix. 1 ff., which seems to belong to the same series, can hardly be interpreted as a simile—at least not in the same sense as the others. But the prophets were obviously imaginative persons; and we are not clear how far they distinguished between actual experiences and figures of speech.

The Song of Songs contains a good deal of descriptive matter; but it belongs more properly to the next section—if indeed it comes within the scope of our work at all.

Riddles seem to be of rare occurrence in early Hebrew literature. The only instance which we can recall is that which Samson proposes to his Philistine guests in Judg. xiv. 14. But we have little doubt that they were cultivated. The wisdom of the Proverbs has something in common with riddle-wisdom—a combination of knowledge or observation with rhetorical skill. Some sentences indeed look like answers to riddles; we may cite especially xxx. 15 f. The same seems to be true of the wisdom traditionally attributed to Solomon. The 'hard questions' asked by the Queen of Sheba (I Kings x. 1 ff.) may mean something in the nature of riddles; the same word (*ḥīdāh*) is used.

III. Saga relating to unspecified individuals occurs in more than one form. We may first take the fictitious story, which is composed for a purpose. An early example of this is to be found in the story told by Nathan to David (II Sam. xii. 1 ff.) of the rich man who robbed the poor man of his only lamb. The story is invented to bring home to the king the character of his dealings with Uriah. A variant form of this type of story is told in the first person, as an experience of the narrator. We may instance the story told by the wise woman of Tekoa (*ib.* xiv. 5 ff.), which is invented at Joab's instigation, in order to induce David to relent from his treatment of Absalom.

Next we may take stories which are not represented as fictitious. Among these may be included the narrative of the Levite and his concubine who was mishandled by the men of Gibeah, found in Judg. xix ff. The only person mentioned by name is Phinehas, son of Eleazar (xx. 28); but he plays no part in the story, and this passage has the appearance of a scribal addition. The story itself—or at least the account of the war to which it leads—is difficult to believe, unless it has been very greatly exaggerated. Yet it would seem to have been current even in Hosea's time, and to have been regarded by him as an important landmark in the national history. At all events this appears to be the most likely interpretation of Hosea x. 9, though other explanations have been proposed.

Another instance may be found in the story, told in I Kings xiii, of the prophet who came from Judah to Beth-el, to prophesy the profanation of the sanctuary by Josiah. This story, it is true, is not wholly nameless; for Jeroboam, the founder of the northern kingdom, is said to have been present, and to have had his hand injured, and subsequently healed at the prophet's intercession. But no name is given to either of the prophets who play the chief parts in the story. In its present form the story must of course date from a time at least three centuries after Jeroboam's reign. As to its origin, the resemblance between the first part of it and the incident related in Amos vii. 10 ff. is obvious enough, though most scholars, we believe, are inclined to regard it as merely accidental. In both cases the scene is laid in the sanctuary of Beth-el, and the prophet comes from Judah. The two kings have the same name, though one lived more than a century and a half after the other. It is true that Jeroboam II is not present at the incident related in Amos, though he, or at least his family, is involved in it. If the two stories were originally identical, we must assume that the king and the priest have been amalgamated in the story of the nameless prophet; and this is the kind of simplification to which stories preserved by oral tradition are liable. We must also assume that the story was preserved and developed in circles where Amos' prophecies were not known, except by a vague report. As to the fate of the prophet on his return journey we are without information in Amos' case; possibly this incident might be due to the influence of folktale. On the whole then we are inclined to regard the identification as possible, but no more than a possibility. If it is true it affords an interesting illustration of the growth of the nameless type of story.

Stories wholly or mainly derived from folktales are not easy to demonstrate. The story of the 'Fall of Man' (Gen. iii) seems to belong to this class, though its original form is not clear (cf. p. 709 f.). Its affinities are widespread; but it is probably of Mesopotamian rather than Hebrew origin. Apart from the Mesopotamian element in the early chapters in Genesis, traces of folktales are apparently to be found only in the stories of characters, historical or unhistorical, who are known to us in other connections; and it is generally questionable whether these stories are not influenced by folktales, rather than folktales transferred *in toto*. The stories in which elements of folktales seem to be most prominent are those of Samson. It may be noted that for one of his exploits—his single-handed slaughter of a host of Philistines—(Judg. xv. 15 ff.) analogies are to be found in incidents related of other Israelite heroes with somewhat similar names (*ib.* iii. 31; II Sam. xxiii. 11 f.).

Timeless nameless poems of Type B, i.e. speeches in character by unspecified individuals (cf. pp. 223 ff., 402 ff., 562), seem to be rare. We have not found any instances in the early prophets; and those which occur in the Psalms and the Proverbs are as a rule very short, e.g. Ps. liii. 1. Occasionally, however, we meet with a longer passage of this kind, as in Prov. vii. 14 ff., where after an introduction, partly narrative and partly descriptive, the speech of the harlot is given at some length.

The Song of Songs has been interpreted as a single piece of dramatic character, in which the principals are Solomon, a girl whom he is courting, and a rival lover, apparently a shepherd. But now it is more generally believed to be a collection of love-songs, or perhaps rather wedding-songs, some of which are in the form of dialogues. There are said to be wedding-songs now sung in Syria, just as in Russia (cf. p. 236), in which the bridegroom is described as a king; and the name Solomon is thought to be used in this sense. In that case the songs are to be re-garded as belonging to the category now under discussion. The form is that of Type B; but if they really belong to the celebration of social ritual, we should assign them rather to Type D (DB). The collection is commonly believed to be very late, on linguistic grounds; but in poetry of this kind the language may well be modernised. Indeed such poetry may be traditional in its general form, though subject of course to modification from time to time in detail; and we have therefore thought fit to mention it here, though we are not able to discuss it at length. It may be noted that very similar poetry was cultivated in Egypt, apparently from c. B.C. 1300 onwards.[1]

Poetry connected with the celebration of social or political ritual (Type D) seems to be preserved in some of the Psalms. Ps. xlv is generally believed to have been composed for the wedding of a king. But no individual names have been preserved; and consequently we may perhaps infer that it was maintained in use for similar occasions. Ps. lxxii gives the impression of having been composed for use at the inauguration of a king. We may compare the examples from the Rgveda

---

[1] Examples are given by Erman, *op. cit.* p. 242 ff.; Peet, *Comparative Study of the Literatures of Egypt, Palestine and Mesopotamia*, p. 92 ff.

referred to on p. 565. Ps. xxi would also seem to have been composed for some state occasion. The dating of all these poems is quite uncertain; none of the suggestions which we have seen appear to us in any way convincing. But we find it difficult to doubt that they have come down from the age of kingship.

In conclusion a word may be said here with regard to fables. Stories of animals seem not to be represented in early Hebrew literature; but a good instance in which the characters are trees occurs in Judg. ix. 8 ff. The fable is related by Jotham, son of Gideon, to the men of Shechem with reference to their choice of Abimelech as king. It does not stand quite isolated; in II Kings xiv. 9 there is a passage which points to familiarity with compositions of this kind. Amaziah, king of Judah, has sent a challenge to Jehoash, king of Israel; and the latter replies by referring to the dealings of a cedar and a thistle.

CHAPTER IX

THE TEXTS

RECITATION AND COMPOSITION

IN the foregoing chapters we have several times had occasion to notice that two passages are more or less identical or seem to be of common origin. Thus Micah iv. 1–3 is almost identical with Is. ii. 2–4, though in the former the prophecy is continued, while in the latter it stops short. The differences in this case are so slight that both passages may well be derived from a common MS. original, though the prophecies are attributed to different authors. Among the other prophecies attributed to these prophets there are a number of examples which must be later than their times. The explanation generally given is that single prophecies or short collections of prophecies were preserved in MSS. without indication of their authorship. In later times, when this was forgotten, they were attributed conjecturally to this or that prophet. The Book of Isaiah has also incorporated a good deal of matter—including narratives and a poem of King Hezekiah (xxxviii. 10 ff.)—which is more or less closely connected with the prophet's personal history.

It is instructive in this respect to compare the Books of Isaiah and Jeremiah. Considerably less than half of the former can be the work of the prophet himself. On the other hand the latter contains few prophecies which are not generally admitted to be by Jeremiah, while even the narratives seem to be either his work or that of persons closely connected with him. Jeremiah's prophecies are not consistently arranged in chronological order; but they are obviously much better preserved than those of the earlier prophets. Individual prophecies, and apparently also series of prophecies, were dictated by the author himself; and the circumstances are often carefully recorded. The conditions of the time were as unfavourable as possible; but the use of written literature was evidently much more advanced. Isaiah's lifetime also falls within what we may call the literary period; but the recording of prophecies—and presumably also other compositions—would seem to have been still more or less accidental. It is not certain that Isaiah himself wrote or dictated any of his prophecies, though in a few cases the use of the first person suggests that he did so.

Passages which recur with slight variants, as in the example noted above, are very frequent in the Old Testament; and it is often difficult to determine how they are to be explained. Where such parallels are limited to a single stanza, and the context is unaffected, as in the Proverbs, they may generally be ascribed to oral tradition. But how is one to account for the relationship between (e.g.) Ps. xiv and Ps. liii, or between Ps. xviii and II Sam. xxii? In the former case at least, so far as we can see, the variants might be due to oral tradition. But other explanations are possible. One text may come from a scribe who had no written copy, and whose memory was defective. Or the variants may be due to deliberate alteration—attempts to improve the poem. Or again—and this case may be by no means rare—a scribe may know a poem in different forms, say from a MS. copy and from memory, and what he reproduces may be a compromise text.[1] Often, as perhaps in one or both of the cases noted, the true explanation may be clear to those who are familiar with the language and diction of Hebrew poetry. We have not this knowledge, and can therefore do no more than call attention to the problem.

In narrative prose variants would seem often to be due to deliberate change. It is generally agreed, we believe, that where the Chronicles and Kings have parallel accounts, the former are in the main dependent upon the latter; yet differences in the wording are extremely frequent. Sometimes, no doubt, the text of the Chronicles may be derived from an older and better text of Kings, and sometimes it gives additional information from other sources. But, apart from such cases, a comparison of the two texts seems to show that the compilers of the Chronicles did not feel themselves bound to reproduce the text of the older work exactly.

An interesting problem is presented by the first chapter of Judges. One passage (12–15) is almost identical with Josh. xv. 16–19. The passages immediately preceding these, Judg. i. 10 f. and Josh. xv. 13–15, likewise contain common elements; but they are far from identical—indeed they contain statements which seem to be incompatible. Again, a subsequent passage (Judg. i. 20) is in partial agreement with Josh. xv. 13–15 (cf. *ib*. xiv. 6 ff., 13 ff.); but it seems to be incompatible with its own context (Judg. i. 10 f.). The same chapter also contains two other short passages which are apparently irreconcilable with one another. One (i. 8) says that "the children of Judah fought against Jerusalem, and took it, and smote it with the edge of the sword, and set the city on fire"; the other (i. 21) says that "the children of Benjamin did not drive

[1] As in the case of certain Norse poems, cf. Vol. I, p. 511.

out the Jebusites that inhabited Jerusalem; but the Jebusites dwelt with the children of Benjamin in Jerusalem unto this day". The second passage is practically identical with Josh. xv. 63, with the noteworthy exception that the latter has in both cases 'Judah' for 'Benjamin'. Further, it may be noted that i. 27 f. is practically identical in substance—in part also in form—with Josh. xvii. 11–13, while i. 29 is in part identical with Josh. xvi. 10. The end of the chapter (i. 30 ff.) is similar in character to i. 27–29, but has apparently no counterparts in Joshua.

The explanation usually given of this chapter is that it consists of fragments of an old account of the conquest of Canaan, traces of which are preserved also in Joshua. This account—which some believe to have belonged to J—is thought to have differed materially from the account of the conquest which forms the main thread of Joshua; and its historical value is generally rated higher than that of the latter. This may be perfectly correct; but some of the passages noted above are inconsistent with other passages in the chapter itself, as well as with passages in Joshua. Moreover the statement in i. 18 that Judah took Gaza, Ashkelon and Ekron must be regarded with some scepticism, though two of these cities are claimed for Judah also in Josh. xv. 45 ff. But we cannot enter upon a discussion of these questions. Our object is to point out the interest which the chapter possesses as an illustration of textual affinities and discrepancies.

Variant forms of saga occur in the First Book of Samuel, as we have noticed above (p. 635). Certain stories of Elijah and Elisha likewise would appear to have had a common origin (cf. p. 682). A still later example is probably to be found in the two accounts of Sennacherib's invasion given in II Kings xviii f. (cf. p. 663 f.).

Saga-variants seem also to be preserved in Genesis. The story of Abraham's visit to Egypt in cap. xii, when he conceals the fact that Sarah is his wife, is clearly a variant of the story told in cap. xx, where the same patriarch visits Abimelech of Gerar: and Isaac's visit to Abimelech in xxvi. 1–11 seems to be another variant of the same story. The rest of cap. xxvi, recounting Isaac's dealings with Abimelech, can hardly be of different origin from xxi. 22–34, though an editorial attempt has been made to distinguish between the two stories. Again, the two stories related of Hagar, in cap. xvi. and in xxi. 9–21, are by no means identical as they stand; but they have so much in common that they may well have originated as variants of one story.

It may be observed that among the variants just noted one version usually comes from J, and the other from E. In the first case J itself preserves two variants, while the third (cap. xx) is from E; in the other two cases one version comes from each of the two texts. It is of interest to note that the first long section of Genesis which is believed to be derived from E, viz. cap. xx–xxii, consists mainly of narratives of which variants are found in J; only in cap. xxii does E preserve a narrative which is not also found in J. There is good reason for believing that in the stories of the patriarchs E and J consisted largely of the same stories, preserved independently by oral tradition, though variants sometimes occurred in the same text. Similar instances of parallel versions are to be found elsewhere in the Hexateuch, and not only in narratives. Thus the account of the 'Ten Commandments' in Ex. xxxiv is generally believed to be a variant version (from J) of the account of the Ten Commandments contained in *ib.* xx (from E); and the variants are of such a kind as could only arise from oral tradition.

Such parallels are easily intelligible; we have seen that analogies are to be found in many lands. More frequently, however, the text which we have, both in narratives and in other passages, is held to be due to a conflation of two (or more) versions—i.e. to be taken partly from J, and partly from E, perhaps with additions from P also. This postulates a process of composition which is much more difficult to understand. Analogies, more or less exact, for such a process are certainly to be found in chronicles and annals, e.g. in the Saxon Chronicle and in many Latin chronicles and annals belonging to the same period. But the Hexateuch has little or nothing in common with works of this kind. Its chief constituents are stories of the saga type, often more or less detailed, and accounts of institutions. The former at least of these elements does not lend itself readily to the process which is postulated.

In our references to the Hexateuch in previous chapters we have, in accordance with general usage, regarded the principles of analysis and the existence of the hypothetical texts, J, E, D and P as established, though we have seldom had occasion to notice passages in which a minute analysis of the text is of essential importance. But we feel bound to say here that we cannot view without considerable misgiving such analyses as the following.[1] In Gen. xxxvii. 1, 1 *a* are derived from P, 2*b*–11, 19, 20, 22–24, 28*a*, 28*c*–30, 36 from E, 12–18, 21, 25–27, 28*b*, 31–35 from J. Again, in Josh. iv. 1–3, 8, 20 are derived from one source of JE, 4–7, 9–11*a*, 18 from another source of the same, 13, 15–17, 19 from P, 11*b*, 12, 14, 21–24 from a Deuteronomic source. More or less

---

[1] The examples are taken from Driver, *Introduction to the Literature of the Old Testament*, pp. 17, 105.

similar analyses are given for many other chapters. The principle upon which the existing text in such cases is believed to be constructed is that of the scrap-book, just as in annals and chronicles. But is it really probable that such a process was applied to narratives, and at what seems to have been an early phase in the history of written literature?

The evidence upon which the analyses are based consists partly in the use of certain terms, especially *J-h-v-h* and *Elohīm*, and partly in linguistic and stylistic characteristics of various kinds, of which none but experts can judge, as well as in inconsistencies in the narratives. Are these features not capable of any other explanation? In other early literatures which are preserved in late texts inconsistent modernisation is a frequent phenomenon. Sometimes also there seems to be reason for suspecting that a scribe knew from memory a text different from that which he was copying.[1] And there may be other possibilities. But we can do no more than express a feeling of doubt. We are quite ready to believe that extracts from (say) E were copied into a text of J; but the 'scrap-book' theory seems to us to present much greater difficulties.

The conflation of JE with P is perhaps easier to understand, since this must have taken place in much later times. The difficulty here seems to us to lie rather in the character ascribed to P. It appears to be generally agreed that P embraced the whole of the Hexateuch, though it had merely brief summaries or notices of many of the stories. But what was its origin? It can hardly have been wholly independent of JE—or perhaps we should say of both J and E.[2] From what is ascribed to it one would gather that P was a body of antiquarian and priestly learning which grew up round JE. Large portions of it indeed, in Exodus, Leviticus, and Numbers, are such as might well have existed as separate documents; but most of the shorter extracts, especially in Genesis, give us the impression of editorial accretions and changes. Indeed personally we should be inclined to doubt if many of the passages from P in Genesis are strictly of independent origin.[3]

---

[1] Cf. Vol. I, p. 511.

[2] The prevailing opinion seems to be that where P covered the same ground as the older texts it originated as an epitome of JE, and that later it was utilised as a framework, into which extracts from JE were re-introduced. Apparently it is held that in the latter process the different texts were rigidly preserved. For this process also analogies might be found in works of the Dark Ages; but we do not know of any parallels dating back to (say) 300 B.C. Are there any cuneiform or Egyptian analogies?

[3] It is held that the text of P is sometimes preserved intact for long stretches, though numerous insertions from J and E may be introduced into it. A good ex-

Although we know that this view is contrary to the general opinion of Biblical scholars, we find it difficult to escape from the suspicion that the growth of the Hexateuch may have had something in common with that of the Mahābhārata. In both cases the nucleus consists of a story or stories, preserved at first by oral tradition, and frequently showing variant accounts of incidents. The stories of the Hexateuch are not heroic, and writing began here doubtless at a relatively earlier stage than in the Mahābhārata; but these differences are hardly essential. In both cases the stories received in course of time voluminous accretions of didactic matter, both moral didactic and antiquarian didactic—represented in the Hexateuch by D and P respectively. The former would seem to date mainly from the sixth century, and the latter from the fifth and following centuries, though both may have begun somewhat earlier. Indeed the growth of the Hexateuch, as also that of the Mahābhārata, may well have been continuous. Both J and E were probably committed to writing in the eighth century; but the resultant conflate text contains much, especially in the story of Joseph,[1] which seems to be not earlier than the seventh. We give these suggestions of course only for what they are worth. It is to be borne in mind throughout that writing began earlier in the Hexateuch, and also that this is a prose work, while the Mahābhārata is poetry. But all the evidence suggests that the text was not regarded as sacred or inviolable until a very late period.

In Judges we have a collection of stories relating to the beginning of the historical period. Most of them have been heavily edited and to

ample is to be found in the story of Abraham (Gen. xii–xxv), in which there are said to be about ten such insertions, some of them very long. But is this explanation really necessary? We are ready to believe that almost all the passages ascribed to P in this analysis (including the whole of cap. xvii and xxiii) do really belong to that element. But we find it difficult to understand why the short passages are not capable of being explained as editorial additions and alterations, coming from the same element. P—whether it ever existed separately or not—is very fond of chronological calculations and of references to certain rites, such as circumcision. We do not see why (e.g.) xii. 4*b* should not be due to editorial addition and xii. 5 to editorial alteration (re-wording). Again, the complicated history of the text postulated in xxi. 1–6 seems to us more difficult to believe than that P re-wrote the passage in order to introduce the reference to circumcision and the calculation. It may be of course that we have not sufficiently appreciated the force of the linguistic evidence; but we do not understand why the text should be regarded as so rigid.

[1] The Egyptian names in this story are said to belong to Dyn. XXVI, or not much earlier. The writer seems to know Egypt well. It is an interesting question whether he was influenced by Egyptian romances; but we are not able to discuss this.

some extent expanded by a didactic writer. Similar elements are to be found in I Sam. i–xii; and it is believed by many scholars that these chapters, except cap. ix and parts of cap. x f., were originally attached to Judg. xvi. The didactic (religious) element has something in common with Deuteronomic writings, but is usually thought to be slightly earlier—perhaps the seventh century. Some scholars however, distinguish between earlier and later elements in the didactic matter itself; and the former has been brought into connection with E of the Hexateuch. The rest of I Samuel (beginning at cap. ix) and II Samuel consists of stories of Saul and David, some of which show religious influence, which in the earlier chapters may be connected with the previous section. The bulk of the matter, however, is of secular interest and derived from heroic saga. We cannot see any probability in the suggestion that this heroic matter is to be connected with J of the Hexateuch.

Some rearrangement has obviously taken place at the end of II Samuel. The narrative of I Kings i f. is a continuation of II Sam. xx; the chapters (xxi–xxiv) which follow the latter form an appendix, of heterogeneous matter, which interrupts the sequence of the story. It is for textual experts to decide when this rearrangement took place.[1] The absence of religious influence in II Samuel, apart from certain chapters, would lead one to expect that the heroic matter was committed to writing in secular circles. But all that can be said with conviction is that the evidence points to the palace or the temple at Jerusalem, between which the relations were close. The next section of I Kings, cap. iii–x, seems to be derived from the lost Book of the Acts of Solomon, which was evidently a work of very different (antiquarian) character, but of the same provenance. The matter, however, unlike the story of David, has been subjected to a strong religious influence, which appears also throughout the rest of Kings. In the following chapters most of the matter relates to the northern kingdom and may have been cast into historical form there. The interest is centred in prophets; and it would seem that the saga, from which it is evidently derived, was current in prophetical circles. But, as we have it this northern work has been converted into a 'synchronous history'—presumably after foreign models, but under strong religious influence—and continued in Judah (doubtless Jerusalem) down to the end of that kingdom. Oral tradition (saga) seems to be represented even for the time of Hezekiah.

The text of the prophetical books will be noticed briefly below.

---

[1] The question, we understand, depends to some extent upon the relations of the different Greek texts.

Saga must have been long and extensively cultivated, as we have seen; but there is hardly any evidence relating to its recitation or composition. Indeed we cannot recall any reference to recitation for the sake of entertainment. The nearest instances we can think of are the passages (II Sam. xii. 1 ff., xiv. 4 ff.) describing the fictitious stories told to David by Nathan and the wise woman of Tekoa; but these are made up for the purpose of admonishing the king, and produced apparently at private interviews. In stories of specified persons the nearest approach to descriptions of saga is probably to be found in the story of Joseph, especially Gen. xlii ff.; and here the approximation is very close, though the saga consists of first-hand reports of the speakers' experiences. But these again are informal. For formal recitation we know of no better instance than the story of Jotham's fable, related in Judg. ix. 7 ff. The fable is declaimed to the men of Shechem from the top of Mount Gerizim; and in view of Deut. xi. 29, xxvii. 11 f., Josh. viii. 33 ff., the incident may perhaps reflect a custom followed by prophets or orators on public occasions. The traditional phraseology found in such passages as Ps. xliv. 1, lxxviii. 3, would also seem to point to a time when the national traditions were recited, probably in a more or less formal style.[1]

References to the recitation of poetry are more frequent and more specific. First we will take references to secular poetry. Minstrelsy seems to have been much cultivated. Amos (vi. 5) speaks of 'idle songs' sung to the sound of the viol among the practices which he denounces. The context suggests that he is thinking of minstrelsy at feasts—presumably amorous songs like those contained in the Song of Songs and perhaps 'drinking-songs', such as were current in Greece during the seventh and sixth centuries. The same practice is referred to in Isaiah xxiv. 8 f., and probably also in v. 12, though songs are not specifically mentioned in the latter passage. In II Sam. xix. 35 it is implied that singing men and women performed at banquets in the king's palace even in David's time. David himself is said to have been skilled in music (cf. Amos vi. 5), and to have been brought to Saul's court as a harpist (I Sam. xvi. 16 ff.). It is not actually stated that he sang there; but this may be due to accident; for he was well known as a poet. In the same period heroic poetry of Type D, accompanied by dancing, is said to have been cultivated by women (*ib.* xviii. 6 f.).

It is clear from the instances given above that music and minstrelsy were cultivated by both men and women. Evidence to the same effect is supplied by Assyrian records. Sennacherib states that among the

[1] We may compare the passage relating to the Lithuanians quoted in Vol. 1, p. 617.

booty which he carried off from Judah were male and female musicians.[1] The same devotion to minstrelsy seems to have characterised the Phoenicians, possibly to an even greater degree. Isaiah (xxiii. 16) pictures Tyre as a harlot going about the city with a harp and singing many songs. So, at a later date, Ezekiel (xxvi. 13) speaks of the songs and the harps of Tyre. Again, in the Egyptian story of Wenamon, which is many centuries earlier—apparently before 1100—the prince of Byblos has an Egyptian singing woman at his court.

Minstrelsy, however, was not limited to the lighter forms of entertainment and to heroic poetry of Type D. The harp could be used also doubtless as an accompaniment to laments, as is implied in Job xxx. 31. And several passages in the Psalms, especially xlix. 4, suggest that it was employed for gnomic or meditative poetry. But much more often we hear of it in hymns of praise—religious poems of Type D. Instances in the Psalms are frequent. In I Chron. xxv many persons are specified whose duty it was to sing to the harp in the Temple at Jerusalem. And in I Kings x. 12 Solomon is said to have provided harps for the singers, whether in the Temple or the palace or perhaps both. The antiquity of these statements cannot be guaranteed—the former rests on very late authority—but there is no need to doubt that music, both vocal and instrumental, was in use for worship from early times. Amos (v. 23) protests against the use of songs and viols at sacrifices. In II Sam. vi. 5 David and 'all the house of Israel' play harps and other musical instruments, when they set out to bring the Ark from Baale-Judah to Jerusalem. The journey is interrupted; but when it is resumed (ib. 12 ff.) David is said to be lightly clad and to dance with all his might in the procession—for which he is subsequently reproved by his wife Michal. In Ex. xv. 20 f., a passage which is believed to come from E, Miriam and the women of Israel are said to celebrate the destruction of the Egyptian host with timbrels and dancing; and she herself sings a hymn of praise to Jehovah. There can be little doubt then that the Psalms, however late they may be in their present form, represent a genre of poetry which was cultivated in the period of kingship, if not in still earlier times.

Poetry and music are also associated with prophecy. In I Sam. x. 5 f. Samuel tells Saul that when he comes to a certain place—which is not clearly specified—he will meet with a band of prophets coming down from the high place with a harp and other musical instruments, "and they shall be prophesying; and the spirit of Jehovah will come mightily

[1] Cf. Johns, *Ancient Assyria*, p. 126.

upon thee, and thou shalt prophesy with them, and thou shalt be turned into another man." And so it comes to pass. Later in his life Saul again has a similar experience, when he is pursuing David (*ib.* xix. 20 ff.). All the messengers whom he sends begin to prophesy when they arrive at Samuel's abode and see the prophets prophesying. Then the king himself sets out, "and the spirit of God came upon him also...and he also stripped off his clothes, and he also prophesied before Samuel, and lay down naked all that day and all that night". What is meant here by 'prophesying' is not quite clear to us; but it evidently denotes some effect of religious ecstasy. We may compare the description of David's behaviour in II Sam. vi. 14 (see above), when he is bringing the Ark to Jerusalem.

But the most interesting passage in this connection is II Kings iii. 15 ff. The kings of Israel, Judah and Edom have come to Elisha, begging him to save their army, which is threatened with destruction through lack of water. After some hesitation he says: "Bring me a minstrel." "And it came to pass, when the minstrel played, that the hand of Jehovah came upon him.[1] And he said, 'Thus saith Jehovah, Make this valley full of trenches'", etc. This is clearly in the nature of a spell, as we have seen (p. 715). For the use of music in spells we have met with analogies elsewhere (cf. Vol. 1, p. 651).

It cannot be assumed of course that even the earlier prophets, including Elisha himself and Elijah, regularly employed a musical form or musical accompaniment in their utterances. Most of the scenes in which these prophets are introduced are 'conversation scenes', and there is nothing to suggest that they speak otherwise than in prose. It may be, however, that in certain passages the absence of reference to music or singing is due to the nature of our records. Those who were responsible for the final form of the stories may not have cared to notice such details. In such a scene as that of the contest on Mount Carmel, described in I Kings xviii, one would have expected at least a poetic form for the prophet's utterances. In this connection we may refer to the story of Balaam, told in Numb. xxii ff. The seer Balaam has been summoned from afar by Balak, king of Moab, to curse the host of Israel. He tells the king on each occasion to build seven altars and offer sacrifices. Then he goes apart by himself to obtain inspiration from Jehovah. On his return, each time he blesses the invading host, instead of cursing them. There is no mention of instrumental music; but the blessings are declared in verse. In xxiv. 3 f., 15 f. the seer speaks of his vision of the

[1] Some scholars hold that the verb-forms used here imply custom.

Almighty, apparently through a form of trance. Whatever may be the origin of this story, it goes back probably to the eighth century or earlier, since it comes from JE; and it may presumably be taken as representing a rite either practised at that time or at least known from tradition.

The prophecies of the pre-literary prophets, as recorded in the Books of Kings, are usually addressed to kings; but those of the 'literary' prophets seem as a rule to be intended for the general public. It is generally agreed, we believe, that the latter also were spoken before—perhaps long before—they were written down; but we are seldom informed of the time, place, circumstances or manner of their delivery. Though printed as prose in the English translation (R.V.)—which has been much blamed for so doing—the prophecies are usually in poetic form; and this doubtless accounts to some extent for the extravagance of the language. But there is nothing to suggest that they were accompanied by music. They would seem to be rather in the nature of public speeches. On one occasion, or more, Amos (vii. 12 ff.) evidently prophesied in the sanctuary of Beth-el, like the nameless prophet in I Kings xiii. 1 ff., if this is not an account of the same incident, preserved by popular tradition. Otherwise his prophecies seem to supply no evidence bearing upon this question; and the same is true of those of Hosea and Micah.[1] Even from Isaiah we learn little, except in passages which describe his interviews with kings.

Much information, however, is given by Jeremiah. This prophet of course lived at a time when writing was in general use; he himself had his prophecies written down from dictation. But it is clear that many of them were uttered as speeches, and sometimes the circumstances are vividly described. Thus in vii. 2 it is stated that he is to speak to all the men of Judah in the gate of the Temple; in xi. 6 "in the cities of Judah and in the streets of Jerusalem"; in xvii. 19 in the gates of Jerusalem. From xvi. 10 it appears that his prophecies were likely to be questioned by his audiences, while in xiv. 13 ff. we hear of other prophets, who were strongly opposed to him. Disputations with opponents are referred to in xviii. 18. In cap. xix he summons the elders of the people and the elders of the priests to the valley of Topheth, and prophesies to them impending disaster—prophecies which he repeats later in the court of the Temple. For this he is imprisoned (xx. 1 f.) for a day by the chief officer of the Temple. In xx. 7 ff. he complains that he is mocked and denounced

---

[1] Jeremiah (xxvi. 18 f.), however, preserves a notice relating to Micah (Micaiah), to which we shall refer below (p. 757).

by everyone. In xxiii. 9 ff. he again attacks the prophets and priests. In cap. xxvi he stands in the court of the Temple and addresses his prophecies to those who come from the cities of Judah to worship there. The priests arrest him and wish to have him put to death; but the princes intervene on his behalf. From many passages in the latter half of the collection it is plain that Jeremiah's activities were very largely of a political character. He advocates a definite policy—that of submission to Babylon—which was opposed to that of the government. On the other hand he is strongly anti-Egyptian, both in the days of Jehoiakim (cap. xlvi) and after the fall of Jerusalem (cap. xlii ff.). In cap. xxvii he even approaches the envoys of foreign powers in Jerusalem, telling them to advise their kings to submit to Nebuchadnezzar. Eventually he is arrested as a traitor and imprisoned; but when Jerusalem is captured by the Babylonians, he is set free and treated with honour by express orders from Nebuchadnezzar.

For the earlier prophets our information is far less full and definite than for Jeremiah; but we see no reason for doubting that their activities were carried on in much the same way, especially by speeches in public places. In the case of Micah indeed we have the evidence of Jerem. xxvi. 17 ff., where it is stated that, when an attack is made upon Jeremiah, certain of the elders of the land quoted Micah iii. 12 and said that these words were spoken by that prophet "to all the people of Judah". They add that Hezekiah and 'all Judah', far from wishing to put Micah to death, had been persuaded by his preaching. The earlier prophets were perhaps not quite so outspokenly political in their activities as Jeremiah, so far as we can judge from their remains. But it is clear that Isaiah and Hosea share the later prophet's aversion to foreign alliances. In particular opposition to reliance upon Egypt seems to be a constant element in their policy; we may refer especially to Is. xxx. 1 ff., xxxi. 1 ff.

The use of a poetical form in political speeches seems to us strange; but it can be paralleled in Greece during the same period, or not much later. Tyrtaios and Solon are the Greek counterparts of the Hebrew poets, though the religious element is less prominent in their poems. In both cases we are concerned with 'post-heroic' conditions. Kings, where they survive, can no longer act wholly according to their own will. In Jerem. xxviii. 5 Zedekiah admits to the princes that he can do nothing against them; and again (ib. 14 ff.) he interviews Jeremiah privately and begs him not to disclose the subject of their conversation. Under such conditions appeals to the public became almost as important as in Greece. The question why the appeals were made in poetry—

whether for mnemonic convenience or rhetorical effect or other reasons —must for the present be deferred. In any case poetry probably gave more scope for the treatment of the emotional element.

Public speeches in prose are of course by no means unknown. Numerous examples are attributed to Moses, Joshua, Samuel, and other leaders of the past. All of these doubtless date from times much later than those to which they are assigned. Some of them, e.g. Samuel's speeches in I Sam. viii. 11 ff. and xii, show post-heroic characteristics; the latter may be compared with Solon's political poems (cf. Vol. 1, p. 356 f.). It is uncertain indeed whether any of them are as old as the times of the early prophets, at least in their present form. Most of the examples at all events are generally believed to be derived from late sources; and there is no doubt that this form of composition was much cultivated in late times. One cannot safely assume, however, that prose oratory was wholly a product of the times of written literature.[1]

[1] Norse sagas frequently speak of such oratory at public meetings during the Viking Age. The evidence is not strictly contemporary; but we see no reason for discrediting it. A good example may be found in the account of the assembly at Upsala given in St Olaf's Saga (*Heimskr.*), cap. 80 f.

CHAPTER X

THE AUTHOR

SECULAR poetry was evidently cultivated both by professional minstrels and singers and also by persons of various ranks from the king downwards. It was as court musician that David first entered Saul's service, though he was already known as a warrior (I Sam. xvi. 18 ff.). The story does not actually state that he sang to the harp; but in view of his fame as a poet later this may be an accidental omission. He continued to compose elegies (e.g. for Abner) after he became king; and it is unlikely that he would have acquired his reputation as a psalmist unless he also cultivated religious poetry.

In I Kings iv. 32, Solomon is said to have composed a thousand and five songs. The context suggests that he cultivated descriptive poetry. In Isaiah xxxviii. 9 ff., a religious poem, evidently intended for accompaniment on the harp (*ib.* 20), is attributed to Hezekiah. Its authenticity is doubted; but the passage may at least be taken as evidence that the cultivation of minstrelsy by a king was not regarded as strange.

We are uncertain whether we should mention here the 'Blessings' attributed to the patriarchs Isaac and Jacob in Gen. xxvii. 27 ff., 39 f., and xlix. May they be taken as evidence for the cultivation of poetry of this kind by leading men? The patriarchs have a semi-religious character; but these poems themselves are not primarily religious.

In I Sam. xviii. 6 f., when Saul and David return from their victory over the Philistines, they are met by women, who come out of the cities dancing and singing with instruments of music. Their songs are obviously heroic poems of Type D; but it is not clear whether the women were professional minstrels. In II Sam. xix. 35 we hear of singing men and women who perform at David's feasts, and who are presumably professionals. The subjects of their songs are not stated; but it is likely that they were, in part at least, heroic. In Numb. xxi. 27 ff. a quotation is given from a poem, evidently heroic (Type D), on the victories of Sihon, king of the Amorites, who is referred to a much earlier period. The quotation is introduced by the words "they that speak in proverbs say". If the expression used here (*mošlīm*) really means 'reciters of poetry',[1] it would seem on the whole probable, though not certain, that professional reciters are intended.

The use of minstrelsy at convivial gatherings is frequently referred to by the prophets, as we have seen. Sometimes, as in Amos vi. 5, the banqueters themselves sing and play; but as a rule it is not stated who the entertainers were. This kind of minstrelsy was evidently widespread. It is referred to in Gen. xxxi. 27; and it was evidently cultivated in Tyre (cf. Ezek. xxvi. 13), as well as in Israel and Judah. Amorous songs of women are alluded to by Isaiah xxiii. 16, where again the reference is to Tyre. From the same prophet (xvi. 10) we hear of vintage-songs, which may have been similar to those current in ancient Greece (cf. *Il.* xviii. 570 ff.).

Lastly, it may be repeated that evidence for professional minstrelsy at the close of the eighth century is supplied by the records of Sennacherib. Male and female musicians were among the spoils which he carried off from Judah.[2] But we have no reason for supposing that minstrelsy was limited to such persons. On the contrary all the evidence tends to show that it was very widely cultivated, and by both men and women. And in this connection it may be noted that there is early evidence for the cultivation also of religious poetry and minstrelsy by women, as well as by men. We may instance the 'Song of Deborah' (Judg. v), the 'Song of Miriam' (Ex. xv. 21) and the 'Song of Hannah' (I Sam. ii). These, however, will require notice below.

No information seems to be preserved with respect to the composers or reciters of saga. This is the more remarkable in view of its wide distribution and the high artistic level which it frequently attains. The evidence suggests that it was much and carefully cultivated in both secular and religious circles. But we are practically dependent upon inferences from the stories themselves.

The only stories, so far as we know, for which there is any direct evidence for authorship, are the two fictitious narratives related to David in II Sam. xii. 1 ff. and xiv. 5 ff., by the prophet Nathan and the 'wise woman' of Tekoa respectively. To these may perhaps be added the account of Saul's death given by the Amalekite (*ib.* i. 4 ff.), which is likewise in part fictitious. All three stories show a certain rhetorical skill; but this is a characteristic of II Samuel in general. It may be in-

---

[1] Elsewhere the word and its cognates denote the recitation or composition of gnomes and proverbial wisdom; but this meaning seems to be inappropriate here.

[2] Cf. Johns, *Ancient Assyria*, p. 126.

ferred—but even this is somewhat uncertain—that the ability to tell stories was rather widespread. All that is certain, however, is that the art is not regarded as peculiar to men. In the second example Joab chooses for his purpose a 'wise woman'—which must mean one who is a trained speaker, or who has studied rhetoric (cf. p. 737). Another woman of the same kind figures *ib.* xx. 16 ff. Her speeches are not narratives; but it is interesting to note that she seems to have paramount influence in her city. Poetry and minstrelsy then were clearly not the only forms of intellectual activity in which women participated.

In an earlier chapter (p. 649 f.) we noted the predominantly feminine interest of the story of David—an interest which seems to indicate that most of it was composed either by women or for the entertainment of women. The intimacy of the picture frequently suggests that it originated in the royal harem; and in view of the intellectual activities attributed to women in early Israel, as pointed out above, the possibility of such an origin cannot be denied. In this connection it is of interest to compare the story with certain of the 'Sagas of Icelanders', which we believe to be derived in the main from feminine sources (cf. Vol. I, pp. 542, 600). It is true that no individual woman figures so prominently in the story as Guðríðr does in Thorfinns Saga Karlsefnis or Guðrún in the Laxdoela Saga. But the outlook and the general characteristics seem to us very similar, if one makes allowance for the difference in the milieu—between an Oriental court on the one side and the life of a farmer's wife in Greenland or Iceland on the other.

There is one scene in the story—the scene of faction and intrigue depicted in I Kings i f., when the old king is dying—which seems to give a clue to its origin. This scene can hardly be other than an *ex parte* account of the events, in favour of Bath-sheba, who is represented as David's favourite wife. In the earlier portions of the story she has only appeared once, viz. in II Sam. xi f., and even here she does not speak; but the narrative in question is of a peculiar and intimate character, as we have noted (p. 649), and the whole action revolves round her. The feature, however, to which we would call attention is the treatment of Joab.[1] This officer seems to have been loyal to David throughout his life; for his action when the king was dying and the succession was in dispute can hardly be taken as evidence to the contrary. Yet David is

---

[1] This feature, apart from other considerations (cf. p. 646), seems to us fatal to the theory that the story is a romance. A romance could hardly have failed to make Joab into a villain. We think the story must have been composed at a time when Joab's fidelity was still a matter of general knowledge.

said to have left instructions for Joab to be put to death. The reason alleged is not disloyalty—there is no reference to Joab's action in the final scene—but the fact that he had slain Abner and Amasa. It has frequently been questioned by commentators whether David ever gave such instructions; the circumstances suggest that a pretext was wanted for getting Joab out of the way. But it may be noted that the pretext is anticipated in the preceding narrative, where David is repeatedly represented (II Sam. iii. 39,[1] xvi. 10, xix. 22) as cherishing resentment against Joab and his brother, though he continues to make use of their services. It would seem that this motif—David's resentment, not Joab's disloyalty—had been introduced into the story as an excuse for what was to follow.

In I Kings i David has apparently made no public declaration as to his successor. The contest between the rival claimants, which accompanies his last illness, is what would naturally take place in a barbaric court; and likewise the proscription of the unsuccessful party, which follows. But David's court was perhaps just passing beyond this stage; evidently some excuse was felt to be necessary. David himself therefore is made responsible for giving the orders, and Solomon, who is a mere boy, for carrying them out. The queen plays a merely passive rôle, following the instructions of Nathan and pleading for Adonijah at his own request. We think that the account of the transactions comes from her. She must have been a woman of rather exceptional ability to have won over most of the leading men, including the prophet, after such an unpromising beginning to her story.

We would suggest then that a large part, though not the whole, of the story of David is derived from saga inspired by Bath-sheba in Solomon's court. Other parts may have become current in the palace and the Temple from various quarters; and marriages such as that of Jehosheba and Jehoiada would be favourable to the formation of a collection, which eventually came to be written down. Many such sagas relating to kings may of course have been current in the palace. The silence of our authorities proves nothing; for the authors or compilers of Kings did not admit secular stories into their collection.

If our view is correct women must have played a more important part in the intellectual life of early Israel than in that of any of the peoples we have discussed hitherto. Such evidence as we have for the earlier

---

[1] In iii. 28 ff. David is anxious to clear himself of bloodguilt in connection with Abner's death; but this is a different matter from giving posthumous orders for Joab's death, perhaps thirty years later.

part of the kingly period shows at least that queens were often active in religion. Apart from Solomon's wives, we may note Maacah, the mother of Asa, and especially Jezebel and her daughter Athaliah. All of these are regarded by the writers of Kings with hostility, as opponents of the worship of Jehovah. But they were evidently devoted to their own cults; Jezebel indeed seems to have been a fanatic. More definite evidence for intellectual activity is to be found in the case of the queen of Sheba, who is clearly a learned person, though she does not belong to Israel. Here also we may perhaps refer to the 'mother of King Lemuel', to whom gnomic and descriptive wisdom is attributed in Prov. xxxi. Her time and country are unknown. The chapter is generally believed to be late; but there is nothing to show that she is regarded as a person of the present.

It is remarkable that from the end of the ninth century women practically disappear from Hebrew literature. Collectively the women of the upper classes are denounced by the prophets Amos and Isaiah. But as individuals they play no further part in either literature or history. A solitary exception may be found in Hosea's wife, if she is not a mere metaphor; but it does not tend to show that women were respected, intellectually or otherwise. On the other hand the romance of Ruth can hardly be regarded as an exception. It was probably composed after— perhaps long after—this time; but it relates to a very early period, and may well have had some basis in tradition.

In religious literature it will be convenient first to notice the poems attributed to women, since these affect the question which we have just been discussing.

The earliest and most important of these is the 'Song of Deborah' (Judg. v). The introductory words say that the song was sung by both Deborah and Barak; but in the poem itself she seems to be the chief speaker. Little is said of her, though in st. 7 she is called a 'mother in Israel'. According to the saga (*ib.* iv. 4 f.) she was a prophetess and the wife of a certain Lappidoth. She dwelt beneath the palm-tree of Deborah, between Ramah and Bethel; "and the children of Israel came up to her for judgement." She is credited therefore with some kind of judicial position; but it is uncertain whether this passage has been influenced by the editorial scheme, which makes a series of judges to govern Israel in succession.

The 'Song of Miriam' (Ex. xv. 21) is perhaps a fragment of a song of triumph, of essentially religious character, like the poem just discussed.

Miriam is the sister of Aaron and Moses, and is described as a prophetess (*ib.* 20). In the earlier form of the story of Moses (JE) she is a not altogether unimportant character. In this passage she leads the women of Israel, while in Numb. xii. 1 ff. she and Aaron seem to claim equality with Moses, for which she is punished with (temporary) leprosy. She is also perhaps the sister who figures in the story of Moses' birth (Ex. ii. 4 ff.). The prophet Micah (vi. 4) speaks of Moses, Aaron and Miriam, as sent to bring Israel out of Egypt.

The 'Song of Hannah' is said (I Sam. ii. 1 ff.) to be sung by Samuel's mother, when she has brought her child to Shiloh. This attribution is now generally believed to be due to some misunderstanding. The words do not seem to be appropriate to the occasion; and it is thought that the poem was originally composed as a thanksgiving for deliverance from some national calamity. Yet the mistake itself may be taken as showing that the composition of such a poem by a woman of early times was not regarded as anything very strange.

We know of no other religious poems attributed to women; nor are we aware of any evidence showing that they cultivated religious saga. In later times, however, there is the striking case of the prophetess Huldah, who is consulted by the high priest and certain officials of King Josiah, when the book of the Law has been found in the Temple (II Kings xxii. 14 ff.). Her response and her message to the king are quite in accord with the (literary) prophecies of the age. She is a married woman, apparently the wife of a royal official; but nothing further seems to be recorded of her.

In much later times still we hear in Nehem. vi. 14 of a prophetess called Noadiah, who is hostile to Nehemiah. But it is somewhat remarkable that the literary prophets seem never to refer to prophetesses, or even to women who are favourably disposed to their cause. In the stories of the earlier prophets, Elijah and Elisha, women are mentioned not unfrequently, though they are not named—both wives of prophets and other women who befriend the prophets; we may cite in particular the account of the 'great woman' of Shunem, given in II Kings iv. 8 ff. But in the eighth and following centuries such evidence is apparently wanting. Moreover the same peculiarity is to be found in the later portions (D and P) of the Hexateuch. The Book of Deuteronomy frequently refers to the legal position of women; but it seems not to mention any individual woman, apart from the allusion to Miriam's leprosy in xxiv. 9.

This disappearance of women from Hebrew literature is due doubtless in part to the 'post-heroic' characteristics of the literature from the eighth century onwards. No post-heroic literature of the individualistic type, seen in Greece and in the North, has been preserved; but the works of the prophets and other writings of the period have much in common with post-heroic literature of a political character, in which the interest is concentrated in the fortunes of the community or nation. In works relating to earlier times the interest of course lies more in persons. But we are inclined to question whether this change of interest explains everything. In spite of the passage relating to Huldah, which may be taken, so far as it goes, as rather striking evidence to the contrary, it may perhaps be suspected that from the eighth century onwards there was a tendency for women, other than professional minstrels, to withdraw both from public life and from intellectual activities.

What has been said above relates of course only to a minor part of early Hebrew literature. There can be little doubt that the greater part of this literature, and more especially the religious literature, is of male authorship. But unfortunately we have little direct evidence, except in the case of the prophets, as to who the authors were.

The Books of Kings contain a good deal of evidence which seems to indicate that their origin is to be traced to the Temple at Jerusalem. On several occasions detailed accounts are given of events which took place in the Temple; we may instance the stories of Athaliah's death and of Josiah's reforms. More significant than these, however, are the frequent references to spoliations, alterations and repairs of the buildings. Among many other passages which betray an intimate knowledge of it we may perhaps note especially the story of the altar which the priest Urijah constructed for Ahaz (II. xvi. 10 ff.).

These Books, however, have incorporated, or at least drawn very freely from two earlier works. The 'Book of the Acts of Solomon', which seems to have been the source of I. iii–x, may itself have originated in the Temple. But in the rest of Book I (from cap. xi) and the first few chapters of Book II the interest is centred primarily in the northern kingdom, and more especially in the doings of prophets who belonged to that kingdom. The evidence points distinctly to northern prophetic circles, at least for the origin of these stories; and it seems not unlikely that they were brought into a connected historical form in that region.

There is no reason for looking beyond Jerusalem for any part of the story of David, so far as we can see. The greater part is of secular interest, and for this the evidence points to the palace. But before David's time Jerusalem was an alien city, and is not often referred to; and the tribe of Judah seldom plays a prominent part in the stories, though the scene is sometimes laid at localities within its territory. The localities connected with Samuel lie within what seem to have been the territories of Benjamin and the southern part of Ephraim; and the stories may have taken form in that district. But the distance between these places and northern Judah is so small that it is hardly necessary to look beyond the latter. Such evidence as is available rather suggests that they circulated among the 'sons of the prophets'. The stories told of Saul are of more varied character and relate to a wider area. They may well have circulated throughout the country, some among the prophets, others in secular circles. The stories in Judges are even more widely distributed; and these also may not be of uniform provenance. A collection consisting of most of them (cap. ii–xvi) is thought to have been brought into connection at some time with the story of Samuel. When and where this took place seems to be quite uncertain; but we are not aware of any evidence tending to show that it was early—say before the times of written literature. The collection clearly reflects a religious milieu.

The later elements in the Hexateuch, D and P, doubtless have their home in Jerusalem; but the origin of the older elements, J and E, is less certain. It is commonly held that the former belonged to the southern, the latter to the northern kingdom; but there can hardly be any doubt that ultimately they had a common origin. Here again the interest is widely distributed, especially in Genesis. Hebron and Beer-sheba, in the south of Judah, are the homes of Abraham and Isaac; but Shechem, Beth-el and other northern localities are equally prominent in the stories. On the whole the evidence seems to point distinctly to Ephraim. The story of Joseph may be late in its present form; but it is hardly to be doubted that he was always the leading figure of the last generation. Of the other books Exodus and Numbers supply practically no evidence; but Joshua again points to Ephraim, as we have seen (p. 701).

Throughout the Hexateuch the milieu is religious. Some scholars describe J and E as 'prophetical' narratives, in contrast with P, the priestly narrative (cf. p. 718); but on the whole we think this description is better avoided. What we would call attention to is the striking difference between Genesis and the other books—the story of the patriarchs and the story of Moses and Joshua. Both stories doubtless originated in religious circles, and both seem to come from the same district; but they are of essentially different character. In the former the interest lies in the fortunes of individuals, women as well as men, though not quite to the same extent. In the latter it is centred in a community and a religious organisation; interest in individuals is reduced to a minimum, and women seldom come into the picture. We cannot regard the second story as a natural continuation of the first. It seems to us incredible that they should have had the same origin.

From what has been pointed out above it appears probable that the Temple at Jerusalem was largely responsible for the preservation of early Hebrew literature. Indeed there can be little doubt that many stories and poems were collected, edited and written down there. But we have no information as to the persons engaged in these activities.

The priests, of whom one naturally thinks first, belonged to two families which claimed descent respectively from Eleazar and Ithamar, the sons of Aaron. From the time of Zadok, at the close of David's reign, the high-priests seem to have been drawn from the former family; but in David's time the senior priest was apparently Abiathar, a descendant of Eli,[1] who is said to have been sprung from Ithamar. In the Books of Samuel priests figure rather frequently. After David's death they are often referred to in the Chronicles, but comparatively seldom in Kings. We are not aware of any evidence that priests engaged in literary activities; but the silence of the records can hardly be regarded as proving that they did not.

Apart from the priests we hear also of Levites connected with the Temple. The Chronicles mention them very frequently, and represent them as a numerous body.[2] Some of them are singers, or 'prophesy' with harps and other musical instruments; others are door-keepers; others again have charge of the treasuries and other duties connected with the services of the Temple. The fullest references (I Chron. vi, ix, xv f., xxiii ff.) relate to the time of David. Much also is said about Levites and their duties in connection with festivals held by Hezekiah and Josiah (II Chron. xxix, xxxi, xxxv). Apart from these long passages there are a few important, though brief, references. Thus it is stated

---

[1] The prophecy given in I Sam. ii. 35 f. seems to reflect the interest of the line of Zadok, as against this house. Some scholars regard this prophecy as late; but we find it difficult to understand why it should be composed at a time when Zadok's line had long been in unbroken possession. We should be inclined rather to regard it as good evidence for the antiquity of the non-heroic saga preserved in I Samuel.

[2] Extravagant numbers (38,000 in all) are given in I. xxiii. 3 ff.

(xi. 14) that in Rehoboam's time the Levites from the northern kingdom went to settle in Judah and Jerusalem. Again, Jehoshaphat sends Levites with princes and priests to teach in the cities of Judah (*ib.* xvii. 7 ff.); and the same king appoints Levites, with priests and other chief men, to act as judges in Jerusalem. It may be observed here that in I Chron. xxvi. 24 ff. the descendants of Moses are counted among the Levites; but they are not priests, as was the case in Dan (cf. p. 659). In Jerusalem they have charge of the dedicated spoils of war, apparently in accordance with longstanding usage.

Levites are often mentioned also in books relating to very ancient times, especially Numbers; but nearly all the references come from P or (less frequently) from D. On the other hand it is noteworthy that they are seldom referred to in Samuel and Kings, and then only as carrying the sacred Ark.[1] We are therefore left in doubt, not as to their existence but as to the importance of their position. If they were merely minstrels and servants or subordinate officials of the Temple, they would hardly require to be mentioned in Kings. The frequent references to them in the Chronicles may in general[2] be due to the influence of their descendants in the Persian period, who seem to have had more authority. It is possible, however, that their position had begun to improve before the end of the monarchy.

The question which interests us is whether this class took any part in literary activities. The positive evidence to this effect is slight. We hear (II Chron. xxxiv. 13) that in Josiah's time "of the Levites there were scribes and officers and porters". Again, it is stated in I Chron. xxiv. 6 that in David's time Shemaiah "the scribe, who was of the Levites", wrote the register of the priests. It is unnecessary, and indeed absurd, to suppose that all the lists contained in the chronicles are works of the imagination. Lists of Temple officials must surely have been kept from early times; and it is reasonable to expect that the scribes who kept them were Levites or priests. There were probably scribes who were not Levites, like the Jonathan mentioned in I Chron. xxvii. 32, who seems to be a relative[3] of the king; and in other cases the class or tribe to which

---

[1] Cf. I Sam. vi. 15; II Sam. xv. 24; I Kings viii. 4.

[2] In some cases Levites may be introduced without justification. In II Chron. xxiii the revolt against Athaliah is carried out by armed Levites. But in II Kings xi, from which this account is largely derived, there is no reference to Levites; the coup is effected by the guard and the Carites, who are believed to be foreign (perhaps Carian) mercenary soldiers. But the Chronicles may have used another source for the story.

[3] The meaning of the word (*dōd*) seems to be uncertain.

a scribe belonged is not stated. But it is at least not unlikely that 'Hezekiah's scribes' were drawn largely from the Levites.

Lastly, it may be observed that we hear of prophets in Jerusalem, though hardly so often as in the northern kingdom. Sometimes we find them in the Temple; and one at least is the son of a priest— Zechariah, the son of Jehoiada, whose death is described in II Chron. xxiv. 20 ff. Isaiah (cap. vi) has a vision in the Temple; but we do not know his ancestry. It is possible therefore that this class also ought to be taken into account. On the whole, however, the frequent references to the Temple would seem rather to point to those classes who were more closely connected with it.

In those elements of the early literature which Jerusalem appears to have taken over from the northern kingdom (cf. p. 765) the influence of the prophets is much more apparent. It is especially noticeable in the older stratum of Kings, from I. xi onwards. Elijah and Elisha are the the central figures; but it should be observed that the interest is not confined to them, even in stories relating to their times. At the time of Ahab's last adventure both prophets were living; but the only prophet who appears in the story is Micaiah. Other stories are concerned with encounters between Ahab and unnamed prophets. 'Sons of the pro- phets'—which evidently means communities of prophets—are men- tioned at various places. On the other hand there is hardly any reference to sanctuaries or priests. The evidence then, though it is merely in- ferential, would seem to point to prophetic circles or communities for the origin of this element.

As regards the early chapters of I Samuel, one can say no more than that they are of religious provenance; and the same is true of the stories in Judges, as we have them. But both the stories in Judges and the older elements (J and E) in the Hexateuch show a striking contrast to the older element in Kings. References to prophets are rare, whereas sanctuaries are frequently mentioned. Much of the contents of the Hexateuch was certainly familiar to the literary prophets, and may have been known also to their predecessors. But we are inclined to think that the origin of these works is to be sought in a different milieu. The account of Moses and his institutions seems to point to a highly organised sanctuary—presumably the one at Shiloh, which seems to have been moved eventually to Gibeon. Shiloh is said to have had a hereditary priesthood (cf. I Sam. ii. 27 ff.), which claimed descent from Aaron;[1]

[1] According to I Chron. xxiv. 3 ff. (cf. I Sam. xiv. 3, xxii. 20); but the genealogy from Aaron to Eli is apparently nowhere given. It may be remarked that Aaron

and there may have been other Levites attached to the sanctuary.[1] Indeed the Temple at Jerusalem would seem to have been regarded as in some sense its legitimate successor. At all events the elaborate ritual literature (P), which grew up at Jerusalem in later times, is associated with the 'Tent of Meeting', which is usually located at Shiloh. It may be inferred then with probability that the milieu in which the traditions originated was of a priestly character.

In the stories of Genesis also prophets are hardly mentioned,[2] whereas references to sanctuaries are frequent. But here the interest is not centred in one sanctuary, but widely distributed throughout the country. From this one can infer only that the stories had a wide circulation. If they originated in a sanctuary their local associations have been obscured—which might happen in course of time, when the stories spread from one sanctuary to another. It is to be borne in mind that the patriarchs are represented as semi-nomadic.

Yet, in spite of what has been said, the description of the older elements in the Hexateuch as 'prophetical' is not altogether without justification. Many of the stories were certainly known to the earliest of the literary prophets. Moreover, in the times of Elijah and Elisha we hear of communities of prophets at Bethel and Gilgal, which were important sanctuaries, as well as at other places. In I Sam. iii. 1 and 21 it is distinctly implied that the sanctuary at Shiloh was regarded as an oracle, though it was quiescent in Eli's time. It is here that Samuel receives his inspiration, as a child; and later, in Jeroboam's time, we find the prophet Ahijah at the same place.

Indeed the Hexateuch itself, or rather the materials from which it is constructed, may in a sense be regarded as prophecy. We have seen[3] that in various other lands prophecy relates to the past and present, as well as the future—or in other words that the revelation of the (unknown) past and present is as much a function of the prophet as the revelation of the future. Such prophecies regularly take the form of

never has priestly functions attributed to him in J or E; he appears only as Moses' assistant or spokesman. It may be that some of the passages in P, which speak of Aaron as a priest, have displaced or remodelled passages to the same effect in J or E. But the possibility should be taken into account that Eli's family really claimed descent from Moses, like the priests of Dan.

[1] J and E have little to say about Levites, except that Moses and Aaron belonged to this tribe; cf. also Ex. xxxii. 26 ff. Here again the absence of evidence is an uncertain quantity. But the 'Song of Moses' must be taken into account.

[2] In xx. 7 the term is applied to Abraham.

[3] Cf. Vol. i, pp. 451 ff., 473, 635; and above, pp. 582, 591.

historical narratives or statements of fact, though, unlike the Hexateuch, they are usually in poetry. It seems to us that much of the Hexateuch may well have had a similar origin, i.e. in prophecy relating to the past. But so far as we are aware this function of prophecy is never expressly recognised in extant Hebrew literature. And consequently we think it better on the whole not to use the word 'prophetic' in reference to the Hexateuch.

The characteristics of Hebrew prophecy have been discussed to some extent in Ch. VIII. The powers attributed to the prophet may be summarised briefly as follows: (i) he has knowledge of 'the unknown present', i.e. knowledge of what is unascertainable by ordinary means; (ii) he has knowledge of the future; (iii) he can grant blessings and impose curses, which will take effect; (iv) he has power over the forces of nature—e.g. he can produce drought or rain, and work various other miracles.

Examples of (i)–(iii) will be found on p. 716 ff. Sometimes of course an incident may be interpreted in more than one way; a passage may be taken as illustrating either (ii) or (iii), or perhaps as a combination of the two. Thus Ahijah's speech to Jeroboam's wife in I Kings xiv. 6 ff. includes a prophecy of her son's death; but in the main it is virtually a curse upon Jeroboam's family.

Under blessings (iii) we may include the power of granting offspring, which the Hebrew prophet shares with the Brahman (cf. p. 614), though examples are not so common as in India. A good instance may be found in II Kings, iv. 16 f., where Elisha promises a son to the lady of Shunem. We may compare the benediction of Hannah by Eli the priest in I Sam. i. 17, though the nature of the blessing is not specified. It may be observed that in Gen. xviii. 10, Judg. xiii. 3 blessings of this kind are pronounced by Jehovah or his messenger.

The miracles (iv) attributed to Elijah and Elisha are very varied in character. Some of them show a certain resemblance to the spells noticed on p. 715, e.g. when Elijah divides the waters of the Jordan by striking them with his cloak (II Kings ii. 8), or when Elisha makes an iron axe-head to float by throwing a stick into the water after it (*ib.* vi. 6). But as the text stands, we cannot in either case speak of spells; for no words are used.[1] The miracle is due to some divine or magical power

---

[1] In II Kings ii. 14, when Elisha returns after Elijah's departure, he strikes the waters with Elijah's cloak and says "Where is Jehovah, the God of Elijah?"— which may be interpreted as a spell.

possessed by the prophet. In other cases, e.g. I Kings xvii. 20 ff., miracles are accompanied by prayer.

What has been said above applies of course primarily to the pre-literary prophets. The literary prophets seem seldom, if ever, to prophesy of the unknown present. Neither do they work miracles, except on rare occasions.[1] On the other hand they seem to retain the power of cursing and blessing, as well as that of prophesying the future. Examples of the former may be seen in Amos' speech to the priest Amaziah (vii. 17) and in Isaiah's prophecy against Shebna (xxii. 15 ff.). The prophecies of disaster impending upon foreign nations, which occur in Amos, i. 3 ff. and frequently in Isaiah's works, may have their origin in such curses as Balaam was invited to pronounce against Israel. But apart from these traditional features, the works of the literary prophets show also 'post-heroic' (political) characteristics, which have been discussed in Ch. VIII (p. 722 ff.). Here we are concerned rather with the early history of the prophet.

In stories relating to pre-literary times we hear often of the 'sons of the prophets', which evidently means communities of prophets. In I Sam. xix. 20 we find Samuel presiding over such a community, while in II Kings iv. 38, vi. 1 Elisha seems to be in a similar position. These communities are sometimes fairly large; fifty of the 'sons of the prophets', apparently from Jericho, follow Elijah and Elisha to the Jordan (*ib.* ii. 7). The members are, sometimes at least, married (*ib.* iv. 1 ff.). From I Kings xx. 38 ff. it would seem that they wore something distinctive in their hair-dressing, though not in their clothes.

In early times these communities are said to indulge in ecstasy so infectious that secular visitors are overcome by it.[2] In I Sam. xix. 20 ff. Saul sends two parties of messengers to the community at Ramah to arrest David; but when they arrive and find the prophets prophesying, they begin themselves to prophesy. Then Saul arrives and does the same, and strips off his clothes. There can be little doubt that 'prophesying' here means singing—perhaps improvising—religious poetry, with or without musical instruments. On another occasion Saul meets a company of prophets prophesying with musical instruments, and is similarly overcome. We may compare II Kings iii. 15, where Elisha

---

[1] We know only of the incident of the sun-dial, described in II Kings xx. 9 ff., Is. xxxviii. 7 f., and perhaps also Hezekiah's recovery, related in the context of the same passages. Isaiah here acts as a doctor. Was this a regular characteristic of Hebrew prophets? We do not know of any other evidence.   [2] Cf. p. 776, note.

receives inspiration through minstrelsy (cf. p. 715). In II Chron. xxv the Levites are said to prophesy with harps, psalteries and cymbals 'for the service of the house of God'.

It would seem then that religious minstrelsy or singing was in early times synonymous with prophecy. But this meaning cannot have been invariable; the prophet must have been thought of as speaking, as well as singing. His distinctive feature is that he regularly represents himself as the spokesman or mouthpiece of his deity—just as much in the straightforward speeches attributed to prophets in the stories of Kings as in the poetic language of the literary prophets. It is of interest to note the parallelism in these meanings with the Teutonic word (Ang.-Sax.) *þyle*, (Norse) *þulr*, 'spokesman, prophet, (learned) poet' (cf. Vol. 1, p. 618 f.). This parallelism applies not only to the word 'prophet' (*nābī'*) but also to the related verb 'prophesy' (*nābā'*)—in the musical sense—which would seem to be more or less equivalent to Norse *þylja*, 'chant'.

We have seen (p. 718 f.) that the prophet is sometimes called a 'seer', especially in stories relating to early times, and perhaps with special reference to his knowledge of the unknown present. In this respect an analogy is to be found in the Irish *fili*—a word which must originally have denoted 'seer' (cf. Vol. 1, p. 606). The *fili*, as he appears in our records is a learned poet, possessing a great repertoire of sagas and anti-quarian learning; in stories he has also the power of causing injury and even death by his curses. But our records date only from Christian times. There can be little doubt that before the introduction of Christianity his activities had a religious side, and that he had then more in common with the Hebrew prophet.

The contrast between the Hebrew prophet and the seer (*ṛṣi*) of ancient India has been pointed out in Ch. VIII (p. 723). In the Upanishads the latter is more of a speculative philosopher than a prophet. But in Vedic times he is an intermediary between gods and men and a religious poet. In the stories of the Mahābhārata he is often credited with prac-tically unlimited knowledge and with power to do what he wishes, whether by blessings and curses or in other respects.

The Indian seers are frequently surrounded by disciples; and there can be little doubt that Irish *filid* received as pupils at least those who aspired to become *filid*. Analogies are to be found in ancient Gaul and elsewhere. Was there an educational side to the activities of the Hebrew prophets or to the communities of the 'sons of the prophets'? It has been suggested that the preservation and circulation of the (non-heroic) stories of the past was largely due to them. But we know of no definite evidence.

It is somewhat curious that, so far as we are aware, early Hebrew literature preserves no instance of the contests in wisdom or manticism, which are so widespread among other peoples.[1] One may cite the story of the sacrifice on Mount Carmel, related in I Kings xviii. 21 ff.—a story which, like so many of the same kind, ends in tragedy for the vanquished party. But the contest here is represented as being between the deities rather than the prophets themselves. A better example may be found in Ex. vii. 8–viii. 19,[2] where Aaron, instructed by Moses, performs a series of supernatural feats. The three first of these—converting rods into serpents, turning the river into blood, and producing innumerable frogs —are performed also by the Egyptian magicians; but at the fourth round—the production of lice—the Egyptians fail. We do not know, however, of any contests which consist only of speech or verbal wisdom, as in other lands.

Supernatural feats are of course a more or less constant element in stories of prophets everywhere. Actually grotesque features, however, such as we find in Indian and Irish stories, seem to be wanting in the Hebrew records, except in the case of Jonah. But it is to be remembered that these stories usually date from times long after the prophets themselves; and the same is probably true of the story of Jonah—which indeed would be by no means out of place in the Mahābhārata. On the other hand the Hebrew records are entirely free from those disgusting features which occur so frequently in stories of seers in the Mahābhārata.

It may be observed that surprisingly little information is preserved as to the origin of most of the prophets. We do not know whether they were often, or indeed, ever, sons of prophets.[3] In II Chron. xxiv. 20 we hear of a prophet who was a son of the high-priest; but we do not know whether prophets often belonged to priestly families. Again, Indian records frequently speak of seers who were princes, and similar cases are to be found in Europe; but we have apparently no such evidence for Israel. On the other hand we do hear, as in Europe,[4] of seers or prophets who were in the service of kings. Such was the case

---

[1] Cf. Vol. I, pp. 97, 105, 474, 590; and above, p. 503 ff.

[2] It should be noted that all the passages here which speak of the Egyptian magicians and imply a contest are said to come from P, though the bulk of the narrative is believed to be taken from J and E.

[3] A possible case is the Jehu, son of Hanani, mentioned in I Kings xvi. 1, if his father was the seer Hanani, referred to in II Chron. xvi. 7.

[4] Cf. Vol. I, pp. 604, 619.

with Nathan and Gad in David's time. The former seems to have been one of the most influential members of the court, and perhaps the king's chief confidant. Other prophets, such as Elisha, evidently had great influence with kings, though they were not attached to their personal service. Lastly, note is to be taken of prophets like Amos, who were unconnected with any kind of prophetic community and even disclaimed the title of prophet. We do not know whether such persons were numerous.

Although no evidence for heredity is available in the case of the prophets, it is clear enough that the priesthood was a hereditary institution. The priests at Jerusalem claimed descent from Aaron (cf. p. 767); and the same claim is made for those at Shiloh, who in a sense may be regarded as their predecessors. The priests at Dan are said to be descended from Moses. Unfortunately no information as to the origin of the priesthood seems to be supplied by the early texts. In the story of Moses all the evidence apparently comes from P; the older texts, J and E or JE, first mention priests in Josh. iii f., as carrying the sacred Ark across the Jordan.[1]

This absence of an early account of the origin of the priesthood is very remarkable, and would seem to point either to an omission in the early texts or to some change in the tradition. It may be that the references to Aaron and Eleazar in P are ultimately derived from the early texts and that only the form—not the substance—of the story has been changed. On the other hand it is also possible that the tradition from which the early texts are derived gave a different account of the origin of the priesthood—an account which came to be discarded in favour of the claims of the house of Aaron. All that can be said with any confidence is that the hereditary priesthoods at Shiloh and at Dan seem to have been established a good time before the rise of the monarchy. The stories of Gideon (Judg. vi. 25 ff.) and of Micah (ib. xvii. 3 ff.) show that in early times the local chiefs had sanctuaries of their own, just as in Europe.[2] Micah at first made his son priest. In other cases possibly the chief may have acted as priest himself, as in Europe.[3]

---

[1] 'Priests' are mentioned in Ex. xix. 22 ff. (J), before the account of the institution of the priesthood (ib. xxviii f.) is given by P. We believe that the word here is generally interpreted to mean 'princes' or 'chiefs'; and kohēn ('priest') apparently does have some such meaning in certain passages in Samuel and Kings. But this explanation does not seem altogether satisfactory.

[2] Cf. Vol. 1, p. 616, and perhaps also p. 621 f.

[3] Some scholars regard Jethro, 'priest of Midian' (Moses' father-in-law) as a person of this kind.

In early Hebrew literature prophecy is regularly represented as due to inspiration from Jehovah. This is not always specifically stated; and there are frequent instances, like II Kings v. 26, which may be interpreted as meaning that a prophet acquires knowledge through some power of 'vision' inherent in himself, just as in the north of Europe and in India. But we cannot recall any passage in which this is definitely stated. Inspiration is at all events the general rule.[1]

The prophet speaks as the mouthpiece of Jehovah; but usually he does not say how he has received his message. Where this is stated the most frequent form of inspiration is by dreams. Occasionally, however, we hear of direct communication, when the medium is apparently not asleep. The most detailed instance is the story of the call of Samuel, related in I Sam. iii. Here Samuel, who is still a child, or at least very young, comes to Eli three times in the night, thinking that the latter has called him. On the third occasion the priest realises that the voice must be Jehovah's and tells Samuel to answer accordingly. So, when he again hears the voice, he replies: "Speak, for thy servant heareth". Then Jehovah makes known to him the impending ruin of Eli's house.

The scene of Samuel's call is the temple or sanctuary at Shiloh. In this connection we may note that Isaiah's vision—the subject of what is commonly thought to be his earliest prophecy (cap. vi)—seems to take place in the Temple at Jerusalem. The most famous scenes of this kind, however, are located at a sacred mountain, Horeb or Sinai, in the south, far beyond the territories of Israel or Judah. It is to Horeb that Elijah goes in I Kings xix. 8 ff. to receive a message from Jehovah. The message is given by a voice, which is preceded by a high wind, earthquake and fire. At Horeb or Sinai—which may mean the same place, though the precise locality is uncertain—Moses meets Jehovah in Ex. xix, and receives from him the Ten Commandments and the 'Book of the Covenant'. Jehovah's approach is preceded by thunder and lightning, smoke and fire, earthquake, and the sound of a trumpet. It may be noted that in Palestine itself also we hear sometimes of worship offered upon the tops of hills and mountains, though the practice is condemned.

On the other hand there seems to be hardly any evidence in early records for inspiration or divination at springs. An instance of revelation takes place in Gen. xvi. 7 at a fountain, which in view of its name (*ib.* 14) may be a sanctuary. A revelation also takes place at Beersheba

---

[1] On this subject cf. Vol. i, p. 635 ff.; it will require further notice in Vol. iii. It may be noted that the mantic ecstasy of the Welsh *awenyddion* is not said to be infectious, though infectious ecstasy (cf. p. 772) was perhaps known to the ancient Celts, as also to the Greeks and Thracians.

(*ib*. xxvi. 24), where Isaac builds an altar and digs a well. In later times this was apparently a famous sanctuary; but its sanctity may have been due not so much to the well (*b'ēr*) as to its having been the dwelling-place of Abraham and Isaac. In view of the European evidence cited in Vol. i, p. 648 ff., it is rather surprising that the Hebrew records should have so little to say on this subject.

Instances of revelation beneath trees, usually oaks, are more frequent. They may be found both in Genesis, e.g. xii. 6 f. (Shechem), xviii. 1 ff. (Hebron), and in Judges, e.g. vi. 11 ff. Sanctuaries or altars are mentioned at the places indicated. It may be observed that even as late as the time of Ahaz we hear of sacrifices 'under every green tree' (cf. II Kings xvi. 4). It may also be noted that in Judg. iv. 5 the prophetess Deborah is said to have dwelt beneath a palm-tree.

One striking instance of revelation, the story of Jacob's dream (Gen. xxviii. 11 ff.), is connected with a menhir. This is presumably the foundation-story of the sanctuary of Bethel (cf. p. 693).

As regards the accessories of inspiration, discussed in Vol. i, p. 651 ff., the importance of music has been noticed above (p. 754 f.). For other accessories the evidence is very slight. The use of strong drink seems to be unknown. The people of Ephraim are frequently charged by the prophets with drunkenness at their feasts, including perhaps religious feasts; but we have not noted any reference to prophecy in this connection. Neither can we recall the use of any magic or mantic potion, like the cauldron of Ceridwen.

Mantic knowledge seems to be attributed to snakes in the story of the Fall; but we do not know of any further evidence to this effect. At Jerusalem in Hezekiah's time, according to II Kings xviii. 4, incense was offered to a serpent of brass, which was believed to have been made by Moses. From Numb. xxi. 9, with which this passage is clearly to be connected, it would seem probable that the virtue of this object was curative (therapeutic) rather than mantic.

We do not know of any special chair or oracular seat used by prophets or seers. On the other hand the prophet's staff is mentioned not unfrequently. In II Kings iv. 29 ff. Elisha sends his servant with his staff to a dying child, and tells him to lay it upon the child's face, in order to revive it. But it is in the story of Moses that the most numerous and striking examples are to be found. Several of the plagues inflicted upon the Egyptians are brought about by a rod, either his own or Aaron's. Instances occur also later, as in Ex. xvii. 5 f., where he strikes a rock with his rod, in order to obtain water.

INDEX